The Reader's Adviser

The Reader's Adviser
A Layman's Guide to Literature
13th EDITION

Barbara A. Chernow and George A. Vallasi, Series Editors

Volume 1
The Best in American and British Fiction, Poetry, Essays, Literary Biography, Bibliography, and Reference
Edited by Fred Kaplan

Books about Books • Bibliography • Reference Books: Literature • Broad Studies and General Anthologies • British Poetry: Early to Romantic • British Poetry: Middle Period • Modern British and Irish Poetry • American Poetry: Early Period • Modern American Poetry • British Fiction: Early Period • British Fiction: Middle Period • Modern British Fiction • American Fiction: Early Period • Modern American Fiction • Commonwealth Literature • Essays and Criticism • Literary Biography and Autobiography

Volume 2
The Best in American and British Drama and World Literature in English Translation
Edited by Maurice Charney

The Drama • British Drama: Early to Eighteenth Century • Shakespeare • Modern British and Irish Drama • American Drama • World Literature • Greek Literature • Latin Literature • French Literature • Italian Literature • Spanish Literature • Portuguese Literature • German and Netherlandic Literature • Scandinavian Literature • Russian Literature • East European Literatures • Yiddish Literature • Hebrew Literature • Spanish American Literature • African Literature • Middle Eastern Literature • Literature of the Indian Subcontinent • Chinese Literature • Japanese Literature • Southeast Asian and Korean Literature

Volume 3
The Best in General Reference Literature, the Social Sciences, History, and the Arts
Edited by Paula T. Kaufman

Reference Books: General • Dictionaries • General Biography and Autobiography • The Social Sciences • Education • Ancient History • United States History • Western Hemisphere: Canada and Latin America • British History • World History • Music and Dance • Art and Architecture • The Mass Media • Folklore and Humor • Travel and Exploration

Volume 4

The Best in the Literature of Philosophy and World Religions
Edited by William L. Reese

General Philosophy • Greek and Roman Philosophy • Medieval Philosophy •
Renaissance Philosophy • Modern Philosophy • Twentieth-Century Philosophy •
Ancient Religion and Philosophy • Eastern Religion and Philosophy • Judaism •
Early Christianity • Late Christianity • Bibles • Minority Religions

Volume 5

The Best in the Literature of Science, Technology, and Medicine
Edited by Paul T. Durbin

General Science • History of Science, Technology, and Medicine • Philosophy of
Science and Pseudoscience • Mathematics • Statistics and Probability • Information
and Communication Science • Astronomy and Space Science • Earth Sciences •
Physics • Chemistry • Biology • Ecology and Environmental Science • Genetics •
Medicine and Health • Illness and Disease • Clinical Psychology and Psychiatry •
Engineering and Technology • Energy • Ethics of Science, Technology,
and Medicine • Science and Society

THE
Reader's Adviser

A Layman's Guide to Literature
13th EDITION

Volume 2

The Best in American and British Drama
and World Literature in English Translation

Edited by Maurice Charney

Barbara A. Chernow and George A. Vallasi, Series Editors

R. R. BOWKER COMPANY
New York & London, 1986

Published by R. R. Bowker Company,
a division of Reed Publishing USA
245 West 17th Street, New York, NY 10011
Copyright © 1986 by Reed Publishing USA,
a division of Reed Holdings, Inc.

International Standard Book Numbers
0-8352-2145-8 (Volume 1)
0-8352-2146-6 (Volume 2)
0-8352-2147-4 (Volume 3)
0-8352-2148-2 (Volume 4)
0-8352-2149-0 (Volume 5)
0-8352-2315-9 (Volume 6)
International Standard Serial Number 0094-5943
Library of Congress Catalog Card Number 57-13277

The paper used in this publication meets the minimum
requirements of American National Standard for
Information Sciences—Permanence of Papers for
Printed Library Materials, ANSI Z39.48-1984.

Contents

Preface

Over its thirteen editions, and since its first publication in 1921, chapters of *The Reader's Adviser* have been expanded and reorganized and new topics have been introduced, thus better to serve the needs of a growing and more diversified population. The first edition, entitled *The Bookman's Manual*, was based on Bessie Graham's course on book salesmanship given at the William Penn Evening High School in Philadelphia. Graham organized the book so that the chapters corresponded to the general classifications familiar to booksellers and, by providing publishers and prices in her text, she simplified book ordering for the bookseller. Since 1921, however, the book industry has experienced significant changes—comparatively few independent book dealers exist, information on titles is available from a wide variety of printed and computerized sources, and publishers are taking fewer risks by printing just enough copies of a title to meet immediate demands. At the same time that these changes were occurring, *The Reader's Adviser* was finding a broader audience; although still used by booksellers, the librarians, general readers, and high school and college students found that the topical organization of the volume with its annotated bibliographies also met their needs. For the nonspecialist who is interested in reading about a particular subject, *The Reader's Adviser* is a perfect starting point. The six-volume set provides annotated bibliographies arranged by subject, with brief biographies of authors, creative artists, and scientists worthy of special mention; in addition, it informs the reader of a book's availability, price, and purchasing source. Since the set is kept up to date by regular revisions, the volumes also serve as a reflection of the current state of the best available literature in print in the United States.

As a result of the growth of new fields of interest to the reading public and the continuing increase in the number of titles published, *The Reader's Adviser* has expanded with each succeeding edition. For this thirteenth edition, it has grown from three to six volumes. The first three volumes will appear simultaneously in 1986; the final three in 1988. The organization of the first two volumes is similar to that in the twelfth edition: Volume 1 covers mainly American and British fiction and poetry and Volume 2 covers drama, Shakespeare, and world literature in English translation. Volume 3, which covers the best in general reference literature, the social sciences, history, and the arts, has experienced the most significant changes—most chapters have been expanded, virtually new chapters have been created for the arts, and several chapters have been moved to form the nuclei of Volumes 4 and 5. Volume 4 covers the Bible, world religions, and philosophy; Volume 5 is devoted to science, technology, and medicine. Except for Volume 6, containing indexes to the entire set, each of the volumes has been edited by a specialist in the field, the whole project having been coordinated by the series editors.

Although the thirteenth edition of *The Reader's Adviser* retains the essential format and basic structure of the earlier editions, the editors and publisher have made a number of improvements designed to enhance the appearance and usefulness of the volumes. First, the design has been modified to increase readability and provide a more open look. The typeface is easier to read, biographies are printed in a larger face, and the titles in the "books about" sections following the biographies are in alphabetical order according to the authors' surnames. Finally, the authors and anonymous sagas that form the main headings in *The Reader's Adviser* are listed in alphabetical order within the chapters rather than the chronological order of previous editions. In the front matter of each volume, a Chronology of these individuals and works provides the reader with an overview of the development of a particular genre. For each chapter, the editors chose an eminent scholar or librarian with particular expertise in the subject area, so that the selection of bibliographies and main listings would reflect the best-informed judgment of a specialist in the field.

The greatest challenge was that of selection—which titles and authors to include. Since *The Reader's Adviser* is not a research tool for students and scholars, but rather a reference work designed for the nonspecialist, the editors' goal was to include those books generally available to an intelligent reader through the facilities of the library system of a moderately sized municipality. Books must be currently available in English from a publisher or distributor in the United States. Out-of-print titles are included for those major works which, because of their importance in the field, could not be excluded from the list. If a book is not presently available in English or cannot be purchased in the United States, it is considered out of print (o.p.) by the editors. In some disciplines, such as modern American poetry, publishers allow titles to go out of print quickly and the available literature was found to be surprisingly thin. The reader will also note that Volume 2 (the comparative literature volume) reveals how little of the world's non-English literature has been translated into English.

In selecting authors for main entries, contributing editors weighed a number of criteria—historical importance, current popularity as determined by the number of in-print titles, and space limitations. Particularly in American and British fiction, U.S. and world history, and the social sciences chapters, the necessity of adding new authors sometimes required eliminating authors who were previously the subjects of main entries in earlier editions of *The Reader's Adviser*. Most major authors are represented; other authors were selected as examples of particular movements or styles. The latter category is subjective; although these choices are valid, someone else's choices might have been equally valid. The constraints of space impose their own compromises.

The organization of each volume and of each chapter is designed to move the reader from the general to the specific, from reference books, books of history and criticism, and anthologies to specific authors, scientists, and creative artists. Each chapter opens with a brief introduction that provides a framework for the literature of a particular period or discipline, followed by general reading lists and then, with few exceptions, the main entries. In chapters covering more than one area of study, such as the social sciences, or more than one country, such as Southeast Asia, this pattern repeats itself for each major division. Each author selected as a main entry receives a brief biography followed by bibliographies of books by and about him or her. Wherever possible, the date of first publication follows the title of a work mentioned in the short biography or will instead appear, when available, as the first date in the "Books by. . ." entries below. In addition to *Books in Print, The New Columbia Encyclopedia* (1975) has served as the authority in verifying dates. The bibliographies of books by an author are mainly composed of collections of works and in-print titles of individual works in the particular genre covered by the chapter. Other titles may be mentioned in the biography, but only those works relevant to the genre under discussion appear in the bibliographies.

The bibliographic entries are so designed that the reader will be able both to locate a book in a library and to know where it is available for purchase and at what price. The editors have included the following information available or applicable for each title: author; title (translated titles or original titles are given in parentheses following the title); editor; series title; translator; authors of prefaces, introductions, and forewords; edition; number of volumes; reprint data; publisher (if more than one, publishers are listed alphabetically); date of publication; and price. The reader should be cautioned that the accuracy and completeness of information depends in large part on the information publishers supply to the *Books in Print* database and the information listed in individual publishers' catalogs.

If a date is listed directly after a title, this indicates the date of the publication of the first edition, regardless of whether that edition is still in print. For reprints, the date of the particular edition from which it was reprinted is given. If a title consists of more than one volume, and is listed with only one price, this is the price of the entire set. As book pricing changes so rapidly, some prices listed in *The Reader's Adviser* may have already changed. Although the editors considered the possibility of deleting prices from *The Reader's Adviser*, it was decided to retain them as an indication to the reader of the general price category into which an individual title falls and to assist the librarian in acquisition. Finally, the reader should be aware that not all in-print editions of a work are necessarily listed, but rather those selected by the editors because of their quality or special features.

To guide the reader through the volumes, *The Reader's Adviser* includes cross-references in three forms. The "see" reference leads the reader to the appropriate volume and chapter for information on a specific author or topic. "See also" refers the reader to additional information in another chapter or volume. Within any introductory narrative portions, the name of an author who appears as a main listing in another chapter or volume is printed in large and small capital letters. In each case, if the chapter cross-referenced is in a different volume from that being consulted, the volume number is also provided.

Each volume of *The Reader's Adviser* has three indexes—one for names, one for book titles, and one for general subjects. The Name Index includes all authors, editors, compilers, composers, directors, actors, artists, philosophers, and scientists cited in *The Reader's Adviser*. If a name appears as a main listing in the text, the name as well as the first page number of the main listing appear in boldface type. The Title Index includes book titles with two exceptions: collected works or generic titles by authors who receive main listings (e.g., *Selected Prose of T. S. Eliot*) and "books about" titles that follow the main listings and include the name of the main-entry author (e.g., *Booker T. Washington* by Louis R. Harlan). (This does not hold true in the case of Chapter 3, "Shakespeare," in Volume 2, where all works by and about him are included.) Therefore, to ensure locating all titles by and about a main-entry author, the user should look up that author in the Name Index to locate the primary listing.

In preparing the thirteenth edition of *The Reader's Adviser*, the series editors are indebted to a great many people for assistance and advice. We are especially grateful to the many people at R. R. Bowker who have worked with us; in particular, to Olga S. Weber, who provided encouragement, support, and a critical eye in reading manuscripts; to Kathy Kleibacker, for her constant faith in the project; and to Marion Sader, Julia Raymunt, Iris Topel, and Nancy Bucenec for their attention to detail and concern for quality in editing and production. We were fortunate in our choice of volume editors. Fred Kaplan, general editor of Volume 1, The Best in American and British Fiction, Poetry, Essays, Literary Biography, Bibliography, and Reference, is Professor of English at Queens College and at the Graduate Center, City University of New York; he is a distinguished Dickens and Carlyle scholar, the editor of *Dickens Studies Annual*, a member of the board of the Carlyle Papers, and is currently writing a biography of Dickens. The general editor of Volume 2, The Best in American and British Drama and World Literature in English Translation, is Maurice Charney, Distinguished Professor at Rutgers University in the department of English. His published works include *How to Read Shakespeare* and a biography of Joe Orton. Paula T. Kaufman, who served as general editor of Volume 3, The Best in General Reference Literature, the Social Sciences, History, and the Arts, is director of the academic information services group, Columbia University Libraries. Volume 4, The Best in the Literature of Philosophy and World Religions, was developed under the general editorship of William L. Reese. He is Professor of Philosophy at the State University of New York, Albany. His publications include the *Dictionary of Philosophy and Religion*. Paul T. Durbin is general editor of

Volume 5, The Best in the Literature of Science, Technology, and Medicine. He is Professor of Philosophy at the University of Delaware and editor of *A Guide to the Culture of Science, Technology, and Medicine*. All made invaluable suggestions for organizing their volumes, recommended contributing editors, and reviewed each chapter for substantive content. The editors also wish to thank the following individuals for their help in the preparation of *The Reader's Adviser:* Paul Anderer, Columbia University; Mary Brake, Academy Chicago Publishers; Rose Brown, The Crossroad Publishing Company; Mary E. Buhl, Holmes & Meier Publishers, Inc.; Hanna Charney, Hunter College of the City University of New York; Victor Erlich, Yale University; Charling C. Fagan, Columbia University Libraries; Linda Ferraro, Columbia University; Bluma Goldstein, University of California, Berkeley; William E. Harkins, Columbia University; John D. Johannon, Yale University; Tami Joplin, Harcourt Brace Jovanovich, Publishers; Greg Kajtze, Cambridge University Press; Frederick R. Karl, New York University; Andre Lefevere, University of Texas, Austin; Audrey M. Livernois, University of Toronto Press; William McCarthy, Yale University Press; Menachem Mansoor, University of Wisconsin; Barbara Miller, Barnard College; J. Hillis Miller, Yale University; Adolf K. Placzek, Columbia University; Rochelle Shifman, Princeton University; Johan Snapper, University of California, Berkeley; Jacob Stern, Graduate Center, City University of New York; H. Paul Varley, Columbia University. Finally, a special thanks to David B. Biesel, who first brought the project to us, and to Antoinette Boone and Frank Van Orman Brown, who keyboarded all of the chapters, assisted in verifying bibliographic data, and coded material for the indexes.

In the 65 years since *The Reader's Adviser* first appeared, it has grown from a tool for booksellers to a standard reference work. In addition to bibliographic information, the introductions and biographies are enjoyable reading for someone just browsing through the volumes. *The Reader's Adviser* has a distinguished history; it is hoped that these latest volumes will continue in that tradition.

Barbara A. Chernow
George A. Vallasi

Contributing Editors

David Bady, THE DRAMA and MODERN BRITISH AND IRISH DRAMA
Assistant Professor of English at Herbert H. Lehman College, City University of New York

Zachary M. Baker, YIDDISH LITERATURE
Head, Technical Services and Yiddish Department, Jewish Public Library, Montreal

Henryk Baran, RUSSIAN LITERATURE
Associate Professor of Russian literature at the State University of New York, Albany

Richard A. Brooks, FRENCH LITERATURE
Professor of French literature at the Graduate School, City University of New York, and general editor of *A Critical Bibliography of French Literature*

Maurice Charney, BRITISH DRAMA: EARLY TO EIGHTEENTH CENTURY and SHAKESPEARE
Distinguished Professor at Rutgers, the State University of New Jersey, in the department of English; author of such published works as *How to Read Shakespeare* and a biography of Joe Orton

David R. Claussenius, SOUTHEAST ASIAN AND KOREAN LITERATURE
Received a Master of International Affairs degree from Columbia University

Frank Dauster, SPANISH AMERICAN LITERATURE
Professor of Spanish, Rutgers, the State University of New Jersey

Margaret Ann Escher, WORLD LITERATURE
Instructor of English at the John Jay College of Criminal Justice, City University of New York

Leo Hamalian, MIDDLE EASTERN LITERATURE
Professor of English at City College of the City University of New York and editor of *Ararat*, a quarterly magazine of Arts and Letters

Marshall Hurwitz, GREEK LITERATURE
Lecturer in classical languages at City College of the City University of New York

Glenderlyn Johnson, AFRICAN LITERATURE
Special Projects Librarian at the Schomburg Center for Research in Black Culture

Linda P. Lerman, HEBREW LITERATURE
Administrative Librarian for Public Services at the Library of the Jewish Theological Seminary of America and President of the Research Division of the Association of Jewish Libraries

Robin Lewis and Sangita Advani, THE LITERATURE OF THE INDIAN SUBCONTINENT
Lewis is Associate Dean and Lecturer in South Asian Studies, School of International and Public Affairs, Columbia University. Advani has a B.A. from Barnard College in Oriental Studies

Vasa D. Mihailovich, EAST EUROPEAN LITERATURES
Professor of Slavic languages and literature at the University of North Carolina, Chapel Hill, and author of *Contemporary Yugoslav Poetry*

Naomi Moniz, PORTUGUESE LITERATURE
Georgetown University

Jacqueline Mueller, JAPANESE LITERATURE
Visiting Assistant Professor of Japanese literature at Lafayette College, Easton, Pennsylvania

Fred J. Nichols, LATIN LITERATURE
Professor of comparative literature at the City University of New York, and editor and translator of *Anthology of Neo-Latin Poetry*

Anne Paolucci, ITALIAN LITERATURE
Director, Doctor of Arts degree program in English at St. John's University, and editor of the *Review of National Literatures*

Henry Paolucci, ITALIAN LITERATURE
Professor, Government and Politics, St. John's University, and President, the Walter Bagehot Research Council

Pamela Spence Richards, GERMAN AND NETHERLANDIC LITERATURE
Rutgers, the State University of New Jersey

Carole Slade, SPANISH LITERATURE
Assistant Professor of comparative literature at Columbia University and editor of *Approaches to Teaching Dante's Divine Comedy*

Jacobus W. Smit, GERMAN AND NETHERLANDIC LITERATURE
Queen Wilhelmina Professor in the history department and a Professor of Germanic languages at Columbia University

Thomas F. Van Laan, AMERICAN DRAMA
  Professor of English at Rutgers, the State University of New Jersey, and author of *Role Playing in Shakespeare* and *The Idiom of Drama*

Marsha L. Wagner, CHINESE LITERATURE
  East Asian Librarian, C. V. Starr East Asian Library, Columbia University

Donald K. Watkins, SCANDINAVIAN LITERATURE
  Professor of Germanic languages at the University of Kansas, Lawrence

Abbreviations

abr.	abridged	ltd. ed.	limited edition
AHR	*American Historical Review*	MLA	Modern Language Association
Amer.	America(n)	Mod.	Modern
annot.	annotated	*N.Y. Herald Tribune*	*New York Herald Tribune*
bd.	bound		
bdg.	binding	*N.Y. Times*	*New York Times*
Bk(s).	Book(s)	o.p.	out-of-print
Class.	Classic(s)	orig.	original
coll.	collected	pap.	paperback
coll. ed.	collector's ed.	Pr.	Press
comp.	compiled, compiler	pref.	preface
corr.	corrected	pt(s).	parts
Ctr.	Center	*PW*	*Publishers Weekly*
ed.	edited, editor, edition	repr.	reprint
Eng.	English	rev. ed.	revised edition
enl. ed.	enlarged edition	*SB*	*Studies in Bibliography*
fl.	flourished	sel.	selected
fwd.	foreword	Ser.	Series
gen. ed(s).	general editor(s)	*SR*	*Saturday Review*
ill.	illustrated	Stand.	Standard
imit. lea.	imitation leather	Supp.	Supplement
intro.	introduction	*TLS*	*Times Literary Supplement*
lea.	leather		
lg.-type ed.	large-type edition	trans.	translated, translator, translation
Lib.	Library		
lib. bdg.	library binding	Univ.	University
Lit.	Literature	Vol(s).	Volume(s)
LJ	*Library Journal*		

Chronology

Main author entries appear here chronologically by year of birth. Within each chapter, main author entries are arranged alphabetically by surname.

Whiting, John. 1917–1963
Behan, Brendan. 1923–1964
Bolt, Robert. 1924–
Shaffer, Peter. 1926–
Nichols, Peter. 1928–
Friel, Brian. 1929–
Osborne, John. 1929–
Arden, John. 1930–
Pinter, Harold. 1930–
Wesker, Arnold. 1932–
Orton, Joe. 1933–1967
Bond, Edward. 1935–
Gray, Simon. 1936–
Stoppard, Tom. 1937–
Churchill, Caryl. 1938–
Brenton, Howard. 1942–
Hare, David. 1947–

5. American Drama

Kelly, George Edward. 1887–1974
Anderson, Maxwell. 1888–1959
O'Neill, Eugene. 1888–1953
Kaufman, George S. 1889–1961
Rice, Elmer. 1892–1967
Green, Paul. 1894–1981
Barry, Philip. 1896–1949
Wilder, Thornton. 1897–1975
Hellman, Lillian. 1905–1984
Odets, Clifford. 1906–1963
Saroyan, William. 1908–1981
Williams, Tennessee. 1911–1983
Inge, William. 1913–1973
Miller, Arthur. 1915–
Simon, Neil. 1927–
Albee, Edward. 1928–
Hansberry, Lorraine. 1930–1965
Baraka, Imamu Amiri. 1934–
van Itallie, Jean-Claude. 1935–
Kopit, Arthur. 1937–
Wilson, Lanford. 1937–
Rabe, David. 1940–
Shepard, Sam. 1943–

Mamet, David. 1947–
Norman, Marsha. 1947–
Henley, Beth. 1952–
Hwang, David Henry. 1957–

6. World Literature

7. Greek Literature

Hesiod. c.700 B.C.
Homer. c.700 B.C.
Sappho. c.612 B.C.
Aesop. fl. 570 B.C.
Aeschylus. 524–456 B.C.
Pindar. 518–c.438 B.C.
Sophocles. c.496–406 B.C.
Euripides. c.485–c.406 B.C.
Aristophanes. c.450–c.385 B.C.
Demosthenes. 385?–322 B.C.
Theophrastus. c.371–287 B.C.
Menander. 342/341–293/289 B.C.
Callimachus. c.305–c.240 B.C.
Theocritus. c.300–c.260 B.C.
Apollonius Rhodius. 3rd century
    B.C.
Longinus. c.1st century A.D.
Lucian. c.120–c.185
Longus. fl. 2nd or 3rd century A.D.?
Heliodorus of Emesa. fl. 220–250
Makriyannis, John. 1797–1864
Palamas, Kostes. 1859–1943
Cavafy, Constantine P. 1863–1933
Kazantzakis, Nikos. 1885–1957
Seferis, George. 1900–1971
Ritsos, Yannis. 1909–
Elytis, Odysseus. 1911–

8. Latin Literature

Terence. c.190–159 B.C.
Plautus, Titus Maccius. d. c.184 B.C.
Cicero. 106–43 B.C.
Lucretius. c.94 or 99–c.55 B.C.
Catullus. 84?–54? B.C.
Virgil. 70–19 B.C.

Horace. 65–8 B.C.

Propertius. c.50–c.16 B.C.

Tibullus. 48?–19 B.C.

Ovid. 43 B.C.–A.D. 17

Seneca, Lucius Annaeus. c.3 B.C.–
A.D. 65

Persius. 34–62

Quintilian. c.35–c.95

Lucan. 39–65

Martial. 40?–104

Statius, Publius Papinius. c.45–c.96

Juvenal. 60?–140?

Pliny the Younger. c.61–c.112

Petronius. d.65

Suetonius. c.69–c.140

Apuleius, Lucius. 114–?

9. French Literature

The Song of Roland. end of 11th
century

Tristan and Iseult. c.1160–1170

Chrétien de Troyes. c. end of 12th
century

Aucassin and Nicolette. 13th
century (first half)

Villon, François. 1431–1465?

Rabelais, François. 1494?–1553?

Ronsard, Pierre de. 1524–1585

Montaigne, Michel Eyquem de.
1533–1592

Corneille, Pierre. 1606–1684

La Rochefoucauld, François, Duc
de. 1613–1680

La Fontaine, Jean de. 1621–1695

Molière. 1622–1673

Sevigne, Mme de. 1626–1696

La Fayette, Marie Madeleine de la
Vergne, Comtesse de. 1634–1693

Racine, Jean. 1639–1699

Marivaux, Pierre Carlet de
Chamblain de. 1688–1763

Voltaire. 1694–1778

Diderot, Denis. 1713–1784

Sade, Comte de. 1740–1814

Laclos, Pierre Ambroise François
Choderlos de. 1741–1803

Chateaubriand, François René,
Vicomte de. 1768–1848

Stendhal. 1783–1842

Balzac, Honore de. 1799–1850

Dumas, Alexandre (père). 1802–
1870

Hugo, Victor Marie. 1802–1885

Baudelaire, Charles. 1821–1867

Flaubert, Gustave. 1821–1880

Dumas, Alexandre (fils). 1824–1895

Zola, Emile. 1840–1902

Mallarmé, Stephane. 1842–1898

France, Anatole. 1844–1924

Verlaine, Paul. 1844–1896

Maupassant, Guy de. 1850–1893

Rimbaud, Arthur. 1854–1891

Rolland, Romain. 1866–1944

Claudel, Paul. 1868–1955

Gide, André. 1869–1951

Proust, Marcel. 1871–1922

Valéry, Paul. 1871–1945

Colette. 1873–1954

Apollinaire, Guillaume. 1880–1918

Giraudoux, Jean. 1882–1944

Mauriac, François. 1885–1970

Romains, Jules. 1885–1972

Saint-John Perse. 1887–1975

Bernanos, Georges. 1888–1948

Cocteau, Jean. 1889–1963

Céline, Louis-Ferdinand. 1894–1961

Giono, Jean. 1895–1970

Breton, André. 1896–1966

Ponge, Francis. 1899–

Green, Julien. 1900–

Saint Exupéry, Antoine de. 1900–
1944

Malraux, André. 1901–1976

Aymé, Marcel. 1902–1967

Sarraute, Nathalie. 1902–

Queneau, Raymond. 1903–1976
Radiguet, Raymond. 1903–1923
Yourcenar, Marguerite. 1903–
Sartre, Jean-Paul. 1905–1980
Beckett, Samuel. 1906–
Char, René. 1907–
Leduc, Violette. 1907–1971
Beauvoir, Simone de. 1908–1986
Simenon, Georges. 1909–
Weil, Simone. 1909–1943
Anouilh, Jean. 1910–
Genet, Jean. 1910–1986
Ionesco, Eugene. 1912–
Camus, Albert. 1913–1960
Simon, Claude. 1913–
Duras, Marguerite. 1914–
Barthes, Roland. 1915–1980
Pinget, Robert. 1919–
Robbe-Grillet, Alain. 1922–
Bonnefoy, Yves. 1923–
Tournier, Michel. 1924–
Butor, Michel. 1926–
Foucault, Michel. 1926–1984
Wiesel, Elie. 1928–

10. Italian Literature
Cavalcanti, Guido. c.1254–1300
Dante Alighieri. 1265–1321
Petrarch. 1304–1374
Boccaccio, Giovanni. 1313–1375
Alberti, Leon Battista. 1407–1472
Poliziano, Angelo. 1454–1494
Bembo, Pietro. 1470–1547
Ariosto, Ludovico. 1474–1533
Castiglione, Baldassare. 1478–1529
Bandello, Matteo. 1485–1561
Aretino, Pietro. 1492–1556
Tasso, Torquato. 1544–1595
Bruno, Giordano. 1548–1600
Vico, Giambattista. 1668–1744
Goldoni, Carlo. 1707–1793
Baretti, Giuseppe. 1719–1789

Parini, Giuseppe. 1729–1799
Alfieri, Count Vittorio. 1749–1803
Foscolo, Ugo. 1778–1827
Manzoni, Alessandro. 1785–1873
Belli, Giuseppe Gioacchino. 1791–1863
Leopardi, Giacomo. 1798–1873
De Sanctis, Francesco. 1817–1833
Carducci, Giosuè. 1835–1907
Verga, Giovanni. 1840–1922
Pascoli, Giovanni. 1859–1912
Svevo, Italo. 1861–1928
D'Annunzio, Gabriele. 1863–1938
Croce, Benedetto. 1866–1952
Pirandello, Luigi. 1867–1936
Deledda, Grazia. 1871–1936
Marinetti, Filippo Tommaso. 1875–1944
Papini, Giovanni. 1881–1956
Ungaretti, Giuseppe. 1888–1970
Montale, Eugenio. 1896–1981
Praz, Mario. 1896–1982
De Filippo, Eduardo. 1900–1984
Silone, Ignazio. 1900–1978
Quasimodo, Salvatore. 1901–1968
Levi, Carlo. 1902–1975
Moravia, Alberto. 1907–
Pavese, Cesare. 1908–1950
Vittorini, Elio. 1908–1966
Bassani, Giorgio. 1916–
Ginzburg, Natalia Levi. 1916–
Morante, Elsa. 1918–1985
Levi, Primo. 1919–
Pasolini, Pier Paolo. 1922–1975
Calvino, Italo. 1923–1985
Fo, Dario. 1926–

11. Spanish Literature
The Cid, Poem of. c.1140
Ruíz, Juan. 1283?–1350?
Rojas, Fernando de. 1475?–1538?
Teresa of Jesus, St. 1515–1582

John of the Cross, St. 1542–1591

Alemán, Mateo. 1546–1614

Cervantes Saavedra, Miguel de.
1547–1616

The Life of Lazarillo de Tormes.
1554

Góngora y Argote, Luis de. 1561–
1627

Lope de Vega Carpio, Félix. 1562–
1635

Quevedo y Villegas, Francisco
Gómez de. 1580–1645

Tirso de Molina. 1584–1648

Calderón de la Barca, Pedro. 1600–
1681

Gracián, Baltasar. 1601–1658

Valera y Alcalá Galiano, Juan.
1827–1905

Alarcón, Pedro Antonio de. 1833–
1891

Bécquer, Gustavo Adolfo. 1836–
1870

Pérez Galdós, Benito. 1843–1920

Pardo Bazán, Emilia. 1851–1920

Unamuno y Jugo, Miguel de. 1864–
1936

Benavente, Jacinto. 1866–1954

Blasco Ibáñez, Vicente. 1867–1928

Baroja y Nessi, Pío. 1872–1956

Machado y Ruiz, Antonio. 1875–
1939

Pérez de Ayala, Ramon. 1880–1962

Jiménez, Juan Ramón. 1881–1958

Salinas, Pedro. 1891–1951

Guillén, Jorge. 1893–

Barea, Arturo. 1897–1957

Alonso, Dámaso. 1898–

García Lorca, Federico. 1899–
1936

Alberti, Rafael. 1902–

Sender, Ramón J. 1902–1982

Hernández, Miguel. 1910–1942

Cela, Camilo José. 1916–

Gironella, José María. 1917–

Goytisolo, Juan. 1931–

12. Portuguese Literature

Vicente, Gil. 1465?–1537?

Camões, Luís vaz de. 1524?–1580

Machado de Assis, Joaquim Maria.
1839–1908

Quental, Antero de. 1842–1891

Eça de Queiroz, José Maria. 1843–
1900

Cunha, Euclydes da. 1866–1909

Pessoa, Fernando. 1888–1935

Ramos, Graciliano. 1892–1953

Andrade, Mário de. 1893–1945

Freyre, Gilberto de Mello. 1900–

Rosa, João Guimarães. 1908–1967

Queiros, Raquel de. 1910–

Amado, Jorge. 1912–

Ribeiro, Darcy. 1922–

Lispector, Clarice. 1924–1977

Ângelo, Ivan. 1936–

Brandão, Ignácio de Loyola. 1936–

Scliar, Moacyr. 1937–

Lobo Antunes, Antonio. 1942–

Souza, Márcio. 1946–

Ribeiro, João Ubaldo. ?–

Telles, Lygia Fagundes. ?–

13. German and Netherlandic Literature

Ruodlieb. c.1050

Reynard the Fox. 12th century

Hartmann von Aue. c.1160–c.1220

Gottfried von Strassburg. 1170?–
1210?

Wolfram von Eschenbach. 1170?–
1220?

Hadewijch c.1200–1250

The Nibelungenlied. c.1200

Johannes von Saaz. c.1350–c.1414

Brant, Sebastian. 1457?–1521

Sachs, Hans. 1494–1576

Bredero, Gerbrand A. 1580–1617

Grimmelshausen, Hans Jakob Christoffel von. 1620?–1676

Lessing, Gotthold Ephraim. 1729–1781

Herder, Johann Gottfried von. 1744–1803

Goethe, Johann Wolfgang von. 1749–1832

Schiller, Friedrich von. 1759–1805

Hölderlin, Friedrich. 1770–1843

Novalis. 1772–1801

Hoffman, E. T. A. 1776–1822

Kleist, Heinrich von. 1777–1811

Chamisso, Adelbert von. 1781–1838

Grimm, Jacob. 1785–1863

Grimm, Wilhelm. 1786–1859

Eichendorff, Joseph, Freiherr von. 1788–1857

Grillparzer, Franz. 1791–1872

Heine, Heinrich. 1797–1856

Büchner, Georg. 1813–1837

Hebbel, Friedrich. 1813–1863

Fontane, Theodor. 1819–1898

Keller, Gottfried. 1819–1890

Multatuli. 1820–1887

Emants, Marcellus. 1848–1923

Revius, Jacobus. 1856–1658

Eeden, Frederick van. 1860–1932

Hauptmann, Gerhart. 1862–1946

Schnitzler, Arthur. 1862–1931

Wedekind, Frank. 1864–1918

George, Stefan. 1868–1933

Mann, Heinrich. 1871–1950

Hofmannsthal, Hugo von. 1874–1929

Mann, Thomas. 1875–1955

Rilke, Rainer Maria. 1875–1926

Schendel, Arthur van. 1876–1946

Hesse, Hermann. 1877–1962

Döblin, Alfred. 1878–1957

Kaiser, Georg. 1878–1945

Musil, Robert. 1880–1942

Zweig, Stefan. 1881–1942

Elsschot, Willem. 1882–1960

Kafka, Franz. 1883–1924

Feuchtwanger, Lion. 1884–1958

Benn, Gottfried. 1886–1956

Broch, Hermann. 1886–1951

Werfel, Franz. 1890–1945

Toller, Ernst. 1893–1939

Jünger, Ernst. 1895–

Ostaijen, Paul van. 1896–1928

Brecht, Bertolt. 1898–1956

Remarque, Erich Maria. 1898–1970

Vestdijk, Simon. 1898–1971

Alberts, A. 1905–

Canetti, Elias. 1905–

Frisch, Max. 1911–

Kirst, Hans Hellmut. 1914–

Weiss, Peter. 1916–1982

Böll, Heinrich. 1917–1985

Schierbeek, Bert. 1918–

Borchert, Wolfgang. 1921–1947

Dürrenmatt, Friedrich. 1921–

Wolkers, Jan. 1925–

Grass, Günter. 1927–

Lind, Jakov. 1927–

Mulisch, Harry. 1927–

Ruyslinck, Ward. 1929–

Wolf, Christa. 1929–

Hochhuth, Rolf. 1931–

Johnson, Uwe. 1934–1984

Handke, Peter. 1942–

14. Scandinavian Literature

Sturluson, Snorri. 1179–1241

The Poetic Edda. 12th or 13th century

The King's Mirror (Speculum Regale). 13th century

Völsunga Saga. 13th century

Eyrbyggja Saga. 1230–1280

Laxdaela Saga. c.1250

Njál's Saga. c.1280
Sturlunga Saga. c.1300
Holberg, Ludvig. 1684–1754
Andersen, Hans Christian. 1805–1875
Ibsen, Henrik. 1828–1906
Jacobsen, Jens Peter. 1847–1855
Strindberg, August. 1849–1912
Lagerlöf, Selma. 1858–1940
Hamsun. Knut. 1859–1952
Nexö, Martin Andersen. 1869–1954
Jensen, Johannes V. 1873–1950
Rölvaag, Ole Edvart. 1876–1931
Sandel, Cora. 1880–1974
Sigurjónsson, Jóhann. 1880–1919
Undset, Sigrid. 1882–1949
Dinesen, Isak. 1885–1962
Sillanpää, Frans Eemil. 1888–1964
Gunnarsson, Gunnar. 1889–1975
Thórdarson, Thorbergur. c.1889–1974
Lagerkvist, Pär. 1891–1974
Olsson, Hagar. 1893–1978
Bengtsson, Frans Gunnar. 1894–1954
Paludan, Jacob. 1896–
Vesaas, Tarjei. 1897–1970
Moberg, Vilhelm. 1898–1973
Munk, Kaj. 1898–1944
Boye, Karin. 1900–1941
Heinesen, William. 1900–
Johnson, Eyvind. 1900–1976
Laxness, Halldór Kiljan. 1902–
Branner, Hans Christian. 1903–1966
Ekelöf, Gunnar. 1907–1968
Waltari, Mika Toimi. 1908–1979
Hansen, Martin A. 1909–1955
Hauge, Alfred. 1915–
Bjørneboe, Jens. 1920–1976
Stigen, Terje. 1922–
Andersen, Benny. 1929–

Brandt, Jørgen Gustava. 1929–
Rifbjerg, Klaus. 1931–
Tranströmer, Tomas. 1931–
Gustafsson, Lars. 1936–
Saarikoski, Pentti. 1937–

15. Russian Literature

Karamzin, Nikolai. 1766–1826
Krylov, Ivan. 1769–1844
Aksakov, Sergei. 1791–1859
Pushkin, Aleksandr. 1799–1837
Gogol, Nikolai. 1809–1852
Goncharov, Ivan. 1812–1891
Herzen, Aleksandr. 1812–1870
Lermontov, Mikhail. 1814–1841
Turgenev, Ivan. 1818–1883
Pisemsky, Aleksei. 1820–1881
Dostoevsky, Fedor. 1821–1881
Nekrasov, Nikolai. 1821–1878
Ostrovsky, Aleksandr. 1823–1886
Saltykov-Shchedrin, Mikhail. 1826–1889
Chernyshevsky, Nikolai. 1828–1889
Tolstoy, Leo. 1828–1910
Leskov, Nikolai. 1831–1895
Korolenko, Vladimir. 1853–1921
Garshin, Vsevolod. 1855–1888
Chekhov, Anton. 1860–1904
Sologub, Fedor. 1863–1927
Gorky, Maxim. 1868–1936
Bunin, Ivan. 1870–1953
Kuprin, Aleksandr. 1870–1938
Andreyev, Leonid. 1871–1919
Prishvin, Mikhail. 1873–1954
Kuzmin, Mikhail. 1875–1936
Remizov, Aleksei. 1877–1957
Bely, Andrei. 1880–1934
Blok, Aleksandr. 1880–1921
Gladkov, Fyodor. 1883–1958
Tolstoy, Alexey Nikolaevich. 1883–1945
Zamyatin, Yevgeny. 1884–1937

Khlebnikov, Velimir. 1885–1922
Akhmatova, Anna. 1889–1966
Pasternak, Boris. 1890–1960
Bulgakov, Mikhail. 1891–1940
Ehrenburg, Ilya. 1891–1967
Furmanov, Dmitry. 1891–1926
Mandelstam, Osip. 1891–1938
Fedin, Konstantin. 1892–1977
Paustovsky, Konstantin. 1892–1968
Tsvetaeva, Marina. 1892–1941
Mayakovsky, Vladimir. 1893–1930
Babel, Issac. 1894–1941
Pilnyak, Boris. 1894–1937?
Tynyanov, Yury. 1894–1943
Esenin, Sergei. 1895–1925
Ivanov, Vsevolod. 1895–1963
Zoshchenko, Mikhail. 1895–1958
Ilf, Ilya. 1897–1937
Kataev, Valentin. 1897–
Leonov, Leonid. 1899–
Nabokov, Vladimir. 1899–1977
Olesha, Yury. 1899–1960
Platonov, Andrei. 1899–1951
Kaverin, Veniamin. 1902–
Petrov, Evgeny. 1903–1942
Ostrovsky, Nikolai. 1904–1936
Panova, Vera. 1905–1973
Sholokhov, Mikhail. 1905–1984
Grekova, Irina. 1907–
Shalamov, Varlam. 1907–1982
Simonov, Konstantin. 1915–1979
Solzhenitsyn, Aleksandr. 1918–
Soloukhin, Vladimir. 1924–
Sinyavsky, Andrei. 1925–
Strugatsky, Arkady. 1925–
Trifonov, Yury. 1925–1981
Aitmatov, Chingiz. 1928–
Iskander, Fazil. 1929–
Shukshin, Vasily. 1929–1974
Aksyonov, Vassily. 1932–
Voinovich, Vladimir. 1932–

Strugatsky, Boris. 1933–
Voznesensky, Andrei. 1933–
Yevtushenko, Yevgeny. 1933–
Brodsky, Joseph. 1940–

16. East European Literatures
Pasek, Jan Chryzostom. 1630–1701
Donelaitis, Kristijonas. 1714–1780
Fredro, Alexander. 1793–1876
Mickiewicz, Adam Bernard. 1798–
   1855
Krasiński, Zygmunt. 1812–1859
Njegoš, Petar Petrović. 1813–1851
Ševčenko, Taras. 1814–1861
Kuliš, Pantelejmon. 1819–1897
Madách, Imre. 1823–1864
Petöfi, Sándor. 1823–1849
Jókai, Mór. 1825–1904
Baranauskas, Antanas. 1835–1902
Prus, Bolesław. 1845–1912
Sienkiewicz, Henryk. 1846–1916
Eminescu, Mihail. 1850–1889
Vazov, Ivan. 1850–1921
Franko, Ivan. 1856–1916
Ukrajinka, Lesja. 1871–1913
Dučić, Jovan. 1874–1943
Ady, Endre. 1877–1919
Pelin, Elin. 1877–1949
Moricz, Szigmond. 1879–1942
Arghezi, Tudor. 1880–1967
Sadoveanu, Mihail. 1880–1961
Yovkov, Yordan. 1880–1937
Krėvė, Vincas. 1882–1954
Hašek, Jaroslav. 1883–1923
Under, Marie. 1883–
Lukács, György. 1885–1971
Rebreanu, Liviu. 1885–1944
Witkiewicz, Stanisław Ignacy.
   1885–1939
Čapek, Karel. 1890–1938
Andrić, Ivo. 1892–1975
Kuliš, Mykola. 1892–1942

Krleža, Miroslav. 1893–1981
Tuwim, Julian. 1894–1953
Parandowski, Jan. 1895–1978
Lengyel, Jozsef. 1896–1975
Németh, László. 1901–1975
Pidmohylny, Valerian. 1901–1941
Seifert, Jaroslav. 1901–1986
Illyés, Gyula. 1902–1983
Stancu, Zaharia. 1902–1974
Gombrowicz, Witold. 1904–1969
József, Attila. 1905–1937
Gliauda, Jurgis. 1906–
Vaičiulaitis, Antanas. 1906–
Eliade, Mircea. 1907–
Kangro, Bernard. 1910–
Djilas, Milovan. 1911–
Miłosz, Czesław. 1911–
Dygat, Stanislaw. 1914–
Hrabal, Bohumil. 1914–
Rannit, Aleksis. 1914–1985
Honchar, Oleksander. 1918–
Herling, Gustaw. 1919–
Mňačko, Ladislav. 1919–
Ćosić, Dobrica. 1921–
Lem, Stanisław. 1921–
Różewicz, Tadeusz. 1921–
Białoszewski, Tadeusz. 1922–1984
Borowski, Tadeusz. 1922–1951
Popa, Vasko. 1922–
Holub, Miroslav. 1923–
Bykaŭ, Vasil. 1924–
Dumitriu, Petru. 1924–
Landsbergis, Algirdas. 1924–
Škvorecký, Josef. 1924–
Konwicki, Tadeusz. 1926–
Vaculík, Ludvík. 1926–
Juhász, Ferenc. 1928–
Kohout, Pavel. 1928–
Mihalić, Slavko. 1928–
Pavlović, Miodrag. 1928–
Kundera, Milan. 1929–

Mrożek, Sławomir. 1930–
Hlasko, Marek. 1934–1969
Kiš, Danilo. 1935–
Havel, Václav. 1936–
Kadare, Ismail. 1936–

17. Yiddish Literature
Jacob ben Isaac of Janow. d.1620?
Gluckel of Hameln. 1645–1724
Nahman of Bratslav. 1772–1811
Zunser, Eliakum. 1835–1913
Mendele Moykher Sforim. 1836–
   1917
Linetski, Isaac Joel. 1839–1915
Peretz, Yitskhok Leybush. 1852–
   1915
Sholom Aleichem. 1859–1916
Cahan, Abraham. 1860–1951
Rosenfeld, Morris. 1862–1923
Ansky, S. 1863–1920
Pinsky, David. 1872–1959
Shapiro, Lamed. 1878–1948
Blinkin, Meir. 1879–1915
Asch, Sholem. 1880–1957
Bergelson, David. 1884–1952
Halpern, Moyshe-Leyb. 1886–1932
Opatoshu, Joseph. 1886–1954
Kreitman, Esther. 1891–1954
Singer, I. J. 1893–1944
Glatstein, Jacob. 1896–1971
Korn, Rokhl. 1898–1982
Rabon, Israel. 1900–1941
Singer, I. B. 1904–
Tsanin, Mordecai. 1906–
Grade, Chaim. 1910–1982
Bryks, Rachmil. 1912–1964
Sutzkever, Abraham. 1913–

18. Hebrew Literature
Ahad Ha-am. 1856–1927
Berdichevsky, Micha Joseph. 1865–
   1921

Bialik, Hayyim Nachman. 1873–1934

Feierberg, Mordecai Zeeb. 1874–1899

Tchernichovski, Saul. 1875–1943

Brenner, Joseph Hayyim. 1881–1921

Agnon, Samuel Joseph. 1888–1970

Barash, Asher. 1889–1952

Hazaz, Haim. 1898–1973

Goldberg, Leah. 1911–1970

Gilboa, Amir. 1917–

Tammuz, Benjamin. 1919–

Megged, Aharon. 1920–

Shamir, Moshe. 1921–

Amichai, Yehuda. 1924–

Kishon, Ephraim. 1924–

Carmi, T. 1925–

Shaham, Nathan. 1925–

Shahar, David. 1926–

Bartov, Hanoch. 1928–

Kaniuk, Yoram. 1930–

Pagis, Dan. 1930–

Zach, Nathan. 1930–

Appelfeld, Aaron. 1932–

Yehoshua, A. B. 1936–

Oz, Amos. 1939–

19. Spanish American Literature

Cruz, Sor Juana Ines de la. 1648–1695

Sarmiento, Domingo Faustino. 1811–1888

Hernández, José. 1834–1866

Martí, José. 1853–1895

Darío, Rubén. 1867–1916

Azuela, Mariano. 1873–1952

DeLisser, Herbert. 1878–1944

Quiroga, Horacio. 1878–1937

Rivera, José Eustasio. 1888–1928

Mistral, Gabriela. 1889–1957

McKay, Claude. 1890–1948

Vallejo, César. 1892–1938

Huidobro, Vicente. 1893–1948

Asturias, Miguel Angel. 1899–1974

Borges, Jorge Luis. 1899–1986

Arlt, Roberto. 1900–1942

Gorostiza, José. 1901–1973

Guillén, Nicolás. 1902–

Mallea, Eduardo. 1903–

Carpentier, Alejo. 1904–1980

Neruda, Pablo. 1904–1973

Yáñez, Agustin. 1904–1980

Mais, Roger. 1905–1955

Roumain, Jacques. 1907–1944

Mittelholzer, Edgar. 1909–1965

Onetti, Juan Carlos. 1909–

Arguedas, Jose Maria. 1911–1969

Gomes, Albert M. 1911–1978

Sábato, Ernesto. 1911–

Reid, V. S. 1913–

Bioy Casares, Adolfo. 1914–

Cortázar, Julio. 1914–1984

Parra, Nicanor. 1914–

Paz, Octavio. 1914–

Arreola, Juan José. 1918–

Rulfo, Juan. 1918–1986

Marqués, René. 1919–1979

Garro, Elena. 1920–

Harris, Wilson. 1921–

Selvon, Samuel. 1923–

Carballido, Emilio. 1925–

Cardenal, Ernesto. 1925–

Donoso, José. 1925–

Wolff, Egon. 1926–

Lamming, George. 1927–

García Márquez, Gabriel. 1928–

Salkey, Andrew. 1928–

Cabrera Infante, Guillermo. 1929–

Fuentes, Carlos. 1929–

Lihn, Enrique. 1929–

Brathwaite, Edward Kamau. 1930–

Walcott, Derek. 1930–

Anthony, Michael. 1932–
Naipaul, V. S. 1932–
Padilla, Heberto. 1932–
Puig, Manuel. 1932–
Vargas Llosa, Mario. 1936–
Valenzuela, Luisa. 1938–
Pacheco, José Emilio. 1939–
Aridjis, Homero, 1940–
Skármeta, Antonio. 1940–
Arenas, Reinaldo. 1943–
Dorfman, Ariel. 1943–
Goldemberg, Isaac. 1945–

20. African Literature
Paton, Alan. 1903–
Senghor, Léopold Sédar. 1906–
Abrahams, Peter. 1919–
Mphahlele, Ezekiel. 1919–
Tutuola, Amos. 1920–
Ekwensi, Cyprian. 1921–
Gordimer, Nadine. 1923–
Ousmane, Sembène. 1923–
Laye, Camara. 1928–1980
Bâ, Mariama. 1929–1981
Oyono, Ferdinand. 1929–
Achebe, Chinua. 1930–
Nwapa, Flora. 1931–
Beti, Mongo. 1932–
Okigbo, Christopher. 1932–1967
Soyinka, Wole. 1934–
Awoonor, Kofi. 1935–
Head, Bessie. 1937–1986
Ngugi Wa Thiong'o. 1938–
Armah, Aki Kwei. 1939–
Coetzee, J. M. 1940–
Omotoso, Kole. 1943–
Emecheta, Buchi. 1944–

21. Middle Eastern Literature
Firdawsī. c.934–c.1020
Omar Khayyam. c.1021–1122

Niẓāmī, Ganjavī. c.1141–1209
'Aṭṭār, Farīd al-Dīn. 1142–c.1229
Rūmī, Jalāl al-Dīn. 1207–1273
David of Sassoun. Late medieval
  period
Kouchag, Nahabed. d.1592
Baronian, Hagop. 1842–1891
Shirvanzadeh. 1858-1935
Zohrab, Krikor. 1861–1915
Odian, Yervant. 1869–1926
Issahakian, Avedick. 1875–1957
Tekeyan, Vahan. 1878–1948
Yessayan, Zabel. 1878–1943
Jubran, Khalil. 1883–1931
Edip, Halide. 1884–1964
Zarian, Gostan. 1885–1969
Charents, Eghishe. 1897–1937
al-Hakim, Tawfiq. 1902–1976?
Hikmet, Nazim. 1902–1963
Hidāyat, Ṣādiq. 1903–1951
'Alavī, Bezorg. 1907–
Antreassian, Antranig. 1908–
Maḥfūẓ, 'Najīb. 1911–
Zaroukian, Antranik. 1913–
Dağlarca, Fazil Hüsnü. 1914–
Anday, Melih Cevdat. 1915–
Nesin, Aziz. 1915–
Gaboudigian, Sylva. 1920–
Kemal, Yaşar. 1922–
Idrīs, Yūsuf. 1927–
Salih, Al-Tayib. 1929–
Adonis. 1930–
Farrokhzad, Forough. 1935–1967
Kanafani, Ghassan. 1936–1972
Ibrahim, Sanallah. 1937–
Behrangi, Samad. 1939–1968

22. The Literature of the Indian Subcontinent
Kālidāsa. 376–c.454?
Ghalib, Mirza Asadullah Khan.
  1797–1869

Tagore, Sir Rabindranath. 1861–1941

Iqbal, Sir Muhammad. c.1873–1939

Premchand. 1880–1936

Narayan, R. K. 1906–

Pillai, Thakazhi Sivasankara. 1914–

Jhabvala, Ruth Prawer. 1927–

Desai, Anita. 1937–

Nirala. ?–1961

23. Chinese Literature

The Book of Songs (Shih Ching)

Ch'ü Yüan. 343?–278 B.C.

Ts'ao Chih. 192–232

Juan Chi. 210–263

T'ao Ch'ien. 365–427

Hsiao Kang. 505–555

Meng Hao-jan. 689–740

Han Shan. fl. early 8th century?

Li Po. 701–762

Wang Wei. 701–761

Kao Shih. 702?–765

Tu Fu. 719–770

Han Yü. 768–824

Po Chü-yi. 772–846

Liu Tsung-yüan. 773–819

Li Ho. 791–817

Li Shang-yin. 813–858

Wei Chuang. 836–910

Mei Yao-ch'en. 1002–1060

Ou-Yang hsiu. 1007–1072

Su Tung-p'o. 1037–1101

Li Ch'ing-chao. 1084–c.1151

Yang Wan-li. 1124–1206

Lu Yu. 1125–1210

Fan Ch'eng-ta. 1126–1193

Chiang K'uei. 1155?–1235?

Wang Shih-fu. fl. 13th century

Kuan Han-ch'ing. c.1220–c.1300

Lo Kuan-chung. c.1330–1400

Kao Ch'i. 1336–1374

Shih Nai-an. fl. before 1400

Wu Ch'eng-en. 1500–1582

Wang Shih-cheng. 1526–1590

T'ang Hsien-tzu. 1550–1617

Feng Meng-lung. 1574–1646

Li Yü. 1611–1680

Ts'ao Hsüeh-ch'in. 1715–1763

Liu T'ieh-yün. 1857–1909

Lu Hsün. 1881–1936

Hu Shih. 1891–1962

Mao Tse-tung. 1893–1976

Lin Yutang. 1895–1976

Mao Tun. 1896–1981

Lao She. 1899–1966

Rou Shi. 1901–1931

Pa Chin. 1904–

Ting Ling. 1904–1986

Ai Ch'ing. 1910–

Ts'ao Yü. 1910–

Ch'ien Chung-shu. 1911–

Hsiao Hung. 1911–1941

Chen Jo-hsi, 1938–

24. Japanese Literature

Ki Tsurayuki. d.945 or 946

The Mother of Fujiwara Michitsuna. d.955

Sei Shōnagon. fl. late 10th century

Izumi Skikibu. fl. c.1000

Murasaki Shikibu. fl. c.1000

Nijō, Lady. late 13th–early 14th century

Kenkō Yoshida. c.1283–c.1352

Ihara Saikaku. 1642–1693

Bashō. 1644–1694

Chikamatsu Monzaemon. 1653–1724

Yosa Buson. 1716–1784

Ueda Akinari. 1734–1809

Kobayashi Issa. 1763–1827

Mori Ōgai. 1862–1922

Futabatei Shimei. 1864–1909
Natsume Sōseki. 1867–1916
Higuchi Ichiyō. 1872–1896
Shimazaki Tōson. 1872–1943
Nagai Kafū. 1879–1959
Shiga Naoya. 1883–1971
Tanizaki Jun'ichirō. 1886–1965
Kawabata Yasunari. 1889–1972
Akutagawa Ryūnosuke. 1892–1927
Ibuse Masuji. 1898–

Enchi Fukimo. 1905–
Dazai Osamu. 1909–1948
Endō Shūsaku. 1923–
Abe Kōbō. 1924–
Mishima Yukio. 1925–1970
Ariyoshi Sawako. 1931–
Ōe Kenzaburō. 1935–

25. Southeast Asian and Korean Literature

Introduction

This volume of the thirteenth edition of *The Reader's Adviser* appears approximately ten years after the twelfth edition, which was published in 1977. Although somewhat longer than the twelfth edition, it is still attempting the almost impossible feat of accounting for the history of English and American drama as well as all of world literature in a single volume. The ground rules of the previous edition have been followed in concentrating on books that are in print and in English.

Only four of the previous contributors appear again in this volume: David Bady, Henryk Baran, Glenderlyn Johnson, and Carole Slade. We have tried not only to bring all entries up to date, but also to make the volume more comprehensive and to address ourselves to the needs of students and librarians as well as the general reader. One could, for example, begin the study of a subject like Portuguese literature by consulting the chapter in this volume. As general editor of this volume, I have been impressed by the passionate intensity of experts writing on their subjects.

This volume is organized somewhat differently from the twelfth edition. More space is devoted to British Drama and to Shakespeare, with an appeal to more advanced students. In the sections on modern British and American drama, one will find up-to-the-minute information on popular playwrights whose plays are being performed in the theater.

The introduction to "World Literature" is much longer than its predecessor, and it addresses itself to the question of what is comparative literature. The French literature section is somewhat shorter than it was in the twelfth edition, partly because Canadian, African, and Caribbean literature in French has been separated out. In general, this volume has a much stronger ethnic consciousness than the previous edition: Portuguese literature now has its own section, Netherlandic literature has been included with German, where it logically belongs, but Yiddish literature is now a separate chapter immediately preceding Hebrew. The East European literatures are included together in a special section rather than in the catch-all category of "other European literature." African literature is considerably expanded, as is Middle Eastern literature. Asian literature, a single chapter in the last edition, has now doubled in size and is divided into four separate chapters: "The Literature of the Indian Subcontinent," "Chinese Literature," "Japanese Literature," and "Southeast Asian and Korean Literature." This brief rundown of chapters should indicate that the divisions are more practicable than those in the twelfth edition, with much more attention being devoted to the literatures of emerging Third World countries.

Following a general cultural trend, the thirteenth edition of *The Reader's Adviser* is oriented more to the practical use of readers and researchers. It is user-friendly. If our intentions have been successful, the thirteenth edition should be accurate, helpful, and stimulating for students, general readers, book lovers who enjoy browsing in libraries, and for all those whose intellectual curiosity is insatiable.

Maurice Charney

The Reader's Adviser

CHAPTER 1

The Drama

David Bady

Stage-Director: Do you know who was the father of the dramatist?
Playgoer: No, I do not know, but I suppose he was the dramatic poet.
Stage-Director: You are wrong. The father of the dramatist was the
dancer. . . . The first dramatists were children of the theatre.
—E. GORDON CRAIG, *The Art of the Theatre*

What a reader wants, of course, is great plays. There is no shortage of masterpieces—but that can be a problem. Drama has had many "golden ages" in many places: in classical Athens; in late sixteenth- and early seventeenth-century England and Spain; in the France of Louis XIV; in the German states at the end of the eighteenth century; and, 100 years later, in a number of improbable corners of Europe—Norway, Sweden, czarist Russia, and Ireland. A serious reader following the migrations of Dionysus will have to make at least another half-dozen stopovers, from Plautus's Rome to Brecht's Berlin and Beckett's Paris. Until fairly recently, the itinerary was too intimidating for many, who found themselves at the mercy of hard-to-locate editions of outdated translations.

The modern drama anthology—usually a softcover college text—has changed all that. The books listed in the Anthologies of Plays section of this chapter gather great handfuls of international plays, in recent English versions, many of which have made themselves standard—the Sophocles of Fitts and Fitzgerald, Richard Wilbur's Molière, Reinhart's (or Fjelde's) Ibsen, Stark Young's Chekhov, Bentley's Brecht. These collections, moreover, impose a shape on their subject. Through the choice of plays, the anthology editor, as much as any scholar or stage producer, has formed the current idea of what the dramatic tradition is. Happily, many of these editors, from Cleanth Brooks and Robert Heilman in the forties to Robert Corrigan and Alvin Kernan today, have been critic-teachers eager to introduce neglected plays to the undergraduate, and to discuss their choices in introductory essays.

It would be hard to overestimate the importance of these humble anthologies. But for that reason, the dependent reader must be wary. Insisting on successful formulas, some publishers work toward the repetition of a narrow selection of plays. The student or teacher will have trouble finding a work of Calderon or Corneille, Schiller or Kleist, in any school anthology. So the national literature chapters of *The Reader's Adviser*, with their lists of individual translations, remain an essential adjunct to the reading of drama.

1

But even the most complete anthology is a document in discontinuity. As we have already noticed, drama flourishes and then vanishes in one country, only to reappear, apparently out of nothing, in another. Literature alone cannot provide the connection. Written drama, for instance, all but disappears from Europe with the fall of Rome. In 500 years, the only new plays are efforts of a nun, Hrotswitha, inspired by the manuscripts in her convent library. Yet before another 500 years have passed, the cities are again filled with drama, new and nonclassical varieties of plays ranging from saints' lives to the magnificent, ungainly polyptychs of the Cycles. Scholars like Hunningher and Hardison (in books listed below) argue the causes of this unexpected renewal. But one credible hypothesis is that while Latin drama died, Latin *theater* did not—that mimes, jongleurs, and folk players maintained through the Dark Ages a tradition of Roman performance, and that this vital art, encountering the first faltering tropes arising from the Christian Mass, produced the burgeoning religious drama of the later Middle Ages.

Again, when the fifteenth- and sixteenth-century humanists strenuously wrote plays in imitation of classical tragedy and comedy, they failed to produce a renaissance of drama. Rebirth waited until their *commedia erudita* had been contaminated with the *commedia dell'arte*, the improvised theater of the actors (which, arguably, carried the virus of ancient comedy). Or until their Senecan tragedy had collided with the romances, histories, and jigs of the popular Elizabethan stage.

Great drama, in other words, seems to come not from playwrights reading other playwrights, but from the meeting of literary impulse and the fertility of theater. The continuous traditions of acting and staging are the matrix of drama, its history and "culture." The anthologies of masterpieces necessarily ignore the theater (which often manages to enjoy its own "golden ages"—for example, in nineteenth-century England—just when written drama seems most moribund). But readers cannot finally understand plays without knowing their medium. They will want to look into the magisterial surveys of theater history by Nicoll and Gassner, the studies of physical theater by Southern and Nagler (and Leacroft's fascinating picturebook), some of the modern appreciations of the *commedia*, and perhaps even the notebooks of directors and sketchbooks of stage designers (noted in the section on "Technique").

Some forceful writers listed under "Theory: Contemporary"—Antonin Artaud, Peter Brook, and Richard Schechner, for example—urge us to go beyond both plays and theater, toward a "performance art" alternately explained as therapy, rite, vision, and community. But readers will find that, in general, the selections of "Theory" and "Criticism" enrich their sense of the creative duality of drama. In collections of historical criticism, for example, they can follow a 2,300-year-long (and ongoing) dialogue, begun by Aristotle, concerning the formal characteristics of tragedy. Entirely different, but complementary, are the immediate responses of the journalist reviewers from Shaw to Tynan, who provide the best description of what actually happens onstage, the life of the theater.

REFERENCE BOOKS

Anderson, Michael, and others. *Crowell's Handbook of Contemporary Drama.* Crowell 1971 $10.00. Dramatic literature (but not theater) since World War II. Long discussions of selected plays.

Bowman, Walter P., and Robert H. Ball. *Theatre Language: A Dictionary.* Theatre Arts 1976 pap. $4.95. A dictionary of some 3,000 terms in English of the drama and stage from medieval to modern times.

Cartmell, Van H., ed. *Plot Outlines of One Hundred Famous Plays.* Peter Smith $10.25

Esslin, Martin, ed. *The Encyclopedia of World Theater.* Scribner 1977 $25.00. Heavily illustrated; short entries.

Gassner, John, ed. *Reader's Encyclopedia of World Drama.* Ed. by Edward Quinn, Crowell 1969 $17.26. Includes an appendix of basic documents in dramatic theory. Illustrated.

Hartnoll, Phyllis, ed. *Concise Oxford Companion to the Theatre.* Oxford 1972 $19.95
————. *Oxford Companion to the Theatre.* Oxford 4th ed. 1983 $49.95. "The most valuable reference tool yet to be published in the theatre world" (*LJ*). The newest edition, which uses an extensive system of cross-references, includes a full bibliography and many illustrations.

Herbert, Ian, ed. *Who's Who in the Theatre.* Gale 2 vols. 17th ed. 1981 vol. 1 $115.00 vol. 2 $85.00 set $200.00. Biographies of living theater personalities. Recent London-New York stage credits, long-run statistics, theater descriptions.

Hochman, Stanley, ed. *McGraw-Hill Encyclopedia of World Drama.* Pref. by Daniel Gerould, McGraw-Hill 5 vols. 2d ed. 1983 $295.00. Entries focus mainly on playwrights.

Kienzle, Siegfried. *Modern World Theatre: A Guide to Productions in Europe and the United States since 1945.* Trans. by Alexander Henderson and Elizabeth Henderson, Ungar 1970 $17.50. Synopses and brief comments on 578 plays.

La Beam, Dennis. *Theatre, Film and Television Biographies Master Index.* Gale 1979 o.p. Index to entries in the standard biographical dictionaries.

Loney, Glenn M. *Twentieth Century Theater.* Facts on File 2 vols. 1983 ea. $60.00. Data on all major and many minor U.S. and British productions since 1900. Has an index and photographs.

Matlaw, Myron. *Modern World Drama: An Encyclopedia.* Dutton 1972 $25.00. Articles on national dramas, playwrights, plays, and technical terms, with an index of characters.

New York Times Directory of the Theater. Intro. by Clive Barnes, Times Bks. 1973 $25.00. Index to theater reviews printed in the *N.Y. Times* from 1920 to 1970.

The New York Times Theatre Reviews, 1920–1980. Times Bks. 13 vols. $1,580.00

Notable Names in the American Theatre. J. T. White 2d ed. 1977 lib. bdg. $69.00. Detailed biographies, with New York production records, theater descriptions, and other useful information.

Rae, Kenneth, and Richard Southern. *An International Vocabulary of Technical Theatre Terms.* Theatre Arts o.p. A total of 637 terms used in the English, U.S., German, Italian, French, Spanish, Dutch, and Swedish theaters.

Shipley, Joseph T. *The Crown Guide to the World's Great Plays: From Ancient Greece to Modern Times.* Crown 1985 $24.95. Contains information on 750 plays: synopsis, production history, cast lists, analysis, and critical opinion. "Invested with scholarship, discernment and relish" (*Christian Science Monitor*).

Sobel, Bernard. *The New Theatre Handbook and Digest of Plays.* Crown 1959 o.p.

Taylor, John R. *The Penguin Dictionary of the Theatre.* *Reference Ser.* Penguin 1966 pap. $6.95

Vaughan, Jack. *Drama A to Z: A Handbook.* Ungar 1978 $11.95 pap. $5.95

Vinson, James, and Daniel Kirkpatrick, eds. *Contemporary Dramatists. Contemporary Writers Ser.* St. Martin's 3d ed. 1982 $55.00. Lists more than 300 playwrights writing in English. Includes biographies, playlists, production data, critical essays, and other relevant material. Supplement on screenwriters, librettists, etc. Appendix of significant writers who have died since 1950. Index of plays.

——. *Great Dramatists. Great Writers of the Eng. Language Ser.* St. Martin's 1979 $50.00. English dramatists of all historical periods.

BIBLIOGRAPHIES AND INDEXES

Adelman, Irving, and Rita Dworkin. *Modern Drama: A Checklist of Critical Literature on 20th-Century Plays.* Scarecrow Pr. 1967 o.p. A guide to critical articles and selections of books, but not reviews.

Baker, Blanche M. *Theatre and Allied Arts.* Ayer repr. of 1953 ed. $43.50. Comprehensive annotated bibliography dealing with all aspects of the theater. Based on *Dramatic Bibliography*, published in 1933, the material has been entirely rewritten and reorganized. Approximately 6,000 volumes published between 1885 and 1950 have been included.

Berquist, G. William, ed. *Three Centuries of English and American Plays: A Checklist—England: 1500–1800; United States: 1714–1830.* Hafner 1963 o.p.

Breed, Paul F., and Florence M. Sniderman. *Dramatic Criticism Index: Bibliography of Commentaries on Playwrights from Ibsen to the Avant Garde.* Gale 1972 $60.00. More than 300 playwrights, most from the twentieth century.

Chicorel Index Series. Amer. Lib. various prices. Vols. 1–3, *Chicorel Theater Index to Plays in Anthologies, Periodicals, Discs and Tapes;* Vol. 3A, *Chicorel Bibliography to the Performing Arts;* Vol. 8, *Chicorel Theater Index to Plays in Periodicals, Discs, and Tapes;* Vol. 9, *Chicorel Theater Index to Plays for Young People;* Vol. 21, *Chicorel Theater Index to Drama Literature.*

Coleman, Arthur, and Gary Tyler. *Drama Criticism.* Ohio Univ. Pr. (Swallow) 1966–70 2 vols. ea. $18.00. Vol. 1, *A Checklist of Interpretation since 1940 of English and American Plays;* Vol. 2, *A Checklist of Interpretation since 1940 of Classical and Continental Plays.*

Connor, John M., and Billie M. Connor. *Ottemiller's Index to Plays in Collections: An Author and Title Index to Plays Appearing in Collections Published between 1900 and Early 1975.* Scarecrow Pr. 6th ed. rev. & enl. 1976 $23.00

Cumulated Dramatic Index, 1909–49. G. K. Hall 2 vols. repr. 1965 $615.00. Cumulates 41 volumes of *Dramatic Index*, an annual subject index to books and articles about drama and theater subjects.

Drury, Francis K. W. *Drury's Guide to Best Plays.* Ed. by James M. Salem, Scarecrow Pr. 3d ed. 1976 $16.00. Provides dates of production or printing, editions, description, plot, and other useful information.

Hunter, Frederick J. *Drama Bibliography: A Short-Title Guide to Extended Reading in Dramatic Art for the English-Speaking Audience and Students in Theatre.* G. K. Hall 1971 $25.00

Index to Full-Length Plays, 1895–1925. Comp. by Ruth G. Thomson, Faxon 1956 lib. bdg. $11.00

Index to Full-Length Plays, 1926–1944. Comp. by Ruth G. Thomson, Faxon 1946 o.p.

Index to Full-Length Plays, 1944–1964. Comp. by Norma O. Ireland, Faxon 1965 o.p.

Index to One-Act Plays, 1900–1924. Comp. by Hannah Logasa and Winifred Ver Nooy, Faxon 1924 o.p. Supplement, 1924–31 (1932) $11.00; Second Supplement,

1932–40 (1941) o.p.; Third Supplement, 1941–48 (1950) o.p.; Fourth Supplement, 1948–57 (1958) $12.00; Fifth Supplement, 1958–64 (1966) $11.00. The index covers 5,000 one-act plays; the 1932 supplement covers 7,000. Indexed by title, author, and subject; states the number of characters in each play. The second supplement includes more than 500 collections, many separate plays from pamphlets and periodicals. The fourth and fifth volumes provide information on characters, setting, background, suitability for school production, etc. The last three supplements are by Hannah Logasa.

Keller, Dean H. *Index to Plays in Periodicals.* Scarecrow Pr. rev. & enl. ed. 1979 $42.50

Litto, Fredric M. *American Dissertations on the Drama and Theatre: A Bibliography.* Kent State Univ. Pr. 1969 $17.00

New York Public Library, Research Libraries. *Bibliographic Guide to Theatre Arts, 1975– .* G. K. Hall annual 1976–to date $55.00. Annual supplement to the NYPL catalog, listing newly entered material.

———. *Catalogue of the Theatre and Drama Collection.* G. K. Hall part 1 (1967) 6 vols. $895.00; part 2 (1967) 9 vols. $720.00; part 3 (1976) 30 vols. $3,485.00; supplement to part 1 (1973) $105.00; supplement to part 2 (1974) 2 vols. $270.00. Entries for editions of more than 120,000 plays, 23,500 volumes of works relating to aspects of theater; 44,000 entries for programs, photographs, clippings, etc.

Palmer, Helen H., and Jane Dyson. *European Drama Criticism, 1900–1975. Drama Explication Ser.* Shoe String 2d ed. 1977 $35.00

Play Index. Wilson 6 vols. 1953–83 ed. by Dorothy H. West and Dorothy M. Peake, vol. 1 1949–52 (1953) $12.00; ed. by Estelle A. Fidell and Dorothy M. Peake, vol. 2, 1953–60 (1963) $17.00; ed. by Estelle A. Fidell, vol. 3, 1961–67 (1968) $20.00; vol. 4, 1968–72 (1973) $25.00; vol. 5, 1973–77 (1978) $33.00; vol. 6, 1978–82 (1983) $40.00. Indexed by author, title, and subject, with cast analysis and publisher.

Salem, James M. *A Guide to Critical Reviews, 1901–1982.* Scarecrow Pr. part 1 (1984) 3d ed. $42.50; part 2 (1967) $9.00; part 3 (1979) 2d ed. $27.50; part 4 (1971) 2 vols. $30.00. Indexes reviews of productions. Part 1, *American Drama, 1901–1982;* Part 2, *The Musical from Rodgers and Hart to Lerner and Loewe;* Part 3, *British and Continental Drama from Ibsen to Pinter;* Part 4, *The Screenplay from the Jazz Singer to Dr. Strangelove.*

Samples, Gordon. *The Drama Scholar's Index to Plays and Filmscripts: A Guide to Plays and Filmscripts in Selected Anthologies, Series and Periodicals.* Scarecrow Pr. 2 vols. 1974–80 ea. $15.00–$32.50. Particularly useful for European sources not listed in other bibliographies.

———. *How to Locate Reviews of Plays and Films: A Bibliography of Criticism from the Beginnings to the Present.* Scarecrow Pr. 1976 $13.00

Stratman, Carl J. *Bibliography of English Printed Tragedy, 1565–1900.* Southern Illinois Univ. Pr. 1966 $17.50

———. *Bibliography of Medieval Drama.* Ungar 1972 $80.00

Vowles, Richard B. *Dramatic Theory: A Bibliography.* NYPL 1956 o.p.

Whalon, Marion K., ed. *Performing Arts Research: A Guide to Information Sources.* Gale 1976 $58.00

YEARBOOKS

The Best Plays of 1894–1983: The Burns Mantle Yearbook of the Theater. Dodd 1920– to date. Consult publisher's catalog for annual volumes and prices. The "ten best plays of the year" produced in New York, represented by a summary of the plot illustrated with dialogue excerpts, together with critical comments. Recent volumes also provide details about all other plays produced in New York, both on- and off-Broadway, with information about regional and festival productions throughout the United States, the London and Continental seasons, "vital statistics of productions, prizes, people, and publications," and a necrology. First published in 1920, the annual was edited until 1948 by Burns Mantle. Successive editors have been John Arthur Chapman, Louis Kronenberger, Henry Hewes, and Otis Guernsey. The series also includes three retrospective volumes, which carry the records back to 1894, where they connect with the last volume (1894) of G. C. Odell's *Annals of the New York Stage.* There are two indexes to *The Best Plays*, both out of print: *Index to the Best Play Series, 1899–1950* and *The Index to the Best Play Series, 1949–1960.*

Theatre World. 1975–to date. Ed. by John Willis, Crown vols. 30–40 vol. 30, 1973–74 (1974) $10.95; vol. 31, 1974–75 (1975) $12.95; vol. 32, 1975–76 (1976) $14.95; vol. 33, 1976–77 (1977) $15.95; vol. 34, 1977–78 (1978) $15.95; vol. 35, 1978–79 (1979) $18.95; vol. 36, 1979–80 (1981) $25.00; vol. 37, 1980–81 (1982) $30.00; vol. 38, 1981–82 (1983) $25.00; vol. 39, 1982–83 (1984) $25.00; vol. 40, 1983–84 (1985) $24.95. *Theatre World* has appeared continuously under various publisher's imprints and titles since 1945. Devoted mainly to credits and photographs of Broadway productions, it also provides off-Broadway, resident, and touring company information.

Theatre Year. Photographs by Donald Cooper, intro. by Michael Coveney, Methuen annual 1983 pap. $11.95. Photographic record of the London theater season, with brief credit lists and an introduction.

ANTHOLOGIES OF PLAYS

Many of these anthologies, following the pioneering example of Brooks' and Heilman's *Understanding Drama*, provide introductions to the reading of plays. Some contain extensive critical and biographical material.

Bain, Carl E., and others, eds. *The Norton Introduction to Literature: Drama.* Norton 3d ed. text ed. 1981 pap. $15.95. Includes Ibsen, *Wild Duck;* Shakespeare, *Hamlet;* Sophocles, *Oedipus Tyrannus;* Pirandello, *Six Characters in Search of an Author;* Bullins, *A Son, Come Home;* Williams, *Glass Menagerie* and *Long Goodbye;* Euripides, *Bacchae;* Wilde, *Importance of Being Earnest;* Chekhov, *Three Sisters.* An introduction to the methods of dramatic criticism.

Barnet, Sylvan, ed. *Eight Great Comedies: Clouds, Mandragola, Twelfth Night, Miser, Beggar's Opera, Importance of Being Earnest, Uncle Vanya, Arms and the Man.* New Amer. Lib. pap. $4.95. Plays by Aristophanes, Machiavelli, Shakespeare, Molière, Gay, Wilde, Chekhov, and Shaw.

———. *Eight Great Tragedies: Prometheus Bound, Oedipus the King, Hippolytus, King Lear, Ghosts, Miss Julie, On Baile's Strand, Desire under the Elms.* New Amer. Lib. pap. $3.50. Plays by Aeschylus, Sophocles, Euripides, Shakespeare, Ibsen, Strindberg, Yeats, and O'Neill.

Barnet, Sylvan, and William Burto. *Types of Drama: Plays and Essays.* Little, Brown 4th ed. text ed. 1984 pap. $17.95. Twenty-one plays—tragedies, comedies, and tragicomedies—including Beckett's *Happy Days*, Fugard's *Master Harold*, Norman's *Night Mother*, and Bergman's *Wild Strawberries*. With additional material on genre theory.

Bentley, Eric, ed. *The Classic Theatre*. Peter Smith 4 vols. $27.75. Vol. 1: *Six Italian Plays*, containing Machiavelli, *The Mandrake*; Beolco, *Ruzzante Returns*; Goldoni, *Servant of Two Masters* and *Mirandolina*; Gozzi, *King Stag*; Anonymous, *The Three Cuckolds*. Vol. 2: *Five German Plays*, containing Goethe, *Egmont*; Schiller, *Don Carlos* and *Mary Stuart*; Kleist, *Penthesilea* and *The Prince of Homburg*. Vol. 3: *Six Spanish Plays*, containing Rojas, *Celestina*; Cervantes, *The Siege of Numantia*; Lope de Vega Carpio, *The Trickster of Seville*; Calderon, *Love after Death* and *Life Is a Dream*. Vol. 4: *Six French Plays*, containing Corneille, *The Cid*; Molière, *Misanthrope*; Racine, *Phaedra*; Le Sage, *Turcaret*; Marivaux, *The False Confessions*; Beaumarchais, *Figaro's Marriage*.

———. *The Dramatic Repertoire*. Applause 2 vols. 1985 pap. ea. $8.95. Vol. 1, *Before Brecht: Four German Plays*; Vol. 2, *Life Is a Dream and Other Spanish Classics*.

———. *From the Modern Repertoire*. Indiana Univ. Pr. 2 vols. $39.95. Contains Becque, *La Parisienne*; Brecht, *The Threepenny Opera*; Büchner, *Danton's Death*; Cocteau, *The Infernal Machine*; Musset, *Fantasio*; Eliot, *Sweeny Agonistes*; Lorca, *The Love of Don Perlimplin*; Schnitzler, *Round Dance*; Sternheim, *The Snob*; Yeats, *A Full Moon in March*; Brecht, *Galileo*; Cummings, *him*; Fergusson, *The King and the Duke*; Giraudoux, *Electra*; Grabbe, *Jest, Irony, and Satire*; MacNeice, *The Dark Tower*; Mirabeau, *The Epidemic*; Obey, *Venus and Adonis*; Ostrovsky, *Easy Money*; Wedekind, *The Marquis of Keith*; Anouilh, *Cecile*; Brecht, *Saint Joan*; Büchner; *Leonce and Lena*; Cocteau, *Intimate Relations*; Musset, *A Door Should Be Either Open or Shut*; Jeffers, *The Cretan Woman*; Pinero, *The Magistrate*; Romains, *Dr. Knock*; Schnitzler, *Anatol*; Zola, *Thérèse Racquin*.

———. *The Modern Theatre*. Peter Smith 6 vols. $63.00. Vol. 1: Büchner, *Woyzeck*; Verga, *Cavalleria Rusticana*; Becque, *Woman of Paris*; Brecht, *Threepenny Opera*; Giraudoux, *Electra*. Vol. 2: Musset, *Fantasio*; Ostrovsky, *Diary of a Scoundrel*; Schnitzler, *La Ronde*; Yeats, *Purgatory*; Brecht, *Mother Courage*. Vol. 3: Gogol, *Gamblers*; Labiche and Marc-Michel, *Italian Straw Hat*; Conrad, *One Day More*; Giraudoux, *Judith*; Anouilh, *Thieves' Carnival*. Vol. 4: Fitch, *Captain Jinks*; Mitchell, *New York Idea*; Wilder, *Pullman Car* and *Hiawatha*; Saroyan, *Man with His Heart in the Highlands*; Burrows, Loesser, and Swerling, *Guys and Dolls*. Vol. 5: Gogol, *The Marriage*; Büchner, *Danton's Death*; Ghelderode, *Escurial*; Anouilh, *Medea*; O'Casey, *Cock-a-Doodle Dandy*. Vol. 6: Musset, *Lorenzaccio*; Wedekind, *Spring's Awakening*; Sternheim, *Underpants*; Beerbohm, *Social Success*; Brecht, *Measures Taken*.

Bermel, Albert. *Six One-Act Farces*. Oracle Pr. 1982 $9.95

Bevington, David. *Medieval Drama*. Houghton Mifflin 1975 text ed. $31.95

Booth, Michael. *Hiss the Villain: Six American and English Melodramas*. Blom 1965 $8.95

Brockett, Oscar G., and Lenyth Brockett. *Plays for the Theatre: An Anthology of World Drama*. Holt 4th ed. text ed. 1984 pap. $17.95

Brockett, Oscar G., and Mark Pape. *World Drama*. Holt text ed. 1984 pap. $18.95

Brooks, Cleanth, and Robert B. Heilman, eds. *Understanding Drama: Twelve Plays*. Irvington 1948 text ed. $38.50. A forerunner of today's teaching anthologies, still one of the best introductions to the critical reading of drama.

Caputi, Anthony, ed. *Modern Drama: Annotated Texts*. *Norton Critical Eds.* text ed. 1966 pap. $11.95. Ibsen, *Wild Duck*; Chekhov, *Three Sisters*; Shaw, *Devil's Disci-*

ple; Strindberg, *Dream Play;* O'Neill, *Desire under the Elms;* Pirandello, *Henry IV.*
Includes biographies, background, and critical information.

Cerf, Bennett. *Twenty-Four Favorite One-Act Plays.* Doubleday 1958 $6.95. The moderns, including Miller, Williams, Inge, Wilder, and O'Neill.

Clark, Barrett H. *World Drama.* Peter Smith 2 vols. $16.00. Vol. 1: Ancient Greece, Rome, India, China, Japan, Medieval Europe, and England; Vol. 2: Italy, Spain, France, Germany, Denmark, Russia, and Norway. Along with the standards, Clark includes some drama rarely found in translation, including works by Chikamatsu, Ruzzante, Goldoni, Alfieri, Calderon, Hugo, Lessing, Holberg, and Ostrovsky.

Clurman, Harold, ed. *Nine Plays of the Modern Theater: Waiting for Godot; The Visit; Tango; The Caucasian Chalk Circle; The Balcony; Rhinoceros; American Buffalo; The Birthday Party; Rosencrantz and Guildenstern Are Dead.* Grove 1981 pap. $11.95

Corrigan, Robert W., and Glenn M. Loney, eds. *Comedy: A Critical Anthology.* Houghton Mifflin text ed. 1971 pap. $17.50. Includes Aristophanes, *Lysistrata;* Shakespeare, *Twelfth Night;* Jonson, *Volpone;* Molière, *Tartuffe;* Sheridan, *School for Scandal;* Wilde, *Importance of Being Earnest;* Chekhov, *Cherry Orchard;* Synge, *Playboy of the Western World;* Shaw, *Misalliance;* Giraudoux, *Madwoman of Chaillot;* Brecht, *Puntila;* Bellow, *Last Analysis.* Theory and criticism, including Bergson, Freud, and Suzanne Langer.

———. *Forms of Drama.* Houghton Mifflin text ed. 1972 pap. $17.50. Includes Sophocles, *Antigone;* Shakespeare, *Othello;* Ibsen, *Ghosts;* Webster, *Duchess of Malfi;* Büchner, *Woyzeck;* Miller, *View from the Bridge;* Molière, *The Miser;* Congreve, *Way of the World;* Shaw, *Arms and the Man;* Plautus, *Menaechmi;* Labiche and Marc-Michel, *Italian Straw Hat;* Jellicoe, *The Knack.*

Dent, Anthony, ed. *International Modern Plays.* Biblio Dist. (Everyman's) repr. of 1950 ed. 1973 pap. $2.50. Includes Čapek, *The Life of the Insects;* Chiarelli, *The Mask and the Face;* Cocteau, *The Infernal Machine;* Hauptmann, *Hannele;* Strindberg, *Miss Julie.*

Dickinson, Thomas H. *Chief Contemporary Dramatists: Second Series.* AMS Pr. repr. of 1921 ed. $47.50

———. *Chief Contemporary Dramatists: Twenty-Two Plays from the Recent Drama of England, Ireland, the U.S., Germany, France, Belgium, Norway, Sweden, and Russia.* AMS Pr. repr. of 1915 ed. $47.50; Richard West repr. of 1915 ed. 1979 $30.00

Gassner, John, ed. *A Treasury of the Theatre.* Simon & Schuster 3 vols. 1951 ea. $24.95. Vol. 1, *Aeschylus to Ostrovsky;* Vol. 2, *Ibsen to Sartre;* Vol. 3, *Wilde to Ionesco.*

———. *Twenty Best European Plays on the American Stage, 1915–1955.* Crown 1957 $22.50

Goldstone, Richard A. *Contexts of the Drama.* McGraw-Hill text ed. 1968 $24.95

Goldstone, Richard A., and A. Lass, eds. *Mentor Book of Short Plays.* New Amer. Lib. (Methuen) pap. $3.95

Hubenka, Lloyd, and Garcia Reloy. *The Design of Drama: An Introduction.* Longman text ed. 1973 pap. $8.95. Extensive introductory materials and exercises. Shakespeare, *Othello;* Sophocles, *Oedipus Rex;* Aristophanes, *Lysistrata;* Ibsen, *A Doll's House;* Strindberg, *The Ghost Sonata;* Rice, *Adding Machine;* Shaw, *Saint Joan;* Anouilh, *The Lark;* Harrison, *Tabernacle;* Bergman, *Seventh Seal.*

Kernan, Alvin B., ed. *Character and Conflict: An Introduction to Drama.* Harcourt 2d ed. text ed. 1969 pap. $15.95. Ibsen, *Hedda Gabler;* Anonymous, *Everyman;* Brecht, *Mother Courage and Her Children;* Wilder, *The Skin of Our Teeth;* Sophocles, *Antig-*

one; Strindberg, *The Stronger;* Chekhov, *The Cherry Orchard;* Synge, *Riders to the Sea;* Molière, *The Misanthrope;* Giraudoux, *Tiger at the Gates;* Arrabal, *Picnic on the Battlefield.* Excellent critical discussions accompany the first six plays.

————. *Classics of the Modern Theater: Realism and After.* Harcourt text ed. 1965 pap. $15.95. Ibsen, *Ghosts;* Strindberg, *The Father;* Chekhov, *The Cherry Orchard;* Shaw, *Arms and the Man;* Pirandello, *Six Characters in Search of an Author;* Strindberg, *The Ghost Sonata;* Lorca, *Blood Wedding;* Brecht, *Mother Courage and Her Children;* Betti, *Corruption in the Palace of Justice;* Ionesco, *The Chairs;* Albee, *The Zoo Story.*

Kriegel, Harriet, ed. *Women in Drama: An Anthology.* New Amer. Lib. (Methuen) 1975 pap. $4.95. Euripides, *Medea;* Aristophanes, *Lysistrata;* Middleton, *Women Beware Women;* Ibsen, *Lady from the Sea;* Strindberg, *Miss Julie;* Shaw, *Mrs. Warren's Profession;* Glaspell, *Trifles;* Terry, *Approaching Simone.*

Levin, Richard. *Tragedy: Plays, Theory and Criticism.* Harcourt text ed. 1960 pap. $10.95. Sophocles, *Oedipus Rex;* Shakespeare, *Othello;* Ibsen, *Ghosts;* O'Neill, *The Hairy Ape.* With sources, critical and theoretical essays.

Miller, Jordan Y. *Heath Introduction to Drama.* Heath 2d ed. 1984 pap. $7.95

Moon, Samuel, ed. *One Act: Eleven Short Plays of the Modern Theatre.* Peter Smith $10.25. Strindberg, Yeats, Pirandello, Wilder, Saroyan, Williams, O'Casey, Anouilh, MacLeish, Miller, and Ionesco.

Perrine, Laurence. *Dimensions of Drama.* Harcourt text ed. 1973 pap. $15.95. Strindberg, *The Stronger;* Chekhov, *The Brute;* Anonymous, *Everyman;* Ibsen, *Enemy of the People;* Lorca, *Blood Wedding;* Shakespeare, *Othello;* Molière, *The Misanthrope;* Shaw, *Candida;* Williams, *Glass Menagerie;* Miller, *Death of a Salesman.* With elaborate study materials.

Plays for a New Theater: Playbook 2. New Directions 1966 $7.50 pap. $2.95. Plays by Corrado Alvaro, Yvan Goll, John Hawkes, Robert Hivnor, and Boris Vian.

Reinert, Otto, and Peter Arnott, eds. *Thirteen Plays: An Introduction.* Little, Brown text ed. 1978 pap. $13.95. Shakespeare, *Hamlet;* Molière, *Tartuffe;* Sophocles, *Oedipus Rex;* Ibsen, *A Doll's House;* Chekhov, *Cherry Orchard;* Shaw, *Major Barbara;* Strindberg, *The Ghost Sonata;* Pirandello, *Six Characters in Search of an Author;* Miller, *Death of a Salesman;* Beckett, *Act without Words II;* Pinter, *Dumbwaiter;* Albee, *Virginia Woolf;* Baraka, *Dutchman.*

————. *Twenty-Three Plays: An Introductory Anthology.* Little, Brown text ed. 1978 pap. $16.95. Adds to the playlist of *Thirteen Plays:* Anonymous, *Everyman;* Racine, *Phaedra;* Etherege, *The Man of Mode;* Gilbert, *Trial by Jury;* Wilde, *The Importance of Being Earnest;* Synge, *Riders to the Sea;* Yeats, *Purgatory;* O'Neill, *Ah, Wilderness;* Brecht, *The Caucasian Chalk Circle;* Weiss, *Marat/Sade.*

Richards, Stanley, ed. *The Best Short Plays.* 1971–to date. *Best Short Plays Ser.* Chilton annual ea. $7.95–$12.95

————. *Twenty One-Act Plays: An Anthology for Amateur Performing Groups.* Doubleday 1978 $9.95

Six Great Modern Plays. Dell 1964 pap. $2.95. Chekhov, *Three Sisters;* Ibsen, *The Master Builder;* Shaw, *Mrs. Warren's Profession;* O'Casey, *Red Roses for Me;* Miller, *All My Sons;* Williams, *The Glass Menagerie.*

Sullivan, Victoria, and James Hatch, eds. *Plays by and about Women.* Random (Vintage) pap. $5.95. Includes Gerstenberg, *Overtones;* Hellman, *Children's Hour;* Boothe, *The Women;* Lessing, *Play with a Tiger;* Terry, *Calm Down Mother;* Ginzburg, *The Advertisement;* Duffy, *Rites;* Childress, *Wine in the Wilderness.*

Wandor, Michelene, ed. *Plays by Women.* Methuen 4 vols. 1982–85 pap. ea. $8.50–$8.95. Vol. 1: Churchill, *Vinegar Tom;* Gems, *Dusa, Fish, Stas and Vi;* Page, *Tis-*

sue; Wandor, *Aurora Leigh.* Vol. 2: Luckman, *Trafford Tanzi;* Goldenberg, *Letters Home;* Duffy, *Rites;* Wymark, *Find Me.* Vol. 3: Gems, *Aunt Mary;* Horsfield, *Red Devils;* Pollock, *Blood Relations;* Wakefield and others, *Time Pieces.* Vol. 4: Churchill, *Objections to Sex and Violence;* Dayley, *Rose's Story;* Lochhead, *Blood and Ice;* Lyssa, *Pinball.* Each play has an afterword by its author.

Warnock, Robert. *Representative Modern Plays: Ibsen to Tennessee Williams.* Scott, Foresman 1964 pap. $9.95. Ibsen, *Master Builder;* Strindberg, *Miss Julie;* Chekhov, *The Seagull;* Shaw, *Doctor's Dilemma;* Synge, *Riders to the Sea;* O'Casey, *Juno and the Paycock;* O'Neill, *Desire under the Elms;* Maugham, *Constant Wife;* Behrman, *Biography;* Williams, *The Glass Menagerie;* Fry, *A Phoenix Too Frequent.*

Watson, E. Bradlee, and Benfield Pressey, eds. *Contemporary Drama: Eleven Plays.* Scribner text ed. 1956 pap. $16.95. Plays by Shaw, Connelly, Wilder, Coward, Saroyan, Anouilh, Williams, Giraudoux, Hellman, Miller, and Fry.

———. *Contemporary Drama: Fifteen Plays.* Scribner text ed. 1959 pap. $16.95. Plays by Ibsen, Wilde, Chekhov, Strindberg, Shaw, Synge, Pirandello, O'Neill, Lorca, Eliot, O'Casey, Wilder, Inge, Miller, and Frings.

Weiss, Samuel A., ed. *Drama in the Modern World.* Heath text ed. 1974 pap. $12.95. Fourteen plays, including Giraudoux's *Ondine;* Brecht's *Good Woman of Setzuan;* and Alexei's *It Happened in Irkutsk.*

DRAMA AND THEATER HISTORY

This section includes general surveys of theater history, as well as discussions of the origins of dramatic performance. Since the major periods of theater art are identified with particular national literatures, the reader must refer to other chapters of this volume for studies of the Elizabethan and Jacobean stage in England, the Spanish Golden Age, the neoclassic drama of France, and German and French romantic plays. However, the reader will find listed here some guides to international moments and movements—classical and medieval drama, modern drama, and the popular performance tradition.

Barranger, Milly S. *Theatre Past and Present: An Introduction.* Wadsworth text ed. 1984 pap. An unusually complete and well-designed introductory textbook.

Beaumont, Cyril W. *History of Harlequin.* Ayer repr. of 1926 ed. 1967 $18.00

Bentley, Eric. *The Playwright as Thinker.* Harcourt 1967 pap. $6.95. A foundation of the criticism of modern European drama. Traces the development of realism and expressionism, Wagnerism and Ibsenism, modern tragedy and comedy.

Bieber, Margaret. *History of the Greek and Roman Theater.* Princeton Univ. Pr. rev. ed. 1980 $60.00 pap. $17.50

Brockett, Oscar G. *History of the Theatre.* Allyn & Bacon 4th ed. text ed. 1981 $37.14

Brockett, Oscar G., and R. Findlay. *Century of Innovation: A History of European and American Theatre and Drama, 1870–1970.* Theater and Drama Ser. Prentice-Hall 1973 $37.95

Chambers, E. K. *The Medieval Stage.* Oxford (Clarendon) 2 vols. 1903 o.p.

Cheney, Sheldon. *Stage Decoration.* Ayer repr. of 1928 ed. 1967 $20.00. Development from ancient Athens to the twentieth century.

———. *The Theatre: Three Thousand Years of Drama, Acting and Stagecraft.* 1903. McKay new ed. 1972 o.p.

Driver, Tom F. *Romantic Quest and Modern Query: A History of the Modern Theatre.* Univ. Pr. of Amer. repr. of 1970 ed. 1980 lib. bdg. $23.50 text ed. pap. $12.95

Duchartre, Pierre L. *The Italian Comedy*. Trans. by Randolph T. Weaver, Dover repr. of 1925 ed. 1966 pap. $7.95. The nature and influence of the *commedia dell'arte*, the improvised theater of the Renaissance.

Else, Gerald F. *The Origin and Early Form of Greek Tragedy*. Harvard Univ. Pr. 1965 $3.75; *Norton Lib.* repr. of 1967 ed. 1972 pap. $2.45. A brief, learned attack on the ritual theory of the origin of tragedy.

Esslin, Martin. *Theatre of the Absurd*. Penguin 3d ed. 1983 pap. $5.95. Establishes "the absurd" as a common ground for playwrights as diverse as Beckett, Genet, Pinter, and Albee, and studies its tradition in drama.

Freedley, George, and John A. Reeves. *History of the Theatre*. Crown rev. ed. 1968 $10.00. With an extensive bibliography.

Gassner, John. *Form and Idea in Modern Theatre*. Dryden 1956 o.p.

——. *Masters of the Drama*. Dover 3d ed. 1953 $10.00. Reviews the entire history of the drama—800 dramatists, 2,000 plays.

——. *The Theatre in Our Times*. Crown 1954 $7.50

Gaster, Theodor H. *Thespis: Ritual, Myth, and Drama in the Ancient Near East*. Fwd. by Gilbert Murray, Gordian 2d ed. rev. 1975 $16.00. Evidence for the ritual theory of dramatic origins.

Gilder, Rosamond. *Enter the Actress*. *Essay Index Repr. Ser.* Ayer repr. 1931 ed. $24.50. A history of women in the theater from ancient Greece to modern times.

Gillespie, Patti P., and Kenneth M. Cameron. *Western Theatre: Revolution and Revival*. Macmillan text ed. 1984. Theater history textbook considers the changing relation between stage, actor, and audience through Western history.

Hardison, O. B. *Christian Rite and Christian Drama in the Middle Ages: Essays in the Origin and Early History of Modern Drama*. Greenwood repr. of 1965 ed. 1983 lib. bdg. $55.00. Essays in the origin and early history of modern drama.

Harsh, Philip W. *A Handbook of Classical Drama*. Stanford Univ. Pr. 1944 $35.00 pap. $10.95. A play-by-play analysis, with material on the theater and bibliographies.

Hartnoll, Phyllis. *Concise History of the Theatre*. Scribner 1973 pap. $8.95; *World of Art Ser.* Thames & Hudson 1985 pap. $9.95

Hunningher, Benjamin. *The Origins of the Theater*. Greenwood repr. of 1961 ed. 1978 $22.50. Challenges the theory that the modern theater had its origins in church festivals.

Kernodle, George, and Portia Kernodle. *Invitation to the Theatre*. Harcourt 3d ed. abr. 1985 pap. $21.95. A college text.

Krutch, Joseph W. *Modernism in Modern Drama: A Definition and an Estimate*. Cornell Univ. Pr. 1966 pap. $3.95

Leacroft, Richard, and Helen Leacroft. *Theatre and Playhouse: An Illustrated Survey of Theatre Buildings from Ancient Greece to the Present Day*. Methuen 1984 $39.95 pap. $13.95. Leacroft's isometric cutaways of theater buildings from all periods make this book uniquely valuable for the student.

MacGowan, Kenneth, and William Melnitz. *The Living Stage: A History of World Theatre*. Prentice-Hall 1955 $38.33

MacGowan, Kenneth, and William Melnitz. *Golden Ages of the Theater*. Prentice-Hall (Spectrum Bks.) 1959 o.p.

Malpede, Karen, ed. *Women in Theatre: Compassion and Hope*. Drama Bk. 1983 pap. $19.95; *Limelight Eds.* 1985 $9.95. Selections from the writing of women in drama, from the medieval playwright Hrotswitha to Martha Graham and Judith Malina.

Mantzius, Karl. *History of Theatrical Art in Ancient and Modern Times*. Intro. by W.

Archer, Peter Smith 6 vols. $72.00. Translation of a fundamental work of theater history, which first appeared in 1897–1916.

Melchinger, Siegfried. *Concise Encyclopedia of Modern Drama.* Ed. by Henry Popkin, trans. by George Wellwarth, Horizon Pr. 1965 o.p. Contains an analytic glossary of dramatic theory and many photographs.

Nagler, Alois M. *The Medieval Religious Stage: Shapes and Phantoms.* Yale Univ. Pr. 1976 $20.00

——. *A Source Book in Theatrical History.* Dover 1952 pap. $8.50; Peter Smith $15.25. More than 300 items provide an essential documentary background for an understanding of each major period of theater history. "An indispensable complement to the study of the drama" (*Educational Theatre Journal*).

Nicoll, Allardyce. *The Development of the Theatre: A Study of Theatrical Art from the Beginnings to the Present Day.* Harcourt 5th ed. rev. 1967 o.p. Well-illustrated survey concerned mainly with physical aspects of the stage.

——. *Masks, Mimes and Miracles.* Cooper Square Pr. repr. of 1931 ed. $30.00

——. *World Drama: From Aeschylus to Anouilh.* Barnes & Noble 2d ed. rev. & enl. text ed. 1976 $45.00. A commanding survey, "planned skillfully and written with clarity and grace" (*N.Y. Times*).

——. *The World of Harlequin.* Cambridge Univ. Pr. 1976 $58.00 pap. $18.95

Pickard-Cambridge, A. W. *Dithyramb, Tragedy and Comedy.* 1927. Oxford 2d ed. rev. 1968 o.p. Presents evidence concerning the origins of classical drama.

Smith, Winifred. *Commedia Dell'arte.* Ayer rev. ed. repr. of 1912 ed. $30.00. "The basic book on the subject published in English" (*LJ*).

Southern, Richard. *Medieval Theatre in the Round.* Theatre Arts enl. ed. 1975 $11.35

——. *The Seven Ages of the Theatre.* Hill & Wang 1961 pap. $5.95. A history of theater buildings and playing spaces, "of the first importance in its field" (Eric Bentley).

Styan, J. L. *Modern Drama in Theory and Practice.* Cambridge Univ. Pr. 3 vols. 1981 ea. $29.50 set $79.50. Vol. 1, *Realism and Naturalism;* Vol. 2, *Symbolism, Surrealism, and the Absurd;* Vol. 3, *Expressionism and Epic Theatre.* Profusely illustrated history of drama from Ibsen to the present.

Valency, Maurice. *The Flower and the Castle: An Introduction to Modern Drama. Making of Modern Drama Ser.* Schocken 1982 $20.00 pap. $9.95. Excellent review of the bourgeois dramatic tradition in Europe, culminating in a play-by-play study of Ibsen and Strindberg.

Wagenknecht, Edward. *Seven Daughters of the Theatre.* Univ. of Oklahoma Pr. 1964 $12.95; *Quality Pap. Ser.* Da Capo repr. of 1964 ed. 1981 pap. $7.95. Jenny Lind, Sarah Bernhardt, Ellen Terry, Julia Marlowe, Isadora Duncan, Mary Garden, and Marilyn Monroe.

Wellwarth, George. *The Theater of Protest and Paradox: Developments in Avant Garde Drama.* New York Univ. Pr. rev. ed. 1971 $25.00

ORIENTAL DRAMA

Arlington, Lewis C. *The Chinese Drama.* Ayer repr. of 1930 ed. $42.00

Bowers, Faubion. *Theatre in the East. Dance Ser.* Ayer repr. of 1956 ed. 1980 lib. bdg. $53.00

Brandon, James R. *Asian Theatre: A Study Guide and Annotated Bibliography.* Amer. Theatre Association 1980 o.p.

——. *Kabuki: Five Classic Plays.* Harvard Univ. Pr. 1975 $27.50. Well-illustrated.

————. *Theater in Southeast Asia*. Harvard Univ. Pr. 1967 $15.00 1974 pap. $8.95.
"Linguistic skill and a talent for dedicated research have produced this authoritative, fact-filled compendium. . . . The book's magnificent bibliography, copious notes, glossary, and index make it an invaluable source of information" (*LJ*).

Halford, Aubrey S., and Giovanna M. Halford. *Kabuki Handbook: A Guide to Understanding and Appreciation*. Tuttle 1955 pap. $6.95

Horrwitz, Ernest P. *Indian Theatre: A Brief Survey of Sanskrit Drama*. Ayer repr. of 1912 ed. 1967 $15.00

Izumo, Takeda, and others. *Chushingura: The Treasury of Loyal Retainers*. Trans. by Donald Keene, Columbia Univ. Pr. 1971 pap. o.p. A puppet play. The most famous of the Kabuki texts, with notes and an introduction.

Kalidasa. *Theater of Memory: The Plays of Kalidasa*. Ed. by Barbara Stoler Miller, trans. by Edwin Gerow and others, Columbia Univ. Pr. 1984 $30.00 pap. $12.00. New translations of *Sakuntala* and two other plays, with essays on Sanskrit drama and Indian theater.

Kincaid, Zoe. *Kabuki: The Popular Stage of Japan*. Ayer repr. of 1925 ed. $38.50. Criticism.

Leiter, Samuel L. *Kabuki Encyclopedia: An English Language Adaptation of Kabuki Jiten*. Greenwood 1979 lib. bdg. $45.00

Liu June-en, trans. *Six Yuan Plays*. Penguin 1972 pap. $3.95. The earliest form of Chinese drama.

MacKerras, Colin. *The Chinese Theatre in Modern Times: From 1840 to the Present Day*. Univ. of Massachusetts Pr. 1975 $17.50

Pound, Ezra, ed. *Classic Noh Theatre of Japan*. Notes by Ernest Fenollosa, intro. by William Butler Yeats, New Directions 1959 pap. $4.95

Scott, A. C. *The Theatre in Asia*. Macmillan 1973 o.p.

————. *Traditional Chinese Plays*. Univ. of Wisconsin Pr. 3 vols. pap. ea. $6.95–$10.00

Waley, Arthur. *The Nō Plays of Japan*. Grove 1957 pap. $7.95; Tuttle 1976 pap. $7.25. Translations of 20 plays, summaries of others. Still the definitive anthology in English.

Wells, Henry W. *The Classical Drama of the Orient*. Asia Publishing House 1965 o.p.

————. *Six Sanskrit Plays in English Translation*. Asia Publishing House 1964 $10.95

Zeami. *On the Art of the No Drama: The Major Treatises of Zeami*. Trans. by J. Thomas Rimer and Masakazu Yamazaki, Princeton Univ. Pr. $32.50 pap. $15.00

Zung, Cecilia S. *Secrets of the Chinese Drama: A Complete Explanatory Guide*. Ayer repr. of 1937 ed. $23.00; Gordon $59.95. Includes synopses of fifty classic plays.

THEORY

After listing some introductions to the reading and viewing of plays, this section considers general theories of the drama, both modern and historical. A special group of these is concerned with the perennial problem of defining the dramatic genres. The last section, "Theory: Contemporary," also brings to the reader's attention some stage innovators of this century—Artaud, Brecht, Brook, Craig, Meyerhold, and Stanislavsky—who are influential in today's theater practice.

Introduction to Drama

Ball, David. *Backwards and Forwards: A Technical Manual for Reading Plays.* Southern Illinois Univ. Pr. 1983 pap. $6.95

Dawson, S. W. *Drama and the Dramatic. Critical Idiom Ser.* Methuen 1970 pap. $5.25

Esslin, Martin. *An Anatomy of Drama. Drama Bk. Ser.* Hill & Wang 1977 $7.50 pap. $4.95

Hayman, Ronald. *How to Read a Play.* Grove (Everyman's) 1977 pap. $4.95

Styan, J. L. *Drama, Stage and Audience.* Cambridge Univ. Pr. 1975 $37.50 pap. $10.95

——. *Dramatic Experience.* Cambridge Univ. Pr. 1965 $27.95 pap. $11.95

——. *Elements of Drama.* Cambridge Univ. Pr. text ed. 1960 $39.50 pap. $11.95

Williams, Raymond. *Drama in Performance.* Basic Bks. 1968 o.p.; Penguin rev. ed. 1972 o.p. Useful analyses of plays as productions: *Antigone,* medieval drama, *Antony and Cleopatra, The Seagull,* Bergman's film *Wild Strawberries,* and others.

Theory: Historical

Adams, Henry H., and Baxter Hathaway, eds. *Dramatic Essays of the Neoclassic Age. Drama Bk. Ser.* Norton $25.50

Aristotle. *Aristotle's Poetics.* Trans. by S. H. Butcher, intro. by Francis Fergusson, Hill & Wang 1961 pap. $3.95. Includes a brief, but important, essay.

——. *Aristotle's Theory of Poetry and Fine Art.* Trans. by S. H. Butcher, Peter Smith $12.00. The Peter Smith reprint contains the original Greek text and a long essay. For other commentaries on Aristotle, see works on tragedy listed under "Theory: Genre."

Carlson, Marvin. *Theories of the Theatre: A Historical and Critical Survey, from the Greeks to the Present.* Cornell Univ. Pr. 1984 $45.00

Clark, Barrett H. *European Theories of the Drama.* Ed. by Henry Popkin, Crown rev. ed. 1965 $19.95. Anthology of writings on dramatic theory from Aristotle to the present. Contains many translations not available elsewhere.

Dukore, B. F. *Dramatic Theory and Criticism.* Holt text ed. 1974 $21.95. Major documents of dramatic theory. Includes an intelligent selection of related material from philosophers, psychologists, and social theorists.

Gassner, John, and Ralph G. Allen. *Theater and Drama in the Making.* Houghton Mifflin 2 vols. 1964 o.p.

Gilbert, Allan H. *Literary Criticism: Plato to Dryden.* 1940. Wayne State Univ. Pr. 1962 o.p. Important for classical and Renaissance theory. Excellent index.

Theory: General

Abel, Lionel. *Metatheatre: A New View of Dramatic Form.* Hill & Wang 1963 o.p. Shakespeare, Brecht, Genet, and Beckett viewed as makers of self-conscious drama.

Beckerman, Bernard. *Dynamics of Drama. Drama Bk.* text ed. 1979 pap. o.p.

Bentley, Eric. *The Life of the Drama.* Peter Smith 1984 $15.50. "A remarkable exploration of the roots and bases of dramatic art, the most far-reaching and revelatory we have had" (*Book Week*).

Fergusson, Francis. *Idea of a Theater: A Study of Ten Plays—The Art of Drama in Changing Perspective.* Princeton Univ. Pr. repr. of 1949 ed. 1968 $27.50 pap. $8.95. A central work of modern criticism. Plays by Sophocles, Wagner, Racine, Shakespeare, Ibsen, Shaw, and others read in the light of neo-Aristotelean theory.

Goldman, Michael. *The Actor's Freedom: Toward a Theory of Drama.* Viking 1975 $8.95

Nicoll, Allardyce. *The Theatre and Dramatic Theory.* Greenwood repr. of 1962 ed. 1978 lib. bdg. $29.75

———. *Theory of Drama.* Ayer repr. of 1931 ed. 1967 $20.00

Theory: Genre

Bermel, Albert. *Farce: From Aristophanes to Woody Allen.* Simon & Schuster 1982 $20.75 pap. $9.95

Charney, Maurice. *Comedy High and Low: An Introduction to the Experience of Comedy.* Oxford text ed. 1978 $17.95

Corrigan, Robert W. *Comedy: Meaning and Form.* Harper 2d ed. text ed. 1981 pap. $12.85

———. *Tragedy: Vision and Form.* Harper 2d ed. 1981 pap. $12.85. More than 30 selections of theory and criticism, emphasizing twentieth-century contributions to the definition of genre.

David, Jessica M. *Farce. Critical Idiom Ser.* Methuen pap. $5.50

Guthke, Karl S. *Modern Tragicomedy: An Investigation into the Nature of the Genre.* Philadelphia Bk. text ed. 1966 pap. o.p.

Heilman, Robert B. *The Iceman, the Arsonist, and the Troubled Agent: Tragedy and Melodrama on the Modern Stage.* Univ. of Washington Pr. 1973 $17.50

———. *Tragedy and Melodrama: Versions of Experience.* Univ. of Washington Pr. 1968 $20.00

———. *The Ways of the World: Comedy and Society.* Univ. of Washington Pr. 1978 $25.00

Herrick, Marvin T. *Comic Theory in the Sixteenth Century. Studies in Language and Lit. Ser.* Univ. of Illinois Pr. repr. of 1950 ed. 1964 pap. $7.50. A clear formulation of Roman-Renaissance ideas of comic form.

Hirst, David L. *Tragicomedy. Critical Idiom Ser.* Methuen 1984 pap. $5.50

Hoy, Cyrus. *The Hyacinth Room: An Investigation into the Nature of Comedy, Tragedy, and Tragicomedy.* Knopf 1964 $6.95

Jones, John. *On Aristotle and Greek Tragedy.* Oxford repr. of 1962 ed. 1968 pap. $3.50

Kerr, Walter. *Tragedy and Comedy.* Simon & Schuster (Touchstone Bks.) 1968 pap. o.p.

Leech, Clifford. *Tragedy. Critical Idiom Ser.* Methuen 1969 pap. $5.25

Lucas, F. L. *Tragedy: Serious Drama in Relation to Aristotle's "Poetics."* Barnes & Noble rev. & enl. ed. 1981 pap. $8.95

Merchant, Moelwyn. *Comedy. Critical Idiom Ser.* Methuen 1972 pap. $5.25

Olson, Elder. *Tragedy and the Theory of Drama.* Wayne State Univ. Pr. 1961 pap. $5.95

Steiner, George. *The Death of Tragedy.* Faber 1963 $13.95 pap. $8.95; Oxford repr. of 1961 ed. 1980 pap. $9.95

Styan, J. L. *Dark Comedy: The Development of Modern Comic Tragedy.* Cambridge Univ. Pr. 2d ed. $42.50 pap. $12.95

Sypher, Wylie, ed. *Comedy: An Essay on Comedy by George Meredith and Laughter by Henri Bergson.* Johns Hopkins Univ. Pr. repr. of 1956 ed. 1980 pap. $6.95. Contains Sypher's useful essay on the meanings of comedy.

Williams, Raymond. *Modern Tragedy.* Stanford Univ. Pr. 1966 pap. $5.95

Theory: Contemporary

Artaud, Antonin. *Selected Writings of Artaud.* Ed. by Susan Sontag, trans. by Helen
Weaver, Farrar 1976 $20.00 pap. $9.95
———. *Theater and Its Double.* 1938. Trans. by Mary C. Richards, Grove (Every-
man's) 1958 pap. $4.95. The work of this revolutionary French theorist (1896–
1948), father of the "theater of cruelty," is discussed in Esslin's *Antonin Artaud.*
Barrault, Jean-Louis. *Reflections on the Theatre.* Trans. by Barbara Wall, Hyperion
repr. of 1951 ed. o.p.
———. *The Theatre of Jean-Louis Barrault.* 1959. Trans. by Joseph Chiari, Hill &
Wang 1961 o.p. Actor, director, friend of Artaud, Barrault was a major presence
in the innovative French theater of the 1940s and 1950s.
Bentley, Eric, ed. *The Brecht Commentaries, 1943–1980.* Grove 1981 $17.50 pap.
$9.50
———. *The Theory of the Modern Stage.* Penguin 1976 pap. $7.95. An anthology of
statements by "ten makers of modern theatre," accompanied by important his-
torical and critical essays.
Braun, Edward. *The Theatre of Meyerhold: Revolution on the Modern Stage.* Drama
Bk. text ed. 1979 pap. $10.00
Brecht, Bertolt. *Brecht on Theatre.* Ed. and trans. by John Willett, Hill & Wang 1964
pap. $6.95. Brecht's principle of "alienated" staging has been as influential as
his drama, written in an anti-Aristotelean, epic mode. For discussion of Brecht,
see Chapter 13 and Bentley's *Brecht Commentaries.*
Brecht, Stefan. *The Original Theatre of the City of New York: From the Mid-60s to the
Mid-70s.* Methuen 9 vols. 1978, write publisher for individual volumes and
prices. A "sympathetic observer's" careful record of the nonliterary theater work
of Robert Wilson, Robert Foreman, Joseph Chaikin, and others. Extensive quota-
tion of theoretical statements.
Brook, Peter. *The Empty Space.* Atheneum 1978 pap. $4.95. Four versions of the con-
temporary theater—the "deadly," the "holy," the "rough," and the "immediate."
Brook, the most experimental of contemporary English directors, is famous for
his preparatory work with actors. The log of an important Brook production is
Selbourne's *Making of a Mid-Summer Night's Dream.*
Craig, Edward Gordon. *Craig on Theatre.* Ed. by J. Michael Walton, Methuen 1983
pap. $9.95. Craig (1872–1966), son of the actress Ellen Terry, was a visionary de-
signer whose illustrated books have had more influence than his infrequent ac-
tual productions. Reprints of Craig's books are listed under "Technique."
Elam, Keir. *The Semiotics of Theatre and Drama.* Methuen 1980 $18.95 pap. $8.95
Esslin, Martin. *Antonin Artaud. Modern Masters Ser.* Penguin 1977 pap. $4.95
Grotowksi, Jerzy. *Towards a Poor Theatre.* Simon & Schuster 1968 $10.95. Theoreti-
cal statements by the Polish director who centers his theater on ritual confrontation of actors and audience.
Marranca, Bonnie. *Theatrewritings.* Performing Arts 1985 $19.95 pap. $8.95. Among
these essays are studies of avant-garde performance groups, contemporary play-
wrights, and modern drama theory.
Meyerhold, Vsevolod. *Meyerhold on Theatre.* Ed. and trans. by Edward Braun, Hill &
Wang 1969 pap. $9.95. At one time a director at the Moscow Art Theatre,
Meyerhold (1874–1942) ended by formulating an anti-Stanislavskian theory of
"biomechanical" acting. His remarkable stage work is discussed by Braun in
The Theatre of Meyerhold.
Pavis, Patrice. *Languages of the Stage: Essays in the Semiology of Theatre.* Performing
Arts 1982 $19.95 pap. $9.95

Schechner, Richard. *The End of Humanism: Writings on Performance.* Performing
    Arts 1982 $18.95 pap. $6.95
——. *Environmental Theater.* Hawthorne Bks. 1973 pap. $3.95
——. *Essays on Performance Theory, 1970–76.* Drama Bk. 1977 pap. o.p.
——. *Public Domain.* Bobbs 1970 o.p. Schechner, founder-director of the Perfor-
    mance Group and professor at New York University, is an important exponent
    of "performance art."
Selbourne, David. *The Making of a Mid-Summer Night's Dream: An Eye-Witness Ac-
    count of Peter Brook's Production from First Rehearsal to First Night.* Methuen
    1982 pap. $11.95
Stanislavsky, Konstantin. *Stanislavsky on the Art of the Stage.* Faber 1967 pap. $9.95;
    trans. by David Magarshack, Hill & Wang 1962 pap. $4.50. Developer of the fa-
    mous method of training actors, Stanislavsky (1863–1938) founded the Moscow
    Art Theatre. Aspects of his production technique are described by Toporkov in
    Stanislavsky in Rehearsal. Stanislavsky's acting treatises appear under "Tech-
    nique."
Toporkov, Vasily O. *Stanislavsky in Rehearsal: The Final Years.* Trans. by Christine
    Edwards, Theatre Arts 1979 $12.95
Turner, Victor. *From Ritual to Theatre: The Human Seriousness of Play.* Performing
    Arts 1982 $17.95 pap. $7.95. Anthropological study of the interpenetration of
    theater and everyday life.
Wiles, Timothy J. *The Theater Event: Modern Theories of Performance.* Trans. by
    Fruma Gottschalk, Univ. of Chicago Pr. 1980 lib. bdg. $17.50. Theories of Stanis-
    lavsky, Brecht, Artaud, and Grotowski.

CRITICISM

This section includes work by both academic and journalistic critics of
drama. See also Adelman and Dworkin, Breed and Sniderman, Coleman
and Tyler, Palmer and Dyson, Salem, and Samples under "Bibliographies."

Agate, James E., ed. *The English Dramatic Critics: An Anthology, 1660–1932.* AMS Pr.
    repr. of 1958 ed. $32.50. Agate (1877–1947) was himself "the most influential
    critic of his time" (Martin Esslin), reviewing for the *Sunday Times* of London
    from 1923 to 1947.
Beerbohm, Max. *Around Theatres.* Greenwood repr. of 1924 ed. 1969 $24.50
——. *Last Theatres.* Ed. by Rupert Hart-Davis, Taplinger 1970 $15.00. In 1898,
    Beerbohm succeeded Shaw as dramatic critic of the English *Saturday Review.*
Bentley, Eric. *In Search of Theatre.* Atheneum text ed. 1975 pap. $4.95
——. *Theatre of Commitment.* Atheneum 1967 $5.00
——. *The Theatre of War: Modern Drama from Ibsen to Brecht.* Viking 1972 o.p.
——. *What Is Theatre?* Atheneum 1968 pap. $4.95; Limelight Eds. repr. of 1968 ed.
    1984 pap. $10.95. For 20 years, the Brander Matthews Professor of Drama at Co-
    lumbia University, as well as working critic (*New Republic*), director, play-
    wright, and performer, Bentley has been called "the greatest critic of the drama
    now writing in English" (Jacques Barzun). *What Is Theatre?* collects 104 of his re-
    views and articles, originally published from 1944 to 1967.
Bermel, Albert. *Contradictory Characters: An Interpretation of the Modern Theatre.*
    Dutton 1973 pap. $4.95; Univ. Pr. of Amer. repr. of 1973 ed. text ed. 1984 pap.

$13.50. Bermel received a George Jean Nathan Award for drama criticism in 1974.

Blau, Herbert. *Blooded Thought: Occasions of Theatre.* Performing Arts 1982 $18.95 pap. $6.95

———. *The Impossible Theatre.* Macmillan 1966 o.p.

———. *Take Up the Bodies: Theater at the Vanishing Point.* Univ. of Illinois Pr. 1982 $16.95. Blau, cofounder of the Actor's Workshop in San Francisco and once head of Lincoln Center's Vivian Beaumont Company, is known for his personal and imaginative critical style.

Brustein, Robert. *Critical Moments: Reflecting on Theater and Society.* Random 1980 $9.95

———. *Revolution as Theatre: Essays on Radical Style.* Liveright 1970 pap. $1.95

———. *Seasons of Discontent: Dramatic Opinions, 1959–65.* Simon & Schuster 1965 $5.95

———. *The Theatre of Revolt: An Approach to the Modern Drama.* Little, Brown 1964 pap. $8.95. *The Theatre of Revolt* uses Ibsen, Chekhov, Shaw, Brecht, and others to illustrate the idea that "revolt is the energy which drives the modern theatre, just as faith drove the theatre of the past."

———. *Third Theatre.* Simon & Schuster (Touchstone Bks.) 1970 pap. $2.95. Director of the American Repertory Theatre at Harvard and former dean of the Yale Drama School, Brustein is also a practical critic (*New Republic*, London *Observer*).

Clurman, Harold. *The Divine Pastime: Theatre Essays.* Macmillan 1974 o.p.

———. *The Naked Image: Observations on the Modern Theatre.* Macmillan 1966 o.p. First a pupil of Jacques Copeau, later a founder of the Group Theatre (1931–41), Clurman went on to an impressive career as producer and director, and as drama critic for *The Nation.*

Comtois, M. F., and Lynn F. Miller. *Contemporary American Theatre Critics: A Dictionary and Anthology of Their Works.* Scarecrow Pr. 1977 $45.00

Corrigan, Robert. *The Theatre in Search of a Fix.* Delacorte 1973 $10.00. Essays on classical, modern, and postmodern theater.

Gilman, Richard. *The Making of Modern Drama.* Farrar 1974 pap. $4.50. Büchner and Handke receive attention along with more familiar heresiarchs. "The best single study of the astonishing transformations dramatic art has undergone in the last century or so" (*N.Y. Times Book Review*).

Kerr, Walter. *The God on the Gymnasium Floor and Other Theatrical Adventures.* Dell 1973 o.p.

———. *Journey to the Center of the Theater.* Knopf 1979 $12.95

———. *Pieces at Eight.* Simon & Schuster 1957 o.p.

———. *The Theatre in Spite of Itself.* Simon & Schuster 1963 o.p. Winner of a George Jean Nathan Award.

———. *Thirty Plays Hath November: Pain and Pleasure in the Contemporary Theater.* Simon & Schuster (Touchstone Bks.) 1970 pap. $2.95. Review collections by the Sunday drama critic of the *N.Y. Times,* former daily critic for the *N.Y. Herald Tribune,* the dean of U.S. journalist reviewers.

Kott, Jan. *The Theatre of Essence and Other Essays.* Northwestern Univ. Pr. $19.95 pap. $9.95

Lahr, John. *Astonish Me: Adventures in Contemporary Theatre.* Viking 1973 o.p.

———. *Up Against the Fourth Wall: Essays on Modern Theatre.* Grove 1970 o.p.

Lahr, John, and Jonathan Price. *Lifeshow: How to See Theatre in Life and Life in Theatre.* Viking 1973 o.p.

Nathan, George J. *The Critic and the Drama.* Intro. by Charles Angoff, Fairleigh Dickinson Univ. Pr. 1972 $16.50
——. *The Magic Mirror: Selected Writings on Theatre.* Ed. by Thomas Quinn Curtiss, Knopf 1960 o.p.
——. *Materia Critica.* Intro. by Charles Angoff, Fairleigh Dickinson Univ. Pr. 1971 $20.00; Richard West repr. of 1924 ed. 1975 $25.00
——. *Passing Judgments.* Intro. by Charles Angoff, *Essay Index Repr. Ser.* Ayer repr. of 1935 ed. $15.00; Fairleigh Dickinson Univ. Pr. 1970 $20.00; Greenwood repr. of 1935 ed. lib. bdg. $15.00; Johnson Repr. repr. of 1935 ed. 1969 $17.00
——. *Theatre of the Moment.* Ed. by Charles Angoff, Fairleigh Dickinson Univ. Pr. 1971 $20.00. Nathan (1882–1958) began reviewing for the *N.Y. Herald* in 1905; at the end of his career, he was writing for *Esquire* and *Newsweek.* He is best known as drama critic of the *American Mercury,* which he cofounded with H. L. Mencken.
Shaw, George B. *Shaw's Dramatic Criticism from the Saturday Review 1895–1898.* Ed. by John F. Matthews, Peter Smith $5.00
Tynan, Kenneth. *Curtains.* Atheneum 1961 o.p.
——. *Show People.* Simon & Schuster 1980 $11.95
——. *The Sound of Two Hands Clapping. Quality Pap. Ser.* Da Capo repr. of 1975 ed. 1982 pap. $7.95
——. *Tynan Right and Left: Plays, Films, Places, People and Events.* Atheneum 1967 o.p. Tynan was an eloquent critic, best known in the United States for his work in the *New Yorker,* a playwright and producer, and, from 1963 to 1973, literary manager of England's National Theatre.
Valency, Maurice. *The End of the World.* Oxford 1980 $27.50; *Making of Modern Drama Ser.* Schocken 1983 pap. $11.95. Completes a series of books on the makers of modern drama: *The Flower and the Castle* (Ibsen/Strindberg); *The Cart and the Trumpet* (Shaw); and *The Breaking String* (Chekhov).
Williams, Raymond. *Drama from Ibsen to Brecht.* Oxford 1969 $6.50
Young, Stark. *The Flower in Drama and Glamour: Theatre Essays and Criticism.* Octagon repr. of 1955 ed. 1973 lib. bdg. $19.00
——. *Immortal Shadows.* Octagon repr. of 1948 ed. 1973 lib. bdg. $20.50. Young was for many years drama editor of the *New Republic.*

TECHNIQUE: ACTING, DIRECTING, PLAYWRITING, STAGE DESIGN

Archer, William. *Playmaking: A Manual of Craftsmanship.* Norwood repr. of 1913 ed. $45.00. Archer was an early collaborator with Shaw and a translator of Ibsen.
Baker, George P. *Dramatic Technique. Theatre, Film and the Performing Arts Ser.* Da Capo repr. of 1919 ed. 1971 lib. bdg. $39.50 1976 pap. $8.95; Greenwood repr. of 1919 ed. lib. bdg. $22.50; Richard West repr. of 1919 ed. 1975 $16.50. A classic of U.S. dramaturgy. Baker (1866–1935), first professor of dramatic literature at Harvard, worked with O'Neill and other important writers in his Workshop 47.
Boleslavski, Richard. *Acting: The First Six Lessons.* Theatre Arts 1949 $9.95
Braun, Edward. *The Director and the Stage: From Naturalism to Grotowski.* Holmes & Meier text ed. 1982 $19.75 pap. $12.50
Clurman, Harold. *On Directing.* Macmillan 1972 $13.95; Macmillan (Collier Bks.) 1974 pap. $8.95
Cole, Toby. *Playwrights on Playwriting.* Intro. by John Gassner, *Drama Bk. Ser.* Hill

& Wang 1961 pap. $5.95. Essays by major playwrights from Ibsen and Zola to Osborne and Ionesco. Bibliography.

Cole, Toby, and Helen K. Chinoy, eds. *Actors on Acting*. Crown rev. ed. 1970 $8.95. Theories, techniques, and practices in the actors' own words; with introductions and biographical sketches.

———. *Directors on Directing*. Bobbs rev. ed. 1963 pap. $13.24. Includes a valuable historical study of the emergence of the director, essays by 15 directors from Antoine to Logan, and excerpts from rehearsal notes for famous productions.

Craig, Edward Gordon. *The Art of the Theatre*. Theatre Arts 1956 o.p.

———. *Scene*. Ayer repr. of 1923 ed. 1968 $18.00

———. *Theatre Advancing*. Ayer repr. of 1919 ed. $12.50

———. *Toward a New Theatre: Forty Designs for Stage Scenes*. Blom repr. of 1913 ed. $35.00

Dean, Alexander, and L. Carra. *Fundamentals of Play Directing*. Holt 3d ed. 1974 text ed. $14.95

Egri, Lajos. *The Art of Dramatic Writing*. Simon & Schuster (Touchstone Bks.) 1972 pap. $9.95

Gassner, John, and Philip Barber. *Producing the Play, with the New Scene Technician's Handbook*. Holt rev. ed. text ed. 1953 $14.95

Gielgud, John. *An Actor in His Time*. Penguin 1982 pap. $4.95

Goodman, Randolph. *Drama on Stage*. Holt 2d ed. text ed. 1978 pap. $21.95. Production studies of six plays representing various periods and styles.

———. *From Script to Stage: Eight Modern Plays*. Holt 1971 o.p. Production studies with commentary by theater professionals.

Gorelick, Mordecai. *New Theatres for Old*. Octagon repr. of 1940 ed. 1975 $37.50. A spirited "Brechtian" view of theater history.

Grebanier, Bernard. *Playwriting: How to Write for the Theater*. Apollo Eds. Barnes & Noble repr. of 1961 ed. 1979 pap. $5.29; Crowell pap. $4.95

Hainaux, Rene, and Yves Bonnat. *Stage Design throughout the World since 1935*. Theatre Arts 1950 o.p. Pictorial survey of experiments in opera, ballet, drama, 1935–50. Contains 176 photographs.

———. *Stage Design throughout the World since 1950*. Theatre Arts 1963 $32.50. Stage design in 33 countries with 192 pages of black-and-white illustrations and 16 pages of color; includes a "Stage Designers' Who's Who."

———. *Stage Design throughout the World since 1960*. Theatre Arts o.p.

Heffner, Hubert C., and Samuel Selden. *Modern Theatre Practice: A Handbook of Play Production*. Prentice-Hall 5th ed. 1973 $32.95. "A standard, authoritative text" (*Guide to Reference Books*).

Jones, Robert E. *Dramatic Imagination*. Theatre Arts 1941 $7.95. Jones, with Lee Simonson and Norman Bel Geddes, led the modernist movement in U.S. scenic design.

Kerr, Walter. *How Not to Write a Play*. Writer 1955 text ed. $10.00

Komisarjevsky, Theodore, and Lee Simonson, eds. *Settings and Costumes of the Modern Stage*. Ayer repr. of 1933 ed. $33.00

Laver, James. *Costume in the Theatre*. Farrar 1965 o.p.

Lawson, John H. *Theory and Technique of Playwriting*. Farrar 1960 o.p. "Beyond doubt the most incisive and illuminating treatment of playwrighting as a dynamic art" (John Gassner).

Le Gallienne, Eve. *The Mystic in the Theatre: Eleonora Duse*. Southern Illinois Univ. Pr. 1973 pap. $6.95

Lewis, Robert. *Advice to the Players*. Intro. by Harold Clurman, Harper text ed. 1980 pap. $14.50. A comprehensive text for actors, in a workshop format.

———. *Method or Madness*. French 1958 $6.50

MacGowan, Kenneth, and Robert Edmund Jones. *Continental Stagecraft*. Blom repr. of 1922 ed. 1964 o.p. An important response to European influences by leading figures in the U.S. art theater of the 1920s.

———. *A Primer of Playwriting*. Random 1941 o.p.

Matthews, Brander, ed. *Papers on Acting*. Farrar 1958 o.p. Comments by nineteenth-century actors: Talma, Booth, Irving, and others.

———. *Papers on Playmaking. Essay Index Repr. Ser*. Ayer repr. of 1957 ed. $19.00. Particularly useful for its view of dramaturgy on the threshold of the modern era: essays by Augier, Sardou, W. S. Gilbert, and others.

Mielziner, Jo. *Designing for the Theatre: A Memoir and a Portfolio*. Potter 1965 o.p. Mielziner (1901–76) established a second generation of modern U.S. stage design with his sets for *Streetcar Named Desire* (1947) and *Death of a Salesman* (1949).

Moussinac, Leon, ed. *New Movement in the Theatre*. Ayer repr. of 1931 ed. 1967 $75.00. Many illustrations.

Olivier, Laurence. *Confessions of an Actor: An Autobiography*. Simon & Schuster 1982 $17.95; Penguin 1984 pap. $5.95

Redgrave, Michael. *Mask or Face: Reflections in an Actor's Mirror*. Intro. by Harold Clurman, Theatre Arts 1958 o.p.

Saint-Denis, Michel. *Theatre: The Rediscovery of Style*. Intro. by Laurence Olivier, Theatre Arts repr. of 1960 ed. 1968 pap. $5.95

———. *Training for the Theatre*. Ed. by Suria Saint-Denis, Theatre Arts 1982 pap. $10.95. Trained in the acting disciplines of Copeau's Vieux Colombier, Saint-Denis (1897–1971) came to England as a teacher and director in 1936. A major influence on postwar British theater, he was later connected with New York's Juilliard School and the Royal Shakespeare Company.

Simonson, Lee. *Stage Is Set. New Repr. in Essays and General Lit. Index Ser*. Ayer repr. of 1932 ed. 1975 $48.50; Theatre Arts 1963 pap. $4.95

Stanislavsky, Konstantin. *An Actor Prepares*. 1930. Trans. by Elizabeth R. Hapgood, intro. by John Gielgud, Theatre Arts 1948 $14.95

———. *An Actor's Handbook*. Trans. by Elizabeth R. Hapgood, Theatre Arts 1963 pap. $4.95. An alphabetical arrangement of statements about theater.

———. *Building a Character*. Trans. by Elizabeth R. Hapgood, intro. by Joshua Logan, Theatre Arts 1949 pap. $14.95

———. *My Life in Art*. 1924. Trans. by J. J. Robbins, Theatre Arts 1948 pap. $10.95

———. *Stanislavski's Legacy: A Collection of Comments on a Variety of Aspects of an Actor's Life and Art*. Ed. and trans. by Elizabeth R. Hapgood, Theatre Arts rev. ed. 1968 pap. $4.95

Sterne, Richard L. *John Gielgud Directs Richard Burton in Hamlet: A Journal of Rehearsals*. Random 1967 o.p. Includes the playing version of *Hamlet* with descriptions of stage business, interviews with principals.

Styan, J. L. *Max Reinhardt*. Oxford 1982 $10.95. Reinhardt (1873–1943) was internationally famous for his exquisitely engineered stage spectacles.

CHAPTER 2

British Drama: Early to Eighteenth Century

Maurice Charney

Art a painter? Canst paint me a tear, or a wound, a groan, or a sigh?
—THOMAS KYD, *The Spanish Tragedy*

PRE-SHAKESPEAREAN DRAMA: MEDIEVAL, TUDOR, AND EARLY ELIZABETHAN

This catch-all category carries us from the beginnings of British drama to about the birth of Shakespeare and Marlowe in 1564. The authoritative *The Revels History of Drama in English* divides the subject into medieval drama in volume 1, then the Tudor and early Elizabethan periods from 1500 to 1576 in volume 2. Medieval and Tudor drama are two distinct subjects, although there is a fair amount of chronological overlap. The medieval mystery plays based on biblical events and performed by the craft guilds were still being presented in Shakespeare's boyhood at the same time as the newer interludes and moralities. The connection between drama and the church was weakening, and troupes of professional actors (like those who appear in *Hamlet*) were traveling from place to place and presenting their entertainments in banquet halls and innyards.

History and Criticism

Axton, Richard. *European Drama of the Early Middle Ages.* Univ. of Pittsburgh Pr. 1975 $16.95

Bevington, David M. *Tudor Drama and Politics: A Critical Approach to Topical Meaning.* Harvard Univ. Pr. 1968 $22.50. Focuses on the relations of drama and society.

Boas, Frederick S. *An Introduction to Tudor Drama.* AMS Pr. repr. of 1933 ed. $14.00; Greenwood repr. of 1933 ed. 1977 lib. bdg. $24.75. A useful book for students.

Bond, Richard W., ed. *Early Plays from the Italian.* Ayer repr. of 1911 ed. $29.00. Many Tudor plays were based on Plautus or Terence through an Italian intermediary.

Clemen, Wolfgang. *English Tragedy before Shakespeare: The Development of Dramatic Speech.* Methuen 1980 $42.00. Very good on style.

Craik, T. W., and others. *The Revels History of Drama in English, 1500–1576*. Methuen 1980 vol. 2 $55.00. Contributions by Norman Sanders, Richard Southern, T. W. Craik, and Lois Potter. Good bibliography.

Davidson, Clifford. *Drama and Art: An Introduction to the Use of Evidence from the Visual Arts for the Study of Early Drama. Early Drama, Art, and Music Ser.* Medieval Institute 1977 pap. $4.95. This is a subject of great importance that needs further work.

————. *From Creation to Doom: The York Cycle of Mystery Plays. Studies in the Middle Ages* AMS Pr. 1984 $32.50

Gardner, John C. *The Construction of the Wakefield Cycle.* Southern Illinois Univ. Pr. 1974 $8.95

Green, A. Wigfall. *Inns of Court and Early English Drama.* Elliots Bks. 1931 $49.50. The inns of court, or law schools, were a nurturing place for drama.

Hardison, O. B. *Christian Rite and Christian Drama in the Middle Ages: Essays in the Origin and Early History of Modern Drama.* Greenwood repr. of 1965 ed. 1983 lib. bdg. $55.00; Johns Hopkins Univ. Pr. 1965 $22.00 pap. $5.95. An important book.

Helterman, Jeffrey. *Symbolic Action in the Plays of the Wakefield Master.* Univ. of Georgia Pr. 1981 $18.50

Hogrefe, Pearl. *The Sir Thomas More Circle: A Program of Ideas and Their Impact on Secular Drama.* Univ. of Illinois Pr. 1959 $27.50. The Humanist circle around Sir Thomas More was active in ethical and didactic drama.

Kahrl, Stanley J. *Traditions of Medieval English Drama.* Univ. of Pittsburgh Pr. 1975 $13.95

Kolve, V. A. *The Play Called Corpus Christi.* Stanford Univ. Pr. 1966 $27.50 pap. $8.95. Advances interesting notions about staging.

Lucas, F. L. *Seneca and Elizabethan Tragedy. Studies in Comparative Lit.* Folcroft repr. of 1923 ed. lib. bdg. $17.50; Haskell repr. of 1922 ed. 1969 lib. bdg. $39.95

Motter, Thomas H. V. *The School Drama in England.* Associated Faculty Pr. repr. of 1929 ed. 1968 $25.50; Richard West repr. of 1929 ed. 1975 $20.00

Nagler, A. M. *The Medieval Religious Stage: Shapes and Phantoms.* Yale Univ. Pr. 1976 $21.00. By a leading theater historian.

Potter, Lois. *The Revels History of Drama in English: Medieval Drama.* Methuen 1983 vol. 1 $55.00. Contributions by A. C. Cawley, Marion Jones, Peter F. McDonald, and Davis Mills. Impressive bibliography. Conveys an excellent sense of the new directions in the study of medieval drama.

Reed, A. W. *Early Tudor Drama.* Octagon repr. of 1926 ed. 1969 lib. bdg. $19.50. An excellent introduction.

Rossiter, Arthur P. *English Drama from Early Times to the Elizabethans.* Folcroft repr. of 1950 ed. 1978 lib. bdg. $20.00

Salter, Frederick M. *Medieval Drama in Chester.* Folcroft repr. of 1973 ed. lib. bdg. $17.50

Southern, Richard. *Medieval Theatre in the Round.* Theatre Arts enl. ed. 1975 $11.35. Highly original and suggestive on staging.

————. *The Staging of Plays before Shakespeare.* Theatre Arts 1973 $19.95

Tydeman, W. *The Theater in the Middle Ages: Western European Stage Conditions c.800–1576.* Cambridge Univ. Pr. 1979 $49.50 pap. $13.95

Wilson, Frank. *The English Drama, 1485–1642. Oxford History of Eng. Lit. Ser.* 1969 $35.00. An excellent survey.

Woolf, Rosemary. *The English Mystery Plays.* Univ. of California Pr. 1980 pap. $7.95

Editions of Pre-Shakespearean Drama

Students are advised to consult the many reprints and facsimile editions that have become available. The Early English Text Society publishes scholarly editions as does the Malone Society. John S. Farmer and others edited 151 volumes in *The Tudor Facsimile Texts Series* (1906–14). The *Medieval Drama Facsimiles Series*, edited by A. C. Cawley and S. Ellis, has been publishing texts at Leeds since 1973. The excellent periodical *Research Opportunities in Renaissance Drama*, edited by David Bergeron, has had a medieval supplement since 1970.

Beadle, Richard, ed. *The York Plays*. Edward Arnold text ed. 1982 $98.50

Beadle, Richard, and Pamela M. King, eds. *The York Mystery Plays*. Oxford 1984 $29.95 pap. $12.95

Bevington, David, ed. *The Macro Plays*. Folger $42.00; Johnson Repr. 1972 $50.00

———. *Medieval Drama*. Houghton Mifflin text ed. 1975 $30.95. An outstanding textbook.

Cawley, A. C., ed. *Everyman and Medieval Miracle Plays*. Biblio Dist. (Everyman's) $9.95

———. *The Wakefield Pageants in the Towneley Cycle*. Barnes & Noble repr. of 1958 ed. 1975 pap. $10.95

Cawley, A. C., and Martin Stevens, eds. *The Towneley Cycle*. Huntington Lib. 1976 pap. $12.00

Eccles, Mark, ed. *The Macro Plays: The Castle of Perseverance, Wisdom, Mankind*. Early Eng. Text Society Ser. Oxford 1969 $17.95

Greenberg, Noah, and W. H. Auden, eds. *The Play of Daniel: A Thirteenth-Century Musical Drama*. Oxford 1959 pap. $5.95. A graceful edition of a play made popular by the Pro Musica group, directed by Noah Greenberg.

Happé, Peter, ed. *English Mystery Plays*. Penguin Eng. Lib. Ser. 1976 pap. $6.95

———. *Four Morality Plays*. Penguin 1980 pap. $6.95

Hussey, Maurice, ed. *The Chester Mystery Plays*. Heinemann text ed. 1975 pap. $5.00; Theatre Arts 2d ed. 1975 pap. $3.50

Lumiansky, R. M., and David Mills, eds. *The Chester Mystery Cycle*. Huntington Lib. 1980 pap. $25.00; Early Eng. Text Society Ser. Oxford 1975 $29.00

Rose, Martial, ed. *The Wakefield Mystery Plays*. Norton Lib. 1969 pap. $10.95

Smith, Lucy T., ed. *The York Plays: The Plays Performed on the Day of Corpus Christi in the 14th, 15th, and 16th Centuries*. Russell repr. of 1885 ed. 1963 $21.00

ELIZABETHAN DRAMA

History and Criticism

The word "Elizabethan" is used generally for the drama from 1558, when Elizabeth came to the throne, through 1642 when the theaters were closed. A more exact usage is to call the drama during the reign of James I "Jacobean" (1603–25). "Caroline" is used for that part of Charles I's reign from his accession in 1625 to the closing of the theaters in 1642. After the death of Shakespeare in 1616 the theaters gradually became more elitist and patronage shifted from the public theaters to the more expensive private playhouses. Shakespeare is, of course, the most notable Elizabethan dramatist, but he has a chapter to himself (see Chapter 3 in this volume). Many of the references here and in Chapter 3 apply equally to Shakespeare *and* Elizabethan drama.

This period represents the greatest creativity in the history of English drama.

Everything seemed to concur to make the drama an enormously popular medium of entertainment. The typical Elizabethan play as described by Doran (see below) was extremely vigorous in its language and action and sacrificed classical unity for complex and episodic plots. It gobbled up materials from foreign sources, especially Italian; from sensational events of the time; and from the themes and conventions of romantic poetry, especially in relation to love. It had an unbounded appetite for new ideas, new forms, and new styles, and expanded the possibilities of the English language as a medium of dramatic expression.

Renaissance Drama is a periodical devoted to this area, with annual issues based on themes. *Research Opportunities in Renaissance Drama* is a more informal publication with attention to research projects and papers. *Medieval and Renaissance Drama in England*, edited by J. Leeds Barroll, has just been published in two volumes. *Studies in Philology* published an annual bibliography until 1978. *Studies in English Literature* has a long discussion article in its spring issue devoted to the most notable studies of the year. Elizabethan drama is included in the annual bibliography of the Modern Language Association.

Bentley, Gerald E. *The Jacobean and Caroline Stage.* AMS Pr. 7 vols. repr. of 1968 ed. 1982 $297.50. A magisterial account of the period that continues Edmund K. Chambers, *The Elizabethan Stage*, and improves on it.

Bowers, Fredson. *Elizabethan Revenge Tragedy, 1587–1642.* Peter Smith 1958 $11.75. A standard account of the subject.

Bradbrook, Muriel C. *Artist and Society in Shakespeare's England.* Barnes & Noble text ed. 1982 $26.75

———. *The Growth and Structure of Elizabethan Comedy.* Humanities Pr. text ed. 1955 $17.55

———. *The Rise of the Common Player.* History of Elizabethan Drama Ser. Cambridge Univ. Pr. 1979 pap. $12.95

———. *Themes and Conventions of Elizabethan Tragedy.* History of Elizabethan Drama Ser. Cambridge Univ. Pr. 2d ed. 1980 $49.50 pap. $16.95. An excellent brief account of a large subject.

Butler, Martin. *Theatre and Crisis, 1632–1642.* Cambridge Univ. Pr. 1984 $39.50

Chambers, Edmund K. *The Elizabethan Stage.* Oxford 4 vols. 1923 $139.00. Special index volume by Beatrice White (includes Chambers, *William Shakespeare*).

Creizenach, Wilhelm. *English Drama in the Age of Shakespeare.* Folcroft repr. of 1916 ed. lib. bdg. $45.00; Haskell repr. of 1916 ed. 1969 lib. bdg. $49.95

Dessen, Alan C. *Elizabethan Stage Conventions and Modern Interpreters.* Cambridge Univ. Pr. 1984 $29.95

Doran, Madeleine. *Endeavors of Art: A Study of Form in Elizabethan Drama.* Univ. of Wisconsin Pr. text ed. 1954 pap. $10.95. A book of first importance for all students of the period. Studies dramaturgic assumptions of Elizabethan playwrights.

Eliot, T. S. *Elizabethan Essays.* Gordon 1973 lib. bdg. $69.95; Haskell repr. of 1934 ed. 1969 lib. bdg. $39.95. Most of these essays were originally written as reviews. They are still trenchant and have a knack for quoting apt passages.

Ellis-Fermor, Una M. *The Jacobean Drama: An Interpretation.* AMS Pr. repr. of 1958 ed. $32.50. An excellent introduction to the subject.

Ford, Boris, ed. *The New Pelican Guide to English Literature: A Guide for Readers.* Penguin 1984 pap. $5.95. Has perceptive essays on the drama.

Fordyce, Rachel, ed. *Caroline Drama: A Bibliographic History of Criticism.* G. K. Hall 1978 lib. bdg. $28.50

Freer, Coburn. *The Poetics of Jacobean Drama.* Johns Hopkins Univ. Pr. text ed. 1982 $26.00

Gibbons, Brian. *Jacobean City Comedy*. Methuen 2d ed. 1981 pap. $13.95

Greenfield, Thelma N. *The Induction in Elizabethan Drama*. Univ. of Oregon Bks. 1970 $6.00. The "induction" was a special extradramatic piece that preceded a play.

Hallett, Charles A., and Elaine S. Hallett. *The Revenger's Madness: A Study of Revenge Tragedy Motifs*. Univ. of Nebraska Pr. 1980 $24.95

Harbage, Alfred. *Annals of English Drama, 975–1700*. Ed. by S. Schoenbaum, Univ. of Pennsylvania Pr. rev. ed. 1964 $18.00. This is a crucial book that attempts to date plays year-by-year.

Hassel, R. Chris, Jr. *Renaissance Drama and the English Church Year*. Univ. of Nebraska Pr. 1979 $17.95. An original approach on the relation of plays to occasions of church festivity.

Hattaway, Michael. *Elizabethan Popular Theatre: Plays in Performance*. *Theatre Production Studies* Routledge & Kegan 1982 $29.95 1985 pap. $12.95

Hillebrand, Harold N. *Child Actors: A Chapter in Elizabethan Stage History*. Russell repr. of 1926 ed. 1964 $8.50. An older book that is still very useful.

Kaufmann, Ralph J., ed. *Elizabethan Drama: Modern Essays in Criticism*. Oxford 1961 pap. $7.95. A valuable collection.

Leech, Clifford, and T. W. Craik. *The Revels History of Drama in English, 1576–1613*. Methuen 1975 vol. 3 $55.00. Contributions by J. Leeds Barroll, Alexander Leggatt, Richard Hosley, and Alvin Kernan.

Levin, Richard. *Multiple Plot in English Renaissance Drama*. Univ. of Chicago Pr. 1971 $22.00. A detailed and practical study.

———. *New Readings vs. Old Plays: Recent Trends in the Reinterpretation of English Renaissance Drama*. Univ. of Chicago Pr. 1979 lib. bdg. $24.00 1982 pap. $8.95. Many cogent objections to the ahistorical, thematic trends in modern scholarship and criticism.

Logan, Terence P., and Denzell S. Smith, eds. *The Later Jacobean and Caroline Dramatists*. *Survey and Bibliography of Recent Studies in Eng. Renaissance Drama Ser.* Univ. of Nebraska Pr. 1978 $21.50

———. *The New Intellectuals*. *Survey and Bibliography of Recent Studies in Eng. Renaissance Drama Ser.* Univ. of Nebraska Pr. 1977 $25.95

———. *The Popular School*. *Survey and Bibliography of Recent Studies in Eng. Renaissance Drama Ser.* Univ. of Nebraska Pr. 1975 $22.95

———. *The Predecessors of Shakespeare*. *Survey and Bibliography of Recent Studies in Eng. Renaissance Drama Ser.* Univ. of Nebraska Pr. 1973 $24.95. Logan and Smith's four volumes are indispensable for anyone working in this area.

Lucas, F. L. *Seneca and Elizabethan Tragedy*. *Studies in Comparative Lit.* Folcroft repr. of 1923 ed. lib. bdg. $17.50; Haskell repr. of 1922 ed. 1969 lib. bdg. $39.95

Mehl, Dieter. *The Elizabethan Dumb Show*. Methuen 1982 $40.00

Nicoll, Allardyce. *Stuart Masques and the Renaissance Stage*. Ayer repr. of 1938 ed. $37.15

Orgel, Stephen, and Roy Strong. *Inigo Jones: The Theatre of the Stuart Court*. Univ. of California Pr. 2 vols. 1973 $250.00. Concerned with the chief architect of masques and royal entertainments in the Stuart period.

Ornstein, Robert. *The Moral Vision of Jacobean Tragedy*. Greenwood repr. of 1960 ed. 1975 lib. bdg. $24.50. A much used study.

Penninger, F. Elaine, ed. *English Drama to 1660 (Excluding Shakespeare): A Guide to Information Sources*. *Amer. Lit., Eng. Lit., and World Lit. in Eng. Information Guide Ser.* Gale 1976 $60.00

Potter, Lois. *The Revels History of Drama in English, 1613–1660*. Methuen 1983 vol. 4

$55.00. Contributions by Philip Edwards, Gerald E. Bentley, Kathleen McLuskie, and Lois Potter. Studies a period generally neglected in literary history. Good bibliography.

Ribner, Irving. *The English History Play in the Age of Shakespeare.* Octagon repr. of 1957 ed. 1979 lib. bdg. $23.00. Important study of the genre.

————. *Jacobean Tragedy: The Quest for Moral Order.* Rowman repr. of 1962 ed. 1979 $20.00. Strongly Christian and ethical in its premises.

Ribner, Irving, and Clifford C. Huffman. *Tudor and Stuart Drama. Goldentree Bibliographies in Language and Lit. Ser.* Harlan Davidson 2d ed. text ed. 1978 $24.95 pap. $14.95

Salomon, Brownell. *Critical Analyses in Renaissance Drama: A Bibliographic Guide.* Bowling Green 1979 pap. $6.95. Arranged alphabetically by author and play. Enormously helpful comments on books and authors.

Shapiro, Michael. *Children of the Revels: The Boy Companies of Shakespeare's Time and Their Plays.* Columbia Univ. Pr. 1977 $29.00. An authoritative statement on this special topic.

Shepherd, Simon. *Amazons and Warrior Women: Varieties of Feminism in 17th-Century Drama.* St. Martin's 1982 $25.00

Tokson, Elliot. *The Popular Image of the Black Man in English Drama, 1550–1688.* G. K. Hall 1982 lib. bdg. $20.00

Tomlinson, Thomas B. *Study of Elizabethan and Jacobean Tragedy.* Cambridge Univ. Pr. 1964 $49.50

Wells, Stanley, ed. *English Drama (Excluding Shakespeare) Select Bibliographical Guides.* Oxford text ed. 1975 pap. $10.95

Welsford, Enid. *The Court Masque: A Study in the Relationship between Poetry and the Revels.* Russell repr. of 1927 ed. 1962 $22.00

————. *The Fool: His Social and Literary History.* Peter Smith $11.25. A much consulted book on a popular topic of social and dramatic significance.

Editions and Anthologies of Elizabethan Plays

The Revels Plays, modeled on the Arden edition of Shakespeare, is the most important edition of Elizabethan and pre-Shakespearean drama. Thirty-four volumes have been published, and the present editors are F. David Hoeniger, E. A. J. Honigmann, and J. R. Mulryne. *The Regents Renaissance Drama Series,* under the general editorship of Cyrus Hoy, is also of high quality. It has published at least 39 volumes. The old Mermaid editions of Elizabethan dramatists, published from the 1880s to the early 1900s, make available some hard-to-find texts. The series has been re-edited since 1956 in single volumes called *New Mermaid Series* under the general editorship of Philip Brockbank and Brian Morris. Many of the better known plays appear in *Crofts Classics Series.* Facsimile reprints of Tudor and Elizabethan plays are available from the Malone Society and *The Tudor Facsimile Texts Series* edited by Farmer. The Scolar Press has published photographic facsimiles of many English Renaissance plays. Under the editorship of Stephen Orgel, Garland Publishers has undertaken an extensive *Renaissance Drama* series, especially of lesser known plays.

Bald, Robert C., ed. *Six Elizabethan Plays.* Houghton Mifflin 1963 pap. $5.95

Beckerman, Bernard, ed. *Five Plays of the English Renaissance.* New Amer. Lib. 1983 pap. $5.95

Brooke, Charles F., and Nathaniel B. Paradise. *English Drama, 1580–1642.* Heath text ed. 1933 $24.95

Fraser, Russell A., and Norman Rabkin. *Drama of the English Renaissance.* Macmillan 2 vols. 1976 consult publisher for price. The best of the big student anthologies.

Gomme, A. H., ed. *Jacobean Tragedies. Oxford Pap. Ser.* 1969 pap. $7.95

Harrier, Richard C., ed. *An Anthology of Jacobean Drama. Stuart Eds. Ser.* New York Univ. Pr. 2 vols. 1963 ea. $32.00

Lamb, Charles. *Specimens of English Dramatic Poets Who Lived about the Time of Shakespeare.* 1808. *Lib. of Lit., Drama, and Criticism* Johnson Repr. 2 vols. repr. of 1893 ed. 1970 $60.00. This anthology of poetic passages was extremely influential for the study of Elizabethan drama in the nineteenth century.

Lawrence, Robert G., ed. *Early Seventeenth-Century Drama.* Biblio Dist. (Everyman's) repr. of 1963 ed. 1970 $12.95

McIlwraith, Archibald K., ed. *Five Elizabethan Comedies. World's Class. Ser.* Oxford 1934 $5.95

———. *Five Elizabethan Tragedies.* Greenwood repr. of 1938 ed. 1981 lib. bdg. $42.50; *Oxford Pap. Ser.* repr. of 1938 ed. 1971 pap. $5.95

Salgado, Gamini, ed. *Three Jacobean Tragedies.* Penguin 1965 pap. $3.95

Spencer, Hazelton. *Elizabethan Plays.* Heath text ed. 1945 $22.95. An excellent big anthology.

Wine, Martin. *Drama of the English Renaissance.* Modern Lib. 1969 pap. $7.95; Random text ed. 1969 pap. $7.95

BEAUMONT, FRANCIS. c.1584–1616, and JOHN FLETCHER. 1579–1625

Beaumont and Fletcher are the best known collaborators of Elizabethan literature. John Aubrey reports that when they lived together they shared one wench and one cloak between them, and everything encourages the myth of literary twins. The collaboration, however, could not have lasted for more than five years, beginning in 1608 and ending in 1613, when Beaumont married a rich heiress. After that time, Fletcher collaborated with other dramatists such as Massinger, Middleton, Shirley, and perhaps Shakespeare. We do not yet understand how to untangle the various shares in Elizabethan dramatic collaborations. A Beaumont and Fletcher play was generally understood to be a tragicomedy with a complex and swiftly moving plot, a good deal of spectacle, upper-class and genteel characters contrasted with low characters (as love is with lust), sentimental effusions, and a smoothly articulated, elegant, and fluent style. *A King and No King*, which is and is not about royal incest, is typical. Beaumont and Fletcher were extremely inventive in setting up actions based on some improbable assumption. The play then became an exercise in disproving the original proposition.

BOOKS BY BEAUMONT AND FLETCHER

The Works of Beaumont and Fletcher. Ed. by A. H. Bullen, AMS Pr. 4 vols. repr. of 1912 ed. 1976 $105.00; ed. by A. R. Waller and A. Glover, Octagon 10 vols. repr. of 1912 ed. 1969 lib. bdg. $230.00

The Dramatic Works in the Beaumont and Fletcher Canon. Ed by Fredson Bowers, Cambridge Univ. Pr. 4 vols. 1983 $95.00–$125.00. The individual plays have separate editors in this splendid modern edition.

A King and No King. 1611. *Eng. Experience Ser.* Walter J. Johnson repr. of 1619 ed.

$15.00; ed. by Robert K. Turner, *Regents Renaissance Drama Ser.* Univ. of Nebraska Pr. 1964 $13.95

The Knight of the Burning Pestle. Ed. by Benjamin W. Griffith, Jr. Barron text ed. 1963 pap. $2.95; *Eng. Experience Ser.* Walter J. Johnson repr. of 1613 ed. 1969 $8.00; ed. by Sheldon P. Zitner, *Revels Plays Ser.* Longwood 1985 $35.00; ed. by Michael Hattaway, *New Mermaid Ser.* Norton 1976 pap. $2.95; ed. by Andrew J. Gurr, *Fountainwell Drama Texts* Univ. of California Pr. 1968 pap. $5.75; ed. by John Doebler, *Regents Renaissance Drama Ser.* Univ. of Nebraska Pr. 1967 $13.95

The Maid's Tragedy. 1619. Ed. by Andrew J. Gurr, *Fountainwell Drama Texts* Univ. of California Pr. 1969 $6.00 pap. $2.95; ed. by Howard B. Norland, *Regents Renaissance Drama Ser.* Univ. of Nebraska Pr. 1968 pap. $13.95 pap. $4.25

Philaster: Or, Love Lies a-Bleeding. 1620. Ed. by Andrew J. Gurr, *Revels Plays Ser.* Longwood repr. of 1969 ed. 1973 pap. $6.50; ed. by Dora J. Ashe, *Regents Renaissance Drama Ser.* Univ. of Nebraska Pr. 1974 $15.95

Books about Beaumont and Fletcher

Appleton, William W. *Beaumont and Fletcher: A Critical Study.* Folcroft repr. of 1956 ed. 1974 lib. bdg. $15.00

Bald, Robert C. *Bibliographical Studies in the Beaumont and Fletcher Folio of 1647.* Folcroft repr. of 1938 ed. lib. bdg. $15.00

Cone, Mary. *Fletcher Without Beaumont: A Study of the Independent Plays of John Fletcher. Salzburg Studies in Eng. Lit., Jacobean Drama Studies* Humanities Pr. 1976 pap. $25.50

Gayley, Charles W. *Francis Beaumont, Dramatist: A Portrait with Some Account of His Circle, Elizabethan and Jacobean, and of His Association with John Fletcher.* Richard West repr. of 1914 ed. 1973 $35.00

Hatcher, Orie L. *John Fletcher: A Study of Dramatic Method.* Folcroft repr. of 1905 ed. lib. bdg. $9.50; Haskell repr. of 1905 ed. 1973 lib. bdg. $49.95

Hensman, Bertha. *The Shares of Fletcher, Field and Massinger in Twelve Plays of the Beaumont and Fletcher Canon. Salzburg Studies in Eng. Lit., Jacobean Drama Studies* Humanities Pr. 2 vols. text ed. 1974 pap. $50.75

McKeithan, Daniel M. *The Debt to Shakespeare in the Beaumont and Fletcher Plays.* AMS Pr. repr. of 1938 ed. $9.50; Gordian repr. of 1938 ed. text ed. 1970 $10.00

Oliphant, Ernest H. *Plays of Beaumont and Fletcher.* AMS Pr. repr. of 1927 ed. $12.50; Phaeton repr. of 1927 ed. 1970 $12.00; Scholarly repr. of 1927 ed. 1971 $10.00

Pearse, Nancy C. *John Fletcher's Chastity Plays: Mirrors of Modesty.* Bucknell Univ. Pr. 1973 $22.50

Sprague, Arthur C. *Beaumont and Fletcher on the Restoration Stage.* Ayer repr. of 1926 ed. $24.50

Thorndike, Ashley H. *Influence of Beaumont and Fletcher on Shakespeare.* AMS Pr. repr. of 1901 ed. $12.50

Waith, Eugene. *The Pattern of Tragicomedy in Beaumont and Fletcher. Yale Studies in Eng. Ser.* Shoe String (Archon) repr. of 1952 ed. 1969 $19.50

Wallis, Lawrence B. *Fletcher, Beaumont and Company.* Octagon repr. of 1947 ed. 1968 lib. bdg. $20.00

Wilson, John H. *The Influence of Beaumont and Fletcher on the Restoration Stage.* Ayer repr. of 1928 ed. 1967 $12.00; Haskell repr. of 1928 ed. 1969 lib. bdg. $46.95

CHAPMAN, GEORGE. c.1559–1634

Chapman had a reputation in his own time for being a learned writer. He translated HOMER's *Iliad* and *Odyssey* and his works are full of humanist scholarship from classical sources. His tragedies are mostly based on contemporary French history. In *Bussy d'Ambois*, the best known of this series, the hero is the aspiring, stoic man who is doomed to extinction in a crass world. Chapman's comedies are much more lighthearted and they experiment in the comedy of "humours" that Jonson was to perfect. The plays are mostly written for the boy companies.

BOOKS BY CHAPMAN

The Tragedies. Ed. by Thomas Marc Parrott, Russell 2 vols. in 1 repr. of 1910 ed. 1961 $30.00

The Comedies. Ed. by Thomas Marc Parrott, Russell 2 vols. repr. of 1914 ed. 1961 $27.50

The Plays of George Chapman: The Comedies. Ed. by Allan Holaday and Michael Kiernan, Univ. of Illinois Pr. 1970 $39.95

All Fools. 1605. Ed. by Frank Manley, *Regents Renaissance Drama Ser.* Univ. of Nebraska Pr. 1968 pap. $2.75

The Widow's Tears. 1605. Ed. by Akihiro Yamada, *Revels Plays Ser.* Johns Hopkins Univ. Pr. text ed. 1975 $18.50; Longwood 1975 $23.50; ed. by Ethel M. Smeak, *Regents Renaissance Drama Ser.* Univ. of Nebraska Pr. 1966 $12.50 pap. $3.50

The Gentleman Usher. 1606. Ed. by John H. Smith, *Regents Renaissance Drama Ser.* Univ. of Nebraska Pr. 1970 $15.95 pap. $3.95

Bussy d'Ambois. 1607. Ed. by Maurice Evans, *Mermaid Dramabook Ser.* Hill & Wang 1966 pap. $3.75; ed. by Nicholas Brooke, *Revels Plays Ser.* Johns Hopkins Univ. Pr. text ed. 1964 14.00; ed. by Nicholas Brooke, *Revels Plays Ser.* Longwood 1964 $24.00 1979 pap. $5.00; ed. by Maurice Evans, *New Mermaid Ser.* Norton 1976 pap. $2.95; ed. by Robert J. Lordi, *Regents Renaissance Drama Ser.* Univ. of Nebraska Pr. 1964 $13.95 pap. $3.25

BOOKS ABOUT CHAPMAN

Bement, Peter. *George Chapman: Action and Contemplation in His Novels. Salzburg Studies in Eng. Lit., Jacobean Drama Studies* Humanities Pr. text ed. 1974 pap. $25.50

Crawley, Derek. *Character in Relation to Action in the Tragedies of George Chapman. Salzburg Studies in Eng. Lit., Jacobean Drama Studies* Humanities Pr. text ed. 1974 pap. $25.50

Ellis, Havelock. *Chapman.* Arden Lib. repr. of 1934 ed. 1979 lib. bdg. $20.00; Folcroft repr. of 1934 ed. lib. bdg. $15.00; Richard West repr. of 1934 ed. $20.00

Goldstein, Leonard. *George Chapman: Aspects of Decadence in Early 17th-Century Drama.* Intro. by James Hogg, *Salzburg Studies in Eng. Lit., Jacobean Drama Studies* Humanities Pr. 2 vols. text ed. 1975 pap. $50.75

Grant, Thomas M. *The Comedies of George Chapman: A Study in Development. Salzburg Studies in Eng. Lit., Jacobean Drama Studies* Humanities Pr. text ed. 1972 pap. $25.50

Ide, Richard S. *Possessed with Greatness: The Heroic Tragedies of Chapman and Shakespeare.* Univ. of North Carolina Pr. 1980 $20.00

Rees, Ennis. *The Tragedies of George Chapman.* Octagon repr. of 1954 ed. 1979 lib. bdg. $18.00

Solve, Norma Dobie. *Stuart Politics in Chapman's Tragedy of Chabot. Eng. Lit. Ser.*
Haskell 1974 lib. bdg. $48.95; Richard West repr. of 1928 ed. $20.00
Swinburne, Algernon C. *George Chapman: A Critical Essay.* Arden Lib. repr. of 1875
ed. 1978 lib. bdg. $27.50; Darby repr. of 1875 ed. 1980 lib. bdg. $22.50; Folcroft
repr. of 1875 ed. 1972 lib. bdg. $22.50; Humanities Pr. repr. of 1875 ed. 1972 text
ed. $10.00
Wieler, John W. *George Chapman: The Effect of Stoicism upon His Tragedies.* Octagon
1968 lib. bdg. $15.50

DEKKER, THOMAS. c.1572–c.1632

Dekker was a popular, prolific writer who had a hand in at least 40 plays,
which he wrote for Philip Henslowe, the theatrical entrepreneur. In the
plays that seem to be completely by Dekker, he shows himself as a realist of
London life, but even his most realistic plays have a strong undertone of romantic themes and aspirations. *The Shoemaker's Holiday,* for example, glori-
fies the gentle craft of the shoemaker, and Simon Eyre speaks in an extravagant, hyperbolic style that is far from realistic. The two parts of *The Honest
Whore* are both vivid and realistic. Dekker also wrote prose pamphlets such
as the *Bellman of London* and *The Gull's Hornbook,* the latter an entertaining account of the behavior of a country yokel and dupe in London.

BOOKS BY DEKKER

The Dramatic Works of Thomas Dekker. Ed. by Fredson Bowers, Cambridge Univ. Pr.
4 vols. 1953–61 ea. $75.00. This is the standard edition in old spelling. The vol-
umes of notes are in preparation.
The Plague Pamphlets of Thomas Dekker. Richard West repr. of 1925 ed. 1978 lib. bdg.
$30.00; Scholarly repr. of 1925 ed. $39.00
The Wonderful Year and Other Pamphlets. Ed. by Eric D. Pendry, *Stratford-upon-Avon
Lib.* Harvard Univ. Pr. 1968 $25.00
The Shoemaker's Holiday. 1600. Ed. by Merritt Lawlis, Barron text ed. 1979 pap.
$3.50; ed. by Stanley Wells, *Revels Plays Ser.* Johns Hopkins Univ. Pr. text ed.
1979 $20.00; ed. by D. J. Palmer, *New Mermaid Ser.* Norton 1976 pap. $4.95
Lanthorne and Candle-Light. Walter J. Johnson repr. of 1608 ed. 1973 $9.50
The Gull's Hornbook. 1609. Ed. by R. B. McKerrow, AMS Pr. repr. of 1904 ed. $14.00;
ed. by R. B. McKerrow, Darby repr. of 1907 ed. 1983 lib. bdg. $45.00; ed. by R.
B. McKerrow, Folcroft repr. of 1905 ed. lib. bdg. $15.00

BOOKS ABOUT DEKKER

Adler, Doris R. *Thomas Dekker: A Reference Guide.* G. K. Hall 1983 lib. bdg. $52.00
Blow, Suzanne K. *A Study of Rhetoric in the Plays of Thomas Dekker. Salzburg Studies
in Eng. Lit., Jacobean Drama Studies* Humanities Pr. text ed. 1972 pap. $25.50
Gregg, Kate L. *Thomas Dekker: A Study in Economic and Social Backgrounds.* Fol-
croft repr. of 1924 ed. lib. bdg. $8.50
Hunt, Mary L. *Thomas Dekker.* Arden Lib. repr. of 1911 ed. 1978 lib. bdg. $27.50; Fol-
croft repr. of 1911 ed. lib. bdg. $25.00
Price, George R. *Thomas Dekker. Eng. Authors Ser.* Irvington 1969 lib. bdg. $15.95
Rhys, Ernest. *Thomas Dekker.* Richard West 1949 $20.00
Shirley, Peggy F. *Serious and Tragic Elements in the Comedy of Thomas Dekker. Salz-
burg Studies in Eng. Lit., Jacobean Drama Studies* Humanities Pr. text ed. 1975
pap. $25.50

Waage, Frederick O. *Thomas Dekker's Pamphlets, 1603–1609 and Jacobean Popular Literature. Salzburg Studies in Eng. Lit., Elizabethan and Renaissance Studies* Humanities Pr. 2 vols. 1977 $50.75

FLETCHER, JOHN. 1579–1625

[SEE UNDER Francis Beaumont.]

FORD, JOHN. 1586–c.1639

Ford's career as a playwright did not begin until 1621, with his collaboration with Dekker on *The Witch of Edmonton*. As a dramatist, Ford was extremely interested in psychology, especially abnormal psychology, and his best-known plays are studies in frustration and quiet suffering. His plots tend to be static and deterministic, with the characters unable to act against a crushing destiny. In *The Broken Heart* all the crucial events are fixed before the play begins, which puts a heavy emphasis on pathos. *'Tis Pity She's a Whore* rewrites *Romeo and Juliet* with brother-sister incest and a violent revenge action. *Perkin Warbeck* is the last of the history plays. The pretender to the throne of Henry VII hardly makes much pretense to establish his legitimate claims. Ford writes in an unusually plain, lyric style that resembles passionate and melancholy speech.

BOOKS BY FORD

The Broken Heart: A Tragedy. 1629. Ed. by T. J. B. Spencer, *Revels Plays Ser.* Johns Hopkins Univ. Pr. 1981 $22.00; *Eng. Experience Ser.* Walter J. Johnson repr. of 1633 ed. 1972 $11.50; ed. by Brian Morris, *New Mermaid Ser.* Norton 1976 pap. $2.95; ed. by Donald K. Anderson, Jr. *Regents Renaissance Drama Ser.* Univ. of Nebraska Pr. 1968 $11.95 pap. $2.95
The Lovers Melancholy. Eng. Experience Ser. Walter J. Johnson repr. of 1629 ed. 1970 $13.00; ed. by R. F. Hill, *Revels Plays Ser.* Longwood 1985 $35.00
The Chronicle Historie of Perkin Warbeck. 1633. *Eng. Experience Ser.* Walter J. Johnson repr. of 1634 ed. 1972 $11.50; ed. by Donald K. Anderson, Jr. *Regents Renaissance Drama Ser.* Univ. of Nebraska Pr. 1965 $10.95 pap. $2.75
'Tis Pity She's a Whore. 1632. Ed. by Mark Stavig, *Crofts Class. Ser.* Harlan Davidson text ed. 1966 pap. $3.75; ed. by Derek Roper, *Revels Plays Ser.* Longwood 1975 $25.00; ed. by Brian Morris, *New Mermaid Ser.* Norton 1978 pap. $2.95; ed. by S. P. Sherman, Richard West repr. 1980 lib. bdg. $25.00; ed. by N. W. Bawcutt, *Regents Renaissance Drama Ser.* Univ. of Nebraska Pr. 1966 pap. $4.25

BOOKS ABOUT FORD

Ali, Florence. *Opposing Absolutes: Conviction and Convention in John Ford's Plays. Salzburg Studies in Eng. Lit., Jacobean Drama Studies* Humanities Pr. text ed. 1974 pap. $25.50
Anderson, Donald K., Jr. *John Ford. Twayne's Eng. Authors Ser.* G. K. Hall lib. bdg. $13.50
Ewing, S. B. *Burtonian Melancholy in the Plays of John Ford.* Octagon repr. of 1940 ed. 1969 lib. bdg. $15.00
Farr, Dorothy M. *John Ford and the Caroline Theatre.* Barnes & Noble text ed. 1979 $28.50

Huebert, Ronald. *John Ford: Baroque English Dramatist.* McGill-Queens Univ. Pr. 1978 lib. bdg. $25.00
Orbison, Tucker. *The Tragic Vision of John Ford. Salzburg Studies in Eng. Lit., Jacobean Drama Studies* Humanities Pr. text ed. 1974 pap. $25.50
Sargeaunt, Margaret J. *John Ford.* Russell repr. of 1935 ed. 1966 $7.50
Sensabaugh, George F. *The Tragic Muse of John Ford.* Ayer repr. of 1944 ed. $17.00
Stavig, Mark. *John Ford and the Traditional Moral Order.* Univ. of Wisconsin Pr. 1968 $25.00

GREENE, ROBERT. 1558–1592

Greene was a notorious figure in his own time, leading a life of excess and debauchery (or at least so he represents himself in his many journalistic pamphlets). His cony-catching exposés of the Elizabethan underworld may or may not be based on real experience. He died, according to his friend Thomas Nashe, from a "banquet of Rhenish wine and pickled herring." Greene wrote many charming prose romances, with interpolated lyric poems. These are like the romantic plots of his plays.

BOOKS BY GREENE

The Life and Complete Works in Prose and Verse of Robert Greene. Ed. by Alexander Grosart, Russell 15 vols. repr. of 1881 ed. 1964 o.p.
Plays and Poems of Robert Greene. Ed. by J. Churton Collins, *Select Bibliographies Repr. Ser.* Ayer 2 vols. repr. of 1905 ed. $36.00
Friar Bacon and Friar Bungay. c.1594. *Malone Society Repr. Ser.* AMS Pr. repr. of 1926 ed. $40.00; ed. by J. A. Lavin, *New Mermaid Ser.* Norton 1976 pap. $2.95; ed. by G. B. Harrison, Richard West repr. of 1927 ed. $17.50
James the Fourth. 1598. *Malone Society Repr. Ser.* AMS Pr. repr. of 1921 ed. $40.00; ed. by Norman Sanders, *Revels Plays Ser.* Longwood 1970 $23.50 pap. $6.50; ed. by J. A. Lavin, *New Mermaid Ser.* Norton 1976 pap. $2.95
The Tragical Reign of Selimus. Ed. by Alexander Grosart, Richard West repr. of 1898 ed. $20.00

BOOKS ABOUT GREENE

Hayashi, Tetsumaro. *Robert Greene Criticism: A Comprehensive Bibliography. Author Bibliographies Ser.* Scarecrow Pr. 1971 $16.50
Jordan, John C. *Robert Greene.* Octagon 1965 lib. bdg. $18.50

HEYWOOD, THOMAS. c.1573–1641

Heywood is a good example of the professional dramatist who worked for Philip Henslowe, the theatrical manager, both as a playwright and an actor. By his own admission, Heywood claimed to have "either an entire hand or at least the main finger" in 220 plays, of which less than 30 survive. His best known play, *A Woman Killed with Kindness,* exemplifies domestic tragedy, in which sentiment and homely details are equally mingled. Heywood wrote an eloquent defense of the theater against Puritan attack called *An Apology for Actors.*

BOOKS BY HEYWOOD

Dramatic Works of Thomas Heywood. Ed. by R. H. Shepherd, Russell 6 vols. repr. of 1874 ed. 1964. $85.00

A Woman Killed with Kindness. 1603. Ed. by R. W. van Fossen, *Revels Plays Ser.* Johns Hopkins Univ. Pr. text ed. 1961 o.p.

An Apology for Actors. 1612. *Eng. Stage Ser.* Garland 1973 lib. bdg. $61.00; Johnson Repr. repr. of 1612 ed. $32.00; Scholars' Facsimiles 1978 $30.00

The Captives: Or, the Lost Recovered. 1624. *Malone Society Repr. Ser.* AMS Pr. repr. of 1953 ed. $40.00; ed. by Alexander C. Judson, Norwood repr. of 1921 ed. 1977 lib. bdg. $30.00

The Fair Maid of the West. c.1631. Ed. by Brownell Salomon, *Salzburg Studies in Eng. Lit., Jacobean Drama Studies* Humanities Pr. text ed. 1976 part 1 pap. $25.50; *Eng. Experience Ser.* Walter J. Johnson 2 pts. repr. of 1631 ed. 1973 $20.00; ed. by Robert K. Turner, Jr. *Regents Renaissance Drama Ser.* Univ. of Nebraska Pr. 2 pts. 1967 pap. $4.95

The English Traveller. 1633. *Eng. Experience Ser.* Walter J. Johnson repr. of 1633 ed. 1973 $8.00

The Escapes of Jupiter. AMS Pr. repr. of 1976 ed. $40.00

The Late Lancashire Witches. Ed. by Laird H. Barber and Stephen Orgel, *Renaissance Drama Ser.* Garland 1979 $45.00

BOOKS ABOUT HEYWOOD

Boas, Frederick S. *Thomas Heywood.* Folcroft 1973 lib. bdg. $15.00; Phaeton repr. of 1950 ed. 1974 $8.50; Somerset repr. of 1950 ed. $19.00

Clark, Arthur M. *Thomas Heywood: Playwright and Miscellanist.* Russell repr. of 1931 ed. 1967 $9.00

Cromwell, Otelia. *Thomas Heywood: A Study in the Elizabethan Drama of Everyday Life. Yale Studies in Eng. Ser.* Shoe String (Archon) repr. of 1928 ed. 1969 $17.50

Johnson, Marilyn L. *Images of Women in the Works of Thomas Heywood. Salzburg Studies in Eng. Lit., Jacobean Drama Studies* Humanities Pr. text ed. 1974 pap. $25.50

Velte, F. Mowbray. *The Bourgeois Element in the Dramas of Thomas Heywood. Studies in Drama* Haskell repr. of 1922 ed. 1969 lib. bdg. $49.95

JONSON, BEN. 1572?–1637

Next to Shakespeare, Jonson was the most creative and energetic playwright and poet of the Elizabethan-Jacobean period. He was learned in the classics, especially Latin literature, and throughout his career he attempted to apply neoclassical principles to his writing. In *The Alchemist,* for example, he strictly adheres to unity of time and place. In his critical opinions expressed in *Timber* and in his conversations with William Drummond of Hawthornden, he is constantly attacking romantic assumptions and a failure to observe classical precedent. His great comedies—*Volpone, Epicoene, The Alchemist,* and *Bartholomew Fair*—are satirical and display an enormous energy in language and characterization. Jonson developed the "humours" theory of comedy in *Every Man in His Humour* and *Every Man Out of His Humour.* The purpose of comedy is to purge eccentricity and whimsical monomania. Jonson wrote two classical tragedies, *Sejanus* and *Catiline,* strongly founded on classical sources. His comedies after *The Devil*

Is an Ass (o.p.) in 1616 represent a decline and are sometimes unfairly referred to as his "dotages." The excellent Yale edition of Jonson, published in individual volumes, is the most fully annotated now available.

BOOKS BY JONSON

Work of Ben Jonson. Ed. by C. H. Herford and others, Oxford 11 vols. 1925–52 ea. $47.00–$49.00

The Works of Ben Jonson, with a Memoir by William Gifford. Telegraph Bks. repr. of 1838 ed. 1982 lib. bdg. $100.00

The Complete Plays of Ben Jonson. Ed. by G. A. Wilkes, Oxford 4 vols. 1981 ea. $79.00–$99.00

The Complete Masques. Ed. by Stephen Orgel, Yale Univ. Pr. 1969 $52.00

Ben Jonson: The Complete Poems. Ed. by George Parfitt, *Eng. Poets Ser.* Yale Univ. Pr. text ed. 1982 $42.00 pap. $10.95

Ben Jonson's Plays and Masques. Ed. by Robert M. Adams, *Norton Critical Eds.* 1979 $22.95 text ed. pap. $5.95

Three Comedies. Ed. by Michael Jamieson, *Penguin Eng. Lib. Ser.* 1966 pap. $3.95

Ben Jonson and the Cavalier Poets. Ed. by Hugh MacLean, *Norton Critical Eds.* 1975 $12.50 pap. $6.95

Every Man in His Humour. 1598. *Malone Society Repr. Ser.* AMS Pr. repr. of 1920 ed. $40.00; ed. by M. Seymour-Smith, *New Mermaid Ser.* Norton 1976 pap. $4.95; ed. by J. W. Lever, *Regents Renaissance Drama Ser.* Univ. of Nebraska Pr. 1971 $23.95

Every Man Out of His Humour. 1600. *Malone Society Repr. Ser.* AMS Pr. repr. of 1920 ed. $40.00

Sejanus. 1603. Ed. by W. D. Briggs, Arden Lib. repr. of 1911 ed. 1977 lib. bdg. $27.50; ed. by W. F. Bolton, *New Mermaid Ser.* Norton 1976 pap. $1.95; ed. by Jonas A. Barish, Yale Univ. Pr. 1965 $23.00

Volpone. 1606. Ed. by Jonas A. Barish, *Crofts Class. Ser.* Harlan Davidson text ed. 1958 pap. $3.75; ed. by R. B. Parker, *Revels Plays Ser.* Longwood 1983 $30.00; ed. by David Cook, Methuen 1967 pap. $6.95; ed. by Philip Brockbank, *New Mermaid Ser.* Norton 1976 pap. $4.95; pref. by Richard B. Young, Yale Univ. Pr. 1962 $26.00 1963 pap. $6.95

Epicoene. 1609. Ed. by R. V. Holdsworth, *New Mermaid Ser.* Norton 1979 pap $7.95; ed. by L. A. Beaurline, *Regents Renaissance Drama Ser.* Univ. of Nebraska Pr. 1966 $15.95 pap. $4.50; ed. by Edward B. Partridge, Yale Univ. Pr. 1972 $23.00

The Alchemist. 1610. Ed. by H. C. Hart, Arden Lib. repr. of 1903 ed. 1978 lib. bdg. $45.00; ed. by John I. McCollum, Jr., Barron 1965 $6.75 pap. $3.50; ed. by J. B. Steane, Cambridge Univ. Pr. text ed. 1967 $7.95; ed. by Gerald E. Bentley, *Crofts Class. Ser.* Harlan Davidson text ed. 1947 pap. $4.75; ed. by H. De Vocht, Kraus 1950 pap. $24.00; ed. by F. H. Mares, *Revels Plays Ser.* Longwood 2d ed. 1979 pap. $4.75; ed. by Douglas Brown, *New Mermaid Ser.* Norton 1976 pap. $4.95; *Eng. Experience Ser.* Walter J. Johnson repr. of 1612 ed. 1971 $14.00; ed. by Alvin B. Kernan, Yale Univ. Pr. 1974 $24.00 pap. $8.95

Catiline. 1611. Ed. by W. F. Bolton and Jane Gardner, *Regents Renaissance Drama Ser.* Univ. of Nebraska Pr. 1973 $17.95

Bartholomew Fair. 1614. Ed. by E. A. Horsman, *Revels Plays Ser.* Johns Hopkins Univ. Pr. text ed. 1960 $17.50; Longwood repr. of 1960 ed. 1965 $23.50; ed. by George Hibbard, *New Mermaid Ser.* Norton 1977 pap. $4.95; ed. by Edward B. Partridge, *Regents Renaissance Drama Ser.* Univ. of Nebraska Pr. 1964 $5.95; ed. by Eugene M. Waith, Yale Univ. Pr. 1963 pap. $7.95

The Staple of News. 1625. Ed. by Devra R. Kifer, *Regents Renaissance Drama Ser.*
  Univ. of Nebraska Pr. 1975 $16.95
The New Inn. 1629. Ed. by Michael Hattaway, *Revels Plays Ser.* Longwood 1985
  $35.00
Timber: Or Discoveries. 1640. Ed. by Ralph S. Walker, Greenwood repr. of 1953 ed.
  1976 lib. bdg. $18.75
The Case Is Altered. Ed. by W. E. Selin, Elliots Bks. 1917 pap. $39.50
The Gypsies Metamorphosed. Ed. by G. Cole, Kraus repr. of 1931 ed. $24.00

Books about Jonson

Bamborough, J. B. *Ben Jonson. Eng. Lit. Ser.* Humanities Pr. text ed. 1970 pap. $5.25
Barish, Jonas A. *Ben Jonson and the Language of Prose Comedy.* Norton Lib. repr. of
  1967 ed. 1970 pap. $2.45. An important and influential study.
Barton, Anne. *Ben Jonson: Dramatist.* Cambridge Univ. Pr. 1984 $54.50 pap. $17.95
Baskerville, Charles R. *English Elements in Jonson's Early Comedy.* Gordian repr. of
  1911 ed. 1967 $12.50; Johnson Repr. repr. of 1911 ed. pap. $20.00
Bates, Steven L., and Sidney D. Orr. *Concordance to the Poems of Ben Jonson.* Ohio
  Univ. Pr. 1978 $48.00
Baum, Helena W. *The Satiric and the Didactic in Ben Jonson's Comedy.* Russell repr.
  of 1947 ed. 1971 $12.00
Beaurline, Lester A. *Jonson and Elizabethan Comedy: Essays in Dramatic Rhetoric.*
  Huntington Lib. 1978 $16.00. Well-informed criticism.
Bentley, Gerald E. *Shakespeare and Jonson, Their Reputations in the Seventeenth Cen-
  tury Compared.* Univ. of Chicago Pr. 2 vols. in 1. 1965 $27.50
Blisset, William, and others. *A Celebration of Ben Jonson.* Univ. of Toronto Pr. 1974
  pap. $7.50
Bradley, Jesse F., and Joseph Q. Adams, eds. *The Jonson Allusion-Book: A Collection
  of Allusions to Ben Jonson from 1597 to 1700.* Russell repr. of 1922 ed. 1971
  $17.00; Scholarly repr. of 1922 ed. 1971 $16.00
Brock, D. Heyward, and James M. Welsh. *Ben Jonson: A Quadricentennial Bibliogra-
  phy, 1947–1972. Author Bibliographies Ser.* Scarecrow Pr. 1974 $16.50
Chalfant, Fran C. *Ben Jonson's London: A Jacobean Placename Dictionary.* Univ. of
  Georgia Pr. 1978 $20.00
Champion, Larry S. *Ben Jonson's "Dotages": A Reconsideration of the Late Plays.*
  Univ. Pr. of Kentucky 1967 $15.00
Chan, Mary. *Music in the Theatre of Ben Jonson.* Oxford 1980 $74.00
Cruickshank, A. H. *Ben Jonson.* Folcroft repr. of 1912 ed. lib. bdg. $8.50
Davis, Joe L. *Sons of Ben: Jonsonian Comedy in Caroline England.* Wayne State Univ.
  Pr. 1967 $10.95
Di Cesare, Mario A., and Ephim Fogel, eds. *A Concordance to the Poems of Ben Jon-
  son.* Cornell Univ. Pr. 1978 $62.50
Dick, Aliki L. *Paideia through Laughter: Jonson's Aristophanic Appeal to Human Intel-
  ligence.* Mouton text ed. 1974 pap. $22.00
Dunn, Esther C. *Ben Jonson's Art.* Arden Lib. repr. of 1925 ed. 1980 lib. bdg. $30.00
Dutton, Richard. *Ben Jonson: To the First Folio. British and Irish Authors Ser.* Cam-
  bridge Univ. Pr. 1984 $29.95 pap. $9.95
Evans, Willa M. *Ben Jonson and Elizabethan Music.* Da Capo repr. of 1929 ed. 2d ed.
  1965 $19.50
Gilbert, Allan H. *Symbolic Persons in the Masques of Ben Jonson.* AMS Pr. repr. of
  1948 ed. $23.00

Hyland, Peter. *Disguise and Role-Playing in Ben Jonson's Drama. Salzburg Studies in Eng. Lit., Jacobean Drama Studies* Humanities Pr. text ed. 1977 pap. $25.50

Jagendorf, Zvi. *The Happy End of Comedy: Shakespeare, Jonson, Molière.* Univ. of Delaware Pr. 1984 $24.50

Johnston, George B. *Ben Jonson: Poet.* Octagon repr. 1970 lib. bdg. $18.50

Judkins, David C. *Ben Jonson's Non-Dramatic Works: A Reference Guide.* G. K. Hall 1982 lib. bdg. $33.50

Juneja, Renu. *Recent Research on Ben Jonson. Salzburg Studies in Eng. Lit., Jacobean Drama Studies* Humanities Pr. text ed. 1978 pap. $25.50

Kerr, Mina. *Influence of Ben Jonson on English Comedy, 1598–1642.* Phaeton repr. of 1912 ed. 1967 $9.00

Knoll, Robert E. *Ben Jonson's Plays: An Introduction.* Univ. of Nebraska Pr. 1965 $17.95. An excellent introduction.

Linklater, Eric. *Ben Jonson and King James.* Associated Faculty Pr. repr. of 1931 ed. 1972 $24.00

Loewenstein, Joseph. *Responsive Readings: Versions of Echo in Pastoral, Epic, and the Jonsonian Masque. Yale Studies in Eng. Ser.* text ed. 1984 $17.50

McEuen, Kathryn A. *Classical Influence upon the Tribe of Ben.* Octagon 1968 lib. bdg. $20.50

Meagher, John C. *Method and Meaning in Jonson's Masques.* Univ. of Notre Dame Pr. 1969 pap. $6.95. Good for interpretation.

Musgrove, S. *Shakespeare and Jonson: The Macmillan Brown Lectures.* AMS Pr. repr. of 1957 ed. $11.50

Nason, Arthur H. *Heralds and Heraldry in Ben Jonson's Plays, Masques and Entertainments.* Arden Lib. repr. of 1907 ed. 1978 lib. bdg. $35.00; Folcroft repr. of 1907 ed. lib. bdg. $25.00; Gordian repr. of 1907 ed. 1968 $12.50

Noyes, Robert G. *Ben Jonson on the English Stage, 1660–1775.* Ayer repr. of 1935 ed. $18.00

Orgel, Stephen. *The Jonsonian Masque.* Columbia Univ. Pr. 1981 $25.00 pap. $10.50. The main authority on Jonson's masques.

Parfitt, George. *Ben Jonson: Public Poet and Private Man.* Barnes & Noble text ed. 1976 $22.50

Partridge, Edward B. *The Broken Compass: A Study of the Major Comedies of Ben Jonson.* Greenwood repr. of 1958 ed. 1976 lib. bdg. $37.50. An important study.

Peterson, Richard S. *Imitation and Praise in the Poems of Ben Jonson.* Yale Univ. Pr. 1981 $24.50

Randall, Dale B. *Jonson's Gypsies Unmasked: Background and Theme of the Gypsies Metamorphos'd.* Duke Univ. Pr. 1974 $15.00

Sackton, Alexander H. *Rhetoric as a Dramatic Language in Ben Jonson.* Octagon repr. 1967 lib. bdg. $16.50

Schelling, Felix E. *Ben Jonson and the Classical School. Studies in Drama* Haskell repr. of 1898 ed. 1970 lib. bdg. $22.95

Small, Roscoe A. *A Stage-Quarrel Between Ben Jonson and the So-Called Poetasters.* AMS Pr. repr. of 1889 ed. $17.00

Smith, G. Gregory. *Ben Jonson.* Folcroft repr. of 1919 ed. lib. bdg. $18.50; Scholarly repr. of 1919 ed. 1972 $19.00

Sturmberger, Ingeborg. *The Comic Elements of Ben Jonson's Drama. Salzburg Studies in Eng. Lit., Jacobean Drama Studies* Humanities Pr. 2 vols. text ed. 1975 pap. $50.75

Summers, Claude J., and Ted Larry Pebworth. *Ben Jonson. Twayne's Eng. Authors Ser.* G. K. Hall 1979 $13.50

Swinburne, Algernon C. *Study of Ben Jonson. Studies in Drama* Haskell repr. of 1889 ed. 1969 lib. bdg. $49.95; ed. by Howard B. Norland, Univ. of Nebraska Pr. 1969 pap. $3.65

Symonds, John A. *Ben Jonson.* AMS Pr. repr. of 1886 ed. $10.00; Folcroft 1973 lib. bdg. $12.50

Townsend, Freda L. *Apologie for Bartholomew Fayre.* Kraus repr. of 1947 ed. pap. $10.00

Trimpi, Wesley. *Ben Jonson's Poems: A Study of the Plain Style.* Stanford Univ. Pr. 1962 $25.00

Wheeler, Charles F. *Classical Mythology in the Plays, Masques, and Poems of Ben Jonson.* Associated Faculty Pr. repr. of 1938 ed. 1970 $21.50

Williams, Mary C. *Sources of Unity in Ben Jonson's Comedy. Salzburg Studies in Eng. Lit., Jacobean Drama Studies* Humanities Pr. text ed. 1972 pap. $25.50

Witt, Robert W. *Mirror Within a Mirror: Ben Jonson and the Play-Within-the-Play. Salzburg Studies in Eng. Lit., Jacobean Drama Studies* Humanities Pr. text ed. 1976 pap. $25.50

Woodbridge, Elizabeth M. *Studies in Jonson's Comedies.* Gordian repr. of 1898 ed. 1966 $7.50

Zwager, Nicholas. *Glimpses of Ben Jonson's London.* Arden Lib. repr. of 1926 ed. 1980 lib. bdg. $30.00; Folcroft 1973 lib. bdg. $20.00

KYD, THOMAS. 1558–1594

Kyd is best known as the author of *The Spanish Tragedy*, an extremely popular revenge tragedy of the late 1580s. This is the most parodied of Elizabethan plays. He may also have written the lost *Hamlet* play that precedes Shakespeare's. Kyd's only acknowledged authorship is the translation of Robert Garnier's Senecan tragedy, *Cornélie*, in 1594. Although Kyd's balanced rhetoric seems old fashioned, *The Spanish Tragedy* is notable for its searing passions and intensely dramatic rendering of revenge-tragedy themes.

Book by Kyd

The Spanish Tragedy. c.1586. Ed. by Frederick Boas, AMS Pr. repr. of 1592 ed. $40.00; ed. by Charles T. Prouty, *Crofts Class. Ser.* Harlan Davidson text ed. 1951 pap. $3.50; ed. by Philip Edwards, *Revels Plays Ser.* Longwood 1981 pap. $5.00; ed. by J. R. Mulryne, *New Mermaid Ser.* Norton 1974 pap. $2.95

Book about Kyd

Murray, Peter B. *Thomas Kyd. Twayne's Eng. Authors Ser.* o.p.

LYLY, JOHN. c.1554–1606

Lyly wrote eight elegant and refined comedies for the boy companies. His witty and elaborate prose style, drawing many allusions from classical mythology, was influenced by his prose romance, *Euphues: The Anatomy of Wit* (1578), and its sequel, *Euphues and His England* (1580). This is the basis for the "euphuistic" style. His comedies are notable for their graceful and incisive portraits of women.

BOOKS BY LYLY

Complete Works. Ed. by R. Warwick Bond, Oxford 3 vols. 1902 $110.00
Endymion: The Man in the Moon. Ed. by George P. Baker, Folcroft repr. 1977 lib. bdg. $20.00
Mother Bombie. 1594. *Malone Society Repr. Ser.* AMS Pr. repr. of 1939 ed. $40.00; ed. by Harriette Andreadis, *Salzburg Studies in Eng. Lit., Elizabethan and Renaissance Studies* Humanities Pr. text ed. 1975 pap. $25.50
Gallathea (and *Midas*). Ed. by Anne B. Lancashire, *Regents Renaissance Drama Ser.* Univ. of Nebraska Pr. 1970 $15.95

BOOKS ABOUT LYLY

Jeffrey, Violet M. *John Lyly and the Italian Renaissance.* Russell repr. of 1928 ed. 1969 $7.50
Saccio, Peter. *The Court Comedies of John Lyly: A Study in Allegorical Dramaturgy.* Princeton Univ. Pr. 1969 $27.50
Scragg, Leah. *The Metamorphosis of Galathea: A Study in Creative Adaptation.* Univ. Pr. of Amer. 1982 lib. bdg. $22.00 text ed. pap. $8.75
Wilson, John D. *John Lyly.* Haskell repr. of 1905 ed. 1969 lib. bdg. $39.95

MARLOWE, CHRISTOPHER. 1564–1593

Marlowe was born in the same year as Shakespeare and by the time of his early death in 1593 his achievement towered over that of his longer-lived contemporary. Marlowe burst into the theatrical scene around 1588 with the two parts of *Tamburlaine,* a grand conqueror play whose mighty hero threatens the world "with high astounding terms." Marlowe's blank verse—his "mighty line"—was strong and passionate and offered a model for later dramatists. All of Marlowe's seven plays test limits or show a protagonist striving against a humdrum and uncomprehending world. Doctor Faustus is a typically Marlovian hero who dares damnation to achieve a more than human scope. Marlowe himself during his lifetime was accused of atheism and homosexuality. He seems to have been a secret agent in the government service, and he was killed in a tavern brawl at Deptford under mysterious circumstances. There is a Marlowe Society in the United States that puts out a regular periodical with reviews.

BOOKS BY MARLOWE

The Complete Works of Christopher Marlowe. Ed. by Fredson Bowers, Cambridge Univ. Pr. 2 vols. 2d ed. 1981 $150.00. This is the standard scholarly edition.
Works. Ed. by C. F. Tucker Brooke, Oxford 1910 $49.95
The Works and Life of Christopher Marlowe. Ed. by R. H. Case, Gordian 6 vols. repr. of 1933 ed. 1966 $75.00
Complete Plays of Christopher Marlowe. Ed. by Irving Ribner, Irvington text ed. 1963 $24.50
Complete Plays and Poems. Ed. by E. D. Pendry and J. C. Maxwell, Biblio Dist. (Everyman's) repr. of 1976 ed. text ed. 1983 pap. $7.50
Marlowe's Poems. Ed. by L. C. Martin, Gordian repr. of 1931 ed. 1966. $12.50
Tamburlaine the Great. 1590. Ed. by U. M. Ellis-Fermor, Gordian 2 vols. repr. of 1930 ed. 1966 $12.50; ed. by J. S. Cunningham, *Revels Plays Ser.* Johns Hopkins Univ. Pr. text ed. 1981 $25.00; ed. by J. W. Harper, *New Mermaid Ser.* Norton 1976

pap. $4.95; ed. by John D. Jump, *Regents Renaissance Drama Ser.* Univ. of Ne-
braska Pr. 2 pts. 1967 pap. $6.50

Edward the Second. 1594. *Malone Society Repr. Ser.* AMS Pr. repr. of 1594 ed. $40.00;
ed. by W. Moelwyn Merchant, *New Mermaid Ser.* Norton 1976 pap. $3.95

Doctor Faustus. 1604. AMS Pr. repr. of 1914 ed. $49.50; ed. by Frederick Boas, Gor-
dian repr. of 1932 ed. 1966 $12.50 pap. $9.75; ed. by Paul H. Kocher, *Crofts
Class. Ser.* Harlan Davidson text ed. 1950 pap. $3.25; ed. by John D. Jump,
Holmes & Meier text ed. pap. $6.50; ed. by John D. Jump, *Methuen Eng. Class.*
1965 pap. $4.95; ed. by Sylvan Barnet, New Amer. Lib. (Signet Class.) 1969 pap.
$2.50; ed. by Roma Gill, *New Mermaid Ser.* Norton 1976 pap. $4.95; ed. by Irving
Ribner, Odyssey Pr. 1966 pap. $8.40; ed. by Louis B. Wright and Virginia A. La-
Mar, Washington Square Pr. pap. $3.95

The Jew of Malta. 1633. Ed. by H. S. Bennett, Gordian repr. of 1931 ed. 1966 $12.50;
ed. by N. W. Bawcutt, *Revels Plays Ser.* Johns Hopkins Univ. Pr. text ed. 1978
$16.50; Longwood repr. of 1977 ed. 1983 pap. $5.00; ed. by T. W. Craik, *New Mermaid Ser.* Norton 1976 pap. $4.95; ed. by Richard W. van Fossen, *Regents Renais-
sance Drama Ser.* Univ. of Nebraska Pr. 1964 $12.95 pap. $3.95; *Eng. Experience
Ser.* Walter J. Johnson repr. of 1633 ed. 1971 $11.50

BOOKS ABOUT MARLOWE

Ando, Sadao, ed. *A Descriptive Syntax of Christopher Marlowe's Language.* Columbia
Univ. Pr. 1976 $65.00

Bakeless, John E. *The Tragicall History of Christopher Marlowe.* Greenwood 2 vols.
repr. of 1942 ed. lib. bdg. $37.50

Benaquist, Lawrence M. *Tripartite Structure of Christopher Marlowe's Tamburlaine
Plays and Edward II. Salzburg Studies in Eng. Lit., Elizabethan and Renaissance
Studies* Humanities Pr. text ed. 1975 pap. $25.50

Birringer, Johannes. *Marlowe's "Dr. Faustus" and "Tamburlaine": Theological and Theatrical Perspectives.* Peter Lang text ed. 1983 pap. $40.55

Clark, Eleanor G. *Raleigh and Marlowe: A Study in Elizabethan Fustian.* Russell repr.
of 1941 ed. 1965 $11.50

Cole, Douglas. *Suffering and Evil in the Plays of Christopher Marlowe.* Gordian repr. of
1962 ed. text ed. 1971 $12.50

Eccles, Mark. *Christopher Marlowe in London.* Octagon repr. 1967 lib. bdg. $18.50

Fanta. *Christopher G. Marlowe's Agonists: An Approach to the Ambiguity of His Plays.*
Harvard Univ. Pr. 1970 pap. $2.50

Fehrenbach, Robert J., and others, eds. *A Concordance to the Plays, Poems, and Translations of Christopher Marlowe.* Cornell Univ. Pr. 1982 $80.00. An important refer-
ence book in the *Cornell Concordance Series.*

Fieler, Frank B. *Tamburlaine, Part One, and Its Audience.* Univ. Pr. of Florida 1961
pap. $3.50

Friedenreich, Kenneth. *Christopher Marlowe: An Annotated Bibliography of Criticism
Since 1950.* Fwd. by Richard Levin, Scarecrow Pr. 1979 $16.50

Godshalk, W. L. *The Marlovian World Picture. Studies in Eng. Lit.* Mouton text ed.
1974 pap. $32.00

Heller, Otto. *Faust and Faustus: A Study of Goethe's Relation to Marlowe.* Cooper
Square Pr. repr. of 1931 ed. 1972 lib. bdg. $20.00

Hotson, J. Leslie. *The Death of Christopher Marlowe.* Russell repr. of 1925 ed. 1967
$7.50. Hotson discovered the sensational circumstances of Marlowe's death.

Howe, James R. *Marlowe, Tamburlaine, and Magic.* Ohio Univ. Pr. 1976. $15.00

Ingram, John H. *Christopher Marlowe and His Associates.* Cooper Square Pr. repr. of 1904 ed. 1970 lib. bdg. $25.00

———. *Marlowe and His Poetry. Poetry and Life Ser.* AMS Pr. repr. of 1914 ed. $7.25; Arden Lib. repr. of 1914 ed. 1978 lib. bdg. $17.50; Folcroft 1972 lib. bdg. $25.00

Kocher, Paul H. *Christopher Marlowe: A Study of His Thought, Learning and Character.* Russell repr. of 1946 ed. 1962. $19.00

Leech, Clifford. *Christopher Marlowe: Poet for the Stage.* AMS Pr. 1985 $32.50

Levin, Harry. *The Overreacher: A Study of Christopher Marlowe.* Peter Smith $11.25. Insightful criticism, especially on style.

Lom, Herbert. *Enter a Spy: The Double Life of Christopher Marlowe.* Rowman 1978 $11.50. Romantic biography.

MacLure, Millar, ed. *Marlowe: The Critical Heritage, 1588–1896.* Routledge & Kegan 1979 $27.95

Masinton, Charles G. *Christopher Marlowe's Tragic Vision: A Study in Damnation.* Ohio Univ. Pr. 1972 $15.00

Meehan, Virginia M. *Christopher Marlowe: Poet and Playwright.* Mouton text ed. 1974 pap. $13.20

O'Neill, Judith, ed. *Critics on Marlowe.* Univ. of Miami Pr. 1970 $5.95

Pinciss, Gerald M. *Christopher Marlowe. Lit. and Life Ser.* Ungar 1975 $12.95 1984 pap. $7.95

Poirier, Michel. *Christopher Marlowe.* Shoe String (Archon) repr. of 1951 ed. 1968 $16.50

Roehrman, Hendrik. *The Way of Life.* AMS Pr. repr. of 1952 ed. $5.00

Sanders, Wilbur. *The Dramatist and the Received Idea.* Cambridge Univ. Pr. 1968 $59.50 1980 pap. $17.95

Sims, James H. *Dramatic Uses of Biblical Allusions in Marlowe and Shakespeare.* Univ. Pr. of Florida 1966 pap. $3.50

Smith, Marion B. *Marlowe's Imagery and the Marlowe Canon.* Arden Lib. repr. of 1939 ed. 1978 $30.00

Smith, Mary E. *Love Kindling Fire: A Study of Christopher Marlowe's The Tragedy of Dido, Queen of Carthage. Salzburg Studies in Eng. Lit., Elizabethan and Renaissance Studies* Humanities Pr. text ed. 1977 pap. $25.50

Steane, J. B. *Marlowe: A Critical Study.* Cambridge Univ. Pr. 1964 pap. $15.95. A good introduction.

Summers, Claude J. *Christopher Marlowe and the Politics of Power. Salzburg Studies in Eng. Lit., Elizabethan and Renaissance Studies* Humanities Pr. text ed. 1974 pap. $25.50

Verity, A. W. *Influence of Christopher Marlowe on Shakespeare's Earlier Style.* Folcroft 1886 lib. bdg. $10.00

Weil, Judith. *Christopher Marlowe.* Cambridge Univ. Pr. 1977 $39.50

Wraight, A. D., and Virginia Stern. *In Search of Christopher Marlowe: A Pictorial Biography.* Fwd. by W. Urry, Vanguard 1965 $17.50

Zucker, David H. *Stage and Image in the Plays of Christopher Marlowe. Salzburg Studies in Eng. Lit., Elizabethan and Renaissance Studies* Humanities Pr. text ed. 1972 pap. $25.50

MARSTON, JOHN. c.1575–1634

Marston studied law in the Middle Temple, but abandoned the law to write biting verse satires in the Roman style of Juvenal. His best known satires are *The Scourge of Villainy* and *The Metamorphosis of Pygmalion's Im-*

age. When verse satires were forbidden in 1599, Marston turned his satiric talent to the theater. *The Malcontent* is his best known play. There is a sharp distinction between the banished Altofronto who speaks in verse and his disguise as Malevole, who expresses himself in a scurrilous and misanthropic prose. *The Dutch Courtesan* is preoccupied with sexuality and is at once moralistic, satirical, cynical, and grotesque. These mixtures of tone are part of the passionate attitudinizing of Marston. All of his plays were written for performance by children's companies in the private theaters.

BOOKS BY MARSTON

Works. Ed. by A. H. Bullen, Adler's 3 vols. repr. of 1887 ed. 1970 $116.00
The Plays of John Marston. Ed. by Harvey H. Wood, Arden Lib. 3 vols. repr. of 1934 ed. 1978 lib. bdg. $250.00; ed. by Harvey H. Wood, Somerset 3 vols. repr. of 1934 ed. $225.00
Antonio and Mellida. 1599. Ed. by George K. Hunter, *Regents Renaissance Drama Ser.* Univ. of Nebraska Pr. 1965 $9.50 pap. $2.95
Antonio's Revenge. 1599. Ed. by George K. Hunter, *Regents Renaissance Drama Ser.* Univ. of Nebraska Pr. 1965 $8.50. *Antonio and Mellida* and *Antonio's Revenge* are two parts of a double play.
The Dutch Courtesan. 1604. Ed. by M. L. Wine, *Regents Renaissance Drama Ser.* Univ. of Nebraska Pr. 1965 $12.95
The Malcontent. 1604. Ed. by George K. Hunter, *Revels Plays Ser.* Longwood 1975 $23.50 pap. $6.50; ed. by Bernard Harris, *New Mermaid Ser.* Norton 1976 pap. $2.95; ed. by M. L. Wine, *Regents Renaissance Drama Ser.* Univ. of Nebraska Pr. 1964 $12.50 pap. $3.95
The Fawn. c.1605. Ed. by Gerald A. Smith, *Regents Renaissance Drama Ser.* Univ. of Nebraska Pr. 1965 $11.95 pap. $2.95

BOOKS ABOUT MARSTON

Allen, Morse S. *The Satire of John Marston. Studies in Drama* Haskell repr. of 1920 ed. 1969 lib. bdg. $45.95
Caputi, Anthony. *John Marston, Satirist.* Octagon repr. of 1961 ed. 1976 lib. bdg. $24.00. An important book.
Colley, John S. *John Marston's Theatrical Drama. Salzburg Studies in Eng. Lit., Jacobean Drama Studies* Humanities Pr. text ed. 1974 pap. $25.50
Geckle, George L. *John Marston's Drama: Themes, Images, Sources.* Fairleigh Dickinson Univ. Pr. 1979 $23.50
Jensen, Ejner. *John Marston, Dramatist. Salzburg Studies in Eng. Lit., Jacobean Drama Studies* Humanities Pr. text ed. 1980 pap. $25.50
Scott, Michael. *John Marston Plays: Themes, Structure and Performance.* Barnes & Noble text ed. 1978 $25.00

MASSINGER, PHILIP. 1583–1640

Massinger is a prolific dramatist who wrote, or had a hand in, more than 50 plays. His specialty was tragicomedy, in which he imitated John Fletcher. His best known play is *A New Way to Pay Old Debts*, based on Middleton's *A Trick to Catch the Old One.* Sir Giles Overreach reflects the historical Sir Giles Mompesson, a notorious capitalist and extortionist, who was tried in 1621. There is a good deal of snobbery in Massinger's play, and the class hatred of Sir Giles is frenzied and passionate. *A New Way* has had an active theatrical history from its own day to the present, especially as a vehicle for the grandly histrionic role of Overreach.

BOOKS BY MASSINGER

Plays of Philip Massinger. Ed. by William Gifford, AMS Pr. 4 vols. 2d ed. repr. of 1813 ed. $160.00

The Plays and Poems of Philip Massinger. Ed. by Philip Edwards and Colin Gibson, *Oxford Eng. Texts Ser.* 5 vols. 1976 $179.00. This is an admirable modern edition of Massinger's extensive works.

A New Way to Pay Old Debts. 1621. Ed. by M. St. Clare Byrne, Greenwood repr. of 1956 ed. 1976 lib. bdg. $19.75; *Royal Shakespeare Company PIT Playtext Ser.* Methuen 1983 pap. $4.95; *New Mermaid Ser.* Norton text ed. 1984 pap. $5.95

City Madam. 1632. *New Mermaid Ser.* Norton text ed. 1984 pap. $5.95; ed. by Cyrus Hoy, *Regents Renaissance Drama Ser.* Univ. of Nebraska Pr. 1964 $10.95 pap. $2.95

BOOKS ABOUT MASSINGER

Cruickshank, Alfred H. *Philip Massinger.* Russell repr. of 1920 ed. 1971 $13.00

Evenhuis, Francis D. *Massinger's Imagery. Salzburg Studies in Eng. Lit., Jacobean Drama Studies* Humanities Pr. text ed. 1973 pap. $25.50

Maxwell, Baldwin. *Studies in Beaumont, Fletcher and Massinger.* Octagon 1966 lib. bdg. $18.50

McManaway, James G. *Philip Massinger and the Restoration Drama.* Folcroft repr. of 1934 ed. lib. bdg. $8.50

MIDDLETON, THOMAS. c.1580–1627

Middleton wrote in a wide variety of genres and styles and is a thoroughly professional dramatist. His comedies are generally based on London life, but are seen through the perspective of Roman comedy, especially Plautus. Middleton is a masterful constructor of plots. *A Chaste Maid in Cheapside* is typical of Middleton's interests. It is biting and satirical in tone; the crassness of the willing cuckold Allwit is almost frightening. Middleton was very preoccupied with sexual themes, especially in his tragedies, *The Changeling*, written with William Rowley, and *Women Beware Women*. The portraits of women in these plays are remarkable. Both Beatrice-Joanna in *The Changeling* and Bianca in *Women Beware Women* move swiftly from innocence to corruption, and Livia in *Women Beware Women* is noteworthy as a feminine Machiavelli and manipulator. In his psychological realism and his powerful vision of evil, Middleton is close to Shakespeare.

BOOKS BY MIDDLETON

The Works of Thomas Middleton. Ed. by A. H. Bullen, AMS Pr. 8 vols. repr. of 1886 ed. $340.00

Three Plays. Ed. by Kenneth Muir, Biblio Dist. (Everyman's) repr. of 1975 ed. 1984 pap. $5.95; ed. by Kenneth Muir, Rowman 1975 pap. $4.75

Best Plays of the Old Dramatists. Scholarly 2 vols. repr. of 1887 ed. $69.00. The old Mermaid edition.

Michaelmas Term. 1607. Ed. by Richard Levin, *Regents Renaissance Drama Ser.* Univ. of Nebraska Pr. 1967 $14.50 pap. $3.25

A Mad World, My Masters. 1608. Ed. by Standish Henning, *Regents Renaissance Drama Ser.* Univ. of Nebraska Pr. 1965 $11.50 pap. $2.95

A Trick to Catch the Old One. 1608. Ed. by C. J. Watson, *New Mermaid Ser.* Norton 1976 pap. $2.95

(and Thomas Dekker). *The Roaring Girl.* 1611. Ed. by A. H. Gomme, *New Mermaid Ser.* Norton 1976 pap. $3.95

Women Beware Women. 1621. Ed. by J. R. Mulryne, *Revels Plays Ser.* Longwood 1975 $23.50 pap. $5.50; ed. by Roma Gill, *New Mermaid Ser.* Norton 1980 pap. $5.95

(and William Rowley). *The Changeling.* 1622. Ed. by N. W. Bawcutt, *Revels Plays Ser.* Longwood 1979 pap. $5.00; ed. by Patricia Thomson, *New Mermaid Ser.* Norton 1976 pap. $4.95; ed. by George W. Williams, *Regents Renaissance Drama Ser.* Univ. of Nebraska Pr. 1966 $11.95 pap. $3.50; ed. by Matthew W. Black, Univ. of Pennsylvania Pr. pap. $8.95

A Game at Chess. 1625. Humanities Pr. text ed. 1980 pap. $25.50; ed. by J. W. Harper, *New Mermaid Ser.* Norton 1976 pap. $2.95

A Chaste Maid in Cheapside. 1630. Ed. by Alan Brissenden, *New Mermaid Ser.* Norton 1976 pap. $2.95

No Wit, No Help Like a Woman's. Ed. by Lowell E. Johnson, *Regents Renaissance Drama Ser.* Univ. of Nebraska Pr. 1976 $14.50

The Widow: A Critical Edition. Ed. by Robert Levine, *Salzburg Studies in Eng. Lit., Jacobean Drama Studies* Humanities Pr. text ed. 1975 pap. $25.50

BOOKS ABOUT MIDDLETON

Asp, Carolyn. *A Study of Thomas Middleton's Tragicomedies. Salzburg Studies in Eng. Lit., Jacobean Drama Studies* Humanities Pr. text ed. 1974 pap. $25.50

Baines, Barbara J. *The Lust Motif in the Plays of Thomas Middleton. Salzburg Studies in Eng. Lit., Jacobean Drama Studies* Humanities Pr. text ed. 1973 pap. $25.50

Barker, Richard H. *Thomas Middleton.* Greenwood repr. of 1958 ed. 1975 lib. bdg. $19.75

Brittin, Norman A. *Thomas Middleton. Twayne's Eng. Authors Ser.* G. K. Hall lib. bdg. $15.95

Cherry, Caroline L. *The Most Unvaluedst Purchase: Women in the Plays of Thomas Middleton. Salzburg Studies in Eng. Lit., Jacobean Drama Studies* Humanities Pr. text ed. 1973 pap. $25.50

Covatta, Anthony. *Thomas Middleton's City Comedies.* Bucknell Univ. Pr. 1974 $18.00

Dunkel, Wilbur D. *Dramatic Technique of Thomas Middleton in His Comedies of London Life.* Russell repr. of 1925 ed. 1967 $6.50

Hallett, Charles A. *Middleton's Cynics. Salzburg Studies in Eng. Lit., Jacobean Drama Studies* Humanities Pr. text ed. 1975 pap. $25.50

Heinemann, Margot. *Puritanism and Theatre: Thomas Middleton and Opposition Drama under the Early Stuarts.* Cambridge Univ. Pr. 1982 $34.50 pap. $13.95

Kistner, A. L., and M. K. Kistner. *Middleton's Tragic Themes.* Peter Lang text ed. 1984 pap. $23.00

McElroy, John F. *Parody and Burlesque in the Tragicomedies of Thomas Middleton. Salzburg Studies in Eng. Lit., Jacobean Drama Studies* Humanities Pr. text ed. 1972 pap. $25.50

Rowe, George E., Jr. *Thomas Middleton and the New Comedy Tradition.* Univ. of Nebraska Pr. 1979 $19.95

Schoenbaum, Samuel. *Middleton's Tragedies*. Gordian repr. of 1955 ed. text ed. 1970 $12.50

Steene, Sara J. *Thomas Middleton: A Reference Guide*. G. K. Hall 1984 lib. bdg. $55.00

PEELE, GEORGE. c.1558–1596?

Peele wrote a variety of plays: *Edward I*, an English Chronicle history; *The Battle of Alcazar*, a foreign history; *The Old Wives' Tale*, a folkloric narration; *The Arraignment of Paris*, a mythological pastoral; and *David and Bethsabe*, a biblical tragedy. Peele is predominantly a courtly dramatist best known for his fluent lyrical gifts.

BOOKS BY PEELE

The Dramatic Works of George Peele. Ed. by Mark R. Benbow, Yale Univ. Pr. 3 vols. 1970 $45.00. This is an excellent scholarly edition.

The Old Wives' Tale. c.1593. *Malone Society Repr. Ser*. AMS Pr. repr. of 1908 ed. $40.00; ed. by Patricia Binnie, *Revels Plays Ser*. Johns Hopkins Univ. Pr. 1980 $14.00

BOOKS ABOUT PEELE

Ashley, L. R. *George Peele*. Irvington text ed. 1970 $24.00

Horne, David H. *The Life and Minor Works of George Peele*. Greenwood repr. of 1952 ed. 1978 lib. bdg. $27.50

TOURNEUR, CYRIL. c.1575–1626

Little is known about the life of Cyril Tourneur. In 1600 he published a verse satire, *The Transformed Metamorphosis*, and the two plays associated with his name—*The Revenger's Tragedy* and *The Atheist's Tragedy*—are both strongly satirical. *The Revenger's Tragedy* is a masterpiece of tragic farce and black comedy, with an impassioned contempt-of-the-world rhetoric. Its authorship has been questioned, with Thomas Middleton the leading candidate. *The Atheist's Tragedy* directly engages the theological theme of atheism; it is both grotesque and homiletic in its proof of the existence of God.

BOOKS BY TOURNEUR

The Plays and Poems of Cyril Tourneur. Intro. and notes by John C. Collins, *Select Bibliographies Repr. Ser*. Ayer 2 vols. repr. of 1878 ed. $34.50

The Revenger's Tragedy. 1607. Ed. by R. A. Foakes, *Revels Plays Ser*. Longwood repr. of 1975 ed. 1980 pap. $5.95; ed. by Brian Gibbons, *New Mermaid Ser*. Norton 1976 pap. $4.95; ed. by Lawrence J. Ross, *Regents Renaissance Drama Ser*. Univ. of Nebraska Pr. 1966 $13.50 pap. $4.50

The Atheist's Tragedy. 1611. Ed. by Brian Morris and Roma Gill, *New Mermaid Ser*. Norton 1976 pap. $2.95

BOOK ABOUT TOURNEUR

Jacobson, Daniel. *The Language of the Revenger's Tragedy*. *Salzburg Studies in Eng. Lit., Jacobean Drama Studies* Humanities Pr. text ed. 1974 pap. $25.50

WEBSTER, JOHN. c.1580–c.1634

Very little is known about Webster's life. He seems to have participated in many dramatic collaborations, but his undisputed work consists of only three plays: *The White Devil* (1612), *The Duchess of Malfi* (1614), and *The Devil's Law-Case* (1623). His two great tragedies, *The White Devil* and *The Duchess of Malfi*, are darkly poetic and brooding, especially in their sardonic villain-spokesmen, Flamineo and Bosola. As critic Robert Dent has shown, Webster plundered other authors for his laborious, jewel-like, sententious, and epigrammatic style, but the overall effect is one of a soaring and passionate poetry. Webster employs the full gamut of violent and sensational effects, especially in *The Duchess of Malfi*, to render a physical sense of horror. His plots are drawn from the political and amorous intrigues of Renaissance Italy.

BOOKS BY WEBSTER

Complete Works of John Webster. Ed. by F. L. Lucas, Gordian 4 vols. repr. of 1927 ed. 1966 $65.00

The Selected Plays of John Webster: The White Devil; The Duchess of Malfi; The Devil's Law-Case. Ed. by Jonathan Dollimore and Alan Sinfield, *Plays by Renaissance and Restoration Dramatists Ser.* Cambridge Univ. Pr. 1983 $42.50 pap. $14.95

Webster: Three Plays. Ed. by D. C. Gunby, *Penguin Eng. Lib. Ser.* 1973 pap. $4.95

The White Devil. 1612. Ed. by John R. Brown, *Revels Plays Ser.* Longwood repr. of 1966 ed. 1979 pap. $5.00; Methuen 1985 pap. $3.95; ed. by Elizabeth M. Brennan, *New Mermaid Ser.* Norton 1976 pap. $5.95; ed. by J. R. Mulryne, *Regents Renaissance Drama Ser.* Univ. of Nebraska Pr. 1969 $15.50 pap. $5.95

The Duchess of Malfi. 1614. Ed. by Fred B. Millett, *Crofts Class. Ser.* Harlan Davidson text ed. 1953 pap. $3.75; ed. by Elizabeth M. Brennan, *Mermaid Dramabook Ser.* Hill & Wang 1966 $3.75; ed. by John R. Brown, *Revels Plays Ser.* Longwood repr. of 1974 ed. 1981 pap. $4.75; ed. by Elizabeth M. Brennan, *New Mermaid Ser.* Norton 2d ed. 1984 pap. $5.95

The Devil's Law-Case. 1623. Ed. by Elizabeth M. Brennan, *New Mermaid Ser.* Norton 1976 pap. $2.95; ed. by Frances A. Shirley, *Regents Renaissance Drama Ser.* Univ. of Nebraska Pr. 1972 $14.95

BOOKS ABOUT WEBSTER

Bliss, Lee. *The World's Perspective: John Webster and the Jacobean Drama.* Rutgers Univ. Pr. 1983 $22.50

Bodtke, Richard. *Tragedy and the Jacobean Temper: The Major Plays of John Webster. Salzburg Studies in Eng. Lit., Jacobean Drama Studies* Humanities Pr. text ed. 1972 pap. $25.50

Bogard, Travis. *Tragic Satire of John Webster.* Russell repr. of 1955 ed. 1965 $18.00. An important study.

Boklund, Gunnar. *The Sources of the White Devil. Essays and Studies on Eng. Language and Lit.* Kraus repr. of 1957 ed. pap. $24.00

Bradbrook, Muriel C. *John Webster.* Columbia Univ. Pr. 1980 $23.00

Corballis, Richard. *A Concordance to the Works of John Webster.* Ed. by J. M. Harding, *Salzburg Studies in Eng. Lit., Jacobean Drama Studies* Humanities Pr. 4 vols. text ed. 1979 pap. $229.50

Dwyer, William W. *A Study of John Webster's Use of Renaissance Natural and Moral*

Philosophy. Salzburg Studies in Eng. Lit., Jacobean Drama Studies Humanities Pr. text ed. 1973 pap. $25.50

Goodwyn, Floyd L., Jr. *Image Pattern and Moral Vision in John Webster. Salzburg Studies in Eng. Lit., Jacobean Drama Studies* Humanities Pr. text ed. 1977 pap. $25.50

Goreau, Eloise K. *Integrity of Life: Allegorical Imagery in the Plays of John Webster. Salzburg Studies in Eng. Lit., Jacobean Drama Studies* Humanities Pr. text ed. 1974 pap. $25.50

Griffin, Robert. *John Webster: Politics and Tragedy. Salzburg Studies in Eng. Lit., Jacobean Drama Studies* Humanities Pr. text ed. 1972 pap. $25.50

Leech, Clifford. *John Webster.* Gordon $59.95; *Eng. Biographies Ser.* Haskell repr. of 1951 ed. 1969 lib. bdg. $39.95

Mahoney, William E. *Deception in the John Webster Plays: An Analytical Study. Salzburg Studies in Eng. Lit., Jacobean Drama Studies* Humanities Pr. text ed. 1976 pap. $25.50

McLeod, Susan H. *Dramatic Imagery in the Plays of John Webster. Salzburg Studies in Eng. Lit., Jacobean Drama Studies* Humanities Pr. text ed. 1977 pap. $25.50

Moore, Don. *Webster: The Critical Heritage. Critical Heritage Ser.* Routledge & Kegan 1982 $26.95. A good account of the enormous volume of Webster criticism.

Morris, Brian, ed. *John Webster. Mermaid Critical Ser.* Verry 1970 $7.00

Murray, Peter B. *A Study of John Webster. Studies in Eng. Lit.* Mouton text ed. 1969 $32.00

Seiden, Melvin. *The Revenge Motive in Websterian Tragedy. Salzburg Studies in Eng. Lit., Jacobean Drama Studies* Humanities Pr. text ed. 1973 pap. $25.50

Sternlicht, Sanford. *John Webster's Imagery and the Webster Canon. Salzburg Studies in Eng. Lit., Jacobean Drama Studies* Humanities Pr. text ed. 1972 pap. $25.50

Stodder, Joseph H. *Moral Perspective in Webster's Major Tragedies. Salzburg Studies in Eng. Lit., Jacobean Drama Studies* Humanities Pr. text ed. 1974 pap. $25.50

Stoll, Elmer E. *John Webster: The Periods of His Work as Determined by His Relations to the Drama of His Day.* Folcroft repr. of 1906 ed. lib. bdg. $9.50; Gordian repr. of 1905 ed. 1967 $8.50; Gordon $59.95

Waage, Frederick O. *The White Devil Discover'd: Backgrounds and Foregrounds to Webster's Tragedy.* Peter Lang text ed. 1984 pap. $19.70

Wang, Tso-Liang. *The Literary Reputation of John Webster to 1830. Salzburg Studies in Eng. Lit., Jacobean Drama Studies* Humanities Pr. text ed. 1976 pap. $25.50

West, Muriel. *The Devil and John Webster. Salzburg Studies in Eng. Lit., Jacobean Drama Studies* Humanities Pr. text ed. 1974 pap. $25.50

Whitman, Robert F. *Beyond Melancholy: John Webster and the Tragedy of Darkness. Salzburg Studies in Eng. Lit., Jacobean Drama Studies* Humanities Pr. text ed. 1973 pap. $25.50

RESTORATION DRAMA

History and Criticism

The restoration of the Stuart monarchy in England in 1660 after the Civil War and the interregnum marked a new period in English history. The return of Charles II and his court from France ushered in an era of pleasure and libertinism that had long been absent. This is evident in the emergence of comedy as the dominant form, and especially a comedy of manners much influenced by MOLIÈRE and the French example. Tragedy was in a sharp decline. The tragedies of Shakespeare that were revived were often radically rewritten, as in the happy ending of *King Lear* in Nahum Tate's version. Heroic tragedy was in the ascendant, a rhetorical and stilted form that turned on the conflict of love and honor. The high-flown conventions of this form were often parodied, as in *The Rehearsal* by George Villiers, Duke of Buckingham.

There is an annual bibliography of Restoration and eighteenth-century literature published in *Philological Quarterly* (to 1970) and, thereafter, as a separate publication in *Eighteenth Century: A Current Bibliography* (of which the volumes from 1970–74 are published in *PQ*). There is also an annual bibliography, as well as articles, in *Restoration and Eighteenth-Century Theatre Research* (volumes 1–16, 1962–77).

Arnott, James F., and J. W. Robinson. *English Theatrical Literature, 1559–1900: A Bibliography.* Johnson Repr. $50.00

Brown, Laura. *English Dramatic Form, 1660–1760: An Essay in Generic History.* Yale Univ. Pr. 1981 $27.00

Craik, T. W. *Revels History of Drama in English, 1660–1750.* Methuen 1980 vol. 5 $55.00. With contributions by John Loftis, Richard Southern, Marion Jones, and A. H. Scouten. Indispensable for the study of the period.

Dobrée, Bonamy. *Restoration Comedy, 1660–1720.* Century Bookbindery 1983 lib. bdg. $40.00; Greenwood repr. of 1924 ed. 1981 lib. bdg. $22.50

Fujimura, Thomas H. *The Restoration Comedy of Wit.* Greenwood repr. of 1952 ed. 1978 lib. bdg. $27.50

Gewirtz, Arthur. *Restoration Adaptations of Early 17th-Century Comedies.* Univ. Pr. of Amer. 1983 lib. bdg. $26.00 text ed. pap. $12.25

Harwood, John T. *Critics, Values, and Restoration Comedy.* Southern Illinois Univ. Pr. 1982 $17.95

Holland, Peter. *The Ornament of Action.* Cambridge Univ. Pr. 1979 $49.50

Hume, Robert D. *The Development of English Drama in the Late Seventeenth Century.* Oxford 1976 $52.00

———. *The Rakish Stage: Studies in English Drama, 1660–1800.* Southern Illinois Univ. Pr. 1983 $25.00

———, ed. *The London Theatre World, 1600–1800.* Southern Illinois Univ. Pr. 1980 $26.95

The London Stage, 1600–1800: A Calendar of Plays, Entertainments and Afterpieces Together with Casts, Box-Receipts and Contemporary Comment. Southern Illinois Univ. Pr. 5 pts. 1963–68 pts. 1–4, 8 vols. o.p.; pt. 5, 3 vols. $100.00. In various parts and volumes all with separate editors. Collects information about performance and production of plays in the period. Indispensable for all students.

Lynch, Kathleen M. *The Social Mode of Restoration Comedy.* Octagon 1965 lib. bdg. $18.50

McCollum, John I., ed. *The Restoration Stage.* Greenwood repr. of 1961 ed. lib. bdg. $18.25

Nicoll, Allardyce. *A History of English Drama, 1660–1900.* Cambridge Univ. Pr. 6 vols. 1959 ea. $65.00–$85.00. The first three volumes cover the Restoration and eighteenth century. An authoritative reference work.

Perry, Henry T. *The Comic Spirit in Restoration Drama.* Russell repr. of 1925 ed. 1962 $7.00

Persson, Agnes V. *Comic Character in Restoration Drama.* Mouton text ed. 1975 pap. $21.00

Rothstein, Eric. *Restoration Tragedy: Form and the Process of Change.* Greenwood repr. of 1967 ed. 1978 lib. bdg. $22.50

Smith, Dane F. *The Critics in the Audience of the London Theater from Buckingham to Sheridan.* Borgo Pr. 1982 lib. bdg. $29.95; Richard West repr. of 1953 ed. 1978 lib. bdg. $25.00

Smith, John H. *The Gay Couple in Restoration Comedy.* Octagon repr. of 1948 ed. 1971 lib. bdg. $18.00

Stratman, Carl J., and others. *Restoration and Eighteenth-Century Theatre Research Bibliography, 1961–1968.* Southern Illinois Univ. Pr. 1971 $25.00; Whitston 1969 $10.50

Summers, Montague. *Bibliography of the Restoration Drama.* Russell repr. of 1934 ed. 1970 $8.00

Van der Weele, Steven. *The Critical Reputation of Restoration Comedy in Modern Times Up to 1950. Salzburg Studies in Eng. Lit., Poetic Drama and Poetic Theory* Humanities Pr. 2 vols. text ed. 1978 pap. ea. $25.50

Wilson, John H. *The Influence of Beaumont and Fletcher on the Restoration Stage.* Ayer repr. of 1928 ed. 1967 $12.00; Haskell repr. of 1928 ed. 1969 lib. bdg. $46.95

Editions of Restoration Drama

Special notice must be taken of the *Regents Restoration Drama Series*, under the general editorship of John Loftis, in which more than 32 well-edited volumes have been published.

Harris, Brice, ed. *Restoration Plays. Modern College Lib. Ser.* Random 1966 pap. $6.00. A popular text.

McMillin, Scott, ed. *Restoration and Eighteenth-Century Comedy. Norton Critical Eds.* 1973 pap. $9.95

Salgado, Gamini. *Three Restoration Comedies.* Penguin 1976 pap. $4.95

Twelve Famous Plays of the Restoration and Eighteenth Century. Somerset 3 vols. repr. of 1933 ed. $150.00

Wilson, John H., ed. *Six Restoration Plays.* Houghton Mifflin 1979 pap. $5.95

CONGREVE, WILLIAM. 1670–1729

Congreve's career as a dramatist ended before he was 30 with *The Way of the World.* Whether he was stung by Jeremy Collier's attack on the theater in *A Short View of the Immorality and Profaneness of the English Stage* or by the lukewarm reception of his play, Congreve must have perceived that times were changing. Interest in the brilliant and artificial world of comedy of manners was waning. There is already something nostalgic and backward-looking about the teasing courtship of Millamant and Mirabell and the scintillating proviso scene for their marriage. Their essential compatibility is expressed by their being able to complete each other's couplets. Congreve's earlier comedies, *The Old Bachelor* (1693), *The Double Dealer* (1693), and *Love for Love* (1695), are all graceful, witty, and poetic, with sparkling, natural dialogue. He wrote one blank verse tragedy, *The Mourning Bride.*

BOOKS BY CONGREVE

The Complete Plays of William Congreve. Ed. by Herbert Davis, Univ. of Chicago Pr. 1967 $35.00

The Comedies of William Congreve: The Old Bachelor, The Double Dealer, Love for Love, The Way of the World. Ed. by Anthony Henderson, *Plays by Renaissance and Restoration Dramatists Ser.* Cambridge Univ. Pr. 1982 $42.50 pap. $14.95

Love for Love. 1695. Ed. by Malcolm Kelsall, *New Mermaid Ser.* Norton 1976 pap. $2.95; ed. by Emmett L. Avery, *Regents Restoration Drama Ser.* Univ. of Nebraska Pr. 1966 $14.50 pap. $3.95

The Way of the World. 1700. Ed. by Henry T. Perry, *Crofts Class. Ser.* Harlan Davidson text ed. 1951 pap. $3.75; ed. by Kathleen M. Lynch, *Regents Restoration Drama Ser.* Univ. of Nebraska Pr. 1965 $13.50 pap. $3.50

BOOKS ABOUT CONGREVE

Bartlett, Laurence. *William Congreve: A Reference Guide.* G. K. Hall 1979 lib. bdg. $25.00

Dobrée, Bonamy. *William Congreve: A Conversation Between Swift and Gay.* Folcroft repr. of 1929 ed. lib. bdg. $6.00

Gosse, Edmund W. *Life of William Congreve.* Folcroft 1973 lib. bdg. $20.00

Hodges, J. C. *William Congreve: The Man.* Kraus repr. of 1941 ed. $18.00

Lynch, Kathleen M. *Congreve Gallery.* Octagon repr. of 1967 ed. lib. bdg. $17.00

Mann, David D., ed. *A Concordance to the Plays of William Congreve.* Cornell Univ. Pr. 1973 $55.00

Mueschke, Paul. *A New View of Congreve's Way of the World.* Folcroft repr. of 1958 ed. lib. bdg. $20.00

Snider, Rose. *Satire in the Comedies of Congreve, Sheridan, Wilde and Coward.* Folcroft repr. of 1937 ed. lib. bdg. $15.00; Phaeton repr. of 1937 ed. text ed. 1971 $9.00

Taylor, D. Crane. *William Congreve.* Folcroft repr. of 1931 ed. lib. bdg. $25.00

Williams, Aubrey L. *An Approach to Congreve.* Yale Univ. Pr. text ed. 1979 $25.00

DRYDEN, JOHN. 1631–1700

Dryden dominates the Restoration period. He worked in all genres and took pleasure in trying out new kinds of plays. In the heroic dramas, *Aureng-Zebe* and *The Conquest of Granada* (1672), Dryden was skillful in tempering the bombast inherent in the genre. Dryden's version of Shakespeare's *Antony and Cleopatra* in *All for Love* is a good example of how far tragedy has moved from individual passion and psychological realism. Dryden is much more interested in psychological types and characteristic situations with moral and ethical overtones of a general nature. Dryden's comedies tend toward the model of tragicomedy developed by Beaumont and Fletcher. *Marriage à la Mode*, for example, is a witty, realistic sexual intrigue that depends on sudden reversals and strong contrasts. (See also Volume 1, Chapter 5.)

BOOKS BY DRYDEN

The Works of John Dryden. Univ. of California Pr. 19 vols. 1956–79 ea. $50.00–$55.00. This will be the standard edition when completed in this projected 21-volume edition.

Dramatic Works. Ed. by Montague Summers, Gordian 6 vols. repr. of 1931 ed. 1968 $150.00

An Essay of Dramatic Poesy and Other Critical Writings. Ed. by John L. Mahoney, Irvington repr. of 1965 ed. text ed. 1982 pap. $7.95
Aureng-Zebe. 1675. Ed. by Frederick M. Link, *Regents Restoration Drama Ser.* Univ. of Nebraska Pr. 1971 $13.50 pap. $4.95
Marriage à la Mode. 1671. Ed. by Mark S. Auburn, *Regents Restoration Drama Ser.* Univ. of Nebraska Pr. 1981 $14.95 pap. $4.95
All for Love. 1677. Ed. by Nicholas J. Andrew, *New Mermaid Ser.* Norton 1976 pap. $4.95; ed. by David M. Vieth, *Regents Restoration Drama Ser.* Univ. of Nebraska Pr. 1972 pap. $4.25

BOOKS ABOUT DRYDEN

Allen, Ned B. *The Sources of John Dryden's Comedies.* Gordian repr. of 1935 ed. 1967 $10.00; Richard West repr. of 1935 ed. 1978 lib. bdg. $25.00
Alssid, Michael W. *Dryden's Rhymed Heroic Tragedies: A Critical Study of the Plays and of Their Place in Dryden's Poetry. Salzburg Studies in Eng. Lit., Poetic Drama and Poetic Theory* Humanities Pr. 2 vols. text ed. 1974 pap. $50.75
Hall, James M. *John Dryden: A Reference Guide.* G. K. Hall 1984 lib. bdg. $50.00
Hughes, Derek. *Dryden's Heroic Plays.* Univ. of Nebraska Pr. 1980 $26.50
Kinsley, James, and Helen Kinsley, eds. *Dryden: The Critical Heritage.* Routledge & Kegan 1971 $38.00
Kirsch, Arthur C. *Dryden's Heroic Drama.* Gordian repr. of 1965 ed. text ed. 1972 $8.50
Larson, Richard L. *Studies in John Dryden's Dramatic Technique. Salzburg Studies in Eng. Lit., Poetic Drama and Poetic Theory* Humanities Pr. text ed. 1975 pap. $25.50
Latt, David J., and Samuel H. Monk. *John Dryden: A Survey and Bibliography of Critical Studies, 1895–1974.* Univ. of Minnesota Pr. rev. ed. 1976 $15.00
Russell, Trusten W. *Voltaire, Dryden and Heroic Tragedy.* AMS Pr. repr. of 1946 ed. $12.50
Sherwood, Margaret P. *Dryden's Dramatic Theory and Practice.* Russell repr. of 1898 ed. 1966 $7.00
Swedenberg, H. T., Jr., ed. *Essential Articles for the Study of John Dryden. Essential Articles Ser.* Shoe String (Archon) 1966 $25.00
Zamonski, John A. *An Annotated Bibliography of John Dryden: Text and Studies, 1949–1973.* Garland 1974 lib. bdg. $25.00

ETHEREGE, SIR GEORGE. c.1635–c.1691

Etherege helped to develop the comedy of manners, or society comedy, in which the brilliant world of wits and fops is both portrayed and satirized. In his best known comedy, *The Man of Mode*, Dorimant is hardly a model for how the young man about town should behave. Etherege is a cool observer of manners. Sir Fopling Flutter is clearly a Frenchified fop and dandy, yet he is also lovable. Harriet is a prototype of the witty, liberated woman, coquettish, teasing, and intelligent. Etherege's other comedies are *The Comical Revenge, or Love in a Tub* and *She Would If She Could.*

BOOKS BY ETHEREGE

The Dramatic Works of Sir George Etherege. Ed. by H. F. Brett-Smith, Scholarly 2 vols. repr. of 1927 ed. 1971 $39.00

The Plays of Sir George Etherege. Ed. by Michael Cordner, *Plays by Renaissance and Restoration Dramatists Ser.* Cambridge Univ. Pr. 1982 $42.50 pap. $15.95
The Works of Sir George Etherege. Ed. by A. W. Verity, Folcroft 1974 lib. bdg. $48.50
The Letters of Sir George Etherege. Ed. by Frederick Bracher, Univ. of California Pr. 1974 $38.50
She Would If She Could. 1668. Ed. by Charlene M. Taylor, *Regents Restoration Drama Ser.* Univ. of Nebraska Pr. 1971 pap. $3.95
The Man of Mode. 1676. Ed. by John Barnard, *New Mermaid Ser.* Norton 1979 pap. $7.95; ed. by W. B. Carnochan, *Regents Restoration Drama Ser.* Univ. of Nebraska Pr. 1966 $15.50 pap. $4.50

BOOKS ABOUT ETHEREGE

Jantz, Ursula. *Targets of Satire in the Comedies of Etherege, Wycherley and Congreve. Salzburg Studies in Eng. Lit., Poetic Drama and Poetic Theory* Humanities Pr. text ed. 1978 pap. $25.50
Mann, David D. *Sir George Etherege: A Reference Guide.* G. K. Hall 1981 lib. bdg. $25.00
McCamic, Frances S. *Sir George Etherege.* Folcroft repr. of 1931 ed. lib. bdg. $15.00

FARQUHAR, GEORGE. 1678?–1707

Farquhar was Irish by birth and education and he brought to English comedy a fresh good humor and an emphasis on country settings. *The Recruiting Officer,* which Brecht rewrote, is a lively takeoff on the author's own military experiences. His best known play, *The Beaux' Stratagem,* engages the marriage debate and the difficulty of divorce, drawing on Milton's divorce tracts. It is a lively, very natural comedy of sensibility. Farquhar wrote *Discourse upon Comedy in a Letter to a Friend,* in which he defended the genre as "a well-framed tale, handsomely told, as an agreeable vehicle for counsel or reproof."

BOOKS BY FARQUHAR

Complete Works. Ed. by Charles Stonehill, Gordian 2 vols. repr. of 1930 ed. 1967 $50.00
The Recruiting Officer. 1706. Heinemann text ed. 1969 $4.00; pref. by Peter Dixon, *Revels Plays Ser.* Longwood 1985 $35.00; ed. by John Ross, *New Mermaid Ser.* Norton 1977 pap. $4.95; ed. by Michael Shugrue, *Regents Restoration Drama Ser.* Univ. of Nebraska Pr. 1965 $13.50 pap. $3.25
The Beaux' Stratagem. 1707. Ed. by Michael Cordner, *New Mermaid Ser.* Norton pap. $2.95

BOOK ABOUT FARQUHAR

Connely, Willard. *Young George Farquhar.* Arden Lib. repr. of 1949 ed. 1980 lib. bdg. $25.00

OTWAY, THOMAS. 1652–1685

Otway was probably the best writer of tragedies in the period. His *Venice Preserved* is rivaled only by Dryden's *All for Love.* As the Royal Shakespeare Company's recent production so well demonstrated, *Venice Preserved* is still a dark and passionate play. The love versus honor conflict echoes the heroic drama, but Jaffier's vacillation between the demands of a friend and a wife reflects the somberness of a world in chaos—a Jacobean tragic theme. Otway's *The Orphan* set the fashion for a serious play based on pathos, if not actual tears.

BOOKS BY OTWAY

Complete Works. Ed. by Montague Summers, AMS Pr. 3 vols. repr. of 1926 ed. $180.00

The Orphan. 1680. Ed. by Aline M. Taylor, *Regents Restoration Drama Ser.* Univ. of Nebraska Pr. 1976 $12.50

Venice Preserved. 1682. Ed. by Malcolm Kelsall, *Regents Restoration Drama Ser.* Univ. of Nebraska Pr. 1969 $11.95

BOOKS ABOUT OTWAY

Armistead, J. M. *Four Restoration Playwrights: A Reference Guide to Thomas Shadwell, Aphra Behn, Nathaniel Lee, and Thomas Otway.* G. K. Hall 1984 lib. bdg. $65.00

Pollard, Hazel M. *From Heroics to Sentimentalism: A Study of Thomas Otway's Trage-dies. Salzburg Studies in Eng. Lit., Poetic Drama and Poetic Theory* Humanities Pr. text ed. 1974 pap. $25.50

Schumacher, Edgar. *Thomas Otway.* Burt Franklin repr. of 1924 ed. 1970 lib. bdg. $18.50

Taylor, Aline M. *Next to Shakespeare.* AMS Pr. repr. of 1950 ed. $17.50

Warner, Kerstin P. *Thomas Otway. Twayne's Eng. Authors Ser.* G. K. Hall 1982 lib. bdg. $16.95

VANBRUGH, SIR JOHN. 1664–1726

Vanbrugh was an architect as well as a playwright, and his massive style of building provoked the following mock-epitaph: "Lie heavy on him, Earth! for he/ Laid many heavy loads on thee!" Vanbrugh is best known for two comedies. In *The Relapse*, which is a sequel to the sentimental play of Colley Cibber, *Love's Last Shift*, Vanbrugh questions the essential goodness of man, especially when presented in the form of an inveterate rake. The foppish Lord Foppington in this play is a memorable character. In *The Provoked Wife*, Vanbrugh has fun with the serious issue of marital incompatibility. Sir John Brute, played with great success by Garrick, is a caricature of a drunken, dim-witted, loutish aristocrat. Brute's attitudinizing is admirably rendered on stage.

BOOKS BY VANBRUGH

Complete Works. Ed. by Bonamy Dobrée and Geoffrey Webb, AMS Pr. 4 vols. repr. of 1928 ed. $225.00

The Relapse. 1696. Ed. by Bernard Harris, *New Mermaid Ser.* Norton 1976 pap. $2.95; ed. by Curt A. Zimansky, *Regents Restoration Drama Ser.* Univ. of Nebraska Pr. 1970 $15.95 pap. $4.50

The Provoked Wife. 1697. Ed. by Antony Coleman, *Revels Plays Ser.* Longwood 1983 $35.00; ed. by James L. Smith, *New Mermaid Ser.* Norton pap. $2.95; ed. by Curt A. Zimansky, *Regents Restoration Drama Ser.* Univ. of Nebraska Pr. 1970 $13.95 pap. $3.95

BOOKS ABOUT VANBRUGH

Anthony, John. *Vanbrugh*. Seven Hills Bks. 1983 pap. $3.50
Bingham, Madeleine. *Masks and Facades: Sir John Vanbrugh, the Man and His Setting*. Rowman 1974 $23.50
Whistler, L. *Sir John Vanbrugh, Architect and Dramatist, 1664–1726*. Kraus repr. of 1938 ed. $23.00

WYCHERLEY, WILLIAM. 1640–1715

Wycherley is much in vogue at the moment for his dark comedy, which is strong, ironic, and complex. The character of Manly in *The Plain Dealer* was taken to be a portrait of the author, although Manly is clearly based on Alceste in MOLIÈRE's *Misanthrope*. *The Country Wife*, Wycherley's most popular play, has a cynical vitality. Taking a hint from a comedy by Terence, Horner pretends to impotence in order to have his way with the ladies, but his success does little to please him. The play demonstrates curious contrasts between truth-speakers and feigners, neither of which can be classified as entirely good or bad. Wycherley's other comedies are *Love in a Wood* (1671) and *The Gentleman Dancing Master* (1672).

BOOKS BY WYCHERLEY

Complete Plays of William Wycherley. Ed. by Gerald Weales, *Norton Lib.* 1972 pap. $5.95
The Plays of William Wycherley. Ed. by Arthur Friedman, *Oxford Eng. Texts Ser.* 1979 $85.00
The Country Wife. 1675. Ed. by John D. Hunt, *New Mermaid Ser.* Norton 1976 pap. $4.95; ed. by Thomas H. Fujimura, *Regents Restoration Drama Ser.* Univ. of Nebraska Pr. 1965 $14.95 pap. $3.50
The Plain Dealer. 1676. Ed. by James L. Smith, *New Mermaid Ser.* Norton, 1980 pap. $7.95; ed. by Leo Hughes, *Regents Restoration Drama Ser.* Univ. of Nebraska Ser. 1967 $16.50 pap. $3.50

BOOKS ABOUT WYCHERLEY

Connely, Willard. *Brawny Wycherly*. Associated Faculty Pr. repr. of 1930 ed. $28.25; Richard West repr. of 1930 ed. $30.00
McCarthy, B. Eugene. *William Wycherley: A Reference Guide*. G. K. Hall 1985 lib. bdg. $47.50
Thompson, James. *Language in Wycherley's Plays: Seventeenth-Century Language Theory and Drama*. Univ. of Alabama Pr. 1984 $17.75

EIGHTEENTH-CENTURY DRAMA

History, Criticism, and Editions

Jeremy Collier's attack on the stage, *A Short View of the Immorality and Profaneness of the English Stage* (1698), signaled a shift in sensibility away from the satirical and often biting Restoration comedy of manners—a licentious and libertine drama in Collier's eyes—to a new sensibility in the early eighteenth century. Restoration drama was middle-class, gentle, genial, and often overtly sentimental. Farquhar's

The Beaux' Stratagem was already moving strongly in this direction. On the opposite side, the eighteenth century also shows a profusion of parodies, farces, burlesques, and dramatic satires, all very self-conscious of literature as separate from real life. John Gay's *The Beggar's Opera* is a wonderfully exuberant burlesque of seriousness, in general, and many other things (including Italian opera), in particular. With the mock-heroic, as in HENRY FIELDING's (see Vol. 1) *The Tragedy of Tragedies; or The Life and Death of Tom Thumb the Great,* the eighteenth century mocked its own pretensions. (The previous section on Restoration Drama lists many books and editions that are also relevant to the eighteenth century.)

Bernbaum, Ernest. *The Drama of Sensibility: A Sketch of the History of English Comedy and Domestic Tragedy.* Peter Smith $11.50

Boas, Frederick S. *An Introduction to Eighteenth Century Drama, 1700–1780.* Greenwood repr. of 1953 ed. 1978 lib. bdg. $27.50

Hampden, John, ed. *The Beggar's Opera and Other 18th-Century Plays.* Biblio Dist. (Everyman's) repr. of 1928 ed. 1975 pap. $2.95

Hughes, Leo. *The Drama's Patrons: A Study of the Eighteenth-Century London Audience.* Univ. of Texas Pr. 1971 $12.95

Krutch, Joseph W. *Comedy and Conscience after the Restoration.* Columbia Univ. Pr. rev. ed. 1924 pap. $12.00. An important study of the change in sensibility.

Leech, Clifford, and T. W. Craik, eds. *The Revels History of Drama in English, 1750–1880.* Methuen vol. 6 1975 $19.95. With contributions by Michael R. Booth, Richard Southern, Frederick Marker, Lise-Lone Marker, and Robertson Davies. Very useful book with a strong theater orientation.

Loftis, John. *Comedy and Society from Congreve to Fielding.* AMS Pr. repr. of 1959 ed. $16.50

Nelson, Bonnie. *Serious Drama and the London Stage, 1729–1739. Salzburg Studies in Eng. Lit., Poetic Drama and Poetic Theory* Humanities Pr. text ed. 1981 pap. $25.50

Pedicord, Harry W. *Theatrical Public in the Time of Garrick.* Southern Illinois Univ. Pr. 1966 lib. bdg. pap. $2.65

Sherbo, Arthur. *English Sentimental Drama.* Michigan State Univ. Pr. 1957 $5.75. An authoritative study.

Smith, Dane F., and M. L. Lawhon. *Plays about the Theatre in England, 1737–1800, or the Self-Conscious Stage from Foote to Sheridan.* Bucknell Univ. Pr. 1979 $25.00

Stone, George W., Jr., and George M. Kahrl. *David Garrick: A Critical Biography.* Southern Illinois Univ. Pr. 1979 $60.00

GAY, JOHN. 1685–1732

Gay is a highly original poet and dramatist who experimented in various forms and genres. His *The What D'Ye Call It: A Tragi-Comical Pastoral Farce* is a burlesque of high seriousness, as is also *Three Hours after Marriage* which he wrote with POPE (see Vol. 1) and Arbuthnot. *The Beggar's Opera* is his best known work. It started the vogue for ballad operas, with tunes drawn from popular airs (Gay's are mostly from D'Urfey's *Pills to Purge Melancholy,* a popular source book for ribald songs). *The Beggar's Opera* satirizes gentility, and its topical political allusions are so direct that the government forbade its sequel *Polly.* BRECHT caught the spirit of the work in his *Threepenny Opera.*

BOOKS BY GAY

Poetical, Dramatic, and Miscellaneous Works. Pref. by S. Johnson, AMS Pr. 6 vols. repr. of 1795 ed. $180.00

Poetry and Prose. Ed. by Charles E. Beckwith and Vinton A. Dearing. *Oxford Eng. Texts Ser.* 2 vols. 1974 $69.00

(and John Fuller), eds. *John Gay: Dramatic Works. Oxford Eng. Texts Ser.* 2 vols. 1983 ea. $95.00

The Beggar's Opera. 1728. Ed. by Benjamin W. Griffith, Jr. Barron text ed. 1962 pap. $3.95; ed. by Edgar V. Roberts, *Regents Restoration Drama Ser.* Univ. of Nebraska Pr. 1969 $19.95 pap. $5.95

Polly—An Opera: Being the Second Part of the Beggar's Opera. 1729. Fwd. by Oswald Doughty, Richard West repr. of 1922 ed. $20.00

BOOKS ABOUT GAY

Armens, Sven M. *John Gay: Social Critic.* Octagon 1966 lib. bdg. $21.50

Gay, Phoebe F. *John Gay: His Place in the Eighteenth Century.* Richard West repr. of 1938 ed. 1973 $16.50

Herbert, Alan P. *Mr. Gay's London.* Greenwood repr. of 1948 ed. 1975 lib. bdg. $22.50

Irving, William H. *John Gay's London, Illustrated from the Poetry of the Time.* Darby repr. of 1928 ed. lib. bdg. $50.00

Kidson, Frank. *The Beggar's Opera: Its Predecessors and Successors.* Greenwood repr. of 1922 ed. lib. bdg. $18.25; Johnson Repr. repr. of 1922 ed. 1969 $14.00

Klein, Julie T. *John Gay: An Annotated Checklist of Criticism.* Whitston 1973 $7.50

Melville, Lewis S. *Life and Letters of John Gay.* Folcroft repr. of 1921 ed. lib. bdg. $20.00

Pearce, Charles. *Polly Peacham: The Story of Lavinia Fenton and the Beggar's Opera.* Ayer repr. of 1913 ed. 1968 $20.00; Richard West 1973 $25.00

Schultz, William E. *Gay's Beggar's Opera: Its Content, History and Influence.* Elliots Bks. repr. of 1923 ed. $9.50

GOLDSMITH, OLIVER. 1728–1774

Goldsmith's ideas about comedy are well expressed in his *An Essay on the Theatre; or, A Comparison Between Laughing and Sentimental Comedy.* Goldsmith attacks sentimental and weeping comedy as a form of bastard tragedy, in which characters make up in feeling for what they lack in humor. Instead, Goldsmith insists on the natural and easy comedy of his own *The Good Natur'd Man* (1768) and *She Stoops to Conquer* where we are made to laugh at vices and foibles in human character. *She Stoops to Conquer* has been enormously popular. In its own time its scenes of "low" life were considered a novelty and gave offense to some. (See also Volume 1, Chapter 10.)

BOOKS BY GOLDSMITH

The Miscellaneous Works. Ridgeway Bks. 7 vols. repr. of 1791 ed. $250.00

Collected Letters. Ed by Katharine C. Balderston, Richard West repr. of 1928 ed. 1980 lib. bdg. $20.00

New Essays. Ed. by Ronald S. Crane, Greenwood repr. of 1927 ed. lib. bdg. $18.75

Complete Poetical Works. Somerset repr. of 1911 ed. $49.00

The Good Natur'd Man and She Stoops to Conquer. Ed. by George P. Baker, intro. by Austin Dobson, Arden Lib. repr. of 1905 ed. 1979 lib. bdg. $25.00

She Stoops to Conquer. 1773. Ed. by Katharine C. Balderston, *Crofts Class. Ser.* Harlan Davidson text ed. 1951 pap. $3.75; ed. by J. A. Lavin, *New Mermaid Ser.* Norton 1980 pap. $6.95; ed. by Harry Shefter, *Enriched Class. Ed. Ser.* Washington Square Pr. pap. $2.95

BOOKS ABOUT GOLDSMITH

Balderston, Katharine C. *A Census of the Manuscripts of Oliver Goldsmith.* Arden Lib. 1978 lib. bdg. $15.00; Folcroft 1976 lib. bdg. $16.50

Danziger, Marlies K. *Oliver Goldsmith and Richard Brinsley Sheridan. Lit. and Life Ser.* Ungar 1978 $13.95

Dobson, Austin. *The Life of Oliver Goldsmith. Select Bibliographies Repr. Ser.* Ayer repr. of 1888 ed. $18.00; Richard West repr. of 1888 ed. 1973 $15.50

Forster, John. *The Life and Times of Oliver Goldsmith.* Arden Lib. 2 vols. repr. of 1877 ed. 1979 lib. bdg. $50.00; Scholarly repr. of 1890 ed. 1972 $40.00

Freeman, John. *Oliver Goldsmith.* Folcroft repr. of 1952 ed. lib. bdg. $25.00

Ginger, John. *The Notable Man: The Life and Times of Oliver Goldsmith.* David & Charles 1978 o.p.

Gwynn, S. *Oliver Goldsmith.* Folcroft repr. of 1935 ed. lib. bdg. $35.00; *Eng. Lit. Ser.* Haskell 1974 lib. bdg. $49.95

Hopkins, Robert H. *The True Genius of Oliver Goldsmith.* Johns Hopkins Univ. Pr. 1969 $19.50

Hudson, William H. *Johnson and Goldsmith and Their Poetry. Poetry and Life Ser.* AMS Pr. repr. of 1918 ed. $7.25; Arden Lib. repr. of 1918 ed. 1978 lib. bdg. $10.00; Folcroft repr. of 1918 ed. lib. bdg. $20.00

Krans, Horatio S. *Oliver Goldsmith: A Critical Biography.* Folcroft repr. of 1918 ed. lib. bdg. $17.50

Pitman, James H. *Goldsmith's Animated Nature: A Study of Goldsmith.* Shoe String (Archon) repr. of 1924 ed. 1972 $16.50

Rousseau, G. S. *Goldsmith: The Critical Heritage.* Routledge & Kegan 1974 $35.00 1985 pap. $15.00

Scott, Temple. *Oliver Goldsmith: Bibliographically and Biographically Considered.* Folcroft repr. of 1928 ed. 1974 lib. bdg. $50.00

Swarbrick, Andrew P., ed. *The Art of Oliver Goldsmith.* Barnes & Noble 1984 $27.50

———. *Oliver Goldsmith: His Reputation Re-Assessed.* State Mutual Bk. 1984 $60.00

Woods, Samuel H., Jr. *Oliver Goldsmith: A Reference Guide.* G. K. Hall 1982 lib. bdg. $29.50

SHERIDAN, RICHARD BRINSLEY. 1751–1816

Like Goldsmith, Sheridan also attacks "The Sentimental Muse" of weeping comedy. In his best known play, *The School for Scandal*, Sheridan revives the Restoration comedy of manners with its portrait of the *beau monde* and its deflation of hypocrisy. The play is indebted to Congreve as well as to Molière, and the picture of society is based on Bath and London. In *The Rivals*, Sheridan amuses himself with the language games of Mrs. Malaprop and her "nice derangement of epitaphs." The allusions are consistently literary, as in her simile "as headstrong as an allegory on the banks of the Nile." Sheridan's acute ear for banalities and truisms are best seen in *The Critic* (1779), a burlesque of sentimental and inflated plays as well as self-important criticism. The play ridicules "false Taste and brilliant Follies of modern dramatic Composition." Sheridan's sparkling dialogue, lively scenes, and masterful dramatic construction have proved enduringly popular.

BOOKS BY SHERIDAN

Dramatic Works of Richard Brinsley Sheridan. Ed. by Cecil Price, *Oxford Eng. Texts Ser.* 2 vols. 1973 $84.00

Sheridan's Plays. Ed. by Cecil Price, *Oxford Stand. Authors Ser.* 1975 pap. $7.95

Letters of Richard Brinsley Sheridan. Ed. by Cecil Price, Oxford 3 vols. 1966 $105.00

The Rivals. 1775. Ed. by Alan S. Downer, *Crofts Class. Ser.* Harlan Davidson text ed. 1953 pap. $3.75; ed. by J. Lavin, *New Mermaid Ser.* Norton 1980 pap. $6.95; ed. by Cecil Price, Oxford 1968 pap. $6.95

The School for Scandal. 1777. Ed. by John Loftis, *Crofts Class. Ser.* Harlan Davidson text ed. 1966 pap. $3.75; ed. by F. W. Bateson, *New Mermaid Ser.* Norton 1979 pap. $6.95; ed. by Cecil Price, Oxford 1971 pap. $6.95

BOOKS ABOUT SHERIDAN

Auburn, Mark S. *Sheridan's Comedies: Their Contexts and Achievements.* Univ. of Nebraska Pr. 1977 $18.50

Darlington, William A. *Sheridan.* Haskell 1974 lib. bdg. $39.95

Durant, Jack D. *Richard Brinsley Sheridan. Twayne's Eng. Authors Ser.* G. K. Hall 1975 lib. bdg. $12.95

———. *Richard Brinsley Sheridan: A Reference Guide.* G. K. Hall 1981 lib. bdg. $33.50

Foss, Kenelm. *Here Lies Richard Brinsley Sheridan.* Folcroft repr. of 1940 ed. lib. bdg. $20.00

Gibbs, Lewis. *Sheridan.* Richard West repr. of 1947 ed. 1973 $13.00

Loftis, John. *Sheridan and the Drama of Georgian England.* Harvard Univ. Pr. 1977 $11.00. Probably the best book on the subject.

Rae, W. Fraser. *Sheridan.* Richard West 2 vols. repr. of 1896 ed. 1973 $100.00

Sadler, Michael T. *The Political Career of Richard Brinsley Sheridan: The Stanhope Essay for 1912.* Folcroft repr. of 1912 ed. 1974 lib. bdg. $15.00

CHAPTER 3

Shakespeare

Maurice Charney

Renowned Spenser, lye a thought more
    nye
To learned Chaucer, and rare Beaumont
    lye
A little neerer Spenser to make roome
For Shakespeare in your threefold
    fowerfold Tombe.
> —William Basse, in E. K. Chambers, *William Shakespeare*

Shakespeare has managed to maintain his popularity better than any other dramatist. In his own time, however, and in the later seventeenth century, it is probable that Ben Jonson's reputation was higher and that many discerning persons thought that Beaumont and Fletcher were more fluent and articulate dramatists. The great period of Shakespeare idolatry did not begin until the mid-eighteenth century. Since that time, Shakespeare has been steadily mythologized as the author par excellence of everyone's imagination. The persistent rumors that deny Shakespeare the authorship of his works are in some way a tribute to his mythical status. Actually, we are fairly well informed about Shakespeare's life, but no amount of biographical information can account for soaring genius and creativity. That must remain astonishing in its own right.

Shakespeare was closely attached to the theater as an actor, a dramatist, and a "sharer" in the repertory company with which he was connected—the Lord Chamberlain's Men which later became the King's Men. As a sharer in the joint-stock company, he was entitled to a fixed share of the receipts from performances at the Globe and later at the Blackfriars Theater. He apparently became prosperous through his theatrical activities, since he bought land in Stratford and also New Place, the splendid building on the main street of his native town. Presumably, he spent time in Stratford when the theaters were not open (for example, because of the plague) and retired there. Many allusions to Stratford and its environs have been found in his plays and poems.

It is not the purpose of this survey to account for the flourishing Shakespeare industry, but rather to suggest ways of approaching the study of Shakespeare's works. We cannot know for sure whether Shakespeare was extremely learned or a natural genius who worked by inspiration. Ben Jonson, a contemporary dramatist, twitted Shakespeare for never blotting a line, but Jonson's own methods of composition were slow and laborious. Shakespeare must have worked quickly, since he turned out approximately two plays a year at the height of his career. He may also have been doing other things, such as writing verses for tombstones and heraldic shields, as legend claims. In his works, Shakespeare was both highly imitative of what his fellow dramatists were doing and extremely inventive. Except for the English history plays, he never wrote the same kind of play twice. He seems to have had a good deal of fun in trying out every kind of play he could think of. He was not always completely successful. His one attempt at a play based on contemporary middle-class life, *The Merry Wives of Windsor*, cannot compete with the brilliant city comedies being written by Middleton, Jonson, Dekker, and Heywood. The most notable quality of Shakespeare's career is its amazing variety.

The study of Shakespeare has been highly institutionalized, especially in relation to university instruction. Most colleges have at least one "Shakespeare man or woman" on their staff, and there is a Shakespeare Society of America with annual conventions in different parts of the United States and Canada. *Shakespeare Quarterly* is more or less the official publication for Shakespeare in the United States; *Shakespeare Survey* is its British status equivalent. Both of these publish excellent annual bibliographies. There is also an annual bibliography in the *Publications of the Modern Language Association* and a bibliographic essay in *Studies in English Literature*. *Shakespeare Studies* may be more adventurous in the kinds of articles it publishes. *Shakespeare Newsletter* is a gossipy, informational source under the idiosyncratic aegis of Louis Marder. The *Shakespeare Bulletin*, associated with the Shakespeare Seminar at Columbia University and edited by James P. Lusardi and June Schlueter at Lafayette College, recently began publication. There seems to be no end in sight to Shakespearean publications. They are thriving, as are productions of Shakespeare in the theater and on film and television.

BIBLIOGRAPHIES

Berman, Ronald. *A Reader's Guide to Shakespeare's Plays: A Discursive Bibliography.* Scott, Foresman 2d ed. 1973 pap. $8.65. Good discussion of the items listed.

Bevington, David, ed. *Shakespeare. Goldentree Bibliographies in Language and Lit. Ser.* Harlan Davidson text ed. 1978 pap. $14.95

Ebisch, Walther, and Levin Schucking, comps. *Shakespeare Bibliography.* Ayer repr. of 1930 ed. 1968 $24.50. With a supplement for the years 1930–1935. The standard Shakespeare bibliography, continued by Gordon Ross Smith (see below).

Jacobs, Henry E., and Claudia D. Johnson, comps. *An Annotated Bibliography of Shakespearean Burlesques, Parodies and Travesties. Reference Lib. of the Humanities* Garland 1975 lib. bdg. $41.00. An entertaining collection of Shakespearean humor.

Jaggard, William. *Shakespeare Bibliography.* Wofsy Fine Arts 1971 $50.00. An important reference book that is continued by Ebisch and Schucking and Gordon Ross Smith.

McLean, Andrew M. *Shakespeare: Annotated Bibliographies and Media Guide for Teachers.* National Council of Teachers of Eng. 1980 pap. $12.00

McManaway, James G., and Jeanne A. Roberts, comps. *Selective Bibliography of Shakespeare: Editions, Textual Studies, Commentary.* Special Publications Ser. Folger 1978 $15.00 pap. $5.95

Parker, Barry M. *The Shakespeare Folger Filmography: A Directory of Feature Films Based on the Works of Shakespeare.* Folger 1979 pap. $5.95

Quinn, Edward, and others. *The Major Shakespearean Tragedies: A Critical Bibliography.* Macmillan (Free Pr.) 1973 $12.95

Raven, Anton A. *Hamlet Bibliography and Reference Guide, 1877–1935.* Russell repr. of 1936 ed. 1966 $9.00. This volume gives some notion of the enormous quantity and variety of studies of a single play.

Smith, Gordon Ross, ed. *Classified Shakespeare Bibliography, 1936–1958.* Pennsylvania State Univ. Pr. 1963 $49.50. Continues Jaggard and Ebisch and Schucking. An important reference work.

REFERENCE WORKS

Abbott, E. A. *A Shakespearian Grammar. Studies in Shakespeare* Haskell repr. of 1870 ed. 1972 lib. bdg. $59.95. An elaborate and ingenious work based on Latin grammar.

Andrews, John F. *William Shakespeare: His World, His Work, His Influence.* Scribner 3 vols. 1985 $180.00. A splendid, new reference book with illustrations.

Brown, Ivor J., and George Fearon. *This Shakespeare Industry: Amazing Monument.* Greenwood repr. of 1939 ed. lib. bdg. $19.75; *Studies in Shakespeare* Haskell repr. of 1939 ed. 1970 lib. bdg. $52.95

Cercignani, Fausto. *Shakespeare's Works and Elizabethan Pronunciation.* Oxford 1981 $95.00

Cohn, Ruby. *Modern Shakespeare Offshoots.* Princeton Univ. Pr. 1975 $43.00 pap. $15.50. An attractive study of contemporary literature that uses Shakespeare.

Dent, R. W. *Shakespeare's Proverbial Language: An Index.* Univ. of California Pr. 1981 $35.00. The modern reader will be surprised at how many expressions in Shakespeare are proverbial in origin.

Halliday, F. E. *The Cult of Shakespeare.* Darby repr. of 1957 ed. 1982 lib. bdg. $35.00; Telegraph Bks. repr. of 1957 ed. 1981 lib. bdg. $30.00

The Harvard Concordance to Shakespeare. Harvard Univ. Pr. (Belknap Pr.) 1974 $75.00. A single-volume abridgment of the nine-volume work. This is quite adequate for the needs of students.

Ingleby, C. M., and others, eds. *The Shakespeare Allusion-Book: A Collection of Allusions to Shakespeare from 1591 to 1700. Select Bibliographies Repr. Ser.* Ayer 2 vols. repr. of 1932 ed. $55.00. Suggests the wide range of interest in Shakespeare from his own time onward.

Kökeritz, Helge. *Shakespeare's Names: A Pronouncing Dictionary. Shakespeare's Supplements Ser.* Yale Univ. Pr. 1959 $9.50. A standard work based on lexicographical principles. Expresses very conservative views on the possibilities of puns and wordplay.

Lewis, Benjamin R. *Shakespeare Documents: Facsimiles, Transliterations, Translations and Commentary.* Greenwood 2 vols. repr. of 1940 ed. 1968 o.p. A valuable reference book, which may be compared with Schoenbaum's documentary life of Shakespeare (see below under "Shakespeare's Life").

Magill, Lewis M., and Nelson A. Ault. *Synopses of Shakespeare's Complete Plays. Quality Pap. Ser.* Little, Brown repr. of 1952 ed. 1968 pap. $3.95

Marder, Louis. *His Exits and His Entrances: The Story of Shakespeare's Reputation.* Arden Lib. repr. of 1963 ed. 1983 lib. bdg. $35.00

Onions, Charles T. *Shakespeare Glossary.* Oxford 2d ed. rev. 1919 pap. $15.00. An indispensable small lexicon based on the *Oxford English Dictionary.*

Schmidt, Alexander. *Shakespeare Lexicon: A Complete Dictionary of All the English Words, Phrases and Constructions in the Work of the Poet.* Ed. by Gregor Sarrazin, Ayer 2 vols. repr. of 1901 ed. 1968 $95.00; De Gruyter 2 vols. rev. & enl. ed. 6th ed. 1971 $78.00. A much larger Shakespeare dictionary than that by Onions, with fuller illustrations from Shakespeare's work.

Spevack, Marvin, ed. *A Complete and Systematic Concordance to the Works of Shakespeare.* Adler's 9 vols. 1968–70 $898.00. This computer-generated concordance, based on *The Riverside Shakespeare* (see below under "Modern Editions"), replaces the old concordance by John Bartlett, which is incomplete and inaccurate.

Stevenson, Burton, ed. *The Standard Book of Shakespeare Quotations.* Folger repr. of 1953 ed. 1979 $16.95

Sugden, Edward H. *Topographical Dictionary to the Works of Shakespeare and His Fellow Dramatists.* Adler's repr. of 1925 ed. 1969 $66.75. A most ingenious book, with full geographical references even to mythical places.

INTRODUCTIONS, HANDBOOKS, AND BACKGROUND READING

Barnet, Sylvan. *A Short Guide to Shakespeare.* Harcourt 1974 pap. $4.95

Brown, John R. *Discovering Shakespeare: A New Guide to the Plays.* Columbia Univ. Pr. 1981 $25.00. Strong theatrical orientation.

Charney, Maurice. *How to Read Shakespeare.* McGraw-Hill 1971 pap. $4.95. A practical approach through character, dramatic convention, structure, language, and style.

Evans, Gareth L., and Barbara L. Evans. *The Shakespeare Companion.* Scribner 1978 $5.95

Frye, Roland M. *Shakespeare: The Art of the Dramatist.* Allen & Unwin repr. of 1970 ed. text ed. 1981 $12.50; Houghton Mifflin text ed. 1970 pap. $6.75

———. *Shakespeare's Life and Times: A Pictorial Record.* Princeton Univ. Pr. 1967 $33.00 pap. $12.50. A lively and entertaining collection of illustrations with commentary.

Goddard, Harold C. *The Meaning of Shakespeare.* Univ. of Chicago Pr. 2 vols. 1951 $33.00 1960 pap. $11.00

Granville-Barker, Harley. *Prefaces to Shakespeare.* Princeton Univ. Pr. 2 vols. vol. 1 $27.50 pap. $11.50 vol. 2 $27.50 pap. $9.95. Contains essays on *Hamlet, King Lear, The Merchant of Venice,* and *Antony and Cleopatra* in Vol. 1. Volume 2 has *Othello, Coriolanus, Julius Caesar, Romeo and Juliet,* and *Love's Labour's Lost.* These are masterful analyses of the plays in performance.

Granville-Barker, Harley, and George B. Harrison. *A Companion to Shakespeare Studies.* Cambridge Univ. Pr. 1934 $69.50

Granville-Barker, Harley, and Edward M. Moore. *More Prefaces to Shakespeare.*

Princeton Univ. Pr. 1974 $16.50 pap. $7.95. Essays on *A Midsummer Night's Dream, The Winter's Tale, Twelfth Night, Macbeth,* and *From Henry V to Hamlet.*

Harbage, Alfred. *William Shakespeare: A Reader's Guide.* Farrar 1963 pap. $8.50; Octagon 1985 lib. bdg. $30.00

Harrison, George B. *Introducing Shakespeare.* Penguin (Pelican) rev. ed. 1950 pap. $2.50; Somerset repr. of 1939 ed. $39.00

Lee, Sidney, and Charles T. Onions, eds. *Shakespeare's England: An Account of the Life and Manners of His Age.* Oxford 1917 o.p. Profusely illustrated. There are many helpful references to Shakespeare's works. A highly informative book.

Muir, Kenneth, and S. Schoenbaum, eds. *A New Companion to Shakespeare Studies.* Cambridge Univ. Pr. 1971 $47.50. Essentially a different book from the collection by Granville-Barker and Harrison.

Schoenbaum, S. *Shakespeare: The Globe and the World.* Oxford 1979 $35.00. This is the catalog for the traveling exhibition prepared by the Folger Library. A lucid, readable book with many illustrations.

Van Doren, Mark. *Shakespeare.* Greenwood repr. of 1939 ed. 1982 lib. bdg. $42.50. A personal, idiosyncratic account of the plays, still very stimulating.

Wilson, John D. *Life in Shakespeare's England.* Folcroft repr. of 1913 ed. 1976 lib. bdg. $35.00

Zesmer, David M. *Guide to Shakespeare.* Barnes & Noble text ed. 1976 $16.50 pap. $7.95. A practical, popular book.

SHAKESPEARE'S LIFE

Quite a good deal is known about Shakespeare's life. One fruitful way of pursuing the subject is indirectly, through the lives of people Shakespeare knew and worked with in Stratford and London. The antiquarian researches of such scholars as Fripp and Eccles help to recreate the local history of Stratford and its environs as Shakespeare must have known it in his boyhood. Schoenbaum deals very successfully with the myths and legends that surround Shakespeare.

Chute, Marchette. *Shakespeare of London.* Dutton 1957 pap. $8.95. Although somewhat fictionalized, this readable biography is well researched and accurate in detail.

Dowden, Edward. *Shakespeare: A Critical Study of His Mind and Art.* 1875. Gordon $59.95. Develops many of the romantic myths about Shakespeare's life.

Eccles, Mark. *Shakespeare in Warwickshire.* Univ. of Wisconsin Pr. 1961 $15.00 pap. $6.50

Fripp, Edgar I. *Shakespeare Studies: Biographical and Literary.* AMS Pr. repr. of 1930 ed. $19.00

———. *Shakespeare's Haunts Near Stratford.* AMS Pr. repr. of 1929 ed. $14.00; Folcroft repr. of 1929 ed. 1972 lib. bdg. $15.00

Lee, Sidney. *A Life of William Shakespeare.* 1898. Arden Lib. repr. of 1908 ed. 1978 lib. bdg. $40.00; Dover rev. ed. repr. of 1931 ed. 1969 pap. $4.50; Peter Smith repr. $7.50; Richard West repr. of 1903 ed. 1973 $19.45; Scholarly repr. of 1903 ed. 1971 $39.00. Considered for a long time the standard life of Shakespeare.

Madden, Dodgson H. *Diary of Master William Silence: A Study of Shakespeare and Elizabethan Sport.* Greenwood repr. of 1897 ed. lib. bdg. $18.75; *Studies in Shake-*

speare Haskell repr. of 1897 ed. 1970 lib. bdg. $51.95; Richard West repr. of 1897 ed. 1973 $14.75. An imaginative recreation of the period.

Schoenbaum, S. *William Shakespeare: A Compact Documentary Life.* Oxford 1977 $22.50 pap. $9.95

————. *William Shakespeare: A Documentary Life.* Oxford 1975 $85.00. The standard account of Shakespeare's life for our time, full of carefully reproduced documents.

MODERN EDITIONS

The following is a selection of the more useful editions that are available. Readers are encouraged to read Shakespeare's works in facsimiles of the original editions. Especially recommended are the facsimile of Shakespeare's First Folio of 1623, which was the first edition of his collected works, splendidly reproduced by Norton, and the quarto facsimiles from the Huntington Library. The quartos were cheap paperback editions of individual plays, usually published close to the time of their production. Reading the folio and the quartos makes it clear that some plays exist in different versions (for example, *Hamlet* and *King Lear*) that cannot logically be conflated or put together into a single version, although this is the practice in all modern editions.

Complete Editions in One Volume

Alexander, Peter, ed. *The Complete Works.* Random 1952 o.p. The edition favored by scholars for reference. Alexander is judiciously sensitive to trends in the new editing of Shakespeare.

Barnet, Sylvan, ed. *The Complete Signet Classic Shakespeare.* Harcourt text ed. 1972 $30.95. A light revision of the *Signet Classic Shakespeare* series collected in one volume. Each volume has a separate editor, although one feels the presence of Sylvan Barnet in the overall lucidity and reasonableness of the interpretations.

Clark, William George, and William Aldis Wright, eds. *The Complete Works: Globe Edition.* AMS Pr. repr. of 1864 ed. $75.00. Constantly revised. Although it is completely out of date textually, the Globe edition set a high standard for all modern editors. Most editions follow its line numbering.

Craig, Hardin, ed. *Complete Works.* Rev. by David Bevington, Scott, Foresman text ed. 1980 $28.95. In its various revisions, this is now primarily the work of Bevington. The introductions and commentaries are especially useful to students.

Evans, G. Blakemore, ed. *The Riverside Shakespeare.* Houghton Mifflin text ed. 1974 $29.95. Incorporates many of the concerns of modern editors, especially in the proper names, and is rapidly becoming a standard reference work. It is the basis for Spevack's *Concordance.* Has valuable introductions to the major genres by Anne Barton, Herschel Baker, Frank Kermode, and Hallett Smith, and a general introduction by Harry Levin.

Harbage, Alfred, ed. *The Complete Pelican Shakespeare.* Penguin Shakespeare Ser. 1974 $29.95. A distinguished group of editors.

Kittredge, George Lyman. *The Complete Works of William Shakespeare.* Crowell 1966 o.p. Kittredge is wonderfully learned; the elaborate footnotes can be read separately as a commentary on the plays. Kittredge edited 16 plays in great detail.

Editions in Two or More Volumes

Many of the older series, such as the *Laurel Shakespeare*, edited by Francis Fergusson, and the *Yale Shakespeare*, edited by Wilbur L. Cross and others, are now out of print. The following is a selection of annotated editions currently available.

Barnet, Sylvan, and others, eds. *The Signet Classic Shakespeare*. New Amer. Lib. 38 vols. 1963–68 pap. ea. $1.50–$3.50. Complete. A very popular edition with students because of the extensive notes and commentaries. For the one-volume edition, see above.

Brooks, Harold F., Harold Jenkins, and others, eds. *The Arden Shakespeare*. Methuen 39 vols. 1951–82 ea. $30.00–$32.00 pap. ea. $6.95–$9.95. This is actually the "new" Arden Shakespeare, revised from the "old" Arden series begun in 1899. Now complete. The Arden edition has the fullest notes and commentaries and is considered the most authoritative of modern editions.

Furness, Horace Howard, and others, eds. *A New Variorum Edition of Shakespeare*. Dover 14 vols. 1871–1912 consult publisher for prices. Collects notes and commentaries on the plays line-by-line. It is full of odd and eccentric opinions from the history of Shakespeare editing and scholarship. Fourteen titles, published between 1871 and 1912, have been reprinted by Dover. A "new" *New Variorum* edition is now being published by the Modern Language Association, under the general editorship of Robert K. Turner, Jr.

Harbage, Alfred, ed. *The Pelican Shakespeare*. Penguin 29 vols. ea. $1.95–$3.50. Complete. Well edited, with useful notes. For the one-volume edition, see above.

Kittredge, George Lyman, and Irving Ribner, eds. *Complete Works*. This is the Kittredge edition as revised by Ribner in single volumes (see above under "Complete Editions in One Volume").

La Mar, Virginia A., and Louis B. Wright, eds. *The Washington Square Edition of Shakespeare. Folger Lib. Ser.* Washington Square Pr. 39 vols. text ed. 1957–68 pap. ea. $1.95–$3.95. Complete. Very sketchily annotated but popular with high school students.

Quiller-Couch, Sir Arthur, John Dover Wilson, J. C. Maxwell, and others, eds. *The New Shakespeare*. Cambridge Univ. Pr. 39 vols. 1921–66 o.p. Complete. Original and sometimes heterodox interpretations. John Dover Wilson is the guiding spirit. The series is currently being reedited.

Spencer, Terence J. B., ed. *The Penguin Shakespeare*. Penguin 36 vols. 1967–to date ea. $3.75. The series is not quite complete. Very long and complex introductions and notes.

Wells, Stanley, ed. *The Oxford Shakespeare*. Oxford 5 vols. 1984 ea. $19.95. This series attempts to reexamine editorial problems on freshly considered principles.

SHAKESPEARE'S WORKS: THE COMEDIES

The comedies fall into four groups: (1) the early comedies such as *The Comedy of Errors* and *The Taming of the Shrew;* (2) the middle ones such as *Twelfth Night* and *As You Like It;* (3) the late comedies or romances such as *The Winter's Tale* and *The Tempest;* and (4) the problem comedies such as *Measure for*

Measure and *All's Well That Ends Well*. There has been a great deal of interest in the comedies in the past ten years, especially in relation to comic theory. It seems clear that Shakespeare wrote at least twice as many comedies as trage- dies, and the history plays have a great deal of comic material (for example, Falstaff and his companions). The tragedies, too, make important use of the "comic matrix" (Susan Snyder's phrase).

Barber, C. L. *Shakespeare's Festive Comedy*. Princeton Univ. Pr. 1972 pap. $8.95. An original and highly stimulating book based on theories of comic festivity that may be explored in Mikhail Bakhtin's book on Rabelais (see Chapter 9 in this volume).

Bennett, Josephine W. *Measure for Measure as Royal Entertainment*. Columbia Univ. Pr. 1966 $27.50

Berry, Ralph. *Shakespeare's Comedies: Explorations in Form*. Princeton Univ. Pr. 1972 $23.00. An original and stimulating approach to comic form.

Bradbury, Malcolm, and David Palmer, eds. *Shakespearian Comedy*. *Stratford-upon-Avon Studies* Crane Russak 1973 pap. $5.50; Holmes & Meier text ed. 1979 pap. $11.50

Campbell, Oscar J. *Shakespeare's Satire*. Gordian repr. of 1943 ed. text ed. 1971 $12.50. Especially directed to satiric plays like *Troilus and Cressida*.

Carroll, W. *The Great Feast of Language in Love's Labour's Lost*. Princeton Univ. Pr. 1976 $30.00. Very interested in Shakespeare's debt to Ovid and Ovidian transfor- mation.

Champion, Larry S. *The Evolution of Shakespeare's Comedy: A Study in Dramatic Per- spective*. Harvard Univ. Pr. 1970 pap. $4.95

Charlton, H. B. *The Dark Comedies of Shakespeare*. Gordon $59.95; *Studies in Shake- speare* Haskell repr. of 1937 ed. 1970 lib. bdg. $24.95

———. *Shakespeare's Comedies: The Consummation*. Gordon $59.95; *Studies in Shake- speare* Haskell repr. of 1937 ed. 1970 lib. bdg. $22.95

Charney, Maurice, ed. *Shakespearean Comedy: Theories and Traditions*. Fwd. by Ann J. Cook, New York Literary Forum 1980 lib. bdg. $25.00. Includes the text of Donatus's treatise on comedy in Latin and English.

Cole, Howard C. *The All's Well Story from Boccaccio to Shakespeare*. Univ. of Illinois Pr. 1981 $13.50. A source study that deals with what Shakespeare used and what he neglected in the *All's Well* story.

Danson, Lawrence. *The Harmonies of The Merchant of Venice*. Yale Univ. Pr. 1978 $24.50. A complex study of the play.

Felperin, Howard. *Shakespearean Romance*. Princeton Univ. Pr. 1972 $29.00

Foakes, R. A. *Shakespeare: From the Dark Comedies to the Last Plays*. Routledge & Ke- gan 1971 $19.00; Univ. Pr. of Virginia 1971 $13.95. Subtle and suggestive.

Frey, Charles. *Shakespeare's Vast Romance: A Study of The Winter's Tale*. Univ. of Mis- souri Pr. text ed. 1980 $17.00

Frye, Northrop. *A Natural Perspective: The Development of Shakespearean Comedy and Romance*. Columbia Univ. Pr. 1965 $11.00; Harcourt 1969 pap. $4.95. Lays the foundation for an understanding of romance.

Gless, Darryl J. *Measure for Measure: The Law and the Convent*. Princeton Univ. Pr. 1979 $29.00. Very interested in legal questions.

Hassel, R. Chris, Jr. *Faith and Folly in Shakespeare's Romantic Comedies*. Univ. of Georgia Pr. 1980 $23.00

Herbert, T. Walter. *Oberon's Mazed World*. Louisiana State Univ. Pr. 1977 $20.00. About *A Midsummer Night's Dream*.

Hotson, Leslie. *Shakespeare's Motley. Studies in Shakespeare* Haskell repr. of 1952 ed. 1970 lib. bdg. $39.95

Hunter, Robert G. *Shakespeare and the Comedy of Forgiveness.* Columbia Univ. Pr. 1965 $25.00

Huston, J. Dennis. *Shakespeare's Comedies of Play.* Columbia Univ. Pr. 1981 $17.50

Jagendorf, Zvi. *The Happy End of Comedy: Shakespeare, Jonson, Molière.* Univ. of Delaware Pr. 1984 $24.50

Knight, G. Wilson. *The Crown of Life: Essays in Interpretation of Shakespeare's Final Plays.* Methuen 1965 pap. $11.95. An approach through poetic and symbolic themes.

Leggatt, Alexander. *Shakespeare's Comedy of Love.* Methuen 1974 pap. $11.95

McFarland, Thomas. *Shakespeare's Pastoral Comedy.* Univ. of North Carolina Pr. 1972 $18.50

Montrose, Louis A. *Curious Knotted Garden: The Form, Themes and Contexts of Shakespeare's Love's Labour's Lost.* Humanities Pr. text ed. 1977 pap. $25.50

Morgann, Maurice. *Essay on the Dramatic Character of Sir John Falstaff.* AMS Pr. repr. of 1777 ed. $8.50; *Select Bibliographies Repr. Ser.* Ayer repr. of 1912 ed. $18.00; Kelley repr. of 1777 ed. lib. bdg. $17.50; Richard West repr. of 1912 ed. 1973 $8.25. Still of great interest for understanding Falstaff.

Muir, Kenneth, ed. *Shakespeare: The Comedies—A Collection of Critical Essays.* Prentice-Hall 1965 $12.95

———. *Shakespeare's Comic Sequence.* Barnes & Noble text ed. 1979 $28.50 pap. $13.95; State Mutual Bk. 1979 $30.00. A lucid and rational account of the comedies.

Nevo, Ruth. *Comic Transformations in Shakespeare.* Methuen 1981 $26.00 pap. $11.50. A lively account of Shakespearean comedy in relation to classical theories of comedy.

Newman, Karen. *Shakespeare's Rhetoric of Comic Character: Dramatic Convention in Classical and Renaissance Comedy.* Methuen 1985 $16.95

Parrott, Thomas M. *Shakespearean Comedy.* Russell repr. of 1949 ed. 1962 $24.00

Peterson, Douglas L. *Time, Tide and Tempest: A Study of Shakespeare's Romances.* Huntington Lib. 1973 $10.00

Pettet, E. C. *Shakespeare and the Romance Tradition.* Folcroft repr. of 1949 ed. lib. bdg. $11.75; *Studies in Shakespeare* Haskell 1975 lib. bdg. $42.95

Phialas, Peter G. *Shakespeare's Romantic Comedies: The Development of Their Form and Meaning.* Univ. of North Carolina Pr. 1969 pap. $6.95

Presson, Robert K. *Shakespeare's Troilus and Cressida and the Legends of Troy.* AMS Pr. repr. of 1953 ed. $17.50

Richmond, Hugh M. *Shakespeare's Sexual Comedy: A Mirror for Lovers.* Irvington 1971 $24.00

Roberts, Jeanne A. *Shakespeare's English Comedy: The Merry Wives of Windsor in Context.* Univ. of Nebraska Pr. 1979 $15.50. Good background for interpreting this very unusual play.

Salingar, L. G. *Shakespeare and the Traditions of Comedy.* Cambridge Univ. Pr. 1974 $62.00 pap. $17.95. A rich and rewarding book mostly devoted to the classical tradition of comedy.

Smith, Hallett. *Shakespeare's Romances: A Study of Some Ways of the Imagination.* Huntington Lib. 1972 $10.00 pap. $5.00

Spivack, Charlotte. *The Comedy of Evil and Shakespeare's Stage.* Fairleigh Dickinson Univ. Pr. 1979 $18.50

Stevenson, David L. *The Love-Game Comedy.* AMS Pr. repr. of 1946 ed. $14.50

Stoll, Elmer E. *Shakespeare's Young Lovers.* AMS Pr. repr. of 1937 ed. $17.50; Arden Lib. repr. of 1937 ed. 1983 lib. bdg. $45.00

Tillyard, E. M. *Shakespeare's Early Comedies.* Humanities Pr. repr. of 1963 ed. text ed. 1983 $15.45 pap. $9.45

———. *Shakespeare's Last Plays.* Humanities Pr. repr. of 1963 ed. text ed. 1983 $10.45 pap. $6.45

Traversi, Derek A. *Shakespeare: The Last Phase.* Russell Pr. repr. of 1954 ed. 1984 lib. bdg. $40.00; Stanford Univ. Pr. 1955 $20.00

Uphaus, Robert W. *Beyond Tragedy: Structure and Experience in Shakespeare's Romances.* Univ. Pr. of Kentucky 1981 $14.00

Wheeler, Richard P. *Shakespeare's Development and Problem Comedies: Turn and Counter Turn.* Univ. of California Pr. 1981 $24.00

Wilson, John D. *The Fortunes of Falstaff.* Cambridge Univ. Pr. 1943 $27.95 pap. $9.95

SHAKESPEARE'S WORKS: THE HISTORIES

Shakespeare's First Folio of 1623 was divided into comedies, histories, and tragedies, and later critics have puzzled over the history play as a separate genre. The English history plays are based on Holinshed's *Chronicles* (1577) and other historical sources, and they deal with events that the audience would have thought of as not-too-distant history. The history plays, of course, use both comic and tragic materials. Although the Roman history plays, *Julius Caesar, Antony and Cleopatra,* and *Coriolanus,* are based on Plutarch's *Lives* and have affinities with the English plays, they are generally classified with the tragedies.

Blanpied, John W. *Time and the Artist in Shakespeare's English Histories.* Univ. of Delaware Pr. 1983 $29.50

Calderwood, James L. *Shakespearean Metadrama: The Argument of the Play in Titus Andronicus, Love's Labour's Lost, Romeo and Juliet, A Midsummer Night's Dream and Richard 2nd.* Univ. of Minnesota Pr. 1971 $10.95

Campbell, Lily B. *Shakespeare's "Histories": Mirrors of Elizabethan Policy.* Huntington Lib. repr. of 1947 ed. 1978 pap. $7.50. A political and intellectual interpretation.

Coursen, H. R. *The Leasing Out of England: Shakespeare's Second Henriad.* Univ. Pr. of Amer. 1982 $25.25 text ed. pap. $12.25

Kelly, Henry A. *Divine Providence in the England of Shakespeare's Histories.* Harvard Univ. Pr. 1970 $20.00

Porter, J. A. *The Drama of Speech Acts: Shakespeare's Lancastrian Tetralogy.* Univ. of California Pr. 1979 $22.50

Riggs, David. *Shakespeare's Heroical Histories: Henry Six and Its Literary Tradition.* Harvard Univ. Pr. 1971 $15.00

Saccio, Peter. *Shakespeare's English Kings: History, Chronicle, and Drama.* Oxford 1977 $15.95 pap. $9.95. An essential introduction to the history plays. Saccio unscrambles the historical background necessary for the plays.

Smidt, Kristian. *Unconformities in Shakespeare's History Plays.* Humanities Pr. text ed. 1982 $32.25

Tillyard, E. M. *Shakespeare's History Plays.* Humanities Pr. repr. of 1944 ed. text ed. 1983 pap. $10.50. A readable and much-used introduction to the history plays.

Traversi, Derek A. *Shakespeare: From Richard II to Henry V.* Stanford Univ. Pr. 1957 $15.00
Waith, Eugene M., ed. *Shakespeare: The Histories—A Collection of Critical Essays.* Prentice-Hall (Spectrum Bks.) 1965 pap. $3.95
Wilders, John. *The Lost Garden: A View of Shakespeare's English and Roman History Plays.* Rowman 1978 $13.50. By the literary adviser to the BBC-TV Shakespeare series.

SHAKESPEARE'S WORKS: THE TRAGEDIES

Shakespeare's tragedies fall into several distinct groups. The early tragedies such as *Titus Andronicus* and *Romeo and Juliet* are still experimenting with ideas of tragedy derived from Seneca and Ovid. A. C. Bradley has singled out four "great" tragedies of Shakespeare's maturity: *Hamlet, Othello, Macbeth,* and *King Lear.* The Roman plays *Julius Caesar, Antony and Cleopatra,* and *Coriolanus* are all tragedies and have attracted increasing interest in recent years. *Timon of Athens* is most likely Shakespeare's last tragedy, and in it we see a definite movement toward the romances. One problem in speaking about Shakespearean tragedy is how to define "tragedy." Shakespeare does not fit very well into the criteria developed in Aristotle's *Poetics.* It is more fruitful to try to define tragedy in relation to other Elizabethan literature.

Barroll, J. Leeds. *Artificial Persons: The Formation of Character in the Tragedies of Shakespeare.* Univ. of South Carolina Pr. 1974 $14.95 text ed. pap. $5.95. Interesting for its use of contemporary sources.
———. *Shakespearean Tragedy.* Folger 1984 $35.00
Bayley, John. *Shakespeare and Tragedy.* Routledge & Kegan 1981 pap. $9.95
Booth, Stephen. *King Lear, Macbeth, Indefinition, and Tragedy.* Yale Univ. Pr. 1983 $18.00. Very teasing in its interpretive suggestions.
Bradbury, Malcolm, and David Palmer, eds. *Shakespearean Tragedy. Stratford-upon-Avon Studies.* Holmes & Meier text ed. 1984 $32.50 pap. $13.95
Bradley, A. C. *Shakespearean Tragedy.* 1904. Fawcett 1977 pap. $2.95. Still a powerful and challenging account of the bases of Shakespearean tragedy.
Brooke, Nicholas. *Shakespeare's Early Tragedies.* Methuen 1973 pap. $10.95. Original and stimulating. Valuable comments on style.
Brown, John R. *Focus on Macbeth. Critical Essays Ser.* Routledge & Kegan 1982 $21.95. A predominantly theatrical approach to the play that raises contemporary questions about how to understand it.
Brown, John R., and Bernard Harris, eds. *Hamlet. Stratford-upon-Avon Studies* Holmes & Meier text ed. pap. $10.75
Campbell, Lily B. *Shakespeare's Tragic Heroes: Slaves of Passion.* Peter Smith repr. 1960 $15.00. An old-fashioned, unpsychological approach.
Cantor, Paul A. *Shakespeare's Rome: Republic and Empire.* Cornell Univ. Pr. 1976 $26.95
Charlton, Henry B. *Shakespearian Tragedy.* AMS Pr. repr. of 1949 ed. $29.50
Cunningham, J. V. *Woe or Wonder: The Emotional Effect of Shakespearean Tragedy.* Ohio Univ. Pr. (Swallow) 1964 pap. $5.00. A long, poetic essay that challenges the reader to develop a theory of tragedy.

Curry, Walter C. *Demonic Metaphysics of Macbeth. Studies in Shakespeare* Haskell repr. of 1933 ed. 1970 pap. $40.00

Dollimore, Jonathan. *Radical Tragedy: Religion, Ideology, and Power in the Drama of Shakespeare and His Contemporaries.* Univ. of Chicago Pr. 1984 $22.50. Very lively new approach with strongly Marxist assumptions.

Elliott, George R. *Flaming Minister: A Study of Othello as Tragedy of Love and Hate.* AMS Pr. repr. of 1953 ed. $19.50

———. *Scourge and Minister: A Study of Hamlet as Tragedy of Revengefulness and Justice.* AMS Pr. repr. $17.50

Evans, Bertrand. *Shakespeare's Tragic Practice.* Oxford 1979 $34.50

Evans, Robert O. *The Osier Cage: Rhetorical Devices in Romeo and Juliet.* Univ. Pr. of Kentucky 1966 $10.00

Felperin, Howard. *Shakespearean Representation: Mimesis and Modernity in Elizabethan Tragedy.* Princeton Univ. Pr. 1977 $22.00. Very much attuned to trends in contemporary criticism.

Frye, Northrop. *Fools of Time: Studies in Shakespearean Tragedy.* Univ. of Toronto Pr. 1967 pap. $9.95

Frye, Roland M. *The Renaissance Hamlet: Issues and Responses in 1600.* Princeton Univ. Pr. 1984 $28.50

Harbage, Alfred, ed. *Shakespeare: The Tragedies—A Collection of Critical Essays.* Prentice-Hall 1964 $12.95 pap. $3.95

Heilman, Robert B. *Magic in the Web: Action and Language in Othello.* Greenwood repr. of 1956 ed. 1977 lib. bdg. $24.75

———. *This Great Stage: Image and Structure in King Lear.* Greenwood repr. of 1963 ed. 1976 lib. bdg. $33.75. Two important studies of symbolic theme and action in Shakespeare.

———, ed. *Shakespeare—The Tragedies: Twentieth-Century Views, New Perspectives.* Prentice-Hall 1984 $13.95 pap. $3.95

Honigmann, E. A. J. *Shakespeare: Seven Tragedies—The Dramatist's Manipulation of Response.* Barnes & Noble 1978 $26.50 pap. $13.95

Jorgensen, Paul A. *Our Naked Frailties: Sensational Art and Meaning in Macbeth.* Univ. of California Pr. 1971 $25.00. Deals with the violence of the play.

Knight, G. Wilson. *The Imperial Theme: Further Interpretations of Shakespeare's Tragedies Including the Roman Play.* Methuen 3d ed. 1965 pap. $11.95. Knight's most impressive demonstration of the "poetic" approach to Shakespeare through image and symbol.

———. *Shakespearian Production: With Special Reference to the Tragedies.* Routledge & Kegan 1968 pap. $7.95; Univ. Pr. of Amer. repr. of 1964 ed. 1982 lib. bdg. $25.00 text ed. pap. $14.00

Knights, L. C. *Some Shakespearean Themes and an Approach to Hamlet.* Stanford Univ. Pr. 1961 $25.00. Essays by one of the most subtle and elegant of Shakespeare critics.

Leech, Clifford. *Shakespeare—The Tragedies: A Collection of Critical Essays. Midway Repr. Ser.* Univ. of Chicago Pr. repr. of 1965 ed. 1975 pap. $15.00

Levin, Harry. *The Question of Hamlet.* Oxford 1959 $16.95 1970 pap. $5.95. Searching questions about how we should understand the play.

McElroy, Bernard. *Shakespeare's Mature Tragedies.* Princeton Univ. Pr. 1973 $27.50

Muir, Kenneth. *Shakespeare's Tragic Sequence.* Barnes & Noble repr. of 1972 ed. text ed. 1979 $27.50 pap. $11.95; State Mutual Bk. 1978 $30.00. A companion volume to *Shakespeare's Comic Sequence.*

Paul, Henry N. *The Royal Play of Macbeth.* Octagon repr. of 1950 ed. 1971 lib. bdg. $26.00

Proser, Matthew N. *The Heroic Image in Five Shakespearean Tragedies.* Gordian repr. of 1965 ed. 1978 $12.50. A Socratic discussion approach to five plays.

Reibetanz, John. *The Lear World: A Study of King Lear in Its Dramatic Context.* Univ. of Toronto Pr. 1977 $25.00 pap. $8.50

Ribner, Irving. *Patterns in Shakespearian Tragedy.* Rowman repr. of 1960 ed. 1979 $20.00

Siegel, Paul. *Shakespearean Tragedy and the Elizabethan Compromise: A Marxist Study. Select Bibliographies Repr. Ser.* Ayer repr. of 1957 ed. $19.00; Univ. Pr. of Amer. repr. of 1957 ed. text ed. 1983 pap. $13.25. Strong on the relation of the plays to Elizabethan society.

Simmons, J. L. *Shakespeare's Pagan World: The Roman Tragedies.* Univ. Pr. of Virginia 1973 $16.95

Soellner, Rolf. *Timon of Athens: Shakespeare's Pessimistic Tragedy.* Ohio State Univ. Pr. 1979 $15.50. A book-length study of a much-neglected play.

Stirling, Brents. *Unity in Shakespearian Tragedy.* Gordian repr. of 1956 ed. 1966 $10.00

Stoll, Elmer E. *Othello: An Historical and Comparative Study.* Gordian repr. of 1915 ed. 1967 $7.50; *Studies in Shakespeare* Haskell repr. of 1915 ed. 1969 lib. bdg. $39.95. Typical of Stoll's approach through historical and comparative models.

Traversi, Derek A. *Shakespeare: The Roman Plays.* Stanford Univ. Pr. 1963 $20.00

Whitaker, Virgil K. *The Mirror Up to Nature: The Technique of Shakespeare's Tragedies.* Huntington Lib. 1965 $20.25

Wilson, John D. *What Happens in Hamlet.* Cambridge Univ. Pr. 3d ed. 1951 $54.50. At once a practical and an imaginative attempt to reconstruct the action of *Hamlet.*

SHAKESPEARE'S WORKS: SONGS, SONNETS, AND POEMS

Shakespeare's nondramatic works have been generally neglected in relation to the enormous amount of criticism of his plays. The sonnets have attracted a good deal of biographical and autobiographical speculation, much of it pointless and without foundation. The criticism of the sonnets is voluminously recorded in Hyder E. Rollins's two-volume edition for the New Variorum series. Shakespeare's long poems, *Venus and Adonis* and *The Rape of Lucrece,* are elaborately finished and have a close relation to verse narratives of the period. It would be interesting to examine further their relation to the plays Shakespeare was writing at the same time.

Booth, Stephen, ed. *Shakespeare's Sonnets.* Yale Univ. Pr. 1977 $45.00 pap. $14.95. Very intricate and ingenious commentaries on the verbal possibilities of the sonnets.

Giroux, Robert. *The Book Known as Q: A Consideration of Shakespeare's Sonnets.* Atheneum 1982 $17.95; Random (Vintage) pap. $7.95

Hubler, Edward. *Sense of Shakespeare's Sonnets.* Greenwood repr. of 1952 ed. 1976 lib. bdg. $27.50. Shows a good sense of Shakespeare's poetry.

Landry, Hilton. *Interpretations in Shakespeare's Sonnets. Perspectives in Criticism Ser.* Greenwood repr. of 1963 ed. 1976 lib. bdg. $18.50

———, ed. *New Essays on Shakespeare's Sonnets.* AMS Pr. 1976 $27.50

Smith, Hallett. *The Tension of the Lyre: Poetry in Shakespeare's Sonnets.* Huntington
    Lib. 1981 $15.00

THEATER, ACTING, STAGE HISTORY, AND DRAMATURGY

There has been increasing emphasis on Shakespeare as a man of the
theater. He was not only a playwright, but also an actor and part-owner of
various theaters in which his plays were performed. The dramaturgical approach to Shakespeare is relatively new in its effort to understand the plays
as performed rather than as literary texts. The two, of course, cannot be
separated. Our stage history of Shakespearean productions has become
more detailed and more sophisticated, as in the important studies of Marvin Rosenberg.

Baldwin, T. W. *The Organization and Personnel of the Shakespearean Company.* Rus-
    sell repr. of 1927 ed. 1961 $15.00
Bartholomeusz, Dennis. *Macbeth and the Players.* Cambridge Univ. Pr. 1969 $49.50
    pap. $13.95
Barton, John. *Playing Shakespeare.* Methuen 1984 pap. $9.95. Barton is an important
    director for the Royal Shakespeare Company.
Bentley, Gerald E. *Shakespeare and His Theater.* Univ. of Nebraska Pr. 1964 $11.50.
    An authoritative statement on Shakespeare as a man of the theater.
Berry, Ralph, ed. *On Directing Shakespeare: Interviews with Contemporary Directors.*
    Barnes & Noble text ed. 1977 $24.50
Bethell, S. L. *Shakespeare and the Popular Dramatic Tradition.* Octagon repr. of 1945
    ed. 1970 lib. bdg. $16.50. Bethell is one of the pioneers in insisting on Shake-
    speare's relation to popular drama.
Bevington, David. *Action Is Eloquence: Shakespeare's Language of Gesture.* Harvard
    Univ. Pr. text ed. 1984 $16.50. One of the fullest and best studies of stage action
    in Shakespeare.
Brown, John R. *Shakespeare's Dramatic Style.* Heinemann text ed. 1970 pap. $8.50
Coghill, Nevill. *Shakespeare's Professional Skills.* Cambridge Univ. Pr. 1964 $47.50
Egan, Robert. *Drama within Drama: Shakespeare's Sense of His Art in King Lear, The
    Winter's Tale, and The Tempest.* Columbia Univ. Pr. 1975 $16.00. One of the best
    studies of self-reflexiveness in Shakespeare.
Gilder, Rosamond. *John Gielgud's Hamlet: A Record of Performance. Select Bibliogra-
    phies Repr. Ser.* Ayer repr. of 1937 ed. $18.00
Goldman, Michael. *Acting and Action in Shakespearean Tragedy.* Princeton Univ. Pr.
    text ed. 1985 $20.00. A brilliant account of various tragedies from the point of
    view of problems encountered by the actor.
Gurr, Andrew. *The Shakespearean Stage, 1574–1642.* Cambridge Univ. Pr. 2d ed. 1981
    $54.50 pap. $14.95
Hodges, Cyril W. *The Globe Restored: A Study of the Elizabethan Theatre.* Intro. by
    Richard Hosley, *Norton Lib.* rev. ed. 1973 pap. $2.95; Somerset repr. of 1953 ed.
    $39.00. Hodges's reconstruction has been generally accepted by critics as a good
    working model of the Globe.
Holmes, Martin. *Shakespeare and Burbage: The Sound of Shakespeare as Devised to
    Suit the Voice and Talents of His Principal Player.* Rowman 1978 $19.50
Homan, Sidney, ed. *Shakespeare's "More Than Words Can Witness" Essays on Visual
    and Nonverbal Enactment in the Plays.* Bucknell Univ. Pr. 1980 $23.50

Howard, Jean E. *Shakespeare's Art of Orchestration: Stage Technique and Audience Response.* Univ. of Illinois Pr. 1984 $16.95

Jones, Emrys. *Scenic Form in Shakespeare.* Oxford 1971 $28.95 1985 pap. $11.95. An important book on the scene as the basic dramatic unit in Shakespeare.

Jorgens, Jack J. *Shakespeare on Film.* Indiana Univ. Pr. 1977 $20.00 pap. $6.95. The leading book in this area. Well argued discussions of the relation of film to play.

Joseph, Bertram. *Acting Shakespeare.* Theatre Arts 1969 pap. $5.95. Presents a controversial thesis about the relation of acting to oratory, especially in its use of gestures.

King, T. J. *Shakespearean Staging, 1599–1642.* Harvard Univ. Pr. $11.00

Lawrence, William J. *Physical Conditions of the Elizabethan Public Playhouse.* Cooper Square Pr. repr. of 1927 ed. 1968 $13.75. Although more than 50 years old, this is still a valuable introduction to the Elizabethan theater and staging.

McGuire, Philip C., and David A. Samuelson, eds. *Shakespeare: The Theatrical Dimension.* AMS Pr. 1979 lib. bdg. $29.50

Muir, Kenneth, and others, eds. *Shakespeare: Man of the Theater.* Univ. of Delaware Pr. 1983 $28.50

Mullin, Michael, ed. *Macbeth Onstage: An Annotated Facsimile of Glen Byam Shaw's 1955 Promptbook.* Univ. of Missouri Pr. 1976 $26.00 pap. $11.95. A good example of the verbal and pictorial record of a particular production.

Nagler, A. M. *Shakespeare's Stage.* Yale Univ. Pr. enl. ed. 1981 pap. $7.95. An excellent introduction.

Odell, George C. *Shakespeare—From Betterton to Irving.* Intro. by R. H. Ball, Ayer 2 vols. repr. of 1920 ed. $50.00; Dover 2 vols. repr. 1966 pap. ea. $3.50; Peter Smith 2 vols. repr. ea. $8.50. A standard stage history of the period.

Reynolds, George F. *Some Principles of Elizabethan Staging.* AMS Pr. repr. of 1905 ed. $5.00; Folcroft repr. of 1905 ed. lib. bdg. $8.50. A very useful and lucid account.

Rosenberg, Marvin. *The Masks of King Lear.* Univ. of California Pr. 1972 $40.00

———. *The Masks of Macbeth.* Univ. of California Pr. 1978 $50.00. Both books are models of readable stage and acting history.

Shattuck, Charles H. *The Hamlet of Edwin Booth.* Univ. of Illinois Pr. 1969 $22.50

———. *Shakespeare on the American Stage: From the Hallams to Edwin Booth.* Folger 1978 $19.95 pap. $9.95. An admirable account of its subject.

Sprague, Arthur C. *Shakespeare and the Actors: The Stage Business in His Plays, 1660–1905.* Russell repr. of 1944 ed. 1963 $25.00

———. *Shakespearian Players and Performers.* Greenwood repr. of 1953 ed. lib. bdg. $14.50. Two studies by one of our leading stage historians.

Styan, J. L. *Shakespeare's Stagecraft.* Cambridge Univ. Pr. 1967 $47.50 pap. $11.95. An excellent introduction.

Van den Berg, Kent. *Playhouse and Cosmos: Shakespearean Theater as Metaphor.* Univ. of Delaware Pr. 1985 $25.00

LANGUAGE AND STYLE

Shakespeare was remarkably fertile in his use of the English language. The *Oxford English Dictionary* records quite a few first uses of English words by Shakespeare, for example "heartache" in its modern sense. Shakespeare's style is adapted to the plays he is writing. *Julius Caesar,* therefore, has one of the smallest lexicons in the canon, whereas *Hamlet* a few years later has one of the largest. Some of the newer books on Shakespeare's language are devoted to puns and wordplay, especially sexual innuendo.

Armstrong, Edward A. *Shakespeare's Imagination: A Study of the Psychology of Association and Inspiration.* Univ. of Nebraska Pr. 1963 $22.95. This unusual study is devoted to image clusters, such as the dog-licking-candy sequence.

Berry, Ralph. *Changing Styles in Shakespeare.* Allen & Unwin text ed. 1981 $12.95
———. *The Shakespearean Metaphor: Studies in Language and Form.* Rowman 1978 $17.50
———. *Shakespearean Structures.* Barnes & Noble 1981 $28.50

Bradbrook, Muriel C. *Shakespeare the Craftsman.* History of Elizabethan Drama Ser. Cambridge Univ. Pr. 1979 pap. $11.95. By one of the best critics of Shakespeare's style.

Clemen, Wolfgang H. *The Development of Shakespeare's Imagery.* Methuen 2d ed. 1977 $37.00 pap. $14.95. After Spurgeon, the most important study of this topic.

Doran, Madeleine. *Shakespeare's Dramatic Language.* Univ. of Wisconsin Pr. 1976 $29.50

Edwards, Philip, and G. K. Hunter. *Shakespeare's Styles.* Cambridge Univ. Pr. 1980 $39.50

Elam, Keir. *Shakespeare's Universe of Discourse: Language Games in the Comedies.* Cambridge Univ. Pr. 1984 $49.50 pap. $15.95

Hardy, Barbara. *Dramatic Quicklyisms: Malapropic Wordplay Technique in Shakespeare's Henriad.* Humanities Pr. 2 vols. text ed. 1979 pap. $25.50

Hartwig, Joan. *Shakespeare's Analogical Scene: Parody as Structural Syntax.* Univ. of Nebraska Pr. 1983 $19.50

Hawkes, Terence. *Shakespeare's Talking Animals: Language and Drama in Society.* Rowman 1974 $14.50. Applies the newer linguistically oriented criticism to Shakespeare.

Hirsh, James E. *The Structure of Shakespearean Scenes.* Yale Univ. Pr. 1981 $22.00

Homan, Sidney. *When the Theater Turns to Itself: The Aesthetic Metaphor in Shakespeare.* Bucknell Univ. Pr. 1981 $20.00. Deals with metadramatic self-consciousness.

Mahood, M. M. *Shakespeare's Wordplay.* Methuen repr. of 1957 ed. 1968 pap. $8.95. The best study of this subject.

Price, Hereward T. *Construction in Shakespeare.* Folcroft repr. of 1951 ed. lib. bdg. $9.50; Norwood repr. of 1951 ed. 1980 lib. bdg. $10.00

Rubenstein, Frankie. *A Dictionary of Shakespeare's Sexual Puns and Their Significance.* Merrimack 1984 $36.00. Far-fetched but ingenious. Goes far beyond Eric Partridge's *Shakespeare's Bawdy* (1947, o.p.).

Spurgeon, Caroline. *Shakespeare's Imagery.* Cambridge Univ. Pr. 1952 $62.50 pap. $13.95. A pioneering study that influenced all further work on Shakespeare's imagery.

Trousdale, Marion. *Shakespeare and the Rhetoricians.* Univ. of North Carolina Pr. 1982 $19.50. Learned and far-ranging.

PRINTING, EDITING, AND TEXT

There has been renewed interest in the study of Shakespeare's early texts and the implications this has for editing. Critics are beginning to move away from the idea of a final, ideal text in favor of the notion of a more fluid text to suit the purposes of a performed play. The so-called Bad Quartos of Shakespeare's plays are being reexamined for their own sake and without any presuppositions about their relations to Good Quartos and the folio text. Many of these ideas are reflected in the new *Oxford Shakespeare* edited by Stanley Wells.

Baldwin, T. W. *On Act and Scene Division in the Shakespeare First Folio.* Southern Illinois Univ. Pr. 1965 $6.50

Bartlett, Henrietta, and Alfred Pollard. *A Census of Shakespeare's Plays in Quarto, 1594–1709.* AMS Pr. repr. of 1916 ed. $24.50

Bertram, Paul. *White Spaces in Shakespeare.* Bellflower 1981 $12.50 pap. $8.50. Concerned with lineation.

Black, Matthew W., and M. A. Shaaber. *Shakespeare's Seventeenth-Century Editors, 1632–1685.* Kraus repr. of 1937 ed. $37.00

Bowers, Fredson. *Textual and Literary Criticism.* Cambridge Univ. Pr. 1959 $29.95. One of our leading textual critics and editors.

Duthie, George I. *Bad Quarto of Hamlet.* Folcroft repr. of 1941 ed. lib. bdg. $15.00

Greg, Walter W. *Principles of Emendation in Shakespeare.* Folcroft repr. of 1928 ed. $11.00; Scholarly repr. of 1928 ed. 1971 $10.00. Authoritative.

Hart, Alfred. *Stolen and Surreptitious Copies: A Comparative Study of Shakespeare's Bad Quartos.* Folcroft repr. of 1942 ed. lib. bdg. $45.00

Hinman, Charlton. *The Printing and Proof-reading of the First Folio Shakespeare.* Oxford 2 vols. 1963 $110.00; Univ. Pr. of Virginia 2 vols. $90.00. A magisterial study.

Howard-Hill, T. H. *Shakespearian Bibliography and Textual Criticism.* Oxford 1971 $39.50

McKerrow, R. B. *Prolegomena for the Oxford Shakespeare: A Study in Editorial Method.* Folcroft repr. of 1939 ed. lib. bdg. $15.00; Oxford 1939 $5.00. An important statement of textual principles.

Parrott, Thomas M., and Craig Hardin, eds. *The Tragedy of Hamlet: A Critical Edition of the Second Quarto.* Gordian repr. of 1938 ed. 1976 $12.50. A model edition of an early text of *Hamlet*. The editors make clear that this text has some striking differences from the one printed in the First Folio of 1623.

Pollard, Alfred W. *Shakespeare Folios and Quartos: A Study in the Bibliography of Shakespeare's Plays, 1594–1685.* Cooper Square Pr. repr. of 1909 ed. 1970 $25.00. Two works by one of the leading textual critics.

———. *Shakespeare's Fight with the Pirates and the Problems of the Transmission of the Text.* Studies in Shakespeare Haskell 1974 lib. bdg. $39.95

Taylor, Gary, and Michael Warren. *The Division of the Kingdom: Shakespeare's Two Versions of "King Lear."* Oxford 1983 $67.00. New and radical ideas about the relation of the quarto and folio *Lear*.

Urkowitz, Steven. *Shakespeare's Revision of King Lear.* Princeton Univ. Pr. 1980 $21.00. Argues for the strong differences between the quarto and folio texts and insists that they should not be conflated.

Walker, Alice. *Textual Problems of the First Folio.* Arden Lib. repr. of 1953 ed. 1979 lib. bdg. $25.00; Folcroft repr. of 1953 ed. 1976 lib. bdg. $20.00. Detailed and informative.

Wells, Stanley, and Gary Taylor, eds. *Modernizing Shakespeare's Spelling: With Three Studies in the Text of Henry V.* Oxford 1979 $24.95

———. *Re-editing Shakespeare for the Modern Reader.* Oxford 1984 $17.95. Some presuppositions of the new *Oxford Shakespeare*.

Willoughby, Edwin E. *The Printing of the First Folio of Shakespeare.* Arden Lib. repr. of 1932 ed. 1979 lib. bdg. $16.50; Folcroft repr. of 1932 ed. lib. bdg. $12.50

FEMINIST STUDIES

This is a relatively recent field of inquiry. Critics have taken up the neglected topics of women and gender in Shakespeare in the light of larger feminist interests. These are often closely linked with psychoanalysis. Irene Dash's book is specifically devoted to stage history, which opens a fruitful topic of the conception of Shakespeare's women in the theater.

Bamber, Linda. *Comic Women, Tragic Men: A Study of Gender and Genre in Shakespeare.* Stanford Univ. Pr. 1982 $20.00

Dash, Irene G. *Wooing, Wedding and Power: Women in Shakespeare's Plays.* Columbia Univ. Pr. 1981 $25.00 1984 pap. $12.50

Dusinberre, Juliet. *Shakespeare and the Nature of Women.* Barnes & Noble repr. 1979 $24.75. This was the pioneering book on the topic. Later studies have expressed both indebtedness to and disagreement with Dusinberre.

French, Marilyn. *Shakespeare's Division of Experience.* Ballantine 1983 pap. $4.50; Summit 1981 $15.95. A popular, highly polemic study.

Kahn, Coppélia. *Man's Estate: Masculine Identity in Shakespeare.* Univ. of California Pr. 1981 $21.00. An original, psychoanalytically oriented account of masculine identity from a feminist perspective.

Lenz, Carolyn R., and Carol T. Neely, eds. *The Woman's Part: Feminist Criticism of Shakespeare.* Univ. of Illinois Pr. 1980 $22.50 pap. $9.95. An excellent selection of essays with a long bibliography.

Novy, Marianne L. *Love's Argument: Gender Relations in Shakespeare.* Univ. of North Carolina Pr. 1984 $21.00

PSYCHOLOGY AND PSYCHOANALYSIS

The thinking of Freud and other psychoanalytic writers has deeply penetrated the study of Shakespeare, although the number of books specifically dependent on psychoanalysis and psychology is relatively small. Ernest Jones's account of Hamlet and Oedipus is a classic of its kind, whose ideas have been challenged but never completely exploded. The newer psychoanalytic writers go beyond Freud to Erikson, Horney, Klein, Nahler, Kohut, Winnicott, and others.

Erlich, Avi. *Hamlet's Absent Father.* Princeton Univ. Pr. text ed. 1977 $32.00

Holland, Norman N. *Psychoanalysis and Shakespeare.* Octagon repr. of 1964 ed. 1976 lib. bdg. $27.50. This is a lucid, readable account of the history of the subject.

Jones, Ernest. *Hamlet and Oedipus.* Norton Lib. repr. of 1949 ed. 1976 pap. $5.95. Jones develops ideas about Oedipus in Freud and applies them specifically to Hamlet.

Kirsch, Arthur. *Shakespeare and the Experience of Love.* Cambridge Univ. Pr. 1981 $34.50

Schwartz, Murray M., and Coppélia Kahn. *Representing Shakespeare: New Psychoana-*

lytic Essays. Johns Hopkins Univ. Pr. text ed. 1982 pap. $8.95. An excellent sampling of the newer psychoanalytic critics.

Sundelson, David. *Shakespeare's Restorations of the Father.* Rutgers Univ. Pr. text ed. 1983 $20.00

Westlund, Joseph. *Shakespeare's Reparative Comedies: A Psychoanalytic View of the Middle Plays.* Univ. of Chicago Pr. 1984 lib. bdg. $17.50

SOURCE STUDIES AND THE HISTORY OF SHAKESPEARE CRITICISM

These are two related topics, the sources of Shakespeare's plays and the history of Shakespeare criticism. They are associated by their common intellectual interests. The study of sources is complex because much depends on how we conceive Shakespeare. Was he a voracious reader or did he learn a good deal quickly from handbooks, encyclopedias, and general conversation? The history of Shakespeare criticism has tended to project a playwright who was prodigiously learned and wise and to draw on what Babcock has called "Shakespeare idolatry."

Anders, Henry R. *Shakespeare's Books.* AMS Pr. repr. of 1904 ed. $12.50; Richard West repr. of 1904 ed. 1973 $12.00

Babcock, Robert W. *The Genesis of Shakespeare Idolatry, 1766–1799.* AMS Pr. repr. of 1931 ed. $24.50. An intriguing historical study.

Boswell-Stone, W. G. *Shakespeare's Holinshed.* Ayer repr. of 1909 ed. 1967 $30.00. A very useful book for the history plays and some of the tragedies.

Bullough, Geoffrey, ed. *Narrative and Dramatic Sources of Shakespeare.* Columbia Univ. Pr. 7 vols. ea. $40.00. A remarkable collection of literature that Shakespeare either used or was acquainted with. Makes for excellent reading in its own right.

Gesner, Carol. *Shakespeare and the Greek Romance: A Study of Origins.* Univ. Pr. of Kentucky 1970 $21.00

Guttman, Selma. *Foreign Sources of Shakespeare's Works.* Octagon 1968 lib. bdg. $17.00

Muir, Kenneth. *The Sources of Shakespeare's Plays.* Yale Univ. Pr. 1978 $26.00

Noble, Richmond S. *Shakespeare's Biblical Knowledge and Use of the Book of Common Prayer: As Exemplified in the Plays of the First Folio.* Richard West repr. of 1935 ed. 1980 lib. bdg. $25.00. This is a difficult subject since there were so many different translations available to Shakespeare.

Phillips, James E., Jr. *The State in Shakespeare's Greek and Roman Plays.* Octagon repr. of 1940 ed. 1971 lib. bdg. $17.00

Smith, David N. *Shakespeare in the Eighteenth Century.* Folcroft repr. of 1928 ed. lib. bdg. $10.00

Vickers, Brian. *Shakespeare: The Critical Heritage. Critical Heritage Ser.* Routledge & Kegan vols. 1–4 1974 $230.00 vol. 5 1979 $40.00 vol. 6 1981 $55.00. This carries Shakespeare criticism in detail from 1623 to 1801.

Westfall, Alfred R. *American Shakespearean Criticism, 1607–1865.* Ayer 1968 $24.50

SHAKESPEARE AND HIS CONTEMPORARIES

This is a large topic that is widely discussed in the criticism of Shakespeare. One point worth noticing is that Shakespeare's contemporaries, and especially his fellow dramatists, did excellent things that Shakespeare never attempted. City comedy and the drama of social realism are cases in point. On the other side, of course, Shakespeare was a lively imitator of literary and theatrical fashions in his own time.

Bentley, Gerald E. *Shakespeare and Jonson: Their Reputations in the Seventeenth Century Compared.* Univ. of Chicago Pr. 2 vols. in 1 1965 $27.50

Boas, Frederick S. *Shakespeare and His Predecessors.* Gordian repr. of 1902 ed. 1968 $15.00; Greenwood repr. of 1904 ed. 1969 lib. bdg. $22.50; *Studies in Shakespeare* Haskell repr. of 1904 ed. 1969 lib. bdg. $53.95; Scholarly repr. of 1904 ed. 1969 $13.00

Bradbrook, M. C. *Shakespeare and Elizabethan Poetry: A Study of His Earlier Work in Relation to the Poetry of the Time.* Richard West repr. of 1961 ed. 1978 lib. bdg. $30.00

Cruttwell, Patrick. *The Shakespearean Moment and Its Place in the Poetry of the Seventeenth Century.* Columbia Univ. Pr. 1954 $27.50. A good study of Shakespeare in context.

Frost, David L. *The School of Shakespeare.* Cambridge Univ. Pr. 1968 $52.50. Marred by excessive Shakespeare idolatry.

Harrison, G. B. *Shakespeare's Fellows: Being a Brief Chronicle of the Shakespearian Age. Studies in Shakespeare* Haskell repr. of 1923 ed. 1972 lib. bdg. $43.95. A chatty historical account.

Honigmann, E. A. J. *Shakespeare's Impact on His Contemporaries.* Barnes & Noble text ed. 1982 $27.50

Schrickx, W. *Shakespeare's Early Contemporaries.* AMS Pr. repr. of 1956 ed. $22.50

Talbert, Ernest W. *Elizabethan Drama and Shakespeare's Early Plays.* Gordian repr. of 1963 ed. 1973 $15.00

Watkins, Walter B. *Shakespeare and Spenser.* Princeton Univ. Pr. 1950 $15.50 pap. $5.95

CRITICAL STUDIES: COLLECTIONS

Bevington, David, and Jay L. Halio, eds. *Shakespeare, Pattern of Excelling Nature: Shakespearean Criticism in Honor of America's Bicentennial.* Univ. of Delaware Pr. $27.50. Papers from the World Shakespeare Congress in Washington, D.C.

Bloom, Edward A., ed. *Shakespeare, 1564–1964: A Collection of Modern Essays by Various Hands.* Univ. Pr. of New England 1964 $15.00

Dean, Leonard F., ed. *Shakespeare: Modern Essays in Criticism.* Oxford 2d ed. 1967 pap. $9.95. A popular anthology in the Oxford Galaxy series.

Hosley, Richard, ed. *Essays on Shakespeare and Elizabethan Drama: In Honor of Hardin Craig.* Univ. of Missouri Pr. 1962 $26.00

Kermode, Frank, ed. *Four Centuries of Shakespearian Criticism.* Avon 1974 pap. $2.45

Kernan, Alvin B. *Modern Shakespearean Criticism: Essays on Style, Dramaturgy, and Major Plays.* Harcourt text ed. 1970 pap. $13.95

Kettle, Arnold, ed. *Shakespeare in a Changing World: Essays.* Beekman 1971 $12.00;

Richard West repr. of 1964 ed. 1980 lib. bdg. $25.00; State Mutual Bk. 1980 $15.00. Marxist essays.

Siegel, Paul N., ed. *His Infinite Variety: Major Shakespearean Criticism since Johnson. Essay Index Repr. Ser.* Ayer repr. of 1964 ed. $25.50

CRITICAL STUDIES: GENERAL

Alexander, Peter. *Shakespeare's Life and Art.* Greenwood repr. of 1961 ed. 1979 lib. bdg. $27.50; New York Univ. Pr. 1967 pap. $3.95

Barton, Anne. *Shakespeare and the Idea of the Play.* Greenwood repr. of 1962 ed. 1977 lib. bdg. $22.50. One of the best studies of Shakespeare's self-consciousness of his own dramatic medium.

Bono, Barbara J. *Literary Transvaluation: From Vergilian Epic to Shakespearean Tragicomedy.* Univ. of California Pr. 1984 lib. bdg. $32.00

Bradbrook, M. C. *Artist and Society in Shakespeare's England.* Barnes & Noble text ed. 1982 $26.75

Bryant, J. A., Jr. *Hippolyta's View: Some Christian Aspects of Shakespeare's Plays.* Univ. Pr. of Kentucky 1961 $24.00

Calderwood, James L. *Shakespearean Metadrama: The Argument of the Play in Titus Andronicus, Love's Labour's Lost, Romeo and Juliet, A Midsummer Night's Dream and Richard 2nd.* Univ. of Minnesota Pr. 1971 $10.95. A strong statement of the metadramatic approach to Shakespeare.

Clemen, Wolfgang. *Shakespeare's Dramatic Art.* Methuen repr. 1981 $45.00

Coleridge, Samuel T. *Shakespearean Criticism.* Biblio Dist. (Everyman's) 2 vols. repr. of 1960 ed. 1974–80 ea. $12.95. Coleridge was very sensitive to poetic and symbolic values in Shakespeare.

Colie, Rosalie L. *Shakespeare's Living Art.* Princeton Univ. Pr. 1974 $40.00. Shakespeare from the point of view of a brilliant comparatist.

Curry, Walter C. *Shakespeare's Philosophical Patterns.* Peter Smith repr. $12.50

Edwards, Philip. *Shakespeare and the Confines of Art.* Methuen 1981 $27.00. Subtle and intelligent.

Ellis-Fermor, Una. *Shakespeare: The Dramatist.* Folcroft repr. of 1948 ed. lib. bdg. $9.50; Methuen 1973 $28.00

Fairchild, Arthur H. R. *Shakespeare and the Arts of Design: Architecture, Sculpture and Painting.* Ayer repr. of 1937 ed. $17.00. Very helpful introduction to the wide range of allusions in Shakespeare to the arts.

Farrell, Kirby. *Shakespeare's Creation: The Language of Magic and Play.* Univ. of Massachusetts Pr. 1976 $15.00. Strongly metadramatic in approach.

Garber, Marjorie. *Coming of Age in Shakespeare.* Methuen 1981 $30.00. Makes important use of anthropology.

Harbage, Alfred. *As They Liked It: A Study of Shakespeare's Moral Artistry.* Peter Smith repr. $10.25; Univ. of Pennsylvania Pr. 1972 pap. $7.95

———. *Shakespeare without Words and Other Essays.* Harvard Univ. Pr. 1972 $15.00

———. *Shakespeare's Audience.* Columbia Univ. Pr. 1941 pap. $11.00; Peter Smith repr. $20.00. Presents a view of the audience that is popular and socially mixed. This view has been recently challenged by Ann Jennalie Cook.

Hart, Alfred. *Shakespeare and the Homilies.* AMS Pr. repr. of 1934 ed. $10.00; Octagon repr. of 1934 ed. 1970 lib. bdg. $16.00

Hibbard, G. R. *The Making of Shakespeare's Dramatic Poetry.* Univ. of Toronto Pr. 1981 $20.00 pap. $8.95

Johnson, Samuel. *Johnson on Shakespeare*. Vols. 7 and 8 of *The Works of Samuel Johnson*. Ed. by Arthur Sherbo, Yale Univ. Pr. 1968 $80.00. Johnson has many trenchant and witty remarks about the plays that are eminently worth reading.

Jones, Emrys. *The Origins of Shakespeare*. Oxford 1977 $27.95

Jorgensen, Paul A. *Shakespeare's Military World*. Univ. of California Pr. 1974 $40.00

Kastan, David S. *Shakespeare and the Shapes of Time*. Univ. Pr. of New England text ed. 1982 $25.00

Kernan, Alvin B. *The Playwright as Magician: Shakespeare's Image of the Poet in the English Public Theater*. Yale Univ. Pr. 1979 $18.50

Knight, G. Wilson. *Myth and Miracle: Essay on the Mystic Symbolism of Shakespeare*. Arden Lib. repr. of 1929 ed. 1978 lib. bdg. $12.50; Folcroft repr. of 1929 ed. lib. bdg. $12.00; Gordon $59.95

Knights, L. C. *Further Explorations: Essays in Criticism*. Stanford Univ. Pr. 1965 $17.50

———. *Shakespeare's Politics*. Folcroft repr. of 1957 ed. lib. bdg. $9.50. Knights interprets "politics" in the largest ethical sense.

Kott, Jan. *Shakespeare Our Contemporary*. Intro. by Martin Esslin, *Norton Lib.* repr. of 1966 ed. 1974 pap. $6.95. Kott is a Polish expatriate and sees Shakespeare against a very contemporary background of totalitarian terror.

Levin, Harry. *Shakespeare and the Revolution of the Times: Perspectives and Commentaries*. Oxford 1976 $25.00 pap. $9.95. Collects his eloquent and elegant essays.

Long, John H. *Shakespeare's Use of Music*. Univ. Pr. of Florida 3 vols. 1977 ea. $12.00–$27.50. An authoritative account.

Melchiori, Giorgio. *Shakespeare's Dramatic Meditations: An Experiment in Criticism*. Oxford 1976 $34.00

Moulton, Richard G. *Shakespeare as a Dramatic Artist*. Folcroft repr. of 1907 ed. lib. bdg. $30.00

———. *Shakespeare as a Dramatic Thinker*. Folcroft repr. of 1907 ed. lib. bdg. $30.00. Two powerful and well-reasoned studies of structure and dramatic form in Shakespeare.

Muir, Kenneth. *The Singularity of Shakespeare and Other Essays*. Barnes & Noble text ed. 1977 $28.50

Mutschmann, Heinrich, and Karl Wentersdorf. *Shakespeare and Catholicism*. AMS Pr. repr. of 1952 ed. 1970 $31.50

Naylor, Edward W. *Shakespeare and Music*. AMS Pr. repr. of 1896 ed. $7.50; Ayer repr. of 1931 ed. $14.00; Da Capo repr. of 1931 ed. 1965 lib. bdg. $27.50

Noble, Richmond S. *Shakespeare's Use of Song*. Arden Lib. repr. of 1923 ed. 1978 lib. bdg. $30.00; Folcroft repr. of 1923 ed. lib. bdg. $25.00

Rabkin, Norman. *Shakespeare and the Common Understanding*. Macmillan (Free Pr.) 1967 pap. $2.95; Univ. of Chicago Pr. 1984 pap. $9.95

———. *Shakespeare and the Problem of Meaning*. Univ. of Chicago Pr. 1981 lib. bdg. $16.00 pap. $4.95. Lucid and direct engagement with central issues in Shakespeare.

Ranald, Margret L. *Shakespeare and His Social Context: Essays in Osmotic Knowledge and Literary Interpretation*. AMS Pr. 1985 $32.50

Root, Robert K. *Classical Mythology in Shakespeare*. Gordian repr. of 1903 ed. 1965 $9.00. An introduction to an important subject.

Rose, Mark. *Shakespearean Design*. Harvard Univ. Pr. 1972 $8.50 pap. $3.50. Triadic patterns in Shakespeare.

Sanders, Wilbur. *The Dramatists and the Received Idea*. Cambridge Univ. Pr. 1968 $59.50 1980 pap. $17.95

Schucking, Levin L. *Character Problems in Shakespeare's Plays*. Peter Smith repr. $11.50

Scott-Giles, W. *Shakespeare's Heraldry*. AMS Pr. repr. of $34.50; Richard West repr. 1973 $13.95

Shaw, George Bernard. *Shaw on Shakespeare*. Ed. by Edwin Wilson, *Essay Index Repr. Ser.* Ayer repr. of 1961 ed. $36.50. Shaw was a witty and iconoclastic commentator on the plays who is always worth reading.

Stewart, J. I. M. *Character and Motive in Shakespeare*. *Studies in Shakespeare* Haskell 1977 lib. bdg. $75.00. A writer of detective stories ("Michael Innes") with a good sense of absurdity in much character study of Shakespeare.

Stirling, Brents. *The Populace in Shakespeare*. AMS Pr. repr. of 1949 ed. $14.00

Stoll, Elmer E. *Art and Artifice in Shakespeare: A Study in Dramatic Contrast and Illusion*. Arden Lib. repr. of 1951 ed. 1983 lib. bdg. $45.00. Stoll popularized a morphological criticism of Shakespeare in relation to traditions and archetypes.

――――. *Shakespeare Studies: Historical and Comparative in Method*. Century Bookbindery 1980 lib. bdg. $50.00; Telegraph Bks. repr. of 1942 ed. 1980 lib. bdg. $40.00

Thiselton-Dyer, T. F. *Folklore of Shakespeare*. Corner House repr. of 1884 ed. 1978 $20.00

Thomson, J. A. *Shakespeare and the Classics*. Greenwood repr. of 1966 ed. 1978 lib. bdg. $22.75; Richard West repr. of 1966 ed. lib. bdg. $30.00. An excellent account of its subject.

Van Laan, Thomas F. *Role Playing in Shakespeare*. Univ. of Toronto Pr. 1977 $30.00. A carefully reasoned attempt to understand Shakespeare's histrionic self-consciousness.

Watson, Curtis B. *Shakespeare and the Renaissance Concept of Honor*. Greenwood repr. of 1960 ed. 1976 lib. bdg. $37.50

Weimann, Robert. *Shakespeare and the Popular Tradition in the Theater: Studies in the Social Dimension of Dramatic Form and Function*. Ed. by Robert Schwartz, Johns Hopkins Univ. Pr. text ed. 1978 $30.00. A learned and powerful Marxist account of Shakespeare's relation to the popular theater.

CHAPTER 4

Modern British and Irish Drama

David Bady

It is quite true that my plays are all talk, just as Raphael's pictures are all
paint, Michael Angelo's statues all marble, Beethoven's symphonies all
noise....
—GEORGE BERNARD SHAW, "The Play of Ideas," *Theatre Arts*

BRITISH DRAMA

A first deliberate effort to create a British literary drama was made in 1904,
when Harley Granville-Barker and George Bernard Shaw took over the management of London's Court Theatre. The critics and actor-managers, who
had been complaining for decades that there were no original plays, had recently been tempted to accept the weak work of Arthur Pinero and Henry
Jones as a substitute. But now, as a revelation, the Court began staging
John Galsworthy, Arnold Bennett, Greek drama in Gilbert Murray's translations, Granville-Barker, and of course Shaw (who brought 12 plays to the
repertory). Writers of the stature of KIPLING (see Vol. 1), CONRAD (see Vol. 1),
and H. G. WELLS (see Vol. 1) were invited to contribute. And although it
never became the national theater Shaw and Barker had been aiming at,
the Court eventually played three seasons and was surprisingly profitable
and immensely influential.

Just over 50 years later, at the same unfashionable Sloane Square playhouse (which had in the meantime been converted into a movie house and
bombed by the Germans), George Devine established his English Stage Company and began to solicit plays from absurdly young dramatists, often with
no professional connections to theater—teachers, architects, bakers. The
aim was again a repertory that could support new writing. From the stage
of the Royal Court not only John Arden, Arnold Wesker, and John Osborne—the "new wave" of the late 1950s—but later figures such as Edward
Bond, Joe Orton, Howard Brenton, and David Hare made their way into the
London theater. When, in the wake of the Royal Court-led revitalization, England at last attained its National Theatre, it was natural that Devine's (and
Shaw's) ideal should be perpetuated. The NT engaged Kenneth Tynan, most
articulate of critics, as its literary adviser, and under his guidance, from

1963 to 1972, Arden, Osborne, Peter Shaffer, and an unknown Tom Stoppard brought their new plays to the National stages.

There are, of course, other ways in which English culture brings its writers to the theater. The BBC produces more than 400 plays a year, many newly commissioned. The Arts Council, administrator of government subsidies since World War II, awards grants to playwrights and holds prize competitions. A less easily defined influence is the persisting classical repertory, based on Shakespeare, which keeps practical drama and literature constantly in touch.

Not that every important dramatist is a writer in the theater. Sometimes he or she is a theater-writer, a craftsman professional like SOMERSET MAUGHAM (see Vol. 1), Noel Coward, Terence Rattigan, or Alan Ayckbourn, eager to work in the traditional commercial forms. These well-made plays or bedroom farces are often eventually acknowledged as classic by an originally contemptuous literary criticism. And sometimes the playwright refuses to think of him- or herself as literary at all, preferring the title of political agitator or performance artist. (It was the Royal Court Theatre that quite naturally became the target of resentment against the literary establishment in the 1970s. Boycotting a playwrighting conference in its auditorium, Hare, Brenton, Trevor Griffiths, and other radicals set about composing their seminal collective theater piece, *Lay-By*.)

But it is still largely true that, in the plays listed in this chapter, the reader will find the special qualities of literary drama. In them is an unusual openness to foreign influence. Pinter and Stoppard would be impossible without SAMUEL BECKETT, and Bond without BERTOLT BRECHT, just as, in years past, ANOUILH, CHEKHOV, and IBSEN have had as much to do with the making of English drama as any native writer. Then again, this literary drama has serious intentions. Beginning with "problem plays" in the 1890s, the British stage has since made room for philosophical and religious debate, outbursts of social anger and political hatred, poetic introspection, and even the meta-seriousness of nonsense. Literary plays, finally, make language their subject as much as their medium. And from *Pygmalion* to Wesker's *Roots*, from Jimmy Porter's rant to the resonant cliché of Pinter's characters, English drama displays the power of the voice to limit and to liberate.

Bibliography and Reference

Adelman, Irving, and Rita Dworkin. *Modern Drama: A Checklist of Critical Literature on 20th-Century Plays.* Scarecrow Pr. 1967 o.p. A guide to critical articles and sections of books, but not reviews.

Breed, Paul F., and Florence M. Sniderman. *Dramatic Criticism Index: Bibliography of Commentaries on Playwrights from Ibsen to the Avant Garde.* Gale 1972 $60.00. More than 300 playwrights, most from the twentieth century.

Coleman, Arthur, and Gary Tyler. *Drama Criticism.* Ohio Univ. Pr. (Swallow) 2 vols. $18.00. Interpretive criticism from 1940.

Mikhail, E. H. *Contemporary British Drama, 1950–1976.* Rowman 1976 $18.50. A checklist of books and articles.

Nightingale, Benedict. *A Reader's Guide to Fifty Modern British Plays.* Barnes & Noble text ed. 1982 $24.50. General introduction to playwrights and lengthy comments on specific plays, from Barrie's *Admirable Crichton* to Griffith's *Comedians.*

Salem, James M. *A Guide to Critical Reviews Part III: British and Continental Drama from Ibsen to Pinter.* Scarecrow Pr. 2d ed. 1979 $30.00. Indexes reviews of productions, not scholarly or critical studies.

Theatre Year. Intro. by Michael Coveney, photographs by Donald Cooper, Methuen 4th ed. 1984 pap. $11.95. Photographic record of the London theater season, with brief credit lists and an essay.

Thompson, John C. *A Reader's Guide to Fifty British Plays: 1660–1900.* Barnes & Noble 1980 $24.50. Includes biographical information and plot summaries.

Vinson, James, ed. *Contemporary Dramatists.* Pref. by Ruby Cohn, *Contemporary Writers Ser.* St. Martin's 3d ed. 1982 $55.00. Lists more than 300 playwrights writing in English. Includes biography, playlist, production date, bibliography, critical essays, and other relevant material. Supplement of screenwriters, librettists, etc. Appendix of significant writers who have died since 1950. Index of plays.

———. *Great Dramatists.* St. Martin's 1979 $50.00. English dramatists of all historical periods.

Weintraub, Stanley, ed. *Modern British Dramatists, 1900 to 1945. Dictionary of Literary Biography Ser.* Gale 2 vols. 1982 $176.00

———. *British Dramatists Since World War II. Dictionary of Literary Biography Ser.* Gale 2 vols. 1983 $176.00. Long biographical-critical essays, including illustrations, selective bibliographies.

History and Criticism

GENERAL

Agate, James E., ed. *The English Dramatic Critics: An Anthology, 1660–1932.* AMS Pr. repr. of 1958 ed. $32.50. Agate was himself "the most influential critic of his time" (Martin Esslin), reviewing for the *Sunday Times* of London from 1923 to 1947.

Booth, M. R., and others. *The Revels History of Drama in English.* Methuen 1975 vol. 6 $19.95

Hunt, Hugh, and others. *Revels History of Drama in English.* Methuen 1978 vol. 7. $55.00 pap. $19.95. The Revels History volumes survey cultural and social backgrounds, theater architecture and stage practice, as well as discuss playwrights and plays. Each contains a bibliography and chronological table, and is profusely illustrated.

Leacroft, Richard, and Helen Leacroft. *Theatre and Playhouse: An Illustrated Survey of Theatre Buildings from Ancient Greece to the Present Day.* Methuen 1984 $39.95 pap. $13.95. The Leacrofts' isometric cutaways of theater buildings from all periods make this book uniquely valuable to the student.

Nicoll, Allardyce. *British Drama.* Ed. by J. C. Trewin, Barnes & Noble 6th ed. rev. text ed. 1978 $26.50; Richard West repr. of 1925 ed. 1975 $5.00

———. *A History of English Drama, 1660–1900.* Cambridge Univ. Pr. 6 vols. 1959 $65.00–$85.00. Vol. 4: *Early Nineteenth Century Drama, 1800–1850* was originally published in two volumes in 1930 as *A History of Early Nineteenth Century Drama, 1800–1850.* Vol. 5: *Late Nineteenth Century Drama, 1850–1900* was originally published in two volumes in 1946. Vol. 6 is an alphabetical catalog of the plays. Long the standard work. Professor at London and Birmingham, Nicoll was also for a time in charge of the Yale drama department.

NINETEENTH CENTURY

Beerbohm, Max. *Around Theatres.* Greenwood repr. of 1954 ed. 1969 lib. bdg. $27.50; Taplinger 1969 $7.95. Criticism by Shaw's successor on the *Saturday Review.*

Craig, Edward Gordon. *Henry Irving.* Ayer repr. of 1930 ed. $22.00. Craig, one of the founders of theatrical modernism, began as a pupil of the greatest Victorian actor-manager.

Davison, Peter. *Popular Appeal in English Drama to 1850.* Barnes & Noble 1982 $28.50

Lytton, Edward, and William Charles Macready. *Bulwer and Macready: A Chronicle of the Early Victorian Theatre.* Ed. by Charles H. Shattuck, Univ. of Illinois Pr. o.p.

Meisel, Martin. *Shaw and the Nineteenth Century Theatre.* Limelight Edns. repr. of 1963 ed. 1984 pap. $11.95. Excellent introduction to the theatrical conventions and modes of the later century, including opera.

Reynolds, Ernest. *Early Victorian Drama (1830–1870).* Ayer repr. of 1936 ed. $19.00; Richard West repr. of 1936 ed. 1975 $7.25

Rowell, George. *Theatre in the Age of Irving.* Rowman 1981 $22.50

———. *The Victorian Theatre: 1792–1914.* Cambridge Univ. Pr. 2d ed. 1979 $42.50 pap. $14.95. A comprehensive survey by the leading historian of nineteenth-century theater.

Shaw, George Bernard. *Shaw's Dramatic Criticism from the Saturday Review, 1895–1898.* Ed. by John F. Matthews, Peter Smith $5.00. Essential not only to students of late Victorian drama, but to readers concerned with Shaw's ideas.

Stokes, John. *Resistible Theatres: Enterprise and Experiment in the Late Nineteenth Century.* Barnes & Noble 1972 o.p.

Trewin, J. C. *The Edwardian Theatre! Drama and Theatre Studies* Rowman 1976 $17.50

Watson, Ernest B. *Sheridan to Robertson: A Study of the Nineteenth-Century London Stage.* Ayer repr. of 1926 ed. $30.00

TWENTIETH CENTURY

Agate, James E. *A Short View of the English Stage, 1900–1926.* Ayer repr. of 1926 ed. $19.00

Ansorge, Peter. *Disrupting the Spectacle: Five Years of Experimental and Fringe Theatre in Britain.* Wesleyan Univ. Pr. 1975 $15.00 pap. $7.00

Brook, Peter. *The Empty Space.* Atheneum text ed. 1978 pap. $4.95. An analysis of theater conditions and possibilities by England's most important experimental director.

Brown, John Russell. *Modern British Dramatists: A Collection of Critical Essays. Twentieth-Century Views Ser.* Prentice-Hall 1968 o.p. A collection focused entirely on the "new wave" of the 1950s and 1960s.

———. *Modern British Dramatists: New Perspectives.* Prentice-Hall 1984 $12.95 pap. $5.95

———. *A Short Guide to Modern British Drama.* Barnes & Noble text ed. 1983 pap. $9.95

Brown, John Russell, and Bernard Harris, eds. *Contemporary Theatre.* St. Martin's 1962 o.p. Chapters on Wesker and Pinter, verse and prose, televised drama, and other topics.

Bull, John. *New British Political Dramatists. Modern Dramatist Ser.* Grove 1984 $19.50 pap. $7.95. Concentrates on Howard Breton, David Hare, Trevor Griffiths, and David Edgar.

Cook, Judith. *Director's Theatre.* Harrap 1974 o.p. Interviews with John Barton, Peter Brook, John Dexter, Peter Hall, Joan Littlewood, Jonathan Miller, and Trevor Nunn (among others).

Davison, Peter. *Contemporary Drama and the Popular Dramatic Tradition in England.* Barnes & Noble text ed. 1983 $28.50. Explores the important relation of modern British drama and the music hall.

Donoghue, Dennis. *The Third Voice: Modern British and American Verse Drama.* Princeton Univ. Pr. 1959 o.p. Yeats and Eliot are treated as crucial figures. Includes shorter studies of Fry and Auden, among others.

Esslin, Martin. *The Theatre of the Absurd.* Doubleday (Anchor) 1969 pap. $2.95; Overlook Pr. rev. ed. repr. of 1961 ed. 1973 $27.95; Penguin (Pelican) 3d ed. 1983 pap. $5.95. Attempts to assimilate Pinter and Simpson to a Continental dramatic tradition.

Evans, Gareth, and Barbara Evans. *Plays in Review, 1956–1980.* Methuen 1985 $17.95. First-night reviews by a variety of English critics.

Gooch, Steve. *All Together Now.* Methuen 1984 pap. $6.95. A manifesto for the community and touring groups who have rejected both the West End and the subsidized theater.

Hayman, Ronald. *British Theatre since 1955: A Reassessment.* Oxford 1979 $17.50
——. *Playback.* Horizon 1974 $6.95
——. *The Set-Up: An Anatomy of the English Theatre Today.* Methuen 1973 o.p.

Hinchcliffe, Arnold P. *British Theatre, 1950–1970.* Oxford 1974 o.p.

Itzin, Catherine. *Stages in the Revolution: Political Theatre in Britain Since 1968.* Methuen 1981 $11.95

Kennedy, A. *Six Dramatists in Search of a Language.* Cambridge Univ. Pr. 1975 $45.00 pap. $14.95. Discusses Shaw, Pinter, Osborne, and others.

Kerensky, Oleg. *The New British Drama: Fourteen Playwrights since Osborne and Pinter.* Taplinger 1979 $11.95. Valuable mainly for its interview material.

Marowitz, Charles, and others, eds. *New Theatre Voices of the Fifties and Sixties: Selections from "Encore" Magazine 1956–1963.* Intro. by Michael Billington, Methuen 1981 $22.00 pap. $10.95 Articles from *Encore* magazine (1956–63), forum of the anticommercial theater movement.

Marowitz, Charles, and Simon Trussler, eds. *Theatre at Work: Playwrights and Productions of the Modern British Theatre.* Hill & Wang 1968 o.p.

Roy, Emil. *British Drama since Shaw. Crosscurrents Modern Critiques Ser.* Southern Illinois Univ. Pr. 1972 $6.95

Spanos, William V. *Christian Tradition in Modern British Verse Drama: The Poetics of Sacramental Time.* Rutgers Univ. Pr. 1967 $22.00

Taylor, John Russell. *Anger and After: A Guide to the New British Drama.* Methuen 1977 o.p. A thorough journalistic account of the new wave playwrights and their plays. Includes a good survey of London theatrical conditions in the 1950s.
——. *The Rise and Fall of the Well-Made Play.* Hill & Wang o.p.
——. *The Second Wave: British Drama for the Seventies.* Hill & Wang 1971 o.p. Nichols, Bond, Stoppard, Orton, Storey, and others; a successor to *Anger and After.*

Trussler, Simon, ed. *New Theatre Voices of the Seventies: Interviews from "Theatre Quarterly" 1970–1980.* Methuen 1981 $22.00 pap. $11.95

Tynan, Kenneth. *Curtains.* Atheneum 1961 o.p. Reprints Tynan's important views of the 1950s.

————. *Show People.* Simon & Schuster 1980 $11.95. Contains profiles of Tom Stoppard and Ralph Richardson.

————. *The Sound of Two Hands Clapping.* Da Capo repr. of 1975 ed. 1982 pap. $7.95

————. *Tynan Right and Left: Plays, Films, Places, People and Events.* Atheneum 1967 o.p. Some of this book is devoted to reviews of new wave theater.

Wilmut, Roger. *From Fringe to Flying Circus: Celebrating a Unique Generation of Comedy, 1960–1980.* Methuen 1985 pap. $10.95

Worth, Katharine. *Revolutions in Modern English Drama.* Bell 1973 o.p. Locates new wave plays in the continuum of British drama.

Theaters and Companies

Arundell, Dennis. *The Story of Sadler's Wells, 1683–1977.* Rowman 2d ed. 1978 $16.50; Theatre Arts 1966 $3.50

Beauman, Sally. *The Royal Shakespeare Company: A History of Ten Decades.* Oxford 1982 $29.95

Browne, Terry. *Playwright's Theatre: The English Stage Company at the Royal Court.* Beekman 1975 $12.00; Wesleyan Univ. Pr. 1975 $15.00 pap. $7.00

Chambers, Colin. *Other Spaces: New Theatre and the Royal Shakespeare Company.* Methuen 1981 pap. $7.95

The Complete Guide to Britain's National Theatre. Ed. by Richard Findlater and others, Heinemann 1977 pap. $5.00

Findlater, Richard, ed. *At the Royal Court: Twenty-Five Years of the English Stage Company.* Grove 1981 $30.00

McCarthy, Desmond. *The Court Theatre, 1904–1907: A Commentary and Criticism.* Ed. by Stanley Weintraub, Univ. of Miami Pr. 1966 $9.95. Chronicle of a brilliantly successful early experiment in repertory theater.

Recent Collections

[See also Chapter 1 in this volume.]

Booth, Michael R., ed. *English Plays of the Nineteenth Century.* Oxford 5 vols. 1969–76 vols. 3–5 ea. $49.00–$65.00 vols. 1–2 o.p.

Landmarks of Modern British Drama. Intros. by Roger Cornish and Violet Ketels, Methuen 2 vols. 1985 ea. $25.00 pap. ea. $8.95. Vol. 1—*The Sixties:* contains Wesker, *Roots;* Arden, *Serjeant Musgrave's Dance;* Pinter, *The Caretaker;* Osborne, *A Patriot for Me;* Bond, *Saved;* Orton, *Loot;* Barnes, *The Ruling Class.* Vol. 2—*The Seventies:* contains Ayckbourn, *Just Between Ourselves;* Brenton, *Weapons of Happiness;* Stoppard, *Every Good Boy Deserves Favor;* Shaffer, *Amadeus;* Nichols, *Passion Play;* Gray, *Quartermaine's Terms;* Churchill, *Top Girls.*

Rogers, Katherine, ed. *The Signet Classic Book of Eighteenth and Nineteenth Century British Drama.* New Amer. Lib. (Signet Class.) 1979 pap. $2.95. Contains Boucicault, *The Octaroon;* Gilbert, *Ruddigore;* Wilde, *Importance of Being Earnest.*

Rowell, George, ed. *Nineteenth-Century Plays.* Oxford Pap. Ser. 2d ed. 1972 pap. $8.95. Contains Jerrold, *Black Ey'd Susan;* Bulwer-Lytton, *Money;* Reade and Taylor, *Masks and Faces;* Boucicault, *The Colleen Bawn;* Bradon and Hazlewood, *Lady Audley's Secret;* Taylor, *The Ticket-of-Leave Man;* Robertson, *Caste;* Albery, *Two Roses;* Lewis, *The Bells;* and Grundy, *A Pair of Spectacles.*

Wandor, Michelene, ed. *Plays by Women.* Methuen 4 vols. 1982–85 pap. ea. $8.50–$8.95. Vol. 1: Churchill, *Vinegar Tom;* Gems, *Dusa, Fish, Stas and Vi;* Page, *Tis-*

sue; Wandor, *Aurora Leigh*. Vol. 2: Luckman, *Trafford Tanzi*; Goldenberg, *Letters Home*; Duffy, *Rites*; Wymark, *Find Me*. Vol. 3: Gems, *Aunt Mary*; Horsfield, *Red Devils*; Pollock, *Blood Relations*; Wakefield and others, *Time Pieces*. Vol. 4: Churchill, *Objections to Sex and Violence*; Dayley, *Rose's Story*; Lochhead, *Blood and Ice*; Lyssa, *Pinball*. Each play has an afterword by its author.

Warnock, Robert. *Representative Modern Plays: British*. Scott, Foresman 1953 pap. $9.95. Contains Barrie, *The Admirable Crichton*; Shaw, *The Doctor's Dilemma*; Galsworthy, *Loyalties*; Synge, *Riders to the Sea*; O'Casey, *Juno and the Paycock*; Maugham, *The Constant Wife*; Coward, *Blithe Spirit*; Eliot, *Murder in the Cathedral*; Fry, *A Phoenix Too Frequent*.

ARDEN, JOHN. 1930–

John Arden's is a striking case of the alienation that has overtaken a number of the original "angry" playwrights—Wesker and Osborne also come to mind—in an age of subsidized theater and broadly tolerant audiences. Trained as an architect, Arden was one of the Royal Court discoveries. His plays of the 1950s, *Live Like Pigs* and, particularly, *Serjeant Musgrave's Dance*, while not initially successes, have become modern classics. (In 1972, John McGrath's theater company paid *Musgrave* homage by producing a version, updated to a Northern Irish situation, called *Serjeant Musgrave Dances On*.) But Arden today, still a prolific and committed playwright, claims he cannot get an English theater to produce his plays and, with his wife Margaretta D'Arcy, has retreated to Ireland, where most of his recent work has been staged.

The problem apparently lies in the political dogmatism, absorption with Irish problems, and militancy that have entered Arden's drama since 1967, when he became a full-time collaborator in writing with his wife. D'Arcy's dramatic instincts, Arden has admitted, are the opposite of his own: she thinks of a subject needing illustration; he thinks of language and action and characters to suit them. His own plays—from *The Waters of Babylon* (1957) through *Armstrong's Last Goodnight* (1964) and *Left-Handed Liberty* (1965)—are imaginative, often balladlike, and (politically) inconclusive. Poetic qualities are not altogether absent from later plays, such as the Arthurian *The Island of the Mighty* (1975). But typically Arden today demands a sharper emphasis. Arden and D'Arcy bitterly criticized the Royal Shakespeare Company's production of *The Island* as imperialist and corrupted, and actually picketed the performances.

BOOKS BY ARDEN

Three Plays. Intro. by John Russell Taylor, Grove 1966 pap. $2.45. Contains *Live Like Pigs*, *The Waters of Babylon*, and *The Happy Haven*.

Plays: One. Grove pap. $4.95. Contains *Serjeant Musgrave's Dance*, *The Workhouse Donkey*, and *Armstrong's Last Goodnight*.

Left-Handed Liberty: A Play about Magna Carta. 1965. Grove 1966 o.p.

Two Autobiographical Plays: The True History of Squire Jonathan and the Unfortunate Treasure. Methuen 1971 o.p.

To Present the Pretence: Essays on the Theatre and Its Public. Holmes & Meier text ed. 1979 $15.00 pap. $9.00

BOOKS BY ARDEN AND MARGARETTA D'ARCY

The Royal Pardon. Methuen 1967 pap. $6.95
The Hero Rises Up. Methuen 1969 pap. $6.95
The Island of the Mighty. Methuen 1975 pap. $6.95
Vandaleur's Folly: An Anglo-Irish Melodrama. Methuen 1981 pap. $6.95
The Business of Good Government: A Christmas Play. Methuen 2d ed. 1984 pap. $4.95

BOOKS ABOUT ARDEN

Gray, Frances. *John Arden.* Grove (Evergreen Bks.) 1982 pap. $9.95
Leeming, Glenda. *John Arden.* British Bk. Ctr. 1975 o.p.
Trussler, Simon. *John Arden.* Columbia Univ. Pr. 1973 pap. $2.50

BARRIE, SIR JAMES MATTHEW, BART. 1860–1937

From short stories, novels, and journalism—he was a theater critic for a time in Edinburgh—James Barrie began writing drama in 1890, toying with the problem play he found in vogue. He soon turned to the whimsical romanticism for which he is remembered (or, mostly, forgotten). But it would be a mistake to ignore the realistic substratum in his plays. *The Admirable Crichton* (1903), in which shipwrecked aristocrats are forced to acknowledge the natural superiority of their servant, is not very far from the comic fantasies of Barrie's friend Shaw. *What Every Woman Knows* (1908) has been called a Scottish *Candida.* And even *Peter Pan*, the play most often used to characterize Barrie's irrelevance, appears to be an oblique confrontation with the sexual and psychological pathologies of the playwright's life, the subjects of recent biographical studies. Produced at London's National Theatre in 1983 without the usual "travesty" casting of an actress for Peter Pan, the play revealed a real pathos in the situation of a woman confronted with a man's inability to mature.

Outdoing Shaw (who had introduced the readable play text to English publishing), Barrie spent long intervals before publication preparing novelistic stage directions and comments for his plays, and sometimes changing their endings. Consequently, the date of its appearance as a book is often no guide to when one of his plays was originally performed. (See also Volume 1, Chapter 11.)

BOOKS BY BARRIE

The Works of J. M. Barrie. AMS Pr. 18 vols. repr. of 1929–41 ed. ea. $32.50
Plays of J. M. Barrie. Scribner 1928 $8.95. Twenty plays.
The Letters of James Matthew Barrie. Ed. by Viola Meynell, AMS Pr. repr. of 1947 ed. 1976 $18.50
Peter Pan. 1904. Avon 1982 pap. $2.95; Bantam repr. 1985 pap. $2.95; Penguin 1970 pap. $1.50; Putnam 1970 $1.95; ed. by Josette Frank, Random 1983 $7.99 pap. $6.95; ed. by S. Trina, Scribner 1980 $14.95. Performed 1904.

BOOKS ABOUT BARRIE

Roy, James A. *James Matthew Barrie*. Norwood repr. of 1937 ed. $20.00
Walbrook, H. M. *James M. Barrie and the Theatre*. Associated Faculty Pr. repr. of
    1922 ed. 1969 $15.00

BOLT, ROBERT. 1924–

Born in Manchester, where he attended university, Bolt was teaching
school in 1957 when his play *Flowering Cherry*, with Ralph Richardson in
the title role, was staged in London. Its success persuaded him to devote
himself to the theater, and *The Tiger and the Horse*, which like its predecessor concerns the paradoxes of idealism and detachment, appeared three
years later. In the meanwhile, Bolt had written for BBC radio the short play
about Thomas More he was to expand into his international triumph, *A
Man for All Seasons*. Stylistically, the earlier works had been (Bolt concedes)
"uneasily straddled between naturalism and nonnaturalism." But *A Man for
All Seasons* made a double move, projecting the familiar themes upon historical myth, and presenting them in the trappings of a fashionable Brechtian theatricality. The resulting simplification, or clarification, of his ideas
brought Bolt the New York Drama Critics Circle Award in 1962, and, for the
play's film version, several Oscars.

Aside from the schematic but interesting experiment *Gentle Jack*, Bolt's
most important work in the 1960s was done for film. He wrote a series of
screenplays for David Lean (*Lawrence of Arabia, Doctor Zhivago*, and *Ryan's
Daughter*) in which personal melodrama is again played out against roman-
ticized history. The most recent stage works are also histories. *Vivat! Vivat
Regina!* confronts Queen Elizabeth's rigidity with the femininity of Mary of
Scotland. *State of Revolution*, written for the National Theatre, is a portrait
of Lenin as a sensitive leader imprisoned in his ideals.

BOOKS BY BOLT

A Man for All Seasons. 1960. Random 1962 $10.95 1966 pap. $2.95
Gentle Jack. 1963. Heinemann text ed. 1965 $1.95
The Thwarting of Baron Bolligrew. 1965. Heinemann text ed. 1966 pap. $3.00
State of Revolution. Heinemann text ed. 1977 pap. $7.50

BOND, EDWARD. 1935–

Because of its pivotal scene, which involves the stoning to death of a baby
by a gang of young toughs in a London Park, Edward Bond's first major production, *Saved*, was banned in its entirety by the Lord Chamberlain. This
last heroic effort of English stage censorship, whose official life was to end
three years later, necessarily drew attention away from the play's dry rendering of an inarticulate and insensitive existence. Even without the censor,
though, this difficulty remains. A distracting violence is still the center of
Bond's work—the surrealist murders and cannibalism of *Early Morning*, the
mutilations of the Shakespearean travesty *Lear* (1970), the drowning man refused assistance in *The Sea*, or infanticide again in *The Bundle*, a Brechtian
parable that intentionally inverts the humane *Caucasian Chalk Circle*.

Bond's violence is not simply an image of evil or crude dramatic shock. It is meant as something to be come to terms with intellectually, or even—as in *The Bundle*—to be agreed to, as the price of effective action. In its obviousness, Bond's brutality challenges the audience to acknowledge its own hidden, structural ruthlessness. But despite his presumption to a "rational theater," the playwright's ideas often seem inadequately worked out (and are certainly inadequately expressed in prefaces that share nothing of Shaw's vivacity and clarity).

Bond has never lost touch, meanwhile, with an impressive stiff poetry of the stage, clearest in stylistically spare works like *Bingo* (about Shakespeare's last days) and *The Fool* (about the madness of the poet John Clare).

BOOKS BY BOND

Plays. Methuen 2 vols. 1977–78 o.p. Vol. 1: *Saved, Early Morning, The Pope's Wedding.* Vol. 2: *Lear, The Sea, Narrow Road to the Deep North, Black Mass, Passion.*
Theatre Poems and Songs. Methuen 1978 pap. $6.95
War Plays: A Trilogy. Methuen 1985 pap. $4.95. Contains *Red, Black and Ignorant, Tin Can People.*
Saved. 1965. Hill & Wang 1966 pap. $3.45; Methuen 1984 pap. $6.95
Narrow Road to the Deep North. 1968. Hill & Wang 1969 pap. $1.50; Methuen 1981 pap. $6.95
Early Morning. 1968. Hill & Wang 1972 $6.50; Riverrun 1980 pap. $4.95
Bingo and The Sea: Two Plays. Hill & Wang 1975 $10.00
The Fool and We Come to the River. Methuen 1976 pap. $6.95
The Woman. 1978. Hill & Wang 1979 $10.95 pap. $5.95
The Bundle, or The New Narrow Road to the Deep North. Methuen 1978 pap. $6.95
The Worlds: Includes the Activist Papers. 1979. Methuen 1980 pap. $6.95
Restoration and the Cat. Methuen 2d ed. 1982 pap. $7.95
Summer. Methuen 1982 pap. $5.95
Derek and Choruses from "After the Assassinations." Methuen 1984 pap. $4.95

BOOKS ABOUT BOND

Coult, Tony. *The Plays of Edward Bond.* Drama Bk. text ed. 1978 pap. $4.95
Hay, Malcolm, and Philip Roberts. *Bond: A Study of His Plays.* Methuen 1981 pap. $11.95

BRENTON, HOWARD. 1942–

Howard Brenton trained in the fringe theaters of the late 1960s, radical experiments in political consciousness-raising, which dispensed with theatrical scenery, stage venues, and formally constructed, full-length plays. After leaving Cambridge, he worked with a group in Brighton until the London production of *Revenge* in 1969 brought him a commission from Portable Theatre, an important touring agitprop company that had been founded by two other Cambridge graduates, David Hare and Tony Bicat. For them, he wrote *Christie in Love*, a stylistically disorienting confrontation of the Rillington Place murderer and the police. Brenton also participated in a seminal playwrighting collaboration of the early seventies, *Lay-By*, and joined Hare in writing a chronicle of British profiteers, *Brassneck*. In the same year, *Magnificence*, with its famous nihilistic conclusion—an accidental detonation that kills both a radical terrorist and his innocent victim—found its way to the stage of the Royal Court.

The scandal of Brenton's work has since then been raised to a higher power by his insistence on leaving the fringe behind, and finding new scope for his ideas on the stages of the establishment—if not in the commercial West End, then in the subsidized theaters. The National Theatre produced his study of an industrial strike, *Weapons of Happiness*, and, most notoriously, *The Romans in Britain*. Violent scenes in this epic of colonialism, which parallels the Roman occupation of Britain to the English presence in Northern Ireland, drew the wrath of citizens' groups, and a lawsuit. More recent subjects include nuclear arms—in *The Genius*, ironically challenging the optimism of BRECHT's *Galileo* (which Brenton has translated)—and the relationship of power and journalism—in *Pravda*, his latest collaboration with Hare.

BOOKS BY BRENTON

Plays for the Poor Theatre: Five Short Plays. Methuen 1980 pap. $7.95. Contains *The Saliva Milk Shake, Christie in Love, Gum and Goo, Heads, The Education of Skinny Spew*.
Revenge. 1969. Methuen 2d ed. 1982 pap. $6.95
Magnificence: A Play. 1973. Methuen 1980 pap. $6.95
The Churchill Play. Methuen 1974 pap. $6.95
Weapons of Happiness. Methuen 1976 pap. $6.95
Epsom Downs. Methuen 1977 pap. $6.95
Sore Throats and Sonnets of Love and Opposition. Methuen 1979 pap. $4.95
The Romans in Britain: A Play. 1980. Methuen 3d ed. 1982 pap. $3.95
Thirteenth Night and A Short Sharp Rock. 1980. Methuen 1981 pap. $4.95
Hitler Dances. Methuen 1982 pap. $6.95
The Genius. 1983. Methuen 1984 pap. $4.95
(and David Hare). *Pravda*. Methuen 1985 pap. $6.95

CHURCHILL, CARYL. 1938–

In the early 1980s Churchill suddenly became one of the contemporary British dramatists best represented on New York stages, as three of her plays were produced in succession. *Cloud Nine*, directed by Tommy Tune, held the stage for two years and won an Obie (as did *Top Girls*). In England, Churchill's career has been less abrupt, a long migration among the characteristic outlets of the new drama. From 1961 to 1972 she wrote radio plays. *Owners* was her first stage work (aside from college productions), commissioned by the Royal Court, where she became resident dramatist in 1974, and which staged *Objections to Sex and Violence* in 1975. In the next year, Churchill began working with two of the important fringe theater companies—Joint Stock (for which she wrote *Light Shining in Buckinghamshire, Cloud Nine*, and *Fen*) and a feminist group, Monstrous Regiment (*Vinegar Tom*: contributions to the revue *Floorshow*). The Lucille Lortel Theatre (New York) production of *Cloud Nine* in 1981 ushered in the most recent, transatlantic phase of Churchill's career. New York's Public Theater, as well as London's Royal Court, staged versions of *Top Girls* in 1982.

Churchill writes plays of many different sorts—Ortonesque (the grotesques of *Owners*), historical (versions of the seventeenth century in *Light Shining*, about the English Civil War, and *Vinegar Tom*, about witchcraft), expressionist (the cross-sexual casting and doubling in *Cloud Nine*), and formally experimental (the permutations of situation in her dramatic Möbius strip, *Traps*). She is increasingly feminist in outlook. But if her demonstrations of sexual liberation are sometimes pat (as in the second half of *Cloud Nine*), her theatrical adventurousness is always invigorating.

BOOK BY CHURCHILL

Plays: One. Methuen 1985 pap. $5.95. Contains *Owners, Traps, Vinegar Tom, Light Shining in Buckinghamshire, Cloud Nine*.

COWARD, SIR NOEL (PIERCE). 1899–1973

In 1964, when *Hay Fever* (1925) was placed in the repertory of the newly organized National Theatre, Noel Coward professed to be grateful: "Bless you for admitting that I'm a classic." The admission has by now grown to a chorus of affirmation. A week-long series of Coward played on BBC television in 1969; there have been major revivals in London and New York; plays long out of print have been republished in popular collections. At the start of the 1960s, though, Coward's reputation had been at an ebb, as he skirmished with the angry new drama (he called it the "scratch and mumble school"), which in turn classified him with Rattigan as a figurehead of the establishment. Coward had enjoyed no big success since *Blithe Spirit* of 1941—a considerable dry spell for a playwright who had once seen five of his plays staged in a single season.

There have been attempts to assimilate the rehabilitated Coward to contemporary drama. Kenneth Tynan, for instance, professed to see a connection between the playwright's famous bare unepigrammatic dialogue, which depended entirely on the actors for its life, and the style of Harold Pinter. And Coward himself profited from the new freedom when, in 1965, his *Song at Twilight* forthrightly discussed homosexuality, a personal subject which, as John Lahr has recently shown, he had carefully evaded throughout his career.

But there is really no way to take Coward except on his own terms. A juvenile prodigy, he was by turns actor, director, composer, lyricist, autobiographer, and author of nearly 60 theater pieces. Although he specialized in light comedy, he worked in many forms—patriotic spectacle, revue, musical, farce, even the problem play. (He associated *The Vortex*, a particularly overheated example, with Pinero.) *Hay Fever, Blithe Spirit*, and *Private Lives* (1930) have proved the most durable of his comedies, along with nine short plays presented as *Tonight at 8:30*. In each, characters demonstrate the combination of perpetual role-playing, cool hedonism, and the energizing self-absorption—the stance that may be Coward's most enduring creation.

BOOKS BY COWARD

Plays: One. Grove 1981 pap. $9.95. Contains *Hay Fever, Fallen Angels,* and *Easy Virtue.*

Plays: Two. Grove 1981 pap. $9.95. Contains *Private Lives, Bitter-Sweet, The Marquise,* and *Post Mortem.*

Plays: Three. Grove 1981 pap. $9.95. Contains *Design for Living, Cavalcade, Conversation Piece,* and three plays from *Tonight at 8:30* (*Hands across the Sea, Still Life,* and *Fumed Oak*).

Plays: Four. Grove 1981 pap. $9.95. Contains *Blithe Spirit, Present Laughter, This Happy Breed,* and three plays from *Tonight at 8:30* (*Ways and Means, The Astonished Heart,* and *Red Peppers*).

Plays: Five. Grove 1983 pap. $9.95. Contains *Relative Values, Looking after Lulu, Waiting in the Wings,* and *Suite in Three Keys.*

Three Plays. Intro. by Edward Albee, Grove (Evergreen) 1979 pap. $4.50. Contains *Blithe Spirit, Hay Fever,* and *Private Lives.*

The Lyrics of Noel Coward. Overlook Pr. repr. of 1965 ed. 1973 $25.00 pap. $9.95; Penguin 1983 $25.00 pap. $8.95

BOOKS ABOUT COWARD

Lahr, John. *Coward: The Playwright.* Avon 1983 pap. $3.95; Methuen 1983 $15.95

Lesley, Cole. *Remembered Laughter: The Life of Noel Coward.* Knopf 1976 $12.95

Levin, Milton. *Noel Coward.* Twayne's Eng. Authors Ser. G. K. Hall 1969 lib. bdg. $13.50

Morley, Sheridan. *A Talent to Amuse: A Biography of Noel Coward.* Little, Brown 1985 $24.45

Snider, Rose. *Satire in the Comedies of Congreve, Sheridan, Wilde and Coward.* Folcroft repr. of 1937 ed. lib. bdg. $15.00; Phaeton repr. of 1937 ed. text ed. 1971 $9.00

ELIOT, T(HOMAS) S(TEARNS). 1888–1965 (NOBEL PRIZE 1948)

Eliot is the pivotal verse dramatist of this century. He followed the lead of William Butler Yeats in attempting to revive metrical language in the theater, and left to Christopher Fry, after the war, an alternative to realism in dialogue, which nevertheless did not revert to the Shakespeareanizing of the Victorians.

But unlike Yeats (and to an extent Fry), Eliot wanted a dramatic verse that would be self-effacing, an elastic medium capable of expressing the most prosaic passages in a play, an insistent, undetected presence nevertheless capable of elevating itself at a moment's notice. His progression from the pageant *The Rock* (1934) and *Murder in the Cathedral* (1935), written for the Canterbury Festival, through *The Family Reunion* (1939) and *The Cocktail Party* (1949), a West End hit, was thus a matter of neutralizing the obviously poetic effects (such as the chorus of *Murder*) and bringing prose passages (like the Shavian Knights' speeches) into the flow of verse.

Eliot applied this principle of submersion to his dramatic themes also. Again unlike Yeats, he moved toward the conventional theater rather than away from it, crowding the richness of mythological and religious material under its familiar surfaces. His Sweeney "fragment" experimented with music hall routines. And while *Murder in the Cathedral*, despite its Agatha Christie title, retained the formality of Greek tragedy, *The Family Reunion* moved the Orestes story into the realistic drawing room of Maugham and Rattigan. Eliot boasted that none of the critics had been able to detect the Euripidean myth of Alcestis that he had secreted in the conversations, puzzling and banal, of *The Cocktail Party*. Not to be caught napping twice, commentators have perhaps spent too much time tracking down the allusions in both of Eliot's later plays, the "Serious Farce," *The Confidential Clerk*, and the Shakespearean valediction, *The Elder Statesman*. (See also Volume 1, Chapter 7.)

BOOKS BY ELIOT

The Complete Poems and Plays, 1909–1950. Harcourt 1952 $18.95
The Family Reunion. Harcourt 1964 pap. $5.95
The Cocktail Party. Harcourt 1964 pap. $2.95
The Confidential Clerk. Harcourt 1954 $9.95 1964 pap. $6.95
The Elder Statesman. Farrar 1959 $4.95
Murder in the Cathedral. Harcourt 1964 pap. $2.95
The Sacred Wood. Methuen 7th ed. 1960 pap. $10.95. Includes essays on the theory of
    verse drama.

BOOKS ABOUT ELIOT

Chiari, Joseph. *T. S. Eliot: Poet and Dramatist*. Gordian repr. of 1972 ed. 1979 $12.00
Clark, D., ed. *Twentieth-Century Interpretations of Murder in the Cathedral*. Prentice-
    Hall (Spectrum Bks.) 1971 $7.95
Headings, Philip R. *T. S. Eliot. Twayne's U.S. Authors Ser.* G. K. Hall rev. ed. 1982
    lib. bdg. $14.50 1985 pap. $6.95
Jones, David E. *Plays of T. S. Eliot*. Univ. of Toronto Pr. 1960 pap. $2.75
Kenner, H., ed. *T. S. Eliot: A Collection of Critical Essays*. Prentice-Hall (Spectrum
    Bks.) 1962 pap. $4.95
Martin, Mildred. *A Half-Century of Eliot Criticism*. Bucknell Univ. Pr. 1972 $35.00
Smith, Carol H. *T. S. Eliot's Dramatic Theory and Practice*. Gordian repr. of 1963 ed.
    1977 $12.50
Smith, Grover, Jr. *T. S. Eliot's Poetry and Plays*. Univ. of Chicago Pr. 2d ed. 1975 pap.
    $9.50

FRY, CHRISTOPHER (born Christopher Harris). 1907–

Success came to Christopher Fry after 38 years of living close to poverty. He was born in Bristol, where his father, a poor architect, turned to lay missionary work in the slums. In 1940, after alternating between teaching and acting, Fry became the director of the excellent Oxford Playhouse. As a Quaker conscientious objector, he refused to bear arms in World War II.

He was first discovered by critics and connoisseurs in 1946, when a small London theater staged *A Phoenix Too Frequent*, his version of the perennial story of the widow who accepts a new lover while mourning beside her late husband's grave. Three years later, John Gielgud's production of *The Lady's Not for Burning* brought Fry popular success in London and the provinces. This clever medieval conceit was produced in New York, and received the Drama Critics Circle Award for 1950. Sir Laurence Olivier commissioned *Ve-*

nus Observed, a play about middle age, the autumn section of what has come to be a cycle of seasonal plays. The winter play, *The Dark Is Light Enough*, followed two years later. Set in 1848, during the Hungarian revolution against the Austrian empire, it takes a moral stand against any use of violence. (An antiwar morality play, *A Sleep of Prisoners*, had been produced in 1951.) It was more than a decade before Fry's summer comedy, *A Yard of Sun*, was published.

Fry's relation to T. S. Eliot is interesting. Like him, Fry is a Christian verse dramatist. He has set a play (like Eliot) in a church (*A Sleep of Prisoners*); he has written an historical study of Becket and Henry II (*Curtmantle*). And, like Eliot, Fry has achieved a loose, speakable verse. Yet their differences are equally instructive. Fry's verse, unlike Eliot's functional amble, strives to be poetic with flamboyant energy and arresting wit. The same theatricality is evident in, say, his Becket play, where he replaces the introspection of Eliot's martyr with the strong clash of personalities. *The Lady's Not for Burning*—which was performed alongside Eliot's *The Cocktail Party* in 1949—is a downright, if intellectual, comedy, unlike the dry drawing-room enigma of Eliot.

As a translator-adaptor, Fry seems almost singlehandedly responsible for the postwar English vogue of modern French writers. His version of JEAN GIRAUDOUX's *The Trojan War Will Not Take Place* (a transatlantic success in 1959, when it was retitled *Tiger at the Gates*) was revived at the National Theatre in 1984, directed by Harold Pinter. Fry is also a screenwriter (John Huston's *The Bible*, William Wyler's *Ben Hur*) and composer.

BOOKS BY FRY

Three Plays: The Firstborn; Thor, with Angels; A Sleep of Prisoners. Oxford 1965 pap. $3.95

The Lady's Not for Burning, A Phoenix Too Frequent, and an Essay, "An Experience of Critics." Oxford 1977 pap. $6.95

Venus Observed. Oxford 1950 $9.95

Dark Is Light Enough. Oxford 1954 $9.95

A Yard of Sun. Oxford 1970 $9.95

BOOKS ABOUT FRY

Roy, Emil. *Christopher Fry. Crosscurrents Modern Critiques Ser.* Southern Illinois Univ. Pr. 1968 $6.95

Stanford, Derek. *Christopher Fry.* Longman rev. ed. 1954 o.p.

Wiersma, Stanley. *Christopher Fry.* Eerdmans 1970 o.p.

GALSWORTHY, JOHN. 1867–1933 (NOBEL PRIZE 1932)

After a gentlemanly education at Ḥarrow and Oxford, and a training at law (that links him with English playwrights from Pinero to John Mortimer), Galsworthy settled into simultaneous careers as a novelist and a playwright. *The Silver Box*, his first successful drama, was staged in 1906, the year he published the first volume of what was to become *The Forsyte Saga*.

His one-word titles—*Justice, Strife, Loyalties*—suggest the nature of Galsworthy's artistic ambition: to generalize a social indictment, keeping faith with the objective methods of naturalism. Systematically, without any apparent imaginative will toward a particular subject, his drama turns a cold eye on a series of institutional problems: "One law for the rich and one for the poor" (*The Silver Box*); the futility of charity in relieving the "submerged tenth" (*The Pigeon*, 1912); the counterclaims of capital and labor (*Strife*, 1909); the intersections of class, race, family, and friendship (*Loyalties*, 1922); and nationalistic jingoism (*Mob*). In each, Galsworthy favors an austere irony and unresolvable situations, and balanced moral positions are displayed in the cabinetwork of "well-made" playwrighting. Reputed to have led to reforms in its time, his realism today seems contrived to produce aesthetic distance and a sense of resignation that is precisely what contemporary political dramatists strain hardest to avoid. Not surprisingly, critics have come away from recent revivals with the sense that (especially in his spare language) Galsworthy anticipates Pinter, rather than any of today's socially engaged playwrights. (See also Volume 1, Chapter 12.)

BOOKS BY GALSWORTHY

The Plays of John Galsworthy. Richard West repr. of 1929 ed. 1980 lib. bdg. $40.00; Scribner 1928 $12.50

Representative Plays. Scribner 1924 o.p.

Five Plays. Intro. by Benedict Nightingale, Methuen 1984 pap. $5.95

Strife. Methuen 1984 pap. $3.95

BOOKS ABOUT GALSWORTHY

Coats, R. H. *John Galsworthy as a Dramatic Artist*. Folcroft repr. of 1926 ed. lib. bdg. $25.00

Frechet, Alec. *John Galsworthy: A Reassessment*. Trans. by Denis Mahaffey, Barnes & Noble text ed. 1982 $29.50

Mikhail, E. H., ed. *John Galsworthy the Dramatist: A Bibliography of Criticism*. Whitston 1971 $7.50

GILBERT, SIR WILLIAM SCHWENCK. 1836–1911

Born in London, William S. Gilbert served a term as a government clerk and was called to the bar as a barrister before being diverted into the bohemian world of Victorian comic journalism. He first achieved popularity as the author of several volumes of "Bab Ballads" (Beerbohm praised them as "silly"). Moving on to theater, Gilbert contributed to the current rage for travesties of opera and for one-act musical "entertainments" until a blank-verse burlesque of TENNYSON's (see Vol. 1) *Princess* led to commissions and full-length comedies, both mythological and "modern." Still highly regarded by critics, some of these—perhaps *Sweethearts* (1874) and *Engaged* (1877)—should be investigated by today's readers and producers. As it is, their best memorial is the early work of Bernard Shaw, who, although he polemically rejected their cynicism, was clearly influenced by Gilbert's comedies and their inversion of social values.

By the time of *Engaged*, however, a second dramatic career had overtaken Gilbert. Collaboration with the composer Arthur Sullivan, begun in 1871 (*Thespis*), achieved theatrical success with *Trial by Jury* in 1875. In the comic operas that followed, Sullivan's generally allusive music enriched the sometimes shrill pessimism of Gilbert's wit. An unlikely jostle of theatrical parody, contemporary satire, intricate meters, and logical fantasy, the librettos have often been compared with the comedies of Aristophanes, and have influenced English playwrights from Wilde to Stoppard. (Gilbert, too, wrote a *Rosencrantz and Guildenstern.*)

Uncomfortable, often acrimonious, the partnership nevertheless lasted through 25 years and 13 Savoy operas (so called because many were staged by Richard D'Oyly Carte at his Savoy Theatre). Gilbert, whose merely theatrical connections (as opposed to Sullivan's serious musical credentials) held him back from formal honors, was knighted in 1907, only a few years before his death.

BOOKS BY GILBERT

The Complete Plays of Gilbert and Sullivan. Norton Lib. repr. of 1941 ed. 1976 pap. $12.95

The Annotated Gilbert and Sullivan. Ed. by Ian Bradley, Penguin 2 vols. pap. ea. $9.95. Vol. 1: *H.M.S. Pinafore, Pirates of Penzance, Iolanthe, Mikado, Gondoliers.* Vol. 2: *Trial by Jury, The Sorcerer, Patience, Princess Ida, Ruddigore, Yeoman of the Guard.*

Plays by W. S. Gilbert. Ed. by George Rowell, Cambridge Univ. Pr. 1982 $39.50 pap. $10.95

Martyn Green's Treasury of Gilbert and Sullivan. Ed. by Martyn Green, Simon & Schuster 1985 $14.95. Contains the librettos of 11 works, more than 100 songs simply arranged for voice and piano, and a full commentary by Green, comic lead of the D'Oyly Carte Opera Company for more than two decades.

Gilbert before Sullivan: Six Comic Plays. Ed. by Jane W. Stedman, Univ. of Chicago Pr. 1967 o.p. One-act musical "entertainments": *No Cards* (1869); *Ages Ago: A Musical Legend* (1869); *Our Island Home* (1870); *A Sensational Novel in Three Volumes* (1871); *Eyes and No Eyes, or The Art of Seeing* (1875); and *Happy Arcadia* (1872). With a selected bibliography and introductory essay.

New and Original Extravagances. Ed. by Sir Isaac Goldberg, Branden 1931 o.p.

The Bab Ballads. 1869. Ed. by James Ellis, Harvard Univ. Pr. (Belknap Pr.) 1970 $22.50 pap. $9.95

BOOKS ABOUT GILBERT

Allen, Reginald. *W. S. Gilbert: An Anniversary Survey and Exhibition Checklist.* Univ. Pr. of Virginia 1963 $5.50

——. *Gilbert and Sullivan in America.* Pierpont Morgan 1979 pap. $3.00

Dark, Sidney, and Rowland Grey. *W. S. Gilbert: His Life and Letters.* Ayer repr. of 1923 ed. $20.00; Gale repr. of 1923 ed. 1971 $40.00

Dunn, George E. *A Gilbert and Sullivan Dictionary.* Da Capo repr. of 1936 ed. 1971 lib. bdg. $22.95; Folcroft repr. of 1936 ed. 1972 lib. bdg. $25.00

Godwin, A. H. *Gilbert and Sullivan: A Critical Approach to the Savoy Operas.* Associated Faculty Pr. repr. of 1926 ed. 1969 $22.50; Richard West 1926 $20.00

Goldberg, Isaac. *Story of Gilbert and Sullivan.* AMS Pr. repr. of 1928 ed. $20.00; Gordon $59.95; Richard West 1973 $19.50

Hibbert, Christopher. *Gilbert and Sullivan and Their Victorian World.* Putnam 1976 $24.95

Pearson, Hesketh. *Gilbert: His Life and Strife*. Greenwood repr. of 1957 ed. 1978 lib. bdg. $24.75

Searle, Townley. *A Bibliography of Sir William Schwenck Gilbert*. Burt Franklin repr. of 1931 ed. 1967 $21.00

Sutton, Max K. *W. S. Gilbert*. Twayne's Eng. Authors Ser. G. K. Hall 1975 lib. bdg. $13.50

GRAY, SIMON. 1936–

Simon Gray's plays seem to have traced the recent history of British comedy, backwards. He began in 1967 with the outrageous *Wise Child*, which kept Alec Guinness, playing a fugitive criminal, in woman's clothing, an Ortonian *Charley's Aunt*. By 1971 Gray had arrived, in *Butley*, at the nonstop rant of a disaffected provincial university teacher, recalling the tone and temper of Osborne's Jimmy Porter and Kingsley Amis's Lucky Jim. *Otherwise Engaged* was cooler in its wit, more elegantly situated in the world of publishing, but no less a monologue, as Simon Hench detaches himself, with disconcerting reasonableness, from wife, friends, and other claimants, including a suicide. In *Quartermaine's Terms* and *The Common Pursuit*, Gray seems at last to have rediscovered the interplay of character without effacing his bitter vision of isolation and sterility.

Gray has edited a literary review (like the characters in *The Common Pursuit*) and taught English in universities, both major and provincial. He has written television plays and novels, and adapted Dostoevsky's *The Idiot* for the National Theatre. Gray has recently published *An Unnatural Pursuit*, a diary of the London production of *The Common Pursuit*, describing his work with the director, his friend Harold Pinter, who has staged several of his plays.

BOOKS BY GRAY

Otherwise Engaged and Other Plays. Methuen 1984 pap. $5.95; *Penguin Plays Ser.* 1976 pap. $2.50

The Rear Column, Dog Days, and Other Plays. Methuen 1985 pap. $5.50; Penguin 1979 pap. $5.95; Viking 1979 $12.95

Wise Child. 1967. Faber 1968 o.p.

Dutch Uncle. Faber 1969 o.p.

Spoiled. Methuen 1971 o.p.

Butley. Methuen 1971 o.p.

Quartermaine's Terms. Modern Plays Ser. Methuen 1983 pap. $6.95

The Common Pursuit. Modern Plays Ser. Methuen 1984 pap. $6.95

HARE, DAVID. 1947–

David Hare was one of the founders of Portable Theatre and, later, Joint Stock, important companies on the British theatrical left. He has collaborated in two of the seminal radical dramas of the seventies—*Lay-By* and *England's Ireland*. He favors writing with the provocateur Howard Brenton. Yet in notable ways, Hare's drama keeps itself apart from the agitprop, assaultive techniques of the contemporary political theater. His plays are constructions—allusions to, if not actually specimens of, the well-made play. Their dialogue is witty. Without epic ambitions, they seek out small societies (not often working-class) and confined situations—a girls' school (*Slag*), the home of a diplomat (*The Great Exhibition*), May Ball at a Cambridge college (*Teeth n' Smiles*), an international conference on Third-World problems (*A Map of the World*). And in the midst of a theater that largely derides the notion of character, Hare has focused constantly on personal drama.

Not that this is simply classicism, or regression. Hare has kept his political convictions onstage by situating his character studies in an historical perspective—in *Plenty*, *Licking Hitler*, and the film *Wetherby*, testing actions against the moral touchstone of World War II. And in *Fanshen*, the reenactment of the collectivization of a Chinese village, he seems to have deliberately adopted the radical theater's simplicities of language and scene, as well as its subject matter.

But even *Fanshen*, as critics have pointed out, takes a detached and ambivalent view of the radical process it describes. And a sense of the playwright's detachment hovers over many of Hare's works—from the early comedy of feminism, *Slag*, to the recent *Map of the World*, which gives most of its best lines to a conservative novelist deriding the emptiness of utopian idealism. Even in his latest work, *Pravda*—a return to collaboration with the committed Brenton—Hare seems to be as fascinated with the figure of the Machiavellian newspaper czar as he is interested in exposing the mechanics of capitalist exploitation.

BOOKS BY HARE

The Great Exhibition. Faber 1972 o.p.
Fanshen. Faber 1976 pap. $6.95
Teeth n' Smiles. Faber 1976 pap. $5.95
Plenty. New Amer. Lib. (Plume) 1985 pap. $6.95
Dreams of Leaving. Faber 1980 pap. $6.95
Saigon: Year of the Cat. Faber 1984 pap. $7.95
(and Howard Brenton). *Pravda.* Methuen 1985 pap. $6.95

NICHOLS, PETER. 1928–

A Bristol-born former actor and schoolteacher, Peter Nichols got his start writing some 14 plays for television, and has continued to write for that medium even since attaining success in the West End. *A Day in the Death of Joe Egg*, his first stage play, was produced in England in 1967 and on Broadway a year later. *Joe Egg* (as a squeamish American management insisted it be retitled) concerns a couple whose marriage is slowly being destroyed by their attempt to raise a hopelessly spastic daughter (Josephine, alias Joe Egg, their "living parsnip"). They survive in their situation as long as they do by ceaselessly joking about it. But this is not black humor, Nichols insists. The black humorist "sets himself at a distance from his characters and [laughs] at them. The characters [in my play] set themselves at a distance from their own situation. . . ."

This comic distancing, as much as its autobiographical revelation, was to be the common characteristic of Nichols's later plays. *Forget-Me-Not-Lane*, distinctly personal in its middle-aged re-examination of a World War II childhood, has characters stepping back and forth through time and in and out of the dramatic situation. In *Passion Play* Nichols's characters even break away from themselves, each partner in a bickering couple splitting into mutually critical components. *The National Health*, produced to general acclaim at the National Theatre, achieves its distancing through the alternation of realistic scenes of suffering and dying in a hospital ward with episodes of an outrageous medical soap opera, *Nurse Norton's Affair*, shown on a simulated television screen. And in the ironic musical episodes of *Privates on Parade*, the story of an army entertainment troupe in the 1950s, Nichols entered the area of alienating theatricalism explored by Osborne's *The Entertainer* and Joan Littlewood's *Oh, What a Lovely War*.

Privates, a Royal Shakespeare Company hit of 1977, has been made into a film, as have *Joe Egg* and *The National Health*. (Nichols also wrote the screenplay for the 1966 film satire *Georgy Girl*.)

BOOKS BY NICHOLS

A Day in the Death of Joe Egg. Grove 1967 pap. $3.95
The National Health, or, Nurse Norton's Affair. 1969. Grove 1975 pap. $3.95
Forget-Me-Not-Lane. Faber 1971 o.p.
Chez Nous: A Domestic Comedy in Two Acts. Faber 1974 pap. $4.95
The Freeway. 1974. Faber 1975 pap. $4.95
Privates on Parade. Faber 1977 pap. $5.95
Born in the Gardens. Faber 1980 pap. $8.50
Passion Play. Methuen 1981 pap. $6.95
Poppy. Methuen 1982 $6.95

ORTON, JOE. 1933–1967

Joe Orton's shocking murder is too easily made the biographical focus for discussion of his plays, devoted as they are to the grotesque, the perverse, and the violent. A more relevant landmark in the playwright's life might be the jail term he served for the bizarre crime of defacing library books, replacing illustrations with uproarious collages, and rewriting jacket blurbs in "mildly obscene" parodies of journalistic cliché. Assaulting the cultural consumer by transposing his familiar icons and vocabulary was the key to Orton's theatrical method. But it was supplemented by a growing verbal power and stage imagery with aspirations to myth.

As Orton's literary powers grew, so did the outrage of social response. The Pinterian ambiance and language of his first works, *Entertaining Mr. Sloane* and the radio play *The Ruffian on the Stair*, were well received. *Sloane* was chosen best new British play of 1964 and won the blessing of Terence Rattigan himself. But *Loot*, joking with death, religion, sex, and family, proved more disturbing. The first production, directed by Peter Wood, closed on tour without reaching London. It was not until 1966 that the play was staged, to acclaim, in Charles Marowitz's fringe theater. In 1969, *What the Butler Saw* failed in the West End despite a cast of many famous names, including Ralph Richardson. Only the Royal Court revival of 1975 gave Orton's undoubted masterpiece its due. But by then the playwright had been dead for eight years.

In the phallic epiphany with which *Butler* ends, as in his version of EURIPI-DES's *Bacchae, The Erpingham Camp,* Orton calls attention to his Dionysian ambitions—his serious use of farce as a means of disruption and liberation. His last plays, in which violent animal spirits subvert dialogue of extreme—even Victorian—formality and outrageous authority figures, represent the greatest comic achievement of contemporary British drama.

Book by Orton

The Complete Plays. Intro. by John Lahr, Grove 1977 pap. $6.95. Contains *Entertaining Mr. Sloane, Loot, What the Butler Saw,* and four shorter plays (*The Ruffian on the Stair, The Erpingham Camp, The Good and Faithful Servant, Funeral Games*).

Books about Orton

Bigsby, Christopher W. *Joe Orton. Contemporary Writers Ser.* Methuen 1982 pap. $4.25

Charney, Maurice. *Joe Orton.* Grove repr. 1984 $19.50 pap. $7.95

Lahr, John. *Prick Up Your Ears: The Biography of Joe Orton.* Avon 1979 pap. $3.50; Knopf 1978 $15.00

OSBORNE, JOHN. 1929–

John Osborne, it is fairly well known, started the new wave rolling. He had worked intermittently as an actor and journalist, and had had two plays performed outside London, when, at 26, he sent a script to the English Stage Company, George Devine's new repertory group, which hoped to establish a "writer's theatre" in London. With *Look Back in Anger* and its oratorial hero Jimmy Porter, the company at the Royal Court inaugurated a revitalization of the British drama, and gave a name to a generation of young writers and their protagonists—"angry young men." In reviews, Osborne found himself crowded together with Wesker, Storey, Jellicoe, Delaney, and Arden, playwrights with whom he shared little beyond their working-class origins and antiestablishment attitudes.

Osborne went on, however, to write plays about figures definitely not young or even angry, exactly. Archie Rice, of *The Entertainer,* is a faded music-hall comedian whose son has been killed in Cyprus. His squalid life alternates between scenes of aggressive and embittered performances before bored holiday audiences, a brilliantly distancing use of the theatrical that turns Archie's show into a metaphor for waning England. That Rice was played by Laurence Olivier was also significant—a gesture of the establishment theater accepting the new drama, meeting it (symbolically) on the common ground of the music hall, a shared popular dramatic tradition.

Luther might be described as an inconclusive attempt to find an historical analogue for Jimmy Porter. But with *Inadmissible Evidence,* Osborne succeeded in creating the third of his archetypes for the modern stage, the decomposing solicitor Bill Maitland, hallucinating in the shadows of his office as business, daughter, mistress, and self slip through his fingers. As *Look Back* is a defiant inversion of Tennessee Williams's *Streetcar Named Desire*, *Inadmissible Evidence* is Osborne's *Death of a Salesman*. Stylistically, the play joined *Look Back* and *The Entertainer* in defining the three courses to be taken by new wave British theater: socially committed naturalism, theatricalism (influenced by the popular stage), and a shadowy interiority, to be fully realized only a decade later in the work of Pinter. So Osborne did not just begin it all—in a sense, he went through it all as well.

Not that he has ever been anything but himself. Characteristic of all three plays are invective and pleading and aggressive vulnerability, in Osborne's peculiar modern version of Shaw's stage-dominating monologue. If there has been any marked development in the more than 15 plays he has written since 1965, it has been in the direction of engaging the speaker with others, in finding an ensemble of voices, as he tried to do in *The Hotel in Amsterdam* and *West of Suez*. Meanwhile, without real commitment, Osborne has been theatrically experimental (in *A Sense of Detachment*, actors planted in the audience interrupt the performance) and thematically daring. *A Patriot for Me*, the homosexual subject which provoked the Lord Chamberlain's censorship in 1966, was triumphantly revived in 1983 in the very heart of the establishment, moving from the Chichester Festival to the Theatre Royal, Haymarket. Osborne's increasingly reactionary social views have today detached him in everyone's mind from the "angries" into whose ranks he was unfairly conscripted a quarter of a century ago.

BOOKS BY OSBORNE

Four Plays. Dodd 1973 $7.50. Contains *West of Suez, A Patriot for Me, Time Present,* and *The Hotel in Amsterdam.*
You're Not Watching Me, Mommy (and *Try a Little Tenderness*). Faber 1983 $5.95
Look Back in Anger. 1956. Penguin 1982 pap. $4.95
The Entertainer. 1957. Penguin 1983 pap. $4.95
Luther. 1961. New Amer. Lib. (Signet) pap. $3.50
Tom Jones: A Film Script. Faber 1964 $4.95
Inadmissible Evidence. Faber 1964 pap. $6.95
A Patriot for Me. 1966. Faber 1983 pap. $7.95
A Sense of Detachment. 1972. Faber 1983 pap. $7.95
The End of Me Old Cigar and Jack and Jill. 1974–75. Faber 1975 pap. $3.95
Watch It Come Down. 1975. Faber 1975 $5.95

BOOKS ABOUT OSBORNE

Ferrar, H. *John Osborne.* Columbia Univ. Pr. 1973 pap. $2.50
Hayman, Ronald. *John Osborne. Lit. and Life Ser.* Ungar 1979 $12.95
Osborne, John. *A Better Class of Person: An Autobiography.* Dutton 1981 $13.75
Trussler, Simon. *Plays of John Osborne: An Assessment.* Humanities Pr. text ed. 1969 pap. $7.50

PINERO, SIR ARTHUR WING. 1855–1934

Arthur Wing Pinero, a former actor, remained a shrewd judge of theatrical taste. After a period of writing comedies and farces (*Dandy Dick* among the best), in the 1890s Pinero fastened on London's newly aroused interest in social problem plays. But instead of following the difficult example of IBSEN, whose plays were just then beginning to be produced in English translations, Pinero turned to the French playwrights of an earlier generation. The *demimondaine* of Augier and *Dumas fils* became, in plays like *The Second Mrs. Tanqueray* (1893), the "woman with a past." The inevitable (and inevitably effective) theatrical business of recognition and confession led to acts of renunciation—in Mrs. Tanqueray's case, suicide—which permitted characters and audiences to escape the moral problems that had been posed for them. Although Wilde admired and imitated Pinero, Shaw (as a critic) denounced the timid morality and conventional characterization of this supposedly "new" drama.

Pinero's one lasting achievement is not a problem play at all, but the affectionate homage of a theater man to an earlier era of the London stage. *Trelawney of the "Wells"* (1898) has had successful modern productions at London's National Theatre and New York's Lincoln Center.

BOOKS BY PINERO

Social Plays. Ed. by Clayton Hamilton, AMS Pr. 4 vols. repr. of 1922 ed. $150.00. With a general introduction and critical preface to each play by Clayton Hamilton.

Three Plays. Intro. by Stephen Wyatt, Methuen 1985 pap. $5.25. Contains *The Magistrate, The Second Mrs. Tanqueray,* and *Trelawney of the "Wells."*

Dandy Dick. 1887. Heinemann text ed. 1959 pap. $5.00

The Collected Letters of Sir Arthur Pinero. Ed. by J. P. Wearing, Univ. of Minnesota Pr. 1974 o.p.

BOOKS ABOUT PINERO

Dunkel, Wilbur D. *Sir Arthur Pinero: A Critical Biography with Letters.* Associated Faculty Pr. repr. of 1941 ed. $15.00

Lazenby, Walter. *Arthur Wing Pinero. Twayne's Eng. Authors Ser.* G. K. Hall lib. bdg. $10.95

Selle, Carl, ed. *The New Drama: The Liars, by Henry Arthur Jones and the Notorious Mrs. Ebbsmith, by Sir Arthur Wing Pinero.* Univ. of Miami Pr. 1968 pap. $4.95

PINTER, HAROLD. 1930–

Harold Pinter was born in London's poor East End. After attending the Royal Academy of Dramatic Art, he worked as an actor and published poetry. In 1958, his third play, *The Birthday Party*, lasted for only 16 performances in London. Two years later, he had plays running successfully both at the Royal Court Theatre and in the West End.

As the bibliographies listed suggest, Pinter is perhaps the most established of the new dramatists, with almost every one of his plays in print, and one who has eluded final critical definition. This last is not entirely the fault of the critics. Although the earliest attempts at categorization, such as

Irving Wardle's "Comedy of Menace," soon proved inadequate, they did help readers cope with Pinter's plays of intentional ambiguity and mysterious violence, such as *The Dumbwaiter* (1957) and *The Birthday Party*. Then *The Caretaker* (1960), *The Collection* (1962), and the screenplay for *The Servant* seemed to move Pinter into a plainer and more familiar style of playwrighting, one concerned with subtle reversals of power in Strindbergian contests to establish "the stronger."

But by *The Homecoming* (1964), critics could no longer ignore the sense that something more was going on. In Peter Hall's Royal Shakespeare production, Vivien Merchant, then Pinter's wife, played the role of a young woman who crosses the Atlantic with her husband to meet his (entirely male) family, and ends up staying on, by mutual agreement, as their private whore who will do public whoring to support herself. (The apparently unaffected husband amiably returns to their children in America.) Such tribal behavior suggested that a framework of mythic criticism might best contain *The Homecoming* (and related works like *A Slight Ache*, 1961).

But just as articles began to appear elaborating this new explanation, Pinter again shifted style, this time to a dramatic minimalism, announced in the experimental short works *Landscape* (1969) and *Silence* (1969). The full-length plays *Old Times* (1971) and *No Man's Land* (1975), which followed, are intentionally static dramas absorbed with events sometimes literal, sometimes remembered, sometimes imagined, among which the audience cannot definitely discriminate.

These were difficult plays. *Betrayal*, his next major work, was deceptively easy, its disorientation so slight, that playgoers might mistake it for an ordinary triangle of lovers. Criticism had been left behind again.

BOOKS BY PINTER

Complete Works. Grove 4 vols. 1977–1981 pap. ea. $5.95–$6.95. Vol. 1: *The Birthday Party, The Room, The Dumbwaiter, A Slight Ache,* and *A Night Out.* Vol. 2: *The Caretaker, Night School, The Dwarfs, The Collection, The Lover,* five revue sketches, and an essay "Writing for Myself." Vol. 3: *The Homecoming, Landscape, Silence, The Basement,* revue sketches, and other writings. Vol. 4: *Old Times, No Man's Land, Betrayal,* and other writings.

Three Plays. Grove (Evergreen) 1962 pap. $4.95. Contains *A Slight Ache, The Collection,* and *The Dwarfs.*

The Homecoming. Grove (Evergreen) 1966 pap. $4.95

Betrayal. Grove 1979 $10.00 pap. $3.95

BOOKS ABOUT PINTER

Almansi, Guido, and Simon Henderson. *Harold Pinter.* Methuen 1983 pap. $4.75

Bold, Alan, ed. *Harold Pinter: You Never Heard Such Silence. Critical Studies* Barnes & Noble 1984 $27.50

Burkman, Katherine H. *The Dramatic World of Harold Pinter: Its Basis in Ritual.* Ohio State Univ. Pr. 1971 $8.00

Dukore, Bernard F. *Harold Pinter.* Grove (Evergreen) 1982 pap. $7.95

Esslin, Martin. *Pinter: The Playwright.* Methuen 4th ed. 1984 pap. $9.95

Ganz, Arthur, ed. *Pinter: A Collection of Critical Essays.* Prentice-Hall 1972 $12.95

Hayman, Ronald. *Harold Pinter. Lit. and Life Ser.* Ungar 1973 $12.95
Kerr, Walter. *Harold Pinter.* Columbia Univ. Pr. 1976 pap. $2.50
Quigley, Austin E. *The Pinter Problem.* Princeton Univ. Pr. 1975 $26.00

PRIESTLEY, J(OHN) B(OYNTON). 1894–1984

Although J. B. Priestley was like John Galsworthy and Somerset
Maugham, a novelist only partially committed to his playwrighting, he was
the dominant literary figure in the London West End during the 1930s, as
he attempted to make realistically rendered domestic conversation the vehicle for a mature study of personality and emotion. Philosophical theories
about time, Socialist dogmatism (often erupting into sermons), and a taste
for dramatic expressionism may be said to have finally deflected him from
his goal. Priestley's experimental bent nevertheless yielded, among his more
than 25 plays, a number of striking theatrical situations—the soliloquies of
Ever Since Paradise, the reviewed life in *Johnson over Jordan* (1939), the re-
play of àn ill-fated conversational turn in *Dangerous Corner* (his most successful play, 1934), and the supernatural visitation in *An Inspector Calls* (his
acknowledged masterpiece, 1946).

A prolific essayist and reviewer (as well as screenwriter), Priestley often
wrote on the drama. His introduction to his collected plays includes witty
and candid comments on each. A lecture, *The Art of the Dramatist* (1957,
o.p.), has also been published.

BOOK BY PRIESTLEY

The Plays of J. B. Priestley. Harper 1950–52 3 vols. o.p. Vol. 1: *Dangerous Corner, I
Have Been Here Before, Johnson over Jordan, Music at Night, The Linden Tree,
Eden End, Time and the Conways.* Vol. 2: *Laburnum Grove; Bees on the Boat
Deck; When We Are Married; Good Night, Children; The Good Companions; How
Are They at Home?; Ever Since Paradise.* Vol. 3: *Cornelius, People at Sea, They
Came to a City, Desert Highway, An Inspector Calls, Home Is Tomorrow, Summer
Day's Dream.*

BOOKS ABOUT PRIESTLEY

Atkins, John. *J. B. Priestley: The Last of the Sages.* Riverrun 1981 $25.00 pap. $13.95
Braine, John. *J. B. Priestley.* Barnes & Noble text ed. 1979 $24.50
De Vitis, A. A., and Albert E. Kalson. *J. B. Priestley. Twayne's Eng. Authors Ser.* G. K.
Hall 1980 lib. bdg. $13.50

RATTIGAN, SIR TERENCE (MERVYN). 1911–1977

Rattigan, who had been a playwright since leaving Oxford at the age of
22, boasted of his workmanship—"I believe sloppy construction, untidy technique, and lack of craftsmanship to be great faults"—and of his ability to
please the English playgoer, the archetypical "Aunt Edna," a "middle-class,
middle-aged maiden lady with time on her hands." Not surprisingly, he fell
out of favor in the England of the 1960s. (He had never been particularly
popular in the United States, which looked on his work as inspirationally
lacking.) At the time of his death, criticism, still taking him at his word,
faintly praised Rattigan's expositions, his management of interleaving char-

acters (as in *Separate Tables*), and his artful episodic development in *Ross*. But Darlow and Hodson's revelations of Rattigan's tormented personal life have helped readers to acknowledge that, despite imposed or sentimental endings, his plays are often full of genuine anguish—in the relations of parents and children (*Man and Boy*) and obsessed lovers (*The Deep Blue Sea*), in recognition of weakness that vitiates heroism (*Ross*, 1960). And revivals of *The Browning Version* (at the National Theatre) and *The Winslow Boy* (1946) have recently moved the critic Harold Hobson to concede that "there are many things in Rattigan that have not yet been properly perceived."

BOOKS BY RATTIGAN

Plays: One. Grove 1982 pap. $5.95. Contains *French without Tears, The Winslow Boy, Harlequinade,* and *The Browning Version.*
While the Sun Shines. 1945. French $1.75
The Browning Version. 1948. French $1.75
O Mistress Mine. 1949. French $1.75
The Deep Blue Sea. 1952. French $1.75
Separate Tables. 1954. French $1.75
Man and Boy. 1963. French $1.75

BOOKS ABOUT RATTIGAN

Darlow, Michael, and Gillian Hodson. *Terence Rattigan: The Man and His Work.* Charles River Bks. $25.00; Merrimack pap. $12.95
Ruskino, Susan. *Terence Rattigan. Twayne's Eng. Authors Ser.* G. K. Hall 1983 lib. bdg. $19.95

SHAFFER, PETER. 1926–

The psychiatrist Dysart and the composer Salieri, the protagonists of Shaffer's two latest, most successful plays, are overcivilized men, each faced with a figure of tormented inspiration—the horse mutilator Strang and the simpering and sublime MOZART (see Vol. 3). The envy felt by the cultivated and repressed for a mind capable of confronting its own demons (and angels) is a subject that runs back through Shaffer's earlier pairings of liberal and reactionary in *Shrivings*, of Conquistador and Inca in *The Royal Hunt of the Sun.* It may even be traceable, in some way, to Shaffer's own equivocal position in the British drama.

Shaffer burst into public attention at the very moment the new drama found its voice—*Five Finger Exercise* won him a citation as the most promising British playwright in 1958, the same year that Pinter and Wesker had their first London productions. Yet from the start Shaffer was chided for the "impersonality"—the overconstructed and underinspired quality—of his playwrighting. (*Five Finger Exercise* was, as its title suggests, an essay in traditional domestic melodrama.) Director John Dexter made heroic efforts to enrich the texture of *The Royal Hunt of the Sun* with ritual, mime, and music in a grand National Theatre production. Later, more successfully, he brought an onstage audience and horse-head masks to *Equus.* But Dexter's near-collaborative efforts, and the extensive rewriting that marked Peter Hall's production of *Amadeus*, suggest that Shaffer, despite his successes, is still somehow too reticent for the overheated contemporary stage, a Salieri clever enough to acknowledge his own exclusion.

Born in Liverpool, Shaffer spent three years working in coal mines before entering Cambridge, and several more employed by a music publisher and the New York Public Library. The twin of playwright Anthony Shaffer (*Sleuth*), he has written detective novels and music criticism.

BOOKS BY SHAFFER

Five Finger Exercise. Harcourt 1959 o.p.
The Private Ear and the Public Eye. 1962. Stein & Day 1964 o.p.
The Royal Hunt of the Sun. 1964. Stein & Day 1965 o.p.
Equus and Shrivings. Atheneum 1974 $7.95
Amadeus. Harper 1981 $11.49 pap. $5.95; New Amer. Lib. (Signet) 1984 pap. $3.50

BOOK ABOUT SHAFFER

Taylor, John Russell. *Peter Shaffer.* Longman 1974 o.p.

SHAW, GEORGE BERNARD. 1856–1950 (NOBEL PRIZE 1925)

Ten of Shaw's most important plays—including *Arms and the Man, Candida,* and *Caesar and Cleopatra*—were written before the turn of the century. But until 1904, the expatriate Irishman was "an unacted playwright in London." Known as a novelist, reviewer, and pamphleteer, Shaw had added the title of dramatist with the printing of *Plays Pleasant and Unpleasant* in 1898. But only the famous experiment at the Court Theatre at last brought these plays before the English public.

Unmistakably the work of a drama reviewer who made his attacks on theatrical convention inseparable from his criticism of society, the early plays are (at the very least) a wonderful celebration of the theatricalities of the nineteenth-century English stage. Less overtly given to parody, the major works of the next decade and a half remain Shaw's most popular: *Man and Superman, Major Barbara, The Doctor's Dilemma, Pygmalion.* The experience of World War I, as Stanley Weintraub has shown in *Journey to Heartbreak* (o.p.), had a profound effect on the playwright's work. His bitter memorial of the war, *Heartbreak House* (1919), which he apparently considered his favorite play, is in some ways his most difficult. It foreshadows the open-form fantasies and political extravaganzas that largely occupied Shaw for the next three decades. Except for *Saint Joan* (1924), the rich work of this period is unjustly neglected by anthologists and producers today.

During his 60 years of literary activity, Shaw produced a tremendous body of work. Contrary to received opinion, his prefaces, polemics, and press releases are almost as uniformly thoughtful as they are uniformly, magnificently, readable.

BOOKS BY SHAW

The Portable Bernard Shaw. Ed. by Stanley Weintraub, *Viking Portable Lib.* Penguin 1977 pap. $7.95. Contains *Devil's Disciple, Pygmalion, In the Beginning, Heartbreak House,* and *Shakes vs. Shav,* with the "Don Juan in Hell" section of *Man and Superman, The Adventures of the Black Girl,* and other writings.

Four Plays by Bernard Shaw. Pocket Bks. 1968 pap. $.75

Plays: Major Barbara, Heartbreak House, Saint Joan, Too True to Be Good. Ed. by Warren S. Smith, *Norton Critical Eds.* 1970 text ed. pap. $8.95

Plays Unpleasant. Penguin Plays Ser. 1950 pap. $2.95. Contains *Widower's Houses, The Philanderer,* and *Mrs. Warren's Profession.*

Selected One-Act Plays. Penguin Plays Ser. 1976 pap. $3.95. *The Shewing-Up of Blanco Posnet; How He Lied to Her Husband; O'Flaherty V.C.; The Inca of Perusalem; Annajanska; The Bolshevik Empress; A Village Wooing; The Six of Calais; Overruled; Dark Lady of the Sonnets; Great Catherine; Augustus Does His Bit.*

Selected Non-Dramatic Writings of Bernard Shaw. Ed. by Dan H. Laurence, Houghton Mifflin 1965 pap. $5.95. Contains *An Unsocial Socialist, The Quintessence of Ibsenism,* and essays and reviews.

Prefaces by Bernard Shaw. Scholarly repr. of 1934 ed. 1971 $95.00

Major Critical Essays. Scholarly repr. of 1932 ed. 1971 $49.00

Shaw's Dramatic Criticism from the Saturday Review, 1895–1898. Ed. by John F. Matthews, Peter Smith $5.00. Reviews from the London *Saturday Review.*

The Quintessence of Ibsenism. Hill & Wang 1959 pap. $6.25

Shaw on Shakespeare. Ed. by Edwin Wilson, *Essay Index Repr. Ser.* Ayer repr. of 1961 ed. $26.50

The Collected Music Criticism of Bernard Shaw. Vienna House 4 vols. 1973 $75.00

Collected Letters. Ed. by Dan H. Laurence, Viking 3 vols. 1985 ea. $45.00. The letters Shaw wrote are estimated at 250,000.

Bernard Shaw's Letters to Granville Barker. Ed. by C. B. Purdom, Theatre Arts pap. $1.00

Cashel Byron's Profession. 1886. Penguin 1979 pap. $3.95

An Unsocial Socialist. 1887. *Norton Lib.* 1972 pap. $2.95; Scholarly repr. of 1932 ed. 1970 $21.00

Arms and the Man. 1894. Ed. by Henry Popkin, Avon 1967 pap. $.60; ed. by Louis Crompton, Bobbs 1969 pap. $5.50; ed. by Norma Jenckes, Garland 1981 lib. bdg. $61.00; *Penguin Plays Ser.* 1950 pap. $2.95

Candida. 1897. Ed. by Raymond S. Nelson, Bobbs 1973 pap. $3.70; *Penguin Plays Ser.* 1950 pap. $2.95

You Never Can Tell. 1898. Ed. by Daniel J. Leary, Garland 1981 lib. bdg. $94.00

Caesar and Cleopatra. 1899. Ed. by Gale K. Larson, Bobbs 1974 pap. $4.20; ed. by Elizabeth T. Forter, *Crofts Class. Ser.* Harlan Davidson text ed. 1965 pap. $3.95; *Penguin Plays Ser.* 1950 pap. $2.95

Captain Brassbound's Conversion. 1901. Ed. by Rodelle Weintraub, Garland 1981 lib. bdg. $61.00

The Devil's Disciple. 1901. Ed by Robert F. Whitman, Garland 1981 lib. bdg. $61.00; *Penguin Plays Ser.* 1950 pap. $2.95

Man and Superman. 1903. Intro. by N. R. Teitel, *Airmont Class. Ser.* pap. $.95; *Penguin Plays Ser.* 1950 pap. $2.50

Major Barbara. 1905. Ed. by Bernard Dukore, Garland 1981 lib. bdg. $94.00; ed. by Elizabeth T. Forter, *Crofts Class. Ser.* Harlan Davidson text ed. 1971 $10.00 pap. $3.95; *Penguin Plays Ser.* 1950 pap. $2.50

The Doctor's Dilemma. 1911. Ed. by Margery M. Morgan, Garland 1981 lib. bdg. $74.00

Pygmalion. 1913. *Penguin Plays Ser.* 1950 pap. $2.25; Pocket Bks. 1983 pap. $2.95; ed. by Harry Shefter, Washington Square Pr. 1983 pap. $2.95

Androcles and the Lion. Penguin Plays Ser. 1963 pap. $2.95

Heartbreak House. Ed. by Anne Wright, Garland 1981 lib. bdg. $67.00; *Penguin Plays Ser.* 1965 pap. $2.95
Saint Joan. Penguin Plays Ser. 1950 pap. $2.50
The Apple Cart. Penguin Plays Ser. 1956 pap. $4.95
The Millionairess. Penguin Plays Ser. 1961 pap. $3.95

BOOKS ABOUT SHAW

Adam, Ruth. *What Shaw Really Said.* Schocken 1967 $6.00. An admirable slim volume guiding the general reader to Shaw's major themes; includes short synopses of his best-known works.

Bentley, Eric. *Bernard Shaw.* Limelight Eds. 1985 $7.95; *Norton Lib.* repr. of 1947 ed. 1976 pap. $3.95. Shaw called this "the best critical description of my public activities which I have yet come across."

Broad, C. Lewis. *Dictionary to the Plays and Novels of Bernard Shaw: With Bibliography of His Works and of the Literature Concerning Him with the Record of the Principle Shavian Play Productions.* Scholarly repr. of 1929 ed. 1972 $29.00. With a bibliography of his works.

Brown, Ivor J. *Shaw in His Time.* Greenwood repr. of 1965 ed. 1979 lib. bdg. $27.50

Chesterton, G. K. *George Bernard Shaw.* Arden Lib. repr. of 1914 ed. 1978 lib. bdg. $25.00; Folcroft repr. of 1961 ed. 1978 lib. bdg. $30.00; Telegraph Bks. repr. of 1909 ed. lib. bdg. $50.00

Crompton, Louis. *Shaw the Dramatist.* Univ. of Nebraska Pr. 1969 $19.95

Dukore, Bernard F. *Bernard Shaw, Playwright: Aspects of Shavian Drama.* Univ. of Missouri Pr. 1973 $23.00

——. *Money and Politics in Ibsen, Shaw, and Brecht.* Univ. of Missouri Pr. text ed. 1980 $17.00

Ervine, John G. *Bernard Shaw: His Life, Work and Friends.* AMS Pr. repr. of 1956 ed. $57.50

Ganz, Arthur. *George Bernard Shaw.* Grove 1984 $17.50 pap. $9.95

Joad, Cyril E. *Shaw and Society: An Anthology and a Symposium.* Folcroft repr. of 1953 ed. lib. bdg. $25.00; Gordon 1976 lib. bdg. $59.95

Laurence, Dan H. *Bernard Shaw: A Bibliography.* Oxford 2 vols. 1983 $152.00

Mander, Raymond, and Joe Mitchenson. *Theatrical Companion to Shaw: A Pictorial Record of the First Performance of the Plays of Bernard Shaw.* Folcroft lib. bdg. $40.00

Matthews, John F. *George Bernard Shaw. Columbia Essays on Modern Writers Ser.* Columbia Univ. Pr. 1969 pap. $2.50

Meisel, Martin. *Shaw and the Nineteenth-Century Theatre.* Limelight Eds. repr. of 1963 ed. 1984 pap. $11.95

Nethercot, Arthur H. *Men and Supermen: The Shavian Portrait Gallery.* Ayer repr. of 1966 ed. 2d ed. $20.00

Pearson, Hesketh. *George Bernard Shaw: His Life and Personality.* Atheneum 1963 pap. $1.95

Silver, Arnold. *Bernard Shaw: The Darker Side.* Stanford Univ. Pr. 1982 $30.00

Valency, Maurice. *The Cart and the Trumpet: The Plays of George Bernard Shaw.* Oxford 1973 $29.95; Schocken repr. of 1973 ed. 1983 $22.00 pap. $11.95

West, Alick. *A Good Man Fallen Among Fabians: A Study of George Bernard Shaw. Select Bibliographies Repr. Ser.* Ayer repr. of 1950 ed. $18.00; Beekman 1974 pap. $9.95; Folcroft lib. bdg. $20.50. A Marxist critique.

Whitman, Robert F. *Shaw and the Play of Ideas.* Cornell Univ. Pr. 1977 $27.50

Winsten, Stephen. *The Quintessence of GBS.* Richard West 1949 $30.00

STOPPARD, TOM (born Tom Straussler). 1937–

When the National Theatre needed a last-minute substitute for a canceled production of *As You Like It*, Kenneth Tynan decided to stage *Rosencrantz and Guildenstern Are Dead*, a work by an unfamiliar author that had received discouraging notices from provincial critics at its Edinburgh Festival debut. Of course, the play, when it opened in April 1967, met with universal acclaim. In New York the next year it was chosen best play by the Drama Critics Circle.

In such an unlikely way Tom Stoppard came to light. Born in Czechoslovakia, a country he left (for Singapore) when he was an infant, his literary career began as a journalist in Bristol, where play reviewing led to playwrighting. After *Rosencrantz and Guildenstern*, Stoppard's reputation suffered through the production of a number of minor works, whose intellectual preoccupations were shrugged off by reviewers: *Enter a Free Man* ("an adolescent twinge of a play," *N.Y. Times*), *The Real Inspector Hound* ("lightweight," *N.Y. Times*), and *After Magritte*. But in the 1970s, the initial enthusiasms aroused by *Rosencrantz and Guildenstern* were more than vindicated by the production of two full-length plays, *Jumpers* and *Travesties*, whose immense verbal and theatrical inventiveness made them absolute successes on both sides of the Atlantic.

Stoppard's method from the start has been to contrive explanations for highly unlikely encounters—of objects (the ironing board, old lady, and bowler hat of *After Magritte*), characters (Joyce, Lenin, and Tzara in *Travesties*), and even plays (*Hamlet* and *Rosencrantz and Guildenstern*, *The Importance of Being Earnest*, and *Travesties*, Stoppard's antiwar play, and *The Real Thing*). In the 1970s, Tynan called for Stoppard—as a Czech and as an artist—to engage himself politically. But although political subjects have since found their way into pieces from *Every Good Boy Deserves Favor* to *Squaring the Circle* (1985), politics and art seem to have become just two more of the playwright's irreconcilables which meet, but never join, in the logical frames of his comedy. The presence of political material—like the Lenin sections that nearly ruin the second part of *Travesties*—has occasionally strained the structure of the plays. But in *The Real Thing*, his most recent success, Stoppard is comfortable enough with the satire on art and activism to bring a third subject, love, into the mix.

Stoppard has lately been acknowledging his Eastern European heritage nonpolitically, in a series of adaptations of plays by Schnitzler, Nestroy, and Molnar.

Books by Stoppard

Enter a Free Man. Grove (Evergreen) repr. of 1968 ed. 1972 pap. $2.95
Rosencrantz and Guildenstern Are Dead. Grove 1967 $10.00 pap. $3.95
The Real Inspector Hound and After Magritte. Grove (Evergreen) 1969 pap. $5.95
Jumpers. Grove 1974 pap. $6.95
Travesties. Grove 1975 pap. $3.95
Every Good Boy Deserves Favor and Professional Foul. Grove 1978 $8.95 pap. $3.95
Night and Day. Grove 1979 o.p.

On the Razzle. Faber 1983 pap. $4.95. Adaptation of John Nestroy.
The Real Thing. Faber 1984 $15.95 pap. $14.95
Rough Crossing. Faber 1985 $15.95 pap. $7.95. Adaptation of Molnar.
The Dog It Was That Died, and Other Plays. Faber 1983 $14.95 pap. $5.95

BOOKS ABOUT STOPPARD

Corballis, Richard. *Stoppard: The Mystery and the Clockwork.* Methuen 1984 pap.
    $9.95
Dean, Joan F. *Tom Stoppard: Comedy As a Moral Matrix.* Univ. of Missouri Pr. text ed.
    1981 $8.00
Hayman, Ronald. *Tom Stoppard.* Rowman 3d ed. 1979 $12.50
Hunter, Jim. *Tom Stoppard's Plays.* Grove (Evergreen) 1983 pap. $12.50
Londre, Felicia H. *Tom Stoppard. Lit. and Life Ser.* Ungar 1981 $13.95
Whittaker, Thomas. *Tom Stoppard.* Grove $17.50 pap. $9.95

WESKER, ARNOLD. 1932–

Arnold Wesker grew up in London's Stepney, and after time at the London School of Film Technique and in the Royal Air Force, worked at a number of jobs—carpenter's mate, farm laborer, pastry chef, among others—until *Chicken Soup with Barley* was performed on an Arts Council grant in 1958. Transferred from a theater in Coventry to the Royal Court, it was joined in repertory there by *Roots* in 1959 and *I'm Talking about Jerusalem* in 1960. The realistic trilogy centered on the Kahn family and their connections, in London and Norfolk: old Communists, arts-and-crafts idealists, torpid farm workers, young radicals—nothing less than "the working class today." A different sort of play occupied Wesker just before and after the trilogy—the panoramic description of the ordinary activities of a large group of characters. *The Kitchen* (1962) followed the rhythms of calm and crisis in a large restaurant; *Chips with Everything* (1962) dealt with the life of conscripts in an Air Force training camp. Critic Kenneth Tynan and others welcomed Wesker's microcosms as revelations of the nature of authority and work, and the possibility of collective social action.

But *Chips*, produced in London and New York, was Wesker's last major success. After it, he withdrew temporarily from writing to direct Centre 42, an ambitious worker arts project, the failure of which is memorialized in *Their Very Own and Golden City* (1966), the chronicle of an idealistic city planner's destructive compromises. Wesker's alienation from the radical politics of the 1970s severed his connection with the English left, and threatened his relation with the English theater. (Many of his later plays have had their debut abroad, in Sweden and in the United States.) Since *The Four Seasons* (1965), about the growing apart of a couple, Wesker's focus has been personal. *The Merchant* retells the story of Shylock; *Caritas* ends with the martyrdom of a nun; *The Old Ones* are brothers confronting the coming of death.

The change in Wesker's drama has encouraged readers to return to the early plays and recognize that they are less about collective action than its human difficulties. "I would like to think," the playwright explains, "that my plays . . . have a higher proportion of poetry than journalism."

BOOKS BY WESKER

The Plays of Arnold Wesker. Harper 2 vols. 1976–77 ea. $12.50. Vol. 1: *The Kitchen, Chips with Everything, The Wesker Trilogy.* Vol. 2: *The Four Seasons, Their Very Own and Golden City, Menace* (television play), *The Friends, The Old Ones.*
The Merchant. Methuen Student Eds. 1983 pap. $3.95

BOOKS ABOUT WESKER

Hayman, Ronald. *Arnold Wesker. Lit. and Life Ser.* Ungar 1973 $12.95
Leeming, Glenda. *Wesker: The Playwright.* Methuen 1982 pap. $10.95. Discusses the plays since 1971, and reassesses the earlier ones.
Leeming, Glenda, and Simon Trussler. *The Plays of Arnold Wesker: An Assessment.* David & Charles 1971 $13.50; Humanities Pr. text ed. 1974 $6.50

WHITING, JOHN. 1917–1963

John Whiting, an actor, had staged only one previous play, *A Penny for a Song,* when his *Saint's Day* raised a storm of controversy by taking first place in a 1951 Arts Council competition. A difficult parable concerned with sterility and self-destruction, it was succeeded in 1954 by *Marching Song,* which caused no such furor, nor did so well with the public. Upon its closing, Whiting withdrew from London theater for a period of seven years and concentrated on writing screenplays; nine were produced. (A later film, *Young Cassidy,* released after Whiting's death, was an adaptation of Sean O'Casey's autobiographical writings.) In 1961, *The Devils,* based on ALDOUS HUXLEY's (see Vol. 1) historical study *The Devils of Loudon,* was performed by the recently organized London branch of the Royal Shakespeare Company. It became Whiting's only conventional success, called a masterpiece by the critics (with the caveat, intoned by Simon Trussler, that it is the playwright's "least characteristic play"). From 1961 to 1962, Whiting served as drama critic to *The London Magazine.* Meanwhile, in the wake of the success of *The Devils,* the RSC revived *A Penny for a Song.* Since his death, two other unseen Whiting works have reached the stage, *No Why,* a one-acter, and *The Nomads.*

BOOKS BY WHITING

Collected Plays. Ed. by Ronald Hayman, Theatre Arts 2 vols. o.p. Vol. 1: *Conditions of Agreement, Saint's Day, A Penny for a Song, Marching Song.* Vol. 2: *The Gates of Summer, No Why, A Walk in the Desert, The Devils, Noman, The Nomads.*
Marching Song. Theatre Arts pap. $1.00
The Devils. Heinemann text ed. 1972 $4.50

BOOKS ABOUT WHITING

Hayman, Ronald, ed. *The Collected Plays of John Whiting.* Heinemann 2 vols. 1969 $13.50
Trussler, Simon. *The Plays of John Whiting: An Assessment.* Humanities Pr. text ed. 1974 $7.00

WILDE, OSCAR. 1854–1900

For Oscar Wilde, playwrighting was the last (and most successful) of a number of careers, all enclosed in a remarkably—some would say, tragically—brief period. A student of classics at Trinity College in his native Dublin, Wilde became a prize poet at Oxford, and went on to publish, in the 1880s, exceptionally successful volumes of intolerably affected verse. Soon abandoning poetry, he returned to it, in "The Ballad of Reading Gaol," only at the end of his life.

At Oxford, Wilde fell under the influence of John Ruskin and Walter Pater, and subsequently became a publicist for the doctrines of "aestheticism," a cult of the artificial compounded with socialism, delicate hedonism, and a smudge of depravity. With such a broad palette, Wilde could enjoy great success as a lecturer in the American Midwest while simultaneously shocking and delighting readers of *The Yellow Book* and other "decadent" London journals. That there was a core of philosophy in his epigrams and attitudes is evident in his later, durable essays, "The Soul of Man Under Socialism" and "The Decay of Lying."

It was in the early 1890s that Wilde's career as a writer found its focus, first with the novel *The Picture of Dorian Gray,* and then with a determined lurch into drama. *Salome* is the sort of play one would have expected Wilde to write—a verse drama, in French. Sought by Sarah Bernhardt, illustrated by Aubrey Beardsley, and banned in London by the Lord Chamberlain, it is remembered today mainly in Strauss's operatic version.

Wilde's next three plays were suprisingly different, amalgams—mixtures, rather—of wit and earnest French dramaturgy, or epigram and Pinero. To call them insincere would, of course, only please the shade of Wilde. They are guilty of something worse, stylistic inconsistency. It is hard to know, but fascinating to speculate on, what exactly Wilde thought he was doing. Shaw, reviewing *An Ideal Husband,* certainly had it right: Wilde "plays with everything: with wit, with philosophy, with drama, with actors and audience, with the whole theatre." Yet, at the same time, "touching what he himself reverences," Wilde "is absolutely the most sentimental dramatist of the day."

The contradiction was resolved in his last play, the incomparable *The Importance of Being Earnest,* perhaps the most formally perfect modern comedy, in which social criticism, the philosophy of triviality, and literary parody are held in the airiest suspension. (See Volume 1, Chapter 6.)

Books by Wilde

The Complete Works. Collins o.p.
The Portable Oscar Wilde. Ed. by Richard Aldington, *Viking Portable Lib.* Penguin 1981 pap. $6.95. Includes *The Picture of Dorian Gray, The Importance of Being Earnest, De Profundis* (complete), and other selections.
Plays, Prose Works, and Poems. Intro. by Isobel Murray, Everyman's o.p. *Picture of Dorian Gray,* two plays, two essays, other selections.
Selected Plays. Penguin Plays Ser. 1954 pap. $2.95. The five important dramas:

Salome (1894), *Lady Windermere's Fan* (1892), *An Ideal Husband* (1895), *A Woman of No Importance* (1893), *The Importance of Being Earnest* (1895).

The Complete Shorter Fiction of Oscar Wilde. Ed. by Isobel M. Murray, *World's Class. Ser.* Oxford 1979 pap. $3.95

Selected Writings of Oscar Wilde. Ed. by Russell Fraser, Houghton Mifflin (Riverside Eds.) 1969 o.p. Five plays, many poems, essays, other selections.

Essays. Intro. by Hesketh Pearson, *Essay Index Repr. Ser.* Ayer repr. of 1950 ed. $18.00

De Profundis and Other Writings. Penguin Eng. Lib. Ser. 1976 pap. $3.95. With "The Soul of Man Under Socialism" and "The Decay of Lying," and a selection of poems.

Literary Criticism of Oscar Wilde. Ed. by Stanley Weintraub, Univ. of Nebraska Pr. 1969 $21.95

The Selected Letters of Oscar Wilde. Ed. by Rupert Hart-Davis, Oxford 1979 pap. $9.95. A selection from Hart-Davis's major edition (o.p.), including the corrected *De Profundis*, Wilde's apologia written in prison.

The Picture of Dorian Gray and Other Stories. Amereon repr. lib. bdg. $15.95; ed. by Richard Ellmann, *Bantam Class. Ser.* 1983 pap. $2.95; Biblio Dist. (Everyman's) 1976 pap. $3.95; Dell 1956 pap. $2.25; fwd. by G. Weales, New Amer. Lib. 1962 pap. $2.95; ed. by Isobel Murray, *World's Class. Ser.* Oxford 1981 pap. $2.50; Penguin 1949 pap. $2.50

The Importance of Being Earnest and Other Plays. New Amer. Lib. (Signet Class.) 1985 pap. $2.50. With *Salome* and *Lady Windermere's Fan.*

Lord Arthur Savile's Crime and Other Stories. Penguin 1973 pap. $3.95. Includes *The Canterville Ghost, The Happy Prince, The Portrait of Mr. W. H.,* and others.

The Happy Prince and Other Stories. Amereon $10.95. Fairy tales written (often for his own children) in the 1880s.

The Picture of Dorian Gray. 1891. *Airmont Class. Ser.* 1964 pap. $1.75; Biblio Dist. (Everyman's) 1976 pap. $3.95; Dell 1956 pap. $2.95; ed. by Isobel M. Murray, *Oxford Eng. Novels Ser.* 1974 $13.50; Penguin 1949 pap. $2.50

Lady Windermere's Fan. 1893. Methuen 1966 pap. $6.95; *New Mermaids Ser.* Norton 1984 pap. $5.95

Salome. 1894. Branden 1962 pap. $2.50

The Importance of Being Earnest. 1899. Avon 1965 pap. $1.95; Heinemann text ed. 1970 $3.50; Methuen 1983 pap. $3.95; NYPL 2 vols. 1956 $30.00; ed. by Russell Jackson, *New Mermaids Ser.* Norton 1980 pap. $6.95

BOOKS ABOUT WILDE

Beckson, Karl, ed. *Oscar Wilde: The Critical Heritage.* Routledge & Kegan 1970 $40.00 1984 pap. $30.00

Bird, Alan. *The Plays of Oscar Wilde. Critical Studies Ser.* Barnes & Noble 1977 $24.50

Ervine, John G. *Oscar Wilde: A Present Time Appraisal.* AMS Pr. repr. of 1952 ed. $32.50

Harris, Frank. *Oscar Wilde: His Life and Confessions.* Greenwood repr. of 1959 ed. 1978 lib. bdg. $32.50; intro. by Frank MacShane, Horizon Pr. repr. of 1974 ed. 1983 pap. $12.95

Holland, Vyvyan. *Son of Oscar Wilde.* Arden Lib. repr. of 1954 ed. 1979 lib. bdg. $22.50; Norwood repr. of 1954 ed. 1978 lib. bdg. $25.00

Mason, Stuart. *Bibliography of Oscar Wilde.* Haskell 2 vols. repr. of 1914 ed. 1972 lib. bdg. $69.95; Longwood repr. of 1914 ed. 1977 lib. bdg. $25.00; Richard West repr. of 1919 ed. 1973 $30.00

Mikhail, E. H. *Oscar Wilde: An Annotated Bibliography of Criticism.* Rowman 1978
    $25.00
———, ed. *Oscar Wilde: Interviews and Recollections.* Barnes & Noble text ed. 2 vols.
    1979 ea. $27.50
Ryskamp, Charles, ed. *Wilde and the Nineties.* Princeton Lib. 1966 pap. $3.50
Sullivan, Kevin. *Oscar Wilde. Columbia Essays on Modern Writers Ser.* Columbia
    Univ. Pr. 1972 pap. $2.50
Symons, Arthur. *A Study of Oscar Wilde.* Folcroft repr. of 1930 ed. lib. bdg. $15.00
Worth, Katharine. *Oscar Wilde. Modern Dramatists Ser.* Grove 1984 $17.50 pap. $9.95

IRISH DRAMA

It is the custom to group under Irish drama not the writers who were born
in Ireland, which would include Shaw and Wilde (and, it has been contended, most of the important "English" playwrights back to the Restoration), but the writers whose dramas are Irish in subject and setting. Mid-
nineteenth century Ireland had in Dion Boucicault a melodramatist of international reputation who often returned to local themes (*The Colleen Bawn,
The Shaughraun*), and who was later admired by Shaw and O'Casey. But the
serious birth of Irish theater came about with Yeats's decision to turn his
back on IBSEN and prose and use the lives of gods and heroes of ancient Irish
legend as the material for a poetic national drama. Following the Easter Rebellion, however, folklore was largely discarded as O'Casey and others tried
to introduce social and political realism to the Dublin stage.

Ireland's National Theatre, the Abbey, was founded in 1899 by Edward
Martyn, Lady Gregory, and Yeats.

The life of the Abbey has been frequently turbulent. Rioting greeted the
masterpieces of both Synge and O'Casey, and in time the theater became as
well known for the plays it refused—Shaw's *John Bull's Other Island,*
O'Casey's *Silver Tassie,* Yeats's *The Herne's Egg,* Behan's *The Quare Fellow*—
as for those it produced. By 1951, when a fire destroyed the original building, the Abbey had lost most of the prestige it had enjoyed in its first decades, although its acting graduates—Barry Fitzgerald, Cyril Cusack,
Siobhan McKenna—were internationally famous.

History, Criticism, and Anthologies

Clark, William S. *The Early Irish Stage: The Beginnings to 1720.* Greenwood repr. of
    1955 ed. 1973 lib. bdg. $22.50. Well organized, comprehensive, and scholarly.
Corrigan, Robert W., ed. *Masterpieces of Modern Irish Theater.* Macmillan (Collier
    Bks.) 1967 o.p. Includes Yeats: *The Countess Cathleen;* Synge: *The Playboy of the
    Western World, Riders to the Sea;* O'Casey: *The Silver Tassie, Cock-A-Doodle-
    Dandy.*
Ellis-Fermor, Una. *The Irish Dramatic Movement.* Rowman repr. of 1939 ed. 1977
    $23.75. An important study of Yeats, Lady Gregory, Synge, and their contempo-
    raries.
Hogan, Robert. *After the Irish Renaissance: A Critical History of the Irish Drama since*

the Plough and the Stars. Univ. of Minnesota Pr. 1967 $10.95. An excellent commentary by the best informed of U.S. critics of Irish drama.

————. *Since O'Casey: And Other Essays on Irish Drama.* Barnes & Noble text ed. 1983 $28.50

————, ed. *Seven Irish Plays, 1946–1964.* Univ. of Minnesota Pr. 1967 $17.50. Contains Michael Malloy, *The Visiting House;* Seamus Byrne, *Design for a Headstone;* Bryan MacMahon, *Song of the Anvil;* John O'Donovan, *Copperfaced Jack;* James B. Keane, *Sharon's Grave* and *Many Young Men of Twenty;* James Douglas, *The Ice Goddess.*

Kain, Richard M. *Dublin in the Age of William Butler Yeats and James Joyce.* Univ. of Oklahoma Pr. repr. of 1962 ed. 1967 $11.95. Personalities and politics.

Krause, David. *The Profane Book of Irish Comedy.* Cornell Univ. Pr. 1982 $22.50. Traditional comedy in Irish drama.

Malone, Andrew E. *Irish Drama.* Ayer repr. of 1929 ed. $27.50

Maxwell, D. E. *A Critical History of Modern Irish Drama, 1891–1980.* Cambridge Univ. Pr. 1985 $47.50 pap. $15.95

Mercier, Vivian. *The Irish Comic Tradition.* Oxford repr. of 1963 ed. 1969 pap. $4.95. A survey of the comic in Gaelic literature from the ninth century on.

BEHAN, BRENDAN. 1923–1964

A Dublin slum boy, Behan at the age of 16 was arrested in Liverpool with a suitcase full of explosives. Sent to the Borstal (reform school) as an IRA terrorist, he was to be arrested and sentenced several more times, once to deportation, before he settled down, in the mid-1950s, to writing. Plays and books began to appear with regularity, but by 1964 Behan was dead, having escaped, through drink and diabetes, the "bent old legs and twisted buniony toes" of an old age he dreaded.

A "quare fellow" is a condemned man about to be hanged, the absent subject about whom the prison society uneasily stirs in Behan's first play. After rejection by the Abbey, it was staged by a small Dublin theater, the Pike, and brought to England by Joan Littlewood in 1956. (The Abbey recanted after *The Quare Fellow*'s London success.) The British soldier in *The Hostage* (1958) is another condemned prisoner, held in a brothel in exchange for an Irish captive. But after his death—typical of Littlewood's fantastic music-hall staging of the play—the soldier stands up again to lead the cast in song.

Littlewood was criticized for expanding the play with music and improvisations, although Behan's thin text certainly profited from the brilliant theatricality of her Theatre Workshop, whose Brechtian productions were important influences on the next decade of London theater. *Richard Cork's Leg,* Behan's last script, was even more seriously in need of the revisions and additions made by Alan Simpson after the author's death.

BOOKS BY BEHAN

The Complete Plays. Intro. by Alan Simpson, Grove 1978 pap. $4.95

Borstal Boy. Godine repr. of 1959 ed. 1982 pap. $8.95. Autobiography.

Brendan Behan's Island: An Irish Sketch Book. Little, Brown 1985 $14.45 pap. $7.70. Anecdotes, two short stories, a one-act play, and several poems.

BOOKS ABOUT BEHAN

Boyle, Ted E. *Brendan Behan. Twayne's Eng. Authors Ser.* G. K. Hall lib. bdg. $13.50
Mikhail, E. H. *Brendan Behan: An Annotated Bibliography of Criticism.* Barnes & Noble text ed. 1980 $28.50
——, ed. *The Art of Brendan Behan. Critical Studies Ser.* Barnes & Noble text ed. 1979 $28.50
——, ed. *Brendan Behan: Interviews and Recollections.* Barnes & Noble 2 vols. 1982 ea. $28.50
O'Connor, Ulick. *Brendan Behan.* Grove 1973 pap. $1.95. Yet another biography, more comprehensive than most of the others.
Porter, R. *Brendan Behan.* Columbia Univ. Pr. 1973 pap. $2.00

FRIEL, BRIAN. 1929–

A schoolteacher until his stories achieved recognition in *The New Yorker*, Brian Friel has maintained a transatlantic reputation with his plays. His American debut piece was *Philadelphia, Here I Come!*, the story of an Irish youth about to leave, reluctantly, for America. Gar's "public" and "private" faces, hopeful and hopeless, were played by two actors. In the year of *Philadelphia*'s long run, 1966, *The Loves of Cass McGuire* failed in New York, but it became a solid hit the next year in Dublin. Appropriately, it concerns a disillusioned, toping old woman who returns to Ireland after a half-century's stay in America. Friel's 1967–1968 triumph in Dublin was *Lovers*, which ended its run only to make room for the Dublin Drama Festival. Consisting of two one-acters, *Winners* (a sort of tragedy) and *Losers* (called "hilarious"), it opened at Lincoln Center in 1968. Also in that year, *Crystal and Fox*, concerning the private life of a traveling show company, was produced in Dublin and Los Angeles. The Abbey Theatre maintained a deplorable tradition by turning down Friel's next play, *The Munday Scheme*. But the political satire (in which it is proposed that the West of Ireland be converted for profit into an international cemetery) eventually took the stage, both in Dublin and New York, in 1969.

Inevitably, Friel has come to the subject of Northern Ireland's troubles. *The Freedom of the City* (1973) confronts the problem directly, but the playwright's more recent approach has been in the form of an historical analogy. *Translations* represents the encounter of peasants and Royal Engineers on a survey in the Donegal of 150 years ago. A London success, it was transferred from a Hampstead stage to the National Theatre.

BOOKS BY FRIEL

Philadelphia, Here I Come! 1964. Farrar 1966 o.p.
Two Plays. Farrar 1970 $6.50 pap. $2.45
Volunteers. Faber 1980 pap. $6.95
The Faith Healer. Faber 1980 pap. $6.95
Living Quarters. Faber 1978 pap. $4.95
Translations. Faber 1981 pap. $8.50
The Communication Cord. Faber 1983 pap. $7.95

Book about Friel

Maxwell, D. E. S. *Brian Friel. Irish Writers Ser.* Bucknell Univ. Pr. 1973 $4.50 pap.
  $1.95

GREGORY, LADY ISABELLA AUGUSTA. 1852–1932

Lady Gregory was one of the founders of the Irish National Theatre Society, the author of books on Irish folklore, and an important playwright. Her story of the revival of native drama for the Irish stage is told in *Our Irish Theatre* (1913). Her journals reveal her as courageous and honest, with the gift of bringing out the best in the many people she befriended, among them Yeats, whose close friend and collaborator she remained from their meeting in the 1890s. She directed the Abbey Theatre with him until her death, and with him wrote the play *Cathleen Ni Houlihan.* Her own, usually brief, plays were Irish legendary fantasies, patriotic historical dramas, and the comedies of peasant life for which she is best known. Simplicity, which Lady Gregory as a writer always sought, should not be confused with naivety. Her balanced dialogue and "constant stripping away of easy sentiment" have been commented on by her editor, Ann Saddlemyer.

Books by Gregory

Collected Plays. Ed. by Ann Saddlemyer, Oxford 4 vols. 1970 consult publisher for information. Vol. 1, *The Comedies;* Vol. 2, *The Tragedies and Tragi-comedies;* Vol. 3, *The Wonder and Supernatural Plays;* and Vol. 4, *Translations and Adaptations and Her Collaborations with Douglas Hyde and W. B. Yeats.*
Seven Short Plays. Core Collection repr. of 1903 ed. 1976 $18.50; Scholarly repr. of 1909 ed. 1970 $29.00
Irish Folk History Plays. Scholarly 2 vols. repr. of 1912 ed. 1971 $39.50
Three Last Plays. Scholarly repr. of 1928 ed. 1971 $39.00
Lady Gregory's Journals. Ed. by Daniel J. Murphy, NYPL 1978 vol. 1 $39.95
Our Irish Theatre: A Chapter of Autobiography. Oxford text ed. 1972 $29.95
A Book of Saints and Wonders: Put Down Here by Lady Gregory According to the Old Writings and Memory of the People of Ireland. Oxford 1971 $13.95

Books about Gregory

Adams, Hazard. *Lady Gregory. Irish Writers Ser.* Bucknell Univ. Pr. 1973 $4.50 pap.
  $1.95
Coxhead, Elizabeth. *Lady Gregory: A Literary Portrait.* Humanities Pr. repr. of 1961 ed. rev. ed. text ed. 1976 $10.00
Saddlemyer, Ann. *In Defence of Lady Gregory, Playwright.* 1965. Dufour 1967 o.p. "This small volume . . . whets the reader's appetite for a full-scale, modern study of the dramatist. The sections on comedy, use of dialect, and fable are of particular interest to students of drama, but the discussion of Lady Gregory's relationship with Yeats and Synge is regrettably brief" (*LJ*).

O'CASEY, SEAN. 1880–1964

Unlike the directors of the Abbey, Sean O'Casey was slum-born and bred, self-educated, and deeply involved in the political and labor ferment that preceded Irish independence. His famous group of realistic plays produced at the Abbey form, in effect, a commentary on each stage of the independence movement. The melodramatic *The Shadow of a Gunman* (1923), the first to be staged, deals with the guerrilla war conducted by the IRA until the peace treaty was signed in 1921. *Juno and the Paycock* (1925), cast in the mold of classic comedy, describes the civil war and failure of hopes that followed the settlement. And the last to be produced, *The Plough and the Stars* (1926), set of howls of resentment by returning to the Easter 1916 uprising itself, and condemning the vanity of the nationalists and the dogmatism of labor, who squabble while Dublin, in the person of its women, suffers martyrdom. (No less offended was the prudery of the Abbey audience, which responded to the presence of Rosie Redmond, the prostitute, much as it had to Christy Mahon's reference to "shifts" in J. M. Synge's *The Playboy of the Western World.*)

It was expected that the Abbey audience would be unsympathetic. But when even the Abbey management, in the person of Yeats, turned against the antiwar play, *The Silver Tassie* (1928), O'Casey (who had already taken up residence in London and married) determined to remain in "exile." It was an ill-chosen moment to throw himself upon the mercy of a commercial theater, because O'Casey was just embarking on a series of dramatic experiments: *Within the Gates* (1934), whose stylized polyphony of urban activities recalls the panorama of *The Plough and the Stars*, and anticipates more modern works such as Wesker's *Kitchen; The Star Turns Red*, a vision of an antifascist revolution; and *Purple Dust* (1940), a fantasy cleansing of the remnants of imperialism from Ireland. Without an assured theater, these and his later plays were condemned to productions often amateurish and unhelpful to the reviser, sometimes coming years after O'Casey had reluctantly published the text. (An exception was the exemplary New York production of *Within the Gates* in 1934. But Irish playwrights have often done better in New York than London.)

After World War II, O'Casey turned to a third, still more idiosyncratic form of drama, of which his own favorite example was *Cock-A-Doodle-Dandy* (1949). Broadly satirical depictions of rural Ireland in the grip of church and complacency, these were Aristophanic comedies with a great deal of folk culture and music hall in their constitution. Their reception was appropriately divided: *Cock-A-Doodle-Dandy* received its first production at the Royal Court in 1959; *The Drums of Father Ned* was forced out of the Dublin Festival of 1958 (and SAMUEL BECKETT withdrew his own play in protest).

In the 1930s, O'Casey served as a drama critic for London's *Time and Tide*, producing a group of scathing comments on West End conventionality, which have been published as *The Flying Wasp* (1937). Other essays on theater appear in *The Green Crow* (1956), *Under a Colored Cap* (1963), and *Blasts and Benedictions* (1967).

BOOKS BY O'CASEY

Collected Plays. St. Martin's 4 vols. ea. $10.00. Vol. 1: *Juno and the Paycock; The Shadow of the Gunman; The Plough and the Stars; The End of the Beginning; A*

Pound on Demand. Vol. 2: *The Silver Tassie; Within the Gates; The Star Turns Red.* Vol. 3: *Purple Dust; Red Roses for Me; Hall of Healing.* Vol. 4: *Oak Leaves and Lavender; Cock-A-Doodle-Dandy; Bedtime Story; Time to Go.*

Selected Plays of Sean O'Casey. Braziller 1956 $7.50. *The Shadow of a Gunman; Juno and the Paycock; The Plough and the Stars; The Silver Tassie; Within the Gates; Purple Dust; Red Roses for Me; Bedtime Story; Time to Go;* a foreword on playwrighting by the dramatist and an excellent comprehensive introduction by John Gassner.

Five One-Act Plays: The End of the Beginning, A Pound on Demand, Hall of Healing, Bedtime Story, and Time to Go. St. Martin's 1966 pap. $2.25

Three Plays: Juno and the Paycock, The Shadow of a Gunman, and The Plough and the Stars. St. Martin's 1969 pap. $3.95

Three More Plays: Silver Tassie, Purple Dust, and Red Roses for Me. St. Martin's 1965 pap. $3.95

Blasts and Benedictions: Articles and Stories. Ed. by Ronald Ayling, Greenwood repr. of 1967 ed. 1976 lib. bdg. $24.75

The Letters of Sean O'Casey, 1942–1954. Ed. by David Krause, Macmillan 2 vols. 1975–80 ea. $60.00

Books about O'Casey

Ayling, Ronald, ed. *Sean O'Casey.* Aurora repr. of 1968 ed. 1970 text ed. pap. $2.50

Benstock, Bernard. *Sean O'Casey.* Irish Writers Ser. Bucknell Univ. Pr. 1971 $4.50 pap. $1.95

Kilroy, Thomas, ed. *Sean O'Casey: A Collection of Critical Essays.* Prentice-Hall $7.95

Krause, David. *Sean O'Casey and His World.* Encore Ed. Ser. Scribner 1976 $3.95

——, ed. *Sean O'Casey: Centenary Essays.* Ed. by Robert G. Lowery, Barnes & Noble 1981 $29.50

Mikhail, E. H. *Sean O'Casey: A Bibliography of Criticism.* Intro. by Ronald Ayling, Univ. of Washington Pr. text ed. 1972 $25.00

——. *Sean O'Casey and His Critics: An Annotated Bibliography, 1916–1982.* Scarecrow Pr. 1985 $25.00

Simmons, James. *Sean O'Casey. Modern Dramatists Ser.* Grove 1984 $17.50 pap. $9.95

SYNGE, JOHN MILLINGTON. 1871–1909

After graduating from Trinity College, Dublin, Synge left for Europe to write poetry. If Yeats had not discovered him in Paris and persuaded him to return to Ireland and absorb its native traditions, the Irish Renaissance might have lost its best playwright. As it was, Synge's poetry of Celtic romanticism was rather more tempered with a European realism than Yeats and his Renaissance had anticipated.

Yeats sent Synge to the West of Ireland to get to know the peasants there. The result was, in addition to the journal *The Aran Islands* (1907), two short plays for the Abbey: *The Shadow of the Glen* (1903), in which a comic resurrection interrupts a widow's marriage-bargaining, and *Riders to the Sea* (1904), about a mother's loss of her last son, a perfect condensed tragedy and probably the finest one-act play. The poorly received *The Well of the Saints*, whose characters vehemently reject reality for comfortable illusion, offered the Abbey audience a warning of what was to come. This was

Synge's masterpiece, *The Playboy of the Western World*, which touched off rioting at the theater. The playboy is Christy Mahon, a lout who becomes a hero among the Mayo peasantry when he boasts he has murdered his father. Satire on Irish romanticism conceals a parable of the poet's development and estrangement from his public. But Dublin nationalists heard only the people slandered, and Dublin prudery heard only the forbidden word "shifts" on Christy's lips.

Playboy was the last play Synge saw staged. He died of cancer at age 37, never having completed *Dierdre of the Sorrows* (1910), his single work in the Celtic legendary mode.

BOOKS BY SYNGE

The Plays. Ed. by Ann Saddlemyer, Catholic Univ. Pr. 2 vols. ea. $21.95–$30.95 pap. ea. $10.95
The Complete Plays of John M. Synge. Random (Vintage) 1960 pap. $3.95
The Complete Plays. Methuen 1981 pap. $3.95
Plays, Poems, and Prose. Biblio Dist. (Everyman's) repr. of 1941 ed. 1972 pap. $3.50
The Collected Letters of John Millington Synge, 1871–1907. Ed. by Ann Saddlemyer, Oxford 1983 vol. 1 $63.00
Riders to the Sea. 1904. Biblio Dist. 1969 $40.00
The Well of the Saints. 1905. Ed. by Nicholas Grene, Catholic Univ. Pr. 1982 $12.95 pap. $5.95
The Playboy of the Western World. 1907. Allen & Unwin text ed. 1962 pap. $2.95; ed. by Henry Popkin, Avon 1967 pap. $.95; Barnes & Noble 1968 pap. $4.09; ed. by William E. Hart, *Crofts Class. Ser.* Harland Davidson 1966 pap. $3.75; Methuen 1983 pap. $3.95

BOOKS ABOUT SYNGE

Benson, Eugene. *J. M. Synge.* Grove (Evergreen) 1983 pap. $9.95
Bourgeois, Maurice. *John Millington Synge and the Irish Theatre.* Ayer repr. of 1913 ed. $22.00; Haskell repr. of 1913 ed. 1969 lib. bdg. $49.95
Johnston, Denis. *John Millington Synge.* Columbia Univ. Pr. 1965 pap. $2.50
Kopper, Edward A., Jr. *John Millington Synge: A Reference Guide.* G. K. Hall 1979 lib. bdg. $28.50
Levitt, Paul. *John Millington Synge: A Bibliography of Published Criticism.* Biblio Dist. 1974 $10.00
Mikhail, E. H. *J. M. Synge: A Bibliography of Criticism.* Fwd. by Robin Skelton, Rowman 1975 $18.50
———, ed. *J. M. Synge: Interviews and Recollections.* Barnes & Noble 1976 o.p.
Price, Alan. *Synge and Anglo-Irish Drama.* Russell repr. of 1961 ed. 1972 $21.00
Skelton, Robin. *The Writings of J. M. Synge.* Irvington text ed. 1971 $18.95 pap. $9.95
Yeats, W. B. *The Death of Synge.* Biblio Dist. repr. of 1928 ed. 1970 $12.50

YEATS, WILLIAM BUTLER. 1865–1939 (NOBEL PRIZE 1923)

"Before [Yeats] began his work, poetry was virtually unknown in the contemporary theatre. . . . Yeats lived to see poetic drama acclimatized in Ireland, England, and America almost as it had been in Elizabethan England. This was the more remarkable in that Yeats's genius does not appear to have been primarily dramatic" (*Oxford Companion to the Theatre*).

"I believe myself to be a dramatist," Yeats himself insisted. "I desire to show events and not merely to tell of them." The "events" of his early plays were the folk and mythological material of the Irish revival, shared with Lady Gregory, with whom he joined in planning the new Irish Literary Theatre. It opened in Dublin in 1899 with Yeats's *The Countess Cathleen* (1892), a five-act verse drama about a woman who sells her soul for the sake of starving Irish peasants. The failure of his first stage organization brought Yeats into partnership with the actors William and Frank Fay, who helped to found the Irish National Theatre Society, which subsequently established itself in the Abbey Theatre under the control of Yeats, Lady Gregory, and John M. Synge. *Land of the Heart's Desire* (1892), *Cathleen Ni Houlihan* (1902), and *Dierdre* (1907) were Yeats's contributions, although he left off writing for Abbey audiences in disgust after the infamous rioting that greeted Synge's *Playboy of the Western World* in 1907.

Yeats's withdrawal from the public theater was completed under the influence of the Japanese No drama, which had convinced him that the primacy of words could be best preserved in performances that dispensed with the stage and its machinery. His *Plays for Dancers* was intended for intimate chamber presentations.

In the last decade of his life, Yeats wrote some of his most interesting plays, beginning in 1930 with an unusual experiment in realistic style and supernatural subject, *Words Upon the Window Pane*. Other plays maintain connections with Irish mythology, classical literature, and Christian themes, while refining verse into a pliable dramatic medium. *The Death of Cuchulain* (1939) is in a way Yeats's *Oedipus at Colonus* (he had translated Sophocles' play in 1934). *The Herne's Egg*, like so many important Irish plays, was refused by Yeats's own Abbey Theatre, and had its staging delayed until 1950. The late plays have had an energetic afterlife, *The King of the Great Clock Tower* (1934), for instance, successfully produced at the London National Theatre in 1981. (See also Volume 1, Chapter 7.)

BOOKS BY YEATS

Collected Plays. Macmillan 1953 $17.95. Contains all the plays published in the 1934 edition, plus five written after 1934 and printed in the *Last Poems and Plays* (o.p.).

Eleven Plays of William Butler Yeats. Ed. by A. Norman Jeffares, Macmillan (Collier Bks.) 1967 pap. $4.95

Cathleen Ni Houlihan. Gordon $59.95

Two Plays for Dancers. Biblio Dist. repr. of 1920 ed. 1970 $12.50

Explorations. Macmillan (Colliers Bks.) 1973 pap. $2.95. A valuable collection of essays and introductions by Yeats. "The longest section is devoted to 'The Irish Dramatic Movement,' essays written between 1901 and 1919 stating (and restating) his philosophy of theater in general and the Irish theater in particular. . . . As might be expected, all reflect in varying measure Yeats's promotion of romantic tendencies and opposition to rationalities in literature and philosophy, his antidemocratic leanings, and his concern with the great Anglo-Irish tradition and his own place in that tradition" (*LJ*).

BOOKS ABOUT YEATS

Dorn, Karen. *Players and Painted Stage: The Theatre of W. B. Yeats.* Barnes & Noble 1984 $24.95

Ellis-Fermor, Una. *The Irish Dramatic Movement.* Rowman repr. of 1939 ed. 1977 $23.75

Ellmann, Richard. *Yeats: The Man and the Masks.* Norton Lib. rev. ed. 1978 pap. $6.95

Knowland, A. S. *W. B. Yeats: Dramatist of Vision.* Pref. by Cyril Cusack, Barnes & Noble 1983 $29.50

Moore, John R. *Masks of Love and Death: Yeats as Dramatist.* Cornell Univ. Pr. 1971 $24.50

Nathan, Leonard E. *The Tragic Drama of William Butler Yeats: Figures in a Dance.* Columbia Univ. Pr. 1965 $25.00

Parkin, Andrew. *The Dramatic Imagination of W. B. Yeats.* Barnes & Noble text ed. 1978 $28.50

Saul, George B. *Prolegomena to the Study of Yeats' Plays.* Octagon 1970 lib. bdg. $11.50

Taylor, Richard. *The Drama of W. B. Yeats: Irish Myth and the Japanese No.* Yale Univ. Pr. 1976 $33.00

Ure, Peter. *Yeats the Playwright: A Commentary on Character and Design in the Major Plays.* Routledge & Kegan 1963 $16.00

Vendler, Helen H. *Yeats's Vision and the Later Plays.* Harvard Univ. Pr. 1963 $12.50

CHAPTER 5

American Drama

Thomas F. Van Laan

> American drama, as a serious form, is a product of the twentieth cen-
> tury.... [I]t was then [that] American Drama began to attend to its own
> processes, to test its own possibilities.
> —C. W. E. BIGSBY, *A Critical Introduction to Twentieth-Century*
> *American Drama*

The American renaissance in literature that flourished in the middle of the
nineteenth century produced a great deal of serious writing—writing that
demonstrated the literary independence of the United States. But it was fiction, poetry, and the essay that flourished—not drama. The first professionally produced play in the United States was Thomas Godfrey's *The Prince of
Parthia* in 1767, and although Americans produced a good many plays during the next century and a half that are still worth reading, most of them
are slavishly derivative of the drama of England and western Europe.

American dramatists found a new subject in the American Revolution,
new characters in the Yankee and the noble American Indian, and a new
theme in the superiority of the new to the old world, but the plays themselves fell into the familiar patterns of the then fashionable historical verse
drama, melodrama, sentimental comedy, and comedy of manners in the
mode of a considerably watered-down Sheridan. Despite some attempts at
dialect, stage speech was stilted, while characters, plots, and situations
were normally stereotypical and sentimentalized. Plays of continuing interest from this century and a half—those that either made the most of the possibilities within these limitations or introduced new material—include
Royall Tyler's comedy, *The Contrast;* William Dunlap's tragedy of the Revolution, *André;* Augustus Stone's tragedy about the noble American Indian,
Metamora; Anna Cora Mowatt's comedy of manners, *Fashion;* G. H. Boker's
verse tragedy, *Francesca da Rimini;* George L. Aiken's dramatization of *Uncle Tom's Cabin;* Joseph Jefferson's version of *Rip Van Winkle;* and Bronson
Howard's Civil War drama, *Shenandoah.*

The transformation then taking place in European drama, largely
through the influence of IBSEN, had little impact on American drama. James
Herne's *Margaret Fleming,* which deals with a husband's infidelities in a
manner reminiscent of Ibsen, is a remarkable piece for its time, but it was
unsuccessful. For the most part the realism and naturalism that dominated

125

European drama in the last third of the century is evident in American drama only in the carefully detailed scenery produced by such designers as David Belasco and in the urban settings and passing attention to social issues of the melodramas written by dramatists like Dion Boucicault, Augustin Daly, and Clyde Fitch.

American drama did not achieve its renaissance until after World War I, when writers and producers turned to the theater to produce art rather than profit. Their way was paved by George Pierce Baker, whose 47 Workshop at Harvard University was to have such illustrious students as Philip Barry, S. N. Behrman, Sidney Howard, and Eugene O'Neill, and by the "little theater" movement that produced the Provincetown Players, which presented O'Neill's first plays, and the Washington Square Players, which later became the Theatre Guild. The true source of this renaissance, however, was the dramatists' discovery of European drama. Ibsen was finally allowed to exert his valuable influence, and by then his work of making modern drama a major art form had been forwarded by STRINDBERG, CHEKHOV, SHAW, SYNGE, and the German expressionists.

The 1920s was a period of considerable experimentation in American drama. Writers like Barry and Howard helped develop a polished brand of realism in both comedy and serious drama, while others, especially O'Neill and Elmer Rice, alternated between realism and more experimental forms, especially expressionism. O'Neill's experimentation was the most ambitious; besides expressionism he tried poetic fantasy, pageantry, myth, and various kinds of tragedy—in all lengths. Also by the mid-1920s Baker had left Harvard for New Haven to establish the prestigious Yale School of Drama, a source for new theater talent from that time to the present.

The interest in experimentation continued into the 1930s with Maxwell Anderson's attempts to produce modern verse tragedy and with the plays of Thornton Wilder (whose most experimental work, *The Skin of Our Teeth*, was produced as late as 1942). For the most part, however, the dominant style of the drama of the 1930s was realism. In keeping with the times (a decade that began in a depression and ended with the rise of fascism), the preoccupation of the most significant plays of the 1930s (especially those of Paul Green, Lillian Hellman, and Clifford Odets) was social protest.

The mid-1940s, coinciding with the end of another world war, produced a second flowering of American drama, primarily achieved by two towering figures, Tennessee Williams and Arthur Miller. They were the heirs of the 1930s in their use of the modified realism evident in *The Glass Menagerie* and *Death of a Salesman*—one that consistently violates the realistic surface in order to dramatize an experience more effectively. Miller also demonstrated the heritage of the 1930s in the social protest prominent in his work. This second flowering lasted until the late 1950s and received a considerable boost from the posthumous productions of O'Neill's later plays.

The modified realism that triumphed in the 1930s remains the dominant mode of American drama in its Broadway version even today. However, toward the end of the 1950s, it was successfully challenged by two forces. One was the influence of new dramatic currents, particularly those of the French absurdists IONESCO and BECKETT and the Epic Theatre of BERTOLT BRECHT. The other and probably more significant force was the expansion of theater from Broadway to off-Broadway and finally to the lofts, church basements, and cafes of off-off-Broadway. As a result of this expansion, the new influences opened up a degree of experimentation far beyond any that had ever been known previously in the American theater.

Another important development of the 1960s, bringing new life to American drama, has been the flourishing of minority theater. The Black Arts Repertory Company was founded in 1964 by Amiri Baraka (LeRoi Jones), the Negro Ensemble Company in 1966 by Douglas Turner Ward and Robert Hooks, and the New Lafayette Theatre in 1967 by Ed Bullins. Similar developments have occurred in the writing and producing of plays by women, in Chicano theater, and—judging from the work of the Chinese-American David Henry Hwang—in other minority theater as well.

For a while it looked as if off- and off-off-Broadway were going to exist as a separate, alternative theater—a counter-Broadway—and some dramatists, such as Jean-Claude van Itallie, Israel Horovitz, and Richard Foreman, remain at home primarily away from Broadway. As far back as the early 1960s, however, Edward Albee made the transition from off-Broadway to Broadway, and more recent times have seen two fairly consistent patterns emerge, one in which the dramatist starts in the alternative theater and gradually makes the transition to Broadway (a good example is Sam Shepard), the other in which the alternative theater provides the dramatist with an arena to test and revise plays that later move to Broadway (examples are David Mamet and Lanford Wilson). Recently, regional theaters, such as the Actors Theatre of Louisville, have become more important, and it is not unusual for a play to reach Broadway only after prior productions at some regional theater, off-off-Broadway, and off-Broadway.

HISTORY AND CRITICISM

Abramson, Doris E. *Negro Playwrights in the American Theatre, 1925–1959*. Columbia Univ. Pr. 1969 pap. $8.50. Analyzes 20 plays from Garland Anderson's *Appearances* to Lorraine Hansberry's *A Raisin in the Sun*. "The most comprehensive survey of 20th century Negro literature to date" (*Choice*).

The American Theater: A Sum of Its Parts. Intro. by Henry B. Williams, French 1971 $12.00. Excellent collection of essays by theater scholars on the development of U.S. drama.

Atkinson, Brooks. *The Lively Years, 1920–1973*. Da Capo 1985 pap. $9.95. The former drama critic of the *N.Y. Times* comments on 82 dramas, many American, which he covered on opening nights. Accompanied by sketches by the Broadway caricaturist Hirschfeld.

Bentley, Eric. *What Is Theatre?* Atheneum 1968 pap. $4.95; Limelight Eds. repr. of 1968 ed. 1984 pap. $10.95. Reviews written mostly for the *New Republic* by the author of *The Life of the Theatre*.

Bernstein, Samuel J. *The Strands Entwined: A New Direction in American Drama*.

Northeastern Univ. Pr. 1980 $20.95. Emphasizes Rabe's *Sticks and Bones*, Guare's *The House of Blue Leaves*, Bullins's *The Taking of Miss Janie*, Robert Anderson's *Double Solitaire*, and Albee's *Seascape*.

Bigsby, C. W. E. *A Critical Introduction to Twentieth-Century American Drama*. Cambridge Univ. Pr. 3 vols. 1982–85 ea. $39.50 pap. ea. $14.95. Vol. 1 covers U.S. drama from 1900 to 1940; Vol. 2 covers Miller, Williams, and Albee; and Vol. 3 the non-Broadway theater. An important survey by a major British critic of U.S. drama.

Bock, Hedwig, and Albert Wertheim, eds. *Essays on Contemporary American Drama*. Hueber 1981 $10.95. Contains essays on black, female, and Mexican-American drama as well as on specific playwrights. "... a reasonable introduction to America's contemporary dramatists" (David Rinear, *Modern Drama*).

Bogard, Travis, Richard Moody, and Walter J. Meserve. *American Drama*. Vol. 8 in *The Revels History of Drama in English*. Methuen 1977 $55.00 pap. $19.95. The relevant volume in an important series, written by three major authorities on American drama and theater.

Bonin, Jane F. *Prize-Winning American Drama: A Bibliographical and Descriptive Guide*. Scarecrow Pr. 1973 $13.00. Describes plays that have won one or more of the five major American drama awards.

Bordman, Gerald. *The Oxford Companion to American Theatre*. Oxford 1984 $49.95. Three thousand entries on playwrights, plays, performers, producers and directors, lyricists and composers, theaters, etc.

Brockett, Oscar G., and Robert R. Findlay. *Century of Innovation: A History of European and American Theatre and Drama, 1870–1970*. Theater and Drama Ser. Prentice-Hall 1973 $37.95

Bronner, Edwin. *The Encyclopedia of the American Theatre, 1900–1975*. A. S. Barnes 1980 $30.00

Brown, Janet. *Feminist Drama: Definition and Critical Analysis*. Scarecrow Pr. 1979 $15.00. Discusses feminist theater groups and plays by Alice Childress, Rosalyn Drexler, Tina Howe, David Rabe, and Ntozake Shange.

Brown, John Russell, and Bernard Harris, eds. *American Theatre*. Holmes & Meier 1967 pap. $11.75. Covers writers, influences, ideological and social conditions, theatrical idioms. Contributors are British and American.

Buttitta, Tony. *Uncle Sam Presents: A Memoir of the Federal Theatre, 1935–1939*. Fwd. by Malcolm Cowley, Univ. of Pennsylvania Pr. 1982 $25.00. Solid introduction to this WPA-funded project, with interesting primary material.

Clurman, Harold. *The Fervent Years: The Group Theatre and the Thirties*. Intro. by Stella Adler, *Quality Pap. Ser*. Da Capo repr. of 1945 ed. 1983 pap. $8.95; Harcourt repr. of 1945 ed. 1975 pap. $4.95. As one of the founders of the Group Theatre, Clurman offers an articulate record of the group's members, including playwrights Clifford Odets, Irwin Shaw, and William Saroyan.

Cohn, Ruby. *Dialogue in American Drama*. Indiana Univ. Pr. 1971 o.p. An important study of the language of America's leading dramatists by a major scholar.

———. *New American Dramatists, 1960–1980*. Grove 1982 pap. $6.95. Indispensable for the study of the more recent American dramatists.

Cole, Toby, ed. *Playwrights on Playwriting: The Meaning and Making of Modern Drama*. Intro. by John Gassner, *Drama Bk. Ser*. Hill & Wang 1961 pap. $5.95. The American playwrights include O'Neill, Wilder, and Williams.

Cooper, T. G., and Carole Singleton. *On Stage in America*. Drama Jazz House 1985 $9.95. A brief history of the U.S. theater.

Craig, E. Quita. *Black Drama of the Federal Theatre Era: Beyond the Formal Horizons.*

Univ. of Massachusetts Pr. 1980 lib. bdg. $17.50. "... valuable insights into an era and dramatic form" (*Choice*).

Downer, Alan S., ed. *American Drama and Its Critics: A Collection of Critical Essays.* Univ. of Chicago Pr. 1965 pap. $15.00

Dukore, Bernard F. *American Dramatists, 1918–1945.* Grove 1984 $19.50 pap. $7.95. Good brief survey, emphasizing major plays of major dramatists (excluding O'Neill) and productions.

Dunlap, William. *The History of the American Theatre and Anecdotes of the Principal Actors.* Burt Franklin 3 vols. in 1 2d ed. $36.50. The first history of the American theater and its playwrights by the notable nineteenth-century playwright and stage manager.

Eaton, Walter P. *The Theatre Guild: The First 10 Years, with Articles by the Directors.* Ayer repr. of 1929 ed. $26.50; Scholarly repr. of 1929 ed. 1971 $18.00

Eddleman, Floyd E. *American Drama Criticism: Interpretations, 1890–1977.* Shoe String 2d ed. 1979 $32.50 Supplement 1 1984 $29.50

Engel, Lehman. *The American Musical Theatre: A Consideration.* 1967. Macmillan rev. ed. 1975 pap. $5.95. Both a history and an analysis of the making of a musical. Includes a discography and a list of published librettos and vocal scores.

Flanagan, Hallie. *Arena: The History of the Federal Theatre.* Ayer repr. of 1940 ed. $29.00. A first-hand account by the woman who headed the government-established theater. "As exciting as a novel and twice as provocative" (John Gassner, *N.Y. Times*).

Flexner, Eleanor. *American Playwrights, 1918–1938.* Ayer repr. of 1938 ed. $32.00

Garfield, David. *The Actors Studio: A Player's Place.* Pref. by Ellen Burstyn, Macmillan 1984 pap. $9.95. "... a sober, well-balanced study of the place" (John Lahr, *N.Y. Times*).

Goldman, William. *The Season: A Candid Look at Broadway.* Harcourt 1969 $8.95; Limelight Eds. rev. ed. repr. of 1969 ed. 1984 pap. $8.95

Goldstein, Malcolm. *The Political Stage: American Drama and Theater of the Great Depression.* Oxford 1974 $29.95. "... for the most part ... a solidly researched work that will serve as a useful introduction to the American drama and theater of this turbulent decade" (Stephen Grecco, *Modern Drama*).

Green, Stanley. *Broadway Musicals of the 1930's.* 1972. Da Capo 1982 pap. $14.95. Discusses 175 musicals produced on Broadway during the 1930s. Presented chronologically.

——. *The World of Musical Comedy.* A. S. Barnes 4th ed. rev. 1980 $30.00; *Quality Pap. Ser.* Da Capo 4th ed. repr. 1984 pap. $16.95

Hartman, John G. *The Development of American Social Comedy from 1787 to 1936.* Octagon repr. of 1939 ed. 1970 $16.00

Havens, Daniel F. *The Columbian Muse of Comedy: The Development of a Native Tradition in Early American Social Comedy 1787–1845.* Southern Illinois Univ. Pr. 1973 $7.95. For serious students of American playwriting in its early stages.

Heilman, Robert B. *The Iceman, the Arsonist, and the Troubled Agent: Tragedy and Melodrama on the Modern Stage.* Univ. of Washington Pr. 1973 $17.50. Major chapters on O'Neill, Miller, and Williams by an important drama scholar.

Hill, E., ed. *The Theatre of Black Americans.* Prentice-Hall 2 vols. 1979 $12.95. Vol. 1 stresses drama; Vol. 2, theater.

Hirsch, Foster. *A Method to Their Madness: The History of the Actors Studio.* Norton 1984 $18.95

Huerta, Jorge A. *Chicano Theater: Themes and Forms. Studies in the Language and Lit. of U.S. Hispanos* Bilingual Pr. 1982 lib. bdg. $16.95 pap. $10.95. "An excellent account of the first 15 years of the current Chicano theater movement in this country, placing it in theatrical, social, and historic context" (*Choice*).

Hughes, Glenn. *History of the American Theatre, 1700–1950*. French 1951 $9.00. A chronological review of American theater.

Kauffmann, Stanley. *Persons of the Drama: Theatre Criticism and Comment*. Harper 1976 $14.95. More than 80 reviews of productions, most of which originally appeared in the *New Republic*, as well as a group of essays on broader topics.

———. *Theater Criticisms*. Performing Arts 1983 pap. $8.95. Reviews and essays originally published between 1975 and 1983.

Kaye, Phyllis J., and Eugene O'Neill, eds. *The National Playwrights Directory*. Gale 2d ed. 1982 $64.00. Bibliographies of living American playwrights.

Kernan, Alvin, ed. *The Modern American Theater: A Collection of Critical Essays*. Prentice-Hall 1967 $12.95. Includes Tynan on Miller, Guthrie on Wilder, Kaprow on "Happenings," and several essays by and about Albee.

Kernodle, George and Portia Kernodle. *Invitation to the Theatre*. Harcourt 3d ed. abr. 1985 pap. $21.95

Keyssar, Helene. *The Curtain and the Veil: Strategies in Black Drama*. Burt Franklin 1981 $19.95. Analyzes plays by Hughes, Richardson, Ward, Hansberry, Baraka, Bullins, and Shange.

Kinne, Wisner P. *George Pierce Baker and the American Theatre*. Greenwood repr. of 1954 ed. 1968 $20.00. "A real contribution to theatrical history" (*Nation*).

Long, E. Hudson, comp. *American Drama from Its Beginning to the Present. Goldentree Bibliographies in Language and Lit. Ser.* Harlan Davidson 1970 pap. $6.95

Ludlow, Noah M. *Dramatic Life as I Found It*. Intro. by Francis Hodge, Ayer repr. of 1880 ed. 1966 $27.50. The frontier theater of the early nineteenth century.

MacGowan, Kenneth, and Robert Jones. *Continental Stagecraft*. Ayer repr. of 1922 ed. $18.00. This book while obviously not about American drama was influential on American theater and is based on the authors' observations of some 60 productions by Appia, Reinhardt, Craig, Stanislavsky, Copeau, and others.

MacNicholas, John, ed. *Twentieth-Century American Dramatists*. Vol. 7 in *The Dictionary of Literary Biography*. Gale 2 vols. 1981 $160.00. Excellent brief biographies with extensive lists of productions and publications by and about the dramatists.

Mantle, Burns, and others, eds. *The Best Plays*. annual Ayer repr. of 1919–1963 eds. 1976 ea. $25.00–$27.50; Dodd 1978–84 ea. $29.95. Each volume includes a summary and excerpts of the ten best plays of the Broadway season, plus invaluable statistics: complete listings of New York productions with dates, theaters, and casts; important premieres of plays in the United States and Europe; lists of drama awards; necrology. The current editor is Otis Guernsey.

Marranca, Bonnie, and Gautam Dasgupta. *American Playwrights: A Critical Survey*. Drama Bk. 1981 $13.95 pap. $10.00. Discusses 18 contemporary playwrights associated with the off-Broadway theater, including Kopit, Wilson, Guare, van Itallie, Shepard, Baraka, and others. Indispensable for dramatists of the past two decades.

Mathews, Jane D. *The Federal Theatre, 1935–1939: Plays, Relief, and Politics*. Octagon repr. of 1967 ed. 1980 lib. bdg. $21.50. "A consistently engrossing account of the W.P.A. Theatre Project" (*PW*).

Meserve, Walter J. *An Emerging Entertainment: The Drama of the American People to 1828*. Indiana Univ. Pr. 1977 $25.00. An important study by a major historian of American drama.

————. *An Outline History of American Drama.* Rowman 1965 pap. $2.25. From colonial theater to Albee.

Moody, Richard. *America Takes the Stage.* Kraus repr. of 1955 ed. $22.00. An important study of the beginnings of American drama and theater by a major historian of American drama.

Mordden, Ethan. *The American Theatre.* Oxford 1981 $25.00. Selective overview for the general reader.

————. *Broadway Babies: The People Who Made the American Musical.* Oxford 1983 $19.95

Moses, Montrose. *The American Dramatist.* Arno repr. of 1925 ed. 1964 $20.00. Discussion of all major American dramatists from the eighteenth century to the 1920s.

Moses, Montrose, and John Mason Brown. *American Theatre as Seen by Its Critics, 1752–1934.* Cooper repr. of 1934 ed. $22.50

The New York Times Directory of the Theater. Intro. by Clive Barnes, Times Bks. 1973 $25.00. Cites, but does not print, actual reviews and articles on actors, actresses, playwrights, producers, directors, and others, which appeared from 1920 to 1970.

Notable Names in the American Theatre. 1966. Ed. by Walter Rigdon and Raymond D. McGill, Gale 2d ed. 1976 $125.00. Includes sections on New York productions, premieres of American plays—at home and abroad, theater group biographies, theater building biographies, awards, biographical bibliography, necrology, and who's who listings.

Odell, George C. *Annals of the New Stage to 1849.* AMS Pr. 15 vols. repr. of 1927–49 ed. 1970 ea. $95.00 set $1,425.00. A valuable history, covering opera, concerts, burlesque, and circus, as well as theater.

Paris Review. *Writers at Work: Third Series.* Penguin 1977 pap. $7.95. Lively and fascinating interviews with contemporary authors, including Hellman, Miller, and Albee.

Quinn, Arthur Hobson. *A History of the American Drama.* 1923–27. Irvington 2 vols. repr. of 1943–46 rev. ed. 1982 ea. $39.50. A standard history.

Rabkin, Gerald. *Drama and Commitment. Studies in Drama* Haskell repr. of 1964 ed. 1972 lib. bdg. $49.95. Examines theatrical developments during the depression (the Theater Union, the Group Theatre, and the Federal Theatre) as well as the effect of political commitment on five playwrights of the period: Lawson, Odets, Behrman, Rice, and Maxwell Anderson.

Rahill, Frank. *World of Melodrama.* Pennsylvania State Univ. Pr. 1967 $24.95. Scholarly study that follows the development of melodrama in France, England, and the United States, documenting stock characters and situations.

Sarlos, Robert K. *Jig Cook and the Provincetown Players: Theatre in Ferment.* Univ. of Massachusetts Pr. 1982 lib. bdg. $25.00. Winner of the American Theater Association's Barnard Hewett Award for distinguished achievement in theater history. ". . . an important contribution to American theatre history, filling in details about the Provincetown experiment" (Linda Benzvi, *Modern Drama*).

Scanlan, Tom. *Family Drama, and American Dreams.* Greenwood 1978 $27.50. Concentrates on selected plays by O'Neill, Miller, and Williams.

Seller, Maxine S., ed. *Ethnic Theatre in the United States.* Greenwood 1983 lib. bdg. $49.95. Essays and information on the full range of ethnic theater.

Shank, Theodore. *American Alternative Theatre.* Grove 1982 pap. $12.50. Discusses the Living Theatre, the San Francisco Mimes, Schechner's Performance Group, Richard Foreman, etc.

Sievers, David. *Freud on Broadway.* 1955. Cooper 1971 $25.00. The influence of Freud on dramatists from Glaspell to the early plays of Miller and Williams.

Vardac, A. Nicholas. *Stage to Screen: Theatrical Method from Garrick to Griffith.* Ayer repr. of 1949 ed. 1968 $18.00. Shows how American and British theater evolved cinematic methods and production techniques that were borrowed by early filmmakers.

Vinson, James, and Daniel Kirkpatrick, eds. *Contemporary Dramatists. Contemporary Writers Ser.* St. Martin's 3d ed. 1982 $55.00. Articles on many living American playwrights that include a biography, a signed critical comment on the dramatist's work, optional comment by the playwright, and a bibliography.

Willis, John. *Theatre World.* 1973–to date. Crown annual vol. 30 (1973–74) $10.95 vol. 31 (1974–75) $12.95 vol. 33 (1976–77) $15.95 vol. 34 (1977–78) $15.95 vol. 35 (1978–79) $18.95 vol. 36 (1979–80) $25.00 vol. 37 (1980–81) $30.00 vol. 38 (1981–82) $25.00 vol. 39 (1982–83) $25.00 vol. 40 (1983–84) $24.95

Wilson, Garff B. *Three Hundred Years of American Drama and Theatre: From Ye Bear and Ye Cubb to Chorus Line.* Prentice-Hall 2d ed. 1982 $28.95. A popular overview.

Young, Stark. *Immortal Shadows.* Octagon repr. of 1948 ed. 1973 lib. bdg. $20.50. A selection from 25 years of criticism by America's finest drama critic to date.

COLLECTIONS

Ballet, Arthur H., ed. *Playwrights for Tomorrow: A Collection of Plays.* Univ. of Minnesota Pr. 1967–73 vols. 3–4 ea. $7.95 vol. 5 $5.50 vols. 6–11 ea. $10.00 vols. 12–13 (1975) ea. $12.95 pap. $4.95. Volumes 1 and 2 are out of print.

Barlow, Judith, ed. *Plays by American Women: The Early Years.* Avon 1981 pap. $3.95; Limelight Eds. rev. ed. repr. of 1981 ed. 1985 $18.95 pap. $8.95

Clurman, Harold, ed. *Famous American Plays of the Nineteen Thirties.* Dell 1959 pap. $3.50. Odets, *Awake and Sing;* Behrman, *End of Summer;* Sherwood, *Idiot's Delight;* Steinbeck, *Of Mice and Men;* Saroyan, *The Time of Your Life.*

———. *Famous Plays of the Sixties.* Dell pap. $2.75. Lowell, *Benito Cereno;* Alfred, *Hogan's Goat;* Heller, *We Bombed in New Haven;* Horovitz, *The Indian Wants the Bronx;* Crowley, *The Boys in the Band.*

Corbin, Richard, and Miriam Balf, eds. *Twelve American Plays, 1920–1960.* Scribner 1969 pap. $9.95. Albee, *The Sandbox;* Chase, *Harvey;* Hellman, *The Little Foxes;* Kesselring, *Arsenic and Old Lace;* Nash, *The Rainmaker;* O'Neill, *Beyond the Horizon;* Patrick, *The Teahouse of the August Moon;* Rodgers and Hammerstein, *The King and I;* Serling, *Requiem for a Heavyweight;* Sherwood, *There Shall Be No Night;* Wilder, *Our Town;* Williams, *The Glass Menagerie.*

Garza, Roberto J., ed. *Contemporary Chicano Theatre.* Univ. of Notre Dame Pr. 1975 $22.95 pap. $7.95. Valdez, *Los Perdidos* and *Bernabé;* Sierra, *La Raza Pura; or Racial, Racial;* Alurista, *Dawn;* Macias, *The Ultimate Pandejadu* and *Martir Montezuma;* Garza, *No Nos Venceremos;* Portillo, *The Day of the Swallows.*

Gassner, John, ed. *Best Plays of the Early American Theatre: From the Beginning to 1916.* Crown 1967 $27.95. Aiken, *Uncle Tom's Cabin;* Barker, *Superstition;* Boucicault, *The Octoroon;* Fechter, *The Count of Monte Cristo;* Fitch, *The Truth;* Gillette, *Secret Service;* Howells, *The Mouse-Trap;* Mackaye, *The Scarecrow;* Mitchell, *The New York Idea;* Moody, *The Great Divide;* Mowatt, *Fashion;* J. and Irving Payne, *Charles the Second;* Sheldon, *Salvation Nell;* Thomas, *The Witching Hour;* Tyler, *The Contrast;* Walter, *The Easiest Way.*

————. *Best Plays of the Modern American Theatre: 2nd Series, 1939–1946.* Crown 1947 $23.95. Barry, *The Philadelphia Story;* Gow and d'Usseau, *Tomorrow the World;* Hellman, *Watch on the Rhine;* Kanin, *Born Yesterday;* Kaufman and Hart, *The Man Who Came to Dinner;* Kesselring, *Arsenic and Old Lace;* Kingsley, *The Patriots;* Laurents, *Home of the Brave;* Lindsay and Crouse, *Life with Father;* Patrick, *The Hasty Heart;* Rice, *Dream Girl;* Saroyan, *The Time of Your Life;* Sherwood, *Abe Lincoln in Illinois;* Thurber and Nugent, *The Male Animal;* Van Druten, *I Remember Mama* and *The Voice of the Turtle;* Williams, *The Glass Menagerie.*

————. *Best American Plays: 3rd Series, 1945–1951.* Crown 1952 $19.95. Anderson, *Anne of the Thousand Days;* Coxe and Chapman, *Billy Budd;* Euripides, *Medea* (adapted by R. Jeffers); Heggen and Logan, *Mister Roberts;* Hellman, *The Autumn Garden;* Herbert, *The Moon Is Blue;* Inge, *Come Back, Little Sheba;* Kingsley, *Darkness at Noon* and *Detective Story;* Lindsay and Crouse, *State of the Union;* McCullers, *The Member of the Wedding;* Miller, *All My Sons* and *Death of a Salesman;* O'Neill, *The Iceman Cometh;* Van Druten, *Bell, Book and Candle;* Williams, *A Streetcar Named Desire.*

————. *Best American Plays: 4th Series, 1952–1957.* Crown 1958 $19.95. Anderson, *Tea and Sympathy;* Axelrod, *The Seven Year Itch;* Gazzo, *A Hatful of Rain;* Hartog, *The Fourposter;* Inge, *Bus Stop* and *Picnic;* Kaufman and Teichman, *The Solid Gold Cadillac;* Lawrence and Lee, *Inherit the Wind;* Levin, *No Time for Sergeants;* Miller, *The Crucible* and *A View from the Bridge;* O'Neill, *A Moon for the Misbegotten;* Van Druten, *I Am a Camera;* Wilder, *The Matchmaker;* Williams, *Cat on a Hot Tin Roof* and *The Rose Tattoo;* Wouk, *The Caine Mutiny.*

————. *Best American Plays: 5th Series, 1957–1963.* Crown 1963 $19.95. Albee, *Who's Afraid of Virginia Woolf?;* R. Anderson, *Silent Night, Lonely Night;* Chayefsky, *Gideon;* Frings, *Look Homeward, Angel;* Gardner, *A Thousand Clowns;* Gibson, *Two for the See-Saw;* Inge, *The Dark at the Top of the Stairs;* Kerr, *Mary, Mary;* Kopit, *Oh Dad, Poor Dad, Mamma's Hung You in the Closet and I'm Feelin' So Sad;* MacLeish, *J.B.;* Mosel, *All the Way Home;* O'Neill, *A Touch of the Poet;* Saroyan, *The Cave Dwellers;* Vidal, *The Best Man;* Williams, *The Night of the Iguana* and *Orpheus Descending;* Wishengrad, *The Rope Dancers.*

————. *Best American Plays: 6th Series, 1963–1967.* Crown 1971 $19.95. Albee, *Tiny Alice;* Alfred, *Hogan's Goat;* R. Anderson, *You Know I Can't Hear You When the Water's Running;* Baldwin, *Blues for Mister Charlie;* Bellow, *The Last Analysis;* Duberman, *In White America;* Gilroy, *The Subject Was Roses;* Goldman, *The Lion in Winter;* Hanley, *Slow Dance on the Killing Ground;* Hansberry, *The Sign in Sidney Brustein's Window;* L. Jones, *The Toilet;* T. Jones, *The Fantasticks;* Lowell, *Benito Cereno;* Manhoff, *The Owl and the Pussycat;* O'Neill, *Hughie;* Simon, *The Odd Couple;* Stein, *Fiddler on the Roof.*

Gassner, John, and Clive Barnes, eds. *Best American Plays: 7th Series, 1967–1973.* Crown 1975 $19.95. Albee, *All Over;* Allen, *Play It Again, Sam;* Crowley, *The Boys in the Band;* Elder, *Ceremonies in Dark Old Men;* Feiffer, *Little Murders;* Foster, *Tom Paine;* Friedman, *Scuba Duba;* Guare, *The House of Blue Leaves;* Horovitz, *Morning;* Kopit, *Indians;* McNally, *Night;* Miller, *The Price;* Montgomery, *Subject to Fits;* Rabe, *Sticks and Bones;* Sackler, *The Great White Hope;* Simon, *The Prisoner of Second Avenue;* Stone and Edwards, *1776;* Wilson, *Lemon Sky.*

Gassner, John, ed. *Best American Plays: Supplementary Volume, 1918–1958.* Crown 1961 $21.95. Barry, *Here Come the Clowns;* Behrman, *Biography;* Chase, *Harvey;* Colton, *Rain;* Davis and Davis, *Ethan Frome;* Goodrich and Hackett, *The Diary of Anne Frank;* Green, *The House of Connelly;* Howard and DeKruif, *Yellow Jack;*

Kingsley, *Men in White;* Mayer, *Children of Darkness;* Odets, *Awake and Sing;* Osborn, *Morning's at Seven* and *On Borrowed Time;* Patrick, *The Teahouse of the August Moon;* Rice, *The Adding Machine;* Riggs, *Green Grow the Lilacs;* Tarkington, *Clarence.*

———. *Twenty Best Plays of the Modern American Theatre.* Crown 1939 $22.50. Abbott and Holm, *Three Men on a Horse;* Anderson, *High Tor* and *Winterset;* Barry, *The Animal Kingdom;* Behrman, *End of Summer;* Booth, *The Women;* Connelly, *Green Pastures;* Ferber and Kaufman, *Stage Door;* Green, *Johnny Johnson;* Hart and Kaufman, *You Can't Take It with You;* Hellman, *The Children's Hour;* Kingsley, *Dead End;* Kirkland and Caldwell, *Tobacco Road;* MacLeish, *The Fall of the City;* Odets, *Golden Boy;* Reed, *Yes, My Darling Daughter;* Shaw, *Bury the Dead;* Sherwood, *Idiot's Delight;* B. and S. Spewack, *Boy Meets Girl;* Steinbeck, *Of Mice and Men.*

———. *Twenty-Five Best Plays of the Modern American Theatre: Early Series.* Crown 1949 $16.95. M. Anderson and Hickerson, *Gods of the Lightning;* M. Anderson, *Saturday's Children;* Bladerston, *Berkeley Square;* Barry, *Paris Bound;* Beach, *The Clod;* Behrman, *The Second Man;* Conkle, *Minnie Field;* Dunning and Abbott, *Broadway;* Glaspell, *Trifles;* Green, *White Dresses;* Hecht and MacArthur, *The Front Page;* Heyward and Heyward, *Porgy;* Howard, *They Knew What They Wanted;* Kaufman and Connelly, *Beggar on Horseback;* Kelley, *Craig's Wife* and *Poor Aubrey;* Millay, *Aria da Capo;* O'Neill, *Desire under the Elms, The Hairy Ape,* and *Ile;* Rice, *Street Scene;* Sherwood, *The Road to Rome;* Stallings and M. Anderson, *What Price Glory?;* Sturges, *Strictly Dishonorable;* Treadwell, *Machinal.*

Gates, Robert A., ed. *Eighteenth and Nineteenth Century American Drama.* Irvington 1984 $34.50 pap. $19.95

Gaver, Jack, ed. *Critics' Choice: New York Drama Critics' Circle Prize Plays, 1935–55. Play Anthology Repr. Ser.* Ayer repr. of 1955 ed. $43.00. M. Anderson, *Winterset* and *High Tor;* Steinbeck, *Of Mice and Men;* Saroyan, *The Time of Your Life;* Hellman, *Watch on the Rhine;* Kingsley, *The Patriots* and *Darkness at Noon;* Williams, *The Glass Menagerie, A Streetcar Named Desire,* and *Cat on a Hot Tin Roof;* Miller, *All My Sons* and *Death of a Salesman;* McCullers, *The Member of the Wedding;* Van Druten, *I Am a Camera;* Inge, *Picnic;* Patrick, *The Teahouse of the August Moon.*

Gerould, Daniel, ed. *American Melodrama: Plays and Documents.* Performing Arts 1983 $21.95 pap. $8.95. Boucicault, *The Poor of New York;* Aiken, *Uncle Tom's Cabin;* Daly, *Under the Gaslight;* Belasco, *The Girl of the Golden West.*

Halline, Allan G., ed. *American Plays.* AMS Pr. repr. of 1935 ed. $44.50; Century Bookbindery repr. of 1935 ed. 1982 $60.00. Tyler, *The Contrast;* Dunlap, *André;* Paulding, *The Bucktails, or Americans in England;* Barker, *Superstition;* Bird, *The Gladiator;* Willis, *Bianca Visconti;* Mowatt, *Fashion;* Boker, *Francesca da Rimini;* Daly, *Horizon;* Miller, *The Danites in the Sierras;* Howard, *The Henrietta;* Mitchell, *The New York Idea;* Moeller, *Madame Sand;* Barry, *You and I;* Davis, *Icebound;* O'Neill, *The Great God Brown;* Green, *The Field God.*

———. *Six Modern American Plays. Modern Lib. College Ed. Ser.* Random 1966 pap. $3.95. O'Neill, *The Emperor Jones;* M. Anderson, *Winterset;* Kaufman and Hart, *The Man Who Came to Dinner;* Hellman, *The Little Foxes;* Williams, *The Glass Menagerie;* Heggen and Logan, *Mister Roberts.*

Hatch, James V., and Ted Shine, eds. *Black Theater, U.S.A.: Forty-Five Plays by Black Americans, 1847–1974.* 1974. Macmillan (Free Pr.) $29.95. The most balanced collection; includes bibliographies. Aldridge, *The Black Doctor;* Séjour, *The*

Brown Overcoat; Brown, *The Escape; or A Leap for Freedom;* Cotter, *Caleb the Degenerate;* Grimke, *Rachel;* Nelson, *Mine Eyes Have Seen;* Burrill, *They That Sit in Darkness;* Toomer, *Balo;* G. Anderson, *Appearances;* Gaines-Shelton, *The Church Fight;* Johnson, *A Sunday Morning;* Matheus, *'Cruiter;* Livingston, *For Unborn Children;* Richardson, *Flight of the Natives;* Bonner, *The Purple Flower;* M. Miller, *Graven Images;* Richardson, *The Idle Head;* Spence, *Undertow;* Edward, *Job Hunters;* Edmonds, *Bad Man;* Hughes, *Little Ham, Don't You Want to Be Free?* and *Limitations of Life;* Browne, *Natural Man;* Ward, *Big White Fog;* Dodson, *Divine Comedy;* Wright and Green, *Native Son;* Hill, *Walk Hard;* Richards, *District of Columbia;* Sebree, *Dry August;* Peterson, *Take a Giant Step;* Baldwin, *The Amen Corner;* Branch, *In Splendid Error;* Hansberry, *The Drinking Ground;* Jackson and Hatch, *Fly Blackbird;* Baraka, *The Slave;* Mitchell, *Star of the Morning;* Ward, *Day of Absence;* Kennedy, *The Owl Answers;* Bullins, *Goin' a Buffalo;* Ferdinand, *Black Love Song #1;* Childress, *Wine in the Wilderness;* Pawley, *The Tumult and the Shouting;* Charles, *Job Security;* Shine, *Herbert III.*

Hewes, Henry. *Famous American Plays of the 1940s.* Dell 1960 pap. $4.95. *The Skin of Our Teeth; Home of the Brave; All My Sons; Lost in the Stars; The Member of the Wedding.*

Jacobus, Lee, ed. *Longman Anthology of American Drama.* Longman 1982 pap. $18.95. Tyler, *The Contrast;* Mowatt, *Fashion;* Aiken, *Uncle Tom's Cabin;* Boucicault, *The Octoroon;* Howard, *Shenandoah;* Glaspell, *Suppressed Desires;* O'Neill, *The Emperor Jones;* Rice, *The Adding Machine;* Connelly, *The Green Pastures;* Odets, *Waiting for Lefty;* Hellman, *The Little Foxes;* Wilder, *The Skin of Our Teeth;* Inge, *Come Back, Little Sheba;* Williams, *Camino Real;* Miller, *A View from the Bridge;* Hansberry, *A Raisin in the Sun;* van Itallie, *TV;* Bullins, *Clara's Ole Man;* Kopit, *Indians;* Gordone, *No Place to Be Somebody;* Rabe, *The Basic Training of Pavlo Hummel;* Simon, *The Sunshine Boys.*

Kozelka, Paul, ed. *Fifteen American One-Act Plays.* Simon & Schuster 1961 pap. $3.50. Morley, *Thursday Evening;* Goodman, *Dust of the Road;* Ehlert, *The Undercurrent;* Green, *The Man Who Died at Twelve O'Clock;* Millay, *Aria Da Capo;* Duffield, *The Lottery* (from a story by Shirley Jackson); Hughes, *Red Carnations;* Valency, *Feathertop* (from a story by Nathaniel Hawthorne); Fletcher, *Sorry, Wrong Number;* Kaufman, *The Still Alarm;* Glaspell, *Trifles;* Tarkington, *The Trysting Place;* Gale, *The Neighbors;* Mosel, *Impromptu;* Bénet, *The Devil and Daniel Webster.*

Leverett, James, ed. *New Plays U.S.A., No. 1.* Theatre Communications 1982 $17.95 pap. $9.95. Breuer, *A Prelude to Death in Venice;* Cole, *Dead Souls;* Hwang, *FOB;* Mann, *Still Life;* Oyama, *The Resurrection of Lady Lester;* Shank, *Winterplay.*

MacGowan, Kenneth, ed. *Famous American Plays of the Nineteen Twenties.* Dell 1959 pap. $2.50. O'Neill, *The Moon of the Caribbees;* M. Anderson and Stallings, *What Price Glory?;* Howard, *They Knew What They Wanted;* Heyward and Heyward, *Porgy;* Barry, *Holiday;* Rice, *Street Scene.*

Marranca, Bonnie, ed. *The Theatre of Images.* Drama Bk. 1977 pap. $10.00. Foreman, *Pandering to the Masses: A Misrepresentation;* Wilson, *A Letter for Queen Victoria;* Breuer, *The Red Horse Animation.* With introductory essays.

Matlaw, Myron, ed. *Nineteenth-Century American Plays.* Applause 1985 pap. $8.95. Mowatt, *Fashion;* Boker, *Francesca da Rimini;* Boucicault, *The Octoroon;* Jefferson, *Rip Van Winkle;* Barras, *The Black Crook;* Howard, *Shenandoah;* Herne, *Margaret Fleming.*

Moore, Honor, ed. *The New Women's Theatre: Ten Plays by Contemporary American Women.* Random (Vintage) 1977 pap. $6.95. Jacker, *Bits and Pieces;* Russ, *Win-*

dow Dressing; Molinaro, *Breakfast Past Noon;* Howe, *Birth and After Birth;* Moore, *Mourning Pictures;* Childress, *Wedding Band;* Wolff, *The Abdication;* Kraus, *The Ice Wolf;* Lamb, *I Lost a Pair of Gloves Yesterday; Out of Our Father's House* (arranged for the stage by Merriam, Wagner, and Hoffsiss).

Moses, Montrose. *Representative Plays by American Dramatists.* Ayer 3 vols. repr. of 1911 ed. ea. $35.00 set $100.00. Vol. 1 (1765–1819): Godfrey, *The Prince of Parthia;* Rogers, *Ponteach; or The Savages of America;* Warren, *The Group;* Brackenridge, *Battle of Bunkers-Hill;* Leacock, *The Fall of British Tyranny; or American Liberty;* Low, *The Politician Out-Witted;* Tyler, *The Contrast;* Dunlap, *André;* Barker, *The Indian Princess; or La Belle Sauvage;* Noah, *She Would Be a Soldier; or The Plains of Chippewa.* Vol. 2 (1815–58): Hutton, *Fashionable Follies;* Payne, *Brutus; or The Fall of Tarquin;* Brown, *Sertorius; or The Roman Patriot;* Willis, *Tortesa the Usurer;* Jones, *The People's Lawyer;* Conrad, *Jack Cade;* Mowatt, *Fashion;* Aiken, *Uncle Tom's Cabin;* Bateman, *Self;* Tayleure, *Horse-Shoe Robinson.* Vol. 3 (1856–1911): Burke, *Rip Van Winkle;* Boker, *Francesca da Rimini;* Bunce, *Love in '76;* Mackaye, *Paul Kauvar; or Anarchy;* Howard, *Shenandoah;* Thomas, *In Mizzoura;* Fitch, *Moth and the Flame;* Mitchell, *The New York Idea;* Walter, *The Easiest Way;* Belasco, *Return of Peter Grimm.*

Nelson, Stanley, ed. (with Harry Smith). *The Scene One: Plays from Off-Off Broadway.* The Smith 1973 pap. $2.50. Plays by Newgurge, Greth, Gauthier, Bailey, Nelson, Bradford, Lohman, Reinhold, and Garcia.

——. *The Scene Two.* The Smith 1974 pap. $3.50. Plays by McGrinder, Kushner, Ordway, Thie, Sainer, Mandel, and Patrick.

——. *The Scene Three: Annual Anthology of Off-Off Broadway Plays.* The Smith 1975 pap. $4.00. Plays by Houston, Reinhold, Herron, Roth, Bailey, Gilbert, Chappart, Garcia, Somerfeld, Lengyel, Gauthier, Wilbert, O'Reilly, Gonzalez, Joseph Lazarus.

——. *The Scene Four.* The Smith 1977 pap. $5.00. Plays by Vallejo, Horovitz, Tolnay, and Shea. All the plays in the Nelson anthologies have been in recent production off-off-Broadway. The texts include original casts, performance time, and information on performing rights.

New American Plays. Hill & Wang 1965–71 vol. 1 ed. by Robert Corrigan, pap. $7.95 vol. 4 ed. by William Hoffman, 1971 $6.50 pap. $2.45. Vol. 1: Rosenberg, *The Death and Life of Sneaky Fitch;* Levinson, *Socrates Wounded;* Mee, *Constantinople Smith;* Cameron, *The Hundred and First;* Washburn, *Ginger Anne;* Osgood, *Pigeons;* Yerby, *The Golden Bull of Boredom;* Jasudowicz, *Blood Money;* Barlow, *Mr. Biggs;* Fredericks, *A Summer Ghost.* Vol. 4: Yankowitz, *Slaughterhouse Play;* Heide, *At War with the Mongols;* Smith, *Captain Jack's Revenge;* Magnuson, *African Medea;* Rubenstein, *Icarus;* Peluso, *Moby Tick.*

Oliver, Clinton S., and Stephanie Sills, eds. *Contemporary Black Drama: Raisin in the Sun, Purlie Victorious, Funnyhouse of a Negro, Dutchman, Blues for Mister Charlie, Day of Absence, Happy Ending, The Gentleman Caller, No Place to Be Somebody.* Scribner text ed. 1971 pap. $15.95

Richards, Stanley. *The Most Popular Plays of the American Theatre.* Stein & Day 1979 $25.00

Strasberg, Lee, ed. *Famous American Plays of the Nineteen Fifties.* Dell 1963 pap. $3.50. Williams, *Camino Real;* Hellman, *The Autumn Garden;* R. Anderson, *Tea and Sympathy;* Albee, *The Zoo Story;* Gazzo, *A Hatful of Rain.*

Wordplays Two: New American Drama. Performing Arts 1982 $16.95 pap. $6.95. Owens, *Chucky's Hunch;* Shawn, *A Thought in Three Parts;* Jenkens, *Dark Ride;* Kondoleon, *The Brides;* O'Keefe, *All Night Long.*

ALBEE, EDWARD. 1928–

Edward Albee was the pampered adopted son of millionaire parents. An indifferent, rebellious student, he attended various private schools and—briefly—Trinity College, then quit home and schooling at age 21 to live in New York City. For nearly a decade he worked at odd jobs, writing poetry, attempting novels, publishing nothing. Just before his thirtieth birthday, he sat down and wrote *The Zoo Story* (1959) in two weeks. *The Sandbox* (1960), *Fam and Yam, The American Dream,* and *The Death of Bessie Smith* (1960) followed rapidly, and the fame of the young dramatist was established.

Although these one-act plays linked Albee to the Theater of the Absurd, *Who's Afraid of Virginia Woolf?,* his Broadway debut in 1962, was by contrast naturalistic. The evening-long argument between a married couple is a strong denunciation of modern marital relationships, amusingly bitchy on the surface but murderously vicious underneath. "The heart of his technique is an archetypal family unity, in which the defeats, hopes, dilemmas, and values of our society (as Albee sees it) are tangibly compressd" (Lee Baxandall, *The Theater of Edward Albee*).

The Ballad of the Sad Cafe, Albee's adaptation of the novella by CARSON McCULLERS (see Vol. 1), was less successful in 1963, while *Tiny Alice* (1965) had elements of the Theater of the Absurd and appeared to many as an allegory about spiritual versus secular elements. *A Delicate Balance* (1967), a more conventional comedy of serious intent, Albee says, is "about how as you get older the freedom of choices becomes less and less, and you are left only with the illusion of freedom of actions and you become a slave of compromise." *Seascape* (1975), intended as a comedy and a balance to the view of life expressed in *All Over* (1971), has a middle-aged couple at the shore meeting a reptile. Their conversation reveals common problems in life.

Albee won the Pulitzer Prize for drama for *A Delicate Balance* and *Seascape* and the New York Drama Critics Circle Award for *Who's Afraid of Virginia Woolf?*

BOOKS BY ALBEE

The Plays of Edward Albee. Atheneum vol. 2 (1981) pap. $9.95 vol. 3 (1982) pap. $9.95 vol. 4 (1982) pap. $10.95. Vol. 2: *Tiny Alice; A Delicate Balance; Box; Quotations from Chairman Mao.* Vol. 3: *Seascape; Counting the Ways and Listening; All Over.* Vol. 4: *Everything in the Garden* (adapted from a play by Giles Cooper); *Malcolm* (adapted from a novel by James Purdy); *The Ballad of the Sad Cafe* (adapted from a novella by Carson McCullers).

The American Dream (and *The Zoo Story*). New Amer. Lib. (Signet Class.) 1963 pap. $2.50

The Sandbox and (*The Death of Bessie Smith*). New Amer. Lib. (Signet Class.) 1964 pap. $2.95

The American Dream and *The Death of Bessie Smith* and *Fam and Yam.* Dramatists $3.25

Who's Afraid of Virginia Woolf? Atheneum text ed. 1962 pap. $5.95; New Amer. Lib. (Signet Class.) 1983 pap. $3.50

The Lady from Dubuque: A Play in Two Acts. Atheneum 1980 $9.95; Dramatists pap.
    $3.25
The Man Who Had Three Arms. Atheneum 1984 $12.95

BOOKS ABOUT ALBEE

Amacher, Richard E. *Edward Albee. Twayne's U.S. Authors Ser.* G. K. Hall $13.50.
    Rates the one-act plays and the full-length tragedies as the best.
Amacher, Richard E., and Margaret Rule, eds. *Edward Albee at Home and Abroad: A
    Bibliography, 1938–June 1968. AMS Studies in Modern Lit.* repr. of 1973 ed.
    $29.50
Bigsby, C. W. E. *Albee. Writers and Critics Ser.* Chips 1978 $22.50. One of the most as-
    tute critics on Albee.
Green, Charles I. *Edward Albee: An Annotated Bibliography, 1968–1977. AMS Studies
    in Modern Lit.* 1980 $22.50
Paolucci, Anne. *From Tension to Tonic: The Plays of Edward Albee.* Southern Illinois
    Univ. Pr. 1972 $9.95

ANDERSON, MAXWELL. 1888–1959

After some years as a teacher and a newspaperman, Anderson turned to
drama in 1923, achieving his first success with *What Price Glory?* in 1924, a
World War I comedy cowritten with Laurence Stallings. During his long
and successful career as a dramatist (his last play premiered in 1958), Anderson produced historical dramas, patriotic plays, musicals, fantasies, and
a thriller. Perhaps his best piece is *Winterset.* Inspired by the Sacco and Van-
zetti case, it dramatizes the efforts of Mio, the son of a man executed ostensibly for murder but actually for his radical ideas, to clear his father's name.
Anderson's first play was a verse drama, and beginning with *Elizabeth the
Queen* (1940), his most famous historical drama, he employed for many
years an irregular blank verse, typical—like his preoccupation with traditional tragic form—of his attempt to bring high seriousness to the Broadway stage. Critics have not been enthusiastic about Anderson's work, and
his plays are seldom revived today, but in his heyday—especially the
1930s—his plays (verse and all) repeatedly succeeded in the commercial
theater.

Anderson won the Pulitzer Prize for drama for *Both Your Houses* (1933)
and the New York Drama Critics Circle Award for *Winterset* (1935) and *High
Tor* (1937).

BOOKS BY ANDERSON

Dramatist in America: Letters of Maxwell Anderson, 1912–1958. Ed. by Laurence G.
    Avery, Univ. of North Carolina Pr. 1977 $32.50
Four Verse Plays: High Tor, Winterset, Elizabeth the Queen, Mary of Scotland. Har-
    court 1959 pap. $9.95
Elizabeth the Queen. French 1930 $3.50
Mary of Scotland. French 1934 $3.50
Winterset. Dramatists 1935 $3.25
Joan of Lorraine. Dramatists 1946 $3.25
Barefoot in Athens. Dramatists 1951 $3.25

The Bad Seed. Dramatists 1955 $3.25
The Golden Six. Dramatists 1958 $3.25

BOOKS ABOUT ANDERSON

Cox, Martha H. *Bibliography of Maxwell Anderson.* Arden Lib. repr. of 1958 ed. 1980
   lib. bdg. $20.00; Folcroft repr. of 1958 ed. lib. bdg. $15.00; Porter 1977 $20.00
Shivers, Alfred S. *The Life of Maxwell Anderson.* Stein & Day 1983 $25.00. "Shiv-
   ers . . . has caught Anderson as no one has and, in so doing, has added enormously to theater history" (Joshua Logan, *N.Y. Times*).
———. *Maxwell Anderson. Twayne's U.S. Authors Ser.* G. K. Hall 1976 $13.50. Espe-
   cially useful for the new biographical material it provides.

BARAKA, IMAMU AMIRI (LeRoi Jones). 1934–

Born LeRoi Jones in Newark, New Jersey, Baraka graduated from Howard University and then taught at Columbia, the New School, and San Francisco State. Baraka has been involved in a number of theater and education
projects designed to improve conditions for blacks. In 1968, he assumed his
new name and became a minister of the Kawaida faith. In 1974 he re-
nounced black nationalism for international Marxist-Leninist thought.

With *Dutchman,* a one-act play about a provocative white girl who alternately entices and belittles and finally kills a young black in the subway, Baraka emerged as an important black dramatic voice. In *The Slave,* a black
revolutionary confronts his former wife, a white woman, and kills their two
children. In *The Toilet,* a black youth beats a white youth who has made homosexual advances, but in the absence of others, returns to comfort the
white youth. *Slave Ship* is an indictment of white imperialism. *The Motion
of History* is epic drama seeking to write black American history from a
Marxist point of view. Baraka's plays are bold in concept, strong in language, and committed to revolutionary racial and social change, but his later plays tend to be excessively didactic. (See also Volume 1, Chapter 9.)

BOOKS BY BARAKA

Dutchman (and *The Slave*). Morrow 1964 pap. $3.95
The Baptism (and *The Toilet*). Grove 1967 pap. $3.95
The Motion of History and Other Plays. Morrow 1978 $8.95. Includes *Slave Ship* and
   S-1.

BOOKS ABOUT BARAKA

Benston, Kimberly W. *Baraka: The Renegade and the Mask.* Fwd. by Larry Neal, Yale
   Univ. Pr. 1976 $26.50. Examines Baraka's plays as products of two cultural tra-
   ditions, the Western and the Afro-American.
Hudson, Theodore R. *From LeRoi Jones to Amiri Baraka: The Literary Works.* Duke
   Univ. Pr. 1973 $18.75 pap. $9.75
Lacey, Henry C. *To Raise, Destroy, and Create.* Whitston 1981 $15.00
Sollers, Werner. *Amiri Baraka/LeRoi Jones: The Quest for "Popular Modernism."* Co-
   lumbia Univ. Pr. 1978 o.p. An important study by a major black scholar.

BARRY, PHILIP. 1896–1949

Barry, a product of Baker's 47 Workshop, is best remembered for his witty and elegant comedies about marriage among the well-to-do. His most noted play is *The Philadelphia Story*, about a wealthy young woman who on her wedding day switches from a dull social climber to remarry her first husband. Other drawing room successes include *Paris Bound* (1929) and *Holiday*. Barry also wrote plays of greater seriousness, but with less critical and popular success. *Hotel Universe*, in which a group of strangers relive personal crises in their lives, and *Here Come the Clowns* are experimental dramas with a mystical side, reflecting Freudian interpretation of character and existential doubt. In *Tomorrow and Tomorrow* (1931) a man discovers that his mistress, in behavior and love, is more his wife than the woman to whom he is legally married.

Of Barry, Brendan Gill wrote, "No matter how ambitious the intentions of his plays, he kept the plays themselves modest in scale. He wrote often in the now unfashionable genre of high comedy but his comedies strove to be deeper than they were high."

BOOKS BY BARRY

The Youngest. French 1922 $3.50
In a Garden. French 1925 $3.50
Holiday. French 1928 $3.50
Hotel Universe. French 1930 $3.75
Here Come the Clowns. French 1938 $11.95
The Philadelphia Story: A Comedy in Three Acts. AMS Pr. repr. of 1939 ed. $24.50; French 1939 $3.50

BOOK ABOUT BARRY

Roppolo, Joseph P. *Philip Barry. Twayne's U.S. Authors Ser.* G. K. Hall $13.50; *Twayne's U.S. Authors Ser.* New College & Univ. Pr. 1965 pap. $5.95

GREEN, PAUL. 1894–1981

Born on a North Carolina farm, Green studied philosophy at the University of North Carolina. He began writing plays as a freshman under the guidance of Frederic Koch, whose Carolina playmakers staged Green's first works. An important regional dramatist, Green portrays the plight of oppressed Southerners of both the old South and the new. His dramas use interpolations of folk songs along with authentic North Carolina dialect. Among Green's finest achievements are *The House of Connelly* (1931, o.p.) and *Johnny Johnson.* John Gassner described the first as "the most poignant drama of the postbellum South" and the second as "the most imaginative and affecting antiwar full-length play in the American Theatre." *In Abraham's Bosom* (o.p.) shows the failure of a mulatto to achieve status. This later work, performed by the Provincetown Players in New York City, won the Pulitzer Prize for drama in 1926.

Green is also largely responsible for the development of pageants or symphonic dramas, as he terms them, the only dramatic writing he did after

1936. *The Lost Colony* was his first outdoor drama and was written to commemorate the three hundred fiftieth anniversary of Raleigh's colony at Roanoke, Virginia. It has been performed with a cast of 150 every summer since. Other popular Green pageants, derived from the life and history of the people or single individuals from a particular locale, are *The Common Glory* and *The Stephen Foster Story*.

BOOKS BY GREEN

The Field God (and *In Abraham's Bosom*). AMS Pr. repr. of 1927 ed. $29.50
Wide Fields. AMS Pr. repr. of 1928 ed. $14.50; Scholarly repr. of 1928 ed. 1971 $13.00
Roll Sweet Chariot. French 1934 $3.50
Johnny Johnson. French 1936 $3.50
The Lost Colony. French 1937 $8.00
The Highland Call. French 1939 $4.00
(and Richard Wright). *Native Son*. French rev. ed. 1941 $4.50
Hawthorn Tree: Some Papers and Letters on Life and the Theatre. *Essay Index Repr. Ser.* Ayer repr. of 1943 ed. $15.00
The Common Glory. 1947. Greenwood repr. of 1948 ed. 1973 lib. bdg. $24.75
Wilderness Road. French 1956 $4.50
The Founders. French 1957 $4.50
Confederacy. French 1958 $3.50
The Stephen Foster Story. French 1959 $3.75
Texas. French 1967 $3.50
The Honeycomb. French 1972 $3.75
Trumpet in the Land. French 1972 $4.00

BOOKS ABOUT GREEN

Clark, Barrett H. *Paul Green*. *Studies in Drama* Haskell 1974 lib. bdg. $29.95
Kenny, Vincent S. *Paul Green*. *Twayne's U.S. Authors Ser.* G. K. Hall lib. bdg. $13.95; *Twayne's U.S. Authors Ser.* Irvington 1971 lib. bdg. $11.95 text ed. pap. $6.95

HANSBERRY, LORRAINE. 1930–1965

The daughter of a well-to-do Chicago real estate man, Hansberry studied painting before venturing to New York in 1950, where she worked as a salesgirl, cashier, and assistant to an off-Broadway producer. She took courses in playwriting at the New School for Social Research and began writing seriously after her marriage to producer Robert Nemiroff. *A Raisin in the Sun*, which brought her sudden success, was the warmly human story of a black family moving into a white neighborhood (as her father had done when she was eight). The title refers to LANGSTON HUGHES's (see Vol. 1) *Harlem:* "What happens to a dream deferred? Does it dry up like a raisin in the sun?" *The Sign in Sidney Brustein's Window*, about the moral problems of a Jewish intellectual in Greenwich Village, was written during her final illness. She died of cancer.

BOOKS BY HANSBERRY

Lorraine Hansberry: The Collected Last Plays. Ed. by Robert Nemiroff, New Amer. Lib. (Plume) 1983 $8.95
To Be Young, Gifted, and Black: Lorraine Hansberry in Her Own Words. Ed. by Robert

Nemiroff, intro. by James Baldwin, New Amer. Lib. (Signet Class.) 1970 pap. $3.50; ed. by Robert Nemiroff, Prentice-Hall 1969 $8.95

A Raisin in the Sun. 1959. New Amer. Lib. (Signet Class.) 1961 pap. $3.50; Random 1969 $11.50

BOOK ABOUT HANSBERRY

Cheney, Anne. *Lorraine Hansberry. Twayne's U.S. Authors Ser.* G. K. Hall 1984 o.p.

HELLMAN, LILLIAN. 1905–1984

Born in New Orleans, Hellman was educated at New York and Columbia universities and worked as a publisher's reader, book reviewer, and theater publicist before Dashiell Hammett, her long-time friend and companion, encouraged her to write plays. The immediate result was her first success, *The Children's Hour,* which was based on a nineteenth-century Scottish trial and concerned the financial and psychological destruction of two teachers at a girls' boarding school after a malicious child convinces her wealthy grandmother that they are lesbians. In subsequent plays Hellman focuses on anti-labor violence (*Days to Come*) and the threat of fascism (*Watch on the Rhine* and *The Searching Wind*). Her best plays, *The Little Foxes* and *Another Part of the Forest,* brilliantly combine comedy and melodrama to attack greed and rapacity through the avaricious Hubbard clan of the turn-of-the-century South. Hellman's other important plays include *The Autumn Garden,* a Chekhovian play about people with unfulfilled lives, and *Toys in the Attic,* which dramatizes a young man's difficult escape from his possessive sisters. In later years Hellman became a distinguished memoirist. Concerning her plays, Robert Corrigan wrote, "In a realistic style, characteristic of Ibsen, she writes of the conflicts of personal morality and their public consequences. . . . In each of her plays she raspingly attacks both the doers of evil and those who stand by and watch them do it."

Hellman won the New York Drama Critics Circle Award for *Watch on the Rhine* and *Toys in the Attic.*

BOOKS BY HELLMAN

The Collected Plays. Little, Brown 1972 $19.95. Includes *The Children's Hour* (1934); *Days to Come* (1936); *The Little Foxes* (1939); *Watch on the Rhine* (1941); *The Searching Wind* (1944); *Another Part of the Forest* (1946); *Montserrat* (a 1950 adaptation of a play by Emmanuel Robles); *The Autumn Garden* (1951); *The Lark* (a 1955 adaptation of a play by Jean Anouilh); *Candide* (a 1956 book of a coauthored musical); *Toys in the Attic* (1960); *My Mother, My Father and Me* (1963).

Six Plays by Lillian Hellman: The Children's Hour, Days to Come, The Little Foxes, Watch on the Rhine, Another Part of the Forest, The Autumn Garden. Random (Vintage) 1979 pap. $8.95

Three: An Unfinished Woman, Pentimento, Scoundrel Time. Intro. by Richard Poirier, Little, Brown 1979 $16.95 pap. $10.95. The complete texts of her important memoirs, with new commentaries by the author.

BOOKS ABOUT HELLMAN

Estrin, Mark. *Lillian Hellman: Plays, Films, Memoirs—A Reference Guide.* G. K. Hall 1980 lib. bdg. $27.50. An excellent survey, presented chronologically.

Falk, Doris V. *Lillian Hellman. Lit. and Life Ser.* Ungar 1978 $12.95 pap. $6.95. ". . . offers a rapid overview of the plays and memoirs" (Mark Estrin, *Modern Drama*).

Lederer, Katherine. *Lillian Hellman. Twayne's U.S. Authors Ser.* G. K. Hall 1979 $13.50. ". . . supplies admirable correctives to critical misreadings of the plays" (Mark Estrin, *Modern Drama*).

HENLEY, BETH. 1952–

Henley was born in Jackson, Mississippi, and received a B.F.A. in drama from Southern Methodist University. Henley achieved popular and critical success with *Crimes of the Heart*, which was produced at the Actors Theatre in Louisville in 1979, off-Broadway in 1980, and on Broadway in 1981. It concerns a "bad day" in the lives of three eccentric sisters, Meg, Lenny, and Babe, the last of whom has shot her husband because she "didn't like his looks." Henley's blend of naturalism combined with absurdist comedy and off-beat humor is also evident in *The Miss Firecracker Contest*, in which members of a small-town family get embroiled in the efforts of one of them to win a beauty contest. Henley won the Pulitzer Prize for drama and the New York Drama Critics Circle Award for *Crimes of the Heart*.

BOOKS BY HENLEY

Crimes of the Heart. Dramatists 1982 pap. $3.25; Penguin 1982 pap. $4.95; Viking 1982 $12.95

Am I Blue? Dramatists 1982 $1.75

The Wake of Jamie Foster. Dramatists 1982 $3.25

HWANG, DAVID HENRY. 1957–

The son of immigrant Chinese parents, Hwang attended Stanford University and the Yale Drama School and has been a director and a teacher of playwriting. *FOB*, which stands for "Fresh off the boat," explores the conflicts and similarities between two Chinese Americans and a Chinese exchange student still steeped in the customs and beliefs of the old world. It won an Obie Award in 1981. *The Dance and the Railroad* concerns an artist and his fellow workers who stage a strike to protest the inhuman conditions suffered by Chinese railroad workers in the American West in the nineteenth century. Maxine Hong Kingston wrote, "David Hwang has an ear for Chinatown English, the language of childhood and the subconscious, the language of emotion, the language of home."

BOOKS BY HWANG

Broken Promises: Four Chinese American Plays. Intro. by Maxine Hong Kingston, Avon 1983 pap. $3.95. *FOB; The Dance and the Railroad; Family Devotions; The House of Sleeping Beauties.*

The Sound of a Voice. Dramatists 1984 $1.75

INGE, WILLIAM (MOTTER). 1913–1973

Inge was born in Independence, Kansas, attended the University of Kansas and Peabody College in Nashville, Tennessee, and also studied theater with Maude Adams at Stephens College in Columbia, Missouri. He taught drama for some years and then served as drama critic for the St. Louis *Star Times* before becoming a playwright. *Come Back, Little Sheba* (1950), his first success on Broadway, is about an aging couple, the wife clinging to the past, the husband an alcoholic. His next play was *Picnic* (1953, later revised as *Summer Brave*), about a virile young drifter and his effect on women in a small town. *Bus Stop* (1955) involves stranded people—each reveals his loneliness, and in the end an aspiring singer accepts the attention of a naive but rough cowboy. *The Dark at the Top of the Stairs* (1958) concerns itself with a frustrated family in which a new understanding between the mother and father, and more confidence on the part of the son and daughter, eventuate.

Inge was immensely popular in the 1950s. In most of his plays the characters live a humdrum existence, usually in the Kansas-Oklahoma region of 50 years ago. Behind the naturalistic dialogue is an inner softness; and the main figures are prone to confession. His works have been called "psychodramas involving the solution of personal and social problems by introspection and togetherness" (Eric Mottram).

Inge won the Pulitzer Prize for drama and the New York Drama Critics Circle Award for *Picnic*. The later part of Inge's career as a dramatist was not successful. He took his own life in 1973.

Books by Inge

Four Plays by William Inge. Grove 1979 pap. $7.95. *Come Back, Little Sheba; Picnic; Bus Stop; The Dark at the Top of the Stairs.*
A Loss of Roses. Dramatists 1960 $3.25
Summer Brave (Picnic). Dramatists 1962 pap. $3.25
Natural Affection. Dramatists 1963 $3.25
Where's Daddy. Dramatists 1966 $3.25
Eleven One-Act Plays. Dramatists $3.25. *The Boy in the Basement; Bus Riley's Back in Town; An Incident at the Standish Arms; The Mall; Memory of Summer; The Rainy Afternoon; A Social Event; Splendor in the Grass; The Tiny Closet; To Bobolink for Her Spirit; People in the Wind.*

KAUFMAN, GEORGE S. 1889–1961

Kaufman, who was born in Pittsburgh, attended law school for two years, failed as a businessman, and became a humorist for Franklin P. Adams's column before joining the *N.Y. Times*, becoming its drama editor in the 1920s. Kaufman was sole author of one long play and two one-act plays, including the popular *The Butter and Egg Man* (1926, o.p.), but he collaborated on more than 25 plays, most importantly with Moss Hart, but also with Marc Connelly, Edna Ferber, and others, including RING LARDNER (see Vol. 1) and John P. Marquand. These plays range from the hilarious madness of *Cocoanuts* and *Animal Crackers*, two Marx Brothers shows that Kaufman worked on, to the comic pathos of *Stage Door* (with Edna Ferber). In all of them Kaufman's distinctive touch was what Brooks Atkinson called "the destructive wise-crack" or "the verbal ricochet." John Gassner wrote of Kaufman and his col-laborators that they "have been marvelous recorders of American surfaces" but in their critical outlook they "were either disinclined or unable to carry it to conclusions. . . . Their flippancy [was] amusing and at worst just a trifle too empty." Commenting on why he did not write true satire, Kaufman said, "Satire is what closes Saturday night." Kaufman, Morris Ryskind, and Ira Gershwin won the Pulitzer Prize for drama for *Of Thee I Sing* and Kaufman and Hart for *You Can't Take It with You* (1937).

BOOKS BY KAUFMAN

(and Ring Lardner, Edna Ferber, and John P. Marquand). *George S. Kaufman and His Collaborators: Three Plays.* Performing Arts 1984 $19.95 pap. $7.95. *June Moon* (with Ring Lardner); *Bravo* (with Edna Ferber); *The Late George Apley* (with John P. Marquand).

(and Moss Hart). *Once in a Lifetime, You Can't Take It with You, The Man Who Came to Dinner: Three Plays.* Grove 1980 pap. $6.95

(and Marc Connelly). *Dulcy.* French 1921 $3.50

(and Marc Connelly). *Merton of the Movies.* French 1922 $3.50

(and Edna Ferber). *The Royal Family.* French 1928 $3.75

(and Morris Ryskind). *Animal Crackers.* French $3.50

(and Edna Ferber). *Dinner at Eight.* French 1932 $3.75

(and Morris Ryskind and Ira Gershwin). *Of Thee I Sing.* French 1932 $3.50

(and Edna Ferber). *Stage Door.* Dramatists 1936 $3.25

(and Moss Hart). *George Washington Slept Here.* Dramatists 1940 $3.25

(and Leueen Macgrath). *Small Hours.* Dramatists 1951 $3.25

(and Howard Teichmann). *The Solid Gold Cadillac.* Dramatists 1954 $3.25

BOOK ABOUT KAUFMAN

Goldstein, Malcolm. *George S. Kaufman: His Life, His Theater.* Oxford 1979 $29.95. "A substantial, diligently researched work [which] is certain to prove valuable to students of the American theater . . ." (Seymour Peck, *N.Y. Times*).

KELLY, GEORGE EDWARD. 1887–1974

A member of Philadelphia's famous Kelly clan and the uncle of Princess Grace of Monaco, Kelly's reputation was made by three of his plays from the 1920s. *The Torch-Bearers* pokes fun at amateur theater groups; *The Show-Off* is a classic presentation of the bragger; *Craig's Wife* is a study of a woman who loves her home and position more than her husband. "Kelly points out the follies and ludicrous behaviour of his times with a crabbed cynicism that would do credit to BEN JONSON if it did not lack Jonson's rau-cous gusto" (*Sievers*). Kelly won a Pulitzer Prize for drama for *Craig's Wife*.

BOOKS BY KELLY

The Torch-Bearers. French 1922 $3.75

The Show-Off. French 1924 $3.50

Craig's Wife. 1925. French rev. ed. 1949 $3.50

Daisy Mayme. French 1926 $3.75

The Fatal Weakness. French 1947 $3.50

KOPIT, ARTHUR. 1937–

Born in New York, Kopit won a scholarship to Harvard to study electrical engineering, but found his main interest was to be playwriting. Shortly after graduation, he wrote *Oh Dad, Poor Dad, Mamma's Hung You in the Closet and I'm Feeling So Sad,* an absurdist play about an overprotective mother who travels not only with her son, but with two Venus's-flytraps and the remains of her husband, in an obvious parody of Tennessee Williams's *Suddenly Last Summer. Indians,* a more ambitious play, depicts in epic style Buffalo Bill who, as a man caught in an ambivalent position between the government and the Indians, comes to represent the nemesis of the American Indian and the untroubled American conscience. *Wings* concerns a former aviatrix and stunt pilot who suffers a stroke and gradually regains language and through it contact with the world. Kopit has also written the book for the successful musical *Nine* and adapted Ibsen's *Ghosts* for Liv Ullman. Gautam Dasgupta has observed of Kopit, "Like the absurdists before him, he chooses to depict a horrific world where logic holds no sway."

BOOKS BY KOPIT

Oh Dad, Poor Dad, Mamma's Hung You in the Closet and I'm Feeling So Sad: A Pseudoclassical Tragifarce in a Bastard French Tradition. Hill & Wang 1960 pap. $5.25
The Day the Whores Came Out to Play Tennis and Other Plays. Hill & Wang 1965 pap. $4.95. Contains *Chamber Music; The Questioning of Nick; Sing to Me through Open Windows; The Hero; The Conquest of Everest.*
Indians. Hill & Wang 1969 pap. $5.25
Wings. Hill & Wang 1978 pap. $5.25
The End of the World. Hill & Wang 1984 $13.95 pap. $6.95

BOOK ABOUT KOPIT

Auerbach, Doris. *Sam Shepard, Arthur Kopit, and the Off-Broadway Theater. Twayne's U.S. Authors Ser.* G. K. Hall 1982 $14.50. A useful introduction, but uneven and too broad in its coverage.

MacLEISH, ARCHIBALD. 1892–1982

[SEE Volume 1.]

MAMET, DAVID. 1947–

Mamet was born in Chicago, and while still in high school worked as a busboy at Chicago's famed Second City, a comedy improvisation cabaret. He was educated at Goddard College, where, as drama instructor and artist-in-residence, he subsequently produced some of his early plays. Others were produced in Chicago, and he still tends to present his work there first, especially at the Goodman Theatre, for which he became associate director and playwright-in-residence in 1978.

Mamet's work reached New York in 1975 with an off-off-Broadway production of two short plays, *The Duck Variations,* in which two old men sit on a park bench and discuss ducks and life, and *Sexual Perversity in Chicago*, concerned with the fundamental emptiness in the sexual relations of four pseudosophisticated young people. Mamet has subsequently produced a number of significant works, among them *American Buffalo,* in which three small-time crooks plot in a Chicago junkshop to rob a man of his coin collection; *A Life in the Theatre,* in which two actors—one old, the other young— perform, rehearse, discuss, and debate their work; and *Glengarry Glen Ross,* which shows real estate men hustling and competing with one another for sales leads. Most of Mamet's plays exhibit the pervasiveness and destructiveness of the American dream. He has been praised for the economy and marvelous accuracy of his dialogue and faulted for his lack of control over plot and structure.

Mamet won the Pulitzer Prize for drama for *Glengarry Glen Ross* and the New York Drama Critics Circle Award for *American Buffalo.*

BOOKS BY MAMET

Goldberg Street: Short Plays and Monologues. 1981 Grove 1985 $12.95 pap. $5.95. *The Blue Hour: City Sketches; Prairie du Chien; A Sermon; Shoeshine; Litko: A Dramatic Monologue; In Old Vermont; All Men Are Whores: An Inquiry.*
Sexual Perversity in Chicago (and *The Duck Variations*). Grove 1978 $10.00 pap. $3.95
American Buffalo. Grove 1977 $10.00 pap. $3.95
A Life in the Theatre. Grove (Everyman's) 1978 pap. $8.95
The Water Engine (and *Mr. Happiness*). Grove (Everyman's) 1978 $10.00 pap. $3.95
Reunion and Dark Pony: Two Plays. Grove (Everyman's) 1979 pap. $2.95
The Woods. Grove (Everyman's) 1979 $10.00 pap. $3.95
Lakeboat. Grove (Everyman's) 1981 $12.50 pap. $4.95
Edmond. Grove (Everyman's) 1983 $15.00 pap. $6.95
Glengarry Glen Ross. Grove (Everyman's) 1984 $17.50 pap. $6.95

MILLER, ARTHUR. 1915–

The son of a well-to-do New York Jewish family, Miller graduated from high school with poor grades and then went to work in a warehouse. His plays have been called "political," but he considers the areas of literature and politics to be quite separate and has said, "The only sure and valid aim—speaking of art as a weapon—is the humanizing of man." The recurring theme of all his plays is the relationship between a man's identity and the image that society demands of him. After two years, he entered the University of Michigan, where he soon started writing plays.

All My Sons, a Broadway success that won the New York Drama Critics Circle Award in 1947, tells the story of a son, home from the war, who learns that his brother's death was due to defective airplane parts turned out by their profiteering father. *Death of a Salesman,* Miller's experimental yet classical American tragedy, "emotionally moving as it is socially terrifying," received both the Pulitzer Prize and the New York Drama Critics Circle Award in 1949. It is a poignant statement of man facing himself and his failure. In *The Crucible,* a play about bigotry in the Salem witchcraft trials of 1692, he brought into focus "the tragedy of a whole society, not just the tragedy of an individual." It was generally considered to be a comment on the McCarthyism of its time. (Miller himself appeared before the Congressional Un-American Activities Committee and steadfastly refused to involve his friends and associates when questioned about them.)

His cinema-novel *The Misfits*, from a Miller short story, was written for his second wife, actress Marilyn Monroe; *After the Fall* has clear autobiographical overtones and involves the story of this ill-fated marriage. In the one-act *Incident at Vichy*, a group of men are picked off the streets one morning during the Nazi occupation of France. *The Price* is a psychological drama concerning two brothers, one a policeman, one a wealthy surgeon, whose long-standing conflict is explored over the disposal of their father's furniture. *The Creation of the World and Other Business* is a retelling of the story of Genesis, attempted as a comedy. *The American Clock* explores the impact of the depression on the nation and some of its individual citizens.

BOOKS BY MILLER

Collected Plays. Viking 2 vols. 1957–1981 ea. $15.95–$17.95. Vol. 1: *All My Sons; Death of a Salesman; The Crucible; A Memory of Two Mondays; A View from the Bridge* (original one-act version). Vol. 2: *The Misfits* (novelistic screenplay); *After the Fall; Incident at Vichy; The Price; The Creation of the World and Other Business; Playing for a Time* (a screenplay based on a book by Fania Fenelon).

The Portable Arthur Miller. Penguin 1977 pap. $7.95; ed. by Harold Clurman, Viking 1971 $14.95. *Death of a Salesman; The Crucible;* selections from *The Misfits;* essays and poetry; critical introduction, chronology, bibliography, and notes.

The Theater Essays of Arthur Miller. Ed. by Robert A. Martin, Viking 1978 $15.00; Penguin pap. $6.95. Miller's commentary on his own work, the nature of tragedy, theater as an institution, etc.

All My Sons. Dramatists 1947 $3.25

Death of a Salesman. Ed. by Gerald Weales, Penguin text ed. 1977 pap. $7.95; Viking 1949 $10.00

An Enemy of the People. Dramatists 1950 $3.25. Miller's adaptation of Ibsen's play.

The Crucible. 1953. Ed. by Gerald Weales, Penguin text ed. 1977 pap. $7.95

A View from the Bridge. 1957. Bantam 1977 pap. $2.95; Penguin 1977 pap. $2.95

After the Fall. Penguin 1980 pap. $3.50; Viking 1964 $10.95

Incident at Vichy. Dramatists 1964 $3.25

The Price. Dramatists 1968 $3.25

The Creation of the World and Other Business. Dramatists 1973 $3.25

The American Clock. Dramatists 1982 $3.25

Some Kind of Love Story. Dramatists $1.75

Elegy for a Lady. Dramatists $1.75

Up from Paradise. French $3.50. A musical version of *The Creation of the World and Other Business.*

BOOKS ABOUT MILLER

Carson, Neil. *Arthur Miller.* Grove 1982 pap. $6.95

Corrigan, Robert W., ed. *Arthur Miller: A Collection of Critical Essays.* Prentice-Hall 1969 $12.95

Evans, Richard I. *Psychology and Arthur Miller.* 1969. Holt 1981 $27.95. A discussion between a psychologist and the dramatist.

Martin, Robert A., ed. *Arthur Miller: New Perspectives.* Prentice-Hall 1981 vol. 2
    $13.95 pap. $4.95
Martine, James J. *Critical Essays on Arthur Miller.* G. K. Hall 1979 $26.00
Moss, Leonard. *Arthur Miller. Twayne's U.S. Authors Ser.* G. K. Hall rev. ed. 1980
    $11.50. Moss sees Miller as more than a purely "social dramatist," concluding
    that his "effort to unify social and psychological perspectives has been the
    source of his accomplishments and his failures as a dramatist."
Welland, Dennis. *Arthur Miller. Writers and Critics Ser.* International Publishing 1966
    $2.50
——. *Miller: The Playwright.* Methuen 2d ed. 1983 pap. $8.95

NORMAN, MARSHA. 1947–

Norman was born in Louisville and educated at Agnes Scott College, the
University of Louisville, and the Center for Understanding Media in New
York City. She has been a schoolteacher and a journalist as well as a playwright. She wrote her first play, *Getting Out,* a study of a woman ex-convict,
for the Actors Theatre of Louisville, which also produced other plays of
hers, including *Third and Oak* (consisting of two one-act plays, *The Laundromat* and *The Pool Hall*) and *The Circus Valentine.* Her most successful play
has been *'Night, Mother,* in which a mother and a daughter examine the
daughter's determination to kill herself. In 1985, *The Laundromat* was produced as a filmed drama for Home Box Office. Norman won the Pulitzer
Prize for drama for *'Night, Mother.*

BOOKS BY NORMAN

Getting Out. Avon 1979 pap. $2.50
'Night, Mother. Hill & Wang 1983 $13.95 pap. $6.95
Third and Oak: The Laundromat. Dramatists 1978 $1.75

ODETS, CLIFFORD. 1906–1963

With Lillian Hellman, Odets remains one of the foremost dramatists of
the 1930s in the United States. Born in Philadelphia, he became an actor
about 1923 and joined the Group Theatre upon its founding in 1930. From
then until its collapse in 1940, the Group Theatre produced seven plays by
Odets, all of which reflect the depression era in which they were written.
His first play, *Waiting for Lefty,* an agitprop play about strikers, was an enormous success. Most of his other plays of the 1930s, most notably *Awake and
Sing* and *Golden Boy,* concern the economic and psychological plight of poor
New York City Jewish families and heighten middle-class Jewish speech
into a kind of poetry. After the collapse of the Group Theatre, Odets produced only four more plays. Malcolm Goldstein wrote, "The plays of Odets
are marked by a strong social sympathy that tended, no matter the political
fashion of the year, to divide humanity into two classes: the exploiters and
the exploited." Harold Clurman observed that Odets's "central theme was
the difficulty of attaining maturity in a world where money as a tokens of
success . . . plays so dominant a role."

BOOKS BY ODETS

Six Plays of Clifford Odets: Waiting for Lefty, Awake and Sing, Golden Boy, Rocket to the Moon, Till the Day I Die, and Paradise Lost. Intro. by Harold Clurman, Grove 1979 pap. $7.95

The Big Knife. Dramatists 1949 $3.25

The Country Girl. Dramatists 1950 $3.25

The Flowering Peach. Dramatists 1954 $3.25

BOOKS ABOUT ODETS

Murray, Edward. *Clifford Odets: The Thirties and After.* Ungar 1968 $11.00. Three of the early and five of the later plays are examined for structure; probing, original evaluations.

Shuman, R. Baird. *Clifford Odets. Twayne's U.S. Authors Ser.* New College & Univ. Pr. 1962 pap. $3.45

O'NEILL, EUGENE. 1888–1953. (NOBEL PRIZE 1936)

O'Neill was America's first major dramatist and remains its finest—the one American dramatist whose reputation is secure worldwide. Born in New York City, the son of the famous actor James O'Neill, the tormented circumstances of his family life are well known to those familiar with his late, great autobiographical drama *Long Day's Journey into Night.* After being suspended from Princeton University in 1907, O'Neill spent several years in various pursuits, including prospecting for gold, shipping out as a merchant seaman, acting in his father's company, writing for newspapers, and drifting. Some of his disillusionment of this period is captured in *The Iceman Cometh* (1946).

In 1912 O'Neill was hospitalized for tuberculosis, and during his six months in a sanitorium he read widely in the world's dramatic literature. By 1913 he was writing plays of his own, and in 1916 his first plays were produced by the Provincetown Players.

O'Neill's first commercial successes, *Beyond the Horizon* (1920) and *Anna Christie* (1921), were realistic, but most of his plays written in the next 12 or so years were relentlessly experimental, employing expressionistic techniques (*The Emperor Jones,* 1921, and *The Hairy Ape,* 1922), symbolism (*The Fountain,* 1925), masks (*The Great God Brown,* 1925), interior monologues (*Strange Interlude,* 1928), and the like; *Mourning Becomes Electra* (1931) was an attempt to combine Greek tragedy (it is based on Aeschylus's *Oresteia*) and Freudian psychology.

In 1934 O'Neill ceased his direct involvement with the commercial theater and devoted his remaining years to writing a projected mammoth cycle of plays on U.S. history (only *A Touch of the Poet, More Stately Mansions,* and some fragments survive), a projected series of one-act plays (of which only *Hughie* survives), and the intense, brooding autobiographical plays, *The Iceman Cometh, Long Day's Journey into Night,* and *A Moon for the Misbegotten* (1952). The plays O'Neill wrote during this final period constitute his lasting achievement.

John Gassner wrote of O'Neill that "despite his not always trustworthy flair for theatricality . . . much of his best work seemed wrung from him rather than contrived or calculated. In it, a uniquely tormented spirit subsumed much of the twentieth century's dividedness and anguish, largely existential rather than topical."

O'Neill won the Pulitzer Prize for drama for *Anna Christie, Beyond the Horizon, Strange Interlude,* and *Long Day's Journey into Night,* and the New York Drama Critics Circle Award for *Long Day's Journey into Night.*

Books by O'Neill

The Plays of Eugene O'Neill. Modern Lib. 3 vols. 1982 ea. $10.95; Random 3 vols. 1941 ea. $10.00 set $30.00

Selected Plays of Eugene O'Neill. Random 1969 $24.95. *The Emperor Jones; Anna Christie; The Hairy Ape; Desire under the Elms; The Great God Brown; Strange Interlude; Mourning Becomes Electra; The Iceman Cometh.*

Nine Plays of Eugene O'Neill. Modern Lib. 1941 $9.95. *Mourning Becomes Electra; Strange Interlude; The Emperor Jones; Marco Millions; The Great God Brown; All God's Chillun Got Wings; Lazarus Laughed; The Hairy Ape; Desire under the Elms.*

Ten "Lost" Plays. Fwd. by Bennett Cerf, Random 1964 o.p. Includes five plays not contained elsewhere; "apprentice works" that O'Neill did not wish to preserve but that are of value as a record.

Children of the Sea. Ed. by Jennifer Atkinson, Bruccoli 1972 $15.00. Four previously unpublished plays: *Children of the Sea; Bread and Butter; Now I Ask You; Shell Shock.*

The Long Voyage Home: Seven Plays of the Sea. Random (Vintage) 1972 pap. $3.95. *The Moon of the Caribbees; Bound East for Cardiff; The Long Voyage Home; In the Zone; Ile; Where the Cross Is Made; The Rope.*

Six Short Plays of Eugene O'Neill. Random (Vintage) 1965 pap. $3.95. *The Dreamy Kid; Before Breakfast; Diff'rent; Welded; The Straw; Gold.*

Three Plays: Desire under the Elms; Strange Interlude; Mourning Becomes Electra. Random (Vintage) 1959 pap. $3.95

The Later Plays. Ed. by Travis Bogard, Random 1967 pap. $3.95. *Ah, Wilderness!; A Touch of the Poet; Hughie; A Moon for the Misbegotten.*

The Theatre We Worked For: The Letters of Eugene O'Neill to Kenneth MacGowan. Ed. by Jackson R. Bryer, Yale Univ. Pr. 1982 $25.00. "As reflections of the quality of Off-Broadway theatre in the 1920's, these letters are indispensable" (Michael Manheim, *Comparative Drama*).

Anna Christie (and *The Emperor Jones* and *The Hairy Ape*). Random (Vintage) 1973 pap. $3.95

The Emperor Jones. Ed. by Max J. Herzberg, Prentice-Hall 2d ed. 1960 pap. $8.95

The Iceman Cometh. Random (Vintage) 1957 pap. $2.95

A Moon for the Misbegotten. Random (Vintage) 1974 pap. $2.95

A Touch of the Poet. Yale Univ. Pr. 1957 pap. $5.95

Long Day's Journey into Night. Yale Univ. Pr. 1950 $18.50 pap. $3.95

Hughie. Yale Univ. Pr. 1959 pap. $3.95. A one-act play.

More Stately Mansions. Ed. by Donald Gallup, rev. by Karl R. Gierow, Yale Univ. Pr. 1964 abr. ed. 1964 pap. $6.95. This full-length tragedy was to have been the fourth play in the cycle on U.S. history.

The Calms of Capricorn. Ed. by Donald Gallup, Ticknor & Fields 1982 $12.95. Gallup completed this work from a surviving scenario by O'Neill.

Chris Christoffersen: A Play in Three Acts. Random 1982 $15.00. An early version of *Anna Christie.*

Eugene O'Neill at Work: Newly Released Ideas for Plays. Ed. by Virginia Floyd, Ungar 1981 $30.00. "It would be impossible to tally the wealth of information [this book] contains" (Michael Hinden, *Comparative Drama*).

BOOKS ABOUT O'NEILL

Berlin, Normand. *Eugene O'Neill.* Grove (Everyman's) 1982 pap. $9.95. An excellent brief survey. ·

Bogard, Travis. *Contour in Time: The Plays of Eugene O'Neill.* Oxford 1972 $27.50. An important study.

Carpenter, Frederic I. *Eugene O'Neill. Twayne's U.S. Authors Ser.* G. K. Hall rev. ed. 1979 lib. bdg. $13.50; *Twayne's U.S. Authors Ser.* New College & Univ. Pr. 1964 pap. $3.45. Superb brief treatment of O'Neill; highly recommended.

Chothia, Jean. *Forging a Language: A Study of the Plays of Eugene O'Neill.* Cambridge Univ. Pr. 1980 $32.50 1982 pap. $13.95. "Insofar as Chothia aims not so much to offer new evaluations but to explicate the linguistic devices that contribute to O'Neill's success, she admirably fulfills her purpose" (Michael Hinden, *Comparative Drama*).

Falk, Doris V. *Eugene O'Neill and the Tragic Tension: An Interpretive Study of the Plays.* Gordian 2d ed. repr. of 1958 ed. 1982 $12.00; Rutgers Univ. Pr. pap. $10.00. A neo-Freudian interpretation.

Floyd, Virginia. *The Plays of Eugene O'Neill: A New Assessment. Lit. and Life Ser.* Ungar 1984 $19.50 pap. $9.95

Gassner, John, ed. *O'Neill: A Collection of Critical Essays.* Prentice-Hall (Spectrum) 1964 $12.95

Manheim, Michael. *Eugene O'Neill's New Language of Kinship.* Syracuse Univ. Pr. 1982 $24.00 pap. $12.95. "In this reading, every one of O'Neill's plays is, to some degree, disguised autobiography, and so surveying the entire repertoire results in something akin to a psychobiography of the dramatist" (T. Adler, *Comparative Drama*).

Martine, James J. *Critical Essays on Eugene O'Neill.* G. K. Hall 1984 $28.50. All new essays containing valuable new material. "Taken as a group, the essays present an excellent contemporary perspective on O'Neill criticism" (*Choice*).

Miller, Jordan Y. *Eugene O'Neill and the American Critic: A Bibliographical Checklist.* Shoe String rev. ed. 1974 $30.00. Essential for the serious student.

Raleigh, John H. *The Plays of Eugene O'Neill.* Southern Illinois Univ. Pr. 1972 pap. $2.85. Analyzes three periods in O'Neill's career, relating them to specific American cultural strands; a detailed and major study.

Sheaffer, Louis. *O'Neill: Son and Artist.* Little, Brown 1973 pap. $8.95. The second half of the monumental Sheaffer opus.

————. *O'Neill: Son and Playwright.* Little, Brown 1968 pap. $8.95. The most important biography.

Winter, S. K. *Eugene O'Neill: A Critical Study.* 1934. Russell 2d ed. enl. 1961 $17.00. The main ideas behind O'Neill's plays in the context of his times.

RABE, DAVID. 1940–

Born in Dubuque, Iowa, Rabe was educated at Loras College and Villanova. His service in Vietnam has had a major influence on his work, particularly in his early plays. In 1971 both *The Basic Training of Pavlo Hummel,* which traces a soldier's life from basic training to an ugly and ironic death in Vietnam, and *Sticks and Bones*, a slightly absurdist play that combines broad satire of U.S. family life with a realistic portrayal of the suffering of a blind veteran, were produced at Joseph Papp's New York Shakespeare Festival, where Rabe's other plays of the 1970s were also produced. *Streamers*, which won the New York Drama Critics Circle Award, is the most notable of his Vietnam plays. Set in an army barracks, it is a powerful presentation of the destruction that can result from blind, uncontrolled rage. *Hurlyburly*, which concerns the hollow life-style of a group of hip Southern Californians, began a long run on Broadway in 1984.

BOOKS BY RABE

The Basic Training of Pavlo Hummel. Penguin 1978 pap. $5.95
Streamers. Knopf 1977 $6.95
Sticks and Bones. French 1972 $3.50
The Orphan. French 1975 $3.50
In the Boom Boom Room. French 1975 $3.50; Knopf 1975 $5.95
Hurlyburly. Grove 1985 $5.95

RICE, ELMER. 1892–1967

A native of New York City, Rice studied law and passed his bar exams. However, he immediately began writing, and *On Trial*, which employed a flashback technique, made Rice an important playwright at age 22. He proceeded to study under Hatcher Hughes at Columbia University, where he also directed. He helped found the Playwrights' Company in 1938, the Dramatists Guild, and other groups. In 1951 he came to the defense of actors whose allegedly left-wing associations were causing them to lose their jobs. During his 45 years in the theater, Rice wrote 50 full-length plays, 4 novels, film and television scripts, as well as his autobiography, and *The Living Theatre*, appraising the theater in terms of the social and economic forces affecting its development.

His two masterpieces are *The Adding Machine* (1923), an expressionistic comedy wherein the hero remains a cipher in mechanized society, and *Street Scene* (1929), which was originally entitled *Landscape with Figures* because Rice considered "the [tenement] house as the real protagonist of the drama." The plot's *crime passionel* is but one aspect of the crowded panorama of tenement life. Robert Hogan writes in assessing Rice's career, "Rice has produced a remarkable body of work—large, varied, experimental and honest. . . . As a consistently experimental playwright he is rivalled in our theatre only by O'Neill." Rice won the Pulitzer Prize for drama for *Street Scene*.

BOOKS BY RICE

Elmer Rice: Three Plays. Hill & Wang 1965 $5.95. Includes *The Adding Machine, Street Scene*, and *Dream Girl*.
The Subway. French 1929 $3.50
The Left Bank. French 1931 $3.50
Dream Girl. Dramatists 1946 $3.25

The Grand Tour. Dramatists 1952 $3.25
The Winner. Dramatists 1954 $3.25
The Living Theatre. Greenwood repr. of 1959 ed. 1972 lib. bdg. $55.00
Love among the Ruins. Dramatists 1963 $3.25

BOOKS ABOUT RICE

Durham, Frank. *Elmer Rice. Twayne's U.S. Authors Ser.* G. K. Hall $14.50; *Twayne's U.S. Authors Ser.* Irvington repr. of 1970 ed. lib. bdg. $8.95 text ed. pap. $4.95
Hogan, Robert. *Independence of Elmer Rice. Crosscurrents Modern Critiques Ser.* Southern Illinois Univ. Pr. 1965 $6.95
Palmieri, Anthony F. *Elmer Rice: A Playwright's Vision of America.* Fairleigh Dickinson Univ. Pr. 1980 $23.50. "As a critical survey of Rice's plays, this book is not the 'pathfinding project' the author imagines, but it surely has value and offers the kind of insight that renders an author's work more clearly understood and therefore more appreciated" (Walter J. Meserve, *Modern Drama*).

SAROYAN, WILLIAM. 1908–1981

An Armenian-American with little formal education, Saroyan was a dramatist who disparaged the usual conventions of the form: "Plot, atmosphere, style, and all the rest of it," he wrote, "may be regarded as so much nonsense" (*Three Times Three*). His plays have been criticized as formless, and his writing as undisciplined, yet his work is imbued with fondness for the human race and contains an infectious enthusiasm for society's misfits and innocents. Saroyan's dramatic career was launched with *My Heart's in the Highlands,* a fantasy. The following year, *The Time of Your Life* was awarded the Pulitzer Prize (which Saroyan publicly refused on the grounds that commerce had no right to patronize art). This play, undoubtedly Saroyan's one enduring piece, takes place in a waterfront saloon where vivid characters can quite appropriately wander in and out and come into contact with the philosophical Joe, a man of unending generosity.

BOOKS BY SAROYAN

My Heart's in the Highlands. French 1939 $3.50
The Time of Your Life. French 1939 $3.75
The Beautiful People. French 1941 $3.50
Hello Out There. French 1941 $1.75
Get Away Old Man. French 1944 $3.50
The Cave Dwellers. French 1957 $3.50

BOOKS ABOUT SAROYAN

Lee, Lawrence, and Barry Gifford. *Saroyan: A Biography.* Harper 1984 $18.22
Saroyan, Aram. *Last Rites: The Death of William Saroyan.* Morrow 1982 $9.75

SHEPARD, SAM. 1943–

Shepard, the best dramatist currently writing in the United States, was born on an army base in Illinois and grew up mainly on a ranch in California. His first play was produced off-off-Broadway when he was 19, and he won the first of his eight Obie Awards when he was 23. A rock lyricist and a major film actor as well as a dramatist, Shepard has written more than 40 plays, winning the Pulitzer Prize for drama with *Buried Child* in 1978.

Shepard's plays show the impact of a variety of influences, including rock music, old movies, popular myths of the old West, and the 1960s drug culture. His early plays, produced off- and off-off-Broadway, are short, bizarre, surrealistic pieces tending to project images rather than provide ordered reflections of reality and are characterized by compelling monologues. These plays culminate in his early masterpiece *The Tooth of Crime*, a cross between rock concert and classical tragedy, which pits Hoss, the reigning superstar, in a verbal shoot-out against the challenger, Crow.

Shepard's later work has become more realistic and more responsive to such traditional concepts of drama as plot, character, and theme. It has also brought to the forefront his previously occasional concern for the collapse of the American dream. Bonnie Marranca wrote, "Shepard is the quintessential American playwright. His plays are American landscapes reflecting the country's iconography, myths, entertainments, archetypes, and—in a less glowing light—the corruption of its revolutionary ideals, and the disorientation of its times."

BOOKS BY SHEPARD

Seven Plays. Bantam 1981 pap. $4.50. *La Turista; The Tooth of Crime; Curse of the Starving Class; Buried Child; Savage/Love; Tongues; True West.*

Fool for Love and Other Plays. Bantam 1984 pap. $6.95. *Melodrama Play; Cowboy Mouth; Geography of a Horse-Dreamer; Action; Angel City; Suicide in B-Flat; Seduced; Fool for Love.*

Angel City: Curse of the Starving Class and Other Plays. Limelight Eds. 1984 $18.95 pap. $9.95. Also contains *Cowboys 2; Rock Garden; Cowboy Mouth; Action; Killer's Head; Sam Shepard: Nine Random Years* (by Patti Smith).

Buried Child, Seduced, and Suicide in B-Flat. Limelight Eds. 1984 $18.95 pap. $9.95

Chicago and Other Plays. Limelight Eds. 1984 $18.95 pap. $9.95. *Chicago; Icarus' Mother; Fourteen Hundred Thousand; Red Cross; Melodrama Play.*

Four Two-Act Plays. Limelight Eds. 1984 $18.95 pap. $9.95. *La Turista; Operation Sidewinder; Geography of a Horse-Dreamer; The Tooth of Crime.*

The Unseen Hand and Other Plays. Limelight Eds. 1984 $18.95 pap. $9.95. *The 4-H Club; Forensic and the Navigators; The Unseen Hand; The Holy Ghostly; Shaved Splits; Back Bog Beast Bait.*

BOOKS ABOUT SHEPARD

Auerbach, Doris. *Sam Shepard, Arthur Kopit, and the Off-Broadway Theater*. Twayne's U.S. Authors Ser. G. K. Hall 1982 $14.50. A useful introduction, but uneven and too broad in its coverage.

Marranca, Bonnie, ed. *American Dreams: The Imagination of Sam Shepard*. Performing Arts 1981 pap. $8.95. A collection of new and reprinted essays on several Shepard plays.

Mottram, Ron. *Inner Landscapes: The Theater of Sam Shepard*. Univ. of Missouri Pr. 1984 pap. $7.95. The first full-length study devoted to Shepard.

SIMON, NEIL. 1927–

Born in the Bronx, Simon had childhood ambitions to be a doctor, but after attending New York University and the University of Denver, he turned instead to television, writing comedy for Sid Caesar, Phil Silvers, and others. His first play, *Come Blow Your Horn* (1958), about a young rebel who moves into the luxurious apartment of his older brother, is partly autobiographical. Since then, Simon has written many successful comedies. Most are about the middle class, the comedy basically deriving from situations of personal frustration. In recent years Simon's plays, such as *Chapter Two*, *Brighton Beach Memoirs*, and *Biloxi Blues*, have become increasingly autobiographical. His detractors have accused him of superficiality and being essentially a "gag writer." But Walter Kerr defends Simon's artistry in writing that his work "has a much more serious, perceptive, human base to it than ordinary mechanical farce. . . he does have an eye and an ear for the crazy, cruel world about him."

BOOKS BY SIMON

Comedy of Neil Simon. Random 1971 $25.00. *Come Blow Your Horn; The Star-Spangled Girl; Barefoot in the Park; The Odd Couple; Plaza Suite; Last of the Red Hot Lovers; The Gingerbread Lady; The Prisoner of Second Avenue.*
The Collected Plays of Neil Simon. Avon 1980 pap. $7.95; Random 1979 $25.00. *The Sunshine Boys; The Good Doctor; God's Favorite; California Suite; Little Me* (with Carolyn Leigh and Cy Coleman); *Chapter Two.*
Barefoot in the Park. Random 1964 $9.95
The Odd Couple. Random 1966 $10.95
Plaza Suite. Random 1969 $9.95
The Prisoner of Second Avenue. Random 1972 $9.95
The Sunshine Boys. Random 1973 $9.95
California Suite. Random 1977 $9.95
Chapter Two. Random 1979 $9.95
They're Playing Our Song. Random 1980 $9.95
I Ought to Be in Pictures. Random 1981 $9.95
Fools. Random 1982 $10.50
Brighton Beach Memoirs: A Play. Random 1984 $10.95

BOOKS ABOUT SIMON

Johnson, Robert K. *Neil Simon. Twayne's U.S. Authors Ser*. G. K. Hall 1984 $16.95. ". . . an effective attempt to bring Simon's work the serious critical attention it deserves" (*Choice*).
McGovern, Edythe M. *Neil Simon: A Critical Study*. Ungar 1979 $14.50. Contains useful summaries of the plays.
———. *Not So Simple Neil Simon*. Intro. by Neil Simon, Perivale Pr. 1978 pap. $7.95

van ITALLIE, JEAN-CLAUDE. 1935–

Van Itallie was born in Brussels and grew up in Great Neck, New York, which, he says, "left me with a horror of the American suburbs." After graduating from Harvard, he got involved with the Open Theatre group under the direction of Joe Chaikin, producing as a result some of the most stunning and innovative experimental theater work of the 1960s, especially *America Hurrah*, a 1965 trilogy consisting of *Interview, TV*, and *Motel*, and *The Serpent*, a 1968 ritualistic and largely mimed theatrical piece that grew out of improvisations on *Genesis* and juxtaposes biblical events with current ones. Van Itallie's plays of the 1970s, which include *A Fable* and *Bag Lady*, have been more traditional in form and simpler in scope, and he has also adapted several of CHEKHOV's plays. In 1983 he returned to the mode of *The Serpent* in *The Tibetan Book of the Dead*, but with notably less success.

BOOKS BY VAN ITALLIE

Five Short Plays. Dramatists 1967 $3.25. *War; Where Is De Queen; Almost Like Being; The Hunter and the Bird; I'm Really Here*.

Seven Short and Very Short Plays. Dramatists 1973 $3.25. *Eat Cake; Take a Deep Breath; Photographs: Mary and Howard; Harold; Thoughts on the Instant of Greeting a Friend in the Street; The Naked Nun; The Girl and the Soldier*.

Early Warnings: Three Related Short Plays. Dramatists *Sunset Freeway* and *Final Orders* $3.25 *Bag Lady* $1.75

America Hurrah. Dramatists 1965 $3.25

The Serpent. Dramatists 1968 $3.25

Mystery Play. Dramatists 1973 $3.25

A Fable. Dramatists 1976 pap. $3.25

The King of the United States. Dramatists 1976 $3.25

The Tibetan Book of the Dead. Dramatists 1983 $3.25

THURBER, JAMES. 1894–1961

[SEE Volume 1.]

WILDER, THORNTON. 1897–1975

Wilder, also a Pulitzer Prize novelist, was born in Wisconsin and educated at Oberlin College and Yale and Princeton universities. His drama, which consistently celebrates human existence, reflects his vast learning in its allusions, borrowings, and experimentation. But it also captures a basic simplicity that has made one of his plays, *Our Town*, one of the most popular and enduring works of the American theater. He made use of antinaturalistic Eastern and classical dramatic traditions and European mystery plays in order to free his work from the conventions of realism and to experiment with stage space and time.

Our Town (1938) is a tender portrait of small-town people, oblivious, except for the heroine (who dies at the end of the play), to what it is to be alive. *The Matchmaker* (1938), a comedy, later formed the basis for *Hello, Dolly*. *The Skin of Our Teeth* (1942) is an expressionist fantasy depicting a suburban family and its freewheeling maid, surviving through war, the Great Flood, and the Ice Age. Much of the material for this play is derived from JAMES JOYCE's (see Vol. 1) experimental novel *Finnegans Wake*, but Wilder quite reasonably argued that "literature has always more resembled a torch race than a furious dispute among heirs." Wilder won the Pulitzer Prize for *Our Town* and *The Skin of Our Teeth*. See also Volume 1, Chapter 14.

Books by Wilder

The Long Christmas Dinner and Other Plays in One Act. Avon 1980 pap. $2.50. Includes *Queens of France; Pullman Car Hiawatha; Love, and How to Cure It; The Happy Journey to Trenton and Camden.*

Three Plays: Our Town, Skin of Our Teeth, Matchmaker. Harper 1957 $14.95. The author's preface is an important contribution to dramatic technique and theater history.

Our Town. Avon 1975 pap. $2.25; Harper 1960 $13.41

The Alcestiad; or Life in the Sun: A Play in Three Acts with a Satyr Play, The Drunken Sisters. Avon 1979 pap. $2.25; Harper 1977 $8.95 1979 pap. $3.95. The main work is adapted from Euripides' *Alcestis.*

Books about Wilder

Burbank, Rex J. *Thornton Wilder. Twayne's U.S. Authors Ser.* G. K. Hall 2d ed. 1978 lib. bdg. $12.50; *Twayne's U.S. Authors Ser.* New College & Univ. Pr. 1961 pap. $5.95

Goldstein, Malcolm. *The Art of Thornton Wilder.* Univ. of Nebraska Pr. 1965 pap. $4.25. "An excellent book on the highlights of Wilder's thought, but [there is] not enough about his art" (*N.Y. Times*).

Harrison, Gilbert A. *The Enthusiast: A Life of Thornton Wilder.* Ticknor & Fields 1983 $19.95

Stresau, Hermann. *Thornton Wilder.* Trans. by Frieda Schutze, *Lit. and Life Ser.* Ungar 1971 pap. $5.95

Wilder, Amos N. *Thornton Wilder and His Public.* Fortress Pr. 1980 $8.95. This brief book by Wilder's older brother, a Harvard emeritus professor of divinity, contains valuable personal reminiscences and other material not available elsewhere.

WILLIAMS, TENNESSEE. 1911–1983

After O'Neill, Williams is the best dramatist the United States has yet produced. Born in his grandfather's rectory in Columbus, Mississippi, his family later moved to St. Louis. There Williams endured many bad years caused by the abuse of his father and anguish concerning his introverted sister, who was later permanently institutionalized. Williams attended the University of Missouri, and, after time out to clerk for a shoe company and for his own mental breakdown, Washington University of St. Louis and the University of Iowa, from which he graduated in 1938.

Williams began writing plays in 1935. During 1943 he spent six months as a contract screen writer for MGM, but produced only one script, *The Gentleman Caller*, which, when MGM rejected it, Williams turned into his first major success, *The Glass Menagerie.* In this intensely autobiographical play, he dramatizes the story of Amanda, who dreams of restoring her lost past by finding a gentleman caller for her crippled daughter, and of Tom, who longs to escape from the responsibility of supporting his mother and sister.

After *The Glass Menagerie*, Williams wrote his masterpiece, *A Streetcar Named Desire*, and a steady stream of further plays, among them such major works as *Cat on a Hot Tin Roof* and *Suddenly Last Summer.* His plays celebrate the "fugitive kind," the sensitive outcasts whose status allows them to perceive the horror of the world and who often give additional witness to it by becoming its victims. Stephen S. Stanton has summed up Williams's "virtues and strengths" as "a genius for portraiture, particularly of women, a sensitive ear for dialogue and the rhythms of natural speech, a comic talent often manifesting itself in 'black comedy,' and a genuine theatrical flair exhibited in telling stage effects attained through lighting, costume, music, and movements." After *The Night of the Iguana* (1961) Williams continued to write profusely—and constantly to revise his work—but it became more difficult to get productions of his plays and, if they were produced, critical or popular acclaim for them.

Williams won the Pulitzer Prize for drama for *A Streetcar Named Desire* and *Cat on a Hot Tin Roof*. He won the New York Drama Critics Circle Award for these two and for *The Glass Menagerie* and *The Night of the Iguana*.

BOOKS BY WILLIAMS

The Theatre of Tennessee Williams. New Directions 7 vols. 1972–81 ea. $17.95–$21.95. Vol. 1: *Battle of Angels; A Streetcar Named Desire; The Glass Menagerie*. Vol. 2: *The Eccentricities of a Nightingale; Summer and Smoke; The Rose Tattoo; Camino Real*. Vol. 3: *Cat on a Hot Tin Roof; Orpheus Descending; Suddenly Last Summer*. Vol. 4: *Sweet Bird of Youth; Period of Adjustment; The Night of the Iguana*. Vol. 5: *The Milk Train Doesn't Stop Here Anymore; Kingdom of Earth; Small Craft Warnings; The Two-Character Play*. Vol. 6: *This Property Is Condemned; The Purification; The Last of My Solid Gold Watches; Auto-da-Fe; The Strangest Kind of Romance; Twenty-Seven Wagons Full of Cotton; The Lady of Larkspur Lotion; Hello from Bertha; Portrait of a Madonna; Lord Byron's Love Letters; The Long Goodbye; Something Unspoken; Talk to Me Like the Rain and Let Me Listen*. Vol. 7: *In the Bar of a Tokyo Hotel; The Mutilated; Gnädiges Fraulein; I Rise in Flames, Cried the Phoenix; I Can't Imagine Tomorrow; Confessional; Frosted Glass Coffin; Perfect Analysis Given by a Parrot*.
American Blues: Five One-Act Plays. Dramatists 1948 $3.25. *Mooney's Kid Don't Cry; Ten Blocks on the Camino Real; The Case of the Crushed Petunias; The Dark Room; The Long Stay Cut Short*.
Twenty-Seven Wagons Full of Cotton and Other One-Act Plays. 1946. New Directions 3d ed. 1953 pap. $5.95. Same contents as Vol. 6 of *The Theatre of Tennessee Williams*.
Four Plays. New Amer. Lib. (Signet Class.) 1976 pap. $3.95. *Summer and Smoke; Orpheus Descending; Suddenly Last Summer; Period of Adjustment*.
Three by Tennessee Williams. New Amer. Lib. (Signet Class.) 1976 pap. $3.95. *Sweet Bird of Youth; The Rose Tattoo; The Night of the Iguana*.
Dragon Country: Eight Plays. New Directions 1970 $7.50 pap. $5.75. Same contents as Vol. 7 of *The Theatre of Tennessee Williams*.
Tennessee Williams: Memoirs. Doubleday 1975 $14.95; Doubleday (Anchor) 1983 pap. $8.95
Battle of Angels. Dramatists 1940 $3.25
The Glass Menagerie. 1945. New Directions 1949 pap. $3.95
A Streetcar Named Desire. New Amer. Lib. (Signet Class.) repr. of 1947 ed. 1984 pap. $2.50; New Directions 1980 pap. $3.95

The Rose Tattoo. Dramatists 1951 $3.25
Camino Real. 1953. New Directions 1970 pap. $5.95
Cat on a Hot Tin Roof. 1955. New Amer. Lib. (Signet Class.) pap. $2.50; New Directions rev. ed. 1975 pap. $5.95. The New American Library edition contains two versions of Act III: Williams's original version and the version Elia Kazan persuaded him to produce for the first Broadway production.
Sweet Bird of Youth. 1959. New Directions 1975 pap. $4.95
Period of Adjustment. Dramatists 1960 $3.25; New Directions 1960 $6.50
The Milk Train Doesn't Stop Here Anymore. Dramatists 1962 $3.25
The Eccentricities of a Nightingale. Dramatists 1964 $3.25. A revised version of *Summer and Smoke.*
Kingdom of Earth. Dramatists 1968 $3.25
Small Craft Warnings. New Directions 1972 $4.95
The Two-Character Play. New Directions rev. ed. pap. $4.25. Alternative title: *Out Cry.*
Vieux Carré. New Directions 1979 $9.50 pap. $4.95
A Lovely Sunday for Crève Coeur. New Directions 1980 $9.50 pap. $3.95
Something Cloudy, Something Clear. Dramatists 1981 $3.25
Clothes for a Summer Hotel. New Directions 1983 $12.00 pap. $4.95

BOOKS ABOUT WILLIAMS

Falk, Signi L. *Tennessee Williams.* Twayne's *U.S. Authors Ser.* G. K. Hall 1985 pap. $6.95; Twayne's *U.S. Authors Ser.* New College & Univ. Pr. 1961 pap. $3.45
Gunn, Drewey W. *Tennessee Williams: A Bibliography.* Scarecrow Pr. 1980 $17.00. "... a major work, indispensable for any devotee of Williams and his plays" (F. E. Eddleman, *Modern Drama*).
Hirsch, Foster. *A Portrait of the Artist: The Plays of Tennessee Williams.* Associated Faculty Pr. 1979 $12.50. Emphasizes the homosexual dimension in Williams's plays.
Londré, Felicia H. *Tennessee Williams. Lit. and Life Ser.* Ungar 1980 $12.95 1983 pap. $6.95. "... beyond an adequate compilation of the facts about the content, composition, and performances of Williams' drama, the reader comes away with no consistent statement about his characteristics and importance as a playwright" (Ina Rae Hark, *Comparative Drama*).
Nelson, Benjamin. *Tennessee Williams.* Astor-Honor 1961 $10.00. A solid, important study.
Rader, Dotson. *Tennessee: Cry of the Heart.* Doubleday 1985 $16.95. An intimate memoir by a close friend.
Spoto, Donald. *The Kindness of Strangers: The Life of Tennessee Williams.* Little, Brown 1985 $19.45
Stanton, Stephen S., ed. *Tennessee Williams: A Collection of Critical Essays. Twentieth Century Interpretations Ser.* Prentice-Hall (Spectrum) 1977 $12.95 pap. $3.95. An excellent collection of major essays, old and new, on Williams's plays.
Tharpe, Jac L., ed. *Tennessee Williams: Thirteen Essays.* Univ. Pr. of Mississippi text ed. 1980 pap. $2.00
Williams, Dakin, and Shepherd Mead. *Tennessee Williams: An Intimate Biography.* Arbor House 1983 $16.95. An anecdotal account, largely drawn from existing sources, by Williams's brother. "The portrait of Tennessee himself is painted with fraternal charity" (Michael V. Tueth, *America*).

WILSON, LANFORD. 1937–

Wilson was born in Lebanon, Missouri, and began writing plays while at the University of Chicago. In 1969, he helped found the off-Broadway Circle Theatre Company, becoming its chief playwright. He thus has had the rare opportunity to develop his craft in collaboration with a permanent company of actors and a theater in which to try out and, if necessary, revise his plays. Like *The Hot L Baltimore*, which ran for 1,166 performances and set an off-Broadway record for a nonmusical play by an American, most of Wilson's plays are vaguely realistic in manner, emphasize characters over plot, and feature likable misfits and deviants. *The Fifth of July* and *Talley's Folly* are about the same family, the Talleys of Lebanon, Missouri. *Angels Fall* concerns a group of people brought together by a nuclear accident.

Wilson won the Pulitzer Prize for drama and the New York Drama Critics Circle Award for *Talley's Folly*.

BOOKS BY WILSON

Balm in Gilead and Other Plays. Hill & Wang 1965 pap. $6.95. Includes *Home Free* and *Ludlow Fair*.

The Rimers of Eldritch and Other Plays. Hill & Wang 1967 pap. $4.95. Includes *This Is the Rill Speaking; Wandering; Days Ahead; The Madness of Lady Bright*.

The Gingham Dog. Hill & Wang 1969 $5.25

Lemon Sky. Dramatists 1970 $3.25

The Sand Castle (and *Wandering; Stoop;* and *Sextet* [*Yes*]). Dramatists 1970 $3.25

The Hot L Baltimore. Hill & Wang 1973 pap. $4.95

The Great Nebula in Orion (and *The Family Continues; Ikke, Ikke, Nye, Nye, Nye Nye;* and *Victory on Mrs. Dandywine's Island*). Dramatists 1973 $3.25

Serenading Louie. Dramatists 1976 $3.25

The Mound Builders. Hill & Wang 1976 $8.95 pap. $5.95

Brontosaurus. Dramatists 1978 $1.75

The Fifth of July. Hill & Wang 1978 $11.95 pap. $4.95

Talley's Folly. Hill & Wang 1980 pap. $5.25

Thymus Vulgaris: A One Act Play. Dramatists 1982 $1.75

Angels Fall. Hill & Wang 1983 $12.95 pap. $6.45

CHAPTER 6

World Literature

Margaret Ann Escher

This art of the novel . . . came into being . . . because the storyteller's own
experience of men and things, whether for good or ill . . . has moved him
to an emotion so passionate that he can no longer keep it shut up in his
heart. Again and again something in his own life or in that around him will
seem to the writer so important that he cannot bear to let it pass into obliv-
ion.

—LADY MURASAKI, *The Tale of Genji*

The term *world literature* has a history of diverse and changing definitions,
and present attitudes toward it reflect both this history and the critical perspectives that give rise to it. It was coined by Goethe in the nineteenth century, thus making it one of the first articulations of the notion, later to become commonplace, that the intellectual or artistic achievements of diverse
cultures might in some way constitute a "world" group. The enormous upsurge in nationalistic movements at that time in various countries led to
the emergence of the scholarly antecedents of literary internationalism,
namely to the disciplines of aesthetics and literary history. Invented to
serve the cause of nationalism, both of these disciplines soon diversified
into a more general interest in the literary history of many nations. Literary
history gradually ceased to rely for its impetus on the fervor of nationalism
and began to evolve into an autonomous intellectual activity. This in turn
created the conditions needed for the birth of "world literature."

This account shows the genesis of what has come to be regarded as the
self-evident prerogative of modern people to write literary histories of every
nation in the world; to gather them—along with certain general literary information such as descriptions and histories of genres, literary movements,
terms, and so on—into encyclopedias, dictionaries, and handbooks; and to
call the sum total world literature. This is the most common definition of
the term.

In contrast to the "encyclopedic" notion of world literature stands the
comparative approach, which during the course of its development in the
nineteenth and twentieth centuries came to be called "comparative literature." It began to emerge in the nineteenth century in response to the growing recognition of the important role played by international and universal
literary forces in the formation of various national literatures. Scholars in-

terested in this type of research have developed methods for examining the transnational dimensions of literary works, as well as standards for determining what constitutes a valid comparison and for weeding out arbitrary comparisons. Works from different cultures and written in different languages are compared on the basis of their sharing a common theme (e.g., the Faust legend), belonging to the same literary movement or period, or influencing each other. Comparative literature thus contrasts with the activities of the histories of national literatures in that it is a *critical* discipline, not an encyclopedic one.

The absence, until recently, of truly comparative histories reflects the enormity of the challenge of applying international and comparative literary concepts to national literatures in such a way as to come up with truly comprehensive accounts of their histories. However, significant progress is now being made in this area. The International Comparative Literature Association has launched a series of works examining various aspects of comparative literary history. The series, entitled *A Comparative History of Literatures in European Languages*, will eventually consist of approximately thirty volumes.

The term *world literature* has one final definition. It is often used interchangeably with the term *great books*. Every country defines its own literary canon—that broad list, constantly being revised, of works on which it sets special value. It should be no surprise that the canons of most countries are loaded heavily with works written in their native (or colonial) languages or else works from other countries that influenced their own literature. Hence, anthologies of world literature, collections of world masterpieces, and so on, present world literature from the vantage point of the culture in which they are published.

GENERAL REFERENCE AND BIBLIOGRAPHY

Bédé, Jean-Albert, and William Edgerton, eds. *Columbia Dictionary of Modern European Literature*. Columbia Univ. Pr. 2d ed. 1980 $65.00. Fully revised and enlarged from the first edition, which was edited by Horatio Smith. Almost 2,000 entries written by 500 contributors. Includes entries on 1,853 individual late nineteenth- and twentieth-century European authors and 36 European literatures. The authors' entries provide biographies and critical discussions of the principal works, and brief bibliographies. The essays on national and regional literatures provide an overview of the area's history and detailed discussions of individual authors in the context of the larger cultural environment.

Benet, William R., ed. *The Reader's Encyclopedia*. Crowell 2d ed. 1965 $21.63 thumb-indexed $24.52. Brief entries on individual works of literature, biblical characters and themes, authors, national literatures, literary movements and periods, and certain historical events and figures. The emphasis is on western European and U.S. literature and history, as well as on classical literature and the Bible. There are some African and Asian entries. Solidly researched and instructive to the student of literature.

Berthold, Margot. *A History of World Theater*. Trans. by Edith Simmons, Ungar 1972 o.p. An erudite encyclopedic survey of theater, both as performance and as literature, from antiquity to the present. It includes discussions of the theater of ancient Egypt and the ancient East, of Islam, the Indo-Pacific, China, Japan, Greece, Rome, and Byzantium. Beginning with the Middle Ages, the perspective shifts away from divisions by culture to divisions by historical periods.

Daiches, David. *Literature and Western Civilization.* Aldus 6 vols. 1972–76 o.p. These fine volumes contain articles on the literatures of Western nations and general topics in the West.

The Fiction Catalog. Wilson 10th ed. 1980 $70.00. Selected by experienced librarians, this lists works of fiction that have been found most useful in libraries in Canada and the United States. It contains works in translation from all European and Asian and many African languages. It is published every five years with four annual supplements.

Frenz, Horst, ed. *Nobel Prize Lectures: Literature, 1901–1967.* Elsevier 1969 $76.50. Sixty-three Nobel laureates in literature from 22 countries make statements reflecting the shifting tastes and values in world literature during the twentieth century.

Frye, Northrop, and Sheridan Baker. *The Harper Handbook to Literature.* Harper text ed. 1985 pap. $12.95. Short unsigned entries on literary periods, styles, forms, and movements, a glossary of literary terms, and longer essays on many topics. The focus is on literature written in English. The book does, however, include entries on philosophical and critical theories such as phenomenology and structuralism that originated outside the English-speaking world. Of particular interest to students of world literature is the "Chronology of Literature and World Events," by Barbara M. Perkins, at the end of the volume. It consists of three parallel time lines: one devoted to world events, another to events in Britain, and the last to events in the Americas. Unfortunately, the "world" time line is restricted largely to events in continental Europe, with only occasional highlights from the history of Asia.

Hochman, Stanley, ed. *McGraw-Hill Encyclopedia of World Drama.* McGraw-Hill 5 vols. 2d ed. 1983 $295.00. A valuable research tool for both the specialist and the student of drama. It contains signed survey articles on regional, national, and ethnic-linguistic drama; biographies of playwrights; a glossary of dramatic terms, forms, movements, and styles; an extensive index of playwrights, titles, genres, historical periods, theaters; an alphabetical list of titles of plays; articles on directors, performance art, stagecraft, and theater companies; many illustrations. Articles on playwrights include biographies; analytical sections assessing the writers' creative achievements both in relation to their own artistic development and to the history of drama; synopses of major plays; a playlist in which titles are given in the original language and translation; and dates of writing, publication, and original production.

Hornstein, Lillian H., and others, eds. *The Reader's Companion to World Literature.* New Amer. Lib. rev. ed. 1973 pap. $4.95. Short unsigned entries in alphabetical order on authors, works, literary types and terms, mythological figures, and literary periods and movements. This volume makes available an abundance of information in readable, easily accessible form on English, U.S., and French literature and their Greek and Roman antecedents. A few milestones of German, Italian, Russian, Scandinavian, Latin-American, and non-Western literature are included and discussed intelligently and with erudition. But the picture of "world" literature offered here is one drawn from an Anglo-American and to a lesser extent French perspective. The world of literature depicted beyond these boundaries consists of the broad massive forms of giants with little information about lesser-known works and writers.

Ivask, Ivar, and Gero von Wilpert. *World Literature since 1945: Critical Surveys of the Contemporary Literature of Europe and the Americas.* Ungar $35.00. Contains 28 unsigned essays about the national and ethnic literatures and languages of western and central Europe, the Soviet Union, the United States, Canada, and Latin America as well as Yiddish literature. Individual authors are discussed in some depth, with the emphasis on writers whose principal work was published after 1945. Most articles are organized internally by literary genre: novel, poetry, drama.

Klein, Leonard S., ed. *Encyclopedia of World Literature in the Twentieth Century.* Ungar 4 vols. 2d ed. rev. & enl. 1983–84 ea. $100.00–$130.00. Hundreds of scrupulously researched, informative, and insightful signed articles on the literatures of most of the nations of the world, major and minor writers, and literary movements. Critical analysis is usually erudite and perceptive while at the same time accessible to the lay reader. There are no separate articles on genres—the sole criticism of what is otherwise a superb achievement.

Preminger, Alex, ed. *The Princeton Encyclopedia of Poetry and Poetics.* Princeton Univ. Pr. rev. ed. 1974 $72.50 pap. $17.50. Eight hundred signed articles by more than 240 contributors on the history of each of the main bodies of world poetry as well as shorter entries on minor bodies of poetry, on the history of international and national movements in poetry, on poetic technique, on poetics and criticism, and on the interrelationship of poetry and other fields such as fine arts, music, and so on. This is an indispensable reference work and research tool for student and professional alike. The articles are broad enough in their scope to touch on and illuminate any topic related to world poetry, while specific and focused enough to enlighten the specialist.

Samples, Gordon. *The Drama Scholars' Index to Plays and Filmscripts.* Scarecrow Pr. 2 vols. 1974–80 ea. $15.00–$35.00

Seymour-Smith, Martin. *The New Guide to Modern World Literature.* Peter Bedrick 3d ed. 1985 $60.00. A monumental, enormously useful 1,400-page guide to the modern literatures of most of the nations and languages of the world. Chapters are generally divided according to country or clusters of related countries, or geographical area. Each chapter includes a history of the nation's contemporary literary events in relation to the broader historical situation, but is devoted mainly to literary biographies of major and minor writers. A good choice for a home reference library.

Shipley, Joseph T. *Dictionary of World Literature.* Little, Brown rev. ed. repr. of 1968 ed. 1972 pap. $2.50. Encyclopedia of literary terms, forms, techniques, methods, problems, and schools of criticism, with some mention of authors and critics. It includes condensed surveys of literary histories of nations. The information is dated, but even today entries are often informative and valuable.

———. *Encyclopedia of Literature: Criticism, Forms, Technique.* Philosophical Lib. 2 vols. 1946 o.p. Contains condensed surveys of the literary history of nations and biographies of authors.

Steinberg, S. H. *Cassell's Encyclopedia of World Literature.* Morrow 3 vols. 2d ed. rev. 1973 o.p. Volume 1 contains 650 signed articles on the history of national literatures, on general literary subjects such as literary genres and schools, and on subjects of general interest. In addition to articles on western, central, and eastern Europe and North America, there are articles on the literatures of Africa, Latin America, Southeast Asia, India, the Middle East, and the West Indies. Volumes 2 and 3 contain biographies of authors from all periods and continents.

Thompson, George A., Jr. *Key Sources in Comparative and World Literature: An Annotated Guide to Reference Materials*. Ungar 1983 $40.00. Thorough and well-organized annotated bibliography of reference materials and bibliographic sources pertinent to research in comparative and world literature. An invaluable resource, it is divided into chapters according to language. Also included is a chapter on the literature of Asia, one on interdisciplinary fields (e.g., literature and music), and a long, exhaustive opening chapter on comparative, general, and world literature. There are subsections on selected individual authors. Most entries are annotated. Reference works are evaluated with a view to their usefulness to research in comparative and world literature.

Ward, A. C. *Longman Companion to Twentieth Century Literature*. Rev. by Maurice Hussey, Longman 3d ed. 1981 o.p. Contains biographical and bibliographical entries on the greater and lesser writers of the twentieth century—mainly English and Scottish, but also including Commonwealth, African, U.S., Continental, and Slavic writers of international repute whose works exist in English translation. Also included are articles on such topics as autobiography and biography, genre (fiction, poetry, drama, and the essay), summaries of the plots of outstanding novels and plays, definitions of literary terms, and an article containing practical advice to writers.

Shorter Dictionaries and Handbooks

The following five handbooks and dictionaries are all excellent.

Cuddon, J. A. *A Dictionary of Literary Terms*. Doubleday 1977 $17.95; Penguin 1982 pap. $8.95. More than 2,000 terms.

Deutsch, Babette. *Poetry Handbook: Dictionary of Terms*. Barnes & Noble 4th ed. repr. of 1974 ed. 1982 pap. $5.72; Crowell 4th ed. repr. of 1974 ed. 1982 pap. $5.72; Harper 4th ed. 1974 $10.95

Fowler, Roger, ed. *A Dictionary of Modern Critical Terms*. Routledge & Kegan 1973 pap. $7.95

Hartnoll, Phyllis, ed. *The Concise Oxford Companion to the Theatre*. Oxford 1972 $19.95. An excellent shortened handbook to the theater and drama based on the full-length *Oxford Companion to the Theatre*. It contains entries on theater terms, playwrights, plays, actors, theater companies.

Yelland, H. L., and K. S. Easton. *Handbook of Literary Terms*. Writer 1980 $10.00

COMPARATIVE LITERATURE

Alridge, A. Owen. *Comparative Literature: Matter and Method*. Univ. of Illinois Pr. 1969 o.p. Seventeen essays by leading comparatists, grouped into five categories: literary criticism and theory, literary movements, literary themes, literary forms (genres), and literary relations (an enormous category including essays on literary history, history of ideas, influence studies, literature and society, literature and science, cross-cultural relations). Each section is introduced by a brief but quite informative essay by the editor that discusses the traditions, assumptions, and techniques underlying each approach.

Clements, Robert J. *Comparative Literature as Academic Discipline: A Statement of Principles, Praxis, Standards*. MLA 1978 $35.00. Clements reviews prior and current definitions of comparative literature, both theoretical and practical, as well as methods of training students in the field. This volume gives practical guidelines to research, course planning, and the teaching of comparative literature, with concrete advice on putting together a syllabus.

Corstius, Jan Brandt. *Introduction to the Study of Comparative Literature*. Random 1968 o.p. A somewhat dated but still valuable elementary introduction to comparative literature that examines the tradition of Western literary criticism, period by period, demonstrating the way in which aesthetic and other theories have crossed national boundaries and constitute a common Western heritage.

Friedrich, Werner. *Outline of Comparative Literature from Dante Alighieri to Eugene O'Neill*. Johnson Repr. repr. of 1959 ed. 1970 $65.00. "A supranational, truly comparative history of literature, stressing influences, parallels and contrasts. Index of names and topics, but no bibliography" (Stallknecht and Frenz, *Comparative Literature*). Ground-breaking and visionary when first published; now it is somewhat dated.

Jefferson, Ann, and David Robey, eds. *Modern Literary Theory: A Comparative Introduction*. Barnes & Noble 1984 pap. $10.95. A first-rate collection of essays by British scholars that examines both current and older schools of criticism and interpretive approaches. The essays are learned, astute, and up-to-date. Included are pieces on Russian formalism, linguistic criticism, Anglo-American New Criticism, structuralism and poststructuralism (Parisian), psychoanalytic criticism, and Marxist Criticism. Also included are indexes of concepts and of names and an excellent bibliography. Highly recommended.

Jost, François. *Introduction to Comparative Literature*. Pegasus 1974 $14.95. This is a very good practical and theoretical introduction to comparative literature. It explains and demonstrates in detail four basic comparative approaches to literature in the study of literary analogies and influences; literary movements and trends; genres and forms; motifs, types, and themes. Excellent bibliography, although no longer up-to-date.

Nichols, Stephen G., Jr., and Richard B. Vowles, eds. *Comparatists at Work: Studies in Comparative Literature*. Blaisdale 1968 o.p. An excellent comparative "sampler," including essays by Rene Wellek, Claudio Guillen, Harry Levin, Haskell Block, and W. Bernard Fleischmann. The largest group of essays is devoted to analysis of texts, both novels and poetry, from a diversity of perspectives. There is also a group of essays on critical theory. Excellent essays on the history of ideas and on literature and the other arts are included.

Prawer, S. S. *Comparative Literary Studies: An Introduction*. Barnes & Noble 1973 o.p. A learned, exhaustive, and very readable outline and critical examination of the methods and theoretical foundations of comparative literature. Modestly subtitled "an introduction," it is indeed that, but the specialist will find it provocative, too. Prawer knows what other comparatists say about the discipline and how their pronouncements apply in practice to their work. He integrates this knowledge, along with his own keen evaluations and judgments, into each of the ten chapters on the theory and practice of the discipline.

Shaffer, E. S., ed. *Comparative Criticism: A Yearbook*. Cambridge Univ. Pr. 4 vols. 1980–82 ea. $37.50–$49.50. A valuable collection of essays, mainly by British comparatists. "Our intention . . . is to explore the notion of literary canon as it relates to the present situation within literary studies in Britain" (Preface). The collection includes seven impressive essays that examine various facets of the Western and Near Eastern literary tradition.

Stallknecht, Newton P., and Horst Frenz, eds. *Comparative Literature: Method and*

Perspective. Southern Illinois Univ. Pr. rev. ed. 1971 $10.00 1973 pap. $2.85.
Twelve essays on the history and methods of comparative literature by prominent members of the profession. The essays provide important insights into the
assumptions underlying the discipline, although they at times seem dated.

Weisstein, Ulrich. *Comparative Literature and Literary Theory: Survey and Introduction*. Trans. by William Riggan, Indiana Univ. Pr. 1974 $12.50. A learned and
critically astute examination of the basic approaches underlying comparative
literature, seen both in the historical context of their evolution in Western culture and within the discipline, and prescriptively, as they should be conceived
of and applied. Weisstein analyzes in depth the basic approaches to comparative literature: influence; movements, epochs, periods, and generations; genre
studies, the study of themes; interrelationships with the other arts. He examines
and evaluates the ways in which prominent scholars use these approaches in
their own work. His appendixes on the prehistory and history of the discipline
and on the problematics of compiling comparative bibliographies are excellent.

Wellek, Rene. *Discriminations: Further Concepts of Criticism*. Yale Univ. Pr. 1970
$37.50. Wellek advocates in all of his writings and in this book in particular the
need for a "genuinely universal study of world literature." *Discriminations* is a
major study by one of the most influential scholars in the field. It is particularly
accessible to the general reader and to students just beginning to work in comparative literature. Although the essays stand on their own, the book identifies
itself as a sequel to Wellek's 1963 work, *Concepts of Criticism*, which is also
highly recommended.

Wellek, Rene, and Austin Warren. *Theory of Literature*. Harcourt rev. ed. 1956 pap.
$5.95. A rigorous, seminal early work that examines many aspects of the prac-
tice of literary analysis in numerous short essays. It is a systematic discussion of
aspects of literary theory within a general rather than a historical framework.
Entries are terse and pointed, at times reading like outlines intended for future
elaboration. Can be forbidding to an inexperienced reader.

COLLECTIONS AND ANTHOLOGIES: GENERAL

Anderson, G. L., ed. *Masterpieces of the Orient*. Norton 1961 pap. $11.95. "This vol-
ume contains extracts from the literatures of Arabia, Persia, India, China and Japan" (Preface). The only anthology of its kind in the United States.

Dube, Anthony, and others. *Structure and Meaning: An Introduction to Literature*.
Houghton Mifflin 2d ed. text ed. 1983 $21.95. An anthology of fiction, poetry,
drama, and criticism.

Laughlin, James, and Elizabeth Harper, eds. *New Directions in Prose and Poetry*.
New Directions Annual 1985 vol. 49 $19.50 pap. $9.95

Mack, Maynard, ed. *The Norton Anthology of World Masterpieces*. Norton 2 vols. 5th
ed. text ed. 1985 ea. $20.95 pap. ea. $18.95. Volume 1 of this fine anthology is divided into three sections—masterpieces of the Ancient World, of the Middle
Ages, and of the Renaissance—and provides students with a good general introduction to Western literature before the Renaissance. Each section begins with
an admirable general essay and works are preceded by excellent biographical
and critical essays. Volume 2 is a discriminating selection of mostly western European, English, U.S., and Russian literature, with a very small sprinkling of
works from Asia, Africa, and South America. Poetry, prose, and drama are represented. The final selection of the volume, entitled "Contemporary Explorations,"

contains an admirably diverse selection of pieces, each of them "contemporary" in a different way, and possessing the seed of a possible future development in literature.

———. *The Norton Anthology of World Masterpieces: Fourth Continental Edition in One Volume.* Norton 1980 o.p. This volume "is an anthology of Western literature containing only writings from the ancient and modern foreign languages . . . the literatures represented in it include Greek, Latin, Hebrew, Gaelic, French, German, Italian, Spanish, Russian, Norwegian, Swedish and Yiddish" (Preface). The finest one-volume anthology of biblical and European literature published in the United States. Especially notable are the excellent writings from the Middle Ages, which are not readily available in any other form in the United States. This volume is divided into seven sections, each beginning with a fine introductory essay and containing biographical and critical information about the authors, as well as bibliographies related to their work. Works are often footnoted.

Wilkie, Brian, and James Hurt. *Literature of the Western World.* Macmillan 2 vols. text ed. 1984 consult publisher for price. Volume 1 of this excellent new anthology of masterpieces of antiquity and western Europe has very fine comprehensive essays introducing the three periods covered in the volume (antiquity, the Middle Ages, and the Renaissance). Biographical and critical articles precede the writings of each new writer. Of particular value are the annotated bibliographies that follow each writer's works. Finally, the volume includes two parallel world time lines, one following political and social events and the other intellectual and cultural events. The dates of the lives of the authors are given on the facing pages. Volume 2 includes another very good although often too heavily English and American selection of prose and poetry. Here too generous excerpts and often entire works are printed. "Rather than offer sketchy representations of two authors of equal rank, we have occasionally chosen to represent one of them more extensively . . . the result, we hope, is depth as well as breadth of coverage and a series of substantial works or selections" (Preface). The editors' decision to exclude all poetry not originally written in English resulted in the exclusion of such giants as Baudelaire, Rilke, and Neruda, to name just three from the modern era.

COLLECTIONS AND ANTHOLOGIES: PROSE FICTION

Albrecht, Robert C., ed. *World of Short Fiction.* Macmillan (Free Pr.) text ed. 1970 pap. $10.95

Angoff, Charles, and Clarence R. Decker, eds. *Modern Stories from Many Lands.* Manyland 2d ed. enl. 1972 $7.95

Angus, Douglas, ed. *Best Short Stories of the Modern Age.* Fawcett 1978 pap. $2.50

Bonheim, Helmut. *The Narrative Modes: Techniques of the Short Story.* Longwood Pr. text ed. 1982 $30.00. Stories in German, English, French, Italian, and Russian.

Clark, Barrett H., and Maxim Lieber, eds. *Best Short Stories of the World.* Norwood repr. of 1926 ed. 1978 lib. bdg. $50.00

Crane, Milton, ed. *Fifty Great Short Stories.* Bantam pap. $3.95

Eberhart, Richard, and Selden Rodman, eds. *War and the Poet.* Greenwood repr. of 1945 ed. 1974 lib. bdg. $45.00

Gullason, Thomas A., and Leonard Casper, eds. *The World of Short Fiction: An International Collection.* Harper 2d ed. 1971 o.p.

Manguel, Alberto, ed. *Black Water: The Book of Fantastic Literature*. Crown 1984 pap.
  $11.95. Fantastic literature from Latin America, France, Germany, Italy, Russia,
  and Denmark.
Stroud, Theodore Albert, ed. *The Literature of Comedy: An Anthology*. Ginn Pr. 1968
  o.p.

COLLECTIONS AND ANTHOLOGIES: POETRY

Barnstone, Aliki, and Willis Barnstone. *A Book of Woman Poets, Book of Puzzlements:
  From Antiquity to Now*. Schocken 1981 $29.95 pap. $12.95. Poetry in 35 languages. Excellent anthology.
Burnshaw, Stanley, ed. *The Poem Itself*. Harper text ed. 1976 pap. $5.95; Horizon Pr.
  1980 pap. $7.95
Cosman, Carol. *The Penguin Book of Woman Poets*. Penguin Poets Ser. 1979 pap.
  $5.95; Viking 1979 $14.95. Excellent anthology.
Nims, John F. *Sappho to Valery: Poems in Translation*. Princeton Univ. Pr. 1980
  $25.00 pap. $11.95. Nims has done beautiful translations of poetry from antiquity to the early part of the twentieth century, from Greek, Catalan, Provençal,
  Galician, Spanish, French, German, and Italian. Original-language versions of
  poems are included on facing pages.
Tomlinson, Charles, ed. *The Oxford Book of Verse in English Translation*. Oxford 1980
  $37.50 pap. $12.95. Verse from Latin, Greek, French, German, Italian, Spanish,
  Navajo, Chinese, Russian, Polish, Hungarian, and other languages, translated by
  celebrated British and American people of letters from the English Renaissance
  to the present.
Van Doren, Mark. *An Anthology of World Poets*. Harcourt 1936 $45.00
Weissbort, Daniel, and Ted Hughes, eds. *Modern Poetry in Translation*. Persea 1983
  pap. $9.95. An excellent selection of poetry in translation from antiquity to the
  present, spanning all continents. Reviews of translations and books on translation theory, including an excellent review and assessment of current translation
  theory by Andre Lefevere, are also included.

COLLECTIONS AND ANTHOLOGIES: DRAMA

Barnet, Sylvan, and others, eds. *Eight Great Comedies: Clouds, Mandragola, Twelfth
  Night, Miser, Beggar's Opera, Importance of Being Earnest, Uncle Vanya, Arms
  and the Man*. New Amer. Lib. pap. $4.95. Comedies by Aristophanes, Machia-
  velli, Shakespeare, Molière, Gay, Wilde, Chekhov, and Shaw.
Bentley, Eric, ed. *The Classic Theatre*. Doubleday (Anchor) 4 vols. pap. ea. $2.95–
  $7.50; Peter Smith 4 vols. $27.75. An excellent series. These plays are not readily
  available in any other form in the United States.
———. *Modern Theatre*. Peter Smith 6 vols. o.p.
Clark, Barrett H., ed. *World Drama*. Dover 2 vols. pap. ea. $8.95–$9.95; Peter Smith
  2 vols. $16.00. Volume 1 contains 26 plays from the Orient, medieval Europe,
  England, ancient Greece and Rome, and India. Volume 2 contains 20 plays from
  Italy, Spain, France, Germany, Denmark, Russia, and Norway.
Kriegel, Harriet, ed. *Women in Drama: An Anthology*. New Amer. Lib. 1975 pap.
  $4.95. Plays about womanhood from antiquity to early twentieth-century Eu-
  rope.

Nicoll, Allardyce. *World Drama: From Aeschylus to Anouilh*. Barnes & Noble 2d ed. rev. & enl. text ed. 1976 $45.00

TRANSLATION

This bibliography represents the latest and most ground-breaking work now being done in translation theory.

Bassnett-McGuire, Susan. *Translation Studies*. Methuen 1981 $15.95 pap. $7.95. Most recent general introduction to translation theory. Excellent.

Brower, Reuben. *Mirror on Mirror: Translation, Imitation, Parody. Studies in Comparative Lit*. Harvard Univ. Pr. 1974 $15.00. An interesting collection of essays but diffuse.

Kelly, Louis. *The True Interpreter*. Basil Blackwell 1979 o.p. A good history of translation in the West.

Lefevere, Andre. *Translating Literature: The German Tradition from Luther to Rosenzwieg*. Humanities Pr. text ed. 1977 pap. $12.00. This is a collection of historically important texts, from Martin Luther to Walter Benjamin, some of which have never before been translated into English.

Newmark, Peter. *Approaches to Translation: Aspects of Translation*. Pergamon 1980 $23.95 pap. $10.95. Linguistic research in translation theory.

Nida, Eugene A., and C. R. Taber, eds. *The Theory and Practice of Translation*. Amer. Bible Society 1969 $8.00. This is an older but very valuable introduction to translation theory along linguistic and anthropological lines. The writers use the Bible, as well as narratives from West African culture, as material.

Savory, Theodore. *The Art of Translation*. Jonathan Cape 1968 o.p. A layperson's introduction to translation theory that is impressionistic, but fun and good nonetheless.

Steiner, George. *After Babel: Aspects of Language and Translation*. Oxford 1975 pap. $12.95. This is one of the great works on translation, a monument to the subject. According to Steiner, everything pertaining to the use of language is translation. The work is anecdotal, filled with examples. It is somewhat too long, but that is not a serious problem.

Wills, Wolfram. *The Science of Translation: Theoretical and Applicative Aspects*. Benjamins 1982 pap. $24.00. This is the most recent introduction to translation theory on linguistic grounds. Methodical, rigorous.

Zuber, O. *The Languages of Theatre: Problems in the Translation and Transposition of Drama*. Pergamon 1980 $39.00. This is the first study done on the various ways of translating for the theater and of getting translated plays produced. Full of information. A very valuable collection of essays.

CHAPTER 7

Greek Literature

Marshall Hurwitz

Even a noble deed will die, if passed over in silence.

—PINDAR, fragment 121

What has come down to us from ancient Greek literature is a fraction of what once existed. The literary remains of that extraordinary culture have been sifted and filtered through many generations, and only the more successful or most consistently read works have survived. Archaeological discoveries have occasionally supplemented our knowledge, but a host of authors and works still remain known only in the citations of their contemporaries.

Homer, for example, had many anonymous antecedents whose works were orally transmitted. Only by understanding Homer's debt to his predecessors can one understand the high degree of sophistication in the two epics in his name. *The Odyssey* is peopled with memorable characters set in the context of an exciting adventure story. We have the names of some of Homer's contemporaries who also derived from this oral tradition (Arctinus of Miletus, Agias of Trozen, and others), but their works, even though they also employed the Trojan War as a theme, have not survived. From the few fragments and summaries of the works that survive, readers might infer that Homer stood out among these bards.

The greatest loss, however, is in the area of lyric poetry. Surviving fragments of Archilochus, Sappho, Alcaeus, and others are fleeting images or incomplete poems. In the centuries that followed Homer, these poets created a literature of personal emotion in finely polished gems of poetry unlike the longer narratives of Homer's epic or Hesiod's didactic poetry. In choral lyrics they created forms to celebrate weddings (*epithalamia, prothalamia*) and to glorify wine, women, and song (*skolia*). Only the remains of Pindar are extensive enough to let us evaluate firsthand his poetic achievement.

One form of lyric poetry, the dithyramb (a poem dedicated to Dionysus), leads directly into the dramatic form of tragedy. According to the tradition, annual performances of dithyrambs accompanied the Dionysiac festivals. In the sixth century Thespis conceived the idea of having one actor leave the chorus to recite the dialogue, and thus dramatic festivals began. Of the dozens of playwrights whose names are known, the works of only three have been transmitted to us—Aeschylus, Sophocles, and Euripides.

Old Comedy, possibly in imitation of tragedy, was also a part of a festival. The sole representative of this type of comedy whose writings have survived intact, Aristophanes, is full of robust and unrestrained humor. As a social critic and antiwar patriot he mercilessly makes fun of his contemporary political leaders; sex and religion too are subjected to his witty barbs.

The fifth century B.C. witnessed the rise of prose to an art form. Originally used for practical matters, prose was conceived of as purely functional. Its use among historians, philosophers, and orators was intended for something more than mere recording; prose that succeeded in immortalizing thoughts or insights was applauded by the contemporary Greek audience. The study of rhetoric that was promoted by the sophistic movement helped to create an atmosphere in which prose grained new respect.

We have the speeches of some of the great orators of the fifth and fourth centuries B.C.—Antiphon, Andocides, Lysias, Isaeus—but the greatest of these was Demosthenes. He attempted to rouse the Athenians to an awareness of the threat from Macedonia in his *Philippics* and *On the Crown*. He was unsuccessful. Philip came down from Macedonia and his son Alexander conquered the Mediterranean world, thus changing the whole character of Greek civilization.

The next age of Greek literature, the Hellenistic period, is quite different from the period that preceded it. Not only do foreign influences appear, but much of the literature is produced on foreign soil. In Alexandria, Egypt, the poets Theocritus, Bion, and Moschus develop the conventions of pastoral poetry, and Callimachus and his disciples refine the elegant short poem. In Rome POLYBIUS (see Vol. 3) writes a history in straightforward prose, analyzing and describing the rise of Rome as a power in the world. In Judaea and the Jewish diaspora a whole corpus of Greek literature develops (including the Apocrypha, the pseudepigrapha, Philo Judaeus, Josephus, and even the New Testament). Besides the revival of old forms as in the epic *Argonautica* by Apollonius of Rhodes, many new forms are created. Comedy undergoes a major transformation; instead of the robust critique of political, social, and sexual matters found in Aristophanes, New Comedy focuses on family relations (the stern father, the irresponsible son, the tricky slave, and so on). Biography and the novel have precursors in the earlier period but it is in the late Hellenistic times that these forms reach their ancient culmination—biography in Plutarch and novels in Longus and Heliodorus. Satire develops out of the earlier Cynical-Stoic diatribes and reaches its epitome in the dialogues of Lucian. Greek philosophy charts a new course in this period with the birth of Epicureanism and Stoicism and other important movements in the history of Western thought.

The rise of Rome in the political sphere and the rise of Christianity in the spiritual sphere radically transformed the world, and ancient Greece and its literary products became a prized heritage. Only the later European Renaissance was successful in resurrecting the Greek spirit and placing the literary remains of that culture as a foundation for our later cultures.

CLASSICAL LITERATURE

History and Criticism

Bieber, Margaret. *The History of the Greek and Roman Theater.* Princeton Univ. Pr. rev. ed. 1980 $60.00 pap. $17.95. Indispensable for understanding the appearance of ancient theaters.

Bolgar, R. R. *Classical Influences on European Culture, A.D. 500–1500.* Cambridge Univ. Pr. 1971 $59.50. An excellent guide to the classical tradition in European culture after the fall of Rome.

Cambridge Ancient History Series. Cambridge Univ. Pr. 12 vols. consult publisher for prices. The standard history of antiquity; highly recommended for its careful, detailed presentation.

Ceram, C. W. *Gods, Graves, and Scholars: The Story of Archaeology.* Knopf rev. ed. 1967 $20.00. Tells the story of archaeological discoveries in a lively and suspenseful style that makes wonderful reading.

Dover, Kenneth. *Ancient Greek Literature.* Oxford 1980 $17.95 pap. $6.95. A collection of popular essays by such outstanding scholars as Dover, M. L. West, and K. Griffin on different periods of Greek literature.

Eastling, P. E., and B. M. Knox. *Cambridge History of Classical Literature.* Cambridge Univ. Pr. 1985 vol. 1 $85.00. If this volume of essays by many different scholars is as good as the Cambridge University Press volume on Latin literature, edited by E. J. Kenney and W. V. Clausen, then this will be a most important volume.

Ehrenberg, Victor L. *Society and Civilization in Greece and Rome.* Harvard Univ. Pr. 1964 $8.95

Frankel, Hermann. *Early Greek Poetry and Philosophy.* Trans. by James Willis, Harcourt 1975 $25.00; Irvington 1975 $34.50. An excellent discussion of the literature and the intellectual motifs of Greek authors prior to the fifth century B.C.

Grube, G. M. *Greek and Roman Critics.* Univ. of Toronto Pr. 1965 pap. $8.50

Hadas, Moses. *Ancilla to Classical Reading.* Columbia Univ. Pr. 1954 pap. $12.00. A useful companion for the reader of Greek and Latin literature.

Hammond, N. G., and H. H. Scullard, eds. *Oxford Classical Dictionary.* Oxford 2d ed. 1970 $45.00. The experts in all phases of classical scholarship have written articles and supplied short bibliographies on their fields of interest for this volume, which is an invaluable source of learning.

Harvey, Paul, ed. *Oxford Companion to Classical Literature.* Oxford 2d ed. 1937 $35.00 pap. $9.95. A valuable reference work that is comprehensive, concise, and well written.

Havelock, Eric A. *The Literate Revolution in Greece and Its Cultural Consequences.* Princeton Univ. Pr. 1982 $27.50 pap. $11.95. A discussion of the transformation of literature from an oral to a written form and its significance in early Greece.

Highet, Gilbert. *Classical Tradition.* Oxford 1949 $29.95. An admirably rich volume that takes into account the many ways the classical tradition has shaped European and American literature. Scholarly, humanistic, yet never pedantic.

Lempriere, J. A. *A Classical Dictionary.* Gordon 2 vols. lib. bdg. $250.00. Still very useful because of its wealth of anecdotes and literary references.

Luce, T. James, ed. *Ancient Writers: Greece and Rome.* Scribner 2 vols. 1982 lib. bdg. $130.00. Essays by many respected scholars on the major authors of ancient Greece—some pedantic, others full of insights.

Marrou, H. I. *History of Education in Antiquity.* Univ. of Wisconsin Pr. text ed. 1982 pap. $10.95. An indispensable, masterful work.

Rose, Herbert J. *Religion in Greece and Rome.* Harper pap. $6.50. A sophisticated, terse analysis.

Rostovtzeff, Mikhail. *Social and Economic History of the Hellenistic World.* Oxford 3 vols. 1941 $109.00. A definitive study by an eminent historian.

Smith, William, ed. *Dictionary of Greek and Roman Antiquities.* Longwood Pr. 2 vols. repr. of 1890 ed. 1977 lib. bdg. $65.00. All of the Smith dictionaries listed here are valuable reference tools.

——. *Dictionary of Greek and Roman Biography and Mythology.* AMS Pr. 3 vols. repr. of 1890 ed. $245.00

——. *Dictionary of Greek and Roman Geography.* AMS Pr. 2 vols. repr. of 1873 ed. $140.00

Snell, Bruno. *The Discovery of the Mind in Early Greek Philosophy and Literature.* Dover 1982 pap. $6.00; Peter Smith 1983 $13.25. A stimulating view of intellectual history.

Whibley, Leonard. *A Companion to Greek Studies.* Folcroft repr. of 1916 ed. 1979 lib. bdg. $125.00; Hafner 4th rev. ed. repr. of 1931 ed. 1963 $24.95. An older but still useful collection of chapters on different aspects of Greek culture, useful as background for the study of the literature.

Collections

Casson, Lionel, trans. and ed. *Masters of Ancient Comedy: Selections from Aristophanes, Menander, Plautus and Terence.* Crowell 1967 pap. $2.95

MacKendrick, Paul L., and Herbert M. Howe, eds. *Classics in Translation.* Univ. of Wisconsin Pr. 2 vols. text ed. 1952 ea. $13.50. New translations, most of which were made for these volumes. Includes the following Greek plays: Aeschylus, *Agamemnon*, translated by L. MacNeice; Sophocles, *Antigone*, translated by M. F. Neufeld; Euripides, *Medea*, translated by W. R. Agard; Aristophanes, *Frogs*, translated by J. G. Hawthorne.

Murphy, Charles T., Kevin Guinagh, and Whitney J. Oates, eds. *Greek and Roman Classics in Translation.* McKay 1947 o.p. Five complete plays: *Prometheus Bound, Oedipus the King, Hippolytus, The Clouds, The Adelphi;* and selections from Homer, Greek poetry, Herodotus, Thucydides, Plato, Aristotle, Epictetus, Demosthenes, Lucretius, Catullus, Cicero, Virgil, Horace, Livy, Tacitus, and Juvenal.

CLASSICAL GREEK LITERATURE

History and Criticism

Alsop, Joseph W. *From the Silent Earth: A Report of the Greek Bronze Age.* Intro. by Maurice Bowra, Greenwood repr. of 1964 ed. 1981 lib. bdg. $39.00

Bonner, Robert J. *Aspects of Athenian Democracy.* Russell repr. of 1933 ed. 1967 $7.00

——. *Lawyers and Litigants in Ancient Athens: The Genesis of the Legal Profession.* Ayer repr. of 1927 ed. $22.00

Bonner, Robert J., and Gertrude S. Smith. *The Administration of Justice from Homer to Aristotle.* AMS Pr. 2 vols. repr. of 1938 ed. $60.00; Greenwood 2 vols. repr. of 1938 ed. 1969 lib. bdg. $32.50

Bowra, Cecil M. *Early Greek Elegists.* Cooper Square Pr. repr. of 1938 ed. 1969 $11.00

———. *The Greek Experience.* New Amer. Lib. pap. $4.95

Cary, Max. *A History of the Greek World: 323–146 B. C.* Methuen 2d rev. ed. repr. of 1951 ed. 1972 pap. $16.95

Cottrell, Leonard. *The Bull of Minos.* Amereon $15.95

Dickinson, G. Lowes. *The Greek View of Life.* 1896. Quality Lib. 1915 $15.00

Else, Gerald F. *The Origin and Early Form of Greek Tragedy.* Harvard Univ. Pr. 1965 $3.75; *Norton Lib.* repr. of 1967 ed. 1972 pap. $2.45

Finley, Moses I. *The Ancient Greeks: An Introduction to Their Life and Thought.* Penguin (Pelican) 1977 pap. $5.95. A brief history of Greek culture from its beginnings to Roman times.

Flaceliere, Robert. *Love in Ancient Greece.* Trans. by James Cleugh, Greenwood repr. of 1962 ed. 1973 lib. bdg. $22.50. This professor at the Sorbonne and a leading French authority corrects some popular misconceptions regarding Greek attitudes toward love, sex, and marriage. He "wears his erudition lightly. . . . His time-span covers Greek literature from Homer to Menander."

Graves, Robert. *The Greek Myths.* Braziller 1959 $10.00; Doubleday 1982 $25.00; Penguin 2 vols. 1955 pap. ea. $3.95. An idiosyncratic and amusing presentation of the myths.

Guthrie, W. K. *Greek Philosophers: From Thales to Aristotle.* Harper pap. $4.95

———. *The Greeks and Their Gods.* Beacon 1955 pap. $8.95

———. *A History of Greek Philosophy.* Cambridge Univ. Pr. 6 vols. 1975 ea. $79.50 2 vols. 1979 pap. ea. $22.95. Excellent summaries.

———. *Socrates.* Cambridge Univ. Pr. 1971 pap. $13.95

Hadas, Moses. *History of Greek Literature.* Columbia Univ. Pr. 1950 $24.00

Hamilton, Edith. *The Echo of Greece.* Norton Lib. 1964 pap. $6.95. This popular interpretation includes studies of Aristotle, Demosthenes, Alexander the Great, and Menander.

———. *The Greek Way.* Amereon $13.95; Avon 1973 pap. $2.75; Norton 1948 $19.95 1983 pap. $3.95

———. *Mythology.* Little, Brown 1942 $15.45; New Amer. Lib. 1971 pap. $2.95. A standard retelling of the stories.

Harrison, Jane. *Epilegomena to the Study of Greek Religion, and Themis: A Study of the Social Origins of Greek Religion.* Univ. Bks. 1962 $10.00. While she had numerous critics among her academic peers, Harrison also won the support and admiration of such great scholars as Gilbert Murray, who contributed the "Jane Harrison Memorial Lecture" to this volume.

———. *Prolegomena to the Study of Greek Religion.* Ayer repr. of 1922 ed. 1976 $57.50; Humanities Pr. text ed. 1981 $26.50

Huxley, G. L. *Early Sparta.* Biblio Dist. 1972 $17.00. The surviving contemporary accounts concerning their victorious enemy, Sparta, are almost all Athenian. This careful study analyzes primary materials about Sparta from 1200 to 490 B.C.

Jaeger, Werner. *Paideia: The Ideals of Greek Culture.* Trans. by Gilbert Highet, Oxford 3 vols. ea. $35.00. Brilliant analysis of Greek culture by an eminent authority on intellectual history.

Jones, John. *On Aristotle and Greek Tragedy.* Oxford repr. of 1962 ed. 1968 pap. $3.50; Stanford Univ. Pr. repr. of 1962 ed. $20.00 pap. $7.95

Kennedy, George. *The Art of Persuasion in Greece.* Princeton Univ. Pr. 3 vols. 1963 $32.00. An excellent history of Greek oratory.

Kerenyi, Karoly. *The Religion of the Greeks and Romans.* Greenwood repr. of 1962 ed. 1973 lib. bdg. $24.75. Combining Greek and Roman mythology, philology, classic literature, and Jungian psychology, this is a stimulating view of how the Greeks and Romans faced the absolute.

Kitto, Humphrey D. *Form and Meaning in Drama: A Study of Six Greek Plays and of Hamlet.* Methuen 2d ed. text ed. 1979 pap. $10.95

——. *Greek Tragedy: A Literary Study.* Methuen 3d ed. rev. 1966 pap. $13.95

——. *The Greeks.* Penguin 1950 pap. $4.95. "Written in [Kitto's] normally graceful, witty, and also opinionated way, it gives a truly wonderful insight into most aspects of ancient Greek civilization" (*LJ*).

Lattimore, Richmond. *The Poetry of Greek Tragedy.* Johns Hopkins Univ. Pr. 1958 $14.00. Penetrating critical study.

——. *Story Patterns in Greek Tragedy.* Univ. of Michigan Pr. 1964 pap. $3.95

Lesky, Albin. *A History of Greek Literature.* Crowell 1976 $22.07 pap. $9.95. A superb comprehensive history that discusses in detail all literary genres, from very early periods through the Hellenistic, Roman, and early Christian eras. Summaries of major works are very full and the extensive bibliographies are up-to-date.

Lloyd-Jones, Hugh. *The Justice of Zeus.* Univ. of California Pr. 2d ed. 1983 pap. $3.45

MacKendrick, Paul L. *The Greek Stones Speak: The Story of Archaeology in Greek Lands.* Norton 2d ed. 1982 $24.95 1983 pap. $9.95. A polished study with a wealth of detail; covers over 2,000 years from the era of Homeric legend to Roman occupation.

Murray, Gilbert. *History of Ancient Greek Literature.* Folcroft repr. lib. bdg. $30.00; Ungar 1966 $12.50. "Murray combined erudition, imagination, sensitivity, and enthusiasm with an urbane narrative style to make the reading of his book an exciting intellectual adventure" (*LJ*).

——. *The Rise of the Greek Epic.* Oxford Pap. Ser. 1934 pap. $3.95

Pausanias. *Description of Greece.* Loeb Class. Lib. Harvard Univ. Pr. 5 vols. ea. $12.50. A guidebook for tourists, written in the second century A.D.

Pearson, Lionel. *Popular Ethics in Ancient Greece.* Stanford Univ. Pr. 1962 $20.00. Covers ethical attitudes of the marketplace, and concepts found in Homer, Hesiod, Theognis, Solon, and fifth-century dramatists.

Pendlebury, John D. *The Archaeology of Crete.* Biblo & Tannen, $12.00; *Norton Lib.* 1965 pap. $6.95. Firsthand account of the excavation in Crete.

Pickard-Cambridge, A. W. *Dithyramb, Tragedy and Comedy.* 1927. Oxford 2d ed. rev. 1962 o.p. A learned work on the beginnings of Greek drama.

——. *Dramatic Festivals of Athens.* 1953. Rev. by D. M. Lewis and J. P. Gould, Oxford 2d ed. 1968 $23.50. Comprehensive account of the festivals by a foremost scholar.

——. *The Theatre of Dionysus in Athens.* Oxford 1946 $55.00. A history from the earliest days to the time of the Roman Empire.

Polybius. *The Histories of Polybius, Discoursing of the Warres betwixt the Romanes and Carthaginenses.* Trans. by Christopher Watson, Walter J. Johnson repr. of 1568 ed. 1969 $30.00; *Loeb Class. Lib.* Harvard Univ. Pr. 6 vols. ea. $12.50. Records the rapid rise of Rome, as seen by a Greek historian of the second century A.D.

Renault, Mary. *The King Must Die.* Bantam 1974 pap. $4.50; ed. by E. Badian, Pantheon 1958 $15.45. An exciting version of the story of Theseus and Ariadne in Crete.

Richter, Gisela M. *Sculpture and Sculptors of the Greeks.* Yale Univ. Pr. 4th ed. rev. & enl. 1971 $47.50. The standard reference book on Greek sculpture.

Robinson, Charles A., Jr. *Athens in the Age of Pericles.* Univ. of Oklahoma Pr. 1959 pap. $5.95. "Incisive, illuminating and relevant" comments.

Rose, H. J. *A Handbook of Greek Literature.* Dutton rev. ed. 1950 o.p. A brief work, excellent for quick reference.

Snell, Bruno. *Poetry and Society: The Role of Poetry in Ancient Greece.* Select Bibliographies Repr. Ser. Ayer repr. of 1961 ed. $14.00

Ventris, M., and J. Chadwick. *Documents in Mycenaean Greek.* Cambridge Univ. Pr. 2d ed. 1973 $135.00. By deciphering the clay tablets found in the ruins of King Minos's palace at Knossos, Crete, Ventris, a British architect, found the key to one of the last remaining lost languages—that of Homer's heroes.

Vermeule, Emily T. *Greece in the Bronze Age.* Univ. of Chicago Pr. 1964 $32.00 pap. $15.00. "Professor Vermeule ... presents a superb, unhackneyed, up-to-date, overall and detailed view of prehistoric Greek mainland civilization, ca. 6500–1100 B.C. . . . Generously documented and illustrated" (*LJ*).

Warner, Rex. *The Stories of the Greeks.* Farrar 1978 $15.00 pap. $9.95. A one-volume edition of the author's three books on the gods, heroes, and wars of ancient Greece: *Men and Gods, Greeks and Trojans,* and *The Vengeance of the Gods.*

Webster, T. B. L. *Studies in Later Greek Comedy.* Greenwood repr. of 1970 ed. 1981 lib. bdg. $32.50

Collections

GENERAL

Auden, W. H., ed. *The Portable Greek Reader. Viking Portable Lib.* Penguin 1977 pap. $7.95. Thematic selections from Homer to Galen; includes very useful chronological outline of classical Greek civilization.

Edmonds, J. M., trans. *Greek Bucolic Poets: Theocritus, Bion, and Moschus. Loeb Class. Lib.* Harvard Univ. Pr. $12.50

——. *Greek Elegy and Iambus. Loeb Class. Lib.* Harvard Univ. Pr. 2 vols. ea. $12.50

——. *Greek Lyric. Loeb Class. Lib.* Harvard Univ. Pr. 3 vols. ea. $12.50

Gow, Andrew S., and D. L. Page. *The Greek Anthology: Garland of Philip and Other Contemporary Epigrams.* Cambridge Univ. Pr. 2 vols. 1968 $130.00. An admirable anthology done with sympathy and skill. The original collection was made by Constantius Cephales about 925 A.D. The original manuscript was found in the Palatine Library at Heidelberg in the seventeenth century, so that it is frequently referred to as the "Palatine Anthology." It contains more than 6,000 poems classified according to type and subject and written by 320 authors beginning in the seventh century B.C.

Grant, Michael, ed. *Greek Literature: An Anthology. Penguin Class. Ser.* 1977 pap. $5.95. A good recent anthology of judiciously chosen selections.

Hadas, Moses, trans. and ed. *Three Greek Romances.* Bobbs 1964 pap. $6.65; Irvington text ed. 1964 $19.50. Contains Longus: *Daphnis and Chloe;* Xenophon, *The Ephesian Tale;* and Chrysostom, *Hunters of Euboia.*

Higham, Thomas F., and C. M. Bowra, eds. *Oxford Book of Greek Verse in Translation.* Oxford o.p. Comprehensive and skillfully translated.

Jebb, Richard C., ed. *The Attic Orators: Selections from Antiphon, Andocides, Lysias, Isocrates and Isaeus.* Russell 2 vols. repr. of 1875 ed. 1962 $20.00; St. Martin's 2d ed. repr. of 1888 ed. $9.95

Maidment, K. J., and J. O. Burtt, trans. *Minor Attic Orators. Loeb Class. Lib.* Harvard Univ. Pr. 2 vols. ea. $12.00. Includes Antiphon and Andocides; Lycurgus, Dinarchus, Demades, Hyperides.

GREEK DRAMA

Arnott, Peter D., trans. *Three Greek Plays for the Theatre.* Indiana Univ. Pr. 1961 pap. $1.95. *The Cyclops, Medea,* and *The Frogs,* prepared especially for the actor.

Arrowsmith, William, ed. *Greek Tragedies in New Translations.* Oxford 15 vols. 1973–81 ea. $19.95. A series of readable translations with an introduction and notes at the back of each volume.

Cooper, Lane, ed. *Fifteen Greek Plays.* Trans. by Gilbert Murray, Oxford 1943 $11.00. Collection of plays translated as follows. Aeschylus: *Prometheus,* by Whitelaw; Agamemnon: *Choephoroe* and *Eumenides,* by Gilbert Murray; Sophocles: *Oedipus the King,* by Gilbert Murray, *Antigone,* by Whitelaw, *Oedipus at Colonus* and *Electra,* by Lewis Campbell; Euripides: *Electra, Iphigenia in Tauris, Medea,* and *Hippolytus,* by Gilbert Murray; and Aristophanes: *The Clouds, The Birds, The Frogs,* by Rogers.

Fitts, Dudley, ed. *Greek Plays in Modern Translation.* Holt text ed. 1947 $8.95. *The Trojan Women, Agamemnon, Electra, Medea, Hippolytus, Alcestis, King Oedipus, Oedipus at Colonus, Antigone, Prometheus Vinctus, Oresteia.*

Grene, David, and Richmond Lattimore, eds. *The Complete Greek Tragedies.* Univ. of Chicago Pr. 1942–60 o.p.

Hadas, Moses, ed. *Greek Drama. Bantam Class. Ser.* 1982 pap. $3.50. Contains Aeschylus: *Agamemnon* and *Eumenides;* Sophocles: *Antigone, Oedipus the King,* and *Philoctetes;* Aristophanes: *The Frogs;* Euripides: *Hippolytus, Medea,* and *Trojan Women.*

Havelock, E. A., and Maynard Mack, eds. *Drama Series.* Prentice-Hall consult publisher for individual volumes and prices. Individual plays with a good scholarly introduction, and commentaries on the bottom of the page.

Oates, Whitney J., and Eugene O'Neill, Jr., eds., *The Complete Greek Drama.* Random 2 vols. 1938 o.p. All the extant tragedies of Aeschylus, Sophocles, and Euripides, and the comedies of Aristophanes and Menander, in a variety of translations.

———. *Seven Famous Greek Plays.* Random (Vintage) 1955 pap. $4.95. Contains Aeschylus, *Agamemnon* and *Prometheus Bound;* Sophocles: *Oedipus the King* and *Antigone;* Euripides: *Medea* and *Alcestis;* Aristophanes: *The Frogs.*

Robinson, Charles A., Jr., ed. *Anthology of Greek Drama. Rinehart Ed.* Holt text ed. repr. of 1949 ed. pap. $12.95. Vol. 1: *Agamemnon, Oedipus Rex, Antigone, Medea, Hippolytus, Lysistrata.* Vol. 2: *Prometheus Bound, Choephoroe, Eumenides, Philoctetes, Oedipus at Colonus, The Trojan Women, The Bacchae, The Clouds, The Frogs.*

AESCHYLUS. 524–456 B.C.

Aeschylus was born at Eleusis of a noble family. He fought at the Battle of Marathon (490 B.C.) where a small Greek band heroically defeated the invading Persians. At the time of his death, Athens was in its golden age. In all of his extant works, his intense love of Greece and Athens finds expression.

Of the nearly 90 plays attributed to him, only 7 survive. These are *The Persians* (produced in 472 B.C.), *Seven against Thebes* (467 B.C.), *The Oresteia* (458 B.C.)—which includes *Agamemnon, Libation Bearers,* and *Eumenides* (or *Furies*), *Suppliants* (463 B.C.), and *Prometheus Bound* (c.460 B.C.). Six of the seven present mythological stories. The ornate language creates a mood of tragedy and reinforces the already stylized character of the Greek theater.

Aeschylus called his prodigious output "dry scraps from Homer's banquet" because his plots and solemn language are derived from the epic poet. But a more accurate summation of Aeschylus would emphasize his grandeur of mind and spirit and the tragic dignity of his language. Because of his patriotism and belief in divine providence, there is a profound moral order to his plays. Characters such as Clytemnestra, Orestes, and Prometheus personify a great passion or principle. As individuals they conflict with divine will but ultimate justice prevails.

Aeschylus's introduction of the second actor made real theater possible because the two could address each other and act several roles. His successors imitated his costumes, dances, spectacular effects, long descriptions, choral refrains, invocations, and dialogue. Swinburne's enthusiasm for *The Oresteia* sums up all praises of Aeschylus; he called it simply "the greatest achievement of the human mind."

BOOKS BY AESCHYLUS

Tragedies. Trans. by Herbert Weir Smith, *Loeb Class. Lib.* Harvard Univ. Pr. 2 vols. 1922–26 ea. $12.50. Vol. 1 contains *The Suppliant Maidens* (c.463 B.C.); *The Persians* (472 B.C.); *Prometheus* (c.460 B.C.); *Seven against Thebes* (467 B.C.). Vol. 2 contains *Agamemnon, The Libation Bearers,* and *Eumenides* (all 458 B.C.); Fragments.

Aeschylus I: Oresteia, Agamemnon, the Libation Bearers, the Eumenides. Trans. and ed. by David Grene and Richmond Lattimore, *Complete Greek Tragedies* Univ. of Chicago Pr. (Phoenix Bks.) text ed. 1969 pap. $5.50. This and the following volume are excellent and authoritative modern translations that convey the complexity and the metrics of the originals.

Aeschylus II, Four Tragedies: Prometheus Bound, Seven against Thebes, the Persians, the Suppliant Maidens. Trans. by Seth G. Benardete and David Grene, ed. by David Grene and Richmond Lattimore, *Complete Greek Tragedies* Univ. of Chicago Pr. (Phoenix Bks.) text ed. 1969 pap. $6.00

Seven against Thebes. Trans. by Gilbert Murray, Allen & Unwin text ed. repr. of 1935 ed. pap. $3.95; trans. by Anthony Hecht and Helen Bacon, *Greek Tragedy in New Translations* Oxford 1973 $19.95

The Suppliants. Trans. by Janet Lembke, ed. by William Arrowsmith, *Greek Tragedy in New Translations* Oxford 1975 $19.95

Prometheus Bound. Trans. by Gilbert Murray, Allen & Unwin text ed. repr. of 1931 ed. $3.95; ed. by W. R. Connor, Ayer repr. of 1932 ed. 1979 lib. bdg. $17.00; trans. by Warren D. Anderson, Bobbs 1963 pap. $4.24; ed. by Mark Griffith, Cambridge Univ. Pr. 1983 $42.50 pap. $15.95; trans. by James Scully and C. John Herington, ed. by William Arrowsmith, *Greek Tragedy in New Translations* Oxford 1975 $19.95

The Persians. Trans. by Janet Lembke and C. John Herington, ed. by William Arrowsmith, *Greek Tragedy in New Translations* Oxford 1981 $19.95

The Oresteia. Trans. by *K. McLeish,* Cambridge Univ. Pr. 1979 $17.95 pap. $6.95; trans. by Philip Vellacott, *Penguin Class. Ser.* 1956 pap. $2.95; (with the title *The Oresteian Trilogy*) trans. by Robert Fagles, intro. by W. B. Stanford, Viking 1975 $20.00

The House of Atreus: Adapted from the Oresteia. Ed. by John Lewin, Univ. of Minnesota Pr. 1966 $5.95. This adaptation of the trilogy *Agamemnon, The Libation Bearers,* and *The Furies* is for contemporary stage presentation and is the version used by the Minnesota Theater Company for its production at the Tyrone Guthrie Theater in Minneapolis.

Agamemnon. Trans. by Gilbert Murray, Allen & Unwin text ed. repr. of 1920 ed. pap. $3.95; trans. by Hugh Lloyd-Jones, Biblio Dist. 1979 $20.00 text ed. pap. $6.75; ed. by J. D. Denniston and Denys Page, Oxford 1957 $15.95; ed. by Eduard Fraenkel, Oxford 3 vols. $79.00. Fraenkel's introduction, critical edition of the Greek text, English translation, and commentary represent the best of modern scholarship on this most difficult and profound of plays.

BOOKS ABOUT AESCHYLUS

Campbell, Lewis. *Tragic Drama in Aeschylus, Sophocles and Shakespeare: An Essay.* Russell repr. of 1904 ed. 1965 $8.50

Earp, Frank R. *Style of Aeschylus.* Russell repr. of 1948 ed. 1970 $9.00

Finley, John H., Jr. *Pindar and Aeschylus.* Harvard Univ. Pr. 1955 $20.00

Gagarin, Michael. *Aeschylean Drama.* Univ. of California Pr. 1976 $28.50. A study of ideas and themes.

Herington, C. J. *Author of the Prometheus Bound.* Univ. of Texas Pr. 1970 $5.50. An intelligent discussion of problems in the "Prometheus."

McCall, M., Jr., ed. *Aeschylus: A Collection of Critical Essays.* Prentice-Hall 1972 $8.95 pap. $1.95

Murray, Gilbert. *Aeschylus: The Creator of Tragedy.* Greenwood repr. of 1940 ed. 1978 lib. bdg. $27.50

Rosenmeyer, Thomas G. *The Art of Aeschylus.* Univ. of California Pr. 1982 $37.50 pap. $12.95. Focusing on language and character rather than on historical background.

Sheppard, J. T. *Aeschylus and Sophocles: Their Work and Influence.* Cooper Square Pr. repr. of 1930 ed. $18.50

Smyth, Herbert W. *Aeschylean Tragedy.* AMS Pr. repr. of 1924 ed. $7.50; Biblo & Tannen repr. of 1924 ed. 1969 $10.00; Gordon $59.95. Written by an American authority on Aeschylus.

Solmsen, Friedrich. *Hesiod and Aeschylus.* Ed. by W. R. Connor, Johnson Repr. repr. of 1949 ed. $27.00. A sophisticated study of the relationship between the two poets; by a leading Hellenist.

Spatz, Lois. *Aeschylus. Twayne's World Authors Ser.* G. K. Hall 1982 lib. bdg. $16.95

Thomson, George. *Aeschylus and Athens: A Study of Athenian Drama and Democracy.* Beekman 4th ed. 1974 $15.95 pap. $11.95; Haskell repr. of 1940 ed. 1969 lib. bdg. $49.95

AESOP. fl. 570 B.C.

The Greek slave of Samos was said to have composed the animal *Fables,* although the sources of many of them have been traced to earlier literature. He is mentioned by Aristophanes and Socrates. Babrius, a second-century Greek fabulist, and Phaedrus, a Latin from Macedonia who matured at the beginning of the first century, versified Aesop's fables. Their versions were rendered into prose during the Middle Ages.

BOOK BY AESOP

Aesop's Fables. Biblio Dist. repr. of 1961 ed. 1975 $11.00; trans. by S. A. Handford, *Penguin Class. Ser.* 1954 pap. $3.95; ed. by Anne T. White, Random 1964 $7.99; ed. by Ann McGovern, Scholastic pap. $1.95; Viking 1981 $13.50

BOOKS ABOUT AESOP

Jacobs, Joseph, ed. *The Fables of Aesop.* Schocken 1966 $8.95 pap. $4.95. A careful account of the transmission of the fables in antiquity, the Middle Ages, and down to modern times.

Perry, Ben E. *The Ancient Romances: a Literary Historical Account of Their Origins.* Univ. of California Pr. 1967 $32.50. This work places Aesop in the romance tradition.

Perry, Ben E., and Richard M. Dorson, eds. *Aesopica: A Series of Texts Relating to Aesop or Ascribed to Him Closely Connected with the Literary Tradition That Bears His Name.* Ayer repr. of 1952 ed. 1980 vol. 1 lib. bdg. $74.50. This valuable source book has ancient testimonies about Aesop.

APOLLONIUS RHODIUS. 3rd century B.C.

This Greek epic poet was a scholar of some note—a fact reflected in his main work, which is based on the legend of the Argonauts, Jason's search for the Golden Fleece. Somewhat pedantic, *The Argonautica* is enlivened by the character of Medea. Virgil used Apollonius as a source for his portrayal of Dido in the *Aeneid.* Apollonius may have been librarian of the great library of Alexandria built by Ptolemy II and certainly studied in Alexandria with Callimachus. His name is derived from his supposed retirement in Rhodes, probably after a literary feud with Callimachus over the relative merits of the long traditional epic as opposed to short, finished poems.

BOOKS BY APOLLONIUS

The Argonautica. Ed. by W. R. Connor, Ayer repr. of 1928 ed. 1979 lib. bdg. $17.00; trans. in prose by R. C. Seaton, *Loeb Class. Lib.* Harvard Univ. Pr. 1912 $12.50. Text and translation recommended.

Voyage of Argo. Trans. by E. V. Rieu, Penguin 1959 o.p.

BOOK ABOUT APOLLONIUS

Beye, C. R. *Epic and Romance in the Argonautica.* Southern Illinois Univ. Pr. 1982 $22.50

ARISTOPHANES. c.450–c.385 B.C.

Aristophanes is the great master of Athenian Old Comedy. In addition to the 11 of his plays that are extant, there are 32 titles and many fragments. Very little is known of his life. Greek drama had reached its peak and was declining when he began to write. His comedies are full of a peculiar mixture of broad political, social, and literary satire, discussions of large ideas, and boisterous vulgarities. His characters are like normal human beings in absurd and preposterous situations. His Greek is exceptionally beautiful and his idyllic lyrics are delightful.

Edith Hamilton says: "To read Aristophanes is in some sort like reading an Athenian comic paper. All the life of Athens is there: the politics of the day and the politicians; the war party and the anti-war party; pacifism, votes for women, free trade, fiscal reform, complaining taxpayers, educational theories, the current religious and literary talk—everything, in short, that interested the average citizen. All was food for his mockery. He was the speaking picture of the follies and foibles of his day." His sharp barbs were aimed at such targets as Socrates, Euripides, and Aeschylus. He spared no class, no profession, and no age group. His plays provide insights into the position of women, the contemporaneous literary and political fashions, and class relations in fifth-century Athens.

BOOKS BY ARISTOPHANES

Complete Plays. Ed. by Moses Hadas, Bantam 1962 pap. $2.50

The Acharnians. Ed. by W. R. Connor, Ayer repr. of 1909 ed. 1979 lib. bdg. $27.50; ed. by Charles E. Graves, Cambridge Univ. Pr. text ed. repr. of 1905 ed. $6.50

The Knights. Ed. by Alan H. Sommerstein, Bolchazy Carducci 1981 $24.50

The Clouds. Ed. by Alan H. Sommerstein, Bolchazy Carducci 1982 $24.50 pap. $12.00; trans. by Peter D. Arnott, *Crofts Class. Ser.* Harlan Davidson text ed. 1967 pap. $3.75; ed. by William Arrowsmith, New Amer. Lib. 1970 pap. $2.25; ed. by K. J. Dover, Oxford 1968 $32.50

Peace. Ed. by Alan H. Sommerstein, Bolchazy Carducci 1985 $24.50 pap. $12.00; trans. by Robert H. Webb, Univ. Pr. of Virginia 1964 pap. $2.95

The Birds. Trans. by Gilbert Murray, Allen & Unwin text ed. 1950 pap. $2.95; trans. by Peter D. Arnott, *Crofts Class. Ser.* Harlan Davidson text ed. 1958 pap. $3.75; New Amer. Lib. pap. $2.50

Lysistrata. Trans. by Donald Sutherland, Harper 1961 pap. $4.50; trans. by Robert H. Webb, Univ. Pr. of Virginia 1963 $4.95

Ladies' Day (*Thesmophoriazusae*). Trans. by Dudley Fitts, Harcourt 1959 o.p. "An excellent new adaptation . . . which should receive wide production because of its lively nature."

The Frogs. Trans. by Gilbert Murray, Allen & Unwin text ed. repr. of 1908 ed. pap. $3.95; trans. by Richmond Lattimore, New Amer. Lib. 1970 pap. $2.95; ed. by W. B. Stanford, St. Martin's 2d ed. 1963 $16.95; trans. by Richmond Lattimore, Univ. of Michigan Pr. 1962 $4.95

The Congresswomen (*Ecclesiazusae*). Trans. by Richmond Lattimore, New Amer. Lib. 1970 o.p.

BOOKS ABOUT ARISTOPHANES

Dearden, C. W. *The Stage of Aristophanes.* Humanities Pr. text ed. 1976 29.25; Longwood Pr. 1976 $46.50

Dover, Kenneth. *Aristophanic Comedy.* Univ. of California Pr. 1972 o.p.

Ehrenberg, Victor. *The People of Aristophanes: A Sociology of Old Attic Comedy.* Porcupine Pr. 2d ed. rev. & enl. repr. of 1951 ed. lib. bdg. $25.00. A careful study.

Henderson, J., ed. *Aristophanes: Essays in Interpretation.* Cambridge Univ. Pr. 1981 $39.50

Lord, Louis E. *Aristophanes: His Plays and His Influence.* Cooper Square Pr. repr. of 1930 ed. $17.50

McLeish, Kenneth. *The Theatre of Aristophanes.* Taplinger 1980 $11.95

Murray, Gilbert. *Aristophanes: A Study.* Ayer repr. of 1933 ed. 1964 $12.00

Solomos, Alexis. *The Living Aristophanes.* Trans. by Marvin Felheim, Univ. of Michigan Pr. text ed. 1974 $10.00

Whitman, Cedric H. *Aristophanes and the Comic Hero.* Harvard Univ. Pr. 1964 $20.00. "This full-fledged, thoroughly documented, sympathetic and sensitive study of the Aristophanic hero and of the nature of Aristophanic comedy is excellent" (*LJ*).

ARISTOTLE. 384–322 B.C.
[SEE Volumes 3 and 4.]

BABRIUS. fl. 2nd cent. A.D.
[SEE Aesop in this chapter.]

BION. fl. c.100 B.C.
[SEE Theocritus in this chapter.]

CALLIMACHUS. c.305–c.240 B.C.

At Alexandria Callimachus was bibliographer for the great library, teacher of Appolonius Rhodius, and a famous, prolific poet. His beautiful, elegant, and refined epigrams, hymns, elegiacs (the *Aetia* or *Causes*), iambics, and little epic survive in varying degrees of completeness. In his day he was widely admired and later served as a model for Catullus and the Roman elegiac poets, especially Ovid.

BOOKS BY CALLIMACHUS

Aetia, Iambi, Hecale, Minor Epic, and Elegiac Poems: Fragments of Uncertain Location. Loeb Class. Lib. Harvard Univ. Pr. 1958 $12.50.
Hymns and Epigrams. Loeb Class. Lib. Harvard Univ. Pr. 1921 $12.50

DEMOSTHENES. 385?–322 B.C.

Demosthenes, the magnificent orator, is said to have had to conquer an originally ineffective vocal delivery. After years of private law practice, he delivered the first of his three *Philippics* against Philip of Macedon in 351 B.C. He saw danger to Athens in the tyrannical expansion of the Macedonian state, but his passionate and compelling exhortations did not save the Greeks from defeat at Chaeronea in 338 B.C. Exiled in 324 B.C., he was recalled after the death of Alexander the Great in 323 B.C. Again he tried to organize the Greek resistance, but failed and was forced to flee when Athens was taken. He took poison to avoid capture. His speeches are characterized by deep sincerity, prodigious power of verbal suggestion, and intricate structure. His influence on Cicero and the Roman rhetoricians was enormous.

BOOKS BY DEMOSTHENES

All the Orations of Demosthenes. Trans. by Thomas Leland, AMS Pr. repr. of 1757 ed. 2d ed. $37.50
Demosthenes' Public Orations. 1912. Trans. by A. W. Pickard-Cambridge, Biblio Dist. (Everyman's) repr. of 1954 ed. 1967 $7.95. The translator has rendered "the speeches into such English as a political orator of the present day might use."
Private Orations. Trans. by A. T. Murray, *Loeb Class. Lib.* Harvard Univ. Pr. 3 vols. 1936–39 ea. $12.50
Funeral Speech, Erotic Essay, Exordia, and Letters. Ed. by E. H. Warmington, *Loeb Class. Lib.* Harvard Univ. Pr. 1949 $12.50
Demosthenes on the Crown. Ed. by Gregory Vlastos, Ayer repr. of 1901 ed. 1979 lib. bdg. $27.00

BOOKS ABOUT DEMOSTHENES

Adams, Charles D. *Demosthenes and His Influence.* Cooper Square Pr. repr. of 1930 ed. $15.00

Jaeger, Werner. *Demosthenes: The Origin and Growth of His Policy.* Ed. by C. R. Kennedy, Univ. of Nebraska Pr. 1963 lib. bdg. $20.50

Pearson, Lionel. *The Art of Demosthenes.* Scholars Pr. 1981 pap. $18.00

Pickard-Cambridge, A. W. *Demosthenes and the Last Days of Greek Freedom: 384–322 B.C.* Ed. by Gregory Vlastos, Ayer repr. of 1914 ed. lib. bdg. $44.00.

EURIPIDES. c.485–c.406 B.C.

The third of the three great Greek tragedians was born in Attica and lived most of his life in Athens. Out of some 80 plays by him only 19 are extant; the dates of the following plays are known: *Alcestis* (438 B.C.), *Medea* and *Philoctetes* (431 B.C.), *Hippolytus* (428 B.C.), *Hecuba* (c.424 B.C.), *Electra* (417 B.C.), *Troades* (415 B.C.), *Iphigenia in Tauris* (c.413 B.C.), *Helen* (412 B.C.), *Phoenissae* (after 412 B.C. and before 408 B.C.), *Ion* (c.411 B.C.), *Orestes* (408 B.C.), *Bacchus* and *Iphigenia in Aulis* (c.405 B.C.) The *Rhesus*—if indeed it is genuine—is the earliest.

When Gilbert Murray's translations made the dramatist popular in the early 1900s, readers were impressed by the author's modernity of thought and spirit, the feeling for human life and problems of pain. Euripides' attitude toward the gods was iconoclastic and rationalistic; toward humans—notably his passionate female characters—deeply sympathetic.

Euripides separated the chorus from the action, the first step toward the complete elimination of the chorus. He used the prologue as an introduction and explanation and was charged with intemperate use of the "deus ex machina," by which artifice a god is dragged in abruptly at the end to resolve a confusion beyond human powers. He developed the literary devices of reversal, recognition by means of rings and necklaces, substitution of children, and violations of maidens, on all of which New Comedy (see Menander in this chapter) depends. His language is simple and direct, well tuned to the expression of passion. He created some of the most unforgettable psychological portraits.

Despite criticism and satire against him, Euripides did win several prizes for tragedy in his lifetime and shortly after his death his reputation rose and has never diminished.

BOOKS BY EURIPIDES

Works. Trans. by Arthur S. Way, *Loeb Class. Lib.* Harvard Univ. Pr. 4 vols. 1912 ea. $12.50

Euripides I. Ed. by David Grene and Richmond Lattimore, *Complete Greek Tragedies* Univ. of Chicago Pr. (Phoenix Bks.) 1955 pap. $5.50. Contains *Alcestis* (438 B.C.), translated by Richmond Lattimore; *The Medea* (431 B.C.), translated by Rex Warner; *The Heracleidae* (c.427 B.C.), translated by Ralph Gladstone; *Hippolytus* (428 B.C.), translated by David Grene; introduction by Richmond Lattimore.

Euripides II. Ed. by David Grene and Richmond Lattimore, *Complete Greek Tragedies* Univ. of Chicago Pr. (Phoenix Bks.) 1956 pap. $5.50. Contains *The Cyclops* (c.423 B.C.) and *Heracles* (c.422 B.C.), translated by William Arrowsmith; *Iphigenia in*

Tauris (c.413 B.C.), translated by Witter Bynner; *Helen* (412 B.C.), translated by Richmond Lattimore.

Euripides III. Ed. by David Grene and Richmond Lattimore, *Complete Greek Tragedies* Univ. of Chicago Pr. (Phoenix Bks.) 1958 pap. $5.50. Contains *Hecuba* (c.424 B.C.), translated by William Arrowsmith; *Andromache* (c.426 B.C.), translated by John Frederick Nims; *The Trojan Women* (415 B.C.), translated by Richmond Lattimore; *Ion* (c.411 B.C.), translated by Ronald Frederick Willetts.

Euripides IV. Ed. by David Grene and Richmond Lattimore, *Complete Greek Tragedies* Univ. of Chicago Pr. (Phoenix Bks.) 1958 pap. $5.50. Contains *Rhesus*, translated by Richmond Lattimore; *The Suppliant Women* (c.421 B.C.), translated by Frank William Jones; *Orestes* (408 B.C.), translated by William Arrowsmith; *Iphigenia in Aulis* (c.405 B.C.), translated by Charles R. Walker.

Euripides V. Ed. by David Grene and *Richmond Lattimore, Complete Greek Tragedies* Univ. of Chicago Pr. (Phoenix Bks.) 1959 pap. $5.50. Contains *Electra* (417 B.C.), translated by Emily Townsend Vermeule; *The Phoenician Women* (c.409 B.C.), translated by Elizabeth Wyckoff; *The Bacchae* (c.405 B.C.), translated by William Arrowsmith.

Ten Plays of Euripides. Trans. by Moses Hadas and John H. McLean, *Bantam Class. Ser.* 1981 pap. $2.95. Contains *Alcestis; Medea; Hippolytus; Andromache; Ion; The Trojan Women; Electra; Iphigenia among the Taurians; Bacchants; Iphigenia at Aulis*.

Three Plays of Euripides. Trans. by Paul Roche, Norton 1974 pap. $3.95. Contains *Alcestis, Medea,* and *The Bacchae*.

Rhesos. Trans. by Gilbert Murray, Allen & Unwin repr. of 1913 ed. text ed. pap. $3.95; trans. by Richard E. Braun, ed. by William Arrowsmith, *Greek Tragedy in New Translations* Oxford 1978 $19.95

Alcestis. Trans. by Gilbert Murray, Allen & Unwin repr. of 1915 ed. text ed. pap. $3.95; trans. and ed. by William Arrowsmith, *Greek Tragedy in New Translations* Oxford 1974 $19.95; ed. by A. M. Dale, *Plays of Euripides Ser.* Oxford 1954 pap. $10.95

Medea. Trans. by Gilbert Murray, Allen & Unwin repr. of 1910 ed. text ed. pap. $3.95; ed. by Alan Elliott, Oxford 1969 pap. $8.95; ed. by Denys L. Page, Oxford text ed. 1938 pap. $10.95

Medea and Hippolytus. Trans. by Sydney Waterlow, AMS Pr. repr. of 1906 ed. $18.50

Hippolytus. Trans. by Gilbert Murray, Allen & Unwin repr. of 1902 ed. text ed. pap. $3.95; trans. by Robert Bagg, ed. by William Arrowsmith, *Greek Tragedy in New Translations* Oxford 1973 $19.95

Electra. Trans. by Gilbert Murray, Allen & Unwin repr. of 1905 ed. text ed. pap. $3.95; trans. by Moses Hadas, Bobbs pap. $2.95; ed. by J.D. Denniston, Oxford 1973 pap. $14.95

The Trojan Women. Trans. by Gilbert Murray, Allen & Unwin repr. of 1905 ed. text ed. pap. $3.95; ed. and adapted by Jean-Paul Sartre, Random (Vintage) pap. $1.65

Iphigenia at Aulis. Trans. by William Merwin and George Dimock, ed. by William Arrowsmith, *Greek Tragedy in New Translations* Oxford 1978 $19.95

Iphigenia in Tauris. Trans. by Gilbert Murray, Allen & Unwin repr. of 1910 ed. text ed. pap. $3.95; trans. by Richmond Lattimore, ed. by William Arrowsmith, *Greek Tragedy in New Translations* Oxford 1973 $14.95

Ion. Trans. by Gilbert Murray, Allen & Unwin text ed. 1954 pap. $3.95; trans. by D. W. Lucas, Verry 1949 $2.50

The Bacchae. Trans. by Gilbert Murray, Allen & Unwin repr. of 1904 ed. text ed. pap.

$3.95; trans. by Michael Cacoyannis, New Amer. Lib. 1982 pap. $1.95; ed. by
E. R. Dodds, Oxford 2d ed. 1960 $15.95

BOOKS ABOUT EURIPIDES

Conacher, D. J. *Euripidean Drama: Myth, Theme and Structure.* Ed. by W. R. Connor,
Univ. of Toronto Pr. 1967 $25.00. One chapter on each play, a good summary.

Decharme, Paul. *Euripides and the Spirit of His Dramas.* Trans. by J. Loeb, Associated Faculty Pr. repr. of 1906 ed. 1968 $15.00

Dodds, Eric R. *The Greeks and the Irrational.* Univ. of California Pr. 1951 pap. $7.95.
A brilliant analysis of the Dionysian tendencies in Greek letters and thought—
particularly relevant to the "Bacchae."

Lucas, Frank L. *Euripides and His Influence.* Cooper Square Pr. repr. of 1930 ed.
$18.50; Gordon, $59.95

Murray, Gilbert. *Euripides and His Age.* Intro. by H. D. Kitto, Greenwood repr. of
1965 ed. 1979 lib. bdg. $27.50; Telegraph Bks. repr. of 1913 ed. 1983 lib. bdg.
$30.00

Powell, J. U., and E. A. Barber, eds. *New Chapters in the History of Greek Literature.*
Biblo & Tannen repr. of 1929 ed. $10.00

Vellacott, Philip. *Ironic Drama.* Cambridge Univ. Pr. 1975 pap. $14.95

Verrall, Arthur W. *Euripides the Rationalist.* Russell repr. of 1895 ed. 1967 $8.00

Whitman, Cedric H. *Euripides and the Full Circle of Myth. Loeb Class. Monographs
Ser.* Harvard Univ. Pr. text ed. 1974 $10.00

HELIODORUS OF EMESA. fl. A.D. 220–250

One of the earliest and longest of the surviving Greek novels, the
Aethiopica is a romance of two young lovers, Theagenes and Charicleia, set
in the fifth century B.C., which shows considerable insight and narrative
skill. It was much read by the Byzantines and in the sixteenth and seventeenth centuries was translated into many languages. Almost nothing is
known of the author except that he was a native of Emesa in Syria and perhaps later become Bishop of Tricca in Thessaly.

BOOKS BY HELIODORUS

The Aethiopian History. Trans. by Thomas Underdowne, intro. by C. Whibley, AMS
Pr. repr. of 1895 ed. $45.00

Ethiopian Story. Trans. by Walter Lamb, Dutton (Everyman's) 1961 o.p.

HERODOTUS. c.484–c.425 B.C.

[SEE Volume 3.]

HESIOD. c.700 B.C.

Hesiod tells us that his father gave up sea-trading and moved from Ascra
to Boeotia, that as he himself tended sheep on Mount Helicon the Muses
commanded him to sing of the gods, and that he won a tripod for a funeral
song at Chalcis. The poems credited to him with certainty are the *Theogony*,
which is an attempt to bring order into the otherwise chaotic material of
Greek mythology through genealogies and anecdotes about the gods, and
The Works and Days, a wise sermon addressed to his brother Perses, which
presents the injustice of the world with mythological examples and memo-

rable images, and concludes with a collection of folk wisdom. Uncertain attributions are the *Shield of Heracles* and the *Catalogue of Women*. Hesiod is a didactic and individualistic poet who is often compared and contrasted with Homer, as both are representative of early epic style.

BOOKS BY HESIOD

Works of Hesiod. Trans. by Thomas Cooke, AMS Pr. 2 vols. in 1 repr. of 1728 ed. $40.00

Hesiod, Homeric Hymns, Fragments of the Epic Cycle, Homerica. Loeb Class. Lib. Harvard Univ. Pr. $12.50. A careful, highly respected, scholarly translation of Hesiod.

The Works and Days. Ed. by W. R. Connor, Ayer repr. of 1932 ed. 1979 lib. bdg. $17.00; trans. by Richmond Lattimore, Univ. of Michigan Pr. 1959 $9.95. This translation in verse is always readable and never strained, and the excellent introductory essay gives much valuable information about a neglected epic tradition. "Hesiod is earth-bound and dun colored; indeed part of his purpose is to discredit the brilliance and the ideals of heroism glorified in the homeric tradition. But Hesiod too is poetry, though of a different order, and Lattimore's is the only version that makes the English reader aware that it is" (Moses Hadas, *N.Y. Times*).

Theogony. Trans. by Norman O. Brown, Bobbs 1953 pap. $3.56; ed. by M. L. West, Oxford 1966 $49.95. The translator gives a fascinating introduction to the poet.

Hesiod: Theogony, Works and Days. Trans. by Apostolos N. Athanassakis, Johns Hopkins Univ. Pr. 1983 $17.95 pap. $6.95. A new, accurate translation with notes.

Hesiod and Theognis. Trans. by Dorothy Wender, *Penguin Class. Ser.* 1976 pap. $3.95

BOOKS ABOUT HESIOD

Burn, Andrew R. *The World of Hesiod.* Ayer repr. of 1936 ed. 1966 $15.00

Solmsen, Friedrich. *Hesiod and Aeschylus.* Ed. by W. R. Connor, Johnson Repr. repr. of 1949 ed. $27.00. The author is a leading classicist and scholar of Hesiod.

Walcott, P. *Hesiod and the Near East.* Verry 1966 o.p. A study of the interaction between Greece and the Near East in the late eighth and early seventh centuries B.C.

HOMER. c.700 B.C.

Homer is the father of European literature. The Greeks believed that both the *Iliad* and the *Odyssey* were composed by the blind bard Homer but were uncertain of his dates or his birthplace. Seven cities claimed him—Athens, Argos, Chios, Colophon, Rhodes, Salamis, and Smyrna. Now it is conjectured that he was an Ionian, probably from Chios, and that he lived around 700 B.C. Scholars have long disputed his authorship of both poems. But, for the present, the urgency of the "Homeric Question" has given way to general agreement that he was the presiding genius behind both epics. Modern experts have shown that these epics could have been recited without a written score or text to prompt the singer's memory because he would have relied instead on his stock of formulaic phrases or epithets to keep the narrative flowing. And yet, it must be said that, oral or written, real or imaginary, late or early, Homer remains a mysterious figure wrapped in the mists of the ancient past.

The *Iliad*, considered the earlier of the two poems, tells the story of the Trojan War and of its two heroes, Achilles and Hector. The narrative, which begins in the midst of the siege and moves very rapidly toward its tragic conclusion, is often interrupted at a moment of crisis by beautiful similes drawn from nature, farming, and handcrafts. Its language is magnificent and rich and its poetry at the peak of Western literary tradition.

The *Odyssey*, which may have been written in Homer's old age, recounts the wanderings of Odysseus after the Trojan War and his final homecoming to Ithaca, where he found his wife Penelope still faithful to him. It is a fantastical adventure story with a comic tone and a happy ending. Like the *Iliad*, it is noteworthy for its beautiful poetry, simplicity of statement, dramatic plot and postponement, and nobility of character.

Also attributed to Homer are the *Homeric Hymns*, invocations to such gods as Apollo, Aphrodite, and Hermes. They vary in tone from tender to amusing to erotic, but all are expressed in exquisite Homeric language. They were written in the dactylic hexameter style of Homer; in antiquity they were believed by some to be written by Homer.

Homer was a bible, an oracle, the repository of all wisdom for the Greeks. His poetry shaped the Greek character and Greek literature from its beginnings. It was the seminal influence on Latin literature and has continued to dominate European vernacular literature even to the present: Hesiod, Pindar, Aeschylus, Sophocles, Euripides, and Plato; VIRGIL, HORACE, AND OVID; DANTE; CHAUCER (see Vol. 1), SHAKESPEARE, and MILTON (see Vol. 1); and in our time, JOYCE (see Vol. 1) and Kazantzakis. The idea of the hero, of tragedy and comedy, of beginning a story in the middle, dramatic postponement, divine intervention, flashback, and the rich assembly of individual plots and characters—all these fundamentals come from Homer.

BOOKS BY HOMER

THE ILIAD: OLDER VERSIONS

Bryant, William Cullen. *The Iliad*. 1870. o.p. In rhymeless iambic pentameter.

Butler, Samuel. *The Iliad*. 1898. o.p. Prose translation. The author of *Erewhon* and *The Way of All Flesh* translated both the *Iliad* and the *Odyssey* into prose in an effort "to rescue them from the clutches of a blighting academism; for he knew that the terriblest thing Homer, a vital and living artist, has to fight against the fact that his work has been a school book for over two thousand five hundred years."

Chapman, George, trans. *The Iliad, The Odyssey, and the Lesser Homerica*. Ed. by Allardyce Nicoll, *Bollingen Ser.* Princeton Univ. Pr. 2 vols. 2d ed. 1967 $80.00. Translation in rhyming couplets. The first English translation of Homer—the translation that inspired Keats to write his famous sonnet: "Much have I travelled in the realms of gold." Chapman first issued his translation in 1616, the year of Shakespeare's death. For present-day readers, Chapman's translation is rather archaic.

Hobbes, Thomas. *Iliads and Odysseys*. AMS Pr. repr. of 1677 ed. 2d ed. $54.50. The famous philosopher tried his hand at Homer toward the end of his career—more, he claimed, for recreation than for any other reason. His version retains some of the vigor of the author's style as seen in his original prose works.

Lang, Andrew. *The Iliad. Airmont Class. Ser.* pap. $1.25. In prose. Written in biblical diction.

Pope, Alexander. *The Iliads.* Oxford 1934 o.p. In rhyming couplets of 18 syllables. Pope's translation, a literary *tour de force*, remained for many years the standard English version, and as such had a great influence on English poetry as well as on the reputation of Homer.

THE ILIAD: MODERN VERSIONS

Fitzgerald, Robert, trans. *The Iliad.* Doubleday (Anchor) 1974 $15.00. Fluent and graceful and eminently readable.

Graves, Robert. *The Anger of Achilles: Homer's Iliad.* o.p. In prose with occasional ballad-like verse. "He is magnificently and unfailingly readable" (Dudley Fitts, *N.Y. Times*).

Lattimore, Richmond, trans. *The Iliad of Homer.* Univ. of Chicago Pr. 1977 $20.00 pap. $6.95. A new verse translation in a free six-beat line. The most faithful to Homer of all the modern translations, Lattimore's version is highly respected for both its accuracy and its poetry.

Murray, Augustus. *The Iliad. Loeb Class. Lib.* Harvard Univ. Pr. 2 vols. ea. $12.50. In prose, bilingual. The rendering is smooth, fluent, and exact.

Richards, Ivor Armstrong. *Iliad: A Shortened Version. Norton Lib.* 1958 pap. $2.75. A very readable modern version of strong continuing action has been made by cutting many passages and omitting entirely Books 2, 10, 13, and 17.

Rouse, William Henry Denham. *The Iliad.* New Amer. Lib. 1954 pap. $2.25. In prose. This is a readable and vigorous rendering.

THE ODYSSEY: OLDER VERSIONS

Bryant, William Cullen. *The Odyssey.* 1871–72 o.p. In blank verse. Rhymeless iambic pentameter similar in excellence to his *Iliad.*

Butler, Samuel. *The Odyssey.* 1900 o.p. In prose.

Chapman, George. *The Odyssey.* 1616. Translation in rhyming couplets. Chapman's *Odyssey* is in all features like his *Iliad.* The only change was the use of a line of five accented syllables instead of seven accented syllables as in the *Iliad.* The ballad style remains the same.

Cowper, William. *The Odyssey.* 1791 o.p. In blank verse. Although Cowper translated the *Iliad* also, he was not nearly so successful with it as with the *Odyssey.* His version of the *Iliad* is found only in his collected poetical works. His attempt to render Homer in Miltonic blank verse is slow and elaborate.

Pope, Alexander. *Odyssey of Homer.* Ed. by Maynard Mack, Yale Univ. Pr. 2 vols. 1967 $92.00. In rhyming couplets. See also Pope, *The Iliads.*

THE ODYSSEY: MODERN VERSIONS

Cook, Albert. *The Odyssey.* Norton 1967 $6.00 pap. $5.95. The author has made a "literal translation following the original line for line. These lines scan easily and move rapidly, thus reproducing one of the special delights of Homeric style. It is always a real pleasure to read a translation which [reflects] faithfully what the poet says" (Francis D. Lazenby).

Fitzgerald, Robert. *The Odyssey.* Harper 1968 pap. $4.33. This new blank-verse translation by an American poet, who worked on it for seven years, has been called a "masterpiece." "One of the great merits of Fitzgerald's book is its rendering of

Homer's heroic dignity, his moral force, his religious spirit—and this without loss of narrative, clarity and action. . . . One never forgets that Homer was a poet, a poet of serious purpose and austere imagery" (*N.Y. Times*).

Lattimore, Richmond, trans. *The Odyssey of Homer: A Modern Translation*. Harper 1967 $12.95. "Lattimore's [verse] translation . . . is the most eloquent, persuasive and imaginative I have seen. It reads as few translations ever do—as if the poem had been written originally in English, and in language idiomatic, lively, and urgent" (Paul Engle).

Murray, Augustus Taber. *The Odyssey. Loeb Class. Lib.* Harvard Univ. Pr. 2 vols. ea. $12.50. In prose.

Rieu, Emil. *The Odyssey. Penguin Class. Ser.* pap. $19.50. In prose. After several experiments and many years, Rieu evoked an easy, unaffected, and rapid style. It is a genuine translation, as is his *Iliad* (o.p.).

Rouse, W. H. *The Odyssey*. New Amer. Lib. 1971 pap. $1.95. A prose translation; recommended.

Shaw, T. E. (Lawrence of Arabia). *The Odyssey*. Oxford 1932 pap. $5.95. This rendering of the *Odyssey* by Lawrence of Arabia is written in straightforward, compelling prose and is faithful to the intent of the original. It reads better than the other modern translations and comes with a brilliant, eccentric introduction.

HOMERIC HYMNS

These poems are short narratives about the gods, embedded in the context of a prayer to the god. The Homeric Hymn to Apollo, for example, tells the story of Leto's search for a place to give birth and how Artemis and Apollo were born; the Homeric Hymn to Demeter tells how Demeter's daughter was abducted by Hades and the subsequent quest of the mother for the daughter. Other poems tell of Aphrodite's love of mortal man or Hermes' theft of Apollo's cattle and many other such tales. Perhaps the attribution of these songs to Homer helped preserve them.

Athanassakis, Apostolos N. *Homeric Hymns*. Johns Hopkins Univ. Pr. 1976 $12.00. An attractive, readable translation with notes.

Evelyn-White, H. G. *Hesiod and the Homeric Hymns. Loeb Class. Lib.* Harvard Univ. Pr. 1914 $12.50. Literal translation in a bilingual edition.

BOOKS ABOUT HOMER

Arnold, Matthew. *On Translating Homer*. AMS Pr. repr. of 1905 ed. $16.25. Arnold believed that Homer is eminently rapid, eminently plain and direct in expression, eminently simple and direct in ideas, and eminently noble.

Austin, Norman. *Archery at the Dark of the Moon: Poetic Problems in Homer's Odyssey*. Univ. of California Pr. 1975 $32.50 pap. $9.95

Bespaloff, R. *On the Iliad. Bollingen Ser.* Princeton Univ. Pr. 1970 $12.00 pap. $2.45. Engaging analysis showing the relationship of Homer's characters and ethical ideas to the present day.

Beye, Charles R. *The Iliad, the Odyssey, and the Epic Tradition*. Gordian repr. of 1966 ed. 1976 $12.50; Peter Smith $14.25

Bowra, C. M. *Tradition and Design in the Iliad*. Greenwood repr. of 1930 ed. 1977 lib. bdg. $29.75. Argues that the poem was constructed by one poet using traditional sources and adding new material of his own.

Bradford, Ernle. *Ulysses Found*. Harcourt 1964 o.p. Since the age of 19, Bradford has sailed the Mediterranean in search of the route of Ulysses and has found Homeric geography to bear out in fact—"it is the very authenticity of the winds and weathers, ports and harbors, which acts as a solid backbone to the poem." "*Ulysses Found* is highly literate, full of wit and wry, a delight from start to finish" (Francis D. Lazenby, *LJ*).

Butler, Samuel. *The Authoress of the Odyssey.* 1897. Univ. of Chicago Pr. 1967 o.p. This heterodox study of the epic argues that it was written more than two centuries after the *Iliad* and that its author was a young Sicilian woman of Trapan; it is worth reading.

Carpenter, Rhys. *Folk Tale, Fiction and Saga in the Homeric Epics.* Univ. of California Pr. 1974 $24.50

Clarke, Howard. *The Art of the Odyssey.* Prentice-Hall 1967 o.p. Five essays intended for readers of Homer in translation. There is an interesting chapter on the history and problems of English translation. "A welcome addition to the ever-increasing Homeric literature" (*LJ*).

———. *Homer's Readers: A Historical Introduction to the Iliad and the Odyssey.* Univ. of Delaware Pr. 1980 $26.50

Cunliffe, Richard J. *A Lexicon of the Homeric Dialect.* Univ. of Oklahoma Pr. 1977 pap. $14.95. For English-speaking readers of Homer in the original, this reprint based on the Oxford Classical Text editions includes all words except, unfortunately, names. "The author's scholarship is matched by his (and the printer's) accuracy."

Finley, John H., Jr. *Homer's Odyssey.* Harvard Univ. Pr. 1978 $16.50. Interesting essays on various themes and characters.

Finley, Moses I. *The World of Odysseus.* Pref. by Mark Van Doren, Viking 1954 o.p. A background book on the ways of the Homeric world for the delight and enlightenment of all readers.

Gordon, Cyrus H. *Homer and Bible: The Origin and Character of East Mediterranean Literature.* Ventnor 1967 pap. $2.95. Explores the connections and interactions of the Mediterranean cultures.

Kazantzakis, Nikos. *The Odyssey: A Modern Sequel.* Simon & Schuster (Touchstone Bks.) 1961 pap. $12.95. The author takes up the story where Homer left off.

Kirk, Geoffrey S. *Homer and the Epic.* Cambridge Univ. Pr. abr. ed. pap. $11.95. A shortened version of *Songs of Homer.*

———. *Songs of Homer.* Cambridge Univ. Pr. 1962 $62.50

Lord, Albert B. *The Singer of Tales.* Pref. by H. Levin, Atheneum text ed. 1965 pap. $3.95; Harvard Univ. Pr. text ed. 1981 $7.95. Using the parallel case of Yugoslavian oral epic, this work explains why Homer may have been an oral poet. A landmark in Homeric studies.

Mireaux, Emile. *Daily Life in the Time of Homer.* Trans. by Iris Sells, Macmillan 1959 o.p. Good background reading.

Nagler, Michael. *Spontaneity and Tradition: A Study in the Oral Art of Homer.* Univ. of California Pr. 1975 $32.00

Nilsson, Martin P. *Homer and Mycenae.* Cooper Square Pr. repr. of 1933 ed. 1968 $30.00; Univ. of Pennsylvania Pr. repr. of 1933 ed. 1972 pap. $8.95. A compelling theological and anthropological study.

Page, Denys L. *History and the Homeric Iliad.* Univ. of California Pr. 1959 $23.50. A heavily annotated and exhaustive study of the preclassical world, based on recent archaeological finds.

Redfield, James M. *Nature and Culture in the Iliad: The Tragedy of Hector.* Univ. of Chicago Pr. (Phoenix Bks.) repr. of 1975 ed. 1978 pap. $5.95

Scott, John A. *The Unity of Homer.* Biblo & Tannen 1921 $10.00

Stanford, William B. *Ulysses Theme.* Univ. of Michigan Pr. 1968 pap. $9.95

Wace, Alan J. B., and Frank H. Stubbings, eds. *A Companion to Homer*. Macmillan 1963 o.p. "Started before 1939, having lost by death editor Wace and three others, but having gained from new excavations and the decipherment of Linear B, the publication of this giant in every sense is an important event. The list of 17 contributors resembles a Homeric Who's Who, the contents a Homeric What's What. Though intended chiefly for those reading Homer in Greek, this Companion has much to do for those reading him in English" (*LJ*).

Weil, Simone. *Iliad, or the Poem of Force*. Pendle Hill 1956 pap. $2.30. This was written by a victim of the Nazi concentration camps who brings her original mind to bear on the meaning of force in the *Iliad*.

Whitman, Cedric H. *Homer and the Heroic Tradition*. Norton Lib. Bobbs 1965 pap. $4.95. Chiefly devoted to the *Iliad* (the *Odyssey* is considered in the final chapter), the book presents arguments, both historical and contemporary, with objectivity; valuable for Whitman's judgments resulting from recent discoveries.

Willcock, Malcolm L. *A Companion to the Iliad*. Trans. by Richmond Lattimore, Univ. of Chicago Pr. 1976 $20.00; Univ. of Chicago Pr. (Phoenix Bks.) 1976 pap. $7.95. Annotations geared to the English text of Lattimore's translation.

JOSEPHUS, FLAVIUS. 37–95

[SEE Volume 3.]

LONGINUS. c.1st century A.D.

"Longinus" is the author assigned to *On the Sublime*, a treatise that defines the sublime in literature, using Homer, PLATO (see Vol. 4), and Demosthenes as the chief examples. Translated by Boileau in 1674, this greatly influenced literary theory until the early nineteenth century and is of lasting importance as a brilliant critique of classical literature.

BOOK BY LONGINUS

On Sublimity. Ed. by D. A. Russell, Oxford 1968 $9.95; (with the title *On the Sublime*), trans. by G. M. A. Grube, Bobbs 1957 pap. $2.40

LONGUS. fl. 2nd or 3rd century A.D.?

The pastoral *Daphnis and Chloe*, the best of the ancient Greek romances, is attributed to Longus. Nothing is known of his life. His passionate love story of two foundlings raised together by shepherds on Lesbos is sweetly told and has been persistently admired for its bucolic charm.

BOOK BY LONGUS

Daphnis and Chloe (and *Love Romances, Parthenius*, and *Fragments of the Ninus Romance*). Trans. by Moses Hadas, rev. by J. M. Edmonds, *Loeb Class. Lib.* Harvard Univ. Pr. $12.00

BOOKS ABOUT LONGUS

Hagg, Thomas. *The Novel in Antiquity*. Univ. of California Pr. text ed. 1983 $30.00. Excellent survey of the whole field.

Heiserman, Arthur. *The Novel before the Novel: Essays and Discussions about the Beginnings of Prose Fiction in the West*. Univ. of Chicago Pr. text ed. 1980 pap. $8.00. A useful introduction.

McCulloh, William E. *Longus. World Authors Ser.* Irvington 1970 lib. bdg. $15.95
Perry, Ben E. *The Ancient Romances: A Literary Historical Account of Their Origins.* Univ. of California Pr. 1967 $32.50. This work places Longus in the context of the romance tradition.

LUCIAN (Lucianus Samosatensis). c.120–c.185 A.D.

Lucian, the wit and satirist, was a brilliant Greek writer in the time of the Roman Empire. He was born in Samosata, Syria; traveled and lectured in Italy, Asia Minor, and Gaul; and in later life held a government position in Egypt. Of nearly 80 works, the most important and characteristic are his essays, written in dialogue form. "Dialogues of the Gods," "Dialogues of the Dead," and "The Sale of Lives" show his knowledge of classical Greek and ancient mythology. He is a good critical source for ancient art and for information about his literary contemporaries. The *True History*, a nonsense fantasy and parody of adventure stories, influenced Rabelais and Swift.

BOOKS BY LUCIAN

The Works of Lucian of Samosata. Trans. by H. W. Fowler and F. G. Fowler, Oxford 1905 o.p. Classic translation of Lucian by the authors of the original *Modern English Usage.*
Selected Works. Trans. by B. P. Reardon, Bobbs 1965 pap. $5.65
Selected Satires of Lucian. Norton Lib. 1968 pap. $8.95
Dialogues. Loeb Class. Lib. Harvard Univ. Pr. 8 vols. ea. $12.50
True History and Lucius or the Ass Trans. by Paul Turner, Indiana Univ. Pr. repr. of 1958 ed. $5.95 pap. $1.95

BOOKS ABOUT LUCIAN

Allinson, Francis G. *Lucian, Satirist and Artist.* Cooper Square Pr. repr. of 1930 ed. $15.00
Jebb, Richard C. *Essays and Addresses.* Longwood Pr. repr. of 1907 ed. 1973 $30.00. Contains a chapter on Lucian.
Robinson, Christopher. *Lucian and His Influence in Europe.* Univ. of North Carolina Pr. 1979 $22.50

MENANDER. 342/341–293/289 B.C.

The late fourth century gave rise to New Comedy—a comedy of manners that was more refined and lacked the robustness of Old Comedy. Until the latter part of the nineteenth century, Menander's plays were known only through adaptations and translations made by the Roman dramatists Plautus and Terence, and by the comments of OVID and PLINY (see Vol. 3). Menander wrote approximately 100 plays and the few extant in the Greek text were found on papyrus rolls in the rubbish heaps of Roman Egypt. However *The Dyskolos*, the first complete Menander New Comedy to be discovered intact, turned up on papyrus in a private Swiss collection. His comedies are skillfully constructed, his characters well delineated, his diction excellent, and his themes mostly the trials and tribulations of young love with conventional solutions.

Menander was born in Athens of the upper class, and studied under the philosopher-scientist Theophrastus, the successor of Aristotle.

BOOKS BY MENANDER

Menander. Trans. by *W. G. Arnott, Loeb Class. Lib.* Harvard Univ. Pr. 1982 vol. 1 $12.50. First of three volumes replacing the older Allison translation.
Comedies. Trans. by Frank G. Allinson, *Loeb Class. Lib.* Harvard Univ. Pr. $12.50
The Girl from Samos. Trans. by E. G. Turner, Athlone text ed. 1972 pap. $14.95
Menander: The Principal Fragments. Trans. by Frank G. Allinson, Greenwood repr. of 1921 ed. lib. bdg. $24.75

BOOKS ABOUT MENANDER

Gomme, A. W., and F. H. Sandbach. *Menander: A Commentary.* Oxford 1973 $69.00. Based on the Oxford Classical Texts of *Dyskolos*, and *Reliquiae Selectae* also edited by Sandbach.
Webster, T. B. *The Birth of Modern Comedy of Manners.* Folcroft 1959 lib. bdg. $10.00; Humanities Pr. 1959 pap. $2.00

MOSCHUS. fl. 150 B.C.

[SEE Theocritus in this chapter.]

PHILO JUDAEUS. fl. c. A.D. 1

[SEE Volume 4.]

PINDAR. 518–c.438 B.C.

Pindar, a Boeotian aristocrat who wrote for aristocrats, lived at Thebes, studied at Athens, and stayed in Sicily at the court of Hieron at Syracuse. His epinicians or choral odes in honor of victors at athletic games, survive almost complete and are divided into four groups dependent on whether they celebrate victory at the Olympian, Pythian, Nemean, or Isthmian games. It is surmised that these are representative of his other poetry—such as the hymns, processional songs, dirges—that is extant in fragments.

The odes joyfully praise beautiful, brilliant athletes who are like the gods in their moment of triumph. Bold mythological metaphor, dazzling intricacy of language, and metrical complexity together create sublimity of thought and of style. Pindar was famous in his lifetime and later throughout the Hellenistic world, as is attested by the story that Alexander the Great in 335 B.C. ordered the poet's house spared when his army sacked Thebes.

The "Pindaric ode" form used in England in the seventeenth and early eighteenth centuries was based on an incorrect understanding of Pindar's metrical schemes and was characterized by grandiose diction. Abraham Cowley published his *Pindarique Odes* in 1656, and the form was used by DRYDEN (see Vol. 1), POPE (see Vol. 1), SWIFT (see Vol. 1), and others. Cowley's odes were paraphrases rather than translations, according to his preface; he said that "if a man should undertake to translate Pindar word for word, it would be thought that one madman had translated another." Sir John E. Sandys's prose translation is "scholarly and dignified." The free-verse renderings used by Richmond Lattimore in an effort to suggest

Pindar's own meters give us a version that is "clear and lucid, except when Pindar himself is otherwise, and then Mr. Lattimore, like a true translator, reproduces the obscurity of the original by an obscurity transferred to the English" (David Grene, *Poetry*).

BOOKS BY PINDAR

Odes and Fragments. Trans. by Sir John E. Sandys, *Loeb Class. Lib.* Harvard Univ. Pr. 1915–19 $12.50

The Odes of Pindar. Trans. by C. M. Bowra, Penguin 1982 pap. $4.95; trans. by Richmond Lattimore, Univ. of Chicago Pr. (Phoenix Bks.) repr. of 1947 ed. 2d ed. 1976 pap. $6.95. An adequate version.

Pindar's Victory Songs. Trans. by Frank J. Nisetich, Johns Hopkins Univ. Pr. text ed. 1980 $30.00 pap. $8.95. A very good translation with a useful scholarly introduction.

Pindar's Odes. Trans. by Roy A. Swanson, Irvington text ed. repr. 1974 pap. $3.95. Includes some famous imitations of Pindar in English.

Songs and Action: Victory Odes of Pindar. Trans. by Kevin Crotty, Johns Hopkins Univ. Pr. 1982 o.p.

BOOKS ABOUT PINDAR

Bowra, C. M. *Pindar*. Ed. by Basil L. Gildersleeve, Oxford 1964 $32.50. Indispensable for understanding the difficult poetry of Pindar.

Burton, R. W. B. *Pindar's Pythian Odes*. Oxford 1962 o.p. A classic study.

Finley, John H., Jr. *Pindar and Aeschylus*. Oxford 1962 o.p. An important study of the relationship between the two poets, who met at Hieron's court in Syracuse.

Norwood, Gilbert. *Pindar*. Univ. of California Pr. 1974 $32.00

PLATO. c.429–347 B.C.

[SEE Volume 4.]

PLUTARCH. c.46–c.125

[SEE Volume 3.]

POLYBIUS. c.200–c.118 B.C.

[SEE Volume 3.]

PROCOPIUS. c.500–c.565

[SEE Volume 3.]

SAPPHO. c.612 B.C.

Sappho, whom PLATO (see Vol. 4) called "the tenth Muse," was the greatest of the early Greek lyric poets. She was born at Mytilene on Lesbos and was a member, perhaps the head, of a group of women who honored the Muses and Aphrodite. Her brilliant love lyrics, marriage songs, and hymns to the gods are written in Aeolic dialect in many meters, one of which is named for her—the Sapphic. Only fragments survive. Her verse is simple and direct, exquisitely passionate and vivid. Catullus, OVID, and SWINBURNE (see Vol. 1) were among the many later poets influenced by her.

BOOKS BY SAPPHO

The Poems of Sappho. Trans. by J. M. Edmonds, *Loeb Class. Lib.* Harvard Univ. Pr. 3
vols. ea. $12.50. Sometimes obscure, but generally faithful translation.
Sappho: A New Translation. Trans. by Mary Barnard, Univ. of California Pr. 1958
pap. $3.95
Greek Lyrics. Trans. by D. A. Campbell, *Loeb Class. Lib.* Harvard Univ. Pr. 1982
$12.50. Greek text with English translation, superseding Edmonds' erratic trans-
lations. Complete with succinct notes.

BOOKS ABOUT SAPPHO

Bowra, C. M. *Greek Lyric Poetry from Alcman to Simonides.* Oxford 2d ed. 1962 o.p. A
sensitive critique of Sappho's lyrics and of problems associated with the text.
Burnett, Anne P. *Three Archaic Poets: Archilochus, Alcaeus, Sappho.* Harvard Univ.
Pr. text ed. 1983 $25.00. Close and perceptive reading of fragments, especially
good on Sappho.
Page, Denys L. *Sappho and Alcaeus.* Oxford 1955 pap. $19.95. Text, translation, and
commentary with an introductory essay to the two poets from Lesbos. This distinguished book is required reading for the serious student.
Robinson, David M. *Sappho and Her Influence.* Cambridge Univ. Pr. repr. of 1930 ed.
$18.50

SOPHOCLES. c.496–406 B.C.

Sophocles, born to a wealthy family at Colonus, near Athens, was admired as a boy for his personal beauty and musical skill. He served faithfully as treasurer and general for Athens when it was expanding its empire
and influence. In the dramatic contests, he defeated Aeschylus in 468 B.C.
for first prize in tragedy, wrote a poem to Herodotus, and led his chorus
and actors in mourning for Euripides just a few months before his own
death. He wrote approximately 123 plays, of which 7 tragedies are extant as
well as a fragment of his satiric play, *Ichneutae (Hunters).* His plays were
produced in the following order: *Ajax* (c.450 B.C.), *Antigone* (441 B.C.), *Oedipus Tyrannus* (c.430 B.C.), *Trachiniae* (c.430 B.C.), *Electra* (between 418 and
410 B.C.), *Philoctetes* (409 B.C.), and *Oedipus at Colonus* (posthumously in 401
B.C.). With Sophocles, Greek tragedy reached its most characteristic development. He added a third actor, made each play independent, that is not dependent on others in a trilogy, increased the numbers of the chorus, introduced the use of scenery, shifted the focus from religious to more philosophical issues, and brought language and characters, though still majestic,
nearer to everyday life. His finely delineated characters are responsible for
the tragedy that befalls them and accept it heroically. Aristotle states that
Sophocles said he portrayed people as they ought to be; Euripides, as they
are. His utter command of tragic speech in the simple grandeur of his choral odes, dialogues, and monologues encourages the English reader to compare him to SHAKESPEARE.

BOOKS BY SOPHOCLES

The Tragedies of Sophocles. Trans. by Richard C. Jebb, *Select Bibliographies Repr. Ser.*
Ayer repr. of 1904 ed. $19.00

The Complete Plays. Trans. by Richard C. Jebb, ed. by Moses Hadas, Bantam pap.
$2.95. A newly revised edition of the famous Jebb translations.

Tragedies. Trans. by Francis Storr, *Loeb Class. Lib.* Harvard Univ. Pr. 2 vols. ea.
$12.50. Volume 1 contains *Oedipus the King, Oedipus at Colonus, Antigone.* Vol-
ume 2 contains *Ajax, Electra, Trachinae, Philoctetes,* and a bibliography of editions and translations.

Sophocles I. Univ. of Chicago Pr. (Phoenix Bks.) 1954 pap. $6.00. Contains *Oedipus
the King,* translated by David Grene; *Oedipus at Colonus,* translated by Robert
Fitzgerald; *Antigone,* translated by Elizabeth Wyckoff.

Sophocles II. Univ. of Chicago Pr. (Phoenix Bks.) 1957 pap. $6.00. Contains *Ajax,*
translated by John Moore; *The Women of Trachis,* translated by Michael Jameson; *Electra* and *Philoctetes,* translated by David Grene.

Three Theban Plays. Trans. by Theodore H. Banks, Oxford 1956 pap. $4.95; trans. by
Robert Fagles, intro. by Bernard Knox, *Penguin Class. Ser.* 1984 pap. $2.95

Three Tragedies: Antigone, Oedipus the King, and Electra. Trans. by H. D. Kitto, Oxford text ed. 1962 pap. $4.95

Antigone. Trans. by Michael Townsend, Harper text ed. 1962 pap. $4.50; trans. by
Richard E. Braun, ed. by William Arrowsmith, *Greek Tragedy in New Translations* Oxford 1973 $19.95

Oedipus the King. Trans. by Peter D. Arnott, *Crofts Class. Ser.* Harlan Davidson text
ed. 1960 pap. $3.75; trans. by *Diskin Clay* and Stephen Berg, ed. by William Ar-
rowsmith, *Greek Tragedy in New Translations* Oxford 1978 $19.95; trans. by Rob-
ert Bagg, Univ. of Massachusetts Pr. 1982 lib. bdg. $10.00 text ed. pap. $5.00;
trans. by Anthony Burgess, intro. by Michael Langham and Anthony Burgess,
Drama Eds. Ser. Univ. of Minnesota Pr. 1972 $5.95 pap. $3.45; ed. by Harry
Shefter, *Enriched Class. Ed. Ser.* Washington Square Pr. pap. $2.95

Oedipus Rex. Ed. by R. D. Dawe, Cambridge Univ. Pr. 1982 $39.50 pap. $13.95

Women of Trachis. Trans. by C. K. Williams and Gregory W. Dickerson, ed. by William Arrowsmith, *Greek Tragedy in New Translations* Oxford text ed. 1978 $19.95

Electra. Trans. by Lewis Theobald, AMS Pr. repr. of 1714 ed. $20.00; trans. by Rich-
ard C. Jebb, intro. by J. F. Charles, Bobbs 1950 pap. $1.80; trans. by E. F. Wat-
ling, *Penguin Class. Ser.* 1953 pap. $2.95

Electra: A Version for the Modern Stage. Trans. by Francis Fergusson, Theatre Arts
1938 pap. $3.50

Oedipus at Colonus. Trans. by Gilbert Murray, Allen & Unwin text ed. 1948 pap.
$3.95; trans. and ed. by Peter D. Arnott, *Crofts Class. Ser.* Harlan Davidson text
ed. 1975 pap. $3.50

BOOKS ABOUT SOPHOCLES

Bates, William N. *Sophocles, Poet and Dramatist.* Ed. by Richmond Lattimore, Russell repr. of 1940 ed. 1969 $10.00

Bowra, C. M. *Sophoclean Tragedy.* Oxford 1944 pap. o.p. A sensitive and comprehensive study.

Campbell, Lewis. *Tragic Drama in Aeschylus, Sophocles and Shakespeare: An Essay.*
Russell repr. of 1904 ed. 1965 $8.50

Earp, Frank R. *Style of Sophocles.* Russell repr. of 1944 ed. 1972 $12.00

Ehrenberg, Victor. *Sophocles and Pericles.* Humanities Pr. 1954 o.p. The author describes the friendship between these two great Athenians.

Grene, David. *Reality and the Heroic Pattern: Last Plays of Ibsen, Shakespeare, and
Sophocles.* Univ. of Chicago Pr. 1967 o.p. A "basic and lucid study" (*LJ*) by the

noted editor of *The Complete Greek Tragedies;* three of ten essays included treat Sophocles' *Ajax, Philoctetes,* and *Oedipus at Colonus.*

Kirkwood, G. M. *A Study of Sophoclean Drama.* Johnson Repr. o.p. An illuminating and important analysis.

Knox, Bernard M. *The Heroic Temper: Studies in Sophoclean Tragedy.* Univ. of California Pr. 1983 pap. $7.95. A perceptive study by a foremost scholar of Sophocles.

Reinhardt, Karl. *Sophocles.* Trans. by Hazel Harvey and David Harvey, intro. by Hugh Lloyd-Jones, Barnes & Noble text ed. 1979 $25.00. A classic study.

Segal, Charles. *Tragedy and Civilization: An Interpretation of Sophocles.* Harvard Univ. Pr. text ed. 1981 $32.50. A significant series of lectures.

Sheppard, J. T. *Aeschylus and Sophocles: Their Work and Influence.* Cooper Square Pr. repr. of 1930 ed. $18.50

Waldock, Arthur J. *Sophocles the Dramatist.* Cambridge Univ. Pr. pap. $9.95

Webster, T. B. *An Introduction to Sophocles.* 1936. Richard West, o.p. An excellent, basic study.

Whitman, Cedric H. *Sophocles: A Study of Heroic Humanism.* Harvard Univ. Pr. 1951 $20.00. This author analyzes the plays as "literary monuments, social documents . . . philosophical treatises."

Winnington-Ingraham, R. P. *Sophocles: An Interpretation.* Cambridge Univ. Pr. 1980 $62.50 pap. $19.95. A good introduction to the playwright.

THEOCRITUS. c.300–c.260 B.C.

Regarded as the creator of pastoral poetry, Theocritus was a native of Syracuse and lived in Alexandria. About 30 idylls and a number of his epigrams are extant. His genuine love of the country lends freshness and great beauty to the idylls; his bucolic characters are realistic and alive. He is a master of dramatic presentation, description, and lyrical refinement. He has had many imitators, among them VIRGIL and SPENSER (see Vol. 1). The surviving works of two other pastoral poets are often included with those of Theocritus: Bion and Moschus of Syracuse, who lived in the second century B.C. and is best known for his *Lament for Adonis.* The Andrew Lang translation (o.p.) in prose of these three poets is considered an English classic.

BOOKS BY THEOCRITUS

The Greek Bucolic Poets. Trans. by J. M. Edmonds, *Loeb Class. Lib.* Harvard Univ. Pr. 1912 $12.50. An accurate version; recommended.

Theocritus. Trans. by Charles S. Calverley, *Select Bibliographies Repr. Ser.* Ayer repr. of 1869 ed. $17.00. Appealing versions by an accomplished Victorian poet-translator.

Poems. Ed. by K. J. Dover, *Penguin Class. Ser.* text ed. 1972 $12.95. Beautifully produced textual edition and translation with an excellent introduction and commentary by a foremost scholar.

The Poems of Theocritus. Trans. by Anna Rist, Univ. of North Carolina Pr. 1978 $20.00. Good translations with a useful introduction.

Poems. Trans. by A. S. Gow, Cambridge Univ. Pr. 2 vols. 1952 $145.00

Idylls of Theocritus. Select Bibliographies Repr. Ser. Ayer repr. of 1919 ed. $24.50

Greek Pastoral Poetry: Theocritus, Bion and Moschus. Trans. by A. Holden, Johns Hopkins Univ. Pr. 1974 o.p.

BOOKS ABOUT THEOCRITUS

Kerlin, Robert T. *Theocritus in English Literature*. Ed. by E. H. Warmington, Folcroft
    repr. of 1910 ed. lib. bdg. $25.00
Rosenmeyer, Thomas G. *The Green Cabinet: Theocritus and the European Pastoral
    Lyric*. Univ. of California Pr. 1969 $34.50. A literary critique of Theocritus and
    his later influence.

THEOPHRASTUS. c.371–287 B.C.

The pupil and successor of Aristotle as head of the Peripatetic school of
philosophy wrote on a variety of subjects—botany, metaphysics, physics,
and law—but is best known for his *Characters*, 30 satiric sketches of different character types. These were imitated by English writers of the seventeenth century and by La Bruyère in his famous *Caractères*.

BOOKS BY THEOPHRASTUS

Characters. Loeb Class. Lib. Harvard Univ. Pr. $12.50
Moral Characters of Theophrastus. Trans. by Eustace Budgell, AMS Pr. repr. of 1714
    ed. $28.00
Enquiry into Plants, and Minor Works on Odours and Weather Signs. Trans. by Arthur
    Hort, *Loeb Class. Lib.* Harvard Univ. Pr. 2 vols. 1916 ea. $12.50
Menander Plays and Fragments and Theophrastus Characters. Trans. by P. Vellacott,
    Penguin Class. Ser. 2d ed. 1973 o.p.

THUCYDIDES. c.470–c.400 B.C.

[SEE Volume 3.]

XENOPHON. c.434?–c.355? B.C.

[SEE Volume 3.]

MODERN GREEK LITERATURE

Modern Greece, a designation commonly used to refer to the Greek nation
from the War of Independence (1821–33) to the present, is something of a
cultural phenomenon. The accomplishments of the ancient Greeks had been
mostly forgotten during the four centuries of Turkish domination, but with
the War of Independence came a consciousness of the past and a renaissance, which combined elements of ancient Greece and the Byzantine empire with modern elements to produce a unique literature. This consciousness of the past, amounting almost to an obsession with some authors, pervades modern Greek literature.

The vigorous cultural life of modern Greece—which has recently produced two Nobel Prize winners, George Seferis and Odysseus Elytis—was in
1967 being stifled by the severities of a military "reform" dictatorship that
had set the usual machinery in motion: books were banned, and writers, musicians, artists, and editors arrested and jailed, or deprived of their citizenship. The arrest of the 58-year-old poet Yannis Ritsos was vigorously protested by 100 French writers of all political complexions in the summer of

1967, and Stanley Kauffmann wrote bitterly in the *New Republic* of the failure of the U.S. government, as well as its traveling performers and artists, to show effective disapproval. With the restoration of the democracy in 1974 conditions in Greece have once again returned to normal, and the Greek government has shown an interest in fostering the arts.

Barnstone, Willis, ed. *Eighteen Texts: Writings by Contemporary Greek Authors.* Harvard Univ. Pr. 1972 $14.50. Published during the rule of the Junta.

Dalven, Rae, ed. *Modern Greek Poetry.* Pref. by Mark Van Doren, Russell 2d ed. enl. repr. of 1949 ed. 1971 $27.50

Dimaras, C. T. *History of Modern Greek Literature.* Trans. by Mary P. Gianos, State Univ. of New York 1973 $36.00 pap. $11.00. Originally published in 1948 and a classic study, but the translation is flawed.

Friar, Kimon, ed. *Modern Greek Poetry: Translation, Introduction, an Essay on Translation, and Notes by Kimon Friar.* Simon & Schuster 1973 $20.00. Includes a full introduction and an essay on translating modern Greek.

Gianos, Mary P., ed. *Introduction to Modern Greek Literature.* Irvington text ed. repr. 1969 $29.50 pap. $16.50. Limited to authors born between the years 1850 and 1914. Fiction and drama translated by Gianos, poetry by Kimon Friar.

Keeley, Edmund, and Peter Bien, eds. *Modern Greek Writers. Princeton Essays in Lit. Ser.* 1972 $25.00

Keeley, Edmund, and Philip Sherrard, trans. and eds. *Six Poets of Modern Greece.* Knopf 1961 o.p. "The selections stress the burning consciousness these poets share of their heritage. Something almost Delphic broods over the six who project their own personal vision": Cavafy, Sikelianos, Seferis, Antoniou, Elytis, Gatsos.

———. *Voices of Modern Greece: Selected Poems by Cavafy, Sikelianos, Seferis, Elytis, Gatsos.* Princeton Univ. Pr. rev. & enl. ed. 1981 $20.00 pap. $6.95

Lorenzatos, Zissimos. *The Lost Center and Other Essays in Greek Poetry.* Trans. by Kay Cicellis, *Princeton Essays in Lit. Ser.* 1980 $21.00

Politis, Linos. *A History of Modern Greek Literature.* Oxford 1973 $36.00. More up-to-date than the history of Dimaras, but lacking some of the elegance of the earlier study.

Sherrard, Philip. *The Marble Threshing Floor. Select Bibliographies Repr. Ser.* Ayer repr. of 1956 ed. $22.00

Spencer, Terence J. *Fair Greece, Sad Relic: Literary Philellenism from Shakespeare to Byron.* Octagon 1972 lib. bdg. $20.50; Scholarly repr. of 1954 ed. 1971 $19.00

CAVAFY, CONSTANTINE P. (Konstantinos Petrou Kabaphēs). 1863–1933

Cavafy was born and died in Alexandria, and he has always been closely associated with that city. During his lifetime he was considered *the* poet of Alexandria, and today his name is identified primarily with Lawrence Durrell's characterization of him in *The Alexandria Quartet.* "As a writer he starts with the ordinary life of his own city, which he knew at all levels from the most to the least reputable. From this, with its complex mixture of West and East, . . . he formed his own outlook on life and sense of values. . . . As a result, his indulgent cynicism, his understanding disillusion, can often bring historical subjects right home today. . . . Cavafy's subtle use of language, his mixture of common speech, officialese, and self-deflating formalisms to produce complex overtones of immediacy, irony and detachment, are not more than hinted at in the existing translations; but his awareness of life, and his attitudes to it, have a rich place in the modern world" (*Modern World Literature*).

BOOKS BY CAVAFY

Complete Poems of Cavafy. Intro. by W. H. Auden, Harcourt enl. ed. 1976 pap. $6.75. This volume presents new translations. "They make genuine poetry, supple, sensitive and civil, as Cavafy's Greek required, and they often catch something of his characteristic 'demotic' touches. The translator has added useful notes on the poet's life and style and on some of the historical allusions" (*Manchester Guardian*). Auden's introduction is excellent.
Collected Poems. Trans. by Philip Sherrard, Princeton Univ. Pr. 1975 $40.00 pap. $8.95

BOOK ABOUT CAVAFY

Bien, Peter. *Constantine Cavafy. Columbia Essays on Modern Writers Ser.* 1964 pap. $1.50

ELYTIS, ODYSSEUS (Odhiseas Alepoudhellis). 1911–   (NOBEL PRIZE 1979)

Odysseus Elytis, poet, painter, and translator, was born in Crete and educated in Athens and Paris. As a young poet he "turned away from the poetry of the damned . . . the nostalgia of autumnal landscapes foreign to Greece, and embraced the tenets of surrealism as a liberating force" (Friar, Modern Greek Poetry).

BOOKS BY ELYTIS

The Axion Esti. Trans. by Edmund Keeley and George Savidis, *Pitt Poetry Ser*. Univ. of Pittsburgh Pr. 1974 $8.95 1979 pap. $5.95. Greek and English on facing pages. " 'The Axion Esti' has been named by poets and Greek scholars alike as one of the major Greek poems of this century."
The Sovereign Sun: Selected Poems. Trans. by Kimon Friar, Temple Univ. Pr. 1974 $19.95 1979 pap. $9.95

KAZANTZAKIS, NIKOS. 1885–1957

The distinguished novelist, poet, and translator was born in Crete and educated in Athens, Germany, Italy, and Paris, where he studied under Henri Bergson. He found time to write some 30 novels, plays, and books on philosophy, to serve his government, and to travel widely. He ran the Greek ministry of welfare from 1919 to 1921 and was minister of state briefly in 1945.

Kazantzakis "has created in Zorba one of the great characters of modern fiction. The novel reflects Greek exhilaration at its best" (*TLS*). A film version of 1965, starring Anthony Quinn, made Kazantzakis widely known in the West. Intensely religious, he imbued his novels with the passion of his own restless spirit, "torn between the active and the contemplative, between the sensual and the aesthetic, between nihilism and commitment" (*Columbia Encyclopedia*). Judas, the hero of *The Last Temptation of Christ*

(1951), is asked by Christ to betray him so that he can fulfill his mission through the crucifixion. For this book Kazantzakis was excommunicated from the Greek Orthodox Church. John Ciardi called *The Odyssey: A Modern Sequel* (1938)—Odysseus transformed into a revolutionary saint—"a monument of the age" (*SR*). The reverent fictional biography *Saint Francis* (1953), which follows the historical account closely, is told simply and with a cumulative emotional impact. *The Fratricides*, Kazantzakis's last novel, portrays yet another religious hero, a priest caught between Communists and Royalists in the Greek Civil War. Marc Slonim says that "throughout his work Kazantzakis remained true to the Hellenic tradition: his heroes are harmoniously developed individuals who feel a strong bond with their physical environment; the author's poetic imagination is of the kind that created legends and myths to explain man and the universe" (*N.Y. Times*).

BOOKS BY KAZANTZAKIS

Rock Garden. Simon & Schuster 1963 $5.95; Simon & Schuster (Touchstone Bks.) 1969 pap. $3.95. One of his earliest novels, it tells of a European caught in the Sino-Japanese wars of the 1930s.

The Odyssey: A Modern Sequel. Simon & Schuster (Touchstone Bks.) 1961 pap. $12.95. This takes up the story of Odysseus where Homer left off and "is a major achievement" (Moses Hadas, *N.Y. Herald Tribune*).

The Greek Passion. Simon & Schuster 1953 $9.95; Simon & Schuster (Touchstone Bks.) 1959 pap. $9.95

Zorba the Greek. Simon & Schuster 1953 $12.95; Simon & Schuster (Touchstone Bks.) 1971 pap. $7.95

The Last Temptation of Christ. Simon & Schuster 1960 $14.95; Simon & Schuster (Touchstone Bks.) 1966 pap. $9.95

Saint Francis. Simon & Schuster (Touchstone Bks.) 1963 pap. $9.95

Freedom or Death. Simon & Schuster (Touchstone Bks.) 1983 pap. $8.95

The Saviors of God. Trans. by Kimon Friar, Simon & Schuster 1960 $5.95; Simon & Schuster (Touchstone Bks.) 1969 pap. $7.95

The Fratricides. Simon & Schuster (Touchstone Bks.) 1985 pap. $8.95

Report to Greco. Simon & Schuster (Touchstone Bks.) 1975 pap. $10.75

BOOKS ABOUT KAZANTZAKIS

Bien, Peter. *Kazantzakis and Linguistic Revolution in Greek Literature.* Princeton Essays in Lit. Ser. 1972 $28.00

———. *Nikos Kazantzakis.* Columbia Univ. Pr. 1972 pap. o.p.

Kazantzakis, Helen. *Nikos Kazantzakis.* Simon & Schuster 1970 o.p.

———. *Nikos Kazantzakis: A Biography Based on His Letters.* Trans. by Amy Mims, Creative Arts Bks. 1983 pap. $12.95. "The intimate and moving account of the life, the work, the thoughts, the loves of this major literary figure, author of 'Zorba the Greek' and other works of fiction and nonfiction. His wife has woven into her text hundreds of his unpublished letters, from those of his school days to the last notes he wrote on his deathbed" (*PW*).

Prevelakis, Pandelis. *Nikos Kazantzakis and His Odyssey.* Trans. by Philip Sherrard, pref. by Kimon Friar, Simon & Schuster 1961 o.p.

MAKRIYANNIS, JOHN. 1797–1864

A hero in the War of Independence, Makriyannis is also one of the greatest figures in modern Greek demotic literature. When he was 32 years old he taught himself to write in order to record his memoirs, by which he hoped to justify his life and politics in the early years of the new nation. The result was a document of great artistic importance. Makriyannis's manuscript was not published until 1907, 43 years after his death, and the effect on the Greek literary world was enormous. Seferis, for example, regarded Makriyannis as the "humblest and also the steadiest" of his teachers.

BOOK BY MAKRIYANNIS

Makriyannis: The Memoirs of General Makriyannis, 1797–1864. Trans. by H. A. Lidderdale, Oxford, o.p.

PALAMAS, KOSTES. 1859–1943

Palamas is the central figure of the New School of Athens and "is a milestone in the history of Greek literature, for his works are the outburst, the catharsis of the long drama of more than 2,000 years, which from the days when the Alexandrian poets ceased to sing had not found the great personality who would give voice to the national sufferings and aspirations, agonies and glories, in works of full magnitude" (Trypanis, *Medieval and Modern Greek Poetry*).

BOOK BY PALAMAS

The Twelve Words of the Gypsy. Trans. by Theodore Stephanides and George Katsimbalis, Memphis State Univ. text ed. 1975 $15.00 pap. $6.95; intro. by Frederic Will, Univ. of Nebraska Pr. 1964 $17.95. An epico-lyric poem of a gypsy musician, who as a "symbol of freedom and art," "develops into the Greek patriot," and finally into the "Hellene, citizen of the world" (Trypanis).

BOOK ABOUT PALAMAS

Maskaleris, Thanasis. *Kostis Palamas. Twayne's World Authors Ser.* G. K. Hall lib. bdg. $16.95

RITSOS, YANNIS. 1909–

Ritsos, imprisoned by the Greek dictatorship, has repeatedly suffered from his strong revolutionary sentiments. "Haunted by death, driven at times to the edge of madness and suicide, Ritsos throughout his life has been upheld by his obstinate faith in poetry as redemption, and in the revolutionary ideal" (Friar, *Modern Greek Poetry*).

BOOKS BY RITSOS

Exile in Return: Selected Poems. Trans. by Edmund Keeley, Ecco Pr. 1985 $17.50
The Fourth Dimension: Selected Poems of Yannis Ritsos. Trans. by Rae Dalven, Godine 1977 $15.00
Eighteen Short Songs of the Bitter Motherland. Trans. by Amy Mims, Nostos 1974 $15.00

SEFERIS, GEORGE (Georgios Sepheriadēs). 1900–1971 (NOBEL PRIZE 1963)

Seferis, who was Greece's ambassador to London in 1961, has done much to "unite the distinctive heritage of Greek tradition with the avant-garde developments in European poetry." He is regarded as one of the greatest poets of his time. Born in Smyrna, he moved to Athens at age 14. He studied in Paris at the end of World War I and afterward joined the Greek diplomatic service. "Eminent as he is as a European poet," wrote Rex Warner, "Seferis is preeminently a Greek poet, conscious of the Greek tradition which shaped, and indeed created the tradition of Europe. Throughout the poetry of Seferis one will notice his profound consciousness of the presences of the past and its weight." His themes show a constant awareness of both the dignity and the inevitable sorrow of man. His images, the voyage, the search, and the ruins that become alive and yet suggest death, are universal, his treatment of them contemporary. His language has a disciplined power and simplicity. In addition to the "Poems," selections from his poetry appear in Keeley and Sherrard's *Six Poets of Modern Greece*. "The 18-member Royal Swedish Literary Academy said Mr. Seferis was awarded the $51,158 [Nobel] prize 'for his eminent lyrical writing, inspired by a deep feeling for the Hellenic world of culture' " (*N.Y. Journal American*).

BOOKS BY SEFERIS

Collected Poems, 1924–1955. Trans. by Philip Sherrard, Princeton Univ. Pr. 3d ed. enl. 1981 $46.00 pap. $12.95. Bibliography, notes.

Poems. Trans. by Rex Warner, Godine 1979 pap. $5.95. "These beautiful, disturbing poems are reports on a journey that never ends, through a landscape that is half modern Greece and half the darkest recesses of the human mind" (*Atlantic*). Drawing on the richness of mythology, Seferis "expresses most powerfully the eternally tragic in the living present. . . . Most persistent of his themes is the Odyssey myth, stemming no doubt from his own personal experience of exile."

Three Secret Poems. Trans. by Walter Kaiser, Harvard Univ. Pr. 1969 $5.95

A Poet's Journal: Days of 1945–1951. Trans. by Athan Angnostopoulos, intro. by Walter Kaiser, Harvard Univ. Pr. (Belknap Pr.) 1974 pap. $5.95

CHAPTER 8

Latin Literature

Fred J. Nichols

Go, little book, my little tragedy!
God grant thy maker, ere his ending day,
May write some tale of happy poetry!
But, little book, of any poet's lay
Envy of heart here shalt thou not display,
But kiss the steps where pass through ages spacious,
Vergil and Ovid, Homer, Lucan and Statius.
—CHAUCER, *Troilus and Cresseyde*

Latin literature must always be seen in light of its Greek antecedents and of contemporary Roman history. "Arma virumque cano" ("Of arms and the man I sing"), the opening words of Virgil's *The Aeneid*, tell the reader that the poem will comment on HOMER's *Iliad* (the arms) and *Odyssey* (the man). Viewed in another way, however, these words mean the Roman Empire and the Emperor Augustus. The poem is both the noblest Roman epic and the imperially sanctioned history of Rome.

The early poets Livius Andronicus, Naevius, and Ennius (their works survive only in fragments) adapted Homer and the Greek tragedians in lustrous Latin verse and thereby laid the foundations of the literature. Influenced by Greek New Comedy and native Italian farce, Plautus was a popular playwright when Rome was expanding in the Mediterranean and developing a taste for Hellenic culture. As Greek fashions took firm hold in the second century B.C., particularly in the brilliant circle associated with Scipio Africanus Minor, Terence was admired for his polished romantic comedies written after the style of his Greek predecessor MENANDER.

The first century B.C., an era of debilitating civil wars at home and conquest abroad, when Rome had replaced Athens and Alexandria as the political and intellectual center of the Mediterranean world, boasted very great literary artists. Cicero was preeminent as orator, philosopher, and statesman. He translated the eloquence of DEMOSTHENES and the logic of PLATO (see Vol. 4) to Latin letters, which he dominated thereafter. The philosopher EPICURUS (see Vol. 4) was interpreted by Lucretius in his melancholy hexameter poem *De Rerum Natura* (*On the Nature of the Universe*). Lucretius's metrical skill and beautiful phrases were imitated by

Virgil, Horace, and Catullus. This last celebrated his loves and his hates in a manner suggestive of the Greek Alexandrian poets, who preferred a personal statement in short, elegant verse to the "swollen" epic. Republican Rome ended with the assassination of JULIUS CAESAR (see Vol. 3), himself an intelligent propagandist of his own military acumen in the *Commentaries.*

The Augustan or the Golden Age of Roman literature (c.44 B.C. to A.D. 17) acclaimed the political harmony achieved by the Emperor Augustus after almost a century of civil strife. Its brightest light was Virgil, whose *Aeneid* immortalized the Roman genius for ruling the world with law, establishing the custom of peace, sparing the conquered, subduing the proud. Virgil's friend Horace sang of Roman virtues, such as moderation and patriotism, with technical virtuosity and self-mocking wit. Also at the emperor's court was Ovid, whose clever elegiac treatises on love's vagaries and fantastical *Metamorphoses* gently mocked imperial Rome. The elegiac poets Tibullus and Propertius proclaimed their personal—even idiosyncratic—loves.

LIVY's (see Vol. 3) anecdotal histories were to prose what Virgil's epic was to poetry in the Augustan epoch. Writing nearly a century later, TACITUS (see Vol. 3) never shared Livy's optimism. Rather, his *Annals* emphasized the loss of liberty and the resulting moral weakness caused by the absolutism of the Empire. His acute and pessimistic analysis was reminiscent of SALLUST (see Vol. 3), a historian of Cicero's age. And the thread of Tacitus's narrative was taken up again in the fourth century A.D. by AMMIANUS MARCELLINUS (see Vol. 3), who was the last great chronicler of Rome.

Phaedrus, a Greek freedman attached to Augustus's household, composed beast fables for advice and entertainment. The despotic political climate of the age took its toll of writers. The urbane Petronius, author of *The Satyricon;* Seneca, the Stoic philosopher and mordant playwright; and the epic poet Lucan all died for political offenses against the emperors. Persius and Juvenal, like Horace before them, developed satire as an original Roman genre. Juvenal was the most incisive of these. He chafed under the tyranny of the Emperor Domitian, and he suffered for speaking the truth. Others in the first century A.D. (known as the Silver Age of Latin literature) chose not to satirize their own era. Quintilian's manual of rhetoric was a valuable, wise guide to teaching the art of oratory. Pliny's letters offered a fascinating picture of contemporary Roman life and a tactful account of current politics. Suetonius looked back in time to the private lives of the Caesars, and Statius wrote of mythological heroes and wars in epic verse. Martial's epigrams could be biting, cruel, and sexually explicit, but their wit and polish made them models of their kind.

Apuleius, whose engaging prose *Metamorphoses* is more commonly known in English as *The Golden Ass,* flourished in the second century A.D. His was the time of the *pax Romana,* before the collapse of the Empire. Donatus and Servius, the biographer and the commentator of Virgil, recalled the past glories of the Augustan Age. Priscian's grammar became a source book for the Middle Ages, Martianus Capella codified the liberal arts for centuries to come, and Macrobius wrote influential commentaries on Cicero and Virgil.

Christian doctrine ruled the literary imagination from the third century onward to the Fall of Rome in the fifth century. Tertullian used his training in Roman rhetoric to champion Christianity and was really the first Latin advocate of the new religion. The most classical of all the early apologists was Lactantius, the Christian Cicero. Later, in the fourth century, Prudentius unified classical poetry with Christian thought in his allegory of the soul, which was modeled on Virgil.

The fifth century, dark days for Rome, was illuminated by Christian thinkers. Trained in classical rhetoric, Christian theology, Greek, Hebrew, and with a mastery of Cicero, Virgil, and Horace, St. Jerome made a fresh translation of the scriptures from the original Hebrew and Greek into a literary Latin called the Vulgate, thereby shaping Christian thought and expression for all time. St. Augustine's knowledge of Latin writers and of Neoplatonism deepened his presentation of Christianity in the seminal *Confessions* and *City of God*.

After the Fall of Rome in the fifth century, Latin continued to be the official language of the West. It survived when Greek was forgotten. Vernacular European authors regarded extant Latin works, especially those of Cicero, Virgil, Horace, and Ovid, as paragons. These models of perfection from antiquity stimulated fertile literary activity, just as the Greek masters had for the Romans centuries earlier. Virgil interpreted Homer and Roman history in sublime Latin verse, and, in turn, fed the genius of Dante and Milton (see Vol. 1), the consummate poets of Christianity. Cicero transmitted a Latinate Plato to the church fathers and medieval apologists. These two, and their Greek predecessors, are the pillars of European and American thought and letters. (See also Chapter 7 in this volume, and Volume 3, Chapter 6.)

HISTORY AND CRITICISM

Appian. *Roman History*. Trans. by H. E. White, *Loeb Class. Lib.* Harvard Univ. Pr. 4 vols. ea. $12.50. A fascinating, anecdotal account written by a Greek living in Rome at the time of Antoninus Pius.

Beare, William. *The Roman Stage*. Rowman repr. of 1950 ed. 1977 $29.50

Bury, J. B. *A History of the Later Roman Empire: From the Death of Theodosius to the Death of Justinian*. 1889. Dover 2 vols. 1957 pap. ea. $7.00. This is the foremost history of the Empire in the fourth, fifth, and sixth centuries.

Carcopino, Jerome. *Daily Life in Ancient Rome: The People and the City at the Height of the Empire*. 1940. Trans. by E. O. Lorimer, ed. by Henry T. Rowell, Yale Univ. Pr. 1960 pap. $7.95

Cary, M., and H. H. Scullard. *A History of Rome*. St. Martin's 3d ed. text ed. 1976 $21.95

Christ, Karl. *The Romans: An Introduction to Their History and Civilization*. Trans. by

Christopher Holme, Univ. of California Pr. 1984 $19.95. An excellent, clear introduction, with illustrations.

Coffey, Michael. *Roman Satire.* Methuen 1976 $16.95

D'Alton, John F. *Roman Literary Theory and Criticism.* 1931. Russell 1962 o.p. A valuable outline of the literary canons that influenced Roman writers.

Dudley, Donald R. *The Romans, 850 B.C.–A.D. 337.* Knopf 1970 o.p. Detailed, dense, and thorough, but quite readable.

Duff, John W. *A Literary History of Rome: From the Origins to the Close of the Golden Age.* 1928. Ed. by A. M. Duff, Harper 3d ed. 1953 o.p. A reset edition of a standard work with a supplementary bibliography of writings that have appeared since 1909. Includes a preliminary study of the origins, language, and character of the Romans, and a history of Latin literature from the earliest times to the death of Augustus.

———. *A Literary History of Rome in the Silver Age: Tiberius to Hadrian.* 1927. Ed. by A. M. Duff, Greenwood repr. of 1964 ed. 3d ed. 1979 lib. bdg. $42.50

Fowler, Warde. *The Religious Experience of the Roman People: From the Earliest Times to the Age of Augustus.* 1911. Cooper 1971 o.p. Respected and authoritative.

Frank, Tenney, *Life and Literature in the Roman Republic.* Univ. of California Pr. 1930 pap. $3.95

Giannelli, Guilio, ed. *The World of Ancient Rome.* Putnam 1967 o.p. An excellent discussion of Roman life by 12 noted classical scholars of Italy, France, and England. "Both text and pictures make this book a welcome companion to all studies in the history, language and literature of Rome" (*LJ*).

Gibbon, Edward. *The Decline and Fall of the Roman Empire.* 1776–88. Biblio Dist. (Everyman's) 6 vols. repr. of 1910 ed. 1978 ea. $9.95; Modern Lib. 3 vols. 1932 ea. $8.95. The classic analysis of Roman history, famous for its incisive observations and impressive prose style.

Grant, W. Leonard. *Neo-Latin Literature and the Pastoral.* Univ. of North Carolina Pr. 1965 o.p. Includes a good, brief survey of the Latin literature of the Renaissance.

Hadas, Moses. *A History of Latin Literature.* Columbia Univ. Pr. 1952 $45.00. The distinguished classical authority who died in 1966 drew on modern scholarship and newer techniques of analysis and appreciation for his interpretations of the classics.

Hamilton, Edith. *The Roman Way.* Avon 1973 pap. $2.95

Highet, Gilbert. *Poets in a Landscape.* Greenwood repr. of 1962 ed. 1979 lib. bdg. $25.00. Seven Latin poets: Catullus, Virgil, Propertius, Horace, Tibullus, Ovid, and Juvenal. The career and work of each are discussed, with generous quotation. "A delightful book by a scholar in whose mind the ancient world has evidently remained vividly alive" (*New Yorker*).

Ijsewijn, Jozef. *Companion to Neo-Latin Studies.* Elsevier 1977 $51.00. A useful introduction to Renaissance Latin literature.

Johnston, Harold W. *Private Life of the Romans. Select Bibliographies Repr. Ser.* Ayer repr. of 1903 ed. $32.00

Johnston, Mary. *Roman Life.* Scott, Foresman text ed. 1957 $20.95. Successor to the author's father's *Private Life of the Romans,* long a standard reference work. Much revised and enlarged, with a wealth of illustrative material, this volume is recommended for the general reader. The bibliography is especially comprehensive.

Kennedy, George. *The Art of Rhetoric in the Roman World, 300 B.C.–A.D. 300.* Princeton Univ. Pr. 3 vols. repr. of 1973 ed. 1982 $110.00. A first-rate study of a subject of central importance in Latin literature.

Kenney, E. J., ed. *Latin Literature.* Vol. 2 in *The Cambridge History of Classical Literature.* Cambridge Univ. Pr. 2 pts. 1983 ea. $12.95. Standard and definitive, with full bibliographies.

Konstan, David. *Roman Comedy.* Cornell Univ. Pr. 1983 $22.50. Good critical analysis of key plays in terms of social relations.

Löfstedt, Einar. *Roman Literary Portraits: Aspects of the Literature of the Roman Empire.* Greenwood repr. of 1958 ed. 1978 lib. bdg. $19.00

Lück, Georg. *The Latin Love Elegy.* Rowman repr. of 1969 ed. 2d ed. 1979 $19.50. Illuminates the poetry of Catullus, Ovid, Propertius, and Tibullus.

MacKendrick, Paul. *The Mute Stones Speak: The Story of Archaeology in Italy.* Norton 2d ed. 1983 $25.50 pap. $9.95

Nash, Ernest. *Pictorial Dictionary of Ancient Rome.* Hacker 2 vols. repr. of 1968 ed. 1980 lib. bdg. $150.00. An essential reference work, valuable to classicists, archaeologists, and informed laypeople, this is a systematic pictorial survey of all Roman buildings and monuments, with old etchings, plans, and drawings to document the original appearance of destroyed or altered monuments; thorough bibliography.

Ogilvie, R. M. *Roman Literature and Society.* Barnes & Noble 1980 $27.50; Penguin 1980 pap. $5.95. A brief introductory survey.

Plutarch. *Lives.* Trans. by Thomas North, AMS Pr. 6 vols. repr. of 1896 ed. $270.00; *Loeb Class. Lib.* Harvard Univ. Pr. 11 vols. ea. $12.50; trans. by John Dryden, Modern Lib. 1967 $10.95. Wonderfully entertaining biographies of the elite of antiquity written in graceful English prose.

Putnam, Michael C. *Essays on Latin Lyric, Elegy, and Epic.* Princeton Univ. Pr. 1982 $33.00 pap. $11.95. Incisive revisionist criticism.

Quinn, Kenneth. *Texts and Contexts: The Roman Writers and Their Audience.* Routledge & Kegan 1979 o.p. A good introductory survey of major works for the contemporary reader.

Richlin, Amy. *The Garden of Priapus: Sexuality and Aggression in Roman Humor.* Yale Univ. Pr. text ed. 1983 $28.00. A thorough approach to an interesting subject.

Rostovtzeff, Mikhail. *Social and Economic History of the Roman Empire.* 1926. Ed. by P. M. Frazer, Oxford 2 vols. 2d ed. 1957 $115.00. Authoritative and widely respected.

Rowell, Henry Thompson. *Rome in the Augustan Age.* Univ. of Oklahoma Pr. 1971 pap. $5.95. Interesting and authoritative material; excellent index and bibliography.

Sellar, William Young. *The Roman Poets of the Augustan Age.* Memoir of the author by Andrew Lang, Biblo & Tannen pt. 1 repr. of 1892 ed.; pt. 2 repr. of 1908 ed. 3d ed. $15.00. Each of Seller's studies is thorough and learned.

———. *The Roman Poets of the Republic.* Biblo & Tannen repr. of 1889 ed. 3d ed. o.p.

Syme, Ronald. *The Roman Revolution.* Oxford 1964 $10.95. A sophisticated scholar examines the changeover from republic to monarchy after the death of Caesar in convincing and devastating detail.

Wilkinson, L. P. *Golden Latin Artistry.* Cambridge Univ. Pr. 1963 o.p. Analyzes Latin literature of the Golden Age with sensitivity and understanding.

Williams, Gordon. *Figures of Thought in Roman Poetry.* Yale Univ. Pr. 1980 $32.00. Described as "about the technique of poetry"; provocative and intelligent.

———. *Tradition and Originality in Roman Poetry.* Oxford 1968 o.p. An important, seminal study.

COLLECTIONS

Brittain, Frederick, trans. and ed. *The Penguin Book of Latin Verse*. Penguin 1962 o.p.
  Plain prose translations of selections from all periods.
Davenport, Basil, ed. *The Portable Roman Reader*. *Viking Portable Lib*. Penguin 1977
  pap. $7.95
Duckworth, George E., ed. *The Complete Roman Drama*. Random 2 vols. 1942 o.p. All
  the extant comedies of Plautus and Terence and the tragedies of Seneca in a vari-
  ety of translations.
Grant, Michael, ed. *Latin Literature*. *Penguin Class. Ser*. 1979 pap. $4.95. A collection
  of verse and prose with introductions discussing the authors and their influence.
Guinagh, Kevin, and Alfred P. Dorjahn, eds. *Latin Literature in Translation*. Century
  Bookbindery repr. of 1942 ed. lib. bdg. $35.00. Selections from 28 authors,
  among them Plautus, Terence, Caesar, Cicero, Catullus, Virgil, Horace, Livy,
  Ovid, Seneca, Pliny, Tacitus, Juvenal, and St. Augustine; some short bibliogra-
  phies, a map, and glossary.
Harsh, Philip W., ed. *An Anthology of Roman Drama*. Holt text ed. 1960 pap. $11.95
Isbell, Harold, ed. *The Last Poets of Imperial Rome*. Penguin Class. Ser. 1983 pap.
  $5.95. Selections from nine poets from the second to the fifth centuries, includ-
  ing Ausonius, Prudentius, and Nemesianus.
Mackail, John W. *Latin Literature*. Ungar 1966 $12.50. History, criticism, and selec-
  tions.
Nichols, Fred J., trans. and ed. *An Anthology of Neo-Latin Poetry*. Yale Univ. Pr. text
  ed. 1979 $70.00 pap. $24.95. A selection of Renaissance poetry in Latin ranging
  from Petrarch to Milton with a critical introduction.
Waddell, Helen, trans. and ed. *Mediaeval Latin Lyrics*. *Norton Lib*. 1977 pap. $4.95. A
  standard anthology, well chosen and translated.
Warmington, E. H., ed. *Minor Latin Poets*. *Loeb Class. Lib*. Harvard Univ. Pr. $12.00
Wedeck, Harry E., ed. *Classics of Roman Literature*. Littlefield 1964 pap. $4.95. Anno-
  tated, with many new translations.
Wender, Dorothea, trans. and ed. *Roman Poetry from the Republic to the Silver Age*.
  Southern Illinois Univ. Pr. 1980 $9.95. Lively translations with a good introduc-
  tory essay.
Whicher, George F., trans. and ed. *The Goliard Poets: Medieval Latin Songs and Sat-
  ires*. Greenwood repr. of 1949 ed. 1979 lib. bdg. $21.00. An entertaining selec-
  tion, energetically translated.

APULEIUS, LUCIUS. 114–?

Apuleius, of African birth, was educated in Carthage and Athens. His most
famous work, *The Golden Ass*, is the tale of a young philosopher who transformed himself not into a bird as he had expected, but into an ass. After
many adventures he was rescued by the goddess Isis. The episode of "Cupid
and Psyche," told with consummate grace, is the most celebrated section.
This romance of the declining Empire influenced the novels of BOCCACCIO,
CERVANTES, FIELDING (see Vol. 1), and SMOLLETT (see Vol. 1); Heywood used
the theme for a drama and WILLIAM MORRIS (see Vol. 1) used some of the material in *The Earthly Paradise*. The early translation (1566) by William
Adlington is graceful. Robert Graves's "translation abandons the aureate

Latinity of Apuleius for a dry, sharp, plain style— which is itself a small masterpiece of twentieth-century prose" (Kenneth Rexroth, *SR*).

BOOKS BY APULEIUS

The Golden Ass, or Metamorphoses. c.150. Trans. by Robert Graves, Farrar 1967 o.p.; trans. by William Adlington, *Loeb Class. Lib.* Harvard Univ. Pr. $12.50; trans. by Jack Lindsay, Indiana Univ. Pr. 1962 pap. $4.95

Apologia and Florida. Trans. by H. E. Butler, Greenwood repr. of 1909 ed. lib. bdg. $15.00

BOOKS ABOUT APULEIUS

Haight, Elizabeth H. *Apuleius and His Influence.* Cooper Square Pr. repr. of 1930 ed. 1963 $20.00; Folcroft repr. of 1927 ed. 1978 lib. bdg. $10.00; Telegraph Bks. repr. of 1927 ed. 1983 lib. bdg. $12.50

Neumann, Erich. *Amor and Psyche: The Psychic Development of the Feminine.* Trans. by Ralph Manheim, Princeton Univ. Pr. 1956 pap. $5.95. A commentary on the tale by Apuleius.

Tatum, James. *Apuleius and the Golden Ass.* Cornell Univ. Pr. 1979 o.p. An introductory work aimed at the general reader.

Walsh, P. G. *Roman Novel.* Cambridge Univ. Pr. 1973 $37.50

CAESAR, JULIUS. 100 B.C.–44 B.C.

[SEE Volume 3, Chapter 6.]

CATULLUS (Gaius Valerius Catullus). 84? B.C.–54? B.C.

Catullus was born in Verona of a wealthy family, but spent much of his short life in Rome. He moved in fashionable society there and was captivated by a woman he called Lesbia, who has been identified as Clodia, a notorious aristocrat. His 25 poems to her tell the story of his tormented love. These together with his other verse—occasional, satiric, epiclike, and epigrammatic—have been widely imitated. The Latin poets Horace, Virgil, Propertius, and Martial were all indebted to him, and he has been translated into English by such eminent poets as CAMPION (see Vol. 1), JONSON (see Vol. 1), BYRON (see Vol. 1), and TENNYSON (see Vol. 1). By his successors he was called *doctus* (learned) because of his ideal of technical perfection, development of new literary forms (miniature epic, elegy, and epigram), and erudition.

BOOKS BY CATULLUS

Poems. Trans. by Frederic Raphael and Kenneth McLeish, Godine 1978 $8.95; trans. by Peter Whigham, Univ. of California Pr. repr. bilingual ed. text ed. 1983 $25.00; trans. by Frank Copley, Univ. of Michigan Pr. 1957 pap. $5.95. The translation by Raphael and McLeish is in the contemporary mode.

Works of Catullus and Tibullus. Trans. by F. W. Cornish, *Loeb Class. Lib.* Harvard Univ. Pr. rev. ed. 1935 $12.50

Catullus. Ed. by Elmer T. Merrill, Harvard Univ. Pr. repr. of 1893 ed. 1965 $16.50

Odi et Amo: The Complete Poetry of Catullus. Trans. by Roy A. Swanson, Bobbs 1959 pap. $5.99

Carmina. Ed. by R. A. Mynors, Oxford 1958 $9.95

BOOKS ABOUT CATULLUS

Duckett, Eleanor S. *Catullus in English Poetry.* Richard West repr. of 1925 ed. $25.00; Russell repr. of 1925 ed. 1972 $13.00. A careful compilation of English poems that imitate Catullus, this includes some of the most beautiful of English lyrics.

Harrington, Karl P. *Catullus and His Influence.* Cooper Square Pr. repr. of 1930 ed. $18.50

Havelock, Eric Alfred. *The Lyric Genius of Catullus.* Russell repr. of 1939 ed. 1967 o.p. A penetrating critical analysis that includes the Latin text of the poems with free translations by the author; bibliography.

McPeek, James A. *Catullus in Strange and Distant Britain.* Russell repr. of 1939 ed. 1972 $20.00

Quinn, Kenneth. *The Catullan Revolution.* Univ. of Michigan Pr. 1971 o.p. An effective critical approach.

————. *Catullus: Poems—A Commentary.* St. Martin's 1971 $18.95. Quinn examines the literary, political, and social aspects of the poems with passionate interest. All of his studies are good reading.

Small, Stuart G. P. *Catullus: A Reader's Guide to the Poems.* Univ. Pr. of Amer. text ed. 1983 lib. bdg. $23.00 pap. $11.50. Straightforward, basic introduction for a reader new to the poems.

CICERO or TULLY (Marcus Tullius Cicero). 106 B.C.–43 B.C.

Cicero was Rome's great prose stylist. Of his speeches, 58 are extant, as well as approximately 900 of his letters, many political and philosophical writings, and rhetorical treatises. As a youth he studied law, oratory, Greek literature, and philosophy. He became consul in 63 B.C., uncovered the conspiracy of Catiline, and aroused the people by his famous "Orations against Cataline." His political career was long, stormy, and often inconsistent. When out of favor or banished, he devoted himself to literary composition, writing many revealing letters and such well known essays as "On Friendship," "On Duties," and "On Old Age," which together with the "Tusculans" and the "Dream of Scipio" have deeply influenced European thought and literature.

During the civil war he sided with Pompey, but after Pompey's decisive defeat at the Battle of Pharsalus in 48 B.C., Cicero became reconciled with Caesar. After Caesar's assassination, Cicero attacked Antony in his *Philippics.* When the Second Triumvirate was established, Antony demanded the head of his enemy. Cicero escaped but was overtaken by soldiers. He died courageously; at Antony's command, his head and hands were displayed over the orators' rostra in Rome. Cicero is one of the subjects of Plutarch's *Lives.* (See also Volume 3, Chapter 6.)

BOOKS BY CICERO

Works. Loeb Class. Lib. Harvard Univ. Pr. 28 vols. 1912–58 ea. $12.50. Excellent edition.

Selected Works. Trans. by Michael Grant, *Penguin Class. Ser.* 1960 pap. $4.95

Selected Political Speeches. Trans. by Michael Grant, *Penguin Class. Ser.* 1977 pap. $4.95. Includes some of the most famous orations.

Select Letters. Ed. by D. R. Shackleton Bailey, Cambridge Univ. Pr. 1980 $42.50 pap.
  $15.95; ed. by W. W. How, Oxford 2 vols. 1925–26 ea. $16.95–$24.00
Letters to Atticus. Trans. by D. R. Shackleton Bailey, *Penguin Class. Ser.* 1978 pap.
  $5.95
Murder Trials. Trans. by Michael Grant, *Penguin Class. Ser.* 1975 pap. $4.95
On the Good Life. Trans. by Michael Grant, *Penguin Class. Ser.* 1971 pap. $4.95
The Offices and Select Letters. Trans. by Thomas Cockman and W. Melmouth, Biblio
  Dist. (Everyman's) 1953 $9.95. A solid piece of work.
On the Commonwealth. c.51 B.C. Trans. by George H. Sabine and Stanley B. Smith,
  Bobbs 1959 pap. $8.40
Brutus (and *Orator*). 46 B.C. *Loeb Class. Lib.* Harvard Univ. Pr. $12.50
De Officiis. 43 B.C. *Loeb Class. Lib.* Harvard Univ. Pr. 1930 $12.50

Books about Cicero

Boissier, Gaston. *Cicero and His Friends: A Study of Roman Society in the Time of Cae-
  sar.* Trans. by Adnah D. Jones, Cooper Square Pr. repr. of 1897 ed. 1970 lib. bdg.
  $25.00. Well known and respected.
Gotoff, Harold C. *Cicero's Elegant Style: An Analysis of the Pro Archia.* Univ. of Illinois
  Pr. 1979 $15.00. Detailed introduction to one of Cicero's most remarkable works
  for the modern reader.
Mitchell, Thomas N. *Cicero: The Ascending Years.* Yale Univ. Pr. 1979 $25.00
Petersson, Torsten. *Cicero: A Biography.* Biblo & Tannen 1920 $15.00
Rawson, Elizabeth. *Cicero: A Portrait.* Cornell Univ. Pr. 1984 $25.00 pap. $9.95
Rolfe, John C. *Cicero and His Influence.* Cooper Square Pr. repr. of 1930 ed. $18.50
Shackleton Bailey, D. R. *Cicero. Class. Life and Letters Ser.* Biblio Dist. 1979 $40.50
  pap. $12.00
Strachan-Davidson, J. L. *Cicero and the Fall of the Roman Republic.* AMS Pr. repr. of
  1894 ed. $30.00; Richard West repr. of 1894 ed. $19.50
Wooten, Cecil W. *Cicero's Philippics and Their Demosthenic Model: The Rhetoric of Cri-
  sis.* Univ. of North Carolina Pr. 1983 $20.00

HORACE (Quintus Horatius Flaccus). 65 B.C.–8 B.C.

Horace's father was an ambitious "freedman of modest circumstances,"
who gave his son the best available education. While a student in Athens,
Horace met Brutus and fought in the Battle of Philippi. After that defeat he
returned to Italy to find his farm confiscated, became a clerk in the civil service, and started writing. Through Virgil he met Maecenas, the great patron
of literature, who gave him the Sabine farm that Horace celebrated in his
poetry. His circumstances improved as his friendship with Maecenas and
the Emperor Augustus grew, and the sarcasm and occasional obscenity of
the *Epodes* and *Satires* gave way to the more genial and mellow mood of the
Odes and *Epistles.* He is acknowledged as one of Rome's greatest poets because of his perfection of verse technique, his candid self-portraiture, urbane wit, sincere patriotism, and sensible commendation of the golden
mean. He made the Rome of his day come alive in street scenes, private banquets, love affairs, country weekends, and in personalities great and small,
rich and poor. The literary canons set forth in his *Ars Poetica* dominated literary criticism throughout the Middle Ages and into the eighteenth century.
His impeccable and very quotable use of language has been widely admired

and his influence on English letters extensive. Poetic translations of Horace into English include those by JONSON (see Vol. 1), DRYDEN (see Vol. 1), MILTON (see Vol. 1), CONGREVE, and POPE (see Vol. 1).

BOOKS BY HORACE

Works. Trans. into English prose by David Watson, rev. by W. Crakelt, AMS Pr. 2 vols. repr. of 1792 ed. 1976 $87.50

Complete Works. Trans. by Charles E. Passage, Ungar 1983 $28.50. A clear and faithful translation in the original meters.

The Essential Horace: Odes, Epodes, Satires and Epistles. Trans. by Burton Raffel, fwd. and afterword by W. R. Johnston, North Point Pr. 1983 $22.50 pap. $13.50. A very modern translation that often catches the tone.

Satires, Epistles, and Ars Poetica. Trans. by H. Rushton Fairclough, *Loeb Class. Lib.* Harvard Univ. Pr. rev. ed. 1926 $12.50. A standard translation; faithful to the original.

Satires (35–30 B.C.) and *Epistles* (20–13 B.C.). Trans. by Smith P. Bovie, Univ. of Chicago Pr. (Phoenix Bks.) 1959 pap. $6.50. "Documented and based on a sound text, thorough scholarship, and poetic sensitivity" (*LJ*).

Horace Talks: The Satires. Trans. by Henry H. Chamberlain, *Select Bibliographies Repr. Ser.* Ayer repr. of 1940 ed. $17.00. "All the elements of Horace's art, both in its spirit and in its form, come to life again in Chamberlain's translation" (E. K. Rand, Preface).

Odes (23–13 B.C.) and *Epodes* (30 B.C.). Trans. by John Marshall, AMS Pr. repr. of 1907 ed. $27.00; trans. by C. E. Bennett, *Loeb Class. Lib.* Harvard Univ. Pr. rev. ed. 1914 $12.50; trans. by Joseph P. Clancy, Univ. of Chicago Pr. (Phoenix Bks.) 1960 pap. $8.95

Ars Poetica (The Art of Poetry) (13–8 B.C.). AMS Pr. repr of 1783 ed. $23.00

BOOKS ABOUT HORACE

Commager, Steele. *The Odes of Horace: A Critical Study.* Yale Univ. Pr. 1962 o.p. "This is good modern criticism, finely calibrated to a classical writer and sustained by firm and conscientious, if somewhat showy, scholarship.... The great, compelling virtue of Commager's study is that it restores to Horace the features of a man; that in place of the silly, moralizing Sabine Micawber of philosophy, it gives us at last a credibly complex picture of a great poet" (*N.Y. Times*).

Fraenkel, Eduard. *Horace.* Oxford 1957 pap. $25.95. This is a basic and comprehensive work by a first-rate scholar; any serious student of Horace must consult it.

Frank, Tenney. *Catullus and Horace: Two Poets in Their Environment.* 1928. Russell 1965 o.p. A vivid and sensitive portrait of the two poets.

Perret, Jacques. *Horace.* Trans. by Bertha Humez, fwd. by Jotham Johnson, New York Univ. Pr. 1964 o.p. Mr. Perret is a professor of Latin at the Sorbonne. His "analysis is fresh, wise, perceptive, with excellent insights.... The lover of Horace will like this eye-opener; the newcomer will find it a handsome introduction to the poet" (*LJ*).

Sedgwick, Henry D. *Horace: A Biography.* Russell repr. of 1947 ed. 1967 $7.50

Shackleton Bailey, D. R. *Profile of Horace.* Harvard Univ. Pr. 1982 $17.50. "He gives us a believable portrait of Horace, but of special importance are his elucidations of the poems" (*Choice*).

Showerman, Grant. *Horace and His Influence.* Cooper Square Pr. repr. of 1930 ed. $18.50. A careful and detailed study.

Verrall, A. W. *Studies Literary and Historical in the Odes of Horace.* Associated Faculty Pr. repr. of 1884 ed. 1969 $19.50
Wilkinson, L. P. *Horace and His Lyric Poetry.* Cambridge Univ. Pr. 1957 pap. $8.50. This sensitive and scholarly study is highly recommended.

JUVENAL (Decimus Junius Juvenalis). 60?–140?

The 16 *Satires* of Juvenal, which contain a vivid picture of contemporary Rome under the Empire, have seldom been equaled as biting diatribes. The satire was the only literary form that the Romans did not copy from the Greeks. Horace merely used it for humorous comment on human folly. Juvenal's invectives in powerful hexameters, exact and epigrammatic, were aimed at lax and luxurious society, tyranny (Domitian's), criminal excesses, and the immorality of women. Juvenal was so sparing of autobiographical detail that we know very little of his life. He was desperately poor at one time and may have been an important magistrate at another.

His influence was great in the Middle Ages; in the seventeenth century he was well translated by DRYDEN (see Vol. 1), and in the eighteenth century he was paraphrased by JOHNSON (see Vol. 1) in his *London* and *The Vanity of Human Wishes.* He inspired in Swift the same savage bitterness.

BOOKS BY JUVENAL

Satires (and Persius's *Satires*). c.110–127. Trans. by John Dryden, AMS Pr. repr. of 1735 ed. $37.50. Some of the Juvenal *Satires* were translated by hands other than Dryden.
Satires (and Persius's *Satires*). 1918. Trans. by G. G. Ramsay, *Loeb Class. Lib.* Harvard Univ. Pr. rev. ed. 1950 $12.50
Satires. Trans. by Thomas Sheridan, AMS Pr. repr. of 1739 ed. $40.00; trans. by William Gifford, Jr., AMS Pr. repr. of 1906 ed. $27.00; trans by William Gifford, Jr., Biblio Dist. 1954 $9.95; trans. by R. Humphries, Indiana Univ. Pr. 1958 pap. $4.95
Sixteen Satires. Trans. by Peter Green, *Penguin Class. Ser.* 1967 pap. $3.95

BOOKS ABOUT JUVENAL

Highet, Gilbert. *Juvenal the Satirist: A Study.* Oxford 1954 o.p. For the general reader and the more advanced student.
Jenkyns, Richard. *Three Classical Poets: Sappho, Catullus and Juvenal.* Harvard Univ. Pr. 1982 text ed. $20.00

LIVY (Titus Livius). c.59 B.C.–C.A.D. 17

[SEE Volume 3, Chapter 6.]

LUCAN (Marcus Annaeus Lucanus). 39–65

Grandson of Seneca the Rhetorician and nephew of Seneca the Philosopher, Lucan was born in Spain and educated in rhetoric in Rome. He was a favorite at Nero's court until the emperor took offense at his precocious literary talent and prevented him from displaying it in public. Lucan then joined a conspiracy against the monarch and was forced to commit suicide. His epic poem *Bellum Civile* (*Civil War*), also called *Pharsalia*, sided with Pompey in his fatal struggle with Julius Caesar. His complex rhetorical style was acclaimed in the Middle Ages; Dante and Chaucer ranked him high as a poet.

BOOK BY LUCAN

Civil War. Trans. by J. D. Duff, *Loeb Class. Ser.* Harvard Univ. Pr. 1928 $12.50

BOOKS ABOUT LUCAN

Ahl, Frederick. *Lucan: An Introduction. Studies in Classical Philology.* Cornell Univ. Pr. 1976 $32.50

Morford, M. P. O. *The Poet Lucan: Studies in Rhetorical Epic.* Oxford 1967 o.p.

LUCRETIUS (Titus Lucretius Carus). c.94 or 99 B.C.–55 B.C.

Almost nothing is known of Lucretius's life, but legends have attached themselves to him. Donatus said that Virgil assumed the toga of manhood the very day Lucretius died (that is, October 15, 55 B.C.); and Jerome stated that the poet was poisoned by a love potion, wrote his *De Rerum Natura* at lucid intervals, and then commited suicide. He may have been one of the Lucretii, an aristocratic Roman family, or a native of Campania who studied Epicureanism in Naples. It is certain, however, that he was a friend or dependent of C. Memmius (who was also the patron of Catullus) to whom the poem is dedicated.

De Rerum Natura (*On the Nature of the Universe*), Lucretius's only work, written in six books, expounds the philosophy of Epicurus. Because the universe and all things in it are made up of atoms swirling about in different combinations, the human soul perishes with the body. Lucretius was intent on proving this so that he might persuade his audience to give up their fear of death and of punishment in the afterlife and their belief in divine intervention. His exposition of the mechanical nature of the universe shows intensity of thought and feeling and is expressed in beautiful, vivid images. His invocation to Venus in Book I and his denunciation of women and the passion of love in Book IV are famous and their influence enduring.

BOOKS BY LUCRETIUS

On the Nature of Things. Trans. by W. H. D. Rouse, *Loeb Class. Lib.* Harvard Univ. Pr. rev. ed. 1975 $12.50. Prose translation; highly recommended.

On the Nature of the Universe. Trans. by Ronald E. Latham, *Penguin Class. Ser.* 1951 pap. $2.95

Lucretius: The Way Things Are. Trans. by Rolfe Humphries, Indiana Univ. Pr. 1968 pap. $4.95. A translation of *On the Nature* in English blank verse.

Lucretius: The Nature of Things. Trans. by Frank O. Copley, Norton 1977 $10.95 pap. $3.95. A clear translation close to the texture of the Latin.

BOOKS ABOUT LUCRETIUS

Bailey, Cyril, ed. *Lucretius: De Rerum Natura.* Oxford 3 vols. 1947 o.p. Volume 1 is a superb introduction to the poet—his life, philosophy, and poetic technique; volumes 2 and 3 are the Latin text with commentary.

De Witt, Norman W. *Epicurus and His Philosophy.* Greenwood repr. of 1954 ed. 1973 lib. bdg. $20.75. Clarifies Lucretius's relationship to Epicurus.

Festugière, André M. *Epicurus and His Gods.* Trans. by C. W. Chilton, Russell repr.
    of 1955 ed. 1969 $7.50. A basic analysis of the Greek philosopher and Lucretius's
    indebtedness to him.
Hadzsits, George D. *Lucretius and His Influence.* Cooper Square Pr. repr. of 1930 ed.
    1963 $28.50. Valuable for its careful presentation of Lucretius's later influence.
Minadeo, Richard. *The Lyre of Science: Form and Meaning in Lucretius' De Rerum
    Natura.* Wayne State Univ. Pr. 1969 $10.95. A clear and solid critical study.
Santayana, George. *Three Philosophical Poets.* Cooper Square Pr. repr. of 1910 ed.
    1971 lib. bdg. $25.00
Sikes, Edward E. *Lucretius: Poet and Philosopher.* Russell repr. of 1936 ed. 1971
    $12.00. An important critical study of the poet.

MARTIAL (Marcus Valerius Martialis). 40?–104

Martial's 12 books of *Epigrams* were written for the most part in elegiac
couplets modeled on Ovid and Catullus. They show Martial's acute observation of Roman life in the last third of the first century and were written
with wit and brevity, often postponing the point or sting until the end. They
are frequently insulting and obscene. Not much is known of Martial's life,
except that he left his home in Bilbilis, Spain, in 64 to live by his writing
and his wits in Rome. He courted the favor of the rich and powerful, was a
friend of Seneca, Lucan, Juvenal, and Quintilian, and Pliny the Younger la-
mented his death. The *Epigrams* have been read and imitated throughout
the centuries; one of them was translated as the memorable "I do not love
thee, Dr. Fell."

BOOKS BY MARTIAL

Epigrams. 80–84. Trans. by Walter C. A. Kerr, *Loeb Class. Lib.* Harvard Univ. Pr. 2
    vols. 1919–20 ea. $12.50
Selected Epigrams. Trans. by Ralph Marcellino, Irvington text ed. 1968 pap. $3.25
Sixty Poems. Trans. by Dudley Fitts, Harcourt bilingual ed. 1967 o.p. "Free para-
    phrases of the original [Latin] by a contemporary poet and critic."
Epigrams from Martial: A Verse Translation. Trans. by Barriss Mills, Purdue Univ. Pr.
    1969 $6.75. These translations have the verve and liveliness of the originals.

BOOKS ABOUT MARTIAL

Murray, Philip. *Poems after Martial.* Wesleyan Univ. Pr. 1967 $15.00. Free adapta-
    tions of some 70 epigrams in all. "A few of the renderings are brilliant," many
    are "witty and urbane" (*LJ*).
Nixon, Paul. *Martial and the Modern Epigram.* Cooper Square Pr. repr. of 1930 ed.
    $17.50
Whipple, Thomas K. *Martial and English Epigram from Sir Thomas Wyatt to Ben Jon-
    son.* Phaeton repr. of 1925 ed. 1970 $10.00

OVID (Publius Ovidius Naso). 43 B.C.–A.D. 17

Born of an equestrian family in Sulmo, Ovid was educated in rhetoric in
Rome but gave it up for poetry. He counted Horace and Propertius among
his friends and wrote an elegy on the death of Tibullus. He became the leading poet of Rome but was banished in A.D. 8 by an edict of Augustus to re-

mote Tomis on the Black Sea because of a poem and an indiscretion. Miserable in provincial exile, he died there ten years later.

His brilliant, witty, fertile elegiac poems include *Amores* (*Loves*), *Heroides* (*Heroines*), and *Ars Amatoris* (*The Art of Loving*), but he is perhaps best known for *Metamorphoses*, a marvelously imaginative compendium of Greek mythology where every story alludes to a change in shape. Ovid was admired and imitated throughout the Middle Ages and Renaissance; CHAUCER (see Vol. 1), SPENSER (see Vol. 1), SHAKESPEARE, and JONSON (see Vol. 1) knew his works well. His mastery of form, gift for narration, and amusing urbanity are irresistible.

BOOKS BY OVID

The Erotic Poems. Trans. by Peter Green, Penguin 1983 pap. $4.95

Heroides (c.5 B.C.–A.D. 8) and *Amores*. Trans. by Grant Showerman, *Loeb Class. Lib.* Harvard Univ. Pr. rev. ed. 1977 $12.50

Amores. c.3 B.C. Ed. by E. J. Kenney, Oxford 1961 $12.95

The Art of Love. c.1 B.C. Trans. by J. H. Mozley, *Loeb Class. Lib.* Harvard Univ. Pr. 1929 $12.50; trans. by Rolfe Humphries, Indiana Univ. Pr. 1957 pap. $4.95

Metamorphoses. c.A.D. 2. Trans. by F. J. Miller, *Loeb Class. Lib.* Harvard Univ. Pr. 2 vols. rev. ed. 1977–84 ea. $12.50; trans. by Rolfe Humphries, Indiana Univ. Pr. 1955 $15.00 pap. $5.95; trans. by Horace Gregory, New Amer. Lib. pap. $3.95; trans. by Mary Innes, *Penguin Class. Ser.* 1955 pap. $3.95

The Fasti. c.A.D. 8. Trans. by James George Frazer, *Loeb Class. Lib.* Harvard Univ. Pr. 1931 $12.50

Tristia (9–12) and *Ex Ponto* (13–17). Trans. by Arthur Leslie Wheeler, *Loeb Class. Lib.* Harvard Univ. Pr. rev. ed. 1985 $12.50

Tristia. Trans. by L. R. Lind, Univ. of Georgia Pr. 1975 $6.95

BOOKS ABOUT OVID

Barsby, John. *Ovid, Greece and Rome.* Oxford 1978 o.p.

Boas, Frederick S. *Ovid and the Elizabethans.* Haskell 1970 pap. $11.95

Evans, Harry B. *Publica Carmina: Ovid's Books from Exile.* Univ. of Nebraska Pr. 1983 $23.50. Careful and thorough introduction for the general reader.

Galinsky, G. Karl. *Ovid's Metamorphoses: An Introduction to the Basic Aspects.* Univ. of California Pr. 1975 $33.50

Jacobson, Howard. *Ovid's Heroides.* Princeton Univ. Pr. 1974 o.p. Interpretive study with emphasis on character.

Rand, E. K. *Ovid.* Cooper Square Pr. repr. of 1930 ed. $18.50. This is indispensable for understanding Ovid's poetry and his influence on later European literature.

Syme, Ronald. *History in Ovid.* Oxford 1970 $32.50

PERSIUS (Aulus Persius Flaccus). 34–62

Persius was a native of Etruria and was educated in Rome, where he became Lucan's friend. He wrote six satires in a somewhat contorted style, which inculcate Stoic morality. His sanity and wit have direct appeal.

BOOKS BY PERSIUS

Satires (and Juvenal's *Satires*). Trans. by G. G. Ramsay, *Loeb Class. Lib.* Harvard Univ. Pr. rev. ed. 1950 $12.50

The Satires of Persius. Trans. by W. S. Merwin, Associated Faculty Pr. repr. of 1961
    ed. 1973 $22.50. The notes and introduction of W. S. Anderson are recom-
    mended.
The Satires of Horace and Persius. Ed. by W. R. Connor and Basil L. Gildersleeve,
    Ayer repr. of 1903 ed. 1979 lib. bdg. $17.00

PETRONIUS (Gaius Petronius Arbiter). d. 65

Tacitus called this Roman dandy—the director of entertainments at the
Emperor Nero's court—"Arbiter Elegantiae" ("Arbiter of Refined Taste"),
and said further that Petronius was in high favor, having been governor of
Bithynia and consul, but he was finally denounced by Nero's favorite,
Tigellinus, and forced to commit suicide. He is considered to have written
The Satyricon, a satiric picaresque romance, in prose interspersed with
verse, which is extant only in fragments. Its subject is Italian low life, and it
is characterized by "brilliant wit and riotous obscenity." The chief episode
describes the vulgarian-upstart Trimalchio and his banquet for the hero.
William Arrowsmith has made a vigorous, appropriately colloquial American English translation. "We savor the satire and the parodies of practically
every Greek or Roman literary type, and we see the universal applications
behind the catalogue of the vices and excesses of Nero's Rome" (*LJ*).

BOOKS BY PETRONIUS

Works of Petronius Arbiter in Prose and Verse. AMS Pr. repr. of 1736 ed. $34.50
The Satyricon. c.60. Ed. by Evan T. Sage and Brady B. Gilleland, Irvington 2d ed.
    enl. text ed. 1969 pap. $12.95; (and Seneca's *Apocolocyntosis*) trans. by M.
    Heseltine and W. H. D. Rouse, *Loeb Class. Lib.* Harvard Univ. Pr. $12.50; trans.
    by William Arrowsmith, New Amer. Lib. 1983 pap. $2.95; (and Seneca's
    Apocolocyntosis) trans. by J. P. Sullivan, *Penguin Class. Ser.* 1978 $3.95

BOOKS ABOUT PETRONIUS

Bagnani, Gilbert. *Arbiter of Elegance: A Study of the Life and Works of C. Petronius.*
    Univ. of Toronto Pr. 1954 o.p. A sound and scholarly work.
Sullivan, J. P. *The Satyricon of Petronius.* Indiana Univ. Pr. 1968 o.p.
Walsh, P. G. *Roman Novel.* Cambridge Univ. Pr. 1970 $37.50

PHAEDRUS. c.15 B.C.–A.D. 50

[SEE Aesop in Chapter 7, this volume.]

PLAUTUS, TITUS MACCIUS. d. c.184 B.C.

Plautus and Terence used stock characters (the young lovers, the clever
slave, the irate father) and devices (mistaken identity), but each handled
these conventions in his own distinct manner. Plautus was the son of a poor
Umbrian farmer who may have fought in the Second Punic War. The playwright Plautus is said to have been a popular actor, true comedian, jovial,
tolerant, rough of humor. He not only modeled his plays on the Greek New
Comedy, but unhesitatingly inserted long passages translated from the
Greek originals. He was the master of comic irony and, as its originator, copied by MOLIÈRE, CORNEILLE, JONSON (see Vol. 1), DRYDEN (see Vol. 1), and

FIELDING (SEE VOL. 1). SHAKESPEARE's *Comedy of Errors* was based on Plautus's *Menaechmi.* Of more than 100 plays, 21 survive.

BOOKS BY PLAUTUS

Works. Trans. by Paul Nixon, *Loeb Class. Lib.* Harvard Univ. Pr. 5 vols. 1916–38 ea. $12.50. This is the best translation for most of the plays. Volume 5 includes selected fragments and an index to proper names. Volume 1 contains *Amphitryon; The Comedy of Asses; The Pot of Gold; The Two Vacchises; The Captives.* Volume 2 contains *Casina; The Casket Comedy; Curculio; Epicidus; The Two Menaechmuses.* Volume 3 contains *The Merchant; The Braggart Warrior; The Haunted House; The Persian.* Volume 4 contains *The Little Carthaginatinian; Pseudolus; The Rope.* Volume 5 contains *Stichus; Three Bob Day; Truculentus; The Tale of a Travelling Bag* (fragments).
The Darker Comedies. Trans. and ed. by James B. Tatum, Johns Hopkins Univ. Pr. 1983 o.p. Racy translations intended for performance.
Amphitryon and Two Other Plays. Ed. by Lionel Casson, *Norton Lib.* 1971 pap. $5.95
The Menaechmi. Trans. by Frank O. Copley, Bobbs 1956 pap. $5.44; (with the title *The Mechaechmus Twins*) trans. and ed. by Lionel Casson, *Norton Lib.* 1971 pap. $5.95
The Pot of Gold and Other Plays. Trans. by E. F. Watling, *Penguin Class. Ser.* 1965 pap. $3.95
The Rope and Other Plays. Trans. by E. F. Watling, *Penguin Class. Ser.* 1964 pap. $3.95

BOOKS ABOUT PLAUTUS

Norwood, Gilbert. *Plautus and Terence.* Cooper Square Pr. repr. of 1930 ed. $17.50
Segal, Erich. *Roman Laughter: The Comedy of Plautus. Studies in Comparative Lit.* Harvard Univ. Pr. 1968 pap. $14.00. A knowledgeable and entertaining presentation of Plautus by a famous classicist and novelist.

PLINY THE YOUNGER (Gaius Plinius Caecilius Secundus). c.61–c.112

Raised by his uncle Pliny the Elder, who was a scholar and industrious compiler of *Natural History,* Pliny the Younger intended his *Letters* for posterity and polished them with extreme care. He was an orator, statesman, and well-educated man of the world. He wrote with discretion on a variety of subjects, and without the bitterness of his friends TACITUS (see Vol. 3) and Suetonius or the disgust for the social conditions of those troubled times found in the writings of his contemporaries Juvenal and Martial. In the introduction to the Loeb edition, Hutchinson wrote: "Melmoth's translation of Pliny's letters, published in 1746, not only delighted contemporary critics . . . but deservedly ranks as a minor English classic. Apart from its literary excellence, it has the supreme merit of reflecting the spirit of the original. . . . No modern rendering can capture the ease and felicity of Melmoth's; for they came of his living in a world like 'Pliny's own.' "

BOOKS BY PLINY THE YOUNGER

Letters. Trans. by William Melmoth, rev. by W. M. L. Hutchinson, *Loeb Class. Lib.* Harvard Univ. Pr. 2 vols. rev. ed. 1969 ea. $12.50
The Letters of the Younger Pliny. Richard West 2 vols. repr. 1978 $27.50

BOOK ABOUT PLINY THE YOUNGER

Sherwin-White, A. N. *Letters of Pliny: A Historical and Social Commentary.* Oxford 1966 o.p.

PROPERTIUS (SEXTUS). c.50 B.C.–c.16 B.C.

Propertius was deprived of his Umbrian estate in the confiscation of the civil war. He applied his rhetorical education not to the courts, but to poetry. His first book of elegies to "Cynthia" won him the patronage of Maecenas and established his reputation as a passionate, witty, self-absorbed, and learned poet. The three books that followed invoke Cynthia, but carry as well tributes to Maecenas, to Roman greatness, addresses to friends, and antiquarian fragments.

BOOKS BY PROPERTIUS

Propertius. Trans. by H. E. Butler, *Loeb Class. Lib.* Harvard Univ. Pr. 1912 $12.50. A careful, scholarly translation.
Poems. Trans. by Constance Carrier, Peter Smith $11.25

BOOKS ABOUT PROPERTIUS

Commager, Steele. *A Prolegomenon to Propertius.* Univ. of Cincinnati Pr. 1974 o.p.
Hubbard, Margaret. *Propertius.* Biblio Dist. 1979 $34.00 pap. $12.00
Sullivan, J. P. *Propertius: A Critical Introduction.* Cambridge Univ. Pr. 1976 $29.95. Concise, clear, and expert.

QUINTILIAN (Marcus Fabius Quintilianus). c.35–c.95

The *Institutio Oratoria* in 12 books was written by Quintilian, the most famous of the Roman rhetoricians, during his later years. It contains the principles of rhetoric, especially in public speaking, and is a practical treatise on the complete education of a Roman and the best methods used in the Roman schools. It offers, in the tenth book, a famous critique of Greek and Latin authors. Quintilian's ideal orator is a good man skilled in speaking. Quintilian was born in northern Spain but educated in Rome, where he began to teach oratory in 68. He was the first rhetorician to establish a public school and to receive a salary from the state.

BOOKS BY QUINTILIAN

Institutionis Oratoriae (On the Training of an Orator). Trans. by H. E. Butler, *Loeb Class. Lib.* Harvard Univ. Pr. 4 vols. 1953 ea. $12.50
Quintilian as Educator: Selections from the "Institutio Oratoria" of Marcus Fabius Quintilianus. Trans. by H. E. Butler, ed. by Frederic M. Wheelock, Irvington text ed. 1974 lib. bdg. $26.50 pap. $11.95

BOOKS ABOUT QUINTILIAN

Kennedy, George. *Quintilian. Twayne's World Authors Ser.* 1969 o.p. By a leading authority on Roman rhetoric.
Wheelock, Frederic M. *Quintilian as Educator.* Twayne 1974 o.p.

SENECA, LUCIUS ANNAEUS. c.3 B.C.–A.D. 65

Seneca was born in Spain of a wealthy Italian family. His father, Lucius Annaeus Seneca, wrote the well-known *Controversaie* (*Controversies*) and *Suasoriae* (*Persuasions*), which are collections of arguments used in rhetorical training, and his nephew Lucan was the epic poet of the civil war. Educated in rhetoric and philosophy in Rome, he found the Stoic doctrine especially compatible. The younger Seneca became famous as an orator but was exiled by the Emperor Claudius. He was recalled by the Empress Agrippina to become the tutor of her son, the young Nero. After the first five years of Nero's reign, Agrippina was murdered and three years later Octavia, Nero's wife, was exiled. Seneca retired as much as possible from public life and devoted himself to philosophy, writing many treatises at this time. But in 65 he was accused of conspiracy and, by imperial order, committed suicide by opening his veins. He was a Stoic philosopher and met his death with Stoic calm.

Seneca's grisly tragedies fascinated the Renaissance and have been successfully performed in recent years. All ten tragedies are believed genuine, with the exception of *Octavia*, which is now considered to be by a later writer. Translations of the tragedies influenced English dramatists such as JONSON (see Vol. 1), MARLOWE, and SHAKESPEARE, who all imitated Seneca's scenes of horror and his characters—the ghost, nurse, and villain.

BOOKS BY SENECA

Letters from a Stoic. Trans. by Robin Campbell, *Penguin Class. Ser.* 1976 pap. $3.95

The Apocolocyntosis (and Petronius's *Satyricon*). Trans. by J. P. Sullivan, *Penguin Class. Ser.* 1978 $3.95

Seneca's Tragedies. Trans. in prose by Frank Justus Miller, *Loeb Class. Lib.* Harvard Univ. Pr. 2 vols. 1917 ea. $12.50. Volume 1 contains *Hercules Furens; Troades; Medea; Hippolytus; Oedipus.* Volume 2 contains *Agamemnon; Thyestes; Hercules Oetaeus; Phoenissae; Octavia.* Comparative analysis, bibliographies, index with identification of mythological and historical characters included.

Seneca: His Tenne Tragedies. Trans. by Thomas Newton, fwd. by T. S. Eliot, AMS Pr. 2 vols. repr. of 1927 ed. ea. $45.00; Burt Franklin 2 vols. in 1 repr. of 1887 ed. 1966 $45.00

Four Tragedies and Octavia. Trans. by E. F. Watling, *Penguin Class. Ser.* 1974 pap. $3.95

Medea. Ed. by C. D. Costa, Oxford 1953 $15.95

BOOKS ABOUT SENECA

Gummere, R. M. *Seneca, the Philosopher, and His Modern Message.* Cooper Square Pr. repr. of 1930 ed. 1963 $18.50

Pratt, Norman T. *Seneca's Drama.* Univ. of North Carolina Pr. 1983 $25.00. An excellent, helpful critical study.

Sørenson, Villy. *Seneca: The Humanist at the Court of Nero.* Trans. by Glyn Jones, Univ. of Chicago Pr. 1984 $25.00. A provocative and thoughtful analysis of the man and his works.

STATIUS, PUBLIUS PAPINIUS. c.45–c.96

Born in Naples, the son of a schoolmaster, Statius became prominent in Rome for his verse. He was a favorite in the court of the Emperor Domitian, and his lyric verse includes elegies, odes, and poems in praise of the emperor. The *Thebaid* is an epic in 12 books about the struggle of the two sons of Oedipus to rule Thebes. Only fragments are extant and the unfinished *Achilleid* (*The Story of Achilles*). His *Silvae* are pleasant occasional verses to his friends, his wife, and the emperor. His influence continued through the Middle Ages. Dante regarded him as a Christian; CHAUCER (see Vol. 1) imitated his *Thebaid* in *Troilus and Cresseyde* and considered him one of the world's great poets.

BOOK BY STATIUS

Silvae, Thebaid or Thebais, Achilleid. Trans. by J. H. Mozley, *Loeb Class. Lib.* Harvard Univ. Pr. 2 vols. 1955 ea. $12.50. A readable and accurate translation.

BOOKS ABOUT STATIUS

Vessey, David. *Statius and the Thebaid.* Cambridge Univ. Pr. 1973 o.p. An appreciative analysis and evaluation.
Wise, Boyd A. *The Influence of Statius upon Chaucer.* Phaeton repr. of 1911 ed. 1967 $9.00; Richard West repr. of 1911 ed. 1973 $7.00

SUETONIUS (Caius Suetonius Tranquillus). c.69–c.140

Suetonius is noted for *The Lives of the Twelve Caesars*, which survives almost intact. Only fragments remain of his much larger collection *Illustrious Men*. He recorded the most minute details of his subjects' lives in a lively, informative style that became a model for many later biographers. The brief period as secretary to the Emperor Hadrian probably gave him access to official archives, so that his background data are authentic, spiced with the gossip of the times.

The 1606 version by Philemon Holland was influential. Rolfe's version "does not lack the qualities of vigor and lightness; on the contrary it is decidedly readable," J. Wright Duff reported in the *Classical Review*, but the 1914 edition suffered from "defective proofreading, inaccuracies in translation, and neglect of sound English." Of the Robert Graves translation, the *Christian Science Monitor* said: "Astonishing truly, that the stiffly framed Latin language that we learn about in our school texts and grammars is capable of such elasticity and color as we find in this reproduction by Mr. Graves." (See also Volume 3, Chapter 6.)

BOOK BY SUETONIUS

The Lives of the Twelve Caesars. Trans. by Philemon Holland, AMS Pr. 2 vols. repr. of 1899 ed. ea. $45.00; trans. by J. C. Rolfe, *Loeb Class. Lib.* Harvard Univ. Pr. 2 vols. 1914–20 ea. $12.50; trans. by Robert Graves, *Penguin Class. Ser.* 1957 pap. $3.95

BOOK ABOUT SUETONIUS

Wallace-Hadrill, Andrew. *Suetonius: The Scholar and His Caesars.* Yale Univ. Pr. 1984 $22.50. The first book on Suetonius in English analyzes him in his social and political context.

TACITUS, CORNELIUS. c.56–c.112/3

[SEE Volume 3, Chapter 6.]

TERENCE (Publius Tertentius Afer). c.190 B.C.–159 B.C.

Terence was born in Carthage. As a boy, he was the slave of Terentius Lucanus, a Roman senator, who educated him and set him free. He was an intimate friend of the younger Scipio and of the elegant poet Laelius. They were the gilded youth of Rome and Terence's plays were undoubtedly written for this inner circle, not for the vulgar crowd. They were adapted from Menander and other Greek writers of the New Comedy and, in the main, were written seriously on a high literary plane with careful handling of plot and character. The six comedies are all extant.

BOOKS BY TERENCE

Comedies. Trans. by John Sargeaunt, *Loeb Class. Lib.* Harvard Univ. Pr. 2 vols. 1912 ea. $12.50. Volume 1 contains *The Lady of Andros, The Self-Tormentor, The Eunuch.* Volume 2 contains *Phormio, The Mother-in-Law, The Brothers.*
The Comedies of Terence. Trans. by Frank O. Copley, Bobbs 1967 pap. $10.28; ed. by R. Kauer and W. M. Lindsay, Oxford 2d ed. 1926 $15.95. The translations by Copley are elegant, witty, and lucid.

BOOKS ABOUT TERENCE

Norwood, Gilbert. *The Art of Terence.* Russell repr. of 1923 ed. 1965 $7.50
———. *Plautus and Terence.* Cooper Square Pr. repr. of 1930 ed. $17.50

TIBULLUS (ALBIUS). 48 B.C.?–19 B.C.

Tibullus became the poet laureate of the republican literary circle that had as its leader Messalla Corvinus. The chief inspirations of his elegies were his sentimental longing for rustic simplicity and his amorous longing for two women (whom he called Delia and Nemesis) and a boy (Marathus). Tibullus contributed refinement of form and simplicity of language to Roman elegy. The third book of his collection, containing poems not by Tibullus, includes six love elegies by Sulpicia, the only poems we have by a Roman woman.

BOOKS BY TIBULLUS

Works of Catullus and Tibullus with Pervigilium Veneris. Trans. by J. P. Postgate, *Loeb Class. Lib.* Harvard Univ. Pr. rev. ed. 1939 $13.50
The Poems of Tibullus with the Tibullan Collection. Trans. by Philip Dunlop, *Penguin Class. Ser.* 1972 pap. $4.95

BOOK ABOUT TIBULLUS

Putnam, Michael C. *Tibullus: A Commentary.* Univ. of Oklahoma Pr. 1979 pap. $8.95.
   Includes the latest scholarship on the poet; the work of a versatile scholar.

VIRGIL or VERGIL (Publius Vergilius Maro). 70 B.C.–19 B.C.

The reign of Augustus, grandnephew of JULIUS CAESAR (see Vol. 3), who became the first Roman emperor (27 B.C.–A.D. 14), marked the Golden Age of
Latin literature. "The writers of the time were moved to celebrate the greatness of Rome, past, present, and to come. The great monument is, of course,
Virgil's 'Aeneid,' which links the foundation of Rome to the fall of Troy,
traces the ancestry of Julius Caesar to the gods, and makes the greatness of
Rome the subject of divine intervention and prophecy" (Basil Davenport).

Virgil was given a good education by his father, a prosperous farmer living near Mantua. After his studies in Rome and Naples, Virgil completed in
37 B.C. *The Eclogues* or *The Bucolics*, which idealized rural life and was modeled on his Greek predecessor Theocritus. At that time Maecenas, a trusted
counselor of Augustus, became the poet's patron and was introduced by Virgil to Horace. *The Georgics*, a didactic, realistic treatise on farming in the
manner of the Greek poet Hesiod and honoring Maecenas, followed *The Bucolics;* and then Virgil devoted the rest of his life to *The Aeneid.* This epic
poem, derived from Homer's *Iliad* and *Odyssey* and drawing on much of
Greek and earlier Latin literature, revealed the greatness of the Roman Empire and was written with perfection of technique and tenderness and melancholy of mood. Virgil considered it still in need of polishing and revision
at the time of his death and asked his executor to destroy the manuscript,
but his order was rescinded by Augustus. Virgil died in Brindisi and was
buried in Naples, where his tomb was revered thereafter—St. Paul is said to
have wept over it. Master Virgil came to be regarded as a magician and as a
prophet of Christianity. And his poetry, particularly *The Aeneid*, was a dominant influence on later European literature. He was DANTE's guide through
Hell in the *Divine Comedy;* and in English letters, CHAUCER (see Vol. 1), Sur-
rey, SPENSER (see Vol. 1), MILTON (see Vol. 1), DRYDEN (see Vol. 1), POPE (see
Vol. 1), and TENNYSON (see Vol. 1) venerated him.

BOOKS BY VIRGIL

Works. Trans. by Henry Rushton Fairclough, *Loeb Class. Lib.* Harvard Univ. Pr. 2
   vols. rev. 1935 ea. $12.50
The Eclogues. c.40–37 B.C. Verse trans. by Guy Lee, *Penguin Class. Ser.* 1984 pap.
   $4.95. A workmanlike translation with good introduction, notes, and bibli-
   ography.
The Georgics. c.37–29 B.C. Trans. by Smith P. Bovie, Univ. of Chicago Pr. 1966 pap.
   $5.50; trans. by L. P. Wilkinson, Penguin 1983 pap. $3.95
The Aeneid. c.29–19 B.C. Trans. by John Dryden, *Airmont Class. Ser.* 1968 pap. $1.95;
   trans. into Scottish verse by Gawin Douglas, ed. by George Dundas, AMS Pr. 2
   vols. repr. of 1839 ed. $45.00; trans. by Edward F. Taylor, ed. by Edward M. For-
   ster, AMS Pr. repr. of 1906 ed. $30.00; trans. by Frank O. Copley, Bobbs text ed.
   1975 pap. $10.28; trans. by Patric Dickinson, New Amer. Lib. 1961 pap. $2.95;
   trans. by W. F. Jackson Knight, *Penguin Class. Ser.* 1956 pap. $2.95; trans. by
   Robert Fitzgerald, Random 1983 $20.00 1984 pap. $9.95; ed. by R. D. Williams,

St. Martin's 2 vols. 1972–73 ea. $17.95; trans. by Allen Mandelbaum, Univ. of California Pr. 1981 $28.50. The translations by Gawin Douglas and John Dryden are influential renderings by a major Scottish and a great English poet. The W. F. Jackson Knight translation is useful because it is so faithful to the literal sense of the original. The translation by Allen Mandelbaum is effective and expressive. Fitzgerald's translation has been widely acclaimed for its skill in capturing the poetic effect of the original.

BOOKS ABOUT VIRGIL

Alpers, Paul. *The Singer of the Eclogues: A Study of Virgilian Pastoral*. Univ. of California Pr. 1979 $26.50. Introductory; includes a translation.

Camps, W. A. *An Introduction to Virgil's Aeneid*. Oxford 1969 pap. $10.95. A solid and scholarly study of the poem in its Roman context.

Commager, Steele, ed. *Virgil: A Collection of Critical Essays*. Prentice-Hall 1966 o.p. Various approaches to Virgil that are provocative and well written.

Conway, Robert S. *Harvard Lectures on the Vergilian Age*. Biblo & Tannen 1928 $10.00; Richard West repr. of 1928 ed. 1975 $7.25

Cruttwell, Robert W. *Virgil's Mind at Work*. Cooper Square Pr. repr. of 1947 ed. $20.00; Greenwood repr. of 1946 ed. 1971 lib. bdg. $15.00

Di Cesare, Mario. *The Altar and the City: A Reading of Virgil's Aeneid*. Columbia Univ. Pr. 1974 $25.00 pap. $12.00. Thoughtful criticism.

Frank, Tenney. *Vergil: A Biography*. Russell repr. of 1922 ed. 1965 $7.50

Gordon, George. *Virgil in English Poetry*. Folcroft repr. of 1931 ed. 1974 lib. bdg. $10.00

Haber, Tom B. *Comparative Study of the Beowulf and the Aeneid*. Richard West repr. of 1931 ed. 1973 $25.00

Haecker, Theodor. *Virgil: Father of the West*. Trans. by A. Wheen, Johnson Repr. repr. of 1934 ed. $14.00

Highet, Gilbert. *The Speeches in Vergil's Aeneid*. Princeton Univ. Pr. 1972 $33.00

Hughes, Merritt Y. *Virgil and Spenser*. AMS Pr. repr. of 1929 ed. $12.50; Associated Faculty Pr. repr. of 1929 ed. 1969 $19.50

Hunt, J. William. *Forms of Glory: Structure and Sense in Virgil's Aeneid*. Southern Illinois Univ. Pr. 1973 $10.00. Sensitive and intimate criticism.

Johnson, W. R. *Darkness Visible: A Study of Virgil's Aeneid*. Univ. of California Pr. 1976 $26.00 pap. $7.95. Superb criticism; subtle and wide ranging in its approach.

Leach, Eleanor W. *Virgil's Eclogues: Landscapes of Experience*. Cornell Univ. Pr. 1974 $29.50. A solid and intelligent approach.

Lee, M. Owen. *Fathers and Sons in Virgil's Aeneid: Tum Genitor Natum*. State Univ. of New York Pr. 1979 $42.50 pap. $14.95

Mackail, John W. *An Introduction to Virgil's Aeneid*. Folcroft repr. of 1946 ed. 1974 lib. bdg. $6.50. Highly recommended.

———. *Virgil and His Meaning to the World of Today*. Cooper Square Pr. repr. of 1930 ed. $17.50

Putnam, Michael C. *Virgil's Pastoral Art: Studies in the Eclogues*. Princeton Univ. Pr. 1970 o.p.

Quinn, Kenneth. *Virgil's Aeneid: A Critical Description*. Univ. of Michigan Pr. 1968 o.p. A massive and detailed study.

Rand, E. K. *The Magical Art of Virgil*. Harvard Univ. Pr. 1931 o.p. An influential study.

Williams, Gordon. *Technique and Ideas in the Aeneid*. Yale Univ. Pr. text ed. 1983 $30.00

CHAPTER 9

French Literature

Richard A. Brooks

I thought writing was an activity that produced reality.... A book was
something imaginary, but beyond the book there was truth.
—Jean-Paul Sartre

From the Middle Ages arguably, from the Renaissance certainly, French literature has continued to hold a high place in Western civilization and, from the nineteenth century onward, has been a principal representative of occidental culture in the Orient. No other literature has held so consistently high the ideal of thought and expression as inseparable couple; no other civilization has attached so much importance to the purity and good usage of its language. From the sixteenth-century *Défense et illustration de la langue française* by Du Bellay to more recent concerns about the intrusion of other modern languages into French (e.g., *franglais*), the French language has adapted, but slowly and carefully, to contemporary pressures.

Ideas come through, for better or for worse, in translation; the style of their expression much less easily. That is why translation into English produces at best only an approximation of the original, why poetry can be perhaps adapted but surely not brought over from French into English. The English-reading public has been well served in recent years by the admirable achievements of translators like Barbara Bray, Richard Howard, Ralph Manheim, Louise Varèse, Richard Wilbur, and Barbara Wright. It must be remembered that this chapter covers only translations of French literature—prose, poetry, and theater—now in print. The date directly after a title is that of the first publication in French.

As Germaine Brée has written in her recent volume *Twentieth-Century French Literature:* "In our view, the literary movement as a whole is part of a social and historical process reaching beyond the confines of the aesthetic. Even at the very beginning of the century, writers and artists demonstrated their conviction that a new age was coming that would require a new kind of art. The transformation undergone by avant-garde art and literature was accompanied much more swiftly, in fact, than that of a society whose energies were completely mobilized by two wars. This process of transformation, which affected the entire Western world, was known as 'modernism.' In 1920, dada broke with 'futurism' by questioning the cult of the machine and the entire cultural tradition. The first decade of the 'modernist' period, which included surrealism, was rich in its ideas, in theories, and in works, particularly poetic ones. Breton and Cocteau were its spokesmen. During its second decade, the need felt for novelty became social, a spirit of political controversy characterized literature, and modernism calmed down, its gratuity and outrageousness replaced by a social concern favorable to fiction. In about 1950, the modernist spirit began to change and to retreat before the new critical and scientific spirit; we then enter a 'postmodernist' period, which after 1970 appeared to be directed toward a new but as yet imprecise aesthetic."

The *nouveau roman*, or new novel, new in the 1950s, seems to have settled in and the work of its principal authors (Butor, Robbe-Grillet, Sarraute, and Claude Simon) is now established. The work of avant-garde writers for the theater, like Beckett and Ionesco, which seemed so experimental and far-out in the 1950s and 1960s, has also now been canonized by the establishment. Subsequently, the literary scene—particularly in criticism—was occupied by the structuralists and semioticians (e.g., Barthes, Foucault, Genette, and Kristeva) as voices in the creative field—novel and theater—seemed relatively silent. More recently, France has witnessed a return to a more imaginative literature with novelists like Michel Tournier and Jean-Marie Le Clézio.

The theater has always been a strong force in French literature with some of its writers ranking among the most celebrated and respected, for example, Corneille, Molière, Racine. It was in the mid-seventeenth century—with influences from antiquity by way of the Renaissance and from Spain, which was finishing its *siglo de oro*—that notions of French comedy and tragedy were formulated after initial experiment during the sixteenth century and the early years of the seventeenth century. The kind of rigid formality that made the careers of Molière and Racine at the end of the seventeenth century falls under questioning in the eighteenth century with Voltaire writing theater on the established model and Marivaux adding a new dimension. It is above all Diderot, particularly in his theoretical essays on theater, who introduces into France and Europe in general (compare with Lessing in Germany) the new theater that shuns the excess of classic formality and moves toward contemporary realism called drama. Beaumarchais, at the end of the century, will be the most gifted translator of these theories to the stage (*Barber of Seville, Marriage of Figaro*).

The nineteenth century is characterized by the Romantic Theater (already adumbrated by Diderot) from roughly 1815 to 1840 (Hugo, Musset, Vigny, and others) and thereafter by the socially conscious realists, purveyors of the well-made play (Dumas *fils*, Sardou, and Scribe) until the end of the century when neoromantic tendencies (Rostand), symbolist redirection (Maeterlinck, Claudel), and uncharted experiments put an end to the "problem theater" of ideas (Curel, Hervieux, Brieux, Porto-Riche, and others).

A particularly rich moment in French theater comes between the two world wars when Freudian ideas, surrealist disenchantment, and a renaissance of the ideal of classical expression (for example, Gide) all work together as ingredients to produce playwrights like Lenormand, Cocteau, Giraudoux, Montherlant, Anouilh, Aymé, and others, some of whom continued to write after 1950.

French theater in its contemporary form may be said to have its sources (aside from the long tradition beginning at the end of the Renaissance) in reformers like Antoine, Copeau, and the *cartel des quatre* (Baty, Dullin, Jouvet, and Pitoëff), in dramatists like Alfred Jarry, Apollinaire, and the surrealists. Of particular relevance more recently are the writings of Antonin Artaud, specifically *The Theater and Its Double*. The so-called Theater of the Absurd, whose principal contributors have been Adamov, Beckett, Genet, Ionesco, and Pinget, now seems to have come to an end, although some of these dramatists continue to write.

BIBLIOGRAPHY

Brooks, Richard A., and David Clark Cabeen, eds. *A Critical Bibliography of French Literature.* Syracuse Univ. Pr. 6 vols. 1947–85 consult publisher for information about individual volumes

MLA International Bibliography of Books and Articles in Modern Languages and Literatures. 1970 to date. MLA annual consult publisher for information. An essential bibliographical source on every aspect of French and other modern literatures. Its quality and scope have improved greatly in recent years through computerization.

HISTORY AND CRITICISM

Babbitt, Irving. *The Masters of Modern French Criticism.* Intro. by Milton Hindus, Arden Lib. repr. of 1912 ed. 1981 lib. bdg. $40.00. This discussion of the most significant of the nineteenth-century critics in which Babbitt, a noted Harvard professor, describes his own critical position, is still of importance. His insistence that what writers write can be studied independently of their lives helped inspire the New Criticism.

Balakian, Anna. *Literary Origins of Surrealism: A New Mysticism in French Poetry.* New York Univ. Pr. 1966 $15.00 pap. $7.50. An intelligent work on the predecessors of surrealism from the nineteenth century through the dadaists.

Barthes, Roland. *S-Z.* Trans. by Richard Miller, Hill & Wang 1974 $10.95 pap. $7.95
———. *Writing Degree Zero.* Trans. by Annette Lavers and Colin Smith, pref. by Susan Sontag, Hill & Wang 1977 $8.95 pap. $4.95. Some major works by a very influential contemporary French critic who has proposed a "science of literature" grounded in linguistics.

Bédé, Jean-Albert, and William Edgerton, eds. *Columbia Dictionary of Modern European Literature.* Columbia Univ. Pr. 2d ed. 1980 $65.00. Helpful summaries of recent trends in French and other European literatures. Includes brief biographical and critical sketches of leading literary figures.

Bersani, Leo. *Balzac to Beckett: Center and Circumference in French Fiction.* Oxford 1970 $15.95

Brée, Germaine, and Margaret Guiton. *An Age of Fiction: The French Novel from Gide to Camus.* Harcourt 1962 pap. $2.35. An excellent introduction.

Brereton, Geoffrey. *An Introduction to French Poets.* Methuen 2d ed. 1973 pap. $11.95

Brooks, Peter. *Novels of Worldliness: Crébillon, Marivaux, Laclos, Stendhal.* Princeton Univ. Pr. 1969 $32.00

Cazamian, Louis F. *A History of French Literature.* Oxford 1955 o.p. "A comprehensive and thorough account . . . from the earliest times to the present day" (*Manchester Guardian*).

Cobban, Alfred. *A History of Modern France.* Penguin (Pelican) 3 vols. rev. ed. 1957–65 pap. ea. $4.95. "The history of France covered here is so interesting and so well told that the book should be purchased by all libraries, large and small" (*LJ*).

Cruickshank, John, ed. *French Literature and Its Background.* Oxford 6 vols. 1969–70 pap. ea. $9.50. One of the most useful surveys of contemporary French literature.

———, ed. *The Novelist as Philosopher: Studies in French Fiction, 1935–1960.* Greenwood repr. of 1962 ed. 1978 lib. bdg. $24.75

Culler, Jonathan. *Structuralist Poetics: Structuralism, Linguistics and the Study of Literature.* Cornell Univ. Pr. 1976 pap. $8.95. A very helpful introduction to structuralism in literature, a critical theory that has been broadly influential in recent years, especially in France.

Demorest, Jean-Jacques, ed. *Studies in Seventeenth-Century French Literature: Presented to Morris Bishop.* Cornell Univ. Pr. 1962 $19.50

Derrida, Jacques. *Dissemination.* Trans. by Barbara Johnson, Univ. of Chicago Pr. 1981 $26.00 1983 pap. $12.95

———. *Of Grammatology.* Trans. by Gayatri C. Spivak, Johns Hopkins Univ. Pr. 1977 $30.00 pap. $8.95. Two important and difficult works by a currently influential French philosopher and principal figure in the school of "deconstructionism."

Doubrovsky, Serge. *The New Criticism in France.* Trans. by Derek Coltman, Univ. of Chicago Pr. 1973 $20.00

Flanner, Janet. *Paris Journal.* Ed. by William Shawn, Harcourt 2 vols. repr. of 1965–71 ed. 1977 pap. ea. $8.95–$9.95. Well-written accounts of the contemporary French scene by Genêt, the Paris correspondent of the *New Yorker* magazine.

Fowlie, Wallace. *The Age of Surrealism.* 1950. Peter Smith 1960 $6.00. Essays on poets from Rimbaud and Mallarmé to Apollinaire, Eluard, and others.

———. *A Guide to Contemporary French Literature from Valéry to Sartre.* Peter Smith $11.00

Frohock, Wilbur M. *Style and Temper: Studies in French Fiction, 1925–1960.* Harvard Univ. Pr. 1967 $10.00

Gay, Peter. *The Party of Humanity: Essays in French Enlightenment.* Norton repr. of 1964 ed. 1971 pap. $6.95. A major work on the eighteenth century by an outstanding contemporary historian.

Genette, Gerard. *Figures of Literary Discourse.* Columbia Univ. Pr. 1984 $26.00 pap. $11.00.

———. *Narrative Discourse: An Essay in Method.* Fwd. by Jonathan Culler, Cornell Univ. Pr. 1979 $27.50 pap. $8.95. Two widely read works by a leading French practitioner of the structuralist approach to literature.

Goldmann, Lucien. *Toward a Sociology of the Novel.* Methuen 1975 pap. $12.95

Harvey, Paul, and Janet E. Heseltine, eds. *The Oxford Companion to French Literature.* Oxford 1959 $49.50. The most comprehensive one-volume work on French literature.

Havens, George R. *The Age of Ideas: From Reaction to Revolution in Eighteenth-Cen-

tury France. Irvington 1955 $39.50. A lively introduction to major figures and intellectual movements of the French Enlightenment.

Howarth, W. D. *Life and Letters in France: The Seventeenth Century.* Nelson-Hall 1965 o.p. Good introduction to seventeenth-century French literature and society.

James, Henry. *French Poets and Novelists. Essay Index Repr. Ser.* Ayer repr. of 1878 ed. $23.00; Folcroft 1973 lib. bdg. $35.00; Gordon lib. bdg. $59.95; Richard West repr. of 1893 ed. 1980 lib. bdg. $30.00

Klein, Leonard S. *Encyclopedia of World Literature in the Twentieth Century.* Ungar 3 vols. 2d ed. 1982 ea. $100.00. Contains articles on French and Francophone literatures as well as entries on individual authors and movements.

Kohn, H. *Making of the Modern French Mind.* Peter Smith o.p.

Lancaster, H. Carrington. *A History of French Dramatic Literature in the Seventeenth Century.* Gordian 9 vols. repr. of 1942 ed. 1966 $150.00. The major source work on the French theater of the period.

Levin, Harry. *The Gates of Horn: A Study of Five French Realists.* Oxford 1963 $27.50 pap. $6.95. An extremely rich overview of works by Stendhal, Balzac, Flaubert, Zola, and Proust by a major twentieth-century American critic.

A Literary History of France. Ed. by John Fox, I. D. McFarlane, and others. Barnes & Noble 5 vols. consult publisher for information on individual volumes. An overview of French literature, with each period covered by a British authority.

Locher, Frances C., and others, eds. *Contemporary Authors.* Gale 115 vols. 1962– to date, consult publisher for information on individual volumes

Nadeau, Maurice. *A History of Surrealism.* Trans. by Richard Howard, Macmillan (Collier Bks.) 1965 o.p. The origin and history of the surrealist school in literature.

Peyre, Henri. *French Novelists of Today.* Oxford rev. & enl. ed. 1967 pap. $5.50. A valuable and detailed guide to the contemporary French novel from a traditionalist point of view.

Picon, Gaëtan. *Contemporary French Literature: 1945 and After.* Trans. by Kelvin W. Scott and Graham D. Martin, Ungar 1974 $11.50. "A remarkably concise and clear presentation of major trends and authors since 1945 ... written expressly for an Anglo-Saxon audience. Totally objective" (Douglas Alden, *A Critical Bibliography of French Literature*).

Poulet, Georges. *Studies in Human Time.* Trans. by Elliott Coleman, Greenwood repr. of 1956 ed. 1979 lib. bdg. $37.50. Interpretations of French writers from Montaigne to Proust as they are related to the problem of time.

Raymond, Marcel. *From Baudelaire to Surrealism.* Methuen 1970 o.p. Outstanding work on poetry from the time of Baudelaire to 1940.

Reid, Joyce M. H., ed. *The Concise Oxford Dictionary of French Literature.* Oxford 1976 $22.50. Useful for rapid bio-bibliographic information.

Robbe-Grillet, Alain. *For a New Novel: Essays on Fiction. Essay Index Repr. Ser.* Ayer repr. of 1965 ed. $17.00; trans. by Richard Howard, Grove 1966 pap. $2.25. Critical essays by a leading practitioner of the new novel.

Roudiez, Leon S. *French Fiction Today: A New Direction.* Rutgers Univ. Pr. 1972 $35.00. On the new novel.

Saintsbury, George E. *A History of the French Novel to the Close of the 19th Century.* Russell 2 vols. repr. of 1917–19 ed. 1964 $25.00

Sarraute, Nathalie. *The Age of Suspicion: Essays on the Novel.* Trans. by Maria Jolas, Braziller 1963 $5.00. Critical essays by a leading practitioner of the new novel.

Tilley, Arthur Augustus. *The Literature of the French Renaissance: An Introductory Essay.* Folcroft repr. of 1885 ed. 1974 lib. bdg. $20.00

Turnell, Martin. *The Art of French Fiction*. New Directions repr. of 1968 ed. o.p. Perceptive critical analyses of works by Prévost, Stendhal, Zola, Maupassant, Proust, Gide, and Mauriac.

Wilson, Edmund. *Axel's Castle: A Study in the Imaginative Literature of 1870–1930*. Norton repr. of 1931 ed. 1984 pap. $6.95; Scribner 1931 $6.95 text ed. pap. $5.95. On symbolist writers, Valéry, Proust, Rimbaud, and others. Important and illuminating although some of the author's assumptions have been questioned.

COLLECTIONS

Aspel, Alexander, and Donald Justice, eds. *Contemporary French Poetry: Fourteen Witnesses of Man's Fate*. Univ. of Michigan Pr. bilingual ed. 1965 pap. $1.95. Good introduction with bilingual selection of poems and listing of critical works.

Chiari, Joseph. *Contemporary French Poetry*. Essay Index Repr. Ser. Ayer repr. of 1952 ed. $15.00. Study of major French poets of the first half of the twentieth century.

Fowlie, Wallace, trans. and ed. *Mid-Century French Poets*. Twayne's International Studies and Translations Program G. K. Hall 1970 lib. bdg. $15.95. Renderings by various translators of poems by Jacob, Fargue, Supervielle, Saint-John Perse, Breton, and others, with notes and bibliographies.

Gavronsky, Serge. *Poems and Texts: An Anthology of French Poems*. October bilingual ed. 1969 $7.50. Anthology and introduction to six contemporary French poets: Ponge, Frénaud, Bonnefoy, du Bouchet, Roche, and Pleynet.

MacIntyre, C. F., trans. *French Symbolist Poetry*. Univ. of California Pr. bilingual ed. 1958 pap. $4.95

Penguin Book of French Verse. Ed. by Anthony Hartley, *Penguin Poets Ser*. 1975 pap. $5.95

Shapiro, Norman R., trans. *The Comedy of Eros: Medieval French Guides to the Art of Love*. Univ. of Illinois Pr. 1971 $12.50

Taylor, Simon W., and Edward Lucie-Smith, eds. *French Poetry Today: A Bilingual Anthology*. Schocken 1972 $10.00. Covers the period 1955–70.

THEATER

Benedikt, Michael, and George E. Wellwarth, eds. *Modern French Theatre: The Avant Garde, Dada and Surrealism*. Trans. by Michael Benedikt, Dutton 1966 pap. $7.95. A collection of 17 representative plays.

Esslin, Martin. *The Theatre of the Absurd*. Doubleday (Anchor) 1969 pap. $2.95; Overlook Pr. repr. of 1961 ed. rev. ed. 1973 $27.95; Penguin (Pelican) 3d ed. 1983 pap. $5.95. An important guide to the post-World War II Theater of the Absurd in France and elsewhere.

Fowlie, Wallace. *Dionysus in Paris: A Guide to Contemporary French Theatre*. Peter Smith repr. of 1960 ed. 1971 $11.25

Grossvogel, David I. *Twentieth-Century French Drama (The Self-Conscious Stage in Modern French Drama)*. Columbia Univ. Pr. 1958 o.p.; Gordian repr. of 1961 ed. 1966 $12.50. A remarkably comprehensive account, with analyses of the best plays of the twentieth century, including most of those by Adamov, Anouilh, Apollinaire, Beckett, Claudel, Cocteau, Giraudoux, Ionesco, Jarry, and Sartre.

Guicharnaud, Jacques, and June Guicharnaud. *Modern French Theatre: From Girau-*

doux to Genet. Yale Univ. Pr. rev. ed. 1975 pap. $7.95. An extremely useful guide to the post-World War II theater in France. Includes annotated lists of directors, producers, and performances as well as a bibliography of critical works.

Pronko, Leonard C. *Avant Garde: The Experimental Theater in France.* Greenwood repr. of 1962 ed. 1978 lib. bdg. $22.50. Excellent analyses of plays by Beckett, Genet, Ionesco, Schéhadé, and others. Good bibliography.

ANOUILH, JEAN. 1910–

While Paris and most of France were under German occupation, the character of Antigone, from Greek legend, was used symbolically in three new French plays. The most striking, played in modern dress, was Anouilh's. It provided a "rallying point for the aspirations of insurgent youth." His is a distinct and highly original talent. He combines the serious with the fantastic and is "less concerned with making innovations than with returning to a tradition." Anouilh himself groups his works as either *pièces roses*, where the good triumph, or *pièces noires*, where the evil are victorious, in the clash between the symbolic characters prevalent in his drama. His usual themes (said *LJ* in its warm review of *Poor Bitos* [1958]) "are the impossibility of attaining what one once had thought was goodness, the corruptibility of human endeavors, and the pitifulness of the pretenses of those who believe themselves to be distinguished." Anouilh was born in Bordeaux, came to Paris when he was very young, began to study law, then worked for a time in an advertising agency. Always interested in the theater, he became secretary to Louis Jouvet, the famous actor-manager, in 1931, and his first play was produced during the following year.

His moving dramatization of the trial of Joan of Arc, *The Lark*, was first presented in New York in 1955 as adapted by Lillian Hellman. About *The Waltz of the Toreadors* (1951, o.p.), the *N.Y. Times* drama critic Brooks Atkinson said, "Although the manner is antic the substance is melancholy. M. Anouilh and Mr. Richardson (who plays the lead) know how to make a vastly entertaining rumpus of blistering ideas." *Time Remembered* (1942), a romantic love story with satiric overtones and undertones, was Anouilh's first Broadway hit. *Becket,* in which Laurence Olivier and Anthony Quinn exchanged the leading roles, was another in 1960. *Becket* also became a successful film with Richard Burton and Peter O'Toole. *Thieves' Carnival,* "the nicest play about an identity crisis ever written" (Walter Kerr), received an excellent performance in 1967 at the Tyrone Guthrie Theater in Minneapolis, as did *Antigone* (1942) at the American Shakespeare Festival Theater in Stratford, Connecticut.

BOOKS BY ANOUILH

Anouilh: Five Plays. Hill & Wang 2 vols. 1958–59 pap. ea. $5.25–$6.95 Vol. 1: *Romeo and Jeanette, The Rehearsal, Ermine, Antigone;* Vol. 2: *Ardèle, Time Remembered, Mademoiselle Colombe, Restless Heart, The Lark.*

The Lark. 1953. Trans. by Christopher Fry, Oxford 1956 $10.95

Becket. 1959. Trans. by Lucienne Hill, Putnam 1960 pap. $5.95

Dear Antoine. 1966. Trans. by Lucienne Hill, Hill & Wang 1971 $4.95

BOOKS ABOUT ANOUILH

Falb, Lewis W. *Jean Anouilh. Lit. and Life Ser.* Ungar 1977 $13.95
Lenski, B. A. *Jean Anouilh: Stages in Rebellion.* Humanities Pr. text ed. 1974 $10.50
McIntyre, H. G. *The Theatre of Jean Anouilh.* Barnes & Noble 1981 $23.50

APOLLINAIRE, GUILLAUME (pseud. of Guillaume de Kostrowitski). 1880–1918

Apollinaire is one of the most widely read and influential of modern French poets. His important works are two volumes of poems, *Alcools* and *Calligrammes.* Symbolism was still alive when he went to Paris in 1898 and he was to "inherit some of its tenets, enrich its tradition, and by embracing its spirit of liberty, develop from it the new movements, modernism, cubism, dada, surrealism. . . . He studied his time like an anthropologist eager to detect in customs and costumes what, for lack of a better word, he called *l'esprit nouveau*" (René Taupin). His great "technical skill, his varied versification, now free, now classical, his use of traditional phrases in a new composition, his grouping of images, the absence of punctuation, create an original unity of tone that involves not sentimentality but intimacy, the intimacy resulting from the somewhat casual alternating between the contemporary and the classical."

His real name was that of his mother, of Polish origin, and he was born either in Rome, where he was baptized, or in Monaco, where he was educated at the Lycée Saint-Charles. In Paris, he wrote novels, short stories, and plays as well as poetry and "developed his erudition in different ways, including the editorship of rare books and responsibilities as censor during World War I. He edited for the Bibliothèque des Curieux erotic books of repute and helped to catalogue the Enfer de la Bibliothèque Nationale." He became the friend of great cubists including PICASSO (see Vol. 3) and Braque and wrote *The Cubist Painters*, which first defined the nature of cubism. An Apollinaire revival, steadily on the rise in France since the end of World War II, has crossed the Atlantic, marked by the appearance here of new translations, new biographies, and numerous articles.

BOOKS BY APOLLINAIRE

Selected Writings of Apollinaire. Trans. by Roger Shattuck, New Directions rev. ed. 1971 pap. $8.95
The Poet Assassinated and Other Stories. Trans. by Ron Padgett, North Point Pr. 1984 pap. $12.50
Bestiary, or the Parade of Orpheus. 1911. Trans. by Pepe Karmel, Godine 1980 $12.95 pap. $5.95
Alcools. 1913. Ed. by Garnet Rees, Longwood Pr. 1975 pap. $14.95; trans. and annotated by Anne Hyde Greet, Univ. of California Pr. 1966 pap. $8.95
The Cubist Painters. 1913. Trans. by Lionel Abel, Wittenborn 1976 pap. $7.50
Calligrammes. 1918. Trans. by Anne H. Greet, Univ. of California Pr. bilingual ed. 1980 $19.95

BOOKS ABOUT APOLLINAIRE

Bates, Scott. *Guillaume Apollinaire. Twayne's World Authors Ser.* G. K. Hall lib. bdg. $10.95

Breunig, LeRoy C. *Guillaume Apollinaire.* Columbia Univ. Pr. 1969 pap. $2.50

Shattuck, Roger. *The Banquet Years: The Origins of the Avant Garde in France, 1885 to World War One. Essay Index Repr. Ser.* Ayer repr. of 1968 ed. rev. ed. $35.00; Random (Vintage) 1968 pap. $4.95

Stamelman, Richard H. *The Drama of Self in Guillaume Apollinaire's "Alcools."* Univ. of North Carolina Pr. 1976 pap. $13.00

Steegmuller, Francis. *Apollinaire: Poet among the Painters. Biography Index Repr. Ser.* Ayer repr. of 1963 ed. $25.00

AUCASSIN AND NICOLETTE. 13th century (first half)

The charming romance of Aucassin and Nicolette, a love story told with touches of tenderness, irony, and realism, was written in the dialect of Picardy by an unknown author. Its form is that of a *chante-fable*, alternating passages of heptasyllabic verse and longer passages of prose.

Of Aucassin et Nicolette. Trans. by Laurence Housman, Folcroft repr. of 1925 ed. 1974 lib. bdg. $15.00; (with the title *Aucassin and Nicolette and Other Medieval Romances and Legends*) trans. and ed. by Eugene Mason, Arden Lib. repr. of 1910 ed. 1978 lib. bdg. $15.00

AYME, MARCEL. 1902–1967

Aymé was one of France's leading humorous writers. He was "insurance broker, bricklayer, journalist, salesman," then—after 1938—a prolific author. "In M. Aymé's writing fantasy is curiously compounded with an earthy but cheerful cynicism, and he rarely fails to be entertaining. He inclines to beat the drum of his preoccupation too loudly and too long, but in spite of what the green mare says there appears to be plenty of room in his world and his book for other elements—such as kindliness, affection, a strong feeling for, and familiarity with the countryside—as well as sex" (*TLS*). Aymé's plays have been hits on the Parisian stage since 1945. His last, *La Convention Belzébir* (1967), in which permits to kill are sold for large sums, satirizes the absurdities of our world.

BOOKS BY AYMÉ

The Green Mare. 1933. Trans. by Norman Denny, Atheneum 1963 pap. $1.45

Wonderful Farm. Harper 1951 $9.89

BOOK ABOUT AYMÉ

Brodin, Dorothy. *Marcel Aymé.* Columbia Univ. Pr. 1968 pap. $2.50

BALZAC, HONORE DE. 1799–1850

Balzac is often said to be the greatest of French novelists. His greatness is not only in the richness of his work, which is comparable to that of Dickens, but also in its extent. Even though he died at the age of 51, he left, among other writings, 92 novels (out of over 100 he had projected), which taken together form what he called *The Human Comedy*. His purpose in this gigantic undertaking was to make an inventory of all the vices and virtues of French society in the first half of the nineteenth century, and to write a history of the manners and customs of the period. *The Human Comedy* is divided into three parts: Studies of Manners, Philosophic Studies, and Analytic Studies. Studies of Manners is subdivided into Scenes of Private Life, of Provincial Life, of Parisian Life, of Country Life, of Political Life, and of Military Life. It is one of the most ambitious literary plans ever conceived or accomplished; the work contains 2,000 distinctly drawn characters. Among the best known of the novels are *Père Goriot* (*Old Man Goriot*), *Cousin Bette* (1846), and *Eugénie Grandet*. Three stories in the Philosophic Studies form an exceptional psychological trilogy: *La peau de chagrin* (*The Wild Ass's Skin*), *Louis Lambert* (1832, o.p.), and *Séraphita*. The last is a Swedenborgian romance and the most mystical of Balzac's works. *Droll Stories* (1832), written earlier in the vein of Rabelais, contains 30 stories and does not belong to *The Human Comedy*. "Balzac," wrote André Maurois, "was by turns a saint, a criminal, an honest judge, a corrupt judge, a minister, a fop, a harlot, a duchess and always a genius."

BOOKS BY BALZAC

Works: With Introductions by George Saintsbury. Short Story Index Repr. Ser. Ayer 10 vols. repr. of 1901 ed. $550.00

The Letters of Honoré de Balzac to Madame Hanska. Gordon 1976 lib. bdg. $59.95

Balzac: Selected Short Stories. Trans. and ed. by Sylvia Raphael, *Penguin Class. Ser.* 1977 pap. $3.95

The Wild Ass's Skin. 1831. Trans. by Herbert J. Hunt, *Penguin Class. Ser.* 1977 pap. $4.95

Eugénie Grandet. 1833. Trans. by Ellen Marriage, Biblio Dist. (Everyman's) repr. of 1907 ed. 1973 $9.95

Old Goriot. 1834. Biblio Dist. (Everyman's) repr. of 1948 ed. 1970 $12.95; trans. by Marion A. Crawford, *Penguin Class. Ser.* 1951 pap. $3.95

Père Goriot. Modern Lib. College Ed. Ser. Random text ed. 1950 pap. $5.00

Séraphita. 1835 Intro. by G. F. Parsons, *Short Story Index Repr. Ser.* Ayer repr. of 1889 ed. $10.00

Lost Illusions. 1837–43. Trans. by Herbert J. Hunt, *Penguin Class. Ser.* 1976 pap. $5.95

Murky Business. 1841. *Penguin Class. Ser.* 1978 pap. $3.95

Ursule Mirouet. 1841. Trans. by Donald Adamson, *Penguin Class. Ser.* 1976 pap. $4.95

Cousin Pons. 1845. Trans. by Herbert J. Hunt, *Penguin Class. Ser.* 1978 pap. $4.95

BOOKS ABOUT BALZAC

Barthes, Roland. *S-Z.* Trans. by Richard Miller, Hill & Wang 1974 $10.95 pap. $7.95

Bersani, Leo. *Balzac to Beckett: Center and Circumference in French Fiction.* Oxford 1970 $15.95

Bertault, Philippe. *Balzac and the Human Comedy.* Trans. by Richard Monges, *Gotham Lib.* New York Univ. Pr. 1963 $10.00 pap. $3.95

Brooks, Peter. *The Melodramatic Imagination: Balzac, Henry James, Melodrama and the Mode of Excess.* Columbia Univ. Pr. repr. of 1976 ed. 1984 $30.00 pap. $12.50; Yale Univ. Pr. 1976 $25.00

Dargan, E. Preston, and Bernard Weinberg. *The Evolution of Balzac's "Comédie Humaine."* Cooper Square Pr. repr. of 1942 ed. 1973 lib. bdg. $23.50

Hunt, Herbert J. *Honoré de Balzac: A Biography.* Greenwood repr. of 1957 ed. lib. bdg. $18.75

James, Henry. *The Question of Our Speech: Lesson on Balzac.* Folcroft repr. of 1905 ed. lib. bdg. $22.00

Kanes, Martin. *Balzac's Comedy of Words.* Princeton Univ. Pr. 1975 $33.00

Maurois, André. *Prometheus: The Life of Balzac.* Carroll & Graf 1983 pap. $11.95

Rodin and Balzac: Bronzes from the Cantor, Fitzgerald Collection, Inc. Norton Art 1973 pap. $4.00

Stowe, William W. *Balzac, James and the Realistic Novel.* Princeton Univ. Pr. 1983 $23.00

Taine, Hippolyte A. *Balzac: A Critical Study.* Arden Lib. repr. of 1906 ed. 1980 lib. bdg. $25.00; Haskell repr. of 1906 ed. 1973 lib. bdg. $49.95

BARTHES, ROLAND. 1915–1980

One of the most influential French critics of his generation. Roland Barthes's writing first appeared in the newspaper *Combat*. He taught at universities in Bucharest and Alexandria and subsequently joined the Centre National de Recherche Scientifique in Paris where he did research on symbols and social signs. In 1962, he was named director of studies at the Ecole des Hautes Etudes and in 1976 to a chair at the Collège de France. His importance as a critic was hailed with the publication in 1953 of his *Le degré zéro de l'écriture*, and he became one of the most important of the French New Critics with a strong influence on the *Tel Quel* group. He was a prolific writer, and his other notable works include *Mythologies*—a work in which he applied the principles of structuralism to everyday phenomena—*Eléments de Sémiologie, Système de la mode, Essais critiques, Sur Racine, S-Z,* and *Le plaisir du texte.* He avoided literary criticism that involved reduction of the meaning of a work to any single statement. Barthes's criticism was wide ranging and cannot be reduced to a single system or method. He was interested not only in structuralist and semiotic approaches to literature, but also in literature and social criticism, psychoanalysis, and theories of "text production."

Books by Barthes

Writing Degree Zero. 1953. Trans. by Annette Lavers and Colin Smith, pref. by Susan Sontag, Hill & Wang 1977 $8.95 pap. $4.95

Mythologies. Trans. by Annette Lavers, Hill & Wang 1972 pap. $4.25; Peter Smith 1983 $13.25

Critical Essays. 1964. Trans. by Richard Howard, Northwestern Univ. Pr. 1972 $20.95 pap. $9.95

Elements of Semiology. 1967. Trans. by Annette Lavers and Colin Smith, Hill & Wang 1977 $8.95 pap. $3.95

The Fashion System. 1967. Trans. by Matthew Ward and Richard Howard, Hill & Wang 1983 $20.50 pap. $7.95

Sade-Fourier-Loyola. Trans. by Richard Miller, Hill & Wang 1976 o.p.

New Critical Essays. Trans. by Richard Howard, Hill & Wang 1980 $10.95 pap. $4.95

On Racine. 1972. Octagon repr. of 1977 ed. lib. bdg. $18.00; Performing Arts 1983
  pap. $7.95
Roland Barthes. 1975. Trans. by Richard Howard, Hill & Wang 1977 $8.95 pap. $7.25
A Lover's Discourse: Fragments. 1977. Trans. by Richard Howard, Hill & Wang 1979
  $10.00 pap. $7.25
The Grain of the Voice: Interviews, 1962–1980. 1981. Trans. by Linda Coverdale, Farrar 1985 $24.95 pap. $9.95

BOOKS ABOUT BARTHES

Champagne, Roland A. *Literary History in the Wake of Roland Barthes: Re-Defining
  the Myths of Reading.* Summa 1984 pap. $13.00
Culler, Jonathan. *Roland Barthes.* Oxford 1983 $19.95 pap. $5.95
Lavers, Annette. *Roland Barthes: Structuralism and After.* Harvard Univ. Pr. $25.00
Thody, Philip. *Roland Barthes: A Conservative Estimate.* Humanities Pr. text ed. 1977
  $23.75; Univ. of Chicago Pr. 1984 pap. $7.95

BAUDELAIRE, CHARLES. 1821–1867

Baudelaire was the poet of decadence of his period. His collected poems,
Les fleurs du mal (*Flowers of Evil*), celebrate "the pursuit of lust, the faculty
of self-torment in love, and moral anarchy." Their literary form is so polished as to be almost faultless. In 1857 he was tried on charges of obscenity
for this volume, and six of the more controversial poems had to be deleted
before it could be sold. "It is Baudelaire's painting of the pleasures and resulting horrors of vice which so scandalised the critics. Yet he was a moralist in the Christian tradition, who expresses revolt against the lure of the
flesh, and the horror of the pleasures which leave a bitter taste of ashes in
the mouth" (Enid Starkie). Throughout the years, in numerous Baudelaire
revivals, different aspects of his work have been hailed: the symbolic, the
decadent, the erotic, the cynical, and the spiritual. Now he is "probably the
poet most widely read all over the world. . . . At the distance of a century [it
is] as if he had written for the present generation with a knowledge of its
problems and interests" (Starkie). He was also a perceptive literary and art
critic, extolling artists like Courbet, Corot, and MANET (see Vol. 3) at a time
when they were objects of general derision. He translated POE's (see Vol. 1)
tales into French. The American's love of horror and mystery had a strong
influence on Baudelaire's prose writings.

Born to a bourgeois family, Baudelaire for a while lived the modish life of
a literary dandy on an inheritance from his father, reluctantly joining the
"Paris *bohème*" when his fortune ran dry. "His character," wrote Morris
Bishop, "is perverse and fascinating. Critics see in him a conflict of many
dualisms: he was both Catholic and satanist, debauchee and mystic, cynical
sensualist and yearner for purity. . . . Unable to excel in virtue, he made himself a legend of vice."

BOOKS BY BAUDELAIRE

Les fleurs du mal. 1857. Trans. by Richard Howard, Godine 1983 $25.00 pap. $15.95
Flowers of Evil. Trans. by Edna St. Vincent Millay, Harper 1936 o.p.; ed. by Jackson
  Mathews and Marthiel Mathews, New Directions rev. ed. 1962 $18.95

Paris Spleen. 1869. Trans. by Louise Varèse, New Directions 1970 pap. $4.95

Art in Paris, 1845–1862: Review of Salons and Other Exhibitions. Ed. by Jonathan Mayne, Cornell Univ. Pr. 1981 pap. $12.95

Baudelaire: A Self Portrait. Ed. by Lois B. Hyslop and Francis E. Hyslop, Jr., Hyperion Pr. repr. of 1957 ed. 1981 $24.00

Baudelaire as Literary Critic. Trans. by Lois B. Hyslop and Francis E. Hyslop, Jr., Pennsylvania State Univ. Pr. 1964 $27.50

Baudelaire on Poe: Critical Papers. Trans. by Lois B. Hyslop and Francis E. Hyslop, Jr., Pennsylvania State Univ. Pr. 1952 $19.75

Selected Poems. Trans. by Geoffrey Wagner, intro. by Enid Starkie, Grove repr. of 1947 ed. 1974 pap. $2.95

Eugene Delacroix: His Life and Works. Ed. by Sydney J. Freedberg, Garland 1979 lib. bdg. $29.00

Intimate Journals. City Lights 1983 pap. $4.95; trans. by Christopher Isherwood, Fertig repr. of 1930 ed. 1977 $19.75

Letters of Charles Baudelaire to His Mother, 1833–1866. Ed. by Arthur Symons, Ayer repr. of 1927 ed. $22.00; ed. by Arthur Symons, Haskell repr. of 1928 ed. 1971 lib. bdg. $52.95

The Mirror of Art: Critical Studies. Ed. by Jonathan Mayne, AMS Pr. repr. of 1955 ed. $32.50

My Heart Laid Bare and Other Essays. Ed. by Peter Quennell, Haskell 1974 lib. bdg. $49.95

The Painter of Modern Life and Other Essays. Ed. by Sydney J. Freedberg, Garland 1979 lib. bdg. $34.00

Selected Critical Studies of Baudelaire. Ed. by D. Parmee, AMS Pr. repr. of 1949 ed. $21.00

Selected Writings on Art and Artists. Trans. by P. E. Charvet, Cambridge Univ. Pr. 1981 pap. $19.95

BOOKS ABOUT BAUDELAIRE

Bersani, Leo. *Baudelaire and Freud.* Univ. of California Pr. 1978 $18.50

Gilman, Margaret. *Baudelaire the Critic.* Octagon repr. of 1943 ed. 1971 lib. bdg. $20.00

Hemmings, F. W. J. *Baudelaire the Damned.* Scribner text ed. 1982 $17.95

Hyslop, Lois B. *Baudelaire: Man of His Time.* Yale Univ. Pr. 1980 $24.50

Lloyd, Rosemary. *Baudelaire's Literary Criticism.* Cambridge Univ. Pr. 1981 $62.50

Poulet, Georges. *Exploding Poetry: Baudelaire-Rimbaud.* Trans. by Françoise Meltzer, Univ. of Chicago Pr. 1984 lib. bdg. $15.00

Quennell, Peter. *Baudelaire and the Symbolists. Essay Index Repr. Ser.* Ayer repr. of 1954 ed. $16.00

Sartre, Jean-Paul. *Baudelaire.* Trans. by Martin Turnell, New Directions 1950 pap. $6.95

Soupault, Philippe. *Baudelaire.* AMS Pr. repr. of 1931 ed. $29.00

Starkie, Enid. *Baudelaire.* New Directions 1958 $12.50

Swinburne, Algernon C. *Les Fleurs du Mal and Other Studies.* Ed. by Edmund Gosse, AMS Pr. repr. of 1913 ed. $22.50

Symons, Arthur. *Charles Baudelaire: A Study.* Richard West repr. of 1920 ed. 1978 lib. bdg. $20.00

Turnell, Martin. *Baudelaire: A Study of His Poetry.* New Directions 1972 pap. $3.45

BEAUVOIR, SIMONE DE. 1908–1986

Simone de Beauvoir and the existentialist philosopher and writer Jean-Paul Sartre were among the leading French intellectuals following World War II. She grew up in Paris, received her doctorate in philosophy from the Sorbonne, and taught in *lycées* in Marseilles, Rouen, and Paris until 1943, after which she turned to literature. She has written novels, essays, and plays. Her most important novels include *Le sang des autres* (*The Blood of Others*), *L'invitée* (*She Came to Stay*), and *Les mandarins* (1954). The last novel is a fictional recreation of life in French intellectual circles during the 1940s. Her two-volume essay *The Second Sex* is one of the leading feminist documents of our time.

Simone de Beauvoir has written an extensive series of autobiographical memoirs that have won critical acclaim. Her *Memoirs of a Dutiful Daughter* is a fascinating account of her transformation from an obedient middle-class girl to a fiercely independent, nonconformist opponent of bourgeois morality, hypocritical idealism, and second-class citizenship for women. Later volumes in the series include *The Prime of Life* (1960, o.p.), *Force of Circumstance* (1963, o.p.), *A Very Easy Death* (1964, o.p.), and *All Said and Done* (1972, o.p.). On Sartre, who died in 1980 and with whom she had a liaison of many years, she wrote shortly before she died *Adieux: A Farewell to Sartre*.

BOOKS BY BEAUVOIR

The Blood of Others. 1944. Trans. by Roger Senhouse and Yvonne Moyse, Pantheon 1984 pap. $7.95

The Ethics of Ambiguity. 1947. Citadel Pr. 1962 pap. $4.95

The Second Sex. 1949. Trans. by H. M. Parshley, Knopf 1953 $25.00; trans. by H. M. Parshley, Random (Vintage) 1974 pap. $5.95

Memoirs of a Dutiful Daughter. 1958. Harper repr. of 1959 ed. 1974 pap. $7.64

Brigitte Bardot and the Lolita Syndrome. 1960. Ayer repr. of 1960 ed. 1972 $20.00

A Very Easy Death. 1964. Pantheon 1985 pap. $4.95

Adieux: A Farewell to Sartre. 1984. Trans. by Patrick O'Brian, Pantheon 1985 pap. $8.95

BOOKS ABOUT BEAUVOIR

Bieber, Konrad. *Simone de Beauvoir. Twayne's World Authors Ser.* G. K. Hall 1979 lib. bdg. $14.50

Cottrell, Robert D. *Simone de Beauvoir. Lit. and Life Ser.* Ungar 1975 $12.95

Keefe, Terry. *Simone de Beauvoir: A Study of Her Writings.* Barnes & Noble text ed. 1983 $18.50

Marks, Elaine. *Simone de Beauvoir: Encounters with Death.* Rutgers Univ. Pr. 1973 $18.00

Whitmarsh, Anne. *Simone de Beauvoir and the Limits of Commitment.* Cambridge Univ. Pr. 1981 $39.50

BECKETT, SAMUEL. 1906–

Samuel Beckett, who is most widely known here for his play *Waiting for Godot*, was born in Dublin and educated at Trinity College. He lectured in Paris at the Ecole Normale Supérieure and then at Dublin University. He returned to settle in Paris permanently in 1937 and eventually abandoned English for French in his writing. He is the author of a number of novels: *Murphy, Molloy, Malone Dies, Watt* (1953), and *The Unnamable*. Except for the first work, all of the novels were written in French and translated into English by the author. Beckett shares with Sartre and Camus an "intense sense of the pervasiveness of misery, solitude, paralysis of will, and above all, the horror of nothingness. His obscure and difficult style is peculiarly suited to the portrayal of a world where, amidst obscenity and occasional blasphemy, the characters create their personal hells in the prisons of their own dark minds" (*Manchester Guardian*). Other plays of Beckett that have won critical acclaim include *Krapp's Last Tape* (1959), *Endgame* (1958), and *Happy Days*.

BOOKS BY BECKETT

The Collected Works of Samuel Beckett. Grove 29 vols. 1981 $175.00
Collected Poems in English and French. Grove 1977 $10.00 pap. $3.95
Proust. 1931. Grove 1957 $10.00
Murphy. 1938. Grove 1970 $12.50
Malone Dies. 1951. Trans. by Samuel Beckett, Grove 1956 $10.00 pap. $3.95
Molloy. 1951. Trans. by Samuel Beckett and Patrick Bowles, Grove 1970 $12.50
Waiting for Godot. 1952. Trans. by Samuel Beckett, Grove 1970 $10.00
The Unnamable. 1953. Grove 1970 $10.00
Stories and Texts for Nothing. 1958. Grove 1970 $10.00
Happy Days. 1960. Grove 1961 $10.00 pap. $4.95
Krapp's Last Tape and Other Dramatic Pieces. Grove 1960 $10.00 pap. $6.95
How It Is. 1961. Trans. by Samuel Beckett, Grove 1970 $12.50
Film: A Film Script. 1966. Fwd. by Alan Schneider, Grove 1969 pap. $6.95
An Examination of James Joyce. Haskell 1974 lib. bdg. $44.95

BOOKS ABOUT BECKETT

Bair, Deirdre. *Samuel Beckett: A Biography.* Harcourt 1980 pap. $7.95
Cohn, Ruby, ed. *A Casebook on Waiting for Godot.* Grove 1967 pap. $4.95
Esslin, Martin. *Mediations: Essays on Brecht, Beckett and the Media.* Grove 1980 $22.50 1982 pap. $9.95
Fletcher, John, and Walter Bachem. *A Student's Guide to the Plays of Samuel Beckett.* Faber 2d ed. 1985 $19.95 pap. $9.95
Fletcher, John, and John Spurling. *Beckett the Playwright.* Hill & Wang rev. ed. pap. $6.95
Friedman, Melvin J., ed. *Samuel Beckett Now: Critical Approaches to His Novels, Poetry, and Plays.* Univ. of Chicago Pr. (Phoenix Bks.) 2d ed. pap. $3.95
Rabinovitz, Rubin. *The Development of Samuel Beckett's Fiction.* Univ. of Illinois Pr. 1984 $17.50

BERNANOS, GEORGES. 1888–1948

A Catholic novelist and essayist, Bernanos was preoccupied in his novels with the theme of the struggle between good and evil within saintly individuals. He traced the unknowing submission of his characters, after some early disappointing experience, to the forces of Satan and the subsequent destruction of their moral selves. His most famous work is *The Diary of a Coun-*

try *Priest*. Both *The Diary of a Country Priest* and *Mouchette* (1937, o.p.), a short novel, are set in bleak villages, untouched by the twentieth century. "In different ways [these books] treat of pride and innocence, those two states of mind and soul that struggle within us for command of whatever destiny we may have in this universe. [They] are suffused with spiritual concerns, but the mystery of Christianity, of salvation and damnation, remains almost austerely beyond analysis or even speculation" (Robert Coles, *New Republic*). Both works were made into films by Robert Bresson.

Bernanos's condemnation of the Franco regime and the Spanish church during the period of the Spanish Civil War is contained in his widely known essay *Les grands cimetières sous la lune*, which was translated as *Diary of My Times* (1938, o.p.). After the signing of the Munich agreement, Bernanos emigrated to Brazil where he continued to write during the war. His last work, completed shortly before his death, is the filmscript of the *Dialogues of the Carmelites* (1949), which is the basis of Poulenc's opera.

BOOKS BY BERNANOS

The Diary of a Country Priest. 1936. Carroll & Graf 1984 pap. $7.95; Doubleday 1974 pap. $2.95; trans. by Pamela Morris, Macmillan 1962 pap. $1.95
Last Essays. Greenwood repr. of 1955 ed. 1968 lib. bdg. $18.75

BOOKS ABOUT BERNANOS

Cooke, John E. *Georges Bernanos: A Study of Christian Commitment.* Humanities Pr. text ed. 1981 $38.50
O'Sharkey, Eithne M. *The Role of the Priest in the Novels of Georges Bernanos.* Vantage 1983 $10.00

BONNEFOY, YVES. 1923–

The work of Bonnefoy, a poet, critic, and translator, is philosophical in nature and difficult to penetrate. He has written meditations on the themes of the immobility of matter and the power of language. Influenced by such German philosophers as HEGEL (see Vol. 4) and HEIDEGGER (see Vol. 4), his poetry reflects a sense of tragic anguish, often through the use of the implied or the understatement. His principal poetic works include *On the Motion and Immobility of Douve*, a philosophical meditation on the value of language, and *Words in Stone*. He has written essays on art history and poetry in *L'improbable* and *La seconde simplicité*. As a translator, he is well known for his renditions of SHAKESPEARE into French: *Hamlet, Julius Caesar, Henry IV*, and *A Winter's Tale*. "Bonnefoy's work reveals a poet who is difficult, who is primarily heir to the Mallarmé tradition, and who ranks with the foremost poets of his generation" (Germaine Brée).

BOOKS BY BONNEFOY

Poems, 1959–1975. Trans. by Richard Pevear, Random (Vintage) 1985 $7.95
On the Motion and Immobility of Douve. 1953. Trans. by Galway Kinnell, Ohio Univ. Pr. bilingual ed. 1968 $10.00
Words in Stone: Pierre Ecrite. 1959. Trans. by Susanna Lang, Univ. of Massachusetts Pr. bilingual ed. 1976 lib. bdg. $13.00

BOOKS ABOUT BONNEFOY

Caws, Mary Ann. *The Inner Theatre of Recent French Poetry: Cendrars, Tzara, Peret, Artaud, Bonnefoy.* Princeton Univ. Pr. 1972 $23.50

———. *Yves Bonnefoy.* Twayne's World Authors Ser. G. K. Hall 1984 lib. bdg. $18.95

Naughton, John T. *The Poetics of Yves Bonnefoy.* Univ. of Chicago Pr. 1984 lib. bdg. $20.00

BRETON, ANDRE. 1896–1966

At the time of Breton's death, his novel *Nadja,* about a young dreamer in love with a "hallucinated and ethereal heroine ... his brightest literary jewel ... was finally reaching beyond the limited circle of friends and coterie disciples ... to a new generation of youth" (Anna Balakian, *SR*). Breton, dynamic personage, poet, novelist, philosophical essayist, and art critic, was the father—he was often called the "pope"—of surrealism. From World War I to the 1940s he was at the forefront of the numerous avant-garde activities that centered in Paris. A prolific producer of pamphlets and manifestoes, he also edited two surrealist periodicals. "Automatic writing," defined by Breton in his *Manifestoes of Surrealism* as a process "by which one strives to express ... the genuine functioning of the mind in the absence of all control exercised by reason," was his method of creation. The manifesto implied that "surrealism was not simply a reform in prosody or in the techniques of the artist but a reformation of the mental process of the writer and the artist, and by the same token of the reader and the viewer" (Balakian). Breton's influence on the art and literature of the twentieth century has been enormous. PICASSO (see Vol. 3), Derain, Magritte, Giacometti, Cocteau, Eluard, and Gracq are among the many whose work was affected by his thinking. From 1927 to 1933 he was a member of the Communist party, but thereafter he opposed communism. He said in *L'amour fou* (1937), "I had ... willed never to become unworthy of the power which, in the direction of eternal love, had made me see and granted me the privilege, even more rare, of making others see. I had never been undeserving of it, I have never ceased to make into one the flesh of the being I love and the snow of the summits in the rising sun."

BOOKS BY BRETON

Poems of André Breton: A Bilingual Anthology. Trans. by Jean-Pierre Cauvin and Mary Ann Caws, Univ. of Texas Pr. text ed. 1982 $27.50 pap. $12.95

Manifestoes of Surrealism. 1924 1930. Trans. by Richard Seaver and Helen R. Lane, Univ. of Michigan Pr. 1972 pap. $8.95

Nadja. 1928. Trans. by Richard Howard, Grove (Evergreen) 1960 pap. $5.95

What Is Surrealism? 1934 1936. Haskell repr. of 1936 ed. 1973 lib. bdg. $49.95

What Is Surrealism? Selected Writings. Studies in Comparative Lit. Haskell repr. of 1936 ed. 1973 lib. bdg. $49.95; ed. by Franklin Rosemont, Monad Pr. 1978 lib. bdg. $35.00 pap. $14.95

Fata Morgana. Trans. by Clark Mills, Black Swan 1982 pap. $3.95

BOOKS ABOUT BRETON

Balakian, Anna. *André Breton: Magus of Surrealism.* Hawkshead Bk. 1971 $10.00

Carrouges, Michel. *André Breton and the Basic Concepts of Surrealism.* Trans. by Maura Prendergast, Univ. of Alabama Pr. 1974 $18.50

Caws, Mary Ann. *André Breton. Twayne's World Authors Ser.* G. K. Hall 1971 o.p.

BUTOR, MICHEL. 1926–

Butor's early education was with the Jesuits, and he subsequently received degrees from the Sorbonne in philosophy. His thesis for his *diplôme d'études supérieures* was on *Mathematics and the Idea of Necessity.* He has taught in Egypt, England, and Greece as well as in the United States. He is currently a professor of literature at the University of Geneva.

Although closely associated with the new novelists, Butor has enjoyed considerable general popularity. *A Change of Heart* (o.p.) was awarded the Prix Théophraste Renaudot, one of the major French literary prizes, in 1957 and put Butor before the general public. The subject of his novels is consciousness, frequently presented in the form of an interior monologue and described in painstaking detail. *Degrees* (1960) is, according to Leon Roudiez, "a complex novel. . . . Though the story line is usually buried within snatches and bits of dialogue and detail, and though the numerous flashbacks from three points of view occasionally puzzle the reader, the interwoven strands of the book provide a brilliant picture of the perennial schoolboy—and the perennial teacher."

Butor has written a number of stereoscopies, works on different levels in which the reader must participate actively. Among these are *Mobile* and *Niagara: A Stereophonic Novel* (o.p.). *Mobile* is a sort of verbal photomontage of catchwords recalling many areas of the United States in which unique typographical arrangements substitute for conventional syntax in connecting words and phrases, and also signify various themes. "It is not, most people would agree, a novel. Some people in France wondered if it was even a book" (Roudiez). In the same vein of experimentation, Butor has produced with the painter Jacques Monory *USA 76*, which Germaine Brée has described as "a case made out of blue altuglas . . . and containing a collection of objects, serigraphs, and texts designed to stimulate the activity of the reader." Butor's literary and art criticism are contained in *Repertoire I to IV* and *Illustrations I to IV* respectively.

BOOKS BY BUTOR

Passing Time. 1956. Trans. by Jean Stewart, Riverrun 1980 pap. $4.95

Mobile: Study for a Representation of the United States. 1962. Trans. by Richard Howard, Simon & Schuster 1963 o.p.

Letters from the Antipodes. Trans. by Michael Spencer, Ohio Univ. Pr. 1981 $21.95

BOOKS ABOUT BUTOR

McWilliams, Dean. *The Narratives of Michel Butor.* Ohio Univ. Pr. 1978 $13.00

Spencer, Michael. *Michel Butor. Twayne's World Authors Ser.* G. K. Hall 1974 o.p.

CALVIN, JOHN. 1509–1564

[SEE Volume 4.]

CAMUS, ALBERT. 1913–1960 (NOBEL PRIZE 1957)

Albert Camus, the novelist, playwright, and essayist, who won the Nobel Prize for literature in 1957, died in 1960 in a car accident near Sens, France. The second youngest man in history to receive the Nobel honor, Camus was also a member of the French Academy.

As one of the leading authors in the French Resistance, he wrote daily outspoken articles in the underground *Combat*, which became an important daily newspaper in France after the war. He was a native of Algeria and lived there until 1940. He was never really committed to the existentialists' view but formulated a modern brand of stoicism: When confronted with the inevitable absurdities of life, man can do nothing but courageously face up to them in full awareness of his situation. This philosophical position is set forth in his essay *The Myth of Sisyphus*. As Camus himself once put it: "The aim is to live lucidly in a world where dispersion is the rule."

His two novels that have had the widest impact are *The Stranger*, a brilliant short work that deals with the theme of the absurd from the social, metaphysical, and religious points of view, and *The Plague* (1947), a defense of the concept of human dignity and a thinly disguised allegory of the French situation during the World War II under the German occupation. Since his death, his *Notebooks* have been published.

"Camus was a versatile writer, with a mastery of style almost unique among his contemporaries. 'The last of the heirs of Chateaubriand,' Sartre called him. His language is rich in imagery and highly controlled. He was a 'Latin.' . . . 'Every artist, no doubt [he wrote], is in quest of his truth. If he is great, each work brings him closer to it, or, at least, gravitates more closely to that central hidden sun, where all, one day, will be consumed' " (Germaine Brée).

BOOKS BY CAMUS

Notebooks. Harcourt 2 vols. 1978 vol. 1 pap. $3.95; Modern Lib. 1965 $3.95. Volume 2 is out of print.
Youthful Writings: Cahiers Two. Trans. by Eileen Kennedy, intro. by Paul Viallaneix, Knopf 1976 $10.95; Random (Vintage) 1977 pap. $2.95
The Stranger. 1942. Amereon $13.95; trans. by Stuart Gilbert, Random (Vintage) 1954 pap. $2.95; trans. by Kate Griffith, Univ. Pr. of Amer. 1982 lib. bdg. $21.75 text ed. pap. $9.00
The Myth of Sisyphus and Other Essays. 1942. Knopf 1955 $7.95; Random (Vintage) 1959 pap. $1.95
Resistance, Rebellion and Death. 1945. Random (Vintage) 1974 pap. $3.95
The Rebel: An Essay on Man in Revolt. 1951. Trans. by Anthony Bower, Knopf 1954 $13.50; intro. by H. Read, Random (Vintage) 1956 pap. $3.95
The Fall 1956. Knopf 1957 $10.95; trans. by Justin O'Brien, Random (Vintage) 1963 pap. $1.95
The Exile and the Kingdom. 1957. Random (Vintage) 1965 pap. $3.95

BOOKS ABOUT CAMUS

Brée, Germaine. *Camus and Sartre: Crisis and Commitment*. Delacorte 1972 $7.95

Cruickshank, John. *Albert Camus and the Literature of Revolt*. Greenwood repr. of 1959 ed. 1978 lib. bdg. $42.50

Fitch, Brian T. *The Narcissistic Text: A Reading of Camus' Fiction*. Univ. of Toronto Pr. 1982 $20.00

Lottman, Herbert. *Albert Camus: A Biography*. Braziller 1981 pap. $8.95; Doubleday 1979 $19.95

McCarthy, Patrick. *Camus*. Random 1982 $17.95

Quilliot, Roger. *Sea and Prisons: A Commentary on the Life and Thought of Albert Camus*. Trans. by Emmett Parker, Univ. of Alabama Pr. 1970 $17.50

Rhein, Phillip H. *Albert Camus*. Twayne's World Authors Ser. G. K. Hall 1969 lib. bdg. $13.95

Showalter, English, Jr. *Exiles and Strangers: A Reading of Camus's "Exile and the Kingdom."* Ohio State Univ. Pr. 1984 $15.00

CELINE, LOUIS-FERDINAND (pseud. of Louis-Ferdinand Destouches). 1894–1961

Céline, an imaginative, "shocking" writer, horrified his readers in *Journey to the End of Night* and *Death on the Installment Plan*, which are to a great extent autobiographical; nevertheless, these novels were translated into all European languages. Céline's world as portrayed in these books is brutal and violent—a place of filth, perversion, obscenity, perfidy, and crime, but there is "fierce sincerity" in his writing. "The great snarling cascade of whores and pimps and cretins . . . from souped-up colors, the hallucinatory slides from the real to the dream, the mad polar swings from blackness to cascades of life, the taking of truth to the tenth power, the 'improvement' on reality, the prose that flies along at treetop level—all are Céline's trademarks, an innovative earthquake in French letters" (Bruce Jay Friedman, *N.Y. Times*). He wrote in the slang of the French underworld, which he called "the language of hatred."

A violent anti-Semite, he was a known collaborationist during the German occupation of France. Fleeing to Denmark after the German collapse, he was imprisoned and later permitted to return to France, mentally unstable and partly paralyzed. Céline's work has enjoyed a great revival; seen in perspective, his influence on contemporary literature eclipses his warped personality.

BOOKS BY CÉLINE

Journey to the End of Night. 1932. Trans. by Ralph Manheim, New Directions 1983 $19.95 pap. $8.95

Death on the Installment Plan. 1936. Trans. by Ralph Manheim, New Directions repr. of 1947 ed. 1971 pap. $9.95

Guignol's Band. 1944. New Directions 1969 pap. $7.95

North. 1954. Delacorte 1972 $10.00; trans. by Ralph Manheim, Penguin 1976 pap. $2.95

Rigadoon. 1969. Delacorte 1974 $8.95; trans. by Ralph Manheim, intro. by Kurt Vonnegut, Jr., Penguin 1975 pap. $4.95

BOOKS ABOUT CÉLINE

Hayman, David. *Louis-Ferdinand Céline*. Columbia Univ. Pr. 1965 pap. $2.50

Matthews, J. H. *The Inner Dream: Céline as Novelist.* Syracuse Univ. Pr. 1978 $22.95
McCarthy, Patrick. *Céline: A Biography.* Penguin 1977 pap. $3.50; Viking 1976 $15.00
Merlin, Thomas. *Louis-Ferdinand Céline.* New Directions 1980 $16.50
Ostrovsky, Erika. *Céline and His Vision. Gotham Lib.* New York Univ. Pr. 1967 $10.00
    pap. $3.95

CHAR, RENE. 1907–

Albert Camus said: "I consider René Char our greatest living poet. . . .
This poet of all times speaks immediately to our own. He is in the midst of
the fight. He formulates for us both our suffering and our survival." Char
speaks in the rhythms of Provence, where he was born, where he grew up,
and where he still often resides. He studied at the *lycée* in Avignon and at
the university in Aix. "But it was the war and his experiences as the leader
of a Maquis group in Provence that have most deeply affected his work—
channeled his major themes, furnished the substance and many of the subjects of his later poems. The privation, the hunger, the moral suffering of
those years were somehow turned into the passionate economy of his style,
his rage to compress everything into aphorisms and short bursts of prose"
(Editor's note, *Hypnos Waking*, 1956, o.p.).

BOOKS BY CHAR

Poems of René Char. Trans. by Mary Ann Caws and Jonathan Griffin, Princeton Univ.
    Pr. 1976 o.p.
No Siege Is Absolute. Trans. by Franz Wright, Lost Roads bilingual ed. 1983 pap.
    $5.95

BOOKS ABOUT CHAR

Caws, Mary Ann. *The Presence of René Char.* Princeton Univ. Pr. 1976 $37.50
———. *René Char. Twayne's World Authors Ser.* G. K. Hall 1977 o.p.
La Charité, Virginia A. *The Poetics and Poetry of René Char.* Univ. of North Carolina
    Pr. 1968 pap. $13.50
Lawler, James R. *René Char: The Myth and the Poem.* Princeton Univ. Pr. 1978 $20.00

CHATEAUBRIAND, FRANÇOIS RENE, VICOMTE DE. 1768–1848

The work of Chateaubriand, writer and statesman, is a remarkable early
example of romanticism in France. In his *Essai historique, politique et moral
sur les révolutions* (1797), he took a stand as a mediator between royalist
and revolutionary ideas and as a Rousseauistic freethinker in religion.
Atala, ou les amours de deux sauvages dans le désert is memorable for its
lush descriptions of nature. The poetic *Génie du Christianisme, ou les
beautés de la religion chrétienne* (1802), appealing to the emotions rather
than to reason, tried to show that all progress and goodness stemmed from
the Christian religion. *René*, a short novel that is largely autobiographical,
is taken from this work. His *mal du siècle*, reminiscent of the profound mal-
aise described earlier by Goethe in *The Sorrows of Young Werther*, is a literary characteristic of the period. Chateaubriand's posthumously published
autobiographical *Mémoires d'outre-tombe* (*Memoirs from Beyond the Grave*,
1849) is considered by many critics to be his masterpiece. A selection under

the title *Memoirs of Chateaubriand* was translated and edited by Robert Baldick in 1961 but is currently out of print.

BOOKS BY CHATEAUBRIAND

Atala (and *René*). 1801 1802. Trans. by Irving Putter, Univ. of California Pr. 1952 o.p.

The Natchez: An Indian Tale. 1826. Fertig 3 vols. repr. of 1827 ed. lib. bdg. $55.00

Chateaubriand's Travels in America. Trans. and ed. by Richard Switzer, Univ. Pr. of Kentucky 1969 $22.00

BOOKS ABOUT CHATEAUBRIAND

Maurois, André. *Chateaubriand: Poet, Statesman, Lover.* Trans. by Vera Fraser, Greenwood repr. of 1938 ed. lib. bdg. $16.25

Painter, George D. *Chateaubriand: The Longed for Tempests, 1768–93.* Knopf 1978 vol. 1 $17.50

Porter, Charles A. *Chateaubriand: Composition, Imagination and Poetry.* Anma Libri 1978 pap. $25.00

Switzer, Richard. *Chateaubriand. Twayne's World Authors Ser.* Irvington 1971 lib. bdg. $15.95

CHRETIEN DE TROYES. c. end of 12th century

A French poet about whom practically nothing is known, Chrétien de Troyes lived at the court of Marie de Champagne, daughter of Eleanor of Aquitaine, at Troyes and wrote outstanding Arthurian romances, including *Erec et Enide, Yvain, Lancelot,* and *Perceval.* Chrétien was one of the first to compose after models established by the troubadours of southern France. His romances, two of which were written for patrons, were intended to entertain an elegant and sophisticated court society. The unfinished *Perceval, or the Grail* is generally regarded as the earliest work on the theme of the Holy Grail. Chrétien was a gifted storyteller and a true poet. It was he who first took the odd bits and pieces of the Arthurian material and molded them into coherent and individually brilliant works of literary art.

BOOKS BY CHRÉTIEN DE TROYES

Arthurian Romances. Trans. by W. W. Comfort, intro. by D. D. Owen, Biblio Dist. (Everyman's) repr. of 1914 ed. 1976 pap. $3.95

Lancelot: The Knight of the Cart. Trans. by Deborah W. Rogers, Columbia Univ. Pr. 1984 $25.00 pap. $12.00

Perceval: The Story of the Grail. Trans. by Nigel Bryant, Rowman text ed. 1982 $47.50

Yvain, or The Knight with the Lion. Trans. by Ruth H. Cline, Univ. of Georgia Pr. 1975 pap. $6.95

BOOKS ABOUT CHRÉTIEN DE TROYES

Frappier, Jean. *Chretién de Troyes: The Man and His Work.* Trans. by Raymond J. Cormier, Ohio Univ. Pr. 1982 lib. bdg. $22.95

Guyer, Foster E. *Chrétien de Troyes: Inventor of the Modern Novel.* AMS Pr. repr. of 1957 ed. $19.50

Holmes, Urban T. *Chrétien de Troyes. Twayne's World Authors Ser.* Irvington 1970 lib. bdg. $15.95

Kelly, Douglas, ed. *The Romances of Chrétien de Troyes: A Symposium.* French Forum 1985 pap. $25.00
Pickens, Rupert T., ed. *The Sower and His Seed: Essays on Chrétien de Troyes.* French Forum 1983 pap. $12.50
Uitti, Karl D. *Story, Myth & Celebration in Old French Narrative Poetry 1050–1200.* Princeton Univ. Pr. 1973 $29.00

CLAUDEL, PAUL. 1868–1955

Claudel was a poet, dramatist, essayist, and religious thinker of great power and originality whose works are suffused with his ardent Catholicism. He also had a distinguished career in the French consular and diplomatic service, which enabled him to spend many years abroad in the Far East, North and South America, and Europe. Almost all of Claudel's work embodies an expression of his deep Roman Catholic faith and is an attempt to impress others with its truth. To understand his work requires a comprehension of and a feeling for the themes and concerns of that faith. His poetic expression is at once symbolic and lyrical, expressing the joy, beauty, and mystery of existence. Among his most important plays are *The City, The Break of Noon, The Tidings Brought to Mary* (1912), and *The Satin Slipper.*

BOOKS BY CLAUDEL

The Book of Christopher Columbus: A Lyrical Drama in Two Parts. 1927. Elliots Bks. 1930 $49.50
The Satin Slipper, or the Worst Is Not the Surest. 1928–39. Elliots Bks. 1931 $42.50
Claudel on the Theatre. Trans. by Christine Trollope, Univ. of Miami Pr. 1972 $10.00
Poetic Art. Associated Faculty Pr. repr. of 1948 ed. 1969 $19.00; Philosophical Lib. $2.75
Ways and Crossways. Associated Faculty Pr. repr. of 1933 ed. 1968 $19.50; trans. by Fr. J. O'Conner, *Essay Index Repr. Ser.* Ayer repr. of 1933 ed. $20.00

BOOKS ABOUT CLAUDEL

Chaigne, Louis. *Paul Claudel: The Man and the Mystic.* Greenwood repr. of 1961 ed. 1978 lib. bdg. $24.75
Chiari, Joseph. *Poetic Drama of Paul Claudel.* Gordian repr. of 1954 ed. text ed. 1969 $12.50
Knapp, Bettina L. *Paul Claudel. Lit. and Life Ser.* Ungar 1982 $16.95
Watson, Harold M. *Claudel's Immortal Heroes: A Choice of Deaths.* Rutgers Univ. Pr. 1971 $20.00

COCTEAU, JEAN. 1889–1963

This versatile, sophisticated, eccentric, exuberant poet-dramatist-novelist experimented with almost every literary and artistic form: novels, plays, poems, film scenarios, ballet, criticism, drawing, painting. "Prodigal son of a wealthy notary," he became the spokesman for literary modernism and surrealism. His artist friends and collaborators included PICASSO (see Vol. 3), DIAGHILEV (see Vol. 3), and RILKE. His career is said to have been sparked by Diaghilev's request that he do something "astonishing"; Cocteau became adept at it. Generous and alert for fresh talent, he "launched a number of gifted adolescents like Raymond Radiguet or outlaws like Genet on their paths to fame" (Henri Peyre). Among the nonliterary achievements of this extraordinary man are the decoration of the city hall of Menton and the fisherman's chapel at Villefranche, both on the French Riviera.

Francis Fergusson considered Cocteau one of the most dexterous and resourceful "poets of the theatre" in our time. "He is a master of the make-believe; of the glamour and the trickery of the stage. But, as he himself explains, he composes his theatrical effects with the rigor of a *symboliste* poet, putting together the words of a small subtle lyric. Sometimes he will play with ancient legends, as in *Antigone* (1926) and *Orphée* (1926); sometimes with themes from contemporary fiction or the contemporary theatre, as in *The Eagle with Two Heads* (1946), *Intimate Relations* (1938), and *The Holy Terrors*. But he always catches the familiar figures in unexpected light, that of his own, unique, poetic intelligence." (See also Volume 3, Chapter 13.)

BOOKS BY COCTEAU

Cocteau: Five Plays. Hill & Wang 1961 pap. $4.50

Cocteau's World: An Anthology of Major Writings by Jean Cocteau. Trans. and ed. by Margaret Crosland, Humanities Pr. text ed. 1972 $21.75

Call to Order. 1926. *Studies in French Lit.* Haskell 1974 lib. bdg. $49.95

The Holy Terrors. 1929. New Directions 1957 pap. $5.95

The Infernal Machine and Other Plays. Trans. by W. H. Auden, Albert Bermel, E. E. Cummings, Dudley Fitts, Mary Hoeck, and John Savacool, New Directions repr. of 1967 ed. pap. $10.95

The Beauty and the Beast: Diary of a Film. 1946. Dover repr. of 1950 ed. 1972 pap. $5.95; Peter Smith $14.00

Cocteau on the Film: Conversations with Jean Cocteau Recorded by André Fraigneau. Garland 1985 lib. bdg. $25.00

BOOKS ABOUT COCTEAU

Ashton, Dore, and others. *Jean Cocteau and the French Scene.* Ed. by Arthur K. Peters, Abbeville Pr. 1984 $19.95

Crosland, Margaret. *Jean Cocteau.* Darby repr. of 1955 ed. 1981 lib. bdg. $30.00

Oxenhandler, Neal. *Scandal and Parade: The Theater of Jean Cocteau.* Rutgers Univ. Pr. 1957 $15.00

Peters, Arthur K. *Jean Cocteau and André Gide: An Abrasive Friendship.* Rutgers Univ. Pr. 1973 $35.00

COLETTE (SIDONIE-GABRIELLE) (Colette Willy, pseud.). 1873–1954

"*La grande* Colette," "romancière, short-story writer, playwright, journalist, editor, actress, dramatic critic, fashion columnist, book reviewer, feature writer, wife and nurse" received the "greatest honor possible for a woman writer in France: the presiding chair in the Goncourt Academy." Her early "Claudine" novels were published in collaboration with her first husband, the notorious "Willy," pseudonym of Henry Gauthier-Villers, whom she had married at 20 and divorced when she was 33. Under M. Willy's "editorship" she became a master craftsman. During her varied, active life, reflected in her novels, she became known for her subtle psychological insight and masterly style. The "Claudine" series is taken from her youth, *The Vagabond* from her days as a music-hall dancer, and *Chéri* from an affair with a "dissolute" young man. "She was her own most interesting character, and beneath her attempts at fictional delineation of a Claudine, a Lea, a Gigi was Colette's palpitating heart, faintly veiled, disarming in its candid subjectivity" (Anna Balakian, *SR*). Gide praised her, and Proust wept on reading *Mitsou*. A Grand Officer of the Legion of Honor, she was accorded a formal state funeral, and in 1967 Paris named a street in her honor.

BOOKS BY COLETTE

The Collected Stories. Ed. by Robert G. Phelps, trans. by Matthew Ward, Antonia White, and Anne-Marie Callimachi, Farrar 1983 $19.95 pap. $9.95
Letters from Colette. Trans. and ed. by Robert G. Phelps, Farrar 1980 $12.95
Earthly Paradise: An Autobiography of Colette Drawn from Her Lifetime Writings. Ed. by Robert G. Phelps, Herma Briffault, and Derek Coltman, Farrar 1966 pap. $10.95
The Complete Claudine. 1900–1903. Trans. by Antonia White. Farrar 1976 pap. $10.95
Retreat from Love. 1907. Trans. by Margaret Crosland. Harcourt 1980 pap. $4.95
The Vagabond. 1911. Trans. by Enid McLeod, Farrar 1975 $8.95 pap. $4.95
Mitsou (and *Music-Hall Sidelights*). 1913 1918. Trans. by Raymond Postgate and Anne-Marie Callimachi, Farrar new ed. 1976 pap. $2.95
Chéri (and *The Last of Chéri*). 1920 1926. Ballantine 1982 pap. $2.50; trans. by Roger Senhouse, Farrar 1976 $7.95
My Mother's House (and *Sido*). 1922 1929. Trans. by Una V. Troubridge and Enid McLeod, Farrar 1975 $7.95 pap. $6.95
The Ripening Seed. 1923. Trans. by Roger Senhouse, Farrar 1975 $7.95 pap. $5.95
Break of Day. 1928. Trans. by Enid McLeod, Farrar 1974 pap. $5.25
My Apprenticeships. 1936. Trans. by Helen Beauclerk, Farrar 1978 $10.00 pap. $4.95
Gigi, Julie de Carneilhan, Chance Acquaintances. 1941 1944. Trans. by Roger Senhouse and Patrick Fermor, Farrar 1976 $11.95 pap. $7.95
The Blue Lantern. 1949. Trans. by Roger Senhouse, Farrar 1977 $10.00 pap. $2.95

BOOKS ABOUT COLETTE

Cottrell, Robert D. *Colette. Lit. and Life Ser.* Ungar 1974 $12.95
Crosland, Margaret. *Colette: The Difficulty of Loving.* Dell 1985 pap. $4.95
Marks, Elaine. *Colette.* Greenwood repr. of 1960 ed. 1982 lib. bdg. $27.50
Richardson, Joanna. *Colette.* Watts 1984 $17.95

CORNEILLE, PIERRE. 1606–1684

Corneille is the first French dramatist to write plays according to modern notions of French drama. He achieved the establishment of a pattern that was to be followed by successive generations of dramatists, including Racine. His plays deal with noble characters, in closely defined situations of high moral intensity, developed within the limits of the "three unities"—a term derived from Aristotle's *Poetics* and interpreted to mean that the dramatic action must transpire in the same locality (unity of place), within the span of time covered by the stage presentation (unity of time), and in a coherent sequence of events (unity of action). Corneille's greatest dramatic success was *Le Cid*, adapted from Guillen de Castro's three-day comedy *La mocedades del Cid*. It vividly represents the dominant theme of his tragedies—the inner struggle between duty and passion—a theme that Racine was later to treat after his own fashion. Some of Corneille's other major tragedies include *Horace* (1640), *Cinna* (1640), and *Polyeuctus* (1643). In his shaping of language and form to his dramatic purposes, Corneille had a great effect on the development of French literature; more specifically, it can be said that he gave form and aim to French neoclassicism. Far from being cold masterpieces of the past, Corneille's plays live today in the French theater, where they are regularly performed and enthusiastically received.

BOOKS BY CORNEILLE

Chief Plays of Corneille. Trans. by L. Lockert, Princeton Univ. Pr. 1957 $38.00

Rodogune: The French Text with a Facing English Translation. Trans. and ed. by William G. Clubb, Univ. of Nebraska Pr. 1974 $14.50

Le Cid. 1636–37. Trans. by John C. Lapp, *Crofts Class. Ser.* Harlan Davidson text ed. 1955 pap. $3.25

The Cid, Cinna, the Theatrical Illusion. Trans. by John Cairncross, *Penguin Class. Ser.* 1976 pap. $3.95

Polyeuctus, The Liar, Nicomedes. Trans. by John Cairncross, *Penguin Class. Ser.* 1980 pap. $4.95

BOOKS ABOUT CORNEILLE

Barnwell, H. T. *The Tragic Drama of Corneille and Racine: An Old Parallel Revisited.* Oxford 1982 $42.00

Broome, J. H. *A Student's Guide to Corneille.* Heinemann text ed. 1971 pap. $5.00

Mallinson, G. J. *The Comedies of Corneille: Experiments in the Comic.* Longwood Pr. 1984 $35.00

Nelson, Robert J. *Corneille: His Heroes and Their Worlds.* Univ. of Pennsylvania Pr. 1963 $8.50

Pocock, Gordon. *Corneille and Racine.* Cambridge Univ. Pr. 1973 $49.50 pap. $13.95

Segall, J. B. *Corneille and the Spanish Drama.* AMS Pr. repr. of 1902 ed. $16.00; Gordon 1976 lib. bdg. $59.95

Turnell, Martin. *The Classical Moment: Studies of Corneille, Molière, and Racine.* Greenwood repr. of 1948 ed. 1971 lib. bdg. $29.75

DERRIDA, JACQUES. 1930–

[SEE Volume 4.]

DESCARTES, RENE. 1596–1650

[SEE Volume 4.]

DIDEROT, DENIS. 1713–1784

After about a century and a half of neglect by critics, Diderot is now considered one of the most original minds of the Enlightenment and is ranked along with MONTESQUIEU (see Vol. 3), Voltaire, and ROUSSEAU (see Vol. 3) as one of the prime figures of the period. He was coeditor with D'Alembert of the *Encyclopédie*, one of the major intellectual monuments of the eighteenth century whose purpose was not only to assemble and disseminate knowledge but also to change the general way of thinking. A philosopher, playwright, novelist, essayist, and literary theoretician, he left behind him works of genius that were appreciated properly only long after his death. *D'Alembert's Dream* (1769) is a statement of his philosophic thought through the experimental form of a dialogue—for he was as interested in literature as in ideas. Perhaps his most engaging satire is *Rameau's Nephew*, a philosophic dialogue in which Diderot examines the problem of morality in a corrupt society, the Paris of his day. His dramatic theories were taken up by later generations in France (starting with Beaumarchais) and influenced ideas about the theater in Germany starting with Lessing. Diderot's two masterpieces in the novel are *The Nun*, an examination of convent life and female sexuality, and *Jacques the Fatalist*, a lively and digressive work somewhat in the manner of Sterne's *Tristram Shandy* that deals with the philosophic problem of individual morality and determinism. His correspondence (particularly with Sophie Volland) provides a valuable portrait of contemporary society. Diderot's *Salons* (1757–81), reviews of painting exhibitions in Paris, are an outstanding example of eighteenth-century art criticism.

BOOKS BY DIDEROT

The Nun. 1760. Trans. by Leonard Tancock, *Penguin Class. Ser.* 1974 pap. $4.95
Rameau's Nephew and Other Works. 1762. Trans. by Jacques Barzun and Ralph H. Brown, Irvington 1964 $26.50
Rameau's Nephew and D'Alembert's Dream. *Penguin Class. Ser.* 1976 pap. $5.95
Encyclopedia: Selections. 1765. Trans. by Nelly S. Hoyt, Bobbs 1965 pap. $8.80
Diderot's Pictorial Encyclopedia of Trades and Industry. 1765. Ed. by Charles C. Gillispie, Dover 2 vols. 1959 ea. $25.00
Jacques the Fatalist and His Master. 1773. Trans. by J. Robert Loy, *Norton Lib.* repr. of 1979 ed. pap. $6.95
Diderot, Interpreter of Nature: Selected Writings. Trans. by Jean Stewart and Jonathan Kemp, ed. by Jonathan Kemp, Hyperion Pr. repr. of 1937 ed. 1981 $29.15
Diderot's Early Philosophical Works. Ed. by Margaret Jourdain, intro. by J. P. Siegel, AMS Pr. repr. of 1916 ed. $15.00; ed. by Margaret Jourdain, Burt Franklin repr. of 1916 ed. 1972 lib. bdg. $20.50
Diderot's Writings on the Theatre. Ed. by F. C. Green, AMS Pr. repr. of 1936 ed. $26.00

BOOKS ABOUT DIDEROT

Fontenay, Elisabeth de. *Diderot: Reason and Resonance*. Trans. by Jeffrey Mehlman, Braziller 1982 $14.95
France, Peter. *Diderot*. Oxford 1983 $12.95 pap. $3.95
Fredman, Alice G. *Diderot and Sterne*. Octagon repr. of 1972 ed. lib. bdg. $22.00
Morley, John. *Diderot and the Encyclopaedists*. Gale 2 vols. repr. of 1923 ed. 1971 $42.00; Richard West 2 vols. repr. of 1878 ed. $19.25
Vartanian, Aram. *Diderot and Descartes: A Study of Scientific Naturalism in the Enlightenment*. Greenwood repr. of 1953 ed. 1975 lib. bdg. $19.25
Wilson, Arthur M. *Diderot*. Oxford 1972 $45.00

DUMAS, ALEXANDRE (père). 1802–1870

Perhaps the most broadly popular of French romantic novelists was Alexandre Dumas, who published during his lifetime some 1,200 volumes. These were not all written by him, however, but were the works of a body of collaborators known as "Dumas & Co." Some of his best works were plagiarized, e.g., *The Three Musketeers* (1844) was taken from the *Memoirs of Artagnan* by an eighteenth-century writer, and *The Count of Monte Cristo* (1845) from Penchet's *A Diamond and a Vengeance*. *My Memoirs* (1852–54), one of Dumas's most entertaining works, is available only in an abridged version, and only a few of his travel journals are in print today.

BOOKS BY DUMAS (PÈRE)

The Three Musketeers. Trans. by Lowell Bair, Bantam 1984 pap. $3.95; Biblio Dist. repr. of 1906 ed. 1977 $14.95; Dodd 1984 illus. $11.95; Penguin 1982 pap. $5.95
The Count of Monte Cristo. Trans. by Lowell Bair, Bantam abr. ed. 1981 pap. $3.50; Dodd 1984 illus. $12.95
My Memoirs. Ed. and trans. by A. Craig Bell, Greenwood repr. of 1961 ed. 1975 lib. bdg. $19.75

BOOKS ABOUT DUMAS

Bell, A. Craig. *Alexandre Dumas: A Biography and Study.* Arden Lib. repr. of 1950 ed. 1980 lib. bdg. $49.50
Maurois, André. *The Titans: A Three-Generation Biography of the Dumas.* Trans. by Gerard Hopkins, Greenwood repr. of 1957 ed. 1971 lib. bdg. $27.50

DUMAS, ALEXANDRE (fils). 1824–1895

Dumas (fils), the playwright, was the son of Dumas (père), the author of popular historical romances. He was the author of plays dealing with social and domestic problems, the best known of which is *La dame aux Camélias* (1852), based on his own novel, and made famous through the opera version by Verdi, *La Traviata*, and a motion picture version, *Camille*.

BOOK BY DUMAS (FILS)

Camille. 1856. Trans. by Matilde Heron, Ayer repr. of 1856 ed., facsimile ed. $11.50; NAL 1972 pap. $3.50

DURAS, MARGUERITE (pseud. of Marguerite Donnadieu). 1914–

Born in Indochina, Marguerite Duras went to Paris at the age of 17 and studied at the Sorbonne. During World War II, she joined the Resistance and published her first books. After the liberation, she was drawn to politics and became a member of the Communist party (from which she was expelled in 1955). Her fame in literature dates from *The Sea Wall*—about white settlers in Vietnam. Duras has many novels to her credit—all "setting powerful subconscious mechanisms in motion behind a screen of trivia" (*SR*). Seeking meaning and fulfillment, the characters in her novels are sacrificed to the ever-flowing tide of existence, and life is perhaps over before they are fully aware of what has been happening. She is usually grouped with the (in fact, widely disparate) new novelists. In 1959, she wrote her first film scenario, *Hiroshima, Mon Amour*, and has since been involved in a number of other films, including *India Song, Baxter, Vera Baxter,* and *Le camion* (*The Truck*). Of her work, Germaine Brée has written: "Novel, play, or film, Duras's work conforms to no genre except that of a muted conversation on the dual theme of love and death."

BOOKS BY DURAS

Four Novels. Trans. by Sonia Pitt-Rivers and others, intro. by Germaine Brée, Grove (Evergreen) 1965 pap. $9.95. Contains *The Square, Moderato Cantabile, Ten-Thirty on a Summer Night,* and *The Afternoon of Mr. Andesmas.*

The Sailor from Gibraltar. 1952. Trans. by Barbara Bray, Riverrun 1980 pap. $6.95

The Sea Wall. 1953. Trans. by Herma Briffault, Farrar 1985 $7.95

Whole Days in the Trees. 1953. Trans. by Anita Barrows, Riverrun 1984 pap. $5.95

Hiroshima, Mon Amour. 1959. Trans. by Richard Seaver, Grove (Evergreen) 1961 pap. $7.95; Peter Smith $7.50

Destroy, She Said. 1969. Trans. by Barbara Bray, Grove 1970 pap. $11.50

India Song. 1975. Trans. by Barbara Bray, Grove (Evergreen) 1976 pap. $3.95

The Lover. Trans. by Barbara Bray, Pantheon 1985 $11.95

BOOKS ABOUT DURAS

Cismaru, Alfred. *Marguerite Duras. Twayne's World Authors Ser.* G. K. Hall 1971 o.p.

Mercier, Vivian. *The New Novel: From Queneau to Pinget.* Farrar 1971 pap. $2.95

FLAUBERT, GUSTAVE. 1821–1880

Flaubert's masterpiece, *Madame Bovary,* is a study of a woman of romantic temperament and upbringing who ruins herself in her thirst for romantic experience. (With the subtitle *Provincial Morals,* it caused a scandal, though Flaubert was declared innocent of offense against public and religious morality in a court case.) *The Sentimental Education* has a similar theme—with a male protagonist. A novel in quite another vein, intended to shock, was *Salammbô,* a story of sex and violence in ancient Carthage. It leaves "an overwhelming impression" of "nightmarish brutality," even "sadism" (Victor Brombert). A year after Flaubert's death appeared his colossal work, *Bouvard and Pécuchet,* "a precious wilderness of wonderful reading," as H. G. Wells called it. Flaubert was possibly the most painstaking writer in all literature. He wrote slowly and laboriously, and his books followed one another at long intervals. *Madame Bovary* took him 6 years; *Bouvard and Pécuchet* remained unfinished after 13 years of work. His tireless search for the right word and his habit of reading aloud every sentence until its cadence was perfect to the ear have earned for him a reputation as perhaps the greatest stylist of all time. He prided himself on being a scrupulously objective literary realist who described life as he saw it (in minute detail), but as a serious artist he became involved with his characters: "I am myself Madame Bovary."

Flaubert despised the bourgeoisie and bourgeois thinking, and compiled a witty book of clichés, *The Dictionary of Accepted Ideas* (also published with the title *A Dictionary of Platitudes: Being a Compendium of Conversational Clichés, Blind Beliefs, Fashionable Misconceptions and Fixed Ideas*). The *Nation* said of his *Selected Letters:* "They are among the finest literary letters in the whole of epistolary literature, and Francis Steegmuller . . . has edited them with discretion after translating them with authority."

BOOKS BY FLAUBERT

Letters: Gustave Flaubert. Arden Lib. repr. 1980 lib. bdg. $40.00

Selected Letters. Trans. by Francis Steegmuller, *Biography Index Repr. Ser.* Ayer repr. of 1953 ed. $17.50

The Letters of Gustave Flaubert, 1830–1857. Trans. and ed. by Francis Steegmuller, Harvard Univ. Pr. (Belknap Pr.) 1981 pap. $5.95

Madame Bovary. 1857. Trans. by Lowell Blair, ed. by Leo Bersani, *Bantam Class. Ser.* 1981 pap. $2.50; trans. by Francis Steegmuller, Modern Lib. repr. of 1957 ed. 1981 pap. $3.50; trans. by Mildren Marmur, fwd. by Mary McCarthy, New Amer. Lib. (Signet Class.) 1964 pap. $2.50; ed. by Paul De Man, *Norton Critical Eds.* text ed. 1965 pap. $5.95; trans. by Alan Russell, *Penguin Class. Ser.* 1951 pap. $2.95

Salammbô. 1862. Trans. by A. J. Krailsheimer, *Penguin Class. Ser.* 1977 pap. $3.95

The Sentimental Education. 1869. Trans. by Robert Baldick, *Penguin Class. Ser.* 1964 pap. $3.95

The First Sentimental Education. Trans. by Douglas Garman, intro. by Gerhard Gerhardi, Univ. of California Pr. 1972 $29.50

The Temptation of St. Anthony. Trans. by Kitty Mrosovsky, *Penguin Class. Ser.* 1983 pap. $4.95

Three Tales. 1877. Trans. by Robert Baldick, *Penguin Class. Ser.* 1961 pap. $2.95

Bouvard and Pécuchet. 1881. Trans. by T. W. Earp and G. W. Stonier, intro. by Lionel Trilling, Greenwood repr. of 1954 ed. 1979 lib. bdg. $27.50; trans. by A. J. Krailsheimer, *Penguin Class. Ser.* 1976 pap. $4.95

The Dictionary of Accepted Ideas. Trans. and ed. by Jacques Barzun, New Directions rev. ed. 1954 pap. $4.95

BOOKS ABOUT FLAUBERT

Barnes, Hazel E. *Sartre and Flaubert.* Univ. of Chicago Pr. $25.00 1982 pap. $10.95

Bernheimer, Charles. *Flaubert and Kafka: Studies in Psychopoetic Structure.* Yale Univ. Pr. 1982 $25.00

Brombert, Victor. *The Novels of Flaubert: A Study of Themes and Techniques.* Princeton Univ. Pr. 1967 $32.00 pap. $11.95

Culler, Jonathan. *Flaubert: The Uses of Uncertainty.* Cornell Univ. Pr. rev. ed. text ed. 1985 pap. $12.95

Giraud, Raymond. *The Unheroic Hero in the Novels of Stendhal, Balzac and Flaubert.* Octagon 1969 lib. bdg. $19.00

Green, Anne. *Flaubert and the Historical Novel: Salammbô Reassessed.* Cambridge Univ. Pr. 1982 $44.50

Kenner, Hugh. *The Stoic Comedians: Flaubert, Joyce and Beckett.* Univ. of California Pr. repr. of 1962 ed. 1975 pap. $2.65

Lowe, Margaret. *Towards the Real Flaubert: A Study of Madame Bovary.* Ed. by A. W. Raitt, Oxford 1984 $22.00

Nadeau, Maurice. *The Greatness of Flaubert.* Trans. by Barbara Bray, Open Court 1972 pap. $9.95

Sartre, Jean-Paul. *The Family Idiot: Gustave Flaubert, 1821–1857.* Trans. by Carol Cosman, Univ. of Chicago Pr. 1981 $25.00

Schor, Naomi, and Henry F. Majewski, eds. *Flaubert and Postmodernism.* Univ. of Nebraska Pr. 1984 $22.50

Sherrington, R. J. *Three Novels by Flaubert: A Study of Techniques.* Oxford 1970 $37.50

Steegmuller, Francis. *Flaubert and Madame Bovary: A Double Portrait.* Univ. of Chicago Pr. 1977 pap. $5.95

FOUCAULT, MICHEL. 1926–1984

An outstanding philosopher and intellectual figure on the contemporary scene, Foucault, particularly with *The Order of Things* and *The Archaeology of Knowledge,* has been influential in the recent interpretation of literature. A professor of philosophy at the universities of Clermont-Ferrand, Tunis, and Vincennes, he was named to a chair at the Collège de France in 1970. He also taught in various departments of French literature as a visiting professor in the United States. Until 1968, he was a major figure in the critical movement known as structuralism. In both *The Order of Things* and *The Archaeology of Knowledge* he was interested in the organization of human knowledge and in the transformations of intellectual categories. The fundamental question of the methods, limits, and themes proper to the history of ideas are the concern of the latter work. Foucault was actively interested in the question of penal reform in France. The last work he published before his death was *A History of Sexuality.*

BOOKS BY FOUCAULT

Language, Counter Memory, Practice: Selected Essays and Interviews. Trans. by Sherry Simon, ed. by Donald F. Bouchard, Cornell Univ. Pr. 1977 $27.95 1980 pap. $7.95
Madness and Civilization: A History of Insanity in the Age of Reason. 1961. Trans. by Richard Howard, Random (Vintage) 1973 pap. $4.95
The Order of Things: An Archaeology of the Human Sciences. 1966. Pantheon 1970 $10.00; Random (Vintage) 1973 pap. $5.95
The Archaeology of Knowledge. 1969. Trans. by A. M. Sheridan-Smith, Harper 1976 pap. $4.95
A History of Sexuality. Trans. by Robert Hurley, Pantheon vol. 1 1978 $8.95 vol. 2 1985 $17.95
Discipline and Punish: The Birth of the Prison. 1975. Trans. by Alan Sheridan, Pantheon 1978 $10.95; trans. by Alan Sheridan, Random (Vintage) 1979 pap. $6.95

BOOKS ABOUT FOUCAULT

Cooper, Barry. *Michel Foucault: An Introduction to the Study of His Thought.* Mellen 1982 $39.95
Racevskis, Karlis. *Michel Foucault and the Subversion of Intellect.* Cornell Univ. Pr. 1983 $21.50
Sheridan, Alan. *Michel Foucault: The Will to Truth.* Methuen 1980 $26.00 pap. $10.95

FRANCE, ANATOLE (pseud. of Anatole-François Thibault). 1844–1924
(NOBEL PRIZE 1921)

Anatole France was the only son of a bookseller. His literary criticism records "the adventures of his soul among masterpieces" and often appears, together with autobiographical elements, under a thin disguise of fiction. Some of the best of this genre are *On Life and Letters, My Friend's Book,* and *The Opinions of Mr. Jerome Coignard. The Crime of Sylvester Bonnard* (1881, o.p.), France's first success, has enjoyed great popularity. His fiction covers a wide range of subjects and historical periods. Widely respected as a distinguished "prince of letters" and "the leading exemplar of French intelligence, wisdom and wit," he was elected to the French Academy.

BOOKS BY FRANCE

The Works of Anatole France. Gordon 40 vols. 1975 $2,700.00

My Friend's Book. 1885. Trans. by Rosalie Feltenstein, Barron text ed. 1950 pap. $2.95

Thais. 1890. Trans. by Basia Gulati, intro. by Wayne C. Booth, Univ. of Chicago Pr. pap. $3.95

At the Sign of the Reine Pedauque. 1893. Biblio Dist. (Everyman's) repr. of 1941 ed. 1969 $8.95

The Opinions of Mr. Jerome Coignard. Folcroft repr. of 1893 ed. lib. bdg. $8.50

Crainquebille. 1901. Trans. by Winifred Stephens, *Short Story Index Repr. Ser.* Ayer 1922 $14.50

Penguin Island. 1908. Rivercity Pr. lib. bdg. $18.95

The Gods Will Have Blood. 1912. Trans. by Frederick Davies, *Penguin Class. Ser.* 1980 pap. $3.95

On Life and Letters. Ed. by Frederic Chapman, *Essay Index Repr. Ser.* Ayer 4 series repr. of 1910–24 ed. ea. $21.00–$22.00

BOOKS ABOUT FRANCE

Brousson, Jean J. *Anatole France Himself.* Trans. by John Pollock, R. West 1973 $20.00

Segur, Nicolas. *Conversations with Anatole France.* Gordon Pr. 1977 lib. bdg. $59.95

Virtanen, Reino. *Anatole France. Twayne's World Authors Ser.* 1969 o.p.

GENET, JEAN. 1910–1986

Many of his contemporaries consider Genet one of France's greatest writers, as did Sartre. While serving one of his many prison sentences for theft, Genet produced his first novel, *Our Lady of the Flowers.* Tom F. Driver (*SR*) called another autobiographical novel, *Miracle of the Rose,* "a major achievement of modern literature.... Genet transforms experiences of degradation into spiritual exercises and hoodlums into the bearers of the majesty of love." His *Thief's Journal,* an account of "Genet's adolescence and young manhood as a beggar, homosexual, convict, and petty thief, is perverse in every sense of the word [but] a literary creation of great importance and midnight beauty" (*LJ*). According to Sartre, Genet then "turned dramatist because the falsehood of the stage is the most manifest and fascinating of all."

Genet was born in Paris in 1910, an illegitimate child who never knew his parents. Abandoned to public welfare, he was adopted by a peasant family in the Morvan. At ten he was sent to a reformatory for stealing. After many years in institutions he escaped and joined the Foreign Legion, but soon deserted. In traveling through Europe he begged, thieved, smuggled, and was imprisoned in almost every country he visited. He escaped life imprisonment in France in 1948 when the president of the Republic, petitioned by a group of eminent writers and artists, granted him a pardon.

Genet's plays, in their lack of plot and other such conventions of the prewar theater, have many elements of the Theater of the Absurd. But his "theatre is, profoundly, a theatre of social protest. Yet . . . it resolutely rejects political commitment, political argument, didacticism, or propaganda. In dealing with the dream world of the outcast of society, it explores the human condition, the alienation of man, his solitude, his futile search for meaning and reality" (Martin Esslin).

BOOKS BY GENET

Complete Poems. Man Root 1980 pap. $8.95
Our Lady of the Flowers. 1944. Trans. by Bernard Frechtman, intro. by Jean-Paul Sartre, Grove 1976 pap. $3.95
The Maids. 1948. Trans. by Bernard Frechtman, intro. by Jean-Paul Sartre, Grove (Evergreen) pap. $4.50
Funeral Rites. 1948. Trans. by Bernard Frechtman, Grove (Evergreen) 1969 pap. $5.95
The Thief's Journal. 1949. Trans. by Bernard Frechtman, intro. by Jean-Paul Sartre, Grove (Evergreen) 1982 pap. $9.95
Miracle of the Rose. 1950. Trans. by Bernard Frechtman, Grove 1971 pap. $7.95
The Balcony. 1956. Trans. by Bernard Frechtman, Grove (Evergreen) 1958 pap. $5.95
The Blacks: A Clown Story. 1958. Trans. by Bernard Frechtman, Grove (Evergreen) 1960 pap. $7.95
The Screens. 1961. Trans. by Bernard Frechtman, Grove (Evergreen) 1962 pap. $4.95

BOOKS ABOUT GENET

Cetta, Lewis T. *Profane Play, Ritual and Jean Genet.* Univ. of Alabama Pr. 1974 $10.50
McMahon, Joseph H. *The Imagination of Jean Genet.* Greenwood repr. of 1963 ed. 1980 lib. bdg. $27.50; Yale Univ. Pr. 1963 $18.50
Savona, Jeannette L. *Jean Genet.* Grove 1984 $19.50 pap. $9.95

GIDE, ANDRE. 1869–1951 (NOBEL PRIZE 1947)

Gide, the reflective rebel against bourgeois morality and one of the most important and controversial figures in modern European literature, published his first book anonymously at the age of 18. As a young man he was an ardent member of the symbolist group, but the style of his later work is more in the tradition of classicism. Much of his work is autobiographical, and the story of his youth and early adult years and the discovery of his own sexual tendencies is related in *Si le grain ne meurt (If it die . . .).* *Corydon* deals with the question of homosexuality openly. Gide's reflections on life and literature are contained in his *Journals*, which span the years 1889 to 1949.

He was a founder of the influential *Nouvelle revue française*, in which the works of many prominent modern European authors appeared, and he remained a director until 1941. He resigned when it passed into the hands of the collaborationists. Gide's sympathies with communism prompted him to travel to Russia, where he found the realities of Soviet life less attractive than he had imagined. His accounts of his disillusionment were published as *Return from the U.S.S.R.* and *Afterthoughts from the U.S.S.R.* Always preoccupied with freedom, a champion of the oppressed, a skeptic, he remained an incredibly youthful spirit.

Gide himself classified his fiction into three categories: satirical tales with elements of farce, like *Les caves du vatican* (*Lafcadio's Adventures*), which he termed *soties;* ironic stories narrated in the first person and related from a single point of view, like *The Immoralist* and *Strait Is the Gate*, which he called *récits;* and a more complex narrative related from a multi-faceted point of view, which he called a *roman* (novel). The only example of the last category that he published was *The Counterfeiters*.

Throughout his career, Gide maintained an extensive correspondence with such figures as Valéry, Claudel, RILKE, and others.

BOOKS BY GIDE

The Immoralist. 1902. Trans. by Richard Howard, Modern Lib. $7.95; trans. by Richard Howard, Random (Vintage) 1970 pap. $3.95

Strait Is the Gate. 1909. Trans. by Dorothy Bussy, Bentley repr. of 1924 ed. 1980 lib. bdg. $12.50; trans. by Dorothy Bussy, Random (Vintage) 1956 pap. $2.45

Lafcadio's Adventures. 1914. Trans. by Dorothy Bussy, Bentley repr. of 1925 ed. 1980 lib. bdg. $12.50; trans. by Dorothy Bussy, Random (Vintage) 1925 pap. $2.95

Corydon. 1923. Trans. by Richard Howard, Farrar 1983 $16.95 pap. $7.95

Dostoevsky. 1923. Greenwood repr. of 1961 ed. 1979 lib. bdg. $22.50; Telegraph Bks. repr. of 1925 ed. 1981 lib. bdg. $25.00

The Counterfeiters. 1926. Trans. by Dorothy Bussy, Random (Vintage) 1973 pap. $4.95

Return from the U.S.S.R. (and *Afterthoughts on My Return*). 1937 1938. Trans. by Richard Howard, Farrar 1985 $15.95

Self-Portraits: The Gide-Valéry Letters, 1890–1942. Trans. by June Guicharnaud, ed. by Robert Mallet, Univ. of Chicago Pr. 1966 o.p.

BOOKS ABOUT GIDE

Brée, Germaine. *Gide.* Greenwood repr. of 1963 ed. 1985 lib. bdg. $49.75

Guérard, Albert J. *André Gide.* Harvard Univ. Pr. rev. ed. 1969 $20.00

Hytier, Jean. *André Gide.* Trans. by Richard Howard, Ungar pap. $2.95

O'Brien, Justin. *Portrait of André Gide.* Octagon repr. of 1953 ed. 1976 lib. bdg. $29.00

Rossi, Vinio. *André Gide: The Evolution of an Aesthetic.* Columbia Univ. Pr. 1968 pap. $2.50; Rutgers Univ. Pr. 1967 $12.50

Schlumberger, Jean. *Madeleine and André Gide: The Platonic Marriage of Saint and Homosexual.* Trans. by Richard H. Akeroyd, Portals Pr. 1981 $12.50

GIONO, JEAN. 1895–1970

"When Giono's first novel, *Colline* (*Hill of Destiny*) appeared in 1929, it struck a fresh, new note.... After Proust and Gide, Duhamel and Romains, Cocteau and Giraudoux, what could be more restful than a world of wind and sun and simple men who apparently had never heard of psychological analysis, never confronted any social problems, never read any books.... For Giono the world of his imagination was undoubtedly a refuge.... Brought up by his father, a shoemaker, in the small town of Manosque, Giono, except for one brief interval, had never left home before 1914" (Germaine Brée and M. Guiton, *An Age of Fiction*). When, as a boy of 19, he was sent to the front with the infantry, he was totally unprepared.

"Four years later, when release came, his revolt was complete; he fled from the modern world and banished it from his novels." After the shock of World War II his novels seemed to gain in stature. One of his best is *Horseman on the Roof*, his chronicle of the great cholera epidemic of 1838. "Giono's vast frescoes reflect his fundamental optimism and love of life, his deliberate refusal to deal with the complications of human psychology" (Brée and Guiton).

BOOKS BY GIONO

Harvest. 1930. Trans. by Henri Fluchère and Geoffrey Myers, North Point Pr. 1984 pap. $9.00

To the Slaughterhouse. 1931. Dufour $14.95

Blue Boy. 1932. Trans. by Katherine A. Clarke, North Point Pr. repr. of 1946 ed. 1981 pap. $9.50

The Song of the World. 1934. Trans. by Henri Fluchère and Geoffrey Myers, North Point Pr. repr. of 1937 ed. 1981 pap. $11.00

Ennemonde. 1968. Dufour $14.95

Joy of Man's Desiring. 1935. Trans. by Katherine A. Clarke, North Point Pr. repr. of 1940 ed. 1980 pap. $12.50

Horseman on the Roof. 1951. Trans. by Jonathan Griffin, North Point Pr. repr. of 1954 ed. 1982 pap. $12.50

The Man Who Planted Hope and Grew Happiness. 1954. Friends Nature pap. $2.00

Ennemonde. 1968. Dufour $14.95

The Straw Man. Trans. by Phyllis Johnson, North Point Pr. 1982 pap. $14.00

The Man Who Planted Trees. Chelsea Green 1985 $13.50

BOOKS ABOUT GIONO

Goodrich, Norma L. *Giono: Master of Fictional Modes*. Princeton Univ. Pr. 1973 $32.00

Redfern, Walter D. *The Private World of Jean Giono*. Duke Univ. Pr. 1967 $12.75

GIRAUDOUX, JEAN. 1882–1944

A novelist, playwright, and critic, Giraudoux entered the diplomatic service in 1910 and, with the exception of World War I, he pursued that career until his retirement in 1940. He rose from the rank of consular attaché to that of cabinet minister. Giraudoux traveled widely (he was always fascinated by Germany) and had published about 30 titles, most of them novels, before becoming a dramatist at age 46. His novels are noted for their preciosity of language and their poetic and mythical qualities. His plays are highly stylized and poetic, generally avoiding "psychological realism." They are frequently confrontations of ideas or contrasts of opposing attitudes toward human experience. He was "more interested in ideas than in dramatic action, more interested in conversation than in ideas." His was a "baroquely opulent dialogue. [He] could skate across a polished verbal mirror with emotional and intellectual freight, as in his *Electra* [1937] and *Judith* [1938], no less gracefully and provocatively than when he brought his audiences the light comic fantastication of *Amphitryon 38* [1937]" (Gassner). *La guerre de Troie n'aura pas lieu* was produced successfully on Broadway in 1955 as *Ti-*

ger at the Gates (1935). Its French title (which means "the Trojan War will not take place") explains the dramatist's wry but grand theme—Hector's "fierce and fruitless effort" to prevent the Trojan War. *Time* said of it: "Just how good an orthodox play is this sunburst of dialectics and wit may be open to question; beyond question the play exhibits the elegance, the light-fingered thoughtfulness, the ironic lyricism of the most civilized playwright of the era between the wars. And Christopher Fry's translation not only does brilliantly by the play but may even be Fry's solidest writing for the theater." Two of Giraudoux's plays won the New York Drama Critics Circle Award: *Ondine* in 1954 and *Tiger at the Gates* in 1956.

BOOKS BY GIRAUDOUX

Four Plays. Adapted by Maurice Valency, Hill & Wang 1958 pap. $6.25. Contains *Ondine, The Enchanted, The Madwoman of Chaillot,* and *The Apollo of Bellac.*
Three Plays. Trans. by Phyllis LaFarge and Peter H. Judd, Hill & Wang 1964 pap. $6.95. Contains *Siegfried, Amphitryon 38,* and *Electra.*
Three Plays. Trans. by Christopher Fry, intro. by Harold Clurman, Oxford 1963 $10.95. Contains *Judith, Tiger at the Gates, Duel of Angels.*
Suzanne and the Pacific. 1921. Trans. by Ben R. Redman, Fertig repr. of 1923 ed. 1975 $25.00
My Friend from Limousin. Trans. by L. C. Willcox, Fertig repr. of 1923 ed. 1977 $22.50
Racine. Folcroft repr. of 1938 ed. lib. bdg. $9.50; Richard West repr. of 1938 ed. 1980 lib. bdg. $10.00

BOOKS ABOUT GIRAUDOUX

Cohen, Robert. *Giraudoux: Three Faces of Destiny.* Univ. of Chicago Pr. (Phoenix Bks.) 1970 pap. $2.45
Mankin, Paul A. *Precious Irony: The Theatre of Jean Giraudoux. Studies in French Lit.* Mouton text ed. 1971 pap. $20.80
Raymond, Agnes. *Jean Giraudoux: The Theatre of Victory and Defeat.* Univ. of Massachusetts Pr. 1966 pap. $8.00

GREEN, JULIEN. 1900–

Julien Green, who writes in French, was born in Paris of American parents. He spent his childhood in France, returning to the United States only to study at the University of Virginia and to serve in both world wars. American life is the background for his two novels, *Mont-Cinère* (1926, o.p.) and *Moïra* (1950, o.p.). French provincial life is the setting for *Adrienne Mesurat* (*The Closed Garden*, 1927, o.p.), and also for *Léviathan* (*The Dark Journey*). *The Transgressor*, set in a French provincial town, was described by the London *Sunday Times* as "rare and memorable." *Each in His Darkness* (1961, o.p.) is a novel about a Frenchman and his dying uncle in America. In his diary, Julien Green reveals his "sensitive, poetic nature" and provides insights into the obsessive, nightmarish atmosphere of his works as well as into the major conflicts of his life—Catholicism versus Protestantism, and "the struggle between spiritual energy and sensual emotion" (Justin O'Brien, *SR*).

BOOKS BY GREEN

The Dark Journey. 1929. Trans. by Vyvyan Holland, Greenwood repr. of 1929 ed. lib.
    bdg. $22.50
Memories of Happy Days. Greenwood repr. of 1942 ed. lib. bdg. $18.75; ed. by Jean-
    Pierre Piriou, Univ. Pr. of Virginia 1976 $14.95
Memories of Evil Days. Ed. by Jean-Pierre Piriou, Univ. Pr. of Virginia 1976 $14.95
God's Fool: The Life of Francis of Assisi. Harper 1985 $16.30

BOOKS ABOUT GREEN

Dunaway, John M. *The Metamorphoses of the Self: The Mystic, the Sensualist, and the
    Artist in the Works of Julien Green.* Univ. Pr. of Kentucky 1978 $12.00
Kostis, Nicholas. *The Exorcism of Sex and Death in Julien Green's Novels.* Mouton
    text ed. 1973 pap. $12.00

HUGO, VICTOR MARIE. 1802–1885

The figure of Victor Hugo dominates the landscape of French literary history. Like a vast colossus he bestrides the century, from the time that it was
two years old until the sunset years of the eighties. In the realms of poetry,
criticism, drama, and fiction, he left an indelible mark.

The revolutionary song of his *Odes et ballades* (1826) and *Les orientales*
(1829) is alive with music and rich in words and images. *Les châtiments* is
a collection of invectives directed against Louis Napoleon from Hugo's exile
on the island of Guernsey. *La légende des siècles* (1859, 1877, and 1883) is a
vast poetic vision of world history from the creation to the present and beyond. Hugo's poems are perhaps the greatest of his works, and among the
greatest productions of modern literature. It is unfortunate that of all his
work, this part has proved least amenable to translation into English.

In the realm of drama, his *Cromwell* and *Hernani* (1830) won him notoriety for breaking away from the French neoclassic traditions of the drama.
His defense, the "Preface to Cromwell," is one of the essential documents in
the history of criticism.

To English-speaking readers, Hugo is probably best known as the author
of *Notre Dame de Paris* (*The Hunchback of Notre Dame*) and of *Les misérables,*
an immense tale of human courage and social oppression set in the era of the
first Napoleon. Both novels were made into classic motion pictures.

When Hugo returned from exile in 1870, at the collapse of the empire of
Napoleon III, he was welcomed and propelled into the arena of politics,
where he remained a controversial voice to the last. When he died in 1885,
all of France went into mourning, as if not an author, but a national hero
had passed from the scene.

BOOKS BY HUGO

Journal, 1830–1848. Greenwood repr. of 1954 ed. lib. bdg. $22.50
Victor Hugo's Intellectual Autobiography. Haskell repr. of 1970 ed. 1975 lib. bdg.
    $49.95
Cromwell. 1827. Greenwood repr. of 1935 ed. lib. bdg. $18.75
The Hunchback of Notre Dame. 1831. Intro. by R. R. Canon, *Airmont Class. Ser.* pap.
    $1.95; trans. by Walter J. Cobb, New Amer. Lib. (Signet Class.) pap. $1.95

Les Misérables. 1862. Fawcett 1979 pap. $2.95; trans. by Charles E. Wilbur, Modern Lib. $9.95; trans. by Norman Denny, *Penguin Class. Ser.* 1982 pap. $8.95

William Shakespeare. 1864. Trans. by Melville B. Anderson, AMS Pr. repr. of 1906 ed. $17.50

BOOKS ABOUT HUGO

Affron, Charles. *A Stage for Poets: Studies in the Theatre of Hugo and Musset.* Princeton Univ. Pr. 1972 $28.00

Brombert, Victor. *Victor Hugo and the Visionary Novel.* Harvard Univ. Pr. text ed. 1984 $20.00

Brown, Nathalie B. *Hugo and Dostoevsky.* Ardis 1978 $15.00 pap. $5.00

Grant, Elliott M. *Career of Victor Hugo.* Kraus repr. of 1945 ed. $32.00

Houston, John P. *Victor Hugo. Twayne's World Authors Ser.* G. K. Hall 1974 lib. bdg. $13.95

Maurois, André. *Victor Hugo.* Trans. by Gerard Hopkins, Arden Lib. repr. of 1956 ed. 1984 lib. bdg. $35.00

Peyre, Henri. *Victor Hugo: Philosophy and Poetry.* Trans. by Roda P. Roberts, Univ. of Alabama Pr. 1980 $12.75

Swinburne, Algernon. *A Study of Victor Hugo.* Folcroft repr. of 1866 ed. 1976 lib. bdg. $17.50

IONESCO, EUGENE. 1912–

The Rumanian-born French dramatist first attracted critical notice when *The Chairs* (1952) was produced in New York. Wildly improbable, hilarious, and wholly original, all his plays combine and contrast the comic and the tragic, the possible and the unlikely. He ranks with Beckett and Adamov among the contemporary leading exponents of the experimental European theater.

In January 1960, for the first time, an avant-garde author was performed in a French national theater. It was Ionesco's thirteenth play, *Rhinoceros.* The crowded theater was the Théâtre de France, the director Jean-Louis Barrault. (Ten years before, Ionesco's first play, *The Bald Soprano*, had been performed at the Théâtre des Noctambules with three persons in the audience on opening night.) *Exit the King*, an allegory about a king who has reigned for several centuries over a now decaying nation and must prepare to die, was produced by the APA Phoenix Repertory Company in New York in 1968. "It is the most personal and moving of all Ionesco's plays," wrote Clive Barnes in the *N.Y. Times*, "and . . . incomparably his greatest work." *Soif et faim* (*Thirst and Hunger*) received mixed reviews (but drew 24 curtain calls) when performed at the Comédie Française in the summer of 1966. Ionesco has adapted several plays from his short stories.

BOOKS BY IONESCO

Four Plays. Trans. by Donald M. Allen, Grove (Evergreen) 1958 pap. $4.95. Contains *The Bald Soprano, The Lesson, Jack, or the Submission,* and *The Chairs.*

The Killer and Other Plays. Trans. by Donald Watson, Grove (Evergreen) 1960 pap. $3.95. Includes *Improvisations, or the Shepherd's Chameleon, Maid to Marry,* and *The Killer.*

Three Plays. Trans. by Donald Watson, Grove (Evergreen) 1958 pap. $3.95. Contains *Amédée, The New Tenant,* and *Victims of Duty.*

Rhinoceros and Other Plays: The Leader, The Future Is in Eggs. Trans. by Derek Prouse, Grove (Evergreen) 1960 pap. $4.95; trans. by Derek Prouse, Peter Smith $14.75

Hunger and Thirst and Other Plays. Trans. by Donald Watson, Grove (Evergreen) 1969 pap. $3.95. Includes *The Picture, Anger,* and *Salutations.*

Killing Game. 1957. Trans. by Helen G. Bishop, Grove (Evergreen) 1974 pap. $2.95

Notes and Counternotes. 1962. Trans. by Donald Watson, Grove (Evergreen) 1964 pap. $18.50; trans. by Donald Watson, Riverrun pap. $9.95

Exit the King. 1963. Trans. by Donald Watson, Grove (Evergreen) 1967 pap. $2.95

Fragments of a Journal. 1967. Trans. by Jean Pace, Grove (Evergreen) 1968 pap. $12.00

Present Past, Past Present. 1970. Trans. by Helen R. Lane, Grove (Evergreen) 1971 pap. $1.95

Macbett. 1972. Trans. by Charles Marowitz, Grove (Evergreen) 1973 pap. $5.95

Man with Bags. Trans. by Israel Horowitz, Grove (Evergreen) 1977 pap. $3.95

The Hermit. Trans. by Richard Seaver, Grove 1980 pap. $4.95

Journeys among the Dead. Trans. by Barbara Wright, Riverrrun 1984 pap. $8.95

BOOKS ABOUT IONESCO

Coe, Richard N. *Eugene Ionesco.* Grove 1968 pap. $1.50; Peter Smith $7.25

Grossvogel, David I. *Four Playwrights and a Postscript: Brecht, Ionesco, Beckett, Genet.* Greenwood repr. of 1962 ed. 1976 lib. bdg. $45.00

Lamont, Rosette C., ed. *Ionesco: A Collection of Critical Essays. Twentieth-Century Views Ser.* Prentice-Hall 1973 $10.95 pap. $1.95

———. *The Two Faces of Ionesco.* Ed. by Rosette C. Lamont and Melvin J. Friedman, pref. by Henri Peyre, Whitston 1978 $15.00

Lewis, Allan. *Ionesco. Twayne's World Authors Ser.* G. K. Hall lib. bdg. $13.50

LACLOS, PIERRE AMBROISE FRANÇOIS CHODERLOS DE. 1741–1803

Les liaisons dangereuses (1784) by Laclos is, by common agreement, one of the key French novels of the eighteenth century. A military man by profession, Laclos's fame rests on this one literary work. A novel of adultery and seduction, the work is structured in the form of a series of letters written by the principal characters. Its brilliant analysis of the strategies and illusions of love and sensuality is presented from a multiple viewpoint that utilizes effectively its epistolary form.

BOOK BY LACLOS

Les liaisons dangereuses. Trans. by P. W. Stone, *Penguin Class. Ser.* 1961 pap. $4.95; (with the title *Dangerous Acquaintances*) trans. by Richard Aldington, AMS Pr. repr. of 1952 ed. $37.50

BOOKS ABOUT LACLOS

Brooks, Peter. *Novels of Worldliness: Crebillon, Marivaux, Laclos, Stendhal.* Princeton Univ. Pr. 1969 $32.00

De Jean, Joan. *Literary Fortifications: Rousseau, Laclos, Sade.* Princeton Univ. Pr. 1984 text ed. $36.50

Rosbottom, Ronald C. *Choderlos de Laclos. Twayne's World Authors Ser.* G. K. Hall 1978 $16.95
Turnell, Martin. *The Novel in France: Mme. de Lafayette, Laclos, Constant, Stendhal, Balzac, Flaubert, Proust. Essay Index Repr. Ser.* Ayer repr. of 1951 ed. $30.00

LA FAYETTE, MARIE MADELEINE DE LA VERGNE, COMTESSE DE. 1634–1693

The first great female novelist in France, La Fayette wrote in an age when women were constrained to conceal their authorship. She was married at the age of 21 to an army officer many years her elder, and the couple lived apart for many years. Mme de La Fayette was part of a small literary circle that included Mme de Sévigné and La Rochefoucauld. Her great novel, *La princesse de Clèves,* is a work of acute psychological analysis that focuses on the problem of an extramarital passion that shatters an otherwise apparently happy marriage.

BOOK BY MME DE LA FAYETTE

The Princess of Clèves. 1678. Greenwood repr. of 1951 ed. 1977 lib. bdg. $27.50

BOOKS ABOUT MME DE LA FAYETTE

Haig, Stirling. *Madame de La Fayette. Twayne's World Authors Ser.* Irvington 1970 lib. bdg. $15.95
Kaps, Helen. *Moral Perspectives in La Princesse de Clèves.* Univ. of Oregon Pr. 1968 $5.00
Kuizenga, Donna. *Narrative Strategies in "La Princesse de Clèves."* French Forum 1976 pap. $9.50

LA FONTAINE, JEAN DE. 1621–1695

Although he had a degree to practice law, La Fontaine does not seem to have done so, but rather spent his life in Paris depending on aristocratic patrons. His principal contribution to literature was his 12 books of *Fables,* to which he devoted 30 years of his life. They were published from 1668 to 1694 and are universally appreciated in France by children and adults alike. In drawing on a tradition of the fable going back to Aesop, La Fontaine created a portrait of human life and French society through the representations of animals. His moral position resembles that of Molière: the prudence of the middle road.

BOOKS BY LA FONTAINE

Fables. Trans. by Marianne Moore, Viking 1954 o.p.
Selected Fables. Trans. by James Mitchie, Penguin 1982 pap. $3.95

BOOKS ABOUT LA FONTAINE

Guiton, Margaret. *La Fontaine: Poet and Counterpoet.* Brown Bk. 1970 $5.00
Lapp, John C. *Esthetics of Negligence: La Fontaine's Contes.* Cambridge Univ. Pr. 1971 $44.50

Sutherland, Monica. *La Fontaine: The Man and His Work.* Folcroft repr. of 1953 ed.
     1974 lib. bdg. $27.50; Richard West repr. of 1953 ed. 1973 $20.00
Wadsworth, Philip A. *Young La Fontaine.* AMS Pr. repr. of 1952 ed. 1970 $21.50

LA ROCHEFOUCAULD, FRANÇOIS, DUC DE. 1613–1680

La Rochefoucauld was one of the great classical French moralists, and his
entire literary reputation is based on the small volume *Maxims,* originally
published in 1665 and in many editions since. In his *Maxims,* La Rochefoucauld pares down the limits of literary expression to the finely balanced
measure of a sentence, or a brief paragraph. Carefully, he points out the hypocrisies of mankind. All human behavior, good, evil, or merely ordinary is,
in his eyes, tainted by self-interest. The views expressed in the maxims were
the bitter fruit of the author's years as a courtier. When his expectations of
favor were at last disappointed, he retired from the royal circle, and enjoyed the company and conversation of talented and sympathetic writers
such as Mme de Sévigné and Mme de Lafayette.

BOOK BY LA ROCHEFOUCAULD

The Maxims. Foundation Class. 1984 $118.45

BOOK ABOUT LA ROCHEFOUCAULD

Mourgues, Odette de. *Two French Moralists. Major European Authors Ser.* Cambridge
     Univ. Pr. 1978 $39.50

LEDUC, VIOLETTE. 1907–1971

Violette Leduc had been publishing works of an autobiographical nature
in France since 1945 but, aside from the enthusiastic support of Simone de
Beauvoir, Sartre, and certain other intellectuals, she had gone unnoticed until the publication of *La bâtarde* propelled her to fame—in part, no doubt,
for "the candor in the totally uninhibited descriptions of [her] Lesbian
loves. . . . This, the story of [her] first forty years, is a courageous confession and a work of art, . . . a weird mixture of burning, naive, lucid, and
unadorned sincerity . . . and of poetic inner monologue" (Henri Peyre, *SR*).

BOOKS BY LEDUC

La bâtarde. Trans. by Derek Coltman, fwd. by S. de Beauvoir, Farrar 1965 pap.
     $9.95
Mad in Pursuit. 1970. Trans. by Derek Coltman, Farrar 1971 $8.95
The Taxi. 1971. Trans. by Helen Weaver, Farrar 1972 $4.95

BOOK ABOUT LEDUC

Courtivron, Isabelle de. *Violette Leduc. Twayne's World Authors Ser.* G. K. Hall 1985
     lib. bdg. $22.95

LEVI-STRAUSS, CLAUDE. 1908–

[SEE VOLUME 3, CHAPTER 4.]

MALLARME, STEPHANE. 1842–1898

Mallarmé is one of the most seminal of modern poets, and his influence
has been felt not only in French, but in English and American poetry as

well. He is also a difficult poet who, after a brief early period, generally strove to express a quintessential ideal beyond the world of reality. The concentrated language that Mallarmé used to express this quintessential ideal compounds the difficulty of his writing for the reader. Moreover, this ideal was to be found in the arena of the intellect rather than the emotions. Poetry was his life's work, and he was able to support his efforts by his practical work as a teacher of English, a writer of essays, and a translator.

BOOKS BY MALLARMÉ

Poems. Trans. by Roger Fry, AMS Pr. repr. of 1936 ed. $32.00
Selected Poems. Trans. by C. F. MacIntyre, Univ. of California Pr. bilingual ed. 1957 pap. $3.95
Selected Poetry and Prose. Ed. by Mary Ann Caws, New Directions 1982 $15.00 pap. $6.95
Herodias. 1864. Trans. by Clark Mills, AMS Pr. repr. of 1940 ed. $16.50
Igitur. 1867–70. Trans. by Jack Hirschman, Press Pegacycle 1974 pap. $10.00

BOOKS ABOUT MALLARMÉ

Bersani, Leo. *The Death of Stéphane Mallarmé.* Cambridge Univ. Pr. 1982 $22.95
Bowie, Malcolm. *Mallarmé and the Art of Being Difficult.* Cambridge Univ. Pr. 1978 $29.95
Chiari, Joseph. *Symbolism from Poe to Mallarmé: The Growth of a Myth.* Fwd. by T. S. Eliot, Gordian repr. of 1956 ed. 1970 $18.50
Cohn, Robert G. *Toward the Poems of Mallarmé.* Univ. of California Pr. 1965 pap. $6.95
Fowlie, Wallace. *Mallarmé.* Univ. of Chicago Pr. 1962 pap. $2.45

MALRAUX, ANDRE. 1901–1976

Man's Fate, the first of Malraux's three war novels of great emotional intensity, deals with the Shanghai revolution of 1927. It won the Prix Goncourt. *Man's Hope,* about the civil war in Spain, was made into a stirring film. *Days of Wrath* tells of the horrors of a concentration camp in Germany. These novels have little plot; they are crowded with characters and read like firsthand historical testimonies of the events they narrate. Malraux's heroes are men of action passionately devoted to their cause. And though it was Sartre who was to preach *l'engagement* (involving oneself in the moral struggles of mankind), Malraux "practised commitment in a much more impressive way. . . . He also expressed the concepts of the 'Absurd' and 'Existentialist Man' well in advance of the time when these terms became part of common parlance" (*N.Y. Review of Bks.*). In committing himself, Malraux lived many lives. Airplane pilot, explorer, and guerrilla revolutionary in China and Spain, he later served under General de Gaulle in the French Resistance. A radical novelist—read by radicals—in his youth, he later became an art critic, an art historian, and de Gaulle's minister for cultural affairs. *The Voices of Silence* has been hailed as his masterpiece. It is a survey of the whole history of art in relation to man's religious beliefs and aspirations.

Books by Malraux

The Conquerors. 1928. Trans. by Stephen Becker, Grove (Evergreen) 1977 pap. $3.95;
Holt 1976 $7.95

Man's Fate. 1933. Trans. by Haakon M. Chevalier, Modern Lib. 1965 pap. $4.50; Random (Vintage) 1969 pap. $4.95 pap. $4.50

Days of Wrath. 1936. Trans. by Haakon M. Chevalier, Arden Lib. repr. of 1936 ed. lib.
bdg. $20.00

Man's Hope. 1937. Trans. by Stuart Gilbert and Alastair MacDonald, Modern Lib.
$10.95

The Voices of Silence: Man and His Art. 1951. Trans. by Stuart Gilbert, Princeton
Univ. Pr. repr. of 1953 ed. 1978 $57.50 pap. $12.95

Lazarus. 1974. Trans. by Terence Kilmartin, Grove (Evergreen) 1978 pap. $2.95;
trans. by Terence Kilmartin, Holt 1977 $7.95

Books about Malraux

Blumenthal, Gerda. *André Malraux: The Conquest of Dread.* Greenwood repr. of 1960
ed. 1979 lib. bdg. $22.50

Frohock, Wilbur M. *André Malraux and the Tragic Imagination.* Stanford Univ. Pr.
1952 $15.00 pap. $5.95

Kline, Thomas J. *André Malraux and the Metamorphosis of Death.* Columbia Univ. Pr.
1973 $26.00

Lacouture, Jean. *André Malraux.* Pantheon 1975 $12.95

Thompson, Brian, and Carl Viggiani. *Witnessing André Malraux: Visions and Revisions.* Wesleyan Univ. Pr. 1984 $32.50

Wilkinson, David O. *Malraux: An Essay in Political Criticism.* Harvard Univ. Pr. 1967
$15.00

MARIVAUX, PIERRE CARLET DE CHAMBLAIN DE. 1688–1763

Marivaux was an outstanding playwright and novelist, noted particularly
for his witty and "precious" plays centered around subtle analyses of the
theme of love. Two of the most famous and still performed today in France
are *Le jeu de l'amour et du hasard* (*The Game of Love and Chance*, 1730) and
Les fausses confidences. Marivaux found his home in the literary salons of
the day, and his style, termed *marivaudage*, reflects the delicate nuances of
such social existence. Marivaux is also known for two unfinished novels, *La
vie de Marianne*, interesting for its depiction of female life in the eighteenth
century, and *Le paysan parvenu* (1735–36), the story of the rise in society of
a poor peasant named Jacob.

Book by Marivaux

Seven Comedies. Trans. and ed. by Oscar Mandel and Adrienne Mandel, Irvington
repr. of 1968 ed. 1984 $29.00

Books about Marivaux

Brooks, Peter. *Novels of Worldliness: Crébillon, Marivaux, Laclos, Stendhal.* Princeton
Univ. Pr. 1969 $32.00

Haac, Oscar A. *Marivaux. Twayne's World Authors Ser.* G. K. Hall 1974 lib. bdg.
$14.95; *Twayne's World Authors Ser.* Irvington text ed. 1974 $15.95

Jamieson, Ruth K. *Marivaux: A Study in Sensibility.* Octagon repr. of 1941 ed. 1969
  lib. bdg. $18.00
McKee, Kenneth N. *The Theater of Marivaux.* Pref. by Jean-Louis Barrault, New York
  Univ. Pr. 1958 $10.00
Rosbottom, Ronald C. *Marivaux's Novels: Theme and Function in Early Eighteenth-
  Century Narrative.* Fairleigh Dickinson Univ. Pr. 1975 $22.50

MAUPASSANT, GUY DE. 1850–1893

A disciple of Gustave Flaubert, Maupassant is one of the most popular
writers of the modern short story, of which he published more than 300. He
also wrote six novels, including *Bel-ami* (1885) and *Pierre and Jean.* A native
of Normandy and a former civil servant, Maupassant demonstrated in his
short stories his concern with those two worlds. Among the most famous
are "The Necklace" and "Mademoiselle Fifi." His attitude toward bourgeois
life was a mixture of contempt and pity, and like his master, Flaubert,
Maupassant was a pessimist at heart. Despite his prolific literary output,
Maupassant suffered from mental disease brought on by syphilis, and he
died insane at the age of 43.

BOOKS BY MAUPASSANT

The Life Work of Henri René Guy de Maupassant. Ed. and intro. by Robert Arnot and
  Paul Bourge, Darby 17 vols. repr. of 1903 ed. 1983 lib. bdg. $550.00
The Complete Novels of Guy de Maupassant. Darby repr. of 1928 ed. 1980 lib. bdg.
  $35.00
Best Short Stories of Guy de Maupassant. Intro. by R. R. Canon, *Airmont Class. Ser.*
  pap. $1.50
Selected Stories. Trans. by Andrew R. MacAndrew, intro. by Edward D. Sullivan,
  New Amer. Lib. 1984 pap. $4.95
Pierre and Jean. 1888. Trans. by Leonard Tancock, *Penguin Class. Ser.* 1979 pap. $3.95
Woman's Life. Trans. by H. N. Sloman, *Penguin Class Ser.* 1978 pap. $3.95

BOOKS ABOUT MAUPASSANT

Boyd, Ernest. *Guy de Maupassant: A Biographical Study.* Richard West repr. of 1926
  ed. 1973 $30.00
Steegmuller, Francis. *Maupassant: A Lion in the Path. Select Bibliographies Repr. Ser.*
  Ayer repr. of 1949 ed. $21.00
Sullivan, Edward D. *Maupassant the Novelist.* Greenwood repr. of 1954 ed. 1978 lib.
  bdg. $24.75
Wallace, A. H. *Guy de Maupassant. Twayne's World Authors Ser.* G. K. Hall 1973 lib.
  bdg. $12.50

MAURIAC, FRANÇOIS. 1885–1970 (NOBEL PRIZE 1952)

Most of Mauriac's novels are set in his birthplace, Bordeaux. They reflect
his classical culture and his meditation on the gospels and the Catholic contemplative writers. He is a moralist, presenting always the eternal conflict:
the world and the flesh against Christian faith and charity. "Every one of
his novels is a fresh attempt and an adventure into the unknown, though every one of them ends monotonously with the gift of grace that the novelist
insists upon imparting to his sinners" (Henri Peyre). Mauriac resisted the

Nazi invaders and the Vichy regime consistently and courageously during World War II. He was elected to the French Academy in 1933 and received the Nobel Prize in 1952.

BOOKS BY MAURIAC

Letters on Art and Literature. Trans. by Mario Pei, *Essay and General Lit. Index Repr. Ser.* Associated Faculty Pr. repr. of 1953 ed. 1970 $17.50
Second Thoughts: Reflections on Literature and on Life. Essay Index Repr. Ser. Ayer repr. of 1961 ed. $12.50
Memoirs intérieurs. Trans. by Gerard Hopkins, Farrar 1961 $4.75
Thérèse. 1927. Trans. by Gerard Hopkins, Farrar 1951 o.p.

BOOKS ABOUT MAURIAC

Moloney, Michael. *François Mauriac: A Critical Study.* Ohio Univ. Pr. (Swallow) 1958 $5.00
Scott, Malcolm. *Mauriac's Politics.* Columbia Univ. Pr. 1980 $16.00
Smith, Maxwell A. *François Mauriac. Twayne's World Authors Ser.* Irvington 1970 lib. bdg. $15.95
Stratford, Philip. *Faith and Fiction: Creative Process in Greene and Mauriac.* Univ. of Notre Dame Pr. 1964 pap. $9.95

MOLIERE (pseud. of Jean-Baptiste Poquelin). 1622–1673

The father of French comedy, Molière is by far the most popular of all French playwrights. A master of all comic forms ranging from farce to comedies of the intellect, Molière's brilliant accomplishments as a prolific dramatist were grounded in 12 years of struggles as an actor and as director of his own theater company in the French provinces. The success of his *Les précieuses ridicules* (*The Pretentious Young Ladies*) in 1659 won him the friendship and support of Louis XIV. His theater is distinguished by the expression of universal truths through a comic medium often using exaggerated and artificial plots. Beneath the laughter provoked by Molière's plays, there is usually a serious underlying reality. His ethical position is one that advocates a middle-of-the-road, practical approach to life. His most important plays include *Les précieuses ridicules* (1659), *The School for Wives* (1662), *Tartuffe* (1669), *Don Juan* (1665), *The Misanthrope* (1666), *The Miser* (1668), *The Would-Be Gentleman* (1670), *The Learned Ladies* (1672), and *The Imaginary Invalid* (1673).

BOOKS BY MOLIÈRE

Eight Plays by Molière. Amereon $20.95
One-Act Comedies of Molière. Trans. by Albert Bermel, Ungar repr. of 1961 ed. 1975 pap. $5.95

BOOKS ABOUT MOLIÈRE

Bulgakov, Mikhail. *Molière.* Methuen 1983 pap. $4.95
Eustis, Alvin. *Molière as Ironic Contemplator.* Mouton text ed. 1974 pap. $26.00
Fernandez, Ramon. *Molière: The Man Seen through the Plays.* Octagon repr. of 1958 ed. 1980 lib. bdg. $16.00

Gaines, James F. *Social Structures in Molière's Theatre.* Ohio State Univ. Pr. 1984 $22.50

Gossman, Lionel. *Men and Masks: A Study of Molière.* Johns Hopkins Univ. Pr. repr. of 1963 ed. 1969 pap. $7.95

Gross, Nathan. *From Gesture to Idea: Aesthetics and Ethics in Molière.* Columbia Univ. Pr. 1982 $24.00

Howarth, W. D. *Molière: A Playwright and His Audience. Major European Authors Ser.* Cambridge Univ. Pr. 1982 $54.50 pap. $16.95

Hubert, Judd D. *Molière and the Comedy of Intellect.* Russell repr. of 1962 ed. 1971 $13.50; Univ. of California Pr. 1974 $30.00

Masters, Brian. *A Student's Guide to Molière.* Heinemann text ed. 1970 pap. $5.00

Turnell, Martin. *The Classical Moment: Studies of Corneille, Molière, and Racine.* Greenwood repr. of 1948 ed. 1971 lib. bdg. $29.75

Wadsworth, Philip A. *Molière and the Italian Theatrical Tradition.* Summa 1977 $13.95

MONTAIGNE, MICHEL EYQUEM DE. 1533–1592

Montaigne invented the essay genre and his *Essays* are a vast compendium of his thoughts, sentiments, reflections, and opinions, as they were put down and gathered together by him in the course of a long, peaceful life at his chateau near Bordeaux. A student of the law, he became counselor to the Parlement of Bordeaux. After attending the royal court in Paris and Rouen, he retired to his property at Montaigne in Périgord in 1571, where he dedicated himself to reading and study in his library tower and to the composition of his *Essays.* Aside from a journey to Italy (of which he kept a detailed diary), and two terms as mayor of Bordeaux, the principal occupation of his mature years was the nurturing of his book, which first appeared in 1580, and of which revised editions appeared in 1588 and 1595. In the *Essays*, where his thought evolves from stoicism to skepticism and to epicureanism, Montaigne's principal topic is himself; he presents in intimate detail the changing matter of his daily existence, his thoughts and his emotions, in an attempt to understand his essential being. In so doing, Montaigne created a mirror for all mankind. He is at once a most individual and a most universal author.

BOOKS BY MONTAIGNE

The Complete Works: Essays, Travel Journal, Letters. Trans. by Donald M. Frame, Stanford Univ. Pr. 1957 $42.50. Most accurate and readable modern English translation of Montaigne.

The Essays of Montaigne. Trans. by John Florio, ed. by George Saintsbury, AMS Pr. 3 vols. $135.00. Often inaccurate, Florio's Elizabethan translation nevertheless was the first to popularize Montaigne for English readers. It has both historic flavor and importance.

Montaigne: Selections from the Essays. Trans. by Donald M. Frame, *Crofts Class. Ser.* Harlan Davidson text ed. 1973 pap. $3.75

BOOKS ABOUT MONTAIGNE

Frame, Donald M. *Montaigne: A Biography.* Harcourt 1965 $10.00; North Point Pr. 1984 pap. $15.00

————. *Montaigne's Discovery of Man: The Humanization of a Humanist.* Columbia
Univ. Pr. 1955 $13.50; Greenwood repr. of 1955 ed. 1983 lib. bdg. $32.50

Gide, André. *The Living Thoughts of Montaigne.* Arden Lib. repr. of 1939 ed. 1979 lib.
bdg. $17.50; Richard West repr. of 1942 ed. 1978 $12.50

Hallie, Philip P. *The Scar of Montaigne: An Essay in Personal Philosophy.* Wesleyan
Univ. Pr. 1966 $16.00

Regosin, Richard. *The Matter of My Book: Montaigne's "Essais" as the Book of the
Self.* Univ. of California Pr. 1977 $20.00

Sayce, R. A. *Essays of Montaigne: A Critical Exploration.* Northwestern Univ. Pr. 1972
$19.95

Screech, M. A. *Montaigne and Melancholy.* Susquehanna Univ. Pr. 1984 $24.50

Young, Charles L. *Emerson's Montaigne.* Arden Lib. repr. of 1941 ed. 1980 lib. bdg.
$30.00; Folcroft repr. of 1941 ed. 1976 lib. bdg. $25.00

MONTESQUIEU, CHARLES LOUIS DE SECONDAT, BARON DE LA BREDE ET DE. 1689–1755

[SEE Volume 3, Chapter 4.]

PASCAL, BLAISE. 1623–1662

[SEE Volume 4.]

PINGET, ROBERT. 1919–

Before deciding to write professionally, Pinget practiced law in his native
city of Geneva and studied painting at the Ecole des Beaux Arts in Paris. Of
all the new novelists, he is one of the more abstruse and has seemed little interested in attracting a following. Nevertheless, *The Inquisitory*, awarded
the 1962 Prix des Critiques, became a bestseller in France. It is essentially a
monologue—a deaf old servant's meandering, half-truthful responses to the
terse questions of an interrogator seeking information on a man who has
vanished. As the old man speaks, he brings to light all the vice and corruption of what appears to be a placid provincial town. In 1965, Pinget's
Quelqu'un (*Someone*), about a man's search for a scrap of paper, won the
Prix Femina. In addition to his work as a novelist, Pinget has also written a
number of plays.

BOOKS BY PINGET

Plays. Trans. by Barbara Wright and Samuel Beckett, Riverrun 2 vols. 1981 pap. ea.
$4.95

Three Plays. Hill & Wang 1968 $5.00

Between Fantoine and Agapa. 1951. Trans. by Barbara Wright, Red Dust 1983 $8.95.
A collection of short stories.

Baga. 1958. Trans. by John Stevenson, Riverrun repr. of 1967 ed. 1985 pap. $6.95

The Inquisitory. 1962. Riverrun 1982 pap. $11.95

Someone. 1965. Trans. by Barbara Wright, Red Dust 1984 $12.95

Passacaglia. 1969. Trans. by Barbara Wright, *New French Writing Ser.* Red Dust 1979
$6.95

Fable. Trans. by Barbara Wright, Red Dust 1980 $6.95

That Voice. 1975. Trans. by Barbara Wright, Red Dust 1983 $10.95

Mahu. Trans. by A. M. Sheridan-Smith, Riverrun 1984 pap. $6.95

BOOKS ABOUT PINGET

Henkels, Robert M., Jr. *Robert Pinget: The Novel as Quest.* Univ. of Alabama Pr. 1979
    $17.75
Mercier, Vivian. *The New Novel: From Queneau to Pinget.* Farrar 1971 pap. $2.95

PONGE, FRANCIS. 1899–

A poet long unread, Ponge has come into his own since the 1950s with admirers from Sartre to Sollers. Sartre considered him the poet of existentialism, and Ponge's emphasis on phenomenology and the priority and autonomous existence of things has attracted him to writers of the new novel and
to the group of semiotic critics centered around the literary review *Tel Quel.*
Among his major collections are *Le parti pris des choses* (*The Voice of
Things*), *Le grand recueil* (*The Big Collection*, 1961), and *Le savon* (*Soap*,
1967).

BOOKS BY PONGE

The Voice of Things. 1942. Trans. by Beth Archer, McGraw-Hill repr. of 1974 ed. con-
    sult publisher for information
Sun Placed in the Abyss and Other Texts. Trans. by Serge Gavronsky, Sun 1977 pap.
    $8.00

BOOKS ABOUT PONGE

Derrida, Jacques. *Signeponge Signsponge.* Trans. by Richard Rand, Columbia Univ.
    Pr. 1984 $21.00
Sorrell, Martin. *Francis Ponge. Twayne's World Authors Ser.* G. K. Hall 1981 $15.95

PROUST, MARCEL. 1871–1922

Proust is one of the most important seminal figures in modern literature.
In the last decade of the nineteenth century, he was already a famous Paris
socialite who attended the most fashionable *salons* of the day. With the
death of his parents in the early years of the twentieth century, Proust became a recluse who confined himself to his cork-lined bedroom on the Bou-
levard Haussmann where he concentrated on the composition of his great
masterpiece, *Remembrance of Things Past.* In recent years, it was discovered
that he had already prepared a first draft of the work in the 1890s in *Jean
Santeuil*, which was only published posthumously in 1952.

Remembrance of Things Past is a complex work that resists summary. In it
the narrator, who bears the same first name as the author, attempts to reconstruct his life from early childhood to middle age. In the process, he surveys French society at the turn of the century and describes the eventual decline of the aristocracy in the face of the rising middle class. The foibles and
hypocrisies of each are set forth through the medium of fiction. The process
of reconstruction of Marcel's past life is made possible by the psychological
device of involuntary memory; according to this theory, all of our past lies
hidden within us only to be rediscovered and brought to the surface by
some unexpected sense perception. In the final volume of the work, the nar-

rator, who has succeeded in recapturing his past, resolves to preserve it through the Work of Art, his novel.

BOOKS BY PROUST

Marcel Proust: Selected Letters, 1880–1903. Trans. by Ralph Manheim, ed. by Philip Kolb, Doubleday 1984 pap. $9.95

Marcel Proust: Letters to His Mother. Ed. by George D. Painter, Greenwood repr. of 1956 ed. 1973 lib. bdg. $18.75

Pleasures and Days: And Other Writings. Trans. by Louise Varèse, Gerard Hopkins, and B. Dupee, Fertig repr. of 1957 ed. 1978 $24.50

Remembrance of Things Past. 1913–27. Trans. by C. K. Scott-Moncrieff, Terence Kilmartin, and Andreas Mayor, Random 3 vols. 1981 ea. $25.00 1982 pap. 3-vol. set $40.00. The definitive Pléiade edition. Includes: *Swann's Way, Within a Budding Grove, The Guermantes Way, The Cities of the Plain, The Captive, The Fugitive,* and *The Past Recaptured.*

BOOKS ABOUT PROUST

Albaret, Céleste. *Monsieur Proust: A Memoir.* McGraw-Hill 1977 pap. $4.95

Ellison, David R. *The Reading of Proust.* Johns Hopkins Univ. Pr. 1983 $22.50

Fowlie, Wallace. *A Reading of Proust.* Peter Smith $11.00; Univ. of Chicago Pr. 2d ed. 1985 pap. $14.00

Hindus, Milton. *Proustian Vision.* Southern Illinois Univ. Pr. 1967 lib. bdg. $7.00 pap. $2.45

Houston, John P. *The Shape and Style of Proust's Novel.* Wayne State Univ. Pr. 1982 $14.95

Maurois, André. *Proust: Portrait of a Genius.* Carroll & Graf 1984 pap. $10.95

Painter, George. *Marcel Proust: A Biography.* Random 2 vols. 1978 ea. $12.95 pap. ea. $4.95

Peyre, Henri. *Marcel Proust.* Columbia Univ. Pr. 1970 pap. $2.50

Pierre-Quint, Léon. *Marcel Proust: His Life and Work.* Darby repr. of 1927 ed. 1984 lib. bdg. $50.00

Poulet, Georges. *Proustian Space.* Trans. by Elliott Coleman, Johns Hopkins Univ. Pr. 1977 $12.00

Price, Larkin B., ed. *Marcel Proust: A Critical Panorama.* Univ. of Illinois Pr. 1973 $24.95

Shattuck, Roger. *Marcel Proust. Modern Masters Ser.* Penguin 1974 pap. $2.95; Princeton Univ. Pr. repr. of 1974 ed. 1982 $22.50 pap. $6.95

Spalding, Philip A. *A Reader's Handbook to Proust.* Folcroft repr. of 1959 ed. 1974 lib. bdg. $35.00

QUENEAU, RAYMOND. 1903–1976

This author of treatises on mathematics and other scholarly works has made his reputation writing comic novels. Queneau (through one of his characters) once defined humor as "an attempt to purge lofty feelings of all the baloney." Roger Shattuck interprets his philosophy: "Life is of course absurd and it is ludicrous to take it seriously; only the comic is serious." Life is so serious to Queneau that only laughter makes it bearable. He has written a play, screenplays, poetry, numerous articles, and many novels—the first of which, *Le chiendent* (*The Bark Tree*), was published in 1933. In *Exercises in Style*, he tells a simple anecdote 99 different ways.

"*The Blue Flowers*," says *Life*, "represents Queneau at his best. . . . The jokes, puns, double-entendres, deceptions, wild events, tricky correspondences—and always the bawdy language growing in fields of glorious rhetoric—make it a feast of comic riches." The influence of CHARLIE CHAPLIN (see Vol. 3) as well as JAMES JOYCE (see Vol. 1) is detectable in Queneau's fiction.

BOOKS BY QUENEAU

Selected Poems. Trans. by Teo Savory, Unicorn Pr. bilingual ed. $15.00 pap. $5.00
The Bark Tree. 1933. Intro. by Barbara Wright, New Directions 1971 pap. $3.95
Exercises in Style. 1947. Trans. by Barbara Wright, New Directions 2d ed. 1981 $12.95 pap. $5.95
We Always Treat Women Too Well. 1947. Trans. by Barbara Wright, intro. by Valerie Caton, New Directions 1981 $14.95 pap. $5.95
The Sunday of Life. 1952. Trans. by Barbara Wright, New Directions 1977 $12.00 pap. $3.95
Zazie in the Metro. 1959. Trans. by Barbara Wright, Riverrun 1982 $13.95 pap. $7.95
The Blue Flowers. 1965. Trans. by Barbara Wright, New Directions 2d ed. 1985 pap. $8.95

BOOKS ABOUT QUENEAU

Guicharnaud, Jacques. *Raymond Queneau*. Columbia Univ. Pr. 1965 pap. $2.50
Mercier, Vivian. *The New Novel: From Queneau to Pinget*. Farrar 1971 pap. $2.95

RABELAIS, FRANÇOIS. 1494?–1553?

One of the leading humanist writers of the French Renaissance, Rabelais was at first a Franciscan and then a Benedictine monk, a celebrated physician and professor of anatomy, and later curé of Meudon. The works of Rabelais are filled with life to the overflowing. His principal protagonists, Gargantua and his son, Pantagruel, are appropriately giants—not only in size, but also in spirit and action. The five books of their adventures are separate works, containing, in different measure, adventures, discussions, farcical scenes, jokes, games, satires, philosophical commentaries, and anything else that a worldly, learned man of genius such as Rabelais could pour into his work. His style is innovative and idiosyncratic, marked by humorous neologisms made up from the learned languages, Greek and Latin, side by side with the most earthy, humble, and rough words of the street and barnyard. His *Gargantua*, published in 1534, satirizes the traditional education of Parisian theologians and, in the Abbé de Thélème episode, recommends a free, hedonistic society of handsome young men and women in contrast to the restrictive life of monasticism. The gigantic scope of Rabelais's work also reflects the Renaissance thirst for encyclopedic knowledge.

BOOKS BY RABELAIS

The Portable Rabelais. Ed. by Samuel Putnam, *Viking Portable Lib.* Penguin 1977 pap. $7.95
Gargantua and Pantagruel. AMS Pr. 3 vols. repr. of 1900 ed. $135.00; trans. by Thomas Urquhart and Peter A. Motteux, Beil text ed. $40.00; Biblio Dist. 2 vols.

repr. of 1929 ed. 1980 ea. $12.95; trans. by John M. Cohen, *Penguin Class. Ser.* 1955 pap. $6.95

BOOKS ABOUT RABELAIS

Bakhtin, Mikhail. *Rabelais and His World.* Trans. by Helene Iswolsky, intro. by Michael Holquist, fwd. by Krystyna Pomorska, Indiana Univ. Pr. 1984 $29.50 pap. $10.95

Coleman, Dorothy. *Rabelais: A Critical Study in Prose Fiction.* Cambridge Univ. Pr. 1971 pap. $13.95

Febvre, Lucien. *The Problem of Unbelief in the Sixteenth Century: The Religion of Rabelais.* Trans. by Beatrice Gottlieb, Harvard Univ. Pr. text ed. 1982 $35.00 1985 pap. $9.95

Frame, Donald M. *François Rabelais.* Harcourt 1977 $12.95

Screech, M. A. *Rabelais.* Cornell Univ. Pr. 1980 $49.50

RACINE, JEAN. 1639–1699

Racine is considered the greatest of French tragic dramatists. His themes are derived from Greco-Roman, biblical, and oriental sources and are developed in the neoclassic manner: keeping to few characters, observing the "three unities" (see above, under Corneille), and writing in regular 12-syllable verses called "alexandrines." In contrast to Corneille, Racine relies on greater simplicity of action, the principle of verisimilitude, and the reduction of his plays to the conflict of inner emotions rather than external incidents. As a Jansenist who believed that man deprived of grace was subject to the tyranny of his instincts, Racine was interested in portraying human passions—particularly the passion of love—in a state of crisis. Racine is also one of the greatest of all French poets, and his plays are a challenge to any translator. His major tragedies include *Andromaque, Britannicus* (1669), *Bérénice* (1670), *Iphigénie* (1674), and *Phèdre.*

BOOKS BY RACINE

Best Plays of Racine: Andromaque, Britannicus, Phaedra, Athalia. Trans. by Lacy Lockert, Princeton Univ. Pr. 1936 pap. $11.95

Four Greek Plays; Andromache, Iphigenia, Phaedra, Athaliah. Trans. by R. C. Knight, Cambridge Univ. Pr. 1982 $39.50 pap. $15.95

Racine: Five Plays. Trans. by Kenneth Muir, Hill & Wang 1969 pap. $7.95

Racine's Mid-Career Tragedies. Trans. by Lacy Lockert, Princeton Univ. Pr. 1958 $29.00

Andromache and Other Plays. Trans. by John Cairncross, *Penguin Class. Ser.* 1976 pap. $3.95

Andromache. 1667. Trans. by Richard Wilbur, Harcourt 1984 pap. $6.95

Phedre. 1677. Trans. by Margaret Rawlings, Dutton bilingual ed. 1962 pap. $6.95; (with the title *Phaedra*) trans. by Robert Lowell, Octagon 1972 lib. bdg. $12.00

BOOKS ABOUT RACINE

Barthes, Roland. *On Racine.* Octagon repr. 1977 lib. bdg. $10.00; Performing Arts 1983 pap. $7.95

Bowra, Maurice. *The Simplicity of Racine.* Arden Lib. repr. of 1956 ed. 1978 lib. bdg. $10.00

Butler, P. F. *A Student's Guide to Racine.* Heinemann text ed. 1974 pap. $5.00
Giraudoux, Jean. *Racine.* Folcroft repr. of 1938 ed. lib. bdg. $9.50; Richard West repr. of 1938 ed. 1980 lib. bdg. $10.00
Goldmann, Lucien. *The Hidden God.* Trans. by Philip Thody, Humanities Pr. text ed. 1976 $24.00
Knight, R. C., ed. *Racine.* Aurora 1970 $2.50
Lapp, John C. *Aspects of Racinian Tragedy.* Univ. of Toronto Pr. 1955 $22.50
Mourgues, Odette de. *Racine: Or the Triumph of Relevance.* Cambridge Univ. Pr. 1967 o.p.
Muir, Kenneth. *Last Periods of Shakespeare, Racine, Ibsen.* Darby repr. of 1961 ed. lib. bdg. $40.00; Wayne State Univ. Pr. 1961 $5.00
Turnell, Martin. *Jean Racine: Dramatist.* New Directions 1972 $17.75
Weinberg, Bernard. *The Art of Jean Racine.* Univ. of Chicago Pr. (Phoenix Bks.) 1969 pap. $3.45
Yarrow, P. J. *Racine.* Rowman 1978 $17.50

RADIGUET, RAYMOND. 1903–1923

This genius died of typhoid fever at 20, leaving one volume of unpublished poems, *The Devil Within,* and two novels, *Devil in the Flesh* (1923) and *Count d'Orgel* (1924). He was a close friend of Cocteau, who said of him: "One is rather appalled by a boy of twenty who publishes the sort of book that can't be written at his age." Radiguet's novels depict the new *mal du siècle* that had broken out during the years following World War I. He combines ingeniously a formal elegance with a licentious content. Radiguet's works deserve reading, both for their inherent excellence and for their influence on Cocteau and others of his generation.

BOOKS BY RADIGUET

Devil in the Flesh. Trans. by A. M. Smith, Boyars text ed. 1968 pap. $7.50
Count D'Orgel. Grove 1970 pap. $1.25

RIMBAUD, (JEAN NICOLAS) ARTHUR. 1854–1891

Rimbaud, a symbolist poet and visionary, abandoned literature at 19. He was shot and wounded in a quarrel with the poet Verlaine, left France, wandered in many countries, and finally became a trader in Abyssinia. He returned to France to die in 1891.

Roger Shattuck has written in the *New York Review of Books* that Rimbaud's work divides itself "naturally into three parts. There are the poems, highly personal and written in more or less regular verse . . . from 1870 to 1872. Then there is the autobiographical prose work, *A Season in Hell,* thirty intense and loosely connected pages composed in four months beginning April 1873. Passing harsh judgment on his past, Rimbaud appears to bid farewell to the long turbulent relationship with Verlaine and to the 'madness' that Rimbaud had cultivated in order to achieve a new level of living and writing. Thirdly, there is the miscellaneous collection of prose poems called *Illuminations* (probably written 1872–74). In *Illuminations,* he appears finally to make peace with the world and to seek, by name, the order and reason he had scorned earlier." Shattuck believes that the secret of Rimbaud's brilliantly concentrated brief life in literature was the result of precociously swift emotional and mental development, which allowed intelligence to separate itself from emotion—a mark of maturity—at a very early age. This produced a poetic harvest "incredibly rich and convincing." Rimbaud has fascinated English-speaking poets from HART CRANE (see Vol. 1) and POUND (see Vol. 1) to the present generation. The preoccupations "fused" in his poetry were, wrote Shattuck, adventure, magic, alchemy, drugs, the "abominations" fostered by the decadents, and a form of "messianic evolutionism that proclaimed a world made new through the mechanics of history."

BOOKS BY RIMBAUD

Complete Works. Trans. by Paul Schmidt, Harper 1976 pap. $6.25
Complete Works with Selected Letters. Trans. by Wallace Fowlie, Univ. of Chicago Pr. repr. of 1967 ed. pap. $8.95
Illuminations and Other Prose Poems. Trans. by Louise Varèse, New Directions bilingual ed. 1957 pap. $5.95
A Season in Hell (and *Illuminations*). Trans. by Enid R. Peschel, Oxford 1973 pap. $8.95
A Season in Hell (and *The Drunken Boat*). Trans. by Louise Varèse, New Directions bilingual ed. 1961 pap. $3.95

BOOKS ABOUT RIMBAUD

Ahearn, Edward J. *Rimbaud: Visions and Habitations.* Univ. of California Pr. text ed. 1983 $34.50
Chadwick, Charles. *Arthur Rimbaud.* Humanities Pr. text ed. 1978 pap. $13.00
Cohn, Robert G. *The Poetry of Rimbaud.* Princeton Univ. Pr. 1973 $42.50
Hackett, C. A. *Rimbaud: A Critical Introduction.* Cambridge Univ. Pr. 1981 $42.50 pap. $14.95
Houston, John P. *The Design of Rimbaud's Poetry.* Greenwood repr. of 1963 ed. 1977 lib. bdg. $22.50
Miller, Henry. *Time of the Assassins: A Study of Rimbaud.* New Directions 1962 pap. $6.95
Perloff, Marjorie. *The Poetics of Indeterminacy.* Northwestern Univ. Pr. repr. 1981 pap. $9.95
Poulet, Georges. *Exploding Poetry: Baudelaire-Rimbaud.* Trans. by Françoise Meltzer, Univ. of Chicago Pr. 1984 lib. bdg. $15.00
Starkie, Enid. *Arthur Rimbaud.* New Directions rev. ed. 1968 pap. $9.95

ROBBE-GRILLET, ALAIN. 1922–

Robbe-Grillet, one of the leading practitioners of the French new novel, began his career as an agricultural expert and spent time in Africa and the French Antilles doing research on tropical fruits. With his early novel *The Erasers,* he established his importance as an avant-garde writer. Generally, he avoids traditional use of character and plot in the novel and places emphasis on the "objectification of things." In *Jealousy* (1957), a romantic triangle is interpreted with utter subjectivity through a "privileged witness," a husband whose suspicions have driven him to the brink. Germaine Brée has written, "His theory was that the writer should thoroughly cover the phenomenology of the object, appealing to the reader to make the act of reading part of the total creative process." Other works in which he employed this theory include *Le voyeur* (1955) and *In the Labyrinth*. He has also applied the use of extremely detailed description in such films as *Last Year at Marienbad*, *L'immortelle* (1962), and *Trans Europe Express* (1966). Robbe-Grillet has written lucidly on literary theory in his *For a New Novel*.

BOOKS BY ROBBE-GRILLET

Two Novels: Jealousy and In the Labyrinth. Trans. by Richard Howard, Grove 1960 pap. $4.95

The Erasers. 1953. Trans. by Richard Howard, Grove (Evergreen) 1964 pap. $9.95

The Voyeur. Trans. by Richard Howard, Grove (Evergreen) 1958 pap. $4.95

In the Labyrinth. 1959. Trans. by Richard Howard, Grove 1978 pap. $2.95

Last Year at Marienbad: Text for the Film by Alain Resnais. 1961. Trans. by Richard Howard, Grove (Evergreen) 1962 pap. $4.95

For a New Novel: Essays on Fiction. 1963. *Essay Index Repr. Ser.* Ayer repr. of 1965 ed. $17.00; trans. by Richard Howard, Grove 1966 pap. $2.25

La maison de rendez-vous. 1965. Trans. by Richard Howard, Grove 1982 pap. $6.95

Project for a Revolution in New York. Trans. by Richard Howard, Grove (Evergreen) 1972 pap. $3.95

Djinn. Trans. by Yvonne Lenard, Grove (Evergreen) 1982 $10.95 pap. $4.95

BOOKS ABOUT ROBBE-GRILLET

Armes, Roy. *The Films of Alain Robbe-Grillet*. Benjamins North Am. 1981 $28.00

Fletcher, John. *Alain Robbe-Grillet. Contemporary Writers Ser.* Methuen 1983 pap. $4.75

Leki, Ilona. *Alain Robbe-Grillet. Twayne's World Authors Ser.* G. K. Hall 1983 lib. bdg. $17.95

Stoltzfus, Ben. *Alain Robbe-Grillet: The Body of the Text*. Fairleigh Dickinson Univ. Pr. 1985 $27.50

Van Wert, William F. *The Film Career of Alain Robbe-Grillet*. G. K. Hall 1977 pap. $7.80; ed. by Ronald Gottesman, Redgrave 1979 pap. $8.90

ROLLAND, ROMAIN. 1866–1944 (NOBEL PRIZE 1915)

Rolland was a novelist, playwright, biographer, and critic. Professor of the history of music at the Sorbonne, he wrote a number of books about music and musicians, as well as one on the great ambition of his life, the establishment of a people's theater. *Essays on Music* (1948) has been translated by David Ewen. His *Prophets of New India* has been published in two volumes as *The Life of Ramakrishna* and *The Life of Vivekananda* (o.p.). *Jean-Christophe* is a fine example of the "biographical" novel, a form of fiction in which the narrative follows exactly the sequence of events in the hero's life. It was the first great novel about a musical genius and contains interesting reflectons on music, art, and letters. On completion of *Jean-Christophe*, Rolland was awarded the Grand Prize in Literature by the French Academy (1913) and the Nobel Prize (1915).

BOOKS BY ROLLAND

Hermann Hesse and Romain Rolland: Correspondence, Diary. Trans. by M. G. Hesse,
    Humanities Pr. text ed. 1978 $15.00
Richard Strauss and Romain Rolland: Correspondence, Diary and Essays. Ed. by Rollo
    Myers, Univ. of California Pr. 1968 o.p.
Jean-Christophe. 1904–12. Trans. by Gilbert Cannan, Avon 3 vols. 1969 o.p.
Handel. 1916. AMS Pr. repr. of 1916 ed. $18.50; Johnson Repr. repr. of 1916 ed.
    $17.00
Musical Tour through the Land of the Past. 1922. Trans. by B. Miall, *Essay Index Repr.
    Ser.* Ayer repr. of 1922 ed. $17.00
Life of Ramakrishna. Vedanta Pr. 1952 $4.50

BOOKS ABOUT ROLLAND

Starr, William T. *Romain Rolland and a World at War.* AMS Pr. repr. of 1956 ed.
    $27.00
Zweig, Stefan. *Romain Rolland: The Man and His Works.* Ayer repr. of 1921 ed. 1973
    lib. bdg. $24.50; *Studies in French Lit.* Haskell repr. of 1921 ed. 1970 lib. bdg.
    $58.95

ROMAINS, JULES (pseud. of Jules Louis Farigoule). 1885–1972

Romains first appeared in English as a medical researcher, with his scientific work *Eyeless Sight: A Study of Extra-Retinal Vision and the Paroptic Sense.* He then became known as a dramatist. His first novel, *The Death of a Nobody,* is still considered by many his masterpiece. The serial novel *Men of Good Will* begins in 1933, with its political unrest recalling the sixth of October 1908, six years before World War I, the day on which the first volume opens. The narrative combines imaginary events with historical, and fictitious characters with actual. This epic novel, with its vast canvas and mass of characters, is an expression of the author's "unanimist" conception of life, a theory that defines society through the individual's relation to masses or groups, and contends that a group of people with a unanimous emotion (such as good will) can develop a mass power superior to any other force. Romains was international president of PEN from 1938 to 1941 and was elected to the French Academy in 1946.

BOOKS BY ROMAINS

The Death of a Nobody. 1911. Trans. by D. MacCarthy and S. Waterlow, Fertig repr.
    of 1944 ed. 1977 $17.50
Eyeless Sight. 1923. Intro. by Leslie Shepard, Citadel Pr. 1978 pap. $4.95
Knock, or the Triumph of Medicine: A Comedy in Three Acts. 1923. Trans. by Betty
    Scherr Sacks, Vantage 1984 $7.95

BOOK ABOUT ROMAINS

Boak, Denis. *Jules Romains. Twayne's World Authors Ser.* 1974 o.p.

RONSARD, PIERRE DE. 1524–1585

Ronsard is one of the principal originators of European poetic tradition as it has existed since the Renaissance. Dissatisfied with native French poetic models, and taken with the example of Greek, Latin, and Italian poetry, he set about to make French poems according to their models. He was the first to imitate systematically forms such as the ode, the sonnet, the epic, the eclogue, and the elegy. He attracted a circle of sympathetic poets; since the group amounted to seven, they called themselves the *Pléiade*, after the seven-starred constellation. Their professed aim was to go back to the original foundations, and they found these in the poetry of early Italy, and ancient Greece and Rome. Their manifesto was an essay by Joachim du Bellay called "Défense et illustration de la langue française," the first significant work of French literary criticism.

Of Ronsard's large and varied literary works (including his lyric Odes, his *Amours* or love poems addressed to Cassandre, and his *Sonnets pour Hélène*, a new series of love poems), the best known are his sonnets, rich in image and delicate of construction.

BOOKS BY RONSARD

Poems of Pierre de Ronsard. Ed. by Nicholas Kilmer, Univ. of California Pr. 1979 $22.00

Songs and Sonnets of Pierre de Ronsard. Trans. by Curtis H. Page, Hyperion Pr. repr. of 1924 ed. 1978 $15.00

Sonnets pour Hélène by Pierre de Ronsard. Trans. by Humbert Wolfe, Richard West repr. of 1934 ed. $25.00

BOOKS ABOUT RONSARD

Armstrong, Elizabeth. *Ronsard and the Age of Gold.* Cambridge Univ. Pr. 1968 $38.50

Hanisch, Gertrude S. *Love Elegies of the Renaissance: Marot, Louise Labé and Ronsard.* Anma Libri 1979 pap. $25.00

Jones, K. R. W. *Pierre de Ronsard. Twayne's World Authors Ser.* G. K. Hall $12.50; *Twayne's World Authors Ser.* Irvington 1970 lib. bdg. $15.95

Lewis, Wyndham D. B. *Ronsard.* Norwood repr. of 1946 ed. $25.00

Quainton, Malcolm. *Ronsard's Ordered Chaos: Visions of Flux and Stability in the Poetry of Pierre de Ronsard.* Barnes & Noble 1980 $28.50

ROUSSEAU, JEAN JACQUES. 1712–1778

[SEE Volume 3, Chapter 4.]

SADE (DONATIEN ALPHONSE FRANÇOIS), COMTE DE (called Marquis de Sade). 1740–1814

A French novelist and playwright, the Marquis de Sade is largely known for his pathological sexual views and ethical nihilism. In recent years, his literary work has reached a larger public, reflecting freer sexual attitudes and the almost total relaxation of censorship. Typical of his output is his novel *Justine* (1791), which presents the theme of vice triumphant over virtue, and depicts the molestation of a virtuous girl and orgies of sexual perversion in a monastery. Other well-known works of Sade include *Philosophy in the Bedroom* (1795), *Juliette* (1797), and *Aline and Valcourt or The Philosophic Novel.*

Books by Sade

One Hundred Twenty Days of Sodom and Other Writings. Ed. by Austryn Wainhouse and Richard Seaver, Grove 1966 pap. $12.50

Juliette. Trans. by Austryn Wainhouse, Grove (Evergreen) 1968 pap. $14.95

Justine. Trans. by Richard Seaver and Austryn Wainhouse, intro. by Maurice Blanchot, Grove 1971 pap. $12.50. Includes *Philosophy in the Bedroom, Eugénie de Franval*, and other writings.

Books about Sade

Barthes, Roland. *Sade-Fourier-Loyola*. Trans. by Richard Miller, Hill & Wang 1976 o.p.

Bloch, Iwan. *Marquis de Sade: The Man and His Age*. Trans. by James Bruce, AMS Pr. repr. of 1931 ed. $15.00

De Jean, Joan. *Literary Fortifications: Rousseau, Laclos, Sade*. Princeton Univ. Pr. text ed. 1984 $36.50

Lynch, Lawrence W. *The Marquis de Sade. Twayne's World Authors Ser.* G. K. Hall 1984 lib. bdg. $16.95

SAINT EXUPERY, ANTOINE DE. 1900–1944

After escaping death in several accidents while flying as a pilot over the most dangerous sections of the French airmail service in South America, Africa, and the South Atlantic, Saint Exupéry was reported missing over southern France in 1944. He was mourned as a hero who had caught the imagination of men and women throughout the world. His books are written in beautifully simple poetic prose, exalting man's courage and heroic hope. He had a rare gift for coining unusual images. *Night Flight* was introduced by André Gide and was at once proclaimed a masterpiece. *Wind, Sand and Stars* is a series of tales, interspersed with philosophical reflections on the earth as a planet and on the nobility of the common man. *Flight to Arras* is the author's own account of a hopeless reconnaissance sortie during the tragic days of May 1940. He probes the meaning of death and war with a courageous belief in the final victory of love and good.

Books by Saint Exupéry

Airman's Odyssey. 1939. Trans. by Lewis Galantiere, Harcourt 1984 pap. $6.95. Includes *Wind, Sand and Stars*, trans. by Lewis Galantiere; *Night Flight*, trans. by Stuart Gilbert; and *Flight to Arras*, trans. by Lewis Galantiere.

Southern Mail. Trans. by Curtis Cate, Harcourt repr. of 1929 ed. 1972 pap. $2.95

Night Flight. 1931. Trans. by Stuart Gilbert, Harcourt repr. of 1932 ed. 1974 pap. $2.95

Wind, Sand and Stars. 1939. Harcourt 1967 pap. $3.95

Flight to Arras. Trans. by Lewis Galantiere, Harcourt repr. of 1942 ed. 1969 pap. $2.95

The Little Prince. 1943. Trans. by Katherine Woods, Harcourt 1982 pap. $4.95

The Wisdom of the Sands. 1948. Trans. by Stuart Gilbert, intro. by Wallace Fowlie, Univ. of Chicago Pr. 1979 pap. $10.95

BOOKS ABOUT SAINT EXUPÉRY

Breaux, Adele. *Saint Exupéry in America, 1942–1943: A Memoir.* Fairleigh Dickinson Univ. Pr. 1971 $16.50

Robinson, Joy M. *Antoine de Saint Exupéry.* Twayne's World Authors Ser. G. K. Hall 1984 lib. bdg. $14.95

SAINT-JOHN PERSE (pseud. of Alexis Saint-Léger Léger). 1887–1975 (NOBEL PRIZE 1960)

Anabasis, the work that established Saint-John Perse as the symbolist successor to Arthur Rimbaud, was generally considered his masterpiece until the publication of the long poem *Seamarks.* The *New Republic* said that this, "a moving celebration set in the ambience of the sea, establishes him once again as the major poet of our time in any language." *Birds,* a meditation on flight illustrated by his close friend Braque, "contains some of the poet's finest lines" (*LJ*).

Saint-John Perse managed to combine poetry with diplomacy most of his life. Born on a small family-owned island of Guadeloupe, he became a member of the French diplomatic corps and was permanent secretary of foreign affairs after Briand's death and until the Germans invaded France. Refusing to become a collaborationist, he fled to England, then Canada, and, at the request of Archibald MacLeish, came to the United States to act as consultant on French poetry to the Library of Congress. Manuscripts left behind when he left France were destroyed by the Nazis. He received the Nobel Prize in 1960.

BOOKS BY SAINT-JOHN PERSE

Collected Poems. Trans. by W. H. Auden, Princeton Univ. Pr. 1982 $60.00

Éloges and Other Poems. Trans. by Louise Varèse, Princeton Univ. Pr. 1956 $20.00

St.-John Perse: Letters. Ed. by Arthur J. Knodel, Princeton Univ. Pr. 1979 $38.50 pap. $12.95

Anabasis. 1924. Trans. by T. S. Eliot, Harcourt repr. of 1938 ed. 1970 pap. $2.95

Exile and Other Poems. Trans. by Denis Devlin, Princeton Univ. Pr. 2nd ed. 1953 o.p.

Birds. 1962. Trans. by Robert Fitzgerald, Princeton Univ. Pr. bilingual ed. 1966 $37.50

BOOK ABOUT SAINT-JOHN PERSE

Galand, René. *Saint-John Perse.* Twayne's World Authors Ser. G. K. Hall lib. bdg. $13.95

SARRAUTE, NATHALIE. 1902–

Nathalie Sarraute is the "thinker" among the practitioners of the new novel. In her essay on the art of fiction, *The Age of Suspicion,* she condemned the techniques used in the novel of the past and took a stand beside Robbe-Grillet as a leader of the avant-garde. The novel, she feels, must express "that element of indetermination, of opacity, and mystery that one's own actions always have for the one who lives them." Her works have now become known to an international public. Her ability to render fleeting awareness and the psychological states underlying articulate speech has won both praise and disdain. Janet Flanner has called Sarraute "the only one among the New Novel experimenters who appears finally to have struck her own style—intense, observational, and personal."

Of her novels, *The Golden Fruits*—about the Paris literary fortunes of an imaginary novel called "The Golden Fruits"—is "the most barren of extraneous decor, the most accomplished from the standpoint of her esthetic aims" (*SR*). *Tropisms*, her earliest (very brief) book, contains "all the raw material I have continued to develop in my later works." Her "tropisms," she says, are instinctive "sensations," or even "movements," "produced in us by the presence of others, or by objects from the outside world. [They hide] l neath the most commonplace conversations and the most everyday gestures." She regards her novels as composed of a series of tropisms of varying intensity.

Books by Sarraute

Collected Plays. Trans. by Maria Jolas and Barbara Wright, Braziller 1981 pap. $5.95
Tropisms. 1939. Trans. by Maria Jolas, Braziller 1957 pap. $4.95
Martereau. 1953. Trans. by Maria Jolas, Braziller 1959 o.p.
The Age of Suspicion: Essays on the Novel. 1956. Braziller $5.00
The Planetarium. 1959. Trans. by Maria Jolas, Riverrun 1980 pap. $4.95
The Golden Fruits. 1963. Trans. by Maria Jolas, Riverrun 1980 $10.95 pap. $4.95
Between Life and Death. 1968. Trans. by Maria Jolas, Riverrun 1980 $14.95 pap. $4.95
Do You Hear Them? 1970. Trans. by Maria Jolas, Braziller 1973 pap. $2.95
Fools Say. Braziller 1976 $7.95
The Use of Speech. 1980. Trans. by Barbara Wright, Braziller 1983 $10.95 pap. $5.95
Childhood. 1983. Trans. by Barbara Wright, Braziller 1984 $14.95 1985 pap. $8.95

Books about Sarraute

Besser, Gretchen R. *Nathalie Sarraute. Twayne's World Authors Ser.* G. K. Hall 1979 lib. bdg. $14.50
Minogue, Valerie. *Nathalie Sarraute: The War of the Words.* Columbia Univ. Pr. 1981 $22.00
Watson-Williams, Helen. *The Novels of Nathalie Sarraute.* Humanities Pr. text ed. 1981 pap. $20.50

SARTRE, JEAN-PAUL. 1905–1980

In his ironic autobiographical essay *The Words*, Sartre described the illusions and idealistic pretensions of the bourgeois family into which he had been born and his subsequent transformation into a writer. A graduate of the prestigious Ecole Normale Supérieure with an *agrégation* in philosophy, Sartre has been a major figure on the literary and philosophical scenes since the late 1930s. Widely known as an atheistic proponent of existentialism, he emphasized the priority of existence over preconceived essences and the importance of human freedom. In his first and best novel, *Nausea*, Sartre contrasted the fluidity of human consciousness with the apparent solidity of external reality, and satirized the hypocrisies and pretensions of bourgeois idealism. Sartre's theater is also highly ideological, emphasizing the importance of personal freedom and the commitment of the individual to social and political goals. His first play, *The Flies* (1943), was produced during the German occupation, despite its underlying message of defiance. One of his most popular plays is the one-act *No Exit* (1944), in which the traditional theological concept of hell is redefined in existentialist terms. In *Red Gloves* (*Les mains sales*, 1948), Sartre examines the pragmatic implications of the individual involved in political action through the mechanism of the Communist party and a changing historical situation.

Sartre has also made significant contributions to literary criticism in his ten-volume *Situations* and in works on Baudelaire, Genet, and Flaubert (*The Family Idiot*). (See also Volume 4.)

BOOKS BY SARTRE

Nausea. 1938. Trans. by Lloyd Alexander, Bentley repr. of 1949 ed. 1979 lib. bdg. $12.50; trans. by Lloyd Alexander, New Directions 1959 pap. $5.25

The Wall: Intimacy. 1939. Trans. by Lloyd Alexander, New Directions 3d ed. 1969 pap. $5.25

No Exit and Three Other Plays. Random (Vintage) 1955 pap. $3.95

Baudelaire. 1947. Trans. by Martin Turnell, New Directions 1950 pap. $6.95

Saint Genet: Actor and Martyr. 1952. New Amer. Lib. (Plume) pap. $4.95

The Words. 1964. Fawcett 1977 pap. $1.50; Random (Vintage) 1981 pap. $3.95

The Family Idiot: Gustave Flaubert, 1821–1857. Trans. by Carol Cosman, Univ. of Chicago Pr. 1981 vol. 1. $25.00

Essays on Language and Literature. Arden Lib. repr. of 1947 ed. 1982 consult publisher for information

Politics and Literature. Riverrun $12.95

Sartre on Theater. Trans. by Frank Jellinek, ed. by Michel Contat and Michel Rybalka, Pantheon 1976 $10.95 1978 pap. $5.95

Situations. Braziller bilingual ed. 1965 o.p.

BOOKS ABOUT SARTRE

Barnes, Hazel E. *Sartre and Flaubert.* Univ. of Chicago Pr. (Phoenix Bks.) 1982 pap. $10.95

Brée, Germaine. *Camus and Sartre: Crisis and Commitment.* Delacorte 1972 $7.95

Brosman, Catherine S. *Jean-Paul Sartre.* Twayne's World Authors Ser. G. K. Hall 1983 lib. bdg. $13.50 1984 pap. $5.95

Champigny, Robert R. *Stages on Sartre's Way, 1938–52.* Kraus 1959 $20.00

Goldthorpe, Phiannon. *Sartre: Literature and Theory.* Cambridge Univ. Pr. 1984 $42.50

Jameson, Fredric. *Sartre: The Origins of a Style.* Columbia Univ. Pr. repr. of 1961 ed. 1984 pap. $8.95

McCall, Dorothy K. *The Theatre of Jean-Paul Sartre.* Columbia Univ. Pr. 1969 $27.50 pap. $11.00

SEVIGNE, MME DE (Marie de Rabutin-Chantal, Marquise de Sévigné). 1626–1696

Mme de Sévigné's letters (written mostly to her daughter from 1648 to 1696) "reflect so accurately the spirit of the time in which they were written and the character and spirit of the woman who wrote them that the reader lives for a while in 17th century France." "They provide vivid pictures of French society in the age of Louis XIV, of the life of the aristocracy in Paris, at court, and in the provinces: and in them figure many of the great personages of the time." Mme de Sévigné is noted for "the unaffected elegance of her style" and "the acuteness of her observations."

BOOKS BY MME DE SÉVIGNÉ

Letters of Madame de Sévigné to Her Daughter and Her Friends. Intro. by Richard Aldington, Folcroft 2 vols. repr. of 1927 ed. 1974 lib. bdg. $85.00
Madame de Sévigné: Selected Letters. Ed. by L. W. Tancock, Penguin 1982 pap. $5.95

BOOKS ABOUT MME DE SÉVIGNÉ

Allentuch, Harriet R. *Madame de Sévigné: A Portrait in Letters.* Greenwood repr. of 1963 ed. 1978 lib. bdg. $22.50
Mossiker, Frances. *Madame de Sévigné: A Life and Letters.* Columbia Univ. Pr. repr. 1985 pap. $14.50; Knopf 1983 $22.95

SIMENON, GEORGES. 1909–

The prolific Belgian-born writer Georges Simenon has produced hundreds of fictional works under his own name and 17 pseudonyms in addition to more than 70 books about Inspector Maigret, long "the favorite sleuth of highbrow detective-story readers" (*SR*). More than 50 "Simenons" have been made into films. In addition to his mystery stories, since 1936 he has been writing what he calls "hard" books, the serious psychological novels now numbering well over 100. The autobiographical *Pedigree*, set in his native town of Liege, is perhaps his finest work. The recent publication of Simenon's intimate memoirs has attracted considerable attention. Simenon himself once said that he would never write a "great novel." Yet Gide called him "a great novelist, perhaps the greatest and truest novelist we have in French literature today," and Thornton Wilder found that Simenon's narrative gift extends "to the tips of his fingers."

The following are some of Simenon's novels, exclusive of the Maigret detective stories, that are in print.

BOOKS BY SIMENON

Aunt Jeanne. Trans. by Geoffrey Sainsbury, Harcourt 1983 $13.95
The Blue Room. Trans. by Eileen Ellenbogen, Harcourt repr. of 1965 ed. 1978 pap. $2.95
The Cat. Trans. by Bernard Frechtman, Harcourt 1976 pap. $2.95
The Iron Staircase. Harcourt 1981 pap. $2.95
The Lodger. Trans. by Stuart Gilbert, Harcourt repr. of 1934 ed. 1983 $12.95
The Long Exile. Trans. by Eileen Ellenbogen, Harcourt 1982 $15.95
The Reckoning. Trans. by Emily Read, Harcourt 1984 $12.95
Sunday. Trans. by Nigel Ryan, Harcourt 1976 pap. $2.50
The Venice Train. Trans. by Alastair Hamilton, Harcourt 1974 $6.50
Intimate Memoirs. Harcourt 1984 $22.95

BOOKS ABOUT SIMENON

Becker, Lucille F. *Georges Simenon. Twayne's World Authors Ser.* G. K. Hall 1977 lib.
    bdg. $14.50
Bresler, Fenton. *The Mystery of Georges Simenon: A Biography.* Stein & Day 1985
    pap. $9.95
Young, Trudee. *Georges Simenon: A Checklist of His "Maigret" and Other Mystery Nov-
    els and Short Stories in French and in English Translations. Author Bibliographies
    Ser.* Scarecrow Pr. 1976 $16.50

SIMON, CLAUDE. 1913–   (NOBEL PRIZE 1985)

Claude Simon, whose novels were influenced by both Faulkner and Camus, creates a universe dominated by fatality and pervaded with doom. His
heroes are outsiders like Meursault and testify to Simon's leaning toward
the philosophy of the absurd. Simon makes great use of the interior monologue and consciously maintains a single point of view in his novels. In *The
Flanders Road*, three French POWs in a German camp pass the time by recalling incidents, trivial and otherwise—"all in precise detail, dissecting
each component, then synthesizing it into one vast jumble of incidents and
impressions—a sort of stream-of-consciousness technique with its intermi-
nable sentences and indeterminable scenes." Of *The Palace* (1962, o.p.),
Henri Peyre wrote: "Nothing happens in this novel, made up of shadowy dialogues and Proustian reminiscences. . . . The chief concern of the novelist,
who no longer relates a story or presents images of real people, is to devise
a language which may be true to his purely subjective vision."

BOOKS BY SIMON

The Flanders Road. 1960. Trans. by Richard Howard, Riverrun 1985 pap. $9.95
Conducting Bodies. 1971. Trans. by Helen R. Lane, Riverrun 1980 pap. $4.95
The World about Us. 1975. Trans. by Daniel Weissbort, pref. by Mark W. Andrews,
    Ontario Review Pr. 1983 $14.95 pap. $7.95
Georgics. 1981. Trans. by John Fletcher, Riverrun 1985 $19.95

BOOKS ABOUT SIMON

Fletcher, John. *Claude Simon and Fiction Now.* Boyars 1978 pap. $7.95
Gould, Karen L. *Claude Simon's Mythic Muse.* Summa 1979 $14.95
Loubere, J. A. *The Novels of Claude Simon.* Cornell Univ. Pr. 1975 $19.50

THE SONG OF ROLAND (Chanson de Roland). End of 11th century

The Song of Roland is the oldest and most famous of the surviving medieval *chansons de geste* or "songs of heroic exploits," a type of narrative poem
written during the period extending from the end of the eleventh century to
the fourteenth. The oldest of the seven manuscripts of the text may be consulted at the Bodleian Library at Oxford; the Oxford manuscript consists of
4,002 decasyllabic assonanced verses by a great but unknown poet, perhaps
the Turoldus referred to at the end of the poem. The poem, considered to be
the first great monument of French literature, is based on historical incidents going back to the year 778 when Charlemagne invaded Spain. Ver-

sions of the work also exist in other medieval literatures, notably in Basque, Provençal, German, Scandinavian, and Latin.

The Song of Roland. Trans. by Patricia Terry, intro. by H. March, Bobbs 1965 $7.87; trans. by Jessie Crosland, Cooper Square Pr. 1926 $16.50; trans. by Robert Harrison, New Amer. Lib. 1970 $2.95; trans. by Frederick Goldin, Norton 1978 $5.95; trans. by Dorothy L. Sayers, *Penguin Class. Ser.* 1957 $2.95; (with the subtitle *An Analytic Edition*) trans. and ed. by Gerard J. Brault, Pennsylvania State Univ. Pr. 2 vols. 1978 ea. $19.50–$27.50; trans. by C. K. Scott-Moncrieff, Univ. of Michigan Pr. 1959 $4.95

STENDHAL (pseud. of Henri Beyle). 1783–1842

One of the great French novelists of the nineteenth century, Stendhal describes his unhappy youth with acute sensitivity and intelligence in the autobiography of his early years, *The Life of Henri Brulard*, written in 1835–36 but published in 1890, long after his death. The son of a provincial Grenoble lawyer with aristocratic pretensions and a single-minded passion for money, Stendhal sought to escape very early from this stifling bourgeois environment. With the help of his cousin, he obtained a position in the ministry of war and was sent to Italy, a country in which he lived for a considerable time and which he loved. But he never lost his yearning for Paris, a city to which he returned frequently. His novels, whose heroes reject any form of authority that would repress their sense of individual freedom, are a fascinating amalgam of romantic sensibility and a lucid intelligence characteristic of eighteenth-century rationalism. Stendhal's major novels are novels of alienation, as their initial premise is a hero out of sorts with contemporary society. Stendhal also wrote some 30 volumes of biography, travel, and art and music criticism.

BOOKS BY STENDHAL

To the Happy Few: Selected Letters of Stendhal. Trans. by Norman Cameron, Hyperion Pr. repr. of 1952 ed. 1980 $27.50

A Life of Napoleon. 1817–38. Fertig repr. of 1956 ed. 1977 $21.50

Love. 1822. Trans. by Suzanne Sale and Gilbert Sale, Dufour 1957 $10.00; trans. by Suzanne Sale and Gilbert Sale, *Penguin Class. Ser.* 1975 pap. $4.95

Life of Rossini. 1822. Trans. and ed. by Richard N. Coe, Riverrun 1982 pap. $14.95; trans. and ed. by Richard N. Coe, Univ. of Washington Pr. 1972 pap. $3.95

The Red and the Black. 1830. Trans. by C. K. Scott-Moncrieff, *Black and Gold Lib.* Liveright 1954 $8.95; trans. by Lloyd C. Parks, New Amer. Lib. (Signet Class.) 1970 pap. $3.95; (with the subtitle *An Annotated Text with Critical Essays*) ed. by Robert M. Adams, *Norton Critical Eds.* 1969 pap. $10.95

Scarlet and Black. Trans. by M. R. Shaw, *Penguin Class. Ser.* 1953 pap. $3.95

Stendhal: Memoirs of an Egotist. Trans. by David Ellis, Horizon Pr. 1975 $6.95

Lucien Leuwen. 1834–35. Trans. by L. Varèse, New Directions 1950 pap. $5.00

Memoirs of a Tourist. 1838. Trans. by A. Seager, Northwestern Univ. Pr. 1962 $18.95

The Charterhouse of Parma. 1839. Trans. by C. K. Scott Moncrieff, New Amer. Lib. (Signet Class.) repr. of 1925 ed. pap. $4.95; trans. by M. R. Shaw, *Penguin Class. Ser.* 1958 pap. $5.95

Lamiel. 1839–42. Trans. by Jacques LeClercq, Fertig repr. of 1929 ed. 1978 $19.75

BOOKS ABOUT STENDHAL

Brombert, Victor, ed. *Stendhal: A Collection of Critical Essays.* Prentice-Hall (Spectrum Bks.) 1962 $12.95

Caraccio, Armand. *Stendhal.* Trans. by Dolores Bagley, New York Univ. Pr. 1965 pap. $4.95

Hazard, Paul. *Stendhal: Henri Beyle.* Trans. by Eleanor Hard, Arden Lib. repr. of 1929 ed. 1979 lib. bdg. $20.00

Hemmings, Frederick W. *Stendhal: A Study of His Novels.* Oxford 1964 $14.95

Levin, Harry. *Toward Stendhal.* Haskell repr. of 1945 ed. 1975 lib. bdg. $46.95

May, Gita. *Stendhal and the Age of Napoleon: An Interpretive Biography.* Columbia Univ. Pr. 1977 $28.50

Strickland, Geoffrey. *Stendhal: The Education of a Novelist.* Cambridge Univ. Pr. 1974 pap. $12.95

Tenenbaum, Elizabeth B. *The Problematic Self: Approaches to Identity in Stendhal, D. H. Lawrence, and Malraux.* Harvard Univ. Pr. 1978 $14.00

Wood, Michael. *Stendhal.* Ed. by Graham Hough, Cornell Univ. Pr. 1971 $19.50 pap. $5.95

TOCQUEVILLE, ALEXIS (CHARLES HENRI MAURICE CLEREL) DE. 1805–1859

[SEE Volume 3, Chapter 7.]

TOURNIER, MICHEL. 1924–

The novelist and essayist Michel Tournier has had a varied career as a producer and director for Radio Television Française, as a journalist, and as director of literary services for the French publishing firm Editions Plon. He was awarded the Grand Prix du Roman by the French Academy in 1967 for his first novel, *Friday*, a takeoff on DEFOE's (see Vol. 1) *Robinson Crusoe*. Tournier's novels are highly complex, revealing a philosophical turn of mind through intricate sets of symbolic allusions. The French title of his second novel, *Le roi des aulnes*, is from GOETHE's poem on the Erl-King and has been translated into English as *The Ogre*. The book won Tournier international attention and the Prix Goncourt. More recently he has written *The Four Wise Men*, a retelling of the nativity story. Although Tournier's novels have been translated into almost 20 languages, he was not, as Roger Shattuck has noted, a part of the French literary establishment of the 1960s and 1970s with its emphasis on "antihumanistic, neo-scientific endeavors based on linguistics and communications theory."

BOOKS BY TOURNIER

Friday. 1967 1978. Trans. by Norman Denny, Pantheon 1985 pap. $7.95

The Ogre. 1970. Trans. by Barbara Bray, *Modern Writers Ser.* Pantheon 1984 pap. $8.95

Gemini. 1975. Trans. by Anne Carter, Doubleday 1981 $14.95

The Four Wise Men. 1980. Trans. by Ralph Manheim, Doubleday 1982 $14.95; Random (Vintage) 1984 pap. $8.95

The Fetishist. Trans. by Barbara Wright, Doubleday 1984 $13.95

A Garden at Hammamet. Trans. by Barbara Wright, Lord John's 1985 $75.00

Cloonan, William. *Michel Tournier*. *Twayne's World Authors Ser.* G. K. Hall 1985 lib.
    bdg. $19.95

TRISTAN AND ISEULT. c.1160–1170

The story of Tristan and Iseult has held the romantic imagination more
strongly perhaps than any other of the medieval legends. There are numerous medieval versions of *Tristan*. The earliest poems of consequence are by
Thomas of Britain and by Béroul, a French author. Their poems are known
to us only in fragments. Gottfried von Strassburg composed a magnificent
version in German; a less accomplished but undeservedly neglected version
was composed in Middle English by a poet named Thomas. In modern
times, many poets including MATTHEW ARNOLD (see Vol. 1), A. C. SWINBURNE
(see Vol. 1), and ALFRED TENNYSON (see Vol. 1) have turned their hands to the
theme. The best-known modern version is by RICHARD WAGNER (see Vol. 3),
Tristan and Isolde, for which he wrote the poetic text (1859) and then the music (1861). His music drama represents the culmination of the view of romantic love as the highest source of human inspiration.

The Romance of Tristan and Iseult as Retold by Joseph Bédier. Trans. by Hilaire Bel-
    loc and Paul Rosenfeld, intro. by Padraic Colum, Random 1965 pap. $2.95.
    Bédier was a brilliant, learned scholar of medieval French literature, and a bril-
    liant prose stylist in his own right. He took the various fragmentary remains of
    the Tristan legend and recast them into a version that is part translation into
    modern French, and part a literary masterpiece in itself. It has been for several
    generations the principal avenue of introduction to the story for French- and En-
    glish-speaking readers alike.
The Romance of Tristan and Isolt. Trans. by Norman B. Spector, Northwestern Univ.
    Pr. text ed. 1973 $14.95

Ferrante, Joan M. *The Conflict of Love and Honor: The Medieval Tristan Legend in
    France, Germany and Italy*. Mouton text ed. 1973 pap. $17.60
Loomis, Gertrude. *Tristan and Isolt: A Study of the Sources of the Romance*. Burt
    Franklin 2 vols. in 1 2d ed. 1970 $32.50

VALERY, PAUL. 1871–1945

Harry T. Moore has written in *Twentieth Century French Literature to
World War II*: "Paul Valéry, who published his most important verse between 1917 and 1922, is the greatest French poet the twentieth century has so
far produced. . . . Few modern poets . . . have presented richer experience
through their verses. Valéry . . . could handle abstractions with a living
and always poetic concreteness, and put them into comparable verse-music."
He was also a critic and aesthetic theorist, interested in art, architecture, and
mathematics. His skepticism, malice, and learning brought him both admiration and hostility. Valéry had been a member of the Mallarmé circle in the
1890s and wrote much symbolist poetry at that time, but an unhappy love affair caused him to fall poetically silent (he earned his living as a journalist)

until Gide and others persuaded him, 20 years later, to publish some of his youthful work. He had thought to add a short new poem and instead wrote *La jeune parque* (*The Young Fate*, 1917), several hundred lines in length. It is technically "superb," "deals movingly with the problems all mankind must face" (Moore), and it won him instant recognition in poetic circles. Several collections of his earlier poems were published in the 1920s, as well as the great *Cimetière marin* (*Graveyard by the Sea*). From then until his death in 1945 he wrote chiefly aesthetic theory, criticism, and an unfinished play (*My Faust*). He helped to revive lively interest in the symbolists and had a pervading influence on French culture generally, though his poetry is not easy for the casual reader. He was elected to the French Academy in 1925. His *Collected Works* have been published in expert translations by the Bollingen Foundation.

Books by Valéry

Collected Works of Paul Valéry. Ed. by Jackson Matthews, *Bollingen Ser.* Princeton Univ. Pr. 15 vols. 1971–75 consult publisher for information about individual volumes

Selected Writings. New Directions bilingual ed. 1964 pap. $6.95. Various translators. Includes poetry, essays, dialogues, and critiques.

Self-Portraits: The Gide-Valéry Letters, 1890–1942. Trans. by June Guicharnaud, ed. by Robert Mallet, Univ. of Chicago Pr. 1966 o.p.

Le cimetière marin. 1920. Trans. and ed. by Graham D. Martin, Univ. of Texas Pr. 1971 $7.95

Charmes. 1922. Trans. by James L. Brown, Forsan 1983 pap. $8.75

Books about Valéry

Arnold, A. J. *Paul Valéry and His Critics. Studies in French Lit.* Haskell repr. of 1970 ed. 1972 lib. bdg. $68.95

Crow, Christine. *Paul Valéry and the Poetry of Voice*. Cambridge Univ. Pr. 1982 $54.50

Grubbs, Henry A. *Paul Valéry. Twayne's World Authors Ser.* Irvington 1968 lib. bdg. $15.95

Ince, W. N. *Poetic Theory of Paul Valéry: Inspiration and Technique*. Humanities Pr. 2d ed. text ed. 1970 pap. $6.00

Lawler, James R. *The Poet as Analyst: Essays on Paul Valéry*. Univ. of California Pr. 1974 $36.00

Mackay, Agnes E. *The Universal Self: A Study of Paul Valéry*. State Mutual Bk. 1982 $39.00; Univ. of Toronto Pr. 1961 $15.00

Stimpson, Brian. *Paul Valéry and Music: A Study of the Techniques of Composition in Valéry's Poetry*. Cambridge Univ. Pr. 1984 $49.50

Suckling, Norman. *Paul Valéry and the Civilized Mind*. Greenwood repr. of 1954 ed. 1978 lib. bdg. $24.75

VERLAINE, PAUL. 1844–1896

The dissolute, erratic leader of the decadents and one of the early symbolists, Verlaine wrote 18 volumes of verse in alternating moods of sensuality and mysticism. He and the poet Rimbaud, ten years his younger, wandered over Europe together, until their relationship ended when Verlaine shot his companion in Brussels in 1873 and was imprisoned for two years. *Sagesse*, his collection of religious poems of great melodic and emotional beauty, is generally considered his finest volume. In his famous poem *Art poétique*, Verlaine stressed the primary importance of musicality in poetry over description. Mallarmé called the collection in which it appears, *Jadis et naguère* (1884), "almost continuously a masterpiece ... disturbing as a demon's work," and described Verlaine's skill as that of a guitarist.

Books by Verlaine

Selected Poems. Trans. by C. F. MacIntyre, Univ. of California Pr. bilingual ed. 1948 pap. $4.95

Confessions of a Poet. Trans. by Ruth S. Wolf and Joanna Richardson, intro. by Martin L. Wolf, Darby repr. of 1950 ed. 1981 lib. bdg. $30.00; trans. by Joanna Richardson, intro. by Peter Quennell, Hyperion Pr. repr. of 1950 ed. 1980 $19.75

Baudelaire, Rimbaud and Verlaine: Selected Verse and Prose Poems. Ed. by Joseph M. Bernstein, Citadel Pr. repr. 1983 pap. $6.95

Four French Symbolist Poets: Baudelaire, Rimbaud, Verlaine, Mallarmé. Trans. by Enid R. Peschel, Ohio Univ. Pr. text ed. 1981 $31.95 pap. $16.95

Royal Tastes: Erotic Writings of Paul Verlaine. Trans. by Alan Stone, Crown 1984 $12.95

Books about Verlaine

Carter, A. E. *Verlaine: A Study in Parallels*. Univ. of Toronto Pr. 1969 $20.00

Chadwick, C. *Verlaine*. Longwood Pr. 1973 $32.50 pap. $14.95

VILLON, FRANÇOIS (François de Moncorbier). 1431–1465?

Villon is one of the first great French lyric poets, and one of the greatest French poets of any age. His "testaments" are mock wills, written in a racy blend of French and underworld slang. Scattered here and there among the ironic items of bequest are exquisite ballads and lyrics, some crystallizing classic themes of medieval literature. After a checkered career at the Sorbonne, Villon embarked on mad bouts of drinking, whoring, and thieving in the Paris underworld, writing poems when he had a bellyful, some paper, and some fuel (so that the ink in the well was not frozen solid). He was at various times arrested, imprisoned, tortured, and nearly put to death; his final sentence was commuted to exile by King Louis XI on his accession to the throne, when he declared amnesties of all sorts, according to the usual practice of the time. It is not known how Villon spent his last years, after his release from prison. Villon's poetry has been translated by Rossetti (see Vol. 1), Synge, and Swinburne (see Vol. 1).

Books by Villon

The Poems of François Villon. Ed. by Galway Kinnell, Univ. Pr. of New England repr. of 1977 ed. 1982 pap. $9.95

Book of François Villon: The Little Testament and Ballads. Trans. by Algernon C. Swinburne, Branden pap. $2.50

Books about Villon

Fox, John. *The Poetry of Villon*. Arden Lib. repr. of 1962 ed. 1981 lib. bdg. $35.00; Greenwood repr. of 1962 ed. 1976 lib. bdg. $19.75

Lewis, Wyndham D. B. *François Villon*. Richard West repr. of 1928 ed. $25.00

Vitz, Evelyn B. *The Crossroad of Intentions: A Study of Symbolic Expression in the Poetry of François Villon*. Mouton text ed. 1974 pap. $16.80

VOLTAIRE (pseud. of François-Marie Arouet). 1694–1778

A leading freethinker of his time and an opponent of political and religious oppression, Voltaire was instrumental in popularizing serious philosophical, religious, and scientific ideas that were frequently derived from liberal thinkers in England, where he lived for two years after his imprisonment in the Bastille. Voltaire's writings are wide-ranging: He wrote plays in the neoclassic style (e.g., *Oedipus*); philosophical essays in a popular vein like *Letters on England*, which has been referred to as the first bomb hurled against the Ancien Régime; and the *Philosophical Dictionary*, a catalog of polemical ideas on a large variety of subjects, particularly religion and philosophy. Voltaire was one of the most prolific letter writers in the entire history of literature, and his correspondence has been published in a French edition of 107 volumes. For the twentieth-century reader, Voltaire is best known for his philosophical tale *Candide*, a masterpiece of satire that is both an attack on the philosophy of metaphysical optimism elaborated earlier in the century by the German philosopher LEIBNIZ (see Vol. 4) and a compendium of the abuses of the Ancien Régime as the author ponders the general problem of evil.

BOOKS BY VOLTAIRE

The Selected Letters of Voltaire. Trans. and ed. by Richard A. Brooks, New York Univ. Pr. 1973 o.p.

Letters on England. 1734. Trans. by Leonard Tancock, *Penguin Class. Ser.* 1980 pap. $4.95

The Elements of Sir Isaac Newton's Philosophy. 1738. Trans. by John Hanna, Biblio Dist. 1967 $35.00

Mahomet the Prophet, or Fanaticism. 1741. Trans. by Robert L. Myers, Ungar pap. $3.95

Voltaire: The Age of Louis XIV and Other Selected Writings. 1751. Intro. by J. H. Brumfit, Irvington text ed. 1963 $24.50

Candide. 1759. Trans. by Lowell Blair, intro. by André Maurois, *Bantam Class. Ser.* 1981 pap. $2.25

Russia under Peter the Great. 1759. Trans. by M. F. Jenkins, Fairleigh Dickinson Univ. Pr. 1983 $35.00

Philosophical Dictionary. 1764. Trans. by Theodore Besterman, *Penguin Class. Ser.* 1984 pap. $4.95

The Philosophy of History. 1765. Citadel Pr. 1965 pap. $3.45

BOOKS ABOUT VOLTAIRE

Brumfit, J. H. *Voltaire: Historian*. Greenwood repr. of 1958 ed. 1985 lib. bdg. $35.00

Mason, Haydn T. *Voltaire: A Biography*. Johns Hopkins Univ. Pr. 1981 $18.50

Mitford, Nancy. *Voltaire in Love*. David & Charles 1984 pap. $9.95; Dutton repr. of 1957 ed. 1985 pap. $8.95; Greenwood repr. of 1957 ed. lib. bdg. $18.75

Morley, John. *Voltaire*. Burt Franklin repr. of 1903 ed. 1973 lib. bdg $23.50; Century Bookbindery repr. of 1913 ed. 1982 lib. bdg. $40.00; Richard West repr. $22.50

Torrey Norman L. *The Spirit of Voltaire*. Russell repr. of 1938 ed. 1968 $11.00
Wade, Ira O. *The Intellectual Development of Voltaire*. Princeton Univ. Pr. 1969 $40.00
———. *Voltaire and Madame du Châtelet: An Essay on the Intellectual Activity at Cirey*.
    Octagon repr. of 1967 ed. lib. bdg. $17.00

WEIL, SIMONE. 1909–1943

A twentieth-century Pascal, this ardently spiritual woman in search of certitude was also a social thinker aware of the human lot. Jewish by birth and Greek by aesthetic choice, she has influenced religious thinking profoundly in the years since her death. "Humility is the root of love," she said (in *La connaissance surnaturelle*), as she questioned traditional theologians and held that the apostles had badly interpreted Christ's teaching. Christianity was, she thought, to blame for the heresy of progress.

BOOKS BY WEIL

The Notebooks. Trans. by Simone Wills, Routledge & Kegan 2 vols. repr. of 1976 ed.
    1984 pap. ea. $20.00
The Need for Roots.1949. Harper pap. $4.95; Octagon repr. of 1952 ed. 1979 lib. bdg.
    $21.50
Iliad, or the Poem of Force. 1953. Pendle Hill 1956 pap. $2.30
Oppression and Liberty 1955. Trans. by Arthur Wills and John Petrie, intro. by F. C.
    Ellert, Univ. of Massachusetts Pr. 1973 pap. $7.95

BOOKS ABOUT WEIL

Dunaway, John. *Simone Weil. Twayne's World Authors Ser.* G. K. Hall 1984 lib. bdg.
    $18.95
Hellman, John. *Simone Weil: An Introduction to Her Thought*. Fortress Pr. 1984 pap.
    $6.95; Humanities Pr. text ed. 1982 $15.45
McFarland, Dorothy T. *Simone Weil. Lit. and Life Ser.* Ungar 1983 $13.95

WIESEL, ELIE. 1928–

Born in Hungary, Elie Wiesel was deported with his family to Birkenau. His father died in Buchenwald, and his mother and sisters at Auschwitz. He was subsequently brought up in France and completed his education at the Sorbonne. Now living in New York, he has been not only a major writer since the publication of his first book, *Night* (which recounts in starkly simple prose the author's own experience as a child during the Nazi Holocaust), but a literary critic and journalist as well. As a writer steeped in the Hasidic tradition and concerned with the Holocaust he survived, Wiesel has written on the problem of persecution and the meaning of being a Jew. *Dawn* is an illuminating document about terrorists in Palestine.

BOOKS BY WIESEL

Night. 1958. Trans. by Stella Rodway, Avon 1972 pap. $2.25
Dawn. 1960. Trans. by Frances Frenaye, Bantam 1982 pap. $2.95
The Accident. 1961. Trans. by Ann Borchardt, Avon 1970 pap. $1.75; Bantam 1982
    pap. $2.50; trans. by Ann Borchardt, Hill & Wang 1985 pap. $6.95
The Gates of the Forest. 1964. Trans. by Frances Frenaye, Schocken repr. of 1966 ed.
    1982 pap. $5.95

The Jews of Silence: A Personal Report on Soviet Jewry. New Amer. Lib. (Plume) pap.
$1.95
The Town beyond the Wall. 1967. Avon 1969 pap. $1.75; trans. by Stephen Becker,
Schocken repr. of 1967 ed. 1982 pap. $5.95
Zalman, or the Madness of God. 1968. Random 1985 $6.95
One Generation After. Random 1970 $8.95; Schocken repr. of 1970 ed. 1982 pap.
$6.95
Souls on Fire: Portraits and Legends of Hasidic Masters. 1972. Random (Vintage) 1973
pap. $1.65; trans. by Marion Wiesel, Summit 1982 $17.50 pap. $7.95
The Oath. 1973. Avon 1974 pap. $2.50; Random 1973 $7.95; Schocken repr. 1986 pap.
$8.95
The Fifth Son. Summit 1984 $15.95
A Beggar in Jerusalem. Pocket Bks. 1978 pap. $2.50; Random 1969 $8.95; Schocken
1985 pap. $8.95
Messengers of God: Biblical Portraits and Legends. Pocket Bks. 1977 pap. $1.95; Ran-
dom 1976 $8.95; Summit 1985 $16.95 pap. $6.95

BOOKS ABOUT WIESEL

Abrahamson, Irving. *Against Silence: The Voice and Vision of Elie Wiesel.* Schocken 3
vols. 1984 ea. $20.00
Berenbaum, Michael. *The Vision of the Void: Theological Reflections on the Works of
Elie Wiesel.* Wesleyan Univ. Pr. 1978 $17.50
Fine, Ellen S. *Legacy of Night: The Literary Universe of Elie Wiesel. Modern Jewish Lit.
and Culture Ser.* State Univ. of New York 1982 $39.50 pap. $13.95
Stern, Ellen. *Elie Wiesel: Witness for Life.* Ktav 1982 $12.95

YOURCENAR, MARGUERITE (pseud. of Marguerite de Crayencour). 1903–

A French novelist, playwright, and essayist born in Belgium, Marguerite
Yourcenar has been a resident of the United States for many yers. She has a
strong humanistic background and has translated the ancient Greek poet
PINDAR and the poems of the modern Greek CONSTANTINE CAVAFY. She has
translated American Negro spirituals and works of VIRGINIA WOOLF (see Vol.
1) and HENRY JAMES (see Vol. 1). Her novels include *Alexis* and *Coup de
Grace.* A collection of poems, *Fires,* was published in 1936. She is particularly known for *Hadrian's Memoirs* (1954), a philosophical meditation in the
form of a fictional autobiography of the second-century Roman emperor.
"With great erudition and great psychological insight, Marguerite
Yourcenar constructed a body of work that is a meditation on the destiny of
mankind" (Germaine Brée). She is the first woman ever elected to the
French Academy (1981).

BOOKS BY YOURCENAR

Four Plays. Trans. by Dori Katz, Performing Arts 1984 consult publisher for informa-
tion
Alexis. 1929 1952. Trans. by Walter Kaiser, Farrar 1984 $12.95 pap. $6.95
A Coin in Nine Hands. 1934 1971. Trans. by Dori Katz, Farrar 1982 $11.95
Fires. 1936. Trans. by Dori Katz, Farrar 1981 $12.95 pap. $8.25
Coup de Grace. 1939. Trans. by Grace Frick, Farrar 1957 $15.00 pap. $5.95

Memoirs of Hadrian. 1951. Farrar 1963 $17.95 pap. $9.95; Modern Lib. 1984 $10.95;
    Pocket Bks. 1977 pap. $3.50
The Abyss. 1968. Trans. by Grace Frick, Farrar 1976 $15.00 pap. $9.95
With Open Eyes: Conversations with Matthieu Galey. Trans. by Arthur Goldhammer,
    Beacon 1984. $19.95 1986 pap. $10.95

BOOK ABOUT YOURCENAR

Horn, Pierre L. *Marguerite Yourcenar. Twayne's World Authors Ser.* G. K. Hall 1985
    lib. bdg. $21.95

ZOLA, EMILE. 1840–1902

Zola was the spokesperson for the naturalist novel in France and the
leader of a school that championed the scientific approach to literature. The
theoretical claims for such an approach, which are considered simplistic today, were outlined by Zola in his *Le roman expérimental* (*The Experimental
Novel*). He was the author of the series of 20 novels called *The Rougon-
Macquart*, in which he attempted to trace scientifically the effects of hered-
ity through five generations of the Rougon and Macquart families. Three of
the outstanding volumes are *L'Assommoir*, a study of alcoholism and the
working class; *Nana* (1880), a story of a prostitute who is a *femme fatale;*
and *Germinal*, a study of a strike at a coal mine. All gave scope to Zola's gift
for portraying crowds in turmoil. Today Zola's novels have been appreciated by critics for their epic scope and their visionary and mythical qualities. His newspaper article "J'accuse," written in defense of Alfred Dreyfus,
launched Zola into the public limelight.

BOOKS BY ZOLA

Thérèse Raquin. 1867. Trans. by Leonard Tancock, *Penguin Class. Ser.* 1962 pap.
    $3.95
L'Assommoir. 1877. *Penguin Class. Ser.* 1970 pap. $4.95
The Experimental Novel and Other Essays. 1880. Trans. by Belle M. Sherman, Haskell
    repr. of 1893 ed. lib. bdg. $49.95
Germinal. 1885. Trans. by Leonard W. Tancock, *Penguin Class. Ser.* 1954 pap. $3.95
The Earth (La terre). 1887. Trans. by Douglas Parmee, *Penguin Class. Ser.* 1980 pap.
    $5.95
La bête humaine. 1890. Trans. by Leonard Tancock, *Penguin Class. Ser.* 1977 pap.
    $4.95
The Debacle. 1892. Trans. by Leonard Tancock. *Penguin Class. Ser.* 1973 pap. $5.95

BOOKS ABOUT ZOLA

Bédé, Jean-Albert. *Emile Zola.* Columbia Univ. Pr. 1974 pap. $2.50
Friedman, Lee M. *Zola and the Dreyfus Case.* Haskell repr. of 1937 ed. 1970 consult
    publisher for information
Grant, Elliott M. *Emile Zola. Twayne's World Authors Ser.* G. K. Hall 1966 lib. bdg.
    $14.50
Hemmings, F. W. J. *The Life and Times of Zola.* Scribner 1977 $4.95
Josephson, Matthew. *Zola and His Time.* Richard West repr. of 1929 ed. lib. bdg.
    $50.00
Schor, Naomi. *Zola's Crowds.* Johns Hopkins Univ. Pr. text ed. 1978 $20.00

CHAPTER 10

Italian Literature

Anne Paolucci and Henry Paolucci

Giuseppe Prezzolini, one of the most distinguished Italian critics of his generation, believed that the Italians, in unifying their country (1861), deprived cultured Europeans of their second fatherland; Italy became a little competitor among other nations, and no longer the dream nation of those who already had their own country. It must be added that Italy has had barely a century to build up a truly native literature.

—MARTIN SEYMOUR-SMITH, *Funk and Wagnall's Guide to Modern World Literature*

The History of Italian Literature of Francesco De Sanctis is still the best introduction to the subject, even though, when it appeared in 1871, united modern Italy had not yet completed its first decade of existence. A literary masterpiece in its own right, it was hailed by Benedetto Croce as the first truly intimate history of Italy as a whole, because "all of Italian life, religious, political, and moral, is represented in it." De Sanctis had been inspired by the critical essays, written mostly in English, of the romantic poet-critic Ugo Foscolo, who had in turn drawn upon the ideas of Giambattista Vico. De Sanctis divided the history of Italian literature into five major overlapping periods. The first began in the late Middle Ages with the earliest significant use of an Italian dialect for literary purposes. During the twelfth and thirteenth centuries, literary centers flourished first in the German imperial court in Sicily, then in ST. FRANCIS OF ASSISI's (see Vol. 4) "sacred Umbria" and the university town of Bologna, and finally in prosperous Florence, where the period quickly culminated in the towering achievement of Dante's *Divine Comedy*, the great medieval epic that at once took its place among the greatest masterpieces of world literature.

Petrarch and Boccaccio inaugurated the second period, which extends from the fourteenth through sixteenth centuries, with an abrupt rejection of the cultural world that had been summed up in Dante. The literary masterpieces of this period, which for a long time eclipsed Dante's achievement, are Petrarch's sonnets and songs, Boccaccio's *Decameron*, Ariosto's mock epic *Orlando Furioso*, Machiavelli's *Prince* and *Mandragola*, and Tasso's chivalric epic *Gerusalemma Liberata*.

The first 200 years of this period of Italian Renaissance humanism—from Petrarch's birth in 1304 to the deaths of Angelo Poliziano and Pico della Mirandola in 1494—were characterized by an extraordinary mood of secular optimism. Educated Italians, studying and imitating classical Latin works, thought of themselves increasingly as citizens not of a politically divided Italy but rather of an ideal cosmopolitan Republic of Letters knowing no national boundaries. However, during the same time, most of the other major European countries were completing their political consolidation into powerful nation-states. When France and Spain marched their armies into Italy late in the fifteenth century, Italian optimism abruptly collapsed. Machiavelli witnessed the event; but his desperate plea for Italian unity remained unheeded for another 250 years.

The mood of the third period is perhaps best typified by the wildly adventurous lives of those Italians who fled Italy to seek a measure of freedom and patronage in foreign lands, or who, if they remained at home, abandoned themselves to unbridled individualism. On a calmer level of literary activity, this period is one in which content came more and more to be sacrificed to conventions of fashionable literary form, with rival styles rapidly succeeding one another. The period produced some exceptionally serious figures, like Vico and Antonio Muratori, but for the most part, its mood of estrangement from reality found its most satisfying expression in the universally popular *commedia dell'arte* and enjoyed a final flowering at the close of the century in the marvelous melodramas of Pietro Metastasio.

Although the fourth period began at the close of the eighteenth century with the national theatrical reforms initiated by Carlo Goldoni and Corlo Gozzi, the great promise of these reforms was fulfilled by Giuseppe Parini and Vittorio Alfieri. Their message was simple. If an Italy degraded for centuries under foreign rule was ever to assume a respected place among the modern nations, Italians in large numbers would have to become self-consciously ashamed of the way of life they had accustomed themselves to accept. That inspired Ugo Foscolo to review the history of Italian literature from a truly national perspective.

In the last decades of the nineteenth century the romantic ideal of nationhood faced up to the challenge of political realities. Unification, the new writers found, actually had the effect of bringing Italy down several notches in international standing. As Giuseppe Prezzolini pointed out, "In an Italy divided up into little states and oppressed by foreign nations, Alfieri, Foscolo, Manzoni, and Leopardi had been European voices: in the new united Italy the one real poet, Carducci, found no echo, then or later, in foreign lands."

Giosuè Carducci proved the very opposite in temperament from both Manzoni and De Sanctis. They had tried by literary means to form a united and educated Italian people to accompany national unification. Carducci, on the contrary, was an aristocratic, elitist, classical scholar who despised the novel as a literary genre and who sought to revive a more humanistic, antihistorical approach to literary studies. In 1906, Carducci became the first Italian to be awarded a Nobel Prize for literature. But even the fiction writers of the period felt constrained to reject the romantic idealism of Manzoni and De Sanctis. What such novelists as Luigi Capuana, Verga, and Pirandello preferred was the fashionable scientific positivism and naturalism or realism that already reigned in France and England and much of the rest of Europe.

By the turn of the century, the tension between elitism in poetry and naturalism in fiction had already given rise to a literature of so-called decadence, which soon refracted itself into a colorful spectrum of "isms" that extends into the contemporary period—neobohemianism, futurism, hermeticism, neorealism, and experimentalism. Out of the foment of such "isms," twentieth-century Italian literature has produced a host of literary talents. Since Carducci four other Italians have been awarded the Nobel Prize for literature—Deledda, Pirandello, Quasimodo, and Montale. However, contemporary Italian literature shows its greatest promise in its professed experimentalism, which applies to the work of contemporary novelists, playwrights, and even critics, as well as poets.

After decades of neglect in American universities, the leading contemporary Italian poets are now being taught and studied in fairly good translations. From another perspective, the twentieth century has been an age of criticism for Italian literature, with interest in the creative process providing the subject matter of some of the best poetry, novels, and plays. Such an age could hardly lack literary critics to carry on the tradition of Foscolo, De Sanctis, and Carducci. Benedetto Croce has of course been the towering figure among critics; but the reader must not ignore the labors of his brilliant colleague Giovanni Gentile, or those of the extraordinary journalist-scholar Giuseppe Prezzolini, who saw it all, living through the length of an entire century, and offering his criticism from a truly international perspective.

HISTORY AND CRITICISM

Apollonio, Umbro, ed. *Futurist Manifestos*. Viking 1973 $17.95

Baron, Hans. *Humanistic and Political Literature in Florence and Venice at the Beginning of the Quattrocento: Studies in Criticism and Chronology*. Russell repr. of 1955 ed. 1968 $9.50

Barzini, Luigi. *The Italians*. Atheneum 1977 pap. $8.95; Peter Smith $16.25

Bernardo, Aldo S., and Anthony L. Pellegrini, eds. *Dante, Petrarch, Boccaccio: Studies in the Italian Trecento in Honor of Charles S. Singleton*. Medieval & Renaissance Texts & Studies 1983 $25.00

Biasin, Gian Paolo. *Literary Diseases: Theme and Metaphor in the Italian Novel*. Univ. of Texas Pr. 1975 $12.50

Burckhardt, Jacob. *The Civilization of the Renaissance in Italy*. Intro. by C. Trinkaus, Harper 2 vols. pap. ea. $4.76; Merrimack 1983 $13.95; intro. by Hajo Holborn, Modern Lib. 1954 $6.95; Peter Smith 2 vols. $28.00

Caesar, Michael, ed. *Writers and Society in Contemporary Italy: A Collection of Essays*. Ed. by Peter Hainsworth, St. Martin's 1984 $25.00. "This book includes useful bibliographies, of both English and Italian works. . . . The authors considered in detail include theorist and novelist Umberto Eco, poet Andrea Zanzotto, playwright Dario Fo, and activist-writer Leonardo Sciascia" (*Choice*).

Corrigan, Beatrice, ed. *Italian Poets and English Critics, 1755–1859: A Collection of Critical Essays*. Univ. of Chicago Pr. 1969 pap. $3.45

Devoto, Giacomo. *The Languages of Italy.* Trans. by V. Louise Katainen, Univ. of Chicago Pr. 1978 lib. bdg. $30.00

Donadoni, Eugenio. *A History of Italian Literature.* Trans. by Richard Monges, *Gotham Lib.* New York Univ. Pr. 2 vols. 1969 $18.50 pap. $7.95

Foligno, Cesare. *Epochs of Italian Literature.* Associated Faculty Pr. repr. of 1920 ed. 1970 $15.00

Gardner, Edmund G. *Italian Literature.* Folcroft repr. of 1927 ed. 1979 $10.00; Norwood repr. of 1927 ed. 1980 lib. bdg. $15.00

Garin, Eugenio. *Italian Humanism: Philosophy and Civic Life in the Renaissance.* Trans. by Peter Munz, Greenwood repr. of 1965 ed. 1976 lib. bdg. $19.25

Garnett, Richard. *A History of Italian Literature.* Richard West repr. of 1898 ed. 1973 $45.00

Gatt-Rutter, J. A. *Writers and Politics in Modern Italy.* Holmes & Meier 1979 $13.50 text ed. pap. $9.50

Grillo, Ernesto. *Studies in Modern Italian Literature.* Richard West repr. of 1930 ed. 1973 $25.00

Haydn, Hiram C. *The Counter-Renaissance.* Peter Smith repr. of 1950 ed. $13.75

Heiney, Donald. *America in Modern Italian Literature.* Rutgers Univ. Pr. 1965 $25.00. Considered the "best history" of the influence of American writing on such Italian authors as Vittorini, Pavese, Calvino, Soldati, and Silone.

Houston, John P. *The Rhetoric of Poetry in the Renaissance and Seventeenth Century.* Louisiana State Univ. Pr. text ed. 1983 $32.50

Howells, William D. *Modern Italian Poets. Essay Index Repr. Ser.* Ayer repr. of 1887 ed. 1972 $26.50; Russell repr. of 1887 ed. 1973 $20.00

Kristeller, Paul O. *Renaissance Thought and Its Sources.* Ed. by Michael Mooney, Columbia Univ. Pr. 1979 $37.00 pap. $13.50

Luciani, Vincent. *A Brief History of Italian Literature.* Vanni 1967 $10.00

McLeod, Addison. *Plays and Players in Modern Italy.* Associated Faculty Pr. repr. of 1912 ed. 1970 $24.50. Commentary on playwrights such as Butti, Rovetta, Rasi, Bracco, Benelli, and players such as Duse, Borelli, Galli, Salvini, Ruggieri, Falconi, Novelli, and Zacconi.

Pacifici, Sergio. *A Guide to Contemporary Italian Literature: From Futurism to Neorealism.* Southern Illinois Univ. Pr. pap. $9.95

——. *The Modern Italian Novel.* Southern Illinois Univ. Pr. 3 vols. 1967–79 vol. 1 (1967) o.p. vol. 2. (1973) $10.95 vol. 3 (1979) $16.95

Praz, Mario. *The Flaming Heart: Essays on Crashaw, Machiavelli and Other Studies from Chaucer to T. S. Eliot. Norton Lib.* repr. of 1958 ed. 1973 pap. $3.95; Peter Smith 1958 $11.75

——. *The Romantic Agony.* Trans. by Angus Davidson, *Oxford Pap. Ser.* 2d ed. text ed. 1951 pap. $12.95

Ragusa, Olga. *Narrative and Drama: Essays in Modern Italian Literature from Verga to Pasolini.* Mouton text ed. 1976 pap. $24.00

Riccio, Peter. *Italian Authors of Today. Essay Index Repr. Ser.* Ayer repr. of 1938 ed. $15.00

Rimanelli, Giose, and Kenneth J. Archity, eds. *Italian Literature: Roots and Branches.* Yale Univ. Pr. 1976 $37.00

Rossetti, Dante Gabriel, trans. *The Early Italian Poets.* Folcroft repr. of 1905 ed. lib. bdg. $30.00; Foundation Class. 2 vols. repr. of 1911 ed. 1985 $237.50; intro. by John Wain, Univ. of California Pr. 1982 $16.95. A history and an anthology.

Sandys, John Edwin. *A History of Classical Scholarship.* Hafner 3 vols. repr. of 1920 ed. 2d ed. 1967 o.p. An indispensable work for students of Italian Renaissance humanism.

Sells, Arthur L. *Italian Influence in English Poetry from Chaucer to Southwell.* Greenwood repr. of 1955 ed. 1971 lib. bdg. $24.75

Snell, F. J. *Primer of Italian Literature.* Richard West repr. of 1893 ed. 1978 lib. bdg. $20.00

Symonds, J. A. *Italian Literature: From Ariosto to the Late Renaissance.* Peter Smith $7.50

————. *The Renaissance in Italy.* Peter Smith 3 vols. $32.25

Tedeschi, John A. *The Literature of the Italian Reformation.* Newberry 1971 pap. $1.25

Thayer, William R. *Italica: Studies in Italian Life and Letters. Essay Index Repr. Ser.* Ayer repr. of 1908 ed. $19.00; Richard West repr. of 1908 ed. 1973 $25.00

Trail, Florence. *A History of Italian Literature.* Haskell repr. of 1903 ed. 1972 lib. bdg. $53.95; Richard West repr. of 1914 ed. 1973 $14.75

Trinkaus, Charles. *Adversity's Noblemen.* Octagon rev. ed. 1965 lib. bdg. $15.00

————. *In Our Image and Likeness.* Univ. of Chicago Pr. 2 vols. 1970 o.p.

Valency, Maurice. *In Praise of Love: An Introduction to the Love Poetry of the Renaissance.* Octagon repr. of 1958 ed. 1976 lib. bdg. $24.00; Schocken repr. 1982 $18.95 pap. $9.95. Troubadour and other traditions of love poetry to the time of Dante.

Venturi, Franco. *Italy and the Enlightenment: Studies in a Cosmopolitan Century.* Ed. by Stuart Woolf, New York Univ. Pr. 1972 $14.50

Vittorini, Domenico. *The Age of Dante.* Greenwood repr. of 1957 ed. 1975 lib. bdg. $22.50

————. *The Modern Italian Novel.* Russell repr. of 1930 ed. 1967 $8.50

Weinberg, Bernard. *A History of Literary Criticism in the Italian Renaissance.* Univ. of Chicago Pr. repr. of 1961 ed. 1974 pap. o.p.

Weiss, Roberto. *Dawn of Humanism in Italy. World History Ser.* Haskell repr. of 1947 ed. 1970 lib. bdg. $22.95

Whitfield, John H. *A Short History of Italian Literature.* Greenwood repr. of 1960 ed. 1976 lib. bdg. $24.75; Longwood 1980 pap. $6.50

Wilkins, Ernest H. *A History of Italian Literature* Ed. by Thomas G. Bergin, Harvard Univ. Pr. rev. ed. text ed. 1974 $30.00

COLLECTIONS

Bentley, Eric, ed. *The Classic Theatre: Six Italian Plays.* Peter Smith o.p. Contains Machiavelli, *The Mandrake;* Beolco, *Ruzzante Returns from the Wards;* Anon, *The Three Cuckolds;* Gozzi, *The King Stag;* Goldoni, *The Servant of Two Masters* and *Mirandolina.*

Bond, Richard W., ed. *Early Plays from the Italian.* Ayer repr. of 1911 ed. $29.00. Includes Ariosto, *Supposes;* Grazzini, *The Bugbears.*

Butler, Arthur J., ed. *The Forerunners of Dante: A Selection from Italian Poetry before 1300.* Gordon 1977 lib. bdg. $59.95

Caetani, Marguerite, ed. *Anthology of New Italian Writers: Selections from Botteghe Oscure.* Greenwood repr. of 1950 ed. lib. bdg. $24.75

Cassirer, Ernst, ed. *Renaissance Philosophy of Man.* Univ. of Chicago Pr. (Phoenix Bks.) 1956 pap. $10.95. Includes Petrarch, *On His Own Ignorance;* Valla, *Dia-*

logue on Free Will; Ficino, *Five Questions Concerning the Mind;* Pico della Mirandola, *Oration on the Dignity of Man;* Pompanazzi, *On the Immortality of the Soul.*

De'Lucchi, Lorna, ed. and trans. *An Anthology of Italian Poems: 13th–19th Century.* Intro. by Cesare Foligno, Darby repr. of 1922 ed. 1981 lib. bdg. $40.00

Garrett, George, ed. *The Botteghe Oscure Reader.* Wesleyan Univ. Pr. 1974 $17.50 pap. $8.95

Goldin, Frederick, ed. and trans. *German and Italian Lyrics of the Middle Ages: An Anthology and a History.* Peter Smith $8.00

Golino, Carlo L., and Salvatore Quasimodo, eds. *Contemporary Italian Poetry: An Anthology.* Greenwood repr. of 1962 ed. 1977 lib. bdg. $24.75

Guercio, Francis M., ed. *Anthology of Contemporary Italian Prose.* Associated Faculty Pr. repr. of 1931 ed. 1970 $21.00

Howells, William D. *Modern Italian Poets. Essay Index Repr. Ser.* Ayer repr. of 1887 ed. 1972 $26.50; Russell repr. of 1887 ed. 1973 $20.00

Lind, L. R., ed. *Twentieth-Century Italian Poetry: A Bilingual Anthology.* Bobbs 1974 pap. $10.50

Marchione, Margherita, trans. *Twentieth-Century Italian Poetry: A Bilingual Anthology.* Pref. by Charles Angoff, Amer. Institute of Italian Studies 1974 $10.00

Painter, William M. *The Palace of Pleasure.* Ed. by Hamish Miles, AMS Pr. 4 vols. repr. of 1929 ed. $240.00; ed. by Joseph Jacobs, Dover 3 vols. text ed. 1966 ea. $4.00; ed. by Joseph Jacobs, Peter Smith 3 vols. 4th ed. ea. $13.25

Rebay, Luciano, ed. *Italian Poetry: A Selection from St. Francis of Assisi to Salvatore Quasimodo.* Peter Smith $6.00

Rendel, Romilda. *An Anthology of Italian Lyrics from the 13th Century to the Present Day.* Arden Lib. repr. of 1926 ed. lib. bdg. $30.00

Scott, Mary A. *Elizabethan Translations from the Italian.* Burt Franklin 1969 $32.50

Shields, Nancy C. *Italian Translations in America.* Gordon $59.95

Smarr, Janet L., trans. *Italian Renaissance Tales.* Solaris Pr. 1983 pap. $13.95

Smith, Lawrence R., ed. *The New Italian Poetry, 1945 to the Present: A Bilingual Anthology.* Univ. of California Pr. 1981 $30.00 pap. $8.95

Spatola, Adriano, and Paul Vangelisti, eds. *Italian Poetry, 1960–1980: From Neo to Post Avant-Garde.* Red Hill Pr. 1982 $15.00 pap. $7.50

Trevelyan, Raleigh, ed. *Italian Short Stories.* Penguin 1965 pap. $2.50

ALBERTI, LEON BATTISTA. 1407–1472

Born in Venice, of a Florentine family in exile, Alberti was truly the "universal man" of the Renaissance: a superb gymnast, architect, painter, sculptor, poet, and scholar who wrote treatises, in Latin and Italian, on statics (physics), building, and mathematics. His most important work in Italian is his dialogue in four books *On the Family,* the title of which literally translates the Greek term *economia.* It treats the education of children, matrimony, acquiring wealth and ensuring family prosperity by gaining a monopoly over the means of satisfying family needs, virtues and vices, bodily exercise, and the cultivation of friendships. Alberti's Italian prose is fresh and colorful. He could write classical Latin so well that he passed off many of his works as recently discovered ancient originals. He perfected himself as a living work of art, all his abilities cultivated to constitute a harmonious whole.

BOOKS BY ALBERTI

The Albertis of Florence: Leon Battista Alberti's Della Famiglia. 1435–36. Trans. by Guido Guarino, Bucknell Univ. Pr. 1971 $30.00. This work takes its title from Xenophon's Socratic dialogue *Economics (Oeconomicus)*. Alberti's treatment of the subject ranks in importance with Machiavelli's *Prince* as a contribution to the founding of modern economic, social, and political sciences.

The Family in Renaissance Florence: A Translation of I Libri Della Famiglia. Trans. by Renee Neu Watkins, Univ. of South Carolina Pr. 1969 $17.95

BOOK ABOUT ALBERTI

Gadol, Joan. *Leon Battista Alberti: Universal Man of the Early Renaissance.* Univ. of Chicago Pr. 1969 $20.00 1973 pap. $5.95

ALFIERI, COUNT VITTORIO. 1749–1803

Born in Asti in the Italian Piedmont, Alfieri came into great wealth at age 14. He roamed across Europe, until his meeting with the Princess of Albany, the wife and then the widow of England's Young Pretender, changed his life. Originally, Alfieri wrote in French as well as Italian, but as he became conscious of what appeared to him to be the tragic fate of Italy in the modern world, he devoted himself to perfecting his mastery of the Italian language and to making use of it as a national literary prophet. Alfieri came to be seen as the embodiment of a long-suppressed dream of Italian renewal, hailed as such in Italy even before his death, and accepted in that role with great enthusiasm by many in England as well as in the United States. Alfieri saw himself as Italy's fifth greatest poet, after Dante, Petrarch, Ariosto, and Tasso, with two centuries of utter decline that was worse than silence separating him from Tasso. Because of the high austerity of his poetry, many like THOMAS BABINGTON MACAULAY (see Vol. 1), for instance, saw him instead as linked directly to Dante, as a return, over the heads of Tasso, Ariosto, and Petrarch, to the fountainhead of Italian poetry. Macaulay accepted the view that Petrarch, the humanist, led Italy astray by departing from Dante's vernacular-directed course. Alfieri wrote almost two dozen tragedies, six comedies, many sonnets, satires, and odes, including five on American independence, and a posthumously published autobiography that has gradually come to overshadow his purely literary works as an expression of his presence in Italy's spiritual and literary history.

BOOKS BY ALFIERI

Tragedies of Vittorio Alfieri. Trans. by Edgar Alfred Bowring, Greenwood 2 vols. repr. of 1876 ed. lib. bdg. $37.50. A great improvement over the translation done in 1815 by Charles Lloyd.

The Prince and the Letters. Trans. by Beatrice M. Corrigan and Julius A. Molinaro, Univ. of Toronto Pr. 1972 $22.50

Of Tyranny. 1777. Trans. by Julius A. Molinaro and Beatrice M. Corrigan, Univ. of Toronto Pr. 1961 $10.00. A political treatise.

BOOK ABOUT ALFIERI

Betti, Franco. *Vittorio Alfieri. Twayne's World Authors Ser.* G. K. Hall 1984 lib. bdg. $18.95

ARETINO, PIETRO. 1492–1556

Born in the province of Arezzo, hence "the Aretine," Aretino wrote several comedies, tragedies, satires, and "other works of a scandalous or licentious character." He acquired an international reputation, especially in England, being differently appraised in different periods. Nashe wrote of him as a thing: "It was one of the wittiest knaves God ever made." And MILTON (see Vol. 1) spoke of him as "that notorious ribald of Arezzo." TITIAN (see Vol. 3) was his friend and painted his portrait. He was called the "Scourge of Princes."

BOOKS BY ARETINO

Dialogues. Trans. by Raymond Rosenthal, Stein & Day 1971 o.p.
Selected Letters. Trans. by George Bull, Penguin 1976 o.p.

BOOKS ABOUT ARETINO

Cleugh, James. *The Divine Aretino.* Stein & Day 1964 o.p.
Hutton, Edward. *Pietro Aretino: The Scourge of Princes.* 1922. Constable 1940 o.p.

ARIOSTO, LUDOVICO. 1474–1533

Born in Reggio, Ariosto lived most of his life in Ferrara, enjoying the patronage first of Cardinal Ippolito and then of the cardinal's brother, Alfonso, Duke of Este, who had been his inseparable companion in youth, and who protected him against the wrath of such powerful enemies as Pope Julius II. In addition to his mock epic *Orlando Furioso,* Ariosto wrote many lyric poems in Latin and Italian, 7 satires in *terza rima,* and 5 comedies in unrhymed lines of 11 syllables. His satires were read and imitated by Thomas Wyatt, and one of his comedies, *I suppositi* (o.p.), was translated and adapted into English by George Gascoigne and performed at Gray's Inn in 1566, providing Shakespeare with much of the content and inspiration for his *The Taming of the Shrew.* The mock epic of chivalry *Orlando Furioso,* versions of which appeared in 1516 and 1521 before the definitive edition of 1532, is undoubtedly the "major literary achievement of the Italian Renaissance." Ariosto, HEGEL (see Vol. 4) observed, prepared the way for the treatment of chivalry in CERVANTE's Don Quixote and SHAKESPEARE's Falstaff, and does so in "the gently veiled humor, the brilliantly disarming ease, the charm, wit, grace, and artful naivete with which he brings on the self-dissolution of all that is in itself essentially fantastical, absurd, or nonsensical." In so doing, Ariosto "highlights and reaffirms all that is truly noble and grand in knighthood, in courage, love and honor." A translation by Sir John Harrington, in English "heroical verse," was published in 1591, but by then Edmund Spenser had already sought to "overgo" Ariosto's great epic in his own *Faerie Queene.* A translation by John Hoole of 1783 was read by WALTER SCOTT (see Vol. 1) and Robert Southey, and BYRON (see Vol. 1) drew on it—as also on the mock epics of Luigi Pulci and Francesco Berni—for his *Don Juan*.

BOOKS BY ARIOSTO

Orlando Furioso. Trans. by Guido Waldman, *World's Class. Ser.* Oxford 1983 pap. $12.95; trans. by Barbara Reynolds, Penguin 2 vols. 1975–77 ea. $9.95–$14.95; trans. by Allan Gilbert, Vanni 2 vols. 1954 $45.00; *English Experience Ser.* Walter J. Johnson repr. of 1591 ed. $51.00. The Reynolds version "in rhymed-verse octaves is most welcome; it is lucid, lively and eminently readable and, one hopes, will assure greater appreciation for a masterwork long neglected in the English-speaking world" (*Choice*). "Waldman's complete and very readable prose translation, which faithfully captures all of the narrative line and much of the magic and majesty of the *Furioso*, renders an invaluable service to students and scholars, and especially to the general readership" (*Choice*).

Ariosto's Seven Planets Governing Italie, or His Satyrs. English Experience Ser. Walter J. Johnson repr. of 1611 ed. 1977 lib. bdg. $11.50

BOOKS ABOUT ARIOSTO

Cameron, A. V. *The Influence of Ariosto's Epic and Lyric Poetry on Ronsard and His Group*. Johnson Repr. repr. of 1930 ed. 1973 $19.00

Chesney, Elizabeth A. *The Countervoyage of Rabelais and Ariosto: A Comparative Reading of Two Renaissance Mock Epics*. Duke Univ. Pr. 1982 $22.00

Gardner, E. G. *King of the Court Poets: A Study of the Work, Life and Times of Lodovico Ariosto*. Haskell repr. of 1906 ed. 1969 lib. bdg. $54.95

Griffin, Robert. *Ludovico Ariosto*. *Twayne's World Authors Ser.* G. K. Hall 1974 lib. bdg. $15.95

McMurphy, Susannah J. *Spenser's Use of Ariosto for Allegory*. Folcroft repr. of 1924 ed. lib. bdg. $9.50

Rodino, Robert J., and Salvatore DiMaria. *Ludovico Ariosto: An Annotated Bibliography of Criticism, 1956–1980*. Univ. of Missouri Pr. 1984 $32.00. Updates Giuseppe Fatini's indispensable annotated bibliography for the period 1510–1956.

BANDELLO, MATTEO. 1485–1561

One of the best collections of Italian short stories, Bandello's tales, which were written and published between 1554 and 1573, furnished subjects for Massinger, SHAKESPEARE, and others. Shakespeare's *Much Ado about Nothing* and *Twelfth Night* and Webster's *The Duchess of Malfi* owe their plots to Bandello.

BOOK BY BANDELLO

Certain Tragical Discourses of Bandello. Trans. by Geffraie Fenton, intro. by R. Douglas, AMS Pr. 2 vols. repr. of 1898 ed $90.00

BARETTI, GIUSEPPE. 1719–1789

An adventurer, Baretti spent many years in England where he became a close friend of SAMUEL JOHNSON (see Vol. 1), in whose company he mastered English as well as the art of dictionary making. His Italian-English, English-Italian dictionaries remained standard until the twentieth century. Between long periods in England, he edited the notorious Italian magazine *Frustra*

Letteraria (*Literary Lash*). Inspired by Johnson, he became the first Italian critic to defend Shakespeare against the attacks of VOLTAIRE. Baretti had himself criticized Dante on grounds similar to those of Voltaire—for having offended classical tastes with his medieval literary barbarism; but, under Johnson's tutelage, Baretti revised his tastes and then wrote in French his famous discourse on Shakespeare and Voltaire, which was first published in London in 1777. In 1769 he had stabbed a man to death in the streets of London in self-defense, and his acquittal was gained through the intervention of his many English friends, including painters, politicians, and actors of the caliber of Reynolds, Burke, and Garrick, as well as Johnson.

BOOK BY BARETTI

A Journey from London to Genoa. State Mutual Bk. 1983 $90.00

BOOK ABOUT BARETTI

Collison-Morley, Lacy. *Giuseppe Baretti: With an Account of His Literary Friendships and Feuds in Italy and in England in the Days of Dr. Johnson.* Richard West repr. of 1909 ed. $30.00

BASSANI, GIORGIO. 1916–

The main theme of Giorgio Bassani's novels and short stories, which have earned him wide acclaim outside Italy, has been the advent of anti-Semitism in a provincial Italian city, Ferrara, during World War II. He had earlier had a very successsful career as an editor with a major publishing house, being credited with having helped to bring to public notice Tomasi di Lampedusa's *The Leopard.* He also edited a major literary magazine and was director of the Italian radio-television network. His first collection of short pieces was *A City on the Plain* (o.p.), written under the pseudonym Giacomo Marchi. He also published much poetry, in several small volumes, finally collected in 1963. The stories and novels that were to make him famous abroad began to appear in the 1950s. They include *A Prospect of Ferrara* (five stories), *The Gold Rimmed Spectacles* (o.p.), and *The Garden of the Finzi-Continis* (1962), Vittorio De Sica's film version of which has become a public television classic.

BOOKS BY BASSANI

Five Stories of Ferrara. 1960. Harcourt 1971 $5.95
The Garden of the Finzi-Continis. Trans. by William Weaver, Harcourt 1977 pap. $4.95
Behind the Door. 1962. Trans. by William Weaver, Harcourt 1976 pap. $2.25
The Heron. 1968. Harcourt 1970 $5.95
The Smell of Hay. 1972. Harcourt 1975 $7.95

BELLI, GIUSEPPE GIOACCHINO. 1791–1863

Author of more than 2,000 sonnets in the modern Roman dialect, Belli produced what has been called a *comédie humaine* that refashions the stories of the Bible, the history of Rome, both ancient and modern, and the actual lives, hopes, fears, prejudices, loves, and hatreds of literally hundreds of typical residents of Rome, including popes and cardinals, ghetto Jews, prostitutes, thieves, and beggars, and the lowest of street people. It was Frances Trollope, the mother of ANTHONY TROLLOPE (see Vol. 1), who first wrote of Belli's art for English readers.

BOOK BY BELLI

Sonnets of Giuseppe Belli. Trans. by William Miller, Louisiana State Univ. Pr. 1981 $17.50

BEMBO, PIETRO. 1470–1547

This truly "Renaissance man" was the most influential cultural figure of his time. He knew all the men of letters of his age, was a lover of Lucrezia Borgia, and a favorite of Popes Leo X, Clement VII, and Paul II, who finally made him a cardinal in 1539. Bembo wrote in both Latin and Italian, modeling himself on Petrarch. For his important literary work, a dialogue on love entitled *Gli Asolani*, he took inspiration from PLATO's (see Vol. 4) *Symposium*, but modeled his style on Petrarch's Tuscan. Bembo put out classic editions of Dante and Petrarch and defended their use of Tuscan Italian.

BOOK BY BEMBO

Gli Asolani. 1505. Trans. by Rudolf B. Gottfried, *Select Bibliographies Repr. Ser.* Ayer repr. of 1954 ed. $18.00

BOCCACCIO, GIOVANNI. 1313–1375

Although a Tuscan—like Petrarch and Dante—Boccaccio was raised and educated in Naples, where he wrote his first works under the patronage of its French Angevin rulers. After his return to Florence in 1340, he witnessed the outbreak of the great plague, or Black Death, in 1348. This provided the setting for his most famous work, the vernacular prose masterpiece *Il Decamerone* (*Decameron*)—a "framed" collection of 100 short stories, told by ten Florentines who leave plague-infested Florence for the neighboring hill town of Fiesole, the beauty of which is repeatedly described in the tales. Each of the ten tells a tale a day through a cycle of ten days. The highly finished work exerted a tremendous influence on all the other modern European literatures even as it established itself as the great classic of Italian fictional prose. Although CHAUCER (see Vol. 1) did not mention Boccaccio's name, his *Canterbury Tales* are clearly modeled on the *Decameron*. Besides the *Decameron*, Boccaccio's Italian works include: a short life of Dante and commentaries on the *Divine Comedy;* a prose romance, *Filocolo* (1340); *Filostrato,* his best known work after the *Decameron; Story of Theseus* (1340–41, o.p.), his only attempt to write an epic, and which Chaucer translated as his "Knight's Tale"; his pastoral comedy *L'Ameto; Amorous Fiametta; The Nymph of Fiesole;* and his last work written in Italian, the gloomy cautionary tale *The Corbaccio.* The *Nymph Song,* as a counterpiece for the *Decameron,* demonstrates that it is possible to read the *Decameron* as an allegory, with the plague representing the "spiritual plague" of medieval Christianity, viewed from the vantage point of Renaissance humanism. Many of the *Decameron* tales are indeed paganized versions of medieval sermons about sin and damnation with the morals reversed. After 1363 Boccaccio concentrated on trying to gain enduring fame by writing, in Latin, a series of "lives" of memorable men and women, and a genealogy of the pagan gods.

BOOKS BY BOCCACCIO

The Decameron. 1348–53. Biblio Dist. 2 vols. repr. of 1930 ed. 1973 ea. $8.95; ed. by Charles S. Singleton, Johns Hopkins Univ. Pr. 1974 $75.00; New Amer. Lib. 1982 pap. $5.95; trans. by Mark Musa and Peter Bondanella, intro. by Thomas G. Bergin, Norton 1983 $29.95; ed. by Mark Musa and Peter Bondanella, *Norton Critical Eds.* 1977 $15.95 pap. $8.95; trans. by G. M. McWilliam, *Penguin Class. Ser.* 1972 pap. $6.95; trans. by John Payne, Univ. of California Pr. 3 vols. 1983 $125.00

The Filostrato. 1335. Trans. by Nathaniel E. Griffin and Arthur B. Myrick, Octagon repr. 1973 lib. bdg. $40.00. Boccaccio's *Filostrato* served as a model for Chaucer's *Troilus and Criseyde.*

The Nymph of Fiesole. 1340–45. Trans. by Daniel J. Donno, Greenwood repr. of 1960 ed. 1974 lib. bdg. $24.75

Amorous Fiametta. 1343–44. Trans. by Bartholomew Young, Greenwood repr. of 1926 ed. 1970 lib. bdg. $19.75

The Corbaccio. 1355. Trans. by Anthony K. Cassell, Univ. of Illinois Pr. 1975 $15.95. Excellent first translation of this controversial work.

Fates of Illustrious Men. 1355–74. Trans. by Louis B. Hall, Ungar o.p.

L'Ameto. Trans. by Judith Serafini-Saudi, Garland 1985 $23.00

BOOKS ABOUT BOCCACCIO

Almansi, Guido. *The Writer as Liar.* Routledge & Kegan 1975 $22.50

Bergin, Thomas G. *Boccaccio.* Viking 1981 $25.00. "Learned, lucid, an indispensable volume for students of the Renaissance" (A. Bartlett Giamatti, book jacket).

Branca, Vittore. *Boccaccio: The Man and His Works.* Trans. by Richard Monges, New York Univ. Pr. 1976 $32.50 pap. $15.00

Chubb, Thomas C. *The Life of Giovanni Boccaccio.* Associated Faculty Pr. repr. of 1930 ed. 1969 $21.50; Richard West repr. of 1930 ed. 1979 lib. bdg. $40.00

Hutton, Edward. *Giovanni Boccaccio.* Richard West repr. of 1910 ed. $40.00

Sauli, Judith P. *Giovanni Boccaccio. Twayne's World Authors Ser.* G. K. Hall 1982 lib. bdg. $16.95

Symonds, John A. *Giovanni Boccaccio as Man and Author.* AMS Pr. repr. of 1895 ed. $10.00

BRUNO, GIORDANO. 1548–1600

This truly cosmopolitan figure of the late Italian Renaissance—often called "the Nolan" after his birthplace near Naples—wandered restlessly across Europe preaching his doctrine of cosmic consciousness and publishing it in dialogues and poetry that read today like volcanic spiritual upheavals. With Tommaso Campanella, author of the utopian *City of the Sun* and a controversial *Defense of Galileo*, Bruno represents the "crisis and dissolution of humanistic philosophy," heralding the birth of modern natural science at the hands of GALILEO (see Vol. 5) and FRANCIS BACON (see Vol. 1). His major writings, attacking the Roman Catholic church and celebrating the poetic frenzy of creative geniuses, have inspired writers of a similar temperament down to the days of JAMES JOYCE (see Vol. 1), who drew on Bruno, as well as Vico, for *Finnegans Wake*.

BOOK BY BRUNO

The Heroic Enthusiasts. Gordon 1976 lib. bdg. $59.95

BOOKS ABOUT BRUNO

Yates, Frances. *Giordano Bruno and the Hermetic Tradition.* Univ. of Chicago Pr. text ed. 1979 pap. $17.00
———. *Lull and Bruno: Collected Essays.* Routledge & Kegan 1982 vol. 1 $26.95

CALVINO, ITALO. 1923–1985

Born in Cuba of Italian parents, Calvino was soon brought to San Remo, near Genoa. After the fall of Mussolini in 1943, he spent some months with a Communist partisan brigade in the mountains and remained a member of the Communist party until 1957 when he left in protest against the Soviet invasion of Hungary. In 1947 he joined the large publishing house of Einaudi—which later published his books—and rose to a top editorial position. His literary sponsors at the start of his career were writers like Cesare Pavese and Elio Vittorini, who were already publishing-house executives. They saw to the publication of Calvino's first novel, *The Path to the Nest of Spiders*, a child's view of the antifascist resistance, which was hailed as one of the main novels of the postwar neorealistic genre. But, even in that work, Calvino showed a tendency to move into a realm of what has since come to be called "magic realism." Thus, in Calvino's short stories fable alternates with realism, with a tendency toward fusion of the two. Almost total fusion occurs in his three allegorical novels, *The Cloven Viscount, The Baron in the Trees*, and *The Nonexistent Knight*. According to Seamus Heaney, Calvino's split-level storytelling cycle is a piece of "marvelous binary blarney," and he marvels that Calvino is able to "get away with it" again in *Mr. Palomar* (o.p.), which Heaney later praised as a "high-wire" performance that gives one a thrilling "sense of the safety net being withdrawn at the end" (*N.Y. Times*).

BOOKS BY CALVINO

The Path to the Nest of Spiders. 1947. Ecco Pr. 1976 pap. $4.95. Calvino's first novella.
The Watcher and Other Stories. 1963. Trans. by William Weaver and Archibald Colquhoun, Harcourt 1975 pap. $3.95
Cosmicomics. 1965. Trans. by William Weaver, Harcourt 1976 pap. $2.95
T Zero. 1967. Trans. by William Weaver, Harcourt 1976 pap. $3.95
Invisible Cities. 1972. Trans. by William Weaver, Harcourt 1978 pap. $3.95. "The brilliant Italian fantasist, Italo Calvino . . . , leaves outer space for a trip through human history, the yearnings and disasters of city life everywhere, and the accumulative pressures of 20th century life." (*PW*).
The Nonexistent Knight and The Cloven Viscount. 1959 1952. Ed. by J. Ferrone and H. Wolff, Harcourt 1977 pap. $4.95
The Baron in the Trees. Trans. by Archibald Colquhoun, Harcourt 1977 pap. $4.95

The Castle of Crossed Destinies. Harcourt 1979 pap. $4.95
If on a Winter's Night a Traveler. Trans. by William Weaver, Harcourt 1982 pap.
     $5.95.
Italian Folktales. Trans. by George Martin, Harcourt repr. of 1956 ed. 1980 $27.50;
     Pantheon 1981 pap. $9.95. "Impossible to recommend too highly" (John Gard-
     ner, *N.Y. Times*)
Difficult Loves. Trans. by William Weaver, Harcourt 1984 $14.95 1985 pap. $4.95

CARDUCCI, GIOSUÈ (Joshua). 1835–1907 (NOBEL PRIZE 1906)

When he received Italy's first Nobel Prize for literature in the year before
his death, Carducci was not only Italy's leading poet but also its first ranking critic and classical scholar. He has been called the "prophet of Italy in
its finest hour," even as Vittorio Alfieri had been prophet of an "Italy yet to
be." Carducci celebrated Italy's classical heritage "at the expense of Romanticism and the Church." But he mellowed with age, accepting a constitutional monarchy instead of a republic and showing a fine aesthetic appreciation of Italy's medieval Catholic heritage. His best poems are in his *Rime
Nuove, Odi Barbare* (*Barbarian Odes*), and *Rime e ritmi*. The *Odes* were experiments in recovering the quantitative metrical-rhythmical structure of
classical poetry for modern Italian. He produced critical studies and scholarly editions of classical Italian as well as Latin and Greek authors.

BOOKS BY CARDUCCI

The Best Poems of Joshua Carducci. Trans. by Montgomery Trinidad, Amer. Class.
     College Pr. 1979 $47.45
Odi Barbare: Italian Text with English Prose. 1873–89. Trans. by William F. Smith,
     Vanni 1950 $7.50

BOOK ABOUT CARDUCCI

Scalia, S. Eugene. *Carducci: His Critics and Translators in England and America,
     1881–1932.* Vanni 1937 $6.50

CASANOVA (Giovanni Jacopo Casanova de Seingalt). 1725–1798

[SEE Volume 1, Chapter 17.]

CASTIGLIONE, BALDASSARE. 1478–1529

Castiglione is chiefly known for his prose dialogues titled *The Book of the
Courtier,* which passed through more than 40 editions in the century after
its original publication in 1528. Written in Italian based on Dante's Tuscan,
it helped to establish Tuscan as the national literary language. The book
was destined to be celebrated throughout Europe as a manual of courtly
manners, but the attentive reader senses the peculiarly Italian atmosphere
that envelops the four main participants in the dialogue as they avoid talking of the political realities that prompted MACHIAVELLI (see Vol. 3) to write
the *Prince* just a few years before.

BOOK BY CASTIGLIONE

The Book of the Courtier. Trans. by Thomas Hoby, intro. by W. Raleigh, AMS Pr. repr. of 1900 ed. $45.00; trans. by Thomas Hoby, Arden Lib. repr. 1979 lib. bdg. $15.00; trans. by Thomas Hoby, intro. by J. H. Whitfield, Biblio Dist. (Everyman's) 1975 $10.95 pap. $4.95; Doubleday (Anchor) 1959 pap. $6.50; trans. by George Bull, *Penguin Class. Ser.* 1976 pap. $4.95

CAVALCANTI, GUIDO. c.1254–1300

Guido Cavalcanti's father and his father-in-law, Farinati degli Uberti, were heads of feuding factions in Florence, whose differences were conciliated in part through the marriage of Guido to Beatrice degli Uberti. Dante made high poetry of it all in his grand portrayals of Guido's father and father-in-law in the *Inferno.* With his spiritualization of chivalric love, analyzing its psychological depths, Guido Cavalcanti brought to the emergent Italian literary language the last of the important elements necessary for the inspired use Dante would make of it in his *Divine Comedy.*

BOOKS BY CAVALCANTI

Translations. Trans. by Ezra Pound, New Directions 1953 pap. $10.00. Especially interesting to see how Pound renders Cavalcanti, a poet with very similar tastes and sensibilities.
The Sonnets and Ballate of Guido Cavalcanti. Trans. by Ezra Pound, Hyperion Pr. bilingual ed. repr. of 1912 ed. 1980 $24.00

CELLINI, BENVENUTO. 1500–1571

[SEE Volume 3, Chapter 12.]

CROCE, BENEDETTO. 1866–1952

All of Italian literary criticism in the twentieth century, in one way or another, draws on or reflects the influence of Benedetto Croce. Born in L'Aquila of a great landowning family, Croce lived almost his entire life in Naples, raising himself, as a scholar of independent means, to the status of a "cultural institution" of national and then general European importance. In literature, Croce contributed a major revision of the Italian view of poetry, drawing first on Hegel and then on the great Italian-Hegelian literary critic Francesco De Sanctis for a modernistic view of poetry, distinguishing it from the nonpoetic elements often fused with it. Croce's most influential work is his *Aesthetic as Science of Expression and General Linguistic,* which he brilliantly summarized and updated in *Breviario de estetica* and in "Aesthetica in nuce," originally written for the fourteenth edition of the *Encyclopaedia Britannica.* In literary criticism, his best works are his studies of the poetry of Dante and his monograph on Ariosto, SHAKESPEARE, and CORNEILLE.

BOOKS BY CROCE

Philosophy, Poetry, History: An Anthology of Essays. Trans. by Cecil Sprigge, Oxford 1966 o.p.

Aesthetic as Science of Expression and General Linguistic. 1902. Trans. by Douglas
    Ainslie, Peter Smith $6.00
The Philosophy of Giambattista Vico. Trans. by R. G. Collingwood, Russell repr. of
    1913 ed. 1964 $20.00
Guide to Aesthetics. 1913. Trans. by Patrick Romanell, Regnery-Gateway repr. of
    1965 ed. 1979 pap. $3.95; trans. by Patrick Romanell, Univ. Pr. of Amer. repr. of
    1979 ed. text ed. 1984 pap. $5.00
The Poetry of Dante. Trans. by Douglas Ainslie, Appel repr. of 1922 ed. $10.00
European Literature in the Nineteenth Century. Studies in Comparative Lit. Haskell
    repr. of 1924 ed. 1969 lib. bdg. $49.95
An Autobiography. Trans. by R. G. Collingwood, *Select Bibliographies Repr. Ser.* Ayer
    repr. of 1927 ed. $13.00
The Defence of Poetry. Trans. by E. F. Carritt, Folcroft repr. of 1933 ed. lib. bdg. $8.50
Poetry and Literature: An Introduction to the Criticism and History. Trans. by Gio-
    vanni Gullace, Southern Illinois Univ. Pr. 1981 $24.95

BOOKS ABOUT CROCE

Orsini, Gian N. *Benedetto Croce: Philosopher of Art and Literary Critic.* Southern Illi-
    nois Univ. Pr. 1961 $10.00
Wellek, René. *Four Critics: Croce, Valery, Lukacs, and Ingarden.* Univ. of Washington
    Pr. 1981 $12.50

D'ANNUNZIO, GABRIELE. 1863–1938

Born into a patriarchal family of the Abruzzo, D'Annunzio was sent to
Prato to master Tuscan Italian. At age 16, under the classicizing influence of
Giosuè Carducci, he published his first poems, *Primo Vero* (o.p.), in 1879.
Sent on to Rome, he began to write prose first in the manner of Giovanni
Verga, then in that of Huysmans, and finally in that of NIETSCHE (see. Vol.
4). In 1896 he had sailed the Aegean with Nietsche's *Birth of Tragedy* in
hand and upon his return he began to write poems of a manifestly heightened inspiration, especially after the start of his clamorous love affair with
the actress Eleanora Duse. His best works of the time include the novel *Il
fuoco* (*The Flame of Life,* 1900), the poems of his *Alcyone* (one of the
Pleiades) which are his best, the play *The Dead City* (1898, o.p.), and his masterpiece *The Daughter of Jorio.* In the early years of the twentieth century,
D'Annunzio had indeed become the "most famous writer in the world." Eager to perform on the world's stage in politics and in war as well as art, he
became an ardent nationalist, lost an eye in a wartime flying accident, and
then personally led an assault on Fiume in 1919, annexing it to Italy and ruling it like a Roman proconsul for 16 months. His support of Mussolini has
prompted some critics to treat him as "one of the progenitors of Italian and
therefore European fascism," to be dismissed as "one of the monsters of his
time." He longed to be, but never became, like Shakespeare, the national
poet and playwright of a great state.

BOOKS BY D'ANNUNZIO

The Triumph of Death. Trans. by G. Harding, Fertig repr. of 1898 ed. 1975 $27.50
Francesca da Rimini. Trans. by Arthur Symons, Foundation Class. repr. of 1902 ed.
    1983 $79.85

The Daughter of Jorio: A Pastoral Tragedy. 1904. Trans. by Charlotte Porter, Greenwood repr. of 1907 ed. lib. bdg. $22.50
Tales of My Native Town. Trans. by Rafael Mantellini, Greenwood repr. of 1920 ed.
lib. bdg. $22.50

BOOKS ABOUT D'ANNUNZIO

Antongini, Tom. *D'Annunzio. Select Bibliographies Repr. Ser.* Ayer repr. of 1938 ed.
$31.00; Richard West repr. of 1938 ed. $18.50. The first unveiling of the controversial life of D'Annunzio when the poet was still alive.
Gullace, Giovanni. *Gabriele D'Annunzio in France: A Study of Cultural Relations.* Syracuse Univ. Pr. 1966 $12.95. An intelligent discussion of why "his reputation was
greater in France than in Italy. Written in an easy, pleasant style that is a delight" (*LJ*).
Rhodes, Anthony. *D'Annunzio: The Poet as Superman.* Astor-Honor 1960 $12.50

DANTE ALIGHIERI. 1265–1321

Born in Florence, Dante was the poet destined to give Italy both its greatest literary masterpiece and its national language. As a result of his active,
partisan political life, he was permanently banished from his native city in
1302. Almost all that is known about Dante's personal life is derived from
his works, especially his imaginative works, so that it is virtually impossible to distinguish his literary portrayals of himself from any life based on
so-called nonliterary sources. The works, written in Latin, in which he reveals the most about himself are *De Vulgare Eloquentia* (*On Eloquence in the
Vernaculars*), a defense of his decision to write poetry in Italian rather than
Latin; *De Monarchia* (*On World Government*), written as a partisan of the
claims to "universal empire" of the German imperial house of Hohen-
stauffen; the famous letter dedicating the *Paradiso* to Can Grande della
Scala, the noble ruler of Milan; the *Vita Nuova* (*New Life*, 1292), a collection
of love poems with commentary; *Il Convivio* (*Banquet*, 1304), an incomplete
philosophic treatise; and the *Inferno, Purgatorio,* and *Paradiso* that make up
The Divine Comedy (*Divina Commedia*). At the center of these works is *The
Divine Comedy*, to the understanding of which the others all contribute.
Dante wrote the poem with at least four different "senses" or levels of meaning—the traditional literal, allegorical, moral, and anagogical senses. Dante
invites the reader to try, eventually, to read it on all four levels of meaning
at once. On the literal level there is an epic journey: Dante, as the epic hero,
journeys beyond the grave to arrive at the heights of heaven. On the allegorical level is an epic conflict between the two greatest institutions of the medieval world, the Holy Roman Catholic church and the Holy Roman Empire.
The moral sense of the poem is evident to the reader who seeks in it answers
to personal problems or dilemmas. The anagogical sense helps the reader to
see how all the other meanings can point us toward an understanding of
God's providential design for all things. Read on the first two levels *The Divine Comedy* qualifies as an epic poem, in the sense of Homer's *Iliad* and *Odyssey*. Dante succeeded in combining the two types of epic integrally, offering an epic journey on the literal level and an epic conflict on an allegorical

level. With his moral and anagogical "senses," Dante raised poetry to levels of meaning usually reserved for moral philosophers and clergy.

As Dante conceived the Christian universe, all of human life on earth amounts to a journey in exile and his *Divine Comedy* can be read as an exile's epic journey back to God that takes him first of all through Hell, whose inhabitants experience a permanently frustrated longing for God. Coming out of Hell, he "once again sees the stars." But he first must be cleansed or purged of the "stains of sin," on the seven-storied mountain of Purgatory, before he can become what he in fact becomes on its summit: "purified and disposed to rise to the stars." In the last third of *The Divine Comedy*, the *Paradiso*, Dante has the experience of rising directly upward through the heavens, until he is finally "projected into orbit," as it were, by the power of love, to circle inertially forever with "the sun and the other stars." In 1929, T. S. ELIOT (see Vol. 1) compared Dante to SHAKESPEARE: "Take the *Comedy* as a whole, you can compare it to nothing but the *entire* dramatic work of Shakespeare. The comparison of the *Vita Nuova* with the *Sonnets* is another, and interesting, occupation. Dante and Shakespeare divide the modern world between them."

BOOKS BY DANTE

The Portable Dante. Ed. by Paolo Milano, *Viking Portable Lib.* Penguin rev. ed. 1977 pap. $6.95. *The Divine Comedy* in its entirety, translated by Laurence Binyon; the complete *Vita Nuova* in Rossetti's version; and a selection from Dante's treatises on politics and language *De Monarchia* and *De Vulgare Eloquentia*, as well as from his *Rhymes* and his *Letters*.

Dante's Lyric Poetry. Trans. and ed. by Kenelm Foster and Patrick Boyde, Oxford bilingual ed. 2 vols. 1967 $34.00

Dante's Rime. Trans. by Patrick S. Diehl, Princeton Univ. Pr. 1979 $32.00 pap. $8.95

The Literary Criticism of Dante Alighieri. Trans. and ed. by Robert S. Haller, Univ. of Nebraska Pr. 1974 $19.50 pap. $5.50. "Dante's ideas on poetic art have been culled from his various Italian and Latin works and are brought together . . . in this little book" (*Choice*).

The New Life (and *Il Convivio*). 1292–95. Trans. by Charles E. Norton, Foundation Class. repr. 1985 $88.25. *The New Life* is dedicated to Dante's earliest friend Guido Cavalcanti and has been aptly described as the "first autobiographical work in modern literature." Charles Elliott Norton called it "the proper introduction to the *Divine Comedy*."

Literature in the Vernacular. c.1302–05. Trans. by Sally Purcell, Carcanet pap. $5.95. In defending his decision to use a modified version of his native Florentine dialect to write poetry, Dante provided the first serious Western work of historical philology.

The Divine Comedy. 1302–21. Trans. by J. B. Fletcher, Columbia Univ. Pr. 1951 $34.00; trans. by Thomas G. Bergin, *Crofts Class. Ser.* Harlan Davidson text ed. 1955 pap. $7.95; trans. by H. R. Huse, *Rinehart Ed.* Holt text ed. 1962 $11.95; trans. by Mark Musa, Indiana Univ. Pr. 3 vols. 1971–84 consult publisher for prices of individual volumes; trans. by John Ciardi, Norton 1971 $29.95; trans. by John D. Sinclair, Oxford 3 vols. rev. ed. 1961 pap. $9.95; trans. by Dorothy L. Sayers, *Penguin Class. Ser.* 3 vols. 1950–62 pap. ea. $2.95–$3.95; trans. by Charles S. Singleton, *Bollingen Ser.* Princeton Univ. Pr. 3 vols. 1973–75 ea.

$72.50 set $195.00 pap. set $47.50; intro. by C. H. Grandgent, Random (Vintage) 1955 pap. $4.95; intro. by David H. Higgins, Regnery-Gateway 1981 $16.95; trans. by Geoffrey Bickersteth, Rowman repr. of 1965 ed. rev. ed. 1972 $22.50. The Fletcher translation in rhymed tercets conveys the ruggedness, force, and vigor of the original; it has the drawings that Botticelli made between 1492 and 1495, and the preface compares all the important translations of Dante. Sinclair's is a prose translation with comment. The Bickersteth translation is in the meter of the original.

Il Convivio. 1306–08. Trans. by Christopher Ryan, Anma Libri 1986 pap. $20.00. This unfinished philosophic treatise, consisting for the most part of prose commentaries on poems, is a sort of encyclopedia on almost all of medieval culture. A useful companion to *The Divine Comedy* for what it has to say about Dante's decision to use Italian not only for the poems but also for the commentary.

On World Government. 1310–12. Trans. by H. W. Schneider, intro. by Dino Bigongiari, Bobbs 1957 pap. $5.44; intro. by W. F. Bense, Garland lib. bdg. $46.00. An argument to prove that, because of man's fallen nature, the only way to ensure world peace is through concentration of power in a single center fashioned on the Roman-imperial model, working in harmony with, but not subservient to, the church.

BOOKS ABOUT DANTE

Auerbach, Erich. *Dante: Poet of the Secular World*. Trans. by Ralph Manheim, Univ. of Chicago Pr. repr. of 1961 ed. 1974 o.p. A classic study, first published in Germany in 1929.

Barolini, Teodolinda. *Dante's Poets: Textuality and Truth in the Comedy*. Princeton Univ. Pr. text ed. 1984 $30.00. This English translation appeared long after the first publication of the work in Florence in 1933. The volume is concise and authoritative, with a critical appraisal of the works.

Boccaccio, Giovanni. *Earliest Lives of Dante*. Trans. by Lionardo B. Aretino, Richard West repr. of 1901 ed. 1973 $17.50; trans. by James R. Smith, Russell repr. of 1901 ed. 1968 $5.00

Boitani, Piero. *Chaucer and the Italian Trecento*. Cambridge Univ. Pr. 1985 $17.95 1983 $49.50. "European scholars . . . describe the 14th century counterpoint between Chaucer in England and Dante, Petrarch and Boccaccio in Italy. . . . Each essay is well footnoted" (*Choice*).

Boyde, Patrick. *Dante, Philomythus and Philosopher: Man in the Cosmos*. Cambridge Univ. Pr. 1981 $74.50 1983 pap. $17.95

Cambon, Glauco. *Dante's Craft: Studies in Language and Style*. Univ. of Minnesota Pr. 1969 $10.00

Cassell, Anthony K. *Dante's Fearful Art of Justice*. Univ. of Toronto Pr. 1984 $20.00

Clements, Robert J., ed. *American Critical Essays on "The Divine Comedy."* New York Univ. Pr. 1967 $10.95 pap. $4.50. Sixteen essays for the serious student by such scholars as Erich Auerbach, Thomas G. Bergin, Charles S. Singleton, and the editor.

Cosmo, Umberto. *Handbook to Dante Studies*. Folcroft repr. of 1950 ed. lib. bdg. $17.50

Croce, Benedetto. *The Poetry of Dante*. Appel repr. of 1922 ed. $10.00

Eliot, T. S. *Dante*. Haskell 1974 lib. bdg. consult publisher for information

Ellis, Steve. *Dante and English Poetry: Shelley to T. S. Eliot*. Cambridge Univ. Pr. 1983 $39.50

Fergusson, Francis. *Dante's Drama of the Mind: A Modern Reading of the Purgatorio*.

Greenwood repr. of 1953 ed. 1981 lib. bdg. $27.50. An excellent interpretative study by an extremely intelligent and attentive reader of Dante.

Ferrante, Joan M. *The Political Vision of the Divine Comedy.* Princeton Univ. Pr. text ed. 1984 $35.00

Fletcher, Jefferson B. *Dante.* Richard West 1916 $25.00; Univ. of Notre Dame Pr. 1965 pap. $3.95

————. *Symbolism of the Divine Comedy.* AMS Pr. repr. of 1921 ed. $19.00

Gardner, Edmund G. *Dante and the Mystics: A Study of the Mystical Aspect of the Divina Commedia.* Haskell repr. of 1913 ed. 1969 lib. bdg. $39.95; Octagon repr. of 1913 ed. 1968 lib. bdg. $24.50

————. *Dante's Ten Heavens. Select Bibliographies Repr. Ser.* Ayer repr. of 1900 ed. 2d ed. $20.00; Haskell repr. of 1898 ed. 1970 lib. bdg. $49.95; Richard West repr. of 1898 ed. 1973 $12.75

Gilson, Etienne. *Dante and Philosophy.* Trans. by David Moore, Peter Smith $12.75

Grandgent, Charles H. *Dante.* Folcroft repr. of 1921 ed. lib. bdg. $30.00

Kirkpatrick, R. *Dante's Paradiso and the Limitations of Modern Criticism.* Cambridge Univ. Pr. 1978 $39.50

Lenkeith, Nancy. *Dante and the Legend of Rome.* Richard West repr. of 1952 ed. 1973 $30.00

Mazzaro, Jerome. *The Figure of Dante: An Essay on the Vita Nuova.* Princeton Univ. Pr. 1981 $17.50

Mazzeo, Joseph A. *Medieval Cultural Tradition in Dante's Comedy.* Greenwood repr. of 1960 ed. 1968 lib. bdg. $24.75

————. *Structure and Thought in the Paradiso.* Greenwood repr. of 1958 ed. 1968 lib. bdg. $18.75

Musa, Mark. *Advent at the Gates: Dante's Comedy.* Indiana Univ. Pr. 1974 $17.50

Reynolds, Mary T. *Joyce and Dante: The Shaping Imagination.* Princeton Univ. Pr. 1981 $35.00

Schless, Howard. *Chaucer and Dante.* Pilgrim Bks. 1984 $42.95

Toynbee, Paget. *Concise Dictionary of Proper Names and Notable Matters in the Works of Dante.* Phaeton repr. of 1914 ed. 1968 $25.00

————. *Dante Alighieri: His Life and Works.* Ed. by Charles S. Singleton, Peter Smith $11.75; Richard West repr. of 1910 ed. $17.50. Invaluable reference tool.

Wilhelm, James J. *Dante and Pound: The Epic of Judgement.* National Poetry Foundation 1974 $18.00

DE FILIPPO, EDUARDO. 1900–1984

Eduardo, as he came to be known, started his acting career on the Neapolitan stage at age six. After he and his brother and sister formed their own theater company in the late 1920s, he established himself as Italy's leading comic actor. Before long he was also its best dialect playwright and, after Luigi Pirandello and Ugo Betti, its best dramatic writer. His well-known plays, most of which were made into successful films, include *Filumena* and *Saturday, Sunday, Monday.*

BOOKS BY DE FILIPPO

Saturday, Sunday, Monday. Trans. by Willis Hall, Heinemann text ed. 1974 pap. $5.50

Filumena. Trans. by Keith Waterhouse and Willis Hall, Heinemann text ed. 1978 pap. $6.00

BOOK ABOUT DE FILIPPO

Mignone, Mario B. *Eduardo De Filippo. Twayne's World Authors Ser.* G. K. Hall 1984 lib. bdg. $18.95

DELEDDA, GRAZIA. 1871–1936 (NOBEL PRIZE 1926)

Among the most honored women writers of modern Italy, Deledda wrote naturalistic or realistic novels, drawing upon her Sardinian background for material. Some critics hold, however, that in Deledda's formula often only the names of places and people serve to evoke a Sardinian atmosphere of strangeness, while she tells her romantic tales in a style quite against the main current of the contemporary European novel. Her best works contain excellent portrayals of women, offering probing analyses of motivations that suggest comparison with Antonio Fogazzaro and even DOSTOEVSKY. Much admired and translated, after she received the Nobel Prize in 1926, were *Elias Portolu* (1903), *Cenere* (1904), and, most of all, *The Mother*.

BOOK BY DELEDDA

The Mother. 1920. Berg 1974 lib. bdg. $15.95; trans. by Mary G. Steegman, Larlin new ed. 1982 $16.00

DE SANCTIS, FRANCESCO. 1817–1883

The greatest of Italy's literary critics and literary historians, De Sanctis was the first European or American to hold a professorship in comparative literature. A chair in the new field was especially set up for him at the University of Naples in 1871. During the next 40 years, similar chairs were set up at Harvard, Zurich, Lyon, Columbia, and the Sorbonne. His great *History of Italian Literature* serves both as an introduction to the subject and as a literary masterpiece in its own right. As Giuliano Procacci observed in his *History of the Italian People*, De Sanctis's chief work is "not merely a literary history, but also represents the nearest approach to a general history of Italy that the nineteenth century was able to produce."

BOOKS BY DE SANCTIS

History of Italian Literature. Trans. by Joan Redfern, Basic Bks. repr. of 1931 ed. 1968 o.p.
De Sanctis on Dante. Trans. by Joseph Rossi and Alfred Galpin, Univ. of Wisconsin Pr. 1957 o.p.

FO, DARIO. 1926–

A "theatrical activist" rather than a playwright, Dario Fo has been a successful comedian, performing and writing for radio, television, film, cabaret, and theater for decades. His *Accidental Death of an Anarchist* is still performed, its content constantly updated from a radical Marxist standpoint to reflect current events. It was performed in New York City in 1985. In *Drama Review*, Suzanne Cowan called it "The Throw-Away Theatre of Dario Fo."

BOOKS BY FO

Accidental Death of an Anarchist. 1970. Pluto Pr. 1977 pap. $4.95
We Can't Pay? We Won't Pay! Pluto Pr. 1981 pap. $4.95

FOSCOLO, UGO. 1778–1827

Ugo Foscolo was a truly international literary figure, drawing inspiration from many lands, translating Laurence Sterne's *A Sentimental Journey*, producing a prose masterpiece in his *Last Letters of Jacopo Ortis* (inspired by GOETHE's *Werther*, but infused with a characteristically Italian romantic patriotism that has no counterpart in Goethe's work) and a poetic masterpiece, *On Sepulchres* (1807), which celebrates the great figures of Italy's past on a height of poetic inspiration where, as Giosuè Carducci would later say, there is a "fusing together in a single sublime choral harmony the accents of sermon and hymn, elegy and satire, tragedy and epic."

BOOKS BY FOSCOLO

Last Letters of Jacopo Ortis. Trans. by Douglas Umstead Radcliff, Univ. of North Carolina Pr. 1970 pap. $10.50
On Sepulchres. Trans. by Thomas G. Bergin, Bethany Pr. 1971 o.p. Bergin captures "Foscolo's varying moods of anguish and hope and emulates his faultless classical form" (*Choice*).

BOOK ABOUT FOSCOLO

Cambon, Glauco. *Ugo Foscolo: Poet of Exile.* Princeton Univ. Pr. 1980 $29.00

FRANCIS OF ASSISI, SAINT. 1181/82–1226

[SEE Volume 4.]

GALILEO, GALILEI. 1564–1642

[SEE Volume 5.]

GINZBURG, NATALIA LEVI. 1916–

Born in Palermo, Natalia Ginzburg moved to Turin where her father took a university professorship. She wrote for the Florentine journal *Solaria*, through which she met Elio Vittorini and Cesare Pavese. In 1938 she married the Marxist radical Leone Ginzburg and joined him in his exile as a militant antifascist in a small town in the Abruzzi, an experience mirrored in her first novel, *The Road to the City* (o.p.). Unlike Carlo Levi, who wrote warmly of a similar experience in confinement, Ginzburg's professed intention was that every sentence about the villagers "should be like a whipping or a slap." Briefly freed after Mussolini's fall, Leone Ginzburg was seized by the Germans and died in 1944. Natalia Ginzburg's novels dwell on the theme of the family and are autobiographical even when the subject is a historical figure. One of her earliest novels, *All Our Yesterdays*, has recently been published in English.

BOOKS BY GINZBURG

All Our Yesterdays. 1957. Trans. by Angus Davidson, Carcanet 1985 $14.95. "The late Angus Davidson's 30-year-old translation holds up well and conveys the quality of this writer who is still too little known outside her native Italy."

Family Sayings. 1963. Trans. by D. M. Low, Carcanet $14.95

No Way. Avon 1976 pap. $1.75; trans. by Sheila Cudahy, Harcourt 1974 $5.95. The novel deals with the isolation, fragmentation, and loneliness of an upper-middle class family and its friends and is written mainly in the form of letters exchanged among them.

GOLDONI, CARLO. 1707–1793

Carlo Goldoni, the great Venetian playwright, reformed the Italian theater. In his time, the reigning theatrical genres were the melodrama and the *commedia dell'arte*, the one stressing musicality, the other the antics of familiar "characters" who more often than not improvised their way through a skeletal script. Goldoni's early *Servant of Two Masters* served to put an end to improvised *commedia dell'arte* by supplying a complete script for masterful actors, but in fact, and hardly ironically, the spirit of the old improvisors lives in modern performances of that comedy. In 1752, Goldoni went to Paris to head the Italian Theater and enjoy the patronage of the royal family, which lasted until the revolution of 1789, after which he lived and died in poverty. He wrote comedies of history, intrigue, and exotic romance, but his plays are comedies of characters and manners. Pirandello praised the latter as Goldoni's triumph. Goldoni had learned from MOLIÈRE and SHAKESPEARE, and even MACHIAVELLI (see Vol. 3), how to set living comic protagonists before his audience; but his genius, said Pirandello, consisted rather in taking subordinate characters—a little housemaid, for instance—and suddenly making her the center of a comedy of her own. Among Goldoni's best plays in Italian are *The Liar* and *The Fan* (1763); in the Venetian dialect, *The Tyrants;* and in French, *The Beneficent Bear*, which was produced for the marriage of Louis XIV and Marie Antoinette in 1771, and which gave Goldoni the pleasure of seeing a play of his own performed in French on the stage where Molière's plays had triumphed.

BOOKS BY GOLDONI

Three Comedies: Mine Hostess, The Boors, The Fan. Intro. by Gabriele Baldini, Greenwood repr. of 1961 ed. 1979 lib. bdg. $27.50; Norwood repr. of 1961 ed. lib. bdg. $20.00

Servant of Two Masters. 1745. Trans. by Frederick H. Davies, Theatre Arts 1961 pap. $3.50

The Comic Theatre: A Comedy in Three Acts. 1750. Intro. by D. Cheney, Univ. of Nebraska Pr. 1969 $9.95

The Liar. 1750. Trans. by Frederick H. Davies, Theatre Arts 1963 pap. $3.50

BOOKS ABOUT GOLDONI

Kennard, Joseph S. *Goldoni and the Venice of His Time.* Ayer repr. of 1920 ed. $33.00

Riedt, Heinz. *Carlo Goldoni.* Trans. by Ursule Molinaro, Ungar 1974 $10.95. "This well-informed, stimulating study fills a long-standing void" (*Choice*).

LEONARDO DA VINCI. 1452–1519
[SEE Volume 3, Chapter 12.]

LEOPARDI, GIACOMO. 1798–1873

Although he is the most purely romantic personality Italian culture can boast of, Leopardi was at the same time thoroughly classical in his approach to literature and, in that sense, antiromantic. In the judgment of most critics, he is the second poet of Italy, rivaling Petrarch in the musicality of his melancholy songs of love and death, matching Alfieri in the austerity of his pessimistic passion, and approaching Dante in his capacity to give poetic expression to a most powerfully experienced sense of an entire universe, in his case a godless universe sublimely devoid of meaning. Leopardi is, besides, virtually without a rival in his mastery of philosophic and satiric dialogue and expository prose.

BOOKS BY LEOPARDI

Essays, Dialogues and Thoughts of Giacomo Leopardi. Trans. by James Thomson, ed. by Bertram Dobell, *Lib. of World Lit. Ser.* Hyperion Pr. repr. of 1905 ed. 1979 $25.00

A Leopardi Reader. Trans. by Ottavio M. Casale, Univ. of Illinois Pr. 1981 $24.95. "An excellent and welcome edition" (*Choice*).

The Moral Essays (Operette Morali). Trans. by Patrick Creagh, Columbia Univ. Pr. 1983 $27.50 1985 pap. $12.50; trans. by Giovanni Cecchetti, Univ. of California Pr. 1982 $28.00 1984 pap. $9.50. Creagh's translation presents itself as prepared "with the cooperation of the Leopardi family."

Pensieri. Trans. by W. S. Di Piero, Louisiana State Univ. Pr. 1981 $20.00; trans. by W. S. Di Piero, Oxford repr. of 1981 ed. 1984 pap. $6.95

BOOK ABOUT LEOPARDI

Perella, Nicolas J. *Night and the Sublime in Giacomo Leopardi.* Univ. of California Pr. 1971 pap. $9.00

LEVI, CARLO. 1902–1975

Carlo Levi's book *Christ Stopped at Eboli* is based on his experience as a doctor "confined" to a small town in southern Italy in the mid-1930s because of his agitation against the fascist regime. Although he was released from confinement before Mussolini fell, he had to hide from the Germans because he was a Jew, and he eventually fled to France. In his book, he pictured a peasantry apparently beyond the help of Christianity's God as well as Italy's national government. What comforted the peasants were legendary visions of Robin Hood-like bandits. Noting that Levi had faithfully rendered the fascination of the old bandit myths, Giuseppe Prezzolini praised the whole as a "heartwarming and poetic book . . . greeted with deserved success."

BOOK BY CARLO LEVI

Christ Stopped at Eboli. 1945. Trans. by Frances Frenaye, ed. by Jack Bevan, Farrar 1947 pap. $5.95

LEVI, PRIMO. 1919–

Born in Torino and a lifelong professional chemist, Primo Levi has the distinction of being the first Jewish-Italian writer to make the twentieth-century European Jewish experience the primary focus of his writing. Most notable are his "poignant yet humane memoirs of his experience in Auschwitz" and *The Reawakening* (o.p.). More recent are his chemist's autobiography, *The Periodic Table*, and the novel *If Not Now, When?* which takes its title from the much repeated admonition of Rabbi Hillel.

Books by Primo Levi

Survival in Auschwitz: The Nazi Assault on Humanity. Trans. by Stuart Woolf, Macmillan (Collier Bks.) 1961 pap. $3.95; Summit 1986 $19.95

The Periodic Table. Trans. by Raymond Rosenthal, Schocken 1984 $16.95 1986 pap. $6.95

If Not Now, When? Trans. by William Weaver, Summit 1985 $15.95. "Judaism permeates the account . . . among contemporary Italian writers Giorgio Bassani (*The Garden of the Finzi-Continis*) alone has explored with such mastery the origin they share" (H. Stuart Hughes, *N.Y. Times*).

MACHIAVELLI, NICCOLO. 1469–1527

[See Volume 3, Chapter 4.]

MANZONI, ALESSANDRO. 1785–1873

Born in Milan, the grandson on his mother's side of Cesare Beccaria, world-famous reformer of criminal jurisprudence, Manzoni first established himself as Italy's leading romantic poet, then as its second tragedian, after Vittorio Alfieri, and finally as its greatest novelist. Although he was raised as a Voltairian rationalist, his major writings date from his "return" to Roman Catholicism. Manzoni's lyric poems, which place him on a par with Petrarch and Leopardi, include his *Inni Sacri* (*Sacred Hymns*) and an ode on the death of Napoleon, *Cinque Maggio* (1821), which Goethe translated into German. Manzoni's historical tragedies, *The Count of Carmignola* (1816–20) and *Adelchi* (1822), were influenced by Goethe and Shakespeare. But his singular masterpiece, initially inspired by the novels of Sir Walter Scott, is *The Betrothed*, a novel to be ranked with the major works of Dante, Petrarch, Boccaccio, Ariosto, and Machiavelli (see Vol. 3), and which "has probably had more influence in Italy," as Lacy Collison-Morley said, "than any other novel in any other land." That novel does for modern Italy what Chaucer's (see Vol. 1) tales and Shakespeare's historical plays did for England. Manzoni continued the tradition of literary-linguistic experimentation that began with Dante, while simultaneously providing Italy with a national equivalent of what Homer's epics proved to be for ancient Greece—at once a source of artistic delight and of spiritual education in the broadest sense. Revising his work for its definitive edition of 1840–1842, Manzoni left his native Milan for Dante's Florence, in order to master a form of Italian that would be deeply rooted in the living, local dialect that had produced the greatest Italian masterpieces of the past, while being at the same time fully suited to serve as the "language of newspapers and practical books, of the school and general conversation" for a united modern Italy.

BOOKS BY MANZONI

The Betrothed. 1825–27. Trans. by Archibald Colquhoun, Biblio Dist. (Everyman's) repr. of 1956 ed. text ed. 1983 pap. $7.95; trans. by Archibald Colquhoun, Dutton 1961 pap. $5.75; trans. by Bruce Penman, *Penguin Class. Ser.* 1984 pap. $5.95
On the Historical Novel. Trans. by Sandra Bermann, Univ. of Nebraska Pr. 1984 $15.00. A translation of *Del Romanzo Storico;* includes bibliography and index.

BOOK ABOUT MANZONI

Wall, Bernard. *Alessandro Manzoni.* Elliots Bks. 1954 $29.50. An outstanding biography in English.

MARINETTI, FILIPPO TOMMASO. 1875–1944

Born in Egypt and educated in Paris, Marinetti gained a reputation as a writer in French long before he launched the "futurist movement" with his manifesto of February 20, 1909, in *Le Figaro.* Proclaiming an ideal of "words in liberty," that manifesto elicited high praise from Wyndham Lewis, Guillaume Apollinaire, EZRA POUND (see Vol. 1), and D. H. LAWRENCE (see Vol. 1), as well as the Italians Aldo Palazzeschi, Giovanni Papini, and Ardengo Soffici. After his French works were translated into Italian, he was arrested and spent two months in an Italian jail for immorality. Despite the notoriety of his first manifesto, the subsequent *Technical Manifesto* of 1912 did the abiding work of the movement. As William De Sua correctly wrote: "Of all his works, the *Technical Manifesto* alone should secure his place among such figures as PABLO PICASSO (see Vol. 3), Ezra Pound, IGOR STRAVINSKY (see Vol. 3), and Guillaume Apollinaire as one of the greatest movers and shapers of modern art."

BOOK BY MARINETTI

Marinetti: Selected Writings. Trans. by R. W. Flint and Arthur A. Coppotelli, Farrar 1972 $12.95

MICHELANGELO BUONARROTI. 1475–1564

[SEE Volume 3, Chapter 12.]

MONTALE, EUGENIO. 1896–1981 (NOBEL PRIZE 1975)

Born in Genoa and largely self-educated, Montale was an infantry officer in World War I and then became a spectator, rather than an activist, during the 20 years of fascism, when he wrote some of his best poetry. He lived in Genoa for his first 30 years, where he started his career as a journalist, and then moved to Florence. There he worked first for a publishing house and then as a reference librarian. Finally, after World War II, he settled down in Milan as literary and music critic and special correspondent for Italy's leading newspaper, *Il corriere della sera.* Montale was much influenced by his readings in Russian, French, and Spanish, as well as by Italian authors, and more particularly by his reading and translating of English and American writers such as SHAKESPEARE, HOPKINS (see Vol. 1), HARDY (see Vol. 1), ELIOT (see Vol. 1), MELVILLE (see Vol. 1), TWAIN (see Vol. 1), FAULKNER (see Vol. 1), and O'NEILL. As a poet under the influence of Giuseppe Ungaretti, he broke with the traditional poetic style, steeped in formal eloquence, and took the advice of Salvatore Quasimodo to write poetry in a style stripped of ornaments so as to allow words to recall their "pristine, evocative meaning." His chief books of poems, essays, and translations include *Cuttlefish Bones* (1925), *Occasions* (1939, o.p.), *The Storm and Other Things* (1956), *Diary of 1971 and 1972* (o.p.), and *Translator's Notebook* (o.p.). When he received the Nobel Prize for literature in 1975, he was hailed as the greatest Italian poet of the twentieth century. His poetry is basically "negative" in spirit, unlike Ungaretti's, which is that of a "Christian poet of sorrow." Yet there is a musicality in the best of Montale's verse that recalls and often matches the hauntingly evocative lyricism of Leopardi.

BOOKS BY MONTALE

Selected Poems. Ed. by Glauco Cambon, New Directions 1966 $7.50 pap. $6.25. The first American edition of his work in English translation.

New Poems. Trans. by G. Singh, New Directions 1976 $7.95 pap. $2.95

The Butterfly of Dinard. 1956. Trans. by G. Singh, Univ. Pr. of Kentucky 1971 $16.00

The Storm and Other Poems. Trans. by Charles Wright, Field Translations 1978 $8.95

The Storm and Other Things. Trans. by William Arrowsmith, Norton 1985 $14.95 pap. $6.95

The Second Life of Art: Selected Essays. Trans. and ed. by Jonathan Galassi, Ecco Pr. 1982 $17.50. "... selections from Montale's writings on art, music, literature, cinema, social issues; on Svevo, Eliot, Pound, Valery, Ungaretti, Auden, and others, culminating in the 1975 Nobel Prize speech 'Is Poetry Still Possible?' " (*LJ*).

Otherwise: Last and First Poems of Eugenio Montale. Trans. by Jonathan Galassi, Random 1984 $14.95 pap. $8.95

Bones of the Cuttlefish: Selected Poems in Translation. Trans. by Antonino Mazza, Mosaic Pr. 1984 $12.95 pap. $6.95. "This translation ... finally makes available, in a single source, all of the poems of Montale's first, important collection" (*RSI*).

BOOKS ABOUT MONTALE

Cambon, Glauco. *Eugenio Montale's Poetry: A Dream in Reason's Presence.* Princeton Univ. Pr. 1982 $25.00. "Cambon benefitted greatly from his long acquaintance with Montale" (David Kirby, *LJ*).

Huffman, Claire De C. L. *Montale and the Occasions of Poetry.* Princeton Univ. Pr. 1983 $29.00. "... the author adds a presentation of other critical views followed by her own rebuttals and/or exemplifications, while integrating the poet's own remarks on his work" (*Choice*).

Singh, G. *Eugenio Montale: A Critical Study of His Poetry, Prose, and Criticism.* Yale Univ. Pr. 1973 $18.50. Excellent comprehensive study by the well-known translator of Montale's works. This volume contains some 60 new translations from Montale's poetry.

West, Rebecca J. *Eugenio Montale: Poet on the Edge.* Harvard Univ. Pr. text ed. 1981 $16.50

MORANTE, ELSA. 1918–1985

Married to Alberto Moravia in 1941 (separated in 1962), Elsa Morante was also a successful novelist in her own right. The Marxist critic Gyorgy Lukacs hailed her early *House of the Liars* (o.p.) as "the greatest modern Italian novel," but it was *Arthur's Island* (1959, o.p.) that brought her international fame and an independent income. Her great financial triumph was, however, *History*, which was the first Italian novel to be marketed with high-pressure promotional advertising, making use of publisher, mass media, and political party resources to push sales up to 600,000 in less than six months.

BOOKS BY MORANTE

History: A Novel. Avon 1978 pap. $2.95; Knopf 1977 $12.95; Random (Vintage) 1984 pap. $8.95
Aracoeli. Trans. by William Weaver, Random 1984 $17.45

MORAVIA, ALBERTO (pseud. of Alberto Pincherle). 1907–

Born in Rome of Jewish-Roman Catholic parents, Moravia was not much disturbed under the "fascist racial laws" until Mussolini's fall in 1943 and the consequent German occupation of Rome. Under fascism, Moravia published his first novel, *The Time of Indifference*, at his own expense; yet it was a great success and remains his most characteristic work. He produced nothing to match it until after World War II, when he emerged as the leading Italian neorealist, publishing in rapid order *The Woman of Rome, Disobedience* (o.p.), *The Conformist* (1951, o.p.), *Ghost at Noon* (o.p.), *Roman Tales* (1954, o.p.), and *Two Women*, which many believe is his best novel, telling of the efforts of a shopkeeper and her daughter, raped by Italy's liberators and learning to adapt themselves to the postwar new order. Moravia made a great stir in world literary circles after World War II by announcing his conversion to Roman Catholicism, which had given him solace and protection during the German occupation. Among his more recent publications is *1984*. In 1941 Moravia married the prolific and highly successful novelist, short-story writer, and poet Elsa Morante.

BOOKS BY MORAVIA

The Time of Indifference. 1928. Trans. by Angus Davidson, Greenwood repr. of 1953 ed. 1976 lib. bdg. $16.75; trans. by Angus Davidson, Woodhill repr. of 1974 pap. $1.50. Moravia's first novel.
The Fancy Dress Party. 1941. Trans. by Angus Davidson, Woodhill repr. 1973 pap. $1.50
The Woman of Rome. 1947. Trans. by Lydia Holland, Woodhill repr. 1974 pap. $1.75
Conjugal Love. 1949. Trans. by Angus Davidson, Woodhill repr. 1973 pap. $1.25
Roman Tales. 1954. Woodhill 1974 pap. $1.50
The Bitter Honeymoon. 1952. Trans. by Frances Frenaye and others, Woodhill repr. 1973 pap. $1.25
Two Women. 1957. Trans. by Angus Davidson, Woodhill repr. 1974 pap. $1.50
The Fetish and Other Stories. 1963. Trans. by Angus Davidson, Greenwood repr. of 1965 ed. 1976 lib. bdg. $18.00

The Lie. 1965. Woodhill 1973 pap. $1.25

Command, and I Will Obey You. 1967. Woodhill 1973 pap. $.95

The Red Book and the Great Wall: An Impression of Mao's China. 1967. Trans. by Ronald Strom, Farrar 1968 pap. $1.95

Bought and Sold. 1970. Trans. by Angus Davidson, Farrar 1973 $6.95; Woodhill 1974 pap. $1.50

Two: A Phallic Novel. 1970. Trans. by Angus Davidson, Farrar 1972 $7.95; Woodhill 1973 pap. $1.50

Time of Desecration. Trans. by Angus Davidson, Farrar 1980 $12.95

1984. Trans. by William Weaver, Farrar 1983 $14.50. "Moravia, 75, has taken his ultimate stand against fanaticism" (*Time*).

BOOKS ABOUT MORAVIA

Cottrell, Jane E. *Alberto Moravia. Lit. and Life Ser.* Ungar 1974 $12.95. Generally superficial study of little value to serious students.

Rebay, Luciano. *Alberto Moravia.* Columbia Univ. Pr. 1970 pap. $2.50

Ross, Joan, and Donald Freed. *Existentialism of Alberto Moravia. Crosscurrents Modern Critiques Ser.* Southern Illinois Univ. Pr. 1972 $6.95. "The book should serve as a good introduction to this Italian literary report, with the exception that the writers take their Moravia too seriously" (*Choice*).

PAPINI, GIOVANNI. 1881–1956

With Giuseppe Prezzolini, Papini was a central figure in the pragmatist movement that brought Italy into the mainstream of European culture before World War I. The record of his labors can be read in the journals *Leonardo* and *Regno, La Voce,* and *Lacerba.* A restless spirit, his shifts from pragmatism to futurism, from agnosticism to Roman Catholicism, from critical severity to enthusiastic encouragement of new writers, mirror the revolutionary current of his time. His most famous writings include lives of Christ, ST. AUGUSTINE (see Vol. 4), and Dante, but most characteristic is his world-famous autobiographical novel *The Failure,* which first endeared him to his generation.

BOOK BY PAPINI

The Failure. Trans. by Virginia Pope, Greenwood repr. of 1924 ed. 1972 lib. bdg. $22.50

PARINI, GIUSEPPE. 1729–1799

Born in Milan, and committed to the priesthood at the discretion of others, Parini served for many years as a tutor to young aristocrats in several noble Milanese families. Out of that experience, Parini wrote his most famous poem, *Il giorno* (*The Day,* 1763–1804). In that masterful satire, which respects the ideals of the class of people satirized, Parini presented himself as a tutor guiding a young aristocrat through the rituals of living through an entire day. The result is a mirror held up to the servile Italian upper class that had accommodated itself to living almost mindlessly, or hypocritically, under foreign rule, and paying for the comforts of that accommodation with its moral character. There is an all-pervasive irony and compassion that permitted the poet to universalize his characterizations, and to produce an exquisitely finished masterpiece that takes the cultivated reader in one bound out of the atmosphere of Arcadia and Metastasio across the threshold of the Italian *risorgimento* or national revival. The unrhymed lines of 11 syllables are as close as easily rhyming Italian prosody can come to English blank verse.

BOOK BY PARINI

The Day: Morning, Midday, Evening, Night. Trans. by Herbert M. Bower, Hyperion
    Pr. repr. of 1927 ed. 1977 $16.15

PASCOLI, GIOVANNI. 1859–1912

After a youth filled with more than a normal share of personal sorrows, Pascoli, who was born in Romagna and educated at Bologna, went on to become a classical scholar of the first order, eventually succeeding to the chair held by Giosuè Carducci at the University of Bologna. He has been belatedly recognized as the "major precursor of modernism in Italian poetry." His best poetry—as in the *Myricae* (1891;1903) and the *Songs of Castelvecchio*—is Wordsworthian in its disarming surface simplicity, but has been correctly characterized as a deliberate retreat into the neutral zone of childlike awareness. His Latin poetry won the leading prizes in Europe, and his studies of Italian authors, especially Leopardi and Dante, help to illuminate his own poetics.

BOOK BY PASCOLI

Giovanni Pascoli: Convivial Poems. Trans. by Egidio Lunardi and Robert Nugent,
    Lake Erie College Pr. 2 vols. bilingual ed. 1979–81 pap. ea. $7.50–$12.50

PASOLINI, PIER PAOLO. 1922–1975

Born in Bologna, Pasolini passed most of his childhood at his mother's birthplace in Friuli, where he learned the local dialect that he used in his first, last, and best poetry. He escaped military service in World War II, but his brother's death in a Communist partisan factional feud in Yugoslavia filled him with a sense of guilt. He became a teacher in a local Communist party chapter, but was accused of blatant immorality in 1949, fired from his job, and expelled from the party. With his mother, he went to Rome, spending much time in the slums, mastering the Roman dialect. His novel *The Ragazzi* (1957, o.p.), based on his Roman street experience, established him as the leading neorealistic writer of the day. Again he was charged with public indecency, but that made him the darling of the Communists, who interpreted his conduct, like that of the *Ragazzi* portrayed in his novel, as the effect of capitalist oppression. His second neorealistic novel, *A Violent Life*, brought him greater success. Before long, however, he rejected neorealism and began to live for art's sake. Thereafter, except for what he called his "cat-like" nocturnal prowling for homosexual sex or love, Pasolini "did not lose a moment," as Cecelia Ross aptly said, "in his efforts to lay new directions for literature as well as for theater and television." He poured all his talents and energies into his major films, starting with *The Gospel according to St. Matthew* (1964), which sustains the mood of Bach's (see Vol. 3) music, and running through *The Hawks and the Sparrows* (1966), *Oedipus Rex* (1967), *Pigsty, Medea* (1970), and a trilogy made up of *The Decameron, Canterbury Tales,* and *Arabian Nights.* It is significant that, shortly before he died—murdered in a homosexual encounter with a notorious street prostitute known as Pino the Frog—Pasolini published a revised and enlarged edition of his dialect poems, *La nuova gioventù.* One finds in it an experimental impetus like that of the poets of the dawn of Italian literary history, even though Pasolini had added to it what John Gatt-Rutter has called "bitter new versions of the original poems, sardonic epitaphs to his now vanished 'poetic country,' the Friuli."

Books by Pasolini

Poems. Trans. by Norman MacAfee and Luciano Martinengo, fwd. by Enzo Siciliano, Random 1982 $10.50 pap. $5.95. ". . . based on a selection Pasolini himself made for an edition in 1970" (N. S. Thompson, *TLS*).

Lutheran Letters. Trans. by Stuart Hood, Humanities Pr. text ed. 1983 text ed. $19.50

A Violent Life. Trans. by William Weaver, Carcanet repr. of 1968 ed. 1985 $18.50 pap. $7.50; ed. by Bruce S. Kupelnick, Garland 1978 lib. bdg. $20.00

Books about Pasolini

Allen, Beverly. *Pier Paolo Pasolini: The Poetics of Heresy.* Anma Libri 1982 pap. $25.00

Friedrich, Pia. *Pier Paolo Pasolini.* Twayne's World Authors Ser. G. K. Hall 1982 lib. bdg. $18.95

Siciliano, Enzo. *Pasolini.* Random 1982 $20.00

Stack, Oswald, ed. *Pasolini on Pasolini.* Indiana Univ. Pr. repr. of 1970 ed. o.p.

PAVESE, CESARE. 1908–1950

In Turin in his native Piedmont, Pavese studied English and American literature and wrote a dissertation on Walt Whitman (see Vol. 1). He read and translated Defoe (see Vol. 1), Dickens (see Vol. 1), Joyce (see Vol. 1), Dos Passos (see Vol. 1), Stein (see Vol. 1), and Faulkner (see Vol. 1), and his version of Melville's (see Vol. 1) *Moby Dick* is a classic. Except for his book of poems *Lavorare stanca* (*Work Wearies*), Pavese's chief works are the novels *The Comrade* (1948, o.p.), *The House on the Hill, Before the Cock Crows* (o.p.), *The Beautiful Summer* (o.p.), and his last and best, *The Moon and the Bonfire* (1952, o.p.). During World War II, he was head of the Rome office of the publishing house of Einaudi, and, with Elio Vittorini, did much to encourage young writers. Although a member of the Communist party, he had not joined the antifascist resistance. Unhappy in love, unable to believe in Christ, and disappointed with things in postwar Italy, he finally made good on what he had often urged as the finest of "final solutions" for himself, committing suicide after winning the coveted Strega Prize.

Books by Pavese

Selected Works. Trans. by R. W. Flint, Farrar 1968 o.p. Contains the novels *The Beach, The House on the Hill, Among Women Only,* and *The Devil in the Hills.*

"Now there can be no excuse for not reading Pavese, one of the few essential novelists of the mid-twentieth century. The translations and the introductions are
admirable" (Susan Sontag).

American Literature: Essays and Opinions. Trans. by Edwin Fussell, Univ. of California Pr. 1970 $23.50

Hard Labor. Trans. by William Arrowsmith, Ecco Pr. repr. of 1979 ed. 1986 pap.
$9.50; trans. by William Arrowsmith, Viking 1976 $8.95

BOOKS ABOUT PAVESE

Biasin, Gian Paolo. *Smile of the Gods: A Thematic Study of Cesare Pavese's Work.*
Trans. by Yvonne Freccero, Cornell Univ. Pr. 1969 $17.50

Lajolo, Davide. *An Absurd Vice: A Biography of Cesare Pavese.* Trans. by Mario
Pietralunga and Mark Pietralunga, New Directions 1983 $18.50 pap. $9.25.
"Pavese from boyhood, through the fascist era, forever obsessed with his 'absurd
vice,' the pull toward death, and finally surrendering with suicide in 1950."

Thompson, Doug. *Cesare Pavese: A Study of the Major Novels and Poems.* Cambridge
Univ. Pr. 1982 $49.50

PETRARCH (Francesco Petrarca). 1304–1374

Son of an exiled Florentine notary, Petrarch was born in Arezzo, but
raised at the papal court in Avignon in southern France. He went to study in
Montpellier in 1317 and in Bologna in 1323. Less than a year after he returned to Avignon in 1326, he fell in love with the woman he called Laura in
the Italian lyrics that make up his *Rime* or *Canzoniere* (*Songbook*). Like
Dante, Petrarch turned to the Italian vernacular to express his most intimate feelings; but he did not, like Dante, place any confidence in the notion
that writing in Italian could ever bring lasting fame. Although he approved
of Dante's decision to give up the living Latin of the church as a medium of
literary expression, he believed that a better alternative than the vernacular
for serious literature was a revival of classical Latin, so that a modern
writer could indeed address himself to all educated Europeans, transcending all provincial and national frontiers. Petrarch, first of the great Renaissance humanists, saw himself as "standing at the borderland of two epochs," looking back upon a thousand years of church-dominated neglect or
ignorance of the loftiest human values that the classical civilization of ancient Greece and Rome had cherished, and looking ahead to a bright new
era when neglected *humanitas* would again receive its due. For at least two
centuries, Petrarch's attitude prevailed, even though it was destined in the
long run to fail. What the attitude made possible was, of course, the towering cosmopolitan achievement of Italian humanism and the Italian Renaissance. Among the great Italian humanistic successors of Petrarch in Italy
are to be counted Coluccio Salutati, Leonardo Bruni, Lorenzo Valla,
Marsilio Ficino, Angelo Poliziano, and Pico della Mirandola. Petrarch truly
believed that he would enjoy everlasting fame for his works written in
Latin. His Latin works are still studied by scholars but little read; whereas
his poetry in Italian, which exerted a tremendous influence on the content
as well as the form of all subsequent European literature, and especially English, is still a living force of the first order in Italian literature.

BOOKS BY PETRARCH

Love Rimes of Petrarch. Trans. by Morris Bishop, Greenwood repr. of 1932 ed. 1980 lib. bdg. $22.50

Sonnets and Songs. Trans. by Anna Maria Armi, AMS Pr. repr. of 1946 ed. $34.50. A complete translation.

Petrarch: Selected Sonnets, Odes, Letters. Trans. and ed. by Thomas G. Bergin, *Crofts Class. Ser.* Harlan Davidson text ed. 1966 pap. $4.25

Petrarch's Lyric Poems. Trans. and ed. by Robert M. Durling, Harvard Univ. Pr. 1976 $30.00 pap. $9.95. A prose translation.

Lord Morley's Tryumphes of Fraunces Petrarcke: The First English Translation of the Trionfi. 1356–74. Ed. by D. D. Carnicelli, Harvard Univ. Pr. 1971 $16.50

Petrarch's Secret, or The Soul's Conflict with Passion. 1341–45. Trans. by William H. Draper, Hyperion Pr. repr. of 1911 ed. 1978 $24.45. Fundamental work for an understanding of Petrarch's inner conflict between his love for Laura and his desire for God.

Petrarch the First Modern Scholar and Man of Letters. Trans. and ed. by James H. Robinson and Henry Winchester Rolfe, Greenwood repr. of 1914 ed. lib. bdg. $22.50. Rich selection of writings, including Petrarch's *Secret.*

BOOKS ABOUT PETRARCH

Bergin, Thomas G. *Petrarch. Twayne's World Authors Ser.* G. K. Hall lib. bdg. $10.95. Excellent introduction to the life and works by the eminent Italianist.

Bernardo, Aldo S. *Petrarch, Laura, and the "Triumphs."* State Univ. of New York Pr. 1974 $34.50 pap. $10.00. Brilliant, penetrating study by the eminent Petrarchist on the essentially humanistic inspiration that Laura provided to Petrarch.

———. *Petrarch, Scipio and the "Africa": The Birth of Humanism's Dream.* Greenwood repr. of 1962 ed. 1978 lib. bdg. $24.75

Jasenas, Michael. *Petrarch in America.* Pierpont Morgan 1974 pap. $10.00

Mann, Nicholas. *Petrarch.* Oxford 1984 pap. $3.95

Petrie, Jennifer. *Petrarch: The Augustan Poets, the Italian Tradition and the "Canzoniere."* Biblio Dist. 1983 $35.00

Scaglione, Aldo. *Francis Petrarch, Six Centuries Later.* Univ. of North Carolina Pr. 1976 $26.00. Outstanding essays by well-known scholars in the United States.

Waller, Marguerite R. *Petrarch's Poetics and Literary History.* Univ. of Massachusetts Pr. 1980 lib. bdg. $13.50

Whitfield, J. H. *Petrarch and the Renascence.* Haskell repr. of 1943 ed. 1969 lib. bdg. $49.95; Russell repr. of 1943 ed. 1965 $7.50

Wilkins, Ernest H. *Studies in the Life and Works of Petrarch.* Medieval Academy repr. of 1955 ed. 1977 $12.00. "This historical biography . . . may well be regarded by its eminent author as a fitting culmination of a long and fruitful period of scholarly work. Dr. Wilkins is internationally recognized as the great Petrarch scholar of [this century] . . . . highly readable and enjoyable" (*LJ*).

PIRANDELLO, LUIGI. 1867–1936 (NOBEL PRIZE 1934)

Born in Sicily, Pirandello attended the Universities of Palermo, Rome, and Bonn (where he studied the Sicilian dialect of his native town, Agrigento) before settling in Rome to teach and write. In 1894, he married a Sicilian girl, Antonietta Portulano, who bore him three children before she went mad, and afterwards provided the inspiration for many of his stories and plays. In all, Pirandello wrote six novels, some 250 short stories, and about 50 plays. It was a novel, *Il fu Mattia Pascal* (1904), that first brought him fame. Only in 1920, when he was past 50, did he turn seriously to playwriting. His first stage success had been a comedy, *Liolà*, written in the Agrigento dialect. It took its theme, if not its mood, from the *Mandragola* of Machiavelli. The main body of Pirandello's plays falls into three overlapping categories, the first exploring the nature of the theater, the second the complexities of personality in the etymological or dramatic sense of the term, and the third rising to dramatic representation of the categorical imperatives of social, religious, and artistic community. Besides his world-famous *Six Characters in Search of an Author* (1921), his best plays in the three categories include *Each in His Own Way* (1924), *It Is So (If You Think So)* (1917), *Henry IV* (1922), *The New Colony, Lazarus, As You Desire Me* (1930), and *The Mountain Giants*, written after he had been awarded the Nobel Prize and left incomplete.

Books by Pirandello

Collected Plays. Trans. by Henry Read and Bruce Penman, Riverrun 1984 pap. $6.95; trans. by John Wardle, Riverrun 1986 pap. $7.95
Naked Masks: Five Plays. Ed. by Eric Bentley, Dutton 1957 pap. $6.95. Includes *Liolà; It Is So (If You Think So); Henry IV; Six Characters in Search of an Author; Each in His Own Way.*
Shoot! (Si Gira): The Notebook of Serafino Gubbio Cinematograph Operator. 1915. Trans. by C. K. Moncrieff, Fertig repr. of 1926 ed. 1975 $18.50; ed. by Bruce S. Kupelnick, Garland 1978 lib. bdg. $22.00
Better Think Twice about It: And Twelve Other Stories. Short Story Index Repr. Ser. Ayer repr. of 1934 ed. $26.50
Tales of Madness. Trans. by Giovanni R. Bussino, Dante Univ. of Amer. Pr. 1984 $14.50
Pirandello: On Humor. 1908. Trans. and ed. by Antonio Illiano and Daniel P. Testa, *Studies in Comparative Lit.* Univ. of North Carolina Pr. 1974 $13.00. "The most complete statement of the Italian playwright's aesthetic. . . . The translation is a lucid reading of a difficult text" (*Choice*).
Caps and Bells. 1918. Trans. by John Field and Marion Field, Manyland 1974 $4.00

Books about Pirandello

Bishop, Thomas. *Pirandello and the French Theater.* Fwd. by Germaine Brée, New York Univ. Pr. 1960 $10.00 pap. $3.95
Paolucci, Anne. *Pirandello's Theater: The Recovery of the Modern Stage for Dramatic Art. Crosscurrents Modern Critiques Ser.* Southern Illinois Univ. Pr. 1974 $6.95. An analysis of 14 plays that shows the gradual development of Pirandello's art from Sicilian naturalism to the philosophic bent of the late works.
Radcliff-Umstead, Douglas. *The Mirror of Our Anguish: A Study of Luigi Pirandello's Narrative Works.* Fairleigh Dickinson Univ. Pr. 1978 $27.50
Ragusa, Olga. *Luigi Pirandello.* Columbia Univ. Pr. 1968 pap. $2.50. "If you don't know much about Pirandello, you do well to begin with this book . . . a thorough summing up, a conscientious survey, rich in sympathetic yet shrewd analysis" (Thomas G. Bergin, *World Literature Today*).
Sogliuzzo, A. Richard. *Luigi Pirandello, Director: The Playwright in the Theater.* Scarecrow Pr. 1982 $19.00

Starkie, Walter. *Luigi Pirandello, 1867–1936.* Univ. of California Pr. 3d ed. rev. 1965 pap. $2.25

Vittorini, Domenico. *Drama of Luigi Pirandello.* Fwd. by Luigi Pirandello, Russell repr. of 1957 ed. 2d ed. enl. 1969 $16.00

POLIZIANO, ANGELO (Politian). 1454–1494

Born Angelo Ambrogini in Tuscany, he was called Poliziano or Politian after the Latin name of his birthplace. At the Medicean court, Lorenzo the Magnificent was his friend and patron, and Luigi Pulci and Pico della Mirandola were close companions. His important works in the vernacular are *The Fable of Orpheus* (o.p.), completed in two days, which ranks as the first Italian pastoral written for dramatization, and the *Stanze* in celebration of a courtly tournament, with brilliant scenes of people and events.

BOOK BY POLIZIANO

The "Stanze" of Angelo Poliziano. Ed. by David Quint, Univ. of Massachusetts Pr. 1979 $10.00

POLO, MARCO. 1254?–1324?

[SEE Volume 3, Chapter 15.]

PRAZ, MARIO. 1896–1982

Born and educated in Rome, the distinguished comparatist, traveler, and art connoisseur Mario Praz spent the years 1924–1934 teaching Italian literature in Liverpool and Manchester before returning to Rome as professor of English and comparative literature. He gained international recognition as a comparatist for his *Romantic Agony* and *The Flaming Heart* (1958, o.p.) and scores of other books and major articles.

BOOK BY PRAZ

The Romantic Agony. Trans. by Angus Davidson, *Oxford Pap. Ser.* 2d ed. text ed. 1951 pap. $12.95

QUASIMODO, SALVATORE. 1901–1968 (NOBEL PRIZE 1959)

Born in Sicily and trained as an engineer, Quasimodo was brought into Italian literary circles by his brother-in-law Elio Vittorini, who drew him to Florence and introduced him to Umberto Saba, Eugenio Montale, and other contributors to the modernist journal *Solaria*. In the late 1930s, Quasimodo gave up engineering for journalism and literature, becoming editor in chief of the weekly *Il Tempo* and professor of Italian literature in Milan. His poetic life was divided into a hermetic period that lasted through World War II and a period of open commitment to social-humanistic causes that lasted until his death. To the first period belong the volumes *Waters and Lands*, *Sunken Oboe*, and *Erato and Apollyon*, which together with the "new poems" written after 1936, were collected in *And It Is Suddenly Evening* (o.p.). The collection is characterized by what has been called Quasimodo's "poetics of the word"—a genuine hermeticism that contrasts with the "bareness" of Montale's effort to strip away ornamentation and with Ungaretti's discursive "imaginings." In creating a "myth of Sicily," Quasimodo sought its roots in the ancient Greek lyric poets and in the Roman poets closest to them, like CATULLUS and VIRGIL. That took him into his second poetic period, of disillusionment with his Edenlike mythical image of Sicily, expressed in the volumes *Day after Day, Life Is No Dream*, and *The False and True*, followed later by *The Incomparable Land* and *To Give and to Have* (1966). He was a translator of OVID, SHAKESPEARE, MOLIÈRE, EZRA POUND (see Vol. 1), and E. E. CUMMINGS (see Vol. 1). When he received the Nobel Prize in 1959, it was especially noted that his best poetry expresses "with classic fire . . . the tragic experience of life in our time."

BOOK BY QUASIMODO

The Complete Poems of Salvatore Quasimodo. Trans. by Jack Bevan, Schocken 1984 pap. $8.95

SILONE, IGNAZIO (pseud. of Secondo Tranquilli). 1900–1978

Silone was 15 years old when an earthquake in his native Abruzzi brought death to his mother and five of his brothers. Before he was 20 he had established himself in Rome as editor of a Socialist weekly. In 1921 he went off on the first of many trips to the Soviet Union and became a founding member of the Italian Communist party. Under fascism, he hid at first, and then, in 1930, he fled to Switzerland, at which time, however, he also broke with the Communist party. The novels that made him world famous as an antifascist were *Fontamara* and *Bread and Wine*, first published in English in 1936 and then in 17 other languages as well as in Italian. Silone was virtually unknown in Italy until after World War II, by which time he had undergone a radical spiritual transformation that is explained in his very moving contribution to *The God That Failed*.

BOOKS BY SILONE

Fontamara. 1930. Intro. by Irving Howe, New Amer. Lib. 1981 pap. $4.50; ed. by J. Rawson, Longwood 1977 pap. $5.95
Bread and Wine. 1936. Trans. by Harvey Fergusson, Jr., New Amer. Lib. (Signet Class.) rev. ed. pap. $2.95; trans. by Eric Mosbacher, Norwood repr. of 1937 ed. lib. bdg. $20.00

SVEVO, ITALO (pseud. of Ettore Schmitz). 1861–1928

Born in Austrian Trieste of a Jewish Italian-German family, Svevo spoke German fluently and pursued a business career before taking up fiction under a pseudonym that means "Italus the Swabian" or South German. His Italian had indeed something foreign about it, as did the characterizations of heroes and heroines in his novels. His first novel, *A Life* (1893, o.p.), published at his own expense, and his second, *Senility* (o.p.), were virtually ignored. Svevo might have despaired had it not been for his friendship with the expatriate Irish novelist JAMES JOYCE (see Vol. 1), with whom he exchanged language lessons in Trieste. Joyce's intervention eventually found a foreign audience for Svevo's third and perhaps best novel, *The Confessions of Zeno* (1923), first published and very well received in France. As Svevo's reputation spread, he was called the Italian PROUST in France, the Italian MUSIL in Germany, and the Italian Joyce in England. Italian critics now point out that, despite Svevo's foreign success, it was an Italian, Eugenio Montale, who wrote the first significant critical appraisal in 1925. Still, by then Montale had already steeped himself in foreign literatures and could assume a foreign perspective, while more natively rooted Italian critics, including even Benedetto Croce, continued to discount Svevo as a writer writing to be translated. Since Svevo's time, Italy has produced a series of distinguished Jewish-Italian novelists, as well as poets and journalists.

BOOKS BY SVEVO

As a Man Grows Older. 1898. Greenwood repr. of 1949 ed. 1977 lib. bdg. $22.50. "For once the title in translation is more appropriate than the original" (H. Stuart Hughes, 1983).
Short Sentimental Journey and Other Stories. 1910–28. Univ. of California Pr. 1967 $21.50
The Confessions of Zeno. 1923. Trans. by Beryl de Zoete, Greenwood repr. of 1930 ed. 1973 lib. bdg. $22.50; Random (Vintage) pap. $3.95
James Joyce. 1927. City Lights 1967 pap. $1.25
Further Confessions of Zeno. Trans. by P. N. Furbank, Univ. of California Pr. 1969 $32.50 pap. $2.95. Contains unfinished works all published posthumously: *The Old Man* (1929), *An Old Man's Confession, Umbertino, A Contract, This Indolence of Mine* (last four items 1949), and the play *Regeneration* (1960).

BOOKS ABOUT SVEVO

Furbank, P. N. *Italo Svevo: The Man and the Writer.* Univ. of California Pr. 1966 $18.50. "A very nearly perfect critical biography" (*N.Y. Times*).
Lebowitz, Naomi. *Italo Svevo.* Rutgers Univ. Pr. 1978 $28.00
Moloney, Brian. *Italo Svevo.* Columbia Univ. Pr. 1974 $10.00

TASSO, TORQUATO. 1544–1595

Few poets have had a more anguished life than Italy's Torquato Tasso, about whom GOETHE wrote his celebrated tragedy *Torquato Tasso*. His great chivalric epic of the Christian crusades is *Jerusalem Delivered*. Tasso, who was a critic before he was a poet, sought to make HOMER and VIRGIL his models and Dante his source of Christian poetic inspiration, but the resulting epic, as finally published in 1581, is a work of Petrarchan melancholy far more deeply felt and all-pervasive than the Petrarchan original. Unlike Dante or Ariosto, Tasso did not succeed in objectifying a world in the epic manner. In celebrating the deeds of heroes, he remained subjective and lyric. The reason may be, as some have suggested, that he felt Italy was a long way from becoming a significant united nation capable of sustaining a truly epic enterprise in its literature. Forlorn in love, overwhelmed by melancholy, ever suspicious of intrigues against him, Tasso became self-critical to the point of trying to rewrite his epic to placate its severest critics. He traveled much and was several times confined as insane by patrons and friends who loved him. He died in Rome, where he had been summoned to be honored, like Petrarch, with the poet's laurel. Second to *Jerusalem Delivered*, Tasso's most influential literary work has been his pastoral play *Aminta*, which has been performed and highly praised. As in his epic, the poetic voice is lyric. Modern critics have come to appreciate that, with his all-pervasive lyricism, Tasso could be said to have been far ahead of his times.

BOOKS BY TASSO

Tasso's Jerusalem Delivered. 1575. Trans. by Joseph Tusiani, Fairleigh Dickinson Univ. Pr. 1970 o.p.; trans. by Edward Fairfax, Southern Illinois Univ. Pr. 1962 $19.95. "Tusiani's aim is a translation of Tasso's octave into acceptable contemporary English, while remaining close to the original in form and content. . . . The result is a half-slave, half free version of middling success. This is not to say that this first American translation of Tasso is not a very commendable effort. It is readable and useful" (*Choice*). Fairfax's translation of 1600 was a major poetic feat with lasting influence; John Dryden praised the work in the following way: "For Spenser and Fairfax both . . . saw much farther into the Beauties of our Numbers, than those who immediately followed them."

Discourses on the Heroic Poem. 1594. Ed. by Mariella Cavalchini and Irene Samuel, Oxford 1973 $45.00. An excellent translation of an important work of literary history, in which Tasso presented the theory of his own epic, *Gerusalemma Liberata*, and discussed other contemporary critical theories.

Creation of the World. Trans. by Joseph Tusiani, notes by Gaetano Cipolla, Medieval and Renaissance Texts & Studies 1982 $13.00

Tasso's Dialogues: A Selection, with the Discourse on the Art of the Dialogue. Trans. by Carnes Loard and Dain A. Trafton, Univ. of California Pr. 1983 $18.50 pap. $7.95

BOOKS ABOUT TASSO

Boulting, William. *Tasso and His Times.* Haskell repr. of 1907 ed. 1969 lib. bdg. $54.95. "This scholarly, well-written study of Tasso's life and work constitutes a significant contribution to both Italian and English literary criticism" (*LJ*).

Hasell, E. J. *Tasso.* Richard West repr. of 1882 ed. 1973 $15.00

Kates, Judith A. *Tasso and Milton.* Bucknell Univ. Pr. 1983 $24.50

UNGARETTI, GIUSEPPE. 1888–1970

Born in Egypt of Tuscan parents, Ungaretti went to Paris in 1912 to complete his education, attending the lectures of Henri Bergson and forming friendships with distinguished members of the avant-garde, including PICASSO (see Vol. 3), Modigliani, and Apollinaire. For a time he was swept up by the futurist movement of Filippo Tommaso Marinetti, affected more by its nationalistic spirit, however, than by the new poetics. His World War I experiences in the Italian army inspired his earliest poetry, first in Italian, *Il porto sepolto*, and then in French, *La guerre*. A 1923 edition of the former included a preface by Benito Mussolini. In 1936, Ungaretti left Italy to teach Italian literature in Brazil, out of which grew his subsequently published critical essays on Dante, Petrarch, Vico, and Leopardi, but he returned to Italy in 1942. After Italy's defeat in the war, he was widely honored in Italy, spent the year 1964 teaching at Columbia University, and returned to Milan, where he died. *Allegria de naufragi* (*The Joy of Shipwrecks*) has been the very Leopardian title of a number of editions of his poems. A translator of SHAKESPEARE, BLAKE (see

Vol. 1), GONGORA, RACINE, and MALLARMÉ, Ungaretti was for a long time the leading poet of the so-called hermetic school; but, in retrospect, it becomes clear that his chief models for the craft of poetry were Leopardi and Petrarch.

BOOK BY UNGARETTI

Selected Poems. Trans. by Allen Mandelbaum, Cornell Univ. Pr. 1975 $29.95; trans. by Patrick Creagh, *Penguin Poets Ser.* 1972 pap. $3.50

BOOKS ABOUT UNGARETTI

Cambon, Glauco. *Giuseppe Ungaretti.* Columbia Univ. Pr. 1968 pap. $2.50
Cary, Joseph. *Three Modern Italian Poets: Saba, Ungaretti, and Montale.* New York Univ. Pr 1969 $15.00

VERGA, GIOVANNI. 1840–1922

A Sicilian, like Luigi Capuana and Luigi Pirandello, Verga was educated as a writer in Florence and Milan, but drew on Sicily for the subject of his chief novels, plays, and short stories. In 1895, he returned permanently to Catania, his Sicilian birthplace, but by then he had already written his best novels of fictional realism (*verismo*), *The House by the Medlar Tree* and *Mastro-don Gesualdo* (*Master don Gesualdo*, 1889), the first dealing with a family of poor Sicilian fishermen, the second with the social climbing of a stonemason who has made a fortune. Of greater international fame has been Verga's short story *Cavalleria Rusticana* (*Rustic Chivalry*, 1880), which provided the libretto for Mascagni's famous opera.

BOOKS BY VERGA

The House by the Medlar Tree. 1881. Trans. by Eric Mosbacher, Greenwood repr. of 1953 ed. 1975 lib. bdg. $24.75; trans. by Raymond Rosenthal, intro. by Giovanni Cecchetti, Univ. of California Pr. text ed. 1983 $24.00 pap. $6.95. The Rosenthal translation is the first complete version in English and a good one, "conveying [well] the color of the language of the Sicilian fishermen and peasants.... A valuable edition" (*Choice*).
The She-Wolf and Other Stories. 1880–83. Trans. by Giovanni Cecchetti, Univ. of California Pr. 2d ed. rev. pap. $6.95
Mastro-don Gesualdo. 1923. Trans. by D. H. Lawrence, Greenwood repr. of 1955 ed. 1976 lib. bdg. $37.50; trans. by D. H. Lawrence, Hippocrene Bks. 1985 pap. $5.95; trans. by Giovanni Cecchetti, Univ. of California Pr. 1979 $22.50 1983 pap. $7.95. Cecchetti's translations are accurate, critically sound in every way, and a great improvement over those of Lawrence.
Little Novels of Sicily. 1925. Trans. by D. H. Lawrence, Greenwood repr. of 1953 ed. 1975 lib. bdg. $19.75
Cavalleria Rusticana and Other Stories. 1926. Trans. by D. H. Lawrence, Greenwood repr. of 1928 ed. 1975 lib. bdg. $22.50

BOOKS ABOUT VERGA

Bergin, Thomas G. *Giovanni Verga.* Elliots Bks. 1931 $13.50; Greenwood repr. of 1931 ed. lib. bdg. $18.75
Lucente, Gregory L. *The Narrative of Realism and Myth: Verga, Lawrence, Faulkner and Pavese.* Johns Hopkins Univ. Pr. text ed. 1981 $19.00

VICO, GIAMBATTISTA. 1668–1744

Born in Naples of a relatively poor family, Vico studied privately and became a professor in rhetoric in the prestigious university of his native city. Learned in jurisprudence, philosophy, history, philology, politics, aesthetics, and literary criticism, he anticipated with brilliant insights the thought of the profoundest thinkers of later times, from HERDER (see Vol. 4), KANT (see Vol. 4), and HEGEL (see Vol. 4) down to the modern existentialists. His greatest work is the *Principles of a New Science on the Nature of Nations*, soon to be called simply *The New Science*. "It is generally known," wrote Giuseppe Prezzolini, "that the aesthetics of De Sanctis and Croce have their origin in Vico," while it is "to Croce that we owe the most illuminating expositions of Vico's thought as well as the launching of a series of editions and studies that have given Vico the leading position he deserves in the history of human thought." Vico traced a pattern in the development of all human culture consisting of repeated cycles (*corsi* and *ricorsi*), passing through three phases: theocratic or hieroglyphic, heroic or metaphoric, and human or analytical. More recently, JAMES JOYCE (see Vol. 1) made extensive use of Vico's pattern of cycles for *Finnegans Wake*, challenging his readers to read the work repeatedly, or cyclically, in a Vichean spirit. Long before Joyce, however, Italy's greatest novelist, Alessandro Manzoni, had written an appreciative passage noting how Vico constantly "inspires you with a feeling of having been led to those regions in which alone one may ever hope to find the truth."

BOOKS BY VICO

Vico: Selected Writings. Trans. and ed. by Leon Pompa, Cambridge Univ. Pr. 1982 $39.50 pap. $14.95

The New Science of Giambattista Vico. 1725. Trans. by Thomas G. Bergin and Max H. Fisch, Cornell Univ. Pr. 1984 pap. $12.95. "A must for all students of the humanities and social sciences" (*Choice*).

The Autobiography of Giambattista Vico. 1725–31. Trans. by Thomas G. Bergin, Cornell Univ. Pr. 1963 pap. $7.95

BOOKS ABOUT VICO

Caponigri, A. Robert. *Time and Idea: The Theory of History in Giambattista Vico.* Univ. of Notre Dame Pr. 1968 pap. $6.95

Manson, Richard. *The Theory of Knowledge of Giambattista Vico: On the Method of the New Science Concerning the Common Nature of the Nations.* Shoe String (Archon) 1969 $12.50

Pompa, Leon. *Vico: A Study of the New Science.* Cambridge Univ. Pr. 1975 $34.50

Tagliacozzo, Giorgio, ed. *Vico and Marx.* Humanities Pr. text ed. 1983 $35.45

Verene, Donald P. *Vico's Science of Imagination.* Cornell Univ. Pr. 1981 $24.95

VITTORINI, ELIO. 1908–1966

Scholars admit that "few writers have exerted such a continuous domination on the literary life of their country as the Italian novelist Elio Vittorini." With Cesare Pavese, Vittorini helped to create Italy's modern "myth of America" between 1930 and 1939 as a means of relieving the anguish of writers constrained, like themselves, to pursue success under fascist tyranny. Under fascism, Vittorini managed to rise to a position of great power in publishing that enabled him to help literally hundreds of young writers to get their writings published—something he continued to be able to do after the war. What he could not continue to do, however, was to write books as good as he had written under fascism. Martin Seymour-Smith explained this by suggesting, for instance, that Vittorini's *Conversation in Sicily* (o.p.) is, ironically, his very best book precisely "because the existence of the fascist censorship forced him on to a metaphorical, a more personal plane." Yet, as Giose Rimanelli pointed out, one has finally to face up to the perplexing question of "how the most important books of twentieth-century Italian literature could have been written just by those people in a fascist state."

BOOKS BY VITTORINI

A Vittorini Omnibus: The Twilight of the Elephant and Other Novels. Trans. by Cinina Brescia and others, New Directions 1973 $9.50

The Red Carnation. 1948. Greenwood repr. of 1952 ed. 1972 lib. bdg. $18.75

Women of Messina. 1949. Trans. by Frances Frenaye and Frances Keene, New Directions 1973 $9.50 pap. $3.75. "Vittorini's own disillusionment in the Communist solution is mirrored in this, his last novel. It is an uneven book but an important one for anyone interested in a more complete understanding of post-war Italy and modern Italian literature" (*Choice*).

CHAPTER 11

Spanish Literature

Carole Slade

And yet a definition of the exceptional aspect of Spanish literature cannot
be based solely on the nationalistic character of its theatre, but rather in
the continual renovation of its historical legends.... Each of its heroic
themes is developed in epic; in historical chronicles; in collections of ballads; in Golden Age theatre; in neoclassical, romantic and modern drama;
in the lyric poetry of many periods; in the novel.
—RAMÓN MENÉNDEZ PIDAL, *Los Españoles en la Literatura*

Spain's geographical situation as a peninsula effectively divided from Europe by the Pyrenees and a few miles across the Straits of Gibraltar from Africa has influenced its history as well as its literature. Spain has been inhab-
ited since prehistoric times by a succession of peoples—Greeks, Cartha-
ginians, Phoenicians, and Romans—all of whom sought to take advantage
of its location. What is perhaps the first Spanish literature is usually attributed to the Romans, for Seneca the Younger, Lucan, Martial, and Quintilian
were born in Spain.

The Poem of the Cid was widely considered to be the first extant Spanish
literature until 1948, when M. S. Stern discovered in a Cairo synagogue 20
poems in Hebrew, the final verses of which were in Spanish, dated around
1040. Since that time 50 such poems have come to light, and they constitute
the oldest known lyric poetry in a Romance language. These anonymous
verses, born out of a mixture of Arabic, Hebrew, and Spanish cultures, are
an appropriate beginning for Spanish literature, which is characterized by
its popular roots and deeply affected by eight centuries of occupation by the
Arabs.

The Poem of the Cid, Spain's only complete epic poem, was fed by the
popular tradition of ballads recounting contemporary events, weddings,
and battles. Many other epics are considered to have been lost; their fragments remain in ballad form. Spontaneity, brevity, and dramatic substitution of narration with dialogue characterize these ballads, which have inspired Spanish writers for centuries. During the twelfth to the fourteenth
centuries in the northwest sector of Spain, a tradition of stylized love poetry
and bawdy, satiric songs in *gallego,* a combination of Spanish and Portuguese, developed that also influenced the style and substance of Spanish poetry. King Alphonse X, known as Alphonse the Wise, wrote a volume of po-

etry in *gallego*. Alongside the ballad and minstrel tradition existed a priestly school represented by Gonzalo de Berceo, the first author known by name.

The Renaissance came late to Spain, which had first to expel the Arabs before turning to intellectual pursuits. The Catholic monarchs, Ferdinand and Isabel, under whom the nation was finally united, sponsored intellectual inquiry and commissioned the first grammar of a modern language. Due to the history and character of Spain, however, the Renaissance never completely manifested itself there. Nevertheless, Spain enjoyed a period of renewal, termed the Golden Age, which ran from 1530 and the poetry of Garcilaso de la Vega to 1681 and the death of Calderón de la Barca.

The Golden Age saw important developments in poetry and the novel and in the theater. Toward the end of the Golden Age, Spanish literature became highly ornamented, convoluted, and intellectually oriented. Luis de Góngora represented this baroque style in poetry, and gongorism or culteranism came to mean an embellished poetic style characterized by extravagant metaphors, neologisms, twisted syntax, and mythological allusions. The school of culteranism was opposed by that of conceptism, a movement that called for concise language and use of the conceit, a philosophic paradox postulated through elaborate and strained metaphors.

The Spanish novel was born during the Golden Age with the anonymous *Lazarillo de Tormes*, which spawned a succession of picaresque novels. The picaresque novels became increasingly satiric and pessimistic while the style became more conceptionist. Miguel de Cervantes's *Don Quijote*, although it shares some elements of the picaresque tradition as well as of the pastoral novel and the novel of chivalry, transcended all its precursors.

For Spanish theater the Golden Age was a period of development and plenitude comparable to that of Elizabethan England. Lope de Vega not only produced an extraordinary number of dramas but also provided the theoretical basis for the development of a uniquely Spanish national theater. Tirso de Molina and Calderón de la Barca developed Spain's national theater of the Renaissance.

In the eighteenth century, the neoclassical period, Spain stagnated both politically and culturally. The literature of the century demonstrates French influence, particularly in the spirit of rationalism. The literary values of the age were defined by the newly founded Royal Academy of Spain. The result was a dry, lifeless formalism. By the end of the century, however, such authors as Gaspar Melchor Jovellanos began to restore vitality to the literature, and the initial signs of romanticism were seen.

While much of Spanish literature may be designated romantic, romanticism itself lived a relatively brief life in Spain, from 1833 to 1848. The movement in Spain was characterized by nationalism and an emphasis on Spain's history and literature.

During the second half of the nineteenth century the Spanish novel entered an extraordinary period of development, beginning with a romantic novel in the *costumbrista* tradition, *The Sea Gull* by Fernán Caballero. From these roots grew the novelistic tradition that culminated in the majestic realistic and historical novels of Benito Pérez Galdós, the regional novels of Juan Valera and José María de Pereda, and the naturalistic novels of Leopoldo Alas and Vicente Blasco Ibáñez.

A new era began in the year 1898 with Spain's defeat in Cuba, an event that called attention to its decline over the centuries. A group of writers, the so-called Generation of 1898, collected around their common concerns of the resurrection of the true spirit of Spain, a *fin-de-siècle* pessimism and anguish, a desire to renew the Spanish language, and a reaction against the scientific and mechanistic.

The early years of the twentieth century brought an important renovation in poetry with the Generation of 1927, which tended toward gongorism, surrealism, and "pure poetry," the elimination of all nonpoetic elements. A later generation, sometimes labeled the Generation of 1936, rejected their aestheticism in favor of clarity, directness, and the expression of social concerns.

The Spanish civil war (1936–1939) marked a break in the development of Spanish literature, for many writers were killed, imprisoned, or exiled, and those who remained in Spain were effectively silenced by stiff censorship. The Spanish novel entered a period of renewal with the publication of Camilo José Cela's *The Family of Pascual Duarte* in 1942. That novel initiated a movement called *tremendismo*, a style of naturalism focusing on the grotesque and violent that has been continued by Miguel Delibes and Ana María Matute. A network of underground dramatists developed, of whom Alfonso Sastre was perhaps the best known. Since the death of dictator Francisco Franco in 1978, restrictions on free speech have been lifted, many exiled writers have returned to Spain, and a new generation of writers is emerging.

HISTORY AND CRITICISM

General

Bell, Aubrey F. *A Castilian Literature.* Russell repr. of 1938 ed. 1968 $8.00. An attempt to define the literary genius of Spain for the English-language reader. Concentrates on medieval, Renaissance, and baroque periods.

Bennassar, Bartolomé. *The Spanish Character: Attitudes and Mentalities from the Sixteenth to the Nineteenth Century.* Trans. by Benjamin Keen, Univ. of California Pr. 1979 $30.00

Benson, Frederick R. *Writers in Arms: The Literary Impact of the Spanish Civil War.* New York Univ. Pr. 1967 o.p. Benson "skillfully interweaves literary criticism with political análysis: he includes a useful chronology and . . . an excellent selective bibliography" (*LJ*).

Bourland, Caroline B. *The Short Story in Spain in the Seventeenth Century, with a Bibliography of the Novella from 1576–1700.* Burt Franklin repr. of 1927 ed. $21.00; Folcroft repr. of 1927 ed. lib. bdg. $14.75. Brief essay on the Italian influence on the Spanish short story in the seventeenth century.

Brenan, Gerald. *The Literature of the Spanish People from Roman Times to the Present*

Day. 1951. Cambridge Univ. Pr. 1953 o.p. Although Brenan's treatment is highly subjective and his value judgments and omissions sometimes controversial, his work is always interesting.

Butt, John. *Writers and Politics in Modern Spain. Writers and Politics Ser.* Holmes & Meier 1978 $14.50 text ed. pap. $9.50

Chandler, Richard E., and Kessel Schwartz. *New History of Spanish Literature.* Louisiana State Univ. Pr. text ed. 1961 $37.50. Authoritative volume covering poetry, drama, fiction, and nonfiction with a succinct discussion of Spanish history and culture; appendixes and classified bibliography.

Crow, John A. *Spain: The Root and the Flower.* Harper rev. ed. 1975 $16.95; Univ. of California Pr. 3d ed. rev. 1985 $18.50 pap. $9.95. Spanish culture, particularly during the Golden Age, is interestingly treated here.

Diaz Plaja, Guillermo. *A History of Spanish Literature.* Trans. by Hugh A. Harter, New York Univ. Pr. 1971 $27.00. A valuable introduction with substantial excerpts from each author by an eminent Spanish historian.

Dunn, Peter N. *The Spanish Picaresque Novel. Twayne's World Authors Ser.* G. K. Hall 1979 lib. bdg. $16.95. Analysis of the genre from *Lazarillo de Tormes* to *Estebanillo González.*

Entwistle, William S. *The Arthurian Legends in the Literatures of the Spanish Peninsula.* Kraus repr. of 1925 ed. 1975 $21.00; Phaeton repr. of 1925 ed. 1975 $12.50

Eoff, Sherman H. *The Modern Spanish Novel: Comparative Essays Examining the Philosophical Impact of Science on Fiction. Gotham Lib.* New York Univ. Pr. 1961 pap. $4.95. A study of the modern Spanish philosophical novel through comparisons with works in other European literatures. Compares novelists in the nineteenth and twentieth centuries in the light of their common intellectual background.

Green, Otis H. *Spain and the Western Tradition: The Castilian Mind in Literature from El Cid to Calderón.* Univ. of Wisconsin Pr. 4 vols. 1963 pap. ea. $7.95. Green interprets the essential ideas of Spanish literary texts from the twelfth through the seventeenth centuries. Topics treated include love, reason, free will, fortune and fate, death, and religion.

Keller, John E., and Richard P. Kinkade. *Iconography in Medieval Spanish Literature.* Univ. Pr. of Kentucky 1984 $50.00

Ley, Charles D. *Spanish Poetry since 1939.* Catholic Univ. Pr. 1962 $13.95. A valuable critical analysis with translations.

Litvak, Lily. *A Dream of Arcadia: Anti-Industrialism in Spanish Literature, 1895–1905.* Univ. of Texas Pr. 1975 $17.50

Madariaga, Salvador de. *The Genius of Spain and Other Essays on Spanish Literature. Essay Index Repr. Ser.* Ayer repr. of 1923 ed. $14.75

McClelland, I. L. *The Origins of the Romantic Movement in Spain.* Humanities Pr. repr. of 1937 ed. text ed. 1975 $15.00. Using a broad definition of romanticism, the author explores romantic tendencies and theories as they apply to the many periods in Spanish literature.

Miller, Beth, ed. *Women in Hispanic Literature: Icons and Fallen Idols.* Univ. of California Pr. text ed. 1984 $30.00 pap. $9.95

Monteser, Frederick. *The Picaresque Element in Western Literature. Studies in the Humanities* Univ. of Alabama Pr. 1975 $11.50

Morris, C. B. *A Generation of Spanish Poets, 1920–1936.* Cambridge Univ. Pr. 1969 $49.50 pap. $13.95. A comprehensive study of this period of transition and change in Spanish poetry.

———. *Surrealism and Spain, 1920–1936.* Cambridge Univ. Pr. 1979 pap. $12.95. A complex study intended for the reader of Spanish and French; includes appendixes of documents of Spanish and French surrealism.

——. *This Loving Darkness: Silent Films and Spanish Writers, 1920–1936.* Oxford 1980 $39.50

Muste, John M. *Say That We Saw Spain Die: Literary Consequences of the Spanish Civil War.* Univ. of Washington Pr. 1966 $14.50

Northrup, George T., and Nelson B. Adams, eds. *An Introduction to Spanish Literature.* Univ. of Chicago Pr. (Phoenix Bks.) 3d ed. enl. 1960 pap. $3.95. An easy-to-read outline of Spanish literature.

Parker, A. A. *The Philosophy of Love in Spanish Literature.* Columbia Univ. Pr. 1985 $12.00

Parks, George B., and Ruth Z. Temple, eds. *Romance Literatures. Lit. of the World in Eng. Translation* Ungar 2 vols. 1970 $110.00. Bibliographies of English translations of Spanish, Spanish-American, Portuguese, and Brazilian literatures.

Pattison, Walter T., and Donald W. Bleznick, eds. *Representative Spanish Authors.* Oxford 2 vols. 3d ed. text ed. 1971 ea. $20.95–$22.00

Peers, Edgar A. *The Spanish Tragedy, 1930–1936.* Greenwood repr. of 1936 ed. 1975 lib. bdg. $16.00

Perez Firmat, Gustavo. *Idle Fictions: The Hispanic Vanguard Novel, 1926–1934.* Duke Univ. Pr. text ed. 1982 $24.75

Post, Chandler R. *Medieval Spanish Allegory.* Gordon 1984 lib. bdg. $90.00

Rivers, Elias L. *Quixotic Scriptures: Essays on the Textuality of Hispanic Literature.* Indiana Univ. Pr. 1983 $17.50

Shaw, Donald L. *The Generation of 1898 in Spain.* Barnes & Noble text ed. 1975 $15.00. Concludes that writers of the Generation of 1898 mistakenly relied on abstract and philosophical perspectives in treating the practical and concrete issues of the time in which they wrote.

Shepard, Sanford. *Lost Lexicon: Secret Meanings in the Vocabulary of Spanish Literature during the Inquisition. Hispanic Studies Collection* Ediciones 1982 pap. $19.95

Stamm, James R. *A Short History of Spanish Literature: Revised and Updated Edition. Gotham Lib.* New York Univ. Pr. 1979 $35.00 pap. $16.50

Ward, Philip. *The Oxford Companion to Spanish Literature.* Oxford 1978 $39.95

Wilson, Edward M. *Spanish and English Literature of the Sixteenth and Seventeenth Centuries.* Ed. by Don Cruickshank, Cambridge Univ. Pr. 1980 $42.50

Spanish Drama

Cook, John A. *Neo-Classic Drama in Spain.* Greenwood repr. of 1959 ed. 1974 lib. bdg. $75.00. A well-documented history of the development of neoclassical drama through the failures of romanticism.

Crawford, J. Wickersham. *Spanish Drama before Lope de Vega.* Greenwood repr. of 1967 ed. 1975 lib. bdg. $82.50. A standard critical work. Traces the development of drama from pre-Encina times to the religious drama, tragedy, and comedy of the late sixteenth century.

——. *The Spanish Pastoral Drama.* Folcroft repr. of 1915 ed. lib. bdg. $22.50. Pastoral plays from the period before Juan del Encina until the seventeenth century, including those of Lope de Vega and Calderón.

Fiore, Robert L. *Drama and Ethos: Natural Law Ethics in Spanish Golden Age Theater. Studies in Romance Languages* Univ. Pr. of Kentucky 1975 $13.00

McKendrick, Melveena. *Woman and Society in the Spanish Drama of the Golden Age.* Cambridge Univ. Pr. 1974 $59.50

Peers, Edgar A., ed. *Spanish Golden Age in Poetry and Drama.* AMS Pr. repr. of 1946 ed. $25.00; Phaeton repr. of 1946 ed. 1974 $10.00

Rennert, Hugo A. *The Spanish Stage in the Time of Lope de Vega.* Kraus repr. of 1909 ed. $39.00. Discusses major playwrights, the origins of comedy and other types of plays, famous theaters, staging, and notable actors. A classic study of the important characteristics and historical development of the Spanish stage.

Shoemaker, William H. *The Multiple Stage in Spain during the Fifteenth and Sixteenth Centuries.* Greenwood repr. of 1935 ed. 1973 lib. bdg. $22.50

Wellwarth, George E. *Spanish Underground Drama.* Pennsylvania State Univ. Pr. 1972 $22.50. A critical study of Spanish playwrights forced "underground" under the censorship of the Franco regime.

Ziomek, Henryk. *A History of Spanish Golden Age Drama. Studies in Romance Languages* Univ. Pr. of Kentucky 1984 $25.00 pap. $10.00

Spanish Fiction

Chandler, Frank W. *Romances of Roguery: The Picaresque Novel in Spain.* Burt Franklin repr. of 1899 ed. 1961 $29.00; Gordon 1977 lib. bdg. $59.95. The social and literary antecedents and the development of the picaresque novel in Spain.

Fox-Lockert, Lucia. *Women Novelists in Spain and Spanish America.* Scarecrow Pr. 1979 $22.50

Johnson, Scott. *The Hero and the Class Struggle in the Contemporary Spanish Novel, 1931–1976.* Gordon 1976 $69.95

Patchell, Mary. *Palmerín Romances in Elizabethan Prose Fiction.* AMS Pr. repr. of 1947 ed. $17.00

Rico, Francisco. *The Spanish Picaresque Novel and the Point of View.* Cambridge Univ. Pr. 1984 $34.50 pap. $12.95

Sole-Levis, Amadey. *Spanish Pastoral Novel. Twayne's World Authors Ser.* G. K. Hall $14.50

Spires, Robert C. *Beyond the Metafictional Mode: Directions in the Modern Spanish Novel.* Univ. Pr. of Kentucky 1984 $18.00

Thomas, Henry. *Spanish and Portuguese Romances of Chivalry.* Kraus repr. of 1920 ed. $22.00

Spanish Poetry

Bergmann, Emilie L. *Art Inscribed: Essays on Ekphrasis in Spanish Golden Age Poetry.* Harvard Univ. Pr. 1980 $20.00

Cobb, Carl W. *Contemporary Spanish Poetry, 1898–1963. Twayne's World Authors Ser.* G. K. Hall 1976 lib. bdg. $14.50. Useful introduction to twentieth-century Spanish poetry.

Compton, Linda F. *Andalusian Lyrical Poetry and Old Spanish Love Songs: The "Muwashshah" and Its "Kharja."* New York Univ. Pr. 1976 $25.00

Cummins, J. G. *The Spanish Traditional Lyric.* Pergamon 1977 pap. $10.25

Daydi-Tolson, Santiago. *The Post-Civil War Spanish Social Poets. Twayne's World Authors Ser.* G. K. Hall 1984 $20.95

Debicki, Andrew P. *Poetry of Discovery: The Spanish Generation of 1956–1971.* Univ. Pr. of Kentucky 1982 $22.00

Fajardo, Salvador J., and John Wilcox, eds. *At Home and Beyond: New Essays on*

Spanish Poets of the Twenties. Society of Spain and Spanish Amer. 1983 pap. $20.00

Foster, David W. *The Early Spanish Ballad. Twayne's World Authors Ser.* G. K. Hall lib. bdg. $14.50

Goldstein, David, trans. *The Jewish Poets of Spain. Penguin Class. Ser.* 1983 pap. $5.95

Keller, John E. *Pious Brief Narrative in Medieval Castilian and Galician Verse: From Berceo to Alfonso X. Studies in Romance Languages* Univ. Pr. of Kentucky 1978 $16.00

McCormick, Robert. *The Concept of Happiness in the Spanish Poetry of the Eighteenth Century. Hispanic Studies Collection* Ediciones 1980 pap. $19.95

Morris, C. B. *Generation of Spanish Poets, 1920–1936.* Cambridge Univ. Pr. 1969 $49.50 pap. $13.95

Salinas, Pedro. *Reality and the Poet in Spanish Poetry.* Trans. by Edith F. Helman, Greenwood repr. of 1966 ed. 1980 lib. bdg. $24.75

SPANISH LITERATURE COLLECTIONS IN ENGLISH

Adams, Agatha B., and others. *Contemporary Spanish Literature in English Translation.* Darby repr. of 1929 ed. 1983 lib. bdg. $15.00; Norwood repr. of 1929 ed. 1978 lib. bdg. $10.00

Chandler, Richard E., and Kessel Schwartz, eds. *New Anthology of Spanish Literature.* Louisiana State Univ. Pr. 2 vols. text ed. 1967 $27.50

Pattison, Walter T., and Donald W. Bleznick, eds. *Representative Spanish Authors.* Oxford 2 vols. text ed. 1971 ea. $20.95–$22.00

Peers, Edgar A. *The Mystics of Spain.* Gordon 1977 lib. bdg. $59.95. Excerpts from the writings of 15 Spanish mystics translated and introduced by Peers. Study of the evolution of mystical thought from St. Ignatius of Loyola to mysticism after St. Teresa.

Ratliff, William F. *A Spanish Literary Reader.* Random 1981 pap. $7.95

Resnick, Seymour, and Jeanne Pasmantier, eds. *Anthology of Spanish Literature in English Translation.* Ungar 2 vols. text ed. 1958 $30.00. Includes works by many of the authors discussed in this chapter, as well as selections from authors not currently available in English translation.

———. *The Best of Spanish Literature in English Translation.* Ungar 1976 pap. $5.95

Schwartz, Kessel, ed. *Introduction to Modern Spanish Literature.* Irvington text ed. 1969 $19.95

Drama

Bentley, Eric, ed. *The Classic Theatre: Six Spanish Plays.* Doubleday (Anchor) pap. $7.50. Contains Fernando de Rojas, *Celestina;* Miguel de Cervantes, *Siege of Numantia;* Lope de Vega, *Fuente Ovejuna;* Tirso de Molina, *Trickster of Seville;* and Calderón de la Barca, *Love after Death* and *Life Is a Dream.*

Clark, B. H., ed. *Masterpieces of Modern Spanish Drama.* Kraus repr. of 1928 ed. $17.00

Wellwarth, George E., ed. *The New Wave Spanish Drama: An Anthology. Gotham Lib.* New York Univ. Pr. 1970 pap. $3.95. Contains J. Ruibal, *The Man and the Fly* and *The Jackass;* J. M. Bellido, *Train to H . . .* and *Bread and Rice, or Geometry in*

Yellow; A. M. Ballesteros, *The Hero and the Best of All Possible Worlds;* and Alfonso Sastre, *Sad Are the Eyes of William Tell.*

Poetry

Cannon, Calvin, ed. *Modern Spanish Poems.* Macmillan 1965 $7.95

Crow, John A., ed. *An Anthology of Spanish Poetry: From the Beginnings to the Present Day, Including Both Spain and Spanish America.* Louisiana State Univ. Pr. text ed. 1979 $25.00 pap. $8.95

Florit, Eugenio, trans. *Spanish Poetry: A Selection from the Cantar de Mío Cid to Miguel Hernández.* Dover 1970 pap. $2.00; Peter Smith $5.50

Turnbull, Eleanor L., trans. *Contemporary Spanish Poetry: Selections from Ten Poets.* Greenwood repr. of 1945 ed. lib. bdg. $22.50. Selections from José Morena Villa, Pedro Salinas, Jorge Guillén, Gerardo Diego, Federico García Lorca, Rafael Alberti, Emilio Prados, Vicente Aleixandre, Luis Cernuda, and Manuel Altolaguirre.

———. *Ten Centuries of Spanish Poetry: An Anthology in English Verse with Original Texts from the Tenth Century to the Generation of 1898.* Intro. by Pedro Salinas, Johns Hopkins Univ. Pr. bilingual ed. 1955 pap. $10.95

ALARCÓN, PEDRO ANTONIO DE. 1833–1891

An anticlerical radical in his youth, Alarcón became religious and conservative after an opponent in a duel spared his life. He is best known for his novella, *The Three-Cornered Hat* (1874), which Emilia Pardo Bazán called "the king of Spanish tales." The plot, reminiscent of many of Boccaccio's tales, involves a jealous miller who disguises himself to revenge what he supposes to be his wife's infidelities with the *corregidor* of the village. *The Three-Cornered Hat*, in which Alarcón skillfully combined humor, picaresque elements, the popular tradition, and a polished style, has served as the basis for operas in French, German, and English, and a ballet by Manuel de Falla.

BOOK BY ALARCÓN

The Three-Cornered Hat. Trans. by H. F. Turner, Dufour 1965 pap. $3.50

ALBERTI, RAFAEL. 1902–

Alberti began his career as a painter, exhibiting his own work in Madrid before age 20. Forced to rest because of poor health, he turned to reading and writing poetry and published his first volume, *Marinero en la tierra,* a book of lyrics evoking lost childhood, in 1924. His poetry remained controversial until 1927, when he wrote *Cal y canto* (published in 1929), poems in the gongorist style dominated by intricate and incongruous images. Alberti said of that volume, "Formal beauty took hold of me until it almost petrified my feelings." In 1929 he published the volume considered his most important, *Concerning the Angels,* a difficult, surreal work dealing with the good and bad angels inhabiting modern shattered psyches. At the same time he was becoming active politically, founding a communist newspaper,

Octubre, in 1934. His poetry during the 1930s became more political than aesthetic, as for example in *El poeta en la calle.* After fighting on the side of the republic during the civil war, he was forced to flee Spain. Since then he has lived in Argentina and Italy. His poetic imagination, revived by the birth of a daughter in 1941, surfaced in *The Painting* (1945, o.p.), a series of odes and sonnets addressed to painters. Of *Selected Poems* (1944), *Library Journal* said, "Alberti's tumultuous spiritual pilgrimage is well defined by the selections in this volume." Interspersed are sections of his autobiography, *A Vanished Grove.*

BOOKS BY ALBERTI

Concerning the Angels. Ohio Univ. Pr. (Swallow) 1967 $6.50
The Lost Grove: Autobiography of a Spanish Poet in Exile. Trans. by Gabriel Berns, Univ. of California Pr. 1977 $21.00 pap. $5.95
The Other Shore: 100 Poems by Rafael Alberti. Trans. by Paul Martin, Kosmos text ed. 1981 $20.00 pap. $7.95
The Owl's Insomnia: Poems. Trans. by Mark Strand, Atheneum 1973 pap. $7.95

ALEMÁN, MATEO. 1546–1614

Mateo Alemán spent much of his life in a kind of picaresque existence, going from the Universities of Salamanca and Alcalá to small government jobs to debtor's prison. It was perhaps in a Seville jail that he wrote the *First Part of the Life of the Pícaro Guzmán de Alfarache,* published in Madrid in 1599; the second part, written by an imitator, was published in Lisbon in 1604. Using some formal aspects of *Lazarillo de Tormes*—autobiographical, the lower-class hero, his service to several masters, and portraits of diverse classes and characters—Alemán developed the picaresque genre by taking his character, Guzmán, through adulthood, when he becomes a gambler, thief, and beggar. Thus he contributes to the corruption of society rather than merely being its victim, as is Lazarillo. Guzmán draws a bitter moral lesson from his experiences: Life is cruel, hunger is the rule, and honor cannot be preserved.

BOOK BY ALEMÁN

The Rogue; or The Life of Guzmán de Alfarache. Trans. by James Mabbe, intro. by J. Fitzmaurice-Kelly, AMS Pr. 4 vols. repr. of 1924 ed. $180.00

BOOKS ABOUT ALEMÁN

McGrady, Donald. *Mateo Alemán. Twayne's World Authors Ser.* Irvington 1968 lib. bdg. $15.95
Rico, Francisco. *The Spanish Picaresque Novel and the Point of View.* Cambridge Univ. Pr. 1984 $34.50 pap. $12.95

ALONSO, DÁMASO. 1898–

Although the major portion of Alonso's work is literary history and criticism, he established himself as a very reputable poet with *Children of Wrath* (1944). The metaphysical and religious poetry of this volume deals with the despair of modern life and man's search for salvation. The poetic form is free verse, adopted by Alonso in the belief that considering the state of the world aesthetic preoccupations are irrelevant.

BOOK BY ALONSO

Children of Wrath. Trans. by Elias L. Rivers, Johns Hopkins Univ. Pr. 1971 $6.95

BAREA, ARTURO. 1897–1957

An exile who died in England, Barea achieved international acclaim for his trilogy, *The Forging of a Rebel*, which was published in English prior to its publication in Spanish in 1952. The first two volumes consist of a novelistic treatment of the events that led him to become a socialist, while the third volume is a powerful narrative of actual events of the civil war, more properly labeled a history than a novel.

BOOK BY BAREA

The Forging of a Rebel. 1940–1946. Trans. by Ilsa Barea, Viking 1974 o.p.

BAROJA Y NESSI, PÍO. 1872–1956

Pío Baroja, whose works were admired by HEMINGWAY (see Vol. 1), was one of Spain's foremost twentieth-century novelists. A socially conscious writer whose mission was to expose injustices, Baroja chose as central characters those who live outside society—bohemian vagabonds, anarchists, degenerates, persons from the lower classes, and tormented intellectuals. In *The Restlessness of Shanti Andía*, Baroja used Basque sailors as protagonists to dramatize his view of life as a constant struggle for survival and to present a shipboard world that functions outside society's laws. In *The Tree of Science*, medical student Andrés Hurtado sees his intelligence as a disease and an incapacitating disgrace. For its treatment of *abulia* (lack of will) Valbuena Prat called this "the novel most typical of the Generation of 1898." Baroja's view that the concepts of beginning and end are human inventions to satisfy unattainable desires for meaning influences the form of his novels, often a series of episodes without cause and effect that end with unresolved problems.

Baroja studied medicine, a discipline reflected in his works by an interest in the pathological. During the 1920s he was popular in the United States, where many of his novels appeared in translation. In 1936 he was elected to the Spanish Academy. Franco later banned all but one of his nearly 100 books, but Baroja continued to live and write, although less assertively, in Spain until his death.

BOOKS BY BAROJA

The Restlessness of Shanti Andía and Other Writings. 1911. Trans. by Anthony Kerrigan, Univ. of Michigan Pr. 1959 o.p.
The Tree of Knowledge. 1911. Trans. by Aubrey F. G. Bell, Fertig repr. of 1928 ed. 1975 o.p.
Caesar or Nothing. Trans. by Louis How, Darby repr. of 1919 ed. 1983 $25.00; Richard West repr. of 1919 ed. 1980 $16.50

BOOK ABOUT BAROJA

Barrow, Leo L. *Negation in Baroja: A Key to His Novelistic Creativity.* Univ. of Arizona
   Pr. 1971 pap. $2.00

BÉCQUER, GUSTAVO ADOLFO (pseud. of Gustavo Adolfo Domínguez
   Bastida). 1836–1870

Bécquer was the archetypal romantic poet, devoting his life to poetry
and dying at 34 of tuberculosis and the effects of his bohemian life of poverty. *The Rhymes,* published during his lifetime in newspapers and collected
by friends in a volume a year after his death, is characterized by subjectivity, musicality, and the traditional romantic themes of love, death, the idealized past, and evocative landscapes. Bécquer uses the metaphor of yearning for an unattainable woman, first an imaginary muse and then a real
woman who rejects him, to describe the spiritual quest of the poet for ineffa-
ble beauty and inspiration. Bécquer's poetry has been called plastic and
painterly for its emphasis on color, light, and architecture. Influences on
The Rhymes are said to be primarily foreign—HEINE, BYRON (see Vol. 1), GOE-
THE, SCHILLER, Musset, and Lamartine. An atmosphere of magic and fantasy pervades the romantic *Legends* (1860–64), which are set in distant
places, such as India, and remote times, primarily the Middle Ages.
Dámaso Alonso called Bécquer's work the beginning of contemporary poetry, and Bécquer was admired deeply for his lyric poetry by the Generation of 1927: Guillén, Salinas, García Lorca, and Alberti.

BOOKS BY BÉCQUER

Romantic Legends of Spain. Trans. by Cornelia F. Bates and Katharine L. Bates,
   Short Story Index Repr. Ser. Ayer repr. of 1909 ed. $19.50
The Inn of the Cats. Trans. by J. R. Carey, Rogers 1945 o.p.
The Rimas of Gustavo Bécquer. Trans. by Jules Renard, Gordon 1976 lib. bdg. $59.95
A Flower on a Volcano. Trans. by Susanne Dubroff, Ally Pr. 1980 pap. $2.50 pap.
   $5.00

BOOK ABOUT BÉCQUER

Ruiz-Fornells, Enrique. *Concordance to the Poetry of Gustavo Adolfo Bécquer.* Univ. of
   Alabama Pr. 1970 $18.50

BENAVENTE, JACINTO. 1866–1954 (NOBEL PRIZE 1922)

Benavente, recipient of the Nobel Prize in 1922, marked the beginning of
modern Spanish drama for his break with the melodrama and affectation of
the previous style, represented by another Nobel Prize winner, José
Echegaray. Benavente called Lope de Vega, Calderón, SHAKESPEARE, IBSEN,
and Perez Galdós his masters, but beside their works his seem bland and
static. He was noted for elegant dialogues, and indeed he used conversation
to relate action that takes place offstage. He excelled in the use of social satire, ironic presentations of human weaknesses, and psychological penetration of character. *The Bonds of Interest* (1907), considered his best play, utilizes puppet figures, "the same grotesque masks of that Italian *commedia*

dell'arte, but not as gay as they were, for in all this time they have thought a great deal," Crispín explains in his introduction. Crispín contrives to secure a financially advantageous marriage for his poverty-stricken master, Leonardo, with Sylvia, daughter of the city's richest man. His thesis that the bonds of money are stronger than those of love seems disproved by the hints of love present in the marriage he finally arranges, but is confirmed in the sequel, which reveals that Leonardo's love waned soon after the marriage.

BOOK BY BENAVENTE

The Bonds of Interest. Ed. by Hymen Alpern and J. G. Underhill, Ungar bilingual ed. 1967 o.p.

BOOK ABOUT BENAVENTE

Peñuelas, Marcelino C. *Jacinto Benavente. Twayne's World Authors Ser.* Irvington 1968 lib. bdg. $15.95

BLASCO IBÁÑEZ, VICENTE. 1867–1928

Blasco Ibáñez is considered the last of the nineteenth-century realistic and naturalistic novelists, even though he actually produced most of his work in the twentieth century. Although he was more than a regional novelist, his finest works, for example *Reeds and Mud* (1902) and *The Cabin* (1898), are set in his native Valencia, depicting the harsh and brutal existence of peasant farmers and fishermen. In *Blood and Sand* (1908), made into a popular film in the United States, he attacked the Spanish passion for bullfighting as primitive. He is most famous abroad for *The Four Horsemen of the Apocalypse* (1916), a naturalistic novel on the horrors of war provoked by the Battle of Marne in which he predicted the involvement of the United States in World War I.

BOOKS BY BLASCO IBÁÑEZ

Last Lion and Other Stories. Trans. by Mariano J. Lorente, Branden pap. $2.50
The Cabin. Trans. by F. H. Snow, Fertig repr. of 1919 ed. 1975 $21.50
Reeds and Mud. Trans. by Lester Beberfall, Branden 1966 pap. $4.00
Blood and Sand. Intro. by Isaac Goldberg, Ungar pap. $4.95
The Four Horsemen of the Apocalypse. Buccaneer Bks. repr. of 1982 lib. bdg. $24.95; Dutton 1918 $8.95

CALDERÓN DE LA BARCA, PEDRO. 1600–1681

Calderón de la Barca was master of the Spanish stage from Lope de Vega's death until his own, serving as court poet to King Philip IV. While lacking Lope's spontaneity and vitality, he surpassed him in profundity of thought and in depicting interior conflicts in his characters. Much of Calderón's work probes metaphysical questions about free will, predestination, and the brevity of life. In addition, he provided theoretical interpretations of many of the same themes—honor, religion, the monarchy—that were presented dramatically by Lope. His style differs from Lope's in being more condensed, symbolic, and decorative, sharing characteristics of both culteranism and conceptism.

Calderón's piece *Life Is a Dream* (c.1635) deals with the same kind of prophecy about an infant that is found in the Oedipus myth. A king, told that his son would step on his head, locks him away from all contact with the world. When the youth awakes, he struggles with his instincts for revenge, finally moderating them. *The Mayor of Zalamea* (c.1642) is a reworking of a play by Lope on the theme of honor. *The Phantom Lady* (1629, o.p.) is a romantic intrigue, while *Devotion to the Cross* (1633, o.p.) is an example of the religious play, *auto sacramental*, a form Calderón perfected. He led a comparatively quiet life and after his ordination in 1651, he retired from the world, writing only two religious plays a year for the city of Madrid and some plays on mythological themes for the court's entertainment.

Books by Calderón de la Barca

Life Is a Dream. Trans. by Edwin Honig, Hill & Wang 1970 $4.50
Beware of Still Waters. Trans. by David Gitlitz, Trinity Univ. Pr. text ed. 1984 $25.00 pap. $12.00
Four Comedies by Pedro Calderón de la Barca. Trans. by Kenneth Muir, Univ. Pr. of Kentucky 1980 $26.00
The Mayor of Zalamea. Methuen 1983 pap. $7.95

Books about Calderón de la Barca

Gerstinger, Heinz. *Pedro Calderón de la Barca*. Trans. by Diana S. Peters, *Lit. and Life Ser.* Ungar $12.95
Hesse, Everett W. *Calderón de la Barca. Twayne's World Authors Ser.* G. K. Hall 1968 lib. bdg. $16.95
Hilborn, Harry W. *A Chronology of the Plays of Don Pedro Calderón de la Barca*. Gordon 1980 $55.00
Honig, Edwin. *Calderón and the Seizures of Honor*. Harvard Univ. Pr. 1972 $17.50
Maraniss, James E. *On Calderón*. Univ. of Missouri Pr. 1978 $15.00
McGaha, Michael D., ed. *Approaches to the Theater of Calderón*. Univ. Pr. of Amer. 1982 lib. bdg. $27.25 text ed. pap. $13.25
McGarry, M. Frances. *Allegorical and Metaphorical Language in the Autos Sacramentales of Calderón*. AMS Pr. repr. of 1937 ed. $23.00
Sullivan, Henry W. *Calderón in the German Lands and the Low Countries: His Reception and Influence, 1654 to 1980*. Cambridge Univ. Pr. 1983 $59.50
Ter Horst, Robert. *Calderón: The Secular Plays*. Univ. Pr. of Kentucky 1982 $24.00
Trench, R. C. *Calderón*. Haskell repr. of 1886 ed. 1970 lib. bdg. $39.95; Richard West repr. of 1886 ed. 1973 $25.00

CELA, CAMILO JOSÉ. 1916–

In Cela's first novel, *The Family of Pascual Duarte*, a condemned criminal relates in letters published after his execution the degrading circumstances that led him to commit a series of brutal murders, including that of a mare, his pet dog, his sister's lover, and his mother. Ironically, he receives the death sentence not for these murders but for killing a local boss. Narrative techniques employed by Cela are epistolary form, stream of consciousness, rupture of chronological sequence, and perspectivism. Cela produced no novel of real literary value after *The Family of Pascual Duarte* (1942) until *The Hive* in 1951, a portrait of the sordid world of the lower class of Madrid, and *Mrs. Caldwell Speaks to Her Son* (o.p.) in 1953. In the latter, a mother writing notes to her dead son tries to reconstruct his life as she gradually lapses into insanity and senility: "Mr. Cela narrates it in a beautiful, stylized way, with a tone of surrealistic casualness and a dash of old-fashioned, good-hearted cynicism" (*New Yorker*). *Journey to the Alcarria* (1948), a description of Cela's walking tour through Spain in the 1940s, is "recommended for larger travel or literature collections" (*LJ*).

BOOKS BY CELA

The Family of Pascual Duarte. Avon 1972 pap. $2.95
Journey to the Alcarria. 1948. Trans. by Francis M. López-Morillas, Univ. of Wisconsin Pr. 1964 $21.50
The Hive. Intro. by Arturo Barea, Ecco Pr. repr. of 1965 ed. 1983 pap. $6.95

BOOKS ABOUT CELA

Kirsner, Robert. *The Novels and Travels of Camilo José Cela. Studies in the Romance Languages and Lit.* Univ. of North Carolina Pr. 1964 pap. $9.50
McPheeters, D. W. *Camilo José Cela. Twayne's World Authors Ser.* Irvington 1969 lib. bdg. $15.95

CERVANTES SAAVEDRA, MIGUEL DE. 1547–1616

The son of a poor apothecary-surgeon, Cervantes believed that "two roads lead to wealth and glory, that of letters and that of arms." He first tried that of arms, seeing service with the Spanish-Venetian-papal fleet in the Battle of Lepanto, in which the Turkish invasion of Europe was thwarted. After being captured by Turkish pirates and held for ransom, he returned to Spain, where he attained a post as commissary of the Spanish Armada and tax collector. He was imprisoned when a banker to whom he entrusted government funds went bankrupt.

His first attempts at the road of letters having proved unsuccessful, for he could not compete with Lope de Vega in the theater, he began writing his satiric novel *Don Quijote* in 1603 while still in prison. In the novel, Alonso Quijano, his head turned from excessive reading, can no longer distinguish between everyday reality and that depicted in the novels of romance and chivalry in fashion during his day. Dubbing himself Don Quijote, he sets out on his bony nag, Rocinante, determined to restore justice to the world. He acquires the rotund peasant Sancho Panza as his squire and a barber's basin for a helmet. One of his most famous adventures involves combat with a giant who turns out to be a windmill, thereby originating the expression "to tilt at windmills." His further efforts are equally "quixotic," but he emerges as a tragic figure striving to maintain his illusions. Under his gaze the most basic reality becomes idealized: A homely servant girl becomes a princess, and all whom Don Quijote encounters must swear to her beauty. Part Two, completed in 1615, continues the narrative and introduces philosophic observations on human nature. At the end of Part Two Cervantes has a disillusioned and humbled Don Quijote die as a precaution against imitations of his work. Sancho, however, now shares Don Quijote's faith and will continue his mission.

This first modern novel, dealing with the nature of reality and truth, is said to have been translated into more languages than any other book except the Bible. It appeared in English in 1612–20, French in 1614–18, Italian in 1622–25, German in 1683, and Russian in 1769. Kenneth Rexroth wrote of *Don Quijote*, "Many people, not all of them Spanish, are on record as believing that *Don Quijote* is the greatest prose fiction ever produced in the Western World. . . . It epitomizes the spiritual world of European man at mid-career as the *Odyssey* and *Iliad* do at his beginnings and *The Brothers Karamazov* does in his decline" (*SR*).

The Exemplary Novels (1613, o.p.) are short stories with a moral that have provided plots for the plays of FLETCHER and MIDDLETON. The *Interludes*, one-act theatrical sketches, represent Cervantes's most successful attempts at writing drama.

BOOKS BY CERVANTES

Early Translations of *Don Quixote*
(Trans. by Thomas Shelton). 1612–20. AMS Pr. 4 vols. repr. of 1896 ed. ea. $35.00. The first translation in English; nearly contemporaneous with *Don Quijote*.
(Trans. by Pierre Motteux). 1690. Ed. by John G. Lockhart, Darby 4 vols. repr. of 1880 ed. 1983 $100.00. Pierre Motteux was born in France but fled to England upon revocation of the Edict of Nantes. His conquest of the English language was rapid, complete, and expert. His version of *Don Quixote* is known as "the ribald rendering," because he translated it freely, often in slang, sparing no pains to make it diverting and peppering it with contemporary allusion.
Modern Translations of *Don Quixote*
(Trans. by J. M. Cohen). Ed. by Olive Jones, Methuen 1980 $10.95. A strong translation in modern English that is faithful to the Spanish, by an eminent translator of Spanish literature.
(Trans. by Samuel Putnam). Modern Lib. 1949 $10.95. A translation from the Spanish, with a critical text based on the first editions of 1605 and 1615; includes variant readings, variorum notes, and an introduction by the translator.
(Trans. by Walter Starkie). New Amer. Lib. (Signet Class.) 1964 pap. $4.95. "Starkie is an eminent Hispanist whose publications on Spanish literature, life and lore are well known throughout the English-speaking world. . . . It is a close translation and, to the average American reader, may seem a bit more stiff in places than that of Putnam. The translation is, however, pleasantly readable and clearly and compactly presented in a single and inexpensive volume. Helpful and excellent introduction and selected bibliography" (*Choice*).
(Trans. by Joseph R. Jones and Kenneth Douglas). *Norton Critical Eds.* 1981 $29.95 pap. $9.95
Other Works
The Portable Cervantes. Trans. by Samuel Putnam, *Viking Portable Lib.* Penguin 1977 pap. $7.95
Three Exemplary Novels. Trans. by Samuel Putnam, Greenwood repr. of 1950 ed.

1982 $23.50. Contains *Rinconete and Cortadillo, Man of Glass,* and *The Colloquy of the Dogs.*

Two Humorous Novels: A Diverting Dialogue between Scipio and Bergansa and the Comical History of Rinconete and Cortadillo. Trans. by Robert Goadby, AMS Pr. repr. of 1741 ed. $49.50

BOOKS ABOUT CERVANTES

Bleznick, Donald W. *Studies on Don Quixote and Other Cervantine Works.* Spanish Lit. Publications 1984 $12.00

Byron, William. *Cervantes: A Biography.* Beekman 1979 $29.95

Calvert, Albert F. *The Life of Cervantes.* Folcroft repr. of 1905 ed. 1976 lib. bdg. $20.00

Close, A. *The Romantic Approach to Don Quixote.* Cambridge Univ. Pr. 1978 $52.50

Crooks, Esther. *The Influence of Cervantes in France in the Seventeenth Century. Studies in Comparative Lit.* Porcupine Pr. repr. of 1931 ed. lib. bdg. $22.50

Duran, Manuel. *Cervantes. Twayne's World Authors Ser.* G. K. Hall 1974 lib. bdg. $13.50

El Saffar, Ruth. *Beyond Fiction: The Recovery of the Feminine in the Novels of Cervantes.* Univ. of California Pr. 1984 lib. bdg. $19.00

———. *Novel to Romance: A Study of Cervantes' Novelas Ejemplares.* Johns Hopkins Univ. Pr. 1974 $12.50

Fitzmaurice-Kelly, J. *The Life of Miguel de Cervantes Saavedra: A Biographical, Literary, and Historical Study of a Tentative Bibliography from 1585 to 1892, and an Annotated Appendix on the Canto de Galiope.* Folcroft repr. of 1892 ed. text ed. $45.00; Richard West 1973 $45.00

Flores, Angel, and M. J. Benardete. *Cervantes across the Centuries: A Quadricentennial Volume.* Gordian repr. of 1947 ed. text ed. 1969 $15.00

Forcione, Alban K. *Cervantes and the Humanist Vision: A Study of Four Exemplary Novels.* Princeton Univ. Pr. 1982 $40.00

———. *Cervantes and the Mystery of Lawlessness: A Study of El Casamiento Engañoso y El Coloquio de los Perros.* Princeton Univ. Pr. 1984 $35.00

———. *Cervantes, Aristotle, and the Persiles.* Princeton Univ. Pr. 1970 $37.50

———. *Cervantes' Christian Romance: A Study of Persiles y Segismundo. Princeton Essays in Lit. Ser.* 1972 $21.00

Johnson, Carroll B. *Madness and Lust: A Psychoanalytic Approach to Don Quixote.* Univ. of California Pr. 1983 $22.50

Madariaga, Salvador de. *Don Quixote: An Introductory Essay in Psychology.* Greenwood repr. of 1935 ed. 1980 $22.50

Nabokov, Vladimir. *Lectures on Don Quixote.* Ed. by Fredson Bowers, Harcourt 1983 $17.95 1984 pap. $7.95

Nelson, L., Jr. *Cervantes: A Collection of Critical Essays.* Prentice-Hall (Spectrum Bks.) 1969 $12.95

Predmore, Richard L. *The World of Don Quixote.* Harvard Univ. Pr. 1967 $8.95. *Library Journal* called this an "indispensable study"; a useful work, "whatever the level of the reader's sophistication."

Weiger, John G. *The Individuated Self: Cervantes and the Emergence of the Individual.* Ohio Univ. Pr. 1979 $15.95

Williamson, Edwin. *The Half-Way House of Fiction: Don Quixote and Arthurian Romance.* Oxford 1984 $34.95

THE CID, POEM OF. c.1140

The manuscript of *The Poem of the Cid* was transcribed in 1307 by Pedro Abad and lay undiscovered in the monastery of Vicar until 1779. This epic poem recounts in 3,730 lines of verse the character and adventures of a Castilian soldier and nobleman, Rodrigo Díaz de Vivar or El Cid (d.1099). While the inspiration of the poem has been attributed to a variety of sources—Germanic, French *chansons de geste*, and Arabic—the Castilian spirit pervades the poem. According to Menéndez Pidal's theory of the gathering of the epic, the songs originated close to the dates of the events related and were transmitted orally through many voices, giving the poem a collective, popular flavor characteristic of much Spanish literature. Around 1140, a Spaniard, thought to be a Christian living in Moslem territory, integrated the tales to create this manuscript as it now exists.

El Cid, sent into exile by Alfonso VI of León after being accused of withholding some of the tribute money due the king, eventually recaptured the city of Valencia for Castilla, thereby giving the Spaniards access to the Mediterranean. Depicted as a protective father, a loving husband, a loyal vassal, and a servant of God, he remains a human being, rather than becoming a superhuman or mythical figure. Although the reality of his deeds is somewhat idealized, the Spanish epic is considerably more grounded in reality and history than the *Song of Roland*, for example.

Some of the unique qualities of *The Poem of the Cid* are realism, powerful description, spontaneity, poetic terseness, and vitality. The democratic spirit, respect for the law, political and social consciousness, and religious spirit reflect the Castilian society of the Middle Ages. In his *History of Spanish Literature* (o.p.), Ticknor wrote, "During the thousand years which elapsed from the time of the decay of Greek and Roman culture, down to the appearance of the *Divina Commedia*, no poetry was produced so original in its tone, or so full of natural feeling, picturesqueness, and energy." The figure and story of the Cid have been developed by Corneille (*Le Cid*), Herder, Southey, Hugo, Heredia, Leconte de Lisle, and Manuel Machado.

The Poem of the Cid. Trans. by Janet Perry, ed. by Michael Ian, Barnes & Noble text ed. 1975 $22.50; trans. by Archer M. Huntington, Kraus repr. of 1942 ed. $18.00; trans. by W. S. Merwin, New Amer. Lib. 1975 pap. $7.95; trans. by R. Hamilton and Janet Perry, *Penguin Class. Ser.* 1985 pap. $4.95; trans. by Lesley Byrd Simpson, Univ. of California Pr. 1957 pap. $3.95

BOOKS ABOUT THE POEM OF THE CID

Christopherson, Merrill G., and Adolfo León. *Cidean Ballads: Ballads about the Great Spanish Hero, El Cid. Comparative Lit. Ser.* Westburg pap. $10.00

Smith, Colin. *The Making of the "Poema de Mío Cid."* Cambridge Univ. Pr. 1984 $49.50

Waltman, Franklin M. *Concordance to the Poema de Mío Cid.* Pennsylvania State Univ. Pr. 1972 $36.00

GARCÍA LORCA, FEDERICO. 1899–1936

García Lorca is perhaps the best known of modern Spanish writers, partly because of his brutal execution outside Granada by Franco's army at the beginning of the civil war, but primarily because of his genius for poetry and drama. In 1928 Lorca published *Gypsy Ballads*, which won him immediate success and is considered one of the most important volumes of poetry of the century. Attracted to the gypsies for their exotic folklore, primitive sexual vitality, and their status as a group on the fringe of Spanish society, Lorca enlarged the gypsy people and their traditions to mythical proportions. Nature takes on human form while reality acquires a dreamlike quality in this powerful transformation of the world into a myth. The verse is colorful, rhythmic, dramatic, symbolic, and suggestive. Lorca's visit to New York in 1929 produced in him a deep despair from his confrontation with a mechanical and dehumanized society, and he saw in the black the only hope for revitalization of that world. The volume *Poet in New York* shows the influence of Negro spirituals and the poets WALT WHITMAN and T. S. ELIOT (see Vol. 1).

Although García Lorca was interested in drama throughout his life, he did not produce much of significance until the 1930s. Most important is his trilogy of Spanish rural life, *Blood Wedding* (1933), *Yerma* (1934), and *The House of Bernarda Alba* (1936), all tragedies with women as protagonists. In each play, the fall of the heroine, and of those around her whom she pulls down, is caused by frustrations produced by society. *Blood Wedding* demonstrates the sterility of the traditional code of honor. *Yerma* reveals the emptiness of a traditional marriage in which the woman must bear her husband children to prove her fidelity, and *The House of Bernarda Alba* dramatizes the destructive nature of Bernarda's dictatorial rule over her house, a microcosm of Spain. *The Butterfly's Evil Spell* (1919) is Lorca's first play; *The Shoemaker's Prodigious Wife* (1931) and *Don Perlimplín* (1931) are farces; *The Billy-Club Puppets* (1931) is a puppet play.

BOOKS BY GARCÍA LORCA

The Gypsy Ballads of García Lorca. Trans. by Rolfe Humphries, Indiana Univ. Pr. 1953 $10.00 pap. $4.95

Poet in New York. Trans. by Ben Belitt, Peter Smith bilingual ed. $12.75

Five Plays: Comedies and Tragicomedies. Intro. by Francisco García Lorca, Greenwood repr. of 1963 ed. 1977 lib. bdg. $24.75

Three Tragedies: Blood Wedding, Yerma, Bernarda Alba. Trans. by James Lujan Graham, Greenwood repr. of 1955 ed. 1977 lib. bdg. $25.00

Lament for the Death of a Bullfighter: And Other Poems. Trans. by A. L. Lloyd, AMS Pr. repr. of 1937 ed. bilingual ed. 1977 $13.50; Greenwood repr. of 1937 ed. 1977 lib. bdg. $18.75

Tree of Song. Trans. by Alan Brilliant, Unicorn Pr. 2d ed. rev. bilingual ed. 1973 $10.00 pap. $4.00

BOOKS ABOUT GARCÍA LORCA

Adams, Mildred. *García Lorca: Playwright and Poet*. Braziller 1977 $8.95

Allen, Rupert C. *Psyche and Symbol in the Theater of Federico García Lorca: Perlimplín, Yerma, Blood Wedding*. Univ. of Texas Pr. 1974 $14.50

Anderson, Reed. *Federico García Lorca. Modern Dramatists Ser.* Grove 1984 $19.50
    pap. $7.95
Barea, Arturo. *Lorca: The Poet and His People.* Cooper Square Pr. repr. of 1949 ed.
    1973 lib. bdg. $18.50
Craige, Betty Jean. *Lorca's "Poet in New York": The Fall into Consciousness.* Univ. Pr.
    of Kentucky 1977 $11.00
Duran, Manuel, ed. *Lorca: A Collection of Critical Essays.* Greenwood repr. of 1962
    ed. 1977 lib. bdg. $15.00
Edwards, Gwynne. *Lorca: The Theater beneath the Sand. Critical Appraisals Ser.* M.
    Boyars 1982 $20.00 pap. $9.95
Higginbotham, Virginia. *The Comic Spirit of Federico García Lorca.* Univ. of Texas
    Pr. 1976 $13.95
Honig, Edwin. *García Lorca.* Octagon rev. ed. repr. of 1963 ed. 1980 lib. bdg. $18.00
Londre, Felicia H. *Federico García Lorca. Lit. and Life Ser.* Ungar 1985 $13.50
Stanton, Edward F. *The Tragic Myth: Lorca and Cante Jondo.* Univ. Pr. of Kentucky
    1978 $14.00
Trend, John B. *Lorca and the Spanish Poetic Tradition.* Russell repr. of 1956 ed. 1971
    $12.00

GIRONELLA, JOSÉ MARÍA. 1917–

Gironella is best known for his trilogy *The Cypresses Believe in God, One
Million Dead* (1961), and *Peace after War*, about Spanish life from the final
years of the republic to the present day. *The Cypresses Believe in God* deals
with social and political activities leading up to the civil war as they affect
life in the Catalan city of Gerona. The point of view is that of its hero, Igna-
cio de Alvear, who in his contacts with people from various political parties
and social classes views a wide spectrum of Spanish society. Gironella
claims to be objective and impartial, but critics have noted, particularly in
the second volume, a gentleness toward the Falange, and indeed he has
been labeled a *"Franquista."* Others have suggested that perhaps he has
moderated his views to prevent censorship of his work.

Born in Gerona and educated in primary school and an ecclesiastical
seminary until he was 13, Gironella worked in a series of odd jobs until the
Spanish civil war, when he served at the front in Franco's army from 1936
to 1939. His first novel, *Un Hombre*, 1946, won the Nadal Prize.

BOOKS BY GIRONELLA

The Cypresses Believe in God. 1953. Trans. by Harriet de Onís, Knopf 1955 o.p.
Peace after War. 1966. Trans. by Joan MacLean, Knopf 1969 o.p.

GÓNGORA Y ARGOTE, LUIS DE. 1561–1627

Born in Córdoba, Luis de Góngora studied for the priesthood there and
then served as private chaplain to King Philip III in Madrid. As a member
of the court, he became involved in the literary controversy of his day, the
antagonism between the exponents of conceptism, led by Quevedo and
Gracián, and culteranism, led by Góngora himself. Both schools were manifestations of the baroque spirit, culteranism being characterized by neolo-
gism, hyperbaton, and use of metaphors as a poetic substitution for reality,

and conceptism relying on conceits and philosophic paradoxes. While Góngora's early poetry consists of relatively simple sonnets, his second period, that of the *Solitudes*, reveals the culteranistic style at its extreme. The *Solitudes* are characterized by pastoral subject matter, artificial language, intricate metaphors, mythological allusions, and musical verse. The French symbolist poets of the late nineteenth century and the Spanish poets of the Generation of 1927 have praised the poetry of Góngora, finding there "delicate imagery, poetic insight, and a heightened awareness of the descriptive capacities of the Spanish language" (Stamm).

BOOKS BY GÓNGORA

Solitudes of Luis de Góngora. Trans. by Gilbert E. Cunningham, Johns Hopkins Univ. Pr. 1968 o.p.
Poems. Trans. by R. O. Jones, Cambridge 1966 o.p.
Fourteen Sonnets and Polyphemus. Trans. by Mack Singleton, Hispanic Seminary 1975 pap. o.p.

BOOKS ABOUT GÓNGORA

Beverly, John. *Aspects of Góngora's Soledades.* Benjamins 1980 $21.00
Richards, Ruth M. *Concordance to the Sonnets of Góngora.* Hispanic Seminary 1982 $15.00
Woods, M. J. *The Poet and the Natural World in the Age of Góngora.* Oxford 1978 $34.95

GOYTISOLO, JUAN. 1931–

Goytisolo first became known in the United States for his novel *The Young Assassins* (1954, o.p.), the story of juvenile delinquents corrupted by social conditions during and immediately after the Spanish civil war. His depictions of the spiritual emptiness and moral decay of Spain under the Franco regime led to the censorship of some of his works there, and he moved to Paris in 1957. *Count Julian* is an exile's view of Spain, with Spanish history, literature, and language derisively viewed across the narrow straits of Tangiers for the purpose of destroying them so that they might be reinvented. Formally, it is a "new novel" along the lines of ROBBE-GRILLET's formulations.

BOOK BY GOYTISOLO

Count Julian. 1970. Trans. by Helen R. Lane, Viking 1974 o.p.

GRACIÁN, BALTASAR. 1601–1658

A Jesuit priest, Baltasar Gracián was the theoretician of conceptism and the great moralistic and didactic writer of his day. In *The Oracle*, he presented examples of ideal men of several types—the hero, the discreet man, and the politician—examples needed to correct man's cruel and barbaric nature. *The Art of Worldly Wisdom* is an explanation and defense of conceptism, in which Gracián advocated extreme brevity of expression.

BOOKS BY GRACIÁN

The Oracle: A Manual of the Art of Discretion. 1647. Trans. by L. B. Walton, Dutton
(Everyman's) 1953 o.p.
The Art of Worldly Wisdom. 1648. Ungar o.p.
Gracián's Manual: A Truth-Telling Manual and the Art of World Wisdom. Trans. by
Martin Fischer, Charles C. Thomas 2d ed. 1979 $7.95

BOOKS ABOUT GRACIÁN

Foster, Virginia R. *Baltasar Gracián. Twayne's World Authors Ser.* G. K. Hall 1975 lib.
bdg. $12.95; Irvington text ed. 1975 $15.95
Welles, Marcia L. *Style and Structure in Gracián's El Criticón. Studies in the Romance Languages and Lit.* Univ. of North Carolina Pr. 1976 pap. $13.00

GUILLÉN, JORGE. 1893–

Guillén's poetry celebrates this life and things of this world. In *Cántico,*
first published in 1928 and then substantially revised numerous times by the
poet, he exalted the pure joy of being: "To be, nothing more. And that suffices." This enthusiasm for life was sustained until *Clamor* (three volumes
published in 1957, 1960, and 1963), when the brutal realities of the modern
world broke into his joyous vision. Even so, Guillén remained optimistic
about the future, and in his poem *Goodbye, Goodbye, Europe,* he spoke of escaping the old decaying world to an "innocent new world," a reference to the
United States where he has taught in universities since 1936. Guillén's style
is concentrated, economical, disciplined, and polished, showing the influence of classical forms as well as of the gongorist style. His is a "pure poetry"
from which he has attempted to remove all nonpoetic elements, such as narrative and anecdote. He has translated Valéry and Claudel into Spanish.

BOOKS BY GUILLÉN

Affirmation: A Bilingual Anthology, 1919–1966. Univ. of Oklahoma Pr. repr. of 1968
ed. 1971 $14.95
Guillén on Guillén: The Poetry and the Poet. Trans. by Anthony L. Geist, Princeton
Univ. Pr. 1979 pap. $7.95

BOOKS ABOUT GUILLÉN

MacCurdy, C. Grant. *Jorge Guillén. Twayne's World Authors Ser.* G. K. Hall 1981 lib.
bdg. $16.95
Yudin, Florence. *The "Vibrant Silence" in Jorge Guillén's Aire Nuestro. Studies in the
Romance Languages and Lit.* Univ. of North Carolina Pr. 1974 pap. $6.00

HERNÁNDEZ, MIGUEL. 1910–1942

Little educated, Hernández studiously imitated the style of Góngora in
his first volume of poetry, published in 1933. In his best volume, *El rayo que
no cesa* (1936), he found his own voice, expressing powerful emotion in classical sonnet form. After fighting for the republic during the civil war, Hernández was imprisoned in a concentration camp, where he died of tuberculosis at age 32 in spite of international protests for his freedom. *The
Songbook of Absences* (1938–1941), written during his years as a political

prisoner, is a painful record of his suffering on separation from his wife, his sorrow at the death of his son, and yearning for the simple country life of his youth.

BOOK BY HERNÁNDEZ

The Songbook of Absences. Trans. by Tom Jones, Charioteer 1980 $7.50

JIMÉNEZ, JUAN RAMÓN. 1881–1958 (NOBEL PRIZE 1956)

On receiving the Nobel Prize in 1956, Juan Ramón Jiménez was praised for "his lyrical poetry, which constitutes an inspiring example in the Spanish language of spirituality and artistic purity." Jiménez's works have indeed provided inspiration for many younger Spanish poets—Federico García Lorca, Pedro Salinas, and Jorge Guillén among them—as well as for Latin American poets. His poetic world is both aesthetic and spiritual. Through poetry Jiménez endeavored not only to express his interior reality but also to reach the highest levels of spiritual experience.

Jiménez's early work is marked by a short period of modernism followed by a rejection of it in favor of simpler forms, particularly that of traditional Spanish ballads. The turmoil and anxiety produced by his sea voyage to the United States to marry an American, Zenobia Camprubí, and their return as newlyweds began his second period. That phase was characterized by increasing subjectivity and purification of his poetry, a process furthered by Zenobia, who protected him from intrusions of the world. His use of woman to symbolize the object of his desires to know and experience reveals the influence of Bécquer. In his final stage, he embarked on a mystical search for the absolute. His revelation was that "God desired" and "God desiring" reside within his own soul.

Platero and I (1914), a poignant and charming story in poetic prose about a silver-gray donkey named Platero, is popular with children. Jiménez did not intend it for children exclusively, however, but rather as a celebration of the essence of the child, "a spiritual island fallen from heaven."

BOOKS BY JIMÉNEZ

Platero and I. Intro. by W. H. Roberts, New Amer. Lib. (Signet Class.) pap. $.95; trans. by Eloise Roach, Univ. of Texas Pr. 1983 pap. $6.95
Naked Music: Poems of Juan Ramón Jiménez. Trans. by Dennis Maloney, White Pine 2d ed. 1984 $2.00
Three Hundred Poems, 1903–1953. Trans. by Eloise Roach, intro. by Ricardo Gullón, Univ. of Texas Pr. 1962 $20.00. A representative collection including those poems that the poet and his wife considered his best. The translator selected them from the Nobel Prize collection *Libros de Poesía* and from books published between 1903 and 1914.

BOOKS ABOUT JIMÉNEZ

Olson, Paul R. *Circle of Paradox: Time and Essence in the Poetry of Juan Ramón Jiménez.* Johns Hopkins Univ. Pr. 1967 $25.00
Young, Howard T. *Juan Ramón Jiménez.* Columbia Univ. Pr. 1967 pap. $2.50

————. *The Line in the Margin: Juan Ramón Jiménez and His Readings in Blake, Shelley and Yeats*. Univ. of Wisconsin Pr. 1980 $27.50

JOHN OF THE CROSS, ST. (Juan de Yepes y Alvarez). 1542–1591

St. John of the Cross represents the pinnacle of Spanish mysticism. In contrast to St. Teresa's works, which refer frequently to things of this world, St. John's poetry works on a purely spiritual, abstract plane. His poems consist of allegorical descriptions of the journey of his spirit through mortification of earthly appetites, illumination, and purification of the soul to union with God. In his prose commentaries on his own poems he laments the insufficiency of language to communicate his mystical experiences and his interior life.

A disciple of St. Teresa, he became the spiritual director of her convent at Avila in 1572 and was responsible for carrying out many of her rigorous new programs for the Carmelite Order. Objections to his extreme reforms led to a period of imprisonment and torture in Toledo. During this time, according to tradition, he wrote *Spiritual Canticle*. His concentrated symbolic poetry has been studied with enthusiasm by such modern poets as T. S. ELIOT (see Vol. 1), PAUL VALÉRY, and Jorge Guillén.

BOOKS BY ST. JOHN OF THE CROSS

The Collected Works of St. John of the Cross. Trans. by Kieran Kavanaugh and Otilio Rodriguez, I.C.S. Publications 1979 $14.95 pap. $7.95

The Dark Night of the Soul. Trans. by Benedict Zimmerman, Attic Pr. 1974 pap. $10.95

Poems of Saint John of the Cross. Trans. by Willis Barnstone, New Directions bilingual ed. 1972 pap. $4.95

Spiritual Canticle. Trans. by Edgar Allison Peers, Doubleday 1975 pap. $4.95

Ascent of Mount Carmel. Trans. by Edgar Allison Peers, Doubleday 1973 pap. $5.95

The Living Flame of Love. Trans. by Edgar Allison Peers, Doubleday 1971 pap. $4.50

BOOKS ABOUT ST. JOHN OF THE CROSS

Cugno, Alain. *St. John of the Cross: Reflections on Mystical Experience*. Trans. by Barbara Wall, Winston Pr. 1982 pap. $13.95

Frost, Bede. *St. John of the Cross*. Gordon 1977 $59.95

Hardy, Richard P. *The Search for Nothing: The Life of John of the Cross*. Crossroads 1982 $10.95

Icaza, Rosa M. *Stylistic Relationship between Poetry and Prose in the Cántico Espiritual of San Juan de la Cruz*. AMS Pr. repr. of 1957 ed. 1969 $21.00

MacDonald, James M. *The Life and Writing of St. John of the Cross*. Gordon 1977 $59.95

Mallory, Marilyn M. *Christian Mysticism: Transcending Techniques: A Theological Reflection on the Empirical Testing of the Teaching of St. John of the Cross*. Humanities Pr. text ed. 1977 pap. $35.75

Palacios, Miguel A. *Saint John of the Cross and Islam*. Trans. by Elmer H. Douglas, Vantage 1980 $7.95

Thompson, Colin P. *The Poet and the Mystic: A Study of the Cántico Espiritual of San Juan de la Cruz*. Oxford 1977 $36.95

THE LIFE OF LAZARILLO DE TORMES. 1554

The composition of *The Life of Lazarillo de Tormes*, published in Burgos, Alcalá, and Antwerp in 1554, has been placed between 1525 and 1550; both the date and the identity of the author remain unknown. The novel gained immediate popularity and is the prototype of the picaresque novel, a genre episodic in form that features the adventures of an antihero, usually young, matching his wits against cruel masters and an indifferent, corrupt society. Among the innovations of *The Life of Lazarillo de Tormes* are the first-person narrative technique, concentration of interest on lower-class figures, and the rejection of chivalric and sentimental literature. Lazarillo, "born in the river Tormes" to a thieving father and a mother of questionable reputation, serves a crafty blind man, a greedy and hypocritical priest, and a starving gentleman striving to keep his appearance of wealth. In each situation the boy must struggle continually for food to stay alive. Lazarillo accepts his fate with resignation, drawing no moral generalizations from his experiences. Fortune, which he naively considers to be good, brings him a marriage with the mistress of the archpriest and a job as a bellringer. The author, however, strips the church, Spain, and human nature in general of its illusions of grandeur, and the next picaresque novel to appear, *Guzmán de Alfarache* by Mateo Alemán, is considerably more bitter in tone and pessimistic in outlook.

Life of Lazarillo de Tormes. Trans. by Harriet de Onís, Barron text ed. 1959 pap. $3.95; trans. by J. Gerald Markley, Macmillan text ed. 1954 pap. consult publisher for price; trans. by W. S. Merwin, Peter Smith $12.00

BOOK ABOUT LAZARILLO DE TORMES

Fiore, Robert L. *Lazarillo de Tormes. Twayne's World Authors Ser.* G. K. Hall 1984 lib. bdg. $15.95

LOPE DE VEGA CARPIO, FÉLIX. 1562–1635

Lope de Vega was the creator of the national theater in Spain, and his achievements in drama are comparable in many respects to those of Shakespeare in England. Lope embraced all of Spanish life in his drama, combining strands of previous Spanish drama, history, and tradition to produce a drama with both intellectual and popular appeal. A prodigious writer whom Cervantes called the "monster of nature," Lope is attributed by his biographer with nearly 2,000 plays, 400 religious dramas, and hundreds of pieces of poetry and literature in every form. He was also involved throughout his life in numerous amorous and military adventures and was ordained as a priest in 1614. In his didactic poem *New Art of Writing Plays* (1609), Lope defined his primary purpose as entertainment of the audience. He recommended a three-act play in which the outcome is withheld until the middle of the third act, when the *dénouement* should be swiftly developed. Maintaining that the possibilities of classical theater had been exhausted, he advocated casting Terence and Plautus aside, that is, abandoning the classical unities. His definition of drama was eclectic, admitting combinations of comedy and tragedy, noble and lower-class characters, a variety of

verse forms as demanded by different situations, and a wide panoply of
themes—national, foreign, mythological, religious, heroic, pastoral, historical, and contemporary. His major strength was the execution of plot; he created no character of the depth or complexity of Shakespeare's major figures. He captured the essence of Spanish character with his treatment of
the themes of honor, Catholic faith, the monarchy, and jealousy. In *Peribáñez* (1610?), a lower-class hero is shown to be more honorable than a
nobleman. King Henry the Just, a fictional creation, pardons Peribáñez
for his revenge killing of the nobleman who contrived to dishonor him by
abusing his new bride. In *Fuente Ovejuna*, a play based on an event narrated
in the Spanish chronicles, the people resist a cruel overlord, refusing to join
the army he tries to mount against Ferdinand and Isabel. After the overlord
interrupts a village wedding, the townspeople of Fuente Ovejuna collec-
tively murder him and finally receive pardon and gratitude from the Catholic kings.

Toward the end of his life Lope lost popularity, but all of Madrid attended
his funeral, and his death was mourned throughout Spain. ALBERT CAMUS
adapted his play *The Knight of Olmedo* (1623?) for French-speaking audiences.

BOOKS BY LOPE DE VEGA

The Knight of Olmedo. Trans. by William F. King, Univ. of Nebraska Pr. 1972 $16.95
Five Plays. Trans. by Jill Booty, ed. by R. D. F. Pring-Mill, Drama Bk. 1961 $2.45.
    *Peribáñez, Fuente Ovejuna, The Dog in the Manger, The Knight of Olmedo, Jus-
    tice without Vengeance.*

BOOKS ABOUT LOPE DE VEGA

Drake, Dana, and Jose A. Madrigal. *Studies in the Spanish Golden Age: Cervantes and
    Lope de Vega*. Ediciones 1978 pap. $10.00
Fitzmaurice-Kelly, J. *Lope de Vega and Spanish Drama. Studies in European Lit. Ser.*
    Haskell repr. of 1902 ed. 1970 lib. bdg. $22.95
Flores, Angel. *Lope de Vega: Monster of Nature*. Associated Faculty Pr. repr. of 1930
    ed. 1969 $19.50; Greenwood repr. of 1930 ed. lib. bdg. $18.75
Gerstinger, Heinz. *Lope de Vega and Spanish Drama*. Trans. by Samuel Rosenbaum,
    Lit. and Life Ser. Ungar 1974 $12.95
Larson, Donald R. *The Honor Plays of Lope de Vega*. Harvard Univ. Pr. 1977 $16.50
McCrary, William C. *The Goldfinch and the Hawk: A Study of Lope de Vega's "El
    Caballero de Olmedo." Studies in the Romance Languages and Lit.* Univ. of North
    Carolina Pr. 1966 pap. $10.50
Morley, S. G., and C. Bruerton. *Chronology of Lope de Vega's Comedies*. Kraus repr. of
    1940 ed. $35.00
Picerno, Richard A. *Lope de Vega's "Lo Que Pasa en Una Tarde": A Critical Annotated
    Edition of the Autograph Manuscript. Studies in the Romance Languages and Lit.*
    Univ. of North Carolina Pr. 1971 pap. $10.50
Rennert, Hugo A. *Life of Lope de Vega*. Ayer repr. of 1904 ed. 1968 $27.50
Trueblood, Alan S. *Experience and Artistic Expression in Lope de Vega: The Making of
    La Dorotea*. Harvard Univ. Pr. 1974 $40.00

MACHADO Y RUIZ, ANTONIO. 1875–1939

Machado's great love for Castile, nourished during his years as a teacher of French in Soria, is the source of much of his poetry. Rejecting modernism and gongorism, he wrote simple, natural, and spare verses. Sadness and melancholy were his dominant moods, deriving from the somber, barren atmosphere of the Castilian landscape, the death of his young wife in 1912, his own solitary nature, and the pessimism of his generation about Spain. In *Campos de Castilla* (o.p.), generally considered to mark his poetic height, his themes are lost youth, time, death, religion, and Spain. Machado believed that memory, capable of transforming and reliving experience, is man's only defense against time. His preoccupation with the concept of time as a stream carrying man to his end in nothingness may have developed from his study of Henri Bergson. In *Juan de Mairena*, Machado the poet carries on a dialogue with Machado the philosopher discussing philosophy, metaphysics, and the anguish of existence, topics that characterize him as a member of the Generation of 1898.

Books by Machado

Canciones. Trans. by Robert Bly, Coffee House $30.00 pap. $4.00
I Never Wanted Fame. Trans. by Robert Bly, Ally Pr. 1979 pap. $2.50
Juan de Mairena: Epigrams, Maxims, Memoranda, and Memoirs of an Apocryphal Professor. Trans. by Ben Belitt, Univ. of California Pr. 1963 pap. $1.50
Selected Poems. Trans. by Antonio Machado and Alan S. Trueblood, Harvard Univ. Pr. 1982 $25.00
Selected Poems of Antonio Machado: A Dialogue with Time. Trans. by Betty Craige, Univ. of New Mexico Pr. 1969 $22.50

Book about Machado

Hutman, Norma L. *Machado: A Dialogue with Time—Nature as an Expression of Temporality in the Poetry of Antonio Machado.* Irvington text ed. 1969 $22.50

ORTEGA Y GASSET, JOSÉ. 1883–1955

[SEE Volume 4.]

PARDO BAZÁN, EMILIA. 1851–1920

The Countess Emilia Pardo Bazán introduced the French naturalistic movement to Spain with *The Burning Question* (1881, o.p.). While she recognized the excesses of naturalism in its exclusive concentration on the sordid aspects of life, she saw in it possibilities for directing the Spanish novel to social and political issues. *The Son of the Bondwoman* (*Los Pasos de Ulloa*, 1886), which deals with the degeneration of an aristocratic family, is naturalistic in subject and in its deterministic conclusion.

Book by Pardo Bazán

The Son of the Bondwoman. Trans. by E. H. Hearn, Fertig repr. of 1908 ed. 1976 o.p.

BOOK ABOUT PARDO BAZÁN

Hemingway, Maurice. *Emilia Pardo Bazán: The Making of a Novelist.* Cambridge
    Univ. Pr. 1983 $39.50

PÉREZ DE AYALA, RAMÓN. 1880–1962

Pérez de Ayala experimented with a variety of novelistic forms. His controversial novels have been criticized by some as pedantic, nihilistic, and
pornographic, while others have praised their intellectual orientation, realistic portrayal of human weaknesses, and frank treatment of sex. *Belarmino
and Apolonio* is a novelistic treatment of the philosophy of perspectivism. At
least two versions of an event are narrated, and characters are described
from many angles and given more than one name. In *Honeymoon,
Bittermoon* Pérez de Ayala constructed a grotesque, stylized world through
skillful use of poetic language, symbol, and caricature, attacking hypocritical prudishness with the story of a young man's initiation into amorous adventures.

BOOKS BY PÉREZ DE AYALA

Belarmino and Apolonio. 1921. Trans. by Murray Baumgarten, Univ. of California Pr.
    1971 $24.95 pap. $5.95
Honeymoon, Bittermoon. 1923. Trans. by Barry Eisenberg, Univ. of California Pr.
    1972 $30.00

BOOK ABOUT PÉREZ DE AYALA

Weber, Frances W. *The Literary Perspectivism of Ramón Pérez de Ayala. Studies in
    the Romance Language and Lit.* Univ. of North Carolina Pr. 1966 pap. $7.00

PÉREZ GALDÓS, BENITO. 1843–1920

Pérez Galdós was Spain's outstanding nineteenth-century novelist. In
scope, purpose, and achievement he was comparable to DICKENS (see Vol. 1)
and BALZAC, two writers he acknowledged as models. At a time when most
Spanish novelists were limited by their regional backgrounds, Galdós
possessed the intellect and vision to embrace the Spanish people as a nation.
In 1873 he began the *National Episodes,* a 46-volume series of historical novels
in which he was concerned less with details and facts of history than with their
impact on the lives of ordinary people.

His works are sometimes divided into two periods: novels of the first period and contemporary Spanish novels. His early novels, *Doña Perfecta*
(1876), *Gloria* (1877), *Marianela* (1878), and *The Family of Leon Roch* (1879,
o.p.), may be characterized as realistic with touches of romanticism. The
novels are united by common characters and themes in the manner of
Balzac's *Human Tragedy. Doña Perfecta* is a denunciation of intolerance.
Marianela explores the irony and tragedy of the destruction of love by scientific progress. *Fortunata and Jacinta* (1886–1887, o.p.), a four-volume masterpiece of the second period, contrasts two women—Jacinta, wife of a wealthy
middle-class man, and Fortunata, wife of a lower-class man. Both are admirable characters, but it is Fortunata who bears a son, demonstrating the vi-

tality of the lower classes. The character of Maxi reveals Galdós's interest in mental illness and his naturalistic strain.

Born and educated in the Canary Islands, Pérez Galdós studied law briefly and spent most of his adult life in Madrid. His study of lower-class Spanish life and his attempts to improve it led him to the advocacy of more equal distribution of wealth and outspoken opposition to the Catholic church. While always popular with the people, he fared less well in literary circles. In 1889 he sought admission to the Royal Academy, an honor he was refused until 1897, and the Nobel Prize went to a contemporary, José Echegaray, a writer of considerably less talent. Galdós died poor and blind. Although the government refused him a state funeral, the entire Spanish nation mourned him. English translations of his novels now out of print are *The Disinherited Lady* (1881), *Miau* (1888), *Compassion* (1897), and *Tristana*.

BOOKS BY PÉREZ GALDÓS

Doña Perfecta. Trans. by Harriet de Onís, Barron 1960 pap. $5.50
Gloria. Trans. by C. Bell, Fertig 2 vols. in 1 repr. of 1882 ed. 1975 $32.50
Marianela. Trans. by H. Lester, Fertig repr. of 1892 ed. 1975 o.p.
The Shadow. Trans. by Karen O. Austin, Ohio Univ. Pr. 1980 $10.95
The Spendthrifts. Arden Lib. repr. of 1952 ed. 1978 lib. bdg. $30.00

BOOKS ABOUT PÉREZ GALDÓS

Engler, Kay. *The Structure of Realism: The Novelas Contemporáneas de Benito Pérez Galdós. Studies in the Romance Languages and Lit.* Univ. of North Carolina Pr. 1977 $14.50
Walton, Leslie B. *Pérez Galdós and the Spanish Novel of the Nineteenth Century.* Gordian repr. of 1927 ed. 1970 $10.00

QUEVEDO Y VILLEGAS, FRANCISCO GÓMEZ DE. 1580–1645

Born into an aristocratic family and educated in classics at the Universities of Madrid and Alcalá, Quevedo spent much of his adult life in the court of Madrid. His experiences in the court of the declining Spanish monarchy contributed to his skepticism and bitterness. In *The Swindler* (1626), Don Pablos narrates his picaresque adventures of the most brutal sort, and unlike the naive Lazarillo or the philosophizing Guzmán, this *pícaro* is completely amoral and misanthropic. The language of the work, densely filled with complex puns, jokes, and obscure allusions, amplifies the confusion of the world portrayed. In *Visions* (1627), Quevedo satirized and ridiculed the foibles and defects of man and society. For his nihilism and pessimism he has been compared to SWIFT (see Vol. 1), DOSTOEVSKY, KAFKA, and the twentieth-century existentialists.

BOOKS BY QUEVEDO

Two Picaresque Novels. Trans. by Michael Alpert, *Penguin Class. Ser.* 1969 pap. o.p.
Choice Humorous Satirical Works. Trans. by John Stevens, *Lib. of World Lit. Ser.* Hyperion Conn repr. of 1926 ed. $27.50
The Comic Works of Don Francisco de Quevedo. Trans. by John Stevens, AMS Pr. repr. of 1709 ed. 2d ed. $69.50

BOOKS ABOUT QUEVEDO

Baum, Doris L. *Traditionalism in the Works of Francisco de Quevedo y Villegas. Studies in the Romance Languages and Lit.* Univ. of North Carolina Pr. 1970 pap. $11.50

Bleznick, Donald W. *Quevedo.* Irvington repr. of 1972 ed. text ed. 1984 $22.50

Ettinghausen, Henry. *Francisco de Quevedo and the Neostoic Movement.* Oxford 1972 $29.95

ROJAS, FERNANDO DE. 1475?–1538?

Fernando de Rojas, thought to be of Jewish parentage and a convert to Christianity during the Inquisition, is generally considered to have written all but the first act of *Celestina.* This drama, or novel in dialogue, first appeared in 1499 as *The Comedy of Calisto and Melibea*, then in 1502 as *Tragi-Comedy* with five additional acts, and finally in 1519 as *Celestina* in the version now read. While grounded in medieval morality and conventions of courtly love, the work has been designated by Menéndez y Pelayo as marking the birth of the Spanish Renaissance for its tragic lovers Calisto and Melibea whose passions lead to their own destruction, its use of elegant language, the individualization of its characters, its glorification of the pleasures of this life, and its emphasis on luck as the law of the universe. Celestina, a worldly wise old schemer who is totally preoccupied with procuring sexual love, once for herself and now for others, is the grand creation of the work. The most important source for the character of Celestina is Juan Ruíz's *The Book of Good Love;* the influence of BOCCACCIO (through the archpriest of Talavera) as well as Greek and Latin works may also be detected. Some critics consider *Celestina* to be surpassed in Spanish literature only by *Don Quijote.*

BOOK BY ROJAS

Celestina; or The Tragicke-Comedy of Calisto and Melibea. Trans. by James Mabbe, intro. by J. Fitzmaurice-Kelly, AMS Pr. 1894 $45.00; (with the title *La Celestina: A Novel in Dialogue*) trans. by Lesley Byrd Simpson, Univ. of California Pr. 1955 pap. $4.95; (with the title *Celestina: A Play in Twenty-One Acts Attributed to Fernando de Rojas*) trans. by Mack H. Singleton, Univ. of Wisconsin Pr. 1958 pap. $9.75

BOOKS ABOUT ROJAS

Deyermond, A. D. *The Petrarchan Sources of "La Celestina."* Greenwood repr. of 1961 ed. 1975 lib. bdg. $18.75

Gilman, Stephen. *The Art of La Celestina.* Greenwood repr. of 1956 ed. 1977 lib. bdg. $24.75

RUÍZ, JUAN. 1283?–1350?

Little is known of the life of Juan Ruíz, often described as Spain's greatest writer of the Middle Ages and likened to CHAUCER (see Vol. 1) and BOCCACCIO. In his term as archpriest of Hita, a small Castilian town east of

Madrid, he apparently collected his own verses and songs into book form around 1330 and then revised and expanded it during a term in prison under sentence by the archbishop of Toledo. In the prose introduction to *The Book of Good Love*, Ruíz defined two categories of love: "good love" or the love of God and "crazy love" or carnal love. While avowing that his purpose was to expose the evils of worldly love and to lead his readers to the exclusive love of God, he admitted that his text may provide those who reject divine love with useful knowlege of the other sort of love. Thus the ironic tone of the book, as well as its humorous, satiric, and didactic nature, become apparent in this introduction. Juan Ruíz's self-consciousness as a writer and his awareness of the qualities of his art provide a glimpse of the Renaissance spirit. The primary literary source for *The Book of Good Love* is *Pamphilus and Galatea*, an anonymous twelfth-century play in Latin by a French poet. Américo Castro and others have suggested the possible influence of Arabic models as shown by the work's composite form, ambiguousness, and sensual elements. In its anticlerical attitudes, the book reflects the crisis of faith facing the Catholic church toward the end of the Middle Ages, a crisis complicated in Spain by the necessity of maintaining the religious fervor of the reconquest.

BOOKS BY RUÍZ

The Book of Good Love. Trans. by Elisha K. Kane, intro. by John E. Keller, Univ. of North Carolina Pr. 1968 $25.00; trans. by Mario A. Di Cesare, State Univ. of New York Pr. 1970 pap. $14.95

The Book of the Archpriest of Hita. Trans. by Mack Singleton, Hispanic Seminary $7.50

The Book of True Love. Intro. by Saralyn R. Daly, Pennsylvania State Univ. Pr. bilingual ed. 1978 $29.95 text ed. pap. $14.95

SALINAS, PEDRO. 1891–1951

Pedro Salinas was one of several modern Spanish poets who have sustained themselves in exile with university teaching. After leaving Spain in 1936, Salinas had a distinguished career as a professor at Cambridge, the University of Puerto Rico, Wellesley, and Johns Hopkins University. While Salinas also wrote criticism, essays, drama, and fiction, he is remembered chiefly as a poet. Love is one of his principal subjects, and in *To Live in Pronouns* (1933), his love for a woman is transformed into the quest for spiritual love, which symbolizes his attempt to reconcile the interior and exterior worlds. Salinas regarded love as the power to create a stable inner reality as protection against the chaos of the world. In this treatment of love and his idealization of women he resembled Bécquer and Jiménez, two of his masters. In *El contemplado* (*Sea of Puerto Rico*, 1946), he discovered peace through a contemplation of the waters of Puerto Rico. In his final volume, *The Incredible Bomb* (1950), he asserted faith in love against the destruction of the nuclear age.

BOOKS BY SALINAS

To Live in Pronouns: Selected Love Poems. Trans. by Edith Helman and Norma
    Farber, Norton 1974 $12.50 pap. consult publisher for information
My Voice Because of You. Trans. by Willis Barnstone, prologue by Jorge Guillén,
    State Univ. of New York Pr. 1976 $19.50
Reality and the Poet in Spanish Poetry. Intro. by Jorge Guillén, Greenwood repr. of
    1966 ed. 1980 lib. bdg. $24.75; intro. by Jorge Guillén, Johns Hopkins Univ. Pr.
    1966 pap. $4.95

BOOK ABOUT SALINAS

Allen, Rupert C. *Symbolic Experience: A Study of Poems by Pedro Salinas.* Univ. of Ala-
    bama Pr. text ed. 1982 $20.00

SENDER, RAMÓN J. 1902–

Seven Red Sundays (1932), involving radical labor movement activities
that culminate in a strike, reflects Sender's left-wing political views. In
1935 he won Spain's national prize for literature with *Mr. Witt among the
Rebels* (o.p.), a novel set in 1873 during Spain's first republic. He escaped to
France after the fall of the second republic in 1936, then fled to Mexico, and
finally settled in the United States, becoming an American citizen in 1942.

BOOK BY SENDER

Seven Red Sundays. Macmillan 1961 o.p.

TERESA OF JESUS, ST. 1515–1582

St. Teresa recorded her extraordinary mystical experiences through metaphor ("the soul is a castle with seven rooms enclosing it") and paradox ("I
die because I do not die"). At the same time, her style is simple, clear, and
marked by archaisms and illiterate expressions. Personal, rather than literary, she derived her poetry from experience. She was known for her practi-
cality and attention to everyday realities ("the Lord requires works"). She
successfully reformed the Carmelite Order, founding 17 convents, against
opposition from both ecclesiastical and secular powers. One of her contemporaries called her "a very great woman as regards the things of this world
and, as regards the things of the next, greater still." She is one of the saints
in GERTRUDE STEIN's (see Vol. 1) play *Four Saints in Three Acts.*

BOOKS BY ST. TERESA

The Collected Works of St. Teresa of Avila. Trans. by Kieran Kavanaugh and Otilio Ro-
    dríguez, I.C.S. Publications 3 vols. 1976–85 pap. ea. $5.95–$7.95
The Letters of St. Teresa. Ed. by Cardinal Gasquet, Gordon 4 vols. 1977 lib. bdg.
    $400.00
The Interior Castle. Trans. by Edgar A. Peers, Doubleday 1972 pap. $4.50; trans. by
    Kieran Kavanaugh and Otilio Rodríguez, Paulist Pr. 1979 $11.95 pap. $8.95
Way of Perfection. Trans. by Edgar A. Peers, Doubleday 1964 pap. $4.95
The Life of Teresa of Jesus: The Autobiography of St. Teresa of Avila. Trans. by Edgar
    A. Peers, Doubleday 1960 pap. $5.50

BOOKS ABOUT ST. TERESA

Clissold, Stephen. *St. Teresa of Avila.* Winston Pr. 1982 pap. $8.95
Glynn, Joseph. *The Eternal Mystic: St. Teresa of Avila, the First Woman Doctor of the Church.* Vantage 1982 $7.95
Sullivan, John. *Centenary of Saint Teresa.* I.C.S. Publications 1984 $6.95
Whalen, James. *The Spiritual Teachings of Teresa of Avila and Adrian Van Kaam.* Univ. Pr. of Amer. 1984 lib. bdg. $24.75 text ed. pap. $15.50

TIRSO DE MOLINA (Fray Gabriel Téllez). 1584–1648

Tirso de Molina, a priest active in the religious order of La Merced, produced more than 400 plays. Adopting Lope de Vega's principles of dramatic composition, he excelled Lope in character development, most notably in his creation of the Don Juan figure. Although the theme had long been a subject in Spanish folklore and the character had been treated previously by Cervantes and Lope de Vega, Tirso's play *The Trickster of Seville* (1630) brought the Don Juan figure to a stature of such figures as Hamlet, Don Quijote, and Faust. Don Juan, who represents complete devotion to worldly pleasures, refuses to repent for his deceptions, seductions, and finally the murder of Don Gonzalo, always maintaining that he still has sufficient time since, according to Roman Catholic doctrine, even a word of repentance on the deathbed suffices to save the sinner from hell. In the most famous scene of the play, he invites the stone statue of Don Gonzalo to supper. The statue comes to life and surprises him with death by poison. Don Juan dies unrepentant and descends into hell for his punishment. The Don Juan theme and figure have been developed by MOLIÈRE, BYRON (see Vol. 1), Zorrilla, SHAW, and CAMUS, among many others.

BOOK BY TIRSO DE MOLINA

Don Juan: The Beguiler from Seville and the Stone Guest. Trans. by Max Oppenheimer, Jr., Coronado Pr. 1976 $6.50

BOOKS ABOUT TIRSO DE MOLINA

Rank, Otto. *The Don Juan Legend.* Ed. by David G. Winter, Princeton Univ. Pr. 1975 $13.00
Weinstein, Leo. *Metamorphoses of Don Juan.* AMS Pr. $21.50

UNAMUNO Y JUGO, MIGUEL DE. 1864–1936

Philosopher, essayist, poet, and novelist, Unamuno was a central figure of the Generation of 1898. His primary concerns were individual destiny, Spain, the nature of human relationships, and renewal of artistic forms. In his major philosophical work, *The Tragic Sense of Life* (1912), Unamuno struggled with his uncertainty about immortality, for him the ultimate problem, since he believed that if man dies completely then nothing in life has meaning. The only possible solution Unamuno saw was a desperate resignation and struggle for an irrational faith that would permit him to live, a solution often compared to Kierkegaard's "leap of faith." Man, then, must conduct himself "passionately well" in order to deserve immortal life. Loving other human beings is the key to living well and the only possibility for salvation: The shoemaker who would mourn the death of a client does a religious work. Reevaluating the figure of Don Quijote, Unamuno saw him as a model for the new man who would save the world, for he acts by faith and love rather than by reason. In *The Agony of Christianity* (1925), Unamuno described the struggle to believe and the agony involved in the preservation of Christian faith.

Many of Unamuno's novels exemplify his philosophic and religious ideas. *Mist* (1914), dealing with the theme of immortality, is also an important work for its contributions to the theory of the modern novel. Asserting his autonomy as a character, Augusto Pérez protests to the author of the work about the decision to have him die. *Abel Sánchez* (1917), a novel on the Cain and Abel theme, develops the existentialistic theme of "the other," the theory that envy is self-hatred, and that the envied person inevitably participates in the envy. Unamuno's poetry covers the range of his contradictory ideas and emotions, but it is in the poetry, particularly the verses evoking his homeland written during his exile in France, that the aspect of the author which has been called "the contemplative Unamuno" (Blanco-Aguinaga) is found. Rejecting modernism and aestheticism, he subordinated form to ideas in his poetry.

The dictator Primo de Rivera sent Unamuno into exile on the Canary Islands in 1934, but he soon escaped to Paris where he remained until 1930, when he returned to Spain. In 1936 he was placed under house arrest when he spoke against anti-intellectualism, and he died on the final day of that year.

BOOKS BY UNAMUNO

Selected Works. Trans. by Anthony Kerrigan, *Bollingen Ser.* Princeton Univ. Pr. 7 vols. consult publisher for information

Perplexities and Paradoxes. Trans. by Stuart Gross, Greenwood repr. of 1945 ed. lib. bdg. $15.00

Three Exemplary Novels. 1920. Trans. by Angel Flores, intro. by Angel del Río, Grove (Evergreen) 1971 $9.95

The Life of Don Quixote and Sancho: According to Miguel de Cervantes Saavedra Expounded with Comment. Trans. by Homer P. Earle, Arden Lib. repr. of 1927 ed. 1983 $60.00

BOOKS ABOUT UNAMUNO

Basdekis, Demetrios. *Miguel de Unamuno.* Columbia Univ. Pr. 1969 pap. $2.50

———. *Unamuno and Spanish Literature.* Borgo Pr. repr. of 1967 ed. 1983 lib. bdg. $19.95

Ferrater Mora, José. *Unamuno: A Philosophy of Tragedy.* Trans. by Philip Silver, Greenwood repr. of 1962 ed. 1982 lib. bdg. $18.75

Foster, David W. *Unamuno and the Novel as Expressionistic Conceit.* Inter-Amer. Univ. Pr. 1973 pap. $2.50

Huertas-Jourda, José. *Existentialism of Miguel de Unamuno.* Univ. Pr. of Florida 1963 pap. $3.50

Marías, Julián. *Miguel de Unamuno.* Trans. by Frances M. López-Morillas, Harvard
    Univ. Pr. 1966 $16.00
Ouimette, Victor. *Reason Aflame: Unamuno and the Heroic Will.* Yale Univ. Pr. 1974
    $27.00
Rudd, Margaret. *The Lone Heretic.* Gordian repr. of 1963 ed. 1976 $15.00
Young, Howard T. *The Victorious Expression: A Study of Four Contemporary Spanish
    Poets—Unamuno, Machado, Jiménez, and Lorca.* Univ. of Wisconsin Pr. 1964
    pap. $7.95

VALERA Y ALCALÁ GALIANO, JUAN. 1827–1905

A realistic and regional novelist, Valera is best known for his creation of
Andalusian atmosphere, sensual themes, and psychological depth. *Pepita Jiménez,* an ironic novel in epistolary form, explores the inner turmoil of
Luis, a young seminarian distracted from his religious study by Pepita Jiménez, who is engaged to his own widower father. A moralist concerned
with correct behavior, Valera indicated through his conclusion to the novel
that Luis's romantically inspired religious faith is hollow and that service
to God may take the form of human, as well as spiritual, love. *Doña Luz*
deals with the same themes.

BOOKS BY VALERA

Pepita Jiménez. 1874. Trans. by Harriet de Onís, Barron 1965 o.p.
Doña Luz. 1879. Trans. by M. J. Serrano, Fertig 1891 o.p.

BOOK ABOUT VALERA

Lott, Robert E. *Language and Psychology in Pepita Jiménez.* Univ. of Illinois Pr. 1970
    $22.50

CHAPTER 12

Portuguese Literature

Naomi Moniz

Leave me, all sweet refrains my lip hath made.
—Luís Vaz De Camões, *Sonnet*

LITERATURE OF PORTUGAL

A considerable part of Portugal's early history witnessed its struggle for independence and autonomy, either against neighboring Spain or the presence of the Moors. Yet from such a tumultuous beginning a long and venerable literary tradition has emerged, one that is an essential component of the artistic history of the Iberian Peninsula. From its very first manifestations to the works being written today, Portuguese literature has strived for and indeed has maintained the independence and originality so fervently sought when the very boundaries of the country were being born. The uniqueness of Portuguese literature cannot be underestimated, and the reader who approaches it for the first time will find that the writings of Portuguese authors constitute some of Europe's most remarkable literary products.

Portugal is an ancient country whose literary history begins in the form of verse—as is the case with so many other European countries—during the later years of the Middle Ages. The roots of Portuguese literature reach back to the Galician-Portuguese lyric poems—the *cantigas de amor, cantigas de amigo*, and *cantigas de escárnio e mal-dizer*—which were being composed and performed on the peninsula at the end of the twelfth century. These three types of oral literature (the poems—which, incidentally, were sung with musical accompaniment—were committed to writing at a later date in songbooks, or *cancioneiros*) are unique to Galician-Portuguese, although the *cantigas de amor* have ancestral ties to the poetry of the troubadors. The *cantigas de amor* and *cantigas de amigo* are lovers' songs—perhaps more appropriately complaints, because the subject of these poems centers on the anguished separation of two lovers—where the former is generally characterized as being sung by a man and the latter by a woman. The *cantigas de escárnio e mal-dizer*, on the other hand, are satiric compositions written by poets of exceptional wit and are often quite acrid in their criticisms of those who are the object of satire; in many instances the poems are blatantly obscene.

Portuguese literature remained essentially a literature of poetry until the appearance of the historical chronicles of Fernão Lopes in the fifteenth century. Lopes's easily readable yet erudite and well-cultivated prose marks an important period in the flowering and codification of Portuguese as a major literary language. Contemporary with Lopes was Gil Vicente, the undisputed founder of Portuguese theater and drama. Vicente, who wrote in Spanish as well as in Portuguese, wrote plays of religious, allegorical, and comical themes in which he revealed himself to be an extraordinarily astute observer of customs, mannerisms, and language.

With the coming of the Portuguese Renaissance in the sixteenth century and the concomitant interest in classical antiquity and the literary forms and ideas of Italy, Portugal experienced one of the greatest periods of its literature. Such a golden age was all the more remarkable when the reader considers that it was virtually the work of a single man, the poet Luís de Camões. A true product of humanism, Camões (both a scholar and a soldier in the Renaissance tradition) captured the spirit of his adventurous country in the epic poem *Os Lusíadas* (*The Lusiads*), an encomium to the Portuguese spirit and a literary epic of the highest rank. Camões's activities also included the writing of many poems, which are, as well, products of a perceptive and extremely skilled lyric poet.

Following the splendid literary output of the late 1500s and early 1600s, the next period of considerable literary production in Portugal was the nineteenth century, highlighted by the novels of Eça de Queiroz. Eça de Queiroz, whose contemporaries included FLAUBERT, HUGO, and DICKENS (see Vol. 1), was Portugal's major proponent of realistic fiction. Throughout most of his career, Eça's work revealed a bitter disappointment with the state of Portuguese society. This disappointment was intensified by a fascination with French society and culture, to which he constantly compared the state of affairs in Lisbon. The majority of his writings, then, are social criticisms, characterized by penetrating and many times deriding satire.

In the early twentieth century a group of poets founded a magazine called *Orpheu*, whose ideologies would continue to influence Portuguese poetry long after its short run of only two issues. The salient figure of the *Orpheu* group was Fernando Pessoa, a poet whose writings are second only to those of Camões. In Pessoa's works, the reader finds people's identity and fate questioned, expressed through disquieting poems of existential doubt.

General Bibliography

Consigliere Pedroso, Zophimo. *Portuguese Folk Tales*. 1882. Trans. by Henriqueta Monteiro, Blom 1969 $10.00. A pleasing collection of fairy tales common to Europe, but recorded in Portugal.

Longland, Jean R. *Selections from Contemporary Portuguese Poetry*. Harvey 1966 o.p. Reviewers considered the 43 poems by 28 modern poets a good introduction to Portuguese poetry, "a quiet delight ... faithfully translated ... [and] finely designed" (*LJ*). Its poetry is "well chosen and will appeal to both teenagers and adults" (*Commonweal*).

Preminger, Alex, ed. *The Princeton Encyclopedia of Poetry and Poetics*. Princeton Univ. Pr. rev. ed. 1974 $72.50 pap. $17.50

Wohl, Helmut. *Portugal*. Pref. by John Train, Scala Bks. 1983 $29.95

CAMÕES, LUÍS VAZ DE (also Luís de Camoens). 1524?–1580

Luís de Camões was Portugal's greatest Renaissance poet, whose profoundly humanistic works have influenced Portuguese literature ever since their appearance in the sixteenth century. In 1572 the epic poem *Os Lusíadas* (*The Lusiads*)—Camões's masterpiece and lasting contribution to European literature—was published in Lisbon. By centering on the landmark 1497–98 voyage of Vasco da Gama to India, Camões exalted the Portuguese spirit in *Os Lusíadas* by recounting the glorious deeds of Portuguese history. Modeled after VIRGIL's *Aeneid* and written in *ottava rima*, the Italian metric form used by Ariosto in *Orlando Furioso*, *Os Lusíadas* continues to be the hallmark of Portuguese classics.

Camões's other poetry (*Rimas*) was published in 1595. In it Camões shows himself to be, in addition to the epic poet, an intensely lyric and sensitive man.

BOOKS BY CAMÕES

Camões: Some Poems. Small Pr. Dist. 1976 pap. $2.00

The Lusiads. 1572. Garland 1980 $80.00; Gordon $75.00; trans. by William C. Atkinson, Penguin 1981 $3.95. The translation by Atkinson is the only prose rendering of the poem.

BOOKS ABOUT CAMÕES

Freitas, William. *Camoens and His Epic*. California Institute for International Studies 1963 pap. $4.00

Hart, Henry H. *Luís de Camoens and the Epic of The Lusiads*. Univ. of Oklahoma Pr. 1962 $21.50. This book of research about the poet-soldier relates his story in detail, presents translations of his lyrics in a chronological arrangement, and includes descriptive information of the poet's era and the place where he spent his life; it is enjoyable as well as informative.

EÇA DE QUEIROZ, JOSÉ MARIA. 1843–1900

Eça de Queiroz was unquestionably Portugal's greatest novelist. He was a constant innovator in the Portuguese literary world of his day, beginning his career in the 1860s writing for newspapers and magazines. He participated in the realist-naturalist revolt against the romantics who were headed by the poet António Feliciano de Castilho and who dominated the era. The two main manifestations of this revolt were the Coimbra Uproar of 1865 (*A Questão Coimbrã*) and the Democratic Speeches at the Lisbon Casino in 1871.

With *The Sin of Father Amaro* (1876, o.p.) Eça introduced realistic and naturalistic techniques into Portuguese fiction. This is a long, tedious novel about provincial life, pettiness, ignorance, and corrupt clergy. Much of its detail comes from Eça's experience as a low-level bureaucrat in Leiria, the locale of the novel. His second novel, *Cousin Bazílio*, is *Madame Bovary* set in Lisbon. It is much quicker reading than *The Sin* and lends itself to dramatization. Of Eça's works in translation, *The Maias* (1888) follows in the realistic-naturalistic vein of Queirosian prose. It is Eça's greatest work, a final attempt to create a Portuguese *Human Comedy*. It is an "undeniable masterpiece, a chronicle of the decay which [has] affected Portuguese society in [read "since"] the last quarter of the nineteenth century" (*N.Y. Herald Tribune*). Although critics have referred to the work of Eça de Queiroz in terms of social criticism and protest, he was, instead, an "imaginative, critical, and witty observer of people" (Guerra da Cal). Of course, faithful portrayals of late nineteenth-century types were, in themselves, literary indictments of the society and of the times.

Another side of Eça de Queiroz appears in *The Mandarin* (1880, o.p.), *The Relic* (1886, o.p.), *The Illustrious House of Ramires*, and *The City and the Mountains* (1901, o.p.). All but the third have humor, fantasy, wit, social criticism, and didactic purposes in common. Eça, in his preface to *The Mandarin*, maintained that fantasy is the true nature of the Iberian temperament. The first two books tell the reader that honesty, frankness, hard work, and courage are the keys to happiness and success. *The City and the Mountains* advocates a return of the educated upper class to the soil, to regenerate, in a paternalistic fashion, a national dynamic among the folk. The protagonist of *The Illustrious House of Ramires* ransoms his family's prestige through colonial enterprise. It must be remembered that the last two novels were written after the humiliating ultimatum delivered by Great Britain in 1890, which forced Portugal to give up its claim to the central African territory between Angola and Mozambique.

BOOKS BY EÇA DE QUEIROZ

Letters from England. Trans. by Ann Stevens, Ohio Univ. Pr. 1970 $12.00. This is a collection of Eça's correspondence with Brazilian and Portuguese newspapers during his stay in England as consul, 1874–88.

Cousin Bazílio. 1878. (With the title *Dragon's Teeth*) trans. by Mary J. Serrano, Greenwood repr. of 1899 ed. 1972 $20.75

The Illustrious House of Ramires. 1897. Trans. by Ann Stevens, Ohio Univ. Pr. 1969 $15.00

BOOK ABOUT EÇA DE QUEIROZ

Coleman, Alexander. *Eça de Queiróz and European Realism.* New York Univ. Pr. 1980 $20.00

LOBO ANTUNES, ANTONIO. 1942–

Lobo Antunes, a psychiatrist and a soldier in the Portuguese colonial wars in Angola, was born in Lisbon in 1942. *South of Nowhere*, his second novel, published in 1980, became the center of controversy in view of its daring content and the novelties of its structure. The objective action of the novel is very brief: it lasts only one night. The narrator tells a silent woman companion his impressions about his experience as a medical doctor in the An-golan war of liberation against Portuguese colonialism. The novel also makes allusions to the epic of great Portuguese discoveries, *The Lusiads*, and its allegorical intentions. It denounces with lucid sarcasm the failure of Portuguese colonization in Africa.

BOOK BY LOBO ANTUNES

South of Nowhere. 1980. Trans. by Elizabeth Love, Random 1983 $11.95

PESSOA, FERNANDO. 1888–1935

Pessoa remains the poetic genius of twentieth-century Portugal. His creation is such that he is ranked among the worldwide greats of this century: PICASSO (see Vol. 3), STRAVINSKY (see Vol. 3), JOYCE (see Vol. 1), Braque, and Le Corbusier (*N.Y. Review of Books*). He was unusual within the Portuguese context for having received a British education in Durban, South Africa, where he excelled as a student and as a young English-language poet. He received the Queen Victoria Prize for his entrance exam at the University of Cape Town. Never graduating from a university (he enrolled at the University of Lisbon), he worked for various commercial concerns in Lisbon as a foreign correspondent until his death in 1935.

Pessoa is singular in the history of poetics for having written verse not only in terms of his own poetic outlook, but also in terms of the outlooks of fictitious poets he created. His heteronyms (not to be confused with pseudonyms) were Ricardo Reis, Alberto Caseiro, and Álvaro de Campos. Each poet had a separate life history, and each wrote from a separate philosophical and aesthetic point of view.

BOOKS BY PESSOA

Selected Poems. Trans. and ed. by Peter Rickard, Univ. of Texas Pr. 1971 $15.00. Includes poems written under his heteronyms, as well as some of his English sonnets and selections from his letters. This collection is valuable because it makes available to English readers Pessoa's letters explaining his reasons for creating heteronymic poets. The translations, both of the poetry and Ottavio Paz's introduction (in Spanish), have been criticized as awkward.
The Keeper of the Sheep. Trans. by Guardador de Rehahnhos, intro. by Edward Honig, Sheep Meadow bilingual ed. 1986 $15.50 pap. $9.50

QUENTAL, ANTERO DE. 1842–1891

The poet Antero de Quental, of Azorian origin, was the high priest of the rebellious Generation of 1870, which attacked the reigning romantics in the Coimbra Uproar and in the Democratic Speeches at the Lisbon Casino (see Eça de Queiroz earlier in this section). His poetic creation spanned three decades and encompassed romanticism, socialism, rationalism, metaphysical pessimism, and mysticism.

BOOK BY QUENTAL

Sonnets and Poems of Antero de Quental. Trans. by Griswald Morley, Greenwood repr. of 1922 ed. 1973 $15.00. When Morley's translation first appeared in English it was hailed as "the best translation to date from this important Portuguese poet" (*Nation*). Morley accomplished this by "not lapsing into the impossible . . . [yet] retain[ing] the sonnet form" (*New Statesman*).

VICENTE, GIL. 1465?–1537?

Gil Vicente was the founder of Portuguese theater and a central figure in Spanish literary history. His plays are masterpieces of drama, farce, and allegory. His works retain a popularity to the present day.

BOOK BY VICENTE

Four Plays. Trans. by A. F. Bell, Kraus repr. of 1920 ed. bilingual ed. $15.00

LITERATURE OF BRAZIL

The history of Brazilian literature is usually divided into two main periods, colonial and national, with the declaration of Brazil's independence from Portugal in 1822 as the dividing line. However, Brazil's bonds to Europe were even more durable than those of Spanish American countries. King John VI, then prince regent of Portugal, fled to Brazil in 1807, just prior to the Napoleonic invasion, and established court in Rio de Janeiro. When he returned to Portugal in 1820 he left his son Pedro as regent. Pedro I declared Brazil's independence in 1822 and he and his son, Pedro II, reigned until 1889. Brazil was thus effectively governed by the Portuguese almost up to the twentieth century.

Literature in Brazil began in the sixteenth century with the narratives of explorers and missionaries, as, for example, the Jesuit priest José de Anchieta, who wrote dramas to educate the Indians and lyric poetry. It was only in 1640 that Portugal regained its independence from Spain, after 60 years of domination, and Brazil's writers of the seventeenth century, often either born or educated in Europe, imitated both Spanish and Portuguese gongorist poets. The eighteenth century saw the establishment of academies that sponsored the writing of histories and the transplantation of neoclassical influences.

Romanticism dominated Brazilian literature from 1836, the date of the manifesto published in Paris by a group of Brazilians, to the 1880s. The romantic movement helped Brazil toward a consciousness of its identity by freeing literature from European forms and subjects and admitting the expression of Brazilian themes. Many writers, such as the poet António Gonçalves Dias, turned to Indian themes. José Martiniano de Alencar's novel *O Guarani* (*The Guarani Indian*) is significant not only for its focus on the Indians but also for its portrayal of landscape and its stylistic achievements. These innovations and others were gathered and perfected by Brazil's great novelist Machado de Assis. Reactions against romanticism took the form of Parnassianism in poetry and the realistic novel in fiction.

The modernist movement, connoting in Brazilian letters the literary and linguistic renovation that began in the 1920s rather than Spanish and Spanish American aestheticism, started with Modern Art Week in 1922, a week-long presentation of modern painting, sculpture, and music organized by Mário de Andrade and others. The modernists' purpose was to free the Brazilian language from classical Portuguese roles and syntax and to create a uniquely Brazilian language and literature. With the modernists Brazil finally achieved literary autonomy, and no subsequent writer discussed in this chapter is without debt to this nationalistic literary movement.

Literary Criticism and History

Coutinho, Alfranio. *An Introduction to Literature in Brazil.* Trans. by Gregory Rabassa, Columbia Univ. Pr. 1969 $30.00

Goldberg, Isaac. *Brazilian Literature.* Intro. by J. D. Ford, *Essay Index Repr. Ser.* Core Collection 1978 $24.50; Gordon $69.95

Hulet, Claude L. *Brazilian Literature.* Georgetown Univ. Pr. 3 vols. lib. bdg. 1974–75 $8.95 pap. $4.95

Martins, Wilson. *The Modernist Idea: A Critical Survey of Brazilian Writing in the Twentieth Century.* Trans. by Jack E. Tomlins, Greenwood repr. of 1970 ed. 1979 lib. bdg. $32.50; trans. by Jack E. Tomlins, New York Univ. Pr. 1971 pap. $5.95

Moog, Clodomir V. *An Interpretation of Brazilian Literature.* Trans. by John Knox, Greenwood repr. of 1951 ed. lib. bdg. $18.75

Patai, Daphne. *Myth and Ideology in Contemporary Brazilian Fiction.* Fairleigh Dickinson Univ. Pr. 1983 $29.50

Putnam, Samuel. *Marvelous Journey: A Survey of Four Centuries of Brazilian Writing.* Century Bookbindery repr. of 1948 ed. 1977 $15.00; Octagon repr. of 1948 ed. 1971 lib. bdg. $20.50

Veríssimo, Érico. *Brazilian Literature: An Outline.* Greenwood repr. of 1945 ed. lib. bdg. $18.75

Collections

Bishop, Elizabeth, ed. *An Anthology of Twentieth-Century Brazilian Poetry.* Trans. by Paul Blackburn, Wesleyan Univ. Pr. 1972 pap. $8.95. Selections with biographical introductions from 14 poets.

Grossman, William L., ed. *Modern Brazilian Short Stories.* Univ. of California Pr. 1974 $23.50 pap. $2.25. Short stories written during Brazil's modernist period, a literary revival beginning in 1922.

AMADO, JORGE. 1912–

Elected to the Brazilian Academy of Letters, Jorge Amado possesses a talent for storytelling as well as a deep concern for social and economic justice. For some critics, his early works suffer from his politics: Fred Ellison wrote, "He reacted violently at times, and some of his books have been marred by extreme partisanship to the left." In the works represented in English translation, however, his literary merits prevail. *The Violent Land* chronicles the development of Brazilian territory and struggles for its resources, memorializing the deeds of those who built the country. *Gabriela, Clove and Cinnamon*, which achieved critical and popular success in both Brazil and the United States, is still more artistic, relating a sensual love story of a Syrian bar owner and his beautiful cook whose skin is the color of the spices that enliven her food. *Home Is the Sailor* concerns Captain Vasco Moscoso de Aragão, a comic figure in the tradition of Don Quijote, who poses as a retired sea captain and must suddenly command a ship in an emergency. In *Doña Flor*, Amado introduced the folk culture of shamans and Yorube gods who resuscitate Doña Flor's first husband during her marriage to the second. The protagonists of *The Shepherds of the Night* are Bahia's poor, and "Amado has given us a deeply moving and funny picture of life in the slums" (*Nation*).

BOOKS BY AMADO

Jubiabá. 1935. Trans. by Margaret A. Neves, Avon 1984 pap. $4.50

Sea of Death. 1936. Trans. by Gregory Rabassa, Avon 1984 pap. $4.50

The Violent Land. 1942. Trans. by Samuel Putnam, Avon 1979 pap. $2.75; trans. by Samuel Putnam, Knopf 1965 $10.00

Gabriela, Clove and Cinnamon. 1958. Trans. by James L. Taylor and William L. Grossman, Avon 1974 pap. $4.95

Home Is the Sailor. 1962. Trans. by Harriet de Onís, Avon 1979 pap. $2.75

Shepherds of the Night. 1964. Trans. by Harriet de Onís, Avon 1978 pap. $3.95

Doña Flor and Her Two Husbands. 1966. Trans. by Harriet de Onís, Avon 1977 pap. $3.95

Tent of Miracles. 1969. Trans. by Barbara Shelby, Avon 1978 pap. $3.95

Teresa Batista: Home from the Wars. 1977. Trans. by Barbara Shelby, Avon 1978 pap. $3.95

Tieta. Avon 1980 pap. $4.95; trans. by Barbara S. Merello, Knopf 1979 $12.95

The Two Deaths of Quincas Wateryell. Avon 1980 pap. $2.50

The Swallow and the Tom Cat: A Love Story. Trans. by Barbara S. Merello, Delacorte 1982 $10.95

Pen, Sword, Camisole: A Fable to Kindle a Hope. Godine 1985 $15.95

ANDRADE, MÁRIO DE. 1893–1945

Mário de Andrade, born in São Paulo, was one of the founders of the modernist movement of Brazil. His purpose was to review the Brazilian language and to awaken his countrypeople to the need for social change. He wrote one of the most important works in twentieth-century Brazilian poetry and a large volume of literary, music, and art criticism. His novel, *Macunaíma*, is one of the masterworks of Brazilian literature—"inventive, blessedly unsentimental" (*Kirkus Review*), and is considered by some critics as a precursor of Latin American magical realism.

BOOK BY ANDRADE

Macunaíma. 1928. Trans. by E. A. Goodland, Random 1984 $14.95

ÂNGELO, IVAN. 1936–

Ivan Ângelo was born in Minas Gerais, Brazil. He is a journalist and the managing editor of an influential evening daily in São Paulo. *The Celebration* is a controversial novel of modern Brazil under censorship in the 1970s and a winner of the Brazilian Publisher's Prize.

BOOK BY ÂNGELO

The Celebration. 1976. Trans. by Thomas Colchie, Avon 1982 pap. $2.95

BRANDÃO, IGNÁCIO DE LOYOLA. 1936–

Brandão was born in the state of São Paulo, Brazil. He started his career in journalism at a very young age writing movie reviews in his hometown. Later he moved to São Paulo where he worked for the major newspapers and wrote some novels. *Zero* was finished in 1969 but was only published five years later in Italy, followed by its publication in Brazil in 1975. Although the book was received with critical acclaim and given literary prizes, it was banned in 1976 by the Ministry of Justice. The censorship was lifted in 1979 and, soon after, *Zero* became a bestseller. *And Still the Earth* is often mentioned as a modern Orwellian novel in the manner of *1984*. The author presents a shocking vision of the future in Brazil: the destruction of the natural environment; the scarcity of water; the crowds in the city oppressed by the brutality of an omnipotent government that controls every one of its subjects.

BOOKS BY BRANDÃO

Zero. 1975. Trans. by Ellen Watson, Avon 1983 pap. $4.50
And Still the Earth. 1982. Trans. by Ellen Watson, Avon 1985 pap. $4.95

CUNHA, EUCLYDES DA. 1866–1909

Cunha accompanied Brazilian government forces on a series of four military expeditions in 1896–97 to put down a rebellion started by a religious fanatic, Antonio the Counsellor, who had proclaimed himself the Messiah. *Rebellion in the Backlands*, Cunha's account of the battles, originally published as newspaper stories, is an inquiry into the condition of the Brazilian people, embellished with descriptions of landscape and living conditions. The work has been described as "the first literary work in Brazil . . . to face Brazilian social problems adequately and with imagination" (Seymour-Smith). The book may be marred for the modern reader by its doctrine of racial superiority and an overly complex style.

BOOK BY CUNHA

Rebellion in the Backlands. 1902. Trans. by Samuel Putnam, Univ. of Chicago Pr. 1957 pap. $9.95

FREYRE, GILBERTO DE MELLO. 1900–

Gilberto Freyre, winner of the 1967 Aspen Award for outstanding contribution to the humanities, has been influential in changing the way Brazilians see themselves and their country. By relating Brazilian history to modern life and by demonstrating how the Portuguese, blacks, and Indians have mingled to form a unique culture and a great nation, Freyre has destroyed the nation's inferiority complex. Alexander Coleman wrote of *The Masters and the Slaves*, "His is a Proustian history, a rich web of counterpoint between formative cultural factors and psychological and biological predisposition, all made living once again within the reconstituted 'tone' of the period." Freyre, whose sophisticated writings have had a pervasive influence on modern Brazilian fiction, termed his *Mother and Son* (o.p.) a "semi-novel." The political and social currents of late nineteenth-century Brazil move against the portrait in the foreground of an overbearing mother and her effeminate son destined for the priesthood: "There is a special charm in this book, in its combination of the earthy and the spiritual, of warmth and intellectuality" (*SR*).

A popular public figure in Brazil, Freyre is affectionately known as Gilberto. He has served as a member of Brazil's U.N. delegation and in its Chamber of Deputies. In 1967, Columbia University, where he once taught, appointed him to a panel to consider the problems of cities and city planning.

BOOKS BY FREYRE

The Masters and the Slaves. 1933. Knopf 1964 $17.50
The Mansions and the Shanties: The Making of Modern Brazil. 1936. Trans. by Harriet de Onís, Greenwood repr. of 1963 ed. 1980 lib. bdg. $42.50
New World in the Tropics: The Culture of Modern Brazil. Greenwood repr. of 1959 ed. rev. ed. 1980 lib. bdg. $27.50
Order and Progress: Brazil from Monarchy to Republic. Trans. by Rod Horton, Greenwood repr. of 1970 ed. 1980 lib. bdg. $42.50

LISPECTOR, CLARICE. 1924–1977

Clarice Lispector was born in the Ukraine and was taken to Brazil as a young child. She was a law student, editor, translator, and newswriter, who traveled widely, spending eight years in the United States.

Family Ties is a collection of short stories revealing Lispector's existentialist view of life and demonstrating that even family ties and social relationships are temporary. Although tied to each other and to the outside world, the characters are finally totally alone and separate. Lispector received praise from American critics for *The Apple in the Dark* (1967, o.p.), a novel about a guilt-ridden man's search for the ultimate knowledge (Eve's apple), which he believes will bring him hope: "Lispector is a superb writer, an artist of vivid imagination and sensitivity, with a glorious feeling for language and its uses" (*SR*). Lispector's books are being translated into various languages in Europe, especially in France, where the critic Hélène Cixous is one of her great admirers and a promoter of her works.

BOOK BY LISPECTOR

Family Ties. 1960. Trans. by Giovanni Pontiero, *Texas Pan-Amer. Ser.* Univ. of Texas Pr. 1984 pap. $6.95

MACHADO DE ASSIS, JOAQUIM MARIA. 1839–1908

Machado de Assis's achievement in both the novel and poetry make him Brazil's paradigm of a writer. His novels are characterized "by a psychological insight as well as a broad view of social conditions in Brazil and the world. The seriousness of the realistic view is highlighted with ironic humor" (*SR*). Beginning as a romantic, Assis developed a style that embraced realism, naturalism, and symbolism. *Epitaph for a Small Winner* reveals his essential pessimism, as the only consolation for Bras Cubas is that he has not passed on his misery to any offspring. About his writing in *Dom Casmurro*, it was said "No satirist, not even Swift, is less merciful in his exposure of the pretentiousness and the hypocrisy that lurk in the average good man and woman" (*New Republic*).

Born in the slums of Rio de Janeiro, Machado de Assis was orphaned early in life. He advanced from typesetter to proofreader and finally to journalist before entering the Brazilian civil service. He was the author of nine novels, more than 200 short stories, opera libretti, drama, and lyric poetry.

BOOKS BY MACHADO DE ASSIS

Helena. 1876. Trans. by Helen Caldwell, Univ. of California Pr. 1984 $14.95
Epitaph for a Small Winner. 1881. Trans. by William Grossman, Avon 1977 pap. $3.50
Dom Casmurro. 1900. Trans. by Helen Caldwell, Univ. of California Pr. 1966 pap. $3.95
Philosopher or Dog? 1981. Avon 1982 pap. $3.95

BOOKS ABOUT MACHADO DE ASSIS

Caldwell, Helen. *The Brazilian Othello of Machado de Assis: A Study of D. Casmurro.* Univ. of California Pr. o.p.
———. *Machado de Assis: The Brazilian Master and His Novels.* Univ. of California Pr. 1970 $27.50
Nunes, Maria Luísa. *The Craft of an Absolute Winner: Characterization and Narratology in the Novels of Machado de Assis. Contributions in Afro-Amer. and African Studies.* Greenwood 1983 lib. bdg. $29.95

QUEIRÓS, RAQUEL DE. 1910–

Raquel de Queirós gained national recognition at age 20 with her first novel *The Year Fifteen* (o.p.), which won the Graça Aranha Foundation Prize. A realistic account of the 1915 drought in the Brazilian Northeast, the novel also reveals the immaturity of the author as an artist. In *The Three Marias*, however, Queirós triumphed artistically. Although demonstrating women's subordinate and degrading roles in an unsympathetic society, the novel at the same time reveals the author's compassion for men's predicaments as well. Fred Ellison wrote of her work, "Simplicity, sobriety, and directness are characteristic of her writing, but are most highly refined in *The Three Marias* . . . . And as an artist, one of the most gifted of the present generation, she has been able to give beautiful form to her tragic inspiring vision."

BOOKS BY QUEIRÓS

The Three Marias. 1939. Trans. by Fred Ellison, Univ. of Texas Pr. 1985 pap. $7.95
Dora, Doralina. 1975. Trans. by Dorothy Scott Loos, Avon 1984 $4.50

RAMOS, GRACILIANO. 1892–1953

Ramos was one of many leftist intellectuals purged by President Getulio Vargas's government during the 1930s. *Barren Lives* examines the psychology of poverty during the drought in the interior of northeastern Brazil. The novel is narrated through the minds of several members of a family who due to their lack of education and primitive natures rarely communicate verbally. Of Ramos's technical accomplishments, Morton Dauwen Zabel wrote in *Nation*, "Graciliano Ramos is notable among the contemporary Brazilian writers for a severity of style, an accuracy of social and moral observation, and an intensity of tragic sensibility which derive as much from fidelity to native experience as from the stylists—PROUST, JOYCE [see Vol. 1], and, more relevantly, Céline—whom his American publisher mentions as models."

BOOKS BY RAMOS

Barren Lives. 1938. Trans. by Ralph E. Dimmick, *Texas Pan-Amer. Ser.* Univ. of Texas Pr. 1965 $10.95 pap. $5.95
São Bernardo. Trans. by R. L. Buccleuch, Taplinger 1979 $7.95

RIBEIRO, DARCY. 1922–

Darcy Ribeiro was born in Minas Gerais, Brazil, in 1922. World-renowned anthropologist, minister of education, and personal adviser to President Goulart, Ribeiro lived in exile after the military coup of 1964. Since his return to Brazil, he has added another dimension to his image of Renaissance man—educator, distinguished statesman, lieutenant governor of Rio de Janeiro, anthropologist, and now a man of letters.

Maíra is the most acclaimed of his novels with translations in French, German, Spanish, and Italian. The novel's major character is Isaías, a young Amazon Indian who attended a Catholic seminary in Rome and returns to his tribe to become its chieftain. Alma, a young white woman in search of her own spiritual fulfillment, joins a group of missionaries that work among the Maírum, Isaías's people. Their stories of return and of discovery, respectively, become a metaphor for the irreconcilable conflict between the rich and complex culture of the Indians and the modern technological Western civilization. *Maíra* is an elegy of a culture that is disappearing.

BOOK BY DARCY RIBEIRO

Maíra. 1978. *Lib. of Contemporary World Lit.* Random (Vintage) 1983 pap. $7.95

RIBEIRO, JOÃO UBALDO. ?–

João Ubaldo Ribeiro was born in the northeastern state of Bahia, Brazil. He has an M.A. degree in political science, but has been mostly involved in journalism. He lives on his native island of Itaparica, near Salvador, where he is the editor in chief of the *Tribuna da Bahia.* He writes weekly columns for *Istoé* magazine, as well as fiction. *Vivo o Povo Brasileiro*, his last novel, was well received by the critics and public alike. *Sergeant Getúlio* is like an epic journey through the *sertões*, the backlands of Euclydes da

Cunha's classic account. Getúlio, a police officer, is a prototype of the anti-hero of the Brazilian Northeast—a brutish, cruel man guided by a primitive sense of honor: "Overriding in violence . . . is the memorable portrait of the hero-narrator" (*Chicago Tribune*). "Getúlio will offend everyone and yet take most readers prisoner and carry them all the way to the explosive conclusion of his journey" (*Los Angeles Times*).

BOOK BY JOÃO UBALDO RIBEIRO

Sergeant Getúlio. 1971. Fwd. by Jorge Amado, Avon 1984 pap. $2.95; fwd. by Jorge Amado, Houghton Mifflin 1978 $7.95

ROSA, JOÃO GUIMARÃES. 1908–1967

Many critics consider João Guimarães Rosa to have been the best Brazilian novelist since Machado de Assis. *The Devil to Pay in the Backlands* is a Faustian quest for self-knowledge and identity with a northeastern bandit, Riobaldo, as protagonist. "But," as Emir Rodríguez Monegal pointed out, "this is a modern morality tale, and therefore not a simple one, so Rosa's angel and his devil are not always clearly distinguishable." The devil in fact turns out to be Riobaldo's unconscious and submerged instincts. A *New York Times* reviewer wrote of the novel, "He entrances the readers with the beauty and grandeur of these backlands. But his descriptions of outer nature are always subordinate to a poignant inner realism, which remains local in flavor while presenting the elemental contrasts of human nature everywhere." The artistic achievement of the novel was defined in the *Times Literary Supplement*: "To the Brazilian public *Big Backlands: Narrow Paths* [the literal translation of the title] was remarkable above all because it signified a linguistic revolution. The language was compounded from archaic Portuguese, from dialects and neologisms."

Rosa was a country doctor in his native state. He took part in the revolution and civil war of 1930–32, then embarked on a diplomatic career, serving in Hamburg, Bogota, and Paris. He was elected to the Brazilian Academy of Letters in 1963 but postponed his investiture "because he feared 'the emotion of the moment' " (*N.Y. Times*), until a few days before his unexpected death from a heart attack in November 1967.

BOOK BY ROSA

The Devil to Pay in the Backlands. 1956. Trans. by James L. Taylor and Harriet de Onís, Knopf o.p.

SCLIAR, MOACYR. 1937–

Scliar was born and still lives in Rio Grande do Sul, Brazil. A physician since 1962, Scliar started his career as a writer telling stories about his experiences as a young doctor. He is a prolific writer and has produced more than ten novels, many of which have won literary prizes. He studied at the Yiddish College in Porto Alegre and went to a Catholic school for his secondary studies. This childhood experience provided the imaginative background for many of his stories. His writing has much of what he called "his

Jewishness": "As much as possible I live in peace with my Jewishness. I have extracted from it what it has of the best: fantasy, ethical substance, and above all, humor" (*Escrever and Viver*). *The Centaur in the Garden* is a story about a centaur who is Brazilian and Jewish, a fantasy of the half-horse, half-human child who grows into adulthood in search of his identity.

BOOK BY SCLIAR

The Centaur in the Garden. 1980. Ballantine pap. $5.95

SOUZA, MÁRCIO. 1946–

Souza was born in the northern state of Amazonas, Brazil. He studied social sciences at the University of São Paulo in the South. It was during that period that Souza decided to write about his native region, the Amazon, feeling that very little was known about its history and culture. *The Emperor of the Amazon*, his first novel, was an extraordinary bestseller and was well received in France and in the United States. It is about the adventures of a latter-day conquistador in the heart of the jungle, involved by accident in a mock epic tale of conquest and revolution. *Mad Maria* is a novel set again in the Amazon region, with a group of people determined to cut a railroad through the forest.

BOOKS BY SOUZA

The Emperor of the Amazon. 1977. Avon 1980 pap. $2.95
Mad Maria. 1980. Trans. by Tomas Colchie, Avon 1985 pap. $4.95

TELLES, LYGIA FAGUNDES. ?–

Telles was born in São Paulo and spent most of her childhood in the small towns of the state. She holds degrees in law and physical education, and started publishing in the 1940s when she was very young. Since then, she has published three novels, a half dozen novellas, and seven short-story collections. In 1969 she was awarded the Cannes Prix International des Femmes for her short story "Before the Green Masquerade." In 1973, *The Girl in the Photograph* won her various literary prizes. Today, she is considered one of the finest women writers in Brazil and has been elected to the Brazilian Academy of Letters.

BOOK BY TELLES

The Girl in the Photograph. 1973. Avon 1982 pap. $3.95

CHAPTER 13

German and Netherlandic Literature

Jacobus W. Smit and Pamela Spence Richards

> German literature is troublesome material for those who like to make trim
> patterns out of untidy realities. Because of its richness and diversity, it fits
> awkwardly into a scheme of periods and movements. . . . Writers in the
> German language have rarely been supported, or constrained, by well-
> established native traditions and have veered, since they lacked this stabi-
> lizing influence, from one extreme to another; they have either set the
> pace or followed in the wake of literary fashion, striving to overhaul their
> contemporaries elsewhere in Europe.
>
> —C. P. MAGILL, *German Literature*

GERMAN LITERATURE

This bibliography deals with all literature written in the German language
in the territories that now comprise West and East Germany, Austria (with
its pre-1918 territories), and Switzerland.

The earliest examples of literature in German date from the early Middle
Ages (c.750), but the highest achievements of medieval literature are found
in the so-called Middle High German period (c.1000–1300). The genres of
that literature are similar to what are found in other European literatures.
Walther von der Vogelweide (c.1200) is the great representative of courtly
love poetry. Hartmann von Aue (*Erec*), Wolfram von Eschenbach (*Parzival*),
and Gottfried von Strassburg (*Tristan*) reflect in their courtly epics the social and moral tensions of feudal society. This feudal orientation shifts in
the fourteenth to sixteenth centuries to a literature that is more representative of the concerns of the upcoming urban middle classes. Those concerns
express themselves in a strong didactic interest as well as in a remarkable
mystical and moralistic religious literature, such as Johannes von Tepl's
The Plowman from Bohemia and the mystics Meister Eckhart and Johannes
Tauler.

In the sixteenth century, the artisanal and middle-class views of the
world found expression in the poetry and plays of the Meistersinger like
Hans Sachs, an often crude but comically earthy playwright from Nuremberg, later celebrated by Richard Wagner in his *Meistersinger*. Of great im-
port for the development of the German language and literature were Mar-

tin Luther's translation of the Bible (1522–34) and his other writings. The tremendous influence of his translation helped toward the creation of a standard German language by preparing the victory of High German as the dominant vehicle for literature.

In the beginning of the seventeenth century an important change took place. The original accented verse of the Middle Ages was replaced by a metered classicist verse, inspired by the work of the French Pléiade poets Du Bartas and PIERRE DE RONSARD. Crucial to this change was the treatise on German versification by Martin Opitz, who had translated the Dutch poets who had earlier pioneered this shift in their own work. The rich baroque language of the important playwright Andreas Gryphius is built on this innovation. The period of the Baroque is very much underrepresented in translation. Only the works of Hans von Grimmelshausen are available. His grimly comical *Simplicissimus* portrays the misery of the wars that devastated Germany in the first half of the seventeenth century.

After the peaks of the seventeenth century, German literature did not reach new heights until the second half of the eighteenth century, when in a new outburst of creativity it established itself as one of the commanding influences on all of European culture and education. In that period the reader can witness the conflict between the enlightened rationalism of such writers as Gotthold Lessing and the writers of the upcoming current of Sturm and Drang (Storm and Stress)—the early romantics. In their earlier years, the towering figures of Wolfgang von Goethe and Friedrich Schiller were leaders of this revolution, but in their later works they returned to more classical and restrained forms of expression. The emotionalism and mysticism of the romantic movement, although a general European phenomenon, had a stronger and more specific impact on German literature than on others.

Goethe, however, in spite of his later classicism, remained the fountainhead of most nineteenth- and twentieth-century literature in Germany. As a playwright (*Faust*), a poet, as well as a novelist (*Werther, Wilhelm Meister*), and creator of the German educational novel, his influence was unmatched by any other writer. The development of German idealistic philosophy (KANT, HEGEL, FICHTER [see Vol. 4]), its preoccupation with the tensions between the ideal and the real, perfection and imperfection, becoming and being, finds resonances in the works of most of the important German authors well into the present. Another powerful philosophical influence came (but not really before the beginning of the twentieth century) from the fiercely critical and deeply antirationalist Friedrich Nietzsche.

Novelistic literature also showed strong reactions to the irrational, emotional character of earlier romantic writing: this is particularly notable in the realistic and naturalistic currents. Theodor Fontane is the greatest representative of this kind of social realism. He analyzed the turmoil of the social and political transformation of German society. The political unification of Germany and the battles between the aristocracy and the rising middle classes and workers' movements are the great events that make themselves felt in literature.

Realism and naturalism came under attack from several sides, from symbolist as well as neoromantic writers. Neoromanticism is most prominently represented by the Austrian Hugo von Hoffmannsthal and in poetry by Rainer Maria Rilke. In this same period appeared the first novelists who came to dominate German literature in the twentieth century: Thomas Mann, Franz Kafka, and Robert Musil.

In poetry and the theater important work was produced under the influence of expressionist theory: its stark, alienating artistic forms were designed to shock the reader or the audience into spiritual transformation. Austria maintained a distinct character, best represented by the nostalgic cynicism of Arthur Schnitzler and the works of Hoffmannsthal and Musil.

The shock of the German defeat in World War I, compounded by social and poitical struggles, the postwar crisis, and finally the rise of National Socialism, colors all literature written in the interwar period. Older writers like Thomas Mann, younger ones like the leftist Bertolt Brecht, or the nihilistic nationalist Ernst Jünger were marked by the same experiences.

Equally strong were the writers' reactions to World War II. The preoccupation with the phenomenon of National Socialism and with postwar realities like the division of Germany is constantly present in the work of writers like Günter Grass, Uwe Johnson, and Peter Handke. One of the most interesting aspects of German literature in recent times is the rise of a really important contribution by East German writers, of whom Christa Wolf is a most impressive example.

Background Reading

Barraclough, Geoffrey. *The Origins of Modern Germany.* Norton repr. of 1946 ed. 1984 pap. $12.95. A clear and detailed presentation of German history from the earliest periods to the middle of the twentieth century. The chapters on the medieval centuries are especially noteworthy.

Bruford, Walter H. *Germany in the Eighteenth Century.* Cambridge Univ. Pr. 1935 $49.50 pap. $14.95. One of the most important and original studies in the field of German literature, it has as its task the definition of the sociological background of the period known as the Age of Goethe.

Gay, Peter. *Weimar Culture: The Outsider as Insider.* Greenwood repr. of 1968 ed. 1981 lib. bdg. $24.25; Harper 1970 pap. $5.95

Jay, Martin. *The Dialectical Imagination: A History of the Frankfurt School and the Institute of Social Research, 1923–1950.* Little, Brown 1973 pap. $8.70

Mosse, George L. *The Crisis of German Ideology: Intellectual Origins of the Third Reich.* Putnam 1964 pap. $3.95

———. *The Nationalization of the Masses: Political Symbolism and Mass Movements in Germany from the Napoleonic Wars through the Third Reich.* New Amer. Lib. 1977 pap. $4.95

Pfeiler, William K. *War and the German Mind.* AMS Pr. repr. of 1941 ed. $19.50. Recent reprint of this investigation into the Germans' pre-World War II psychological conditioning. "Pfeiler's extremely fair study will increase our understanding of . . . modern Germany" (Hans Kohn, *Nation*).

Schorske, Carl E. *Fin-de-Siècle Vienna: Politics and Culture.* Knopf 1980 $16.95; Random (Vintage) 1981 pap. $9.95

Steiner, Jean François. *Treblinka*. Anti-Defamation League repr. pap. $3.50; New Amer. Lib. 1979 pap. $3.95. A "nonfiction novel" re-creating the horrors of the Polish concentration camp. Based on diaries, documents, and interviews with the 40 survivors of the 600 who escaped on August 2, 1943. "A powerful, unforgettable book" (*PW*), which has also proved controversial.

History and Criticism

Bennett, E. K. *A History of the German Novelle*. Ed. by H. M. Waidson, Cambridge Univ. Pr. rev. ed. 1961 $52.50 pap. $12.95. Bennett's study still remains a classic of Novelle scholarship and is among the best in either German or English.

Boeschenstein, Hermann. *German Literature in the Nineteenth Century*. St. Martin's 1969 $19.95

Cernyak-Spatz, Susan E. *German Holocaust Literature*. Peter Lang text ed. 1985 $19.00

Demetz, Peter. *Postwar German Literature: A Critical Introduction*. Irvington text ed. 1970 $27.50; Schocken repr. of 1970 ed. 1972 pap. $2.95

Emrich, Wilhelm. *The Literary Revolution and Modern Society and Other Essays*. Ungar 1971 o.p.

Francke, Kuno. *History of German Literature as Determined by Social Forces*. AMS Pr. repr. of 1901 ed. 4th ed. $37.50. A seminal work by the most distinguished Germanist of the twentieth century.

Fuerst, Norbert. *The Victorian Age of German Literature: Eight Essays*. Pennsylvania State Univ. Pr. 1965 $23.50. Readably describes the biographical, historical, and philosophical factors affecting the literature of 1820 through 1880.

Gerber, Margy, and Judith Pouget. *Literature of the German Democratic Republic in English Translation*. Univ. Pr. of Amer. 1984 lib. bdg. $22.50 text ed. pap. $9.75

Gray, Ronald. *German Poetry: A Guide to Free Appreciation*. Cambridge Univ. Pr. 1976 $29.50 pap. $10.95

————. *The German Tradition in Literature, 1871–1945*. Cambridge Univ. Pr. 1966 $49.50 pap. $19.45. Analyzes the tradition that flourished in Goethe's time through what the author considers its aberration in the early 20th century. "[A] wealth of stimulating observations and suggestions" (*LJ*).

Gropius, Walter, ed. *The Theater of the Bauhaus*. Trans. by Arthur S. Wensinger, Wesleyan Univ. Pr. 1971 pap. $12.95. The book is for readers experienced with the theater. The three contributors are Oscar Schlemmer, Laszlo Moholy-Nagy, and Farkas Molnar. The avant-garde Bauhaus, a school devoted to all the arts in the Munich of the 1920s, had a vast influence on theater throughout the world and on such artists as Robert Edmond Jones and Frank Lloyd Wright.

Haile, H. G. *The History of Doctor Johann Faustus*. Univ. of Illinois Pr. 1965 o.p. The anonymous *Story of Dr. Faustus* (1587) illuminates the beliefs and superstitions of its century. Haile describes how "a quite simple reality turned into one of the most striking sagas of the Germanic world" (*LJ*).

Hamburger, Michael. *A Proliferation of Prophets: Essays on German Writers from Nietzsche to Brecht*. Humanities Pr. 2 vols. text ed. 1983–84 ea. $32.00; St. Martin's 1984 $22.50

Hatfield, Henry. *Clashing Myths in German Literature: From Heine to Rilke*. Harvard Univ. Pr. text ed. 1974 $16.50

Heller, Erich. *In the Age of Prose: Literary and Philosophical Essays.* Cambridge Univ. Pr. 1984 $39.50 pap. $12.95

Hutchinson, Peter. *Literary Presentations of Divided Germany.* Cambridge Univ. Pr. 1977 $32.50

Kayser, Wolfgang. *The Grotesque in Art and Literature.* Trans. by Ulrich Weisstein, Columbia Univ. Pr. 1981 $24.00; trans. by Ulrich Weisstein, Peter Smith $7.50

Lange, Victor. *The Classical Age of German Literature, 1740–1815.* Holmes & Meier text ed. 1983 $29.50 pap. $17.50; State Mutual Bk. 1982 $60.00 pap. $30.00

Pickering, F. P. *Essays on Medieval German Literature and Iconography.* Cambridge Univ. Pr. 1980 $44.50

Ritchie, J. M. *German Literature under National Socialism.* Barnes & Noble 1983 $28.50. "A handbook for the study of pre-Nazi, Nazi, and post-Nazi literature. Useful for every level." (*Choice*).

Robertson, John G. *The Literature of Germany.* Richard West repr. of 1962 ed. $10.00; Russell Pr. 1985 lib. bdg. $40.00. There is no finer general literary history of German available in English.

Samuel, Richard, and Thomas R. Hinton. *Expressionism in German Life: Literature and the Theatre.* Sayer repr. of 1939 ed. 1983 $12.50

Schrader, Richard J. *God's Handiwork: Images of Women in Early Germanic Literature.* Greenwood 1983 lib. bdg. $25.00

Silbermann, Marc D. *Literature of the Working World: A Study of the Industrial Novel in East Germany.* Peter Lang 1977 pap. $16.30

Silz, Walter. *Realism and Reality.* AMS Pr. repr. $27.00. Silz's work is the classic study of the nineteenth century Novelle of German Realism.

Sokel, Walter H. *The Writer in Extremis: Expressionism in Twentieth-Century German Literature.* Stanford Univ. Pr. 1959 $20.00

Stern, J. P. *Re-Interpretations: Seven Studies in Nineteenth-Century German Literature.* Cambridge Univ. Pr. $49.50

Taylor, Archer. *The Literary History of Meistergesang.* Kraus repr. of 1937 ed. $12.00

Thalmann, Marianne. *The Literary Sign Language of German Romanticism.* Trans. by Harold A. Basilius, Wayne State Univ. Pr. 1972 $9.95

Zipes, Jack. *Breaking the Magic Spell: Radical Theories of Folk and Fairy Tales.* Methuen 1984 pap. $9.95; Univ. of Texas Pr. text ed. 1979 $15.00

———. *The Great Refusal: Studies of the Romantic Hero in German and American Literature.* Adler's 1970 $21.90

Collections

Engel, Eva L., ed. *German Narrative Prose.* Dufour $15.95

Flores, Angel. *An Anthology of German Poetry from Holderlin to Rilke in English Translation.* Peter Smith 1960 $11.50

Francke, Kuno, ed. *German Classics.* AMS Pr. 20 vols. repr. of 1914 ed. $900.00

Gode, Alexander, and Frederick Ungar, eds. *Anthology of German Poetry through the Nineteenth Century.* Ungar 2d ed. rev. 1963 $14.50 pap. $5.95

Hamburger, Michael, ed. *East German Poetry: An Anthology.* Trans. by Gisela Brotherston, Humanities Pr. 1979 $14.75

Waidson, H. M., ed. *German Short Stories.* Cambridge Univ. Pr. 3 vols. text ed. ea. $5.50–$6.95

BENN, GOTTFRIED. 1886–1956

"Benn was a striking figure in his time. . . . He has been a powerful influence on recent younger Germanic poets" (Harry T. Moore). The publication of his first volume of poems, *Morgue* (o.p.), in 1912, established him as a member of the European avant-garde and an enfant terrible of expressionism. A Berlin physician, Benn brought to his early poems a medically based obsession with the phenomena of physical and mental decay and a radical disillusionment with the bourgeois world.

BOOK BY BENN

Primal Vision, Selected Writings. Trans. by Michael Hamburger and others, M. Boyars 1985 $15.00

BOOK ABOUT BENN

Alter, Reinhard. *Gottfried Benn: The Artist and Politics (1910–1934).* Peter Lang 1976 pap. $18.25

BÖLL (or BOELL), HEINRICH. 1917–1985 (NOBEL PRIZE 1972)

Although Böll had won three literary prizes in Germany and had had earlier novels in translation published in the United States (now o.p.), it was not until *Billiards at Half-Past Nine* that he became established abroad as one of the most important German novelists to have emerged since World War II. *The Clown,* his story of the antihero who cannot make a go of life but continues ruefully to try, is intensely cynical about modern Germany in a lighthearted way. Of a Gauleiter who had "protected" a radical in the Hitler period, who in turn was bound to swear to a "denazification" court that he owed his life to that "swine," Böll writes, "Needless to say he [the Gauleiter] didn't hold his protective hand over everyone, not over Marx the leather merchant and Krupe the Communist. They were murdered. And the Gauleiter is doing all right today. He has a construction business."

Absent without Leave (1964) and *Enter and Exit* are "essential reading for all who care about the contemporary German conscience, consciousness, and literary sensibility" (*SR*). "With his sensitive, tight, allusive prose, shorn of sentimentality, Mr. Böll turns the German soldier into a portrait of every soldier" (*LJ*). *18 Stories,* written over a period of 20 years, "satirizes the indignities and absurdities of making a living in postwar Germany. . . . A shrewd and skillful translation" (*SR*).

The son of Victor Böll the sculptor, Heinrich was born in Cologne. He was drafted in 1938 shortly after finishing his schooling and served several years in the infantry before his demobilization in 1945. "Böll reminds one of Thomas Mann at his peak as an uncompromising foe of conventionality and political faddism, as well as a writer who in many respects courts the label of 'old-fashioned' by putting narrative ahead of experimentation. Equally unusual is Böll's dedication to literary art, his conviction that it is one of the few contemporary means of free expression" (*N.Y. Times*).

In *The Lost Honor of Katharina Blum* (1974), Böll continues to focus on modern German society and the destructive possibilities latent in it. "What is strong and attractive here, as in Böll's other novels, is the sense of the faint weirdness of daily life in a conformist country. Everything so aspires to order that the very slightest deviation smacks of a disturbing anarchy" (*N.Y. Times*).

In the 1960s and 1970s, Böll became involved in the German peace movement and in the effort to stop the deployment of U.S. nuclear missiles on West German soil.

BOOKS BY BÖLL

And Never Said a Word. 1954. Trans. by Leila Vennewitz, McGraw-Hill 1978 $8.95 pap. $5.95

Irish Journal. 1957. Trans. by Leila Vennewitz, McGraw-Hill 1967 pap. $4.95. Seventeen sketches of Ireland in the mid-1950s updated with an epilogue. "Böll has an affinity for Ireland and things Irish, a fresh outlook and an uncluttered style" (*PW*).

Billiards at Half-Past Nine. 1959. Avon 1975 pap. $3.95; McGraw-Hill repr. of 1962 ed. 1973 pap. $5.95; Peter Smith 1983 $12.50

The Bread of Those Early Years. 1959. Trans. by Leila Vennewitz, McGraw-Hill 1976 $7.95

The Clown. 1963. Avon 1975 pap. $4.95; trans. by Leila Vennewitz, McGraw-Hill 1971 pap. $5.95. A good translation. "An engaging and distinguished novel" (*SR*).

18 Stories. Trans. by Leila Vennewitz, McGraw-Hill 1966 consult publisher for information.

Children Are Civilians Too. Trans. by Leila Vennewitz, McGraw-Hill repr. of 1970 ed. 1977 pap. $5.95

Group Portrait with Lady. 1971. Avon 1974 pap. $3.95; trans. by Leila Vennewitz, McGraw-Hill 1973 $8.95

Missing Persons. Trans. by Leila Vennewitz, McGraw-Hill 1977 $9.95

The Safety Net. 1979. Knopf 1982 $13.95; trans. by Leila Vennewitz, Penguin 1983 pap. $4.95

What's to Become of the Boy? Trans. by Leila Vennewitz, Knopf 1984 $11.95; *Penguin Fiction Ser.* 1985 pap. $4.95

BOOKS ABOUT BÖLL

Conrad, Robert C. *Heinrich Böll. Twayne's World Authors Ser.* G. K. Hall $15.95

Reid, James H. *Heinrich Böll: Withdrawal and Re-emergence.* Humanities Pr. text ed. 1975 $11.00

BONHOEFFER, DIETRICH. 1906–1945

[SEE Volume 4.]

BORCHERT, WOLFGANG. 1921–1947

Borchert grew up under the Nazi regime. During the war he was imprisoned and even sentenced to death for his "defeatist" attitude. He died at the age of 26, the night before the Hamburg premiere of his great success, *The Outsider* (*The Man Outside*). Surrealistic in technique, the play concerns the return of a maimed German prisoner of war who finds everything destroyed, all hope shattered, even the symbolic "God" perplexed. The only one who flourishes is the undertaker. The hero's pitiful efforts to make a place for himself end in failure. "If there is one word that could possibly sum up the spirit of *The Outsider*," says Wellwarth in his introduction to *Postwar German Theater*, "it is outrage. The play is . . . a graphic and mercilessly unrestrained excoriation of the sinister and diabolical system that had destroyed Germany so completely, both morally and physically. [It] remains important first because it is an excellent drama itself, the only completed play by one of Germany's greatest modern poetic geniuses; second, because it is the most perfect expression of postwar German youth's disillusionment with the system which had ruined their country and their own best years; and third, because it is the only really successful re-creation of the World War I art form known as Expressionism."

BOOK BY BORCHERT

The Man Outside. 1947. Trans. by A. D. Porter, New Directions rev. ed. 1971 pap. $6.95

BRANT (or BRANDT), SEBASTIAN. 1457?–1521

Sebastian Brant was born in Strassburg and studied at Basel, where he became a lecturer. When Basel joined the Swiss Confederacy, he returned to Strassburg and became the town clerk. He was author of a number of political and religious pamphlets. KATHERINE ANNE PORTER (see Vol. 1) drew on *Das Narrenschiff* for her novel *Ship of Fools*.

His famous parody of the late medieval period depicts life as a paradise for simpletons. It is a series of rhymed sermons excoriating sin and folly with grotesque satire. The crew of a seabound vessel is made up of 112 fools, each representing a "fashionable foible" of man. In their foolishness, they perish. Although of secondary literary merit, the book became immensely popular. It was translated into Low German, Latin, French, and English. A famous early edition of the work was translated by Alexander Barclay in 1509.

BOOK BY BRANT

Ship of Fools. 1497. Trans. by Alexander Barclay, AMS Pr. 2 vols. repr. of 1874 ed. $75.00; (with the title *Shyp of Folys of the Worlde*), trans. by Alexander Barclay, Walter J. Johnson repr. of 1609 ed. $76.00

BRECHT, BERTOLT. 1898–1956

"The German avant-garde in drama is Brecht. . . . His work is fresh, vital, and pertinent enough to give a new direction to theatrical history" (Eric Bentley). He left Germany because of Hitler in 1933, and many of his vigorous plays, radio scripts, and poems were written against Hitlerism. He was one of the editors of a short-lived anti-Nazi magazine in Moscow (1936–39) and came to the United States in 1941. In 1949 his wife, Helen Weigel, starred successfully in his play *Mother Courage and Her Children*, "a Brecht masterpiece and a relentless Marxist indictment of the economic motives behind internal aggression" (Robert Brustein). Many of Brecht's plays are produced regularly on the U.S. stage. Brecht has also found a large audience as librettist for Kurt Weill's *Threepenny Opera*, an adaptation of John Gay's *Beggar's Opera*. His most ambitious venture in verse drama, *Saint Joan of the Stockyards*, was written in Germany shortly before Hitler came to power.

Brecht was "a playwright with a point of view not only toward society but toward the theater. He saw the stage as a platform for the promulgation of a message. His aim . . . was to 'develop the means of entertainment into an object of instruction and to change certain institutions from places of amusement into organs of public communication' " (*N.Y. Times*). He called himself an epic realist. Howard Taubman has defined the Berlin Epic Theater concept, developed by Brecht and the director Erwin Piscator, in its simplest terms (it involved a good deal more than this and had a tremendous impact on world drama) as a theater "which aims to make one think rather than feel."

Brecht's only piece of long fiction is the *Three Penny Novel* (o.p.). Brecht was the subject of Günter Grass's play *The Plebeians Rehearse the Uprising*, which portrays him as betraying his own ideals but is generally acknowledged to have distorted the facts of the true episode.

At the height of the Cold War, Brecht settled in East Berlin, where he died in 1956 of a heart attack. Martin Esslin has cited evidence that, although he was certainly a radical and accepted assistance in his theatrical efforts from the East German government, his heart belonged to no government or ideology. On his 1947 American visit he was summoned to Washington by the House Un-American Activities Committee, before which he testified as to his right of Marxist dissent. He firmly denied that he had ever been a member of the Communist Party. How radical Brecht really was has been the subject of considerable controversy; but, for literary purposes, his politics need only be judged as they contributed to his artistry.

In his final years Brecht experimented powerfully with his own theater and company—the Berliner Ensemble—which put on his plays under his direction and which continued after his death with the assistance of his wife. Brecht's fecundity, originality, and versatility were matched by his genius, which still looms immense over Europe.

BOOKS BY BRECHT

Collected Plays. Ed. by Ralph Manheim and John Willett, Random (Vintage) 9 vols. 1971–73 pap. ea. $3.95–$7.95

Bertolt Brecht, Poems, 1913–1956. Ed. by John Willett and Ralph Manheim, Methuen 2d ed. 1980 $29.95 pap. $13.95

Jungle of Cities and Other Plays. Trans. by Verschoyle N. Goold, Grove 1966 pap. $3.95. Contains *Drums in the Night* and *Roundheads and Peakheads*.

The Jewish Wife and Other Short Plays. Trans. by Eric Bentley, Grove 1965 pap. $2.95. Contains *The Informer, In Search of Justice, The Exception and the Rule, The Measure Taken, The Elephant Calf*, and *Salzburg Dance of Death*.

Parables for the Theatre: Two Plays by Bertolt Brecht. 1948. Trans. by Eric Bentley,

Univ. of Minnesota Pr. 1965 $10.95. Two "epic" plays: *The Caucasian Chalk Circle* and *The Good Woman of Setzuan.*

Edward II: A Chronicle Play. 1924. Trans. by Eric Bentley, Grove 1970 pap. $1.95

Manual of Piety. 1926. Trans. by Eric Bentley, notes by Hugo Schmidt, Grove bilingual ed. 1966 o.p.

Threepenny Opera. 1928. Trans. by Eric Bentley and Desmond Vesey, Grove 1964 pap. $2.45

The Mother. 1932. Grove 1978 pap. $2.95. Brecht's dramatic adaptation of Gorky's novel.

The Rise and Fall of the City of Mahoganny. 1930. Trans. by W. H. Auden and Chester Kallman, Godine 1976 $12.95 pap. $6.95

Saint Joan of the Stockyards. 1933. Indiana Univ. Pr. 1970 $15.00 pap. $3.95

Mother Courage and Her Children. 1941. Trans. by Eric Bentley, Grove 1963 pap. $2.45

Galileo. 1942. Trans. by Eric Bentley, Grove 1966 pap. $3.50

The Good Woman of Setzuan. 1943. Trans. by Eric Bentley, Grove 1966 pap. $2.95

The Caucasian Chalk Circle. 1947. Trans. by Maja Apelman, Grove 1971 pap. $2.95

Brecht on Theatre. Trans. by John Willett, Hill & Wang 1964 pap. $6.95. His own ideas on the theater and aesthetics.

BOOKS ABOUT BRECHT

Cook, Bruce. *Brecht in Exile.* Holt 1983 $17.95

Dickson, Keith A. *Towards Utopia: A Study of Brecht.* Oxford 1978 $49.95

Gray, Ronald D. *Brecht the Dramatist.* Cambridge Univ. Pr. 1976 $42.50 o.p.

Hayman, Ronald. *Brecht: A Biography.* Oxford 1983 $24.95

Lyon, James K. *Bertolt Brecht in America.* Princeton Univ. Pr. 1980 $33.00 pap. $9.95

BROCH, HERMANN. 1886–1951

Born in Vienna, this novelist, philosopher, and playwright came to the United States in 1938, was awarded a Guggenheim Fellowship (1941–42), a membership in the American Institute of Arts and Letters (1942), and a Rockefeller Fellowship for Philosophical and Psychological Research at Princeton (1942–44). He had been a mathematician, engineer, and director of a Viennese textile concern. His remarkable prose trilogy describing three stages in the disintegration of modern European society, *The Sleepwalkers*, is "a striking example of a new type of European cultural portraiture in which scientific speculation and poetic imagination are combined to represent the incoherent variety of contemporary experience" (Victor Lange). *The Death of Virgil*, whom Broch regarded "as a prototype of the modern man . . . depicts the last eighteen hours of Virgil's life—an obvious parallel to Joyce's work. . . . Broch's vision of the immanence of death will probably be regarded as his most original contribution to human experience. His evocation of the totality and simultaneity of life is his greatest achievement in literature" (Theodore Ziolkowski).

BOOKS BY BROCH

The Sleepwalkers: A Trilogy of Hermann Broch. 1932. Trans. by Edwin Muir, North Point Pr. repr. of 1964 ed. 1985 pap. $16.50; Octagon repr. of 1947 ed. 1980 lib. bdg. $54.50

The Death of Virgil. 1945. Trans. by Jean S. Untermeyer, North Point Pr. repr. of
      1945 ed. 1983 pap. $15.50; intro. by Hannah Arendt, Peter Smith $15.75

BOOK ABOUT BROCH

Simpson, Malcolm R. *The Novels of Hermann Broch*. Peter Lang 1977 o.p.

BÜCHNER, GEORG. 1813–1837

"Büchner's genius, though it had no time to mature fully, is unsurpassed
in German literature after Goethe's death, but his reputation is entirely a
product of the years since about 1910." The life of Georg Büchner was
short, intense, and tragic—and extremely significant for the development of
modern drama. He started a literary revolution that is continuing still. His
three modern plays, *Danton's Death* (1835), *Leonce and Lena* (1850), and
Woyzeck (1850), were greatly ahead of their time in their penetrating dramatic and psychological treatment. They served as an impetus for contemporary schools of drama as different as the Ionesco's Theater of the Absurd
and Brecht's Epic Theater. Alban Berg based the libretto of his opera
Wozzeck on *Woyzeck*. *Danton's Death*, a powerful drama of the French Revolution, is, like *Woyzeck*, still popular.

BOOKS BY BÜCHNER

Georg Büchner: Complete Plays and Prose. Trans. by Carl R. Mueller, Hill & Wang
      1963 pap. $5.95
Plays of Georg Büchner. Trans. by Victor Price, Oxford 1971 pap. $5.95. Includes *Dan-
      ton's Death*, *Leonce and Lena*, and *Woyzeck*.
Leonce and Lena. Trans. by Hedwig Rappolt, TSL Pr. text ed. 1983 pap. $4.00
Woyzeck. Trans. by John MacKendrick, Methuen 1980 pap. $6.95
Danton's Death. Trans. by Howard Brenton, Methuen 1983 pap. $6.95; trans. by Hed-
      wig Rappolt, TSL Pr. text ed. 1983 pap. $4.00

BOOKS ABOUT BÜCHNER

Benn, M. B. *The Drama of Revolt: A Critical Study of Georg Büchner*. Cambridge Univ.
      Pr. 1976 $54.50 pap. $15.95
Hilton, Julian. *Georg Büchner*. Grove (Evergreen) 1982 pap. $8.95
Richards, David G. *Georg Büchner*. State Univ. of New York Pr. 1977 $44.50

CANETTI, ELIAS. 1905–   (NOBEL PRIZE 1981)

Born in Bulgaria into a Sephardic Jewish family, Canetti was educated in
Germany, Switzerland, and Austria. He holds a Ph.D. from the University of
Vienna (1929) and, since 1938, he has been a resident of England. Canetti became known first for his novel *Auto-da-Fé* and for his plays. More recently a
good many of his essays have been translated. A dominant theme in his
work is the conflict between the attempt at individual self-definition and
the autonomous life and driving force of the masses.

Canetti has been awarded the Vienna Prize (1966), the Critics Prize (Germany 1967), the Great Austrian State Prize (1967), the Büchner Prize (1972),
the Sachs Prize (1975), the Hebbel Prize (1980), and the Nobel Prize for Literature (1981).

BOOKS BY CANETTI

Auto-da-Fé. 1938. Trans. by D. V. Wedgewood, Continuum 1984 $17.50 pap. $11.95
Crowds and Power. 1960. Continuum 1982 $17.50 pap. $11.95; trans. by Carol Stewart, Farrar 1984 pap. $8.95
Comedy of Vanity and Life Terms. 1965. Trans. by Gitta Honegger, Performing Arts 1983 $18.95. A play.
The Voices of Marrakesh: A Record of a Visit. 1967. Continuum 1978 $9.95 1982 pap. $5.95; trans. by J. A. Underwood, Farrar 1984 pap. $5.95
Kafka's Other Trial: The Letters to Felice. 1969. Trans. by Christopher Middleton, Schocken 1982 $11.95 pap. $5.95
The Human Province, Notes 1942–1977. 1973. Trans. by Joachim Neugroschel, Continuum 1978 $12.95 1985 pap. $9.95
The Conscience of Worlds. 1975. Trans. by Joachim Neugroschel, Continuum 1979 $12.95; Farrar 1984 pap. $7.95
The Tongue Set Free: Remembrance of a European Childhood. 1977. Trans. by Joachim Neugroschel, Continuum 1980 $14.95 1983 pap. $9.95
The Torch in My Ear. 1980. Trans. by Joachim Neugroschel, Farrar 1982 $16.50 pap. $9.95
The Plays of Elias Canetti. 1984. Trans. by Ralph Manheim, Farrar 1986 $17.95 pap. $12.95

CHAMISSO, ADELBERT VON (LOUIS CHARLES ADÉLAIDE DE CHAMISSO). 1781–1838

This German romantic writer and naturalist was born in France and forced to flee at the time of the French Revolution. He was a member of the literary circle of Mme. de Staël near Geneva. Some of his verse was set to music by Schumann. He is best known for his humorous tale of *Peter Schlemihl*, the man who sold his shadow to the devil.

BOOK BY CHAMISSO

Peter Schlemihl: The Shadowless Man. 1814. Intro. by Joseph Jacobs, Telegraph Bks. repr. 1981 lib. bdg. $35.00

DÖBLIN, ALFRED. 1878–1957

Novelist, playwright, poet, essayist, Alfred Döblin was one of the most prolific writers of his time. He was also a practicing physician in the working-class district of Alexanderplatz. His novel of this name is considered his best work, and represents, in its montage technique, Döblin's experimental attitude toward prose writing. Döblin fled the Nazi regime in 1933 and lived for a while in the United States. Later he became a French citizen and a convert to the Roman Catholic Church.

BOOKS BY DÖBLIN

Berlin, Alexanderplatz: The Story of Franz Biberkopf. 1930. Trans. by Eugene Jolas, Ungar 1984 pap. $9.95
Karl and Rosa, November 1918: A German Revolution. Trans. by John E. Woods, Fromm Intl. Pub. 1983 $19.95 pap. $10.95
Men without Mercy. 1935. Trans. by Phyllis Blewitt, Fertig repr. of 1937 ed. 1976 $32.50

DÜRRENMATT (or DUERRENMATT), FRIEDRICH. 1921–

Dürrenmatt was born near Bern, Switzerland, the son of a Protestant clergyman. He studied philosophy and theology and originally planned to become a painter. "All of a sudden," he has said, "I began to write, and I just had no time to finish my University degree." He has called his first play, *It Is Written* (1947, o.p.), "a wild story of Anabaptists during the Reformation." When it was first produced in Zurich, it caused a minor theatrical scandal because of its somewhat unorthodox sentiments. *The Marriage of Mr. Mississippi*, his first successful comedy, was produced in Munich in 1952, and, as adapted by Maximillian Slater with the title *Fools are Passing Through*, had a brief off-Broadway production in 1958. With this play he became established as one of the most popular European dramatists writing in German. His seventh play, *The Visit* (1956, o.p.), which starred Alfred Lunt and Lynn Fontaine on Broadway, received the N.Y. Drama Critics Circle Award in 1959. Brooks Atkinson called it "devastating. A bold, grisly drama of negativism and genius."

Dürrenmatt, in his nondramatic work, turns out "some of the most wry and bitter writing of this wry and bitter time." In an interview published in *Esquire*, the author was asked what reaction he most preferred his audiences to have to his work. "Fright!" he replied. "That is the modern form of empathy." *The Judge and His Hangman* is the best of the detective stories qua mystery, lacking the explicit moral concern that informs his other books of this genre.

BOOKS BY DÜRRENMATT

Plays and Essays. Continuum 1982 $19.50 pap. $8.95
The Judge and His Hangman (and *The Quarry*). 1952, 1953. Godine 1983 pap. $7.95
The Physicists. 1962. Trans. by James Kirkup, Grove (Evergreen) 1964 pap. $3.95

BOOKS ABOUT DÜRRENMATT

Fickert, Kurt J. *To Heaven and Back: The New Morality in the Plays of Friedrich Dürrenmatt.* Univ. Pr. of Kentucky 1972 $8.00
Tiusanen, Timo. *Dürrenmatt: A Study in Plays, Prose, Theory.* Princeton Univ. Pr. 1977 $40.00
Whitton, Kenneth S. *The Theatre of Friedrich Dürrenmatt.* Humanities Pr. text ed. 1979 $20.75 1980 $21.25

EICHENDORFF, JOSEPH, FREIHERR VON. 1788–1857

Born in Silesia, Eichendorff studied in Breslau, Halle, Heidelberg, and Vienna. A devout Roman Catholic, he expresses a serene attitude toward life in all his writings. His poems are beautifully balanced lyrics that embody the romantic and transcendental fashions of his time. Among his Novellen, *Aus dem Leben eines Taugenichts* (*Memoirs of a Good-for-Nothing*) is especially delightful in its lighthearted spontaneity.

BOOK BY EICHENDORFF

Memoirs of a Good-for-Nothing. 1821. Trans. by Leopold von Lowenberg-Wertheim, Riverrun 1981 pap. $3.95

BOOK ABOUT EICHENDORFF

Radner, Lawrence R. *Eichendorff: The Spiritual Geometry.* Purdue Univ. Pr. 1971
    $8.75

FEUCHTWANGER, LION (pseud. of J. L. Wetcheek). 1884–1958

Feuchtwanger, novelist and dramatist, was born in Munich, the son of a
wealthy Jewish manufacturer. The rise of the Nazis drove him to France,
and after the collapse of that country he escaped with great difficulty to
Spain; he reached the United States in 1940. A major work is his trilogy on
the Jewish historian: *Josephus* (1932), *The Jew of Rome* (1935, o.p.) and *Josephus and the Emperor* (1942, o.p.). He was best known in Germany as a dramatist, but his international success was due to his revival of the historical
novel written with modern psychological understanding.

BOOKS BY FEUCHTWANGER

The Oppermanns. 1923. Carroll & Graf 1983 pap. $8.95
The Jew Suss. 1925. Carroll & Graf 1984 $18.95 pap. $8.95
Success: Three Years in the Life of a Province. Carroll & Graf 1984 pap. $10.95; trans.
    by Edwin Muir, Norwood repr. of 1930 ed. lib. bdg. $25.00
Josephus: A Historical Romance. 1932. Atheneum repr. 1972 pap. $10.95

BOOK ABOUT FEUCHTWANGER

Kahn, Lothar. *Insight and Action: The Life and Work of Lion Feuchtwanger.* Fairleigh
    Dickinson Univ. Pr. 1976 $28.50

FONTANE, THEODOR. 1819–1898

Fontane's fictional studies of nineteenth-century Berlin society, written in
his late maturity, secured him a firm place in literature as the first master
of the German realist novel; his declared aim was to show "the undistorted
reflection of the life we lead." "He introduced his people in spirited conversations at picnics and banquets, and developed a broad and yet intimate
perspective of background conditions; he was less interested in plots, and often would make a point by silence" (Ernst Rose). *Effi Briest*, his masterpiece, is a revealing portrait of an individual victimized by outmoded standards. Fontane, on whom SIR WALTER SCOTT (see Vol. 1) had made a deep impression, traveled to England as a journalist and wrote two books based on
his experiences: *A Summer in London* and *Across the Tweed.* He also wrote
historical novels, poetry, and dramatic criticism.

BOOKS BY FONTANE

Short Novels and Other Writings. Fwd. by Peter Demetz, Continuum 1982 $19.50 pap.
    $8.95
A Man of Honor. 1883. Trans. by E. M. Valk, Ungar 1975 $12.50 pap. $4.95
Jenny Treibel. 1892. Trans. by Ulf Zimmermann, Ungar 1977 pap. $4.95
Effi Briest. 1895. Trans. by Douglas Parmee, *Penguin Class. Ser.* 1976 pap. $3.95

BOOKS ABOUT FONTANE

Bance, Alan. *Theodor Fontane: The Major Novels.* Cambridge Univ. Pr. 1982 $47.50

Garland, Henry. *The Berlin Novels of Theodor Fontane.* Oxford 1980 $45.00
Robinson, A. R. *Theodor Fontane: An Introduction to the Man and His Work.* Verry
     o.p.

FRISCH, MAX. 1911–

Max Frisch has been for some 30 years one of the outstanding literary figures in Europe. He is a Swiss architect by profession and a dramatist and
novelist by avocation. His important dramatic works, *The Chinese Wall*
(1947), *The Firebugs* (1958), and *Andorra* (1961) are out of print. The latter
created a sensation in Europe through its portrayal of anti-Semitism.

Of his novels, *Stiller* remains his masterpiece. *Man in the Holocene* and
Bluebeard are his latest works of fiction.

Books by Frisch

I'm Not Stiller. 1954. Random (Vintage) 1958 pap. $3.95. This novel is an "elaborate
     and powerful illustration of Kierkegaard's thesis that man's road to freedom
     lies through self-acceptance. . . . What gives it stature as a novel is Frisch's dis-
     section of the tormented and tormenting relationship between Stiller and his
     wife. The real heart of the situation—and of the book—lies in the fifty-page post-
     script by the public prosecutor" (*N.Y. Herald Tribune*).
Homo Faber. 1957. Trans. by Michael Bullock, Harcourt repr. of 1959 ed. 1971 pap.
     $4.95; ed. by Paul K. Ackermann, Houghton Mifflin text ed. 1973 pap. $13.50
Gantenbein. 1964. Trans. by Michael Bullock, Harcourt repr. of 1965 ed. 1982 $7.95
Sketchbook. 1966–71. Trans. by Geoffrey Skelton, Harcourt 2 vols. 1974–77 ea.
     $10.00–$12.95 pap. ea. $8.95; Peter Smith 2 vols. 1984 ea. $16.75
Triptych. 1978. Trans. by Geoffrey Skelton, Harcourt 1980 $9.95
Man in the Holocene. 1979. Trans. by Geoffrey Skelton, Harcourt 1980 $9.95 1981
     pap. $4.95
Bluebeard. 1982. Trans. by Geoffrey Skelton, Harcourt 1983 $10.95 1984 pap. $4.95

Book about Frisch

Butler, Michael. *The Novels of Max Frisch.* Humanities Pr. text ed. 1976 $17.50

GEORGE, STEFAN. 1868–1933

Aristocratic and recondite, George deliberately wrote difficult poetry for
those few destined to understand him. Gathered about him was a group of
gifted, often physically beautiful young men, the so-called George Kreis
(George Circle), to whom he charged the spreading of his ideas. George's poems continue to influence young writers—not so much for their themes as
for their austere formal style and perfection of diction, a diction expanded
by his vast knowledge of languages ancient and modern. Many young poets
today would aspire to Bithell's praise: "George paints with vowels or plays
on them just as a pianist plays on keys; he tangles his construction; he
swathes the inner meaning of the poem in a floating veil of symbol."

Book by George

The Works of Stefan George. Trans. by Olga Marx and Ernst Morwitz, Univ. of North
     Carolina Pr. 2d ed. 1974 $27.50. Faithful and readable translations.

GOETHE, JOHANN WOLFGANG VON. 1749–1832

Johann Wolfgang von Goethe, "Europe's last universal man," belongs with the most remarkable writers of all time. Poet, dramatist, critic, novelist, artist, and scientist, he once remarked that all his works were "fragments of a great confession." In 1775, at the time of his *Werther* success, he was invited to the court of Weimar, where he became adviser to the young duke. Here he settled, engaging in political and cultural activities and eventually becoming the object of cultural pilgrimage himself. To Weimar, in time, came Schiller, and the two pursued their fruitful friendship. Goethe's love affairs, which he managed to combine with a stable marriage, continued throughout his long life, and provided him with literary material as well as inspiration.

With his play *Götz von Berlichingen* and his novelette *The Sorrows of Young Werther*, Goethe became the standard bearer of the Sturm and Drang movement, which represents a youthful, idealistic revolt against the constraints of European neoclassicism, particularly French rationalism. His plays *Iphigenia in Tauris* and *Torquato Tasso* are representative of the classical rigor of his second phase.

His last period, when he was the great and somewhat lonely Olympian of world literature, produced creative work of amazing vitality and diversity: novels, narrative poems, autobiographical works, and the monumental poetic drama *Faust*, which represents the best thought of 60 years of Goethe's life.

In *Faust*, with its breadth of vision and grandeur of poetic expression, the emphasis is on a man's constant striving toward the full range of human experience—cultural, intellectual, and spiritual—beyond the search for mere abstract knowledge or purely physical pleasures. The earliest manuscript of *Faust*, the *Urfaust*, was not discovered until 1887. *Faust Part I* was completed in two stages in 1775 and 1790, and it was not published until after Goethe's death in 1832.

Goethe's greatness lay in his combination of intellectual energy, modesty, and "reverence for life" (Albert Schweitzer's key phrase) and in his continual protest against the rationalization and mechanization of the cosmos, including man.

BOOKS BY GOETHE

Götz von Berlichingen. 1773. Trans. by Charles E. Passage, Ungar pap. $4.75. Drama.
The Sorrows of Young Werther. 1774. Trans. by Victor Lange, Holt 3 bks. in 1 1949 pap. $10.00; (with the title *The Sufferings of Young Werther*), trans. by Baryard Quincy Morgan, Ungar 1957 pap. $4.50; Amer. Class. College Pr. 1984 $55.75
Egmont: A Play. 1778. Ed. by H. M. Waidson, Basil Blackwell repr. of 1960 ed. 1974 pap. $9.95; trans. by Charles E. Passage, Ungar 1985 pap. $5.95
Iphigenia in Tauris. 1779. Trans. by Charles E. Passage, Ungar pap. $3.95
Roman Elegies and Venetian Epigrams. 1794, 1795. Trans. by L. R. Lind, Univ. Pr. of Kansas 1974 $22.50
Wilhelm Meister. 1795–96. Trans. by H. M. Waidson, Riverrun 6 vols. 1982 ea. $7.95

Hermann and Dorothea. 1797. Trans. by Daniel Coogan, Ungar bilingual ed. pap.
    $3.95. A provincial epic.
Faust. 1808–32. *Anchor Literary Lib.* Doubleday pap. $7.95; trans. by Walter Arndt,
    ed. by Cyrus Hamlin, *Norton Critical Eds.* text ed. 1976 pap. $10.95; trans. by
    Barker Fairley, Univ. of Toronto Pr. 1970 pap. $6.00. The legend of Dr. Johann
    Faust is as much a part of Western literary tradition as is that of King Arthur.
    Its most famous treatments have been the version of the chapbooks, and those
    by Christopher Marlowe and Goethe. Goethe has taken the basic tale of a
    scholar who strikes a bargain with the devil but changes the object of Faust's de-
    sire from power to knowledge. Nor does Goethe's drama set a time limit—Meph-
    istopheles can claim Faust's soul at whatever time Faust can say he is satisfied.
    After the death of Gretchen in Part I and of his son Euphorion (from his union
    with Helen of Troy) in Part II, Faust turns his energies toward improving the lot
    of his fellow man, and it is while he is engaged in clearing a marsh that he sees
    the purpose of earthly existence—namely, that only the man who constantly
    strives deserves the privilege of life and freedom. This moment of insight pro-
    vides him with the satisfaction he has been seeking and he dies. Mephistopheles,
    believing he has won the wager, summons his demons, but the angels of God ap-
    pear and take Faust's soul into heaven. As they take his soul they sing, "He who
    constantly strives is worthy of salvation," thus confirming Faust's ultimate in-
    sight. Faust's salvation is also a major departure from the traditional Faust leg-
    end. Instead of providing a warning to all Christians, which the chapbook ver-
    sion hoped to accomplish with its vivid description of Faust's inglorious end,
    Goethe instead investigates the meaning of human existence, and, more impor-
    tantly, provides an answer.
Elective Affinities. 1809. Greenwood repr. of 1963 ed. 1976 lib. bdg. $24.75; *Penguin
    Class. Ser.* 1978 pap. $4.95; trans. by Elizabeth Mayer and Louise Bogan,
    Regnery-Gateway repr. pap. $5.95; trans. by J. A. Froude and R. D. Boylan, Un-
    gar pap. $4.95. An "extraordinary and unforgettable novel . . . about the elemen-
    tal power of love" (*SR*).
Theory of Colours. 1810. Trans. by C. L. Eastlake, Biblio Dist. 1967 $35.00; Gordon
    lib. bdg. $79.95; MIT 1970 pap. $9.95
Goethe's World View: Presented in His Reflections and Maxims. Trans. by Heinz
    Norden, ed. by Frederick Ungar, Ungar pap. $4.50
The Autobiography of Johann Wolfgang von Goethe. Univ. of Chicago Pr. (Phoenix
    Bks.) 2 vols. pap. ea. $15.00

BOOKS ABOUT GOETHE

Abbe, Derek van. *Goethe: New Perspectives on a Writer and His Time.* Bucknell Univ.
    Pr. $18.00
Blackall, Eric A. *Goethe and the Novel.* Cornell Univ. Pr. 1976 $57.50
Boyd, James. *Goethe's Knowledge of English Literature.* Haskell repr. of 1932 ed. 1972
    lib. bdg. $49.95
Butler, E. M. *Goethe and Byron.* Folcroft repr. of 1949 ed. $8.50
Carlson, Marvin A. *Goethe and the Weimar Theatre.* Cornell Univ. Pr. 1978 $29.95
Crawford, Mary C. *Goethe and His Women Friends.* Haskell repr. of 1911 ed. 1972
    $72.95
Croce, Benedetto. *Goethe.* Associated Faculty Pr. repr. of 1923 ed. 1970 $19.50
Gearey, John. *Goethe's "Faust": The Making of Part I.* Yale Univ. Pr. 1981 $23.50

Glehn, M. E. von. *Goethe and Mendelssohn.* Haskett repr. of 1874 ed. $49.95
Gray, Ronald D. *Goethe: A Critical Introduction.* Cambridge Univ. Pr. text ed. pap. $16.95
Hammer, Carl, Jr. *Goethe and Rousseau: Resonances of the Mind.* Univ. Pr. of Kentucky 1973 $20.00
Hoyer, Walter. *Goethe's Life in Pictures.* Adler's 1963 $1.95; Dufour 1967 $6.00
Lukacs, Georg. *Goethe and His Age.* Trans. by Robert Anchor, Fertig repr. of 1968 ed. 1978 o.p. A sociological discussion.
Steiner, Rudolf. *Goethe's Conception of the World.* Haskell repr. of 1932 ed. 1972 lib. bdg. $49.95
Trevelyan, Humphry. *Goethe and the Greeks.* Fwd. by H. Lloyd Jones, Cambridge Univ. Pr. 1981 $52.50 pap. $18.95; Octagon repr. of 1941 ed. 1972 lib. bdg. $20.50
Wheeler, Kathleen M. *The Romantic Ironists and Goethe.* Cambridge Univ. Pr. 1984 $49.50 pap. $14.95

GOTTFRIED VON STRASSBURG. 1170?–1210?

Little is known about Gottfried von Strassburg, the greatest stylist of the medieval German period. Only one work of his, *Tristan and Isolde*, has been preserved (indeed, it may well be the only one he ever wrote), and it is incomplete. Gottfried did not identify himself as the poet, and it is only through later sources that his name is linked with *Tristan*. Internal evidence in *Tristan* suggests that Gottfried stopped working on it around 1210 and it is assumed that he died shortly thereafter.

Gottfried, probably a native of Strassburg, was a very learned man, well versed in Latin, French, and German. Unlike his brother poets, Hartmann von Aue and Wolfram von Eschenbach, Gottfried was not a knight, but a member of the urban patrician class. He was urbane, sophisticated, learned—more cannot be said of this great poet.

BOOK BY GOTTFRIED VON STRASSBURG

Tristan. Trans. by Arthur T. Hatto, Penguin 1960 pap. $3.95. Gottfried based his *Tristan* on the *Tristan* of a Latin poet named Thomas, who tells of the ill-fated lovers Tristan and Isolde. In his prologue Gottfried makes clear that he is writing a love story for those who truly understand love. He calls those people the "noble hearts" and emphasizes that they are not necessarily noble by birth, but rather in attitude. In *Tristan* Gottfried moves far beyond the conventions of courtly love and examines the phenomenon of love in great detail, so that love assumes an individuality of its own and is viewed as a powerful, independent, mystical force in the world, on a level with religion. In *Tristan* Gottfried also presents a view of the poets of his day. In the famous "Literary Excursus," he praises Hartmann von Aue for his clarity of style and criticizes an unnamed poet whom he calls "the companion of the hare, leaping willy-nilly over the word heath." It is generally accepted that Gottfried is taking his colleague Wolfram von Eschenbach to task, for if there is any medieval German poet who lacks those qualities of clarity that Gottfried prizes, it is Wolfram.

Books about Gottfried von Strassburg

Jackson, William T. *Anatomy of Love: A Study of the Tristan of Gottfried von Strass-burg.* Columbia Univ. Pr. 1971 $26.00
Picozzi, Rosemary. *A History of Tristan Scholarship.* Peter Lang 1971 pap. $22.85

GRASS, GÜNTER. 1927–

The outspoken Günter Grass is West Germany's outstanding contemporary writer, its wunderkind. He is a poet, novelist, painter, and sculptor. He won an immediate and enormous audience in Europe and the United States with his first novel, *The Tin Drum,* the "allegorical" story of Oskar Matzerath, who decides at the age of three to stop growing, thereby absolving himself of the responsibility of making adult decisions. He is the rogue, the picaresque outsider, who communicates only by banging his ever-present little drum. The story of Oskar's fantastic progress is a scandalous, sardonic satire of Nazi Germany. In *Cat and Mouse* (1961), Grass again journeys into the realm of the grotesque to tell the story of Joachim Mahlke, another antihero—a youth with an enormous Adam's apple, an outsider because of his peculiarity. In the 1967 German film version of *Cat and Mouse,* Lars Brandt, son of foreign minister Willy Brandt, played the leading role. The Interior Ministry, which subsidized the film, threatened to withdraw its funds because of a scene in which Brandt toys with the Iron Cross, one of Germany's highest wartime decorations. "For Grass, the scene symbolizes young Germany playing on the wreck of Hitler's Reich" (*N.Y. Times*).

The Tin Drum, Cat and Mouse, and *Dog Years* form a kind of trilogy. *Dog Years,* Grass's most ambitious work, is "the story of an incredible odyssey through the jungle of life in Germany just before, during, and after the Hitler era. . . . Monstrous, magnificent, and unforgettable" (*SR*). It concerns a Jew who creates weird scarecrows—the symbols on which Grass again builds his grimly humorous picture of modern man violating all the standards of decency to which he gives lip service.

In his more recent works it is evident that the former enfant terrible is approaching middle age and becoming more moderate. Grass is now facing up to a new generation of Germans, unburdened by guilt and impatient. Rather than barging ahead, he is now advocating slow, deliberate progress as desirable. In his *Aus dem Tagebuch einer Schneck* (*From the Diary of a Snail,* 1972), Grass presents the snail as a model worthy of imitation.

Grass was born in Danzig, the son of a grocer, and was once a member of the Hitler Youth; at 16 he was drafted for World War II. Taken prisoner, and released after the war, he became first a farm laborer and stonecutter and eventually a sculptor and stage designer, until writing claimed all his time. He was awarded an honorary doctorate by Harvard University in 1976. Grass makes his home in West Berlin, where since 1983 he has been president of the Academy of Art.

Books by Grass

The Tin Drum. 1959. Trans. by Ralph Manheim, Random 1971 $10.95 pap. $5.95
Dog Years. 1963. Fawcett 1979 pap. $2.95

The Flounder. 1977. Fawcett 1979 pap. $2.95; trans. by Ralph Manheim, Harcourt 1978 $12.00

In the Egg and Other Poems. Trans. by Michael Hamburger and Christopher Middleton, Harcourt 1977 pap. $5.95

Headbirths; Or, the Germans Are Dying Out. 1980. Fawcett 1983 pap. $2.95

The Meeting at Teltge. Fawcett 1982 pap. $3.50; Harcourt 1981 $9.95

BOOKS ABOUT GRASS

Hollington, Michael. *Günter Grass: The Writer in a Pluralist Society.* Boyars 1980 $16.00 1982 pap. $8.95

Lawson, Richard H. *Günter Grass. Lit. and Life Ser.* Ungar 1984 $12.95

O'Neill, Patrick. *Günter Grass: A Bibliography, 1955–1975.* Univ. of Toronto Pr. 1976 $17.50

Thomas, Noel. *The Narrative Works of Günter Grass.* Benjamins North Amer. 1983 $42.00

GRILLPARZER, FRANZ. 1791–1872

Grillparzer was the first Austrian writer to achieve international standing. He was born and lived in a Vienna where music was all important and literature was strictly controlled by the church and the imperial court. His career as a playwright and as a minor government official was beset by difficulty. His plays repeatedly state his personal conviction that to be involved in love or in political power is to invite disaster. He never married his fiancée, though he never released her from their betrothal, and died her lodger.

An ardent patriot, he sought to glorify Austria in his historical plays but met with censorship from Prince Metternich's government. After the failure of his play *Weh Dem, Der Lügt* (*Thou Shalt Not Lie*) in 1838, he permitted no new play to be performed or published, though he continued to write for more than 30 years.

BOOKS BY GRILLPARZER

Medea. 1818. Trans. by Arthur Burkhard, M. S. Rosenberg pap. $5.00

King Ottocar: His Rise and Fall. 1825. Trans. by Arthur Burkhard, M. S. Rosenberg pap. $5.00

Hero and Leander: The Waves of the Sea and of Love. 1831. Trans. by Arthur Burkhard, M. S. Rosenberg pap. $5.00

The Jewess of Toledo. 1855. Trans. by Arthur Burkhard, M. S. Rosenberg $5.00

Sappho. Trans. by Arthur Burkhard, Register Pr. 1953 pap. $5.00; St. Martin's 1965 $6.95

BOOK ABOUT GRILLPARZER

Yates, Douglas. *Franz Grillparzer: A Critical Biography.* Folcroft repr. of 1946 ed. $22.00; Norwood repr. of 1946 ed. 1980 lib. bdg. $25.00

GRIMM, JACOB (LUDWIG KARL), 1785–1863, and WILHELM (KARL) GRIMM. 1786–1859

A persistent element in the German romantic movement was the nationalism that found expression in collections of folksongs and folktales. One of the first was *Des Knaben Wunderhorn* (*The Boy's Magic Horn*), 1805, edited by two poets of the later romantic literary circle, Clemens Brentano and Achim von Arnim. In 1812, the brothers Grimm published their collection of *Kinder-und Hausmärchen* (*Household Tales*), which has become a staple of world literature.

This interest in the past, and especially the Germanic past, gave impetus to the field of Germanic philology. The Grimms and those inspired by them worked feverishly to collect and edit manuscripts of Germanic heroic tales and to produce a grammar of the German language, and the Grimms themselves began work on the monumental *Deutsches Wörterbuch* (*German Dictionary*), which was not finished until 1961. They departed from the indiscriminate patriotic fervor of the early romanticists and insisted that the past and its literary monuments be approached in a strict, scientific way. This is their greatest legacy.

BOOKS BY THE GRIMMS

Grimm's Household Tales. 1884. Trans. by Margaret Hunt, Gale 2 vols. repr. of 1884 ed. 1968 $58.00; Gordon $59.95

Household Stories from the Collection of the Bros. Grimm. Trans. by Lucy Crane, Peter Smith repr. of 1886 ed. $8.95. These editions, illustrated by Walter Crane, the pre-Raphaelite painter, have a charming, antique atmosphere about them.

The Complete Grimm's Fairy Tales. Pantheon 1974 $17.00

German Fairy Tales. Fwd. by Bruno Bettelheim, Continuum 1984 $24.50 pap. $10.95

Grimm: Selected Tales. Trans. by Wilhelm Grimm and David Luke, Penguin 1983 pap. $3.95

Hansel and Gretel. Oxford 1981 $9.95; Prentice-Hall 1985 $11.95

Teutonic Mythology. Trans. by James S. Stallybrass, Peter Smith 4 vols. 4th ed. $60.00. An examination of the roots of German law and religion.

BOOK ABOUT THE GRIMMS

Ellis, John M. *One Fairy Tale Too Many: The Brothers Grimm and Their Tales.* Univ. of Chicago Pr. 1983 $17.50

GRIMMELSHAUSEN, HANS JAKOB CHRISTOFFEL VON. 1620?–1676

A popular didactic novel of the Reformation period, Grimmelshausen's *Simplicissimus* has been called "undoubtedly the greatest novel of the seventeenth century." It is an early example of the picaresque genre. The hero of the novel, who shares some of his creator's adventures, is no conventional "fool" reflecting on the follies of mankind, but a real soldier of fortune in the Thirty Years' War. The misery he experiences forces him to search for an answer to the riddle of human existence. One of the sequels to *Simplicissimus* is *Landstörtzerin Courasche*, a bawdy, picaresque tale of a woman camp follower in an ugly world, "a symbol of the age and a lively individual [who] comes out on top in any situation with unimpaired self-assurance if not virtue" (*LJ*). Bertolt Brecht drew on this source for his play *Mother Courage and Her Children. The False Messiah* (1672), in which a thief poses as the Prophet Elijah, "paints an equally grotesque picture of the world. . . . It is hard to comprehend how the Victorians could have made a religious author out of Grimmelshausen" (*SR*).

BOOKS BY GRIMMELSHAUSEN

The Adventurous Simplicissimus. 1669. Trans. by A. T. Goodrick, pref. by E. Bentley, Univ. of Nebraska Pr. (Bison) 1962 pap. $7.95
The Runagate Courage. 1670. Pref. by E. Bentley, Univ. of Nebraska Pr. 1965 $16.95. Good introductory essay linking the work to Brecht's drama *Mother Courage and Her Children.*

BOOK ABOUT GRIMMELSHAUSEN

Hayens, Kenneth C. *Grimmelshausen.* Ridgeway Bks. repr. of 1932 ed. $25.00

HANDKE, PETER. 1942–

An Austrian playwright and novelist, Handke was born in Carinthia. In both his plays and novels, Handke protests against established literary conventions and experiments with new forms: his first production, *Offending the Audience,* had neither characters nor plot. His novels of the 1970s are largely autobiographical. Handke was awarded the Büchner Prize in 1973 and in 1979 refused to accept the Kafka Prize. A graduate of the University of Graz, he has lived in West Berlin and Paris and now makes his home in Salzburg.

BOOKS BY HANDKE

Kaspar and Other Plays. Trans. by Michael Roloff, Farrar 1970 pap. $6.95. Includes *Kaspar, Offending the Audience,* and *Self-Accusation.*
Short Letter, Long Farewell. 1972. Trans. by Ralph Manheim, Farrar 1974 $7.95
A Sorrow Beyond Dreams. 1972. Trans. by Ralph Manheim, Farrar 1975 $6.95. Addresses the suicide of Handke's mother.
The Left-handed Woman. 1976. Trans. by Ralph Manheim, Farrar 1978 $7.95
A Moment of True Feeling. Trans. by Ralph Manheim, Farrar 1977 $7.95
Short Homecoming. 1979. Trans. by Ralph Manheim, Farrar 1985 $16.95

BOOKS ABOUT HANDKE

Hern, Nicholas. *Peter Handke. Lit. and Life Ser.* Ungar 1971 $12.95
Schulueter, June. *The Plays and Novels of Handke.* Univ. of Pittsburgh Pr. 1981 pap. $7.95

HARTMANN VON AUE. c.1160–c.1220

Born in Swabia, Hartmann von Aue is generally credited with having introduced Arthurian romance into German literature. It seems evident that he attended a monastery school and visited France during his youth. He entered service with a lord of Aue to whom he was deeply attached. When his master died, Hartmann joined the crusade of Henry VI in 1197. He wrote epics, love songs, and crusading lyrics, as well as a "Büchlein," a lover's complaint in the form of a debate between the heart and the body. His *Erec* is the first known Arthurian romance in German. It closely follows its French model, the *Eric* of CHRÉTIEN DE TROYES. Hartmann's *Der Arme Heinrich* and his *Iwein* are famous and influential romances.

In the poem *Gregorius,* Hartmann virtually created a new genre, the so-called courtly legend, in which an edifying story is told with all the refinements of courtly style. *Gregorius* is a moral tale of sin and suffering in which penance is followed by reward. The hero is the child of an incestuous union of brother and sister. The boy is abandoned, discovered, raised by monks, becomes a knight-errant, saves a lady in distress, and marries her. Later he discovers that she is his mother. In despair he undertakes a prolonged and bitter expiation. His penance is at last accepted, his virtue recognized, and he is crowned pope. Hartmann's version of the ancient Oedipus legend became the source for Wolfram's *Parzival* and for Thomas Mann's *The Holy Sinner.*

BOOK BY HARTMANN

Gregorius. c.1195. Trans. into rhyming couplets by Edwin H. Zeydel and Bayard Q. Morgan, AMS Pr. repr. $18.50; trans. by Sheema Zeben Buehne, intro. by Helen Adolf, Ungar 1966 $11.50 pap. $5.95

HAUPTMANN, GERHART (JOHANN ROBERT). 1862–1946
(NOBEL PRIZE 1912)

Hauptmann, Germany's outstanding playwright of the naturalist school, was by nature an experimenter. He was a strange mixture: sometimes a revolutionary, as in his greatest play, *The Weavers* (1892); sometimes the compassionate creator, as in *Hannele* (1893), about a beggar girl dreaming of heaven. *The Sunken Bell* (1897), his most famous drama, is an allegorical verse play on the quest for an ideal, similar in theme to Ibsen's *Peer Gynt.* Hauptmann won the Nobel Prize in 1912, and was given an honorary degree by Columbia University in 1932, at which occasion he delivered an oration on Goethe.

Hauptmann ranks in Germany after Schiller, Goethe, and Brecht as the most widely performed German playwright. He stands as a landmark between the classic and the modern theater. "The heroes of his plays were not from either the ruling class or the bourgeoisie, but almost always from the masses. . . . By 1913, Hauptmann's naturalism was known throughout the world" (*N.Y. Times*).

Hauptmann deserves no less fame as a writer of prose. His earlier works, such as *Thiel the Crossing Keeper* (1888), show him at his strongest in the naturalistic mode. His characters are enslaved by their environment and by their own drives, especially the sex drive. In the *Heretic of Soana* (1918) Hauptmann concentrates on the power of the sexual urge in man in the story of the priest who gave up his church for the love of a woman, but he has moved away from the brooding excesses of naturalism.

Frowned upon by the Nazis for having been a prominent figure under the Republic, which once favored nominating him for the presidency, Hauptmann never spoke out against Nazi tyranny, but shook hands with Goebbels and accepted a medal. Yet when he died at his home in the Silesian Mountains, he had been about to move to East Berlin at the invitation of the Soviet Military Government. These events were forgotten or ignored during the 1962 centennial celebrations of his birth in the two Germanys. During the memorial week in Cologne, seven different plays of his were performed—three of them by Cologne's own repertory theater and the others by companies from Munich, Düsseldorf, Hamburg, and Göttingen. In West Germany alone, more than 20 of Hauptmann's plays were presented in theaters throughout the country.

BOOKS BY HAUPTMANN

The Fool in Christ, Emmanuel Quint. 1910. Trans. by T. Seltzer, Fertig repr. of 1911 ed. $25.00

Three Plays: The Weavers, Hannele, The Beaver Coat. Trans. by Horst Frenz and Miles Waggoner, Ungar repr. of 1951 ed. 1978 pap. $5.95

BOOK ABOUT HAUPTMANN

Maurer, Warren. *Gerhart Hauptmann. Twayne's World Authors Ser.* G. K. Hall 1982 lib. bdg. $18.95

HEBBEL, FRIEDRICH. 1813–1863

Hebbel, a North German by birth, lived abroad most of his life. The son of a stonemason and a servant girl, his childhood was passed in dire poverty, and his later travels, though sponsored in part by the Danish King Christian VIII, were marked by financial difficulties. His education was scanty and largely self-achieved. His ties to his early patroness, the novelist Amelia Schoppe, and to Elsie Lensing, a woman some years his senior, caused constant stress. Only in Vienna, where he married the well-known actress Christine Enghaus, did he settle down to a reasonably peaceful existence.

Hebbel wrote plays, short stories, lyric poems, an epic poem, and a great deal of criticism and dramatic theory. His plays are linked with those of the Viennese Franz Grillparzer as examples of late classicism.

BOOK BY HEBBEL

Herod and Mariamne. 1850. Trans. by Paul H. Curts, AMS Pr. repr. of 1950 ed. $27.00. A tragedy in five acts.

BOOK ABOUT HEBBEL

Flygt, Sten G. *Friedrich Hebbel. Twayne's World Authors Ser.* Irvington 1968 lib. bdg. $15.95

HEINE, HEINRICH. 1797–1856

Heinrich Heine is the best-known representative of the political and intellectual movement of the nineteenth century called Young Germany. Son of a Düsseldorf merchant, Heine's early years were ones of misadventure and failure. Born a Jew, he converted to Christianity in order to receive his law degree from the University of Göttingen in 1825. But his first love did not lie with law, and with the publication of the *Travel Sketches* (1826–31) he became a full-time writer. True to the spirit of the Young Germans, Heine idolized things French and eventually settled in Paris in 1831. There he was active as a journalist and attempted to interpret Germany and events in Germany to his French readers. He never lost his love for Germany, however, and some of his most beautiful poetry reveals the depths of his longing and love for his native land. From 1848 until his death in 1856 he was almost totally paralyzed, but he continued to produce some of the most sensitive poetry in the German language during those years. Brilliant, mercurial in both poetry and prose, he combined romanticism and sentiment with irony and satire. Abroad, his fame equaled Goethe's. Many of his poems have been set to music by Schubert, Schumann, and Brahms.

The Bibliothèque Nationale in Paris in 1966 acquired a collection of Heine's manuscripts, which includes "more than 2,500 unpublished pages written by Heinrich Heine and another 2,500 pages of letters to the poet and documents about him" (*N.Y. Times*).

Books by Heine

The Works of Heinrich Heine. Trans. by Charles G. Leland, AMS Pr. 20 vols. repr. of 1906 ed. ea. $20.00
Lyric Poems and Ballads. Trans. by Ernst Feise, Univ. of Pittsburgh Pr. repr. of 1968 ed. bilingual ed. pap. $4.95
The North Sea. Trans. by Howard M. Jones, Open Court $4.95
Heinrich Heine's Memoirs. Ed. by Gustav Karpeles, Ayer 2 vols. in 1 repr. of 1910 ed. $44.00
The Prose Writings of Heinrich Heine. Ed. by Havelock Ellis, Ayer repr. of 1887 ed. $26.50

Books about Heine

Butler, Eliza M. *Heinrich Heine.* Century Bookbindery repr. of 1956 ed. 1981 lib. bdg. $30.00; Greenwood repr. of 1956 ed. lib. bdg. $19.75
Sammons, Jeffrey L. *Heinrich Heine: A Selected Critical Bibliography of Secondary Literature, 1956–1980.* Garland 1982 lib. bdg. $36.00. A sensitive study by one of the foremost Heine scholars in this country.

HERDER, JOHANN GOTTFRIED VON. 1744–1803

Herder, humanist philosopher, poet, and critic, was born in Mohrungen in East Prussia. He suffered a deprived childhood but managed to attend the University of Königsberg, where he soon abandoned medical studies for theology. It was then that he came under the aegis of Kant (see Vol. 4), an influence that led to Herder's revolutionary approach to history. In his major work, *Ideas on a Philosophy of Human History* (1784–91), he proclaimed "humanity to be the essence of man's character as well as the irrevocable aim of history" (Ernst Rose). He had a tremendous influence on German romanticism. Herder later broke with Goethe and with most of his other followers. His last years were spent in bitterness, intellectual isolation.

Books by Herder

God: Some Conversations. Trans. by Frederick Burkhardt, Irvington text ed. 1940 pap. $5.95
Spirit of Hebrew Poetry. Trans. by James Marsh, Allenson-Breckenridge 2 vols. in 1 1971 $35.00

BOOK ABOUT HERDER

Mayo, Robert S. *Herder and the Beginnings of Comparative Literature.* Univ. of North Carolina Pr. 1969 $13.00

HESSE, HERMANN. 1877–1962 (NOBEL PRIZE 1946)

When this German novelist, poet, and essayist publicly denounced the savagery and hatred of World War I, he was considered a traitor. He moved to Switzerland where he eventually became a naturalized citizen. He warned of the advent of World War II, predicting that cultureless efficiency would destroy the modern world. His theme is the conflict between the elements of a person's dual nature and the problem of spiritual loneliness. His first novel, *Peter Camenzind,* was published in 1904. His masterpiece, *Death and the Lover* (1930, o.p.), contrasts a scholarly abbot and his beloved pupil, who leaves the monastery for the adventurous world. *Steppenwolf* (1927), a European bestseller, was published when defeated Germany had begun to plan for another war. It is the story of Haller, who recognizes in himself the blend of the human and wolfish traits of the completely sterile scholarly project. Hesse won the Nobel Prize in 1946.

BOOKS BY HESSE

Stories of Five Decades. Ed. by Theodore Ziolkowski and Ralph Manheim, Farrar 1973 pap. $7.95

Peter Camenzind. 1904. Trans. by Michael Roloff, Farrar 1969 $7.95

Beneath the Wheel. 1906. Bantam 1970 pap. $3.95; trans. by Michael Roloff, Farrar 1968 pap. $5.95

Gertrude. 1910. Trans. by Hilda Rosner, Farrar 1969 pap. $2.25

Rosshalde. 1914. Trans. by Ralph Manheim, Farrar 1970 pap. $1.95

Demian: The Story of Emil Sinclair's Youth. 1919. Bantam pap. $1.95; Harper 1965 $12.45. "Portrays a young boy's discovery of the chaos that lies beneath the surface respectability of everyday life" (*SR*).

Klingsor's Last Summer. 1920. Trans. by Richard Winston and Clara Winston, Farrar 1970 $6.50

Wandering. 1921. Trans. by James Wright, Farrar 1972 pap. $5.95

Siddhartha. 1922. Bantam pap. $2.95; Buccaneer Bks. repr. 1983 lib. bdg. $16.95; trans. by Hilda Rosner, New Directions 1951 $14.95 pap. $3.00. A novel inspired by Hesse's travels in India.

Steppenwolf. 1927. Bantam pap. $3.95; Buccaneer Bks. repr. 1983 lib. bdg. $16.95; Holt rev. ed. 1970 $9.95; *Rinehart Ed.* Holt text ed. 1963 pap. $10.95

Wandering. 1927. Trans. by James Wright, Farrar 1972 pap. $5.95

Narcissus and Goldmund. 1930. Bantam 1971 pap. $3.95; trans. by Ursule Molinaro, Farrar 1968 pap. $8.25

The Journey to the East. 1932. Trans. by Hilda Rosner, Farrar 1956 $1.45

Magister Ludi: The Glass Bead Game. 1943. Bantam 1970 pap. $3.95

If the War Goes On: Reflections on War and Politics. Trans. by Ralph Manheim, Farrar 1971 pap. $1.95

Strange News from Another Star. Trans. by Denver Lindley, Farrar 1972 pap. $4.95; G. K. Hall repr. 1973 $6.95

Reflections. Trans. by Ralph Manheim, ed. by Volker Michels, Farrar 1974 pap. $2.65

Autobiographical Writings. Trans. by Denver Lindley, ed. by Theodore Ziolkowski, Farrar 1972 $8.95 pap. $3.95
Hours in the Garden and Other Poems. Trans. by Rika Lesser, Farrar 1979 pap. $4.95
Knulp: Three Tales from the Life of Knulp. 1915. Trans. by Ralph Manheim, Farrar 1971 pap. $4.95
Pictor's Metamorphoses and Other Fantasies. Ed. by Theodore Ziolkowski, Farrar 1982 $15.95 pap. $8.25
Tales of Student Life. Ed. by Theodore Ziolkowski and Ralph Manheim, intro. by Theodore Ziolkowski, Farrar 1976 $8.95 pap. $4.95

BOOKS ABOUT HESSE

Freedman, Ralph. *Hermann Hesse: Pilgrim of Crisis.* Pantheon 1979 $15.00
Marrer-Tising, Carlee. *The Reception of Hermann Hesse by Youth in the United States.* Peter Lang 1982 $51.60
Mileck, Joseph. *Hermann Hesse: Biography and Bibliography.* Univ. of California Pr. 2 vols. 1977 $90.00

HOCHHUTH, ROLF. 1931–

When *The Deputy,* an epic drama in the manner of Schiller, was simultaneously first published and performed on stage by Erwin Piscator's company in Berlin in 1963, it created a furor. "It is almost certainly the largest storm ever raised by a play in the whole history of drama," said Eric Bentley (*The Storm over The Deputy*). Reading "like a German doctoral dissertation in verse," (Robert Brustein, *New Republic*), it is a searing indictment of Pope Pius XII, "God's deputy" on earth, for not having intervened publicly when Hitler organized and carried out the massacre of six million Jews. A Jesuit priest, the only invented character, reasons with the Pope in the play and in despair "becomes" a Jew and goes off to his death at Auschwitz. "To me," said Hochhuth, "Pius is a symbol, not only for all leaders but for all men . . . who are passive when their brother is deported to death."

The storm raged—with bannings, picketings, and riots in various parts of the world, and countless articles pro and con. Cardinal Spellman and Pope Paul VI were only two of the Catholic churchmen who came to the defense of Pope Pius, the latter on the ground that had he spoken out he "would have been guilty of unleashing on the already tormented world still greater calamities involving innumerable innocent victims." This conclusion is also in part that of Pinchas E. Lapide, an "Orthodox Jewish scholar and former Israeli diplomat," whose book *Three Popes and the Jews* (o.p.) is "scholarly, thorough and well balanced," wrote Bernhard E. Olson (*SR*).

Unfortunately, this work is no longer in print, nor is Hochhuth's almost as controversial play *The Soldiers,* in which WINSTON CHURCHILL (see Vol. 3) is accused of being personally responsible for the death of the Polish general Vladislav Sikorski. Hochhuth now lives in Basel, Switzerland.

BOOKS BY HOCHHUTH

A German Love Story. 1978. Trans. by John Brownjohn, Little, Brown 1980 $10.95. The basis for the movie, *A Love in Germany.*
Tell Thirty-Eight. Little, Brown 1984 $15.45

BOOK ABOUT HOCHHUTH

Taeni, Rainer. *Rolf Hochhuth.* Humanities Pr. 1977 $9.75

HOFFMANN. E(RNST) T(HEODOR) A(MADEUS). 1776–1822

Hoffmann was among the foremost raconteurs of the late romantic period in Germany. His Gothic influence was felt widely throughout France, England, and America—in the works of Musset, BAUDELAIRE, WALTER SCOTT (see Vol. 1), and POE (see Vol. 1), among others. Offenbach used three of his stories for the opera *Tales of Hoffmann.* Fascinated by the morbid and the grotesque, Hoffmann breathed life into his imaginary world and made it seem quite real. "His writing is . . . plastic, a quality which is conspicuous in his power of endowing with reality the supernatural phantasms of his brain" (J. G. Robertson).

Although he was musically productive in his early years, Hoffmann turned to literature for financial reasons and published his first work, *Weird Tales* (o.p.), with a preface by Jean Paul (Richter), in 1814–1815. He settled in Berlin, where his literary circle, the Serapionsabende, included Chamisso and provided material for *The Serapion Brethren* (1819–21, o.p.), a collection of stories supposed to have been told by a similar group of friends. The gruesome and chilling *Devil's Elixir* (1815–16, o.p.), a novel, is interesting for its psychological insights. The tales told by Hoffmann's fictional counterpart, the musician Kreisler, in *Weird Tales*, as well as the novel *Murr the Tomcat* (1820–22, o.p.), are in part autobiographical.

BOOKS BY HOFFMANN

Selected Writings of E. T. A. Hoffmann. Fwd. by R. Wellek, Univ. of Chicago Pr. 2 vols. 1969 $30.00
The Tales of Hoffmann. Penguin 1982 pap. $4.95; trans. by Michael Bullock, Ungar 1963 pap. $4.95
The Best Tales of Hoffmann. Ed. by E. F. Bleiler, Dover 1963 pap. $6.95
Three Märchen of E. T. A. Hoffmann. Trans. by Charles E. Passage, Univ. of South Carolina Pr. 1971 $19.95
The Strange Child. Trans. by Anthea Bell, Neugebauer Pr. 1984 $12.95
The Nutcracker and the Mouse King. Trans. by Anthea Bell, Neugebauer Pr. 1983 $12.95

BOOKS ABOUT HOFFMANN

Hewett-Thayer, Harvey. *Hoffmann: Author of the Tales.* Octagon 1970 $29.00
McGlathery, James M. *Mysticism and Sexuality: E. T. A. Hoffmann.* Peter Lang 3 vols. 1981–84 pap. ea. $21.60–$30.00

HOFMANNSTHAL, HUGO VON. 1874–1929

Hofmannsthal wrote the libretti for Richard Strauss's *Der Rosenkavalier, Ariadne auf Naxos,* and *Die Frau ohne Schatten.* Both men of genius, they preferred to work miles apart and depend upon the mail. Their divergent personalities emerge through their letters: "Strauss, genial, calm and absolutely insistent upon stageworthy librettos; von Hofmannsthal, introspective, sensitive, and possessed of his own high literary standards. Each recognized in the other his opposite number and determined to make the partnership work," as it did in many instances.

Hofmannsthal's plays are all written in verse and most of them are modernized adaptations from other dramatists. His masterpiece, *Electra* (1903), a modern treatment of the Greek tragedy, was set to music by Richard Strauss. Dramas such as *Jedermann* (1911) and *The Tower* (1925, o.p.) showed him to be a serious and responsible social critic. Their "deep symbolism is pervaded by an uncanny insight into the demonic forces and potentialities of our century" (*LJ*). With Max Reinhardt he helped to found the Salzburg Festival of music and theater, which still occurs annually. In his poetry he proved himself to be the most socially sensitive of the Viennese poets of the 1890s.

BOOK BY HOFMANNSTHAL

Selected Writings. Bollingen Ser. Princeton Univ. Pr. 3 vols. 1952–63 ea. $37.50–$50.00. Vol. 1 includes tales, novellas, essays, notes on his travels, and the unfinished novel *Andreas*. Vol. 2 includes *Death and the Fool, The Emperor and the Witch, The Little Theater of the World, The Mine at Fauln, The Marriage of Zobeide*, and the prologue to the *Antigone of Sophocles*. Vol. 3 includes three plays and three libretti, chosen to show the range of his theatrical writings.

BOOKS ABOUT HOFMANNSTHAL

Broch, Hermann. *Hugo von Hofmannsthal and His Time: The European Imagination, 1860–1920.* Ed. by Michael P. Steinberg, Univ. of Chicago Pr. 1984 $28.00 pap. $13.95
Hamburger, Martin. *Hofmannsthal: Three Essays.* Princeton Univ. Pr. 1970 pap. $6.95. Recommended.
Norman, F., ed. *Hofmannsthal Studies in Commemoration.* Humanities Pr. text ed. 1963 $22.75; State Mutual Bk. 1963 $50.00. Useful scholarly volume, but recommended for those with some knowledge of Hofmannsthal.

HÖLDERLIN, (JOHANN CHRISTIAN) FRIEDRICH. 1770–1843

Only during the last 50 years has Hölderlin come to be recognized as a great lyric poet. Except for his philosophical novel *Hyperion* (1797–99) and translations of two of SOPHOCLES' plays, his works were published by friends after he became hopelessly insane in his thirties. He spent his early life as a private tutor. Hellenic in feeling, his poetry is written in the classical meters or in free verse on Greek themes. Hölderlin knew and wrote of the tragic elements in life, but his poems encompass and transcend these in a vision of ultimate harmony. "He aimed at balance even in his rhythms, matching ascending units with descending ones and uniting many voices in a symphony. . . . He has become a guidepost for moderns" (Ernst Rose).

BOOKS BY HÖLDERLIN

Poems and Fragments. Trans. by Michael Hamburger, Cambridge Univ. Pr. bilingual ed. 1980 pap. $19.95. The largest selection of his poems available. Includes two fragments of the tragedy "The Death of Empedocles."

Selected Poems of Friedrich Hölderlin and Eduard Morike. Trans. by Christopher Middleton, Univ. of Chicago Pr. 1973 pap. $3.75
Hymns and Fragments. Trans. by Richard Sieburth, Princeton Univ. Pr. 1984 $27.50 pap. $9.95

BOOKS ABOUT HÖLDERLIN

Shelton, Roy C. *The Young Hölderlin.* Peter Lang 1973 $31.30
Unger, Richard. *Friedrich Hölderlin. Twayne's World Authors Ser.* G. K. Hall 1984 lib. bdg. $18.95

JOHANNES VON SAAZ (or VON TEPL). c.1350–c.1414

Johannes von Saaz was born in the village of Schüttwa and studied at the University of Prague. From 1383 he was town clerk, headmaster, and archepiscopal notary in Saaz. His young wife Margaretta died in 1400, and *The Plowman* is her literary memorial. Written as a legal debate between the plowman as plaintiff and Death as the accused, it forms a perfect miniature play. "This little book in dialogue form is the first really important work of prose literature in the German language," writes M. O'C. Walshe (*Medieval German Literature*). It was the fruit of an early wave of humanism in Bohemia.

BOOK BY JOHANNES VON SAAZ

The Plowman from Bohemia. Trans. by Alexander Henderson and Elizabeth Henderson, Ungar 1966 pap. $3.95

JOHNSON, UWE. 1934–1984

"Contemporary Germany is Johnson's all-purpose, modern symbol of confused human motives, social forces that drive people frantic, and frustrations in communication that finally choke men into silence" (Webster Schott, *N.Y. Times*). *The Third Book about Achim* (o.p.), winner of the $10,000 International Publishers' Prize in 1962, is a novel about divided Germany. It addresses one of the crucial philosophical problems of any age, but particularly the present: What is objective truth? Is there such a thing at all? Johnson's style is difficult: "bewildering time-sequences; abrupt and arbitrary shifts in point of view; shadowy characters; huge, eccentrically punctuated sentences; tortured syntax; esoteric excursions; oceanic digressions" (*SR*). Joachim Remak, in *Harper's*, says, "It is an easy book to dislike at first [but] in the course of the novel all the annoying traits suddenly vanish or become unimportant. For this is a great book; literary award judges can be right."

The novel was catharsis for Johnson's own personal conflicts: he had reluctantly left his home in East Germany in 1959 in order to have his first novel published without censorship. This first novel, *Speculations about Jacob*, was praised for a style that defies the traditional structure of the novel and indeed of language. In his *Anniversaries*, Johnson again treats pressing moral and political issues by having the scene of the novel switch from New York City during the Vietnam War to Mecklenburg, Germany, in the Nazi period. One of the major themes of the book is the failure of liberalism in the United States in the 1960s and in Germany in the 1930s. Johnson's work is consistent, never pedestrian, and sometimes brilliant. In 1971 Johnson received the Büchner Prize. He died in March 1984.

BOOKS BY JOHNSON

Speculations about Jacob. 1959. Trans. by Ursule Molinaro, Harcourt 1972 pap. $2.95
Anniversaries: From the Life of Gesine Cresspahl. 1970–73. Trans. by Leila Vennewitz,
    Harcourt 1975 $10.00

BOOK ABOUT JOHNSON

Buolby, Mark. *Uwe Johnson. Lit. and Life Ser.* Ungar 1974 $12.95

JÜNGER, ERNST. 1895–

One of the most enduring figures of modern German literature, Jünger published his war diary, *The Storm of Steel,* in 1920 at the age of 25. The recipient of the Pour le Mérite, Germany's highest award for bravery in the field, Jünger was lionized by his generation for his celebration of the "purifying" experience of war. His "heroic nihilism" was further articulated in his *War as a Spiritual Experience* (*Der Kampf als Innerer Erlebnis*), published in 1922. His allegorical *On the Marble Cliffs* is sometimes seen as an attack on Nazism. Nonetheless, Jünger served as an officer in the Reichswehr in Paris during World War II. Since the war he has become involved in the conservation movement, and the defense of nature has been the subject of his later writing. He remains primarily known for his early works, and his romanticization and aestheticizing of war now elicit much criticism. His recent receipt of a prestigious literary prize was the subject of considerable controversy.

BOOKS BY JÜNGER

The Storm of Steel. 1920. Trans. by B. Creighton, Fertig repr. of 1929 ed. 1975 $25.00
On the Marble Cliffs. 1939. Trans. by Stuart Hood, intro. by George Steiner, Penguin
    1984 pap. $4.95

KAFKA, FRANZ. 1883–1924

Kafka, a Czech who wrote in German, is now known for his "surpassing originality as an innovator in creative method." Very little of his work was published during his lifetime. The first three uncompleted novels form what Max Brod, his close friend, called a "trilogy of loneliness." "Like every other work, they reflect in a profoundly religious sense the experience of human isolation and the pathos of exclusion." He was born in Prague of middle-class Jewish parents and seems to have suffered early serious personality difficulties as the son of a domineering father. He took a law degree at the German University of Prague, then obtained a position in the workmen's compensation division of the Austrian government. Always neurotic, enigmatic, and obsessed with a sense of inadequacy, failure, and sinfulness, his writing was a quest for fulfillment. He spent several years in sanatoriums and died of tuberculosis in a hospital near Vienna. Before his death he asked Max Brod to burn all his manuscripts. But Brod disregarded this injunction and was responsible for the posthumous publication of Kafka's longer narratives, which have brought him worldwide fame in the past 25 years. The nightmare world of *The Castle* and *The Trial*, in which the little man is at the mercy of heartless forces that manipulate him without explanation, has become frighteningly relevant to the period of the modern mammoth (or authoritarian) state, in which ordinary citizens find themselves increasingly helpless.

The publication of Kafka's letters to his fiancée, Felice Bauer, will help to demystify him somewhat. Kafka's writings seem to have universal application, and when reading much of the literary criticism on Kafka, one is often unable to determine whether one is reading about Kafka and his neuroses or those of the critic.

BOOKS BY KAFKA

The Complete Stories. Ed. by N. N. Glatzer, Schocken 1976 $14.50 pap. $7.95

Letters to Milena. Schocken 1962 pap. $5.95

Letters to Friends, Family, and Editors. Trans. by Richard Winston and Clara Winston, Schocken 1977 $24.50 pap. $7.95

Letters to Ottla and the Family. Trans. by Richard Winston and Clara Winston, ed. by N. N. Glatzer, Schocken 1982 $15.95

Parables and Paradoxes. Schocken bilingual ed. 1961 pap $5.95. A selection from his works.

The Metamorphosis. 1916. Trans. by Stanley Corngold, *Bantam Class. Ser.* text ed. 1981 pap. $3.95; Schocken bilingual ed. 1968 pap. $3.95; Vanguard 1985 $9.95

In the Penal Colony: Stories and Short Pieces Including the Metamorphosis. 1920. Trans. by Willa Muir and Edwin Muir, Schocken 1961 $12.95 pap. $6.95

The Trial. 1925. Buccaneer Bks. repr. 1983 lib. bdg. $17.95; Knopf rev. ed. 1937 $13.50; Random (Vintage) 1985 pap. $4.95; Schocken 1968 pap. $5.45

The Castle. 1926. Knopf rev. ed. 1954 $12.95; Modern Lib. 1969 $4.95; Random (Vintage) 1985 pap. $5.95; commentary by Thomas Mann, Schocken repr. 1976 pap. $8.95

Amerika. 1927. Trans. by Edwin Muir, New Directions 1962 pap. $5.95; trans. by Edwin Muir, Schocken 1962 $10.00 pap. $5.95

The Great Wall of China: Stories and Reflections. 1931. Trans. by Willa Muir and Edwin Muir, Schocken repr. of 1946 ed. 1970 pap. $4.95

Description of a Struggle and Other Stories. Schocken 1958 $7.50. More than a dozen very short pieces, three stories, and a dramatic piece.

I Am a Memory Come Alive: Autobiographical Writings. Ed. by Nahum N. Glatzer, Schocken 1976 pap. $5.95

BOOKS ABOUT KAFKA

Brod, Max. *Franz Kafka: A Biography.* Schocken 2d ed. 1963 pap. $5.95. Kafka's lifelong friend and literary executor, the man who knew him as well as anyone, wrote this intimate biography, which Alfred Kazin described as "invaluable to anyone at all interested in the mind of the genius."

Canetti, Elias. *Kafka's Other Trial: The Letters to Felice.* Trans. by Christopher Middleton, Schocken 1982 $11.95 pap. $5.95. This critical study of the letters shows how the correspondence and the situation from which it arose greatly inspired Kafka's writings. This book can be considered essential.

Emrich, Wilhelm. *Franz Kafka*. Trans. by Sheema L. Buehme, Ungar 1968 $28.50. "An illuminating study of Franz Kafka's writings, examining Kafka's philosophic design by the square inch. . . . A remarkable study" (*PW*).

Flores, Angel, ed. *Franz Kafka Today*. Ed. by Homer Swander, Gordian repr. of 1958 ed. 1977 $13.50. Eighteen essays on the short stories, novels, letters, and diaries.

———. *The Kafka Problem: An Anthology of Criticism about Franz Kafka*. Gordian repr. of 1963 ed. 1976 $17.50

Gray, Ronald. *Franz Kafka*. Cambridge Univ. Pr. 1973 pap. $12.95

Hayman, Ronald. *Kafka: A Biography*. Oxford 1982 $22.50 pap. $8.95

Heller, Erich. *Franz Kafka*. Princeton Univ. Pr. repr. of 1974 ed. 1982 $23.00 pap. $7.95. "Heller's is one of the more enlightened Kafka studies of recent years" (*N.Y. Times*).

Hughes, Kenneth, ed. *Franz Kafka: An Anthology of Marxist Criticism*. Univ. Pr. of New England text ed. 1981 $25.00

Neumeyer, Peter F., ed. *Twentieth-Century Interpretations of The Castle*. Prentice-Hall (Spectrum Bks.) 1969 pap. $1.25

Pascal, Roy. *Kafka's Narrators: A Study of His Stories and Sketches*. Cambridge Univ. Pr. 1982 $44.50 pap. $13.95

———. *A Nightmare of Reason: A Life of Franz Kafka*. Farrar $25.50

Politzer, Heinz. *Franz Kafka: Parable and Paradox*. Cornell Univ. Pr. rev. & enl. ed. 1966 pap. $8.95

Taubert, Herbert. *Franz Kafka: An Interpretation of the Works*. Gordon repr. of 1948 ed. $75.00

KAISER, GEORG. 1878–1945

In the "GAS trilogy" (*The Coral, Gas I*, and *Gas II*) Kaiser's fundamental theme, the regeneration of man, is presented in terms of contemporary social conflicts. The cycle of plays encompasses the entire evolution of capitalism within an abstract scheme. In essence it is a morality play.

Kaiser was the leading playwright of German expressionism, and exponent of its meager settings, violent contrasts, and love of the grotesque and shocking—all aimed at arousing in the beholder an intense "awareness of life." His more than 50 plays include every variety of style and subject matter, including social drama, comedy, farce, romance, legend, and history. His characters are types shorn of individual subtleties, embodiments of ideas pure and simple. Kaiser stands as one of the boldest and most fascinating of the older generation of modern dramatists, and his impact on the contemporary theater, both inside and outside Germany, has been considerable. "A brilliant technician, he called his plays thought dramas. They deal chiefly with social themes and were not of a kind to please the Nazis, upon whose rise to power Kaiser left Germany." He died in Switzerland.

BOOKS BY KAISER

Plays. Trans. by B. J. Kenworthy, Riverrun 2 vols. 1980–82 pap. ea. $6.95

The Coral: A Play. 1917. Trans. by Winifred Katzin, Ungar pap. $3.95

Gas I: A Play. 1918. Trans. by Herman Scheffauer, Ungar pap. $3.95

Gas II: A Play. 1920. Trans. by Winifred Katzin, Ungar pap. $3.75

BOOKS ABOUT KAISER

Benson, Renate. *German Expressionist Drama: Ernst Toller and Georg Kaiser.* Grove 1984 $19.50 pap. $7.95

Tyson, Peter. *The Reception of Georg Kaiser.* Peter Lang 1984 $51.60

KELLER, GOTTFRIED. 1819–1890

This Swiss German-language poet and novelist, born in Zurich, is known for his widely read realistic short stories of Swiss provincial life. The *Saturday Review* wrote of his autobiographical *Green Henry*, "The book's instantly captivating quality is the charm with which a quietly sequential life of curiosity and perception is narrated in the pellucid recollection of the mature poet. Keller's eye for the colorful scene and his skill in endowing the concrete particular with something like archetypal significance make him an artist of rare integrity." His best work, *A Village Romeo and Juliet,* "tells of the tragic fate of two youthful lovers who are prevented from making an honest marriage by the sins of their fathers" (Ernst Rose).

BOOKS BY KELLER

Green Henry. 1854–55. Trans. by A. M. Holt, Riverrun 1985 pap. $16.95

People of Seldwyla (and *Seven Legends*). 1856. Trans. by M. D. Hottinger, *Short Story Index Repr. Ser.* Ayer repr. of 1929 ed. $16.00. These two collections are Keller's most famous. The first takes a nonsentimental but gentle view of the events (sometimes tragic) that take place in the lives of "typical" Swiss people in his mythical village of Seldwyla. The second pokes gentle fun at the Virgin Mary and other inhabitants of heaven.

A Village Romeo and Juliet. 1876. Trans. by Paul B. Thomas, Ungar $6.00 pap. $3.95

The Banner of the Upright Seven and Ursula. 1878. Trans. by Bayard Q. Morgan, intro. by Gerda Breit, Ungar repr. of 1914 ed. 1974 pap. $3.95

Martin Salander. 1886. Trans. by Kenneth Halwas, Riverrun 1981 pap. $4.95

Legends of Long Ago. 1911. Trans. by Charles H. Handchen, *Short Story Index Repr. Ser.* Ayer repr. of 1911 ed. $12.00

The Misused Love Letters and Regula Amrain and Her Youngest Son. Trans. by Michael Bullock and Anne Fremantle, Ungar 1974 $8.50 pap $3.95

KIRST, HANS HELLMUT. 1914–

Kirst drew on his experiences as a soldier and officer in World War II to become "the number one chronicler of the German military mind" (*SR*). He has been a farmer, playwright, and critic and is now one of Germany's most successful novelists; his work has been translated into 24 languages.

BOOK BY KIRST

The Night of the Long Knives. Putnam 1976 $8.95

KLEIST, HEINRICH VON. 1777–1811

This German dramatist, poet, and novelist of a Prussian military family disliked the army and resigned his commission to become a journalist and pamphleteer. None of his literary works had any real success in his short lifetime and none of his eight plays was performed. Poverty stricken and despondent, he killed himself and a newfound, seriously ill friend, Frau Vogel, by mutual agreement. Yet *The Broken Jug* is one of the funniest comedies in German literature, a realistic picture of village life in which a slovenly local judge is exposed. *Amphitryon*, also a comedy, studies the dilemma of a young matron whom Jupiter seduces in the guise of her husband. Kleist's tragedy *The Prince of Homburg* (1810, o.p.) is generally considered his masterpiece. Of his novelettes, *Michael Kohlhaas* (1810, o.p.) is outstanding. In Kleist was embodied the great conflict between classicism and romanticism, and his general theme was the conflict between individual human feelings—often erratic—and the impersonal harshness of man-made law, which he saw as nevertheless necessary for the functioning of society.

BOOKS BY KLEIST

Amphitryon: A Comedy. 1807. Trans. by Marion Sonnenfeld, Ungar pap. $4.95
The Broken Jug. 1808. Trans. by John T. Krumpelmann, Ungar pap. $3.45
The Marquise of O and Other Stories. 1810–11. Trans. by David Luke and Nigel Reeves, *Penguin Class. Ser.* Penguin 1978 pap. $3.95; pref. by Thomas Mann, Ungar repr. of 1960 ed. 1973 $15.95 pap. $5.95
An Abyss Deep Enough: The Letters of Heinrich von Kleist with a Selection of Essays and Anecdotes. Trans. by Philip B. Miller, Dutton 1982 $16.95

BOOKS ABOUT KLEIST

Burckhardt, Sigurd. *The Drama of Language: Essays on Goethe and Kleist.* Johns Hopkins Univ. Pr. 1970 $17.50
Dyer, Denys. *The Stories of Kleist: A Critical Study.* Holmes & Meier text ed. 1977 $32.50
Ellis, John M. *Heinrich von Kleist: Studies in the Character and Meaning of His Writings.* Univ. of North Carolina Pr. 1979 $17.50
Maas, Joachim. *Kleist: A Biography.* Trans. by Ralph Manheim, Farrar 1983 $22.50
Richardson, Frank C. *Kleist in France.* AMS Pr. repr. of 1962 ed. $27.00
Silz, Walter. *Heinrich von Kleist: Studies in His Works and Literary Character.* Greenwood repr. of 1962 ed. 1977 lib. bdg. $24.75

LESSING, GOTTHOLD EPHRAIM. 1729–1781

Lessing, one of the outstanding literary critics of all time, was "the first figure of European stature in modern German literature." The son of a Protestant pastor, he was educated in Meissen and at Leipzig University, then went to Berlin as a journalist in 1749. While employed as secretary to General Tauentzien (1760–65), he devoted his leisure to classical studies. This led to his critical essay *Laocoon*, in which he attempted to clarify certain laws of aesthetic perception by comparing poetry and the visual arts. He fought always for truth and combined a penetrating intellect with shrewd common sense.

He furthered the German theater through his weekly dramatic notes and theories, found mainly in the *Hamburg Dramaturgy*, which he wrote during his connection with the Hamburg National Theater as critic and dramatist (1768–69). His plays include *Miss Sara Sampson*, important as the first German prose tragedy of middle-class life; *Minna von Barnhelm* (o.p.), his finest comedy and the best of the era; and his noble plea for religious tolerance, *Nathan the Wise*.

BOOKS BY LESSING

Laocoon: An Essay on the Limits of Painting and Poetry. 1776. Biblio Dist. repr. of 1930 ed. 1970 $12.95; trans. by Edward A. McCormick, Johns Hopkins Univ. Pr. 1984 pap. $9.95; trans. by Robert Phillimore, Longwood repr. of 1874 ed. 1978 lib. bdg. $40.00

Minna von Barnhelm. 1767. Trans. by Kenneth J. Northcott, Univ. of Chicago Pr. 1972 $10.00

Hamburg Dramaturgy. 1769. Dover pap. $2.75

Emilia Galotti: A Tragedy in 5 Acts. 1772. Trans. by Anna G. von Aesch, Barron text ed. 1959 pap. $2.95

Nathan the Wise: A Dramatic Poem in 5 Acts. 1779. Trans. by Walter F. Ade, Barron text ed. 1972 pap. $3.95; trans. by Bayard Q. Morgan, Ungar pap. $4.50

Lessing's Theological Writings: Selections in Translation. Trans. by Henry Chadwick, Stanford Univ. Pr. repr. of 1957 ed. pap. $3.25

BOOKS ABOUT LESSING

Haney, John D. *Lessing's Education of the Human Race.* AMS Pr. repr. of 1908 ed. $22.50

Lamport, F. J. *Lessing and the Drama.* Oxford text ed. 1981 $39.00

Robertson, John G., ed. *Lessing's Dramatic Theory.* Ayer repr. of 1939 ed. $33.00. Lessing's analysis of "the theory of tragedy and the nature of drama." Includes some selections from other Lessing works and from those of European contemporaries.

Rolleston, Thomas W. *The Life of Gotthold Ephraim Lessing.* Associated Faculty Pr. repr. of 1889 ed. 1971 $21.00; Richard West repr. of 1889 ed. $11.50

Wellbery, David E. *Lessing's Laocoon: Semiotics and Aesthetics in the Age of Reason.* Cambridge Univ. Pr. 1984 $49.50

LIND, JAKOV. 1927–

An Austrian Jew whose parents were exterminated during World War II, Lind has translated the bitter memories of his youth into grotesque tales illustrating the horror of the Nazi years. The title story from *Soul of Wood* (1962, o.p.), actually a short novel, concerns the fate of a paralytic Jewish boy, the son of Nazi victims. He is left on a mountaintop by his guardian, who then vies with others to reclaim the boy for exploitation; all the horrors of Nazism are encountered as events transpire. *Journey through the Night* (o.p.), another story, describes with black humor the bizarre intellectual game between an admitted cannibal and his proposed victim in a railway compartment. "Lind's stories are fluid, inventive, surrealistic, and fantastic, though based in reality, bitter, and grimly savage. Expert, well-translated nightmares" (*LJ*).

BOOKS BY LIND

Travels to the Enu: The Story of a Shipwreck. St. Martin's 1982 $11.95

The Stove. 1982. Sheep Meadow 1983 $13.95 pap. $7.95

LUTHER, MARTIN. 1483–1546

[See Volume 4.]

MANN, HEINRICH. 1871–1950

Heinrich Mann wrote about artists and poets and voluptuaries, for whom art is a "perverse debauch." His novels set in Germany are usually grotesque caricatures with political implications; those set in Italy tend to be "riotous paeans of life lived at fever heat in a world where common sense and goodness and pity do not count." His *Professor Unrat* (1905, o.p.) was made into the famous film *The Blue Angel. The Little Town* (1909, o.p.) is perhaps his most benign novel.

Heinrich Mann, like his brother Thomas, fled Nazi Germany and came to the United States. He died in California. His literary reputation is stronger in Europe. In the United States his reputation is clouded partly by the rancour of his brilliant, hectic prose, and partly by his admiration of the Soviet Union.

Books by Heinrich Mann

Young Henry of Navarre. 1935. Trans. by Eric Sutton, Overlook Pr. 1984 $18.95
Man of Straw. Penguin 1984 pap. $6.95

Books about Heinrich Mann

Gross, David. *The Writer and Society: Heinrich Mann and Literary Politics in Germany, 1890–1940.* Humanities Pr. text ed. 1980 $18.00
Hamilton, Nigel. *The Brothers Mann.* Yale Univ. Pr. 1979 $35.00 pap. $11.95

MANN, THOMAS. 1875–1955 (Nobel Prize 1929)

Although Mann suffered some diminution in popularity after his death, his hundredth anniversary and the general renewed interest in Germany and German literature have succeeded in bringing Mann again to the fore of literary discussion.

His achievement remains tremendous. *Buddenbrooks*, his first novel, was published when Mann was just 26 years old. An intricate panoramic history of the decline of a German mercantile family not unlike Mann's own, it introduced (in the persons of several family members) what were to be Mann's dominant themes, with variations—the isolation of the artist in society, intellectualism versus the life of the emotions and senses, decay and death as sharpeners of life, and the relationship of all these to the political and social climate in which Mann found himself. In *The Magic Mountain* he studied the fringe world of a tuberculosis sanatorium. *Doctor Faustus*, his culminating masterpiece, describes the life of a composer who sells his soul to the devil as the price of his genius. The stories *Death in Venice* and *Mario the Magician*, about two different varieties of artist, portray with consummate skill and dramatic tension an atmosphere of mounting evil.

Mann's tone was ironic; his concern was with the ideas that move the intellectual man. Though early in life he claimed to be "unpolitical," the harsh realities of Germany before and throughout World War II drove him eventually to devote much of his time to lecturing and writing against the Hitler government. The "Joseph" tetralogy is "implicitly related to the experiences of that time in being Mann's tribute to the national life and religious spirit of the Jews in their darkest hour" (J. P. Stern).

An anti-Nazi from the beginning, Mann fled Germany in 1933. He lived the life of an exile in the United States during the period in which his worldwide reputation reached its zenith. He left in the McCarthy era for Switzerland, and lectured in both zones of Occupied Germany.

BOOKS BY THOMAS MANN

Thomas Mann's Diaries. Ed. by Richard Winston and Clara Winston, Abrams 1982 $29.95

Stories of Three Decades. Knopf 1936 $17.95; trans. by H. T. Lowe-Porter, Modern Lib. $6.95

Past Masters, and Other Papers. 1933. Trans. by H. T. Lowe-Porter, *Essay Index Repr. Ser.* Ayer repr. of 1933 ed. $15.20

Buddenbrooks. 1901. Knopf 1964 $15.00; Random (Vintage) 1984 pap. $5.95

Royal Highness. 1909. Buccaneer Bks. repr. of 1983 ed. lib. bdg. $18.95; Random (Vintage) 1983 pap. $7.95

Death in Venice. 1912. Trans. by Erich Heller, *Modern Lib. College Ed. Ser.* Random 1970 pap. $2.50

Reflections of a Non-Political Man. 1918. Trans. by Walter Morris, Ungar 1983 $29.50

The Magic Mountain. 1924. Buccaneer Bks. repr. 1983 lib. bdg. $17.95; Knopf 1956 $20.50; trans. by H. T. Lowe-Porter, Random text ed. 1969 pap. $6.95

Nocturnes. 1934. *Short Story Index Repr. Ser.* Ayer repr. of 1934 ed. $9.00

Joseph and His Brothers. Knopf 1948 $35.00

The Beloved Returns: Lotte in Weimar. Random (Vintage) 1983 pap. $7.95

The Transposed Head: A Legend of India. 1940. Random 1959 pap. $1.95

The Order of the Day. 1942. *Essay Index Repr. Ser.* Ayer repr. of 1942 ed. $18.75

Dr. Faustus: The Life of the German Composer, Adrian Leverkühn, as Told by a Friend. 1947. Knopf 1948 $15.00; Random 1971 pap. $6.95

The Holy Sinner. 1951. Random (Vintage) 1984 pap. $7.95. The retelling of a medieval legend.

The Black Swan. 1953. Trans. by Willard R. Trask, Harcourt repr. of 1954 ed. 1980 pap. $2.95; Knopf 1954 $11.50

The Confessions of Felix Krull, Confidence Man: The Early Years. 1954. Knopf 1955 $12.50; Random (Vintage) 1969 pap. $4.95. A continuation of the short story, "Felix Krull," about a handsome nineteenth-century swindler. "A self-sufficient masterpiece of story telling . . . clear-cut in structure and swift-moving in pace . . . one of the most intricate examples of Mann's craft" (*New Republic*).

Last Essays. Trans. by Richard Winston and Clara Winston, Century Bookbindery repr. of 1959 ed. 1984 lib. bdg. $25.00

BOOKS ABOUT THOMAS MANN

Apter, T. E. *Thomas Mann: The Devil's Advocate.* New York Univ. Pr. 1979 $25.00

Berendsohn, Walter A. *Thomas Mann: Artist and Partisan in Troubled Times.* Trans. by George C. Buck, Univ. of Alabama Pr. 1973 $20.00

Bergsten, Gunilla. *Thomas Mann's Doctor Faustus: The Sources and Structure of the Novel.* Trans. by Krishna Winston, Univ. of Chicago Pr. 1969 $14.00

Burgen, Hans, and Hans-Otto Mayer. *Thomas Mann: A Chronicle of His Life.* Trans.
by Eugene Dobson, Univ. of Alabama Pr. rev. ed. pap. $7.50

Feuerlicht, Ignace. *Thomas Mann. Twayne's World Authors Ser.* G. K. Hall 1969 lib.
bdg. $13.50

Hatfield, Henry. *From "Mountain": Mann's Later Masterpieces.* Cornell Univ. Pr. 1979
$24.50

Heller, Erich. *Thomas Mann: The Ironic German.* Appel 1958 $12.00; Regnery-Gate-
way repr. of 1961 ed. 1979 pap. $6.95

Hollingdale, R. J. *Thomas Mann: A Critical Study.* Bucknell Univ. Pr. 1971 $20.00

Jonas, Ilsedore B. *Thomas Mann and Italy.* Trans. by Betty Crouse, Univ. of Alabama
Pr. 1979 $17.75

Jonas, Klaus W. *Fifty Years of Thomas Mann Studies: A Bibliography of Criticism.*
Kraus repr. of 1955 ed. 1969 $15.00

Kaufmann, Fritz. *Thomas Mann: The World as Will and Representation.* Cooper
Square Pr. repr. of 1957 ed. 1973 lib. bdg. $22.50. Mann's philosophy as a forma-
tive element in his art.

Lukacs, Georg. *Essays on Thomas Mann.* Trans. by S. Mitchell, Humanities Pr. repr.
of 1964 ed. pap. $6.75

Mann, Erika. *The Last Year of Thomas Mann.* Trans. by Richard Graves, Ayer repr. of
1958 ed. $14.00

Reed, T. J. *Thomas Mann: The Uses of Tradition.* Oxford 1974 pap. $11.95

Stern, Joseph P. *Thomas Mann.* Columbia Univ. Pr. 1967 pap. $2.50. A good, concise
analysis of Mann's major works and present significance.

Weigand, Hermann J. *The Magic Mountain.* 1933. AMS Pr. repr. of 1965 ed. $18.50.
Authoritative study.

Williamson, James R. *Brother Artist: A Psychological Study of Thomas Mann's Fiction.* Univ. Pr. of Amer. 1983 $28.75 pap. $16.75

Winston, Richard. *Thomas Mann: The Making of an Artist, 1875–1911.* Afterword by
Clara Winston, Knopf 1981 $17.95

MUSIL, ROBERT. 1880–1942

The Man without Qualities, Musil's magnum opus (1930–42, o.p.), is a
novel about the life and history of prewar Austria. It was unfinished when
Musil died, though he had labored over the three-volume work for ten years
and it fills three volumes. Encyclopedic in the manner of PROUST and DOSTO-
EVSKY, "it is a wonderful and prolonged fireworks display, a well-peopled
comedy of ideas" (V. S. Pritchett)—and a critique of contemporary life. It
made Musil's largely posthumous reputation. "Musil's whole scheme pro-
phetically describes the bureaucratic condition of our world, and what can
only be called the awful, deadly serious, and self-deceptive love affair of one
committee for another" (Pritchett).

Young Törless is a novel of troubled adolescence set in a military school,
modeled on the one attended by both Musil and Rainer Maria Rilke. It was
his first book and was immediately successful. He then abandoned his studies in engineering, logic, and experimental psychology and turned to writing. He was an officer in the Austrian army in World War I, lived in Berlin
until the Nazis came to power, and finally settled in Geneva. He also wrote
plays, essays, and short stories.

BOOKS BY MUSIL

Young Törless. 1906. *Modern Class. Ser.* Pantheon 1982 pap. $5.95
The Enthusiasts. Trans. by Andrea Simon, Performing Arts 1983 $15.95 pap. $5.95
Three Short Stories. Ed. by Hugh Sacker, Oxford 1970 pap. $7.95

BOOKS ABOUT MUSIL

Hickman, Hannah. *Robert Musil.* Open Court 1984 $24.95
Luft, David S. *Robert Musil and the Crisis of European Culture, 1880–1942.* Univ. of California Pr. 1980 $33.00 pap. $8.95
Peters, Frederick G. *Robert Musil, Master of the Hovering Life: A Study of the Major Fiction.* Columbia Univ. Pr. 1978 $28.00

THE NIBELUNGENLIED. c.1200

The *Nibelungenlied* is the most powerful and dramatic work of the courtly period. It was also one of the most popular works, and complete or partial versions appear in more than 30 manuscripts. Although the ultimate sources of the epic are to be found in ancient Germanic heroic songs, the medieval German poet, whose identity is still not known and probably never will be, took the matter of these ancient legends and rearranged them to fit his own contemporary situation. The *Nibelungenlied* is a strong criticism of aspects of the political system of feudalism, especially that of taking revenge, a custom that had great currency in the poet's world.

In the nationalistic nineteenth century, this aspect of the *Nibelungenlied* was overlooked, and instead the warrior ethos of battle and victory at any price was glorified. This outlook persisted through the Third Reich. The reasons for this misunderstanding are complex, and the reader is advised to refer to George Mosse, *The Nationalization of the Masses.* It is only recently that the humane strivings of the *Nibelungen* poet have been recognized and emphasized in scholarship. The tragedy of the *Nibelungen* has attracted the fancy of many German writers and composers. Most noteworthy is Friedrich Hebbel, who adapted the legend well in his dramatic trilogy *Die Nibelungen.*

The Nibelungenlied. Trans. by D. G. Mowatt, Biblio Dist. (Everyman's) repr. of 1965 ed. 1962 $10.95; trans. by A. T. Hatto, *Penguin Class. Ser.* 1965 pap. $3.95. Hatto's is the preferred translation, with many excellent appendixes, most noteworthy of which is the "Introduction to a Second Reading."

BOOKS ABOUT THE "NIBELUNGENLIED"

Donington, Robert. *Wagner's "Ring" and Its Symbols.* Faber 3d ed. 1974 pap. $8.95
Shaw, George B. *The Perfect Wagnerite: A Commentary on the Niblung's Rings.* Dover 1966 pap. $3.00

NIETZSCHE, FRIEDRICH (WILHELM). 1844–1900

[SEE Volume 4.]

NOVALIS (pseud. of Friedrich Leopold, Freiherr von Hardenberg). 1772–1801

Novalis, one of the early poets of German Romanticism, provided the movement with its best known symbol, the "blue flower," from his fragmentary novel *Heinrich von Ofterdingen*. The blue flower became the symbol for the deep-rooted romantic yearning, the search that would never end. Novalis himself was a Saxon nobleman and a government official who was fated to die young from tuberculosis. His most famous work, *Hymns to the Night*, might strike some readers as an exercise in morbidity. They were written in memory of his fiancée, Sophie von Kuhn, who died in 1797 at the age of fifteen. His *Hymns* eloquently express his grief at the death of Sophie and are a unique mixture of religious, mystical feeling and personal sadness. The *Hymns* were composed in 1800 and the death he so longed for struck him a year later.

Books by Novalis

Hymns to the Night. Trans. by Dick Higgins, McPherson 2d ed. 1984 $12.50 pap. $5.95

Henry von Ofterdingen. 1802. Trans. by Palmer Hilty, Ungar pap. $4.95. An excellent translation of a work expressing "Novalis's own ideas and [those of] early German Romanticism in general" (*LJ*). For the well-informed reader.

Books about Novalis

Birell, Gordon. *The Boundless Present: Space and Time in the Literary Fairy Tales of Novalis and Tieck*. Univ. of North Carolina Pr. 1979 $14.00

Dyck, Martin. *Novalis and Mathematics*. AMS Pr. repr. of 1960 ed. $27.00

Hannah, Richard W. *The Fichtean Dynamic of Novalis' Poetics*. Peter Lang 1981 pap. $23.85

Hiebel, Friedrich. *Novalis: German Poet, European Thinker, Christian Mystic*. AMS Pr. repr. of 1953 ed. $27.00

Neubauer, John. *Bifocal Vision: Novalis' Philosophy of Nature and Disease*. Univ. of North Carolina Pr. 1971 $16.50

Neuberger, John. *Novalis. Twayne's World Authors Ser*. G. K. Hall 1980 $16.95

REMARQUE, ERICH MARIA. 1898–1970

In 1947, after eight successful years in the United States, Remarque became a U.S. citizen. During World War I he was drafted into the German army at the age of 18. After the war he tried various occupations and in his spare time wrote the antimilitaristic *All Quiet on the Western Front* that became a classic of modern warfare but was condemned as "defeatist" by the Nazis. *The Road Back* (1931, o.p.) is the sequel. His later novels deal with World War II; they have had greater popularity than critical success.

Books by Remarque

All Quiet on the Western Front. 1929. Buccaneer Bks. repr. 1981 lib. bdg. $16.95; Fawcett 1979 pap. $2.95

The Black Obelisk. 1956. Trans. by Denver Lindley, Harcourt 1957 $19.95

Bobby Deerfield. Fawcett 1978 pap. $1.95

BOOK ABOUT REMARQUE

Barker, Christine, and Rex W. Last. *Erich Maria Remarque*. Barnes & Noble 1979 $26.50

RILKE, RAINER MARIA. 1875–1926

Germany's greatest modern poet was born in Prague of old Bohemian and Alsatian stock. He lived for many years in Paris, where he was secretary to Auguste Rodin; he then traveled in all parts of Europe. His popularity and influence have been international. In 1911, he began at the castle of Duino in Istria, the ten poems comprising the *Duino Elegies*, his masterpiece, completed in 1922. *Sonnets to Orpheus*, 55 joyous and brilliant songs, followed, and completed his poetic vision of humankind's struggle. Not easy to summarize, Rilke's themes are love and death, expressed in symbols at once subtle and simple, concrete yet mystical and profound. An affirmer of life, he could not bear World War I, in which he was very briefly a soldier. His extraordinary letters form a part of his great literary achievement.

BOOKS BY RILKE

Selected Works: Poetry. Trans. by J. B. Leishman, New Directions vol. 1 $17.95
Ewald Tragy. 1899. Ed. by Inge D. Halpert, Irvington text ed. 1961 pap. $2.95
Rodin. 1903. Haskell 1974 lib. bdg. $39.95
Poems from the Book of Hours. 1905. Trans. by Babette Deutsch, New Directions 1975 pap. $3.95
Poems, 1906–1926. Trans. by J. B. Leishman, New Directions $16.00
New Poems, 1907–1908. Trans. by J. B. Leishman, New Directions bilingual ed. 1964 $16.50. Some 189 of Rilke's poems expertly translated with "a penetrating introduction [on their] origin and nature" (*LJ*).
Poems, 1912–1926. Trans. by Michael Hamburger, Black Swan 1982 $17.50
Translations from the Poetry of Rainer Maria Rilke. Trans. by M. D. Herter, Norton bilingual ed. 1962 pap. $5.95
Selected Poems (Fifty Selected Poems). Trans. by C. F. MacIntyre, Univ. of California bilingual ed. 1940 pap. $5.95
The Lay of the Love and Death of Cornet Christopher Rilke. 1906. Trans. by M. D. Herter, *Norton Lib.* bilingual ed. 1963 pap. $4.95; trans. by Leslie Phillips and Stefan Schimanski, Telegraph Bks. repr. of 1948 ed. 1981 lib. bdg. $20.00
The Notebooks of Malte Laurids Brigge. 1910. Trans. by M. D. Herter, Norton 1964 pap. $4.95. A novel.
The Life of the Virgin Mary. 1913. Trans. by C. F. MacIntyre, Greenwood repr. of 1947 ed. 1972 lib. bdg. $18.75
Duino Elegies. 1923. Trans. by Gary Miranda, Breitenbush 1981 pap. $8.95; trans. by David Young, Norton 1978 $8.95 pap. $4.95; trans. by C. F. MacIntyre, Univ. of California Pr. bilingual ed. 1961 pap. $2.95
Sonnets to Orpheus. 1923. *Norton Lib.* 1962 pap. $4.95; trans. by C. F. MacIntyre, Univ. of California Pr. 1960 pap. $2.95
Visions of Christ: A Posthumous Cycle of Poems. Trans. by Aaron Kramer, ed. by Siegfried Mandel, Colorado Associated Univ. Pr. 1967 $17.50
Letters to a Young Poet. Trans. by Stephen Mitchell, Random 1984 $14.95
Nine Plays. Trans. by Klaus Phillips and John Locke, Ungar 1979 $14.00

Wartime Letters of Rainer Maria Rilke, 1914–1921. Trans. by M. D. Herter, *Norton Lib.*
    1964 pap. $6.45
Letters. Trans. by M. D. Herter and Jane B. Greene, *Norton Lib.* 2 vols. pap. ea. $8.95;
    Peter Smith 2 vols. ea. $16.75

BOOKS ABOUT RILKE

Baron, Frank, ed. *Rilke: The Alchemy of Alienation.* Ed. by Warren R. Maurer and
    Ernst S. Dick, Univ. Pr. of Kansas 1980 $25.00
Bauer, Arnold. *Rainer Maria Rilke. Lit. and Life Ser.* Trans. by Ursula Lamm, Ungar
    1972 $12.95
Brodsky, Patricia P. *Russia in the Works of Rainer Maria Rilke.* Wayne State Univ. Pr.
    1984 $26.00
Butler, Eliza M. *Rainer Maria Rilke.* Octagon repr. of 1941 ed. 1973 lib. bdg. $29.00
Fuerst, Norbert. *Phases of Rilke.* Haskell repr. of 1958 ed. 1972 lib. bdg. $43.95
Graff, Willem L. *Rainer Maria Rilke: Creative Anguish of a Modern Poet.* Greenwood
    repr. of 1956 ed. lib. bdg. $27.50
Holthusen, Hans Egon. *Portrait of Rilke: An Illustrated Biography.* Trans. by W. H.
    Hargreaves, Folcroft repr. of 1952 ed. $12.50. This is a worthwhile introduction
    by the well-known German critic and poet.
Lippmann, Wolfgang. *Rilke: A Life.* Trans. by Russell Stockman, Fromm 1984 $22.95
    pap. $12.95
Peters, H. F. *Rainer Maria Rilke: Masks and the Man.* Gordian repr. of 1960 ed. 1977
    $12.50. In addition to his own views on Rilke's poetry, the author presents those
    of many Rilke scholars, critics, friends, and those of Rilke himself.
Purtscher, Nora. *Rilke: Man and Poet.* Greenwood repr. of 1950 ed. 1972 lib. bdg.
    $22.50
Schwartz, Egon. *Poetry and Politics in the Work of Rainer Maria Rilke.* Trans. by
    David Wellberry, Ungar 1981 $11.95
Webb, Karl E. *Rainer Maria Rilke and Jugenstil.* Univ. of North Carolina Pr. 1978
    pap. $25.00

RUODLIEB. c.1050

Ruodlieb was composed in Latin hexameters sometime in the eleventh century, probably in the Bavarian monastery of Tengernsee. Unfortunately it is
preserved only in fragments. It relates the tale of a young knight, Ruodlieb,
who is forced to leave home because of the actions of his enemies. He places
himself in the service of a foreign monarch known as the "great king," who
becomes involved in a war with the "lesser king." The war is concluded to
the great king's advantage. Presumably all 12 axioms would have been
acted on in dramatic situations in the complete story; only three are extant.

The *Ruodlieb* is surprising in many ways. The rulers, both the great king
and the lesser king, are men of justice and restraint. In place of the ancient
warrior ethic, according to which the greatest honor in battle was to win, a
milder spirit enters here, in which concluding peace to the satisfaction of
both parties is more important. The new aspect points ahead to the romances of the courtly age.

Ruodlieb. Ed. by Gordon B. Ford, Jr., Adler's 1967 pap. $20.00

SACHS, HANS. 1494–1576

The late medieval and sixteenth-century German cities saw the development of a peculiar literature that expressed the taste and interests of the lower and middle bourgeoisie. It is a mixture of the medieval popular genre's ill-digested classical themes and a sharply realistic observation of urban life. Hans Sachs was the most important of those Meistersinger and was as such celebrated in Richard Wagner's opera of that name. Sachs's productivity was enormous: biblical and classical drama takes an important place in it, and more than 1,000 Lent farces (*Fastnachspiele*). He is best in those earthy farces, which excel in satirical observation of the daily scene.

BOOK BY SACHS

Merry Tales and Three Shrovetide Plays. Trans. by William Leighton, *Lib. of World Lit. Ser.* Hyperion Pr. repr. of 1910 ed. 1978 $23.75

SCHILLER, (JOHANN CHRISTOPH) FRIEDRICH VON. 1759–1805

Schiller was the first German dramatist to have his plays translated widely into English. More than 200 such translations were published between 1792 and 1900. Each of his nine dramas is a masterpiece of situation, characterization, subtle psychology, and exalted artistic conception of the dramatic form. *The Robbers* (1781), his first play (prose), was the last of the great works of the German Sturm and Drang period and an immediate success, a rallying cry for the freedom and idealism of youth against tyranny and hypocrisy that the young Schiller found in the times. *Mary Stuart,* one of the great verse dramas of his "classical" maturity, was "a psychological tragedy in a very modern sense" (J. G. Robertson), and has been the Schiller play most often produced abroad. His themes, usually expressed through historical persons and situations, were freedom, justice, heroism—the noblest aspirations of man.

Schiller's life was a struggle against poverty and, in his last years, tuberculosis. His friendship with Goethe was a rewarding one for both writers and led to Schiller's settling in Weimar. "The German classical age attains its culmination in the friendship of Goethe and Schiller," says Robertson. Together they revitalized German poetry and the German stage. "Schiller's view of life was no calm and dispassionate one like Goethe's. [He] was always a partisan, a champion of high ideas. . . . He remains Germany's greatest dramatist and, after Goethe, the poet whose work has had the firmest hold upon the affections of his people" (Robertson).

BOOKS BY SCHILLER

Friedrich Schiller: An Anthology for Our Time. Ed. by Frederick Ungar, Ungar 1976 pap. $4.95. With an account of his life and work by Frederick Ungar.
The Robbers, Wallenstein. Trans. by F. J. Lamport, *Penguin Class. Ser.* 1980 pap. $6.95
The Bride of Messina, William Tell, and Demetrius. Trans. by Charles E. Passage, Ungar 1962 $10.50 pap. $4.95
Don Carlos, Infante of Spain: A Drama in Five Acts. 1787. Trans. by Charles E. Passage, Ungar 1959 $10.50 pap. $4.95

Wallenstein: A Historical Drama in Three Acts. 1798–99. Trans. by Charles E. Passage, Ungar pap. $4.95
Mary Stuart. 1801. Trans. by Charles E. Passage, Ungar pap. $5.95
William Tell. 1804. Silver Burdett 1984 $5.96
On the Aesthetic Education of Man (in a Series of Letters). 1793–95. Trans. by Reginald Snell, Ungar 1965 $10.50 pap. $4.95

BOOKS ABOUT SCHILLER

Carlyle, Thomas. *The Life of Friedrich Schiller.* Richard West repr. of 1901 ed. 1973 $16.50
Dewhurst, Kenneth, and Nigel Reeves. *Friedrich Schiller: Medicine, Psychology and Literature, with the First English Edition of His Complete Medical Writings.* Univ. of California Pr. $42.00
Thomas, Calvin. *Life and Works of Friedrich Schiller.* AMS Pr. repr. of 1901 ed. $17.50; Richard West repr. of 1901 ed. 1973 $17.45
Von Heiseler, Brent. *Schiller.* Trans. by John Bednall, Richard West repr. of 1959 ed. 1973 $20.00

SCHNITZLER, ARTHUR. 1862–1931

Arthur Schnitzler, Viennese playwright, novelist, short story writer, and physician, "caught in his gentle hand the last golden glow of Vienna's setting glory and converted it to art." A sophisticated writer much in vogue in his time, he chose themes of an erotic, romantic, or social nature, expressed with clarity, irony, and subtle wit. *Reigen*, a series of ten dialogues linking people of various social classes through their physical desire for one another, has been filmed many times as *La Ronde.* As a Jew, Schnitzler was sensitive to the problems of anti-Semitism, which he explored in the play *Professor Bernhardi*, seen in New York in a performance by the Vienna Burgtheater in 1968. Henry Hatfield calls Schnitzler "second only to Hofmannsthal among the Austrian writers of his generation and one of the most underrated of German authors. . . . He combined the naturalist's devotion to fact with the impressionist's interest in nuance; in other words, he told the truth" (*Modern German Literature*).

In his most famous story, *Lieutenant Gustl* (1901), Schnitzler employs the stream-of-consciousness technique in a brilliant exposition of the follies and gradual disintegration of society in fin de siècle Vienna. Schnitzler has also been linked with Freud and is credited with consciously introducing elements of modern psychology into his works.

BOOKS BY SCHNITZLER

Plays and Stories. Ed. by Egon Schwartz, Continuum 1983 $19.50 pap. $8.95
Shepherd's Pipe, and Other Stories. Trans. by O. F. Theis, *Short Story Index Repr. Ser.* Ayer repr. of 1922 ed. $11.00
The Round Dance (La Ronde) and Other Plays. Trans. by Charles Osborne, Humanities Pr. text ed. 1982 $15.25; trans. by Charles Osborne, Riverrun 1984 $15.00 pap. $6.95
(and Raoul Auernheimer). *The Correspondence of Arthur Schnitzler and Raoul Auernheimer: With Raoul Auernheimer's Aphorisms.* Ed. by Donald G. Daviau and Jorun B. Johns. Univ. of North Carolina Pr. 1978 $14.00

The Letters of Arthur Schnitzler to Herman Bohr. Univ. of North Carolina Pr. 1978
    $15.00
Anatol. 1893. Trans. by Frank Marcus, Methuen 1982 pap. $6.95
Living House (and *The Green Cockatoo*). 1898. Intro. by Ashley Dukes, Core Collection
    repr. of 1917 ed. 1977 $15.00
Beatrice. 1900. Trans. by Agnes Jacques, AMS Pr. repr. of 1926 ed. $15.00
Berta Garlan. 1900. Darby 1984 $25.00
Viennese Idylls. 1913. Trans. by Frederick Eisemann, *Short Story Index Repr. Ser.*
    Ayer repr. of 1913 ed. 1973 $16.00
Professor Bernhardi. 1913. Trans. by Hetty Landstone, AMS Pr. repr. of 1928 ed.
    $15.00
Dr. Graesler. 1917. Trans. by E. C. Slade, AMS Pr. repr. of 1930 ed. $15.00
Fraulein Else. Trans. by Robert A. Simon, AMS Pr. repr. of 1925 ed. $15.00; trans. by
    Robert A. Simon, Arden Lib. repr. of 1925 ed. 1979 lib. bdg. $12.50; trans. by
    Robert A. Simon, Darby repr. of 1928 ed. 1981 lib. bdg. $15.00
None but the Brave. Trans. by Richard L. Simon, AMS Pr. repr. of 1926 ed. 1972
    $15.00
Rhapsody: A Dream Novel. 1926. Trans. by Otto P. Schinnerer, AMS Pr. repr. of 1927
    ed. $15.00; trans. by Otto P. Schinnerer, Arden Lib. repr. of 1927 ed. 1979 lib.
    bdg. $12.50
Daybreak. 1927. Trans. by William A. Drake, AMS Pr. repr. of 1927 ed. $15.00
Therese. Trans. by William A. Drake, AMS Pr. repr. of 1928 ed. 1972 $15.00
Little Novels. 1929. Trans. by Eric Sutton, AMS Pr. repr. of 1929 ed. $16.00
Casanova's Homecoming. Trans. by Paul Eden and Paul Cedar, AMS Pr. repr. of 1930
    ed. $15.00
Viennese Novelties. AMS Pr. repr. of 1931 ed. $31.50
Undiscovered Country. Trans. by Tom Stoppard, Faber 1981 pap. $5.95
Some Day Peace Will Return: Notes on War and Peace. Trans. by Robert O. Weiss, Un-
    gar 1971 $8.50

BOOKS ABOUT SCHNITZLER

Allen, Richard H. *An Annotated Arthur Schnitzler Bibliography. Studies in the Ger-
    manic Languages and Literatures Ser.* Univ. of North Carolina Pr. 1966 $12.50
Reichert, Herbert W., and Herman Salinger, eds. *Studies in Arthur Schnitzler.* AMS
    Pr. repr. of 1963 ed. $27.00
Urbach, Reinhard. *Arthur Schnitzler.* Trans. by Donald Daviau, *Lit. and Life Ser.* Un-
    gar 1973 $12.95

TOLLER, ERNST. 1893–1939

A German-Jewish dramatist who fought in World War I, Toller was later
imprisoned for trying to stop the war by organizing a strike of the munition
workers. For his part in the Bavarian revolution he was exiled by the Nazis
and his books were burned. He then came to New York. His plays and lectures spoke for the millions of Germans "who have been deprived of their
voices." A radical, he identified strongly with the proletariat. He took his
own life in despair, following the victory of Franco in Spain and the Munich
Pact, perhaps unable to bear the prospect of an inevitable World War II.

BOOKS BY TOLLER

The Swallow Book. 1924. Haskell repr. 1974 $40.95
I Was a German: The Autobiography of Ernst Toller. AMS Pr. $30.00

BOOKS ABOUT TOLLER

Benson, Renate. *German Expressionist Drama: Ernst Toller and Georg Kaiser.* Grove
    1984 pap. $19.50
Oscar, Michael. *Anarchism in the Drama of Ernst Toller.* State Univ. Pr. of New York
    1980 $49.95
Pittock, Malcolm. *Ernst Toller. Twayne's World Authors Ser.* G. K. Hall 1979 lib. bdg.
    $16.95

WEDEKIND, FRANK (BENJAMIN FRANKLIN). 1864–1918

This poet-playwright turned actor in order to produce the effect he
wanted in his plays. Like most innovators, "his has always been the fate of
being misunderstood, misrepresented or misinterpreted by critics." Though
as a young writer he associated himself with the naturalists, "Wedekind was
not a consistent naturalist," says John Gassner (*Treasury of the Theater*). "An
original artist who was not apt to follow fashions, he helped himself to
much naturalistic detail to support his personal crusade for frankness about
the elemental power of the sexual instinct." The earth spirit (*Erdgeist*) was
his symbol for the primitive strain in human beings.

BOOKS BY WEDEKIND

Lulu Plays and Other Sex Tragedies. Trans. by Stephen Spender, Riverrun 1979 pap.
    $5.95
Spring Awakening: A Play. 1908. Trans. by Edward Bond, Methuen 1981 pap. $6.95;
    trans. by Tom Osborn, Riverrun 1979 pap. $5.95

BOOKS ABOUT WEDEKIND

Best, Alan. *Frank Wedekind.* Ed. by R. W. Last, *Modern German Authors Ser.* Humani-
    ties Pr. text ed. 1975 $7.50
Gittleman, Sol. *Frank Wedekind.* Ungar repr. 1980 $11.95

WEISS, PETER. 1916–1982

In December 1965 Peter Weiss's *Marat/Sade*, in a brilliant presentation by
Britain's Royal Shakespeare Company, stormed the Broadway stage, captivating audience and critic alike. The assumption that the play about the
murder of Marat by Charlotte Corday might have been one of the many dramatic pieces written by Sade—and enacted by his fellow inmates for "thera-
peutic" reasons during the Marquis's confinement at Charenton—provided
Weiss (who maintained that "every word I put down is political") with his
framework for the "confrontation of the revolutionary Marat as the apostle
of social improvement and the cynical individualist, the Marquis de Sade"
(*N.Y. Times*).

The Investigation, which Weiss considered his best play, was first presented in 20 theaters in East and West Germany; Ingmar Bergman was its
Swedish director. It was staged in New York in 1966. Taken almost entirely

from the actual proceedings of the 1965 Frankfurt War Crimes Tribunal on Auschwitz, *The Investigation* is a "harrowing but insistently commanding experience" (Walter Kerr, *N.Y. Times*). The audience, in effect, reenacts the role of the original courtroom spectators in this shattering, true account of man's depravity.

Weiss received the Büchner Prize in 1982, the year of his death.

BOOKS BY WEISS

The Persecution and Assassination of Jean-Paul Marat as Performed by the Inmates of the Asylum of Charenton under the Direction of the Marquis de Sade. 1964. Trans. by Geoffrey Skelton, pref. by Peter Brook, Atheneum text ed. 1966 pap. $5.95. Music examples, biographical note.
The Investigation: A Play. 1965. Atheneum text ed. 1966 pap. $6.95

BOOKS ABOUT WEISS

Best, Otto F. *Peter Weiss.* Trans. by Ursule Molinaro, *Lit. and Life Ser.* Ungar 1976 $12.95
Vance, Kathleen. *The Theme of Alienation in the Prose of Peter Weiss.* Peter Lang text ed. 1981 pap. $28.35

WERFEL, FRANZ. 1890–1945

Born in Prague of Jewish parents, Werfel served in World War I, then lived and wrote in Vienna until driven out by the Nazi occupation of Austria. *And the Bridge Was Love: Memories of a Lifetime,* by his wife, Alma Werfel, in collaboration with E. B. Ashton (o.p.), is a deeply personal autobiography of a remarkable life in Vienna by the woman who was married to the composer-conductor Mahler and the architect GROPIUS (see Vol. 3). Werfel escaped to the United States after the fall of France in 1940. He won international recognition for his fiction; he also wrote lyrical poetry and drama. His comedy *Jacobowsky and the Colonel* (o.p.) was successfully produced in New York in 1944. In 1967 the Hamburg Opera presented Giselher Klebe's operatic version of the play at the Metropolitan Opera House in New York.

BOOKS BY WERFEL

The Forty Days of Musa Dagh. 1934. Carroll & Graf repr. 1983 pap. $9.95. Historical novel of the Armenian resistance to the Turks in 1915.
The Song of Bernadette. 1942. Avon 1980 pap. $1.95
Between Heaven and Earth. 1944. *Essay Index Repr. Ser.* Ayer repr. of 1944 ed. $18.00

WOLF, CHRISTA. 1929–

Christa Wolf was born in Landsberg an der Warthe (now Gorzow, Poland) and educated at the universities of Jena and Leipzig between 1949 and 1953. She is distinguished by her recognition in both her home in the Democratic Republic and in the West for her sensitive portrayal of the complexities of life in a divided Germany. Her first novel, *Divided Heaven,* which was critically acclaimed throughout the German-speaking world, is the story of two lovers separated by the decision of one to defect to the

West. While this and Wolf's subsequent work, *The Quest for Christa T,* met with criticism from the Socialist party leadership, Wolf has remained an important literary force in the Democratic Republic and is a member of the German Academy of Sciences. Her essay "The Reader and the Writer" established her as a major literary theorist. She was awarded the Büchner Prize in 1980.

BOOKS BY WOLF

Divided Heaven. 1963. Trans. by Joan Becker, Adler's 1976 pap. $4.95

The Quest for Christa T. 1968. Trans. by Christopher Middleton, Farrar 1970 pap. $6.95. Denounced for its candid portrayal of conformity and hypocrisy in the German Democratic Republic.

A Model Childhood. 1976. Trans. by Ursule Molinaro and Hedwig Rappolt, Farrar 1980 $17.50

No Place on Earth. 1979. Trans. by Jan van Heurck, Farrar 1982 $11.95 pap. $6.95

The Reader and the Writer. 1972. International Pubns. 1978 pap. $1.95. An elaboration of Wolf's theory of "subjective authenticity," which she has been applying to her writing since *Quest for Christa T.*

Cassandra: A Novel and Four Essays. 1983. Trans. by Jan van Heurck, Farrar 1984 $17.95

Patterns of Childhood. Trans. by Ursule Molinaro and Hedwig Rappolt, Farrar 1984 pap. $9.95

BOOK ABOUT WOLF

Ezergailis, Inta. *Women Writers: The Divided Self.* Benjamins North Amer. 1982 $15.00

WOLFRAM VON ESCHENBACH. 1170?–1220?

"I am Wolfram von Eschenbach and I know a little about singing"; thus does perhaps the most unique personality in medieval German literature introduce himself to readers. The second part of the statement is one of the greatest understatements in the realm of literature. He is the author of two works not available in translation, *Willehalm* and *Titurel* (incomplete), and of lyrics—the few songs that have survived all show great innovativeness and skill.

He is best known to general audiences as the author of *Parzival,* a Grail romance of more than 24,000 lines. His main source is the incomplete *Perceval, or the Grail* of Chrétien de Troyes. Whether Wolfram had another source that supplied him with the end of the tale or whether he provided it himself is not definitely known. Wolfram teases his audience on several occasions by a reference to a mysterious Kyot who supposedly transmitted the tale and who was Wolfram's chief source. Modern scholars have given up the search for Kyot, and most now assume that the completion of the *Parzival* story is by Wolfram himself.

The basic theme of *Parzival* is like that of the other German courtly romances, examining how a person can so arrange his life that he is pleasing to both God and man. As in other tales, the answer lies in compassion.

Wolfram's *Parzival* also provided the material used in Wagner's libretto for *Parsifal.*

BOOK BY WOLFRAM

The Parzival of Wolfram von Eschenbach. AMS Pr. repr. of 1951 ed. $18.50

BOOKS ABOUT WOLFRAM

Green, D. H. *The Art of Recognition in Wolfram's "Parzifal."* Cambridge Univ. Pr. 1982 $69.50

Rachbauer, M. A. *Wolfram von Eschenbach.* AMS Pr. repr. of 1934 ed. $28.00

ZWEIG, STEFAN. 1881–1942

Born in Vienna, the prolific Zweig was a poet in his early years. In the 1920s, he achieved fame with the many biographies he wrote of famous people including BALZAC, DOSTOEVSKY, DICKENS (see Vol. 1), and FREUD (see Vol. 3). Erasmus, with whom he closely identified, was the subject of a longer biography. He also wrote the novellas *Amok* (o.p.) and *The Royal Game* (1944). As Nazism spread, Zweig, a Jew, fled to the United States and then to Brazil. He hoped to start a new life there but the haunting memory of Nazism, still undefeated, proved too much for him, and he died with his wife in a suicide pact.

BOOKS BY ZWEIG

Emile Verhaeren. 1910. Trans. by Jethro Bithell, *Select Bibliographies Repr. Ser.* Ayer repr. of 1914 ed. $16.00

Romain Rolland: The Man and His Works. 1920. Ayer repr. of 1921 ed. 1973 lib. bdg. $24.50; Haskell repr. of 1921 ed. 1970 lib. bdg. $58.95

Passion and Pain. Trans. by Paul Eden and Paul Cedar, *Short Story Index Repr. Ser.* Ayer repr. of 1925 ed. $15.00

Mental Healers: Franz Anton Mesmer, Mary Baker Eddy, and Sigmund Freud. Arden Lib. repr. of 1931 ed. 1983 lib. bdg. $35.00; Ungar pap. $6.95

Marie Antoinette: The Portrait of an Average Woman. 1932. Trans. by Paul Eden and Paul Cedar, Century Bookbindery repr. of 1933 ed. 1983 lib. bdg. $30.00; Crown 1984 pap. $8.95

Erasmus of Rotterdam. 1934. Richard West repr. $30.00

The Story of Magellan. 1938. Century Bookbindery repr. 1983 lib. bdg. $35.00

Beware of Pity. 1939. Crown 1983 $3.98; trans. by Phyllis Blewitt and Trevor Blewitt, New Amer. Lib. (Plume) 1984 pap. $7.95

The World of Yesterday: An Autobiography. Arden Lib. repr. of 1943 ed. 1977 lib. bdg. $30.00; intro. by Harry Zohn, Univ. of Nebraska Pr. repr. of 1943 ed. 1964 pap. $6.95. This intensely moving document eloquently expresses Zweig's bitter disappointment with the changes that Nazism brought about not only externally but also, and more importantly, in the souls of people.

The Royal Game and Other Stories. Crown 1981 $3.98; Dutton 1983 pap. $7.95

BOOK ABOUT ZWEIG

Klawiter, Randolph J. *Stefan Zweig: A Bibliography.* Univ. of North Carolina Pr. 1965 $15.00. Lists more than 3,400 items and includes an essay on Zweig's life and personality.

NETHERLANDIC LITERATURE

The adjective Netherlandic is used here to denote all literature in the Dutch language, in the Netherlands as well as in Belgium, where Flemish is the mother tongue of 60 percent of the population. There are only some slight dialect differences between Dutch and Flemish, and most writers in the Netherlands and Belgium use the standard version of Netherlandic. This is not to deny, though, that important differences exist in political, religious, and social experiences, which express themselves in different characteristics of Netherlands and Belgian literature.

Netherlandic literature began in the twelfth century, although some earlier texts are known. The genres in the Netherlandic medieval texts are roughly the same as in France and Germany. There are the traditional Frankish, Carolingian tales, courtly literature on Celtic and classical themes, translations from French epics, religious texts, and theater. The marked urban and nonfeudal, or sometimes antifeudal, character of this society comes to the fore in a strong concentration on didactic genres, history, moralistic religious texts, and lay mysticism. The antifeudal character expresses itself brilliantly in the animal epic *Reynard the Fox*, a satire on the injustices of feudal society and the greed of its power establishment. Among the mystical texts two stand out: Jan van Ruysbroek's *Spiritual Espousal* and the remarkable transformation of worldly love poetry into expressions of mystical love by the nun Hadewijch.

By the sixteenth century the Netherlands (including present-day Belgium) had become one of the wealthiest and most urbanized areas of Europe, heavily centered on the industrial and commercial cities of Flanders and Brabant. The growing strength of the urban middle and artisanal classes showed itself in an original, although qualitatively unimpressive, literature produced for and by the burghers in their literary societies, known as Chambers of Rhetoric. It was also in the sixteenth century that those urban populations, stimulated also by the religious conflicts of the Reformation, started the Revolt of the Netherlands against their subordination to the Hapsburg King of Spain. The revolt had important consequences for the future of Netherlandic literature. The most advanced part of the country, the area of present-day Belgium, was reconquered by the Spanish, and its language and literature shrank to the level of a local patois; it was not revived until the nineteenth century.

The center of the Netherlandic culture moved to the north, to the free and protestant Republic of the United Netherlands, with Amsterdam as its booming economic and cultural center. A brilliant cultural life blossomed there, best known for its painting. Dutch poets, also very active, reformed Netherlandic versification and adapted the language to the classical meter. Very little of this rich literary life can be read in translation, not even the work of the greatest poet, Pieter Corneliszoon. Hooft, an elegant Marinist lyricist and historian, and Joost van den Vondel have either never been translated or are long out of print. The latter poet achieved in his immense oeuvre a nobility of diction and a richness of descriptive power that make him comparable to a more sensual, more baroque Milton. Religious poetry was as important as one can expect in a Protestant country; the work of Jacobus Revius gives a good impression of its high status.

Literary creativity began to weaken and succumbed to French classicism in the late seventeenth and the eighteenth centuries. Literary production remained second-rate throughout most of the nineteenth century as well, with the great exception of Multatuli, whose passionate attacks on the whole of contemporary society sent shock waves through staid Dutch society. Around 1880 a programmatic movement for a break with the past became the fountainhead of a renewed literature inspired by such great foreign models as Verlaine and naturalist writers like Zola. The most important writer to come out of this movement was the novelist Louis Couperus.

This period also saw Flemish literature begin to make a comeback, stimulated by the growing Flemish nationalist reaction against francophone domination of Belgium. For a while many Flemish authors tried to propagate a distinct Flemish language, but more and more they adopted the standard Netherlandic language. Both in the north and the south, the twentieth century witnessed a remarkable revitalization of literature, most visibly so in poetry. Novelistic work after Couperus remained too often in the sphere of petty realism. The writers who rallied around the review *Forum* in the 1930s, notably M. ter Braak, Simon Vestdijk, Willem Elsschot, and Edgar Du Perron, brought about an interesting revolt against formalism and aestheticism, rallying around a program for a literature of engagement in social and political life.

Contemporary Netherlandic literature is still strongly under the influence of the war experience. Unfortunately the most important writers of the war generation have either not been translated or have been long out of print. Some of the work of W. F. Hermans and G. Reve is available in anthologies. *The Assault*, the most recent novel of the third important writer of this generation, Harry Mulisch, was just published in translation. Another important writer, whose works are now out of print, is Louis-Paul Boon, whose experiments with the novel form (as in his *Chapel Road*) are interesting means of expressing his views of present Belgian society.

While the amount of material in translation is thus meager, an exception must be made for the excellent collection of Dutch colonial literature appearing in the series *Library of the Indies*, published by the University of Massachusetts Press.

Background

Geyl, Pieter. *The Revolt of the Netherlands*. Barnes & Noble 1980 $21.50

Goudsblom, Johan. *Dutch Society*. Random 1967 pap. $2.95; Peter Smith $4.25

Huizinga, Johan. *The Waning of the Middle Ages: A Study of the Forms of Life, Thought and Art in France and in the Netherlands in the XIVth and XVth Centuries*. Doubleday 1977 pap. $5.95

Motley, J.L. *The Rise of the Dutch Republic*. 1900. AMS Pr. 6 vols. ea. $17.50

Wilson, Charles. *The Dutch Republic and the Civilization of the Seventeenth Century.* McGraw-Hill 1968 pap. $3.95

Literary Studies

Allison, Henry E. *Benedict De Spinoza. Twayne's World Authors Ser.* G. K. Hall 1975 lib. bdg. $14.95

Best, Thomas W. *Macropedius. Twayne's World Authors Ser.* G. K. Hall lib. bdg. $15.95

King, Peter. *Multatuli. Twayne's World Authors Ser.* G. K. Hall lib. bdg. $15.95

Meijer, Reinder P. *Literature of the Low Countries: A Short History of Dutch Literature in the Netherlands and Belgium.* Irvington text ed. 1978 $39.50 pap. $12.95; Kluwer Academic 1978 pap. $14.00. The best available literary history of Netherlandic literature from its beginnings to the modern era.

Warnke, Frank J. *European Metaphysical Poetry.* Yale Univ. Pr. 1975 pap. $7.95

Weevers, Theodor. *Poetry of the Netherlands in Its European Context: 1170–1930.* Humanities Pr. text ed. 1960 $20.00

Collections

Angoff, Charles, ed. *Stories from the Literary Review.* Fairleigh Dickinson Univ. Pr. 1969 $20.00

Krispyn, Egbert, ed. *Modern Stories from Holland and Flanders.* G. K. Hall 1973 lib. bdg. $10.50. Short prose by leading writers from the 1950s and 1960s, rendered into English by various translators.

Murphy, Henry C., ed. *Anthology of New Netherland or Translations from Early Dutch Poetry of New York.* Friedman repr. of 1865 ed. 1969 $14.00; Irvington repr. of 1865 ed. 1972 $12.00 text ed. pap. $6.50. Annotated edition of memoirs and poems by Jacob Steendam, Henricus Selyns, and Nicasius de Sille, who during the seventeenth century lived and worked in New Amsterdam.

Nieuwenhuys, Rob, ed. *Memory and Agony: Dutch Stories from Indonesia.* G. K. Hall 1979 lib. bdg. $14.50

Rich, Adrienne, ed. *Necessities of Life: Poems, 1962–1965.* Norton 1966 o.p. A bilingual collection of works by a half dozen of this century's leading poets, several of whom had actually died before the period indicated in the title.

Smith, William J., and James Holmes. *Dutch Interior: Postwar Poetry of the Netherlands and Flanders.* Columbia Univ. Pr. 1984 $25.00

Wolf, Manfred, trans. *Change of Scene: Modern Dutch and Flemish Poetry.* Twowindows Pr. 1969 pap. $2.50. A small but good selection of texts by 13 poets who made their name in the 1950s.

———. *Ten Flemish Poems.* Twowindows Pr. 1972 pap. $2.25. A slender volume containing works by five poets.

ALBERTS, A. 1905–

Alberts, who was a civil servant in the Indies before World War II, writes incisive and ironic stories about the contradictory relationships in a colonial situation.

BOOK BY ALBERTS

The Islands. Trans. by Hans Koning, ed. by E. M. Beekman, *Lib. of the Indies Ser.*
   Univ. of Massachusetts Pr. 1983 lib. bdg. $13.00

BREDERO, GERBRAND A. 1580–1617

Bredero was the most important comedy writer of the Dutch seventeenth
century and one of the most important literary figures overall. His play *The
Spanish Brabanter* ridicules the manners of a self-styled nobleman from Antwerp with his Spanish behavior. It is also important for the sharp ear
Bredero had for the language and sensibilities of the people.

BOOK BY BREDERO

The Spanish Brabanter. 1617. Trans. by H. David Brumble III, Medieval & Renaissance Texts 1982 $13.00

EEDEN, FREDERIK VAN. 1860–1932

In his turn-of-the-century novel about a woman's sexual urges, the author's handling of the topics of erotic passion, drug abuse, and prostitution
reveals his training as a psychiatrist.

BOOKS BY EEDEN

The Deeps of Deliverance. Trans. by Margaret Robinson, Twayne 1975 o.p.
Paul's Awakening. Trans. by H. S. Lake, Hunter House 1985 $6.95

ELSSCHOT, WILLEM. 1882–1960

Elsschot was a Flemish advertising agent who wrote in his spare time.
The two novels *Soft Soap* and *The Leg* (of the 1920s and 1930s) are hard-bitten,
cynical accounts of the seamier side of business life. The third text in the volume, *Will-o'the-Wisp,* is a novella rather than a novel. It evokes the melancholy
mood of a rainy evening in Antwerp as experienced by some foreign sailors.

BOOK BY ELSSCHOT

Three Novels. British Bk. Ctr. 1965 o.p.

EMANTS, MARCELLUS. 1848–1923

Emants's *A Posthumous Confession* is the first-person account of a social
misfit who murders his wife. In spite of Emants's awkward style, it created
a sensation when it appeared in 1894. To the author's dismay, the public
tended to identify him with the protagonist.

BOOK BY EMANTS

A Posthumous Confession. 1894. Trans. by J. M. Coetzee, G. K. Hall 1975 lib. bdg.
   $9.95

ERASMUS, DESIDERIUS. 1469–1536

[SEE Volume 4.]

FRANK, ANNE. 1929–1945

[SEE Volume 3, Chapter 3.]

HADEWIJCH. c.1200–1250

Hadewijch is one of the most powerful mystical poets in medieval literature. She uses the forms and conventions of courtly love poetry to convey a most intense feeling of rejection and acceptance by the divine lover.

BOOK BY HADEWIJCH

The Complete Works. Trans. by Columba Hart, Paulist Pr. 1980 o.p.

MULISCH, HARRY. 1927–

Mulisch is, with W. F. Hermans and G. Reve, one of the most talented novelists of his generation. As in the work of the other two, the experiences of World War II play an important part in his work. In *The Assault* the postwar consequences of the killing of a Nazi by members of the underground are painfully analyzed.

BOOK BY MULISCH

The Assault. Trans. by Claire White, Pantheon 1985 $12.95

MULTATULI (pseud. of Eduard Douwes Dekker). 1820–1887

Multatuli is the most important Netherlandic novelist of the nineteenth century. His best-known work is *Max Havelaar,* which was based on his experiences as a government official in the Dutch East Indies. In it, he lambasts the colonial regime for its alleged exploitation and maltreatment of the native population. The book's documentary value is open to question, but in literary and aesthetic terms it was far ahead of its time.

BOOKS BY MULTATULI

Max Havelaar: Or the Coffee Auctions of the Dutch Trading Company. 1860. Trans. by Roy Edwards, intro. by D. H. Lawrence, afterword by E. M. Beekman, Univ. of Massachusetts Pr. 1982 lib. bdg. $17.50 pap. $11.00
The Oyster and the Eagle: Selected Aphorisms and Parables. Trans. by E. M. Beekman, Univ. of Massachusetts Pr. 1974 o.p. Some of Multatuli's minor writings.

BOOK ABOUT MULTATULI

King, Peter. *Multatuli. Twayne's World Authors Ser.* G. K. Hall lib. bdg. $15.95

OSTAIJEN, PAUL VAN. 1896–1928

Ostaijen was a Flemish avant-garde writer who led the expressionist movement in Flemish literature. He wrote stories, poems, and criticism.

BOOKS BY OSTAIJEN

Patriotism, Inc. and Other Tales. Trans. by E. M. Beekman, Univ. of Massachusetts Pr. 1971 o.p.
Feasts of Fear and Agony. 1920. Trans. by H. van Ameyden van Duym, New Directions 1976 $5.95

REVIUS, JACOBUS. 1856–1658

This strongly Calvinist poet is noted for his synthesis of the traditions of popular Netherlandic poetry with the forms and conventions developed in Renaissance Italy.

BOOK BY REVIUS

Selected Poems of Jacobus Revius, Dutch Metaphysical Poet. Trans. by Henrietta Ten Harmsel, Wayne State Univ. Pr. 1968 $8.95

REYNARD THE FOX. 12th century

The well-known main actors in the collection of stories known as the Reynard cycle are a clever, smooth-talking, unprincipled fox, and his constant adversary, a stupid, coarse-mannered, equally unprincipled wolf named Ysengrim. The tales appear to have originated in the Netherlands, where they became the vehicle for lively comic scenes and sharp satires of the church and the court. Their influence has been worldwide, and parallel versions of the tales may be found in the literature of nations far removed from the Low Countries. There are many other versions of the Reynard cycle than that listed below. Perhaps the most brilliant of them all is the Latin poem *Ysengrimus* by Novardus of Ghent, whose keen-witted verse has been translated into Dutch and German, but not yet into English.

The History of Reynard the Fox. Trans. by William Caxton, ed. by N. F. Blake, Oxford text ed. 1970 $21.95. An illustrated edition of the text, which became an English classic in the hands of its translator and publisher, the man who brought the art of printing to England.

RUYSLINCK, WARD (pseud. of R. K. M. de Belser). 1929–

The title of this author's first novel, *The Depraved Sleepers*, sums up the theme. His fifth novel, *Golden Ophelia*, deals with the fate of the sensitive outsider in our mechanized society.

BOOK BY RUYSLINCK

The Depraved Sleepers (and *Golden Ophelia*). Trans. by R. B. Powell and David Smith, G. K. Hall 1978 lib. bdg. $11.50

SCHENDEL, ARTHUR VAN. 1876–1946

Arthur van Schendel was the leading figure in the Dutch neoromantic movement of the beginning of the twentieth century. In his later work he turns from romantic nostalgia and a fascination with Italy to a confrontation with his roots in Dutch culture and history.

BOOK BY SCHENDEL

John Campagnie. Trans. by Fr. van Rosevelt, ed. by E. M. Beekman, Univ. of Massachusetts Pr. 1983 lib. bdg. $16.00

SCHIERBEEK, BERT. 1918–

Schierbeek is one of the most difficult and unconventional of Dutch experimental poets, composing his incantations in a hypnotic prose verse.

BOOK BY SCHIERBEEK

Shapes of the Voice. G. K. Hall 1977 lib. bdg. $10.00. An anthology from his most important work.

SPINOZA, BARUCH (or BENEDICTUS DE). 1632–1677

[SEE Volume 4.]

VESTDIJK, SIMON. 1898–1971

Vestdijk has the distinction of having tried his hand, with respectable results, at nearly every genre of literature. He published 50 novels, 7 volumes of short stories, 22 volumes of poetry, and 33 collections of essays and critical prose. Furthermore, he distinguished himself as a translator of American and British writers into Dutch.

BOOKS BY VESTDIJK

Rum Island. 1940. Riverrun pap. $5.95
New Writers, No. 2, 1980. Riverrun pap. $6.00

WOLKERS, JAN. 1925–

Especially through the film version of *Turkish Delight*, Wolkers has received much publicity and critical attention. He is a very typical representative of the explicit eroticism of the 1960s, but there are also subtle and compassionate tones in his work that set it apart from the run-of-the-mill literary titillations.

BOOK BY WOLKERS

Turkish Delight. Trans. by Greta Kilburn, Boyars repr. of 1974 ed. 1983 pap. $7.50

CHAPTER 14

Scandinavian Literature

Donald K. Watkins

Our time, in its lack of balance, its heterogeneity, and through the violent expansion of its conflicting forces, is baroque and fantastic, much more fantastic than naturalism is able to portray it. In our daily lives we scarcely possess the feeling of security which naturalism's form gives, but rather an acute need of finding expression for all the anguish we feel as life wells up against us. It is here that we are left in the lurch—when we try to understand ourselves and our own time.

—PÄR LAGERKVIST, *Modern Theatre*

At the beginning of Scandinavian literacy 1,000 years ago, the contour of artistic culture quickly rose to a high plateau of poetic and narrative craft, especially on Iceland, which had been colonized by people from Norway beginning in the ninth century. Eddic and skaldic verse preserved unique views of religious and social life at a time when Christian and pagan ways vied in northern Europe. The wealth of Old Norse-Icelandic sagas, their readability as fresh now as then, realistically depict folk and court ways in medieval Scandinavia. For much later northern writers, especially in the nineteenth century, the sagas gave substance to the national pedigrees of the adamantly independent but culturally kindred countries. In the case of non-Germanic Finland, a similar statement of national spirit was forged in *Kalevala*.

The late medieval and early modern literatures of Denmark, Norway, and Sweden expressed a vigorous folk tradition in ballads and the needs of religiosity, and established Lutheranism in hymns, a major genre of poets. Norway, a province of Denmark until 1814, virtually lacked a separate literary presence before Henrik Wergeland's championship of national identity. Finland had been culturally repressed under both Swedish and Russian rule for 800 years before it gained independence in 1917. With justification it is said that Iceland did not leave its Middle Ages until the twentieth century. Denmark, by contrast, fostered Scandinavia's most cosmopolitan literature (Ludvig Holberg, Hans Christian Andersen, Søren Kierkegaard) before the great Ibsen and Strindberg startled their European and American contemporaries. Nationalistic self-assertion limits the appeal today of many writers whose countries were coming into their own little more than 100 years ago.

Realism and naturalism, aiming at detailed description and evaluation of the individual and society, dominated the decades around 1900 (Ibsen, Jens Peter Jacobsen, Strindberg). Brilliant criticism permeates the works of Bjørnstjerne Bjørnson, Hermann Bang, and Knut Hamsun, while Pär Lagerkvist exemplifies the power of Swedish expressionism to face existential and religious questions and to attack the evils of totalitarian times. Major writers since 1900 have been deeply concerned with the history and fate in industrial society of working people (Eyvind Johnson, Vilhelm Moberg, Martin A. Hansen). Their concerns, however different in detail, illustrate the power of literature to underpin and speak for democratic sensibilities. Scandinavia was spared the convulsions, human and literary, of World War I, but since the 1920s it has shared the general European disillusionment. Dissatisfaction with the drab, if not threatening, here and now of the atomic era has not produced a single direction in literature, but rather a brilliant variety of voices in prose and poetry, including such individualists as Isak Dinesen, Gunnar Ekelöf, and Tarjei Vesaas.

GENERAL READING AND REFERENCE

Bédé, Jean-Albert, and William Edgerton, eds. *Columbia Dictionary of Modern European Literature.* Columbia Univ. Pr. 2d ed. 1980 $60.00

Bredsdorff, Elias, and others. *Introduction to Scandinavian Literature.* Greenwood repr. of 1951 ed. lib. bdg. $24.75

Buchanan-Brown, J., ed. *Cassell's Encyclopedia of World Literature.* Morrow 3 vols. rev. ed. 1977 o.p.

Eggenberger, David, and others, eds. *The McGraw-Hill Encyclopedia of World Drama.* McGraw-Hill 4 vols. 1972 o.p.

Klein, Leonard S., ed. *Encyclopedia of World Literature in the 20th Century.* Ungar 4 vols. 2d ed. rev. & enl. 1983–84 ea. $100.00–$130.00 index $35.00

Kvamme, Janet, and Edwin Brownrigg. *Index Nordicus: A Cumulative Index to English-Language Periodicals on Scandinavian Studies.* G. K. Hall 1978 o.p. Covers the period 1911–1975.

Matlaw, Myron. *Modern World Drama: An Encyclopedia.* Dutton 1972 $25.00

Rossel, Sven. *A History of Scandinavian Literature: 1870 to 1980.* Trans. by Anne C. Ulme, Univ. of Minnesota Pr. 1982 $25.00

SCANDINAVIAN DRAMA

The figures of Henrik Ibsen and August Strindberg loom in the background as one views the development of Scandinavian drama in the twentieth century. Of Ibsen it can be said that his realistic plays of the period 1877–1883 created a norm for many Scandinavian dramatists who followed him. For others, the Ibsen tradition became a stale convention to be avoided. The second main dramatic tradition was created by the egocentricity of Strindberg. Rather than the outer, social reality of Ibsen's problem plays, Strindberg cultivated the subjective reality of an inner consciousness where no natural laws can be observed.

For all the power of Scandinavian theater at the turn of the century, it must be said that the real strength of Scandinavian literature since Ibsen and Strindberg has been in prose and poetry. Few are the dramatists who are not better known as novelists (e.g., Pär Lagerkvist and Vilhelm Moberg in Sweden, Hans Christian Branner and Isak Dinesen in Denmark, Tarjei Vesaas in Norway), and with few exceptions the theater has not had great masters in recent decades. Yet there are very talented dramatists in Scandinavia today, and the theater does have a large and loyal audience.

The student of film is also aware that Ingmar Bergman is essentially an excellent and complex dramatist whose medium happens to be photographic. Literature by and on Bergman, including published scripts of his films, is abundant.

Friis, Erik J., ed. *Modern Nordic Plays: Denmark. Lib. of Scandinavian Lit.* Irvington 5 vols. text ed. 1973–74 ea. $29.50 1982 pap. ea. $10.95. Volume 1 on Finland contains Paavo Haavikko, *The Superintendent;* V. V. Järner, *Eva Maria;* Eeva-Liisa Manner, *Snow in May;* Veijo Meri, *Private Jokinen's Marriage Leave.* Volume 2 on Iceland contains Halldór Laxness, *The Pigeon Banquet;* Jökull Jakobsson, *The Seaway to Baghdad;* Erlingur E. Halldórsson, *Mink;* Oddur Björnsson, *Ten Variations* and *Yolk-life.* Volume 3 on Sweden contains Lars Forssell, *The Madcap;* Folke Fridell, *One Man's Bread;* Lars Görling, *The Sandwiching;* Björn-Erik Höijer, *Isak Juntti Had Many Sons.* Volume 4 on Norway contains Johan Borgen, *The House;* Finn Havrevold, *The Injustice;* Tarjei Vesaas, *The Bleaching Yard;* Axel Kielland, *The Lord and His Servants.* Volume 5 on Denmark contains Hans Christian Branner, *Thermopylae;* Ernst Bruun Olsen, *The Bookseller Cannot Sleep;* Klaus Rifbjerg, *Developments;* Peter Ronild, *Boxing for One.*

Haugen, Einar, and G. M. Gathorne-Hardy, eds. and trans. *Fire and Ice: Three Icelandic Plays.* Univ. of Wisconsin Pr. 1967 $20.00 pap. $6.00. Includes Jóhann Sigurjónsson, *The Wish;* David Stefánsson, *The Golden Gate;* Agnar Thördarson, *Atoms and Madams.*

DANISH LITERATURE

Billeskov-Jansen, F. J., and P. M. Mitchell, eds. *Anthology of Danish Literature.* Southern Illinois Univ. Pr. 2 vols. 1971 ea. $25.00 1972 pap. ea. $10.95

Bodelson, Anders. *Straus.* Trans. by Nadia Christensen and Alexander Taylor, Harper 1974 o.p. Realistic depiction of contemporary society characterizes the many novels in which Bodelson describes social and inner conflict.

Bredsdorff, Elias. *Danish Literature in English Translation.* Greenwood repr. of 1950 ed. 1973 lib. bdg. $18.75. Covers the period 1533–1950.

Brønner, Hedin. *Three Faroese Novelists: An Appreciation of Jørgen Frantz Jacobsen, William Heinesen and Hedin Brú. Lib. of Scandinavian Lit.* Irvington 1973 $19.50

Brú, Hedin. *Old Man and His Sons.* Trans. by John F. West, Eriksson 1970 $5.95. Along with William Heinesen, Brú is one of the leading writers of the Faroe Islands. This novel shows the generation gap in Faroese terms.

Contemporary Danish Plays. Trans. by Elias Bredsdorff, *Play Anthology Repr. Ser.* Ayer repr. of 1953 ed. $21.50

Contemporary Danish Poetry. Ed. by Line Jensen and others, G. K. Hall (Twayne) 1977 lib. bdg. $13.00

Contemporary Danish Prose. Trans. by Elias Bredsdorff, intro. by F. J. Billeskov-Jansen, Greenwood repr. of 1958 ed. 1974 lib. bdg. $22.50

Dal, E. *Danish Ballads and Folk Songs.* Trans. by H. Meyer, Amer.-Scandinavian Foundation 1967 $7.50. Dal's knowledge of medieval Danish literature is expert. This fine collection of early verse does not include music.

Ditlevsen, Tove. *Complete Freedom and Other Stories.* Trans. by Jack Brondum, Curbstone 1982 pap. $7.00. Drawing from her own youth in a working-class neighborhood of Copenhagen, Ditlevsen deals in novels, short stories, and poetry with the experience of children and women. The Brondum translation received the PEN/American-Scandinavian Translation Award.

Grundtvig, Svendt. *Danish Fairy Tales.* Dover repr. of 1919 ed. 1972 pap. $4.50; Peter Smith $7.75

Harder, Uffe. *Paper Houses.* Trans. by Uffe Harder and Alexander Taylor, Curbstone 1982 pap. $4.00. Harder, known in Denmark as a surrealistic poet and translator, here appears for the first time in English.

Hein, Piet. *Grooks.* Doubleday 5 vols. 1969–73 ea. $1.45–$2.50. The mathematician Hein is famous for his modern aphorisms, which he called "grooks."

Larsen, Marianne. *Selected Poems.* Trans. by Nadia Christensen, Curbstone 1982 pap. $5.00. Brilliant poetry and fierce social criticism.

Mitchell, P. M. *History of Danish Literature.* Intro. by Mogens Hausted, Amer.-Scandinavian Foundation 1971 $17.50; Kraus repr. 1971 $22.00

——, trans. *The Royal Guest: And Other Classical Danish Narrative.* Trans. by Kenneth H. Ober, Univ. of Chicago Pr. 1977 lib. bdg. $15.00. Selections from works by M. Goldschmidt, J. P. Jacobsen, H. Pontoppidan, and H. Bang.

Nordbrandt, Henrik. *Armenia.* Trans. by Henrik Nordbrandt and Alexander Taylor, Curbstone pap. $7.50

——. *God's House.* Trans. by Henrik Nordbrandt and Alexander Taylor, Curbstone 1979 pap. $3.50

——. *Selected Poems.* Trans. by Henrik Nordbrandt and Alexander Taylor, Curbstone pap. $7.50

Panduro, Leif. *Kick Me in the Traditions.* Trans. by Carl Malmberg, Eriksson text ed. 1985 $13.95. Panduro frequently deals with problems of puberty and identity in his many novels and plays; his humor and satire have earned him a prominent place in current Danish literature.

Schade, Jens August. *The Selected Poems of Jens August Schade.* Trans. by Alexander Taylor, Curbstone 1984 pap. $7.50

Schnack, Asgar. *Aqua.* Trans. by Asgar Schnack and Alexander Taylor, Curbstone 1982 pap. $4.00

Sonne, Jørgen. *Flights.* Trans. by Jørgen Sonne and Alexander Taylor, Curbstone 1981 pap. $4.00

Thorup, Kirsten. *Baby: A Novel.* Trans. by Nadia Christensen and Alexander Taylor, Louisiana State Univ. Pr. 1980 $14.95

Willumsen, Dorrit. *If It Really Were a Film.* Trans. by Anne M. Rasmussen, Curbstone 1982 pap. $7.00. "Willumsen, the 1981 recipient of the Danish Academy's Grand Prize, makes her debut in English with these psychological suspense-filled short stories" (*Choice*).

ANDERSEN, BENNY. 1929–

A talented jazz pianist, composer, highly popular poet, and writer of short stories, Benny Andersen has also written television plays, children's books, film scripts, and two novels. Andersen's poetry, with its irony, humor, and wordplay, suggests comparison with E. E. Cummings. Andersen is a critic of social norms and the large and small brutalities that modern society inflicts on the individual striving for an authentic life, and individual, often bizarre experience, is the focus of Andersen's intense scrutiny. His intriguing blend of the humorous and the utterly serious shows an artist intent on shaping values through literature.

BOOKS BY BENNY ANDERSEN

Selected Poems. Trans. by Alexander Taylor, Curbstone 1983 pap. $6.00; Princeton Univ. Pr. 1975 $17.00 pap. $5.95
Selected Stories. Trans. by Donald K. Watkins and others, intro. by Leonie A. Marx, Curbstone 1982 pap. $6.00
The Pillows. 1965. Curbstone 1983 $7.50

BOOK ABOUT BENNY ANDERSEN

Marx, Leonie A. *Benny Andersen: A Critical Study.* Greenwood 1983 $25.00

ANDERSEN, HANS CHRISTIAN. 1805–1875

Fairy tales comprise only a rather small part of Andersen's lifework—his novels and travel books were more warmly received by his contemporaries. During his lifetime, his talent was more esteemed in other countries than it was in his native Denmark—Dickens called the Dane "a great writer." Andersen complained bitterly about the lack of encouragement for his first volume of *Fairy Tales, Told for Children,* published in 1835. In 1843, he began the series called *New Adventures* and the title no longer addressed itself exclusively to children. Other volumes followed until Andersen's death. "There is no longer any doubt that Andersen was born so he could write these fairy tales and stories: they are his contribution to world history" (Fredrik Böök). "My fairy tales are written as much for adults as for children," said Andersen in his old age. "Children understand only the trimmings, and not until they are mature will they see and comprehend the whole."

BOOKS BY HANS CHRISTIAN ANDERSEN

The Complete Fairy Tales and Stories. Ed. by Eric Haugaard, Doubleday $24.95
Tales and Stories by Hans Christian Andersen. Trans. by Patricia Conroy and Sven H. Rossel, Univ. of Washington Pr. 1980 $22.50 pap. $9.95
It's Perfectly True: And Other Stories. Trans. by Paul Leyssac, Harcourt 1938 $7.50. Twenty-eight stories.
Eighty Tales. Trans. by R. P. Keigwin, Random 1982 $14.95 pap. $7.95
The Story of My Life. 1867. Trans. by Mary B. Howitt, Folcroft o.p.

BOOKS ABOUT HANS CHRISTIAN ANDERSEN

Böök, Fredrik. *Hans Christian Andersen: A Biography.* Trans. by George C. Schoolfield, Univ. of Oklahoma Pr. 1962 $4.50. An authoritative biography, "persevering in hunting the true Andersen."
Bredsdorff, Elias. *Hans Christian Andersen.* Scribner 1975 $10.00

Gronbech, Bo. *Hans Christian Andersen. Twayne's World Authors Ser.* G. K. Hall 1980 lib. bdg. $13.50
Spink, Reginald. *Hans Christian Andersen and His World.* Putnam 1972 $6.95
———. *Hans Christian Andersen: The Man and His Work.* Vanous 1975 pap. $6.00

BRANDT, JØRGEN GUSTAVA. 1929–

Since his first publication in 1949, Brandt's great and acclaimed production has been primarily in poetry, of which some two dozen collections have been published. He also writes essays, stories, and novels. His approach to experience is mystical and his style reflective and vigorous as he speaks to the human condition in a flawed, beautiful world.

BOOKS BY BRANDT

Tête-à-Tête. Trans. by Jørgen Gustava Brandt and Alexander Taylor, Curbstone 1978 pap. $4.00
Selected Longer Poems. Curbstone 1983 pap. $6.00

BRANNER, HANS CHRISTIAN. 1903–1966

Freudian psychoanalysis, existentialism, and modern humanism are the driving forces in Branner's fine short stories and novels. While the psychological view of human personality presented in Branner seems very simplistic today, his symbolism is intriguing as he describes with great finesse the erotic awakening of youth and adult sexual relationships. *The Story of Börge* is one of Branner's best studies of child psychology. *The Riding Master*, published in 1949 (no U.S. edition), his most famous novel, prompted a spirited public reaction by Isak Dinesen, who found fundamental fault with Branner's concept of "humanism."

BOOKS BY BRANNER

The Story of Börge. 1942. Intro. by Thomas L. Markey, *Lib. of Scandinavian Lit.* Irvington 1973 lib. bdg. $27.50
Two Minutes of Silence: Selected Short Stories. 1944. Trans. by Vera Lindholm Vance, intro. by Richard B. Vowles, Univ. of Wisconsin Pr. 1966 $17.50. Includes a detailed bibliography.

BOOK ABOUT BRANNER

Markey, Thomas L. *H. C. Branner. Twayne's World Authors Ser.* G. K. Hall 1973 lib. bdg. $15.95

DINESEN, ISAK (pseud. of Karen Blixen). 1885–1962

Isak Dinesen was a unique figure in the literature of modern Denmark, quite distant from the trends of the 1930s and later. She lived the happiest and most eventful years of her life in Africa rather than Denmark; she wrote primarily in a faultless and yet quite personal variety of literary English; and she found her most receptive audience, not in Denmark, but in the United States. From 1914 to 1931 Karen Blixen—her married name, by which she is known in Europe—struggled to maintain a coffee plantation in the British colony of Kenya. In contrast to the poor prospects of the farm, she was surrounded by a wealth of European and native friends in a relatively un-Westernized land of enormous beauty. *Out of Africa* and its late sequel, *Shadows on the Grass*, are not memoirs in the usual sense. Facts are insignificant as she assesses her African experience; it is the spirit of a primitive and yet noble culture that gives these books their enduring evocative power. Dinesen perceived an Africa where humanity and nature were still one. Here she came to terms with life and acquired a proud, exquisite fatalism. The two African books are definitely a key to greater appreciation of her works of pure fiction. If her pastorals in memory of Kenya helped Dinesen overcome her grief at losing her home there, then her stories, with their finely wrought fantasy, contain undercurrents of the truths she discovered in Africa. Her stories are "eccentric masterpieces; ostensibly Gothic pastiche, their outward form conceals epic wisdom, profound feminine sorrow, and a clean magic almost lost today. She is undoubtedly the princess of modern aristocratic storytellers, a delight and a revelation" (Seymour Smith). In 1957 Dinesen received an honorary membership in the American Academy and National Institute of Arts and Letters, an honor rarely awarded to nonresidents.

BOOKS BY DINESEN

Seven Gothic Tales. 1934. Intro. by Dorothy Canfield, Modern Lib. $6.95; Random (Vintage) 1972 pap. $4.95

Out of Africa. 1938. Modern Lib. $8.95; Random (Vintage) 1985 pap. $4.95

Winter's Tales. 1942. Random (Vintage) 1961 pap. $4.95

The Angelic Avengers. 1944. Univ. of Chicago Pr. 1975 $8.95. Written under the pseudonym Pierre Andrézel.

Last Tales. Random 1957 $8.95; Random (Vintage) 1975 pap. $4.95

Carnival: Entertainments and Posthumous Tales. Univ. of Chicago Pr. 1977 $10.00 1979 pap. $9.95

Daguerrotypes and Other Essays. Trans. by P. M. Mitchell and W. D. Paden, Univ. of Chicago Pr. 1979 $12.95 pap. 1984 $6.95

Letters from Africa, 1914–1931. Trans. by Anne Born, Univ. of Chicago Pr. 1981 $25.00; Univ. of Chicago Pr. (Phoenix Bks.) 1984 pap. $9.95

Anecdotes of Destiny. 1958. Random (Vintage) 1974 pap. $3.95. A collection of five stories.

Shadows on the Grass. Random (Vintage) 1961 pap. $2.95; Univ. of Chicago Pr. $6.95. Four sketches; a sequel to *Out of Africa*.

Ehrengard. 1963. Random (Vintage) 1975 pap. $1.95

BOOKS ABOUT DINESEN

Beard, Peter, ed. *Longing for Darkness: Kamante's Tales from out of Africa*. Harcourt 1975 $19.95

Bjørnvig, Thorkild. *The Pact: My Friendship with Isak Dinesen*. Intro. by William Jay Smith, Louisiana State Univ. Pr. 1983 $16.95

Henriksen, Liselotte. *Isak Dinesen: A Bibliography*. Univ. of Chicago Pr. 1977 $12.50

Langbaum, Robert. *Isak Dinesen's Art: The Gayety of Vision*. Univ. of Chicago Pr. (Phoenix Bks.) 1975 pap. $4.95

Lasson, Frans. *The Life and Destiny of Isak Dinesen*. Univ. of Chicago Pr. (Phoenix Bks.) 1976 pap. $15.95

Thurman, Judith. *Isak Dinesen: The Life of a Storyteller.* St. Martin's 1982 $19.95
    1983 pap. $9.95

HANSEN, MARTIN A. 1909–1955

As a critic of the form and content of civilization since the Middle Ages,
Martin A. Hansen saw a deterioration of humanity and morality as rationalism and scientism became the guiding lights of European culture. Hansen
pointed to the coherent culture of the Danish Middle Ages as the humane
condition society had lost. In his childhood, Hansen personally observed the
disintegration of rural folk culture as economic and agricultural requirements modernized country life. His participation in the Danish Underground during World War II also greatly increased his sense of the failure of
modern times to provide ethical stability. A very learned and Christian romanticism imbues his many novels and stories; he was at times very obtuse
and allegorical. In *Lucky Kristoffer*, a historical novel set in the sixteenth
century, combatants in the strife of Reformation times express both medieval and modern attitudes, both harmony and disharmony. *The Liar*, written in the form of a schoolteacher's diary, presents a psychological critique
of modern times as the teacher experiences a crisis of faith.

Books by Hansen

Lucky Kristoffer. 1945. Trans. by John J. Egglishaw, *Lib. of Scandinavian Lit.* Amer.-
    Scandinavian Foundation 1974 lib. bdg. $8.50; *Lib. of Scandinavian Lit.* Irving-
    ton 1974 lib. bdg. $6.50
The Liar. Trans. by John J. Egglishaw, Twayne 1950 o.p.

Book about Hansen

Ingwersen, Faith, and Niels Ingwersen. *Martin A. Hansen. Twayne's World Authors
    Ser.* 1976 o.p.

HEINESEN, WILLIAM. 1900–

As a young man in the Faroe Islands, William Heinesen thought of a profession in art or music. His early poetry—he writes in Danish rather than
Faroese—from the 1920s demonstrates keen sensitivity to the powerful sensual contrasts of nature in the Atlantic islands. In the 1930s, his elegiac and
ecstatic pantheism received a social awareness. Of novels from this period,
Noatun has appeared in an English translation in London. In this novel, the
reader meets the vital people of a Faroese settlement bravely surviving
storms, sickness, and exploitation as they struggle to establish a *noatun*, or
new town. The individualistic people and sharp beauty of the Faroese are
Heinesen's subjects; his strong satire, humor, and imagination have made
him one of Denmark's finest prose writers. *The Lost Musicians* and *The Kingdom of the Earth* share many of the same characters, created by Heinesen to
depict fantastic events in Torshavn a generation or so ago. In Heinesen's
rich fantasy is an expression of the antinaturalism and unrealism that also
mark the writing of Isak Dinesen and Martin A. Hansen. It is not necessary
to have even heard of the Faroes to enjoy the magic of William Heinesen.

BOOKS BY HEINESEN

The Lost Musicians. 1950. Trans. by Erik J. Friis, intro. by Hedin Brønner, *Lib. of Scandinavian Lit.* Amer.-Scandinavian Foundation 1971 $8.95; Hippocrene Bks. 1972 pap. $3.95; *Lib. of Scandinavian Lit.* Irvington 1971 lib. bdg. $6.95

The Kingdom of the Earth. 1952. Trans. by Hedin Brønner, *Lib. of Scandinavian Lit.* Irvington 1974 lib. bdg. $29.50

The Winged Darkness and Other Stories by William Heinesen. Trans. by William Heinesen, ed. by Hedin Brønner, Irvington 1983 $19.50

BOOKS ABOUT HEINESEN

Brønner, Hedin. *Three Faroese Novelists: An Appreciation of Jørgen Frantz Jacobsen, William Heinesen and Hedin Brú. Lib. of Scandinavian Lit.* Irvington 1973 $19.50

Jones, W. Glyn. *William Heinesen. Twayne's World Authors Ser.* G. K. Hall 1974 lib. bdg. $16.95

HOLBERG, LUDVIG. 1684–1754

Holberg, the outstanding genius of the Danish Enlightenment, contributed in the areas of history, philosophy, and literature. His name stands by that of Molière as a master of European comedy. His 33 comedies created a national repertoire and a theatrical tradition. Holberg's strength in creative writing lay not in extended plot but in the individual scene, the anecdote, the characterization. *Peder Paars*, a mock heroic poem, gave Holberg the framework in which to satirize the government, the church, and the university. The novel *Niels Klim* likewise reported on human foibles. Students of eighteenth-century European literature will want to seek out translations of Holberg's philosophical writing.

BOOKS BY HOLBERG

Seven One-Act Plays. Trans. by Henry Alexander, intro. by Svend Kragh-Jacobsen, Kraus 1950 $15.00. Contains *The Talkative Barber, The Arabian Powder, The Christmas Party, Diedrich the Terrible, The Peasant in Pawn, Sgnarel's Journey to the Land of the Philosophers,* and *The Caged Bridegroom.*

Four Plays by Holberg. Trans. by Harry Alexander, Kraus repr. of 1946 ed. $20.00. Contains *The Masked Ladies, The Fussy Men, The Weathercock,* and *Masquerades.*

Selected Essays. Intro. and trans. by P. M. Mitchell, Greenwood repr. of 1955 ed. 1976 lib. bdg. $18.75

Peder Paars. 1719. Trans. by Bergliot Stromsoe, intro. by Børge Gedsø Madsen, Amer.-Scandinavian Foundation 1962 $8.95

The Journey of Niels Klim to the World Underground. 1741. Ed. by James I. McNelis, Jr., Greenwood repr. of 1960 ed. 1973 lib. bdg. $24.75. This edition is based on a translation published in London in 1742.

BOOK ABOUT HOLBERG

Billeskov-Jansen, F. J. *Ludvig Holberg. Twayne's World Authors Ser.* G. K. Hall 1974 lib. bdg. $15.95. A study by one of the deans of modern Danish literary scholarship.

JACOBSEN, JENS PETER. 1847–1885

Jens Peter Jacobsen, Denmark's foremost novelist of naturalism, expressed in his small body of work his rejection of religion and his enthusiasm for the new doctrine of evolution. In his autobiographical novel *Niels Lyhne*, sometimes called by contemporaries "the bible of atheism," he wrote that "there is no God and man is his prophet." During his troubled life, cut short by tuberculosis, he translated into Danish nearly all of Charles Darwin's writings. His own work—two novels, a book of short stories, and a few poems—strove to "bring into the realm of literature the eternal laws of nature" and to free the concept of nature from the distorted concept of romanticism. The novella *Mogens* was Jacobsen's first publication; it became famous as an example of the new naturalistic current in literature. In it, life is seen as perceptions of the instant, and people are motivated by natural laws and drives. In *Marie Grubbe*, externally a seventeenth-century historical romance, the life of Marie is determined by her erotic needs; although born into nobility, she finally finds happiness in life as the wife of a coarse stableman. Jacobsen's concern with anxiety and inner torment brings to mind the great nineteenth-century Russian novelists, while his naturalism and interest in psychology are reminiscent of Flaubert. Jacobsen's influence on major European writers who followed him, such as Rilke, is well documented.

BOOKS BY JACOBSEN

Mogens: And Other Stories. 1872–85. *Short Story Index Repr. Ser.* Ayer repr. of 1921 ed. $17.00

Marie Grubbe. 1876. Trans. by Hanna Astrup Larsen, pref. by Robert Raphael, *Lib. of Scandinavian Lit.* Amer.-Scandinavian Foundation 2d ed. rev. 1975 lib. bdg. $7.95; G. K. Hall (Twayne) 1975 lib. bdg. $9.95

Niels Lyhne. 1880. Trans. by Hanna Astrup Larsen, intro. by Børge Gedsø Madsen, Norwood repr. of 1921 ed. 1979 lib. bdg. $20.00

BOOK ABOUT JACOBSEN

Jensen, Niels L. *Jens Peter Jacobsen. Twayne's World Authors Ser.* G. K. Hall 1980 lib. bdg. $16.95

JENSEN, JOHANNES V(ILHELM). 1873–1950 (NOBEL PRIZE 1944)

Johannes V. Jensen has had great influence on Danish literature both as a lyric poet and as a novelist. He was born in a village in northwestern Jutland, where his father was a veterinarian and his grandfather a farmer and weaver. He studied medicine in Copenhagen, but did not become a doctor. His great interest in anthropology and biology was concentrated in the theory of evolution. Darwinian philosophy permeates the six novels that comprise his epic *The Long Journey*. His deep sense of science, or all-including nature, was what aroused his imagination.

BOOK BY JENSEN

The Long Journey. 1908–22. Nobel Prize edition 1945 o.p.

KIERKEGAARD, SØREN (AABYE). 1813–1855
[SEE Volume 4.]

MUNK, KAJ (HARALD LEININGER). 1898–1944

Deep religious conviction and love of the heroic, inspired individual were blended in the personality and work of Kaj Munk, perhaps Denmark's most significant dramatist in the twentieth century. As a Lutheran minister he became a magnetic preacher, whose political and cultural criticism had certain philosophical aspects in common with the antirationalism of contemporary European fascism. The irony in this lies in the fact that Munk's heroic ideal was humane and Christian. In the spirit of his heroes, Munk persistently and publicly attacked nazism during the occupation of Denmark and was murdered by the Gestapo in 1944.

In *Before Cannae* (1943), Hannibal, the ruthless empire builder, is opposed by the humanitarian Fabius. In *He Sits at the Melting Pot* (1938), God endows a man with the strength of love with which to do battle against the power-hungry of this world. *The Word* (1932), Munk's greatest success on the stage, confirms that miracles through faith are possible in modern times.

BOOK BY MUNK

Five Plays. Trans. by R. P. Keigwin, Amer.-Scandinavian Foundation 1964. Contains *Herod the King, The Word, Cant, He Sits at the Melting Pot,* and *Before Cannae.*

BOOK ABOUT MUNK

Harcourt, Melville. *Portraits of Destiny.* Twin Circle 1966 o.p.

NEXÖ, MARTIN ANDERSEN. 1869–1954

Martin Andersen Nexö, the first prominent voice in Danish literature of trade unionism and proletarian solidarity, spent an impoverished youth working at various trades in Copenhagen and on the island of Bornholm. After 1901 he supported himself by writing. A Communist and an enemy of injustice, he avoided arrest during the Nazi occupation in World War II by fleeing, first to Sweden and then to the Soviet Union. He died in East Germany. *Pelle the Conqueror* and *Ditte* are Nexö's classic proletarian novels. *Pelle* describes the development of Danish trade unionism in the nineteenth century; its blend of autobiographical insights with a passionate sense of justice cast in epic narrative remind one of Gorky. *Ditte* charts the struggle of a young woman against poverty and cold indifference. *Ditte*'s fate is described in basic moral terms and is not linked with political events; thus it differs rather sharply from *Pelle.*

BOOKS BY NEXÖ

Ditte: Ditte, Daughter of Man. 1920. Trans. by A. G. Chater and Richard Thirsk, Peter Smith 3 vols. in 1 $16.00. This volume also includes *Girl Alive!* and *Towards the Stars.*
Pelle the Conqueror. 1906. Trans. by Jessie Muir and Bernard Miall, Peter Smith 4

vols. in 2 $27.00. The volumes also include *Boyhood, Apprenticeship, The Great Struggle,* and *Daybreak.*

In God's Land. 1929. Trans. by Thomas Seltzer, Peter Smith 1933 o.p.

PALUDAN, (STIG HENNING) JACOB (PUGGAARD). 1896–

Jacob Paludan is a novelist and essayist who began as a pharmacist. He spent part of his youth in Ecuador and New York City. *Jörgen Stein,* his outstanding work, shows Denmark at the outset of World War I and is a scathing indictment of the materialism and complacency of the period. Paludan is known for his acute psychological penetration and fine style.

BOOK BY PALUDAN

Jörgen Stein. 1932–33. Trans. by Carl Malmberg, intro. by P. M. Mitchell, Univ. of Wisconsin Pr. 1966 $25.00 pap. $6.00

RIFBJERG, KLAUS. 1931–

The productivity of Rifbjerg has been continuous and extreme: poetry, novels, stories, and plays for the stage as well as radio and television. Experimenting in all the genres, Rifbjerg deals often with the psychology of the Danish middle classes. In *Anna (I) Anna,* the wife of a diplomat flees her comfortable but trivial life to join a hippie in wandering through central Europe. The 22 poems in *Selected Poems* show "the range of his poetic voice, sardonic or satiric or witty and displaying compassion for his fellow human beings . . . the finest in lyrics" (*Scandinavian-American Bulletin*).

BOOKS BY RIFBJERG

Anna (I) Anna. Trans. by Alexander Taylor, Curbstone 1982 pap. $9.95
Selected Poems. Trans. by Alexander Taylor, Curbstone 3d ed. enl. 1985 pap. $4.50

FINNISH LITERATURE

Ahokas, Jaakko. *A History of Finnish Literature.* Mouton text ed. 1973 pap. $47.00
Binham, Philip, and Richard Dauenhauer, eds. *Snow in May: An Anthology of Finnish Writing, 1945–1972.* Fairleigh Dickinson Univ. Pr. 1975 o.p.
Jansson, Tove. *Finn Family Moomintroll.* Avon 1975 pap. $1.95
———. *Moominland Winter.* Avon 1976 pap. $1.95
———. *Moominpappa at Sea.* Avon 1977 pap. $1.95
———. *The Summer Book.* Trans. by Thomas Teal, Pantheon 1975 $6.95. A Swedo-Finnish writer, Jansson is a master creator of sophisticated children's literature.
Paulaharju, Samuli. *Arctic Twilight: Old Finnish Tales.* Trans. by Allan M. Pitkänen, ed. by Robert W. Matson, Finnish-Amer. Literary Heritage Foundation 1982 $15.00
Schoolfield, George C., ed. and trans. *Swedo-Finnish Short Stories. Lib. of Scandinavian Lit.* Amer.-Scandinavian Foundation 1974 lib. bdg. $13.50; G. K. Hall (Twayne) 1974 lib. bdg. $14.50. "This first collection in English presents a competent and skillful translation of a little-known part of Scandinavian writing" (*LJ*).

THE KALEVALA (THE LAND OF THE HEROES)

The Kalevala (1835–1849), the Finnish national epic of three semidivine brothers living in Kaleva, a mythical land of abundance and happiness, was known to scholars as early as 1733, but was ignored until the nineteenth century. The verses were collected by two Finnish physicians, Zakarias Topelius, who published the first fragments in 1822, and Elias Lönnrot, who continued to travel and sift the folk songs chanted to him by rune singers and who gave the cycle its present form in 1835–1836. His second edition, published in 1849, has remained the definitive version. Rich in mythology and folklore, its influence in all branches of the arts has been great. Sibelius used it in a number of his compositions. Longfellow borrowed its poetic form for *The Song of Hiawatha*. Kenneth Rexroth (*SR*) found the Kirby translation "in rather antiquated language with poor notes." The Lönnrot-Magoun version he called "a fine, scholarly edition." Rexroth said: "Recited in the original language, the *Kalevala* has a gripping sonority and haunting cadences quite unlike any other great poem in any language."

The Kalevala, or The Land of Heroes. Trans. by W. F. Kirby, intro. by J. B. C. Grundy, Biblio Dist. (Everyman's) 2 vols. in 1 1978 $8.95

The Kalevala: Poems of the Kaleva District. Comp. by Elias Lönnrot, trans. by Francis Peabody Magoun, Jr., Harvard Univ. Pr. 1963 $25.00 text ed. 1985 $9.95

OLSSON, HAGAR. 1893–1978

"The formidable Hagar Olsson, critical firebrand of Finnish modernism," as she has been called by Alrik Gustafson, became a foremost expressionist writer and editor in the 1920s. *The Woodcarver and Death* (1940) was based on a legend that has been praised for its poetic simplicity.

BOOK BY OLSSON

The Woodcarver and Death. Trans. by George C. Schoolfield, Univ. of Wisconsin Pr. 1965 $15.00

SAARIKOSKI, PENTTI. 1937–

A student of classical languages and literatures, journalist, social critic, satirist, and translator, Saarikoski has been called the *enfant terrible* of Finnish literature.

BOOKS BY SAARIKOSKI

Collected Poems. Ohio Univ. Pr. (Swallow) 1967 o.p.
Poems, 1958–1980. Trans. by Anselm Hollo, Coffee House 1984 $40.00 pap. $10.00

SILLANPÄÄ, FRANS EEMIL. 1888–1964 (NOBEL PRIZE 1939)

The son of a landless peasant, Sillanpää studied natural science at Helsinki University, but his interest soon shifted to writing. His first novel was published in 1916, and his second, *Meek Heritage*, in 1919, established him as the foremost Finnish writer—entitled to a lifetime pension from the government. His next book to receive international fame was *The Maid Silja*, a novel of the Finnish Civil War of 1918. In 1936 he was made an honorary doctor of philosophy by Finland's State University, and in 1939 received the

Nobel Prize for literature. *"People in the Summer Night,"* said *Choice,* "is written to a Finnish audience largely agrarian.... Sillanpää is good at capturing the smells, textures and colors of Finnish country life."

BOOKS BY SILLANPÄÄ

Meek Heritage. 1919. Eriksson 1972 $5.95
The Maid Silja. 1931. Trans. by Alexander Matson, Berg 1974 $15.95; Larlin 1984 $16.00
People in the Summer Night: An Epic Suite. 1934. Trans. by Alan Blair, intro. by Thomas Warburton, Univ. of Wisconsin Pr. 1966 $15.00

WALTARI, MIKA TOIMI. 1908–1979

The Egyptian, a great success in Europe, where it was translated into many languages, brought Waltari into prominence in other countries. Born in Helsinki, he went to Paris after receiving a university education. There he wrote his first published novel, which was a success. He returned to Helsinki in 1929 and continued to write—poems, plays, novels, and fairy tales. In 1936, he became editor of Finland's principal illustrated weekly, *Suomen Kuvalehti,* and his three-volume historical novel *From Father to Son* appeared the next year. It won the national Literary Prize and was filmed and translated into 14 languages. Unfortunately, none of his works is currently available in English.

BOOKS BY WALTARI

The Egyptian. 1949. Berkley 1978 o.p.
The Secret of the Kingdom. Putnam 1961 o.p.
Roman. Berkley pap. o.p.
The Etruscan. Berkley 1971 o.p.

OLD NORSE-ICELANDIC LITERATURE: SAGAS AND VERSE

In medieval times the island-nation of Iceland produced a body of literature that was unsurpassed in Europe in its quality, variety, and sheer quantity. Although the English use of the word "saga" suggests adventure and dramatic events, the Icelandic word "saga" is a general term for any fictional or nonfictional account. Icelandic narrative prose embraces several kinds of themes. *The Sagas of the Icelanders* tell of local events and personalities from the more recent historical past, although these sagas were not meant and should not be understood to be historically accurate in detail. *Njál's Saga* exemplifies this group, which is the one best represented in English translation. *The Sagas of Antiquity* deal with mythical-heroic figures (e.g., *Völsunga Saga* and *Hrolf's Saga Kraka*), while the *Sagas of the Knights* are the Scandinavian counterpart to the chivalric literature of medieval France and Germany (e.g., *The Saga of Tristram and Isönd*). The *Sagas of the Sturlings* deal with twelfth- and thirteenth-century Icelandic history. The descendants of Sturla Thórdarson, including Snorri Sturluson, played a decisive role in Icelandic politics in this period. *The Sagas of the Kings,* accounts of the lives of western Norse rulers, are best known through the translations of Snorri Sturluson's *Heimskringla.*

The anonymous Eddic lays, first written down in the thirteenth century, vary in content. Some relate directly to the heroic lays of the eastern and southern Germanic peoples (Goths, Burgundians, Franks); others, "songs of the gods," tell of Germanic religion; a third category is aphorisms. Skaldic verse, composed by individual poets from the ninth and fourteenth centuries, is a complex lyric genre, which relies on the poet's mastery of metaphor, meter, assonance, and alliteration. Skaldic poems typically recount the lives of famous men, loves past and present, and specific moments in the poet's life. The good *skald* (poet) was a respected craftsman in medieval Scandinavia, and skaldic verse is often quoted in the prose sagas.

Davidson, H. Ellis. *Gods and Myths of Northern Europe.* Gannon lib. bdg. $10.50; Penguin (Pelican) 1965 pap. $4.95

Hallberg, Peter. *The Icelandic Saga.* Trans. by Paul Schach, Univ. of Nebraska Pr. (Bison) 1962 pap. $2.35

———. *Old Icelandic Poetry: Eddic Lay and Skaldic Verse.* Trans. by Paul Schach and Sonja Lindgrenson, Univ. of Nebraska Pr. 1975 $17.95

Hermannsson, Halldór. *Bibliographical Notes on Icelandic and Old Norse Literature.* Kraus repr. of 1942 ed. $14.00. Hermannsson was author of numerous specialized bibliographies and studies of Old Norse-Icelandic literature. The originals appeared in the series *Islandica,* published by Cornell University Press; several have been reprinted by Kraus.

Hollander, Lee. *Old Norse Poems.* Kraus repr. of 1936 ed. $16.00

———. *Saga of the Jomsvikings.* Ayer repr. of 1955 ed. $12.00

———. *The Sagas of Kormák and the Sworn Brothers.* Kraus repr. of 1949 ed. 1972 o.p.

———. *The Skalds: A Selection of Their Poems with Introduction and Notes.* Univ. of Michigan Pr. 1968 o.p. Hollander was a master interpreter of this Old Norse poetic genre. This book will be of interest to all students of medieval poetry.

———. *Víga-Glúms Saga and the Story of Ögmund Dytt.* Amer.-Scandinavian Foundation $7.50

Ingstad, Helge. *Westward to Vinland.* Trans. by Erik J. Friis, St. Martin's 1969 $8.95. The fascinating story of the Norwegian archaeologist's search for the medieval Norse house sites on the Atlantic coast of North America.

Johnston, George, trans. *Saga of Gisli the Outlaw.* Intro. by Peter Foote, Univ. of Toronto Pr. 1963 pap. $8.95

Jones, Gwyn. *A History of the Vikings.* Oxford repr. of 1968 ed. 1984 pap. $9.95

———, ed. *Eirik the Red and Other Icelandic Sagas.* World Class. Pap. Ser. Oxford 1980 pap. $3.95

Kristjansson, Jonas. *Icelandic Sagas and Manuscripts.* Heinman rev. ed. 1980 $22.50

Magnusson, Magnus, trans. *Vikings.* Dutton 1980 $22.95; State Mutual Bk. 1980 $49.00

———. *Vinland Sagas: The Norse Discovery of America.* Trans. by Hermann Pálsson, *Penguin Class. Ser.* 1965 pap. $3.95

Pálsson, Hermann, and Paul Edwards, trans. *Gongu-Hrolf's Saga.* Univ. of Toronto Pr. 1981 $16.50

———. *Hrafnkel's Saga and Other Stories.* Penguin 1971 pap. o.p.

———. *Hrolf Gautreksson.* Univ. of Toronto Pr. 1971 $15.00

———. *The Orkneyinga Saga.* Merrimack 1978 $14.95; *Penguin Class. Ser.* 1981 pap.

$4.95. Written around 1200, "The Saga of the People of Orkney" recounts the history of the earls of Orkney and their relations with the rulers of Norway and Scotland from 900 to 1171.

Schach, Paul. *Icelandic Sagas*. Twayne's World Authors Ser. G. K. Hall 1984 lib. bdg. $18.95. Excellent survey and bibliography.

Simpson, Jacqueline. *The Viking World*. St. Martin's 1980 $14.95

French and German Chivalric Literature in Old Norse-Icelandic

Icelandic versions of chivalric themes have their origins in medieval French literature. To assign this medieval Scandinavian "literature in translation" to Iceland is somewhat arbitrary, for interest in French courtly culture was officially promoted by the Norwegian king Hákon Hákonarson, who reigned from 1217 to 1263 and saw political value in an emulation of French aristocratic ideals. Courtly literature, through its ideals of knighthood and kingship, reinforced the royal hierarchy of Norway. By way primarily of the western Norwegian cultural center of Bergen, English (Arthurian) and German (the *Nibelungen* theme) literature reached Norway-Iceland.

In 1226 King Hákon assigned to a certain "Brother Robert" the task of translating the *Roman de Tristan et Iseult* by the Anglo-Norman poet Thomas of Brittany. This translation is the earliest of the Norwegian-Icelandic *Sagas of the Knights*. Brother Robert's version of the French original is especially valuable as a complement to the now incomplete French *Tristan and Iseult* and the German version of Gottfried von Strassburg.

The Saga of Tristram and Isönd. Trans. by Paul Schach, Univ. of Nebraska Pr. (Bison) 1973 $14.95 pap. $3.95

Erex Saga and Ívens Saga: The Old Norse Versions of Chrétien De Troye's "Erec" and "Yvain." Trans. by Foster W. Blaisdell, Jr., and Marianne E. Kalinke, Univ. of Nebraska Pr. 1977 $10.95

EYRBYGGJA SAGA. 1230–1280

This "saga of the Icelanders" tells of the people of the farmstead Eyrr and their enemies. The story is told with great interest in local tradition and ancient customs, so the saga is especially valuable for students of early Scandinavian culture.

Eyrbyggja Saga. Trans. by Paul Schach and Lee M. Hollander, Univ. of Nebraska Pr. 1959 $12.95

GUNNARSSON, GUNNAR. 1889–1975

"In the forefront of Icelandic writers . . . who have . . . sought a wider public through the medium of a foreign tongue, stands the novelist Gunnar Gunnarsson. . . . Enormously productive, he is one of the most widely read writers in Scandinavia, and is known far beyond the borders of the northern countries" (Bach, *The History of Scandinavian Literatures*). Novelist, poet, and dramatist, Gunnarsson was prolific in all the creative literary fields, including the short story and historical novel. Like many other Icelandic writers, Gunnarsson spent a period in Copenhagen, returning to Iceland in 1939 and writing in both Danish and Icelandic. He is known as a brilliant interpreter of Icelandic life, particularly that of its humble people, and as a writer of subtle psychological novels of romantic theme. *The Black Cliffs* is one of these, having to do with the involvement of a young couple in a sensational murder case. *The History of the Family at Borg*, translated as *Guest the One-Eyed* (1912–14), and the autobiographical *The Church on the Mountain* (1924–28) are Gunnarsson's best-known works.

BOOK BY GUNNARSSON

The Black Cliffs. 1939. Trans. by Cecil Wood, intro. by Richard N. Ringler, Univ. of Wisconsin Pr. 1967 $17.50

THE KING'S MIRROR (SPECULUM REGALE). 13th century

This didactic work on courtly behavior belongs, strictly speaking, to Old Norwegian literature. Similar works are present in Old French and medieval English literature. Because it illuminates the social concepts illustrated by the Old Norse-Icelandic sagas in many instances, *The King's Mirror* is essential reading for the student of medieval Icelandic literature and for the student of medieval European history in general. In the form of a conversation between a farmer and a son, the relationships of the various social classes to one another and to God are discussed.

The King's Mirror. Trans. by Laurence M. Larson, *Lib. of Scandinavian Lit.* Amer.-Scandinavian Foundation $8.50; *Lib. of Scandinavian Lit.* Irvington 1917 lib. bdg. $7.50

LAXDAELA SAGA. c. 1250

This unforgettable family saga is "a tale of a love triangle with all its subterfuges, vicious insinuations, retaliations, and heartaches, presented with detachment and subtle discernment so typical of the sagas" (Margaret Arent). The story is not tightly knit, yet the numerous subplots do point to the broad design.

Laxdaela Saga. Trans. by Magnus Magnusson and Hermann Pálsson, *Penguin Class. Ser.* 1969 o.p.

LAXNESS, HALLDÓR KILJAN. 1902– (NOBEL PRIZE 1955)

When presenting the 1955 Nobel Prize to Laxness, the Swedish Academy of Letters cited "his vivid writing, which has renewed the Icelandic narrative art." *Independent People* was a bestseller in this country; *Paradise Reclaimed* (1960), based in part on Laxness's own experiences in the United States, is a novel about a nineteenth-century Icelandic farmer and his travels and experiences, culminating in his conversion to the Mormon church. Although Laxness has been by turns a Catholic convert, a Communist, and a target of the radical press, he has described himself as "one who loves the Russians but practices a lot of the American way of life." "Though Laxness came to believe that the novelist's best material is to be found in the proletariat, his rejection of middle-class concerns was never complete, and the ambiguity of his attitude toward the conflict of cultural values accounts for the mixture of humor and pathos that is characteristic of all his novels"

(*SR*). He owes much to the tradition of the sagas, and writes with understated restraint, concentrating almost entirely on external details—from which he extracts, by the manner of his telling, the utmost in absurdity. The *Atlantic* found that *The Fish Can Sing*, the adventures of a young man in 1900 who wants to be a singer, "simmers with an ironic, disrespectful mirth which gives unexpected dimensions to the themes of lost innocence and the nature of art."

BOOKS BY LAXNESS

Salka Valka. 1931–32. Trans. by F. H. Lyon, Allen & Unwin 1963 $8.95. A novel of Socialistic vision and love set in an Icelandic fishing village.
World Light. 1955. Trans. by Magnus Magnusson, Univ. of Wisconsin Pr. 1969 o.p.
The Atom Station. Second Chance repr. of 1948 ed. 1982 $16.95 pap. $8.95
Independent People: An Epic. Trans. by J. A. Thompson, Greenwood repr. of 1946 ed. 1976 lib. bdg. $37.50

BOOK ABOUT LAXNESS

Hallberg, Peter. *Halldór Laxness*. Trans. by Rory McTurk, *Twayne's World Authors Ser.* Irvington 1971 lib. bdg. $15.95; *Twayne's World Authors Ser.* G. K. Hall 1971 $13.00

NJÁL'S SAGA. c.1280

Njál's Saga may well be Iceland's most famous literary work of the Middle Ages. Written by an anonymous author—a situation typical of *Sagas of the Icelanders*—the saga tells of events in southern Iceland in the years 960–1015, the period in which Iceland was formally converted to Christianity. The nuances of characterization achieved by the author are unique in saga literature. The ethical views observed in the story are both heathen and Christian; the two philosophies conflict in a fateful drama. Note that the translation by Dasent is very old and extremely Victorian in style. The edition by Magnusson and Pálsson is superb and equipped with a fine introduction and notes.

The Story of Burnt Njál: From the Icelandic of the Njál's Saga. Trans. by George W. Dasent, Arden Lib. repr. of 1979 ed. lib. bdg. $12.50; Biblio Dist. (Everyman's) repr. of 1911 ed. 1971 $9.95 pap. $3.50
Njál's Saga. Trans. by Magnus Magnusson and Hermann Pálsson, *Penguin Class. Ser.* 1960 pap. $4.95

BOOKS ABOUT NJÁL'S SAGA

Lönnroth, Lars. *Njál's Saga: A Critical Approach*. Univ. of California Pr. 1976 $37.50
Sveinsson, Einar Ol. *Njál's Saga: A Literary Masterpiece*. Ed. by Paul Schach. Univ. of Nebraska Pr. 1971 $12.50. A very useful and important study from 1933.

THE POETIC EDDA. 12th or 13th century

A major source of insight into pagan Germanic religious concepts and cosmology, *The Poetic Edda* (also called *The Elder Edda*, in contrast to *The Prose Edda* of Snorri Sturluson) was written in the twelfth or thirteenth century. Thus it is the product of Christian times but nevertheless gives a glimpse of heathen thought. Serious students of Eddic verse will find it useful to consult all available translations of the original Old Icelandic text.

Norse Poems. Trans. by W. H. Auden and Paul Taylor, Humanities Pr. text ed. 1981 $16.75

The Poetic Edda. Trans. by Lee Hollander, Univ. of Texas Pr. 1962 o.p.

SIGURJÓNSSON, JÓHANN. 1880–1919

Sigurjónsson was one of the best of modern Icelandic dramatists. His recurrent theme was the tragedy inevitable in the lives of those whose passionate ambition drives them to exceed their limitations—the Greek sin of *hubris*. In *The Wish*, Loftur, a student, seeks power through the black art of sorcery, bringing misery to the girl who loves him and death to himself.

Sigurjónsson, scion of a wealthy family, was sent to Copenhagen University to become a veterinarian, but left it to write plays and was the first modern writer of Iceland to receive fame beyond its borders. *Eyvind of the Hills* (1911), first produced in Copenhagen, brought him his initial success and was later performed in Reykjavik and other Scandinavian cities. An early Swedish film was made from it. Sigurjónsson's approach to his characters was lyric and compassionate, but fate in his plays is inexorable.

BOOK BY SIGURJÓNSSON

The Wish (Loft's Wish). 1915. In *Fire and Ice: Three Icelandic Plays*. Ed. by Einar Haugen, Univ. of Wisconsin Pr. 1967 $20.00 pap. $6.00

STURLUNGA SAGA. c.1300

The thirteenth century in Iceland was one of great literary production, especially in the area of biographies of nobility and kings. Both individuals and events in the twelfth and thirteenth centuries contributed to the large collection of accounts entitled *Sturlunga Saga,* so named because of the prominence of the Sturlung family in Icelandic affairs. The heart of this work is formed by Sturla Thórdarson's account of the period 1200–1262, at which time Iceland lost its independence and came under the power of the king of Norway.

Sturlunga Saga. Trans. by Julia H. McGrew and George Thomas, *Lib. of Scandinavian Lit*. Irvington 2 vols. 1970–74 lib. bdg. ea. $40.00

STURLUSON, SNORRI. 1179–1241

Snorri Sturluson's fame as a historian—his main work is the 16 sagas included in *Heimskringla*, a monumental history of Norway from its beginning until 1177—lies both in his critical approach to sources and in his fine, realistic exposition of event and motivation. To this day *Heimskringla* is read with gusto all over Scandinavia, and Norwegians know it as the major source book of their nation's history. *The Prose Edda* by Snorri Sturluson was intended to be a handbook in skaldic poetry; it includes invaluable mythological tales that were on the verge of being forgotten even in Sturluson's time. Many expert Scandinavian medievalists (e.g., Sigurdur Nordal and Björn M. Olsen) have pointed to Sturluson as the author of the anonymous *Egil's Saga*. In spite of the lack of absolute proof, included here under Sturluson's name is this fascinating account of life in Norway, England, and Iceland of the poet-warrior whose skaldic verse is renowned for its unusual emotional and personal qualities. Snorri Sturluson's own life was as eventful as those about which he wrote. Returning to Iceland from exile in 1239, he again became deeply involved in serious power struggles and was murdered in 1241.

BOOKS BY STURLUSON

Egil's Saga. 1200–1230. Trans. by Hermann Pálsson and Paul Edwards, Penguin 1977 pap. $4.95

Heimskringla. Trans. by Samuel Laing, rev. by Jacqueline Simpson, Dutton (Everyman's) 2 vols. 1964 o.p. A "major sourcebook of early Norwegian history in a smooth translation" (*LJ*).

King Harald's Saga: Harald Hardradi of Norway. Trans. by Magnus Magnusson and Hermann Pálsson, Penguin 1976 pap. $3.95

The Prose Edda of Snorri Sturluson: Tales from Norse Mythology. Trans. by A. G. Brodeur, Amer.-Scandinavian Foundation 1916 $12.50; trans. by Jean I. Young, Univ. of California Pr. 1964 pap. $4.95

BOOK ABOUT STURLUSON

Ciklamini, Marlene. *Snorri Sturluson*. *Twayne's World Authors Ser*. G. K. Hall 1978 $16.95

THÓRDARSON, THORBERGUR. c.1889–1974

In Search of My Beloved, a novella by the Icelandic poet, essayist, and novelist Thorbergur Thórdarson, is part of a longer autobiographical novel, *An Iceland Aristocracy*, and "tells of a young poet travelling around Iceland in search of his [dream girl] whom he is too shy to approach. . . . Well written, with a touch of humor, and ably translated" (*LJ*). Thórdarson too was something of a drifter in his youth until he was given a place in the University of Iceland in 1913, where he began to find himself and grew interested in the language and folk culture of Iceland. He devoted himself to "word collecting" for awhile, which meant further wandering, but became interested in mysticism and the supernatural, as well as in social problems, all of which became elements in his work. His essays *A Letter to Laura* created a stir on publication and had an influence on Laxness. In later years he wrote chiefly novels.

BOOK BY THÓRDARSON

In Search of My Beloved. 1938. Trans. by Kenneth G. Chapman, intro. by Kristjan Karlsson, *Lib. of Scandinavian Lit*. Irvington 1967 lib. bdg. $4.75

VÖLSUNGA SAGA. 13th century

The Icelandic prose saga of the Volsungs tells of the ruin of their chief, Sigurd, by Gudrun, his wife. In this saga, Brynhild is the chief of the Valkyries, whom Sigurd had saved and loved. The same poetic materials were used in the German *Nibelungenlied*, where Sigurd became Siegfried, Gudrun is

Kriemhild, and Brynhild is Brunhild or Brünnehilde. Wagner used them in his opera cycle *The Ring of the Nibelungs*, Ibsen in *The Vikings at Helgeland*, and Hebbel in his dramatic trilogy *The Nibelungs*. William Morris made them known to English readers through his Lovers of Gudrun in *The Earthly Paradise* and *Sigurd the Volsung*. His own poetic adaptations do not measure up to his translation.

The Saga of the Volsungs. Trans. by George K. Anderson, Univ. of Delaware Pr. 1982 $29.50

The Saga of the Volsungs, The Saga of Ragnar Lodbrook, together with The Lay of Kraka. Trans. by Margaret Schlauch, AMS Pr. repr. of 1930 ed. $21.50

NORWEGIAN LITERATURE

Asbjörnsen, Peter C., and Jörgen Moe. *Norwegian Folk Tales*. Pantheon 1982 pap. $5.95. Norwegian fairy tales are best known in the form given them by the two nineteenth-century collectors Asbjörnsen and Moe.

Beyer, Harald. *A History of Norwegian Literature*. Trans. by Einar Haugen, Amer.-Scandinavian Foundation 1956 pap. $15.00

Christiansen, Reidar T., ed. *Folktales of Norway*. Trans. by Pat S. Iversen, Univ. of Chicago Pr. 1964 $12.00 pap. $7.95

Christiansen, Sigurd W. *Chaff before the Wind*. Greenwood repr. of 1925–29 ed. 1974 $17.50

———. *Two Living and One Dead*. Greenwood repr. of 1931 ed. 1975 $17.25. Novel depicting ethical and religious conflict in small-town Norway.

Sandemose, Aksel. *Werewolf*. 1958. Trans. by Gustaf Lannestock, intro. by Harald S. Naess, Univ. of Wisconsin Pr. 1966 pap. $6.00. The author's last novel, written in a surrealistic manner. Sandemose is a more important writer than this one translation would suggest. He is concerned with psychological conflict between individual and society. The werewolf symbolizes the spiritual repression that keeps the individual from happiness.

BJØRNEBOE, JENS. 1920–1976

When *The Least of These* appeared as Bjørneboe's second novel, the major critic and author Sigurd Hoel described it as "the most important novel since the war." It has enjoyed great popularity since then. With fine realism—typical of Bjørneboe—the novel describes the brutal treatment received by the little boy Jonas at the hands of teachers who are too stupid and indifferent to realize that the child has dyslexia.

An almost humorous interlude in Bjørneboe's career as a writer of verse, novels, and plays occurred in 1966, when a small publisher of pornography announced *Without a Stitch*, "by a well-known Norwegian author." The detailed and monotonous erotic performances of the heroine prompted the book's confiscation by police and its official condemnation as "indecent" by the courts, even though evidence presented at the trials proved that the official guardians of morality in Norway were very capricious in their treatment of erotic literature.

In contrast, the horrors of recent German history are brought together in the complicated novel *Moments of Freedom*, whose narrator is a bailiff in an Alpine city. The landmarks in this man's experience of life are the atrocities of the twentieth century, and he has consequently begun to write a 12-volume "history of bestiality." In form, the novel is something of a collage with philosophical, psychological, political, and mythological elements, to name a few; its black humor is that of modern history. One of the most important novels of the 1960s in Norway, *Moments of Freedom* was followed in 1969 by a sequel, *The Powder House*. Both suggest that cruelty is a congenital trait of humanity.

BOOKS BY BJØRNEBOE

The Least of These. 1955. Trans. by Bernt Jebsen and Douglas K. Stafford, Bobbs 1960 o.p.

Without a Stitch. 1966. Trans. by Walter Barthold, Grove 1969 o.p.

Moments of Freedom: The Heiligenberg Manuscript. 1966. Trans. by Esther Greenleaf Murer, Norton 1975 o.p.

HAMSUN, KNUT. 1859–1952 (NOBEL PRIZE 1920)

The writing of Knut Hamsun introduced into Norwegian literature a predominant concern with the immediate emotional life of the individual without reference to social programs or abstract "truths." The very title of Hamsun's first major work, *Hunger*, suggests its theme: the psychic ebb and flow of a brilliant young writer who actually starves but who is filled with spontaneity and emotional freedom, which brings both joy and misery. Hamsun sharply criticized naturalist writers for the gray superficial reality they described. He made it his goal, through art and psychology together, to illuminate the mysterious realities of the individual psyche, yet as a poetic philosopher Hamsun was clearly anti-intellectual.

Influences such as Strindberg, Nietzsche, and Georg Brandes were present in Hamsun's development, but his childhood in the intensely dramatic natural world of northern Norway did as much to create his basic mood. The shifting weather and rich colors of his early home were expressed anew in Hamsun's lyric and often ecstatic treatment of a wide range of fictional and yet psychologically credible personalities. Both *Pan* and *Victoria* are rich in the prose, poetry, eroticism, and pantheism that inspired Hamsun throughout his life. His almost mystical admiration for the spontaneous individual living close to nature led Hamsun to despise industrial society and to mythologize traditional rural Norwegian patriarchal families. He saw degeneracy—money grubbers and weak conformists—where others saw progressive industrialism. *Growth of the Soil*, for which Hamsun received the Nobel Prize in 1920, is his gospel of the simple life and by implication a beautiful attack on modern civilization. It is ironic that Hamsun's visionary and violent love of traditional country life coaxed him in the latter part of his life into a fateful intellectual sympathy with Nazi dogma. Although he was scorned and severely punished by his countrymen after World War II, Hamsun's contribution to world literature was great and beyond reproach.

BOOKS BY HAMSUN

The Cultural Life of Modern America. 1889. Trans. and ed. by Barbara C. Morgridge, Harvard Univ. Pr. 1969 $14.00. Hamsun's early views—rather casually documented but firmly espoused throughout his life—on U.S. life and society, based on his experience in the United States in the 1880s.

Hunger. 1890. Trans. by Robert Frye, intro. by Isaac Bashevis Singer, Avon 1975 pap. $2.25; Farrar 1967 pap. $6.95

Mysteries. 1892. Carroll & Graf 1984 pap. $8.95; trans. by Gerry Bothmer, Farrar 1971 $8.95

Pan: From Lieutenant Thomas Glahn's Papers. 1894. Trans. by James W. McFarlane, Farrar 1956 pap. $6.25

Victoria. 1898. Trans. by Oliver Stallybrass, Farrar repr. of 1969 ed. 1969 pap. $2.95

The Wanderer. 1906–09. Trans. by Oliver Stallybrass and Gunvor Stallybrass, Farrar 1975 pap. $3.95

Growth of the Soil. 1917. Trans. by W. W. Worster, Knopf 1953 $16.95; Random (Vintage) 1972 pap. $5.95

The Women at the Pump. 1920. Trans. by Gunvor Stallybrass, Farrar 1978 $10.00 pap. $4.95; Richard West repr. of 1928 ed. 1977 lib. bdg. $12.50

Wayfarers. 1927. Trans. by James W. McFarlane, Berkley 1985 pap. $4.95; Farrar 1980 pap. $10.95

HAUGE, ALFRED. 1915–

Religious problems viewed from a distinctly Christian point of view are the themes of this important writer's recent work, yet his fame in Scandinavia rests on the dramatic historical trilogy *Cleng Peerson*. These carefully researched and exciting novels are in the form of letters written by the poor farmer's son Cleng Peerson, who had become known as "the father of Norwegian emigration" in the early nineteenth century. The original Norwegian version was slightly abridged by the author for the English-language translation. Thanks to its general factual basis and realistic depiction of conditions in Norway and the United States, *Cleng Peerson* has quasi-documentary value as a comment on the making of U.S. society. Hauge has written some 30 other books, 4 in 1975 alone.

BOOK BY HAUGE

Cleng Peerson. 1961–65. Trans. by Erik J. Friis, G. K. Hall (Twayne) 2 vols. 1975 $25.00

IBSEN, HENRIK (JOHAN). 1828–1906

It has now been over a century since the appearance of Ibsen's *The Pillars of Society* (1877), the first of the "social plays" by the Norwegian who has had the most profound influence on the direction and techniques of modern stagecraft. The timelessness of the drama from this period—including *A Doll's House* (1879), *Ghosts* (1881), and *An Enemy of the People* (1882)—is attested to by the many Broadway, television, and repertory productions that pay perennial tribute to Ibsen's incisive characterizations of individuals in conflict. Conflict with self rather than social forces best describes the plays of the next period, 1884–1890: *The Wild Duck, Rosmersholm, The Lady from the Sea*, and *Hedda Gabler*. *A Doll's House* and *Hedda Gabler* present two equally acute views of the price and value of women's liberation. Ibsen clearly did not offer simplistic programs for social groups but rather wrote about unique individuals. Ibsen's last plays, in the years 1892–1899, *The Master Builder*, *Little Eyolf*, *John Gabriel Borkman*, and *When We Dead Awaken*, generally concern the self-destructive aspects of artistic ambition. The symbolism in these plays makes them more demanding and less well known today, as is Ibsen's early work (including *Brand*, 1866, and *Peer Gynt*, 1867), reflecting romantic and nationalistic preoccupations. Nevertheless, Ibsen's genius inspires modern producers to stage *Peer Gynt*, a technical venture that Ibsen himself may never have intended for his dramatic poem.

The reader's needs may serve as a guide when the wealth of Ibsen editions is surveyed. The library and the professional student of modern drama will turn to James W. McFarlane's edition, *The Oxford Ibsen*. Currency of language is very important for an appreciation of Ibsen's major plays, and in recent years the efforts of Una Ellis-Fermor, Rolf Fjelde, Eva Le Gallienne, Michael Meyer, and Peter Watts have provided good translations of the essential plays. In discussing the drama of Ibsen, Eva Le Gallienne is also able to draw from her distinguished career in the theater, both as actress and manager.

F. L. Lucas's treatment of Ibsen, *The Drama of Ibsen and Strindberg*, is still out of print. On the positive side, there is now the translation by Einar Haugen and A. E. Santaniello of the second, revised edition of Halvdan Koht's *Life of Ibsen*. Koht's biography is the most authoritative, but in the United States more publicity has been given to Michael Meyer's *Ibsen, A Biography* (o.p.). The virtue of Meyer's biography is the vast amount of information brought together from other sources, including Koht, yet he does not advance new insights.

Books by Ibsen

The Oxford Ibsen. Ed. by James W. McFarlane, Oxford 8 vols. vols. 1, 2, 5, and 6 (1960–70) o.p. vol. 3 (1962) $25.95 vol. 4 (1963) $32.50 vol. 7 (1966) $36.95 vol. 8 (1971) pap. $9.95

Correspondence of Henrik Ibsen. Ed. by Mary Morrison, Haskell repr. of 1905 ed. 1970 lib. bdg. $49.95

Speeches and New Letters. Haskell repr. of 1910 ed. 1972 lib. bdg. $39.95

Plays. Methuen 4 vols. 1981 pap. ea. $3.95

Eight Plays. Trans. by Eva Le Gallienne, *Modern Lib. College Ed. Ser.* Random rev. ed. text ed. 1982 pap. $4.95. Includes *A Doll's House*, *An Enemy of the People*, *Rosmersholm*, *Hedda Gabler*, *The Master Builder*, *The Wild Duck*, and *The Lady from the Sea*.

Seven Famous Plays. Trans. and ed. by William Archer, Biblio Dist. 1961 $12.95

Four Great Plays. Trans. by Sharp R. Farquharson, intro. by John Gassner, *Bantam Class. Ser.* 1981 pap. $2.50. Contains *A Doll's House*, *An Enemy of the People*, *The Lady from the Sea*, and *John Gabriel Borkman*.

Four Major Plays. Trans. by Rolf Fjelde, New Amer. Lib. (Signet Class.) 2 vols. 1965–70 pap. ea. $2.25–$2.50

Four Major Plays: A Doll's House, Ghosts, Hedda Gabler, The Master Builder. Trans. by James W. McFarlane and Jens Arup, *World's Class. Ser.* Oxford 1981 pap. $4.95

Brand. Trans. by Michael Meyer, Biblio Dist. (Everyman's) 1961 $5.00; Methuen 1967 pap. $6.95

A Doll's House and Other Plays. Trans. by Peter Watts, *Penguin Class. Ser.* 1965 pap. $2.95. Includes *League of Youth* and *The Lady from the Sea.*

Ghosts and Other Plays. Trans. by Peter Watts, *Penguin Class. Ser.* 1964 pap. $3.50. Includes *Public Enemy* and *When We Dead Awaken.*

Hedda Gabler and Other Plays. Trans. by Una Ellis-Fermor, *Penguin Class. Ser.* 1951 pap. $3.50. Includes *Pillars of the Community* and *The Wild Duck.*

The Master Builder and Other Plays. Trans. by Una Ellis-Fermor, *Penguin Class. Ser.* 1959 pap. $3.95. Includes *Rosmersholm, Little Eyolf,* and *John Gabriel Borkman.*

Peer Gynt. Trans. by Sharp R. Farquharson, Biblio Dist. (Everyman's) 1956 $8.95; trans. and ed. by Kai Jurgensen and Robert Schenkkan, *Crofts Class. Ser.* Harlan Davidson 1966 pap. $1.25; trans. by David Rudkin, Methuen 1983 pap. $4.95; ed. by James W. McFarlane, Oxford 1970 pap. $2.25; trans. by Peter Watts, *Penguin Class. Ser.* 1966 pap. $3.50

BOOKS ABOUT IBSEN

Brandes, Georg. *Henrik Ibsen.* Ayer repr. of 1899 ed. $14.00. A discussion of the style and themes, with emphasis on social dramas, by the Danish scholar-critic, a contemporary of Ibsen.

Bull, Francis. *Ibsen: The Man and the Dramatist.* Folcroft 1973 lib. bdg. $8.50

Downs, Brian W. *Ibsen: The Intellectual Background.* Octagon Repr. of 1946 ed. 1969 lib. bdg. $17.00

———. *A Study of Six Plays by Ibsen.* Octagon repr. of 1950 ed. 1972 lib. bdg. $18.50

Firkins, Ina T. *Henrik Ibsen: A Bibliography of Criticism and Biography, with an Index to Characters.* Folcroft 1973 lib. bdg. $10.00

Haugen, Einar. *Ibsen's Drama: Author to Audience.* Univ. of Minnesota Pr. 1979 $15.00 pap. $7.95

Johnston, Brian. *The Ibsen Cycle.* G. K. Hall (Twayne) 1975 lib. bdg. $17.50

Koht, Halvdan. *Life of Ibsen.* Ed. and trans. by Einar Haugen and A. E. Santaniello, Ayer repr. of 1971 ed. $33.00

McFarlane, James W. *Ibsen and the Temper of Norwegian Literature.* Octagon repr. of 1960 ed. 1979 lib. bdg. $18.50

Northam, John. *Ibsen: A Critical Study.* Cambridge Univ. Pr. 1973 $44.50 pap. $14.95

Weigand, Hermann J. *The Modern Ibsen: A Reconsideration. Select Bibliographies Repr. Ser.* Ayer repr. of 1953 ed. $24.50

RÖLVAAG, OLE EDVART. 1876–1931

Norwegian-born Rölvaag emigrated to the United States at age 20 in 1896. Following a college education in Minnesota and Norway, he began the teaching (at St. Olaf College, Minnesota) and writing career that was to bring him fame as an interpreter of the Norwegian-American cultural experience. Rölvaag's understanding of immigrant life on the prairie was the source of novels that have given his name a solid place in both Norwegian and American literature. His first, highly autobiographical work, *The Third Life of Per Smevik,* was published under the pseudonym Paal Morck. Rölvaag's major work, *Giants in the Earth,* is a translation of the first two of four novels dealing with the family of Per Hansa; *Peder Victorious* and *Their*

Fathers' God complete the epic, although these two novels are considered less compelling. A new Norwegian edition of the tetralogy was published in 1975 by the Norwegian Book Club. The fascinating novels of Rölvaag, Alfred Hauge, and Vilhelm Moberg bear witness to the fact that emigration to the United States was a major phenomenon in Scandinavian history.

BOOKS BY RÖLVAAG

When the Wind Is in the South and Other Stories. Trans. by Solveig Zempel, Augustana College 1985 $12.95

The Third Life of Per Smevik. 1912. Trans. by Ella Valborg Tweet and Solveig Zempel, Dillon 1971 $5.95

The Boat of Longing: A Novel. 1921. Trans. by Nora O. Solum, Greenwood repr. of 1933 ed. 1974 lib. bdg. $27.50

Giants in the Earth. 1925. Trans. by Ole Edvart Rölvaag and Lincoln Colcord, Darby repr. 1980 lib. bdg. $20.00; Harper 1965 pap. $3.37

Peder Victorious: A Tale of the Pioneers Twenty Years Later. 1928. Trans. by Nora O. Solum, Darby 1979 lib. bdg. $25.00; trans. by Nora O. Solum, intro. by Gudrun H. Gvale, Univ. of Nebraska Pr. (Bison) repr. of 1929 ed. 1982 pap. $7.50

Pure Gold. Trans. by Sivert Erdahl, Greenwood repr. of 1930 ed. 1973 lib. bdg. $27.00

Their Fathers' God. Trans. by Trygve M. Ager, Greenwood repr. of 1931 ed. 1974 lib. bdg. $27.50; trans. by Trygve M. Ager, Univ. of Nebraska Pr. (Bison) repr. of 1931 ed. 1983 pap. $7.95

BOOK ABOUT RÖLVAAG

Reigstad, Paul. *Rölvaag: His Life and Art.* Univ. of Nebraska Pr. 1972 $13.95

SANDEL, CORA (pseud. of Sara Fabricius). 1880–1974

Alberta Alone, a Norwegian classic, is an autobiographical trilogy (*Alberta and Jacob, Alberta and Freedom,* and *Just Alberta*) in the tradition of Sigrid Undset. Cora Sandel described with insight and honesty the coming to maturity of a small-town Norwegian girl in a "magnificent work of introspection" (*LJ*). "If the book has a fault, it is in being a little too unhurried in its wanderings. Miss Sandel is a stylist, a writer of marvelous delicacy; and the standard trouble with beautiful writers is that not enough happens in their books. Alberta merely exists in Norway, only begins to live in Paris, has a child by a painter, tries sometimes to write. Nothing more. *Alberta Alone* is not one of the very great novels . . . but it is one of those that make you remember certain things you thought you had forgotten. To read it is, in part, to relive the painful experience of growing human" (*SR*). Sandel wrote other novels as well as short stories. Her insight into the psyches of women and artists was especially acute and justly praised.

BOOKS BY SANDEL

Alberta and Jacob. 1926. Trans. by Elizabeth Rokkan, intro. by Linda Hunt, Ohio Univ. Pr. repr. of 1965 ed. 1984 $15.95 pap. $7.95

Alberta and Freedom. 1931. Trans. by Elizabeth Rokkan, intro. by Linda Hunt, Ohio Univ. Pr. repr. of 1965 ed. 1984 $15.95 pap. $7.95

Alberta Alone. 1939. Trans. by Elizabeth Rokkan, intro. by Linda Hunt, Ohio Univ. Pr. repr. of 1965 ed. 1984 $15.95 pap. $7.95

STIGEN, TERJE. 1922–

Stigen, a gifted storyteller influenced by Knut Hamsun, is able to create a narrative climate where reality and fantasy intermingle. In his novels he frequently returns to northern Norway with its powerful and mysterious beauty. In *An Interrupted Passage,* three men and a woman in a fishing boat pass the time in storytelling; their secret thoughts are revealed and their common fate seen. In several works Stigen has dealt realistically with historical themes.

Book by Stigen

An Interrupted Passage. 1956. Trans. by Amanda Langemo, *Lib. of Scandinavian Lit.* Irvington 1974 lib. bdg. $7.00

UNDSET, SIGRID. 1882–1949 (Nobel Prize 1928)

Sigrid Undset is the daughter of archaeologist Ingvald Undset. Her comprehensive knowledge of medieval Scandinavian culture has its literary monuments in *Kristin Lavransdatter* (1920–22) and *The Master of Hestviken* (1925–27), historical novels that depict both the concrete and psychological dimensions of life in the Norwegian Middle Ages. In Norway, Undset's first fiction is categorized according to the time of action: medieval or modern. *Jenny,* an idealistic and tragic love story, is one of the latter novels. Norwegian criticism of Sigrid Undset's writing centers on her religiosity—she became a conservative, almost reactionary Catholic in Lutheran Norway in the 1920s—an intensity of belief rather naturally expressed in the medieval novels. On the polemic side, she wrote works of primarily religious moment. Yet the medieval novels are not polemic. In fact, the central motifs are eroticism, marriage, and family life, in short, the full life of a medieval woman who sees herself in the light of contemporary Christian beliefs. These novels are great, realistic delineations of medieval personalities. Cultural, autobiographical, and religious topics constitute a large and interesting portion of Undset's writing. *Longest Years* and *Stages on the Road* are autobiographical, while *Men, Women and Places* is a collection of essays. *Happy Times in Norway,* also autobiographical, was written in the United States during World War II, when Sigrid Undset escaped the German occupation of Norway.

Books by Undset

Jenny. 1911. Trans. by W. Emme, Fertig 1975 o.p.
Kristin Lavransdatter. Trans. by C. Archer and J. S. Scott, Knopf 1935 $25.00
The Master of Hestviken. 1925–27. Trans. by A. G. Chater, Knopf 4 vols. in 1 1934 $15.00; New Amer. Lib. 1978 pap. $11.95
Stages on the Road. 1933. Trans. by A. G. Chater, *Essay Index Repr. Ser.* Ayer repr. of 1934 ed. $16.50
Longest Years. 1934. Trans. by A. G. Chater, Kraus repr. of 1935 ed. $22.00

Men, Women and Places. 1938. Trans. by A. G. Chater, *Essay Index Repr. Ser.* Ayer
    repr. of 1939 ed. $20.00
Happy Times in Norway. 1942. Trans. by Joran Birkeland, Greenwood repr. of 1942
    ed. 1979 lib. bdg. $27.50
Four Stories. Trans. by Naomi Walford, Greenwood repr. of 1969 ed. 1978 lib. bdg.
    $22.50

BOOKS ABOUT UNDSET

Bayerschmidt, Carl F. *Sigrid Undset. Twayne's World Authors Ser.* 1970 o.p.
Winsnes, Andreas H. *Sigrid Undset: A Study in Christian Realism.* Trans. by P. G.
    Foote, Greenwood repr. of 1953 ed. lib. bdg. $18.75

VESAAS, TARJEI. 1897–1970

By 1934, when *The Great Cycle* appeared, Tarjei Vesaas had published 11
works. In this novel he clearly showed the enduring qualities of his later
work: delicate human portraiture, compelling symbolism and allegory, and
constant sensitivity to universal problems (hope, fear, love) of the human being both alone and in society. By the end of his life Vesaas had written some
35 works of prose and poetry and had received the Venice Triennale Prize in
1952 and the Nordic Council Prize for literature in 1964. Perhaps the foremost writer of novels and short stories of his generation in Norway, he
wrote of common people in rural Norway who represented humanity at its
best and worst. His realism is psychological rather than historical, as in *The
Seed*, which deals with the hatred, fear, and mass psychosis spawned in a
small community by the murder of a girl. It is apparent that the barbarous
acts of the killer's lynchers mirror the hideous transformation of decent people in Fascist Europe of the late 1930s. Children and adolescents occupy a
special place in Vesaas's writing; in both *The Spring Night* and *The Birds* the
reader participates in the inner life of youth observing the adult world. As
for Vesaas's poetry, published rather late in his career, it "has contributed
significantly to the liberation of Norwegian poetry from conventional patterns. His form is modern and international, free from the musical regularity of the popular ballad, and . . . his themes are mostly the things which
gladden his inland heart—the mountain, the snow, and the trees" (Harald
Naess).

BOOKS BY VESAAS

The Great Cycle. 1934. Trans. by Elizabeth Rokkan, intro. by Harald Naess, Univ. of
    Wisconsin Pr. 1967 o.p.
The Seed and The Spring Night. 1940. 1954. Trans. by Kenneth Chapman, Amer.-Scan-
    dinavian Foundation $8.95
Land of Hidden Fires. 1953. Trans. by Fritz Konig and Jerry Crisp, Wayne State
    Univ. Pr. 1973 $9.95
The Birds. 1957. Trans. by Torbjorn Stoverud and Michael Barnes, Morrow 1972
    pap. $2.25
Bridges. 1966. Trans. by Elizabeth Rokkan, Morrow 1970 o.p.
The Boat in the Evening. 1968. Trans. by Elizabeth Rokkan, Morrow 1972 $5.95

Book about Vesaas

Chapman, Kenneth C. *Tarjei Vesaas. Twayne's World Authors Ser.* Irvington 1970 lib. bdg. $15.95

SWEDISH LITERATURE

Almqvist, C. J. *Sara Videbeck and The Chapel.* Trans. by Adolph B. Benson, *Lib. of Scandinavian Lit.* Amer.-Scandinavian Foundation 1972 $6.95. Classical short novels, depicting Swedish folk life, from the older narrative tradition.

Axelsson, Sun. *A Dreamed Life.* Trans. by Ulla Printz-Påhlson, Ohio Univ. Pr. $16.95 pap. $8.95

Bly, Robert, ed. *Friends, You Drank Some Darkness: Three Swedish Poets, Martinson, Ekelöf and Transtromer.* Beacon 1975 pap. $5.95

Enqvist, Per Olov. *The Night of the Tribades: A Play from 1889.* Trans. by Ross Shideler, Hill & Wang 1977 $9.95

Gullberg, Hjalmer. *Gentleman, Single, Refined and Selected Poems, 1937–1959: Poems.* Trans. by Judith Moffett, Louisiana State Univ. Pr. text ed. 1979 $13.95

Gustafson, Alrik. *A History of Swedish Literature.* Univ. of Minnesota Pr. 1961 $25.00. An extensive survey that includes a detailed critical bibliographic guide and list of Swedish literature in translation as of 1961.

Harding, Gunnar, ed. *Modern Swedish Poetry in Translation.* Ed. by Hollo Anselm, intro. by Robert Bly. Univ. of Minnesota Pr. 1979 $15.00 text ed. pap. $7.95

Lundkvist, Artur. *Agadir.* Trans. by William Jay Smith and Leif Sjöberg, Ohio Univ. Pr. 1979 $12.95 pap. $7.95. Author of more than 60 books, Lundkvist is a poet, literary critic, and translator of non-Scandinavian literatures. The poem *Agadir* describes the earthquake that destroyed the Moroccan city in 1960.

Matthias, John, and Göran Printz-Påhlson, trans. *Contemporary Swedish Poetry.* Ohio Univ. Pr. (Swallow) 1980 $18.95 pap. $9.95

Ostergren, Jan. *Rainmaker.* Trans. by John Matthias and Göran Printz-Påhlson, Ohio Univ. Pr. 1983 $13.95 pap. $7.95

Sonnevi, Göran. *The Economy Spinning Faster and Faster.* Ed. by Robert Bly, Sun 1982 $20.00

BENGTSSON, FRANS GUNNAR. 1894–1954

This "gentleman scholar with remarkable sensitive and highly developed literary talents" was best known in his country as an informal essayist in the great English tradition of Lamb and Hazlitt. He was also a lyric poet, biographer, translator, and historical novelist. His prose was "a marvelously virile, precise and flexible medium of expression for a vigorous, many-faceted, and astonishingly learned mind" (*Columbia Dictionary of Modern European Lit.*). *The Long Ships* is his novel of the tenth-century Vikings. "Under the merriment and the fighting there is a great deal of scholarship as sound as it is imperceptible. Reading this marvelously good-humored ale-broth of a book you say: this is how it must have been to be a Viking chief a thousand years ago" (*N.Y. Times*). *The Sword Does Not Jest* (1935, o.p.) is a "biography of the great Swedish military leader Charles XII." "The picture is as rich in detail as Brueghel, and we are thus given not only the tragic story of a great man sur-

rounded by mental midgets and clever foes but the story of his times as well"
(*SR*).

BOOK BY BENGTSSON

The Long Ships: A Saga of the Viking Age. 1941. Trans. by Michael Meyer, Knopf 1954
    o.p.

BERGMAN, INGMAR. 1918–

[SEE Volume 3, Chapter 13.]

BOYE, KARIN. 1900–1941

Karin Boye's poetry and prose from the 1920s and 1930s express her intense search for an understanding of herself in an essentially absurd world.
Turning from the emotionally charged intensity of her youth, Boye never
overcame serious periods of depression when she later tried to find coherence through a radical Marxist and psychoanalytic view of man's nature.
Loneliness and guilt contended with her love of life and belief in religious
truth in her later expressionistic poetry. *Kallocain*, Boye's most important
work of prose, reflects her travels in totalitarian Germany and the Soviet
Union. A society is described in which all human activity is harnessed to
serve the state, and complete enslavement of the individual is assured by
the drug Kallocain. The drug forces one to reveal all thoughts. In this novel,
which is comparable, in some respects, to Franz Kafka's work and to Aldous
Huxley's *Brave New World*, the sanctity of the human spirit is threatened to
the utmost by the Fascist collective state. Boye took her own life in 1941.

BOOK BY BOYE

Kallocain. 1940. Trans. by Gustaf Lannestock, intro. by Richard B. Vowles, Univ. of
    Wisconsin Pr. repr. of 1940 ed. 1966 $17.50

EKELÖF, GUNNAR. 1907–1968

"Ekelöf is a poet of surprising stature, one of the masters of modern poetry, yet little known in America" (*LJ*). Few writers of his eminence are
more difficult to characterize, for the poetry that began to appear in 1932
was Ekelöf's extremely personal and evolving investigation of human consciousness and culture. For Ekelöf, a twentieth-century mystic, all things,
people, and ideas formed a complex interdependent unity; the past was in
the present and reality for the poet was the changing visions he might find
in himself. In their introduction to selections of Ekelöf's work before 1965,
Rukeyser and Sjöberg provide fascinating glimpses of a poet whose love of
nature and music joined with profound loneliness in inimitably lyric poetry. The strength and genuineness of his often bleak voice won him immense popularity in Sweden as well as almost all the literary awards a
Scandinavian poet may receive. The second selection, made by W. H. Auden
and Sjöberg, is taken from two of Ekelöf's last volumes: *Diwan over the
Prince of Emgión* (1965) and *The Tale of Fatuhmeh* (1966). Here Ekelöf ex-
pertly drew from the medieval Greek and Middle Eastern literature and

spirit to create a mystical and visionary search, through and while suffering, for essential human experience.

BOOKS BY EKELÖF

Selected Poems of Gunnar Ekelöf. Trans. by Muriel Rukeyser and Leif Sjöberg, *Lib. of Scandinavian Lit.* Irvington 1971 lib. bdg. $19.50

Selected Poems by Gunnar Ekelöf. Trans. by W. H. Auden and Leif Sjöberg, intro. by Göran Printz-Påhlson, Pantheon 1972 o.p.

Selected Poems. Trans. by Leonard Nahan and James Larson, Princeton Univ. Pr. 1982 $8.95

Guide to the Underworld. Trans. by Rika Lesser, Univ. of Massachusetts Pr. 1980 $10.00

I Do Best Alone at Night. Trans. by Robert Bly, Charioteer 1977 $7.50

BOOK ABOUT EKELÖF

Sjöberg, Leif. *A Reader's Guide to Gunnar Ekelöf's "A Molna Elegy."* Twayne 1973 o.p.
An essential guide for students of Ekelöf.

GUSTAFSSON, LARS. 1936–

Gustafsson's philosophical and linguistic training are central to his work as he probes, in carefully constructed prose, the nature of knowledge and relationships.

BOOKS BY GUSTAFSSON

The Death of a Beekeeper. Trans. by Guntram H. Weber, New Directions 1981 $12.95 pap. $5.95

The Tennis Players. Trans. by Yvonne L. Sandstroem, New Directions 1983 $13.00 pap. $6.25

JOHNSON, EYVIND (OLOF VERNER). 1900–1976 (NOBEL PRIZE 1974)

The Days of His Grace is one of three powerful historical novels Eyvind Johnson wrote between 1949 and 1964. In this book the reader has access to a small but important fraction of a literary career that began in 1924. Johnson combined urgent concern for the psychology of the individual with an interest in historical development; he always was a politically engaged writer. *The Days of His Grace* is set in the empire of Charlemagne; young Italians in their longing for personal and national freedom are overwhelmed by the superior, ruthless force of the totalitarian machine instituted by Charlemagne. Irony, understatement, appropriate variations in language, style, and sound research in the historical background of the period make this a fine novel whose message, however, is timeless.

BOOK BY JOHNSON

The Days of His Grace. 1960. Vanguard 1970 o.p.

BOOK ABOUT JOHNSON

Orton, Gavin. *Eyvind Johnson. Twayne's World Authors Ser.* G. K. Hall lib. bdg. $16.95

LAGERKVIST, PÄR (FABIAN). 1891–1974 (Nobel Prize 1951)

In 1913 Pär Lagerkvist described his goals as a writer: to achieve classical simplicity and dignity as seen in the models of Homer, classical tragedy, the Old Testament, and the Icelandic saga. In the following 60 years Lagerkvist realized his early goal in dramas and prose of great beauty and terrible immediacy. Man the eternal questioner, man the victim and victimizer, man the pilgrim whose baggage is anxiety and uncertainty, these are just a few of the chords struck by Lagerkvist in his internationally recognized work. What was said of *The Holy Land* is true of all of Lagerkvist's work: " 'The Holy Land' rejects all needless words, compels toward a hidden momentous goal, disturbs with cruel symbols, satisfies with symbols. People and things are symbols yet clear to sight and clearly relevant to man" (*Choice*). For many readers, Lagerkvist's most compelling personification is that of *The Dwarf*, who is the evil that lives in all men. There are no easy answers to the questions Lagerkvist posed. His uncertainty concerning the nature of God was expressed in *The Sibyl*, a mystical work that found a particularly enthusiastic audience in the United States.

Books by Lagerkvist

Modern Theatre: Seven Plays and an Essay. Trans. by Thomas R. Buckman, Univ. of Nebraska Pr. 1966 $23.95

The Eternal Smile. Trans. by Erik Mesterton and David O'Gorman, Hill & Wang 1971 pap. $5.95

The Man Who Lived His Life Over. 1928. Trans. by Walter Gustafson, intro. by Henry W. Wells, Twayne 1971 o.p.

The Dwarf. 1944. Trans. by Alexandra Dick, Hill & Wang, 1958 pap. $6.95

Barabbas. 1950. Trans. by Alan Blair, Random (Vintage) o.p.

Evening Land: Aftonland. 1953. Trans. by W. H. Auden and Leif Sjöberg, Wayne State Univ. Pr. 1975 $12.95

The Sibyl. 1956. Trans. by Naomi Walford, Random (Vintage) 1963 pap. $2.95

The Holy Land. 1964. Trans. by Naomi Walford, Random (Vintage) 1982 pap. $2.95. The last of five novels begun in 1950 with *Barabbas*, about the significance of Christ's crucifixion. Each novel is a response to a theme, and each must be viewed in relation to the others.

The Marriage Feast. Trans. by Alan Blair and Carl E. Linden, Hill & Wang 1973 $6.95

Pilgrim at Sea. Random (Vintage) 1982 pap. $2.95

Books about Lagerkvist

Sjöberg, Leif. *Pär Lagerkvist*. Columbia Univ. Pr. 1976 pap. $2.50

Spector, Robert D. *Pär Lagerkvist*. *Twayne's World Authors Ser*. G. K. Hall 1973 lib. bdg. $13.95

White, Ray L. *Pär Lagerkvist in America*. Humanities Pr. text ed. 1980 pap. $19.75

LAGERLÖF, SELMA (OTTILIANA LOVISA). 1858–1940
(Nobel Prize 1909)

Selma Lagerlöf, winner of the Nobel Prize in 1909, was the first woman to be elected a member of the Swedish Academy. Her first novel, *The Story of Gösta Berling* (1891, o.p.), assured her position as Sweden's greatest storyteller. She retold the folktales of her native province, Värmland, in an original and poetic prose. She wrote steadily, but her work was uneven in quality. It "tended to be unashamedly subjective, its characters are moved by impulse and by inner vision, [and] its style often favors rhetorical effects" (Walter Gustafson). *The Wonderful Adventures of Nils* is a delightful fantasy for children. Her charming autobiography, *Marbacka*, is a trilogy. Her correspondence with the Nobel prizewinner Nelly Sachs, whom she assisted and encouraged, will not be released until 1990.

Books by Lagerlöf

From a Swedish Homestead. 1899. Trans. by Jessie Brochner, *Short Story Index Repr. Ser.* Ayer repr. of 1901 ed. $22.00

Jerusalem. 1901. Trans. by Jessie Brochner, Greenwood repr. of 1903 ed. lib. bdg. $22.50

The Wonderful Adventures of Nils. 1913. Pantheon 1947 o.p.

Marbacka. 1922. Trans. by Velma S. Howard, Gale repr. of 1926 ed. 1974 $34.00

Memories of My Childhood: Further Years at Marbacka. 1930. Trans. by Velma S. Howard, Kraus repr. of 1934 ed. 1975 $17.00

The Diary of Selma Lagerlöf. Trans. by Hanna A. Larsen, Kraus repr. of 1936 ed. 1975 o.p.

Book about Lagerlöf

Edström, Vivi. *Selma Lagerlöf. Twayne's World Authors Ser.* G. K. Hall 1984 lib. bdg. $19.95

MOBERG, (CARL ARTUR) VILHELM. 1898–1973

The Emigrants and *Unto a Good Land* provide the first volumes of Moberg's internationally famous tetralogy describing the lives of Swedish emigrants in the nineteenth century. *The Last Letter Home* completes this psychologically penetrating and historically accurate treatment of Swedish settlement in Chisago County, Minnesota. Moberg's strident individualism and enduring empathy with the common man are also seen in *A Time on Earth*, in which the old Swedish-American Albert Carlson assesses his life as death approaches. In Scandinavia, Moberg is famous as a historian and dramatist as well as novelist. His *History of the Swedish People*, of which two volumes were completed when he died in 1973, depicts in characteristically virile language the life of the common people—in sharp contrast to kings and nobility—throughout Sweden's history. One regrets that relatively few of Moberg's some 80 works are currently available to the English-language reader.

Books by Moberg

The Emigrants. 1949. Trans. by Gustaf Lannestock, Warner Bks. 1983 pap. $3.95

Unto a Good Land. 1952. Trans. by Gustaf Lannestock, Warner Bks. 1983 pap. $3.95

The Last Letter Home. 1959. Trans. by Gustaf Lannestock, Warner Bks. 1983 pap. $3.95

A Time on Earth. 1963. Trans. by Naomi Walford, Warner Bks. 1984 pap. $3.50

A History of the Swedish People: From Odin to Engelbrecht. Trans. by Paul Britten Aus-
    tin, Pantheon 2 vols. 1972–74 ea. $6.95
The Settlers. Trans. by Gustaf Lannestock, Warner Bks. 1983 pap. $3.95

BOOK ABOUT MOBERG

Holmes, Philip. *Vilhelm Moberg. Twayne's World Authors Ser.* G. K. Hall 1980 lib.
    bdg. $16.95

STRINDBERG, (JOHAN) AUGUST. 1849–1912

Strindberg was Sweden's greatest dramatist. His pessimism and his fero-
cious hatred of women have won for him the title "the Swedish Schopen-
hauer." "He was an extremely productive writer in many fields; poet, journalist, social critic, historical and 'regional' novelist as well as dramatist
(not to mention his painting); but the Strindberg with whom the world is
mainly concerned is the writer of a dozen or so plays" (Alan Harris). *The Father* (1887), *Miss Julie* (1888), *Creditors* (1888), and *Comrades* contain his severest arraignment of women. He was three times married and three times
divorced, and his woman-hating plays reflect many of his own marital difficulties. In 1967 Britain's National Theater starred its director, Sir Laurence
Olivier, in *The Dance of Death* (1901), another naturalistic play involving
the duel of the sexes. His "stark portrayal of a schizoid, aging Swedish
Army Captain fighting to sustain his ferocity and arrogance with animal disregard for other people was a superb and mysterious creation" (Henry
Hewes, *SR*).

Not all of his work was cynical, however. *Lucky Per* (1912, o.p.), an allegorical play in five acts, is said to have greatly influenced Maeterlinck's *The
Blue Bird. Swanwhite* (1901) is a fairy drama for children, and *The Dream
Play* (1901) is a delicate fantasy. He was a master of the one-act play. *To Damascus* (1898–1904), in which he "abandoned traditional dramatic techniques in order to dramatize his own inferno of soul in his search for religious certainty," has been called the first expressionistic drama, and his
plays in this vein have influenced the plays of O'Neill and other moderns.
Brooks Atkinson, writing about the *Scapegoat* (o.p.) in the *N.Y. Times*,
pointed out that what Strindberg contributed to modern drama was his understanding "that human motives are complex"—he created "individuals"—
and the craftsmanship of virtuoso. "Strindberg," Atkinson concluded, "led a
tragic life. It was squalid, quarrelsome, vindictive and irrational. But those
baleful eyes . . . saw many things that other writers did not see, or evaded
as being in bad taste. 'For my part,' he said, 'I find the joy of life in the hard
and cruel battles of life—and to be able to add to my store of knowledge, to
learn something, is enjoyable to me.' He made that valiant remark in 1888.
It provides a sound prologue to the existentialism of today."

Fascination with the genius of August Strindberg has not slackened since
his death. His enormous influence, along with that of Ibsen, on European
and world literature can hardly be exaggerated. In general, however, English-language readers are perhaps less familiar with Strindberg's autobiographical writing and novels. Strindberg is here no less an entrancing

master of language and alarming self-revelation than in the dozen or so expressionistic plays so frequently cited and produced. In fact, the novel *The Natives of Hemsö* is one of Strindberg's most popular works in Scandinavia, where it has had numerous stage and television dramatizations.

The excellent translations by Walter G. Johnson (*The Washington Strindberg*) will be the standard English-language edition for years to come. The introductions provide a wealth of information, interpretation, and bibliography for further study.

BOOKS BY STRINDBERG

A Dream Play and Four Chamber Plays. Trans. by Walter G. Johnson, *Norton Lib.* repr. of 1973 ed. 1975 pap. $7.95; Univ. of Washington Pr. 1973 $22.00

Pre-Inferno Plays. Trans. and ed. by Walter G. Johnson, *Norton Lib.* 1976 pap. $6.96

Apologia and Two Folk Plays: The Crownbride and Swanwhite. Trans. by Walter G. Johnson, Univ. of Washington Pr. 1981 $25.00

Plays from the Cynical Life. Trans. by Walter G. Johnson, Univ. of Washington Pr. 1983 $25.00

Plays of Confession and Therapy: To Damascus I, To Damascus II, and To Damascus III. Trans. by Walter G. Johnson, Univ. of Washington Pr. 1979 $25.00

Days of Loneliness. Trans. by Arvid Paulson, Irvington text ed. 1971 pap. $9.95

The Dance of Death. Trans. by Arvid Paulson, intro. by Daniel Seltzer, Norton 1976 $7.95 pap. $5.95

World Historical Plays. Trans. by Arvid Paulson, intro. by Gunnar Ollén. *Lib. of Scandinavian Lit.* Amer.-Scandinavian Foundation 1970 $8.50. Includes *The Nightingale of Wittenberg, Through Deserts to Ancestral Lands, Hellas,* and *The Lamb and the Beast;* the main characters are Luther, Moses, Socrates, and Christ.

Six Plays of Strindberg. Trans. by Elizabeth Sprigge, Doubleday (Anchor) 1955 pap. $5.50

Strindberg: Five Plays. Trans. by Harry G. Carlson, New Amer. Lib. (Signet Class.) 1984 pap. $3.95; trans. by Harry G. Carlson, Univ. of California Pr. 1983 $20.00 pap. $8.95

The Chamber Plays. Trans. by Evert Sprinchorn, Seabury Quinn, Jr., and Kenneth Peterson, Univ. of Minnesota Pr. 2d ed. rev. 1981 $15.00 pap. $6.95

In Midsummer Days: And Other Tales. Trans. by Ellie Schleussner, *Short Story Index Repr. Ser.* Ayer repr. of 1913 ed. $18.00

Historical Miniatures. Trans. by Claude Field. *Short Story Index Repr. Ser.* Ayer repr. of 1913 ed. $21.00

Zones of the Spirit. Haskell 1974 lib. bdg. $53.95

Inferno: From an Occult Diary. Trans. by Mary Sandbach, *Penguin Class. Ser.* 1979 pap. $6.95

The Red Room. 1879. Trans. by Elizabeth Sprigge, Biblio Dist. (Everyman's) 1967 $5.00

The Natives of Hemsö. 1889. Trans. by Arvid Paulson, Amer.-Scandinavian Foundation 1965 $6.95; trans. by Arvid Paulson, Liveright 1973 pap. $2.95

A Madman's Defense. 1895. Intro. by Evert Sprinchorn, Peter Smith $11.25; intro. by B. G. Madsen, Univ. of Alabama Pr. 1971 $16.50

Legends: Autobiographical Sketches. 1898. Haskell repr. of 1912 ed. 1972 lib. bdg. $42.95

Fair Haven and Foul Strand. 1902. Haskell repr. of 1914 ed. 1972 lib. bdg. $42.95

The Son of a Servant: The Story of the Evolution of a Human Being, 1849–1867. Intro. by Evert Sprinchorn, Peter Smith $11.25. Autobiographical novel.

BOOKS ABOUT STRINDBERG

Blackwell, Marilyn J., ed. *Structures of Influence: A Comparative Approach to August Strindberg.* Univ. of North Carolina Pr. 1982 $26.00

Carlson, Harry G. *Strindberg and the Poetry of Myth.* Univ. of California Pr. 1982 $23.50

Dahlström, Carl E. *Strindberg's Dramatic Expressionism.* Ayer repr. of 1930 ed. $26.50. The authoritative treatment of Strindberg's post-Inferno, expressionist plays.

Johannesson, Eric O. *The Novels of August Strindberg: A Study in Theme and Structure.* Univ. of California Pr. 1968 $33.00

——. *Strindberg and the Historical Drama.* Univ. of Washington Pr. 1963 $20.00

Lamm, Martin. *August Strindberg.* Ed. by Harry G. Carlson, Ayer repr. of 1971 ed. $25.00. The essential biography of Strindberg.

Ollén, Gunnar. *August Strindberg. Life and Lit. Ser.* Ungar 1984 pap. $7.95

Reinert, Otto, ed. *Strindberg: A Collection of Critical Essays.* Prentice-Hall (Spectrum) 1971 pap. $1.95

Steene, Birgitta. *Greatest Fire: A Study of August Strindberg. Crosscurrents Modern Critiques Ser.* Southern Illinois Univ. Pr. 1973 $6.95

SWEDENBORG, EMANUEL. 1688–1772

[SEE Volume 4.]

TRANSTRÖMER, TOMAS. 1931–

Tranströmer, an occupational psychologist by profession, has regularly published his influential poetry since 1954. His poetic language—admirably reconstructed in the English translations currently available—is the syntax of normal prose bearing strong, often symbolic imagery from a world the reader recognizes as his own as well as the poet's. Basically simple images are wonderfully charged with the power to describe human perceptions of nature and of self.

BOOKS BY TRANSTRÖMER

Windows and Stones: Selected Poems. Trans. by May Swenson and Leif Sjöberg, Univ. of Pittsburgh Pr. 1972 $14.95

Baltics. Oyez 1975 $5.00 pap. $2.50

Truth Barriers: Poems by Tomas Transtömer. Trans. by Robert Bly, Sierra 1980 $9.95 pap. $5.95

Tomas Transtömer: Selected Poems. Trans. by Robin Fulton, Ardis 1981 $15.00 pap. $7.00

CHAPTER 15

Russian Literature

Henryk Baran

> "Paul!" called the Countess from behind the screen. "Send me a new novel,
> will you, but please not the kind they write nowadays."
> "What do you mean, *grand'maman?*"
> "I mean a novel in which the hero does not strangle either his mother or
> his father, and which describes no drowned bodies. I am terribly scared of
> drowned bodies."
> "There are no such novels these days. Would you perhaps like some Rus-
> sian ones?"
> "You don't mean to say there are Russian novels? . . . Send some to me,
> my dear, send some by all means!"
> —ALEXANDER PUSHKIN, *The Queen of Spades*

One of the great world literatures in the modern era, Russian literature began by following in the cultural footsteps of Byzantium after the conversion
to Christianity in the tenth century. In the medieval period, there was little
that would be considered "literary" in a modern sense of the word. The principal genres were religious (saints' lives) and historical (chronicles). The
greatest achievement of medieval Russian literature, the unusual and complex *Tale of Igor's Campaign,* came toward the end of the twelfth century.

Medieval genres continued to flourish long after the West entered the era
of the Renaissance. By the mid-sixteenth century, Moscow celebrated its status in a series of monumental literary compilations. The sheer size, ornamental style, and self-assurance of these works mirrored the insular, conservative world view of the Muscovite state.

A decisive shift came with the reforms of Peter the Great in the early
1700s. Under the impact of Western European languages, the lexicon of Russian was significantly enlarged. There was a fundamental change in poetry.
Mikhail Lomonosov and others established a syllabotonic system of versification as the basis for most later Russian verse. The high poetic genres—the
ode, the tragedy, the epic poem—dominated; Lomonosov and Gavriil
Derzhavin emerged as the two outstanding poets of the eighteenth century.

In the early nineteenth century, the sharply accelerated transmission of
foreign developments led to a remarkable coexistence of literary schools
and world views. Classicism was still present, romanticism made its appearance, and realism was beginning its development. A Golden Age of poetry—
Pushkin was its greatest figure—held sway into the 1840s, when prose

emerged. The literary scene was dominated by writers who made Russian fiction a major force within European literature as a whole: Gogol, Dostoevsky, Tolstoy, Turgenev, and others. The Russia they depicted was sufficiently familiar to Western readers to be understandable, yet sufficiently different to be exotic and fascinating—a combination that has proved enduringly attractive for readers around the world.

The nineteenth century saw the establishment of a tradition that still sharply differentiates Russian literature from its Western counterparts. In a society in which normal means of political expression are not available, literature and its creators become vehicles for voicing society's most urgent conditions.

Poetry again came to the fore in the 1890s. Although important realistic fiction continued to appear, the reading public slowly turned to symbolism—a movement that tried to use art as a bridge to the transcendent. Such symbolist masters as Sologub, Bely, and Blok brought a new poetic Golden Age. In the late 1900s they were joined by members of new poetic groups. There was a renewal of poetic language—new rhythms were added, the boundaries of the lexicon were enlarged, and new forms of composition were discovered.

In the twentieth century, political events have had a major impact on the development of Russian literature. The Bolshevik takeover in October 1917 and the subsequent civil war led to the death or emigration of many literary figures. As a consequence, an émigré literature flourished until World War II in Germany, France, and several other countries.

Initially, the Communist party adopted a generally neutral attitude; still, by the 1920s patterns of political control over literature began to emerge. The First Congress of the Union of Soviet Writers (1934) proclaimed socialist realism as the accepted mode of Soviet literature. Through alternating periods of political relaxation ("thaws") and tightening, this doctrine, which requires a writer to portray Soviet life in an optimistic light, has remained the dominant form of politically orthodox literature in the Soviet Union.

To this day, literature continues to be affected by shifting political currents. During the 1960s and 1970s, a number of writers were involved in the movement for human rights and in the emigration movement. Prevented from publishing some (or all) of their works, writers released them in *samizdat* (the practice of copying and circulating privately published texts not approved by the authorities) or published them in the West without official sanction. Involvement in activities condemned by the state brought retribution for many writers. Punishment has varied, ranging from trials and imprisonment to exile. The presence of so many talented writers and poets in the West has revitalized Russian literature in emigration.

The best of recent Russian literature has sought to escape the shackles of ideology—to deal honestly with the burdens of the country's past and its current social and political problems. At the same time, it has striven to experiment with new fictional forms, to express often unpalatable truths through the fantastic and the grotesque.

HISTORY AND CRITICISM

Alexandrova, Vera. *History of Soviet Literature*. Trans. by Mirra Ginsburg, Greenwood repr. of 1963 ed. 1971 lib. bdg. $37.50. From Gorky to Yevtushenko, with an epilogue on Solzhenitsyn's *One Day in the Life of Ivan Denisovich*.

Andrew, Joe. *Russian Writers and Society in the Second Half of the Nineteenth Century*. Humanities Pr. 1982 $40.00. Introduction to Turgenev, Dostoevsky, Tolstoy, and Chekhov.

——. *Writers and Society during the Rise of Russian Realism*. Humanities Pr. 1980 $28.00

Auty, R., and Dimitri Obolensky, eds. *Companion to Russian Studies: An Introduction to Russian Language and Literature*. Cambridge Univ. Pr. 1981 pap. $18.95

Avins, Carol. *Border Crossings: The West and Russian Identity in Soviet Literature*. Univ. of California Pr. 1983 $28.00

Berlin, Isaiah. *Russian Thinkers*. Ed. by Henry Hardy and Aileen Kelly, Penguin 1979 pap. $5.95. Seven essays by a leading figure in the study of Russian intellectual history and literature. Portraits of Herzen, Belinsky, Turgenev, and Tolstoy. Includes classic comparison of Tolstoy and Dostoevsky.

Berry, Thomas E. *Plots and Characters in Major Russian Fictions*. Shoe String 2 vols. 1977–78 $20.00–$21.50

Brown, Deming. *Soviet Russian Literature since Stalin*. Cambridge Univ. Pr. 1978 $42.50 pap. $10.95

Brown, Edward J. *Major Soviet Writers: Essays in Criticism*. Oxford new ed. 1973 pap. $8.95. A fine critical anthology.

——. *Russian Literature since the Revolution*. Harvard Univ. Pr. rev. & enl. ed. 1982 $25.00 pap. $9.95. Best survey of Soviet literature; fundamental reference tool.

Brown, William E. *A History of Eighteenth-Century Russian Literature*. Ardis 1980 $29.50 pap. $15.00

——. *A History of Russian Literature of the Romantic Period*. Ardis 4 vols. 1985 $150

——. *A History of Seventeenth-Century Russian Literature*. Ardis 1980 $20.00 pap. $10.00

Chyzhevskyi, Dmytro. *A History of Russian Literature from the Eleventh Century to the End of the Baroque*. Hyperion Pr. repr. of 1960 ed. 1981 $38.50. Very detailed; best reference tool on medieval literature.

Cizevskij, Dmitrij. *A History of Nineteenth-Century Russian Literature*. Trans. by Richard N. Porter, ed. by Serge A. Zenkovsky, Vanderbilt Univ. Pr. 2 vols. 1974 ea. $7.95. An excellent history.

Clark, Katerina. *The Soviet Novel: History as Ritual*. Univ. of Chicago Pr. 1981 $20.00. Provocative analysis.

Debreczeny, Paul, and Jesse Zeldin, eds. *Literature and National Identity: Nineteenth-Century Russian Critical Essays*. Univ. of Nebraska Pr. 1970 $16.95

Dunham, Vera. *In Stalin's Time: Middle-Class Values in Soviet Fiction*. Cambridge Univ. Pr. 1976 $42.50 pap. $12.95. Sociologically based study of orthodox Soviet literature.

Eikhenbaum, Boris, and Ray Parrott, eds. *Russian Prose*. Ardis 1985 $22.50 pap. $7.50. Essays by formalist critics of the 1920s on early nineteenth-century prose.

Erlich, Victor, ed. *Twentieth-Century Russian Literary Criticism*. Yale Univ. Pr. 1975 o.p. Very important articles included.

Ermolaev, Herman. *Soviet Literature Theories 1917–1934: The Genesis of Socialist Realism*. Octagon repr. of 1963 ed. 1977 $20.00

Fennell, John, ed. *Nineteenth-Century Russian Literature: Studies of Ten Russian Writ-*

ers. Univ. of California Pr. 1976 $37.00. Uneven, but with a great deal of useful information and provocative discussion.

France, Peter. *Poets of Modern Russia. Cambridge Studies in Russian Lit.* 1983 $37.50 pap. $12.95

Freeborn, Richard. *The Russian Revolutionary Novel: Turgenev to Pasternak.* Cambridge Univ. Pr. 1982 $49.50

Gudzii, Nikolai K. *History of Early Russian Literature.* Octagon repr. 1970 $52.00. Standard Soviet textbook on the medieval period; dull but very thorough.

Gumilev, N. *On Russian Poetry.* Ardis 1977 $15.00 pap. $5.00

Hayward, Max. *Writers in Russia, 1917–1978.* Ed. by Patricia Blake, Harcourt 1983 $22.95. Stimulating essays by a leading critic and translator.

Hingley, Ronald. *Nightingale Fever: Russian Poets in Revolution.* Knopf 1981 $16.50

Hosking, Geoffrey. *Beyond Socialist Realism: Soviet Fiction since Ivan Denisovich.* Holmes & Meier 1980 $29.75

Janecek, Gerald. *The Look of Russian Literature: Avant-Garde Visual Experiments, 1900–1930.* Princeton Univ. Pr. 1984 $47.50

Lavrin, Janko. *From Pushkin to Mayakovsky: A Study in the Evolution of a Literature.* Greenwood repr. of 1948 ed. 1971 lib. bdg. $27.50

Lewanski, Richard C., comp. *The Slavic Literatures.* Vol. 2 in *The Literatures of the World in English Translation.* Ungar 1967 $50.00

Maguire, Robert A. *Red Virgin Soil: Soviet Literature in the Late 1920's.* Princeton Univ. Pr. 1967 $40.00

Mathewson, Rufus W., Jr. *The Positive Hero in Russian Literature.* Stanford Univ. Pr. 2d ed. 1975 $27.50 pap. $8.95

Matich, Olga, and Michael Heim, eds. *The Third Wave: Russian Literature in Emigration.* Ardis 1984 $25.00 pap. $13.50. Proceedings of symposium of émigré writers, Western journalists, and scholars.

Matlaw, Ralph, ed. *Belinsky, Chernyshevsky, and Dobrolyubov: Selected Criticism.* Indiana Univ. Pr. 1976 $12.50 pap. $5.95. Selections from the most influential nineteenth-century Russian critics.

Mersereau, John. *Russian Romantic Fiction.* Ardis 1983 $29.50 pap. $10.00

Mirsky, D. S. *Contemporary Russian Literature, 1881–1925.* Kraus repr. of 1926 ed. $22.00. Superb survey; still unequaled by any other in English.

——. *History of Russian Literature from Its Beginnings to 1900.* Ed. by Francis J. Whitfield, Random 1958 pap. $3.95. Best available one-volume history of pre-twentieth-century Russian literature: accurate, insightful, readable. Contains abridged versions of Mirsky's *History of Russian Literature* and *Contemporary Russian Literature.*

The Modern Encyclopedia of Russian and Soviet Literature (Including Emigré and Non-Russian Literatures). Ed. by Harry B. Weber, Academic International Pr. 6 vols. 1977–to date ea. $32.50

Nabokov, Vladimir. *Lectures on Russian Literature.* Ed. by Fredson Bowers, Harcourt 1981 $19.95 1982 pap. $8.95

Nakhimovsky, Alexander D., and Alice Stone Nakhimovsky, eds. and trans. *The Semiotics of Russian Cultural History: Essays by Iurii M. Lotman, Lidiia Ia. Ginsburg, and Boris A. Uspenskii.* Cornell Univ. Pr. 1984 $29.95 pap. $9.95. Leading scholars explore intersections of history, literature, and biography.

Pomorska, Krystyna. *Russian Formalist Theory and Its Poetic Ambience.* Mouton text ed. 1968 $18.00. An examination of the relationship between futurism and formalist criticism.

Proffer, Carl R., comp. *Nineteenth-Century Russian Literature in English: A Bibliogra-*

phy of Criticism and Translations. Ardis 1985 $39.50. Covers general topics and 65 individual writers; through 1983.

Rabinowitz, Stanley, ed. and trans. *The Noise of Change: Russian Literature and the Critics (1891–1917).* Ardis 1985 $25.00 pap. $9.50. Critical responses in a time of literary transition.

Rzhevsky, Nicholas. *Russian Literature and Ideology: Herzen, Dostoevsky, Leontiev, Tolstoy, and Fadeyev.* Univ. of Illinois Pr. 1983 $18.95. Important treatment of a major topic.

Segel, Harold B. *Twentieth-Century Russian Dramas from Gorky to the Present.* Columbia Univ. Pr. 1979 $40.00 pap. $18.00

Seyffert, Peter. *Soviet Literary Structuralism: Background, Debate, Issues.* Slavica 1985 pap. $17.95

Shneidman, N. N. *Soviet Literature in the Nineteen Seventies: Artistic Diversity and Ideological Conformity.* Univ. of Toronto Pr. 1979 $22.50

Shukman, Ann, ed. *The Semiotics of Russian Culture. Michigan Slavic Contributions* pap. $15.00. Analysis of Russian literature and culture; particularly interesting on premodern period.

Slonim, Marc. *Soviet Russian Literature: Writers and Problems, 1917–1977.* Oxford 2d ed. 1977 $25.00 pap. $10.95

Smith, Gerald Stanton. *Songs to Seven Strings: Russian Guitar Poetry and Soviet "Mass Songs."* Indiana Univ. Pr. 1984 $22.50. Explores a major segment of unofficial literature and culture.

Sokol, Elena. *Russian Poetry for Children.* Univ. of Tennessee Pr. 1984 $24.95

Struve, Gleb. *Russian Literature under Lenin and Stalin, 1917–1953.* Univ. of Oklahoma Pr. 1971 o.p. Most authoritative English-language discussion of this period.

Terras, Victor. *Belinskij and Russian Literary Criticism: The Heritage of Organic Aesthetics.* Univ. of Wisconsin Pr. 1974 $37.50

Terras, Victor, ed. *Handbook of Russian Literature.* Yale Univ. Pr. 1985 $35.00. Best reference work in English. Up-to-date entries by many scholars; bibliographies.

Todd, William M., ed. *Literature and Society in Imperial Russia, 1800–1914.* Stanford Univ. Pr. 1978 $25.00. Important studies.

Trotsky, Leon. *Literature and Revolution.* Univ. of Michigan Pr. 1960 pap. $7.95

Woll, Josephine, and Vladimir Treml. *Soviet Dissident Literature: A Critical Guide.* G. K. Hall 1983 $26.50

COLLECTIONS

Aksyonov, Vassily, and others. *Metropol: A Literary Almanac.* Norton 1983 $24.95. Unauthorized writings from the late 1970s.

Alexander, Alex. *Russian Folklore: An Anthology in English Translation.* Nordland 1974 $25.00 pap. $12.00

Bowra, Cecil M., ed. *A Book of Russian Verse.* Greenwood repr. of 1943 ed. 1971 lib. bdg. $15.00

Brown, Clarence, ed. *The Portable Twentieth-Century Russian Reader.* Penguin 1985 pap. $7.95. Eclectic choices reflect the breadth of twentieth-century Russian literary experience: Zamiatin, Akhmatova, Mandelstam, Pasternak, and others. New translation of Olesha's *Envy.*

Chadwick, Nora, ed. and trans. *Russian Heroic Poetry.* Russell repr. of 1932 ed. 1964 $12.50. Selection of folk epics.

Cooper, Joshua, ed. and trans. *Four Russian Plays*. Penguin 1972 pap. $5.95. Contains Fonvizin, *The Minor;* Griboedov, *Woe from Wit;* Gogol, *The Inspector-General;* Ostrovsky, *Thunder.*

Dobson, Rosemary, and David Campbell, eds. and trans. *Seven Russian Poets: Imitations*. Univ. of Queensland Pr. 1980 $9.95

Fetzer, Leland, ed. and trans. *An Anthology of Pre-Revolutionary Russian Science Fiction (Seven Utopias and a Dream)*. Ardis 1982 $35.00 pap. $6.00. Works from the nineteenth to the early twentieth centuries.

Ginsburg, Mirra. *Last Door to Aiya: A Selection of the Best New Science Fiction from the Soviet Union*. Phillips 1969 $10.95

Glad, John, and Daniel Weissbort, eds. *Russian Poetry: The Modern Period*. Iowa Translations Ser. 1978 $25.00 pap. $12.50. Good selections.

Green, M., ed. and trans. *The Russian Symbolist Theater: An Anthology of Plays and Critical Texts*. Ardis 1985 $37.50 pap. $13.95. Works by nine critics and playwrights.

Guerney, Bernard G., ed. *A Treasury of Russian Literature*. Vanguard repr. of 1943 ed. $17.50

Karlinsky, Simon, and Alfred Appel, Jr. *The Bitter Air of Exile: Russian Writers in the West, 1922–1972*. Univ. of California Pr. rev. ed. 1977 pap $6.95. Important, less known segment of modern Russian literature.

Luker, Nicholas, ed. and trans. *An Anthology of Russian Neo-Realism: The "Znanie" School of Maxim Gorky*. Ardis 1982 $30.00 pap. $7.50. Works by Andreev, Bunin, Kuprin, Artsybashev, and Gorky.

Maddock, Mary, trans. *Three Russian Women Poets*. Intro. by Edward J. Brown, Crossing Pr. 1983 $16.95 pap. $6.95. Akhmatova, Tsvetaeva, Akhmadulina.

Markov, Vladimir, and Merrill Sparks, eds. and trans. *Modern Russian Poetry: An Anthology*. Bobbs bilingual ed. 1967 o.p. Extremely comprehensive, well-chosen.

Morrison, R. H., ed. and trans. *America's Russian Poets*. Ardis 1975 pap. $2.50

Obolensky, Dimitri, ed. *The Heritage of Russian Verse*. Indiana Univ. Pr. repr. of 1962 ed. bilingual ed. 1976 $25.00 pap. $12.50

Pachmuss, Temira, ed. and trans. *A Russian Cultural Revival: A Critical Anthology of Russian Emigré Literature before 1939*. Univ. of Tennessee Pr. 1981 $29.50 pap. $11.95

Peterson, R. E., ed. and trans. *The Russian Symbolists: An Anthology of Critical and Theoretical Writings*. Ardis 1985 $25.00

Proffer, Carl R., ed. *From Karamzin to Bunin: An Anthology of Russian Short Stories*. Indiana Univ. Pr. 1969 pap. $7.95

———. *Russian Romantic Prose: An Anthology*. Translation Pr. 1979 $17.50

Proffer, Carl R., and Ellendea Proffer, eds. *The Ardis Anthology of Russian Futurism*. Ardis 1980 $22.50

———. *The Barsukov Triangle, The Two-Toned Blond and Other Stories*. Ardis 1984 $29.50 pap. $10.50. Works by contemporary writers: Abramov, Maramzin, Okudzhava, Rasputin, and others.

———. *Contemporary Russian Prose: An Anthology*. Ardis 1982 $30.00 pap. $9.95. Includes Trifonov, *The Exchange;* Sokolov, *A School for Fools;* Aksyonov, *The Steel Bird.*

———. *The Twenties: An Anthology*. Ardis 1984 $37.50 pap. $15.00. Prose, poetry, drama, essays, and manifestos.

Pushkin, Alexander. *The Bakhchesarian Fountain and Other Poems by Various Authors*. Trans. by William Lewis, Ardis repr. of 1849 ed. 1985 $19.50. First edition of Pushkin in English. Includes lyric poems by other figures.

Raffel, Burton, ed. *Russian Poetry under the Tsars: An Anthology*. State Univ. of New York Pr. 1971 $19.00

Reavey, George, ed. and trans. *The New Russian Poets*. Scribner bilingual ed. 1981 pap. $9.95

Reavey, George, and Marc Slonim, eds. and trans. *Soviet Literature*. Greenwood repr. of 1934 ed. 1972 lib. bdg. $18.00

Reeve, F. D., ed. and trans. *Contemporary Russian Drama (Recent Russian Plays)*. Irvington 1968 $29.00. Includes Rozov, *Alive Forever;* Pogodin, *Petrarchan Sonnet;* Shvartz, *Naked King;* Panova, *It's Been Ages;* Zorkin, *Warsaw Melody*.

——. *Nineteenth-Century Russian Plays (An Anthology of Russian Plays)*. Norton 1973 pap. $8.95

Richards, David, ed. *The Penguin Book of Russian Short Stories*. Penguin 1981 pap. $4.95. Twenty major writers, from Pushkin to Nabokov and Solzhenitsyn.

Rydel, Christine, ed. *The Ardis Anthology of Russian Romanticism*. Ardis 1984 $42.50 pap. $9.50. Broad, comprehensive selection of poems, prose, and criticism from 1810 to 1840.

Segel, Harold, comp. *The Literature of Eighteenth-Century Russia*. Dutton 2 vols. 1967 o.p. Comprehensive; ample annotations—standard textbook.

Wiener, Leo. *Anthology of Russian Literature*. Gordon repr. 1976 $150.00

Yarmolinsky, Avrahm, ed. *Treasury of Russian Verse*. *Granger Index Repr. Ser.* Ayer repr. of 1949 ed. $21.00

Zenkovsky, Serge A., ed. and trans. *Medieval Russia's Epics, Chronicles, and Tales*. Dutton rev. & enl. ed. 1974 pap. $6.50. An extremely rich anthology of medieval texts (eleventh through seventeenth centuries).

AITMATOV, CHINGIZ. 1928–

Aitmatov has become well known for his Russian-language prose describing the life of his own Kirghiz people. Although he is a member of the Communist party, his works do not follow the narrow canons of socialist realism. With depth and sensitivity, Aitmatov presents the Kirghiz in the throes of societal change, deals very broadly with ethical problems, and takes up topics that are generally avoided in official Soviet literature.

BOOKS BY AITMATOV

Tales of the Mountains and the Steppes. Imported Pubns. 1973 $6.95

(and Kaltai Mukhamedzhanov). *The Ascent of Mount Fuji*. 1975. Farrar 1975 pap. $4.95

The Day Lasts More Than a Hundred Years. 1981. Trans. by John French, Indiana Univ. Pr. 1983 $17.50

Cranes Fly Early. Imported Pubns. 1983 pap. $4.95

AKHMATOVA, ANNA. 1889–1966

Akhmatova began as a creator of simple, yet psychologically deep, lyrics with which she achieved an extraordinary popularity. Together with her first husband, Nikolay Gumilev, she formed part of the Acmeist group, which sought to bring poetry down to earth from its previous Symbolist heights. During the Stalin years, she was almost totally barred from literature; her son, a historian, was arrested and imprisoned several times. In

1946, together with Mikhail Zoshchenko, Akhmatova became the target of a public campaign of vilification led by Zhdanov, then culture "boss" and a close associate of Stalin. Her work began to be published again in the 1960s, and a number of important editions appeared in the 1970s, signaling the poet's acceptance by the literary establishment. Shortly before her death, Akhmatova was awarded the Taormina Prize for poetry in Italy, and an honorary doctorate from Oxford.

Akhmatova has emerged as one of the major figures of twentieth-century Russian poetry. Her themes range from a woman's intimate feelings to the nature of poetic creation and broad issues of Russia's history. In addition to individual lyric poems, she produced two major masterpieces: *Requiem*, a cycle of poems on the suffering of Stalinist terror in the 1930s, and *Poem without a Hero*, a complex, highly allusive narrative on Russian literature and culture.

BOOKS BY AKHMATOVA

You Will Hear Thunder, Akhmatova: Poems. Trans. by D. M. Thomas, Ohio Univ. Pr. 1985 $22.00 pap. $11.00. Includes *Requiem* and *Poem without a Hero*. Selections from each of her major periods; appeared earlier in two separate collections.

Requiem and Poem without a Hero. Trans. by D. M. Thomas, Ohio Univ. Pr. 1976 $10.00 pap. $5.50

Way of All the Earth. Trans. by D. M. Thomas, Ohio Univ. Pr. 1980 $11.95 pap. $6.95

Poems. Trans. by Lyn Coffin, intro. by Joseph Brodsky, Norton 1983 pap. $5.95. Restrained, faithful translations.

Selected Poems. Trans. by Walter Arndt, Robin Kemball, and Carl R. Proffer, Ardis 1976 pap. $6.95

BOOKS ABOUT AKHMATOVA

Haight, Amanda. *Anna Akhmatova: A Poetic Pilgrimage.* Oxford 1976 $18.95. A good biography; fair discussion of the poetry.

Leiter, Sharon. *Akhmatova's Petersburg.* Univ. of Pennsylvania Pr. 1983 $20.00

AKSAKOV, SERGEI. 1791–1859

A close friend of Gogol, Aksakov came from the old landholding nobility. His family background became the subject for a series of reminiscences written late in life. Their objective and precise description of provincial life, their insight and honesty about human psychology, as well as their event-filled contents, have made them enduring classics of nineteenth-century prose.

BOOKS BY AKSAKOV

Memoirs of the Aksakov Family. Trans. by J. D. Duff, Hyperion Pr. 3 vols. repr. of 1917 ed. 1977 ea. $15.00–15.50 pap. ea. $10.00. The three volumes correspond to the three Oxford titles below.

A Russian Gentleman. Trans. by J. D. Duff, ed. by Edward Crankshaw, *World's Class.-Pap. Ser.* Oxford 1982 pap. $6.95

Years of Childhood. Trans. by J. D. Duff, intro. by David Cecil, *World's Class.-Pap. Ser.* Oxford 1983 pap. $7.95

A Russian Schoolboy. Trans. by J. D. Duff, intro. by John Bayley, *World's Class.-Pap. Ser.* Oxford 1983 pap. $6.95

BOOK ABOUT AKSAKOV

Durkin, Andrew R. *Sergei Aksakov and Russian Pastoral.* Rutgers Univ. Pr. 1983 $30.00

AKSYONOV (AKSENOV), VASSILY. 1932–

Aksyonov made his debut during the late 1950s and early 1960s, when he was closely associated with the popular journal *Yunost'* (Youth). His highly original work is distinguished by the use of contemporary idiom, including slang and foreign borrowings—the idiom used by young people whose psychology and social problems are depicted in his works. In the 1970s, Aksyonov increasingly turned toward the fantastic and the grotesque. He was involved in the unofficial *Metropol* collection and was exiled in 1980. Since then he has lived in the United States, where he has published several important novels.

BOOKS BY AKSYONOV

Surplussed Barrelware. 1968. Ed. by Joel Wilkinson and Slava Yastremski, Ardis 1985 $23.50 pap. $5.95
The Burn. 1980. Trans. by Michael Glenny, Houghton Mifflin 1984 $19.95; Random 1984 $19.95
The Island of Crimea. 1981. Trans. by Michael Heim, Random $16.95 1984 pap. $8.95. Political fantasy; excellent translation.

ANDREYEV (ANDREEV), LEONID. 1871–1919

Andreyev's standing as one of the most popular writers of the first decade of the twentieth century was due to his ability to combine modernist and realist techniques, and his willingness to break taboos. His subjects included sexual problems (e.g., venereal disease) and various kinds of abnormality. Such works caused a scandal, but won their author a wide following. In the aftermath of 1905, Andreyev dealt with the moral and psychological dilemmas of the revolutionaries, as in the stunning *The Tale of the Seven Who Were Hanged* (o.p.). Andreyev had a talent for depicting the dark, irrational forces in life; however, his pessimism and mysticism are sometimes undercut by an obvious lack of existential authenticity.

BOOKS BY ANDREYEV

Selected Stories. Ed. by M. H. Shotton, Basil Blackwell text ed. pap. $9.95
Silence. Trans. by W. H. Lowe, ed. by Isaac Goldberg, Branden pap. $3.00
Little Angel and Other Stories. Short Story Index Repr. Ser. Ayer repr. of 1915 ed. $18.00
Plays by Leonid Andreyeff: The Life of a Man, The Black Maskers, The Sabine Women. Trans. by Clarence L. Meader and Fred N. Scott, AMS Pr. repr. of 1915 ed. $29.00
When the King Loses His Head and Other Stories. Trans. by Archibald J. Wolfe, Ayer repr. of 1919 ed. $19.00

He Who Gets Slapped: A Play in Four Acts. Trans. by Gregory Zilboorg, Greenwood
    repr. of 1922 ed. 1975 lib. bdg. $15.00

BOOK ABOUT ANDREYEV

Kun, Alexander. *Leonid Andreyev.* Ayer repr. of 1924 ed. 1969 $20.00

BABEL, ISAAC (ISAAK). 1894–1941

Babel won early success with stories about his native Odessa and about
the exploits of the Soviet cavalry in the Polish campaign of 1920–1921. During the 1930s his output was small, but his talent remained undiminished.
He was arrested in May 1939, during the Great Purge, and his manuscripts
were confiscated. His exact fate is unknown. "Rehabilitated" in 1956, he is
still published only occasionally in the Soviet Union—the very strong Jewish element in his stories, as well as the ambiguous position the author took
on key issues, make his stories uncomfortable for Soviet authorities.

For a Russian reader, the Odessa tales are particularly exotic. Their protagonists, members of the city's Jewish underworld, are presented in romantic, epic terms. The Red Cavalry stories are noted for their account of the
horrors of war. In both cycles Babel relies on precisely constructed short
plots, on paradoxes in the situations the protagonists confront and in how
they respond, and on nonstandard language—be it the combination of Yiddish, slang, and standard Russian in the Odessa tales, or of uneducated Cossack speech and standard Russian in the Red Cavalry cycle. The result of
such features is a literary heritage that is very rare in the history of Russian
literature.

BOOKS BY BABEL

The Collected Stories: Red Cavalry, Tales of Odessa, and Other Stories. Trans. and ed.
    by Walter Morrison, New Amer. Lib. pap. $7.95
You Must Know Everything. Carroll & Graff 1984 pap. $8.95; trans. by Max Hayward,
    ed. by Nathalie Babel, Farrar 1969 $10.95 pap. $6.95
Benia Krik: A Film Novel. Trans. by Ivor Montagu and Sergei Nalbandov, Hyperion
    Pr. repr. of 1935 ed. 1973 $15.00

BOOKS ABOUT BABEL

Falen, James E. *Isaac Babel: Russian Master of the Short Story.* Univ. of Tennessee Pr.
    1974 $17.95
Luplow, Carol. *Isaac Babel's "Red Cavalry."* Ardis 1982 $25.00
Mendelson, Danuta. *Metaphor in Babel's Short Stories.* Ardis 1982 $25.00

BELY (BIELY), ANDREI (pseud. of Boris Bugayev). 1880–1934

A major symbolist poet, Bely was also one of the most important figures
in twentieth-century Russian prose. He initially studied science, but had already started his literary career by the time he graduated from the university. His early poetry was shaped by a set of mystical beliefs associated with
the concept of the Divine Wisdom, Sophia—beliefs shared by Alexander
Blok and other Symbolist poets. In later years, Bely was deeply affected by

the German anthroposophist Rudolf Steiner, whose follower he became in 1912.

Bely's prose continued the stylistic traditions of Gogol. Brilliantly innovative in language, composition, and subject matter, it had a great impact on early Soviet literature. His novels *St. Petersburg* and *The Silver Dove* deal with Russian history taken in broad perspective; another important work, *Kotik Letaev* (1920, o.p.), anticipated stream-of-consciousness techniques in Western fiction in its depiction of the psyche of a developing infant.

BOOKS BY BELY

Complete Short Stories. Ed. by Ronald Peterson, Ardis 1979 $14.00. Minor pieces; readable translation.
Selected Essays of Andrey Bely. Trans. and ed. by Steven Cassedy, Univ. of California Pr. 1985 $35.00
The Silver Dove. 1910. Trans. by George Reavey, intro. by Harrison Salisbury, Grove 1974 pap. $7.95
St. Petersburg. 1916. Trans. by John Cournos, Grove 1959 pap. $7.95; (with the title *Petersburg*) trans. by Robert A. Maguire and John E. Malmstad, Indiana Univ. Pr. 1978 $27.50 pap. $8.95. The Maguire and Malmstad translation is unabridged, annotated, and both faithful and readable.
The First Encounter. 1921. Trans. by Gerald Janecek, Princeton Univ. Pr. bilingual ed. 1979 $15.00

BOOKS ABOUT BELY

Alexandrov, Vladimir E. *Andrei Bely: The Major Symbolist Fiction.* Harvard Univ. Pr. 1985 $22.50
Elsworth, J. D. *Andrey Bely: A Critical Study of His Novels.* Cambridge Univ. Pr. 1984 $39.50
Maslenikov, Oleg. *Frenzied Poets: Andrey Biely and the Russian Symbolists.* Greenwood repr. of 1952 ed. 1968 lib. bdg. $15.00
Mochulsky, Konstantin. *Andrei Bely.* Trans. by Nora Szalawitz, Ardis 1976 $20.00 pap. $5.50
Steinberg, Ada. *Words and Music in the Novels of Andrey Bely.* Cambridge Univ. Pr. 1982 $57.50

BLOK, ALEKSANDR (ALEXANDER). 1880–1921

Blok was one of the most important Russian poets of this century, a lyricist of extraordinary vision and passion, whose life and art were closely intertwined. He started writing early; his first collection, *Verses on the Beautiful Lady* (o.p.), published in 1904, mythologizes his young wife, Lyubov, as the incarnation of a mystical presence. Succeeding collections mirror his abandonment of this ideal; the last volume of a trilogy arranged by the poet himself, including the cycles *Retribution* (o.p.) and *The Terrible World* (o.p.), shows Blok at the height of his powers. Increasingly in his poetry, as well as in his essays and plays, Blok gave way to his premonitions of impending apocalyptic events; few of his generation possessed his perception of the cataclysms the twentieth century would bring.

Blok's best-known work, particularly in the West, is the long poem *The Twelve* (1918), in which a group of revolutionary guardsmen, with Christ at their head, travels through darkened Petersburg. This response to the October Revolution is complex and contradictory, and its changing language and rhythms reflect the many sources and shifting moods of the poem.

BOOKS BY BLOK

Selected Poems: Alexander Blok. Imported Pubns. 1981 $9.00
The Twelve and Other Poems. Trans. by Anselm Hollo, Gnomon Pr. 1977 pap. $4.00
The Twelve and The Scythians. Trans. by Jack Lindsay, Lawrence Hill 1982 pap. $4.50
The Spirit of Music. Trans. by I. Freiman, Hyperion Pr. repr. of 1946 ed. 1973 $8.50

BOOKS ABOUT BLOK

Chukovsky, Kornei. *Alexander Blok as Man and Poet.* 1924. Trans. by Katherine O'Connor, ed. by Diana Burgin, Ardis 1982 $22.00
Hackel, Sergei. *The Poet and the Revolution: Alexander Blok's The Twelve.* Oxford 1975 $49.95
Mochulsky, Konstantin. *Aleksandr Blok.* Trans. by Doris Johnson, Wayne State Univ. Pr. 1983 $30.00
Pyman, Avril. *Aleksandr Blok: A Biography.* Oxford 2 vols. 1979–80 $29.95–$39.95. The most complete treatment of Blok's biography and poetic development.
Reeve, F. D. *Alexander Blok: Between Image and Idea.* Octagon repr. of 1962 ed. 1980 $18.50
Vogel, Lucy, ed. *Aleksandr Blok: An Anthology of Critical Essays and Memoirs.* Ardis 1982 $27.50 pap. $5.50

BRODSKY, JOSEPH. 1940–

Brodsky's first poems appeared mainly in *Syntax,* an underground Leningrad literary magazine. In 1964, he became the object of international concern after being tried and sentenced to five years of administrative exile for "parasitism." As a result of intervention by prominent Soviet cultural figures, he was freed in 1965. In 1972, under pressure from the authorities, he emigrated to the United States, where he has taught at various universities and where he has published a number of collections of poetry.

Brodsky is arguably the best contemporary Russian poet, the inheritor of Akhmatova's mantle. He has written short lyrics and longer poems, and has experimented with various genres and techniques. His concerns are universal. They involve common human experiences and are often nostalgically pessimistic. Brodsky has involved himself in American literary life, writing regularly in English-language magazines. In this, he is an exception among "third-wave" Russian émigrés.

BOOKS BY BRODSKY

Selected Poems. Trans. by George L. Kline, fwd. by W. H. Auden, Harper 1974 $9.95
A Part of Speech. Trans. by Anthony Hecht and others, Farrar 1980 $12.95 pap. $7.95
Roman Elegies. Farrar bilingual ed. 1982 pap. $9.95
Less than One. Farrar 1984 $18.95

BULGAKOV, MIKHAIL. 1891–1940

A practicing physician, like Chekhov, Bulgakov became a popular writer and playwright in the relatively easy time of the 1920s. The civil war and its internecine horrors became one of his major themes, as did the crazy-quiltlike new Soviet society. His early prose is often satiric, with strong elements of the fantastic and grotesque.

Bulgakov wrote a number of important plays that provoked bitter attacks in the press, and he was shut out of the theater and literature in 1929. Only a direct appeal to the Soviet government (that is, to Stalin) changed the situation; intervention by the dictator enabled Bulgakov to resume a professional career. Even then, however, some of his important works, such as the novel *The Life of Monsieur de Molière*, were rejected by publishing houses and theaters.

Bulgakov's masterpiece, written "for the drawer" over a number of years, and only published decades after his death, is the novel *Master and Margarita*. The novel may be read on many levels, from the purely satiric to the allegorical. It has been acclaimed as one of the most important achievements of twentieth-century Russian fiction.

Today, Bulgakov is celebrated for both his drama and his prose. Several of his plays are favorites of the public and standard fare in Soviet theaters.

BOOKS BY BULGAKOV

Heart of a Dog. 1925. Trans. by Mirra Ginsburg, Grove 1968 pap. $2.95
Master and Margarita. Trans. by Mirra Ginsburg, Grove 1967 pap. $4.95; New Amer.
    Lib. (Signet Class.) pap. $4.95. Ginsburg's translation is superior.
Molière. Methuen 1983 pap. $4.95

BOOKS ABOUT BULGAKOV

Belozerskaya-Bulgakova, L. E. *My Life with Mikhail Bulgakov.* Trans. by M. Thompson, Ardis 1983 $18.95
Natov, Nadine. *Mikhail Bulgakov. Twayne's World Author Ser.* G. K. Hall 1985 $19.95
Proffer, Ellendea. *Bulgakov: Life and Work.* Ardis 1984 $45.00 pap. $15.00. Principal study in English.
——. *An International Bibliography of Works by and about Mikhail Bulgakov.* Ardis 1976 $15.00

BUNIN, IVAN. 1870–1953 (NOBEL PRIZE 1933)

Bunin was little known in the United States until he won the Nobel Prize (the first Russian writer to do so). By then, he had decades of literary activity behind him. In the intensely group-oriented literary milieu of turn-of-the-century Russia, Bunin largely remained a loner, working within the realist tradition, but enriching it with a powerful lyric element. He traveled abroad a great deal and used exotic locales as settings for many of his works. He was an outspoken opponent of the Bolsheviks and emigrated to Paris; ironically, since his death, he has been celebrated in the Soviet Union as a major writer.

Bunin's themes are diverse. Born in an impoverished rural gentry family, he often wrote about the decline of the countryside and about the passing of a way of life. Sometimes his depiction of provincial Russia was elegiac; at other times it was tragic. More fundamentally, Bunin was concerned with the problem of man's isolation in suffering. A number of his works, such as the remarkable "The Gentleman from San Francisco" (1916), may be read as allegories. In later years, Bunin grew increasingly preoccupied with problems of sexual attraction and death (e.g., his last collection of stories, *Dark Avenues*).

BOOKS BY BUNIN

In a Far Distant Land. Trans. by Robert Bowie, Hermitage 1983 pap. $8.50
Stories and Poems. Imported Pubns. 1979 $8.95
The Gentleman from San Francisco and Other Stories. Merrimack 1979 $6.95; Octagon repr. of 1934 ed. 1980 $22.00
Dark Avenues and Other Stories. Trans. by R. Hare, Hyperion Pr. 1977 $15.00 pap. $10.00
The Village. 1909–10. Trans. by Isabel F. Hapgood, Fertig repr. of 1923 ed. 1975 $21.00
Fifteen Tales. Trans. by Bernard G. Guerney, Core Collection repr. of 1924 ed. 1978 $21.50
The Well of Days. Trans. by Gleb Struve and Hamish Miles, Fertig repr. of 1933 ed. 1977 $25.00; Hyperion Pr. $13.95 pap. $4.95
Memories and Portraits. Greenwood repr. of 1951 ed. 1968 lib. bdg. $15.00
Grammar of Love. Trans. by John Cournos, Hyperion Pr. 1977 $15.00 pap. $3.50
Velga. Trans. by Guy Daniels, Phillips 1970 $7.95

BOOK ABOUT BUNIN

Woodward, James B. *Ivan Bunin: A Study of His Fiction*. Univ. of North Carolina Pr. 1980 $22.50

CHEKHOV, ANTON (also TCHEKHOV, TCHEKOV, TCHEKHOFF, CHEHOV). 1860–1904

The greatest of Russian dramatists, Chekhov was also a master of the story, and he had a profound influence on world literature in both these areas. Forced to support himself while in medical school, he began in 1880 with trivial comic tales written for humor magazines. By 1884, the first collection of his stories appeared, and by the end of the decade, he was a professional writer.

Chekhov's path to mastery as a dramatist was even more rapid. He moved from one-act plays to four innovative works that are part of the core of modern world theater: *The Sea Gull, Uncle Vanya, Three Sisters,* and *The Cherry Orchard.*

Dead of tuberculosis at age 44, Chekhov left behind a vast literary heritage, much of which was pioneering in both subject matter and techniques. His themes were drawn from all areas of Russian life; he explored the situations and problems of his characters with both sensitivity and clear-minded rationality, never allowing himself to descend into false pathos. Chekhov showed how tragedies result from human beings' inability to communicate their thoughts and emotions. In this, he anticipated a major theme of modern fiction and theater (especially the Absurdist). His dramas eschew the conventions of the well-made play and are notable for the complex interrelationship of their elements: a low-keyed network of minor incidents, moods, and words, all typical of ordinary lives, which builds to an almost unbearable emotional intensity, is the hallmark of Chekhovian theater.

Although there are numerous editions of Chekhov in English, many of his prose tales have not yet been translated. Ronald Hingley's *Oxford Chekhov* series is particularly notable for both its large scope and the high quality of the translations.

BOOKS BY CHEKHOV

The Oxford Chekhov. Trans. and ed. by Ronald Hingley, Oxford 9 vols. 1964–80 ea. $34.95–39.50

The Portable Chekhov. Ed. by Avrahm Yarmolinsky, *Viking Portable Lib*. Penguin 1977 pap. $7.95

Selected Works. Imported Pubns. 2 vols. 1979 $13.50

Best-Known Works. Ayer repr. of 1929 ed. $32.75

Tales of Chekhov. Ecco Pr. 12 vols. 1984–86 pap. ea. $8.50–$9.50 vol. 13 in preparation

Anton Chekhov's Short Stories. Trans. by Constance Garnett, ed. by Ralph Matlaw, *Norton Critical Eds*. 1979 pap. $6.95

Image of Chekhov: Forty Stories in the Order in Which They Were Written. Trans. by Robert Payne, Knopf 1963 $15.00

Chekhov: Selected Stories. Trans. by Ann Dunnigan, New Amer. Lib. (Signet Class.) 1960 pap. $2.95

Seven Short Novels. Trans. by Barbara Makanowitzky, intro. by Gleb Struve, Norton repr. of 1963 ed. 1971 pap. $8.95

Seven Short Stories. Trans. by Ronald Hingley, *Oxford Pap. Ser*. 1974 $6.95

The Russian Master and Other Stories. Trans. by Ronald Hingley, *World's Class. Ser*. Oxford 1984 pap. $5.95

Nine Humorous Tales. Trans. by Isaac Goldberg and Henry T. Schnittking, Ayer repr. of 1918 ed. $13.00

Chekhov: The Early Stories, 1883–88. Trans. by Patrick Miles and Harvey Pitcher, Macmillan 1983 $14.95 1984 pap. $5.95

The Duel and Other Stories. Trans. by Ronald Wilks, Penguin repr. 1984 pap. $4.95

The Kiss and Other Stories. Trans. by R. E. Long, Ayer repr. of 1915 ed. $20.00; Penguin 1982 pap. $3.95

The Black Monk and Other Stories. Trans. by R. E. Long, Ayer repr. of 1903 ed. $17.00

The Party and Other Stories. Trans. by Ronald Wilks, Penguin 1985 pap. $3.95

The Sinner from Toledo and Other Stories. Trans. by Arnold Hinchcliffe, Fairleigh Dickinson Univ. Pr. 1972 $14.50

Lady with Lapdog and Other Stories. Trans. by David Magarshack, *Penguin Class. Ser*. 1964 pap. $3.95

Late-Blooming Flowers and Other Stories. Intro. by I. C. Chertok and Jean Gardner, Carroll & Graf repr. of 1964 ed. 1984 pap. $8.95

The Grasshopper and Other Stories. Trans. by A. E. Chamot, Ayer repr. of 1926 ed. $16.00

My Life and Other Stories. Trans. by S. S. Koteliansky and Gilbert Cannan, Ayer repr. of 1920 ed. $16.00

Rothschild's Fiddle and Other Stories. Trans. by George W. Rickey, Ayer repr. of 1917 ed. $16.00

Steppe and Other Stories. Trans. by Adeline Kaye, Ayer repr. of 1915 ed. $16.00

Russian Silhouettes: More Stories of Russian Life. Trans. by Marian Fell, Ayer repr. of 1915 ed. $21.00

Wild Honey. Trans. by Michael Frayn, Methuen 1984 pap. $6.95

On the Harmful Effects of Tobacco. Quist 1977 $6.95

Anton Chekhov's Plays. Ed. by Eugene K. Bristow, *Norton Critical Eds.* 1977 $7.95

Plays. Trans. by Elisaveta Fen, *Penguin Class. Ser.* 1959 pap. $3.95. All major, several minor plays.

Best Plays. Trans. by Stark Young, Modern Lib. $6.95 1966 pap. $3.95

Chekhov: The Major Plays—Ivanov, Sea Gull, Uncle Vanya, Three Sisters, Cherry Orchard. Trans. by Ann Dunnigan, New Amer. Lib. (Signet Class.) 1964 pap. $2.95

Five Major Plays. Bantam Class. Ser. 1982 pap. $2.50; trans. by Ronald Hingley, Oxford 1977 pap. $4.95

Anton Chekhov: Four Plays. Trans. by David Magarshack, *Mermaid Dramabook Ser.* Hill & Wang 1969 pap. $7.95

The Brute and Other Farces: Seven Short Plays. Ed. by Eric Bentley, Limelight Eds. repr. of 1958 ed. 1985 $15.95 pap. $5.95

The Letters of Anton Chekhov. Ed. by Avrahm Yarmolinsky, Viking 1973 $20.00. Another major edition of the letters.

Anton Chekhov's Life and Thought: Selected Letters and Commentary. Trans. by Michael Heim in collaboration with Simon Karlinsky, selection, commentary, and intro. by Simon Karlinsky, Harper 1973 o.p. A major edition.

The Selected Letters of Anton Chekhov. Trans. by Sidonie K. Lederer, ed. by Lillian Hellman, Farrar 1984 $16.95 pap. $7.95

Life and Letters of Anton Chekhov. Trans. by S. S. Koteliansky and Philip Tomlinson, Ayer repr. of 1925 ed. $26.50. First part of a three-volume set.

Letters of Anton Tchehov to Olga Knipper. Trans. by Constance Garnett, Ayer repr. of 1925 ed. $24.00. Second part of a three-volume set.

Letters on the Short Story, the Drama and Other Literary Topics. Ed. by Louis S. Friedland, Ayer repr. of 1924 ed. 1965 $20.00; Darby 1982 $35.00. Third part of a three-volume set.

The Island: A Journey to Sakhalin. Trans. by Luba Terpak and Michael Terpak, intro. by Robert Payne, Greenwood repr. of 1967 ed. 1977 lib. bdg. $26.50

Anton Tchehov: Literary and Theatrical Reminiscences. Trans. by S. S. Koteliansky, Ayer repr. of 1927 ed. $20.00

Ivanov. 1887. Trans. by Ariadne Nicolaeff, ed. by John Gielgud, Theatre Arts pap. $1.00

The Sea Gull. 1896. Trans. by Fred Eisemann and Oliver F. Murphy, Branden pap. $3.00

The Sea Gull (and *Tragedian in Spite of Himself*). Trans. by Jean-Claude Van Itallie, Harper repr. of 1974 ed. 1977 pap. $1.95

Uncle Vanya. 1899. Ed. by David Magarshack, Basil Blackwell pap. $9.95

Three Sisters. 1901. Trans. by R. Jarrell, Macmillan 1969 $5.95; trans. by Michael Frayn, *Theatre Class. Ser.* Methuen 1983 pap. $6.95

The Cherry Orchard. 1903. Avon 1965 pap. $.95; trans. by Michael Frayn, *Theatre Class. Ser.* Methuen 1978 pap. $6.95; Pluto Pr. 1981 pap. $5.95; ed. by John Gielgud, Theatre Arts 1963 pap. $3.50

BOOKS ABOUT CHEKHOV

Barricelli, Jean-Pierre, ed. *Chekhov's Great Plays: A Critical Anthology.* New York Univ. Pr. 1981 $29.50. Essays by leading scholars of literature and theater.

Bitsilli, Peter. *Chekhov's Art: A Stylistic Analysis.* Trans. by Toby Clyman and Edwina Cruise, Ardis 1983 $25.00 pap. $5.00. Influential essay by a leading Russian émigré critic.

Chudakov, A. P. *Chekhov's Poetics.* Trans. by Edwina Cruise and Donald Dragt, Ardis 1983 $32.50 pap. $7.50. Structuralist analysis; rigorous, provocative.

Hahn, Beverly. *Chekhov. Major European Authors Ser.* Cambridge Univ. Pr. $44.50 pap. $13.95

Kramer, Karl D. *The Chameleon and the Dream: The Image of Reality in Cexov's Stories.* Mouton text ed. 1970 $26.00

Peace, Richard. *Chekhov: A Study of the Four Major Plays.* Yale Univ. Pr. 1983 $18.50

Simmons, Ernest J. *Chekhov: A Biography.* Univ. of Chicago Pr. 1970 pap. $3.95

Styan, J. L. *Chekhov in Performance: A Commentary of the Major Plays.* Cambridge Univ. Pr. 1971 $42.50 pap. $13.95

Van der Eng, Jan, and others. *On the Theory of Descriptive Poetics: Anton P. Chekhov as Storyteller and Playwright—Three Essays.* Benjamins 1978 pap. $22.00

Wellek, Rene, and Nona Wellek, eds. *Chekhov: New Perspectives.* Prentice-Hall 1984 $12.95 pap. $5.95

CHERNYSHEVSKY, NIKOLAI. 1828–1889

Together with Nicolay Dobrolyubov and Dmitry Pisarev, Chernyshevsky was a leading radical thinker of the mid-nineteenth century. He championed materialism, utilitarianism, and a rather naively reasoned idea of social and historical progress, and infused his very influential literary criticism with his views on society. His most important philosophical work is *The Anthropological Principle in Philosophy* (o.p.), where he argued that social environment determines man's behavior, and in favor of a rational egoism. Chernyshevsky's most famous book, *What Is to Be Done?* (1863), was written while he was imprisoned for revolutionary activity. Almost devoid of artistic merit, deliberately unliterary, the novel celebrates female emancipation and the new radical intelligentsia, and offers a vision of a future utopia. It had an enormous impact on Russian intellectuals because of its ideas, and is still regarded as a major classic in the Soviet Union; it also has been mercilessly pilloried, first by Dostoevsky in *Notes from Underground*, and more recently by Nabokov in *The Gift*.

BOOKS BY CHERNYSHEVSKY

What Is to Be Done? Trans. by N. Dole and S. S. Skidelsky, intro. by K. Feuer, Ardis 1985 pap. $6.95

Belinsky, Chernyshevsky, and Dobrolyubov: Selected Criticism. Ed. by Ralph E. Matlaw, Indiana Univ. Pr. 1976 $12.50 pap. $5.95

Selected Philosophical Essays. Hyperion Pr. repr. of 1953 ed. 1981 $45.00

DOSTOEVSKY (DOSTOIEVSKY, DOSTOEVSKII, DOSTOEVSKI,
   DOSTOYEVSKY), FEDOR (FEODOR, FYODOR). 1821–1881

One of the most significant figures in modern world literature, Dostoevsky successfully debuted with *Poor Folk* (1846), a subtle novel about the psychology of the poor and the socially insignificant, a subject of major importance throughout his fiction. In 1849, he and other members of the mildly
socialist Petrashevsky Circle were arrested and charged with political
crimes; after going through a shattering mock execution, they were sentenced to terms of imprisonment and army service in the ranks. Dostoevsky
emerged from a Siberian prison camp in 1854. There, he had become a devout believer in Christianity and Russia. His views were unconventional, opposed to both the radical and reactionary attitudes of the time, and formed
a major stratum of many of his subsequent polemic and fictional works.
Dostoevsky's private life during the 1860s was full of vicissitudes, including
the deaths of his wife and brother, struggles with creditors, and a serious
gambling addiction. A change for the better came with his second marriage
in 1867, which gave him a stable, happy family life. Yet, whatever the private turmoil, this was the start of a period that would produce his greatest
works, including *Notes from Underground*, a profound examination of the
modern consciousness, and the series of major novels, from *Crime and Punishment* to *The Brothers Karamazov*.

During the 1870s, Dostoevsky drew close to religious figures and to conservative governmental circles and wrote a large number of publicistic pieces
on topics ranging from literature to international affairs, often espousing nationalistic, anti-Western views. However, his works were popular with a
public that was often very radical. At the 1880 Pushkin celebrations in Moscow, Dostoevsky's speech was greeted with enthusiasm; the same public display of affection was shown at his funeral in 1881.

Dostoevsky's role in modern literature is manifold. He was a profound innovator in fiction, who transformed realism and created a new brand of psychological novel. His works operate on a number of levels. A gripping plot
becomes the vehicle for examining not only human psyche (his insights are
startlingly contemporary) but also the most profound philosophical and
theological questions. He has been treated as a precursor of the existentialists; he has also been interpreted as a religious thinker. Overall, he was a
writer and thinker of such complexity and so open to the clash of ideas that
readers continue to find in him what they seek.

Almost all of Dostoevsky's writings are now available in English. Constance Garnett's translations have been a standard; however, they do not always capture the subtleties and flavor of Dostoevsky's language.
Magarshack's versions of the great novels are somewhat better in this regard.
The *Norton Critical Editions* are particularly useful. The translations are updated, and key critical materials on the works in question are appended.

BOOKS BY DOSTOEVSKY

Great Short Works of Fyodor Dostoevsky. Trans. by George Bird and others, ed. by
   Ronald Hingley, Harper 1968 pap. $3.80

The Best Short Stories of Dostoyevsky. Trans. by David Magarshack, *Modern Lib. College Ed. Ser.* Random 1950 $6.95 1964 pap. $6.95. Includes *Notes from Underground* and *The Honest Thief.*

Stories. Imported Pubns. 1981 pap. $4.00

Poor Folk and The Gambler. Trans. by C. J. Hogarth, Biblio Dist. (Everyman's) repr. of 1915 ed. 1974 $9.95 pap. $4.95

An Honest Thief and Other Stories. Trans. by Constance Garnett, Greenwood repr. of 1919 ed. 1975 lib. bdg. $42.50

Notes from Underground and Selected Stories: White Nights, Dream of a Ridiculous Man, House of the Dead. Trans. by Andrew R. MacAndrew, New Amer. Lib. (Signet Class.) pap. $2.25

Notes from Underground and The Double. Trans. by Jessie Coulson, *Penguin Class. Ser.* 1972 pap. $2.95

Letters from the Underworld: The Gentle Maiden and The Landlady. Biblio Dist. (Everyman's) repr. of 1913 ed. 1971 $9.95 pap. $3.95

The Gambler, Bobok, A Nasty Story. Trans. by Jessie Coulson, *Penguin Class. Ser.* 1966 pap. $3.95

The Diary of a Writer. Trans. by Boris Brasol, Octagon 2 vols. repr. of 1949 ed. 1973 $86.00

The Unpublished Dostoevsky. Ed. by Carl R. Proffer, Ardis vol. 1 trans. by Thomas Berczynski and others, 1972 $25.00 vol. 2 trans. by Carl R. Proffer and Arline Boyer, 1975 $25.00 vol. 3 trans. by David Lapeza and Arline Boyer, 1976 $25.00

Complete Letters. Ed. by David Lowe and Ronald Meyer, Ardis 1985 vol. 1 $35.00

Dostoevsky: Letters and Reminiscences. Trans. by S. S. Koteliansky and J. Middleton Murray, *Select Bibliographies Repr. Ser.* Ayer repr. of 1923 ed. $23.00

Letters of Dostoevsky. Trans. by Ethel C. Mayne, intro. by A. Yarmolinsky, Horizon repr. of 1961 ed. pap. $11.50

New Dostoyevsky Letters. Trans. by S. S. Koteliansky, Haskell 1974 $49.95

Poor Folk. 1846. Trans. by Robert Dessaix, Ardis 1983 $19.50 pap. $4.50

The Double: Two Versions. 1846. Trans. by Evelyn Harden, Ardis 1985 $19.50 pap. $6.50. Includes first and second editions.

Netochka Nezvanova. 1849. Trans. by Ann Dunnigan, Prentice-Hall 1971 pap. $2.45

Memoirs from the House of the Dead (House of the Dead). 1860–62. Trans. by H. S. Edwards, intro. by N. Andreyev, Biblio Dist. (Everyman's) repr. of 1911 ed. 1975 $9.95 pap $3.95 1979 $7.00 pap. $3.95; trans. by Jessie Coulson, ed. by Ronald Hingley, *World's Class. Ser.* Oxford 1983 pap. $4.95

The Insulted and Injured (The Insulted and the Humiliated). 1861. Trans. by Constance Garnett, Greenwood repr. of 1955 ed. 1975 lib. bdg. $32.50; Imported Pubns. 1976 $6.95

Notes from Underground. 1864. Trans. by Mirra Ginsburg, intro. by Donald Fanger, *Bantam Class. Ser.* 1981 pap. $2.50; trans. by Ralph E. Matlaw, Dutton 1960 pap. $3.95

Notes from Underground (and *The Grand Inquisitor*). Trans. by Serge Shishkoff, ed. by Robert G. Durgy, Univ. Pr. of Amer. repr. of 1969 ed. 1982 pap. $12.25

The Crocodile, an Extraordinary Event. 1865. Trans. by S. D. Cioran, Ardis 1985 $15.00 pap. $3.50

Crime and Punishment. 1866. Intro. by R. R. Canon, *Airmont Class. Ser.* pap. $2.95; trans. by Constance Garnett, *Bantam Class. Ser.* 1981 pap. $2.50; trans. by Constance Garnett, intro. by N. Andreyev, Biblio Dist. repr. of 1955 ed. 1977 pap. $3.75; Buccaneer Bks. repr. 1982 $29.95; trans. by Constance Garnett, intro. by E. J. Simmons, Modern Lib. 1950 $6.95; trans. by Sidney Monas, New Amer. Lib

(Signet Class.) pap. $2.25; trans. by Jessie Coulson, ed. by George Gibian, *Norton Critical Eds.* rev. ed. 1975 pap. $8.95; trans. by Jessie Coulson, intro. by John Jones, *World's Class.-Pap. Ser.* Oxford 1981 pap. $5.95; trans. by David Magarshack, *Penguin Class Ser.* 1952 pap. $3.95; trans. by Constance Garnett, intro. by E. J. Simmons, *Modern Lib. College Ed. Ser.* Random 1950 pap. $5.95

The Gambler. 1867. Trans. by Andrew R. MacAndrew, Norton repr. of 1964 ed. 1981 pap. $3.95; trans. by Victor Terras, ed. by Edward Wasiolek, Univ. of Chicago Pr. 1972 $9.95 pap. $2.95

The Idiot. 1868. Trans. by Constance Garnett, *Bantam Class. Ser.* 1981 pap. $3.50; trans. by Constance Garnett, Modern Lib. $10.95; intro. by H. Rosenberg, New Amer. Lib. (Signet Class.) repr. 1969 pap. $2.25; trans. by David Magarshack, *Penguin Class. Ser.* 1956 pap. $5.95; Imported Pubns. 2 vols. $8.45; trans. by John W. Strahan, Washington Square Pr. pap. $1.25

The Possessed (The Devils). 1872. Trans. by Constance Garnett, ed. by A. Yarmolinsky, Modern Lib. 1936 $7.95; trans. by Andrew R. MacAndrew, New Amer. Lib. (Signet Class.) 1962 pap. $4.50; trans. by David Magarshack, *Penguin Class. Ser.* 1954 pap. $5.95

Stavrogin's Confession and The Plan of the Life of a Great Sinner. Haskell repr. of 1922 ed. 1972 $48.95

The Adolescent (A Raw Youth). 1875. Trans. by Andrew R. MacAndrew, Norton repr. of 1971 ed. 1981 pap. $11.95

The Brothers Karamazov. 1880. Intro. by O. H. Rudzik, *Airmont Class. Ser.* pap. $2.50; trans. by Andrew R. MacAndrew, intro. by Konstantin Mochulsky, *Bantam Class. Ser.* 1981 pap. $2.95; Buccaneer Bks. repr. 1983 $31.95; trans. by Constance Garnett, Modern Lib. 1933 $9.95; ed. by Manuel Komroff-Hill, New Amer. Lib. (Signet Class.) 1971 pap. $2.75; trans. by Constance Garnett, ed. by Ralph E. Matlaw, *Norton Critical Eds.* 1976 $17.50 pap. $10.95; trans. by David Magarshack, Penguin 1982 pap. $5.95; Imported Pubns. 2 vols. 1980 $15.95; trans. by Constance Garnett, intro. by Marc Slonim, *Modern Lib. College Ed. Ser.* Random 1950 pap. $6.00; intro. by Marc Slonim, *Russian Lib. Ser.* Random (Vintage) 1955 pap. $6.95

The Grand Inquisitor. Intro. by A. Fremantle, Ungar pap. $2.45

Grand Inquisitor on the Nature of Man. Trans. by Constance Garnett, intro. by W. Hubben, Bobbs 1948 pap. $4.79

BOOKS ABOUT DOSTOEVSKY

Bakhtin, Mikhail. *Problems of Dostoevsky's Poetics.* Trans. by Caryl Emerson, intro. by Wayne Booth, *Theory and History of Lit. Ser.* Univ. of Minnesota Pr. 1984 $35.00 pap. $14.95. Major contribution to both Dostoevsky criticism and modern literary theory.

Dalton, Elizabeth. *Unconscious Structure in Dostoevsky's "The Idiot": A Study in Literature and Psychoanalysis.* Princeton Univ. Pr. 1979 $24.50

Dostoevsky, Anna. *Dostoevsky: Reminiscences.* Trans. by Beatrice Stillman, intro. by Helen Muchnic, Liveright repr. 1977 pap. $5.95. Dostoevsky's second wife; highly readable account.

Fanger, Donald. *Dostoevsky and Romantic Realism: A Study of Dostoevsky in Relation to Balzac, Dickens, Gogol.* Univ. of Chicago Pr. 1968 pap. $7.00. Dostoevsky and his precursors.

Frank, Joseph. *Dostoevsky: The Seeds of Revolt, 1821–1849.* Princeton Univ. Pr. 1976 $36.00 pap. $9.95. First volume of magisterial four-part study of Dostoevsky's life and writings.

———. *Dostoevsky: The Years of Ordeal, 1850–1859*. Princeton Univ. Pr. 1983 $25.00. Second volume of Frank's study.

Holquist, Michael. *Dostoevsky and the Novel: The Wages of Biography*. Princeton Univ. Pr. 1977 $22.00

Jackson, Robert L. *The Art of Dostoevsky: Deliriums and Nocturnes*. Princeton Univ. Pr. 1981 $30.00. By a leading Dostoevsky scholar.

———. *Dostoevsky's Quest for Form: A Study of His Philosophy of Art*. Physsardt 2d ed. 1978 pap. $8.00

———, ed. *Dostoevsky: New Perspectives*. Prentice-Hall 1983 $12.95 pap. $5.95. Excellent selection of essays.

———, ed. *Twentieth-Century Interpretations of Crime and Punishment. Twentieth-Century Interpretations Ser*. Prentice-Hall 1973 $8.95

Miller, Robin F. *Dostoevsky and "The Idiot": Author, Narrator and Reader*. Harvard Univ. Pr. 1981 $20.00. Stimulating analysis.

Mochulsky, Konstantin. *Dostoevsky: His Life and Work*. Trans. by Michael A. Minihan, Princeton Univ. Pr. 1967 pap. $12.50. Very important for Dostoevsky's philosophical and theological ideas.

Morson, Gary S. *The Boundaries of Genre: Dostoevsky's "Diary of a Writer" and the Traditions of Literary Utopia*. Univ. of Texas Pr. 1981 $25.00. Theoretically innovative analysis.

Shestov, Lev. *Dostoevsky, Tolstoy and Nietzsche*. Trans. by Bernard Martin and Spencer Roberts, Ohio Univ. Pr. 1969 $16.00

Terras, Victor. *A Karamazov Companion: Commentary on the Genesis, Language and Style of Dostoevsky's Novel*. Univ. of Wisconsin Pr. 1981 $30.00 text ed. pap. $12.50

———. *Young Dostoevsky, 1846–1849: A Critical Study*. Humanities Pr. 1969 $43.00

Wasiolek, Edward. *Dostoevsky: The Major Fiction*. MIT 1964 pap. $4.95. A very good introduction.

Wellek, Rene, ed. *Dostoevsky: A Collection of Critical Essays*. Prentice-Hall 1962 pap. $2.95

EHRENBURG (ERENBURG), ILYA. 1891–1967

More widely traveled than any other Soviet literary figure, Ehrenburg was a versatile if uneven writer, poet, and journalist. Familiar with an extraordinary range of people in Russia and Western Europe, he survived the Stalin era to bear witness to the losses suffered by the Soviet culture. Of his novels, the first, *The Extraordinary Adventures of Julio Jurenito*, is usually regarded as the best. It is a biting satire of the West. A later work, *The Thaw* (1954, o.p.), gave its name to the immediate post-Stalin period. Its cautious deviation from Stalinist norms in literature signaled some broader change.

BOOKS BY EHRENBURG

Julio Jurenito. 1922. Trans. by Anna Bostok and Yvonne Kapp, Greenwood repr. of 1958 ed. 1976 lib. bdg. $20.75

A Street in Moscow. Trans. by Sonia Volochova, Hyperion Pr. repr. of 1932 ed. $19.50

BOOK ABOUT EHRENBURG

Greenburg, Anatol. *Ilya Ehrenburg: Writing, Politics, and the Art of Survival*. Intro., postscript, and additional material by Erik de Mauny, Viking $17.95. First major study; excellent on the writer and his times.

ESENIN, SERGEI. 1895–1925

Esenin achieved worldwide notoriety because of his marriage in 1922 to the dancer ISADORA DUNCAN (see Vol. 3). His literary reputation has a more substantive basis. By birth and upbringing the inheritor of peasant traditions, he was initially influenced by the symbolists. His early works are filled with folk and religious themes. After the Revolution, Esenin's hopes for a new Russia brought to his writing strong messianic expectations. He became leader of a group that emphasized striking imagery as the key to poetry. His poems are rough in both language and imagery, and their contents echo Esenin's bohemian life-style (e.g., the poem "Confessions of a Hooligan"). Although very popular, Esenin was often harshly criticized by the authorities and many fellow writers and poets. Personal difficulties and doubts about the Revolution led to his suicide in a Leningrad hotel.

BOOKS BY ESENIN

Selected Poetry. Imported Pubns. 1981 $8.45
Confessions of a Hooligan: Fifty Poems. Trans. by Geoffrey Thurley, Humanities Pr. 1973 $10.50

BOOKS ABOUT ESENIN

Davies, J., ed. *Esenin: A Biography in Memoirs, Letters, and Documents.* Ardis 1982 $30.00
McVay, Gordon. *Esenin: A Life.* Ardis 1976 $15.00
———. *Isadora and Esenin.* Ardis 1980 $17.50 pap. $7.50. Both McVay studies are considered authoritative.

FEDIN, KONSTANTIN. 1892–1977

In his early works, Fedin expressed a certain nostalgia for the passing of the prerevolutionary way of life. *Cities and Years* handles this theme through deft manipulation of time. In later works, trying to comply with the dictates of socialist realism, Fedin became more optimistic. *Early Joys* and *No Ordinary Summer* (1948, o.p.) falsify history and mythologize Stalin; not surprisingly, their author was awarded the Stalin Prize. During the 1960s, as head of the Writers' Union and a committed champion of political orthodoxy, Fedin helped stop the publication of Solzhenitsyn's *Cancer Ward*, an act that was condemned by liberal writers and intellectuals.

BOOKS BY FEDIN

Cities and Years: A Novel. 1924. Trans. by Michael Scammell, Greenwood repr. of 1962 ed. 1975 lib. bdg. $21.25
Early Joys. 1946. Imported Pubns. 1973 $5.95
Carp. Ed. by G. A. Birkett, Irvington 1966 pap. $1.75

FURMANOV, DMITRY. 1891–1926

Furmanov earned a place for himself in Soviet literature with his *Chapayev.* In part a novel, in part a documentary, this work is based on Furmanov's experiences as a political commissar with the forces of Chapayev, a guerilla leader in the Urals. Furmanov glorified his protagonist as a kind of folk hero, successfully capturing his psychology. The book was subsequently made into a successful film.

BOOK BY FURMANOV

Chapayev. 1923. Trans. by George Kittell and Jeanette Kittell, ed. by O. Gorchakov, Hyperion Pr. repr. of 1935 ed. 1973 $25.00; Imported Pubns. 1974 $3.45

GARSHIN, VSEVOLOD. 1855–1888

Although his literary output only consists of about 20 short stories, Garshin was a very talented writer, with a great moral sensitivity and a spirit of compassion for human suffering. These qualities were given a special stimulus by his army experiences during the war with Turkey in 1877. The war is reflected in "Four Days," a popular story of a wounded soldier who for four days remains on the battlefield next to the putrefying corpse of a Turk.

In spite of his literary reputation, Garshin grew increasingly morbid in his last years and ultimately committed suicide by throwing himself down a staircase. Of his stories, the best are the romantic "Attalea Princeps" (a fable about a palm tree) and "The Red Flower" (about the inmate of an insane asylum).

BOOK BY GARSHIN

The Signal and Other Stories. Trans. by Rowland Smith, Ayer repr. of 1915 ed. $21.00

GLADKOV, FYODOR. 1883–1958

Gladkov's literary activity developed after 1922, when he participated in so-called proletarian literary organizations. *Cement,* his most famous work, deals with the transition from the civil war period to the postwar reconstruction of industry and society. Its protagonists are depicted in an idealized, romantic way, but with some vigor and attempt at balance. Over the years, the novel was revised several times. Gladkov, in tune with the prevailing political and literary trends, made its contents increasingly bloodless.

Gladkov subsequently moved away from the romanticism of *Cement.* His later works include a "five-year plan" novel, *Energy,* and a three-volume autobiography.

BOOKS BY GLADKOV

Cement: A Novel. 1925. Trans. by A. S. Arthur and C. Ashleigh, Ungar pap. $9.95
Restless Youth. Trans. by R. Parker and V. Scott, Hyperion Pr. repr. of 1958 ed. 1976 $21.00

GOGOL, NIKOLAI. 1809–1852

A Ukrainian by background, Gogol was one of Russia's greatest writers, unsurpassed in imagination and comic wit. After trying to establish himself in different professions, he achieved a major success with a volume of stories based on Ukrainian life and folklore, *Evenings on a Farm near Dikanka*

(1831). Two additional collections were also successful: *Mirgorod* (1832) and *Arabesques* (1835).

During this early period, Gogol was in close contact with various groups of Russian intellectuals and literary men, including Pushkin. During the years, he drew ever closer to the Slavophiles, sharing their belief that Russia's national salvation lay in preserving patriarchal, pre-Petrine traditions.

His next great success came with the 1836 staging of the comedy *The Inspector-General* (also translated as *The Government Inspector*). Although its satirization of provincial bureaucracy raised a storm of official protest, the play established Gogol as a writer of genius. Soon afterward he left Russia; from 1836 to 1848 he lived almost entirely abroad. During this period, he produced several new works, among them "The Overcoat," perhaps the most influential Russian short story, and the first part of *Dead Souls*.

After 1848 Gogol grew ever more troubled. Certain negative traits began to dominate his personality. A belief in his personal mission to save Russia, faintly present in some early writings, was made explicit in *Selected Passages from Correspondence with Friends*. The book was derided in Russia. Partly in response to this, Gogol turned toward a fanatical brand of Christianity and embraced ascetic practices that ruined his health and upset his mental balance. A tragic result was his burning of most of the second part of *Dead Souls*. Shortly afterward, the combined mental and physical deterioration led to Gogol's death.

Generations of writers, readers, and critics have interpreted Gogol in different, contradictory ways. All these views find support in his literary heritage. Claimed as a founder of realism, he also has been considered a romantic and was an object of special interest for the symbolists. His early collections are infused with folklore, with its lyric and comic stories of devils, witches, and young lovers. Subsequently, the fantastic is transferred to the cold world of St. Petersburg, where the demonic assumes a more serious form. He was a social critic, particularly concerned for the victims of society ("The Overcoat"), yet he was also the creator of grotesque, puzzling plots, which defy rational interpretation ("The Nose"). Claimed for their own by both liberals and conservatives of the time, he was able to express a concern for Russia's future in images that have struck the imagination and have the storehouse of national symbols (the galloping troika of *Dead Souls*).

Finding the English equivalent of Gogol's style is very difficult. Existing translations (e.g., Garnett, Magarshack, MacAndrew, and Wilks) are accurate, but lack the verbal effervescence of the original.

BOOKS BY GOGOL

The Complete Tales of Nikolai Gogol. 1923. Trans. by Constance Garnett, ed. and rev. by Leonard J. Kent, Univ. of Chicago Pr. 2 vols. 1985 pap. ea. $9.95. Modernization of Garnett's classic translation, with annotations.

The Collected Tales and Plays of Nikolai Gogol. Ed. by Leonard J. Kent, Octagon repr. of 1964 ed. 1978 $43.00

The Overcoat and Other Tales of Good and Evil. Trans. by David Magarshack, Bentley repr. of 1965 ed. 1979 $12.50; Norton 1965 pap. $4.95

Diary of a Madman. Trans. by Ronald Wilks, Penguin 1973 $2.95. Includes "The
Nose," "The Overcoat," "How Ivan Ivanovich Quarrelled with Ivan Niki-
forovich," and "Ivan Fyodorovich Shponka and His Aunt."
Diary of a Madman and Other Stories. Trans. by Andrew R. MacAndrew, New Amer.
Lib. (Signet Class.) 1961 pap. $2.50
Nikolai Gogol: A Selection. Imported Pubns. 2 vols. 1980–81 ea. $11.00
The Mantle and Other Stories. Trans. by Claud Field, Ayer repr. of 1916 ed. $15.00
St. John's Eve and Other Stories. Trans. by Isabel F. Hapgood, Ayer repr. of 1886 ed.
$17.00
The Theater of Nikolay Gogol: Plays and Selected Writings. Ed. by Milton Ehre, trans.
by Milton Ehre and Fruma Gottschalk, Univ. of Chicago Pr. 1980 pap. $5.95. Ac-
curate translations; very helpful annotations.
Selected Passages from Correspondence with Friends. 1847. Trans. by Jesse Zeldin,
Vanderbilt Univ. Pr. 1969 $14.95
Arabesques. 1835. Trans. by Alexander Tulloch, intro. by Carl R. Proffer, Ardis 1981
$27.50 pap. $5.00. First translation of all the stories and essays in original collec-
tion.
Taras Bulba. Amereon repr. $9.95; Biblio Dist. (Everyman's) 1977 pap. $1.95
The Government Inspector. 1836. Trans. by D. J. Campbell, Heinemann 1981 pap.
$5.00
Marriage: An Absolutely Incredible Incident in Two Acts. Trans. by Bella Costello,
Barnes & Noble 1969 $8.95
Dead Souls. 1842. Airmont pap. $1.95; trans. by Andrew R. MacAndrew, New Amer.
Lib. (Signet Class.) 1961 pap. $2.95; trans. by George Reavey, intro. by George
Gibian, Norton 1971 pap. $7.95 1985 $29.95; trans. by David Magarshack, Pen-
guin 1961 $3.95

BOOKS ABOUT GOGOL

Fanger, Donald. *The Creation of Nikolai Gogol.* Harvard Univ. Pr. 1979 $20.00 pap.
$7.95. Major study; sophisticated analysis.
———. *Dostoevsky and Romantic Realism: A Study of Dostoevsky in Relation to Bal-
zac, Dickens, Gogol.* Univ. of Chicago Pr. 1968 pap. $7.00.
Frantz, Philip, comp. *Gogol: A Bibliography.* Ardis 1983 $30.00
Gippius, V. V. *Gogol.* Trans. and ed. by Robert A. Maguire, Ardis 1981 $22.50; Univ.
Pr. of New England text ed. 1963 pap. $8.50. By a very good early twentieth-cen-
tury Russian critic.
Karlinsky, Simon. *The Sexual Labyrinth of Nikolai Gogol.* Harvard Univ. Pr. 1976
$20.00
Maguire, Robert A., ed. *Gogol from the Twentieth Century: Eleven Essays.* Princeton
Univ. Pr. 1974 $40.00 pap. $12.50
Nabokov, Vladimir. *Nikolai Gogol.* New Directions 1961 pap. $4.95. Provocative,
Nabokovian.
Peace, Richard. *The Enigma of Gogol.* Cambridge Univ. Pr. 1982 $47.50

GONCHAROV, IVAN. 1812–1891

Goncharov came from a wealthy merchant family. He pursued a career in
the civil service, first in the Ministry of Finance, and later, during more liberal times after 1855, as an official of the censorship. His life was very
placid, troubled only once by an extended sea voyage to Japan. In his later
years, he suffered from paranoia, having become obsessed that Turgenev

and foreign writers (e.g., FLAUBERT) had plagiarized elements of his last work.

Goncharov's reputation as a major realist writer rests on his second novel, *Oblomov*. The fame of this text derives from its unmatched depiction of man's slothfulness and boredom, qualities incarnated in the book's hero, Oblomov, who has become a literary and psychological archetype, while the term "Oblomovism" has entered the language as a designation for indolence and inertia of epic proportions. Goncharov's other works have been somewhat slighted by the critics. *A Common Story* is an entertaining *bildungsroman* about a young man's gradual abandonment of his early ideals. *The Precipice*, on which Goncharov worked for almost 20 years, is a massive portrayal of country life. Although its antiradical plot is not terribly successful, the book contains a gallery of striking social and psychological types: particularly memorable are the novel's women.

BOOKS BY GONCHAROV

A Common Story. 1847. Trans. by Constance Garnett, Hyperion Pr. 1977 $15.00 pap. $10.00; (with the title *Same Old Story*) Imported Pubns. 1975 $7.95
Oblomov. 1859. Trans. by C. J. Hogarth, Bentley repr. of 1915 ed. 1980 $14.00; New Amer. Lib. (Signet Class.) 1981 pap. $3.95; *Penguin Class. Ser.* 1978 pap. $4.95
The Precipice. 1869. Trans. by M. Bryant, Fertig repr. of 1915 ed. $25.00; Hyperion Pr. abr. ed. 1977 pap. $10.00

BOOK ABOUT GONCHAROV

Ehre, Milton. *Oblomov and His Creator: The Life and Art of Ivan Goncharov*. Princeton Univ. Pr. 1974 $31.00

GORKY (GORKI), MAXIM (pseud. of Alexey Peshkov). 1868–1936

Gorky is officially viewed as the greatest Russian writer of the twentieth century—a rank far above the true measure of his talent. Proclaimed as the founder of the doctrine of socialist realism, he has had significant influence on many Soviet writers as well as authors in Europe and the developing world.

His formal education was minimal. From the age of eleven, he had to fend for himself, and he held a variety of jobs along the Volga River. Self-taught, he published his first story in 1892. His first collection, *Sketches and Stories*, is a romantic celebration of the strong outcasts of society—the hobos and the drifters—and helped popularize this type of literary protagonist. *Foma Gordeyev*, Gorky's first novel, gives a picture of generational conflict within the Russian bourgeoisie.

A popular public figure on the left, Gorky was often in trouble with the tsarist government. During the 1900s, he was the central figure in the Znanie publishing house, putting out realist prose with a social conscience. Some of his own works were extremely successful. The play *The Lower Depths* (1902), set in a poorhouse, is not only a staple of Soviet theater but also has been quite well known and influential in the United States: EUGENE O'NEILL's *The Iceman Cometh* is an offshoot of it. The novel *Mother* is an icon of a working-class woman who is transformed into a kind of saint of the Revolution; its optimism in the ultimate triumph of the cause has helped make it a prototype of socialist realist fiction. In the years prior to 1917, Gorky published his memoirs, a trio of works that show his art at its best, and some very lively reminiscences of such writers as Tolstoy and Chekhov. After the October Revolution, although a Bolshevik party member since 1905, he was very critical of the new regime. Very active in various cultural projects, he helped save the lives of many writers, artists, and scholars during the cold and hungry years of the civil war. In 1921, he left Russia for Italy, but returned permanently a decade later, recognized as the grand old man of Soviet literature. He was active on behalf of Stalin's economic policies and presided over the entrenchment of socialist realism. On his death, he left unfinished a major work of considerable interest, the novel *The Life of Klim Samgin* (1927–36).

BOOKS BY GORKY

Collected Works of Maxim Gorky. Imported Pubns. 10 vols. 1979–82 set $76.00

Selected Short Stories. Beekman 1975 $12.95

Selected Stories. Imported Pubns. 1981 pap. $4.00

A Book of Short Stories. Ed. by Avrahm Yarmolinsky and Moura Budberg, Octagon repr. 1972 $27.50

Orloff and His Wife: Tales of the Barefoot Brigade. Trans. by Isabel F. Hapgood, Ayer repr. of 1901 ed. 1973 $29.00

Twenty-Six Men and a Girl and Other Stories. Ayer repr. of 1902 ed. $21.00

Outcasts and Other Stories. Ayer repr. of 1905 ed. $18.00

Tales of Two Countries. Ayer repr. of 1914 ed. $15.00

Stories of the Steppe. Ayer repr. of 1918 ed. $10.00

The Lower Depths & Other Plays. Trans. by Alexander Bakshy and Paul S. Nathan, AMS Pr. repr. of 1945 ed. $17.25; Yale Univ. Pr. 1959 pap. $5.95. Contains *The Lower Depths, Barbarians, Enemies, Queer People, Vassa Zheleznova, The Zykovs, Yegor Bulychev.*

Plays. Imported Pubns. 1975 $6.45

Autobiography of Maxim Gorky. Trans. by I. Schneider, Citadel Pr. repr. of 1949 ed. 1969 pap. $5.95; Peter Smith $13.25. Contains *My Childhood, In the World, My Universities.*

My Apprenticeship; My Universities. Beekman 1975 $16.00; Imported Pubns. 1973 $6.95. Individual prose and theatrical works.

Foma Gordeyev. 1899. Century Bookbindery repr. of 1956 ed. 1981 $25.00; Greenwood repr. of 1956 ed. 1974 lib. bdg. $17.00

The Lower Depths. 1902. Trans. by Edwin Hopkins, Branden pap. $3.00

Enemies: A Play. 1906. Trans. by Jeremy Brooks and Kitty Hunter-Blair, intro. by Edward Braun, Viking 1972 $9.95

Mother. 1906. Trans. by I. Schneider, intro. by Howard Fast, Citadel Pr. 1984 pap. $6.95; trans. by Margaret Wettlin, Imported Pubns. repr. of 1949 ed. 1976 $4.40

My Childhood. 1913. Beekman 1975 $11.95; trans. by Ronald Wilks, *Penguin Class. Ser.* 1966 pap. $3.95; (with the title *Childhood*) Imported Pubns. 1973 $5.45

My Apprenticeship (In the World). 1916. Trans. by Ronald Wilks, *Penguin Class. Ser.* 1974 pap. $4.95

My Universities. 1922. Trans. by Ronald Wilks, *Penguin Class. Ser.* 1979 pap. $3.95

The City of the Yellow Devil. Imported Pubns. 1972 $4.45
Her Lover. Trans. by R. Nisbet, ed. by Isaac Goldberg, Branden pap. $3.00
Decadence. Trans. by Veronica Dewey, Folcroft repr. of 1927 ed. $25.00; trans. by Ve-
    ronica Dewey, fwd. by Irwin Weil, Univ. of Nebraska Pr. 1984 pap. $8.95
Culture and the People. Ayer repr. of 1939 ed. $19.00
Reminiscences of Leo Nikolaevich Tolstoy. Arden Lib. repr. of 1920 ed. 1981 $15.00;
    trans. by S. S. Koteliansky and Leonard Woolf, Folcroft repr. of 1920 ed. 1977
    $15.00
Untimely Thoughts. Trans. by Herman Ermolaev, Eriksson 1968 $6.95. Essays criti-
    cal of the Bolsheviks during 1917–18.
On Literature. Beekman 1975 $12.00; Imported Pubns. 1979 $9.45; Univ. of Washing-
    ton Pr. 1975 pap. $7.95. Selection of reminiscences, articles, letters; lively, well
    translated.
Letters. Imported Pubns. 1973 $4.95
Fragments from My Diary. Folcroft repr. of 1924 ed. $25.00
Bystander. Trans. by Bernard G. Guerney, Folcroft repr. of 1930 ed. $25.00
Reminiscences of My Youth. Trans. by Veronica Dewey, Dynamic Learning Corp.
    1979 $20.00; Richard West repr. of 1924 ed. 1980 $25.00

Books about Gorky

Hare, Richard. *Maxim Gorky: Romantic Realist and Conservative Revolutionary.*
    Greenwood repr. of 1962 ed. 1978 lib. bdg. $19.50
Wolfe, Bertram D. *The Bridge and the Abyss: The Troubled Friendship of Maxim Gorky
    and V. I. Lenin.* Praeger repr. of 1967 ed. 1983 $27.50

GREKOVA, IRINA (pseud. of Elena Venttsel). 1907–

A distinguished professional mathematician, Grekova has been publishing short stories and novellas since 1957. She raises important moral problems: "Ladies' Hairdresser" depicts a young, charmingly naive hairdresser
who approaches his work as a creative artist and is persecuted for this
nonconformism by the management and fellow workers. Grekova's tales are
presented from the point of view of a professional, urban woman—an unusual type of narrator in Soviet prose; the language of her stories is witty
and polished.

Book by Grekova

Russian Women: Two Stories. Trans. by Michael Petrov, Harcourt 1983 $17.95. Con-
    tains "Ladies' Hairdresser" and "The Hotel Manager."

HERZEN, ALEKSANDR. 1812–1870

Herzen's place in literature is linked to his role in Russia's political and
intellectual history. In the 1830s, together with his friend N. Ogaryov, he became the center of a university circle whose members were actively interested in utopian socialist theory. In the 1840s he helped shape the ideas of
Russian Westernism. He also wrote fiction. His novel *Who Is to Blame?* presents a woman caught between two men. All three are unable to find a
place for themselves in Russian society, and, in line with Herzen's ideas
about individual dignity and freedom, are responsible for their own unhappiness.

After leaving Russia in 1847, Herzen became actively involved in European revolutionary movements. Their failure produced *From the Other Shore* (1855), a collection of essays and dialogues on historical subjects. But his masterpiece is his memoirs, *My Past and Thoughts*, which presents Russian society in the first half of the nineteenth century through a combination of reminiscences, analysis, and anecdotes. Yet another achievement was *The Bell* (*Kolokol*), a weekly that Herzen published for a decade, which had an enormous influence on both government and society in Russia from 1857 to 1861.

Like many radical thinkers of the time (Vissarion Belinsky, Nikolay Chernyshevsky, and others), Herzen combined political and literary interests. Unlike them, however, he never lost his sensitivity of feeling and style, and directed his irony at his allies as well as his adversaries. In this, he was exceptional in Russian nineteenth-century letters.

BOOKS BY HERZEN

From the Other Shore. Trans. by Moura Budberg and Richard Wollheim, Hyperion Pr. repr. of 1956 ed. 1980 $21.50; trans. by Moura Budberg, *Oxford Pap. Ser.* text ed. 1979 $6.95

Who Is to Blame? A Novel in Two Parts. 1847. Trans. by Michael R. Katz, Cornell Univ. Pr. 1984 $32.50 pap. $9.95; trans. by Margaret Wettlin, Imported Pubns. 1978 $7.45. Katz's is an award-winning translation.

My Past and Thoughts. 1852–68. Gordon 6 vols. $600.00; trans. by Constance Garnett, ed. by Dwight McDonald, Univ. of California Pr. 1981 $34.00 pap. $9.95. The Gordon edition is complete; the University of California Press edition is a selection.

The Memoirs of Alexander Herzen. Trans. by J. D. Duff, Russell 2 pts. in 1 repr. of 1923 ed. 1967 $10.00. Selection from *My Past and Thoughts.*

Childhood, Youth and Exile: My Past and Thoughts, Parts 1 and 2. Trans. by J. D. Duff, Oxford 1980 pap. $5.95

BOOK ABOUT HERZEN

Carr, Edward H. *The Romantic Exiles.* Octagon repr. of 1933 ed. 1975 $27.50

ILF, ILYA (pseud. of Fainzilberg). 1897–1937, and PETROV, EVGENY (pseud. of Kataev). 1903–1942

The famous collaboration of Ilf and Petrov created the inimitable rogue and confidence man, Ostap Bender, whose adventures, with their frequent satiric thrusts at Soviet life, have become classics of Russian comic literature. In the first novel, *The Twelve Chairs*, Bender searches for a hoard of jewels concealed in a set of dining room chairs. In the second, *The Little Golden Calf*, Bender tries hard and fails to become a millionaire. A six-month car trip in 1935–36 through the United States resulted in a witty travelogue. The collaboration was broken by Ilf's untimely death from tuberculosis; Petrov was killed while working as a war correspondent.

BOOKS BY ILF AND PETROV

The Twelve Chairs (Diamonds to Sit On). 1928. Trans. by John H. Richardson, Pyramid Bks. 1973 o.p.
The Little Golden Calf (The Golden Calf). 1931. Trans. by Charles Malmouth, Ungar
1961 $11.50
Little Golden America. Trans. by Charles Malmouth, Ayer repr. of 1974 ed. $26.50

ISKANDER, FAZIL. 1929–

A native of Abkhazia in the Georgian Republic, Iskander is a noted author
of prose in Russian. Most of his works are set in his native region and are
narrated in the first person with a seemingly guileless comic wit, which allows Iskander to touch on various delicate topics. *The Goatibex Constellation*
is a very funny satire on the bureaucracy and on the misguided yet influential biological fantasies of Trofim Lysenko. Iskander took a different tack in
Sandro of Chegem, a series of tales about an Abkhazian's life from the 1880s
to the 1960s. The protagonist's saga, sometimes witty—sometimes terrifying—allows the author to tell the turbulent story of the Abkhazian people. A
small part of this very large work was published in the Soviet Union; the
complete text has appeared only in the West.

BOOKS BY ISKANDER

Thirteenth Labour of Hercules. Imported Pubns. 1978 pap. $5.45
The Goatibex Constellation. Trans. by H. Burlingame, Ardis 2d ed. 1982 pap. $3.95
Sandro of Chegem. Trans. by Susan Brownsberger, Random 1983 pap. $9.95
The Gospel According to Chegem. Random 1984 pap. $10.95

IVANOV, VSEVOLOD. 1895–1963

Ivanov, one of the most interesting Soviet prose writers, began writing before the October Revolution; his first efforts were encouraged by Gorky. His
well-known novel *Armoured Train 14-69* deals with the civil war and uses a
number of innovative fictional techniques. A very prolific writer, he was
first a member of the Serapion Brotherhood. Subsequently, his highly ornamental style gave way to the more sober practices of socialist realism.
Many of Ivanov's stories are set in distant regions of the Soviet Union and
reflect his interest in the exotic, oriental cultures.

A later work by Ivanov, *The Adventures of a Fakir*, is autobiographical,
very colorful, and quite readable.

BOOKS BY IVANOV

Selected Stories. Imported Pubns. 1983 pap. $4.00
Armoured Train 14-69. 1922. Trans. by Gibson-Cowan and A. T. Grant, Greenwood
repr. of 1933 ed. 1983 lib. bdg. $25.00
The Saga of the Sergeant. Ed. by G. A. Birkett, Irvington repr. of 1932 ed. 1966 pap.
$1.75
The Adventures of a Fakir. 1934–35. Hyperion Pr. repr. of 1936 ed. 1974 $20.35

KARAMZIN, NIKOLAI. 1766–1826

During 1789 and 1790 Karamzin, a young poet and short story writer, toured Western Europe; on his return, he distilled his impressions in the form of travel letters, a genre made popular by LAURENCE STERNE (see Vol. 1). *Letters of a Russian Traveller*, in which Karamzin's impressions are woven into a wealth of information about Western European society and culture, became a favorite of readers and was widely imitated.

The most influential prose writer of the eighteenth century, Karamzin shaped the development of the Russian literary language, introducing many Gallicisms to supplant Slavonic words and idioms, and breaking down the classicist canons of isolated language styles. Appointed court historian by Alexander I, he wrote a 12-volume *History of the Russian State* (1818–24)—a model of Russian prose.

BOOKS BY KARAMZIN

Letters of a Russian Traveller. 1797–1801. Trans. by Florence Jonas, Greenwood repr. of 1957 ed. 1976 lib. bdg. $20.75
Selected Aesthetic Works of Sumarokov and Karamzin. Trans. by Henry M. Nebel, Jr., Univ. Pr. of Amer. 1982 $24.00 pap. $11.75. Good selection, ample annotations.

BOOK ABOUT KARAMZIN

Cross, A. G. *N. M. Karamzin: A Study of His Literary Career, 1783–1803.* Southern Illinois Univ. Pr. 1971 o.p. Most comprehensive study.

KATAEV (KATAYEV), VALENTIN. 1897–

Kataev was a popular novelist in the 1920s, creating works full of humor and parody. He wrote an outstanding comic novel, *The Embezzlers*, aiming his wit at corrupt Soviet officials, and an excellent satiric play about the housing shortage, *Squaring the Circle* (1929, o.p.). In 1933, he wrote *Time Forward!* (o.p.), a novel about the construction of a metallurgical plant, regarded as a classic of socialist realism. Overall, he survived the Stalin years with a minimum of compromise yet fully active professionally. Since the 1960s, Kataev has experimented with semiautobiographical works, playing with time and memory, and paying homage to the many vanished figures of Russian culture.

BOOKS BY KATAEV

The Embezzlers. 1927. Trans. by Leonide Zarine, Hyperion Pr. repr. of 1929 ed. 1973 $21.00
The Small Farm in the Steppe. Trans. by Anna Bostock, Greenwood repr. of 1958 ed. 1976 lib. bdg. $19.75
A Mosaic of Life; or The Magic Horn of Oberon: Memoirs of a Russian Childhood. Trans. by Moura Budberg and Gordon Latta, O'Hara 1976 $15.00. Entertaining anecdotes of childhood; good translation.

KAVERIN, VENIAMIN (pseud. of Veniamin Zil'ber). 1902–

Kaverin began as a member of the Serapion Brotherhood, a loose association of writers united by a belief in the autonomy of art and the freedom of the writer. His early fiction shows the influence of Western authors: E. T. A. Hoffman, EDGAR ALLAN POE (see Vol. 1), ROBERT LOUIS STEVENSON (see Vol. 1). He has a talent for plot and good insight into psychology. Two of his novels are of particular note. *The Troublemaker* (o.p.) portrays the Leningrad literary milieu, in particular parodying the activities of the formalists. *The Unknown Artist* deals with the problem of the artist in the new society. Kaverin's later work has been more conventional, but it has confronted important issues; in the 1960s, it turned increasingly philosophical.

BOOK BY KAVERIN

The Unknown Artist. 1931. Hyperion Pr. repr. of 1947 ed. 1973 $15.00

BOOK ABOUT KAVERIN

Oulanoff, Hongor. *The Prose Fiction of Veniamin A. Kaverin.* Slavica 1976 pap. $11.95

KHLEBNIKOV, VELIMIR (VIKTOR VALDIMIROVICH). 1885–1922

Khlebnikov, who together with Mayakovsky was a principal figure in the futurist group, is famous both as poet and utopian thinker. He is well known for his radical attempts at linguistic theorizing and experimentation, for his idiosyncratic theories of historical recurrence, and for his nomadic, nonmaterialistic style of life. His works are highly complex and rich in meaning, and include a large number of lyric poems, narrative poems, stories, and theoretical articles.

Despite the enormous difficulty of translating Khlebnikov, selections from his work have appeared in many languages. An English translation of his complete writings is in progress.

BOOKS BY KHLEBNIKOV

The King of Time: Poems, Fictions, Vision of the Future. Trans. by Paul Schmidt, ed. by Charlotte Douglas, Harvard Univ. Pr. 1985 $18.50. Selection from forthcoming complete translation of Khlebnikov's works.
Snake Train: Poetry and Prose. Trans. by Gary Kern and others, ed. by Gary Kern, intro. by Edward J. Brown, Ardis 1976 o.p. Wide sampling; translations of prose are better than those of poetry.

BOOK ABOUT KHLEBNIKOV

Markov, Vladimir. *The Longer Poems of Velimir Khlebnikov.* Greenwood repr. of 1962 ed. 1975 lib. bdg. $15.00

KOROLENKO, VLADIMIR. 1853–1921

Of mixed Ukrainian-Polish parentage, Korolenko was exiled for political activity to Siberia (1879–84). He then spent a decade in the provincial city of Nizhny Novgorod, where he produced most of his best work. He returned to the capital in 1895 and was elected a member of the academy in 1900.

A major figure among the Populists, Korolenko fought actively against social and political injustices, writing publicistic pieces about religious persecution, racial discrimination, and other social issues. After the October

Revolution, he was hostile to the Bolshevik government and maintained this attitude until his death.

Korolenko's prose is distinguished by a charming lyricism, an optimistic love of both nature and man, and a wonderful sense of humor. His autobiographical *History of My Contemporary* shows many of these qualities and is perhaps his best work.

BOOKS BY KOROLENKO

Selected Stories. Imported Pubns. 1978 $5.45

The Blind Musician. Gordon repr. of 1890 ed. $34.95; Greenwood repr. of 1890 ed. lib. bdg. $15.00

In a Strange Land. Trans. by Gregory Zilboorg, Greenwood repr. of 1925 ed. 1975 lib. bdg. $15.75

Birds of Heaven and Other Stories. Trans. by Clarence A. Manning, Ayer repr. of 1919 ed. $17.00

Makar's Dream and Other Stories. Trans. by Marian Fell, Ayer repr. of 1916 ed. $17.00

KRYLOV, IVAN. 1769–1844

The greatest of the many classicist writers of verse fables, Krylov began as a journalist; some of his satiric essays are still very effective. The first publication of his fables in book form came in 1809; from then on, his work in this genre enjoyed enormous success both in the salons of St. Petersburg and among a wider reading public.

In his fables, initially modeled on LA FONTAINE and then increasingly original, Krylov criticized human stupidity, arrogance, and other vices. His success is partially due to his use of colloquial language. Many of his epigrammatic formulations are so apt and so pithy that they have solidly entered the corpus of Russian idioms. For this reason, he is very difficult to translate.

BOOKS BY KRYLOV

Krylov's Fables. Trans. by Bernard Pares, Hyperion Pr. 1977 $15.95 pap. $10.00

Kriloff and His Fables. Trans. by C. F. Coxwell, Scholarly repr. of 1869 ed. 1970 $29.00

KUPRIN, ALEKSANDR. 1870–1938

Kuprin was a leading figure in the realistically oriented "Znanie" group of writers. His education in a military academy and his subsequent army service provided the material for many of his early works. The most important of these is the short novel *The Duel*, which deals critically with Russian army life. Its subject and high literary qualities made it very popular. *The Pit* (1909) is also well known for its depiction of the life of prostitutes. In general, Kuprin's forte was the treatment of contemporary social problems; he was less adept at creating plots.

After the October Revolution, Kuprin settled in France. His humorous works in emigration are not as strong as those of the earlier period.

Books by Kuprin

Garnet Bracelet. Imported Pubns. 1982 pap. $4.00

River of Life and Other Stories. Ayer repr. of 1916 ed. $18.00

Gambrinus and Other Stories. Trans. by Bernard G. Guerney, Ayer repr. of 1925 ed.
    $13.00

Slav Soul and Other Stories. Ayer repr. of 1916 ed. $17.00

The Duel. 1905. Hyperion Pr. 1977 $15.00

Yama: The Pit. 1905–15. Trans. by Bernard G. Guerney, Hyperion Pr. 1977 $13.95
    pap. $5.50

KUZMIN, MIKHAIL. 1875–1936

Almost unknown to most Soviet readers, Kuzmin occupied an important place in Russian literature of the early twentieth century. An erudite and talented poet and prose writer, personally close to the symbolists, he developed a distinct aesthetic credo, advocating an abandonment of the symbolists' multilayered "forest of symbols" and a return to the appreciation of the concrete world for its own sake. He presented these views in a 1910 article, which is regarded as a manifesto of acmeism. In general, Kuzmin's writings show his immersion in the world of literature and philosophy, from antiquity to the present. His works often involve a reworking of historical and legendary subjects, as in "The Deed of Alexander of Macedon." Some of his poetic cycles reveal a degree of experimentation and complexity matched only by Mandelstam and Akhmatova. Finally, in both prose and poetry, Kuzmin often freely treated the theme of homosexual love, and was almost unique in Russian literature in this regard.

Books by Kuzmin

Selected Prose and Poetry. Trans. and ed. by Michael Green, Ardis 1980 pap. $6.50.
    Broad selection, including the novel *Wings.* Good introduction; uneven translations.

Travellers by Land and Sea. Trans. by John Barnstead, Ardis 1984 $17.95 pap. $5.00

LEONOV, LEONID. 1899–

Leonov revived the psychological novel of Dostoevsky and his early writing shows the influence of the nineteenth-century master. His popular first novel, *The Badgers,* deals with a revolt of peasants against Red Army grain collectors during the NEP period. *The Thief* (1927, o.p.) portrays the psychological traumas of a former civil war hero. During the Stalin period, Leonov produced a number of works generally in accord with the dictates of socialist realism, but still with unusual features and occasional flashes of dissent from the party line. *The Russian Forest,* featuring a conflict between a proponent of conservation and an advocate of industrialization whatever the cost, contains an interesting commentary on aspects of Stalinism.

Books by Leonov

The Badgers. 1924. Hyperion Pr. 1973 repr. of 1946 ed. $23.50

Skutarevsky. Trans. by Alec Brown, Greenwood 1971 repr. of 1936 ed. lib. bdg. $20.25

Soviet River. Trans. by Ivor Montagu and Sergei Nalbandov, Hyperion Pr. repr. 1981
    $21.50; (with the title *River*) Imported Pubns. 1983 pap. $4.00
The Russian Forest. 1953. Imported Pubns. 2 vols. 1976 $9.95

LERMONTOV, MIKHAIL. 1814–1841

One of Russia's greatest nineteenth-century poets, Lermontov was at first an officer in an elite Guard regiment. Because of the views he expressed in a passionate poem written on the death of Pushkin in 1837, he was arrested, tried, and transferred to the Caucasus. The poem, a passionate condemnation of the St. Petersburg elite for inciting Pushkin's ill-fated confrontation with D'Anthes, brought Lermontov instant fame. He returned to the capital a year later and began to publish regularly; two volumes of poems and the novel *A Hero of Our Time* appeared in 1840. Next year, as punishment for a duel, he was sent again to the army in the Caucasus, where he distinguished himself in battle. He was killed in a duel in July 1841, the result of his own quarrelsome conduct.

Lermontov was strongly influenced by BYRON (see Vol. 1) and SCHILLER. He wrote striking poems that unfolded his own psyche and presented him in the typically romantic posture of defiance toward society. The lyrics of his final years are more reflective and philosophical. There are also his longer narrative poems, derived from Byronic models. The most important is *The Demon*, the story of a fallen angel's love for a woman; it has provided Russian literature and art with a powerful archetype. Besides poetry, Lermontov also wrote plays and prose. Among the prose works, *A Hero of Our Time* is the most important. Made up of several tales by different narrators, the novel centers on Pechorin—an early example of the egotistical nineteenth-century "superfluous man," and a derivative of the Byronic hero. Both the figure of Pechorin and Lermontov's complex narrative technique gave a powerful stimulus to the development of Russian realist fiction.

BOOKS BY LERMONTOV

Major Poetical Works. Trans. by Anatoly Liberman, *Minnesota Publications in the Humanities Ser.* 1984 $39.50
Vadim. Trans. and ed. by Helena Goscilo, Ardis 1984 $17.50. Annotated.
The Demon. 1829–39. Ed. by Dennis Ward, Basil Blackwell pap. $9.95
A Hero of Our Time. 1837–40. Trans. by Vladimir Nabokov and Dmitri Nabokov, Doubleday (Anchor) 1982 pap. $4.95; trans. by Paul Foote, *Penguin Class. Ser.* 1966 pap. $3.95

BOOKS ABOUT LERMONTOV

Eikhenbaum, B. M. *Lermontov.* Trans. by Ray Parrot and Harry Weber, Ardis 1981 $20.00 pap. $6.50
Garrard, John. *Mikhail Lermontov. Twayne's World Authors Ser.* G. K. Hall 1982 $16.95

LESKOV, NIKOLAI. 1831–1895

A writer and journalist, Leskov was the son of a minor government official. His formal education was very limited, but was replaced by extensive reading. For a few years he was employed by the estate manager of a wealthy landowner. This job took him all over Russia and gave him material for the future.

In 1860, Leskov became a journalist. Soon, however, he started writing fiction. His first novel came out in 1864. It was an attack on the radical intelligentsia. In 1865, he produced his famous story "Lady Macbeth of the Mtsensk District," an account of passion and crime within the merchant class. The novel *The Cathedral Folk*, a charming, sympathetic depiction of life among the clergy, appeared in 1872. In the 1880s and 1890s, Leskov, very close to Tolstoy in his views on religion and art, wrote many didactic pieces, often drawing on Byzantine and medieval Russian texts to produce his anecdotes and fables. He also wrote a number of brilliant satires on Russian society.

Leskov's reputation among critics oscillated during his lifetime, but he has always been widely read, ranks among the major prose writers of the nineteenth century, and has been a significant influence on contemporary writers. Such authors as Zamyatin and Zoshchenko have been attracted by his verbal virtuosity, particularly by his use of narrators whose language is made colorful through colloquialisms, dialect words, and idioms (the *skaz* technique). He was also curiously modern in his relative disdain for the realist novel, and in his interest in such peripheral narrative models as the memoir, the anecdote, and the ethnographic account.

BOOKS BY LESKOV

The Sealed Angel and Other Stories. Trans. by K. Lantz, Univ. of Tennessee Pr. 1984 $23.95

The Amazon and Other Stories. Trans. by David Magarshack, Hyperion Pr. 1976 $15.00 pap. $10.00

The Enchanted Pilgrim and Other Stories. Trans. by David Magarshack, Hyperion Pr. 1977 $15.00

The Musk-Ox and Other Tales. Trans. by R. Norman, Hyperion Pr. 1977 pap. $10.00

The Sentry and Other Tales. Trans. by A. Chamot, intro. by Edward Garnett, Hyperion Pr. 1977 $14.85 pap. $10.00

The Cathedral Folk. 1872. Trans. by Isabel F. Hapgood, Greenwood repr. of 1924 ed. lib. bdg. $19.75; Hyperion Pr. 1977 pap. $10.00

BOOK ABOUT LESKOV

McLean, Hugh. *Nikolai Leskov: The Man and His Art.* Harvard Univ. Pr. 1977 $30.00. Exhaustive, scholarly account.

MANDELSTAM (MANDEL'SHTAM), OSIP. 1891–1938

Mandelstam is ranked by the cognoscenti as one of the greatest Russian poets of this century, a status that he has attained gradually, particularly since the rediscovery of his work in the late 1960s. Born into a Jewish merchant family, he was baptized in 1911, but never lost the link with Judaism; at the same time, steeped in Russian and European culture, he made Russia, its literature, and its fate in the modern world his primary concern as a verbal artist.

His total output is relatively modest. It includes several early published collections of poems and a number of later collections that appear only after his death. There is also the poet's prose, including numerous essays on Russian and world literature and experimental masterpieces, such as *The Egyptian Stamp* (o.p.) and *Journey to Armenia*, where the boundary between fiction, autobiography, and essay is obliterated. Mandelstam's early works are steeped in literature, as befitted a member of the classically oriented Acmeist group before the October Revolution. He extensively quoted and alluded to earlier poets and writers, taking up major questions of philosophy and art. The lyricism of works from this period can be broadly appreciated, but a true understanding of the poet's message requires the reader to penetrate Mandelstam's complex cultural universe. His later poetry attains an even higher level of artistry yet becomes simpler. Increasingly, its subject becomes the poet's own life during the Stalin years and his quest to assert the survival of the human spirit and of culture in the face of a totalitarian state.

Mandelstam's creation was inseparable from his life, particularly starting from about 1930. Nonconformist, increasingly isolated within literature and limited in his ability to work professionally, he lived poorly and was subject to persecution. He was arrested and exiled during the early 1930s. In May 1938 he was arrested again, and is said to have died in December of that year in a transit labor camp. His widow Nadezhda and a small group of friends preserved his writings at great personal risk. A number of translators have attempted to convey Mandelstam in English. In general, his prose has fared better at their hands than his poetry.

BOOKS BY MANDELSTAM

Selected Poems of Osip Mandelstam. Trans. by Clarence Brown and others, Atheneum 1984 pap. $6.95
Osip Mandelstam's Stone. Trans. by Robert Tracy, Princeton Univ. Pr. 1980 $23.00 pap. $8.95
Selected Poems. Trans. by David McDuff, Farrar bilingual ed. 1975 $10.00 pap. $3.95. Covers major periods; restrained English versions.
The Complete Prose and Letters of Osip Mandelstam. Ed. by Jane G. Harris and C. Anthony, Ardis 1979 pap. $12.50
Prose of Osip Mandelstam. Trans. by Clarence Brown, Princeton Univ. Pr. 1975 $21.00
Osip Mandelstam: Selected Essays. Trans. by Sidney Monas, Univ. of Texas Pr. 1977 $17.50. Mandelstam on Russian and world poetry; provocative and erudite. Accurate translations.
Journey to Armenia. 1931–32. Trans. by Sidney Monas, Ritchie 1979 $50.00. Experimental prose rendition of the poet's 1930 visit to Armenia.

BOOKS ABOUT MANDELSTAM

Brown, Clarence. *Mandelstam.* Cambridge Univ. Pr. 1973 $39.50 pap. $13.95. Thorough biography; comment on Mandelstam's writings.
Mandelstam, Nadezhda. *Hope Abandoned.* Trans. by Max Hayward, Atheneum 1973

pap. $12.95. Continuation of *Hope against Hope;* memoirs; includes harsh at-
tacks on many personalities of the Stalinist period.
———. *Hope against Hope.* Trans. by Max Hayward, Atheneum 1976 pap. $8.95.
Memoirs of the poet's widow; superbly written.
Taranovsky, Kiril. *Essays on Mandel'stam.* Harvard Univ. Pr. 1976 $14.50. Funda-
mental studies on Mandelstam's poetics; provides the key to the modern understanding of his art.

MAYAKOVSKY, VLADIMIR. 1893–1930

Mayakovsky was one of Russia's most important avant-garde poets. He began as a futurist, one of a group of painters and poets of the 1910s, and became noted for his flamboyance in public life, for his aesthetic iconoclasm,
and for the very real verbal brilliance of his poems. Early involvement with
the Bolsheviks (1908) was followed years later by endorsement of the new
Soviet government. Mayakovsky placed his talents at the service of the Soviet state, although his dreams for drastic cultural changes were rebuffed
by the new rulers, most of whom had relatively conservative tastes in literature. During the civil war and the 1920s, Mayakovsky wrote a great deal of
agitational verse of varying quality; he also wrote film scenarios and two
plays. A notable figure in Soviet life, he had a considerable international
reputation and was allowed to travel abroad. However, he was also harshly
criticized for his deviation from the increasingly rigid Soviet cultural
norms. This, in combination with problems in his personal life, ultimately
led to his suicide at age 36.

Mayakovsky was a great innovator in the realm of versification. His experiments with rhythm, rhyme, and language affected many poets. Verbal
innovation, particularly the use of extravagant metaphor and hyperbole,
went hand in hand with great lyric talent, often refracted through the poet's
various comic and tragic masks. Among his most important achievements
are his long narrative poems, such as *The Cloud in Trousers* (1915), *War and
the World,* and *About That.* Also very good are his plays, *The Bedbug* (1928)
and *The Bathhouse* (1929)—brilliant satires of Soviet philistinism and bureaucracy.

BOOK BY MAYAKOVSKY

The Bedbug & Selected Poetry. Trans. by Max Hayward and George Reavey, ed. by Patricia Blake, Indiana Univ. Pr. 1975 $17.50 pap. $5.95

BOOKS ABOUT MAYAKOVSKY

Brown, Edward J. *Mayakovsky: A Poet in the Revolution.* Princeton Univ. Pr. 1973
$39.00. Excellent, thorough analysis of Mayakovsky's life and art.
Charters, Ann, and Samuel Charters. *I Love: The Story of Vladimir Mayakovsky and
Lili Brik.* Farrar 1979 $17.50. Interesting biographical material, but caution ad-
vised.
Terras, Victor. *Vladimir Mayakovsky. Twayne's World Authors Ser.* G. K. Hall 1983
$18.95. A good introduction.

NABOKOV, VLADIMIR ("Sirin," pseud.). 1899–1977

Nabokov belonged to two literatures, Russian and American. Born into a prominent political family, he emigrated in 1919 and lived in Europe, mostly Germany, until 1940, when he emigrated to the United States. In this country, he taught in several universities and not only wrote but also worked professionally in lepidopterology. At age 60, he moved for the last time to Switzerland.

Nabokov's reputation rests on numerous novels and short stories, both in Russian and English. The former date from his time in Germany and mostly depict life in emigration. The most important of these is *The Gift*, which not only treats the life of émigrés, but through it takes a close look at Russian literature and intellectual history. The English-language novels were written both in America and Switzerland. They include the celebrated *Lolita*, *Ada*, and *Look at the Harlequins!* During this period Nabokov also translated (or supervised the translation of) his Russian novels and stories, so that a large body of his writings, in versions authorized by the author, is accessible in two languages.

A hallmark of Nabokov's art is its deliberate artifice. Nabokov disdained Dostoevsky and admired Gogol and Pushkin; not surprisingly, therefore, his own works are full of complex, puzzlelike plots, in which fantasy plays a major role. Literature itself is a prime subject of Nabokov's fiction; he frequently underscored the "createdness" of his texts through unreliable narrators, and he filled his novels and stories with literary allusions and quotations—a good knowledge of literature is essential to a full understanding of Nabokov.

Besides his fiction, which has made him a major figure in twentieth-century literature, Nabokov also made his mark as a critic and translator. His commented prose rendition of Pushkin's poem *Eugene Onegin* is a hallmark in Pushkin scholarship.

BOOKS BY NABOKOV

The Portable Nabokov. Ed. by Page Stegner, *Viking Portable Lib.* Penguin 1978 pap. $7.95

Nabokov's Dozen. Avon 1973 pap. $2.95; Ayer repr. of 1958 ed. $16.50; Doubleday 1984 pap. $6.95

A Russian Beauty and Other Stories. Trans. by Dmitri Nabokov and Simon Karlinsky, McGraw-Hill 1974 pap. $5.95

Tyrants Destroyed and Other Short Stories. Trans. by Dmitri Nabokov, McGraw-Hill 1975 $8.95 1981 pap. $5.95. Mostly pre-World War II stories.

Details of a Sunset and Other Stories. McGraw-Hill 1980 pap. $4.95. Tales of Russian émigré life.

Poems and Problems. McGraw-Hill 1981 pap. $5.95

The Man from the U.S.S.R. and Other Plays. Trans. by Dmitri Nabokov, Harcourt 1984 $24.95

The Nabokov-Wilson Letters: Correspondence between Vladimir Nabokov and Edmund Wilson. Ed. by Simon Karlinsky, Harper 1979 $16.30. Approximately 250 letters; fascinating intellectual interaction; well edited and annotated.

Lectures on Russian Literature. Ed. by Fredson Bowers, intro. by Simon Karlinsky,

Harcourt 1981 $19.95 1982 pap. $9.95. Witty and idiosyncratic; best read after a
    more balanced historical overview.
Lectures on Don Quixote. Ed. by Fredson Bowers, Harcourt 1983 $17.95 1984 pap.
    $7.95. Personal vision of the great novel.
Lectures on Ulysses: A Facsimile of the Manuscript. Bruccoli 1980 $75.00
Lectures on Literature: British, French and German Writers. Intro. by John Updike,
    Harcourt 1980 $19.95. Seven college lectures; a writer's view of fellow writers.
Mary. 1926. McGraw-Hill 1981 pap. $4.95
King, Queen, Knave. 1928. McGraw-Hill 1980 pap. $5.95
Laughter in the Dark. 1932. New Directions rev. ed. 1960 $12.50 pap. $5.95
Glory: A Novel. 1933. McGraw-Hill 1971 $6.95 1980 pap. $4.95
Invitation to a Beheading. 1938. Putnam 1965 pap. $6.95
Real Life of Sebastian Knight. 1941. Intro. by C. Benner, New Directions 1959 $16.00
    pap. $5.95
Bend Sinister. 1947. McGraw-Hill 1973 pap. $5.95
Lolita. 1955. Berkley Publishing 1984 pap. $3.95; Putnam 1972 $5.95; (with the title
    Annotated Lolita) ed. and intro. by Alfred J. Appel, Jr., McGraw-Hill 1970 pap.
    $6.95
Pnin. 1957. Avon 1973 pap. $3.50; Bentley repr. of 1957 ed. 1982 $12.50; Doubleday
    (Anchor) 1984 pap. $6.95
Pale Fire. 1962. Berkley Publishing 1982 pap. $3.50; Putnam 1980 pap. $6.95
Speak, Memory: An Autobiography Revisited. 1966. Putnam 1970 $7.95
Ada or Ardor: A Family Chronicle. 1969. *McGraw-Hill Pap.* 1980 pap. $6.95
Transparent Things. McGraw-Hill 1972 $9.95
Look at the Harlequins! McGraw-Hill 1974 $7.95 1981 pap. $5.95
Lolita: A Screenplay. McGraw-Hill 1983 pap. $6.95
Notes on Prosody and Abram Gannibal. Bollingen Ser. Princeton Univ. Pr. 1969 pap.
    $7.95
Strong Opinions. McGraw-Hill 1973 $8.95 1981 pap. $6.95

BOOKS ABOUT NABOKOV

Boyd, Brian. *Nabokov's "Ada": The Place of Consciousness.* Ardis 1985 pap. $7.50
Field, Andrew. *Nabokov: His Life in Art.* Little, Brown 1967 o.p.
———. *Nabokov: His Life in Part.* Viking 1977 $18.95
Hyde, George M. *Vladimir Nabokov: America's Russian Novelist.* Humanities Pr.
    1977 $18.75
Johnson, D. Barton. *Worlds in Regression: Some Novels of Vladimir Nabokov.* Ardis
    1985 $25.00 pap. $7.50
Page, Norman, ed. *Nabokov: The Critical Heritage.* Routledge & Kegan 1982 $25.00
Rivers, J. E., and Charles Nicol, eds. *Nabokov's Fifth Arc: Nabokov and Others on His
    Life's Work.* Univ. of Texas Pr. 1982 $30.00. Broad selections; insightful, stimulat-
    ing essays.
Rydel, Christine. *A Nabokov Who's Who: A Complete Guide to Characters and Proper
    Names in the Works of Vladimir Nabokov.* Ardis 1985 $30.00 pap. $15.00

NEKRASOV, NIKOLAI. 1821–1878

Nekrasov entered literature at an early age after his father, a brutal country squire, refused to support him at the university. A very considerable
business ability brought him success in publishing. From 1846 to 1866 he
was the co-owner and editor of *The Contemporary*, and in his hands the jour-

nal became the leading Russian literary organ, which published works by all the major writers. Later, he achieved a similar success with the journal *Notes of the Fatherland.*

Besides his publishing work, Nekrasov was also a poet, a principal representative of the realist school—a movement that, under the influence of radical critics, eschewed the aesthetic in favor of the civic, choosing themes from contemporary Russian life and its many problems. Nekrasov was at his strongest as a satirist. His masterpiece is the vast poem *Who Can Be Happy and Free in Russia?*, in which a group of peasants wanders through the country and shows the reader a vast catalog of evils in Russian life. Not only satire, but also his lyric and narrative poems are deeply influenced by folklore; perhaps his most important work that shows this is the long poem *The Peddlars*, the beginning of which has in turn become a popular song.

Books by Nekrasov

Poems. Trans. by Juliet Soskice, Hyperion Pr. 1977 $11.50 pap. $3.50
Who Can Be Happy and Free in Russia? 1863–78. Trans. by Juliet Soskice, Hyperion Pr. 1977 pap. $4.95
Red-Nosed Frost. Ed. by V. E. Holttum, Basil Blackwell $9.95

Book about Nekrasov

Chukovsky, Kornei. *The Poet and the Hangman: Nekrasov and Muravyov.* Trans. by R. W. Rotsel, Ardis 1977 $10.00 pap. $2.95

OLESHA (OLYESHA), YURY. 1899–1960

Of Polish background, Olesha opted for the new Soviet state and became popular in the early 1920s for his satiric verse. His most important work, *Envy*, deals with the problems of older intellectuals in accepting the new Soviet society, as does the play *A List of Benefits* (o.p.). The novella *The Three Fat Men*, a fairy tale about a revolution, also proved very popular. Olesha wrote a number of excellent short stories as well. During the Stalin period, his work was essentially suppressed; only after his death was *No Day without a Line* put together from his manuscripts.

Although his total output is modest, Olesha was a major figure in modern Russian prose. He was a master of fictional technique, particularly adept at manipulating imagery and at forcing the reader to reexamine personal expectations of what depictions of reality should be like. Among his major themes, the artist's place in contemporary society stands out. It is developed with great detail in *Envy*.

Books by Olesha

Envy and Other Works. Trans. by Andrew R. MacAndrew, Norton 1981 pap. $7.95
Envy. 1927. Trans. by Thomas Berczynski, Ardis 1979 pap. $4.50
Yury Olesha: The Complete Short Stories and The Three Fat Men. Trans. by Aimée Fisher, Ardis 1979 $17.50
The Complete Plays. Trans. and ed. by M. Green and J. Katsell, Ardis 1983 $27.50 pap. $7.50. Moderately interesting, well-translated works.

No Day without a Line. 1965. Ardis 1979 $17.50 pap. $7.00. Literary criticism, memoirs, notes; concise, anecdotal.

BOOK ABOUT OLESHA

Beaujour, Elizabeth K. *The Invisible Land: A Study of the Artistic Imagination of Iurii Olesha.* Columbia Univ. Pr. 1970 $27.00

OSTROVSKY (OSTROVSKII), ALEKSANDR. 1823–1886

Aleksandr Ostrovsky was the major figure in Russian theater thanks to the large number of his plays (about 50, mostly in prose) and to their generally high artistic merit. His work falls into two periods. The first, pre-1861, includes dramas that mostly deal with an area of Russian life Ostrovsky knew quite intimately—the society of merchants and of the lower levels of the government bureaucracy. The treatment this social sphere received at Ostrovsky's hands was quite varied. He exhibited both an attraction and a disgust for certain attitudes and human types he depicted. His masterpiece of this period is *The Storm* (1860), in which social themes provide the background and the motivation for a tragic love story.

After 1861, Ostrovsky devoted himself in part to historical dramas and to plots taken from folklore [for example, his masterpiece, *The Snow Maiden* (1873, o.p.)]. Other plays deal with the gentry in the changed conditions of postemancipation Russia; some of them are staples of the Russian dramatic repertoire.

BOOKS BY ALEKSANDR OSTROVSKY

Without a Dowry and Other Plays. Trans. and ed. by Norman Henley, Ardis 1985 $32.50. Also includes *A Profitable Position, Ardent Heart, Talents and Admirers.*
Easy Money and Two Other Plays: Even a Wise Man Stumbles, and Wolves and Sheep. Trans. by David Magarshack, Greenwood repr. of 1944 ed. lib. bdg. $15.00
Artistes and Admirers. Trans. by E. Hanson, Univ. of Manchester Pr. 1970 pap. $6.50
The Storm. 1860. Trans. and intro. by David Magarshack, Ardis 1985 $15.00 pap. $5.00

OSTROVSKY, NIKOLAI. 1904–1936

Nikolai Ostrovsky was the author of the celebrated inspirational classic, *How the Steel Was Tempered.* Autobiographical, highly simplistic, it deals with the formation and growth of its dedicated Communist hero, Pavel Korchagin. A special aura surrounds the work; its author was blind and bedridden when he wrote it. Since 1935, the book has been used as a propaganda tool in educating Soviet youth.

BOOKS BY NIKOLAI OSTROVSKY

How the Steel Was Tempered. 1932–34. Imported Pubns. $5.95.
Born of the Storm. Trans. by Louise L. Hiler, Hyperion Pr. repr. of 1939 ed. 1975 $19.25. Ostrovsky's second novel about revolution in the Ukraine; unfinished.

PANOVA, VERA. 1905–1973

Panova's first novel, *The Train*, about a hospital train in World War II, won the 1947 Stalin Prize. She won two more Stalin prizes for her work, but was criticized at times by the establishment. After Stalin's death, she was the first to come out with a work, *Span of the Year*, that violated the canons of official literature by focusing on the problems of the individual and by showing the fallibility of party bureaucrats. Her novel stands as a landmark of the "thaw" period. In later years, she wrote finely crafted works about children, as well as a cycle of tales drawn from medieval Russian history.

BOOKS BY PANOVA

Selected Works. Imported Pubns. 1976 $6.45
The Factory. Trans. by Moura Budberg, Hyperion Pr. repr. of 1949 ed. 1977 $20.35
Span of the Year. 1954. Trans. by Vera Traill, Hyperion Pr. repr. of 1957 ed. 1977 $18.75
On Faraway Streets. Trans. by Rya Gabel, Braziller 1968 $3.95

PASTERNAK, BORIS. 1890–1960 (NOBEL PRIZE refused 1958)

Pasternak was acclaimed as a major poet some 30 years before *Dr. Zhivago* made him world famous. After first pursuing promising careers in music and philosophy, he started writing around 1909 and came out with his first collection of verse in 1914. His first genuine triumph came with the collection *My Sister, Life* (1917), in which a love affair stimulates a rapturous celebration of nature. The splendid imagery and difficult syntax of this volume are a hallmark of the early Pasternak.

During the 1920s, Pasternak tried to accept the new historical reality, and moved from the lyric to the epic, taking up historical and contemporary subjects (e.g., the long poem *The Year 1905*). He was tolerated by the literary establishment, but increasingly in the 1930s turned to translation rather than original verse. He was a prolific translator; his versions of major Shakespeare plays have become the standard texts used in Soviet theaters.

From the start, prose was an important focus of Pasternak's efforts. The most notable early work is the story "The Childhood of Luvers" ("Zhenia's Childhood"), which explored a girl's developing consciousness of her surroundings. There is also his artistic and intellectual autobiography, *Safe Conduct*. But Pasternak's greatest prose achievement came later in the novel *Dr. Zhivago*, which was written over a number of years. Its hero, a physician and a poet, confronts the great changes of the early twentieth century and travels a path through life that parallels that of Christ. *Dr. Zhivago* was rejected for publication in the Soviet Union. It appeared in 1957 in the West and won its author worldwide acclaim. A Nobel Prize followed in 1958. This led to a major public campaign against Pasternak in the Soviet Union. Pressure placed on the poet was so extraordinary that he officially turned down the award. After that, he was left in relative peace, and he died within a couple of years. He was the first of many writers in the post-Stalin period to challenge the Soviet state.

BOOKS BY PASTERNAK

Selected Poems. Trans. by Jon Stallworthy and Peter France, Norton 1983 $15.00;
    Penguin 1984 pap. $6.95. Economical, apt translations; good introduction by
    Pasternak's son.
Poems of Boris Pasternak. Trans. by Lydia Pasternak, Allen & Unwin 1984 pap. $4.95
My Sister, Life. Trans. by Mark Rudman, Ardis 1983 $22.50 pap. $7.50
Seven Poems. Trans. by George L. Kline, Unicorn Pr. 1970 $10.00 pap. $3.00
The Correspondence of Boris Pasternak and Olga Freidenberg. Trans. and comp. by Elli-
    ott Mossman, Harcourt 1982 $19.95 pap. $9.95. Moving vision of the two corre-
    spondents and Russian society in the Stalin period.
Letters: Summer 1926. Trans. by Margaret Wettlin and Walter Arndt, ed. by Yevgeny
    Pasternak, Yelena Pasternak, and Konstantin M. Azadovsky, Harcourt 1985
    $24.95. Correspondence between Pasternak, Marina Tsvetayeva, and Rainer Ma-
    ria Rilke.
Zhenia's Childhood. 1922. Schocken 1982 $13.95 pap. $5.95
Dr. Zhivago. Ballantine 1981 pap. $3.50; Pantheon 1958 $17.95; Univ. of Michigan
    Pr. 1959 $24.00
Safe Conduct. 1931. Intro. by Babette Deutsch, New Directions 1958 pap. $6.25
I Remember: Sketch for an Autobiography. Trans. by David Magarshack, Harvard
    Univ. Pr. 1983 pap. $4.95; Peter Smith $11.75
The Poems of Dr. Zhivago. Trans. and ed. by Donald Davie, Greenwood repr. of 1965
    ed. 1977 lib. bdg. $21.00

BOOKS ABOUT PASTERNAK

Conquest, Robert. *The Pasternak Affair: Courage of Genius.* Octagon repr. of 1962 ed.
    1979 $18.00
Davie, Donald, and Angela Livingstone, eds. *Pasternak.* Aurora 1970 pap. $2.50
De Mallac, Guy. *Boris Pasternak: His Life and Art.* Univ. of Oklahoma Pr. 1981 $26.95
Gifford, Henry. *Pasternak: A Critical Study.* Cambridge Univ. Pr. 1977 $42.50 1981
    pap. $17.95
Hughes, Olga R. *The Poetic World of Boris Pasternak.* Princeton Univ. Pr. 1974 $20.00
Ivinskaya, Olga. *A Captive of Time: My Years with Pasternak.* Trans. by Max Hay-
    ward, Beekman 1979 $22.50
Rowland, Mary F., and Paul Rowland. *Pasternak's "Dr. Zhivago."* Southern Illinois
    Univ. Pr. 1968 $10.95 pap. $6.95

PAUSTOVSKY, KONSTANTIN. 1892–1968

Paustovsky's first story was published in 1912; over the years, he developed into one of the best stylists in twentieth-century Russian literature,
and he was nominated for the Nobel Prize in 1965. He wrote many stories,
novels, and plays, and managed to escape being totally bound by the
straightjacket of socialist realism even during the Stalin era. He is known
for his short stories, in which depictions of protagonists who escape from reality into dreams are combined with a sharp eye for realistic detail. *Story of
a Life* (1947–60), his reminiscences of more than 50 years, is often considered his best work and contains a great deal of interesting material.
Paustovsky was very popular during the post-Stalin period and had a great
impact on younger writers. In 1966, he made an appeal for the convicted

writers Daniel and Sinyavsky—an action that won widespread admiration within the Russian intelligentsia.

BOOKS BY PAUSTOVSKY

Selected Stories. Imported Pubns. 1974 $5.45
Story of a Life. Pantheon 1982 $8.95
The Black Gulf. Trans. by Eugenia Schimanskaya, Hyperion Pr. repr. of 1946 ed. 1977 $15.00

PILNYAK, BORIS (pseud. of Boris Vogau). 1894–1937?

Pilnyak was one of the leading writers of the 1920s. He became very popular after the publication of *The Naked Year,* which deals with the Revolution and its impact on Russia. His subsequent career was marred by several scandals. A 1926 story, "The Tale of the Unextinguished Moon," which presents the death of a high-ranking military leader in terms similar to the actual death of a celebrated army commissar Frunze, brought him into difficulties; all copies of the magazine in which the story appeared were confiscated. A more dangerous situation arose when the novel *Mahogany* was published in Germany in 1929: a campaign of villification forced him from the All-Russian Union of Writers. In the 1930s, Pilnyak slowly faded from view. He was arrested during the purges and apparently shot in 1937.

Pilnyak's great impact on literature came largely from his style. Continuing the ornamental tradition of Bely, he created a literary language that combines epic solemnity with lyricism, draws on folklore, and freely creates complex, often highly striking or shocking constructions. The attraction of such techniques was so strong that charges of "Pilnyakism" were leveled against many writers who followed in a similar vein. Pilnyak's works were very carefully constructed; as has been shown in recent criticism, they express complex meanings derived from his views on major philosophical problems.

BOOKS BY PILNYAK

Ivan Moscow. Trans. by A. Schwartzman, Hyperion Pr. repr. of 1935 ed. 1973 $15.00
The Naked Year. 1921. AMS Pr. repr. of 1928 ed. $12.50; trans. by Alexander Tulloch, Ardis 1975 $25.00 pap. $5.95
Tales of the Wilderness. Trans. by F. O'Dempsey, Hyperion Pr. repr. of 1925 ed. 1973 $16.50
Volga Falls to the Caspian Sea. AMS Pr. repr. of 1931 ed. $15.00

BOOK ABOUT PILNYAK

Browning, Gary. *Boris Pilnyak: Scythian at a Typewriter.* Ardis 1985 $25.00. Critical study of life and works.

PISEMSKY (PISEMSKII), ALEKSEI. 1820–1881

A provincial, and ridiculed as such by some, Pisemsky was educated in Moscow, where he began to attract attention with his *Sketches of Peasant Life* (o.p.). In 1858 he became the editor of a major literary journal; the same year, he published his famous novel *One Thousand Souls*, the story of an ambitious man's unscrupulous rise to power and wealth. A year later he came out with another notable work, the play *A Bitter Fate* (1860, o.p.), a tragedy about peasants. In his art and many polemic pieces, Pisemsky was an exponent of Slavophile and nationalist ideas. His writings provide a good perspective on this important strain in Russian life.

BOOKS BY PISEMSKY

One Thousand Souls. 1858. Trans. by Ivy Litvinov, Greenwood repr. of 1959 ed. lib. bdg. $18.50; Hyperion Pr. 1977 pap. $5.95
The Simpleton. Trans. by Ivy Litvinov, Hyperion Pr. 1977 $12.65 pap. $10.00
Nina, the Comic Actor and an Old Friend. Trans. by Maya Jenkins, Ardis 1984 $17.50

BOOK ABOUT PISEMSKY

Moser, Charles A. *Pisemsky: A Provincial Realist*. Harvard Univ. Pr. 1969 $16.50

PLATONOV, ANDREI. 1899–1951

An electrical engineer and land reclamation specialist by background, for a long time Platonov was remembered mainly as a member of the Pereval group of the 1920s and early 1930s. (Pereval was a group of writers influenced by the basically humanistic, cultivated ideas of the critic Voronsky.) A very fine stylist, Platonov was vehemently attacked for his ideological "mistakes" by the more extreme "proletarian" writers, and such assaults eventually forced him to stop publishing. He reemerged during the war, but new attacks once again reduced him to silence. As a result of these persecutions, only a portion of Platonov's real output was known. Within the last few years, however, publication of more of his works has shown him to be an important figure in modern Russian prose. His key novels, *Chevengur* and *The Foundation Pit* (o.p.), have appeared only in the West. Profoundly pessimistic, they reveal him as deeply skeptical of attempts by communism to remold human nature, and sharply critical of the debasement of language that took place in the Soviet Union during the Stalin years.

BOOKS BY PLATONOV

Andrei Platonov: Collected Works. Trans. by Marion Jordon and others, Ardis 1978 $22.50 pap. $5.50
Fierce, Fine World. Trans. by Laura Beraha and others, Imported Pubns. 1983 pap. $4.00
Chevengur. Trans. by Anthony Alcott, Ardis 1978 $17.50 pap. $6.50

PRISHVIN, MIKHAIL. 1873–1954

By training, Prishvin was a specialist in agronomy. His interests, however, were much broader, encompassing ethnography and folklore, linguistics, and ornithology, all of which benefited from his many travels. His first published work was a collection of stories, *In the Land of Unscared Birds* (1907, o.p.). The emphasis on nature in this book is characteristic of much of Prishvin's subsequent prose.

Prishvin was notable for his rich, colorful use of language. In this, as well as in his injection of ethnographic concerns into literature, he was close to his contemporary Remizov, and part of the "neorealist" strain in early twentieth-century prose.

BOOKS BY PRISHVIN

The Lake and the Woods; or Nature's Calendar. Trans. by W. L. Goodman, Greenwood repr. of 1951 ed. lib. bdg. $17.50

Jen Sheng: The Root of Life. Trans. by George Walton and Philip Gibbons, Hyperion Pr. repr. of 1936 ed. 1973 $18.15

PUSHKIN, ALEKSANDR. 1799–1837

Pushkin is acknowledged as the greatest Russian poet—a "national poet"—unsurpassed in his mastery of diverse genres and in the perfection with which he blended contents and form in his works. "Pushkinian simplicity" is a byword in the history of Russian literature. Born in a gentry family, he was educated and made his literary debut in an exclusive school near Petersburg. He was welcomed into the capital's literary society, quickly becoming an intimate of its leading figures, but his rather wild life in Petersburg came to an end in 1820, when he was banished to the South of Russia for some of his political verses. The years of exile were very productive. The Caucasus, the Crimea, and Moldavia, with their exotic, oriental character, stimulated the writing of major works. Equally beneficial was the poet's subsequent restriction to his mother's estate in Mikhailovskoye (1824–26); his confinement there also kept Pushkin from active involvement with the unsuccessful Decembrist revolt in 1825. A new phase in the poet's life began in September 1826, when he was summoned by Emperor Nicholas I, granted a pardon for past offenses, and promised special protection. Yet Pushkin's existence under the eye of his imperial patron and censor proved increasingly restrictive. In addition, although his creative genius was in full flower, his personal life was far from happy. In 1831, after a long courtship, Pushkin married the beautiful but frivolous Nathalie Goncharova. His wife was a success in court circles, and Pushkin was thrust into the company of people whom he scorned and who had little use for him. The final crisis was provoked by Nathalie's friendship with a Frenchman in Russian service, Baron D'Anthès. A series of incidents culminated in a duel between Pushkin and his wife's admirer in January 1837. The poet was wounded and died two days later. At the orders of the authorities, who feared public outrage, he was hastily buried.

Pushkin demonstrated his genius in short lyrics, long narrative poems, plays, and prose. His poems, especially those of his mature period, are extraordinary in their ease, effortless control, and universality of thought and feelings. His narrative poems are of various types. Some, such as "The Fountain of Bakhchisaray," are modeled on BYRON's (see Vol. 1) Eastern tales. *Eugene Onegin,* his single greatest creation, is a brilliant, psychologically subtle "novel in verse" about a Petersburg dandy. An "encyclopedia of Russian life" of the time, it helped establish the tradition of Russian realism. His final long poem, *The Bronze Horseman* (1833), deals with the opposition between the rights of the individual and the demands of the state; in this dramatic and majestic work, the conflict, posed in the context of Russian history, is left unresolved.

Among Pushkin's plays, the Shakespearean *Boris Godunov* (1825) is better known in the West (thanks to the opera!) but yields in depth to a group of extraordinarily concentrated short plays, *The Little Tragedies* (1830s). The poet's prose, which includes the *Tales of Belkin* (1831) and *The Queen of Spades* (1834), was extremely important in the development of Russian fiction. It had a major impact on, among others, Dostoevsky and Tolstoy. Pushkin was also the author of several hundred very lively letters (in the fashion of the time, often intended for a wider audience) and of many critical essays on literature.

Pushkin's witty, precise, yet melodious writing has presented challenges to translators. Vladimir Nabokov's exchanges with Edmund Wilson on translating Pushkin are evidence of the very different methods that may be adopted. Nabokov's own rendition of *Eugene Onegin* is obligatory for anyone with serious interest in Pushkin. Walter Arndt has been very successful in capturing the rhythms, style, and meaning of the poems; Debreczeny's recent translation of the prose is particularly noteworthy.

BOOKS BY PUSHKIN

The Poems, Prose and Plays of Pushkin. Ed. by Avrahm Yarmolinsky, Modern Lib. 1943 $5.95

Collected Narrative and Lyrical Poetry. Trans. and ed. by Walter Arndt, Ardis 1984 $30.00 pap. $9.50. Metrical translations.

The Bronze Horseman: Selected Poems of Alexander Pushkin. Trans. and intro. by D. M. Thomas, *Penguin Class. Ser.* 1983 pap. $5.95; Viking 1982 $15.95. Some excellent renditions, but Thomas's approach has stirred controversy.

Narrative Poems by Alexander Pushkin and by Mikhail Lermontov. Trans. by Charles Johnston, intro. by Kyril FitzLyon, Random (Vintage) 1983 $12.95 pap. $5.95

Selected Works. Imported Pubns. 2 vols. 1974 $8.45

Epigrams and Satirical Verse. Trans. by Cynthia H. Whittaker, Ardis 1984 $15.00

Pushkin's Fairy Tales. Trans. by Janet Dalley, Smith Publications 1979 $12.95

Alexander Pushkin: Complete Prose Fiction. Trans. by Paul Debreczeny, Stanford Univ. Pr. 1983 $38.50. Accurate, elegant translations by a leading Pushkin scholar; excellent introduction and notes.

Complete Prose Tales of Pushkin. Norton 1968 pap. $9.95

Captain's Daughter and Other Stories. Random (Vintage) 1957 pap. $4.95

Captain's Daughter and Other Tales. Trans. by Natalie Duddington, Biblio Dist. (Everyman's) repr. of 1933 ed. 1978 $10.95 pap. $2.95

The Queen of Spades and Other Stories. Trans. and intro. by Rosemary Edmonds, *Penguin Class. Ser.* 1978 pap. $3.95. Includes "The Captain's Daughter" and "Dubrovsky."

Prose Tales. Trans. by T. Keane, Ayer repr. of 1914 ed. $22.00

Letters of Alexander Pushkin. Trans. by J. Thomas Shaw, Univ. of Wisconsin Pr. 3 vols. in 1 1967 pap. $17.50

Boris Godunov. Trans. by Philip L. Barbour, Greenwood repr. of 1953 ed. 1976 lib. bdg. $22.50; trans. by Alfred Hayes, intro. by Peter Ustinov, Viking 1982 $19.95

Eugene Onegin: A Novel in Verse. 1823–31. Trans. by Walter Arndt, Dutton rev. & enl. ed. 1981 pap. $6.25; trans. by Charles Johnston, intro. by John Bayley, *Penguin Class. Ser.* 1979 pap. $3.95; trans. by Vladimir Nabokov, *Bollingen Ser.* Princeton Univ. Pr. bilingual ed. 4 vols. 1981 $120.00 2 vols. pap. $19.95; trans. by Charles Johnston, Viking 1978 $12.50. The Nabokov edition is extremely accurate, has exhaustive commentaries, and is indispensable to students of Pushkin.

The Golden Cockerel. Trans. by Elizabeth C. Hulick, Astor-Honor 1962 $7.95

A Journey to Arzrum. Trans. by Birgitta Ingemanson, Ardis 1974 $7.95

The History of Pugachev. Trans. by Earl Sampson, Ardis 1983 $17.95

BOOKS ABOUT PUSHKIN

Debreczeny, Paul. *The Other Pushkin: A Study of Alexander Pushkin's Prose Fiction.* Stanford Univ. Pr. 1983 $32.50

Jakobson, Roman. *Pushkin and His Sculptural Myth.* Trans. and ed. by John Burbank, Mouton 1975 pap. $15.00

Lednicki, Waclaw. *Pushkin's Bronze Horseman: The Story of a Masterpiece.* Greenwood repr. of 1978 lib. bdg. $24.75

Lezhnev, Abram. *Pushkin's Prose.* Trans. by Roberta Reeder, intro. by Paul Debreczeny, Ardis 1983 $27.95 pap. $6.50

O'Bell, Leslie. *Pushkin's "Egyptian Nights": The Biography of a Work.* Ardis 1984 $21.50

Todd, William M., III. *The Familiar Letter as a Literary Genre in the Age of Pushkin.* Princeton Univ. Pr. 1977 $26.50

Vickery, Walter N. *Alexander Pushkin. Twayne's World Authors Ser.* G. K. Hall $13.50

REMIZOV, ALEKSEI (ALEXEI). 1877–1957

A very prolific prose writer, artist, and calligrapher, Remizov was a paradoxical figure, well known for his love of the grotesque and the comic, in both life and literature. Influenced by symbolism, he still maintained a very personal style, which over the years moved from a continuation of realist traditions, albeit with modernist tendencies into a fictional world of dreams and fantasy, removed from any definable genre. He was fascinated by ethnography and history, particularly Russian, and many of his works are reworkings of medieval and folk texts. He was a superb stylist. His ornamental prose influenced such writers as Zamyatin and Pilnyak. An émigré since the 1920s, Remizov was almost totally ignored in the Soviet Union until a few years ago. Translations of his works have been appearing for a long time in the West, and he has been attracting increasing critical attention and becoming recognized as an important figure in the development of Russian prose.

BOOKS BY REMIZOV

Selected Prose. Ed. by Sona Aronian, Ardis 1985 $25.00 pap. $9.95. Comprehensive collection from various periods; extensive introduction; major bibliography of criticism.

The Clock. Trans. by John Cournos, Hyperion Pr. 1977 $15.00 pap. $3.50

Fifth Pestilence with the History of the Tinkling Cymbal & Sounding Brass: Ivan

Semyonovich Stratilatov. Trans. by Alec Brown, Hyperion Pr. 1977 $15.00 pap. $10.00

On a Field Azure. Trans. by Beatrice Scott, Greenwood repr. of 1946 ed. 1975 lib. bdg. $15.00; Hyperion Pr. 1977 pap. $2.95

SALTYKOV-SHCHEDRIN, MIKHAIL ("Shchedrin," pseud.). 1826–1889

The greatest satirist of the nineteenth century, Saltykov served as a government official until the mid-1860s, when he devoted himself full time to writing. A liberal, interested in Western literature generally, he and his writings suffered the political ups and downs of changing times. As editor of the journal *Notes of the Fatherland*, he was a very influential figure in Russian intellectual life, and particularly in its radical wing, although he had sharp disagreements with other radicals over their social prescriptions for the future.

Many of Saltykov's pieces are too journalistic and topical to be easily accessible today. His major works, however, continue to be read with great interest. Among these is his magnificent satire on Russian history, *The History of a Town* (1869–70), compressed into the story of the town of Foolov. His most important work, however, is a set of stories about the decline of a gentry family, published as a single text under the title *The Golovlyov Family*. The novel, with its unforgettable negative hero, Porfiry Petrovich, ranks among the great creations of Russian realist prose.

BOOKS BY SALTYKOV-SHCHEDRIN

The Golovlyov Family. 1872–76. Trans. by Samuel Cioran, Ardis 1976 $17.50 pap. $5.95; trans. by Natalie Duddington, Hyperion Pr. 1977 $14.85

The History of a Town; or The Chronicle of Foolov. Trans. by Susan Brownsberger, Ardis 1982 $25.00 pap. $7.50

The Pompadours: A Satire on the Art of Government. Trans. and intro. by David Magarshack, Ardis 1985 $24.00 pap. $6.95

Fables. Trans. by Vera Velkhovsky, Greenwood repr. of 1941 ed. 1976 lib. bdg. $19.25; Hyperion Pr. 1977 $15.00 pap. $3.95

SHALAMOV, VARLAM. 1907–1982

Shalamov, a poet and prose writer, spent about 17 years in the Kolyma camps in Siberia, one of the harshest parts of the Soviet camp system. He fixed his experiences and those of other convicts in a cycle of superb short stories. These convey the overwhelming horror of the camps through terse, often one-episode plots, dispassionate narration, and irony. Ideally, the Kolyma cycle should be read in conjunction with Solzhenitsyn's *The Gulag Archipelago*. The selections in the first of the two volumes in English translation are stronger than in the second.

BOOKS BY SHALAMOV

Kolyma Tales. Trans. by John Glad, Norton 1980 $9.95 1982 pap. $5.95
Graphite. Trans. by John Glad, Norton 1981 $14.95

SHOLOKHOV, MIKHAIL. 1905–1984 (NOBEL PRIZE 1965)

For decades a pillar of the Soviet literary establishment, Sholokhov owes his stature principally to *The Quiet Don*, a four-volume epic of the life and fate of the Don Cossacks in the revolution and civil war. Although himself a party member, Sholokhov depicted both sides in the civil war fairly impartially, and showed his hero, Gregory Melekhov, as he was driven by background and fate from one to the other. The novel is very realistic, the exotic Cossack milieu is captured superbly, and the whole works on a scale unseen since *War and Peace*. Among Sholokhov's later works, *Virgin Soil Upturned*, which deals with the collectivization of agriculture, deserves particular mention, but it is far weaker than the great historical novel and shows Sholokhov's submission to the dictates of the party.

Over the years, Sholokhov's authorship of *The Quiet Don* has been questioned, most recently, among others, by Solzhenitsyn. Sholokhov does have strong defenders, both in the Soviet Union and the West. Part of the anger directed against him resulted from his political stance. Very conservative in his politics, Sholokhov made vicious attacks on dissidents and the West, and, aside from his concern for the environment, was a very devoted follower of the party line.

BOOKS BY SHOLOKHOV

Mikhail Sholokhov: Collected Works. Imported Pubns. 1984 vol. 1 $9.95
And Quiet Flows the Don. 1928–40. Imported Pubns. 4 vols. 1974 $14.00; trans. by H. C. Stevens, Random 2 vols. 1965 pap. $7.95
Don Flows Home to the Sea. Trans. by H. C. Stevens, Random 1965 vols. 3 & 4 pap. $6.95
Virgin Soil Upturned. 1932–60. Imported Pubns. 2 vols. 1979 $10.20. Based on a bowdlerized 1952 edition.
At the Bidding of the Heart: Essays, Sketches, Speeches, Papers. Imported Pubns. 1973 $4.45

BOOK ABOUT SHOLOKHOV

Ermolaev, Herman. *Mikhail Sholokhov and His Art*. Princeton Univ. Pr. 1982 $32.00

SHUKSHIN, VASILY. 1929–1974

Shukshin was a popular film actor and director, as well as one of the new generation of "village writers"—authors who celebrate the countryside and search for stable values in the traditional rural society. He published a number of collections, plays, and novels that used colloquial Russian with great effectiveness. His writing has been very popular, but Shukshin's most celebrated achievement is the film *Snowball Berry Red*, the story of a former criminal who tries to reform—Shukshin directed the film, starred in it, and wrote the original story on which it is based.

BOOKS BY SHUKSHIN

I Want to Live: Short Stories. Trans. by Robert Daglish, Imported Pubns. 1973 pap. $3.95

Roubles in Words, Kopeks in Figures and Other Stories. Trans. by Natasha Ward and David Illife, Boyars 1984 $14.95

SIMONOV, KONSTANTIN. 1915–1979

Simonov had a long career as a poet, playwright, and novelist. His poetry includes many love lyrics as well as pieces on historical subjects; some of his poems of the war period became very popular during that time. He was at his best in his prose, particularly the trilogy dealing with the war period: *Days and Nights* (1945, o.p.), *The Living and the Dead*, and *Soldiers Are Not Born* (o.p.). For his work, Simonov received the top Soviet prizes; he was a leading member of the literary establishment.

BOOK BY SIMONOV

The Living and the Dead. 1959–71. Trans. by R. Ainsztein, Greenwood repr. of 1962 ed. 1968 lib. bdg. $25.00

SINYAVSKY, ANDREI ("Abram Tertz," pseud.). 1925–

In February 1966, Sinyavsky and Yuli Daniel were tried in a closed court; in spite of appeals by many writers in Russia and the West, they were sentenced to terms in labor camp for maligning the Soviet Union through "hostile" and "slanderous" writings published illegally abroad in the early 1960s. The trial marked the start of a period of confrontation between Soviet authorities and the nascent human rights movement in the Soviet Union. As Tertz, Sinyavsky wrote a number of satiric, often grotesque and surrealistic prose works, including the short novel *The Trial Begins* (1960) and the essay "On Socialist Realism," a brilliant attack on official Soviet literary dogma. After his emigration to the West in 1973, he published *A Voice from the Chorus*, a hybrid work in which notes and letters from a labor camp are a vehicle for philosophical and literary meditations, and where the author's own voice is joined by a multitude of voices of other inmates. A professor of Russian literature at the Sorbonne, Sinyavsky has been very active in émigré literary life, generally taking a liberal, democratic position on political and cultural matters. He has edited a journal, written many polemic essays, and publised important works of criticism, both under his own name and under his pseudonym. Sinyavsky's many contributions make him one of the most important figures in contemporary Russian letters.

BOOKS BY SINYAVSKY

The Trial Begins. Trans. by Max Hayward and George Denis, Univ. of California Pr. 1982 pap. $6.95. Bound with "On Socialist Realism."
A Voice from the Chorus. Trans. by Kyril FitzLyon and Max Hayward, intro. by Max Hayward, Farrar 1976 $10.00

SOLOGUB, FEDOR (pseud. of Fyodor Kuzmich Teternikov). 1863–1927

Sologub was a representative of the symbolist movement, particularly in its early decadent phase. A schoolteacher for many years, he began to publish in the 1890s. He attracted wide attention with his *The Petty Demon*, in which a brilliant satirical depiction of provincial society is the background for the descent into paranoia of the brutish Peredonov. This novel stands at the transition from realist to modernist fiction and has been widely translated. Sologub's poetry is notable for its economy and lyricism, and has earned him a place among major Russian poets of the early twentieth century. Like much of his prose, it reflects Sologub's pessimistic, dualistic philosophy, which inverts traditional symbols of good and evil.

BOOKS BY SOLOGUB

The Sweet-Scented Name and Other Fairy Tales and Stories. Ed. by S. Graham, Hyperion Pr. 1977 $11.95 pap. $3.95
Bad Dreams. 1896. Trans. by Vassar Smith, Ardis $16.00 pap. $5.50
The Petty Demon. 1907. Trans. by Samuel Cioran, Ardis 1983 $30.00 pap. $6.95. Critical essays on the novel appended.
The Created Legend. 1907–13. Trans. by Samuel Cioran, Ardis 3 vols. 1978–79 ea. $13.00–$17.00 pap. ea. $5.00; trans. by John Cournos, Fertig repr. of 1916 ed. 1975 $13.50; Hyperion Pr. 1977 pap. $10.00. Cioran's translation includes the complete trilogy; Cournos's only includes the first volume.

BOOK ABOUT SOLOGUB

Rabinowitz, Stanley J. *Sologub's Literary Children: Keys to a Symbolist's Prose.* Slavica 1980 $10.95

SOLOUKHIN, VLADIMIR. 1924–

One of the most noted of the "village writers," Soloukhin started publishing in 1946. His prose celebrates the countryside, both nature and the village society. A twentieth-century Slavophile, Soloukhin has been concerned with the destruction of Russia's cultural monuments, particularly churches and icons—e.g., his controversial *Letters from the Russian Museum* (o.p.). Soloukhin has been extremely prolific; *Vladimir Country Roads* (o.p.), the account of a trip in central Russia, is particularly well known.

BOOKS BY SOLOUKHIN

Sentenced and Other Stories. Trans. by D. W. Martin, Ardis $20.00 pap. $6.50
Honey on Bread. Imported Pubns. 1982 pap. $4.00

SOLZHENITSYN, ALEKSANDR. 1918–   (NOBEL PRIZE 1970)

Solzhenitsyn's fame rests on works shaped by his experiences during the Stalin years. In February 1945, while in the army, he was arrested for exchanging with a friend a number of letters critical of Stalin and sentenced to eight years' imprisonment. He served his term in various places, including a prison research institute, such as described in his novel *The First Circle* (1968). Exiled "in perpetuity" in 1953, he taught school in central Asia, overcame stomach cancer (his experiences in an oncological clinic are reflected in *Cancer Ward*), was freed in 1956, and was rehabilitated in 1957.

With this background, Solzhenitsyn became an unmatched chronicler of the Soviet penal system. His novella *One Day in the Life of Ivan Denisovich,* which appeared during Khrushchev's anti-Stalin campaign, was the first to deal honestly with the Soviet "concentration camp universe" and brought instant fame to its author. For a few years, Solzhenitsyn enjoyed some official backing. Things changed by the mid-1960s, when he was stopped from publishing and was subjected to both open and covert harassment. New attacks followed publication in the West of *Cancer Ward* and *The First Circle;* expulsion from the Writers' Union came in 1969.

In 1970, Solzhenitsyn was awarded the Nobel Prize for literature. The final episode in his duel with the state came in December 1973, when the first volume of *The Gulag Archipelago* was published in Paris. Its appearance resulted in Solzhenitsyn's arrest and expulsion from the Soviet Union in February 1974.

Solzhenitsyn's life abroad (in Vermont since 1976) has been secluded, although he had given a number of controversial speeches and interviews concerning Western society and its relationships to the Soviet bloc. He has revised and reissued his earlier works, but his principal writing project has been a series of novels (overall title *The Red Wheel*) dealing with World War I and the coming to power of the Bolsheviks. The first of these is *August 1914* (recently revised); parts of the second, *October 1916*, have appeared in Russian.

Solzhenitsyn continues the traditions of Dostoevsky and Tolstoy, using the narrative vehicle to examine moral and philosophical concerns. He is a master of language, and is particularly noted for his use of very picturesque colloquial Russian (including prison camp slang).

BOOKS BY SOLZHENITSYN

We Never Make Mistakes. Trans. by Paul W. Blackstock, Univ. of South Carolina Pr. repr. of 1963 ed. 1971 $8.95; Norton 1971 pap. $5.95. Includes "Incident at Krechetovka Station" and "Matryona's House."

Nobel Lecture. Trans. by Thomas P. Whitney, Harper 1972 $5.95; trans. by F. D. Reeve, Farrar bilingual ed. 1973 pap. $1.50

Warning to the West. Farrar 1976 $7.95 pap. $5.95. Speeches and interviews during 1975–76, often critical of Western society.

A World Split Apart. Harper 1979 $9.57 pap. $4.76. Text of 1978 controversial commencement address at Harvard: biting critique of Western society and values.

East and West: The Nobel Lecture on Literature, A World Split Apart, Letter to the Soviet Leaders, and a BBC Interview with Aleksandr I. Solzhenitsyn. Harper 1980 pap. $1.95

Detente: Prospects for Democracy and Dictatorship. 1976. Transaction Bks. 2d ed. 1980 $4.95 pap. $3.95. Criticism of U.S. foreign policy; critique of Solzhenitsyn's views included.

The Mortal Danger: How Misconceptions about Russia Imperil America. Harper 2d ed. 1981 pap. $3.95. Strident, often harsh criticism of American policy and policymakers.

One Day in the Life of Ivan Denisovich. 1962. Bantam 1970 pap. $2.95; trans. by Ralph Parker, intro. by M. Kalb, fwd. by A. Tvardovsky, Dutton repr. of 1963 ed. 1971 $4.95; trans. by Gillon Aitken, Farrar 1971 $15.00; New Amer. Lib. (Signet Class.) pap. $2.50

Cancer Ward. 1968. Bantam 1969 pap. $4.95; trans. by Rebecca Frank, Dell 1974 pap. $3.75; trans. by Nicholas Bethell and David Burg, Modern Lib. $10.95

The First Circle. 1968. Bantam 1976 pap. $4.95

August 1914. 1971. Bantam repr. of 1971 ed. 1974 pap. $1.50; trans. by Michael Glenny, Farrar 1972 $10.00

The Gulag Archipelago, 1918–1956: An Experiment in Literary Investigation. 1973. Trans. by Thomas P. Whitney, Harper 1974 $20.14 pap. $1.95. Parts 1 and 2 of the massive chronicle of the Soviet camp system. Fascinating combination of historical analysis, literary craftsmanship, and polemics.

The Gulag Archipelago, Two. Trans. by Thomas P. Whitney, Harper 1975 $20.14 pap. $4.33. Parts 3 and 4.

The Gulag Archipelago, Three. Trans. by Harry T. Willetts, Harper 1978 $20.14 1979 pap. $2.95. Parts 5–7.

The Oak and the Calf: A Memoir. 1975. Trans. by Harry T. Willetts, Harper 1980 $17.26 1981 pap. $8.61. Solzhenitsyn against the Soviet system until his exile; often fascinating; sometimes pretentious.

Lenin in Zurich: Chapters. 1975. Trans. by Harry T. Willetts, Farrar 1976 $8.95. Chapters on Lenin from August 1914 and from forthcoming works in *The Red Wheel* cycle. Plays and poems.

The Love-Girl and the Innocent. Trans. by Nicholas Bethell and David Burg, Farrar 1970 $5.95 pap. $2.95

Candle in the Wind. Trans. by Keith Armes and Arthur Hudgins, Univ. of Minnesota Pr. 1973 $10.00

Prussian Nights. 1974. Trans. by Robert Conquest, Farrar bilingual ed. 1977 $8.95 pap. $2.95. A weak poem about World War II.

BOOKS ABOUT SOLZHENITSYN

Berman, Ronald, ed. *Solzhenitsyn at Harvard: The Address, Twelve Early Responses, and Six Later Reflections.* Ethics & Public Policy Center 1980 $11.00 pap. $7.00. A good sample of commentary on Solzhenitsyn's Harvard speech.

Dunlop, John B., Richard S. Haugh, and Alexis Klimoff, eds. *Aleksandr Solzhenitsyn: Critical Essays and Documentary Materials.* Macmillan 1975 pap. $4.95; Nordland 1974 $47.50. Very important collection on Solzhenitsyn pre-exile.

Dunlop, John B., Richard S. Haugh, and Michael Nicholson, eds. *Solzhenitsyn in Exile: Critical Essays and Documentary Materials.* Hoover Institution 1985 $19.95. New, very important anthology.

Feuer, Kathryn B., ed. *Solzhenitsyn: A Collection of Critical Essays.* Prentice-Hall (Spectrum Bks.) 1976 $12.95. Fine selection of materials.

Kodjak, Andrej. *Alexander Solzhenitsyn.* Twayne's World Author Ser. G. K. Hall 1978 $13.95

Labedz, Leo, ed. *Solzhenitsyn: A Documentary Record, with the Nobel Prize Lecture.* Indiana Univ. Pr. enl. ed. 1973 o.p. Very important collection of documents.

Lakshin, Vladimir. *Solzhenitsyn, Tvardovsky and Novy Mir.* Trans. by Michael Glenny, MIT 1980 $17.50 pap. $5.95. An account of the early Solzhenitsyn, by a participant.

Lukacs, Georg. *Solzhenitsyn.* Trans. by William D. Graf, MIT 1971 pap. $2.95. Discussion of early prose by a leading critic.

Moody, Christopher. *Solzhenitsyn.* Modern Writers Ser. Barnes & Noble 2d ed. rev. 1975 $8.50

Scammell, Michael. *Solzhenitsyn: A Biography.* Norton 1984 $29.95. Most up-to-date, extensive study of Solzhenitsyn's life and writings—a landmark.

STRUGATSKY, ARKADY. 1925–   , and STRUGATSKY, BORIS. 1933–

The Strugatsky brothers are very popular science fiction writers who have regularly used the genre to comment on contemporary society. Some of their works, such as *The Snail on the Slope* and *The Ugly Swans*, have been very controversial.

BOOKS BY ARKADY AND BORIS STRUGATSKY

Hard to Be a God. Seabury 1973 o.p. Negative utopia; commentary on historical theories.
Escape Attempt. Trans. by Roger DeGaris, Macmillan 1982 $14.95
Roadside Picnic. Pocket Bks. 1982 pap. $2.50

TOLSTOY, ALEXEY NIKOLAEVICH. 1883–1945

Alexey Nikolaevich Tolstoy developed from a talented writer at the fringes of symbolism before World War I into a leading figure in Soviet letters and an apologist for the regime during the Stalin period. *Nikita's Childhood* is a moving exploration of the world of a young boy. *Aelita* is a utopia, an early example of this genre in Russia. A trilogy on the Revolution, *Road to Calvary* (1918–23), is uneven, with the first work, *The Sisters* (o.p.), the most successful. Tolstoy's best work is the unfinished novel *Peter the First* (1921–34). Its first two parts have won it a major place in Russian historical fiction. Making deft use of detail and language of the period, Tolstoy portrayed Peter as a great historical figure and painted a striking picture of the reformist emperor and his society.

BOOKS BY ALEXEY NIKOLAEVICH TOLSTOY

Nikita's Childhood. 1920. Imported Pubns. 1977 $6.45
Aelita, or The Decline of Mars. 1922. Trans. by Leland Fetzer, Ardis 1985 $15.00 pap. $5.95

TOLSTOY, LEO (TOLSTOI, LEV). 1828–1910

Tolstoy's biography is characterized by moral and artistic seeking, and by conflict with himself and his surroundings. Of the old nobility, he began by living the usual, dissipated life of a man of his class; however, his inner compulsion for moral self-justification led him on a different path. In 1851 he became a soldier in the Caucasus, and he began to publish while stationed there. Even more significant were his experiences during the Crimean War; the siege of Sevastopol provided the background for his sketches of human behavior in battle in the *Sevastopol Stories*.

After the war, Tolstoy mixed for a time with St. Petersburg literary society, traveled extensively abroad, and married Sophia Bers. The couple were happy for a long time, but his religious conversion in 1879 led to increasing unhappiness and bitter conflict.

Tolstoy's life after his marriage was centered on his family. He celebrated it in the final section of *War and Peace*, the great novel in which he unfolded the stories of families in Russia during the Napoleonic period, and in which he explored the nature of historical causation and of freedom and necessity.

A different note emerged in *Anna Karenina*. Here, too, Tolstoy focused on families, this time emphasizing an individual's conflict with society and its norms. A period of inner crisis culminated in Tolstoy's 1879 conversion to a rationalistic form of Christianity in which moral behavior was supremely important.

Tolstoy then began to proselytize his faith through fiction, publicistic essays, and personal contacts. Between 1880 and 1883 he wrote three major works on religion. A supreme polemicist, he participated in debates on a large number of political and social issues, generally at odds with the government. His advocacy of nonresistance to evil attracted many followers and later had a profound influence on MAHATMA GANDHI (see Vol. 4) and through him MARTIN LUTHER KING, JR. (see Vol. 4). Tolstoy's stature as a writer and public figure was enormous both within Russia and abroad, greater than that of any other Russian writer. When he was excommunicated by the Orthodox Church in 1901, a cartoon depicted him as disproportionately larger in stature than his ecclesiastical judges.

The final years were filled with inner torment. Living as he did on a luxurious estate, Tolstoy felt himself at odds with his own teachings. He also suffered from his conflict with his wife over the disposition of his property, which she wished to safeguard for their children. In 1910, desperately unhappy, the aged writer left home. He did not get far; he caught pneumonia and died of heart failure at a railway station, an event that was headline news throughout the world.

In the course of Tolstoy's career, his art evolved significantly, but it possessed a certain underlying unity. From the beginning, he concentrated on man's inner life. The body of his writing is enormous, encompassing both fiction and a vast amount of publicistic material. Besides his three great novels (including *Resurrection*), there are many superb shorter works. Among these, *The Death of Ivan Ilyich* (1884) stands as a philosophical text of the first order, while the *Hadji Murat* is a gem of narration and plot construction. Tolstoy has been translated extensively. The (Louise and Aylmer) Maude and Garnett translations are institutions (sometimes modernized)— for many works, they are the only versions available—and are used by different publishers. Translations by Edmonds, Magarshack, and Dunnigan are also justifiably popular.

BOOKS BY LEO TOLSTOY

Complete Works of Count Tolstoy. Trans. by Leo Wiener, AMS Pr. repr. of 1905 ed. 24 vols. $900.00

The Portable Tolstoy. Trans. by Louise Maude, Aylmer Maude, and George Kline, ed. by John Bayley, *Viking Portable Lib.* Penguin 1978 pap. $9.95. Chronologically arranged, includes *The Kreutzer Sonata* and *The Power of Darkness*.

Short Novels. Ed. by Ernest J. Simmons, Modern Lib. $6.95

Great Short Works of Leo Tolstoy. Intro. by John Bayley, Harper pap. $3.80

Tolstoy: Tales of Courage and Conflict. Ed. by Charles Neider, Carroll & Graf repr. of 1958 ed. 1985 pap. $11.95. Thirty-six stories arranged chronologically, including "The Death of Ivan Ilyich" and "The Kreutzer Sonata."

The Raid and Other Stories. Ed. by Aylmer Maude and Louise Maude, intro. by P. N. Furbank, *World's Class. Ser.* Oxford 1982 pap. $4.95

Sebastopol: Tales. 1855–56. Trans. by Frank D. Millet, intro. by Philip Rahv, Univ. of Michigan Pr. 1961 pap. $6.95

Tales of Sevastopol: The Cossacks. Imported Pubns. 1982 $10.95

The Cossacks, Sevastopol, The Invaders and Other Stories. Ayer repr. of 1899 ed. $32.00

The Cossacks, Ivan Ilyich, Happy Ever After. Trans. by Rosemary Edmonds, *Penguin Class. Ser.* 1961 pap. $2.95

Prisoner in the Caucasus. Imported Pubns. 1984 pap. $6.95

A Landowner's Morning, Family Happiness and The Devil. Trans. by Kyril FitzLyon and April FitzLyon, intro. by Kyril FitzLyon, Merrimack 1984 $13.95

Master and Man and Other Stories. Trans. by Paul Foote, *Penguin Class. Ser.* 1977 pap. $3.95. Includes "Father Sergius" and "Hadji Murat."

Esarhaddon and Other Tales. Ayer repr. of 1903 ed. $11.00

Master and Man and Other Parables and Tales. Biblio Dist. (Everyman's) repr. of 1910 ed. 1969 $9.95 pap. $5.95

Death of Ivan Ilych and Other Stories. Trans. by Aylmer Maude, New Amer. Lib. (Signet Class.) 1960 pap. $1.95

The Russian Proprietor and Other Stories. Trans. by Nathan H. Dole, Ayer repr. of 1887 ed. $21.00

Father Sergius and Other Stories and Plays. Ayer repr. of 1911 ed. $20.00

The Kreutzer Sonata and Other Stories. Trans. by Benjamin R. Tucker, Ayer repr. of 1890 ed. $19.00

Stories for Children. Trans. by Jacob Guralsky, Imported Pubns. 1977 pap. $1.99

Fables, Tales, Stories. Imported Pubns. 1973 pap. $1.95

Fables and Fairy Tales. New Amer. Lib. (Plume) 1972 pap. $5.95

"Childhood," "Boyhood" and "Youth." Intro. by C. J. Howarth, Biblio Dist. (Everyman's) repr. of 1912 ed. 1976 $9.95; trans. by Rosemary Edmonds, *Penguin Class. Ser.* 1964 pap. $3.95

The Private Diary of Leo Tolstoy, 1853–1857. Trans. by Louise Maude, ed. by Aylmer Maude, Kraus repr. of 1927 ed. $13.00

Last Diaries. Trans. by Lydia Kesich, ed. by Robert Kastenbaum, Ayer repr. of 1960 ed. 1979 $23.00

Tolstoy's Letters. Trans. and ed. by R. F. Christian, Scribner 2 vols. 1978 ea. $9.95. More than 600 letters from 1845 to 1910; excellent translations; detailed annotations.

Essays and Letters. Trans. by Aylmer Maude, *Select Bibliographies Repr. Ser.* Ayer repr. of 1909 ed. 1973 $24.50; Irvington repr. of 1909 ed. $21.00

War, Patriotism, Peace. Intro. by C. Chatfield, Garland 1973 $42.00

Childhood. 1852. Trans. by Leo Wiener, Ardis repr. 1984 $19.50; ed. by B. Faden, Basil Blackwell bilingual ed. pap. $9.95

War and Peace. 1869. Biblio Dist. (Everyman's) 3 vols. 1976 ea. $9.95; trans. by Constance Garnett, *Apollo Eds.* Crowell 1976 pap. $6.95; trans. by Constance Garnett, Modern Lib. 1931 $9.95; trans. by Ann Dunnigan, intro. by John Bayley, New Amer. Lib. (Signet Class.) 1968 pap. $4.95; trans. by Louise Maude and Aylmer Maude, ed. by George Gibian, *Norton Critical Eds.* 1966 pap. $13.95; trans. by Louise Maude and Aylmer Maude, ed. by Henry Gifford, *World's Class.-Pap. Ser.* Oxford 2 vols. 1983 pap. ea. $5.95; trans. by Rosemary Edmonds, Penguin rev. ed. 1982 pap. $8.95; intro. by Clifton Fadiman, Simon & Schuster 1941 $25.50; ed. by Ernest J. Simmons, Washington Square Pr. abr. ed. pap. $3.95

Anna Karenina. 1876. Intro. by R. R. Canon, *Airmont Class. Ser.* pap. $2.50; trans. by Joel Carmichael, intro. by Malcolm Cowley, *Bantam Class. Ser.* 1981 pap. $2.95; Imported Pubns. 2 vols. 1978 $14.00; trans. by David Magarshack, New Amer. Lib. (Signet Class.) pap. $2.95; trans. by Louise Maude and Aylmer Maude, ed. by George Gibian, *Norton Critical Eds.* 1970 pap. $9.95; trans. by Louise Maude and Aylmer Maude, intro by John Bayley, *World's Class. Ser.* Oxford 1980 pap. $5.95; trans. by Rosemary Edmonds, *Penguin Class. Ser.* rev. ed. 1954 pap. $4.95; trans. by Constance Garnett, ed. by Leonard J. Kent and Nina Berberova, *Modern Lib. College Ed. Ser.* Random 1950 pap. $5.50 1965 $9.95; State Mutual Bk. 1982 pap. $10.00

What Men Live By. Peter Pauper $4.95

The Death of Ivan Ilyich. 1884. Trans. by Lynn Solotaroff, intro. by Ronald Blythe, *Bantam Class. Ser.* 1981 pap. $1.95

The Fruits of Enlightenment. Trans. by Michael Frayn, Methuen 1979 pap. $6.95

Master and Man. 1895. Ed. by Eleanor Aitken, Cambridge Univ. Pr. 1969 $14.95

Resurrection. 1899. New Amer. Lib. 1984 pap. $4.95; trans. by Rosemary Edmonds, *Penguin Class. Ser.* 1966 pap. $4.95

Hadji Murat. 1904. Trans. by Susan Layton, Cherry Valley 1985 $17.50 pap. $6.50

Books about Leo Tolstoy

Berlin, Isaiah. *The Hedgehog and the Fox: An Essay on Tolstoy's View of History.* Simon & Schuster (Touchstone Bks.) 1953 o.p. Superb analysis of the theories underlying *War and Peace.*

Chertkov, Vladimir. *The Last Days of Tolstoy.* Trans. by Nathalie A. Duddington, Kraus repr. 1973 $21.00. By Tolstoy's chief disciple.

Christian, Reginald F. *Tolstoy: A Critical Introduction.* Cambridge Univ. Pr. 1970 $52.50 pap. $13.95

Eikhenbaum, Boris. *Tolstoi in the Seventies.* Trans. by A. Kaspin, Ardis 1982 $32.50. Third part of Eikhenbaum's trilogy.

———. *Tolstoi in the Sixties.* Ardis 1982 $25.00. Second of three-volume study; very extensive.

———. *The Young Tolstoy.* Ardis 1972 o.p. Early, provocative discussion by a major Russian critic.

Gifford, Henry. *Tolstoy.* Oxford 1982 $12.95 pap. $3.95

Gorky, Maxim. *Reminiscences of Leo Nikolaevich Tolstoy.* Trans. by S. S. Koteliansky and Leonard Woolf, Folcroft repr. of 1920 ed. 1977 $15.00. Striking picture of the aged writer.

Jones, M., ed. *New Essays on Tolstoy.* Cambridge Univ. Pr. 1979 $37.50

Tolstoy, Alexandra. *Tolstoy: A Life of My Father.* Nordland 1975 pap. $9.95; Octagon repr. of 1953 ed. 1973 $29.00. By Tolstoy's daughter.

Tolstoy, Sophia. *The Final Struggle: Being Countess Tolstoy's Diary for 1910.* Octagon 1972 $27.50. By Tolstoy's wife.

Troyat, Henri. *Tolstoy.* Trans. by Nancy Amphoux, Crown 1980 pap. $6.95. A very readable biography.

Wasiolek, Edward. *Tolstoy's Major Fiction.* Univ. of Chicago Pr. 1978 $6.95. A good introduction.

TRIFONOV, YURY. 1925–1981

The main achievement of Trifonov's three decades in literature are a series of short novels from the late 1960s and 1970s about the Russian intelligentsia. He explores human relationships in the context of an urban existence filled with problems close to the heart of the ordinary Russian reader: exchange of apartments, competition for careers, money troubles, and so on. These are used as the basis for longer-term exploration, through flashbacks and reminiscences, of the Stalin period and its disastrous effects on society. Restrained yet ironic, Trifonov's tales are invaluable for anyone interested in contemporary Russia.

BOOKS BY TRIFONOV

The Impatient Ones. Imported Pubns. 1978 $8.95

The Long Goodbye: A Trilogy. Trans. by Helen Burlingame and Ellendea Proffer, Ardis 1978 $25.00 pap. $7.95. Includes "The Long Goodbye," "The Exchange," and "Taking Stock."

Another Life (and *The House on the Embankment*). Trans. by Michael Glenny, Simon & Schuster 1983 $16.95

The Old Man. Trans. by Jacqueline Edwards and Mitchell Scheider, Simon & Schuster 1984 $16.95

TSVETAEVA (TSVETAYEVA, CVETAEVA), MARINA. 1892–1941

Tsvetaeva, whose first collection appeared in 1911, ranks among the major twentieth-century Russian poets. Her numerous lyrics and longer poems are distinguished by great vigor and passion. These are combined with an astonishing mastery of technical aspects of verse. Tsvetaeva was highly innovative in her use of language and rhythms. Her subject matter varies greatly. Her poetry is often diarylike. She was often concerned with the fate of her generation and did not shy away from difficult topics. In her poetry, she often subsumed herself in other characters, merging dramatic and lyric elements. Particularly striking are her longer poems *Poem of the Mountain*, *Poem of the End*, and *Ratcatcher*, and her later collections *Craft* and *After Russia*. In emigration Tsvetayeva also seriously turned to prose. Drawing on her past, she wrote a number of striking quasi-autobiographical pieces within which she explored in great depth problems of literature and literary creation.

Following the civil war, where her sympathies were on the side of the White forces, Tsvetaeva led a difficult and isolated existence in Prague and Paris during the twenties and thirties. Her eventual return to the Soviet Union, largely for family reasons, ended in tragedy; isolation and humiliation on the part of official Soviet literary figures brought her to suicide in 1941. Ignored for a long time by the Soviet authorities, she has been republished since the 1960s and has attracted an increasing number of readers both in the Soviet Union and abroad. As was the case with her work from the very beginning, poets have been a particularly attentive part of her audience.

BOOKS BY TSVETAEVA

Selected Poems of Marina Tsvetayeva. Trans. by Elaine Feinstein, Oxford rev. & enl. ed. 1981 pap. $14.95. Includes both poetic and literal translations.

A Captive Spirit: Selected Prose. Trans. by Janet M. King, Ardis 1980 $35.00; Merri-

mack 1984 pap. $11.95. Experimental prose, accurately translated and well an-
notated.

(and others). *Three Russian Women Poets*. Trans. by Mary Maddock, Crossing Pr.
$16.95 pap. $6.95

The Demesne of Swans. Trans. by Robin Kemball, Ardis 1980 $15.00 pap. $7.50. Poems on the civil war.

BOOK ABOUT TSVETAEVA

Proffer, Ellendea, ed. *Tsvetaeva: A Pictorial Biography*. Trans. by J. M. King, intro. by
Carl R. Proffer, Ardis 1980 $25.00 pap. $11.00. Striking photographs and accompanying text.

TURGENEV, IVAN. 1818–1883

Turgenev was the first great Russian novelist to win popularity abroad.
Of wealthy aristocratic background, he lived in Europe for a long time and
received honors not only in Russia but also in France and England. (Henry
James included him in a survey of French novelists, and Turgenev was buried in France.) His realistic sketches, first published in the journal *The Contemporary* and later in book form as *Notes of a Hunter* (o.p.), were immediately successful. They depicted the sufferings of the peasants and helped
arouse public opinion concerning the institution of serfdom. The three succeeding novels, *Rudin, A Nest of the Gentry*, and *On the Eve*, helped cement
Turgenev's fame as a major novelist. Another novel, *Fathers and Sons*,
proved very controversial, since it drew fire from all quarters for its pointed
depiction of the conflict between radically inclined young people and their
more conservative parents. Turgenev fled to the West, where he produced
his last two novels, *Smoke* (1867), a satiric depiction of aristocratic circles,
and *Virgin Soil*, a work about the Populist movement of the 1870s.

Taken together, Turgenev's novels form a literary chronicle of major
trends in Russian life during the middle decades of the nineteenth century.
Their plots are generally subdued, and their protagonists are usually rather
aimless, unsure men who are trying to find a role for themselves in society.
The quest by these "superfluous men" is usually unsuccessful. The stories in
Notes of a Hunter are excellent in their realistic depiction. Later short works
are increasingly nostalgic and resigned. Tales from the last period of
Turgenev's life include strong elements of the fantastic and the poetic, as
evidenced by his *Poems in Prose* (alternative title—*Senilia*), and show that
the author continued to evolve in his technique.

BOOKS BY TURGENEV

Novels of Ivan Turgenev. Trans. by Constance Garnett, AMS Pr. repr. of 1899 ed. 15
vols. $400.00; Scholarly 15 vols. $375.00

The Vintage Turgenev. Random (Vintage) 2 vols. pap. ea. $1.95

Fathers and Sons: A Nest of the Gentry. Imported Pubns. 1974 $5.45

First Love and Other Tales (Selected Tales of Ivan Turgenev). Trans. by David
Magarshack, *Norton Critical Lib.* 1968 pap. $7.95

First Love: Three Short Novels—First Love; The Diary of a Superfluous Man; Acia.
Trans. by Constance Garnett, Hyperion Pr. 1977 pap. $4.95

Brigadier and Other Stories. Trans. by Isabel F. Hapgood, Ayer repr. of 1904 ed. $30.00

Desperate Character and Other Stories. Trans. by Constance Garnett, Ayer repr. of 1917 ed. $16.00

Diary of a Superfluous Man and Other Stories. Trans. by Isabel F. Hapgood, Ayer repr. of 1904 ed. $17.00

Dream Tales and Prose Poems. Trans. by Constance Garnett, Ayer repr. of 1897 ed. $20.00

Phantoms and Other Stories. Trans. by Isabel F. Hapgood, Ayer repr. of 1904 ed. $18.00

Reckless Character and Other Stories. Trans. by Isabel F. Hapgood, Ayer repr. of 1904 ed. $20.00

Torrents of Spring, Etc. Trans. by Constance Garnett, Ayer repr. of 1916 ed. $19.00

The Jew and Other Stories. Trans. by Isabel F. Hapgood, Ayer repr. of 1904 ed. $17.00

Stories and Poems in Prose. Imported Pubns. 1982 $11.95

Three Novellas. Trans. by Marion Mainwaring, Farrar 1969 $5.95

The Portrait Game: The Game Played with Imaginary Sketches. Trans. and ed. by Marion Mainwaring, Horizon Pr. 1973 $5.95

Plays of Ivan S. Turgenev. Trans. by M. S. Mandell, intro. by William L. Phelps, Russell 2 vols. in 1 repr. of 1924 ed. 1970 $18.50

Three Famous Plays: A Month in the Country; A Provincial Lady; A Poor Gentleman. Trans. by Constance Garnett, AMS Pr. repr. of 1951 ed. $14.50; Hyperion Pr. 1977 $11.95

Letters in Two Volumes. Trans. and ed. by David Lowe, Ardis 2 vols. 1983 $50.00. Contains 334 letters—excellent translation and notes; best edition of Turgenev's letters in English.

Turgenev's Letters. Trans. and ed. by A. V. Knowles, Scribner 1983 $30.00. Contains 236 letters—well chosen, well translated; good notes.

Diary of a Superfluous Man. 1850. Trans. by David Patterson, Norton 1984 $15.00

A Month in the Country. 1850. Trans. and intro. by Isaiah Berlin, *Penguin Class. Ser.* 1983 pap. $3.95; Heinemann pap. $5.00

Mumu. 1852. Trans. by J. Domb and Z. Shoenberg, Rogers bilingual ed. 1946 $5.00

Sketches from a Hunter's Album. 1852. Trans. by Richard Freeborn, *Penguin Class. Ser.* 1967 pap. $3.95; (with the title *Memoirs of a Sportsman*) trans. by Isabel F. Hapgood, Ayer repr. of 1904 ed. $29.00

Rudin. 1856. Trans. by Richard Freeborn, *Penguin Class. Ser.* 1975 pap. $3.95

Home of the Gentry (A Nest of the Gentry). 1859. Trans. by Richard Freeborn, Gannon $9.50; *Penguin Class. Ser.* 1970 pap. $3.95

First Love. 1860. Trans. by Isaiah Berlin, intro. by V. S. Pritchett, *Penguin Class. Ser.* repr. of 1950 ed. 1978 pap. $3.95; trans. by Isaiah Berlin, intro. by David Cecil, Viking 1982 $14.75

On the Eve. 1860. Trans. by Gilbert Gardiner, *Penguin Class. Ser.* 1950 pap. $4.95

Fathers and Sons (Fathers and Children). 1862. Trans. by Constance Garnett, Airmont pap. $1.25; trans. by Barbara Makanowitzky, *Bantam Class. Ser.* 1981 pap. $1.95; trans. by Avril Pyman, Biblio Dist. (Everyman's) repr. of 1962 ed. 1978 $8.95; ed. by Ernest J. Simmons, Holt 1949 pap. $10.95; trans. by George Reavey, New Amer. Lib. (Signet Class.) pap. $2.25; ed. by Ralph E. Matlaw, *Norton Critical Eds.* 1966 pap. $5.95; trans. by Rosemary Edmonds, *Penguin Class. Ser.* rev. ed. 1965 pap. $2.95; trans. by Bernard G. Guerney, *Modern Lib. College Ed. Ser.* Random 1950 pap. $3.95

Spring Torrents. 1872. Trans. by Leonard Shapiro, *Penguin Class. Ser.* 1980 pap. $3.95

Virgin Soil. 1877. Trans. by Rochelle S. Townsend, intro. by N. Andreyev, Biblio Dist. (Everyman's) repr. of 1911 ed. 1976 pap. $2.95; trans. by Constance Garnett, intro. by V. S. Pritchett, Grove 1977 pap. $3.95

Poems in Prose: In Russian and English. 1879–83. Trans. by Constance Garnett and Roger Rees, ed. by S. Konovalov, intro. by André Mazon, International Univ. Pr. 1951 pap. $25.00

BOOKS ABOUT TURGENEV

Freeborn, Richard. *Turgenev: The Novelist's Novelist—A Study.* Greenwood repr. of 1960 ed. 1978 lib. bdg. $24.75

Kagan-Kans, Eva. *Hamlet and Don Quixote: Turgenev's Ambivalent Vision.* Mouton 1975 pap. $24.00

Lowe, David. *Turgenev's "Fathers and Sons."* Ardis 1983 $23.50

Pritchett, Victor S. *The Gentle Barbarian: The Life and Work of Turgenev.* Random 1977 $11.95; Random (Vintage) 1978 pap. $3.95

Ripp, Victor. *Turgenev's Russia: From "Notes of a Hunter" to "Fathers and Sons."* Cornell Univ. Pr. 1980 $22.50

Schapiro, Leonard. *Turgenev: His Life and Times.* Harvard Univ. Pr. 1982 pap. $9.95; Random 1979 $15.95

Waddington, Patrick. *Turgenev and England.* New York Univ. Pr. 1980 $40.00

Yarmolinsky, Avrahm. *Turgenev: The Man, His Art, His Age.* Richard West repr. of 1926 ed. 1980 $40.00

TYNYANOV, YURY. 1894–1943

Tynyanov was one of the founders of structuralist criticism and made lasting contributions to the study of Pushkin, to the theory of poetic language, and other subjects. His novels tend to embody his theoretical interests. His most important works deal with the oppressive period of Nicholas I. *Death and Diplomacy in Persia* (English-language title of *The Death of Wazir-Mukhtar*) is a biographical novel about the celebrated nineteenth-century satirist Aleksandr Griboedov. Other novels include *Kyukhlya* (1925, o.p.), a work about the Decembrist poet Kyukhelbeker, and the unfinished *Pushkin* (1936–37), which deals with the life of the great poet. Of Tynyanov's short stories, "Sublieutenant Kizhe," an anecdote from the time of Emperor Paul I, has achieved the greatest reknown and was made into a movie in 1934.

BOOK BY TYNYANOV

Death and Diplomacy in Persia. 1927–28. Trans. by A. Brown, Hyperion Pr. repr. of 1938 ed. 1974 $24.75

VOINOVICH, VLADIMIR. 1932–

The best contemporary Russian satirist, Voinovich served in the Soviet Army and worked for a time at a variety of jobs, including that of carpenter. He published his first short story in 1961, which describes life on a collective farm and met with acclaim. He got into trouble with the authorities when he protested the trial of Andrei Sinyavsky and Yuli Daniel, and the expulsion of Solzhenitsyn from the Writers' Union. He himself was barred from literature in 1974. Increasingly under pressure, Voinovich emigrated with his family to West Germany in 1980, and has since come to visit and lecture in the United States.

One of Voinovich's best-known works is *The Ivankiad* (published in 1976 in Russian in the United States), a comic account of his difficulties in getting an apartment and, more broadly, of the plight of an individual in fighting bureaucracy in the Soviet Union. His most important achievement is the satiric novel *The Life and Extraordinary Adventures of Private Ivan Chonkin*, which depicts Soviet society at the start of the German invasion, and is particularly devastating in depicting the gap between official slogans and reality. Chonkin is a peasant-hero in the tradition of ČAPEK's Schweik. His adventures are continued in *Pretender to the Throne*, a grimmer work that, among other topics, satirizes Stalin and the secret police.

Part of Voinovich's appeal lies in his ironic narration and in his skillful recreation of colloquial, often crude speech. He has been well served by his translators; the English-language versions of his works are eminently readable.

BOOKS BY VOINOVICH

In Plain Russian. Trans. by Richard Lourie, Farrar 1979 $11.95. Satiric sketches of Soviet life.
The Ivankiad. 1976. Trans. by David Lapeza, Farrar 1977 $5.95
The Life and Extraordinary Adventures of Private Ivan Chonkin. Trans. by Richard Lourie, Farrar 1976 pap. $7.95
Pretender to the Throne: The Further Adventures of Private Ivan Chonkin. Trans. by Richard Lourie, Farrar 1981 $17.95

VOZNESENSKY, ANDREI. 1933–

Voznesensky initially studied architecture, but abandoned it for literature during the late 1950s. His first two collections of poems, *Mosaic* (o.p.) and *Parabola* (o.p.), appeared in 1960. They displayed great energy, verbal virtuosity, and inventiveness—all of which have since become his hallmarks. During the 1960s, Voznesensky became extremely popular in the Soviet Union. He published several important volumes, including *Antiworlds* (1964) and *Achilles' Heart* (1965, o.p.). He also made many trips to Western Europe and the United States, and achieved wide recognition. His themes—modern urban life, the impact of technology on civilization, freedom of the artist—are appealing to both Russian and foreign audiences. Voznesensky has been in and out of trouble with the Soviet authorities. Although he has enjoyed much more latitude than most Soviet writers, he has been outspoken on the subject of creative freedom and was involved in the unofficial *Metropol* collection.

BOOKS BY VOZNESENSKY

Antiworlds and The Fifth Ace. Trans. by W. H. Auden and others, ed. by Patricia Blake and Max Hayward, Schocken bilingual ed. 1973 pap. $3.95
Dogalypse. City Lights 1972 pap. $1.50

YEVTUSHENKO (EVTUSHENKO), YEVGENY. 1933–

Yevtushenko was born in a small junction on the Trans-Siberian Railroad (subject of his 1956 long poem *Zima Junction*). After Stalin's death in 1953, he emerged as an important poet and became a spokesman for the younger generation.

In 1961, Yevtushenko came out with the poem "Babi Yar," which deals with the notorious wartime massacre of Jews in a ravine near Kiev. The poem made Yevtushenko internationally famous, but the fact that it raised the spectre of domestic anti-Semitism aroused a storm of opposition in official Soviet circles.

During the years, Yevtushenko has become part of the Soviet establishment. His early reputation as a defender of artistic freedom in the Soviet Union was seriously damaged by his willingness to write works in tune with the official line. On occasion, however, he has taken quite liberal positions.

Like Voznesensky, Yevtushenko has traveled extensively abroad and has become very well known. His trips have inspired many topical, sometimes autobiographical, works that have been well received by Western as well as Russian readers. Overall, although sometimes quite effective, his writing lacks true depth.

BOOKS BY YEVTUSHENKO

The Poetry of Yevgeny Yevtushenko. Boyars bilingual ed. 1981 pap. $8.95
A Dove in Santiago. Trans. by D. M. Thomas, Viking 1983 $13.50
The Face behind the Face. Putnam 1979 pap. $4.95
Wild Berries. Trans. by Antonina Bouis, Morrow 1984 $15.95

ZAMYATIN, YEVGENY (EUGENE ZAMIATIN). 1884–1937

Zamyatin studied at the Polytechnic Institute in St. Petersburg and became a naval engineer. His first story appeared in 1908, and he became serious about writing in 1913, when his short novel *A Provincial Tale* (o.p.) was published. He became part of the neorealist group, together with Remizov, Prishvin, and other writers. In 1916 he supervised the construction of icebreakers for the Russian government in England. After his return to Russia, he published two satiric works about English life.

During the civil war and the early 1920s, Zamyatin published fiction and theoretical works. He played a central role in various cultural activities, as an editor, organizer, and teacher of literary craft. He had an important influence on a number of younger writers, such as Olesha and Ivanov.

Zamyatin's prose after the Revolution involved extensive use of ellipses, color symbolism, and elaborate chains of imagery. It is exemplified in such well-known stories as "Mamai" and "The Cave." His best-known work is *We*. This satiric tale of a future antiutopia, a plausible extrapolation from twentieth-century social and political trends, which directly influenced GEORGE ORWELL's (see Vol. 1) *1984*, was published abroad in several translations during the 1920s. In 1927 a shortened Russian version appeared in Prague; the violent press campaign that followed led to Zamyatin's resignation from a writer's organization, and, eventually, to his direct request to Stalin for permission to leave the Soviet Union. This being granted, Zamyatin settled in Paris, where he continued to work until his death. He is not published in the Soviet Union, where he is essentially unknown and unstudied.

BOOKS BY ZAMYATIN

The Dragon. Trans. and ed. by Mirra Ginsburg, Univ. of Chicago Pr. 1976 $20.00 pap. $3.95. Short stories.

We. Trans. by Mirra Ginsburg, Avon 1983 pap. $3.95; trans. by Gregory Zilboorg, Dutton pap. $4.95. Ginsburg's translation is the best.

A Soviet Heretic: Essays by Yevgeny Zamyatin. Trans. and ed. by Mirra Ginsburg, Univ. of Chicago Pr. 1974 pap. $4.95. Comprehensive collection.

BOOK ABOUT ZAMYATIN

Shane, Alex M. *The Life and Works of Evgenij Zamjatin.* Univ. of California Pr. 1968 $39.50. Thorough discussion of biography and art.

ZOSHCHENKO, MIKHAIL. 1895–1958

Born in the Ukraine, Zoshchenko moved with his family to St. Petersburg in 1904. He volunteered for military service in World War I and spent two years at the front, where his health was permanently damaged by poison gas. During the civil war, he volunteered for the Red Army. Later, he held a succession of jobs, including detective, carpenter, telephone operator, militiaman, and actor.

Zoshchenko's first book appeared in 1921. His stories were very successful, and he was extraordinarily popular. He came under political pressure during the 1930s. In 1946, together with Akhmatova, he was singled out for attack by culture "boss" Zhdanov, and was expelled from the Union of Soviet Writers. He did not write much original work, producing mostly translations.

Zoshchenko was an extremely effective satirist, who took his subjects from the paradoxes and incongruities of Russian society in the postrevolutionary period. He depicted human nature, which the new government was trying to change, but which asserted itself nonetheless. His language is fascinating. The stories are often narrated by someone from the lower classes, who speaks in a mixture of the colloquial and of the new Soviet rhetoric—the result is very comic. During the 1930s, Zoshchenko began to explore in fiction various philosophical and theoretical problems. A well-known example of this type of investigation is the 1943 *Before Sunrise*, in which the author analyzed his own psychology, in the process touching on the then-forbidden theories of FREUD (see Vols. 3 and 5).

BOOKS BY ZOSHCHENKO

Nervous People and Other Satires. Trans. by Maria Gordon and Hugh McLean, ed. by Hugh McLean, Indiana Univ. Pr. 1975 pap. $4.95

Scenes from the Bathhouse: And Other Stories of Communist Russia. Trans. by Sidney
      Monas, Univ. of Michigan Pr. 1961 pap. $5.95
The Woman Who Could Not Read and Other Tales. Trans. by E. Fen, Hyperion Pr.
      repr. of 1940 ed. 1973 $13.50
The Wonderful Dog and Other Tales. Trans. by E. Fen, Hyperion Pr. repr. of 1942 ed.
      1973 $14.50
Youth Restored. 1932. Trans. by Joel Stern, Ardis 1985 $20.00

CHAPTER 16

East European Literatures

Vasa D. Mihailovich

O nomen dulce libertatis—O sweet name of liberty.
—CICERO, *Oration against Verres*

All East European literatures have several features in common: They all originated during the process of accepting Christianity and for the purpose of satisfying the needs of the church; they were directly engaged in the struggle for
liberation from various enemies and at various times; they were influenced
by the literary developments in the West; and they all had to struggle
against, and in most instances submit to, political dictates in the aftermath
of World War II. Aside from that, they followed their own timetable of development and the peculiarities of their individual natures. Therefore, it would
be a mistake to treat them as a monolithic bloc, despite the common historical circumstances, for it is through their uniqueness that each has contributed significantly to world literature.

ALBANIAN LITERATURE

Whatever possibilities for the development of culture and literature existed
in Albania before the sixteenth century, they were dashed by the Turkish
conquest and the defeat of Albania's legendary leader Skenderbeg in 1468.
The conquest led to the dispersal of spiritual and cultural leaders, mostly to
Italy and Sicily, where they wrote in the Roman Catholic tradition for the
next 200 years. Almost all writing in this period was of a religious and didactic nature, but there were also dictionaries, encyclopedias, and collections of folk literature. The leading writer was the Calabrian Jeronim de
Rada, who collected fragments of Albanian epics to which he added poems
of his own, which are not devoid of a lyrical quality. Similar romantic and
patriotic works were written in other Albanian conclaves and colonies in
Constantinople, Lebanon, Egypt, Rumania, and the United States.

Writers at home survived mainly because of the help of Roman Catholic
missions. Preoccupied with collecting and imitating folk poetry and influenced by Albanian writings abroad, they kept the romantic spirit alive until
the national awakening swept Albania in the second half of the nineteenth

century, centered around the League of Prizren. There were also attempts at a historical novel and the crude beginnings of the short story.

The romantic and patriotic spirit in literature lasted until independence was won in 1912. Although romanticism still persisted, writers were exposed to other European trends such as realism and symbolism. Çajupi, Gjergj Fishta, and Fran S. Noli were the leading authors in the first decades of this century. By the 1930s socialist and radical ideas began to influence Albanian writers, especially those from the South, the Tosks. Younger writers were much more influenced by modern European trends than the preceding generation. The most prominent among them was Migjeni (an acronym for Millosh Gjergj Nikolla), whose strong social criticism foreshadowed the literature after World War II.

The last four decades have been difficult for writers. The establishment of a communist state in 1944 forced them to accept socialist realism and strict controls. The elimination of dissidents became the order of the day. Consequently, even though language and style have been enriched, higher quality is still lacking. The lone exception is the poet and novelist Ismail Kadare, whose novel *The General of the Dead Army* has been translated and published in more than two dozen countries.

Although works by several Albanian writers have been translated into English, unfortunately few are readily available.

History and Criticism

Skendi, Stavro. *Albanian and South Slavic Oral Epic Poetry. Amer. Folklore Society Memoir Ser.* Kraus repr. of 1954 ed. $21.00
———. *Albanian National Awakening, 1878–1912.* Princeton Univ. Pr. 1967 $25.00

KADARE, ISMAIL. 1936–

Ismail Kadare is the most prominent of contemporary Albanian writers. He has written poetry, short stories, literary criticism, and seven novels. His works have been translated and published in more than two dozen countries. An internationally known figure, he has visited and lectured in many countries. He was also a representative to Albania's People's Assembly.

BOOK BY KADARE

The General of the Dead Army. 1963. Trans. by Derek Coltman, Viking 1972 $7.95. "Not just a revelation of Albanian literature—a revelation in any terms" (*L'Express*).

BULGARIAN LITERATURE

The history of Bulgarian literature goes back to the end of the ninth century, when literary activity was spurred by the disciples of Cyril and Methodius, the two Greek monks chiefly responsible for the dissemination of Christianity among the Slavs by way of a written language they had devised based on a Slavic tongue. This brief but intense flourish laid the foundation of the culture of all Balkan Slavs. The second flourishing occurred in the second half of the fourteenth century, before the country fell to the Turks. During the five-century long occupation, little literature was possible. It was not until 1762 that the Bulgarians attempted to regain their literary consciousness, when a monk from the Hilendar monastery on Mount Athos wrote his history of Bulgaria with the main purpose of awakening the national consciousness of his enslaved people.

Literary activity in the nineteenth century was closely connected with the struggle for liberation. The best writers of the century, the lyric poet Christo Botev and the novelist and poet Ivan Vazov, drew most of their inspiration from this struggle. But when independence was finally won in 1878, writers satirized the shortcomings of their people when they proved unworthy of immense sacrifices during the struggle.

At the turn of the century writers began to widen their horizons and to reflect the influence of modern Western literary movements. Foremost among these was Pencho Slaveykov, whose work shows the degree of modernity reached by Bulgarian writers in a relatively short time. Symbolism also attracted some talented poets (Peyo Yavorov and Todor Trayanov), who stayed away from the romantic and realistic themes of the previous generation, while others flirted with expressionism.

All these trends reappeared in the interwar period, resulting in a rich, multifaceted literary activity. In general, short stories and lyric poetry were the most successful genres. Many of the older authors continued to be a factor, but there was also new blood. Among the former, the most significant were the short-story tellers and novelists Elin Pelin and Yordan Yovkov.

The installment of a communist system in 1944 brought about drastic changes in literature. The dictates of socialist realism resulted in faceless uniformity and atrophy of imagination. Only partial relaxations after 1956 and in the 1960s and 1970s gave young writers a chance to develop their potential, although serious restrictions are still felt. The best writers turn to historical novels, either to escape the present or to compare it with the past.

History and Criticism

Manning, Clarence A., and Roman Smal-Stocki. *History of Modern Bulgarian Literature.* Greenwood repr. of 1960 ed. 1974 lib. bdg. $27.50. A brief survey from the beginnings to the present. Convenient but rather selective and at times unreliable.

Matejic, Mateja. *A Bibliographical Handbook of Bulgarian Authors.* Ed. by K. L. Black, Slavica 1982 $14.95. A very useful and detailed handbook, combining biography with pertinent bibliographic data.

Moser, Charles A. *A History of Bulgarian Literature, 865–1944.* Mouton text ed. 1972 $35.20. A detailed treatment of Bulgarian literature, focusing on the literature of the twentieth century and with an extensive bibliography. The best history available.

Slavov, Atanas. *The "Thaw" in Bulgarian Literature. East European Monographs* East European Quarterly 1981 $20.00

Collections

Kirilov, Nikolai, and Frank Kirk, eds. *Introduction to Modern Bulgarian Literature: An Anthology of Short Stories.* Trans. by Marguerite Alexieva, Irvington 1969 lib. bdg. $14.50. An extensive anthology of short stories by various authors from the late nineteenth century to the present. Though arranged in somewhat haphazard fashion, the collection provides some notion of the character of modern Bulgarian short fiction. Includes a brief introduction.

Moser, Charles A., and Vasa D. Mihailovich, eds. *White Stones and Fir Trees: An Anthology of Contemporary Slavic Literature.* Fairleigh Dickinson Univ. Pr. 1977 $35.00. A collection of poems and short stories.

PELIN, ELIN (pseud. of Dimitūr Ivanov). 1877–1949

Pelin came from the village to the city to earn his living through literature. The two principal collections of his excellent stories appeared in 1904 and 1911, and brought him fame as the bard of the peasants inhabiting the region around Sofia. He also gained renown as a satirist and humorist. After 1922 he wrote very little.

BOOK BY PELIN

Short Stories. Twayne's International Studies and Translations Ser. G. K. Hall o.p. Short works set in the Bulgarian countryside, exploring the intimate human problems of the peasant in his ordinary life.

VAZOV, IVAN. 1850–1921

Vazov dominated the literary scene in Bulgaria at the close of the nineteenth century as a poet, short-story writer, novelist, and playwright. Since then he has been recognized as the patriarch of Bulgarian letters. He lived through the heroic period of his country's liberation from the Turks, chronicled the events of the times, glorified his people's achievements, and agonized over their shortcomings. Through the power of his pen he succeeded in stimulating a sense of nationhood in his fellow Bulgarians.

BOOK BY VAZOV

Under the Yoke. Twayne o.p. The most important Bulgarian novel and Vazov's finest work. Describes the abortive April 1876 uprising, when the Bulgarians rose against hopeless odds in an attempt to drive their Turkish oppressors from their homeland. A central document for an understanding of the Bulgarian historical viewpoint.

YOVKOV, YORDAN. 1880–1937

The best prose craftsman in modern Bulgarian literature, Yovkov filtered the materials provided by real life through his memory to produce extraordinarily delicate small masterpieces. His most characteristic hero is the impractical daydreamer, incapable of dealing with the real world. In the 1930s he turned to writing for the stage.

BOOK BY YOVKOV

Short Stories. Twayne 1965 o.p. Ultimately affirmative stories of the trials and tragedies of life in the Bulgarian countryside.

BOOK ABOUT YOVKOV

Mozejko, Edward. *Yordan Yovkov.* Slavica 1984 pap. $9.95

BYELORUSSIAN LITERATURE

As is the case of all Slavic literature, the beginnings of Byelorussian literature can be traced to the conversion to Christianity in the eleventh and
twelfth centuries. The first literary works were chronicles and other ecclesiastical documents. In the sixteenth century, the Golden Age of Old Byelorussian literature, Francišak Skaryna translated the Bible into Old Byelorussian and several other writers made their appearance. In the first half of
the nineteenth century the romantic movement brought on the revival of
Byelorussian literature through the works of several capable writers, including Francišak Bahusevič. During this period, the Russians prohibited publication of works in Byelorussian, but the ban was not always enforced.

When the ban was permanently lifted at the beginning of the twentieth
century, Byelorussian literature flowered again. This was marked not only
by several prominent writers, but also by the development of various
genres, most notably lyric poetry, the novel, and drama. The two leaders of
the literary revival were Jakub Kołas and Janka Kupała. Another prominent
writer, Maksim Bahdanovič, transcended the still prevalent romantic realism and introduced neoclassicism, impressionism, and symbolism into
Byelorussian poetry. Like their predecessors, all these writers, gathered in a
group called "Adradženstva" (Renaissance), saw their mission not only in
writing literature but also in fighting for a national identity, independence,
and even survival.

This struggle continued after World War I, when the Byelorussians found
themselves divided between Russia and Poland. An added element was a
sharpened ideological difference, which was evident even in the Soviet
Union. There, one group, speaking through the journal *Maladniak* (Sap-
lings), demanded a stronger ideological commitment and advocated revolutionary romanticism and national communism. Another group, gathered
around the journal *Uzvyšča* (Excelsior), strove for high literary standards devoid of nonliterary considerations. The differences were resolved through
the suppression of versatility and independence during the Stalinist regime,
lasting until the mid-1950s. Today, most Byelorussian writers have to adhere to socialist realism, although some are more adept than others at cir-
cumventing it. Despite the limitations, there is a noticeable enhancement of
language and style. Among the leading contemporary authors, mention
should be made of the lyricists Uładzimier Duboŭka and Maksim Tank and
the fiction writers Janka Bryl and Vasil Bykaŭ.

History and Criticism

Adamovich, Anthony. *Opposition to Sovietization in Byelorussian Literature, 1917–1957*. Fwd. by Alexander Dallin, Scarecrow Pr. 1958 o.p. An analysis of Byelorussian literature mainly from 1917 to 1929, the period during which it had to conform to the Soviet views on literature. Based on personal experience. Includes a comprehensive bibliography and short biographies of more than 40 authors.

Bird, Thomas E., ed. *Modern Byelorussian Writing: Essays and Documents*. Queens College Pr. 1976 $10.00. A symposium on various aspects of Byelorussian literature in exile.

Collection

Rich, Vera. *Like Water, Like Fire: An Anthology of Byelorussian Poetry from 1828 to the Present Day*. Crane Russak 1971 $16.00. A pioneering anthology of Byelorussian poetry, the first of its kind in English.

BYKAŬ, VASIL. 1924–

A native of a small Byelorussian village, Bykaŭ served in World War II, studied sculpture, and worked as a newspaper editor. His novels, most of which are about soldiers at war, have been translated into many languages. Bykaŭ is one of the more successful of non-Russian Soviet authors.

BOOKS BY BYKAŬ

The Ordeal. Trans. by Gordon Clough, Dutton 1972 o.p. A brief novel about the guerrilla warfare in Byelorussia in World War II.

Pack of Wolves. Trans. by Lynn Solotaroff, Crowell 1981 $11.49

CZECHOSLOVAK LITERATURE

The first works in Czech literature, written in the fourteenth century, were both religious and secular: hymns, hagiography, epic and lyric poems, drama, and historical and didactic writings. Influenced by Western examples, this activity was interrupted by the Hussite wars, after which an increasingly vernacular literature, especially poetry, began to develop. In the sixteenth century the influence of humanism resulted in the predominance of prose works, culminating in the translation of the Bible. The Thirty Years' War, which resulted in the absorption of Old Bohemia into the Hapsburg empire, put a temporary end to writing in Czech. Only those writers who emigrated continued writing in Czech; among them, Jan Amos Komenský became prominent for his educational and theological works in Latin and Czech.

The national revival did not come until the end of the eighteenth century. One of the first concerns was the renewal of the literary language. Jozef Dobrovský and Jozef Jungmann codified literary Czech, which enabled writers to write in their native language again. Two poets contributed significantly to the resurgence of poetry: Jan Kollar, a Slovak writing in Czech, and Karel Hynek Macha, whose epic poem *Máj* marks the beginning of modern Czech poetry. As the century progressed, the romantic spirit, closely connected with the awakening of national consciousness and with the growing desire to gain independence from Austria, dominated the literary scene.

By the 1890s new realities brought a reaction against romanticism and aligned Czech literature with a more practical and liberal approach regarding the overriding concern of the time—total independence. This movement was inspired by the ideas and writings of Tomáš G. Masaryk, who would later become president of independent Czechoslovakia, and by Jozef Svatopluk Machar and Petr Bezruč. In addition, symbolist lyric poets reflected the increasing influence of Western literature—an influence that has been present in Czech literature from the very beginning.

When independence was finally won in 1918, Czech writers responded to the changed situation in several ways. Some were inspired by the Bolshevik Revolution; others fell under the spell of surrealism; still others wrote novels and short stories with pronounced social overtones. The most famous of these writers did not belong to any of the groups: Jaroslav Hašek, who became world famous for his satirical antiwar and anti-Austrian novel *The Good Soldier Schweik*, and Karel Čapek, whose novels, short stories, and plays are also published in many countries. The poet Jaroslav Seifert went through many phases and settled on pure, unaffected poetry of love and everyday life, for which he received the Nobel Prize in 1984. The interwar period was distinguished above all by a sharpened consciousness of many leading writers, some of whom showed distinct leftist leanings.

It was the writers with radical social views who took over when the communists established their system after 1948. Opponents were silenced or forced into exile. The fluctuation of strict controls and relaxations, however, enabled writers—especially those from the new generation such as the novelists Josef Škvorecký, Ludvík Vaculík, and Milan Kundera, the poet Miroslav Holub, and the playwright Václav Havel—to write defiant works of high quality. These writings were terminated by the crushing of the so-called Prague Spring in 1968, and literature fell once again under the strict controls and deadly effects of socialist realism that still prevail in Czechoslovakia.

If anything was written in Slovak before the eighteenth century, it was not preserved. In the middle of the eighteenth century attempts were made to establish the written form of Slovak, which was finally codified by L'udovit Štúr in the 1840s. The best of the writers who began to write in Slovak was Janko Král, whose ballads and epic and lyric poems reveal the basic inspiration for Slavic writers: their own folk poetry and the romantic poetry of other Slavic nations. The strongest genre in the nineteenth century was lyric poetry, and the two poets who helped establish it were Hviezdoslav and Ivan Krasko.

The flowering of Slovak literature came after World War I, when the Slovaks were finally able to enjoy full cultural freedom. Writers followed modern European trends, many literary journals were started, and publishing in Slovak was unfettered. As a result, Slovak literature was enriched in both theme and style, and new, more accomplished writers appeared. By and large, Slovak authors have shared the fate of their Czech compatriots before, during, and after World War II. Of several promising writers, Ladislav Mňačko has been most successful at home and abroad. After 1968, the Slovaks had to submit to strict party controls, an unsavory situation that still exists.

History and Criticism

Chudoba, F. *Short History of Czech Literature*. Kraus repr. of 1924 ed. $22.00
French, Alfred. *Czech Writers and Politics, 1945–1969. East European Monographs* East European Quarterly 1982 $35.00
———. *Poets of Prague: Czech Poetry between the Wars*. Oxford 1969 $6.95
Harkins, William E. *Russian Folk Epos in Czech Literature, 1800–1900*. Greenwood repr. of 1951 ed. 1971 lib. bdg. $29.75
Harkins, William E., and Paul I. Trensky, eds. *Czech Literature since 1956: A Symposium*. Bohemica o.p.
Kovtun, George J. *Czech and Slovak Literature in English: A Bibliography*. Lib. of Congress 1984 consult publisher for information
Liehm, Antonin J. *The Politics of Culture*. Trans. by Peter Kussi, Grove 1972 o.p. An important collection of interviews with writers who were involved in the Prague Spring.
Lützow, Francis. *History of Bohemian Literature*. Associated Faculty Pr. repr. of 1899 ed. 1970 $25.00
Novák, Arne. *Czech Literature*. Ed. by W. E. Harkins, *Joint Committee on Eastern Europe Publication Ser*. Michigan Slavic Pubns. 1976 $15.00
Selver, Paul. *Czechoslovak Literature: An Outline*. Gordon $69.95
———, trans. *Anthology of Czechoslovak Literature*. Kraus repr. of 1929 ed. $23.00
Součková, Milada. *Literary Satellite: Czechoslovak-Russian Literary Relations*. Univ. of Chicago Pr. 1970 $12.50

Collections

Busch, Marie, and Otto Pick, eds. *Selected Czech Tales. Short Story Index Repr. Ser*. Ayer. repr. of 1925 ed. $14.00
Liehm, Antonin, and Peter Kussi, eds. *The Writing on the Wall: An Anthology of Czechoslovak Literature Today*. Karz Cohl 1983 $25.95

ČAPEK, KAREL. 1890–1938

Karel Čapek is best known abroad for his plays, but at home he is also revered as an accomplished novelist, short-story writer, essayist, and writer of political articles. His bitingly satirical novel *The War with the Newts* reveals his understanding of the possible consequences of scientific advance. The novel *Krakatit*, about an explosive that could destroy the world, foreshadows the feared potential of a nuclear disaster. In his numerous short stories he depicts the problems of modern life and common man in a humorous and whimsically philosophical fashion. The plays of Karel Čapek presage the Theater of the Absurd. *R.U.R.* (Rossum's Universal Robots) was a satire on the machine age. He created the word *robot* (from the Czech noun *robota*, meaning work) for the man-made automatons who in that play took over the world, leaving only one human being alive. *The Insect Comedy*, whose characters *are* insects, is an ironic fantasy on human weakness. *The Makropoulos Secret* (1923, o.p.), later used as the basis for Leoš Janaček's opera, was an experimental piece that questioned whether immortality is really desirable. All the plays have been given successfully in New York. Most deal satirically with the modern machine age or with war. Underlying all his work, though, is a faith in man, truth, justice, and democracy, which has made him one of the most beloved of all Czech writers.

BOOKS BY ČAPEK

Money and Other Stories. 1921. *Short Story Index Repr. Ser.* Ayer repr. of 1930 ed. $18.00

R.U.R. and The Insect Play. 1921 Oxford 1961 pap. $5.95

The Absolute at Large. 1922. Ed. by Lester Del Rey, *Lib. of Science Fiction* Garland 1975 lib. bdg. $21.00

Krakatit. 1924. *Science Fiction Ser.* Ayer repr. of 1925 ed. 1975 $23.00

President Masaryk Tells His Story. Eastern European Collection Ser. Ayer repr. of 1928–35 ed. 1970 $25.50

Intimate Things. Essay Index Repr. Ser. Ayer repr. of 1936 ed. $15.00

The War with the Newts. 1936. Trans. by M. Weatherall and R. Weatherall, AMS Pr. repr. of 1937 ed. $19.00; intro. by Darko Suvin, *Science Fiction Ser.* G. K. Hall repr. of 1937 ed. 1977 lib. bdg. $15.95

BOOKS ABOUT ČAPEK

Masaryk, Tomáš G. *On Thought and Life: Conversations with Karel Čapek.* Trans. by M. Weatherall and R. Weatherall, *Essay Index Repr. Ser.* Ayer repr. of 1938 ed. $16.00

Matuska, Alexander. *Karel Čapek.* Telegraph Bks. repr. of 1964 ed. 1983 lib. bdg. $50.00. A critical examination of his works. Bibliography, index.

HAŠEK, JAROSLAV. 1883–1923

Even though Jaroslav Hašek wrote a large number of short stories, his fame rests mainly on his satirical novel *The Good Soldier Schweik*, in which he created the fat and cowardly dog-catcher-gone-to-war who personified Czech bitterness toward Austria in World War I. The humorous complications in which Schweik becomes involved derive from Hašek's own experience; his work as a journalist was interrupted by war and, like Schweik, he became a soldier. Eventually he was taken prisoner by the Russians. Later he returned to Prague as a communist to work as a free-lance writer. At his death he had completed only four "Schweik" novels of a projected six. Martin Esslin has said, "Schweik is more than a mere character; he represents a basic human attitude. Schweik defeats the powers that be, the whole universe in its absurdity, not by opposing but by complying with them. . . . In the end the stupidity of the authorities, the idiocy of the law are ruthlessly exposed." The character of Schweik made a tremendous impression on Bertolt Brecht, who transformed his name to use him afresh in the play *Schweyk in the Second World War.*

Book by Hašek

The Good Soldier Schweik. 1920–23. Amereon $15.95; trans. by Cecil Parrott, Bentley 1980 lib. bdg. $15.00; trans. by Cecil Parrott, Penguin 1985 pap. $6.95

HAVEL, VÁCLAV. 1936–

Václav Havel, a skillful practitioner of the Theater of the Absurd, lashes out in his plays at the inability of human beings to communicate, stressing people's difficulties in coping with problems engendered by the machine age. Because of his sarcastically critical attitude, his plays have not been performed in Czechoslovakia since 1969, but they are often staged abroad.

Book by Havel

The Memorandum. Trans. by Vera Blackwell, intro. by Tom Stoppard, Grove (Evergreen Bks.) repr. of 1968 ed. 1980 pap. $5.95

HOLUB, MIROSLAV. 1923–

Holub is a distinguished scientist as well as a poet. The noted British critic A. Alvarez sees Holub's main concern as "the way in which private responses, private anxieties, connect up with the public world of science, technology, and machines."

Books by Holub

Selected Poems. Trans. by Ian Milner and George Theiner, Penguin 1967 o.p.
Although. Intro. by A. Alvarez, Grossman 1971 o.p.
Sagittal Section: Poems by Miroslav Holub. Intro. by Charles Simic, Field Translations 1980 $9.95
Interferon: or, On Theater. Intro. by David Young, Field Translations 1982 $10.95 pap. $5.95

HRABAL, BOHUMIL. 1914–

Hrabal worked as a lawyer, clerk, railwayman, traveling salesman, steelworker, and laborer before turning to literature in 1962. In his tragic-comic novels and short stories he concentrates on the everyday lives of ordinary people. Thomas Lask says, "Hrabal shows an offbeat, original mind, a fey imagination and a sure hand in constructing his tales" (*N.Y. Times Bk. Review*). Hrabal's novel *Closely Watched Trains* was made into an internationally successful movie.

Books by Hrabal

The Death of Mr. Baltisberger. Trans. by Michael Henry Heim, Doubleday 1975 o.p. A collection of short stories.
Closely Watched Trains. Writers from the Other Europe Ser. Penguin 1981 pap. $4.95

KOHOUT, PAVEL. 1928–

At first a staunch supporter of the communist regime, the playwright Pavel Kohout later became an outspoken critic of repressive conditions in the literary life of his home country and, as a consequence, is no longer published there.

BOOK BY KOHOUT

White Book. Trans. by Alex Page, Braziller 1977 $8.95

KUNDERA, MILAN. 1929–

One of the foremost contemporary Czech writers, Kundera is a novelist, poet, and playwright. His play *The Keeper of the Keys* (o.p.), produced in Czechoslovakia in 1962, has long been performed in more than a dozen countries. His first novel, *The Joke,* is a biting satire on the political atmosphere in Czechoslovakia in the 1950s. It tells the story of a young communist whose life is ruined because of a minor indiscretion: writing a postcard to his girlfriend in which he mocks her political fervor. *The Joke* has been translated into a dozen languages and was made into a film, which Kundera wrote and directed. His novel *Life Is Elsewhere* won the 1973 Prix de Médicis for the best foreign novel. His books are no longer published in Czechoslovakia. He now lives in Paris.

BOOKS BY KUNDERA

Laughable Loves. Intro. by Philip Roth, Penguin 1975 pap. $6.95. "These are stories of the ways in which people respond—stunned or energized, frightened or amused when their own buried erotic impulses are suddenly released; stories told with subtle grace and an astonishing psychological precision" (Publisher's note).

Life Is Elsewhere. Penguin 1985 pap. $6.95. This internationally acclaimed novel has not been published in Czechoslovakia, or anywhere else, for that matter, in the original Czech. It has been described as a "brilliant, unsparing, and high-comic novel—a portrait of the self-deluded poet defining himself through abstract cliché yet determined to stand out as Hero, whose naive and frenzied venture into the real blood and guts of politics preordains his emergence as fool and informer, setting in motion a tragedy of errors. . . . *Life Is Elsewhere* demonstrates the gifts that have won Kundera the praise of such diverse writers as Sartre, Aragon and Philip Roth."

The Farewell Party. Ed. by Philip Roth, intro. by Elizabeth Pochoda, *Writers from the Other Europe Ser.* Penguin 1977 pap. $5.95. A satirical farce about love in Czech society beset by political and ideological preoccupations.

The Book of Laughter and Forgetting. Knopf 1980 $10.95; trans. by Michael H. Heim, *Writers from the Other Europe Ser.* Penguin 1981 pap. $5.95

The Joke. Trans. by Michael H. Heim, Harper 1982 $14.37; intro. by Philip Roth, *Writers from the Other Europe Ser.* Penguin 1983 pap. $5.95. The travails of a young Czech intellectual willing to support the communist system who is persecuted because of an innocuous practical joke. Fortunately, the ordeal serves him as a purgatory, forcing him to realize deeper and more durable values.

The Unbearable Lightness of Being. Trans. by Michael H. Heim, Harper 1984 $15.34 1985 pap. $6.95. "One of the most original and important voices in contemporary fiction. . . . It demands to be judged not as a work of political or 'dissident' literature, but as a work of art" (*N.Y. Times*). "Kundera has raised the novel of ideas to a new level of dream-like lyricism and emotional intensity" (*Newsweek*).

MŇAČKO, LADISLAV. 1919–

Mňačko is a leading Slovak communist writer and journalist who has earned the highest literary honors his country could bestow, and has received much publicity both for his satirical novel about Czech communist leadership and for his criticism of Czech anti-Semitism and of the Czech pro-Arab position on the Arab-Israeli war. When *The Taste of Power* was published in the United States in August 1967, Mňačko was stripped of his citizenship and the honors he had won and expelled from the Communist party. The book, praised by *Library Journal* as "a work of major significance," exposes "the ironic discrepancies between the public conduct and private motives of . . . [a thinly disguised head of state], a far from attractive yet curiously human figure for whom the taste of power had slowly turned into the taste of gall" (*SR*).

BOOKS BY MŇAČKO

The Taste of Power. Trans. by Paul Stevenson, Praeger 1967 o.p.
The Seventh Night. Dutton 1969 o.p.

SEIFERT, JAROSLAV. 1901–1986 (NOBEL PRIZE 1984)

Seifert published his first book of poetry in 1921 and in the next several decades went through several phases of development. He wrote in an unaffected, down-to-earth style about the everyday concerns and emotions of common man.

BOOKS BY SEIFERT

The Casting of Bells. Trans. by Tom O'Grady, *Outstanding Authors Ser.* Spirit That Moves Us rev. ed. 1984 $15.00 pap. $7.00
Morový Sloup: The Plague Monument. Trans. by Lyn Coffin, Michigan Slavic Pubns. bilingual ed. 1985 pap. $7.00
An Umbrella from Piccadilly. Trans. by Ewald Osers, Parsons Bks. 1985 $12.50 pap. $6.95

ŠKVORECKÝ, JOSEF. 1924–

One of the foremost Czech writers of the postwar generation, Škvorecký is the author of five novels and many filmscripts, and the translator into Czech of FAULKNER (see Vol. 1), HEMINGWAY (see Vol. 1) and Dashiel Hammett. His first novel, *The Cowards*, took an unorthodox look at the events of May 1945 when Czechoslovakia was liberated from the Nazis. The novel was, in its author's words, a *succès scandale*. In spite of a ban by the party, *The Cowards* circulated underground and exerted a powerful influence on young Czech writers before the political thaw set in. *Miss Silver's Past* was the last of his books to appear in Czechoslovakia, where it was published in 1969. *The Tank Corps*, which should have appeared the same year, was banned. Škvorecký left Czechoslovakia in 1968 and now teaches at the University of Toronto. He also publishes books of Czech émigré writers. In 1980 he received the Neustadt International Prize for Literature.

BOOKS BY ŠKVORECKÝ

The Cowards. 1958. Trans. by Jeanne Nemcová, Ecco Pr. repr. of 1970 ed. 1980 pap. $8.95. A compelling novel of the author's youthful experiences during World War II and of his attempts to overcome the grim reality by preferring love and music to war and killing. The novel "transcends the local framework, overshadows political implications, and turns into a bittersweet farewell to youth—an experience as old as man" (*SR*).

The Bass Saxophone. 1967. Trans. by Káča Poláčková-Henley, Knopf 1978 $8.95

Miss Silver's Past. 1974. Intro. by Graham Greene, Ecco Pr. repr. of 1975 ed. 1985 pap. $7.50. This novel "tells a spellbinding story of moral corruption and political cynicism in the guise of a love story that turns into a murder mystery. But beyond a diverting thriller, this novel also offers a remarkable account of life among the privileged few in a communist society, the first book to give us a glimpse of the underworld of intellectual pimp and literary prostitute that rules the cultural establishment" (Publisher's note).

The Engineer of Human Souls. 1977. Trans. by Paul Wilson, Knopf 1984 $17.95; Washington Square Pr. 1985 pap. $9.95. A satirical novel about the U.S. and Canadian societies.

VACULÍK, LUDVÍK. 1926–

One of the outstanding Czech novelists of the postwar generation, Vaculík has been a shoemaker, teacher, soldier, and journalist. His first novel, *The Busy House* (o.p.), appeared in 1963. He edited *Literarni Listy* from 1966 until 1968 when it was suppressed by the government. His novel *The Axe*, published in 1966, made Vaculík famous in Czechoslovakia. He was among the writers who criticized the Novotny regime at the Writers' Union Congress in 1967. He was expelled from the party but was readmitted during the Prague Spring of 1968. At this time Vaculík wrote the *Two Thousand Word Manifesto*, which was signed by thousands and which some believe contributed to the Soviet leaders' decision to intervene militarily. He was expelled from the party a second time and his writings are now banned in Czechoslovakia.

BOOKS BY VACULÍK

The Axe. Trans. by Marian Sling, Okpaku 1973 $7.95. Neal Ascherson describes this novel as "the story of a lonely farmer who deliberately destroys his own family relationships and friendships to bring socialist collectivization to his village in Moravia and who—through the very challenge that his own integrity offers to the corrupt Stalinist bureaucracy of the new order—is himself destroyed."

The Guinea Pigs. Trans. by Káča Poláčková-Henley, intro. by Neal Ascherson, Penguin 1975 o.p. In his introduction to this novel, Neal Ascherson writes: "One could try to discuss *The Guinea Pigs* without bringing up Franz Kafka, but it would be a useless exercise. This is the same world of meaningless, menacing activity broken into by strokes of atrocity delivered by an authority never named or identified."

ESTONIAN LITERATURE

The Estonian language is closely related to the Finno-Ugric group of languages. It is not surprising, therefore, that the first important literary work was the epic *Kalevipoeg* (*The Son of Kalev*), written from 1857 to 1861, in imitation of the Finnish epic *Kalevala*. The early Estonian literature consists almost entirely of epic and lyric folk poetry. It is estimated that this small nation has produced about 400,000 folk songs. Estonians wrote mostly in Latin until 1525, when the church replaced Latin with Estonian. The publication of *Kalevipoeg* signaled the awakening of national consciousness and the rise of romanticism in literature, which prevailed until the end of the nineteenth century. At that time a more realistic trend began to take hold, manifested in the depiction of rural life with social and political overtones. At the same time some authors, who were influenced by the French, introduced symbolism and impressionism. Of greater importance was the emergence of the "Young Estonia" movement, which advocated openness to foreign literatures, stylistic sophistication, and formal excellence. The writers of this movement, for the most part, established the tone of Estonian literature in the interwar period. Gustav Suits and Marie Under, considered the greatest Estonian poets, were leaders in this period. Anton Hansen Tammsaare, with his five-volume novel *Truth and Justice,* and Bernard Kangro brought new approaches to Estonian fiction by way of experimentation, symbolism, and psychological probing.

   The vicissitudes of Estonian national and political life have forced many writers to leave the country on at least two occasions. Consequently, after the takeover of Estonia by the Soviet Union and the establishment of a communist state in 1944, many writers chose to live in exile. In the last few decades two kinds of Estonian literature have existed. The one written at home is shaped and dictated by the tenets of socialist realism. Although some younger poets have been successful in asserting themselves after some relaxation of controls in the post-Stalin period, very little of that literature is above the level of propaganda. The best contemporary writers are in exile. The most representative among them are Suits, Under, Kangro, Karl Ristikivi, Ilmar Jaks, Helga Nōu, and Aleksis Rannit.

History and Criticism

Rubulis, Aleksis. *Baltic Literature: A Survey of Finnish, Estonian, Latvian, and Lithuanian Literatures.* Univ. of Notre Dame Pr. 1970 $8.50

Collections

Maas, Selve. *The Moon Painters and Other Estonian Folk Tales.* Viking 1971 o.p.
Matthews, William Kleesmann, ed. *Anthology of Modern Estonian Poetry.* Greenwood repr. of 1953 ed. 1977 lib. bdg. $19.75

KANGRO, BERNARD. 1910–

A poet, prose writer, playwright, literary historian, and critic, Kangro lives and works in Sweden. He has 14 books of poetry and 6 novels to his credit. His poetry is rich, musical, predominantly elegiac, and delusory, while his novels are experimental and psychological.

BOOK BY KANGRO

Earthbound. Trans. by W. K. Matthews, Estonian House 1951 o.p.

RANNIT, ALEKSIS. 1914–1985

Rannit published his first book of poems in 1937 and later added five more collections. Because he lived the last three decades of his life in the United States, he is perhaps the best-known Estonian poet in the English-speaking world. He defines poetry as a "dance of syllables . . . the consensually pulsating expression of our spirit . . . a kind of sorcery in which metaphorical thinking blends with authentic reality to create a mythical order."

BOOKS BY RANNIT

Donum Estonicum. Elizabeth Pr. 1976 $16.00 pap. $8.00
Cantus Firmus. Trans. by Henry Lyman, Elizabeth Pr. 1978 $50.00

UNDER, MARIE. 1883–

Under, a poet and translator, worked mostly as a free-lance writer in Stockholm. The author of 13 collections of poetry, she is revered as Estonia's greatest lyric poet.

BOOK BY UNDER

Child of Man. Trans. by W. K. Matthews, Estonian House 1955 o.p.

HUNGARIAN LITERATURE

Hungarian literature had its beginnings in the thirteenth century. From then until the early seventeenth century, it manifested itself primarily in such religious works as chronicles and translations of the Bible. Hungarian writers played a very important role in facilitating the conversion to Christianity and in spreading the new religion among the predominantly illiterate populace. Secular literature did not begin to develop until the period of the Enlightenment in the late eighteenth century, when the foundation was laid for the flowering that was to come in the next century. Although literary works were primarily didactic, in tune with the period, there were attempts at a humorous, light-hearted depiction of reality and at the cultivation of national and traditional values as opposed to foreign influences. The first writer of international stature did not appear until the nineteenth century. Sándor Petőfi, one of the greatest, if not the greatest, of Hungarian poets, wrote patriotic, love, and nature poems inspired to a large degree by folk poetry, which, he believed, is the only true poetry. His friend János Arany also contributed significantly to the basically romantic literature around the middle of the century, while Imre Madách wrote dramatic poems of exceptional depth and originality.

Through the nineteenth century, writers came mostly from the ranks of the nobility, while those from lower classes had just begun to make their presence felt. The latter gained full stride early in the twentieth century with the appearance of the revolutionary poet Endre Ady, who is still considered the greatest Hungarian poet of this century. The "modern" movement, centered around an influential magazine, *Nyugat* (The West), replaced the stagnant literature of the preceding decades and ushered in a versatile, socially conscious literature on a higher level, open to Western influences. This versatility and high-spirited activity carried over into the interwar period, in which many prewar writers were joined by new voices. The three consummate poets, Mihály Babits, Attila József, and Gyula Illyés, raised Hungarian poetry to new heights, while Ferenc Molnár, Lajos Zilahy, and Lázsló Németh brought the Hungarian middle class into a sharper focus with their novels and short stories. Throughout this period, and even after World War II, writers either advocated revolutionary social change or took a more neutral stand, making their art the main modus of existence. The former were aided by the theoretical works of a world-famous Marxist critic, Gyorgy Lukács, who gradually changed from a liberal to a communist and became the theoretical leader of the writers on the Left. Other writers wrote about the rural life in various regions of Hungary, representing the populist movement that was demanding social reform. In fact, relatively few writers were able to stay out of political and ideological struggles during the 1930s and 1940s, due primarily to a rather volatile political situation in Hungary at that time. This involvement took a terrible toll among writers during and after World War II. Even Lukács was severely criticized at times by the communists for valuing Western literature above that of socialist realism.

After the communist takeover, socialist realism was installed as the official literary method, but it brought forward few worthy results. Even though it has remained the official method to this day, writers have paid only lip service to it. By the same token, they were not able to fulfill their artistic potential. Nevertheless, new names have entered the literary scene, who along with the established writers provide for a lively literature. Several writers left the country after the events of 1948 and 1956 and continued to write in exile, without repeating their earlier successes. There are also Hungarian minority literatures in Rumania, Yugoslavia, and Czechoslovakia; however they have failed to produce a writer of prominence.

History and Criticism

Czigány, Lóránt. *The Oxford History of Hungarian Literature from the Earliest Times to the Present.* Oxford 1984 $39.95. The most competent and complete history in English.

Klaniczay, Tibor, and H. H. Remak, eds. *A History of Hungarian Literature.* Ungar 1984 $45.00. A Marxist-oriented study, with predictable limitations.

Reményi, Joseph. *Hungarian Writers and Literature.* Ed. by August J. Molnar, Rutgers Univ. Pr. 1964 o.p. The late Hungarian-American author examines the literature of the nineteenth and twentieth centuries. Brilliant essays by a knowledgeable observer.

Tezla, Albert. *Hungarian Authors: A Bibliographical Handbook.* Harvard Univ. Pr. (Belknap Pr.) 1970 $50.00. Extension of the author's *An Introductory Bibliography to the Study of Hungarian Literature* (1964) and to be used in conjunction with that book.

Collections

Cushing, G. F., ed. *Hungarian Prose and Verse. London East European Ser.* Humanities Pr. text ed. 1956 $15.50; Longwood Pr. 1956 $25.00

Duczynszka, Ilona, ed. *The Plough and the Pen: Writing from Hungary, 1930–1956.* Dufour o.p.

Tezla, Albert, ed. *Ocean at the Window: Hungarian Prose and Poetry since 1945.* Univ. of Minnesota Pr. 1981 $25.00

Vajda, Miklós, ed. *Modern Hungarian Poetry.* Intro. by Miklós Vajda and William Jay Smith, Columbia Univ. Pr. 1977 $25.00 pap. $14.00

ADY, ENDRE. 1877–1919

Considered the greatest Hungarian lyric poet of the twentieth century, Ady introduced new vigor into the stagnant, conventional poetry of the turn of the century. His early poetry was revolutionary in both language and content and offended literary and political conservatives. In his later writings, from before and during World War I, he voices his anguish at social injustice and the carnage of war. Ady wrote poetry dealing with love and religion as well as with social and political themes.

BOOK BY ADY

Poems of Endre Ady. Lit. Ser. Hungarian Cultural Foundation 1969 $19.50

ILLYÉS, GYULA. 1902–1983

A poet, dramatist, novelist, essayist, and translator, Illyés published his first volume of poems in 1928. His published works amount to more than 35 volumes in Hungarian. He was one of the leaders of the populist movement in literature, which attempted to "explore the village" and to write about the squalid condition of the peasantry. His largely autobiographical study of the peasantry, *People of the Puszta,* is considered a classic. Illyés always wrote in the "daily language of simple people," drawing on the wealth and rhythms of the Hungarian language.

BOOK BY ILLYÉS

People of the Puszta. Trans. by G. F. Cushing, International Publishing Service 1971 o.p.

BOOK ABOUT ILLYÉS

Kabdebo, Thomas, and Paul Tabori, eds. *Tribute to Gyula Illyés: Poems.* Occidental 1968 o.p.

JÓKAI, MÓR (also MÓRICZ, MAURICE). 1825–1904

Mór Jókai, an author of romances who enjoyed great popularity in his day, was a sort of Jules Verne of Hungary who became known throughout Europe. He wrote more than 100 novels. Though weak in characterization, Jókai was a master of suspense and fantastic—sometimes "scientific"—adventure, which took place in exotic settings and was colored by his own exuberant optimism. *Black Diamonds* (1870) and *The Man with the Golden Touch* (sometimes translated *A Modern Midas*) are his two outstanding tales.

BOOKS BY JÓKAI

Tales from Jókai. Trans. by R. Nisbet Bain, *Short Story Index Repr. Ser.* Ayer repr. of 1904 ed. 3rd. ed. $5.37
The Man with the Golden Touch. 1872. Ungar o.p. A novel.
The Dark Diamonds. Trans. by Frances Gerard, Vanous $5.00

JÓZSEF, ATTILA. 1905–1937

A poet, József was born in poverty and remained poor all his life. In his poetry he protested against the conditions of the working class. He was a contributor to *Nyugat* (The West). His first collection of poems was *Beggar of Beauty* (1922). In the last years of his life he became a poet of national and world stature. His best works are the collections of poems *The Bear's Dance* (1934), *There Is No Pardon* (1936–37), and *Last Poems* (1937). József drew on Hungarian folklore, German expressionism, and French surrealism but integrated these materials into his own powerful poetic style. After being held in disrepute by the communist regime during the Zhdanov period, József is now considered the greatest Hungarian poet.

BOOKS BY JÓZSEF

Works of Attila József. Lit. Ser. Hungarian Cultural Foundation 1973 $9.80
Selected Poems and Texts. Trans. by John Batki, *International Bks.* Univ. of Iowa Pr. pap. $2.50

JUHÁSZ, FERENC. 1928–

Juhász's first book of poems, *The Winged Colt* (1947, o.p.), made his reputation before he was 20. After several works glorifying the new communist regime, Juhász in the early 1950s began to move away from politics and to develop his own original poetic style. The large epic poem *The Prodigal Country*, according to Gomori, introduced a "new epoch in modern Hungarian poetry." Juhász's collection of poems *Battling the White Lamb* (1957, o.p.) contains *The Boy Changed into a Stag Cries Out at the Gate of Secrets*, which W. H. Auden called "one of the greatest poems written in my time." After being in official disfavor in the late 1950s and early 1960s, Juhász is now tolerated by the regime and allowed to travel abroad. Hungarians consider him the greatest poet of his generation and the heir to Atilla József.

BOOKS BY JUHÁSZ

The Boy Changed into a Stag: Selected Poems, 1949–1967. Trans. by Kenneth McRobbie and Ilona Duczynska, Oxford 1970 o.p.
(and Sandor Weores). *Selected Poems.* Trans. by Davis Wevill and Edward Morgan, Peter Smith $11.00

LENGYEL, JOZSEF. 1896–1975

A novelist, memoirist, and short-story writer, Lengyel was an active communist who, in 1937, was arrested and held in Siberia until 1955. In his writings he describes his experiences of this period and tries to understand the debasement of socialism into Stalinism.

BOOKS BY LENGYEL

Confrontation. Trans. by Anna Novotny, Citadel Pr. 1973 $6.95
The Spell (and *From Beginning to End*). Trans. by Ilona Duczynska, Beekman $14.95
The Judge's Chair. Beekman $12.95
Prenn Drifting. Beekman $12.95
Acta Sanctorum. Beekman $12.95

LUKÁCS, GYÖRGY (also GEORG, GEORGE). 1885–1971

George Steiner, in *Language and Silence*, calls Lukács "the one major critical talent to have emerged from the gray servitude of the Marxist world." This well-known writer on European literature combines a Marxist-Hegelian concern for the historical process with great artistic sensitivity. Lukács joined the Hungarian Communist party in 1918, serving in its first government until the defeat of Béla Kun. He spent many years in exile, first in Berlin and then, from 1933 to 1945, in Moscow, writing and studying. He later became a professor of aesthetics in Budapest, but after the 1956 revolution he was stripped of influence because of his too-friendly attitude to non-Marxist literatures. "A Communist by conviction, a dialectical materialist by virtue of his critical method, he has nevertheless kept his eyes resolutely on the past. . . . Despite pressure from his Russian hosts, Lukács gave only perfunctory notice to the much-heralded achievements of 'Soviet Realism.' Instead, he dwelt on the great lineage of eighteenth- and nineteenth-century European poetry and fiction. . . . The critical perspective is rigorously Marxist, but the choice of themes is 'central European' and conservative" (Steiner). Lukács has concentrated mainly on criticism of Russian, French, and German authors, and often writes in German. Robert J. Clements (*SR*) found that Hungarian young people regard him as somewhat passé.

BOOKS BY LUKÁCS

The Historical Novel. 1955. Humanities Pr. repr. of 1962 ed. text ed. 1978 $15.50; trans. by Hannah Mitchell and Stanley Mitchell, Univ. of Nebraska Pr. repr. of 1937 ed. 1983 $8.95

Goethe and His Age. Trans. by Robert Anchor, Fertig repr. of 1968 ed. 1978 $25.00; Humanities Pr. text ed. 1968 pap. $9.00
Solzhenitsyn. Trans. by William D. Graf, MIT 1971 pap. $2.95
Theory of the Novel. Trans. by Ann Bostock, MIT 1971 pap. $6.95
The Meaning of Contemporary Realism. Humanities Pr. text ed. 1980 $13.45 pap. $7.45
Essays on Realism. Trans. by David Fernbach, ed. by Rodney Livingstone, MIT text ed. 1981 pap. $9.95

BOOKS ABOUT LUKÁCS

Bahr, Ehrhard, and Ruth G. Kunzer. *Georg Lukács. Lit. and Life Ser.* Ungar 1972 $12.95
Meszaros, I. *Lukács' Concept of Dialectics: With Biography, Bibliography and Documents.* Humanities Pr. text ed. 1972 $16.25

MADÁCH, IMRE. 1823–1864

Madách's drama in verse, *The Tragedy of Man*, is Faustlike in theme. It begins and ends in heaven, and Adam and Eve are its protagonists, with Lucifer battling God for the possession of their souls. *The Tragedy of Man* is still performed on the Hungarian stage as one of its great classics.

BOOK BY MADÁCH

The Tragedy of Man. 1861. Gordon $59.95; trans. by J. C. Horne, Vanous 8th ed $4.00

MORICZ, SZIGMOND. 1879–1942

Moricz was a novelist, short-story writer, and playwright associated with the literary journal *Nyugat* (The West). In his early works, Moricz described the grim reality of the countryside in a stark, naturalistic manner. His later novels about the upper classes are less forceful than the early ones. Among his best-known novels are *The Torch* (1917) and his historical novels in the trilogy *Transylvania* (1922–35). Moricz is generally recognized as Hungary's first modern writer.

BOOK BY MORICZ

Be Faithful unto Death. Trans. by Susan K. Laszlo, Vanous 1962 o.p.

NÉMÉTH, LÁSZLÓ. 1901–1975

Németh is known as a brooding philosopher and reformer who has written many books on the situation of Hungary in Europe as well as critical works, journalism, and a number of novels. *Revulsion* (1947, o.p.) is an example of the latter. The sensitive story of a young farm girl, set in the Hungary of the late 1930s, it gives a vivid picture of village and rural life. "Written in the tradition of Flaubert and Pasternak by one of Hungary's leading authors and critics . . . this novel can be recommended to every thoughtful person" (*LJ*).

BOOK BY NÉMÉTH

Guilt. Dufour 1966 $13.95

PETÖFI, SÁNDOR. 1823–1849

Considered the greatest lyric poet of nineteeenth-century Hungary, Petöfi takes as the subject for most of his poems the life of Hungarian peasantry. The main themes of his poetry are love and patriotism. He is best known for his poem about peasant life, *Janos the Hero,* and for the "Talpra Magyar," known as the Hungarian "Marseillaise," written during the Hungarian struggle for independence in 1848. Petöfi enlisted in the army in order to take part in this struggle and is believed to have died during the battle of Segesvar in 1849, at the age of 26.

Books by Petöfi

Works. Lit. Ser. Hungarian Cultural Foundation 1973 $13.90
Sixty Poems. Trans. by Emil Delmar, Kraus 1948 o.p.

Book about Petöfi

Tribute to Sándor Petöfi on the 150th Anniversary of His Birth. International Publishing Service 1974 o.p.

LATVIAN LITERATURE

Early Latvian literature consists entirely of folk poetry; more than one million folk songs have been recorded. The Latvians were ruled by the Germans for many centuries and the first literary works in Latvia were written by the German clergy in the sixteenth century. Literature in Latvian originated in the second half of the nineteenth century as a result of the national awakening and the drive toward independence. Poems, stories, novels, and plays show the influence of folk literature. The first important work is a novel about the plight of the peasants, *The Time of the Land Surveyors,* written by the brothers Kaudzītes. By the turn of the century, the influence from abroad, especially that of French symbolism, became more noticeable. In the aftermath of the uprising in 1905 against the German landowners, some writers retained their nationalistic fervor while others turned to Marxism.

Among the authors before the independence of 1918, Jānis Rainis stands out. He was the first to draw the attention of the outside world to Latvian literature with his philosophically tinged poems and plays. Other notables of this period are the poet and fairy tale writer Kārlis Skalbe and the poet Edvards Virza. Most writers in this period were preoccupied with transforming their legacy of folk literature into a more modern idiom under the influence from abroad.

After independence, writers either stayed at home or moved to the Soviet Union. The ratio of published books to the population was among the highest in the world. Most of the writers who emigrated to the Soviet Union perished in the purges of the 1930s; at any rate, they failed to produce works of lasting value. The writers at home fared better, although they produced only one outstanding writer, the poet Aleksandrs Čaks, who was able to influence the younger poets with his formalistic innovations.

The Soviet occupations of 1940 and 1944 brought strict controls and literary dictates. Predictably, few outstanding authors and works have appeared since then, although some younger writers have been able to elude the grip of socialist realism by reconciling tradition with contemporaneity. By far the best Latvian literature is written by émigré writers: in Sweden, the poet Veronika Strēlerte, the novelist Andrejs Irbe, and the most important Latvian playwright, Mārtiņš Zīverts; in London, the poet Velta Snikere and the novelist Guntis Zariņš; and in the United States, the poets Linards Tauns and Astrīda Ivask, and fiction writers Gunars Saliņš, Knuts Lesiņš, and Anšlāvs Eglītis.

It is indeed unfortunate that very little of Latvian literature is available in English.

History and Criticism

Ekmanis, Rolfs. *Latvian Literature under the Soviets, 1940–1975.* Nordland 1977 o.p. A scholarly examination of the difficult conditions of Latvian writers in the Soviet Union.

Rubulis, Aleksis. *Baltic Literature: A Survey of Finnish, Estonian, Latvian, and Lithuanian Literatures.* Univ. of Notre Dame Pr. 1970 $8.50

Collections

Cedrins, Inara, ed. *Contemporary Latvian Poetry.* Intro. by Juris Silenieks, *Iowa Translations Ser.* 1984 pap. $15.00. The best available anthology of Latvian poetry in English.

Straumanis, Alfreds, ed. *Confrontations with Tyranny: Six Baltic Plays. Ethnic Heritage Ser.* Waveland Pr. 1977 $18.00. First in a series of volumes of drama translations. This volume contains two each of Estonian, Latvian, and Lithuanian plays dealing with a common theme.

LITHUANIAN LITERATURE

Unfavorable historical and political conditions prevented Lithuanian literature from asserting itself until the late eighteenth century. At that time Kristijonas Donelaitis wrote poems about the pastoral life, reflecting the strong attachment to nature of many Lithuanian writers. Donelaitis's poetry could not inspire other poets because Polish domination was replaced by that of Russia at the beginning of the nineteenth century. The full awakening of national consciousness engendered a strong desire for independence, expressed most eloquently by the romantic poets, especially by those from neighboring Poland. The forerunner of this romantic enthusiasm was Antanas Baranauskas, whose evocation of the past and of the joys of country life exudes optimism. The patriotic zeal of the romanticists intensified when the Russians forbade the publication of books in Lithuania after the unsuccessful uprising in 1863. The poet Maironis personifies the patriotic spirit toward the end of the nineteenth century. Other writers, forced to print their books abroad and smuggle them into Lithuania, found their models among Western authors, especially the French symbolists.

The lifting of the ban in 1904 greatly increased literary activity, bringing forth many new names. This process continued after Lithuania finally won its independence in 1918 and between the two world wars. The poet Jonas Aistis blended French modernism with native folkloristic elements. Putinas, who was originally influenced by Russian symbolism, enriched Lithuanian poetry and added psychological depth to his novels and plays. Vincas Krėvė, perhaps the best Lithuanian fiction writer, found the strength of his heroes in the myths of Lithuania's past. Antanas Vienulis spanned several periods, finally opting for Soviet Lithuania. In his starkly realistic works he depicts the everyday life of his countrymen forced to accept the dictates of the mighty. Antanas Vaičiulaitis, a master of impressionistic style, wrote novels and short stories about life in the country, as well as fairy tales. The emotional poetry of Bernardos Brazdžionis displays religious overtones of Catholic mysticism.

Most of these writers emigrated when the Soviets returned in 1944, and continued to write about their homeland. Others blossomed after they had emigrated, mostly to the United States. The most outstanding of them, Henrikas Radauskas, blends fantasy and reality through a sure command of his modernistic poetic idiom. Other noteworthy émigré writers are Kazys Braidūnas, Nýka-Niliūnas (pseud. of Alfonsas Čipkus), Antanas Škema, Algirdas Landsbergis, and Kostas Ostrauskas.

The writers who remained, or came later to the fore, in Soviet Lithuania had to work in much harsher conditions and under strict controls. Despite all these difficulties, some authors have succeeded in reconciling their artistic aspirations with the stifling demands of socialist realism. Among those writers are Eduardas Mieželaitis, Juozas Grušas, Justinas Marcinkevičius, Mykolas Sluckis, Icchokas Meras, and Thomas Venclova. Although there has been no work of international acclaim, these writers, especially the younger ones, are at least keeping the hope for a better future alive.

History and Criticism

Šilbajoris, Rimvydas. *Perfection of Exile: Fourteen Contemporary Lithuanian Writers.* Univ. of Oklahoma Pr. 1970 $18.95. Fourteen essays on 14 Lithuanian authors in exile, with a historical survey of Lithuanian literature.
Zobarskas, Stepas. *Lithuanian Short Story: Fifty Years.* Manyland 1977 $12.50

BARANAUSKAS, ANTANAS. 1835–1902

A Roman Catholic bishop, Baranauskas included creative writing among his other hobbies. *The Forest of Anykščiai* was written in response to the challenge to produce poetry in the Lithuanian language that would measure up to the standards of written Polish. This idyllic work, tracing the history and the demise of a small forest grove, met the challenge in exquisite syllabic verse, melodious and expressive to mirror the complex emotional experience of man living in an instinctive harmony with nature.

BOOK BY BARANAUSKAS

The Forest of Anykščiai. Trans. by Nadas Rastenis, Lithuanian Days 1970 o.p. A narrative poem.

DONELAITIS, KRISTIJONAS. 1714–1780

Author of the first important work in Lithuanian, Donelaitis, a village pastor, wrote very little else. *The Seasons* grew out of his efforts to enlist the services of art in his pastoral work. The long narrative poem surveys the course of the seasons in the life of eighteenth-century Lithuanian peasants "plodding the treadmill of time toward a hoped-for eternity in which their plain country virtue is to meet its just reward" (*Perfection of Exile*).

BOOK BY DONELAITIS

The Seasons. Trans. by Nadas Rastenis, Lithuanian Days 1967 o.p.

GLIAUDA, JURGIS. 1906–

When the exigencies of exile deprived Gliauda of his profession as a lawyer, he turned to belles lettres and rapidly developed into a prolific novelist, conservative in terms of moral and ethnic values but often experimental in the structure and language of his work. First written in 1945, *House upon the Sand* pictures the "crime and punishment" of a German landowner just before Hitler's empire crumbled. "Understatement and simplicity of style reveal an ordinary German infected by the dread disease of Nazism and its consequences."

BOOKS BY GLIAUDA

House upon the Sand. Trans. by Raphael Sealey and Milton Stark, Manyland 1963 o.p.
Sonata of Icarus. Trans. by Raphael Sealey, intro. by C. Angoff, Manyland 1968 $5.00
Simas. Manyland 1971 $5.00

KRĖVĖ, VINCAS (MICKIEVIČIUS). 1882–1954

The grand old man of Lithuanian letters, Vincas Krėvė laid the foundation for many levels and styles of Lithuanian prose and drama, greatly extending the powers of spoken Lithuanian to function as an effective written medium. *Legends of the Old People of Dainava* (1912) elevated the heroic Lithuanian in iridescent beauty of quasi-folkloristic language approaching high poetry. The historical plays *Šarūnas* (1912) and *Skirgaila* (1925) depict Lithuanian rulers confronted with tremendous moral and intellectual challenges as they struggle to create and then defend a unified Lithuanian nation. *The Herdsman and the Linden Tree* presents some of the best realistic stories Krėvė wrote.

BOOK BY KRĖVĖ

The Herdsman and the Linden Tree. Manyland 1964 $3.95

LANDSBERGIS, ALGIRDAS. 1924–

Landsbergis began writing in exile, in Germany. His novel *The Journey* (1954, o.p.) "not so much reflects as refracts the realities of wartime existence as a slave laborer in Germany, passing them through the prism of a young man's consciousness" (*Encyclopedia Lithuanica*), which is itself shattered by the loss of home and by the traumatic realization that the entire edifice of civilized Europe is crumbling before his eyes. *Wind in the Willows* (1958, o.p.), a mystery play, turns to a legend about Saint Casimir, the patron saint of Lithuania. *Five Posts* is a soul-searing play about hopeless guerrilla resistance imposing crushing burdens of grim heroics on gentle, creative people for whom peace and freedom have become dreams beyond possibility.

BOOKS BY LANDSBERGIS

Five Posts in a Market Place. Manyland 1968 $4.00
The Last Picnic. Manyland 1977 pap. $4.00

VAIČIULAITIS, ANTANAS. 1906–

Educator, diplomat, and writer, Vaičiulaitis stands among the best Lithuanian prose stylists. He is able to register barely perceptible nuances of feeling and to control complex, brooding mental processes in language that is lucid and elegant, and that appears deceptively simple on the surface. A gentle lyrical touch, an eye for miniature patterns in nature and in human experience, are blended with a quiet, refined sense of irony and humor. His main novel, *Valentina* (1936, o.p.), portrays the unfulfilled love of two fragile souls under a dreamy summer sky filled with dark forebodings. *Noon at a Country Inn* contains a number of Vaičiulaitis's best stories, in which human foibles are depicted with loving wit, and human tragedy with restrained candor.

BOOK BY VAIČIULAITIS

Noon at a Country Inn. Manyland 1965 $3.95

POLISH LITERATURE

In common with the experience of other eastern European countries, the beginnings of Polish literature in the tenth century are tied with the adoption of Christianity. Predominantly religious works—prayers, hymns, the lives of saints, and so on—were in Latin, although there are some works in the vernacular as well. Many such works were written from the tenth to the fifteenth centuries, but there was no outstanding literary figure. The first notable Polish writer was Jan Kochanovski, a poet educated in Italy, who wrote elegies in Latin and highly personal lyric poems in Polish. At this time, as Poland exuded political and military strength and economic prosperity, the Renaissance exerted a strong influence on Polish writers, strengthening their national identity. Since Polish culture has always gravitated toward the West, it is no surprise that literature would follow the next development in Western cultural history, that of the baroque. This period, which lasted until the middle of the eighteenth century, gave rise to lyric poetry replete with formalistic innovations and flowery imagery. It is interesting to note that Polish literature does not have medieval epics or abundant folk literature; instead, it developed historical epics and memoirs, which flourished especially during this period, as exemplified by the memoirs of Jan Chryzostom Pasek.

By the beginning of the eighteenth century, Poland entered a political and economic decline, which was to some degree reflected in literature. However, despite the loss of the country's independence, literature kept pace with the Enlightenment present in western Europe throughout the eighteenth century. The focus shifted toward new ideas, the pursuit of knowledge, and the use of literature for the dissemination of knowledge, as exemplified by the growth of theater. Yet, poetry was not neglected, thanks primarily to the greatest poet of the period, Ignacy Krasicki.

Much of Polish literature has been dictated by historical events. When the uprising against the Russians failed in 1831, many writers emigrated, mostly to France. By that time, romanticism, which had reigned in western Europe since the end of the eighteenth century, was already felt in Poland as well. The best Polish romantic poets—Adam Mickiewicz, Juliusz Słowacki, and Cyprian Norwid—continued to write in the romantic vein abroad, reinforcing, in turn, the romantic spirit of the writers at home. Others who excelled at this time were the playwright Zygmunt Krasiński and Józef Kraszewski, an author of more than 400 volumes of novels, most of which were historical. What united these writers, aside from their allegiance to romanticism, was the idea of messianism, which they found in those nations willing to fight for their independence.

Their influence weakened, however, in the second half of the nineteenth century as, again following the general trend of European literature, Polish writers turned toward realism, called "positivism" and "critical realism." In contrast to the predominance of poetry in the romantic period, the realistic period was dominated by the short story and the novel. Under the influence of AUGUSTE COMTE (see Vol. 4), Hippolyte Taine, JOHN STUART MILL (see Vol. 4), and CHARLES DARWIN (see Vol. 5), writers focused on history and on political and social problems. Of the several significant authors, three should be singled out: Eliza Oreszkowa, Henryk Sienkiewicz, and Bolesław Prus. Didactic and hopeful at first, they later turned toward a gloomier reality of social conflicts in both city and village life. Others embraced the biological determinism of naturalism. It is not surprising that poetry did not fare well in these "un-poetic times," as the critic Julian Krzyzanowski called it.

Toward the end of the century, a new movement, called "Młoda Polska" (Young Poland), came into being. Paralleling similar movements in other literatures, Young Poland reflected the *fin de siècle* pessimistic mood, and the search for new ways in the arts manifested in numerous isms in the first two decades of the twentieth century. The Polish movement was somewhat less pessimistic in that it rejected the utilitarianism of the positivists and demanded a return to former philosophical values and even to romanticism.

The constant struggle for independence undoubtedly had something to do with this optimism. It was a dynamic movement, producing a number of spirited writers, including Władisław Reymont, the recipient of the Nobel Prize in 1924. Their output varied, but their overall impact on Polish literature is unmistakable. Even though the period of the Young Poland closed with the end of World War I, its influence continued to be felt.

The interwar period is characterized by a variety of groups, movements, and approaches to literature. Although many older writers continued to be active, new generations gave the period their own stamp, which is not easily defined because of the high degree of independence of groups and individuals. Poetry again became a dominant genre. The most important group of poets was gathered around the journal *Skamander* and was led by Julian Tuwim, one of the most innovative of modern Polish poets. Another group, led by Jan Przyboś, was represented by the Cracow avant-garde.

After the devastation of World War II, additional difficulties arose from the imposition of a communist system in Poland, which led to a division into émigré writers and those who remained at home. A good number opted for exile, among them the poet Czesław Miłosz and the playwright Sławomir Mrożek. At home there are many excellent writers who are trying to salvage their dignity and freedom of creativity. Two leading contemporary poets, Tadeusz Różewicz and Zbigniew Herbert, are the best guarantee for the ultimate survival of Polish literature. It is interesting to note that, unlike other East European authors, the Polish writers in exile and those at home keep in contact and influence each other.

History and Criticism

Carpenter, Bogdana. *The Poetic Avant-Garde in Poland, 1918–1939.* Univ. of Washington Pr. 1983 $22.50

Ehrlich, Victor, and others, eds. *For Wiktor Weintraub: Essays in Polish Literature, Language and History Presented on the Occasion of His 65th Birthday.* Mouton new ed. text ed. 1975 $86.00. A distinguished collection of scholarly contributions on diverse topics.

Folejewski, Zbigniew, and others, eds. *Studies in Russian and Polish Literature in Honor of Waclaw Lednicki.* Humanities Pr. 1962 o.p.

Guergelewicz, Mieczyslaw. *Introduction to Polish Versification.* Univ. of Pennsylvania Pr. 1970 o.p. A useful introductory study.

Kridl, Manfred. *A Survey of Polish Literature and Culture.* Trans. by Olga Scherer-Virski, Columbia Univ. Pr. 1956 o.p. A discussion of Polish literature up to 1939 by a distinguished literary historian.

Krzyzanowski, Julian. *A History of Polish Literature.* Trans. by Doris Ronowicz, Hippocrene Bks. 1979 $39.95

———. *Polish Romantic Literature. Essay Index Repr. Ser.* Ayer repr. of 1931 ed. $18.00. An eminent Polish scholar's fundamental examination of a major literary period.

Lednicki, Waclaw. *Russia, Poland and the West: Essay in Literary and Cultural History.* Associated Faculty Pr. repr. of 1954 ed. $24.50. Erudite and provocative essays by a distinguished scholar.

Levine, Madeline G. *Contemporary Polish Poetry, 1925–1975. Twayne's World Authors*

Ser. G. K. Hall 1981 lib. bdg. $16.95. An acclaimed survey by an American scholar.

Maciuszko, Jerzy J. *Polish Short Story in English: A Guide and Critical Bibliography.* Wayne State Univ. Pr. 1968 $17.50

Miłosz, Czesław. *The History of Polish Literature.* Univ. of California Pr. rev. ed. text ed. 1983 $32.50 pap. $10.95. A survey of Polish letters and culture from the beginning to modern times by a distinguished modern scholar. The Nobel Prize winner of 1980.

Collections

Coleman, Marion M. *The Polish Land.* Alliance College rev. ed. text ed. 1974 pap. $5.00

Gillon, Adam, and Ludwik Kryzanowski, eds. *Introduction to Modern Polish Literature.* Twayne's International Studies and Translations Ser. G. K. Hall 1963 lib. bdg. $16.95; Hippocrene Bks. 2d ed. 1981 pap. $12.95

Holton, Milne, and Paul Vangelisti, eds. *The New Polish Poetry: A Bilingual Collection.* Pitt Poetry Ser. Univ. of Pittsburgh Pr. 1978 $14.95 pap. $7.95

Miłosz, Czesław. *Postwar Polish Poetry: An Anthology.* Univ. of California Pr. rev. ed. text ed. 1983 $25.00 pap. $6.95. Contains 125 poems by 25 poets, with the emphasis on poetry written after 1956.

Ordon, Edmund, ed. *Ten Contemporary Polish Stories.* Intro. by Olga Virski-Scherer, Greenwood repr. of 1958 ed. 1974 lib. bdg. $24.75

Peterkiewicz, Jerzy, ed. *Five Centuries of Polish Poetry, 1450–1970.* Greenwood repr. of 1970 ed. 1979 lib. bdg. $22.50. A good, representative selection.

BIAŁOSZEWSKI, TADEUSZ. 1922–1984

Białoszewski's first volume of poems, *The Revolution of Things,* appeared in 1956. Deliberately provocative in its use of grotesque imagery, it had a considerable impact. His next book, *Erroneous Emotions* (1961, o.p.), was radically antipoetic in its choice and use of words and sounds. He published two more collections of poetry plus plays and several books of prose, one of which, *A Memoir of the Warsaw Uprising,* describes the horrors of the ill-fated battle seen through the eyes of the civilians.

BOOKS BY BIALOSZEWSKI

The Revolution of Things. 1956. Trans. by Bogdan Czaykowski and Andrzej Busza, Charioteer 1974 $7.50

A Memoir of the Warsaw Uprising. 1970. Trans. and ed. by Madeline G. Levine, Ardis 1977 o.p.

BOROWSKI, TADEUSZ. 1922–1951

Borowski finished his secondary schooling in the underground school system of occupied Warsaw and then began to study at the underground Warsaw University. He published a mimeographed volume of poems in 1942. Subsequently, he was arrested by the gestapo and sent to Auschwitz. Although initially he reacted with skepticism to Marxist ideology, he later became a convert and an ardent champion of socialist realism. A combination of personal and ideological factors apparently led to his suicide in 1951.

BOOK BY BOROWSKI

This Way for the Gas, Ladies and Gentlemen. Penguin 1976 pap. $5.95. A collection of short stories.

DYGAT, STANISLAW. 1914–

Dygat began to publish before 1939. During the war, he was interned for a time in a German concentration camp near Bodensee, an experience that provided him with material for a subsequent antiheroic novel. Among his other novels, *Journey* and *Disneyland* (translated as *Cloak of Illusion*) have been particularly successful.

BOOK BY DYGAT

Cloak of Illusion. Trans. by David Welsh, MIT 1970 $22.50 .

FREDRO, ALEXANDER. 1793–1876

Son of a rich landowner, Fredro participated in the 1812 French campaign against Russia as aide-de-camp to Napoleon. Subsequently, disillusioned with the emperor, he departed from the contemporary romantic tradition by consistently debunking the Napoleonic myth. A prolific comedy writer with a classicist outlook, he spent most of his life quietly on his estate. In his plays, which have become a fixture of Polish theater, he exhibits a keen interest in and sensitivity to human beings. *Maidens' Vows* (1832) and *Vengeance* (1833) are among his most amusing works. In another, *Mr. Jowialski*, Fredro created a memorable figure of a teller of fables and proverbs.

BOOK BY FREDRO

The Major Comedies of Alexander Fredro. Trans. by Harold B. Segel, *Columbia Slavic Studies Ser.* Princeton Univ. Pr. 1969 $42.00

GOMBROWICZ, WITOLD. 1904–1969

Gombrowicz, son of a wealthy lawyer, studied law at Warsaw University and philosophy and economics in Paris. His first novel, *Ferdydurke*, with its treatment of existential themes and a daring use of surrealistic techniques, became a literary sensation in Warsaw. *Yvonne: Princess of Burgundia*, which anticipated many themes of the Theater of the Absurd, was also enormously successful; together with another of his plays, *The Marriage* (1953, o.p.), it has been staged throughout the world.

During the war, Gombrowicz lived in Argentina. In the postwar period, *Ferdydurke* was at first banned by the Polish authorities (continuing a ban imposed by the Nazis). During the "thaw," it was published in Warsaw in 1957 and its author was hailed as the "greatest living Polish writer" by the critic Sandauer. The ban on Gombrowicz's works was reimposed in 1958.

By this time, however, Gombrowicz had achieved a wide reputation in western Europe and the United States. In the sixties, he settled in France.

BOOKS BY GOMBROWICZ

Yvonne: Princess of Burgundia. 1935. Trans. by K. G. Jones and C. Robbins, Grove (Evergreen) o.p.

Three Novels: Ferdydurke, Pornografia, and Cosmos. Trans. by Eric Mosbacher and Alisdair Hamilton, Grove (Evergreen) 1978 pap. $9.95

A Kind of Testament. 1973. Trans. by Alisdair Hamilton, M. Boyars 1982 pap. $8.95; trans. by Alisdair Hamilton, Temple Univ. Pr. 1973 $14.95

Possessed: Or the Secret of Myslotch. Trans. by J. A. Underwood, M. Boyars 1981 $7.95

BOOK ABOUT GOMBROWICZ

Thompson, Ewa M. *Witold Gombrowicz. Twayne's World Authors Ser.* G. K. Hall 1979 lib. bdg. $16.95

HERLING, GUSTAW (HERLING-GRUDZIŃSKI). 1919–

Herling became known as a literary critic shortly before 1939. During World War II, he was imprisoned for a time in a labor camp in the north of Russia. After the war, he lived in England and finally settled in Naples. *A World Apart* is an excellent work on Stalinist camps. A collection of his short stories appeared in English under the title *The Island.*

BOOK BY HERLING

A World Apart. Trans. by Joseph Marek, Greenwood repr. of 1951 ed. 1974 lib. bdg. $29.75

HLASKO, MAREK. 1934–1969

Hlasko began his literary career as a correspondent among workers. His first stories were published in 1955 in literary periodicals; their publication as a single collection under the title *First Step in the Clouds* met with a very favorable reception. He followed up his success with a novella, *The Eighth Day of the Week* (1956, o.p.). While Hlasko's popularity grew during the Polish "thaw," he faced increasing difficulties with the authorities, and defected to the West in 1958. In emigration, his portrayal of life under communism grew harsher; the publication of *The Graveyard* increased the Polish authorities' hostility toward him. He died in Wiesbaden, Germany, at the age of 35.

BOOK BY HLASKO

The Graveyard. Trans. by Norbert Guterman, Greenwood repr. of 1959 ed. 1975 lib. bdg. $22.50

KONWICKI, TADEUSZ. 1926–

Konwicki fought as a young man in the resistance movement against the Nazis, an experience that provided him with material for several novels. He later became preoccupied with psychological and philosophical problems of young people and with lyrical reminiscences of his childhood in Lithuania. His strongly anticommunist novel, *The Polish Complex*, was published without the sanction of the authorities.

BOOKS BY KONWICKI

A Dreambook for Our Time. 1963. Trans. by David Welsh, MIT 1970 $17.50; intro. by Leszak Kolakowski, Penguin 1976 pap. $6.95. "A certain dreamlike quality, a gossamer of things long past yet somehow still clinging to life, pervades Konwicki's facile and poetic narration" (*SR*).
The Polish Complex. 1977. Trans. by Richard Lourie, Farrar 1982 $12.95; intro. by Joanna Clark, Penguin 1984 pap. $5.95
A Minor Apocalypse. Trans. by Richard Lourie, Farrar 1983 $16.95; Random (Vintage) 1984 pap. $7.95
Moonrise, Moonset. Trans. by Richard Lourie, Farrar 1985 $16.95

KRASIŃSKI, ZYGMUNT. 1812–1859

Until World War I, Krasiński was considered, together with Mickiewicz and Slowacki, a national "poet-seer." At present his reputation has been significantly diminished, but he is rightly viewed as a major figure of the romantic period. His best work, the poetic drama *The Undivine Comedy* (1835), deals with the problem of a poet's moral responsibility in a social framework (an important romantic dilemma) and with the problems of revolution. *Iridion* (1836), another poetic drama, is set in third-century Rome.

BOOKS BY KRASIŃSKI

Iridion. Trans. by Florence Noyes, Greenwood repr. of 1927 ed. 1975 lib. bdg. $24.75
The Undivine Comedy. Trans. by Harriette E. Kennedy and Zofia Uminska, Greenwood repr. of 1924 ed. 1976 lib. bdg. $15.00

BOOK ABOUT KRASIŃSKI

Lednicki, Waclaw, ed. *Zygmunt Krasiński, Romantic Universalist: An International Tribute*. Polish Institute of Arts and Sciences 1964 $6.00

LEM, STANISLAW. 1921–

Lem is not only Poland's best science fiction writer, but he has also acquired a solid world reputation. A medical graduate of Cracow University, he is at home both in the sciences and in philosophy, and this broad erudition gives his writings genuine depth. He has published extensively, not only fiction, but also theoretical studies. A trend toward increasingly serious philosophical speculation is found in his later works, such as *Solaris*, which was made into an excellent Soviet film.

BOOKS BY LEM

The Star Diaries. 1957. Avon 1984 pap. $1.75; trans. by Michael Kandel, Continuum 1976 $9.95; trans. by Michael Kandel, Harcourt 1985 pap. $3.95; (with the title *Memoirs of a Space Traveler: Further Reminiscences of Ijon Tichy*) trans. by Joel Stern and Maria Swiecicka-Ziemianek, Harcourt 1983 pap. $3.95

Memoirs Found in a Bathtub. 1961. Trans. by Michael Kandel and Christine Rose, Continuum 1973 $6.95

Return from the Stars. 1961. Avon 1982 pap. $2.95

Solaris. 1961. Berkley Publishing 1976 pap. $1.75

The Cyberiad: Fables for the Cybernetic Age. 1965. Avon 1976 pap. $2.50; Harcourt 1985 pap. $3.95

The Chain of Chance. 1968. Harcourt 1978 $7.95 1984 pap. $2.95

His Master's Voice. 1968. Trans. by Michael Kandel, Harcourt 1983 $12.95 1984 pap. $2.95

Tales of Pirx the Pilot. 1968. Avon 1981 pap. $2.95

The Futurological Congress. 1971. Avon 1976 pap. $2.75; trans. by Michael Kandel, Continuum 1974 $6.95; trans. by Michael Kandel, Harcourt repr. of 1975 ed. 1985 pap. $3.95

Imaginary Magnitude. Trans. by Marc Heine, Harcourt repr. of 1973 ed. 1984 $15.95 1985 pap. $3.95

A Perfect Vacuum. 1979. Trans. by Michael Kandel, Harcourt 1980 $8.95 1983 pap. $3.95

The Cosmic Carnival of Stanislaw Lem: An Anthology of Entertaining Stories by the Modern Master of Science Fiction. Ed. by Michael Kandel, Continuum 1981 pap. $7.95

More Tales of Pirx the Pilot. Trans. by Louis Iribarne, Magdalena Majcherczyk, and Michael Kandel, Harcourt repr. of 1982 ed. 1983 pap. $2.95

MICKIEWICZ, ADAM BERNARD. 1798–1855

Mickiewicz was born in Lithuania to the family of a landless lawyer. He received a solid classical education at Wilno University, then the best in Poland. Arrested in 1823 for suspected revolutionary activities, he was exiled to Russia in 1825. His four and a half years there were a period of poetical and social success: He became a friend of Pushkin and a welcome figure in aristocratic salons. In 1829, Mickiewicz left Russia. During the 1831 uprising, he appeared briefly in Prussian Poland and subsequently joined the Great Emigration in Paris, where he was viewed as the spiritual leader of the exiles. During the early 1840s, Mickiewicz became a follower of the Lithuanian mystic Towiański, a move that finished him as a poet and made him unpopular with most of his fellow exiles. After the outbreak of the Crimean War, his anti-Russian activities brought the poet to Turkey, where he died in late 1855. His remains were transferred to a crypt in Wawel Castle in Cracow in 1890.

Although his education in classical literature left a perceptible trace on his poetic diction, Mickiewicz was both the initiator of the romantic movement and one of its great figures. His literary position was established in 1822 with the publication of a short but striking anthology of poems. His subsequent ballads and historical poems were even finer; however, he reached special heights in his dramatic cycle *Forefathers' Eve* (1823). Mickiewicz's Russian period is distinguished by the creation of sonnets (especially the *Crimean Sonnets* cycle) and of the poem *Konrad Wallenrod* (1826–27).

A period of relative poetic sterility that began after *Konrad Wallenrod* ended in 1832, when Mickiewicz published his *Books of the Polish Nation,* a work in biblical prose that aspired to be the gospel of émigrés and is the clearest example of Polish national messianism. In 1832 Mickiewicz also wrote *Forefathers' Eve, Part III,* which he loosely connected with the earlier dramatic cycle, and in which he considered Poland's relationship with Russia through the prism of an intense personal vision.

Mickiewicz's last masterpiece is *Pan Tadeusz,* which continues the traditions of the epic and to a degree represents a turning away on the poet's part from romanticism. The poem deals with life in Lithuania in 1811 to 1812. A large number of characters, all of whom are basically good, and a wealth of lovingly described details of nature and the country society combine to make *Pan Tadeusz* an extraordinary, if idealized, canvas of everyday life.

BOOKS BY MICKIEWICZ

Poems by Adam Mickiewicz. Ed. by George R. Noyes, Polish Institute of Arts and Sciences 1944 $17.00

Konrad Wallenrod, and Other Writings. Trans. by George R. Noyes, Greenwood repr. of 1925 ed. 1975 lib. bdg. $25.00

Pan Tadeusz. 1834. Ed. by Watson Kirkconnell, Polish Institute of Arts and Sciences 2d ed. 1981 $8.00

BOOKS ABOUT MICKIEWICZ

Gardner, Monica M. *Adam Mickiewicz: The National Poet of Poland. Eastern European Collection Ser.* Ayer repr. of 1911 ed. 1970–71 $19.00

Kridl, Manfred, ed. *Adam Mickiewicz, Poet of Poland: A Symposium.* Greenwood repr. of 1951 ed. lib. bdg. $29.75

Weintraub, Wiktor. *Literature as Prophecy: Scholarship and Martinist Poetics in Mickiewicz's Parisian Lectures.* Humanities Pr. 1959 o.p.

———. *The Poetry of Adam Mickiewicz.* Humanities Pr. 1954 o.p. An excellent readable survey by an eminent scholar.

MIŁOSZ, CZESŁAW. 1911–   (NOBEL PRIZE 1980)

Born in Lithuania, Miłosz published his first volume of poetry in 1933. His next, *Three Winters* (1936), expressed very strongly the "catastrophic" themes current among a number of poets. During World War II he continued his literary activities underground. In 1951 he emigrated from Poland. Miłosz is the author of several prose works, one of which, the well-known study *The Captive Mind* (1953), analyzes East European intellectuals' relationship to Stalinism. He presently teaches at the University of California at Berkeley. In 1978 he received the Neustadt International Prize for Literature, and in 1980 the Nobel Prize.

BOOKS BY MILOSZ

Selected Poems. Intro. by Kenneth Rexroth, Continuum 1973 $9.95; Ecco Pr. rev. ed. repr. of 1973 ed. 1981 pap. $8.95

The Captive Mind. Octagon repr. of 1953 ed. 1981 lib. bdg. $18.50; Random (Vintage)
  repr. of 1953 ed. 1981 pap. $4.95
The Issa Valley. 1955. Trans. by Louis Iribarne, Farrar 1981 $13.95 pap. $7.95. A
  novel about the poet's childhood in Lithuania.
Native Realm: A Search for Self Definition. 1959. Doubleday 1981 $12.95; trans. by
  Catherine S. Leach, Univ. of California Pr. 1981 pap. $7.95
Visions from San Francisco Bay. 1969. Trans. by Richard Lourie, Farrar 1982 $14.95
  1983 pap. $8.00. Essays written, in the words of the poet, "to exorcise the evil
  spirit of contemporary times."
Emperor of the Earth: Modes of Eccentric Vision. Univ. of California Pr. 1977 $19.95
  pap. $7.95
The Land of Ulro. 1977. Trans. by Louis Iribarne, Farrar 1984 $17.95
Bells in Winter. Trans. by Miłosz Czesław and Lillian Vallee, Ecco Pr. 1978 $9.95
  1979 pap. $5.00. A collection of poems.
The Witness of Poetry. Harvard Univ. Pr. 1983 $8.95 1984 pap. $3.95. "By the strength
  of its condensed lucid exposition, *The Witness of Poetry* provides us with a key to
  Miłosz's poetic historiosophy, philosophy, and aesthetics. Of course, Miłosz's entire work offers one of the most profound responses to the dilemmas of our century" (*The New Criterion*).
The Separate Notebooks. Trans. by Robert Hass and others, Ecco Pr. 1984 $17.50

MROŻEK, SŁAWOMIR. 1930–

  Mrożek's plays are well known in eastern Europe, and *Tango* (1964) has
been performed throughout the world. It is the story of an intellectual who
wants to reform his family but falls prey to his own brother, who establishes
a dictatorship. *The Elephant* (1957) is a collection of savage and satiric short
stories. "They are all fantastic, yet they reflect, bitterly and wittily, the realities of life behind the Iron Curtain" (*Times*, London). He "has employed the
techniques of ORWELL [see Vol. 1] and KAFKA to present contemporary man as
terrified and ludicrous. Mrożek's brief fables are grotesque, scathing comments on the new bureaucrats of the People's Democracies." Mrożek is still
performed in Poland, where *Tango* had its sensational first showing in 1966.
Mrożek now works and lives, however, in Genoa, Italy.

BOOKS BY MROŻEK

Six Plays. Trans. by Nicholas Bethell, Grove (Evergreen) 1967 pap. $4.95. Contains
  *The Police, The Martyrdom of Peter Ohey, Out at Sea, Charlie, The Party, En-
  chanted Night.*
Striptease, Tango, Vatzlav: Three Plays. Trans. by Lola Gruenthal and others, Grove
  (Evergreen) 1981 pap. $12.50
The Elephant. Ed. by Konrad Syrop, Greenwood repr. of 1963 ed. lib. bdg. $15.00;
  Grove (Evergreen) 1985 pap. $6.95
Tango. Trans. by Ralph Manheim and Teresa Dzieduszycka, Grove (Evergreen) 1969
  pap. $3.95

PARANDOWSKI, JAN. 1895–1978

  Parandowski, whose literary career began in Lwów and continued in
Warsaw, was president of the Polish P.E.N. Club. A classicist by education,
he concentrated on ancient Greece and Rome in his fiction and essays. His

first published novel, *King of Life* (1921, o.p.), was about Oscar Wilde. His series on classical subjects, among which *The Olympic Discus* is particularly outstanding, is distinguished by exquisite style that continues Roman, French, and Polish Renaissance tradition in prose. After World War II, Parandowski achieved great success with a prose translation of the *Odyssey*.

BOOK BY PARANDOWSKI

The Olympic Discus. 1933. Trans. by A. M. Malecka and S. A. Walewski, intro. by George Harjan, Ungar o.p.

BOOK ABOUT PARANDOWSKI

Harjan, George. *Jan Parandowski. Twayne's World Authors Ser.* o.p.

PASEK, JAN CHRYZOSTOM. 1630–1701

Pasek was an adventurer, soldier, and politician. His many activities, typical of a man of his troubled times, provided him with a wealth of material for his memoirs. Pasek's love and mastery of detail, displayed in a rich, witty, and racy colloquial language, have not only given his writings lasting artistic value, but have also made them a source of ideas and idiom for subsequent poets and writers (Słowacki, Sienkiewicz, and others).

BOOK BY PASEK

Memoirs of the Polish Baroque: The Writings of Jan Chryzostom Pasek, a Squire of the Commonwealth of Poland and Lithuania. Ed. by Catherine S. Leach, University of California Pr. 1977 $43.50 pap. $5.95

PRUS, BOLESŁAW (pseud. of Aleksander Głowacki). 1845–1912

Prus was by profession an extremely productive and highly influential journalist, who won fame with his *Weekly Chronicles*, short pieces on diverse subjects. His work in fiction began with short stories, usually about the Warsaw poor. His first novel, *The Outpost* (1886, o.p.), dealt with village life, focusing in particular on the mechanism of German settlement in Polish lands. In *The Doll* (1890), Prus creates an enormous rich canvas of Warsaw life, into which he weaves the story of his hero, Wokulski, and his doomed passion for the aristocratic Isabella. His third major novel, *The Pharaoh* (1895–96, o.p.), is set in eleventh-century B.C. Egypt, and deals with the unsuccessful struggle of a young pharaoh against the dominant priestly class.

BOOK BY PRUS

The Doll. Trans. by David Welsh, Hippocrene Bks. 1972 pap. $5.95; Polish Institute of Arts and Sciences 1972 $4.50

RÓŻEWICZ, TADEUSZ. 1921–

A soldier in the underground Home Army during the Nazi occupation, Różewicz began to publish immediately after 1945. His first volumes of poetry, *Anxiety* (1947, o.p.) and *The Red Glove* (1948, o.p.), made wide use of war material and deliberately sought to destroy literary conventions. In focusing on man as essentially alone in the universe, the poet approached the conception of the French existentialists. After 1956 Różewicz turned his attention to the stage, writing plays that basically belong to the Theater of the Absurd. He has also published several collections of short stories and a novel.

BOOKS BY RÓŻEWICZ

The Survivor and Other Poems. Trans. by Magnus J. Krynski, Princeton Univ. Pr. 1976 $21.00 pap. $7.95

Conversations with a Prince and Other Poems. Trans. by Adam Czerniawski, Small Pr. Dist. 1982 o.p.

Marriage Blanc (and *The Hunger Artist Departs*). Trans. by Adam Czerniawski, M. Boyars 1983 $13.50. Two plays.

SIENKIEWICZ, HENRYK. 1846–1916 (NOBEL PRIZE 1905)

Far more celebrated than any of his positivist contemporaries, Sienkiewicz began as a journalist and achieved considerable renown with his account of a two-year journey to the United States. Between 1882 and 1888 he wrote three historical novels dealing with political and military events in seventeenth-century Poland: *With Fire and Sword* (o.p.), *The Deluge*, and *Pan Michael*. Although superficial in its analysis of historical events, the trilogy gained enormous popularity both in Poland and in other Slavic countries thanks to Sienkiewicz's masterful use of epic techniques and of the seventeenth-century colloquial idiom. Even more popular, if artistically far weaker, was his *Quo Vadis?*, a novel about Rome in the age of Nero (Sienkiewicz's fame in the West is chiefly based on this work). Another historical novel, *The Teutonic Knights* (1900, o.p.), deals with the fifteenth-century struggle between Poland-Lithuania and the Teutonic Order. Among his other works is *The Połaniecki Family* (1895), a work that extolled the virtues of philistinism and was sharply attacked by the progressive intelligentsia.

BOOKS BY SIENKIEWICZ

Western Septet: Seven Stories of the American West. Alliance College 1973 pap. $5.00

Hania. Ayer repr. of 1876 ed. $26.00

The Deluge: An Historical Novel of Poland, Sweden, and Russia. 1886. Trans. by Jeremiah Curtin, AMS Pr. 2 vols. repr. of 1898 ed. $24.50; Scholarly 2 vols. repr. of 1891 ed. 1971 $22.00

Pan Michael: An Historical Novel of Poland, the Ukraine, and Turkey. 1887–88. Trans. by Jeremiah Curtin, Greenwood repr. of 1898 ed. 1968 lib. bdg. $27.75

Quo Vadis? A Narrative of the Time of Nero. 1896. Airmont Class. Ser. 1968 pap. $2.50; trans. by C. J. Hogarth, Biblio Dist. (Everyman's) repr. of 1941 ed. 1980 $11.95; trans. by Jeremiah Curtin, Little, Brown repr. of 1896 ed. 1943 $6.95

BOOKS ABOUT SIENKIEWICZ

Coleman, Arthur P., and Marion M. Coleman. *Wanderers Twain: Exploratory Memoir on Helen Modjeska and Henryk Sienkiewicz.* Alliance College 1964 $5.00

Giergielewicz, Mieczyslaw. *Henryk Sienkiewicz. Twayne's World Authors Ser.* 1968 o.p.

Lednicki, Waclaw. *Henryk Sienkiewicz.* Humanities Pr. 1960 o.p. A very good survey.

TUWIM, JULIAN. 1894–1953

A Jew by birth, Tuwim was the major figure of the "Skamander" school and a leading poet of interwar Poland. A marvelous innovator of poetic language, he published not only numerous collections of poetry, but also several encyclopedic works on folklore. His best poem is *Ball at the Opera* (1936), in which he presents an apocalyptic vision of a dictatorship. His most ambitious work, *Polish Flowers*, was written mainly during World War II, in exile in Brazil and the United States.

BOOK BY TUWIM

The Dancing Socrates and Other Poems. Twayne 1971 o.p.

WITKIEWICZ, STANISŁAW IGNACY (WITKACY). 1885–1939

Son of an eminent Warsaw art critic, Witkiewicz went through traumatic experiences in Russia during World War I (he served in the Russian army) and the beginning of the Revolution. A prolific writer, he also painted and wrote papers on philosophy. His creative writings consist mainly of novels and dramas (at least 36, of which only 22 have survived). In his plays, Witkiewicz deals with profound social and philosophical problems in a way that makes him a forerunner of the Theater of the Absurd.

BOOKS BY WITKIEWICZ

The Madman and the Nun, and Other Plays. Ed. by C. Durer and Daniel G. Gerould, Univ. of Washington Pr. 1968 $20.00
Tropical Madness: Four Plays. Drama Bk. 1973 pap. $1.95

RUMANIAN LITERATURE

Although the first written documents in Rumania date back to 1527 and the Bible was translated in 1688, Rumanian literature began to develop only in the nineteenth century, when the Rumanians slowly gained independence from multiple foreign domination. There were numerous writers preceding this period, but few of great importance. The romantic movement, coming mainly from France, enlivened the literary scene, awakening an interest in folk poetry and allowing more accomplished writers to appear. Folk literature, which had been handed down orally for centuries, could now be recorded in a written language that more or less corresponded to the oral form. The first collection of folk poetry was published in 1852 by Vasile Alecsandri, the first Rumanian writer who was exposed to foreign influence, during his study in Paris, and whose works, in turn, were translated into French. His poems and plays, but above all his collections of folk poetry, together with the prose works of Heliade Rădulescu, mark the beginning of modern Rumanian literature.

Rumanian literature came of age in the second half of the nineteenth century with the appearance of some of its great writers in almost all genres. Romanticism gave way to realism, bringing literature more in tune with national and social realities. The best poet of that time, indeed of all Rumanian literature, Mihail Eminescu, published a collection of lyric poems in 1884 about love and death in a meditative, highly pessimistic mood, but also with sincere patriotism and simplicity derived from folk songs and ballads. With his poetic power and consummate craftsmanship he strongly influenced the further development of Rumanian poetry. One of the best short-story tellers, Ion Creangă, wrote about the bucolic life in his native Moldavia, idealizing the patriotic world of the past.

By the end of the nineteenth century, the French influence, which has always been strong in Rumanian literature, manifested itself in the impact on symbolist poets, especially Alexandru Macedonski, a versatile author who foreshadowed the modernistic tendencies of the twentieth century. Along with these trends there was a sharp turn toward social criticism, best personified by the prolific fiction writer Mihail Sadoveanu, whose keen interest in social problems moved him to the extreme Left and endeared him to the new regime after World War II. Western influences continued to be reflected after World War I in the works of such prominent writers as Ian Barbu, Lucian Blaga, George Bacovia, and perhaps the best poet of the group, Tudor Arghezi, who combined his foreign experiences (in France and Switzerland) with his rich and experimental idiom.

The interwar period also gave rise to a number of new writers unencumbered with the legacies of the prewar past. Perhaps the most prominent among these is the writer and philosopher Mircea Eliade, who now lives abroad but is published in his own country. Another writer of this group is Zaharia Stancu, a prolific novelist who joined the Communist party and became a high functionary.

Rumanian literature after World War II suffered the same fate as all other East European literatures that have to contend with the dictates of a communist regime. As a result, few writers have been able to rise above mediocrity. However, there are a few writers—the poets Nichita Stanescu, Ion Alexandru, and Marin Sorescu, and the fiction writers Eugen Barnu, Marin Preda, Stefan Banulescu, and Fanus Neagu—whose talent and originality cannot be denied or contained. There is still a younger generation of promising writers, who hold the future of Rumanian literature in their hands; their full development, however, is yet to come.

Collections

Byng, Lucy M., trans. *Roumanian Stories. Short Story Index Repr. Ser.* Ayer repr. of 1921 ed. $18.00

Manning, Olivia, ed. *Romanian Short Stories. World's Class. Ser.* Oxford 1971 $7.95

ARGHEZI, TUDOR. 1880–1967

Arghezi is widely considered Rumania's most important poet after Eminescu. Influenced by French *Symbolisme*, Arghezi developed as a modernist but at the same time as a poet of tradition and ancestral continuity, reconciling in his work the most contradictory spiritual and aesthetic tendencies of his age. It was only after World War II that a series of more or less successful translations won him belated recognition in the West. He has also been translated into Italian by Nobel Prize winner SALVATORE QUASIMODO and into Spanish by RAFAEL ALBERTI and PABLO NERUDA.

BOOK BY ARGHEZI

Selected Poems of Tudor Arghezi. Trans. by Brian Swann, Princeton Univ. Pr. 1976 $30.00 pap. $7.95. While some translations of Arghezi have appeared in journals or anthologies, this is the first time the English-speaking public is offered a representative selection of his poetry in book form.

DUMITRIU, PETRU. 1924–

This author is the Rumanian novelist best known to Americans. Dumitriu's successful early literary career included writing for magazines in Bucharest, winning the Rumanian State Prize for Literature three times, and serving as director of the State Publishing House. In 1960, however, he left Rumania to live in the West, escaping through East Berlin. *Meeting at the Last Judgment* (1962, o.p.), based on his own experiences, presents a revealing picture of the fear-ridden lives of the Rumanian communist elite. *Incognito* "reemphasizes the author's earlier theme: the awesome power with which the communists are able to take over a country once the will of its people has been demoralized" (*LJ*). Its sequel, *The Extreme Occident* (1964, o.p.), shows "the whole of present-day Western Europe as one vast cesspool of aimlessness, desperation, and lost or corrupted values" (*SR*). Dumitriu's books are alive with melodramatic cloak-and-dagger activities, as well as the ideological overtones noted above. He now lives in West Germany.

BOOK BY DUMITRIU

Incognito. 1962. Trans. by Norman Denny, Melvin McCosh 1964 o.p.

ELIADE, MIRCEA. 1907–

Born in Bucharest, Rumania, Mircea Eliade studied at the University of Bucharest and, from 1928 to 1932, at the University of Calcutta with Surendranath Dasgupta. After taking his doctorate in 1933 with a dissertation on Yoga, he taught at the University of Bucharest and, after the war, at the Sorbonne in Paris. Eliade has been a professor of the history of religions at the University of Chicago since 1957. He is "by nearly unanimous consent the most influential student of religion in the world today" (*N.Y. Times Bk. Review*). He is at the same time a writer of fiction, known and appreciated especially in western Europe where several of his novels and volumes of short stories have appeared in French, German, Spanish, and Portuguese. *Two Tales of the Occult* tries "to relate some yogic techniques, and particularly yogic folklore, to a series of events narrated in the genre of a mystery story." Both *Nights at Serampore* and *The Secret of Dr. Honigberger* evoke the mythical geography and time of India. Mythology, fantasy, and autobiography are skillfully combined in Eliade's tales.

BOOKS BY ELIADE

Autobiography: Journey East, Journey West, 1907 to 1937. Trans. by Mac L. Ricketts, Harper 1981 vol. 1 $17.50 pap. $9.57
Tales of the Sacred and the Supernatural. Westminster 1981 pap. $7.95

EMINESCU, MIHAIL. 1850–1889

Rumanians regard Eminescu as their greatest poet. The richness and suggestive verbal power of his poetry have prompted some to compare him with KEATS (see Vol. 1). His influence was so profound that Rumanian poetry and poetic diction have developed along lines that would have been impossible to predict on the basis of their traditions and achievements up to the mid-nineteenth century. "His use of archaisms, dialectal words, and neologisms, together with skillful metaphor, simile and alliteration, enhanced the expressive power of Rumanian and endowed it with a great richness, while the philosophical nature and profundity of his work gave Rumanian poetry a maturity it hitherto lacked" (*Cassell's Encyclopaedia of World Literature*). The complexity of Eminescu's stylistic imagination makes his poetry extremely hard to translate.

BOOKS BY EMINESCU

The Last Romantic: Mihail Eminescu. Trans. by Roy MacGregor-Hastie, Univ. of Iowa Pr. 1972 $12.00. Part of the European Series of the Translations Collection of UNESCO.
Poems. Gordon $69.95

REBREANU, LIVIU. 1885–1944

The eminent novelist, theater critic, playwright, and essayist Liviu Rebreanu was at the height of his influence in the years between the two world wars. An innovator in Rumanian literature, he is remembered particularly for his portrayals of Rumanian villagers living under hardship, and for his treatment of war and revolution. He wrote many short stories before turning to longer fiction. Of the novels, *Ion*, a vast panorama of Transylvanian village life before World War I, is a "landmark in the history of the Rumanian novel" (*Cassell's Encyclopaedia of World Literature*). *The Forest of the Hanged* (o.p.), about that war, and *Uprising*, about a peasants' revolt, are his two other important novels.

BOOKS BY REBREANU

Ion. 1920. Dufour 1965 $15.00
Uprising. 1932. Dufour 1964 $15.00

SADOVEANU, MIHAIL. 1880–1961

Sadoveanu, who wrote more than 120 books, is generally considered to be Rumania's greatest prose writer. His fiction is being published for the first time in this country under a U.S.-Rumanian cultural exchange program.

Tales of War was inspired by the 1877 War of Independence against Turkey. "Although this is a youthful work and some of the tales are scarcely more than anecdotes, it does constitute an authentic record of an heroic people fighting to liberate their country from the tyranny of Ottoman rule." In *Evening Tales* he writes "mostly of simple folk, of innkeepers and bailiffs, highwaymen and gypsies, fishermen and hunters, with the inevitable boyar or landowner supplying the element of conflict." In *The Mud-Hut Dwellers*, "vivid descriptions of peasant life in nineteenth-century Rumania charm and captivate the reader. . . . The novel is an affirmation of man, of the joy and love which can be his in spite of his condition" (*Choice*).

BOOKS BY SADOVEANU

Tales of War. 1905. Irvington 1962 lib. bdg. $22.00
The Mud-Hut Dwellers. 1912. Irvington 1964 $22.00
Evening Tales. Trans. by E. Farca and L. Marinescu, Irvington 1962 lib. bdg. $26.00

STANCU, ZAHARIA. 1902–1974

Stancu began his literary career as a poet. During the 1930s he was active as a journalist and edited such periodicals as *Azi* (*Today*) and *Lumea romaneasca* (*Rumanian World*). After World War II he published a cycle of novels that won him official recognition. He was president of the Rumanian Writers' Union from 1965 until his death.

BOOKS BY STANCU

Barefoot. Ed. by Frank Kirk, Irvington 1971 lib. bdg. $29.50
The Gypsy Tribe. Abelard-Schuman 1973 o.p.

UKRAINIAN LITERATURE

The history of Ukrainian literature goes back to the eleventh century when, during the Kievan Rus, the Ukrainians converted to Christianity and began to write religious literature, notably vitae and chronicles, in Church Slavic, a written language common to all early Slavs. Parallel to these works were epic and lyric songs in oral form, the most outstanding of which is the *Tale of Ihor's Campaign* (the epic is also claimed by the Russians). This remarkable work depicts in a highly poetic fashion a military expedition of one of the early Kievan princes against the nomadic tribes. After the Kievan Rus was destroyed by the Mongols and the Ukrainians were incorporated into the Polish-Lithuanian state, literary activity was confined to the copying of old books and translating the Bible into Ukrainian. In the sixteenth and seventeenth centuries poetry and drama began to develop. After 1654, however, when the Ukraine was absorbed into the Russian empire and writing in Ukrainian was banned, some Ukrainian writers chose to write in Russian. It was not until 1798 that publishing in Ukrainian was restored, beginning with *Eneyida*, a syllabo-tonic verse imitation of Virgil by Ivan Kotlyarevski. For the next century or so Ukrainian writers had to cope with severe restrictions on their use of Ukrainian, but they still managed to produce several great authors: the poet Taras Ševčenko, the novelist Ivan Franko, and the playwrights Lesja Ukrajinka and Mykola Kuliš. By then the romantic movement, which had dominated Ukrainian literature for most of the century, gave way to realism and, at the turn of the century, to modernistic tendencies. In the first two decades of the twentieth century, several notable writers reflected the modern Western trends of symbolism, futurism, and neoclassicism, while other authors experimented with expressionism, impressionism, and other movements.

This lively activity continued in the first decade after the Bolshevik Revolution. At first the Ukrainians were encouraged to develop their culture, which resulted in sort of a national and cultural revival. Many prewar writers continued their work while new faces also appeared. The most influential group was that of VAPLITE (Free Academy of Proletarian Literature), which, enjoying the support of the regime, was trying to uphold high literary standards and to look for models to the West, not in Russia. However, the activity was brought to a tragic halt in the 1930s, as many authors were purged or liquidated. As in all other literatures in the so-called socialist camp, writers had to accept strict controls and socialist realism was the only valid literary method. Very little good literature was produced at this time. After the ravages of World War II, which were especially devastating in the Ukraine, Ukrainian literature continued to exist under restrictive conditions although, during the various periods of relaxation since Stalin's death, writers were able to write somewhat more freely. More importantly, talented new writers have made Ukrainian literature of the last three or so decades artistically more accomplished and colorful. Perhaps the most prominent of these new faces is the novelist Oleksander Honchar, who excelled in his war novels. Among younger writers, the poets Ivan Drach and Vasyl Symonenko should be singled out.

Two other aspects of contemporary Ukrainian literature are worth mentioning: the dissent in the Ukraine manifested primarily through underground publishing (*samvydav*), and the literary activity of numerous émigré writers, gathered mostly in West Germany, Canada, and the United States. Although neither of these phenomena has produced literature of high order, both are indicative of the unsettled conditions under which the Ukrainian writers have to work, as they have done practically throughout their history.

History and Criticism

Čyževskyj, Dmytro. *A History of Ukrainian Literature from the 11th to the End of the 19th Century.* Trans. by D. Ferguson, Ukrainian Academy of Arts and Sciences text ed. 1975 pap. $20.00

Grabowicz, George G. *Toward a History of Ukrainian Literature.* Harvard Univ. Pr. text ed. 1981 pap. $8.50

Luckyj, George S. *Literary Politics in the Soviet Ukraine 1917–1934. Select Bibliographies Repr. Ser.* Ayer repr. of 1956 ed. $22.00. Deals with literary organizations, their histories and conflicts.

Manning, Clarence A. *Ukrainian Literature: Studies of the Leading Authors. Essay In-*

dex Repr. Ser. Ayer repr. of 1944 ed. $18.00. Brief portraits of the major Ukrainian literary figures.

Collections

Andrusyshen, C. H., and Watson Kirkconnell, trans. *The Ukrainian Poets, 1189–1962.* Univ. of Toronto Pr. 1963 o.p. The best anthology of Ukrainian poetry in English, including almost a hundred poets, with critical introductions.

Luckyj, George S., ed. *Modern Ukrainian Short Stories.* Ukrainian Academy of Arts and Sciences bilingual ed. 1973 lib. bdg. $18.50

Zenkovsky, Serge A., ed. *Medieval Russia's Epics, Chronicles, and Tales.* Dutton rev. ed. 1974 pap. $14.95

FRANKO, IVAN. 1856–1916

Franko, a prolific Galician Ukrainian writer, scholar, and journalist, was a master of several genres; his works also show an extraordinary variety of themes. His earliest published works include a series of romantic historical novels and a group of naturalistic portrayals of the conflict of nascent industrialism and labor in the Ukraine. Other works depict the social disintegration of the gentry and the attempts of the new intelligentsia to supplant it. He is perhaps best known for his epic verses, especially the great epic *Moses* (1905), in which he expounds his philosophy of the nation and the role of the charismatic personality.

BOOKS BY FRANKO

Ivan Franko: The Poet of the Western Ukraine, Selected Poems. Trans. by Percival Cundy, Greenwood repr. of 1948 ed. lib. bdg. $19.75

Fox Mykyta. Trans. by Bohdan Melnyk, Tundra 1978 $14.95

HONCHAR, OLEKSANDER. 1918–

Honchar's novels deal with events of World War II, and with aspects of life in the Soviet Union. He is adept at descriptions of nature and is a precise stylist in the Ukrainian literary language.

BOOK BY HONCHAR

Shore of Love. Imported Pubns. 1980 $8.95

KULIŠ, MYKOLA. 1892–1942

Kuliš was an outstanding Soviet Ukrainian dramatist. He first wrote in the vein of ethnographic realism, but went on to compose highly original ethnographic plays. The *Sonata Pathetique* is a vivid representation of the Revolution of 1917, which is allegorically presented as an expressive and profoundly tragic sonata. The play was staged by the two leading theaters in Russia, but its presentation was not allowed on the Ukrainian stage.

BOOK BY MYKOLA KULIŠ

Sonata Pathetique. Trans. by George S. N. Luckyj and Moira Luckyj, intro. by Ralph
   Lindheim, Ukrainian Academic Pr. 1975 lib. bdg. $11.50

KULIŠ, PANTELEJMON (also KULISH). 1819–1897

Kuliš, a scholar as well as a novelist, in *The Black Council* gives a vivid
picture of the different levels of society in seventeenth-century Ukraine. His
theme is the need for people to be motivated by high ideals as they engage
in the "struggle of truth with injustice."

BOOK BY PANTELEJMON KULIŠ

The Black Council. Trans. and abr. by George S. N. Luckyj and Moira Luckyj, intro.
   by Romana Bahrij Pikulyk, Ukrainian Academic Pr. 1973 lib. bdg. $11.50

PIDMOHYLNY, VALERIAN. 1901–1941

Pidmohylny's last novel, *A Little Touch of Drama*, published in 1930,
shows the influence of French writers such as MAUPASSANT. In his earlier
works he experimented with impressionistic psychological stories and with
literary expressionism.

BOOK BY PIDMOHYLNY

A Little Touch of Drama. Ukrainian Classics in Translation Ser. Trans. by George S.
   Luckyj and Moira Luckyj, Ukrainian Academy of Arts and Sciences 1972 lib.
   bdg. $11.50

ŠEVČENKO, TARAS (also SHEVCHENKO). 1814–1861

Ševčenko is the outstanding Ukrainian romantic poet, creator of the
Ukrainian literary language and symbol of the national movement. He was
born a serf and educated in St. Petersburg to serve as a portraitist and artist. His freedom was purchased in 1838 by several of his admirers.
Ševčenko's first eight poems were collected in *The Bandura Player*. The publication of this collection in 1840 was a literary sensation. This collection
was followed in the next three years by *The Haidamaks* and a series of poems based strongly on folk-song rhythms. The writings composed after his
return to the Ukraine in 1843 included strong invectives against serfdom
and the baneful role that Russians played in Ukrainian history.

For a decade after 1847 Ševčenko was exiled to Central Asia for his participation in the Sts. Cyril and Methodius Society. This clandestine organization advocated the union of all Slavs on the basis of independence and
equality. During his exile he wrote several lyrics and novelettes. The poems
of the last four years of his life, including *Neofity* and *Mariya*, are built on
strongly religious themes.

BOOK BY ŠEVČENKO

The Poetical Works of Taras Shevchenko. Trans. by C. H. Andrusyshen and Watson
   Kirkconnell, Univ. of Toronto Pr. 1964 $25.00. A good collection by two veteran
   interpreters of Ukrainian poetry.

UKRAJINKA, LESJA (pseud. of Larysa Petrivna Kvitka, née Kosač). 1871–1913

The earliest works of Ukrajinka were lyric poems with exotic themes and motifs borrowed from remote times and places. After experimenting in prose drama, she wrote a great number of dramatic poems, the genre for which she is most famous.

BOOK BY UKRAJINKA

Spirit of Flame: A Collection of the Works of Lesya Ukrainka. Trans. by Percival Cundy, fwd. by Clarence A. Manning, Greenwood repr. of 1950 ed. 1971 $16.25

BOOK ABOUT UKRAJINKA

Bida, Constantine. *Lesya Ukrainka: Life and Works.* Trans. by Vera Rich, Univ. of Toronto Pr. 1968 $17.50. Contains selections from her work.

YUGOSLAV LITERATURE

Yugoslav literature consists of several separate literatures—Serbian, Croatian, Slovenian, and Macedonian being the main ones—along with a number of minority literatures. After the South Slavs (except Bulgarians) were united in Yugoslavia in 1918, these literatures continued on their own paths. The first literary activity of the South Slavic tribes developed in the ninth century after their conversion to Christianity. At first, literary works were invariably linked with church activity and needs. Even the exquisite biographies of Serbian monarchs and church leaders were the result of religious fervor. Then came a centuries-long domination of the Serbs and Macedonians by the Turks, and of the Croats and Slovenes by the Austrians, during which the only literature possible was in the oral form, resulting in a remarkable body of epic poetry, folk songs, tales, and other oral literature. This imposed hiatus lasted into the nineteenth century. The only exception was the Croatian literature of the city-republic of Dubrovnik, which enjoyed a prosperous independence in the sixteenth and seventeenth centuries and produced literature in the spirit and imitation of the Renaissance. Marko Marulić, Marin Držić, and Ivan Gundulić are the best representatives of this short-lived flourish.

The revival of all Yugoslav literatures in the first half of the nineteenth century was closely connected with the struggle for independence as well as with the somewhat belated influence of Western romanticism. The writer largely responsible for the revival was Vuk Stefanović Karadžić. He reformed the written language, translated the Bible, and published the first dictionary of the Serbian language and collections of folk poetry that were to inspire WALTER SCOTT (see Vol. 1), GOETHE, Mickiewicz, and others to translate some of the ballads. The reform of the language used by most Serbs and Croats immediately brought forth a number of gifted writers, the most important of whom was the Montenegrin prince and bishop Petar Petrović Njegoš, whose writings belong to the most significant works in all of Yugoslav literature. Other noteworthy romantic authors are the Serb Branko Radičević, the Croats Ivan Mažuranić and Petar Preradović, and the Slovene France Prešeren, whose *Poetry* still stands as the best book of poetry in Slovenian literature.

The second half of the nineteenth century saw a shift toward realism as a result of the influence from abroad, especially from Russia and France, and of profound social and political changes in the Balkans. Almost all realists were primarily concerned with rural life. The Serbs Laza K. Lazarević, Janko Veselinović, and Simo Matavulj, among others, created a special subgenre, the "peasant short story." After a brief spell of naturalism, modernistic tendencies from the West, especially France, penetrated all Yugoslav literatures. The modern trend, appropriately called *Moderna*, was particularly strong in Croatia, while in Serbia Jovan Dučić and Milan Rakić revolutionized Serbian poetry and brought it into the twentieth century.

Gallant efforts and enormous sacrifices of all South Slavs in World War I, which led to the independence of some for the first time and the unification of all, created a new climate that was propitious for further development of Yugoslav literature. The interwar period is characterized by great diversity and lively activity. The two most outstanding writers were the Serb Ivo Andrić and the Croat Miroslav Krleža, who set the tone for the entire period, in different ways, to be sure. They would continue to be decisive factors in the postwar era, concluding their careers as the most important Yugoslav literary figures of the century.

After another traumatic experience in World War II, writers found themselves in different political conditions following the establishment of a communist regime. However, after a brief flirt with socialist realism, this method was abandoned and strict controls were removed after 1948. By the early 1950s, writers had earned the right to use any method and to experiment. Since then, all Yugoslav literatures have had a policy of government noninterference in literary affairs and of having ties with Western and other literatures.

Undoubtedly as a result of this freedom, there has been a steady stream of fresh talent, resulting in some remarkable achievements. Andrić published his most important works after the war and received the Nobel Prize in 1961—the only South Slavic author to do so. Crnjanski returned after years of exile and continued to publish, as did many other prewar authors. But it is the new writers who raised Yugoslav literature to new heights, in practically all genres, but especially in poetry. Among the Serbs, one should mention the poets Vasko Popa and Miodrag Pavlović; the fiction writers Meša Selimović, Mihailo Lalić, Dobrica Ćosić, and Danilo Kiš; and the playwright Aleksandar Popović. Among the Croats, the poets Jure Kaštelan, Vesna Parun, and Slavko Mihalić should be singled out, along with prose writers Vladan Desnica, Ranko Marinković, and Mirko Božić. The Slovenes also have several first-rate authors. The Macedonians have gained the right to publish in Macedonian for the first time in centuries, thus ending their underground existence. They have already produced several outstanding poets as well as some noteworthy fiction writers and playwrights. By all indications, the future of Yugoslav literature is bright and promising.

History and Criticism

Barac, Antun. *A History of Yugoslav Literature. Joint Committee on Eastern Europe Publication Ser.* Michigan Slavic Pubns. $15.00. A reliable general survey of all Yugoslav literature, mainly up to 1941. A good source of basic information.

Eekman, Thomas. *Thirty Years of Yugoslav Literature, 1945–1975.* Michigan Slavic Pubns. 1978 $15.00. A complementary survey to that of Barac, filled with facts and cursory analyses of all important authors and works.

Kadić, Ante. *Contemporary Serbian Literature.* Mouton text ed. 1964 pap. $10.00

———. *From Croatian Renaissance to Yugoslav Socialism. Slavistic Printings and Reprintings Ser.* Mouton text ed. 1969 $41.00

Koljević, Svetozar. *The Epic in the Making.* Oxford 1980 $74.00. One of the best treatments of Serbian epic poetry in any language. The author combines the thorough knowledge of a native scholar with sharp critical perception.

Lord, Albert B. *The Singer of Tales.* Pref. by H. Levin, Atheneum text ed. 1965 pap. $3.95; *Harvard Studies in Comparative Lit.* Harvard Univ. Pr. text ed. 1981 pap. $7.95. The classic study, based on field-collected South Slavic epic songs, of the oral theory of epic composition and transmission within a living tradition. Part 2 applies the theory to Homer and to medieval oral epics (*Beowulf, Chanson de Roland*, and *Digenis Akritas*).

Lukić, Sveta. *Contemporary Yugoslav Literature: A Sociopolitical Approach.* Trans. by Pola Triandis, ed. by Gertrude J. Robinson, Univ. of Illinois Pr. 1972 $15.00. A critical analysis by a Marxist revisionist literary critic, especially of the literary scene from 1945 to 1968.

Mihailovich, Vasa D., ed. *Modern Slavic Literatures. Lib. of Literary Criticism Ser.* Ungar 1976 vol. 2 $55.00. The Yugoslav section contains critical excerpts on 47 contemporary Yugoslav authors.

Mihailovich, Vasa D., and Mateja Matejic. *A Comprehensive Bibliography of Yugoslav Literature in English, 1593–1980.* Slavica 1984 $24.95. An all-inclusive bibliography, the first volume of a continuing series.

Subotić, Dragutin P. *Yugoslav Popular Ballads.* Folcroft repr. of 1932 ed. 1976 lib. bdg. $35.00. A solid study of Yugoslav folk poetry, with a treatment of its reception in Germany, France, and English-speaking countries.

Collections

Butler, Thomas. *Monumenta Serbocroatica: A Bilingual Anthology of Serbian and Croatian Texts from the 12th to the 19th Century.* Michigan Slavic Pubns. 1979 $15.00. An excellent collection of many texts presented in English for the first time. With introductions.

Dordevic, Mihailo, ed. *Anthology of Serbian Poetry.* Philosophical Lib. 1984 $19.95. A limited but useful anthology of Serbian poetry at the beginning of the twentieth century.

Holton, Milne, ed. *The Big Horse and Other Stories of Modern Macedonia.* Univ. of Missouri Pr. 1974 $17.00

Holton, Milne, and Graham W. Reid, eds. *Reading the Ashes: An Anthology of the Poetry of Modern Macedonia. Pitt Poetry Ser.* Univ. of Pittsburgh Pr. 1977 $14.95 pap. $7.95

Lenski, Branko, ed. *Death of a Simple Giant and Other Modern Yugoslav Stories.* Vanguard 1964 $10.00. One of the best collections of Yugoslav short stories.

Matejic, Mateja, and Dragan Milivojević. *An Anthology of Medieval Serbian Literature in English.* Slavica 1978 pap. $9.95. Many medieval pieces presented here in English for the first time.

Mihailovich, Vasa D., ed. *Contemporary Yugoslav Poetry.* Intro. by Gertrude G. Champe, *Iowa Translations Ser.* text ed. 1977 $24.00 pap. $12.00. The most complete Yugoslav poetry collection in English.

Mikasinovich, Branko, ed. *Modern Yugoslav Satire.* Cross Cultural 1979 $20.00 pap. $12.00

Mikasinovich, Branko, Dragan Milivojević, and Vasa D. Mihailovich, eds. *Introduction to Yugoslav Literature. Twayne's International Studies and Translations Ser.* G. K. Hall lib. bdg. $10.95. A good collection of writings from the nineteenth and twentieth centuries.

Pennington, Anne, and Peter Levi, trans. *Marko the Prince: Serbo-Croat Heroic Songs.* St. Martin's 1984 $19.95. The best translation and selection of Serbo-Croatian epic poems.

ANDRIĆ, IVO. 1892–1975 (NOBEL PRIZE 1961)

Andrić began to write short stories in 1923 and was one of the most respected writers in Yugoslav literature of the interwar period. He gained worldwide acclaim with his postwar novels, *The Bridge on the Drina* and *The Chronicle of Travnik,* which eventually earned him the Nobel Prize in 1961. Andrić wrote almost exclusively about his native Bosnia and its people, isolated for centuries in a world of myths, legends, hard life, and unfulfilled aspirations. What interested him most was the mixture of races and religions and their attempts, not always successful, at living together in harmony amid the forces constantly tearing the fragile social fabric apart. Andrić's ability to penetrate the heart and the soul of his characters and his meticulous craftsmanship established his reputation as one of the greatest Yugoslav writers of the twentieth century.

BOOKS BY ANDRIĆ

The Pasha's Concubine and Other Tales. Trans. by Joseph Hitrec, Knopf 1968 o.p. This collection includes some of the best of Andrić's stories, skillfully translated.

Bosnian Chronicle. 1945. Trans. by Joseph Hitrec, Knopf 1963 o.p.

The Bridge on the Drina. 1945. Trans. by Lovett Edwards, intro. by William H. McNeill, Allen & Unwin 1959 $13.95; Univ. of Chicago Pr. (Phoenix Bks.) 1977 pap. $8.95

Devil's Yard. Trans. by Kenneth Johnstone, Greenwood repr. of 1962 ed. 1975 lib. bdg. $24.75

ĆOSIĆ, DOBRICA. 1921–

Dobrica Ćosić participated in World War II as a partisan and afterward wrote a novel about his experiences, *Distant Is the Sun* (o.p.). Subsequent novels steadily enhanced his reputation as a skillful writer able to transform his engagé subject matter (all Ćosić's novels are politically tinged) into genuine artistic accomplishments. At the same time Ćosić steadily alienated himself from the power structure, to which he himself had contributed, becoming one of the main dissidents among Yugoslav intellectuals. His ambitious tetralogy, *This Land, This Time,* is an apotheosis of the tragic ordeal and eventual triumph of Serbia, a small nation of peasants that "defeated three empires"—the Turkish, Austro-Hungarian, and German—in World War I. His latest series of novels—the first of which, *The Sinner,* appeared in 1985—debunks the myth of infallibility of the communists before and during World War II, an act that put him again on a collision course with the powers that be, but that also demonstrates his remarkable moral courage.

BOOKS BY ĆOSIĆ

Reach to Eternity. Trans. by Muriel Heppell, Harcourt 1980 $14.95
South to Destiny. Harcourt 1981 $19.95
This Land, This Time. Trans. by Muriel Heppell, Harcourt 4 vols. 1983 $29.95

DJILAS, MILOVAN. 1911–

Milovan Djilas is known as an author of political writings about his experiences as a young communist before and during World War II, as a high functionary after the war, and, finally, as a renegade. His initial ambition, however, was to be a fiction writer but because of the vicissitudes of his life, he has been able to fulfill that ambition only partly—a few short stories and three volumes of his autobiography that reveal all his artistic potential. Ironically, even those few works have been published only in translation into other languages, because he is not allowed to publish in Yugoslavia. In all his works, Djilas cannot get away from his basically political nature, seeing and interpreting everything through the Marxist prism. He has also written a perceptive book on Njegoš.

BOOKS BY DJILAS

Land without Justice. 1958. Harcourt 1972 pap. $8.95
Montenegro. Trans. by Kenneth Johnstone, Harcourt 1963 $9.95
The Leper and Other Stories. Trans. by Lovett Edwards, Harcourt 1964 o.p.
Njegoš: Poet, Prince, Bishop. Trans. by Michael B. Petrovich, Harcourt 1966 o.p.
Under the Colors. Trans. by Lovett Edwards, Harcourt 1971 o.p.
The Stone and the Violets. Trans. by Lovett Edwards, Harcourt 1972 o.p.

DUČIĆ, JOVAN. 1874–1943

Jovan Dučić was a career diplomat and the poet most responsible for the modernization of Serbian poetry at the turn of the century. His poetry was heavily influenced by the French symbolists, but he was able to give it his own touch of a sensitive, refined, and highly articulate poet who paid great attention to his craft. In addition to exquisite lyric poems, he wrote poems in prose, erudite travelogues, pseudo-philosophical essays, and historical prose. Often accused of being aloof, pseudo-aristocratic, and posing, he is nevertheless recognized as a master of poetic mood and a consummate craftsman.

BOOK BY DUČIĆ

Plave Legende—Blue Legends. Trans. by Vasa D. Mihailovich, Kosovo bilingual ed.
1983 $6.00

KIŠ, DANILO. 1935–

Since his first novel in 1963, Danilo Kiš has steadily gained in reputation
as one of the most powerful Serbian writers. He "writes in a distinctly personal, lyrical style with a special knack for evoking childhood, or for suggesting the atmosphere of wartime. In modern Serbian literature his novels
are conspicuous for their naturalness of expression and purity of expression.
Close to the latest currents among the youngest generation of European novelists, Kiš is at the same time faithful to the classic ideals of simplicity and
balance" (*Yugoslav Literary Lexicon*).

BOOKS BY KIŠ

Garden, Ashes. Trans. by William J. Hannaher, Harcourt 1975 $7.95 1978 pap. $2.95
A Tomb for Boris Davidovich. Intro. by Joseph Brodsky, *Writers from the Other Eu-
rope Ser.* Penguin 1980 pap. $5.95
Hourglass. Trans. by Ammiel Alcalay and Klara Alcalay, Farrar 1985 $17.95

KRLEŽA, MIROSLAV. 1893–1981

During his long and fruitful career as a free-lance writer, Miroslav
Krleža tried his pen in several genres: poetry, fiction, drama, essays, and
literary criticism. He was equally at home in all of them. The constant in all
his works is a merciless criticism of bourgeois societies, first in the decomposing Austro-Hungarian empire, then in Yugoslavia between the two
world wars. As a consistent Marxist, he saw revolutionary social change as
the only way out of the "Pannonian morass," as he called it, yet he also advocated freedom of creativity and the preservation of an artist's dignity. Of his
many works, the stories and plays of the Glembay cycle and the multivolume novel *Flags* remain among the most significant achievements not only
in Croatian but in all of Yugoslav literature.

BOOKS BY KRLEŽA

The Return of Philip Latinowicz. 1932. Trans. by Zora Depolo, Vanguard 1968 o.p.
On the Edge of Reason. 1938. Trans. by Zora Depolo, Vanguard 1975 o.p.
The Cricket beneath the Waterfall and Other Stories. Ed. by Branko Lenski, Vanguard
1972 o.p. Includes the best of Krleža's stories.

MIHALIĆ, SLAVKO. 1928–

Slavko Mihalić has published several books of poetry since 1954. In his poems he exhibits neoromantic and intellectualistic inclinations, attempting
to overcome the absurdity of life with his ardent belief in the humanistic
role of a poet. Writing in an idiom remarkable for its simplicity, precision,
and lyrical fluency, he is considered one of the best of contemporary Croatian poets.

BOOK BY MIHALIĆ

Atlantis: Selected Poems, 1953–1982. Trans. by Charles Simic and Peter Kastmiler, Greenfield Review Pr. 1984 pap. $5.00

NJEGOŠ, PETAR PETROVIĆ (Prince-Bishop of Montenegro). 1813–1851

Njegoš, the titular head and the spiritual leader of Montenegro, wrote lyrical poetry, epic poems, and plays in verse. He was primarily concerned about helping his people overcome the backwardness imposed on them by historical events, while at the same time warding off the Turkish attacks. His Miltonian epic *The Ray of Microcosm* expresses his philosophical and religious views, while the verse drama *The Mountain Wreath* echoes his undying commitment to freedom at all costs. *The Mountain Wreath*, revered as the best work in all South Slavic literature, centers on the Montenegrins' coming to grips with their main dilemma—how to deal with those of their people who have accepted Islam and are siding with the enemy.

BOOK BY NJEGOŠ

The Mountain Wreath. 1847. Trans. by Vasa D. Mihailovich, Charles Schlack, Jr. 1986 $29.95. The new translation, adhering to the decasyllabic verse of the original.

PAVLOVIĆ, MIODRAG. 1928–

Miodrag Pavlović appeared on the literary scene in the early 1950s. Together with Popa, Pavlović was most influential in bringing about the revolution toward modernism in Serbian poetry. His poetry has a strong intellectual ring to it and a universal scope. It is technically flawless, showing many innovations and striking metaphors. Its language is rich, economical, precise. Like Popa, Pavlović is searching for old myths, which he finds in many quarters, but mostly in Serbian medieval history. Being one of the first to issue a call for regeneration of poetry, away from romanticism or pragmatic utilitarianism, and toward a more disciplined, analytical, and intellectual approach, he has remained remarkably constant in his stance, charting a new course with every new book.

BOOKS BY PAVLOVIĆ

The Conqueror in Constantinople. Trans. by Joachim Neugroschel, New Rivers Pr. 1976 pap. $1.25

The Slavs beneath Parnassus. Trans. by Bernard Johnson, New Rivers Pr. 1985 pap. $5.50

POPA, VASKO. 1922–

Vasko Popa is the most translated of contemporary Yugoslav poets—his entire poetic opus has been translated into English. He was chiefly responsible for steering Serbian poetry away from stale traditionalism, which came close to being socialist realism, in the early 1950s. His modernism is expressed in terse, aphoristic, elliptical idiom, in beautifully crafted poetic entities that tend to run in cycles, and above all in his efforts to penetrate the essence of the phenomena around him, dead or alive. Popa is a poet's poet, a powerful craftsman of images and metaphors, an incessant seeker of the primeval roots and myths. His eight collections of poems, so far, belong to the most accomplished poetry in all of Yugoslav literature.

BOOKS BY POPA

Collected Poems. Trans. by Anne Pennington, intro. by Ted Hughes, Univ. of Iowa Pr. pap. $5.95

Homage to the Lame Wolf: Selected Poems of Vasko Popa. Trans. by Charles Simic, Field Translations 1979 $8.95

The Little Box. Trans. by Charles Simic, Charioteer 1973 $7.50

Earth Erect. Trans. by Anne Pennington, Univ. of Iowa Pr. pap. $2.50

CHAPTER 17

Yiddish Literature

Zachary M. Baker

> The Yiddish language—a language of exile, without a land, without fron-
> tiers, not supported by any government, a language which possesses no
> words for weapons, ammunition, military exercises, war tactics.... In a
> figurative way, Yiddish is the wise and humble language of us all, the idiom
> of frightened and hopeful humanity.
> —ISAAC BASHEVIS SINGER, *The Nobel Lecture*

Yiddish had its origins in the Middle Ages as the spoken vernacular of Ashkenazic Jews who settled in the Rhineland after migrating there from France
and northern Italy. By 1750 the geographical spread of Yiddish encompassed Jews residing throughout northern, central, and eastern Europe. At
its apogee, before 1939, an estimated 11 million people, spread over 6 continents, were native Yiddish speakers. Now only 2–3 million people worldwide speak Yiddish, and the language is rarely passed on to the younger generation.

The precipitous decline of the language can be attributed above all to the
gradual linguistic assimilation of Yiddish speakers to prevailing national
languages, and to the tragic Nazi onslaught, which eliminated about one-
half of all Yiddish-speaking Jews, including more than 1 million children.
In recent years Yiddish has shown signs of some vitality, particularly
among Hasidic Jews and among university students returning to their ancestral language.

Linguists describe Yiddish as a complex "fusion language," composed of
elements deriving from Middle High German, Hebrew, and Aramaic, and
from various Romance and Slavic languages. Naturally, Yiddish is a product of the culture that nurtured it and is steeped in the rhythms of traditional Jewish prayer, talmudic study, and Hasidic storytelling—what Max
Weinreich labeled "The Way of the Shas" (rabbinically steeped culture).
With the onset of industrialization, urbanization, and massive emigration,
the Yiddish language and its burgeoning secular literature could not help
but be affected by the translation of Eastern European Jewry from an insular, small-town group to a socially and linguistically diversified population
with offshoots the world over.

Yiddish literature is commonly divided into two periods: early and modern. Early Yiddish literature was largely produced and almost exclusively

printed in Western Europe from the sixteenth to the eighteenth centuries. Although many of the works written during this period were religious in nature, this was not universally the case, as is demonstrated by one of the very oldest extant Yiddish books, the *Bove-bukh*, by Elye Bohur Levita Ashkenazi, published in Venice in 1540. This epic poem was a translation from the Italian *Buovo d'Antona*, which in turn was based on the Middle English romance *Sir Bevis of Hampton*.

Nevertheless, the most widely disseminated Yiddish book of the early period was the *Tsene-urene* collection of Bible stories and commentaries, written by Jacob ben Isaac Ashkenazi of Janow at the end of the sixteenth century. Much religious literature in Yiddish was aimed explicitly at a female readership, because it was assumed that women (unlike men) were not literate in Hebrew. Indeed, Yiddish literature did not entirely lose its stigma as a literature of women and unlettered men until the end of the nineteenth century.

The groundwork for modern Yiddish literature was laid in part by the early Hasidim, whose leaders preached, sang, and spun their stories in the everyday language of their followers. The symbolistic *Tales* of Rabbi Nahman of Bratslav, published in 1815, are the outstanding example of this Hasidic literature, and they enjoy a sizable audience to this day.

Half a century after Rabbi Nahman's *Tales* were first published, a new, secular literature arose, under the influence of the *Haskalah* (*Enlightenment*). There were popular "dime novelists" like I. M. Dik and N. M. Shaykevitsh; at the same time, the three great Yiddish literary pioneers, S. Y. Abramovitsh, who adopted the pen name Mendele Moykher Sforim (Mendele the Book Peddler), I. L. Peretz, and S. Rabinovitsh, better known as Sholom Aleichem, now flourished. All three of the Yiddish "classicists" began their literary careers in Hebrew, with Peretz writing in Polish as well.

Peretz was the only one of this literary trio to raise a generation of disciples. From the 1890s until his death, Peretz "held court" in Warsaw, and many writers who achieved fame after his death visited him for words of advice and encouragement. One such writer was Sholem Asch, who until the emergence of I. B. Singer was the Yiddish author whose works were by far the most widely available in English.

Twentieth-century Yiddish literature includes realism, naturalism, neoromanticism, symbolism, futurism, expressionism, stream-of-consciousness, proletarian fiction, and socialist realism. One circle of New York-based modernist poets known as "Di yunge," active during and shortly after World War I, was succeeded by the introspective "Inzikhitsn," one of whose leading exponents was Jacob Glatstein.

The unfolding tragedy of European Jewry put an end to much avantgarde experimentation among the surviving Yiddish authors, who were suddenly deprived of a younger generation of readers. Nevertheless, the post-Holocaust period witnessed a last great flowering of Yiddish fiction and poetry, much of it devoted to an exploration of the catastrophe theme. It was during the two decades after the end of World War II that Abraham

Sutzkever, Rokhl Korn, Chaim Grade, and I. B. Singer were at the peak of their powers, creating enduring poems, short stories, and novels.

The first Yiddish author to have his works translated into English was the New York "sweatshop poet" Morris Rosenfeld, whose *Songs from the Ghetto* was published in 1898. Since then the quantity of translations and authors translated has steadily increased, a trend that has greatly accelerated during the past decade. The recent growth of academic interest in Yiddish studies has seen the emergence of critical editions in translation, aimed at a university-based audience. Students of Yiddish literature, as well as general readers, will clearly benefit, should the current proliferation of translations continue. It is to be devoutly desired, moreover, that publishers will see fit to reissue important titles that have gone out of print all too soon after their initial appearance.

GENERAL READING LIST

Dobroszycki, Lucjan, and Barbara Kirshenblatt-Gimblett. *Image before My Eyes: A Photographic History of Jewish Life in Poland, 1864–1939.* Schocken 1977 $29.95 1979 pap. $19.95. A richly illustrated photo album, including an informative introduction on Polish-Jewish history and culture during the period covered.
Dubnow, Simon. *History of the Jews in Russia and Poland from the Earliest Times until the Present Day.* Trans. by I. Friedlander, intro. by Leon Shapiro, Ktav 3 vols. in 2 o.p. Classic survey of the history of Eastern European Jewry by one of its pioneer historians. Reprinted from the 1916 Jewish Publication Society of America edition.
Howe, Irving. *The World of Our Fathers.* Bantam 1981 pap. $3.95; Harcourt 1976 $14.95; Pocket Bks. repr. 1978 pap. $6.95; Simon & Schuster (Touchstone Bks.) 1983 pap. $12.95. The story of Eastern European Jews in the United States, their struggles, achievements, and contributions to American life. Combines a thorough knowledge of the American scene with an intimate familiarity with American Jewish life and letters.
Vishniac, Roman. *Polish Jews: A Pictorial Record.* Intro. by Abraham J. Heschel, Schocken 1968 $12.00 pap. $7.95. Some 31 photographs by a famous artist-photographer. Many of these photos are reproduced in the author's 1983 album, *A Vanished World,* published by Farrar.
Zborowski, Mark, and Elizabeth Herzog. *Life Is with People: The Culture of the Shtetl.* Intro. by Margaret Mead, Schocken 1962 pap. $7.95. A classic anthropological study of the now-disappeared small-town life of Eastern European Jewry.

HISTORY AND CRITICISM

Abramowicz, Dina, ed. *Yiddish Literature in English Translation: Books Published 1945–1967.* Yivo 2d ed. 1968 pap. $5.00
————. *Yiddish Literature in English Translation: List of Books in Print.* Yivo text ed. 1976 pap. $7.50. Two essential tools for the compilation of a comprehensive bibliography of Yiddish works in English translation.
Birnbaum, S. A. *Yiddish: A Survey and a Grammar.* Univ. of Toronto Pr. 1979 $42.50. Based in part on lectures delivered at the University of London in 1934 and

1938, this work includes a topical overview of Jewish languages, along with a history and a grammar of Yiddish.

Dawidowicz, L. S., ed. *For Max Weinreich on His Seventieth Birthday: Studies in Jewish Language, Literature and Society.* Mouton 1964 $66.00. Contributions to Yiddish linguistics and literature and Jewish sociology, by scholars paying tribute to a major figure in Yiddish studies.

Doroshkin, Milton. *Yiddish in America: Social and Cultural Foundations.* Fairleigh Dickinson Univ. Pr. 1970 $26.50. Covers the period 1880–1920 and concentrates on two major institutions of Eastern European Jewry: the Yiddish press and the *landsmanshaftn*, or fraternal organizations.

Feinsilver, Lillian M. *The Taste of Yiddish.* A. S. Barnes 1980 $14.95 pap. $6.95. Includes observations on the general characteristics of the language, lists of idiomatic expressions with their translations, and a study of mutual influences between Yiddish and English.

The Field of Yiddish: Studies in Yiddish Language, Folklore, and Literature. Ed. by Uriel Weinreich, Lexik House repr. 1954 $12.50 2d collection 1965 o.p.; ed. by Marvin I. Herzog, Wita Ravid, and Uriel Weinreich, Mouton 3d collection 1969 $27.50; ed. by Marvin I. Herzog, Institute for the Study of Human Issues 4th collection 1980 $22.00. Scholarly contributions dealing with the Yiddish language in its historical development, dialects, and onomastics, as well as with Yiddish literature and folklore.

Fishman, Joshua A., ed. *Never Say Die: A Thousand Years of Yiddish in Jewish Life and Letters. Contributions to the Sociology of Language Ser.* Mouton 1981 $47.50. Includes articles on the history of Yiddish and the sociology, culture, and political status of Yiddish-speaking Jews. Most articles are in English; some are in Yiddish.

———. *Yiddish in America: Socio-Linguistic Description and Analysis.* Research Center for Language & Semiotic Studies text ed. 1965 pap. $5.50. Sociocultural background, periodization, and statistical data on Yiddish in the United States.

Geipel, John. *Mame-Loshn: The Making of Yiddish.* Flatiron 1982 $19.50 pap. $9.00. Brief survey of the Yiddish language, its history, and idioms.

Goldberg, Judith. *Laughter through Tears: The Yiddish Cinema.* Fairleigh Dickinson Univ. Pr. 1982 $18.00

Goldman, Eric A. *Visions, Images and Dreams: Yiddish Film Past and Present.* Ed. by Diane Kirkpatrick, *Studies in Cinema* UMI Research 1983 $39.95. Goldberg and Goldman are two academic surveys of Yiddish-language films. Both books include extensive bibliographies and filmographies.

Goldsmith, Emanuel S. *Architects of Yiddishism at the Beginning of the Twentieth Century: A Study in Jewish Cultural History.* Fairleigh Dickinson Univ. Pr. 1976 $27.50. The Yiddish language and cultural movement and its significance for Jewish life.

Kahn, Yitzhak. *Portraits of Yiddish Writers.* Vantage 1979 $7.95. Essays on 22 writers including Mendele, I. L. Peretz, Sholom Aleichem, D. Bergelson, J. Opatoshu, H. Leivick, Ch. Grade, A. Sutzkever, I. Manger, J. Glatstein, R. Korn, E. Greenberg, and others.

Kumove, Shirley. *Words like Arrows: A Collection of Yiddish Folk Sayings.* Schocken 1985 $19.95. Representative collection of Eastern European Jewish proverbs. Bilingual edition (original and transliterated Yiddish, English translations).

Liptzin, Sol. *A History of Yiddish Literature.* Jonathan David 1972 $10.00. Historical survey, covering the development of Yiddish literature from medieval times through the post-World War II period.

Madison, Charles A. *Yiddish Literature: Its Scope and Major Writers*. Ungar 1968 $20.00. After a historical survey of the development of Yiddish literature from the beginning to Mendele "the book . . . treats individually the work of fourteen major writers. . . . Major novels, plays and poems are outlined and discussed critically" (Publisher's note).

Pinsker, Sanford. *Schlemiel as Metaphor: Studies in the Yiddish and American Jewish Novel*. Pref. by H. T. Moore, *Crosscurrents Modern Critiques Ser*. Southern Illinois Univ. Pr. 1971 $6.95. A study of a comic figure who is conceived as a metaphor of the Jewish and human condition. The works of Mendele, Sholom Aleichem, I. B. Singer, and American-Jewish writers are analyzed.

Roback, A. A. *The Story of Yiddish Literature*. Gordon repr. of 1940 ed. 1974 $75.00. The first comprehensive survey in English since 1899. Includes a bibliography of translations and other works in English on the subject.

Rosten, Leo. *Hooray for Yiddish*. Simon & Schuster (Touchstone Bks.) 1984 pap. $6.95.

———. *The Joys of Yiddish*. McGraw-Hill 1968 $19.95; Washington Square Pr. 1970 pap. $3.95. Rosten's books are lexicons of common Yiddish expressions, aimed at a popular readership, that also seek to illuminate "the whole . . . realm of Jewish culture, thought, history, religion, customs, wit" (Publisher's note).

Rubin, Ruth. *Voices of a People: The Story of Yiddish Folksong*. Jewish Publication Society repr. of 1973 ed. 1979 pap. $8.95. Covers historical development from the sixteenth century to the present. Provides content analysis and music to selected songs.

Sandrow, Nahma. *Vagabond Stars: A World History of Yiddish Theater*. Harper 1977 $20.00. "A lively, vital chronicle of the life and times of Yiddish theater, through five continents and more than 300 years" (Publisher's note).

Schulman, Elias. *The Holocaust in Yiddish Literature*. Workmen's Circle 1983 $4.00. Brief survey of a central motif in post-World War II Yiddish literature.

Soltes, Mordecai. *The Yiddish Press: An Americanizing Agency*. Ayer repr. of 1925 ed. 1969 $15.00. Thorough study based on an analysis of primary sources.

Waxman, Meyer. *A History of Jewish Literature*. A. S. Barnes 5 vols. in 6 $50.00; Cornwall Bks. 6 vols. $50.00. Historical survey of Jewish literature in several languages, from biblical times to the twentieth century. Deals extensively with Yiddish literature.

Weinreich, Max. *History of the Yiddish Language*. Trans. by Joshua A. Fishman, Univ. of Chicago Pr. 1980 $60.00; Yivo 1980 $45.00. A seminal work that treats the vocabulary, phonology, and grammar of Yiddish, their historical development, and the symbiotic relationship of the language with the traditional religious culture of Ashkenazic Jewry. This translation is based on the first two volumes of the four-volume Yiddish original, published in 1973, and includes the complete narrative and an exhaustive index, but omits the footnotes and bibliography.

Weinreich, Uriel, and Beatrice Weinreich. *Yiddish Language and Folklore: A Selective Bibliography for Research*. Mouton 1959 o.p. Includes works both in English and Yiddish, and covers books as well as contributions to journals.

Wiener, Leo. *The History of Yiddish Literature in the Nineteenth Century*. Intro. by Elias Schulman, Hermon repr. of 1899 ed. 1973 $14.50. "The first introduction to Yiddish literature for the English reader. . . . Though now slightly dated [it] remains a classic handbook" (Publisher's note).

Wisse, Ruth R. *The Schlemiel as Modern Hero*. Univ. of Chicago Pr. (Phoenix Bks.) 1980 pap. $3.95. Study of a representative motif in modern Yiddish fiction, which reappears in a different disguise in contemporary American literature.

Zinberg, Israel. *A History of Jewish Literature*. Ktav 12 vols. ea. $22.50. Volume 7, *Old Yiddish Literature from Its Origins to the Kaskalah Period*, is described as "... an account of the rich literature produced in this language from its origins in the eleventh century to the dawn of the era of Enlightenment" (Publisher's note). With valuable bibliographic notes edited and supplemented with the newest contributions by the translator, a glossary of Hebrew and other terms, and an index.

COLLECTIONS

Ausubel, Nathan, ed. *A Treasury of Jewish Folklore*. Crown 1948 $14.95; Doubleday 1951 $17.95
———. *A Treasury of Jewish Humor*. Doubleday 1951 $17.50. Both anthologies contain a rich selection of material from Yiddish sources.
Betsky, Sarah Z., ed. and trans. *Onions and Cucumbers and Plums: Forty-six Yiddish Poems in English*. Granger Index Repr. Ser. Ayer repr. of 1958 ed. $16.00; Wayne State Univ. Pr. 1981 $12.50 pap. $6.95. Selections from modern Yiddish poets, with Yiddish and English on opposite pages.
Cooperman, Jehiel B., and Sara H. Cooperman, trans. *America in Yiddish Poetry: An Anthology*. Exposition Pr. 1967 $10.00. Poems about the United States and American life.
Frank, Helena, trans. and comp. *Yiddish Tales*. Ed. by Moses Rischin, Ayer repr. of 1912 ed. 1975 $47.50. Includes stories by 20 Yiddish writers.
Gaster, Moses, trans. *Ma'aseh Book: Book of Jewish Tales and Legends*. Jewish Publication Society 1981 pap. $10.95. A popular collection of talmudic and midrashic tales from early Yiddish literature.
Glatstein, Jacob. *Anthology of Holocaust Literature*. Temple Bks. Atheneum repr. of 1968 ed. text ed. 1972 pap. $6.95. Most of the materials included are translations from the Yiddish.
Goldberg, Isaac, ed. *Six Plays of the Yiddish Theatre*. Gordon 1977 lib. bdg. $59.95
Howe, Irving, and Eliezer Greenberg, eds. *Ashes out of Hope: Fiction by Soviet Yiddish Writers*. Schocken 1978 pap. $4.95. Includes D. Bergelson, "Joseph Schur," "The Hole through Which Life Slips," "Civil War"; Moyshe Kulbak, "Zelmenyaner"; and Der Nister, "Under a Fence."
———. *A Treasury of Yiddish Poetry*. Holt 1972 pap. $4.95; Schocken 1976 pap. $6.95. An important effort, making outstanding Yiddish poets available to the English reader for the first time.
———. *A Treasury of Yiddish Stories*. Schocken 1973 pap. $8.95. Comprehensive selection, covering Yiddish writers of the nineteenth and twentieth centuries, with a valuable introduction by Irving Howe.
———. *Voices from the Yiddish: Essays, Memoirs, Diaries*. Schocken 1975 pap. $5.95; Univ. of Michigan Pr. 1972 $9.95. An anthology arranged by topics, such as "The Founding Fathers," "East European Scene," "A Few Central Themes and Figures," "Jewishness in America," "The Holocaust," "Yiddish: Language and Literature."
———. *Yiddish Stories Old and New*. Avon 1977 pap. $2.50; Holiday 1974 $5.95. Selection of stories by Sholom Aleichem, I. L. Peretz, A. Reisen, I. D. Berkowitz, I. Metzker, I. Manger, J. Opatoshu, and I. B. Singer.
Landis, Joseph C., ed. and trans. *The Great Jewish Plays*. Avon 1974 pap. $3.50; Hori-

zon Pr. 1972 $8.95. Contains S. Ansky, *The Dybbuk;* Hirshbein, *Green Fields;* D. Pinsky, *King David and His Wives;* H. Leivick, *The Golem.*

Leftwich, Joseph, ed. *An Anthology of Modern Yiddish Literature.* Mouton 1974 text ed. pap. $13.60. Includes stories, essays, plays, and poems of 42 Yiddish writers of the pre- and post-1939 period. With an introduction, biographical notes, glossary, and bibliography.

———, trans. and ed. *The Golden Peacock: A Worldwide Treasury of Yiddish Poetry.* A. S. Barnes 2d ed. rev. 1961 o.p. A comprehensive edition, with an introduction by Leftwich.

Lifson, David S., trans. and ed. *Epic and Folk Plays of the Yiddish Theater.* Fairleigh Dickinson Univ. Pr. 1975 $25.00. Contains P. Hirshbein, *Farvorfn vinkl;* H. Leivick, *Hirsh Lekert;* L. Kobrin, *Yankel Boyla;* Y. Aksenfeld, *Recruits.*

Metzker, Isaac, ed. *A Bintel Brief.* Trans. by Bella S. Metzker and Diana S. Levy, Behrman 1982 pap. vol. 1 $5.95; Viking 1981 vol. 2 $10.95. The letters reflect the life and problems of Yiddish-speaking immigrants from Eastern Europe.

Neugroschel, Joachim, trans. and comp. *The Shtetl.* Putnam (Perigee) 1982 $10.95. Includes 20 stories and novellas, in 4 parts: "The Religious Roots," "The Jewish Enlightenment," "Tradition and Modernism," "War, Revolution, Destruction."

———. *Yenne Velt: The Great Works of Jewish Fantasy and Occult.* Pocket Bks. 1978 pap. $6.95. Includes works ranging from the medieval *Ma'aseh Book* to the stories of I. B. Singer. Among other authors represented are A. B. Gotlober, Mendele Moykher Sforim, I. L. Peretz, S. Ansky, Der Nister (Pinkhes Kahanovitsh), M. Kulbak, and D. Bergelson, plus tales of Rabbi Nahman of Bratslav.

Schwartz, Howard, and Anthony Rudolf, eds. *Voices within the Ark: The Modern Jewish Poets.* Avon 1983 pap. $15.95; Pushcart Pr. 1980 $39.50. Among the numerous authors, active on all continents and in many languages, represented in this anthology are 44 Yiddish poets.

Whitman, Ruth. *An Anthology of Modern Yiddish Poetry.* Intro. by Robert Szulkin, pref. by I. B. Singer, Workmen's Circle repr. of 1966 ed. 1979 pap. $4.95. Included in this collection are works by 14 Yiddish poets.

Wisse, Ruth R. *A Shtetl and Other Yiddish Novellas.* Lib. of Jewish Studies Behrman 1973 $6.95. Contains five novels by masters of Yiddish letters. I. M. Weissenberg, *A Shtetl;* D. Bergelson, *At the Depot;* S. Ansky, *Behind a Mask;* J. Opatoshu, *Romance of a Horse Thief;* Mendele Moykher Sforim, *Of Bygone Days.* Translated for the first time into English, with an introduction that traces the development of modern Yiddish literature in the late nineteenth and early twentieth centuries.

ANSKY, S. (pseud. of Shloyme Zaynvil Rapport). 1863–1920

Born in a small town in Belorussia, Ansky was educated in traditional Jewish schools and by self-education. His democratic ideas and love for the poor and underprivileged prompted his interest in folk psychology and its artistic reflection—folklore. His famous play *The Dybbuk* is based on a popular belief in possessed souls to which Ansky gave a highly poetic and symbolic interpretation.

BOOK BY ANSKY

The Dybbuk: A Play. Trans. by S. Morris Engel, Liveright 1972 pap. $3.95; Regnery-Gateway repr. of 1974 ed. 1979 pap. $5.95

ASCH, SHOLEM. 1880–1957

Asch, one of the major figures in Yiddish letters, was born in Kutno, near Warsaw, Poland. He began writing in 1901, first in Hebrew, then in Yiddish. His early, quietly humorous stories of Jewish small-town life brought Yiddish literature to international notice. His epic novels and plays dealt with the contemporary scene and the Jewish experience on a worldwide scale. The range and reach of his talent were wide; his collected works appeared in Yiddish in 29 volumes. Much was translated into English, but some translators are now out of print. A bibliography of English translations of his works was compiled by Libby Okun-Cohen and appeared in the *Bulletin of Bibliography* in 1958.

Books by Asch

In the Beginning: Stories from the Bible. 1914. Trans. by Caroline Cunningham, Schocken 1966 $6.00

Mottke the Thief. 1916. Trans. by Willa Muir and Edwin Muir, Greenwood repr. of 1935 ed. lib. bdg. $27.50

Mother. 1925. Trans. by Nathan Ausubel, pref. by L. Lewisohn, AMS Pr. repr. of 1930 ed. $12.50

Kiddush ha-Shem: An Epic of 1648. Trans. by Rufus Learsi, *Modern Jewish Experience* Ayer repr. of 1926 ed. 1975 $21.00

Sabbatai Zevi. Trans. by Florence Whyte and George R. Noyes, Greenwood repr. of 1930 ed. 1974 lib. bdg. $18.75

Three Cities: Petersburg, Warsaw, Moscow. Trans. by Edwin Muir, Carroll & Graf repr. of 1933 ed. 1983 pap. $10.50

Salvation (Der tilim yid). 1934. Trans. by Willa Muir and Edwin Muir, Schocken 2d ed. 1968 o.p.

Children of Abraham: The Short Stories of Sholem Asch. 1939. Trans. by Maurice Samuel, *Short Story Index Repr. Ser.* Ayer repr. of 1942 ed. $27.50; Irvington repr. of 1942 ed. 1982 lib. bdg. $24.00

The Nazarene (Der man fun Natseres). 1939. Carroll & Graf 1984 $21.95 pap. $10.95. Part 1 of a trilogy; see the last entry in this list.

East River. Trans. by A. H. Gross, Carroll & Graf repr. of 1946 ed. 1983 pap. $8.95

Tales of My People. Trans. by Meyer Levin, *Short Story Index Repr. Ser.* Ayer repr. of 1948 ed. $20.00

Mary, The Nazarene, The Apostle. 1949. Carroll & Graf 1985 pap. $10.95. This is a trilogy; *The Nazarene* is part 1, *The Apostle* is part 2, and *Mary* is part 3.

Book about Asch

Siegel, Ben. *The Controversial Sholem Asch: An Introduction to His Fiction.* Bowling Green 1976 $12.95 pap. $7.95

BERGELSON, DAVID. 1884–1952

One of the masters of modern Yiddish prose, Bergelson was born in Okhrimova, the Ukraine. His works deal with the decline of the small-town Ukrainian Jewish shtetl before and during the Russian Revolution. He left Soviet Russia for Western Europe in 1921, returning there in 1934. On August 12, 1952, along with 23 other notable Soviet Jewish personalities, Bergelson was executed in Moscow. Although some of his shorter works have appeared in anthologies of Yiddish fiction in English translation, only one of his longer novels has been translated.

BOOK BY BERGELSON

When All Is Said and Done (Nokh Alemen). 1913. Trans. by Bernard Martin, Ohio Univ. Pr. 1971 $18.95 pap. $10.00

BLINKIN, MEIR. 1879–1915

A member of the literary group "Di yunge," Blinkin's career was cut short when he died young at 36. The stories contained in the slim volume listed below are examples of stories about life in the shtetl and on the lower east side of New York City.

BOOK BY BLINKIN

Stories. Trans. by Max Rosenfeld, intro. by Ruth R. Wisse, *Modern Jewish Lit. and Culture Ser.* State Univ. of New York Pr. 1984 $10.95

BRYKS, RACHMIL. 1912–1964

Born in a small town near Lodz, Poland, Bryks lived through the terrible experience of the ghetto in Lodz and the concentration camp at Auschwitz. After his liberation, he settled in the United States and began to write works of fiction dealing almost exclusively with the Holocaust period.

BOOK BY BRYKS

Kiddush Hashem: Cat in the Ghetto. Trans. by S. Morris Engel, Behrman text ed. 1977 pap. $3.95

CAHAN, ABRAHAM. 1860–1951

Cahan was the founder and influential editor of the *Jewish Daily Forward*. He was the author of several important immigrant-era novels in English, including *Yekl* and *The Rise of David Levinsky*. His Yiddish-language memoirs offer insight on American-Jewish literature, Yiddish journalism, and the immigrant scene in New York.

BOOK BY CAHAN

The Education of Abraham Cahan. Trans. and intro. by Leon Stein, Schocken 1969 $7.50. Translated from vols. 1 and 2 of his *Bleter fun mayn lebn*.

GLATSTEIN, JACOB. 1896–1971

Born in Lublin, Poland, Glatstein lived in the United States from 1914 until his death. One of the major figures in modern Yiddish poetry, Glatstein cultivated free verse and poetry closely related to the reality of contemporary events and social environment. A master of the Yiddish language, he created poems that became classic expressions of Jewish attitudes and reactions to the tragic events of the Holocaust. He also wrote brilliant prose; especially remarkable are two accounts of his trip to Europe on the eve of World War II.

BOOKS BY GLATSTEIN

The Selected Poems of Jacob Glatstein. Trans. by Ruth Whitman, October 1973 $7.50
  pap. $2.95
Homecoming at Twilight (Ven Yash iz gekumen). 1940. Trans. by Norbert Guterman,
  fwd. by Maurice Samuel, A. S. Barnes 1962 o.p.

BOOK ABOUT GLATSTEIN

Hadda, Janet. *Yankev Glatshteyn.* Twayne 1980 o.p.

GLUCKEL OF HAMELN. 1645–1724

Gluckel of Hameln was a writer and businesswoman who lived in Hamburg, Germany. Her memoirs were first published by her family in 1896
and are considered a classic of early Yiddish literature. They provide a rare
inside look at everyday life during the late seventeenth and early eighteenth
centuries, a period of great turmoil for European Jews.

BOOK BY GLUCKEL OF HAMELN

The Memoirs of Gluckel of Hameln. Trans. by Marvin Lowenthal, intro. by Robert
  Rosen, Schocken 1977 pap. $7.95

GRADE, CHAIM. 1910–1982

Grade was born in Vilna, Poland, where he received a thorough education
in the talmudic academies of the region. He started to write poetry in 1932
and very soon won literary recognition. He escaped the Nazi onslaught as a
refugee in the Soviet Union, only to return and find his mother and wife
killed and his hometown destroyed. His later work, both poetry and prose,
is dedicated to the tragic Holocaust theme and to the re-creation of a world
that is no more. His characters are deeply rooted in Jewish tradition and
the lore of his native land; his poetry is forceful and dramatic, with the pathos of national and personal tragedy.

BOOKS BY GRADE

The Agunah. Trans. and intro. by Curt Leviant, Menorah 1978 pap. $3.95
Rabbis and Wives. Trans. by Harold Rabinowitz and Inna Hecker Grade, Knopf 1982
  $15.95; Random (Vintage) 1983 pap. $5.95
The Well. Trans. by Ruth R. Wisse, Jewish Publication Society 1967 o.p.
The Yeshiva (Tsemakh Atlas). Trans. by Curt Leviant, Bobbs 2 vols. 1976–77 ea.
  $15.00; Menorah 2 vols. repr. 1979 pap. $11.95

HALPERN, MOYSHE-LEYB. 1886–1932

Halpern was born in Zloczow (Galicia) and came to the United States in
1908, where he joined up with the group of modernist New York Yiddish poets known as "Di yunge." His work conveys vivid images of his European
childhood home and the modern American urban scene.

BOOK BY HALPERN

In New York: A Selection. Trans. and ed. by Kathryn Hellerstein, *Jewish Poetry Ser.*
  Jewish Publication Society 1982 $14.95 pap. $9.95

JACOB BEN ISAAC OF JANOW. d.1620?

Very little is known about the author of the seventeenth-century best-seller that has had more than 200 editions since its first known printing in 1622. The book is a collection of rabbinical commentaries and legends on the Bible and reflects faithfully the Jewish folk psyche, its naive piety, its absolute identification with the word of God as transmitted in the Bible, and its stern adherence to the moral principles of its religious tradition. Its influence on later Yiddish literature has been significant.

BOOK BY JACOB BEN ISAAC

Tz'enah ur'enah: The Classic Anthology of Torah Lore and Midrashic Comment. Trans. by Miriam Stark Zakon, intro. by Meir Holder, *ArtScroll Judaica Ser.* Mesorah 3 vols. 1983–84 o.p.

KORN, ROKHL (RACHEL). 1898–1982

Born in Galicia, Rokhl Korn wrote her first poem in Polish, before switching to Yiddish. She published several books in Poland before World War II, and her postwar writing is regarded as some of the finest poetry produced in Yiddish during that period. She received numerous literary prizes for her work. After the war she settled in Montreal.

BOOK BY KORN

Generations: Selected Poems. Ed. by Seymour Mayne, trans. by Rivka Augenfeld, Flatiron 1982 $12.95 pap. $6.95

KREITMAN, ESTHER. 1891–1954

The older sister of I. B. and I. J. Singer, Esther Kreitman was a notable Yiddish author in her own right. "What distinguished her fiction . . . is her portrayal of the woman's, particularly the free thinking woman's, point of view. . . . [Her] works record a young woman's passionate struggle for identity and autonomy" (Joshua A. Fogel, *The Yale Review*). Among her translations is a Yiddish version of *A Christmas Carol* by Charles Dickens.

BOOK BY KREITMAN

Deborah: A Novel. Trans. by Maurice Carr, intro. by Clive Sinclair, St. Martin's 1984 $13.95

LINETSKI, ISAAC JOEL. 1839–1915

The author, a contemporary of the great Yiddish writer Mendele Moykher Sforim, earned his fame with a single book, *Dos poylishe yingl* (*The Polish Lad;* also called *Dos Khsidishe yingl*, or *The Hasidic Lad*), which first appeared in 1867. It is a biting satire on what the author portrayed as the backwardness, fanaticism, ignorance, and superstitions of shtetl life during the mid-nineteenth century.

BOOK BY LINETSKI

The Polish Lad. Trans. by Moshe Spiegel, intro. by Milton Hindus, Jewish Publication Society 1975 $7.95

MENDELE MOYKHER SFORIM (pseud. of Sholem Yankev Abramovitsh). 1836–1917

This writer, known as the grandfather of Yiddish literature, won fame under the pen name Mendele the Book Peddler. A novelist and essayist, he was reared in a small town not far from Minsk, Belorussia, and received a traditional orthodox Jewish education. After his father's death, when he was 14, he set out as a wandering scholar and gained a great fund of experience and insight into Russian Jewish folkways, at the same time falling under the influence of the secularizing trends of the *Haskalah.* His first works were in Hebrew, but for his popular tales he turned to Yiddish as a more suitable vehicle. Later, he translated most of his Yiddish works into Hebrew. He has been called the creator of classical Yiddish, and he was a master of early modern Hebrew prose as well.

BOOKS BY MENDELE MOYKHER SFORIM

The Parasite (Dos kleyne mentshele). 1866. Trans. by Gerald Stillman, Yoseloff 1956 o.p.
Fishke the Lame. 1869. Trans. by Gerald Stillman, Yoseloff 1960 o.p.
The Nag (Di klyatshe). 1873. Trans. by Moshe Spiegel, Beechhurst 1955 o.p. Satiric allegory telling of the adventures of an impoverished scholar and his battered workhorse, symbol of the Jewish people.
The Travels and Adventures of Benjamin the Third. 1878. Schocken 1968 pap. $5.50. "This early classic of Yiddish literature tells the story of two small town innocents who wander out into the world in search of the legendary Red Jews and of the rock-hurling, Sabbath-observing river Sambatyon" (*Judaica Book News*).

BOOKS ABOUT MENDELE MOYKHER SFORIM

Miron, Dan. *A Traveler Disguised: A Study in the Rise of Modern Yiddish Fiction in the 19th Century.* Schocken 1973 o.p. About the contribution of Abramovitsh/Mendele to the development of Yiddish fiction.
Steinberg, Theodore L. *Mendele Mocher Seforim. Twayne's World Authors Ser.* G. K. Hall 1977 lib. bdg. $16.95

NAHMAN OF BRATSLAV. 1772–1811

The grandson of Israel ben Eliezer (Baal Shem Tov), founder of Hasidism, Rabbi Nahman of Bratslav was renowned for his storytelling. After his death a number of his moralistic and symbolic tales were published in a bilingual, Yiddish and Hebrew book. These tales had an important impact on later Yiddish writing and, thanks largely to the efforts of the philosopher MARTIN BUBER (see Vol. 4), were eventually made known to a far wider public. Two recent English translations of *The Tales* exist, one of them published by Rabbi Nahman's present-day disciples.

BOOKS BY NAHMAN OF BRATSLAV

The Tales. 1815. Trans. by Arnold J. Band, pref. by Joseph Dan, Paulist Pr. 1978 o.p.
Rabbi Nachman's Stories. Trans. with notes by Aryeh Kaplan, Breslov Research Institute 1983 o.p.

OPATOSHU, JOSEPH. 1886–1954

One of the greatest Yiddish novelists, Opatoshu was born in Poland and came to the United States in 1907. His first writings were naturalistic stories of contemporary life. He was especially interested in the lower strata and in underworld characters, and described life of the New York ghetto. Later he became a historical novelist par excellence, dealing with such varied periods and places as the Roman Empire, medieval Germany, and nineteenth-century Poland. Several of his historical novels have been translated into English but are now out of print.

BOOKS BY OPATOSHU

In Polish Woods. 1922. Trans. by Isaac Goldberg, Jewish Publication Society 1938 o.p. Set in and around the nineteenth-century Hasidic rabbinical court of Kotsk.
A Day in Regensburg: Short Stories. 1933. Trans. by Jacob Sloan, Jewish Publication Society 1968 o.p. Set in the sixteenth-century German Jewish community of Regensburg.

PERETZ, YITSKHOK LEYBUSH (I. L.). 1852–1915

One of the three founding fathers of Yiddish literature, "I. L. Peretz stands at the intellectual center of Yiddish culture and literature. Born in Poland he was exposed . . . to that conflict of ideas and impulses which was to dominate his . . . life as a writer and intellectual leader: the conflict between traditionalism as embodied in a powerful Hasidic inheritance, and modernism, the new trend of secular-progressivist thought that was beginning to sweep through the world of East European Jewry" (Irving Howe, *A Treasury of Yiddish Stories*). Peretz wrote short stories, plays, and essays. A bibliography of translations of Peretz's works into English was compiled by Uriel Weinreich and appeared in Volume 1 of *The Field of Yiddish.* Unfortunately, many important Peretz translations are now out of print.

BOOKS BY PERETZ

Stories and Pictures. 1906. Gordon $75.00
Bontshe the Silent. Trans. by A. S. Rappoport, *Short Story Index Repr. Ser.* Ayer repr. of 1927 ed. $16.00
Peretz. Ed. and trans. by Sol Liptzin, *Biography Index Repr. Ser.* Ayer repr. of 1947 ed. $21.25. Bilingual (English/Yiddish) edition.
In This World and the Next: Selected Writings. Trans. by Moshe Spiegel, Yoseloff 1958 o.p.
The Book of Fire: Stories. Trans. by Joseph Leftwich, Yoseloff 1960 o.p.
My Memoirs. Trans. by Fred Goldberg, Citadel Pr. 1964 o.p.
Selected Stories. Ed. by Irving Howe and Eliezer Greenberg, Schocken 1975 pap. $4.95
The Seven Good Years and Other Stories. Trans. and adapted by Esther Hautzig, Jew-

ish Publication Society 1984 $10.95. Includes ten stories and a biographical sketch.

BOOKS ABOUT PERETZ

Adler, Ruth. *Women of the Shtetl: Through the Eye of Y. L. Peretz.* Fairleigh Dickinson Univ. Pr. 1979 $17.50
Samuel, Maurice. *Prince of the Ghetto.* 1948. Schocken 1973 pap. o.p. Skillful retelling of Peretz's folk and Hasidic tales.

PINSKY, DAVID. 1872–1959

Born in Mogilev, the Ukraine, Pinsky early became involved in the Labor Zionist activities. In 1898 he emigrated to the United States. His works include novels, short stories, and plays, many of which have been translated into English but are no longer in print. "It is the earliest stories that seem most fresh. . . . The young Pinsky was able to communicate compassionate tenderness in writing about the Jewish poor" (Irving Howe, *A Treasury of Yiddish Stories*).

BOOKS BY PINSKY

Three Plays. Trans. by Isaac Goldberg, *Modern Jewish Experience* Ayer repr. of 1918 ed. $27.00
Temptations: A Book of Short Stories. Trans. by Isaac Goldberg. *Short Story Index Repr. Ser.* Ayer repr. of 1919 ed. $20.00
Ten Plays. 1920. Trans. by Isaac Goldberg, Core Collection 1977 $16.50

RABON, ISRAEL. 1900–1941

Rabon was born in Lodz, Poland, to an impoverished, slum-dwelling family. His literary output was meager, consisting of two volumes of prose fiction and one book of poems. Nevertheless, these works have become recognized for the light they shed on the urban *lumpenproletariat* of pre-Holocaust Poland, as well as for their purely literary qualities. In both style and subject matter, Rabon's fiction is influenced by the works of Knut Hamsun.

BOOK BY RABON

The Street. 1928. Trans. by Leonard Wolf, Schocken 1985 $14.95. A "Jewish soldier returning to Lodz at the end of World War I joins the ranks of unemployed transients in the large city and becomes a street person. . . . A surrealistic and bizarre novel written in the style of avant-garde German expressionism of the 1920's" (*Judaica Book News*).

ROSENFELD, MORRIS. 1862–1923

Born in the Ukraine, Rosenfeld settled in the United States in 1886, where he put in long hours at the needle trades. His famous "sweatshop poems" made him the champion of the immigrant working masses, and he was one of the pioneers of American-Yiddish literature.

BOOK BY ROSENFELD

Songs from the Ghetto. Trans. by Leo Wiener, Irvington repr. of 1898 ed. lib. bdg. $15.00. The first Yiddish book to be translated into English. The translator was professor of Slavic languages at Harvard and author of a history of Yiddish literature, listed in the first section of this bibliography.

SHAPIRO, LAMED. 1878–1948

Lamed Shapiro was born in the Ukraine. He visited the United States in 1905 and returned in 1911. One of the most important short story writers in Yiddish, he was "a successor to the first generation of Yiddish writers . . . but after some early influence he departed radically from their style and subject matter. . . ." (Publisher's note)

BOOK BY SHAPIRO

The Jewish Government and Other Stories. Trans. and ed. by Curt Leviant, Twayne 1971 o.p.

SHOLOM ALEICHEM (pseud. of Sholem Rabinovitsh). 1859–1916

Sholom Aleichem (Hebrew greeting meaning "Peace be unto you!") was born near Pereyaslav, the Ukraine, and settled in the United States two years before his death. The most popular and beloved of all Yiddish writers, he wrote with humor and tenderness about the Yiddish-speaking Jews of Eastern Europe and won the title "the Jewish Mark Twain." "He is the passer-by, the informal correspondent, the post office into which Jews drop their communications to the world. All he does, you understand, is to write down stories people bring him. He invents nothing" (Alfred Kazin, *Contemporaries*). One of his creations, Tevye the Dairyman, has become world famous, thanks to the highly successful Broadway musical *Fiddler on the Roof*, which is based on Sholom Aleichem's Tevye stories. Although he also wrote plays and novels, it is for his short stories and his humorous monologues that Sholom Aleichem will be best remembered.

BOOKS BY SHOLOM ALEICHEM

The Best of Sholom Aleichem. Ed. by Irving Howe and Ruth R. Wisse, Simon & Schuster 1980 pap. $5.95; Washington Square Pr. 1982 pap. $3.95

Favorite Tales of Sholom Aleichem. Trans. by Julius Butwin and Frances Butwin, Avenel 1983 o.p. Reprint of *The Old Country*, published in 1946, and *Tevye's Daughters*, published in 1949.

Selected Stories. Intro. by Alfred Kazin, Modern Lib. 1956 o.p.

Some Laughter, Some Tears: Tales from the Old World and New. Trans. by Curt Leviant, Putnam (Perigee) 1979 pap. $4.95

Stories and Satires. Trans. by Curt Leviant, Macmillan (Collier Bks.) 1970 o.p.; Yoseloff 1959 o.p.

Holiday Tales of Sholom Aleichem. Trans. by Aliza Shevrin, Atheneum 1985 pap. $4.95; Scribner 1979 $10.95. "Seven stories, two available for the first time in English, capture the essence of the Jewish holidays of Passover, Purim, Chanukah or Sukkot" (*Judaica Book News*).

The Nightingale, or The Saga of Yosele Solovey the Cantor (Yosele Solovey). 1889. Trans. by Aliza Shevrin, Putnam 1985 $16.95

The Adventure of Menahem-Mendl. 1892–1913. Trans. by Tamara Kahana, Putnam 1979 pap. $4.95

In the Storm. 1907. Trans. by Aliza Shevrin, New Amer. Lib. 1985 pap. $6.95; Putnam 1984 $15.95

The Adventures of Mottel, the Cantor's Son. 1907–16. Trans. by Tamara Kahana, Macmillan (Collier Bks.) 1961 o.p.

Wandering Star. 1912. Trans. by Frances Butwin, Crown 1952 o.p. Novel about an itinerant Yiddish theatrical troupe.

Marienbad. 1913. Trans. by Aliza Shevrin, Putnam 1982 $13.95

From the Fair: The Autobiography of Sholom Aleichem (Funem yarid). 1916–17. Trans. by Curt Leviant, Viking 1985 $20.00. New, expanded edition of a work earlier translated by Tamara Kahana, under the title *The Great Fair: Scenes from My Childhood* (1955).

Hanukah Money. Trans. and adapted by Uri Shulevitz and Elizabeth Shub, Greenwillow 1978 $11.75

Inside Kasrilevke. Trans. by Isidore Goldstick, Schocken 1968 pap. $4.95

Why Do Jews Need a Land of Their Own? (Oyf vos badarfn yidn a land?). Trans. by Joseph Leftwich and Mordecai S. Chertoff, Cornwall Bks. 1984 $19.95. "Another publication of Beth Sholom Aleichem, Tel Aviv, this volume contains nearly everything that Sholom Aleichem wrote on Zion, Zionism and Palestine as a homeland for the Jews" (*AJL Newsletter*).

BOOKS ABOUT SHOLOM ALEICHEM

Aarons, Victoria. *Author as Character in the Works of Sholom Aleichem*. Mellen 1985 $39.95

Butwin, Joseph, and Frances Butwin. *Sholom Aleichem. Twayne's World Authors Ser.* G. K. Hall 1977 lib. bdg. $12.95

Falstein, Louis. *The Man Who Loved Laughter: The Story of Sholom Aleichem. Covenant Ser.* Jewish Publication Society 1968 $4.25

Gittleman, Sol. *Sholom Aleichem: A Non-Critical Introduction*. Mouton text ed. 1974 pap. $13.60

Miron, Dan A. *Sholem Aleykhem: Person, Persona, Presence*. Yivo 1972 pap. $1.50. About Sholom Aleichem's pseudonyms and their meaning in his work.

Samuel, Maurice. *World of Sholom Aleichem*. Knopf 1943 $10.00. "A pilgrimage through . . . the townlets and villages of the famous Pale of Settlement, recounting the adventures of the chief characters in the works of Sholom Aleichem and recreating the folklore, the outlook and the memories which were in part transplanted to America" (Publisher's note).

Waife-Goldberg, Marie. *My Father, Sholom Aleichem*. Pocket Bks. pap. $1.50

SINGER, I(SAAC) B(ASHEVIS). 1904– (NOBEL PRIZE 1978)

The first Yiddish writer to be awarded the Nobel Prize for literature (1978), I. B. Singer is also the most widely translated of Yiddish authors. Born in Leoncin, Poland, he had a traditional Jewish education and, as the son of a rabbi, attended a rabbinical seminary in Warsaw. His first fiction was written in Hebrew, but most of his work has been in Yiddish. Before coming to the United States in 1935 he worked as a proofreader and a translator in Warsaw. His work was not translated into English until he was 46.

Since his arrival in the United States he has been on the staff of the *Jewish Daily Forward*, where most of his work has been serialized. His books are often marked by elements of fantasy and are distinguished for their lustiness, philosophical insight, and humor. Singer has written a large number of children's books, some of which are listed here. In recent years, stage productions and films have been made of several of his works, including *The Magician of Lublin* and *Yentl*.

In 1964 Singer was elected to the National Institute of Arts and Letters. Eleven years later he received an honorary doctoral degree from the Hebrew University of Jerusalem and the S. J. Agnon Golden Medal Award from the American Friends of the Hebrew University. Since receiving the Nobel Prize he has continued his active literary career. Most of his works appear in book form in translation only.

Books by I. B. Singer

The Collected Stories of Isaac Bashevis Singer. Farrar 1982 $19.95 pap. $9.95. Anthology including 47 previously published stories.

An Isaac Bashevis Singer Reader. Farrar 1971 $17.95 pap. $12.50

Gimpel the Fool and Other Stories. Trans. by Saul Bellow and others, Farrar 1957 $9.95 pap. $4.95; Fawcett 1980 pap. $2.50

The Spinoza of Market Street. 1961. Trans. by Elaine Gottlieb and others, Avon 1963 pap. $1.65; Fawcett 1980 pap. $2.95. An anthology of 11 short stories.

Short Friday and Other Stories. Farrar 1964 $10.95. Sixteen tales that "penetrate life, depth, reality, the supernatural, and have an earthy quality that makes for enjoyable reading" (*LJ*).

Zlateh the Goat and Other Stories. Trans. by I. B. Singer and Elizabeth Shub, Harper 1966 $13.41 1984 pap. $3.80. "Seven short stories coming out of the author's background as a young Jewish boy in Poland before World War I" (Library of Congress card).

The Séance and Other Stories. Farrar 1968 $12.95 pap. $6.95; Fawcett 1981 pap. $2.75

A Day of Pleasure: Stories of a Boy Growing Up in Warsaw. Farrar 1969 pap. $5.95. Episodes from the author's childhood.

A Friend of Kafka and Other Stories. Farrar 1970 $12.95 pap. $5.95

A Crown of Feathers. Farrar 1973 $12.95; Fawcett 1979 pap. $2.95. Winner of a National Book Award.

Passions and Other Stories. Farrar 1975 $8.95; Fawcett 1978 pap. $2.95

Old Love and Other Stories. Farrar 1979 $10.95; Fawcett 1980 pap. $3.25

Stories for Children. Farrar 1984 $13.95. Includes 36 previously published stories and an essay: "Are Children the Ultimate Literary Critics?"

Gifts. Author's Workshop Ser. Jewish Publication Society 1985 $30.00. "New, previously unpublished stories with an introductory essay that describes the author's early passion for writing" (*Judaica Book News*).

The Image and Other Stories. Farrar 1985 $17.95. "The master's new stories range from the old days in Warsaw to recent years in America" (*Judaica Book News*).

Satan in Goray. 1935. Trans. by Jacob Sloan, Farrar 1955 $8.95; Fawcett 1980 pap. $2.50. A story of religious hysteria among persecuted Jews in a small Polish town in the seventeenth century, it portrays the messianic longing for redemption among Jews in the wake of the Chmielnicki massacres of 1648–54.

The Family Moskat. 1950. Farrar 1965 $15.00 pap. $7.95; Fawcett repr. 1975 pap.

$2.95. The first novel by the author, this is the history of a Polish-Jewish family from the early 1900s to World War II.

In My Father's Court. 1956. Trans. by Channah Kleinerman-Goldstein, Elaine Gottlieb, and Joseph Singer, Farrar 1966 pap. $5.95; Fawcett 1979 pap. $2.50. Memoir of the author's childhood in Poland, offering a glimpse of Hasidic life and of his rabbinical family.

The Magician of Lublin. 1960. Fawcett 1979 pap. $2.50. A novel of nineteenth-century Poland.

The Slave. 1962. Trans. by I. B. Singer and Cecil Femley, Avon 1964 pap. $1.95; Fawcett 1980 pap. $2.50. Novel set in a seventeenth-century Carpathian village.

The Manor. Farrar 1967 $6.95. The first volume of a planned trilogy, set in nineteenth-century Poland.

The Estate. 1969. Farrar 1979 $15.00

Joseph and Koza, or The Sacrifice to the Vistula. Farrar 1970 $4.95. Winner of the 1970 National Book Award for children's literature.

Enemies: A Love Story. Farrar 1972 $10.95; Fawcett 1977 pap. $2.95

The Penitent. 1974. Farrar 1983 $13.95; Fawcett 1985 pap. $2.95

Shosha. Farrar 1978 $8.95; Fawcett 1979 pap. $2.95

(and Ira Moskowitz). *A Little Boy in Search of God: Mysticism in a Personal Light*. Trans. by Joseph Singer, Doubleday 1976 $8.95. Memoirs.

A Young Man in Search of Love. Trans. by Joseph Singer, Doubleday 1978 $6.95. Memoirs.

Nobel Lecture. Farrar 1979 $9.95 pap. $3.25

Lost in America. Trans. by Joseph Singer, Doubleday 1981 $17.95. Memoirs.

The Reaches of Heaven: A Story of the Baal Shem Tov. Farrar 1981 $15.00 pap. $8.95

The Golem. Farrar 1982 $11.95

Yentl the Yeshiva Boy. Trans. by Marion Magid and Elizabeth Pollet, Farrar 1983 $10.95

Love and Exile: The Early Years—A Memoir. Doubleday 1984 $17.95. Contains "A Little Boy in Search of God," "A Young Man in Search of Love," "Lost in America," and a new introduction, "The Beginning."

BOOKS ABOUT I. B. SINGER

Allentuck, Marcia, ed. *Achievement of Isaac Bashevis Singer*. Pref. by T. Moore, *Crosscurrents Modern Critiques Ser*. Southern Illinois Univ. Pr. 1969 $9.95

Buchen, Irving H. *Isaac Bashevis Singer and the Eternal Past*. Gotham Lib. New York Univ. Pr. 1968 $15.00 pap. $3.95

Kresh, Paul. *Isaac Bashevis Singer: The Magician of West 86th Street*. Doubleday (Dial) 1979 $14.95

———. *Isaac Bashevis Singer: The Story of a Storyteller*. Jewish Biography Ser. Lodestar Bks. 1984 $13.95

Malin, Irving, ed. *Critical Views of Isaac Bashevis Singer*. Gotham Lib. New York Univ. Pr. 1969 $12.00 pap. $4.95

———. *Isaac Bashevis Singer*. Lit. and Life Ser. Ungar 1972 $12.95

Miller, David Neal. *Fear of Fiction: Narrative Strategies in the Works of Isaac Bashevis Singer*. State Univ. of New York Pr. 1985 lib. bdg. $29.50 text ed. pap. $9.95

Siegel, Ben. *Isaac Bashevis Singer*. Pamphlets on Amer. Writers Ser. Univ. of Minnesota Pr. 1969 pap. $1.25

Sinclair, Clive. *The Brothers Singer*. Schocken 1983 $14.95. Literary biography of Israel Joshua Singer and Isaac Bashevis Singer.

Singer, Isaac Bashevis, and Richard Burgin. *Conversations with Isaac Bashevis*

Singer. Doubleday 1985 $15.95. By the author of *Conversations with Jorge Luis Borges.*

SINGER, I(SRAEL) J(OSHUA). 1893–1944

I. J. Singer, the older brother of Isaac Bashevis Singer, was born in Bilgoraj, Poland, came to the United States in 1934, and was naturalized in 1939. His works include novels, short stories, and plays, and have enjoyed both critical acclaim and widespread popularity.

Books by I. J. Singer

Steel and Iron. 1927. Trans. by Joseph Singer, Crowell 1969 o.p. The impact of World War I and the Russian Revolution on Jewish life.

Yoshe Kalb. 1932. Trans. by Maurice Samuel, intro. by I. B. Singer, Vanguard 1976 $12.95. A portrayal of Hasidic life in nineteenth-century Poland.

The Brothers Ashkenazi. 1936. Trans. by Joseph Singer, Carroll & Graf 1985 pap. $9.95. A panoramic novel about the rise and fall of a family of Jewish industrialists in prewar Poland.

East of Eden. 1938. Trans. by Maurice Samuel, Vanguard 1974 $10.00. The deceived hopes and expectations of Jewish Communists in the Soviet Union.

The River Breaks Up. 1938. Trans. by Maurice Samuel, Vanguard 1976 $10.00. Short stories.

The Family Carnovsky. 1943. Trans. by Joseph Singer, Harper 1973 o.p. Tragedy of assimilated Jewish families in Nazi Germany.

Of a World That Is No More. 1946. Vanguard 1970 o.p. Childhood memoirs, worth comparing with I. B. Singer's *In My Father's Court,* which deals with the same household.

SUTZKEVER, ABRAHAM. 1913–

Sutzkever is a towering figure among Yiddish poets of all ages. He started to write in his native city of Vilna in the 1930s and endured the Nazi occupation of that city. He joined the partisans in 1943 and was called as a witness to the Nuremberg trials of 1946. Now he lives in Israel, where he edits the prestigious Yiddish literary journal *Di Goldene Keyt* (*The Golden Chain*). A great master of word and image, he found his own way of extracting beauty from the somber realities of Jewish life, and his writing eloquently expresses the tragedy and heroism of the Holocaust period.

Books by Sutzkever

Siberia: A Poem. Trans. and intro. by Jacob Sonntag, letter on the poem and drawings by Marc Chagall, Abelard-Schuman 1961 o.p.

Burnt Pearls: Ghetto Poems. Trans. by Seymour Mayne, Mosaic Pr. 1981 o.p.

Book about Sutzkever

Leftwich, Joseph. *Abraham Sutzkever: Partisan Poet.* A. S. Barnes 1971 o.p.

TSANIN, MORDECAI. 1906–

Tsanin, born in Sokolow-Podlaski, Poland, settled in Israel, where he has served as editor-in-chief of the Yiddish daily *Letste nayes.* In addition to his distinguished journalistic activities, he has devoted himself to producing a multivolume fictional panorama of Jewish history, one volume of which has been translated into English.

BOOK BY TSANIN

Artapanos Comes Home. Trans. by I. M. Lask, A. S. Barnes 1980 $12.00. Historical novel.

ZUNSER, ELIAKUM. 1835–1913

Zunser was a famous wedding bard, composing couplets so popular that they passed into the realm of folk poetry and folk song. Both before and after his emigration to the United States in 1889, collections of his rhymes were frequently published, some of which were later translated into English.

BOOK BY ZUNSER

Selected Songs of Eliakum Zunser. Modern Jewish Experience Ayer repr. of 1928 ed. 1975 $24.50

BOOK ABOUT ZUNSER

Liptzin, Sol. *Eliakum Zunser: Poet of His People.* Behrman 1950 o.p.

CHAPTER 18

Hebrew Literature

Linda P. Lerman

Literature responds to the demands of life, and life reacts to the guidance of
literature. The function of literature is to plant the seed of new ideas and
new desires; the seed once planted, life does the rest. The tender shoot is
nurtured and brought to maturity by the spontaneous action of men's
minds, and its growth is shaped by their needs.

—AHAD HA-AM, *The Eternal Light*

Hebrew literature encompasses more than 2,000 years of creativity. It has
been the literary outlet and creative expression of the Jewish people from
the biblical period to the present. When Hebrew ceased to be the spoken language toward the end of the biblical period, it was maintained chiefly in religious literature. By the Middle Ages, Hebrew was known as *leshon ha-
kodesh*, the sacred tongue.

Hebrew was used primarily for liturgical works, codes, and legal texts
(e.g., commentaries, glosses, decisions, judgments), prophetic and wisdom
literature, and responsa. While some of this literature has been translated
into English, the majority remains only in the original Hebrew.

Tenth-century Spain, Provence, and Italy witnessed a growth in Hebrew
secular or quasisecular literature. The poetry of Solomon Ibn Gabirol,
Moses Ibn Ezra, and Judah Halevi are based on biblical and secular themes.
Their works are the primary fruits of the renaissance of Hebrew literature
during the Golden Age of Spain.

Modern Hebrew literature arose from the secular literature of Ashkenazi
Jewry. The exact beginning of the modern Hebrew literary era is disputed
by two prominent schools of thought. There are those who adhere to
Gershom Scholem's view that the close of the seventeenth century is the
starting point, which coincides with the disruption of medieval authority
following Shabbtai Zvi's messianic proclamation and downfall; others view
the German Haskalah movement in the latter part of the eighteenth century
as the impetus for the modern period.

Historians also debate the periodization of modern Hebrew literature. In
the *Encyclopaedia Judaica* Professor Ezra Spicehandler offers the following
generally accepted schema. The European Period (1781–1921) including
Haskalah literature in Europe (1781–1881) and modern Hebrew literature
in Russia and Poland (1881–1920); the Palestinian-Halutzic Period (1905–

1948), which comprises the Ottoman Period (1905–1917) and the Mandate Period (1920–1948); and, lastly, the Israel Period (1948 to the present).

The Haskalah, from the root meaning understanding or intelligence, was a movement committed to reason. Followers called *maskilim* chose those practices and beliefs in Judaism that were in accord with reason. The purpose of their literature was to educate on a moral, social, and aesthetic level.

Except for the poems of Ephraim Luzzatto, no Hebrew lyric poetry or Hebrew narrative prose of this period was especially noteworthy. The major emphasis of the Haskalah was in the area of modern Jewish scholarship, known as *Wissenschaft des Judenthums*.

In the Russian Haskalah the greatest literary figure was the poet, short story writer, and journalist, Judah Leib Gordon. He dominated the literary scene until the 1880s. Abraham Mapu, the first modern Hebrew novelist, wrote in Russia during the mid-1800s.

Political and social events of the 1880s in Europe influenced literary critics who began to demand a more realistic form of literature and the development of social criticism. Hebrew critics voiced similar attitudes and thus an empathy for people—their hopes and life-styles—became the focus of writings. Ahad Ha-Am is considered the most influential intellectual figure of the Modern European Period and is also the father of the modern Hebrew essay.

Mendele Moykher Sforim bridges the period between the Haskalah and the Nationalist era. While he is perhaps better known as the first serious Yiddish writer, he wrote in a new Hebrew literary style that established a standard of imaginative complexity and command of Hebrew prose.

In contrast to Mendele's style of realism, the works of David Frischmann, I. L. Peretz, and Micha Joseph Berdichevsky, all from Warsaw, were neoromantic and impressionistic. Berdichevsky is considered the most skillful proponent of this style. He challenged Ahad Ha-Am's views that a mainstream, unified Judaism existed and also opposed his efforts toward a nationalistic culture. Berdichevsky was a proponent of individualism and secularism rather than traditionalism, themes he reiterated throughout his works. M. Z. Feuerberg's writings, also of the same period, never cross into secularism but remain much like the author was, caught between the loss of faith and reason.

The high point in literary form and content of this European Period is found in the poetry of Hayyim Nachman Bialik. His works were primarily written between 1892 and 1917, a time of great political and social upheaval in Russia. Bialik masterfully strikes the balance between the old traditionalist culture and the new European culture. His style and command of the vast resources of the Hebrew literary tradition cast a shadow and strong influence over most other Hebrew writers of this period.

There were few exceptions to the dominance of Bialik's style and Saul Tchernichovski was the most significant. He introduced a more European style of poetry that stressed individualism, humanism, and universalism.

Hebrew literature in Palestine found its literary voice with the writers who emigrated during the 1880s. Best known among these was Eliezer Ben-Yehuda, the great lexicographer and journalist. Moshe Smilansky wrote realistic stories of Palestinian life and was the first to write about Arab life in Hebrew fiction. The ancient divinely promised land of *Eretz Israel* became the focus of many writers. Hebrew, as a language, was also developing and the literature reflects a growing flexibility in the vocabulary and stylistic use of language.

Following the upheavals of World War I and the Russian Revolution, Palestine became the new center of Hebrew literature as writers like Bialik continued to emigrate. The emigration of 1920–24 brought a new radical expression of literary leadership. Eliezer Steinman and Abraham Shlonsky founded a new literary journal called *Ketuvim* (Writings), which became a principal vehicle for the modernists. These new writers included Yaakov Horowitz, Nathan Alterman, and Leah Goldberg. The leading poets of this period were Shlonsky, his disciples Alterman and Goldberg, and Uri Zvi Greenberg. They experimented with new rhythms and the spoken idiom. The leading prose writers of this period were Samuel Joseph Agnon and Haim Hazaz. Agnon's achievements are considered second only to Bialik's. Typical themes were an idealistic attitude toward Zionism and nostalgic recollections of European childhoods.

The establishment of the State of Israel begins the latest period of modern Hebrew literature. The writers of this generation were native speakers of Hebrew, most having been born in Palestine or emigrated as young children. They are less affected by Yiddish and European linguistic and cultural styles. Many were members of the *kibbutzim* (collective settlements) and favored the collective ideology rather than an individualistic one. By the late 1950s, some writers began to question the collective ideology and expressed their disillusionment through a new individualism and existentialism.

These Israeli writers spoke of the alienation of modern man and of a world becoming more secularized. Whether dealt with directly or appearing on a more subconscious level, the Holocaust became and is one of the major themes in modern Hebrew literature. The major source of spiritual struggle found in the works of Aaron Applefeld, Yonat Sened and Alexander Sened, Moshe Shamir, Hanokh Bartov, Amos Oz, A. B. Yehoshua, and Yehuda Amichai is the Holocaust. Only a small percent of Hebrew literature has been translated into book length form in English. Most of the English translations appear either in anthologies or in periodical literature. See Volume 4 for pre-nineteenth century works in philosophy and religion.

HISTORY AND CRITICISM

Chomsky, William. *Hebrew: The Eternal Language.* Jewish Pubns. 1975 pap. $5.95
Goell, Yohai. *Bibliography of Modern Hebrew Literature in English Translation.* Transaction Bks. 1968 $14.95 supplement Keter 1975 $8.95. An annual supplement is published by the Institute for the Translation of Hebrew Literature.

Halkin, Simon. *Modern Hebrew Literature: From the Enlightenment to the Birth of the State of Israel.* 1950. Schocken 1975 pap. $3.75. An excellent guide to trends and values in Hebrew literature from its beginnings to the 1940s.

Posner, R., and I. Ta-Shema. *The Hebrew Book: An Historical Survey.* Keter 1975 $30.00

Silberschlag, Eisig. *From Renaissance to Renaissance: Hebrew Literature.* Ktav 2 vols. 1971–77 ea. $25.00. Encyclopedic in its survey of Hebrew literature from the end of the medieval Spanish period through modern times. See also Leon I. Yudlik's *Escape into Siege* below.

Yudlik, Leon I. *Escape into Siege.* Fairleigh Dickinson Univ. Pr. 1974 o.p. A survey of contemporary Israeli literature from the 1940s to the early 1970s.
See also Eisig Silberschlag's *From Renaissance to Renaissance* above.

Zinberg, Israel. *A History of Jewish Literature.* Trans. and ed. by Bernard Martin, Ktav 12 vols. ea. $22.50. A monumental work tracing the development of Jewish literature from tenth-century Spain to nineteenth-century Russia. It deals with major Jewish writers of poetry, fiction, and drama, as well as contributors to other fields such as philosophy, history, the Bible, religious law, folklore, and legend.

ANTHOLOGIES

Bargad, Warren, and Stanley F. Chyet, eds. and trans. *Israeli Poetry: A Contemporary Anthology. Jewish Literature and Culture Ser.* Indiana Univ. Pr. 1985 $29.95. Includes a bibliography and index.

Burnshaw, Stanley, ed. *The Modern Hebrew Poem Itself.* Schocken 1960 pap. $5.95. Contains 69 transliterated Hebrew poems; the original Hebrew and literal English translations together with commentaries.

Carmi, T., ed. *The Penguin Book of Hebrew Verse.* Penguin bilingual ed. 1981 pap. $9.95; Viking 1981 $25.00. Winner of the Kenneth B. Smilen/Present Tense Literary Award (1982). This collection spans 4,000 years of Hebrew poetry from biblical verse and poems from the Talmud to the modern poets.

Davidson, Israel. *Thesaurus of Medieval Hebrew Poetry. Lib. of Jewish Class.* Ktav 4 vols. rev. ed. 1970 $150.00

Frank, Bernhard, trans. *Modern Hebrew Poetry.* Pref. by Nieh Hualing, Univ. of Iowa Pr. text ed. 1980 $20.00 pap. $9.95

Glazer, Myra, ed. *Burning Air and a Clear Mind: Contemporary Israeli Women Poets.* Ohio Univ. Pr. 1981 $17.95 pap. $8.95. A collection of works by 18 poets, who range in age from their twenties to their eighties, expressing a remarkably similar vision.

Kravitz, Nathaniel. *Three Thousand Years of Hebrew Literature: From the Earliest Time through the 20th Century.* Ohio Univ. Pr. (Swallow) 1971 $20.00

Lasker-Schuler, Else. *Hebrew Ballads and Other Poems. Jewish Poetry Ser.* Jewish Pubns. 1981 $10.95

Lelchuk, Alan, and Gershon Shaked, eds. *Eight Great Hebrew Short Novels.* New Amer. Lib. 1983 $7.95. Selected solely for their literary merit, these novels display the versatility of modern Hebrew literature. Included are works of U. N. Gnessin, Y. C. Brenner, Y. Shami, S. Y. Agnon, D. Fogel, Amos Oz, J. Knaz, and A. B. Yehoshua.

Leviant, Curt. *Masterpieces of Hebrew Literature: A Treasury of Two Thousand Years of*

Jewish Creativity. Ktav 1969 pap. $14.95. A comprehensive introduction to the mainstream of postbiblical literature.

Mezey, Robert, ed. *Poems from the Hebrew. Poems of the World Ser.* Crowell 1973 $11.49. Includes ancient poems, the poems of Moorish Spain (e.g., Samuel the Prince, Solomon Ibn Gabirol, Moses Ibn Ezra, Judah Halevi), and the modern poets (e.g., Bialik, S. Tchernichovski, Y. Fichman, N. Alterman, L. Goldberg, A. Gilboa, and Y. Amichai).

Michener, James A. *First Fruits: A Harvest of 25 Years of Israeli Writing.* Fwd. by Chaim Potok, Jewish Pubns. 1975 o.p. Fifteen tales representing the first 25 years of Israel's existence as a state, including stories by A. Barash, H. Hazaz, S. Y. Agnon, Amos Oz, and A. Megged.

Millgram, Abraham E. *An Anthology of Medieval Hebrew Literature.* Telegraph Bks. 1982 lib. bdg. $100.00. The collection is divided into the following categories: Poetry of Spain; Prayers; Hymns; Dirges; Ethical Literature; Zohar; Legal Literature; Travelers' Accounts; and Folk Tales.

Mintz, Ruth F., ed. *Modern Hebrew Poetry: A Bilingual Anthology.* Univ. of California Pr. 1982 pap. $9.95; Greenwood repr. of 1968 ed. 1982 lib. bdg. $42.50. "Excellent representatives of the Hebrew Literature of the late 19th and 20th centuries" (*LJ*).

Penueli, S. Y., and A. Ukhmani, eds. *Anthology of Modern Hebrew Poetry.* Keter 2 vols. 1975 pap. set $10.00. A fine selection made under the auspices of the Institute for the Translation of Hebrew Literature.

Schwartz, Howard, and Anthony Rudolf, eds. *Voices within the Ark: The Modern Jewish Poets.* Intro. by Laya Firestone, Avon 1983 pap. $15.95; Pushcart Pr. 1980 $39.50. A one-volume work of selections from the finest poetry written by Jewish poets since the turn of the century; approximately a fifth of the volume contains translated Hebrew poems.

AGNON, SAMUEL JOSEPH (pseud. of Samuel Josef Czaczkes). 1888–1970 (NOBEL PRIZE 1966)

Born in Galicia, in a home influenced by rabbinic and Hasidic traditions and the reviving spirit of European culture, Agnon began writing Hebrew and Yiddish at the age of eight. He contributed poetry and prose to periodicals, such as *Ha-Mizpeh* and *Der Juedische Wecker*. After he immigrated to Palestine in 1907, he no longer wrote in Yiddish. In 1914, he met Salman Schocken and convinced him that someone should undertake the publishing of Hebrew books. Many years later four volumes of Agnon's collected works in Hebrew were published by Berlin Schocken Verlag in 1931. Agnon was awarded the Bialik Prize for Literature in 1934, and in 1936 he was made an honorary doctor of Hebrew Letters by the Jewish Theological Seminary of America. Other honors followed, including the Israel Prize in 1954 and 1958, culminating in the Nobel Prize in 1966.

Agnon often deals with philosophical and psychological problems in a miraculous or supernatural manner. Reality is colored in a dreamlike atmosphere. Agnon is concerned with contemporary problems of a spiritual nature—the disintegration of traditional life, loss of faith and identity, and loneliness.

Creating a unique Hebrew prose style, his works link historic Jewish piety and martyrdom with longing for Israel, and yet they have universal appeal to the modern reader. Agnon himself has said: "I am not a modern writer. I am astounded that I even have one reader. I don't see the reader before me. . . . No, I see before me only the Hebrew letter saying 'write me thus and not thus.' I, to my regret, am like the wicked Balaam. It is written of him that 'the word that God putteth in my mouth, that shall I speak' " (*N.Y. Times*).

BOOKS BY AGNON

The Bridal Canopy. 1931. Trans. by I. M. Lask, Schocken 1967 pap. $8.95. Recognized as one of the cornerstones of modern Hebrew literature, this folk-epic established Agnon as a central writer.

A Simple Story. 1935. Trans. by Hillel Halkin, Schocken 1985 $14.95

In the Heart of the Seas: A Story of a Journey to the Land of Israel. 1947. Trans. by I. M. Lask, Schocken repr. of 1948 ed. 1980 pap. $4.95. The story of the pilgrimage to Palestine of Polish Jews in the early nineteenth century.

Days of Awe. 1948. Intro. by Judah Goldin, Schocken 1965 $8.95. A collection of traditions, legends, and learned commentaries concerning the Jewish High Holy Days.

Betrothed (and *Edo and Enam*). 1965. Trans. by Walter Lever, Schocken 1975 o.p. Two tales.

A Guest for the Night. 1968. Trans. by Misha Louvish, Schocken 1968 $10.00 1980 pap. $8.95. Written after Agnon revisited his home in Galicia in 1930. Agnon has the narrator describe the desolation time has wrought. Originally published in serial form in the magazine *Haaretz* from October 18, 1938 to April 7, 1939.

Twenty-one Stories. 1970. Ed. by Nahum N. Glatzer, Schocken 1971 $10.00 pap. $8.95

BOOKS ABOUT AGNON

Aberbach, David. *At the Handles of the Lock.* Oxford 1985 $29.95

Band, Arnold J. *Nostalgia and Nightmare: A Study in the Fiction of S. Y. Agnon.* Univ. of California Pr. 1968 $42.50. Includes a bibliography.

Fisch, Harold. *S. Y. Agnon. Lit. and Life Ser.* Ungar 1975 $12.95. An overview and informative critique of some of Agnon's work.

Hochman, Baruch. *The Fiction of S. Y. Agnon.* Cornell Univ. Pr. 1970 o.p.

AHAD HA-AM (pseud. of Asher Hirsch Ginzberg). 1856–1927

A self-taught thinker and Hebrew essayist, Ahad Ha-Am (meaning "One of the People") received a traditional Jewish education in his Hasidic home in Skvira, Kiev. Not being able to reconcile his modern rationalist thinking with Hasidism, he first abandoned that way of life and eventually all religious faith. Settling in Odessa in 1884, he became one of the leading members of the Hibbat Zion movement in Russia. Ahad Ha-Am developed an idea of Zionism that was not rooted in completely political ideals. While he did not agree with those who urged the establishment of a national Jewish homeland for the sake of obtaining the survival of many desperate Jews who suffered under the severity of czarist Russia, Ahad Ha-Am placed more emphasis on the need to create a national consciousness by cultural prepara-

tion through education. "Cultural Zionism" developed around the idea of a
Jewish state as the "spiritual center" for all Jews. As editor of *Ha-Shilo'ah*
(1896), the predominant monthly of Hebrew literature and Zionism in Eastern Europe, Ahad Ha-Am contributed to the development of Hebrew literature. After he settled in Palestine in 1922, Ahad Ha-Am continued to ex-
pound his ideas of spiritual and cultural revitalization. It was there that he
published his correspondence and memoirs.

Books by Ahad Ha-Am

Essays, Letters, Memoirs. Trans. and ed. by Leon Simon, East & West Lib. 1946 o.p.
Nationalism and the Jewish Ethic. Trans. by Leon Simon, ed. and intro. by Hans
    Kohn, Schocken 1962 o.p.
Selected Essays of Ahad Ha-Am. Ed. by Leon Simon, Atheneum repr. of 1912 ed. 1970
    pap. $8.95; ed. by Leon Simon, Jewish Pubns. pap. $4.95
Ten Essays on Zionism and Judaism. Ayer repr. of 1922 ed. $26.50

Books about Ahad Ha-Am

Ahad Ha-Am, Asher Ginzberg: A Biography. Jewish Pubns. 1960 o.p.
Kornberg, Jacques, ed. *At the Crossroads: Essays on Ahad Ha'am. Modern Jewish His-
    tory Ser.* State Univ. of New York Pr. 1983 $34.50 pap. $10.95

AMICHAI, YEHUDA. 1924–

Yehuda Amichai was born in Germany and immigrated to Palestine in
1936. His novels and poetry are innovative in their use of Hebrew terms. Following World War II and Israel's War of Independence in 1948, Amichai began to introduce new words of technical, legal, and administrative meaning
into his poetry to replace sacral phrases. His poetry reflects the modernizing of the Hebrew language within the last 45 years. "One of Amichai's most
characteristic effects in his poetry is the mingling of past and present, ancient and modern, person and place: the here and now for him inevitably recalls the past" (*Judaica Book News*). Amichai is one of Israel's most highly regarded poets and in 1981 he shared the Israel Prize for Literature with Amir
Gilboa.

Books by Amichai

Not of This Time, Not of This Place. 1963. Trans. by Shlomo Katz, Biblio Dist. 1973
    $15.00
Poems. Trans. by Assia Gutmann, intro. by Michael Hamburger, Harper 1969 o.p.
Songs of Jerusalem and Myself. 1973. Trans. by Harold Schimmel, Harper 1975 o.p.
    The translator received the Jewish Book Council's Kovner Award for Poetry in
    1974 for this volume, the second collection of his works in English.
Amen. Trans. by Yehuda Amichai and Ted Hughes, Harper 1977 $7.95 pap. $4.95
Travels of a Latter Day Benjamin of Tudela. Cauldron Pr. 1977 o.p.
Time. Trans. by Yehuda Amichai, Harper 1979 $10.53
Love Poems. Harper bilingual ed. 1981 $12.95 pap. $7.25. Poems of longing and sepa-
    ration gathered from earlier collections of the poet's works already published in
    English.
Great Tranquility: Questions and Answers. Trans. by Glenda Abramson and Tudor

Parfitt, Harper 1983 $12.02 pap. $7.64. Poetry reflecting the insights of a man coming to terms with his past.

The World Is a Room. Trans. by Elinor Grumet and others, Jewish Pubns. 1984 $13.95. "With this book—a collection of some of his most poignant short stories, all written in the 1950s—Amichai demonstrates once again that he has equal artistic dexterity in prose as well as poetry" (*Judaica Book News*). Included are stories that expose the conflicts of Israeli society and the struggle for humanity.

APPELFELD, AARON. 1932–

Deported to a concentration camp from his native town of Chernovtsy, Bukovina, Appelfeld immigrated to Palestine in 1947. Since 1959, his novels and stories have become widely recognized for their highly symbolic characterization around the central theme of the Holocaust. His literary work is not a historical retelling, but a remarkable fusion of despair and hope, weakness and strength, cowardice and courage.

BOOKS BY APPELFELD

Badenheim 1939. Trans. by Dalya Bilu, Godine 1980 $12.95; trans. by Dalya Bilu, Washington Square Pr. 1981 pap. $3.50. A novelization of the author's earlier story with the same title. It is "a novel rich in perception, clarity, and understanding of this difficult period" (*Judaica Book News*).

The Age of Wonders. Trans. by Dalya Bilu, Godine 1981 $12.95; Washington Square Pr. repr. 1983 pap. $3.95

Tzili: The Story of a Life. Trans. by Dalya Bilu, Dutton 1983 $12.95; Penguin 1984 pap. $4.95. A surreal novel about the Jewish spirit. Appelfeld's *Tzili* is a collective symbol of exile "particularly as it is expressed in the figure of a woman symbolic of the Jewish people betrothed to God" (*Judaica Book News*).

The Retreat. Trans. by Dalya Bilu, Dutton 1984 $12.95; *Penguin Fiction Ser.* 1985 pap. $5.95. A hotel retreat near Vienna is established to relieve Jews of their ethnic characteristics in order to assimilate into the general population. Escape from the world and from their identities proves to be an experiment in futility.

BARASH, ASHER. 1889–1952

Asher Barash is a major Hebrew novelist and short story writer of historical fiction. His works illustrate the traditional life of Galician Jewry, combining realism and a certain heartiness with a touch of mysticism. Like other authors who immigrated to Israel, his works exhibit a tension of living on two planes, the Diaspora and the Land of Israel.

BOOKS BY BARASH

Though He Slay Me. Trans. by Murray Rosten, Massada 1963 o.p. A collection of short stories.

A Golden Treasury of Jewish Tales. Trans. by Murray Rosten, Massada 1965 o.p. A collection of folklore.

Pictures from a Brewery. Trans. by Katie Kaplan, Bobbs 1974 o.p. A family saga set in a twentieth-century East Galician town in Poland. "The prose in translation is almost poetic; the style tends to offer the reader 'pictures' of people and places" (*AJL Bulletin*).

BARTOV, HANOCH. 1928–

Combining his journalist skills in reporting with his talents as a novelist, Bartov's fiction reflects the traumatic experience of the Holocaust. The Israeli novelist also wrote stories of his travels. He was a cultural attaché at the Israeli Embassy in London from 1966 to 1968.

BOOKS BY BARTOV

The Brigade (Wounds of Maturity). 1965. Trans. by David S. Segal, Holt 1969 o.p. Bartov sketches a portrait of a soldier, a member of the Jewish Brigade of the British Army in World War II, who confronts both the victims and victimizers of the Holocaust. The novel received the Shlonsky Prize and has received additional critical acclaim.

Whose Little Boy Are You? 1970. Trans. by Hillel Halkin, Jewish Pubns. 1979 $9.95. A story of a boy growing up in Palestine during the British Mandate Period. "Imbued with the mysticism of childhood—it is also full of the color of a small village distinctly resembling the author's own Petah Tikvah" (*AJL Bulletin*).

BERDICHEVSKY, MICHA JOSEPH (also known as Bin-Gorion). 1865–1921

This revolutionary figure in modern Hebrew literature rebelled against his Hasidic family of Medzibezh, Podolia, and advocated aestheticism and extreme secularism in Jewish life. He called for a "transvaluation" in the Nietzschean sense, of Judaism and Jewish history that led Hebrew contemporary critics to attach the name "Aher" ("the alien" or "the apostate") to him. Berdichevsky in turn showed little appreciation for outstanding contemporary literary figures. His prolific writings can be divided into four groups: essays, fiction, folklore anthologies, and scholarship. Berdichevsky's works embody the ambivalent attitudes of his time toward traditional Judaism and the European culture of the Jewish intellectuals.

BOOK BY BERDICHEVSKY

Mimekor Yisrael: Classical Jewish Folktales. Trans. by I. M. Lask, ed. by Micha J. Bin-Gorion and Emanuel Bin-Gorion, intro. by Dan Ben-Amos, Indiana Univ. Pr. 3 vols. 1976 $100.00. A collection of national, religious, folk, and oriental tales collected by Berdichevsky. Includes bibliography and index.

BIALIK, HAYYIM NACHMAN (also Chaim). 1873–1934

Born of humble parentage in the Ukraine, Bialik went to Odessa in 1891, where he was a teacher and a publisher. He was influenced by early Zionist ideas, particularly those of Ahad Ha-Am, and lived in various places in Europe, writing and teaching. By the time he settled in Tel Aviv, in 1924, his fame had become legendary. Bialik brought about a revolution in Hebrew poetry, avoiding European trends and drawing inspiration from early Hebrew literature. In prophetic, rhetorical poems of national revival, Bialik identified himself with the fate of his people and called upon Jews to express pride in their heritage and to resist the Russian pogroms. The crises of his generation were not his only themes, however; he wrote many lyric poems of a personal character and songs of nature. He also wrote short stories, translated works by such authors as CERVANTES, SHAKESPEARE, HEINRICH HEINE, and others into Hebrew, and wrote a variety of essays on Hebrew literature, language, style, and culture. Israel's highest literary prize and an Israeli publishing house are named for Bialik.

BOOKS BY BIALIK

Selected Poems. 1926. Ed. by I. Efros, Bloch 1965 o.p.; trans. by Maurice Samuel, Union of American Hebrew Congregations 1972 o.p. Reissue of translations that originally appeared in *New Palestine.*

And It Came to Pass. Hebrew Publishing 1938 $6.95. A collection of retold legends and stories of Kings David and Solomon.

BOOK ABOUT BIALIK

Kurzweil, Baruch. *Bialik and Tshernichovsky.* Schocken 1971 o.p.

BRENNER, JOSEPH HAYYIM. 1881–1921

A novelist and short story writer, Brenner drew upon his years of wandering after leaving his traditional home in Novi Mlini (Ukraine) to focus on the problem of the uprooted fugitives from traditional Judaism. He exposed the anxieties, self-probing, and despair of the self-doubting Jewish intelligentsia. Such despair, ironically, infused his readers with a new creative life. Brenner is viewed as exercising powerful personal influence on his generation and the succeeding one. He was killed during the riots in the spring of 1921 near Tel Aviv.

BOOK BY BRENNER

Breakdown and Bereavement. Trans. by Hillel Halkin, Jewish Pubns. 1975 o.p. This is the last novel written by Brenner. It tells the story of Hefez, who searches for a spiritual home in Palestine. The setting is an agricultural settlement prior to World War I, where many of Brenner's uprooted generation attempted to create a new life for themselves, having left their European ties behind.

BOOK ABOUT BRENNER

Fleck, Jeffrey. *Character and Context: Studies in the Fiction of Abramovitsh, Brenner and Agnon.* Scholars Pr. 1984 pap. $14.00

CARMI, T. (pseud. of Carmi Charny). 1925–

Born in New York City, Carmi grew up in a home where Hebrew was the mother tongue. Having lived as a child in Palestine, he immigrated in 1947. He has taught at Brandeis, Oxford, and Stanford, and was poet-in-residence at the Hebrew University of Jerusalem. Carmi has published ten volumes of poetry in Hebrew. Thus far, three of these works have appeared in English translation. In Israel, he was awarded the Shlonsky Prize for Poetry, the Brenner Prize for Literature, and the Prime Minister's Award for Creative Writing. He was also awarded the 1982 Irving and Bertha Neuman Literary Award of New York University's Institute of Hebrew Culture and Education and the 1982 Kenneth B. Smilen/Present Tense Literary Award for his translation and editing work for *The Penguin Book of Hebrew Verse.*

BOOKS BY CARMI

The Brass Serpent. Trans. by Dom Moraes, Ohio Univ. Pr. 1964 o.p.
Selected Poems of T. Carmi and Dan Pagis. Trans. by Stephen Mitchell, intro. by
    W. L. Rosenthal, Penguin 1976 o.p.
The Penguin Book of Hebrew Verse. Viking 1981 $25.00
At the Stone of Losses. Jewish Pubns. 1983 $13.95; trans. by Grace Schulman, *Jewish
    Poetry Ser.* Univ. of California Pr. bilingual ed. 1983 $13.95 pap. $8.95

FEIERBERG (FEUERBERG), MORDECAI ZEEB. 1874–1899

Born in Russia, Feierberg wrote essays and novels in Hebrew. *Whither?* is
regarded as one of the outstanding achievements in Hebrew fiction.

BOOK BY FEIERBERG

Whither? and Other Stories. Trans. by Hillel Halkin, Jewish Pubns. 1973 $4.95. Re-
    lates the struggles of Eastern European Jewish youths who are disappointed
    with the Enlightenment, yet not content with being traditional Jews.

GILBOA, AMIR. 1917–

Born in Radzywilow, Volhynia (Russia), Gilboa immigrated to Palestine
in 1937. His poetry was first published while serving in the Jewish Brigade
during World War II. His verse blends personal and national motifs reminiscent of Bialik. Gilboa is able to use various levels of language to create a
freshness in his poems of ancient words with the wonder of new experiences. He is considered a leading Israeli poet. In 1981 he shared the Israel
Prize for Literature with Yehuda Amichai.

BOOK BY GILBOA

The Light of Lost Sons. Trans. by Shirley Kaufman with Shlomith Rimmon, Persea
    1979 $10.00 pap. $4.95. Anthology of selected poems.

GOLDBERG, LEAH. 1911–1970

A Lithuanian-born Palestinian poetess and critic, Goldberg arrived in Tel
Aviv in 1935. Shortly afterward, she published her first volume of poetry
with the assistance of Abraham Shlonsky, her mentor, and the mentor of a
circle of other modernist authors. A prolific writer, Goldberg primarily
wrote poetry, but she also wrote several children's works, translated European classics into Hebrew, and was the author of a novel and a play. Her approach to writing was universal and only after the Holocaust did she write
from within a Jewish framework.

BOOKS BY GOLDBERG

Lady of the Castle. Trans. by T. Carmi, Institute for the Translation of Hebrew Lit.
    1974 o.p. A revision of *Lady of the Manor* (1957) also translated by T. Carmi.
Selected Poems of Leah Goldberg. 1976. Trans. by Robert Friend, fwd. by Yehuda
    Amichai, afterword by Gershom Scholem, Panjandrum 1977 pap. $4.50
Russian Literature in the Nineteenth Century. Trans. by Hillel Halkin, Humanities Pr.
    1976 $18.50

HAZAZ, HAIM. 1898–1973

Born in Kiev, Russia, Haim Hazaz moved to Palestine in 1921. His early works are based on themes of village life among European Jews during crucial changes that uprooted the foundations of Jewish existence. However, he is not restricted in era or location in his writings. His fiction encompasses wide geographic, historic, and ethnographic variations, from stories on the biblical period to works dealing with Yemenite and other oriented and nonoriented Jewish settlements in Israel. Hazaz is ranked among the greatest Hebrew authors. He was awarded the Israel Prize for Literature in 1953.

BOOKS BY HAZAZ

Mori Sa'id. Trans. by Ben Halpern, Abelard-Schuman 1956 o.p.

Gates of Bronze. Intro. by Robert Alter, Jewish Pubns. 1975 $7.95. A novel set in a fictional village in Russia during the crisis faced by the Jews who experienced the Bolshevik Revolution.

The End of Days. Trans. by Dalya Bilu, Institute for the Translation of Hebrew Lit. 1982 o.p.

BOOK ABOUT HAZAZ

Bargad, Warren. *Ideas in Fiction: The Works of Hayim Hazaz.* Scholars Pr. 1982 pap. $13.50

KANIUK, YORAM. 1930–

A native Israeli, Kaniuk served in the Haganah and later in the War of Independence. He was in the United States from 1950 to 1961, sharpened his artistic abilities, and developed a nostalgic vision of Tel Aviv and a deep attachment for Jerusalem. He has been called the incurable romantic in love with absurdity projected by bizarre characters.

BOOKS BY KANIUK

The Acrophile. 1960. Trans. by Zeva Shapiro, Atheneum 1961 o.p. A collection of short stories.

Himmo, King of Jerusalem. Trans. by Yosef Shacter, Atheneum 1969 o.p.

Adam Resurrected. 1971. Harper repr. 1978 pap. $4.95

Rockinghorse. Trans. by Richard Flantz, Harper 1977 $12.50. "Eloquent in its descriptive passages" (*AJL Bulletin*).

The Story of Great Aunt Shlomzion. 1978. Trans. by Zeva Shapiro, Harper 1979 $10.95

KISHON, EPHRAIM (formerly Ferenc Kishont). 1924–

An Israeli satirist, playwright, film writer, and director, Kishon is best known in the English-speaking world for his feuilletons. Born in Budapest, Kishon first began publishing humorous essays there. In 1949 he immigrated to Israel and began his columns in the Hebrew daily newspaper *Omer* and later in the daily *Ma'ariv* and the *Jerusalem Post*. Kishon is considered Israel's national humorist. He has been awarded the Israeli Nordau Prize, the Herzl Prize for Literature, and the Sokolov Prize for outstanding journalistic achievement.

BOOKS BY KISHON

Look Back, Mrs. Lot! 1960. Trans. by Yohanan Goldman, Penguin 1964 o.p.

Blow Softly in Jericho. Trans. by Yohanan Goldman, Atheneum 1970 o.p.

Wise Guy, Solomon. Trans. by Yohanan Goldman, Atheneum 1973 o.p. "Kishon continues to carry on his private war with the telephone, TV, taxes, traffic, politics, and women's fashions, to name a few of the targets of his freewheeling, wildly improbable response to the late twentieth century" (Jacket notes).

New York Ain't America. Trans. by Miriam Arad and Yohanan Goldman, Bantam 1982 o.p.

MEGGED, AHARON. 1920–

Megged's family immigrated to Palestine from Wloclavek, Poland, in 1926. Until 1950 he worked on a kibbutz in Haifa. His first short story collection, *Sea Winds* (o.p.), was inspired by his life on kibbutz Sedot Yam. His prose often shows strong autobiographical emphasis. Megged's stories and novels have been translated into many languages.

BOOKS BY MEGGED

Fortunes of a Fool. 1960. Trans. by Aubrey Hodes, Random 1962 o.p. The antihero, tortured by thoughts of his shortcomings and terrified of ridicule, perceives himself the only "good man" among a society of "wicked."

The Living on the Dead. 1970. Trans. by Misha Louvish, McCall 1971 o.p. Describes modern Israeli society in unflattering terms as the unfulfilled society of the first pioneers.

The Short Life: A Novel. Trans. by Miriam Arad, Taplinger 1980 $10.95

Asahel. 1980. Trans. by Robert Whitehill and Susan C. Lilly, Taplinger 1982 $11.95. "The beauty and fine quality of this novel come from the superb characterizations of the three main characters, and the many beautifully drawn surrounding portraits" (*Judaica Book News*).

OZ, AMOS. 1939–

A native Israeli, Oz was the first contemporary Israeli writer to earn an international reputation through his writing. His stories and novels are rooted in the rich life of Israel, frequently revealing a fondness for realistically conveyed history handled with graceful manipulation of plot and character, style, and mood.

BOOKS BY OZ

My Michael. Trans. by Nicholas de Lange, Random 1975 o.p.

Touch the Water, Touch the Wind. Trans. by Nicholas de Lange, Harcourt 1974 $9.95

Unto Death: "Crusade" and "Late Love." Harcourt 1975 $6.95 1978 pap. $3.95. These novellas depict the atmosphere of hate in which Jews live today and as they did in the Middle Ages.

The Hill of Evil Counsel. Harcourt 1978 $7.95. The fading days of the British Mandate in Jerusalem are recreated as the plot advances to the planning for the future and the anticipated revolt leading to the State of Israel. The title story along with the two other stories, *Mr. Levi* and *Longing*, complete this volume.

Elsewhere Perhaps. Trans. by Nicholas de Lange, Harcourt 1973 $7.95 1985 pap. $5.95. Oz captures the essence of kibbutz life in Metsudat, Ram, near the Syrian border in the Golan Heights. He "portrays human relationships movingly, yet with detached, unsentimental realism" (*AJL Bulletin*).

Soumchi. Trans. by Penelope Farmer, Harper 1981 $8.79

Where the Jackals Howl and Other Stories. Trans. by Nicholas de Lange and Philip Simpson, Harcourt 1981 $12.95. As many of his generation, Oz saw the Arab presence as an evil menace. In this volume, the first collection of his stories, the jackal is symbolic of the dispenser of death.

In the Land of Israel. Trans. by Maurie Goldberg-Bartura, Harcourt 1983 $12.95; Random (Vintage) 1984 pap. $5.95. Interviews conducted by Oz with people in all echelons of Israel's society accompanied by his observations and reflections.

A Perfect Peace. Trans. by Hillel Halkin, Harcourt 1985 $16.95. Set on a kibbutz in the mid-1960s, this novel focuses on the immigrant generation that built the country and the following generation making their lives there. "Oz has managed to describe in great detail kibbutz life and the changing ideals from one generation to the next, while detailing the search which every person undergoes at some time in his life. An excellent picture of life in Israel on the kibbutz" (*AJL Newsletter*).

PAGIS, DAN. 1930–

Dan Pagis is a survivor of the Holocaust. Born in Rumania in 1930, he lived through three years in a concentration camp, arrived in Israel in 1946, and now lives in Jerusalem where he is a professor of medieval Hebrew literature at the Hebrew University. As a scholar, Pagis has established himself by publishing distinguished editions of medieval Hebrew poetry. One of the leading poets of this generation, he has mastered and applied the tools of textual criticism to medieval Hebrew poetry. The mastery of the idiom shows itself in his own poems that echo the poets of Spain's Golden Age, such as Judah Halevi, Solomon Ibn Gabirol, and Moses Ibn Ezra. The Holocaust is the outstanding influence in his work. Imaginatively, "his art mirrors the agony of the survivor, resounds with the pangs and poetry of Jewish history, and grapples with genocide, grief, survival, and an attempt to perceive redemption" (*Judaica Book News*).

BOOKS BY PAGIS

Selected Poems. Trans. by Stephen Mitchell, Small Pr. Dist. repr. 1972 pap. $3.50

Selected Poems of T. Carmi and Dan Pagis. Trans. by Stephen Mitchell, intro. by W. L. Rosenthal, Penguin 1976 o.p.

Points of Departure. 1981. Trans. by Stephen Mitchell, intro. by Robert Alter, *Jewish Poetry Ser.* Jewish Pubns. bilingual ed. 1982 $12.95 pap. $8.95. More than 50 poems with English and Hebrew on facing pages.

SHAHAM, NATHAN. 1925–

Born in Tel Aviv, Shaham served in the Palmah and later in the War of Independence. He joined kibbutz Bet Alfa in the 1950s. He has written fiction, plays, and children's stories.

BOOK BY SHAHAM

The Other Side of the Wall: Three Novellas. Trans. by Leonard Gold, Jewish Pubns. 1983 $13.95. "The three tales in the present collection *S/S Cairo City, The Other*

Side of the Wall, and *The Salt of the Earth* offer vivid refractions of Israeli society as experienced through the prism of the kibbutz" (*Judaica Book News*).

SHAHAR, DAVID. 1926–

A fifth generation native of the land of Israel, Shahar is rooted in the sights and sounds of Jerusalem. Few writers can capture as well the multiple ethnicity of the inhabitants of that ancient city. As a writer he is compelling. He has published 15 books, 5 of which have appeared in English or French translation. Shahar received the coveted Prix Médicis for the best foreign literature of the year in 1981 for *Day of the Countess,* the third volume in his trilogy *The Palace of Shattered Vessels.*

Books by Shahar

News from Jerusalem. Trans. by Dalya Bilu and others, Houghton Mifflin 1974 o.p.
    Stories recreating city life in Jerusalem and its people during the past 60 years.
The Palace of Shattered Vessels. Trans. by Dalya Bilu, Houghton Mifflin 1975 o.p.
His Majesty's Agent. Trans. by Dalya Bilu, Harcourt 1980 $14.95. A compelling love
    story as well as an evocation of life in Mandate Palestine and the new State of Israel.

SHAMIR, MOSHE. 1921–

Born in Safed and raised in Tel Aviv, Shamir is a writer of novels, plays, short stories, and contemporary comment. His early works showed strong interest in the human concerns of social and national problems. As he begins to criticize his heroes' motives, he turns his attention to the psychological and social issues facing Israeli society. At one point, Shamir declared that history had usurped the place of religion in Jewish life, so although committed to Israeli life, he frequently returns to the times of the first and second commonwealth. He shows strong narrative talent, writing in a high literary style with elaborate descriptions and dialogues.

Books by Shamir

The King of Flesh and Blood. Trans. by David Patterson, Hebrew Publishing 1958
    pap. $5.95. The original Hebrew version was issued in ten editions.
The Fifth Wheel. Benmir Bks. repr. of 1961 ed. 1986 pap. $8.95
My Life with Ishmael. Biblio Dist. 1970 $18.00
The Hittite Must Die. Trans. by Margaret Benaya, Hebrew Publishing repr. of 1964
    ed. 1978 pap. $5.95

TAMMUZ, BENJAMIN. 1919–

A native of Kharkov, Russia, Tammuz immigrated to Palestine in 1924. He attended a yeshiva in Tel Aviv while also studying at the Herzlia secondary school. He worked as a laborer in the British army camps and was a member of the Palmah. His work as a journalist involved assignments as a press censor for the Mandatory Government and as a reporter for a political party newspaper and later as the editor of the weekend literary supplement of *Haaretz.* His earliest works were short stories of his childhood focusing on the roots of Israeli life. His subsequent novels reflect the theme of social criticism.

BOOKS BY TAMMUZ

Castle in Spain. Trans. by Joseph Shacter, Bobbs 1973 o.p.

Minotaur. Trans. by Kim Parfitt and Mildred Budny, New Amer. Lib. 1981 $11.95 1982 pap. $1.50. "The writing is spare and evocative of another era, a tribute to the translators. A beautiful work" (*AJL Newsletter*).

Requiem for Na'aman. Trans. by Mildred Budny and Yehuda Safran, New Amer. Lib. 1982 $12.95. Spanning the years from 1895 to 1974, the novel dramatizes the counterpoint between sensitive individuals coming to terms with reality and the political emergence of the modern Israeli state.

TCHERNICHOVSKI (TCHERNICHOWSKY), SAUL. 1875–1943

The great modern Hebrew poet grew up in a pious home that was open to the influences of the Haskalah and Hibbat Zion. The religious and secular education he received in his native village of Mikhailovka, Russia, was a source of inspiration to him. His further education in Odessa included the works of the great contemporary poets of his time and also Hebrew literary circles. Tchernichovski published his first poems in 1892, which were characterized by a variety of classical poetic forms. Tchernichovski's poetic works show the strong influences of various periods of his life. From 1905 to 1922, he was strongly influenced by the works of Goethe and Nietzsche. The earlier romantic tendencies of his poetry are replaced by outspoken and universalistic views of life. His personal experiences during World War I and the Bolshevik Revolution left a deep imprint on him. He left for Berlin where his literary work provided a meager living. The Zionist General Council published a ten-volume jubilee edition of his works (1928–34) as a mark of appreciation to him. The years from 1931 to 1943 are considered his Eretz Israel Period. It was there that his lifelong relationship with Schocken Publishing developed. He later moved from Tel Aviv to Jerusalem where he lived the remainder of his life. While Tchernichovski's earlier works were ingrained toward universalism and humanism, his later works proved him to be the poet of the historic Jewish tragedy, the simplicity of Jewish folk life, and the Jewish national rebirth.

BOOK BY TCHERNICHOVSKI

Poems. Trans. by David Kuselewitz, Eked 1978 o.p.

BOOK ABOUT TCHERNICHOVSKI

Silberschlag, Eisig. *Saul Tschernichovsky: Poet of Revolt.* Cornell Univ. Pr. 1968 o.p. This is the most important study of Tchernichovski produced in English. It contains translations by Sholom J. Kahn and others as well as a bibliography.

YEHOSHUA, A(BRAHAM) B. 1936–

Born in Jerusalem, Yehoshua served in the Israeli army and eventually settled in Haifa. Like Amos Oz, his fiction and dramatic works show a subtlety of portraiture and semisurrealist style that place them in the forefront of modern Israeli literature and his popularity among the English reading public continues to grow. He has been called a visionary in writer's garb.

BOOKS BY YEHOSHUA

Three Days and a Child. Trans. by Miriam Arad, Doubleday 1970 o.p. A collection of short stories including "A Poet's Continuing Silence," "Three Days and a Child," "Facing the Forests," "Flood Tide," and "A Long Hot Day, His Despair, His Wife, and His Daughter."

A Night in May. Trans. by Miriam Arad, Institute for the Translation of Hebrew Lit. 1974 o.p. Yehoshua confronts the fates of individuals with the fate of the nation on the eve of the Six Day War.

Early in the Summer of 1970. Doubleday 1977 o.p. A collection of short stories focusing on the emotional violence that pervades the life of the people in Israel. "A very thoughtful picture of life in a beleaguered land" (*AJL Bulletin*).

The Lover. Doubleday 1978 $10.00. Written against the background of the Yom Kippur War, the novel tells of a husband's search for his wife's lover. Each of the main characters is fully developed and the scenes of Israel are vividly portrayed.

Between Right and Right. Doubleday 1981 $11.95. Yehoshua examines the old myths and new realities of Israel in this collection of essays on Zionism. "This is indeed a thought-provoking and challenging book" (*Judaica Book News*).

Late Divorce. Doubleday 1984 $16.95; Dutton 1985 pap. $9.95. A novel about nine days in the lives of the turbulent Kaminka family. The climax of their struggles is an allegory of the modern Israeli condition.

ZACH, NATHAN. 1930–

Originally from Berlin, Zach's family immigrated to Palestine in 1935. He has been known since the mid-1950s as the leader of a Hebrew modernistic revolution. Although he is a major Israeli poet and has received the Bialik Prize, he is not as widely known as Yehuda Amichai. The majority of his works have yet to appear in English.

BOOK BY ZACH

The Static Element, Selected Poems. Trans. by Nathan Zach and Shulamit Yasny-Starkman, Atheneum 1982 $12.95 pap. $7.95

CHAPTER 19

Spanish American Literature

Frank Dauster

The writer proposes symbols. The meaning of those symbols, or the moral
which can be drawn from them, is a matter for critics and readers, and not
the writer.

—JORGE LUIS BORGES, *El escritor y su obra*

The long period of domination of Latin America by Spain and Portugal, lasting until the early nineteenth century, created cultural and economic dependence on the mother countries. The first writings to come from the New
World were the chronicles of explorers. Almost from the Conquest, there
was literary activity, primarily poetry that reflected the currents dominant
in Spain and a theater of religious proselytizing. Although strict prohibi-
tions prevented the importation of fiction, prose romances circulated
widely. Still, there was no creative fiction until the eighteenth century.

The seventeenth and eighteenth centuries were dominated by an extremely mannered baroque style characterized by intricate wordplay and
formal structures, although many cultivated writers also wrote in Indian
languages. By the late eighteenth century, French rationalism exercised a
profound effect. The entire period, with certain major exceptions, was relatively barren of original literary work, with one notable exception—the
Mexican lyric poet and dramatist Sor Juana Inés de la Cruz. The South
American continent developed intellectual autonomy more slowly than did
Mexico, due to the extraordinary distances and difficulty of communication,
but Peru boasts a rich colonial tradition of satiric poetry.

Although still culturally dependent on Europe at the beginning of the
nineteenth century, a uniquely Latin American culture was being created
through the mixture of various ethnic groups, the confrontation with an immense and unique landscape, and the development of native traditions. The
literature of the early nineteenth century was quite naturally preoccupied
with the subjects of revolution and patriotism, as José Joaquín Olmedo's
The Victory of Junín: Song to Bolívar. The end of Spanish domination, however, brought to many countries dictatorships almost as oppressive as European rule. The literary figures of the mid-nineteenth century were largely
concerned with political and social problems. Many writers were exiled for
their outspoken defense of liberty or political beliefs. At the same time,
some were beginning to recognize growing U.S. imperialism as a problem

637

that replaced European colonialism. Possibly due to the need for expressing such ideas, and certainly as a result of the conflict with an overwhelming and varied natural world, the literature of the mid-nineteenth century tended to the essay, diary, realistic novel, and *costumbrismo*, or the sketch of local customs.

This dependence on and preoccupation with everyday realities should not be exaggerated. Modernism, the aesthetic movement that revolutionized twentieth-century Spanish letters, had its origin in Spanish America, and it was introduced into Spain by Rubén Darío. Although in its origins modernism was a blending of French symbolism and Parnassianism, by the beginning of the twentieth century most modernists had developed a strong interest in hemispheric themes. Few writers concerned themselves any longer with the ideal of "art for art's sake." With this event, Spanish American literature may be said to have achieved true independence.

Social and political conditions of the early twentieth century, symbolized by the Mexican Revolution (1910–20), had a profound impact on literature. The violence and suffering of the Revolution and the upheavals that followed it were interpreted in the subgenre known as the "novel of the Revolution." The two world wars, which brought both alliance with and dependence on the United States, and the Spanish civil war (1936–39) had a profound effect on Spanish America in every way; the latter severed the sentimental attachment to Spain that still remained and brought an influx of political refugees who influenced and enriched Spanish American literature. The result has been a period of innovation and creativity. Since World War II an original style best described as magic realism or suprarealism, the integration of the real and the fantastic, has renewed the novel, making it a viable form in Spanish America when it appears to have been exhausted in Europe.

Spanish American literature has been recognized as a major literature and the number of translations of Latin American works is burgeoning; it is impossible to list them all. A number of university presses and several commercial publishers have extensive lists of Spanish American works, and more are appearing at a regular rate. At the same time, translations tend to be very recent works of immediate interest; it is deplorable that such writers as Vicente Huidobro, Alfonsina Storni, José Lezama Lima, and Elena Garro, to mention only a few, should be all but unknown in the English-speaking world. Although the principal bibliographies are out of print, they are readily available in reference libraries, and *Review* and the *Handbook of Latin American Studies* are important additional sources.

LITERARY CRITICISM AND HISTORY

Aldrich, Earl M., Jr. *Modern Short Story in Peru.* Univ. of Wisconsin Pr. 1966 $25.00.
    Includes short excerpts in English and Spanish.
Anderson-Imbert, Enrique. *Spanish American Literature: A History.* Trans. by John V.
    Falconieri, Wayne State Univ. Pr. 2 vols. 2d ed. rev. & enl. 1963 pap. ea. $5.95.

An extraordinarily complete study by an Argentine writer of "keen critical abilities" (*LJ*).

Brotherston, Gordon. *The Emergence of the Latin American Novel*. Cambridge Univ. Pr. 1977 $29.95 text ed. pap. $10.95. A general introduction, including Brazil, and chapters on Arguedas, Asturias, Carpentier, Cortázar, García Márquez, Onetti, Rulfo, and Vargas Llosa.

———. *Images of the New World: The American Continent Portrayed in Native Texts*. Thames & Hudson 1982 $10.95

———. *Latin American Poetry*. Cambridge Univ. Pr. 1975 $39.50 pap. $9.95. An excellent historical introduction.

Brushwood, John S. *Mexico in Its Novel: A Nation's Search for Identity*. Texas Pan-Amer. Ser. Univ. of Texas Pr. 1966 $17.50 pap. $8.95. "A revealing analysis for academic and large public libraries" (*LJ*). Includes an extensive list of novels by date.

———. *The Spanish American Novel: A Twentieth Century Survey*. Texas Pan-Amer. Ser. Univ. of Texas Pr. 1975 $20.00. The best reference source for the field.

Collins, James A. *Contemporary Theater in Puerto Rico: The Decade of the Seventies*. Intro. by Manuel Méndez Ballester, Univ. of Puerto Rico Pr. 1982 pap. $30.00. Collection of reviews and newspaper pieces.

DeCosta, Miriam, ed. *Blacks in Hispanic Literature: Critical Essays*. Associated Faculty Pr. 1976 $15.00. An informative overview of an important topic.

Donoso, José. *The Boom in Spanish American Literature: A Personal History*. Trans. by Gregory Kolovakos, intro. by Ronald Christ, Columbia Univ. Pr. 1977 $16.00. Highly personal view of recent literature by one of its most original and idiosyncratic voices.

Englekirk, John E., and others. *An Outline History of Spanish American Literature*. Irvington 4th ed. text ed. 1981 pap. $12.95. A useful introductory guide with extensive bibliographies of suggested reading, editions, translations, and critical references for each author.

Fein, John M. *Modernismo in Chilean Literature: The Second Period*. Duke Univ. Pr. 1965 $10.75. A historical account of the development of the theoretical bases of modernism.

Fernández Moreno, César, Julio Ortega, and Ivan A. Schulman, eds. *Latin America in Its Literature*. Trans. by Mary G. Berg, Holmes & Meier 1980 $49.50. A good background in social and literary history for recent developments in literature.

Foster, David W. *Currents in the Contemporary Argentine Novel: Arlt, Mallea, Sábato, and Cortázar*. Univ. of Missouri Pr. 1975 $13.00. Chapter 1 outlines the history of the Argentine novel before the authors discussed began to write, and the final chapter discusses more recent novels; includes a substantial bibliography.

———. *Studies in the Contemporary Spanish-American Short Story*. Univ. of Missouri Pr. 1979 $15.50. Structuralist analyses of stories by Benedetti, Borges, Cabrera Infante, Cortázar, García Márquez, and Rulfo in the vein of recent European criticism.

Foster, David W., and Virginia R. Foster, eds. *Modern Latin American Literature*. Lib. of Literary Criticism Ser. Ungar 2 vols. 1975 $120.00. Selections from reviews and critical articles on works by twentieth-century Latin American authors, including Brazilian writers; an excellent reference book.

Franco, Jean. *Introduction to Spanish American Literature*. Cambridge Univ. Pr. 1969 $42.50. A comprehensive, relatively difficult history of Spanish American literature beginning with colonial times.

Freudenthal, Juan R., Jeffrey Katz, and Patricia M. Freudenthal. *Index to Anthologies of Latin American Literature in English Translation.* G. K. Hall 1977 lib. bdg. $20.00. In addition to indexing 116 anthologies, provides bibliographies for further reading in history, criticism, and essay.

Gallagher, D. F., and Nathan Milton. *Modern Latin American Literature.* Oxford 1973 $10.95 pap. $3.95

González Peña, Carlos. *History of Mexican Literature.* 1960. Ed. by Gusta Barfield Nance and Florence J. Dustan, Southern Methodist Univ. Pr. 3d ed. 1968 $15.00 pap. $6.95

Guibert, Rita, ed. *Seven Voices: Pablo Neruda, Jorge Luis Borges, Miguel Angel Asturias, Octavio Paz, Julio Cortázar, Gabriel García Márquez, Guillermo Cabrera Infante.* Knopf 1972 $12.50. Interviews with Pablo Neruda, Jorge Luis Borges, Miguel Angel Asturias, Octavio Paz, Julio Cortázar, Gabriel García Márquez, and Guillermo Cabrera Infante; a very good reference source.

Handbook of Latin American Studies. Univ. Pr. of Florida repr. of 1935–48 ed. 1963 vols. 1–14 ea. $20.00–$25.00; 1956 1958 1961–79 vols. 22, 24, 27–40 ea. $25.00–$47.50; Octagon repr. of 1949–55 1957 1959–1960 eds. vols. 15–21, 23, 25–26 ea. $35.00; Univ. of Texas Pr. 1980–86 vols. 41–46 ea. $65.00. An annual comprehensive, critical bibliography, begun in 1935 by Harvard University Press and edited by noted scholars, has now been reorganized into two volumes—social sciences and humanities—published in alternate years. Includes a thorough section on translations of literary works.

Harss, Luis, and Barbara Dohmann. *Into the Mainstream: Conversations with Latin American Writers.* Harper 1967 o.p. Valuable reference source that discusses Carpentier, Asturias, Borges, Cortázar, Guimarães Rosa, Onetti, Rulfo, Fuentes, García Márquez, and Vargas Llosa.

Langford, Walter M. *The Mexican Novel Comes of Age.* Univ. of Notre Dame Pr. 1971 $19.95 pap. $3.95. A useful study of modern Mexican novelists.

Levine, Suzanne Jill. *Latin American Fiction and Poetry in Translation.* Interbk. 1970 pap. $1.25. A bibliographic reference work.

MacAdam, Albert J. *Modern Latin American Narrative: The Dreams of Reason.* Univ. of Chicago Pr. 1977 $10.95

Menton, Seymour. *Magic Realism Rediscovered, 1917–1981.* Art Alliance 1982 $29.50. The source of a much-used term often applied to Latin American fiction.

———. *Prose Fiction of the Cuban Revolution.* Latin Amer. Monographs Univ. of Texas Pr. 1975 $20.00. The author's purpose in this extensive study is to record and classify the more than 200 volumes of novels and short stories published in Cuba between 1959 and 1975.

Miller, Yvette, and Charles Tatum. *Latin American Women Writers: Yesterday and Today.* Latin Amer. Literary Review Pr. 1977 $7.50

Morris, Robert J. *The Contemporary Peruvian Theater.* Texas Tech Pr. 1977 pap. $6.00. Covers 1946 to the 1970s.

Paz, Octavio. *The Labyrinth of Solitude: Life and Thought in Mexico.* Trans. by Rebecca Philips, Grove (Evergreen) 1985 $22.50. Complementary essays, published some years apart, by one of Spanish America's outstanding poets and intellectuals, that examine the psychology and the creativity of the Mexicans.

Peden, Margaret S., ed. *The Latin American Short Story: A Critical History. Twayne's Critical History of the Modern Short Story Ser.* G. K. Hall 1983 lib. bdg. $18.95

Ramos, Samuel. *Profile of Man and Culture in Mexico.* Trans. by Peter G. Earle, intro. by T. B. Irving, *Texas Pan-Amer. Ser.* Univ. of Texas Pr. 1962 $12.50 pap. $5.95. In this Mexican classic, a philosopher, critic, and professor attempts to explore Mexican culture through the use of Adlerian psychoanalysis.

Schwartz, Kessel. *A New History of Spanish American Fiction.* Univ. Pr. of Miami 2 vols. 1972 ea. $18.95

Schwartz, Ronald. *Nomads, Exiles, and Emigrés: The Rebirth of the Latin American Narrative, 1960–80.* Scarecrow Pr. 1980 $16.00. General introduction with useful bibliographies.

Shaw, Bradley A. *Latin American Literature in English, 1975–1978.* Center for Inter-Amer. Relations 1979 o.p. Supplements the following volume.

———. *Latin American Literature in English Translation: An Annotated Bibliography.* New York Univ. Pr. 1976 $17.75. A good reference source.

Souza, Raymond D. *Major Cuban Novelists: Innovation and Tradition.* Univ. of Missouri Pr. 1976 $20.00. Carpentier, Lezama Lima, and Cabrera Infante.

Terry, Edward D., ed. *Artists and Writers in the Evolution of Latin America.* Univ. of Alabama Pr. 1969 $14.75. Critical essays on Miguel Angel Asturias, Euclydes da Cunha, social protest in the Spanish American novel, art and life in Mexico, José Mariátegui, and Chilean politics.

Unger, Roni J. *Poesía in Voz Alta in the Theater of Mexico.* Univ. of Missouri Pr. text ed. 1981 $18.00

Urbanski, Edmund S. *Hispanic America and Its Civilization.* Trans. by Frances K. Hendricks and Beatrice Berler, Univ. of Oklahoma Pr. 1979 $17.95

Wilgus, A. Curtis. *Latin America, Spain and Portugal: A Selected and Annotated Bibliographical Guide to Books Published 1954–1974.* Scarecrow Pr. 1977 $50.00

Zea, Leopoldo. *The Latin American Mind.* Trans. by James H. Abbott and Lowell Dunham, Univ. of Oklahoma Pr. 1970 pap. $8.95. An eminent Mexican philosopher traces the rise of positivism as the aftermath of romanticism; an important work.

COLLECTIONS

Armand, Octavio, ed. *Toward an Image of Latin American Poetry.* Longbridge-Rhodes 1982 $14.00 pap. $7.00

Bierhorst, John, ed. and trans. *Black Rainbow: Legends of the Incas and Myths of Ancient Peru.* Farrar 1976 $9.95

Blackwell, Alice Stone. *Some Spanish-American Poets.* 1929. Darby repr. of 1937 ed. bilingual ed. 1982 $85.00. Selections by poets from 19 Spanish American countries.

Colecchia, Francesca, and Julio Matas, trans. *Selected Latin American One-Act Plays.* Pitt Latin-Amer. Ser. Univ. of Pittsburgh Pr. 1974 pap. $5.95. Ten plays with an excellent introduction.

Craig, George D., ed. *The Modernist Trend in Spanish American Poetry: A Collection of Representative Poems of the Modernist Movement.* Gordian repr. of 1934 ed. text ed. 1971 $12.50; Gordon 1977 lib. bdg. $59.95

Cranfill, Thomas M., ed. *The Muse in Mexico: A Mid-Century Miscellany.* Univ. of Texas Pr. 1959 $12.50. Poetry, fiction, photographs, and drawings.

Flores, Angel, and Harriet Anderson. *Masterpieces of Latin American Literature.* Macmillan 2 vols. ea. $18.95–$19.95. Excellent introduction to each author and bibliographies.

Franco, Jean, ed. *Short Stories in Spanish.* Penguin 1966 pap. $3.95. The majority of these stories are by Spanish Americans: Onetti, Martínez Moreno, Rulfo, Benedetti, and others.

Frank, Waldo, ed. *Tales from the Argentine.* Trans. by Anita Brenner, *Short Story In-*

dex Repr. Ser. Ayer repr. of 1930 ed. $17.00; Gordon 1977 lib. bdg. $59.95. Stories by Ricardo Güiraldes, Lucio Vicente López, Leopoldo Lugones, Roberto J. Payró, Horacio Quiroga, and Domingo Faustino Sarmiento.

Fremantle, Anne, ed. *Latin-American Literature Today.* New Amer. Lib. 1977 pap. $2.25. Includes a number of less well known authors.

Howes, Barbara, ed. *Eye of the Heart: Short Stories from Latin America.* Avon 1974 pap. $4.95. An excellent selection of 42 short stories by Latin American authors; includes six Brazilian writers.

Jones, Willis Knapp. *Spanish-American Literature in Translation.* Ungar 2 vols. ea. $16.50–$22.50. An extensive collection.

———, trans. *Men and Angels: Three South American Comedies.* Southern Illinois Univ. Pr. 1970 $8.95. Contains J. F. C. Barthes and C. S. Damel, *The Quack Doctor;* J. M. Rivarola Matto, *The Fate of Chipí González;* M. Frank, *The Man of the Century.* Three samples of commercial theater.

Kalechofsky, Robert, and Roberta Kalechofsky, eds. *Echad: An Anthology of Latin American Jewish Writings.* Micah text ed. 1980 pap. $11.00. Poems, a play, fiction, and essays by 24 writers from 12 countries.

Luzuriaga, Gerardo, and Robert S. Rudder, eds. and trans. *Modern One-Act Plays from Latin America.* Univ. of California Latin Amer. Ctr. 1974 pap. $7.50

Mallan, Lloyd, ed. *Three Spanish-American Poets.* Trans. by Mary Wickes, Gordon 1977 $59.95. Pellicer, Neruda, and Carrera Andrade.

Mancini, Pat M., ed. *Contemporary Latin American Short Stories.* Fawcett 1979 pap. $1.95

Marzán, Julio, ed. *Inventing a Word: An Anthology of Twentieth Century Puerto Rican Poetry.* Columbia Univ. Pr. text ed. 1980 $24.50 pap. $10.50. Good introduction to the complicated thrust of Puerto Rican poetry today.

Meyer, Doris, and Margarite Fernández Olmos, eds. *Introductory Essays. Contemporary Woman Authors of Latin America Ser.* Brooklyn College Pr. Vol. 1. 1984 pap. $9.50. A valuable introduction to a flourishing area of Latin American literature.

———. *New Translations. Contemporary Woman Authors of Latin America Ser.* Vol. 2. Brooklyn College Pr. 1984 pap. $12.50.

Oliver, William I., ed. and trans. *Voices of Change in the Spanish American Theater: An Anthology.* Univ. of Texas Pr. 1971 $20.00. Contains E. Carballido, *Loose the Lions;* G. Gambaro, *The Camp;* C. Maggi, *The Library;* E. Buenaventura, *On the Right Hand of God the Father;* L. J. Hernández, *The Mulatto's Orgy;* S. Vodanovic, *Viña* and *Three Beach Plays.*

Paz, Octavio, ed. *An Anthology of Mexican Poetry.* Trans. by Samuel Beckett, Indiana Univ. Pr. 1958 $8.50 pap. $2.45. Paz chose the poems and wrote a historical introduction for this important collection.

Robe, Stanley L. *Hispanic Legends from New Mexico.* Univ. of California Pr. 1977 $30.00

Rodríguez Monegal, Emir, ed. *The Borzoi Anthology of Latin American Literature.* Knopf 2 vols. 1977 pap. ea. $7.95–$9.95. Especially important for the more recent period and for its coverage of Brazil.

Rodríguez-Nieto, Catherine, trans. *Fireflight: Three Latin American Poets.* Oyez 1976 pap. $2.50. Elsie Alvarado de Ricord, Lucha Corpi, and Concha Michel.

Tipton, David, ed. *Peru: The New Poetry.* Red Dust 1977 $10.95. Peruvian poetry by authors born between 1922 and 1947.

Wagenheim, Kal, ed. *Cuentos: An Anthology of Short Stories from Puerto Rico.*

Schocken bilingual ed. 1979 $10.50 pap. $4.95. Stories by authors from both
New York and Puerto Rico.

White, Steven F., ed. and trans. *Poets of Nicaragua: A Bilingual Anthology, 1918–
1979*. Unicorn Pr. 1982 $9.00. Thirteen poets.

Wieser, Nora J., ed. and trans. *Open to the Sun: A Bilingual Anthology of Latin American Women Poets*. Perivale Pr. 1980 pap. $9.95. Includes some newer poets in ad-
dition to the famous figures from the early part of the twentieth century.

ARENAS, REINALDO. 1943–   Cuba

The novel *Hallucinations* recreates in a poetic style, in which time, space,
and character move on multiple planes of fantasy and reality, the life of
Fray Servando Teresa de Mier, a Mexican priest famous for his hatred of the
Spaniards, who denied even that they had brought Christianity to the New
World. Arenas begins with a letter to the friar: "Ever since I discovered you
in an execrable history of Spanish literature, described as the friar who had
traveled over the whole of Europe on foot having improbable adventures; I
have tried to find out more about you." In a dazzling meditation on the nature of fiction, Arenas discovers that he and Servando are the same person,
and author and character become one.

BOOK BY ARENAS

*Hallucinations: Being an Account of the Life and Adventures of Friar Servando Teresa
de Mier*. 1969. Trans. by Gordon Brotherston, Ultramarine 1971 $15.00

ARGUEDAS, JOSE MARIA. 1911–1969   Peru

Arguedas was an ethnologist and teacher, and himself the product of a rural Peruvian world in which Indian and white were inextricably mingled
yet lived separately, with disastrous psychological results for both. In his
prose he created a fusion of the two worlds, which is at the same time a disguised symbolic autobiography, using language that combined elements of
Spanish and Quechua syntax in an effort to express this complex reality. He
was the son of a rural judge and lawyer. The problems created by a dis-
rupted and difficult childhood were exacerbated by the cultural tensions of
his society, and he finally committed suicide.

BOOKS BY ARGUEDAS

Deep Rivers. Trans. by Frances H. Barraclough, Univ. of Texas Pr. 1978 pap. $8.95
Yawar Fiesta. Trans. by Frances H. Barraclough, Univ. of Texas Pr. 1985 $19.95 pap.
$8.95

ARIDJIS, HOMERO. 1940–   Mexico

Like most Latin American writers, Aridjis has had to resort to journalism
for financial support while creating a body of poetry that becomes more impressive with each volume. His is basically a poetry of the search for love
and the love relationship, and through this relationship, of the search for
value and meaning. Love and poetry thus become almost interchangeable,

since poetry is also a unique source of knowledge. *Exaltation of Light* extends this approach to other areas of human experience, and to the ever-present Aztec past, so that the Mexican experience becomes a metaphor for humankind's pursuit of life.

BOOKS BY ARIDJIS

Blue Spaces. Intro. by Kenneth Rexroth, Continuum 1974 $8.95
Exaltation of Light. Trans. by Eliot Weinberger, Boa Eds. 1982 $12.00 pap. $6.00

ARLT, ROBERTO. 1900–1942   Argentina

Arlt has only recently been acknowledged as a seminal figure in the development of the theater and novel in Argentina, in his treatment of madness and the uncertainties of external reality, and in his use of shifting point of view and internal monologue. The seven madmen in the book of that title organize a secret society to be financed by a chain of brothels, with the purpose of changing society. At the same time, each of them pursues his own special fixation. Against this background, the protagonist pursues his own existential search for meaning. Arlt's work is a perceptive comment both on the role of the individual in modern society and of society's destructive effects on that individual.

BOOK BY ARLT

The Seven Madmen. Trans. by Naomi Lindstrom, Godine 1984 $14.95

ARREOLA, JUAN JOSÉ. 1918–   Mexico

Confabulario and Other Inventions is a collection of Arreola's short stories, satiric sketches, and fables published from 1941 to 1961 in several separate volumes. One section comprises his *Bestiary,* 26 fables and allegories, each developing the human qualities and foibles of a particular beast. Arreola is an extraordinarily versatile author, and his tales range from sheer fantasy, through ironic social criticism, to occasional, although rare, overt realism. *The Fair* is a collage of dialogic voices providing a vision of a town. No subject escapes Arreola's pointedly satiric pen in his witty, compact, phantasmagorical stories, in some ways reminiscent of the works of Borges.

BOOKS BY ARREOLA

Confabulario and Other Inventions, 1941–1961. Trans. by George D. Shade, Univ. of Texas Pr. repr. of 1964 ed. 1974 $14.95 pap. $7.95
The Fair. Trans. by John Upton, Univ. of Texas Pr. 1977 $12.95

ASTURIAS, MIGUEL ANGEL. 1899–1974 (NOBEL PRIZE 1967)   Guatemala

Novelist, playwright, poet, translator, and diplomat, Asturias won the Nobel Prize "for his highly colored writing rooted in national individuality and Indian tradition." His first novel, *El Señor Presidente,* a fictional account of the sordid, terror-ridden period of violence and human degradation under the Guatemalan dictator Estrada Cabrera, was completed in 1932 but not published until 1946 for political reasons. It was pioneering in its use of surrealistic structures and Indian myth as integrated parts of the novel's structure. *Mulata* uses a Guatemalan version of the legend of Faust as a point of departure for Asturias's inventive use of Indian myth.

Asturias, who during his first stay in Paris associated with the surrealists ANDRÉ BRETÓN and Paul Eluard, described his process of writing as "automatic." "What I obtain from automatic writing is the mating or juxtaposition of words which, as the Indians say, have never met before," he stated. In 1966, Asturias received the Lenin Peace Prize for writings that "expose American intervention against the Guatemalan people."

Following the 1954 uprising, Asturias was deprived of his citizenship by the new government and lived in exile for eight years. In 1967, on the election of President Julio César Méndez Montenegro, he was restored to his country's diplomatic services as ambassador to Paris and continued to publish. "My work," he said, "will continue to reflect the voice of the peoples, gathering their myths and popular beliefs and at the same time seeking to give birth to a universal consciousness of Latin American problems."

BOOKS BY ASTURIAS

El Señor Presidente. 1946. Trans. by Frances Partridge, Atheneum text ed. 1975 pap. $5.95
Mulata. 1963. Avon 1982 pap. $3.50

AZUELA, MARIANO. 1873–1952   Mexico

After receiving his degree in medicine, Azuela returned to poor districts to practice, a manifestation of his lifelong concern for the *pueblo* of Mexico. During the Mexican Revolution, Azuela joined the forces of Francisco Villa, becoming director of public education in Jalisco under the Villa government. When that government fell, he served as doctor to Villa's men during their retreat northward. From these experiences came his novel *The Underdogs*, which he published in installments in a newspaper after fleeing to Texas in 1915. That novel, which has been called an "epic poem in prose of the Mexican Revolution" (Torres-Rioseco), deals with the Revolution from the point of view of the humble soldiers, examining the circumstances that keep them in poverty, the brutality of the fighting, and the opportunism and betrayal of the Revolution. An admirer of EMILE ZOLA, Azuela stressed the effect of environment on character in many of his novels.

BOOKS BY AZUELA

Two Novels of Mexico: The Flies and The Bosses. Trans. by Lesley B. Simpson, Univ. of California Pr. 1956 pap. $3.95
Three Novels: The Trials of a Respectable Family; The Underdogs; The Firefly. Trans. by Frances K. Hendricks and Beatrice Berler, intro. by Luis Leal, Trinity Univ. Pr. 1979 $15.00

BOOKS ABOUT AZUELA

Leal, Luis. *Mariano Azuela. Twayne's World Authors Ser.* G. K. Hall 1971 $6.95
Robe, Stanley L. *Azuela and the Mexican Underdogs.* Univ. of California Pr. 1979 $30.00

BIOY CASARES, ADOLFO. 1914–   Argentina

Bioy Casares has collaborated with Borges on a number of works, including their *Anthology of Fantastic Literature* (1940), a documentation of the development of Spanish American suprarealism, and the *Six Problems for Don Isidro Parodi*, a playful and inventive variation on the theme of the detective who cannot visit the scene of the crime; in this case, he is imprisoned. Bioy Casares's numerous works are characterized by intelligence and a sense of playful fantasy. *The Invention of Morel* (1953, o.p.), about which Borges stated in his prologue that Bioy Casares has disproven Ortega's theory that no new subject matter exists for the novel, concerns a scientist's illusions about immortality. *Asleep in the Sun* is in the form of a letter from a mental hospital; its tale is so bizarre that ultimately the recipient (and the reader) are left to wonder if, in fact, the puzzle has any solution or whether it is not, like much of Bioy Casares's and Borges's work, an inside joke between author and reader.

BOOKS BY BIOY CASARES

Asleep in the Sun. Trans. by Suzanne Jill Levine, Persea 1978 $8.95
(and Jorge Luis Borges). *Six Problems for Don Isidro Parodi.* 1981. Trans. by Norman Thomas di Giovanni, Dutton 1983 pap. $4.95

BORGES, JORGE LUIS. 1899–1986   Argentina

Born in Buenos Aires, Borges was educated by an English governess and studied in Europe. He returned to Buenos Aires in 1921, where he helped to found several avant-garde literary periodicals. In 1955, after the fall of Juan Perón, whom he vigorously opposed, he was appointed director of the Argentine National Library. With SAMUEL BECKETT he won the $10,000 International Publishers Prize in 1961, thus establishing himself as one of the most prominent writers in the world. He regularly taught and lectured throughout the United States and Europe. His ideas have been a profound influence on writers throughout the Western world and on the most recent developments in literary and critical theory.

Borges was a writer of massive international culture, and his work reflects this, as well as his sense of literature—and life—as a combination of game and puzzle. He regarded all of people's endeavors to understand an incomprehensible world as fiction; hence, his fiction is metaphysical and based on an "esthetics of the intellect," in his words. Some critics have called him a mystic of the intellect. A prolific writer of essays, short stories—they are sometimes difficult to distinguish—and poetry, Borges's concerns are perhaps clearest in his stories, which Jean Franco described as follows: "Each of his stories to which he gave the name '*ficciones*' ["*Ficciones,*" "*El Aleph,*" "*Dreamtigers*"] is a small masterpiece, whose deceptively limpid surface constantly knots the reader into problems. Saturated with literary references, often as near to essay as the conventional idea of short story, the '*ficciones*' nevertheless challenge print culture at a very deep level and perhaps even suggest its impossibility." A central image in Borges's work is the labyrinth, a mental and poetic construct, "a universe in miniature," which man builds and therefore believes he controls but which nevertheless traps him. In spite of Borges's belief that people cannot understand the chaotic world, in his writing he continually attempted to do so, and much of his work deals with people's efforts to find the center of the labyrinth, symbolic of achieving understanding of their place in a mysterious universe. In such later works as *The Gold of the Tigers* he wrote of his lifelong descent into blindness and what this had done to his perceptions of the world around him and himself as a writer. He died in Geneva in 1986.

BOOKS BY BORGES

Selected Poems, 1923–1967. Ed. by Norman Thomas di Giovanni, Delacorte bilingual ed. 1971 $12.50

Borges: A Reader—A Selection from the Writings of Jorge Luis Borges. Ed. by Emir Rodríguez Monegal and Alastair Reid, Dutton 1981 o.p. A comprehensive and balanced selection from Borges's entire production.

Dreamtigers. Trans. by Mildred Boyer and Harold Morland, intro. by Miguel Enguídanos, woodcuts by Antonio Frasconi, Univ. of Texas Pr. 1964 $12.95 1985 pap. $6.95. "A collection of miscellaneous poems, stories, anecdotes, essays, vignettes, all of which add up to a psychic portrait of the author" (*LJ*).

The Aleph and Other Stories, 1933–1969. Dutton 1979 pap. $5.95

The Universal History of Infamy. 1935. Trans. by Norman Thomas di Giovanni, Dutton 1972 $6.95. Short story collection.

Book of Imaginary Beings. 1944. Trans. by Norman Thomas di Giovanni, Dutton 1979 pap. $3.95. A modern bestiary of fantastic monsters and mythical beasts.

Ficciones. 1944. Trans. and ed. by Anthony Kerrigan, Grove (Evergreen) 1962 pap. $4.95

Labyrinths: Selected Short Stories and Other Writings. 1961. Ed. by Donald A. Yates and James E. Irby, pref. by André Maurois, New Directions 2d ed. rev. 1969 pap. $6.95. This contains 22 "fictions," 120 essays, and 8 parables. Among the essays are "The Argentine Writer and Tradition," "The Fearful Sphere of Pascal," "Valéry as Symbol," "Kafka and His Precursors." The parables concern such subjects as Dante's *Divine Comedy, Cervantes and the Quixote,* and various philosophical problems.

A Personal Anthology. 1961. Fwd. by Anthony Kerrigan, Grove (Evergreen) 1967 pap. $6.95. "Composed of twenty-eight prose pieces (stories, essays, parables) and twenty poems, [*A Personal Anthology*] has been translated admirably into English" (*SR*). "The book is both a delight for Borges fans and an introduction for Borges tyros. It splendidly displays the various facets of a remarkable, original literary personality—gravity, skepticism, wit, fantasy, playfulness, and an affectionate, sorrowful concern for the human race" (*New Yorker*).

Other Inquisitions. Trans. by Ruth L. Simms, intro. by James E. Irby, Univ. of Texas Pr. 1964 $14.95 pap. $7.95. Essays.

Introduction to American Literature. 1967. Trans. and ed. by Robert O. Evans and L. Clark Keating, Univ. Pr. of Kentucky repr. of 1967 ed. 1971 $10.00

In Praise of Darkness. 1969. Trans. by Norman Thomas di Giovanni, Dutton bilingual ed. 1974 pap. $5.95

Doctor Brodie's Report. 1970. Trans. by Norman Thomas di Giovanni, Dutton 1979 pap. $2.50. Short stories.

The Book of Sand. Trans. by Norman Thomas di Giovanni, Dutton 1979 pap. $5.95

(and Adolfo Bioy Casares). *Six Problems for Don Isidro Parodi*. 1981. Trans. by Norman Thomas di Giovanni, Dutton 1983 pap. $4.95. Pseudonymous parodic detective stories.

Evaristo Carriego. Trans. by Norman Thomas di Giovanni, Dutton 1984 $16.95 pap. $8.95. A picturesque street poet much appreciated by Borges.

Seven Nights. Intro. by Alastair Reid, New Directions 1984 $14.00 pap. $5.95

BOOKS ABOUT BORGES

Aizenberg, Edna. *The Aleph Weaver: Biblical, Kabbalistic, and Judaic Elements in Borges*. Scripta $25.00

Alazraki, Jaime. *Jorge Luis Borges*. Columbia Univ. Pr. 1971 pap. $2.50

Alifano, Roberto, ed. *Twenty-Four Conversations with Borges: Interviews by Robert Alifano*. Trans. by Noemi Escandell, Grove 1984 $17.95 pap. $8.95

Barnstone, Willis, ed. *Borges at Eighty: Conversations*. Indiana Univ. Pr. 1982 $17.50

Bell-Villada, Gene H. *Borges and His Fiction: A Guide to His Mind and Art*. Univ. of North Carolina Pr. 1981 $19.00 pap. $10.00

Christ, Ronald J. *Narrow Act: Borges' Art of Allusion*. Fwd. by Jorge Luis Borges, New York Univ. Pr. text ed. 1969 $10.95 pap. $4.95. Focuses on Borges's literary device of allusion; a useful critical work with an introduction by Borges.

Dunham, Lowell, and Ivar Ivask. *Cardinal Points of Jorge Luis Borges*. Univ. of Oklahoma Pr. 1972 $13.95 pap. $6.95

MacMurray, George R. *Jorge Luis Borges*. Ungar 1980 $15.50

Sorrentino, Fernando. *Seven Conversations with Jorge Luis Borges*. Trans. by Clark M. Zlotchew, Whitston 1981 $18.50

Stabb, Martin S. *Jorge Luis Borges*. Twayne's World Authors Ser. G. K. Hall 1970 lib. bdg. $13.50; St. Martin's 1975 pap. $4.95

Sturrock, John. *Paper Tigers: The Ideal Fiction of Jorge Luis Borges*. Oxford 1978 $17.50

CABRERA INFANTE, GUILLERMO. 1929–   Cuba

Three Trapped Tigers, winner of the Barcelona Seix Barral Prize in 1964, takes Havana nightlife before the revolution as a symbol of the decadence of the Batista regime. The protagonists are singers, musicians, aristocrats, and intellectuals who live off an American-supported and -dominated entertainment world. The triumph of the novel is in its language, a combination of "Spanglish" and the daily idiom of the Cuban subworld. In his puns and wordplay (the title in Spanish is a tongue twister), Cabrera Infante demonstrates the debt to his acknowledged masters: Lewis Carroll, Nabokov, and Joyce. At the same time, however, he attempts to free Cuban language and literature from constricting foreign influence. *Infante's Inferno*, again a punning title—the original is *La Habana para un infante difunto*, still another pun—is a parody of novels about the writing of novels; at the same time, it is a lament for the author's lost Havana and a search for identity in a world where all anchors have been torn loose. In 1965, Cabrera Infante defected from Cuba to England, where he now resides.

BOOKS BY CABRERA INFANTE

View of Dawn in the Tropics. Trans. by Suzanne Jill Levine, Harper 1978 $8.95

Infante's Inferno. Trans. by Suzanne Jill Levine and Guillermo Cabrera Infante, Harper consult publisher for information.

CARBALLIDO, EMILIO. 1925–   Mexico

Carballido is known primarily as a playwright and one of the leaders of a movement that revitalized Mexican theater during the 1950s and 1960s. Previously, Mexican theater had been derivative of European models. Carballido is responsible for breaking from the traditional realistic drama and introducing a surrealistic, fantastic world (one to which the Mexican novel has already turned) into the theater. At the same time, Carballido probes the nature of reality and of man's responsibility to himself and others. The play *Theseus,* included in the volume *The Golden Thread* (1957), is a twentieth-century version of the Greek myth, in which Theseus takes full responsibility for his actions, willfully neglecting to put up the white sail of victory on his return from killing the minotaur so that his father will hurl himself from the Parthenon and he will become king. *The Clockmaker from Cordoba* is a wryly comic vision of the fallibility of justice and the weakness of mankind. Like all Carballido's work, ultimately it expresses an abiding faith in a weak but essentially striving humanity. *The Norther* is a short novel.

BOOKS BY CARBALLIDO

The Golden Thread and Other Plays. Trans. by Margaret S. Peden, *Texas Pan-Amer. Ser.* Univ. of Texas Pr. 1970 $11.90
The Norther. 1958. Trans. by Margaret S. Peden, Univ. of Texas Pr. 1968 $7.95

BOOK ABOUT CARBALLIDO

Peden, Margaret S. *Emilio Carballido. Twayne's World Authors Ser.* G. K. Hall 1980 lib. bdg. $16.95

CARDENAL, ERNESTO. 1925–   Nicaragua

An ordained priest who lives in Solentiname, a community that he founded, and a member of the Nicaraguan cabinet, Fr. Cardenal is Latin America's best known exponent of what might be called the literature of the theology of liberation. His poetry is the expression of tension between his faith and a strongly rooted sense of reality and the need for drastic change. Influenced heavily by Thomas Merton, by his residence in the Trappist community of Gethsemane, Kentucky, by English and American poetry, Christianity, and the fact of social injustice, Cardenal consciously writes antirhetorical and often didactic poetry. Frequently he uses other sources: newspapers, American-Indian texts, and so on, just as the masses at Solentiname use nontraditional sources as subjects for discussion. *Zero Hour* details the existence of tyranny in America; the *Psalms* are a rewriting of the biblical Psalms of David for a modern world. *The Gospel in Solentiname* is a collection of dialogues or commentaries on the Gospels.

BOOKS BY CARDENAL

Apocalypse and Other Poems. Ed. by Robert Pring-Mill and Donald D. Walsh, New Directions 1977 pap. $4.95

Zero Hour and Other Documentary Poems. Trans. by Donald D. Walsh, New Directions 1980 pap. $5.95

With Walker in Nicaragua and Other Early Poems. Trans. by Jonathan Cohen, Wesleyan Univ. Pr. 1985 $17.00 pap. $8.95

Psalms. Crossroads 1981 pap. $3.95

In Cuba. Trans. by Donald D. Walsh, New Directions 1974 $10.50 pap. $3.95

Homage to an American Indian. Trans. by Monique Altschul and Carlos Altschul, Johns Hopkins Univ. Pr. 1976 o.p.

Love. Crossroads 1981 pap. $4.95

The Gospel in Solentiname. Trans. by Donald D. Walsh, Orbis Bks. 4 vols. 1982 pap. ea. $8.95

CARPENTIER, ALEJO. 1904–1980   Cuba

Carpentier was director of Cuba's National Press, which published many millions of volumes in an ambitious program, and for some years was Cuba's ambassador to France. A composer and musicologist, he consciously applied the principles of musical composition in much of his work. Imprisoned for political activity in 1928, he escaped with the aid of Robert Desnos, a French surrealist poet, to Paris, where he joined the literary circle of surrealists Louis Aragon, Tristan Tzara, and Paul Eluard. Surrealism influenced his style and, according to Carpentier, helped him to see "aspects of American life he had not previously seen, in their telluric, epic, and poetic contexts." Carpentier articulated a theory of marvelous reality, "lo real maravilloso," with an almost surrealistic sense of the appearance in America and relationship of unrelated or antithetical elements, often from distinct ethnic and cultural backgrounds. *The Lost Steps* takes the form of a diary of a Cuban musician and intellectual who seeks escape from civilization during his trip to a remote Amazon village in search of native musical instruments. The three short stories "The Road to Santiago," "Journey to the Seed," and "Similar to Night," and the novel *The Pursuit*, printed in *The War of Time* (the title is an allusion to a line from Lope de Vega defining a man as "a soldier in the war of time"), present time as subjective rather than historical, and capable of remarkable personal variations. *The Kingdom of This World* deals with the period of Henri Christophe and the slave revolts in Haiti. Its circular structure presents the inevitable recurrence of tyranny and the need for eternal struggle against it. *Reasons of State* is another notable addition to the gallery of Latin American fictional portraits of dictators; it uses Carpentier's love for baroque style and parody to raise serious questions about the nature of revolution.

BOOKS BY CARPENTIER

The Kingdom of This World. 1949. Macmillan (Collier Bks.) 1971 pap. o.p.

The Lost Steps. 1953. Avon 1979 pap. $2.50

The War of Time. 1958. Trans. by Frances Partridge, Knopf 1971 $4.95

Reasons of State. 1976. Trans. by Frances Partridge, Writers & Readers 1981 pap. $4.95

Books about Carpentier

González Echeverría, Roberto. *Alejo Carpentier: The Pilgrim at Home.* Cornell Univ. Pr. 1977 $27.50

Janney, Frank. *Alejo Carpentier and His Early Works.* Tamesis 1981 o.p.

CORTÁZAR, JULIO. 1914–1984   Argentina

Cortázar's view that fantasy and reality, the rational and the irrational, exist on both intersecting and identical planes produced his formal experiments with the novel and short story, experiments always in the spirit of philosophical and literary play. His short stories explore from fresh perspectives interchanging identities and intersecting levels of reality and time. *Blow-Up* provided Antonioni with the point of departure for his film of that title. In *Cronopios and Famas* (1962, o.p.) Cortázar created a world filled with imaginary beings who represent the magic of everyday life, the *cronopios*, while *famas* are those seeing only conventional reality. It is this perception of the comic that pervades all Cortázar's work and gives it its special tone.

The Winners uses the classic structure of a voyage with travelers of widely different origins to ask metaphysical questions about human relationships and the purpose of the voyage, representing life. The protagonist of *Hopscotch*, in quest of reality (the heaven or home of a hopscotch game), tries to liberate himself from the restrictions imposed by time, language, and social conventions. The novel has alternative structures on one of which the reader must decide. "I was trying," the author wrote, "to break the habits of readers—not just for the sake of breaking them, but to make the reader free. . . . Space and time are left completely by the wayside. There are moments in it when the reader will not know when or where the action is taking place." *Sixty-two: A Model Kit* (literally translated, *A Model to Be Put Together*, 1968, o.p.) continues the theoretical lines developed in *Hopscotch*. It is an attempt to replace routine psychologizing by alternative modes of presenting inner realities. *A Manual for Manuel* explores the relationship of dream to fiction and to reality, always with a sense of the comic absurdity of existence and of its underlying tragedy.

Books by Cortázar

A Change of Light and Other Stories. Trans. by Gregory Rabassa, Knopf 1980 $11.95. Selections from *Octaedro* (1974) and *Alguien que anda por ahi* (1978).

We Love Glenda So Much and Other Stories. Trans. by Gregory Rabassa, Knopf 1983 $11.95; Random 1984 pap. $8.95

Hopscotch. 1963. Avon 1974 pap. $5.95

A Certain Lucas. Trans. by Gregory Rabassa, Knopf 1984 $12.95

The Winners. Trans. by Elaine Kerrigan, Pantheon 1984 pap. $8.95

BOOKS ABOUT CORTÁZAR

Alazraki, Jaime, ed. *The Final Island: The Fiction of Julio Cortázar*. Ed. by Ivar Ivask, Univ. of Oklahoma Pr. 1978 $17.95
Boldy, Stephen. *The Novels of Julio Cortázar*. Cambridge Univ. Pr. 1980 $34.50
Brody, Robert. *Julio Cortázar: Rayuela*. Tamesis 1976 o.p.

CRUZ, SOR JUANA INÉS DE LA. 1648–1695   Mexico

Born Juana de Asbaje in a small town, Sor Juana became a nun in 1669, probably because her illegitimate birth removed her from consideration for marriage to someone worthy of her. A misfit in a restrictive colonial society that mistrusted such intense intellectual curiosity in a woman, Sor Juana was the finest lyric poet and one of the most interesting dramatists of the Spanish American colonial period. Despite the opposition of the ecclesiastical hierarchy, she carried out scientific experiments, became the confidante of nobility and a correspondent of intellectuals throughout Spanish America. *A Woman of Genius (Respuesta a Sor Filotea)* is an extraordinary document of the intellectual history of a woman who would not be defeated by her circumstances. Ultimately, she sold her books and devoted herself to caring for the sick and poor; she died of an illness contracted while nursing during an outbreak of the plague.

BOOK BY CRUZ

A Woman of Genius: The Intellectual Autobiography of Sor Juana Inés de la Cruz. Trans. and intro. by Margaret S. Peden, Lime Rock Pr. 1982 $37.50 pap. $6.95

DARÍO, RUBÉN (pseud. of Félix Rubén García Sarmiento). 1867–1916   Nicaragua

Darío, a Nicaraguan who traveled widely in the Spanish-speaking world, was the greatest poet of the modernist movement and profoundly influenced twentieth-century poetry in Spanish. *Azul (Azure)* (1888), a volume in three parts consisting of stories, poetic prose, and poetry, is still strongly romantic but also shows Darío's assimilation of French Parnassianism and symbolism. Darío strove for artistic refinement, elegance of expression, and the renovation of poetic language and form. He invented daring neologisms and verse forms, but also renewed forgotten techniques. Initially, his was the world of swans, centaurs, and doves, of art for art's sake. With his *Profane Prose* (1896), he distinguished himself as the true leader of the modernist movement. The title itself reveals his desire to alter the use of the language, for the contents are neither prose nor profane, but rather elegant, aristocratic verse. Here Darío experimented with combinations of rhythms, sounds, accents, and meter, treating such exotic themes as peacocks and princesses with erotic and pagan tones. His next volume, *Songs of Life and Hope* (1905), which contains some of his best verse, shows a turn away from evasion of reality toward meditative introspection on life and death, as well as commitment to the concept of a Spanish America united in a search for freedom, and an intense preoccupation about the power of the United States, as revealed in *To Roosevelt*.

BOOKS BY DARÍO

Selected Poems of Rubén Darío. Trans. by Lysander Kemp, Univ. of Texas Pr. 1965 $6.95

Eleven Poems of Rubén Darío: Bilingual Edition. Trans. by Thomas Walsh and Salomon De la Selva, Gordon 1977 lib. bdg. $59.95

BOOK ABOUT DARÍO

Ellis, Keith. *Critical Approaches to Rubén Darío.* Univ. of Toronto Pr. 1975 $20.00

DONOSO, JOSÉ. 1925– Chile

Donoso has been compared to Henry James for his psychological penetration of characters and to WILLIAM FAULKNER (see Vol. 1) for novelistic technique. His obsessive subject is the decay of the Chilean bourgeoisie, but he vigorously rejects anything reminiscent of traditional realism or the portrayal of regional customs. In *This Sunday* he focuses on a family's activities on Sundays to view the boredom, passions, and misery of Chilean bourgeois society and its servants. *The Obscene Bird of Night* deals with the decline of feudal society through the story of a landholding family in a kaleidoscopic vision of decay and outrageous behavior.

BOOKS BY DONOSO

Charleston and Other Stories. Trans. by Andrée Conrad, Godine 1977 $12.95

This Sunday. Trans. by Lorraine O'Grady Freeman, Knopf 1967 $5.95

The Obscene Bird of Night. 1970. Trans. by Leonard Mades, Godine repr. of 1973 ed. 1979 pap. $9.95

A House in the Country. Trans. by Suzanne J. Levine, Knopf 1984 $16.95; Random (Vintage) 1985 pap. $8.95

BOOK ABOUT DONOSO

McMurray, George R. *José Donoso. Twayne's World Authors Ser.* G. K. Hall 1979 lib. bdg. $16.95

DORFMAN, ARIEL. 1943– Chile

A resident of Holland since being exiled from Chile in 1973 by the military government, Dorfman is a vociferous critic of U.S. economic and political involvement in Latin America. In *The Emperor's Old Clothes*, he saw cultural imperialism in unexpected facets of American society. *Widows* is a parable of military dictatorship. Its setting in Greece after World War II does not hide the fact that it is an extended metaphor for the present Chilean situation. It deals with the problem of the *desaparecidos*, those who have been kidnapped by government agents and simply vanish. The novel was refused publication in Chile.

BOOKS BY DORFMAN

The Emperor's Old Clothes: What the Lone Ranger, Babar, and the Innocent Heroes Do to Our Minds. Pantheon 1983 $14.95 pap. $6.95

Widows. Trans. by Stephen Kessler, Pantheon 1983 $10.95; Random (Vintage) 1985 pap. $6.95

FUENTES, CARLOS. 1929–   Mexico

The most famous Mexican novelist of the twentieth century is probably Carlos Fuentes, also an essayist, journalist, film writer, and diplomat. All of Fuentes's works demonstrate his primary concern, the interpretation of Mexican culture and history. He finds Mexico's search for identity particularly difficult due to its beginning with the annihilation of the Indians. The protagonist of *Where the Air Is Clear*, described by Fuentes as "a synthesis of the Mexican present," is the whole of Mexico City, and a panorama of post-revolutionary Mexican life is presented through a wide range of characters from various classes and professions. *The Death of Artemio Cruz*, which made an international reputation for Fuentes, narrates a dying man's reflections on the crucial decisions of his life as vitality and energy drain from him; its progression from present to past provides a unique perspective on both the individual and the historical process. At the appearance of *A Change of Skin* (1968, o.p.) in English, Robert J. Clements described it as a "great book . . . incorporating every technique of the contemporary novel . . . bursting in energy, capacious in content, gripping in evocation, and humanitarian in its universal tolerance" (*SR*). There are other threads to Fuentes's fiction, however; the theme of doubling of personality and consciousness allied to the persistence of the past, as in *Aura*, or the deliberate parody of spy fiction in *The Hydra Head*. *Terra Nostra* (o.p.) is a massive effort to capture the multiple strands of history, European and American, that have gone to make up the complexities of Mexico; like all Fuentes's work, it struggles to unravel the significance and the forms in which the past shapes the present.

BOOKS BY FUENTES

The Good Conscience. 1959. Trans. by Sam Hileman, Farrar 1961 pap. $6.25
Where the Air Is Clear. 1959. Trans. by Sam Hileman, Farrar 1971 pap. $8.95
The Death of Artemio Cruz. 1962. Trans. by Sam Hileman, Farrar 1964 pap. $6.95
Aura. Trans. by Lysander Kemp, Farrar bilingual ed. 1975 $7.95 pap. $6.95
The Hydra Head. Trans. by Margaret S. Peden, Farrar 1978 $14.95 pap. $9.95
Burnt Water. Trans. by Margaret S. Peden, Farrar 1980 $11.95
Distant Relations. Trans. by Margaret S. Peden, Farrar 1982 $11.95 pap. $7.95

BOOKS ABOUT FUENTES

Brody, Robert, and Charles Rossman, eds. *Carlos Fuentes: A Critical View.* Univ. of Texas Pr. text ed. 1982 $22.50
Durán, Gloria. *The Archetypes of Carlos Fuentes: From Witch to Androgyne.* Shoe String (Archon) 1980 $22.50
Faris, Wendy B. *Carlos Fuentes.* Ungar 1983 $16.50 pap. $6.95

GARCÍA MÁRQUEZ, GABRIEL. 1928–   (NOBEL PRIZE 1982)   Colombia

García Márquez has created a fictional world out of his memories in a town named Macondo, which is the setting for most of his novels and short stories. Earlier works like *No One Writes to the Colonel* and *Leaf Storm* had already examined the dust and rain and boredom of this cultural and economic backwater, but the publication of *One Hundred Years of Solitude* caused a literary sensation. An epic novel covering a one-hundred-year cycle of the town's existence, it traces its founding by José Arcadio Buendía with an incestuous relationship through its destruction by a cyclone. The magical style mingles the fantastic, mythical, and commonplace on multiple levels. The tone and structure have a number of biblical parallels. Although much of the novel is comic, its characters are finally tragic for their self-imposed isolation and destruction. With this work García Márquez established himself internationally as a major novelist and was awarded the Nobel Prize in 1982.

He is not, however, a one-book novelist. *In Evil Hour* and *Leaf Storm* are chilling portraits of the stagnation, broken only by violence, of a provincial dead end. *The Autumn of the Patriarch* is a portrait of a mythical dictator who assumes the characteristics, and some of the historical details, of a series of Latin American tyrants, but with a fine sense of irony. *Confiscated Power* (*Chronicle of Death Foretold*) presents from the inside the disastrous consequences of the male code of honor in Hispanic society, and many of García Márquez's short stories are brilliantly imaginative parables of a world that threatens logic and reason.

Books by García Márquez

Leaf Storm and Other Stories. 1955. Trans. by Gregory Rabassa, Avon 1973 pap. $1.95; Harper 1972 $10.95 1979 pap. $4.76

No One Writes to the Colonel and Other Stories. 1961. Trans. by J. S. Bernstein, Harper 1968 $9.95 1979 pap. $5.72

One Hundred Years of Solitude. 1967. Trans. by Gregory Rabassa, Avon 1971 pap. $3.95; Harper 1970 $18.22

The Autumn of the Patriarch. Trans. by Gregory Rabassa, Harper 1976 $13.41

In Evil Hour. Trans. by Gregory Rabassa, Avon 1980 pap. $2.95; Harper 1979 $11.49

Innocent Erendira and Other Stories. Trans. by Gregory Rabassa, Harper 1978 $11.49 1979 pap. $4.76. A collection ranging from early pieces to the title novella originally conceived as a filmscript.

Books about García Márquez

Janes, Regina. *Gabriel García Márquez: Revolutions in Wonderland.* Univ. of Missouri Pr. text ed. 1981 $7.95

McMurray, George R. *Gabriel García Márquez.* Ungar 1977 $13.95 1984 pap. $7.95

Oberhelman, Harley D. *The Presence of Faulkner in the Writings of García Márquez.* Texas Tech Pr. 1980 pap. $7.00

Williams, Raymond L. *Gabriel García Márquez. Twayne's World Authors Ser.* G. K. Hall 1984 lib. bdg. $14.95 1985 pap. $6.95

GARRO, ELENA. 1920– Mexico

Best known as a dramatist, Elena Garro won the important Premio Xavier Villaurrutia in 1963 for the novel *Recollections of Things to Come*. The interior world of the characters' memories of life in Ixtepec during the Cristero Rebellion of 1926–1928 is narrated dramatically in poetic prose that makes considerable use of Aztec mythology in its creation of a myth of Mexican women. A choreographer, script writer, and journalist, Elena Garro was at one time married to the Mexican poet Octavio Paz.

BOOK BY GARRO

Recollections of Things to Come. 1962. Trans. by Ruth L. Simms, *Texas Pan-Amer. Ser.* Univ. of Texas Pr. 1969 $6.50

GOLDEMBERG, ISAAC. 1945–   Peru

Among the many shifts in Latin American literature during the past few years, one of the most important has been the emergence of a group of writers who chronicle the Jewish immigrant experience. For Goldemberg's characters, growing up Jewish in Peru has been an experience of sorrow and desolation laced with humor. His work is a fascinating document and a source of constant surprises, as in the need to develop a daily idiom built on elements from Spanish, Yiddish, and Quechua, in an effort to harmonize the triple tradition within which they lived.

BOOKS BY GOLDEMBERG

The Fragmented Life of Don Jacobo Lerner. Trans. by Robert S. Picciotto, Persea repr. of 1976 ed. 1985 pap. $8.95. A novel.
Just Passing Through. Trans. by Isaac Goldemberg and David Ungar, Point of Contact bilingual ed. 1981 $7.00. Poetry.

GUILLÉN, NICOLÁS. 1902–   Cuba

Guillén, one of the leaders of the Afro-Antillean school of poetry, was inspired by popular dance, ballads, song rhythms, and speech patterns, all of which show a heavy African influence. In his first volumes, *Motives of Sound* (1930, o.p.) and *Sóngoro Cosongo* (1931, o.p.), meaning is communicated primarily through sound, and many poems are in regional popular dialect. Much of his subsequent poetry reflects his profound social commitment: *West Indies Limited* (1934, o.p.) opposes imperialism, and *Spain* (1937, o.p.) expresses his support for the republic during the Spanish civil war. *Tengo* deals with the Cuban Revolution in a tone aimed at a popular audience. All Guillén's work is an intense effort to relate poetry to the culture of the Cuban people and to political and social protest.

BOOKS BY GUILLÉN

Tengo. 1964. Trans. by Richard J. Carr, intro. by José Antonio Portuondo, Broadside Pr. 1974 $7.25 pap. $4.25
Man-making Words. Trans. by Robert Márquez and David Arthur McMurray, Univ. of Massachusetts Pr. bilingual ed. 1972 $12.00 pap. $6.50
Patria o Muerte: The Great Zoo and Other Poems, 1925–1969. Trans. by Robert Márquez, Monthly Review 1972 $8.50 pap. $3.25

BOOK ABOUT GUILLÉN

Ellis, Keith. *Cuba's Nicolás Guillén: Poetry and Ideology.* Univ. of Toronto Pr. 1983 $27.50

HERNÁNDEZ, JOSÉ. 1834–1866   Argentina

Martín Fierro is a lyric epic poem written in praise of the gaucho way of life at a time when gauchos were looked on as curiosities or nuisances by the European-dominated Buenos Aires society and were being swallowed by industrial and agricultural progress and manipulated by contending political parties. Hernández's primary purpose was to inform people about the vanishing culture of the gaucho; although the first part of the poem portrays the rebellion against society's mistreatment of the gaucho and its restrictions on his freedom to roam as he saw fit, the second part has a more didactic tone and urges a reconciliation. This poem became the voice of the gaucho, but it has also been adopted by all Argentines as an important part of their national tradition.

BOOK BY HERNÁNDEZ

The Gaucho Martín Fierro. Trans. by Norman Mangouni, Scholars' Facsimiles repr. of 1872 ed. bilingual ed. 1974 $25.00; trans. by Frank G. Carrino, Alberto J. Carlos, and Norman Mangouni, State Univ. of New York Pr. 1974 pap. $7.95

HUIDOBRO, VICENTE. 1893–1948   Chile

Virtually unknown in the United States, Huidobro was one of the most important innovators in Latin American poetry of the early twentieth century and an important theoretician of the new art. He lived in Europe for many years, specifically in Paris from 1916 to 1926, where he wrote poetry in French and participated in French poetic movements. He proclaimed himself the inventor of the school that he called Creationism, which he considered the foundation of a new way of conceiving art. For Huidobro the mission of the poet was the creation of new poetic realities. Art was totally free and the poem was free of both its poet-creator and the circumstances in which it was created. Huidobro tended to exaggerate and became a center of polemics, but it is clear that he was one of the first to announce such important avant-garde concepts. His creative work is startling because of the novelty of the metaphors and the formal and verbal experimentation.

BOOK BY HUIDOBRO

The Selected Poetry of Vicente Huidobro. Trans. by Stephen Gredman and others, ed. by David M. Guss, New Directions 1981 $18.95 pap. $6.95

GOROSTIZA, JOSÉ. 1901–1973   Mexico

Death without End, a complex, metaphysical volume, has been called "the most important Mexican poem to appear up to that time in his generation" by Enrique Anderson Imbert. Utilizing ironic contrast with great power, the poem expresses man's unavailing effort to find order and permanence; its central metaphor is the water, symbol of the poet, of mankind, and of all matter, which is momentarily given form by the glass (intelligence and language), but which may be spilled and run into nothingness and chaos, what Margaret S. Peden has called "the paradox of form in formlessness" (*Handbook of Latin American Studies*).

BOOK BY GOROSTIZA

Death without End. 1939. Trans. by Laura Villaseñor, intro. by Salvador Novo, Univ. of Texas Pr. 1969 $10.00

LIHN, ENRIQUE. 1929–   Chile

Lihn is a difficult poet because his sources lie in various traditions of modern Chilean poetry, especially Neruda and Parra, while he rejects traditionalism. He is in the line of neorealism and antipoetry, but is unwilling to settle into schools or a school. His *Poesía de Paso* received the Cuban Casadelas Americas Prize in 1966. He says of his own work, "my poetry postulates, instead of discontinuity, the coherence [delirious, in the best of cases] of a continuous discourse, it tries to become a reflection, it rambles; and although it may integrate linguistic elements of the most diverse origins, signs of a traumatic relation with *Literature* prevail."

BOOKS BY LIHN

The Dark Room and Other Poems. Trans. by Jonathan Cohen and others, ed. by Patricio C. Lerzundi, New Directions 1978 $8.95 pap. $2.45
The Endless Malice. Trans. by William Witherup and Serge Echeverria, Lillabulero Pr. 1969 o.p.

MALLEA, EDUARDO. 1903–   Argentina

Mallea has been associated with Argentina's avant-garde since the late 1920s and for 15 years greatly influenced Argentine letters from his position as literary director of the progressive newspaper *La Nación. History of an Argentine Passion,* a spiritual and intellectual autobiography, has been widely read throughout Latin America. His view of the world basically existentialist, Mallea is concerned with people's loneliness, lack of communication, and alienation. He utilizes stream-of-consciousness techniques and disjunctures of chronological time to portray inner realities. Mallea names as literary influences BLAKE (see Vol. 1), RIMBAUD, KIERKEGAARD (see Vol. 4), UNAMUNO Y JUGO, KAFKA, JOYCE (see Vol. 1), and PROUST, and he was among the first to introduce the techniques of these European novelists to Argentina. Mallea won the Buenos Aires Municipal Prize for prose in 1935 and the National Prize for literature in 1937.

BOOK BY MALLEA

History of an Argentine Passion. Trans. by Yvette E. Miller and Myron Lichtblau, Latin Amer. Literary Review Pr. 1983 pap. $13.95

MARQUÉS, RENÉ. 1919–1979   Puerto Rico

Marqués is the most important of the Puerto Rican dramatists who in the 1950s and 1960s created a theater that revealed a surge in Puerto Rican pride and ethnic identity. His early work is heavily naturalistic, but in later plays he made extensive use of unorthodox time sequences and imaginative lighting to create a symbolic portrait of what he considered his island's problems. In his essays, Marqués examined the identity of the Puerto Rican as he saw it, against the backdrop of a dreaded cultural and linguistic assimilation with the United States.

BOOK BY MARQUÉS

The Docile Puerto Rican. Trans. by Barbara B. Aponte, Temple Univ. Pr. 1976 $19.95

MARTÍ, JOSÉ. 1853–1895 Cuba

Martí is a symbol of Cuban independence, for he campaigned throughout his life for its liberation and finally died in the war against Spain. He was also an important literary figure and one of the founders of modernism. Rejecting the elaborate aestheticism of many modernists, he wrote in a simpler style based largely on folk poetry, as in *Ismaelillo* and *Versos Sencillos*, and much of his poetry deals with the struggle for freedom and his political and emotional exile from his homeland. He was also an accomplished prose stylist in a much more intricate fashion and influenced the later development of the short story and essay. His writings now collected, many of which were originally published in newspapers, are essential for an understanding of the Spanish American independence process.

BOOKS BY MARTÍ

Inside the Monster: Writings on the United States and American Imperialism. Trans. by Elinor Randall, Monthly Review 1975 $16.50 1977 pap. $5.95
Major Poems. Trans. by Elinor Randall, ed. by Philip S. Foner, Holmes & Meier 1982 $22.50 text ed. pap. $12.50
Martí on the U.S.A. Trans. by Luis A. Baralt, Southern Illinois Univ. Pr. 1966 $7.95
On Education: Articles on Educational Theory and Pedagogy, and Writings for Children from "The Age of Gold." Trans. by Elinor Randall, Monthly Review 1979 $14.00 pap. $7.50
On Art and Literature: Critical Writings. Trans. by Elinor Randall, Monthly Review 1982 $18.00 pap. $10.00
Our America: Writings on Latin America and the Struggle for Cuban Independence. Trans. by Elinor Randall, Monthly Review 1978 $16.50 1979 pap $7.50

BOOKS ABOUT MARTÍ

Gray, Richard B. *José Martí: Cuban Patriot.* Univ. Pr. of Florida 1962 $9.50
Kirk, John M. *Martí: Mentor of the Cuban Nation.* Univ. Pr. of Florida 1983 $17.95
Lizaso, Felix. *Martí: Martyr of Cuban Independence.* Greenwood repr. of 1953 ed. 1974 lib. bdg. $15.00
Mañach, José. *Martí: Apostle of Freedom.* Devin $6.50
Zendegui, Guillermo de. *Martí's Circle.* Trans. by Scott Johnson, Gordon 1980 $59.95

MISTRAL, GABRIELA (pseud. of Lucila Godoy y Alcayaga). 1889–1957
(NOBEL PRIZE 1945) Chile

Gabriela Mistral's pen name was formed from those of Frederic Mistral, a Provençal poet, and GABRIELE D'ANNUNZIO, the Italian poet and patriot. Her first major collection of poetry was published in the United States in 1922 under the title *Desolación*. The sonnets of this volume, among her very best, evoke her passion for a young lover and her anguish at his suicide. Critics consider her collection *Tala* (*Felling of Trees*), published in Buenos Aires in 1938, her best work.

Anti-imperialism and a feminist rebellion against a masculine society are among the main themes of Mistral's poetry, but love—physical, religious, humanitarian, and maternal—was her primary subject; an unhappy personal life provided the source of much of her poetic drive. Much of Mistral's time and energy was dedicated to the children of the world; she was an energetic spokeswoman for them and was responsible for the foundation of schools throughout Latin America. On the invitation of the Mexican government, she reorganized that country's school system in the 1920s, and she represented Chile in various posts at the League of Nations, the United Nations, and as a member of the consular service.

BOOKS BY MISTRAL

Selected Poems. Trans. by Langston Hughes, Indiana Univ. Pr. 1957 pap. $1.75
Selected Poems of Gabriela Mistral. Trans. and ed. by Doris Dana, Johns Hopkins Univ. Pr. 1971 o.p.

NERUDA, PABLO (pseud. of Neftalí Ricardo Reyes). 1904–1973
(NOBEL PRIZE 1971)   Chile

Neruda's poetry moved through a variety of periods and styles, beginning with the youthful romanticism of *Crepusculary* (1919, o.p.), which shows the seeds of his later social commitment. In *Twenty Poems of Love and a Song of Despair*, his tone becomes more despairing, a mood amplified in *The Attempt of Infinite Man* (o.p.), an experiment with the avant-garde expressing the painful confrontation with man's limits. The three hermetic volumes of *Residence on Earth* (1933) are surrealistic in style and subject matter, characterized by twisted syntax, audacious metaphors, and truncated phrases that express the chaos of the modern mind and an ontological despair. The *Canto General* (1950) is an effort to capture the epic tone of Latin America's history; highly political in large part, it contains some of the poet's finest work, as in his single greatest work, *The Heights of Machu Picchu*. In later work Neruda ranged from experiments with "conversational" poetry in *Extravagaria* to lyric autobiography to the rapturous contemplation of the natural world's wonders (*Odes*). In volumes such as *Spain in the Heart* (o.p.) and *Intimate Letter to Millions* (o.p.), his verse becomes less hermetic, more accessible, and particularly more political.

In 1927 Neruda entered Chile's diplomatic corps, and after an unpleasant tour in the Orient he became consul to Barcelona and then moved to Madrid in 1935. He devoted himself to the cause of the Spanish republic, and its destruction by Franco's forces led him into political activism and a conversion to communism. He saw as his mission the education of the proletariat, and the pessimism of his early period changed to optimism about man's solidarity and the future of communism. Neruda remained an international figure throughout his life, as well as an important force in Chilean politics. His extraordinary poetic talent and his active social role made him a legendary and symbolic figure for intellectuals, students, and artists from all of

Latin America. "The tension, the repression, the drama of our position in Latin America doesn't permit us the luxury of being uncommitted," he said. Neruda won the Nobel Prize in 1971 "for poetry that, with the action of an elemental force, brings alive a continent's destiny and dreams." He died in Chile shortly after the coup d'état that deposed President Allende in 1973.

BOOKS BY NERUDA

The Captain's Verses. 1952. Trans. by Donald D. Walsh, New Directions bilingual ed. 1972 pap. $5.25

Five Decades: Poems, 1925–1970. Trans. and ed. by Ben Belitt, Grove (Evergreen) bilingual ed. 1974 pap. $8.95

New Poems, 1968–1970. Trans. and ed. by Ben Belitt, Grove (Evergreen) bilingual ed. 1972 pap. $3.95

Residence on Earth and Other Poems. Trans. by Angel Flores, Gordian bilingual ed. 1976 $10.00; trans. by Donald D. Walsh, New Directions 1973 pap. $7.95

Selected Poems of Pablo Neruda. Dell 1973 pap. $12.95

Isla Negra: A Notebook. Trans. by Alastair Reid, afterword by Enrico M. Santi, Farrar bilingual ed. 1981 $18.95 pap. $10.25

Memoirs. Trans. by Hardie St. Martin, Farrar 1977 $11.95; Penguin 1978 pap. $7.95

Twenty Love Poems and a Song of Despair. 1924. Penguin 1976 pap. $4.95

The Heights of Machu Picchu. 1950. Trans. by Nathaniel Tarn, Farrar bilingual ed. 1967 $4.95 pap. $7.25

Extravagaria. 1958. Trans. by Alastair Reid, Farrar bilingual ed. 1974 $8.95

The Splendor and Death of Joaquín Murieta. 1966. Trans. by Ben Belitt, Farrar bilingual ed. 1972 $7.95 pap. $2.95. A play on "a Chilean bandit done injustice in California on July 23, 1853."

We Are Many. Trans. by Alastair Reid, Brossman 1968 $5.00 pap. $2.95

Toward the Splendid City: Nobel Lecture. Farrar bilingual ed. 1974 $4.95

Fully Empowered. Trans. by Alastair Reid, Farrar bilingual ed. 1975 $12.95 pap. $6.95

Passion and Impression. Trans. by Margaret S. Peden, Farrar 1982 $25.00

Elegy. Trans. by Jack Hirschman, West End 1983 pap. $2.00

Still Another Day. Trans. by William O'Daly, Copper Canyon Pr. 1984 pap. $7.00

BOOKS ABOUT NERUDA

Belitt, Ben. *Adam's Dream: A Preface to Translation.* Grove 1978 $12.50 pap. $4.95

Bizarro, Salvatore. *Pablo Neruda: All Poets the Poet.* Scarecrow Pr. 1979 $15.00

De Costa, René. *The Poetry of Pablo Neruda.* Harvard Univ. Pr. text ed. 1982 pap. $5.95. An overall view of Neruda's production, with each period represented by analysis of one crucial work.

Durán, Manuel, and Margery Safir. *Earthstones: The Poetry of Pablo Neruda.* Indiana Univ. Pr. 1981 $22.50

Felstiner, John. *Translating Neruda: The Way to Machu Picchu.* Stanford Univ. Pr. 1986 $20.00 pap. $9.95

Russ, Frank. *The Word and the Stone: Language and Imagery in Neruda's "Canto General."* Modern Language and Lit. Monographs Oxford 1972 $11.25

Santi, Enrico M. *Pablo Neruda: The Politics of Prophecy.* Cornell Univ. Pr. 1982 $25.00

ONETTI, JUAN CARLOS. 1909–   Uruguay

Onetti's subject is the decay and materialism of the modern world, but he presents it in a dense, indirect prose style that creates a world often bordering on nightmare. The narrator of *A Brief Life* creates a number of other existences for himself to escape the boredom and limits, symbolized by his wife's mastectomy, of his own. Ultimately, the created worlds take over supposed reality. *The Shipyard* (o.p.), generally considered his best novel, demonstrates the central character's inability to control his life in an absurd existence. Onetti's characters never cease trying to create meaning, but they flounder helplessly in a world that is beyond their efforts at control.

BOOK BY ONETTI

A Brief Life. 1950. Trans. by Hortense Carpentier, Viking 1976 $14.95

BOOK ABOUT ONETTI

Kadir, Djelal. *Juan Carlos Onetti. Twayne's World Authors Ser*. G. K. Hall 1977 o.p.

PACHECO, JOSÉ EMILIO. 1939–   Mexico

Pacheco, one of Mexico's ablest critics, is also a poet of extraordinarily formal and thematic diversity, preoccupied with the struggle to express social concerns while maintaining artistic integrity. Originally preoccupied with metaphysical concerns, he sees humankind caught in time between poles of a destructive flow; people are trapped in a permanent present as time, somehow, passes. In his questioning of every aspect of existence, even poetry, the poet creates a sense of harmony within flux.

BOOKS BY PACHECO

Signals from the Flames. Trans. by Thomas Hoeksema, Latin Amer. Literary Review Pr. 1980 pap. $8.50. A selection from 13 years of work covering the poet's major development.
Don't Ask Me How the Time Goes By: Poems, 1964–1968. Trans. by Alastair Reid, Columbia Univ. Pr. bilingual ed. 1978 $25.00 pap. $12.00

PADILLA, HEBERTO. 1932–   Cuba

Padilla held a number of bureaucratic, educational, and journalistic positions under the government of Fidel Castro. His outspokenness in cultural affairs caused considerable tension and his collection of poems *Fuera del Juego* won an important Cuban prize but was judged antirevolutionary. Now an exile in the United States, he was the protagonist in the notorious "Padilla Affair," and was accused of subversive activities, causing an international protest. In 1980 he was permitted to leave Cuba. Padilla's poetry is anchored in the real world and tends to satirize abstract theorizing. The poems collected below mark his imprisonment, as well as his taste for Eliot and the breadth of his literary interests.

BOOKS BY PADILLA

Legacies: Selected Poems. Trans. by Alastair Reid and Andrew Hurley, Farrar bilingual ed. 1982 $15.95 pap. $8.95

Subversive Poetry: The Padilla Affair. Georgetown Univ. Cuban Students Association bilingual ed. consult publisher for information. Eighteen poems from *Fuera del Juego.*

Heroes Are Grazing in My Garden. Trans. by Andrew Hurley, Farrar 1984 $16.95. A novel written in the United States.

PARRA, NICANOR. 1914–   Chile

In an effort to transform poetry, Parra invented what he calls the "antipoem," which, he says, "returns poetry to its roots." He uses elements commonly considered ugly or antipoetic, ordinary objects and commonplace language, with a sardonic humor and an unexpected angle of vision. His work is comparable to that of the American Beat poets of the 1950s in its nonpoetic flat tone, direct statement, black humor, and violence, and he intends his poetry as an affront to society. At the same time, he works within a Chilean popular tradition, which gives his work a distinctly original flavor. Parra is a professor of theoretical physics at the University of Chile and an accomplished folk musician. Pablo Neruda called him "one of the great names in the literature of our language."

BOOK BY PARRA

Sermons and Homilies of the Christ of Elqui. Trans. by Sandra Reyes, Univ. of Missouri Pr. 1984 $13.50

PAZ, OCTAVIO. 1914–   Mexico

Octavio Paz's poetic roots are in romanticism and such neoromantics as D. H. Lawrence, but he has been profoundly influenced by Mexican Indian mythology and oriental religious philosophy, particularly Tantric Buddhism. The latter influence came about while he was serving as Mexico's ambassador to India (1962–68), when he resigned to protest the government's treatment of students demonstrating prior to the Olympic Games in Mexico City. He conceives of poetry as a way of transcending barriers of world, time, and individual self. Through poetry he seeks to achieve a state of innocence and a euphoria of the sense bordering on the mystical, and he expresses anguish when language fails him. Much of Paz's poetry is erotic, with women being the vehicle across the abyss to "the other side of the river," where union with universal consciousness is possible. He constantly experiments with form in an effort to break down the traditional forms of poetry; several of his long major works are circular and have coexisting variant readings, and *Renga* is a collaborative poem by poets in four languages.

Poetry for Paz is necessarily in conflict with society because of its potential for transmuting and reforming it, and the poetic imagination is a valuable tool for understanding society. His essays on the Mexican character, history, and traditions, such as *The Labyrinth of Solitude* and *The Other Mexico*, are fundamental to understanding the Mexican society. He has also written extensively on aesthetics, poetics, and the nature of language and poetry.

BOOKS BY PAZ

Early Poems, 1935–1955. Trans. by Muriel Rukeyser and others, Indiana Univ. Pr. 1973 $7.95; New Directions rev. ed. 1973 pap. $6.95

Selected Poems of Octavio Paz. Trans. by Eliot Weinberger, New Directions 1984 pap. $5.95

A Draft of Shadows and Other Poems. Trans. by Eliot Weinberger, New Directions 1979 pap. $6.95

Alternating Current. 1961–67. Trans. by Helen R. Lane, Seaver Bks. 1973 $9.95 1983 pap. $7.95. Essays on poetry, fiction, and philosophy.

The Labyrinth of Solitude, The Other Mexico, and Other Essays. Trans. by Lysander Kemp, Grove 1985 $22.50 pap. $9.95

Children of the Mire: Modern Poetry from Romanticism to the Avant-Garde. Harvard Univ. Pr. 1974 pap. $5.95. The Charles Eliot Norton Lectures for 1971–1972.

Configuration. 1957–67. Intro. by Muriel Rukeyser, New Directions bilingual ed. 1971 pap. $5.95. Includes *Sun Stone* (1957) and *Blanco* (1967), two major long poems.

Conjunctions and Disjunctions. 1969. Trans. by Helen R. Lane, Viking 1974 $7.95 1982 pap. $7.95

The Other Mexico: Critique of the Pyramid. Trans. by Lysander Kemp, Grove (Evergreen) 1972 pap. $2.45. Lectures on Mexican history and culture given at the University of Texas in 1969; continues the brilliant analysis of *The Labyrinth of Solitude.*

Renga: A Chain of Poems. Trans. by Charles Tomlinson, fwd. by Claude Roy, Braziller 1972 $5.95 pap. $2.95. An attempt at a collective poem, originally written in the four languages, with translation.

Eagle or Sun? Trans. by Eliot Weinberger, New Directions bilingual ed. 1976 $8.50 pap. $5.95

Marcel Duchamp. Trans. by Rachel Phillips and Donald Gardner, Seaver Bks. 1981 $14.95 pap. $6.95

The Monkey Grammarian. Trans. by Helen R. Lane, Seaver Bks. 1981 $14.95 pap. $7.95. Essays on the nature and function of poetic language.

On Poets. Trans. by Michael Schmidt, Humanities Pr. text ed. 1983 $31.50

BOOKS ABOUT PAZ

Phillips, Rachel. *Poetic Modes of Octavio Paz. Modern Language and Lit. Monographs* Oxford 1973 $12.00

Wilson, Jason. *Octavio Paz: A Study of His Poetics.* Cambridge Univ. Pr. 1979 o.p.

PUIG, MANUEL. 1932–   Argentina

Puig is fascinated by the variety and richness, and at the same time, by the stultifying effects of pop culture. Most of his novels are technically parodies of some form of pop art while they portray the spiritual emptiness of the characters who are affected by these forms. *Betrayed by Rita Hayworth* is an innovative novel narrating through a variety of techniques the story of a young Argentine boy who lives vicariously through the movies. Puig uses the phenomenon of compulsive movie-going as a symbol for alienation and escape from reality. *Heartbreak Tango* evokes the spiritual emptiness of the

Argentine provincial life of the 1930s and the vulgarity of popular music and the soap opera; *The Buenos Aires Affair* uses the form of the detective novel to parody pop fiction. *Kiss of the Spider Woman* examines political and sexual liberation in novelistic techniques that reject traditional dialogue in favor of various other kinds of texts, and in *Blood of Unrequited Love* a man and a woman relive an old but passionate affair in the Brazilian backlands. *Eternal Curse* is a novelty for Puig in that it consists entirely of dialogue, plus an epilogue in letters. Less obviously parodic and more elliptical, with less reliance on the machinery of pop culture, it demonstrates his constant search for a new form for his novels.

BOOKS BY PUIG

Betrayed by Rita Hayworth. 1968. Trans. by Suzanne J. Levine, Random (Vintage) 1981 pap. $4.95

Heartbreak Tango. 1969. Trans. by Suzanne J. Levine, Dutton 1975 pap. $2.45; Random (Vintage) 1981 pap. $3.50

The Buenos Aires Affair: A Detective Novel. Trans. by Suzanne J. Levine, Random (Vintage) 1980 pap. $3.50

Kiss of the Spider Woman. Trans. by Thomas Colchie, Knopf 1979 $8.95; Random (Vintage) 1980 pap. $3.95

Eternal Curse on the Reader of These Pages. Random 1982 $13.50 1983 pap. $3.95

Blood of Unrequited Love. Trans. by Jan L. Grayson, Random 1984 $7.95

QUIROGA, HORACIO. 1878–1937   Argentina

One of the fathers of the Spanish American short story, Quiroga participated extensively in the modernist movement in Montevideo and later lived in the tropical province of Misiones. Although best known as the author of stories about the jungle that reveal the dangers at every step, he also wrote imaginative fantastic tales among the best of their kind in an area that has produced a great number of such authors. His work, like his life, is filled with violent tragedy and a sense of foreboding.

BOOK BY QUIROGA

The Decapitated Chicken and Other Stories. Texas Pan-Amer. Ser. Univ. of Texas Pr. 1976 $14.95 1984 pap. $6.95

RIVERA, JOSÉ EUSTASIO. 1888–1928   Colombia

After the publication of a book of romantic sonnets entitled *The Promised Land* (1921, o.p.), Rivera wrote his own novel, *The Vortex*, prototype of the Latin American jungle novel. Rejecting the traditional romantic view of the jungle as magnificent landscape peopled by innocent natives, Rivera presented a man-eating, terrifying green trap that closes on the protagonist. The narrator is Arturo Cova, a persona of Rivera, whose memoirs relate his seduction of a young girl, their escape into the jungle, crime and corruption in the rubber industry, and the extreme violence that results when people's instincts are unchecked by civilization. Based on historical data, personal observation, and travel logs, *The Vortex* grew out of the conflict Rivera saw between literary presentations of the jungle and his own experience of it.

Rivera died of diseases contracted in the jungle in the course of his work as member of a commission appointed to settle a boundary dispute between Colombia and Venezuela.

BOOK BY RIVERA

The Vortex. 1924. Trans. by James K. Earl, Fertig repr. of 1935 ed. 1979 $19.50

RULFO, JUAN. 1918–1986   Mexico

Rulfo's collection of short stories, *The Burning Plain*, deals in harsh, colloquial language with the poor peasants of remote areas of the province of Jalisco—their traditions, problems, and passions. His only published novel, *Pedro Páramo*, also based on rural life, treats the theme of the *cacique* or boss of a town. The structure of the novel, influenced in part by Faulkner, involves the juxtaposition and transposition of pieces of narrative, monologue, dialogue, and poetic prose.

BOOKS BY RULFO

The Burning Plain and Other Stories. 1953. Trans. by George D. Schade, *Texas Pan-Amer. Ser.* Univ. of Texas Pr. 1967 $12.95 pap. $6.95
Pedro Páramo: A Novel of Mexico. 1955. Trans. by Lysander Kemp, Grove 1959 pap. $3.95

SÁBATO, ERNESTO. 1911–   Argentina

Sábato's protagonists in his three major novels are all obsessive neurotics trapped in a society that went wrong centuries ago. *On Heroes and Tombs* analyzes the phenomenon of Peronism and the social conditions that caused it, but it is also an anguished examination of what Sábato perceives to be the basic errors of Argentine society from its beginnings. The complex plot integrates the tyranny of Perón with that of Rosas a century earlier. Its principal characters counterpoint the decadence of the old aristocracy with the potential for change of the descendants of the European immigrants. One entire major section is devoted to a schizophrenic episode by a protagonist-villain, Fernando Vidal Olmos, who may also be seen as hero. Sábato's work is difficult to explicate, but reading it is an overwhelming experience.

BOOK BY SÁBATO

On Heroes and Tombs. Trans. by Helen R. Lane, Godine 1981 $17.95

SARMIENTO, DOMINGO FAUSTINO. 1811–1888   Argentina

Born into a humble family, Sarmiento became president of the Argentine republic in 1868. He was a driving force in the effort to Europeanize Argentina and in the struggle against the rural power elite. His reputation in literature is based on *Civilization and Barbarism: Life of Juan Facundo Quiroga*, a combination of essay and history that often approaches the novel in its handling of imaginative narrative. Demonstrating the barbaric actions of both Juan Manuel de Rosas, the dictatorial governor of Argentina, and the gaucho Facundo in *Tiger of the Pampas* (o.p.), Sarmiento advocated the civilizing influences of education and economic progress. His ambivalent feelings and romantic view of the gaucho led him to create a mythical character rather than a historical figure. The narratives and sketches in *Travels* have been described as "a virtual novel" (Anderson Imbert) for their imaginative quality.

BOOKS BY SARMIENTO

Sarmiento Anthology. Trans. by Stuart E. Grummon, ed. by Allison Bunkley, Associated Faculty Pr. 1971 $12.50

Life in the Argentine Republic in the Days of the Tyrants, or Civilization and Barbarism. 1845. Gordon $75.00; trans. by Marty T. Mann, Macmillan (Hafner) pap. $9.95

Sarmiento's Travels in the United States in 1847. Trans. by M. A. Rockland, Princeton Univ. Pr. 1970 $33.00

BOOKS ABOUT SARMIENTO

Bunkley, Allison W. *Life of Sarmiento*. Greenwood repr. of 1952 ed. lib. bdg. $20.00

Crowley, Frances G. *Domingo Faustino Sarmiento. Twayne's World Authors Ser*. G. K. Hall lib. bdg. $16.95

Jones, C. A. *Sarmiento: Facundo*. Tamesis 1974 o.p.

SKÁRMETA, ANTONIO. 1940–   Chile

Skármeta is another of the Chileans profoundly affected by his country's political travail; since 1975, he has lived in Berlin. *The Insurrection* is a novel of the Nicaraguan Revolution just before Somoza's fall; it captures the intensity and extremes of a moment that transforms a whole society. The novel has been translated into seven languages and was made into an award-winning film in Europe. *Chileno!* was written for adolescents drawing on Skármeta's own experience of exile.

BOOKS BY SKÁRMETA

Chileno! Trans. by Hortense Carpentier, Morrow 1979 $10.00

The Insurrection. Trans. by Paula Sharp, Ediciones Norte 1983 pap. $7.50

VALENZUELA, LUISA. 1938–   Argentina

Luisa Valenzuela is one of the many women who have emerged as major voices in Latin American fiction. Her elliptic metaphoric pieces broaden the definitions of short story and novel. *Strange Things Happen Here* is close to an allegory of the Argentine political situation, but it shuns conventional realism to blur reality in a hallucinatory style. Cortázar said of Valenzuela that she lucidly charts "the seldom-chosen course of a woman deeply anchored in her condition, conscious of discriminations that are still horrible all over our continent, but, at the same time, filled with joy in life that permits her to surmount both the elementary stages of protest and an overestimation of women in order to put herself on a perfectly equal footing with any literature—masculine or not."

BOOKS BY VALENZUELA

Clara: Thirteen Short Stories and a Novel. Trans. by Hortense Carpentier and Jorge
    Castello, Harcourt 1976 $12.95
Strange Things Happen Here. Harcourt 1979 $9.95
The Lizard's Tail. Trans. by Gregory Rabassa, Farrar 1983 $16.50
Other Weapons. Trans. by Deborah Bonner, Ediciones Norte 1985 $8.50

VALLEJO, CÉSAR. 1892–1938   Peru

Primarily a poet and one of Latin America's finest of the twentieth century, Vallejo also wrote several novels and plays with a strong social content.
His situation as a *mestizo*, of part Indian blood, his humble social background, and the political and social discrimination to which he was subjected because of these factors, created the profound psychological tensions
and alienation from society that mark his work. His work is permeated with
a sense of the dignity of the oppressed Indian and a spirit of rebellion. In his
first volume, *The Black Heralds,* he used the techniques of symbolism to express bitterness at his suffering and condition of isolation. *Trilce* (1922) is one
of the most original works of modern poetry, with an innovative syntax and
structure that transcend normal logical rules to express the poet's feeling of
solitude and the helplessness of oppressed peoples. After the publication of
Trilce, Vallejo moved to Paris, where he lived in poverty and was harshly
treated because of his political opinions. His posthumously published *Human Poems,* and *Spain, Let This Cup Pass from Me* reveal his anguish over the
Spanish civil war and his sense of solidarity with combatants for peace and
freedom, in poetry of a simpler structure and form.

BOOKS BY VALLEJO

Selected Poems of César Vallejo. Trans. by R. H. Hays, Sachem 1981 $13.50 pap. $6.95
Autopsy on Surrealism. Trans. by Richard Schaaf, Curbstone 1982 pap. $4.00
Poemas Humanos: Human Poems. 1939. Trans. by Clayton Eshelman, Grove bilin-
    gual ed. 1969 $8.50 pap. $3.45
Spain, Let This Cup Pass from Me. 1939. Trans. by Alvaro Cardoña-Hine, Red Hill
    1972 pap. $4.00
César Vallejo: The Complete Posthumous Poetry. Trans. by Clayton Eshelman and José
    R. Barcia, Univ. of California Pr. 1978 pap. $6.95

VARGAS LLOSA, MARIO. 1936–   Peru

Vargas Llosa, who received his doctorate from the University of Madrid
and has lived in London and Paris, now resides in Peru. In addition to novels, he has also written extensively on the modern novel, especially García
Márquez and FLAUBERT, and recently premiered two successful plays.
Vargas Llosa's first novel, *The City and the Dogs* (*The Time of the Hero,* 1966,
o.p.), brought both scandal and fame to its author. A thousand copies were
ceremoniously burned in Peru, where Vargas Llosa was denounced as an enemy of the state, but the novel was published in Spain to high critical acclaim.

The Green House (1968, o.p.), based on memories of experiences in the jungle, contains five interrelated stories fragmented through the five parts of the novel and covering a span of 45 years. Space, time, character, and action are broken and juxtaposed in a marvelous display of novelistic technique. Implicit are critiques of Peru's religious and military establishments. In *Conversation in the Cathedral, La Catedral* being a bar, Vargas Llosa used the conversation between the son of a wealthy man and his father's mulatto chauffeur as a base for a series of juxtaposed pieces of other conversations, again exposing a corrupt society and revealing man's weaknesses and desperate condition. *Captain Pantoja and the Special Service* is Vargas Llosa's first openly comic novel, but it also uses overlapping simultaneous plots and a sardonic approach to the role of the military in Latin American public (and private) life. The humor does not hide the dark underside of a jungle where the unexpected is always waiting. *Aunt Julia and the Scriptwriter* is openly autobiographical, dealing in barely disguised form with his first marriage. It again uses a favorite technique of juxtaposing two distinct narrative threads to satirize the commercialism and hypocrisy of society. In *The War of the End of the World* Vargas Llosa used a popular messianic revolt in the Brazilian backlands at the turn of the century to explore relations between fiction and so-called reality, one of his favorite critical themes.

BOOKS BY VARGAS LLOSA

Conversation in the Cathedral. 1969. Trans. by Gregory Rabassa, Harper 1975 $12.50

Captain Pantoja and the Special Service. Trans. by Ronald Christ and Gregory Kolovakos, Harper 1978 $11.49

The Cubs and Other Stories. Trans. by Gregory Kolovakos and Ronald Christ, Harper 1979 $10.00. Short fiction from the two Spanish collections, *Los Jefes* (1965) and *Los Cachorros* (1967).

Aunt Julia and the Scriptwriter. Trans. by Helen R. Lane, Avon 1983 pap. $3.95; Farrar 1982 $17.50

The War of the End of the World. Trans. by Helen R. Lane, Farrar 1984 $18.95

BOOK ABOUT VARGAS LLOSA

Rossman, Charles, and Alan Warren Friedman, eds. *Mario Vargas Llosa: A Collection of Critical Essays.* Univ. of Texas Pr. 1978 $12.50

WOLFF, EGON. 1926–   Chile

After working as a chemical engineer, Wolff began writing plays in 1958. He is one of a group of playwrights who developed with the support of Chilean university theaters. His plays most often deal with the demise of the guilt-ridden middle class, but he has abandoned overt realism in favor of a series of dramatic images that resist reduction to a simplistic message. *Paper Flowers*, which, in the translator's words, portrays the "destruction of a bourgeoise indifferent to its surrounding social problems," is also a chilling portrait of a psychopathic personality and an investigation of the dynamics of human relationships.

BOOK BY WOLFF

Paper Flowers: A Play in Six Scenes. Trans. by Margaret S. Peden, Univ. of Missouri
    Pr. 1971 $6.50 pap. $5.95

YÁÑEZ, AGUSTIN. 1904–1980   Mexico

An important figure in Mexican public life, Yáñez served as governor of
his state of Jalisco, professor at the National University, and secretary of
public education. Although not well known outside Mexico, he was a
founder of the contemporary novel, and his *The Edge of the Storm*, published
in 1947, has been termed by Walter M. Langford the most single important
work in the history of the Mexican novel. Influenced by DOS PASSOS (see Vol.
1), ALDOUS HUXLEY (see Vol. 1), and JAMES JOYCE (see Vol. 1), Yáñez brought
the Mexican novel into the twentieth century in the areas of narrative technique and psychological penetration. *The Edge of the Storm* is the first of a
trilogy, now including *The Prodigal Land* and *The Lean Lands*.

BOOKS BY YÁÑEZ

The Edge of the Storm. Trans. by Ethel Brinton, *Texas Pan-Amer. Ser.* Univ. of Texas
    Pr. 1963 pap. $7.95
The Lean Lands. 1962. Trans. by Ethel Brinton, *Texas Pan-Amer. Ser.* Univ. of Texas
    Pr. 1968 $6.50

CARIBBEAN LITERATURE

Caribbean literature, although barely known in the United States, is rich
and complex. It is the product of the culture of a number of islands and, by
extension, neighboring shores that represent a variety of ethnic and cultural
strands—English, African, Dutch, French, East Indian, Portuguese, and Hispanic—and is inevitably shaped by its history of imperialism, colonialism,
and discrimination. Exile, voluntary or forced, is a central fact; many Caribbean authors are immigrants from Asia, while others have emigrated from
the West Indies to England, Australia, or other nations. The nostalgia for African roots and the clear sense of cultural identity have led to the publication of a number of studies and collections that include both African and Caribbean authors. Many writers deal with the commonality of background
and situation, despite national, regional, or even linguistic differences.

There is great diversity; although English and to a lesser degree French
are the dominant languages, there are also many regional patois, or folk languages, that are vehicles for literary expression, much like the Scot dialect
in Great Britain. Lamentably, little of this non-English material has been
translated, so that Haitian literature, for example, is almost totally inacces-
sible to the non-French reading public. Writers of such international importance as the Martinican poet and dramatist Aimé Césaire, and the
Guyanese poet Leon-Gontran Damas, among the founders of the important
Negritude movement, are unavailable in English. Even important English-

language texts are soon out of print, although Heinemann's series of Caribbean writers is a healthy step toward remedying the situation.

It was not until nearly the twentieth century that the French- and English-speaking lands began to produce a literature that was not simply the product of transplanted Londoners or Parisians. Shortly after 1900, writers of black and white ancestry alike began to describe the Caribbean experience as something distinct from the European tradition. At present there is a flourishing literature of considerable diversity, with increasing governmental sponsorship, university creative writing workshops, and similar activity.

Literary History and Criticism

Brown, Lloyd W. *West Indian Poetry.* Heinemann 2d ed. text ed. 1984 pap. $15.00; *Twayne's World Authors Ser.* G. K. Hall 1978 lib. bdg. $14.50

Dathorne, O. R. *The Literature of the Black Man in the Caribbean.* Louisiana State Univ. Pr. 1981 o.p.

Gilkes, Michael. *The West Indian Novel. Twayne's World Authors Ser.* G. K. Hall 1981 $14.95

Harris, Wilson. *The Womb of Space: The Cross-cultural Imagination.* Greenwood 1983 $29.95

King, Bruce. *West Indian Literature.* Shoe String (Archon) 1980 $16.50. Essays on the historical background, Mittelholzer, Selvon, Lamming, Walcott, Naipaul, Harris, Brathwaite, and Jean Rhys.

Ramchaud, Kenneth. *The West Indian Novel and Its Background.* Heinemann 2d ed. 1984 pap. $10.00

Collections

Dathorne, O. R. *Caribbean Narrative.* Heinemann 1966 pap. $5.50

———. *Caribbean Verse: An Anthology.* Heinemann 1967 pap. $4.50

Jekyll, Walter. *Jamaican Song and Story.* Intro. by Alice Werner, AMS Pr. repr. of 1907 ed. $28.00; Dover 1966 pap. $4.00; Kraus repr. of 1904 ed. pap. $24.00

Lomax, Alan, ed. *3000 Years of Black Poetry: An Anthology.* Dodd 1984 pap. $7.95

McFarlane, John E. *A Treasury of Jamaican Poetry.* 1966. Gordon 1977 $59.95

———. *Voices from Summerland: An Anthology of Jamaican Poetry.* Gordon 1977 lib. bdg. $59.95

Ramchaud, Kenneth, ed. *West Indian Narrative: An Introductory Anthology.* Humanities Pr. 1966 $5.50

Salkey, Andrew, ed. *West Indian Stories.* Faber 1968 pap. $4.95

Sander, Reinhard W., ed. *From Trinidad: An Anthology of Early West Indian Writing.* Holmes & Meier text ed. 1979 $45.00

Shapiro, Norman R., ed. *Negritude: Black Poetry from Africa and the Caribbean.* October 1970 $7.50 pap. $4.95. Fifty-one poems by 20 Caribbean poets.

Sherlock, Philip M. *West Indian Folk Tales.* Oxford repr. of 1966 ed. 1978 $14.95

Sherlock, Philip M., and Helen Sherlock. *Ears and Tales and Commonsense: More Stories from the Caribbean.* Harper 1974 $10.95

Underwood, Edna. *The Poets of Haiti.* Gordon repr. of 1934 ed. 1977 $34.95

Wolkstein, Diane, ed. *The Magic Orange Tree and Other Haitian Folktales.* Schocken 1980 pap. $5.95

ANTHONY, MICHAEL. 1932–   Trinidad

Anthony avoids the social and the polemic; his work is all a skillful recreation of the rural experiences of his youth in a style that avoids the excesses of political commitment and of avant-gardism. *The Year in San Fernando* is an ironic, first-person narrative of the experience of a year in the city for a twelve-year-old boy.

BOOKS BY ANTHONY

The Games Were Coming. Andre Deutsch 1963 $9.95; *Heinemann Caribbean Writers Ser.* 1977 pap. $4.50
The Year in San Fernando. 1965. *Heinemann Caribbean Writers Ser.* 1970 pap. $4.00
Cricket in the Road. Heinemann Caribbean Writers Ser. 1973 pap. $4.00
Sandra Street and Other Stories. Heinemann Caribbean Writers Ser. 1973 pap. $3.00
All That Glitters. Andre Deutsch 1981 $14.95; *Heinemann Caribbean Writers Ser.* 1983 pap. $5.00

BRATHWAITE, EDWARD KAMAU. 1930–   Barbados

A graduate of Cambridge, Brathwaite has been influenced by his experiences in England and long residence in Ghana, where he taught. Since the 1960s, he has been a historian at the University of the West Indies. Brathwaite is vitally interested in the cultural transmission from Africa to the Caribbean. His poetry makes extensive use of dialect and the fusion-tension between European and African sources, and African oral communal poetry has influenced him. He has also used the blues as an expression of the oppression of the Caribbean people, flavored by African oral tradition and island music and speech rhythms. He appears to regard poetry as a vehicle for communicating an emerging synthetic culture. The result is a vigorous, ironic poetic idiom. He is also a highly regarded novelist; his novel *To Sir, with Love* was made into a much-praised film.

BOOKS BY BRATHWAITE

To Sir, with Love. Jove 1973 pap. $2.75; New Amer. Lib. (Signet) 1982 pap. $1.75
Mother Poem. Oxford 1977 pap. $10.95
The Arrivants. Oxford 1981 pap. $8.95
Sun Poem. Oxford 1982 $11.95

DELISSER, HERBERT. 1878–1944   Jamaica

DeLisser was a newspaper editor and prominent conservative member of white society, but in *Jane's Career* he showed the beginnings of an awareness of the total spectrum of island society. The protagonist is a black girl who emancipates herself economically after a series of predictable dilemmas. His other novels are historical, and the structure of *Jane's Career* is conventional and linear.

BOOK BY DELISSER

Jane's Career. 1914. *Heinemann Caribbean Writers Ser.* 1972 pap. $4.00; Holmes & Meier 1971 $27.50

GOMES, ALBERT M. 1911–1978   Trinidad

Of Portuguese ancestry, Gomes studied in Port-of-Spain and New York. He was active in politics and the union movement, and wrote poetry, novels, and an autobiography. Gomes's political career led to service on the City Council and as deputy mayor of Port-of-Spain, and in the government of Trinidad and Tobago. After the collapse of the Federation of the West Indies in 1962, Gomes settled in England. His poetry is formally traditional and tends toward abstract intellectualism.

BOOK BY GOMES

All Papa's Children. Three Continents 1978 pap. $5.00

HARRIS, WILSON. 1921–   Guyana

Harris's novels deal typically with the metaphoric voyage of self-discovery, often through the Guyanese hinterland or upriver (*Palace of the Peacock*). The heroes of *DaSilva* and *Genesis* both live in London and use the city as a base for the inner exploration of their multiethnic antecedents. Harris sees a relationship between words as the raw material of literature and colors as the material of art; he attempts to use language as a painter uses paints, in layers or shocking contrasts.

BOOKS BY HARRIS

Palace of the Peacock. 1960. Faber 1969 pap. $4.95
Whole Armor and the Secret Ladders. Faber 1973 pap. $5.95
The Eye of the Scarecrow. Faber 1974 pap. $3.95
DaSilva's Cultivated Wilderness and Genesis of the Clowns. Faber 1978 $9.95
The Tree of the Sun. Faber 1978 $10.95
The Angel at the Gate. Faber 1983 $15.95

BOOK ABOUT HARRIS

Gilkes, Michael. *Wilson Harris and the Caribbean Novel.* Univ. Place 1975 $10.00

LAMMING, GEORGE. 1927–   Barbados

Lamming's works are a panorama of West Indian history with a strong sense of nationalism. *In the Castle of My Skin* is at least partially autobiographical in its presentation of the protagonist's growing sense of individuality and the consequent estrangement from the village and folk community. The subsequent exile is told in *The Emigrants*, the return in *Of Age and Innocence*, and the reclamation of the heritage in *Season of Adventure*. Much of Lamming's work deals with the role of the black man in England, where all his books were published.

BOOKS BY LAMMING

In the Castle of My Skin. 1953. Schocken 1983 pap. $6.95

The Emigrants. 1954. Schocken 1980 pap. $6.95
Of Age and Innocence. 1958. Schocken 1981 pap. $7.95
Season of Adventure. 1960. Schocken pap. $6.95

MAIS, ROGER. 1905–1955   Jamaica

Mais spoke for the dispossessed black community of Jamaica. *The Hills Were Joyful Together* is a devastating portrait of degradation and violence, although it uses a complicated symbolic structure. His other works were published after he left Jamaica in 1952, perhaps as a result of the negative reaction to his social voice. They continue his commitment to social conscience, but show as well a growing tension between that concept of the artist's duty and the notion of the individual artistic conscience.

Books by Mais

The Hills Were Joyful Together. 1953. *Heinemann Caribbean Writers Ser.* 1981 pap. $6.50
Black Lightning. Heinemann Caribbean Writers Ser. 1983 pap. $5.00
Bother Man. Heinemann Caribbean Writers Ser. 1974 pap. $5.00

McKAY, CLAUDE. 1890–1948   Jamaica

Born in rural black society in Jamaica, McKay immigrated to New York in 1912. In Harlem, he found the intellectual and creative ferment of the beginnings of the Harlem renaissance and Marcus Garvey's Back-to-Africa movement. His first novel, *Home to Harlem*, was published in New York. Like *Banjo*, it deals with the black man in the white world and exalts blackness. As did many West Indian writers living and working in other lands, McKay felt a need for a real West Indian identity, a quest developed in *Banana Bottom*. In *Banana Bottom* and the short story collection *Gingertown*, McKay caught Jamaican popular attitudes and values. McKay's poetry shows a clear awareness of poverty and inequality. He made extensive use of black folk idiom, although his later work made growing use of Christian imagery and traditional language.

Books by McKay

Selected Poems. G. K. Hall 1971 $11.50
Constab Ballads. Gordon 1977 $59.95
The Dialect Poetry of Claude McKay. Ayer 2 vols. in 1 repr. of 1912 ed. $21.00
Home to Harlem. Chatham repr. of 1928 ed. 1973 $12.95
Banjo. 1929. Harcourt 1970 pap. $5.95
Gingertown. Ayer repr. of 1932 ed. $16.00
Banana Bottom. Chatham repr. of 1933 ed. 1971 $7.95; Harcourt 1974 pap. $6.95
A Long Way from Home. Ayer repr. of 1937 ed. $19.00

Books about McKay

Gayle, Addison. *Claude McKay: The Black Poet at War.* Broadside Pr. pap. $2.50
Giles, James R. *Claude McKay. Twayne's U.S. Authors Ser.* G. K. Hall 1976 $12.50

MITTELHOLZER, EDGAR. 1909–1965 Guyana

Mittelholzer's work represents the personal struggle between a sense of identification with European culture and a sense of identity as a West Indian. He was the first of his generation to emigrate from the West Indies and to attempt to carve a career as a serious novelist in England. In a relatively short life, he published 22 novels, among other volumes. *Corentyne Thunder* is a traditionally written novel, but it deals with the spiritual schizophrenia of a protagonist torn between two conflicting loyalties. *A Morning at the Office* is a coldly objective view of the absurdities of tightly organized hierarchical colonial society.

BOOKS BY MITTELHOLZER

Corentyne Thunder. 1941. *Heinemann Caribbean Writers Ser.* 1970 pap. $5.50
A Morning at the Office. 1948. *Heinemann Caribbean Writers Ser.* 1974 pap. $5.00

NAIPAUL, V(IDIADHAR) S(URAJPRASAD). 1932– Trinidad

Born in Trinidad of Hindu parents, V. S. Naipaul was educated at Oxford and lives in Britain, where he has won a number of literary awards. The *N.Y. Herald Tribune* wrote of the beguiling, warmly humorous *Mystic Masseur:* "The characterizations are vivid and witty. Human truths are revealed, and we are entertained." *Miguel Street* describes the aberrant lives of a mean street in Port-of-Spain, Trinidad. "A particular delight of Mr. Naipaul's writing is the dialogue. The West Indian idiom in his hands is full of color and a rich Elizabethan disregard for conventional correctness" (*TLS*). Naipaul's work, even when he appears to be analyzing a picturesque character, is really an analysis of the entire society of Trinidad. *The Middle Passage* extends this survey of the social order to other areas of the West Indies: Surinam, Martinique, Jamaica, and British Guyana, and finds that "the present character of the regions he visited express their history as colonial territories built on slave labor." In *An Area of Darkness*, Naipaul expressed with sympathy and insight his observations on a trip to India, where he saw the loftiest human values contrasted with the meanest physical suffering.

BOOKS BY NAIPAUL

Mystic Masseur. Heinemann Caribbean Writers Ser. text ed. 1971 pap. $5.00
Miguel Street. Heinemann Caribbean Writers Ser. 1974 pap. $4.95; Penguin 1977 pap. $3.95; Random 1984 pap. $3.95
Guerillas. Knopf 1975 $10.00; Random 1980 pap. $3.95
India: A Wounded Civilization. Knopf 1977 $10.00; Random 1978 pap. $3.95
The Loss of El Dorado. Penguin 1977 pap. $4.50; Random 1984 pap. $4.95
A Bend in the River. Knopf 1979 $10.00; Random 1980 pap. $3.95
The Return of Eva Peron. Knopf 1980 $10.00; Random 1981 pap. $2.95
Among the Believers: An Islamic Journey. Knopf 1981 $15.00; Random 1982 pap. $6.95
An Area of Darkness. Random 1981 pap. $4.95
The Middle Passage: Impressions of Five Societies—British, French, and Dutch—in the West Indies and South America. Random 1981 pap. $5.95

Three Novels. Knopf 1982 $18.95
A House for Mr. Biswas. Knopf 1983 $17.95; Penguin 1976 pap. $4.95
Finding the Center: Two Narratives. Knopf 1984 $13.95

BOOKS ABOUT NAIPAUL

Hamner, Robert D. *A Critical Perspective on V. S. Naipaul.* Three Continents 1977 $24.00 pap. $14.00
———. *V. S. Naipaul. Twayne's World Authors Ser.* G. K. Hall 1973 $14.50
McSweeney, Kerry. *Four Contemporary Novelists: Angus Wilson, Brian Moore, John Fowles, V. S. Naipaul.* McGill-Queens Univ. Pr. 1983 $24.95
Morris, Robert K. *Paradox of Order: Some Perspectives.* Univ. of Missouri Pr. 1975 $7.90
Sudha, Rai. *V. S. Naipaul: A Study in Expatriate Sensibility.* IND-US 1982 $12.00

REID, V. S. 1913–   Jamaica

Reid's historical novel *New Day* (o.p.) is based on the Morant Bay Uprising of 1865 and demonstrates an awareness that there have been armed resistances to oppression, although the novel also shows a certain ambivalence toward this resistance. There is an interesting use of dialect and skillful contrast of two time levels. *The Leopard* presents an African protagonist during the Mau Mau Rebellion in Kenya. The novel is clearly allegorical, but its lyric character and understanding of the African circumstances have been much praised. Both revolts were connected to the inequalities of colonial structures, and Reid's themes show his awareness of the similarity of the colonial experience.

BOOK BY REID

The Leopard. Chatham repr. of 1958 ed. 1972 $7.50; *Heinemann Caribbean Writers Ser.* 1980 pap. $4.00

ROUMAIN, JACQUES. 1907–1944   Haiti

Roumain was one of those educated young who were interested in the revindication of folkways and a national culture, centered around the foundation of *La Revue Indigène* in 1927. The experience generated a movement of social protest as well as literary nationalism. Poet and author of ethnological studies, Roumain also wrote a number of novels. His posthumous novel *The Masters of the Dew* is a powerful realistic vision of life in a peasant community, written in Creolized French, the language of the people and their culture that permeates the novel.

BOOK BY ROUMAIN

The Masters of the Dew. Trans. by Langston Hughes and Mercer Cook, *Heinemann Caribbean Writers Ser.* 1978 pap. $4.50

SALKEY, ANDREW. 1928–   Jamaica

Born in Panama and educated in Jamaica and London, Salkey is an important critic and anthologist who uses African folktales and the variegated West Indian popular culture, such as cultism, as sources for his novels and short stories. He is also a poet. Salkey is a writer attempting to forge a distinctive West Indian personality out of the diversity of the various ethnic sources

BOOKS BY SALKEY

West Indian Stories. Faber 1968 pap. $4.95
Away. Schocken 1980 $11.95
In the Hills Where Her Dreams Live. Black Scholar Pr. 1981 pap. $4.95

SELVON, SAMUEL. 1923–   Trinidad

Largely self-educated, Selvon was first a poet, later a journalist, and then a professional novelist. *Turn Again Tiger* is a sequel to his highly successful first novel, *A Brighter Sun*, whose newly married Indian peasant protagonist is drastically affected by his settlement in a suburban area. In *Turn Again Tiger* the protagonist returns to his community with a deeper sense of place. Both novels explore his relations to his origins and the various layers of Trinidadian society. *Moses Ascending* is a humorous satire of the situation of the West Indian in London. Although his roots are in the nineteenth-century novel, Selvon has created a personal literary language out of the fusion of standard English with Creole folk language, just as he has allied the techniques of European fiction to the West Indian rhythms.

BOOKS BY SELVON

Turn Again Tiger. 1958. *Heinemann Caribbean Writers Ser.* 1980 pap. $4.50
A Brighter Sun. Longman text ed. 1972 pap. $4.95
Moses Ascending. Heinemann Caribbean Writers Ser. repr. of 1975 ed. 1984 pap. $5.50

WALCOTT, DEREK. 1930–   Saint Lucia

Walcott studied at the University of the West Indies and has lived extensively in England and the United States. He is a prolific author of prose, plays, and poetry. Although his island childhood is apparent in his work, he is less rooted in popular language and folklore and rejects a simplistic nostalgia. Unlike many other West Indian writers, Walcott attempts to incorporate the double European-African tradition. He is an individual trying to locate his own place and the place of the Caribbean citizen in a complex world. Much of his work presents vivid images of nostalgia for the distant island and a sense of isolation and alienation. The volume of poetry *Sea Grapes* is a disenchanted warning against self-aggrandizing political leaders. *Another Life* is a picturesque gallery of scenes of Caribbean life, but it also presents life as an odyssey, as a perpetual search for change and growth.

BOOKS BY WALCOTT

Dream of Monkey Mountain and Other Plays. Farrar 1970 pap. $8.95; Univ. Place 1970 $15.00
Sea Grapes. Farrar 1976 $8.95 pap. $4.95
The Joker of Seville and Babylon: Two Plays. Farrar 1978 $15.00 pap. $6.95
The Star-Apple Kingdom. Farrar 1979 $10.00 pap. $5.95

Remembrance and Pantomime. Farrar 1980 $15.95 pap. $7.95
Another Life. Three Continents 1982 $7.50
The Fortunate Traveller. Farrar 1982 $11.95 pap. $7.95
Midsummer. Farrar 1984 $12.50 pap. $7.95
Three Plays: The Last Carnival; Beef, No Chicken; A Branch of the Blue Nile. Farrar
    1985 $22.50 pap. $9.95

CHAPTER 20

African Literature

Glenderlyn Johnson

In talking about African literature, there are two common fallacies we must avoid. The first is to see African literature as so different and special and so removed from the realm of other literatures, that it can share no common approaches with them. The opposite fallacy holds that nothing of real importance separates African literature from, say European literature, against which it is inevitably measured.
—CHINUA ACHEBE, "The Uses of African Literature," *Okike: An African Journal of New Writing*

Modern African literature, rooted in oral tradition and steeped in folklore, is an intimate reflection of the continent's rich culture and complex history. Traditionally, it was the duty of the village *griot* (oral historian) to mentally preserve the history of his particular area, which he was often asked to recite at various social and ceremonial gatherings such as births, circumcisions, and government functions.

By drawing on this oral legacy and combining indigenous folktales, legends, and proverbs, contemporary authors have produced a body of creative prose that has a distinctly African personality, despite the fact that the vast majority is written in the languages of the continent's former colonists. Although Africa's population is composed of a multiplicity of distinct ethnic groups, and African writers are by no means a monolithic body, their works do reveal common themes: colonialism, traditional culture, and politics.

As an established genre, modern African literature is still a very young discipline, emerging on the international scene in the 1950s. Among the pioneers of this period are Chinua Achebe, Amos Tutuola, and the late Guinean author Camara Laye. Prior to the late 1950s, however, several Africans writing in the vernacular had already attracted large domestic audiences, and their works are especially significant within the historical evolution of modern African literature.

According to Albert S. Gérard, "Tiny Lesotho [formerly Basutoland] was the first subsaharan country to produce a sizeable amount of vernacular creative writing in the first two decades of this century" (Brom Weber, ed., *Sense and Sensibility in Twentieth-Century Writing*). A key figure in this flowering was Thomas Mofolo, who is known primarily for his historical novel *Chaka*. Written in Sesotho (southern Sotho) and based on the life of the great nineteenth-century Zulu warrior Chaka, Mofolo's book (which has been widely translated) is famous throughout Africa. "*Chaka* may well be the first major African contribution to contemporary world literature" (Gérard).

Nigerian author D. O. Fagunwa, a master of the Yoruba language, may have, according to some critics, the largest reading audience in Africa. Traditional folktales are Fagunwa's forte, and his works are extremely popular among the approximately 14 million Yorubas living in West Africa. His fertile imagination and engaging style appeal to all age groups. To date, only one of his five novels, *Forest of a Thousand Daemons*, has been translated into English.

Many West African novelists were highly influenced by Fagunwa—Amos Tutuola (*The Palm-Wine Drinkard*) being perhaps the foremost example. Filled with Yoruba myths and folktales, Tutuola's book is generally acknowledged as the first English-language novel from Africa to receive international acclaim. Written in a sort of Pidgin English and "peopled" with ghostlike characters, it remains extremely popular, despite the continuing controversy surrounding Tutuola's use of "wrong" English.

Although Tutuola's novel was highly acclaimed, he does not approach the enduring popularity achieved by Chinua Achebe, Africa's best-known novelist. Achebe is world renowned for writing simple, yet memorable, novels. His first book, *Things Fall Apart*, was an immediate international success and the classic illustration of the tragic culture-conflict theme. Achebe's work laid the foundation for numerous other books depicting the total disruption of African traditions during the period of European colonialism.

Of the many talented francophone African writers of the 1950s and 1960s, the best known is probably the late Guinean author Camara Laye. In his semiautobiographical novel *L'enfant noir*, he poignantly captures day-to-day life in traditional Africa. Laye was one of the early African novelists to gain a measure of recognition outside Africa and, although some nationalists accused him of indulging in colonial nostalgia at a time when most of the continent was on the verge of independence, his book was hailed as a masterpiece and is one of the most celebrated African novels ever written. Ferdinand Oyono is another well-known francophone writer whose works have been widely translated. *Houseboy,* a biting mixture of humor, wit, and satire, is by far his most popular book.

Africa's francophone writers received a degree of international publicity somewhat earlier than their English counterparts. A particularly significant period in African letters occurred in the mid-1930s, when francophone writers (and some black Caribbean artists) developed a new literary movement called négritude. This was a reaction to the cultural assimilation policy of French colonialism. Négritude peaked in the 1940s and 1950s, when the independence fervor was building throughout Africa. The objective was to advance ethnic pride by actively promoting Africa's cultural past. Writers in this tradition consciously incorporated myriad elements of African culture in their works. Nowhere is this more evident than in the poetry of Léopold Sédar Senghor, Africa's quintessential symbol and chief popularizer of the movement. Senghor defines négritude as the "sum total of all the cultural values of Africa."

Following Africa's independence era, there was a noticeable increase in books dealing with politics. Some works expressed a sense of pride in the continent's newly won independence; others were powerful indictments of various African governments. For example, Ayi Kwei Armah's highly controversial novel *The Beautyful Ones Are Not Yet Born* attacks political corruption in neocolonial Africa.

More recently there has been a statistically small but discernible increase in literary works by African women. Focusing generally on women's issues, these authors create characters who are, in the main, modern-day African women whose lives are not bound by tradition. Bessie Head and Flora Nwapa are two of the true pioneers. Their narratives have opened up new vistas, challenging one-dimensional, stereotypical images of the acquiescent African woman by introducing more complete and realistic portraits.

One of the major concerns in African literature today is the language dilemma—a colonial legacy that created a sense of cultural dualism among many African writers. Since the vast majority of contemporary African literature is written in the languages of the ex-colonists, the audience is limited to Africa's educated elite. Desiring a wider audience, many authors have begun to publish in indigenous languages. Some even advocate a national language, perhaps Swahili, for the entire continent. The most outspoken writer on this issue is Kenya's Ngugi wa Thiong'o, who has written fiction and drama in Kikuyu (his mother tongue) to much critical acclaim.

African literature of the 1980s is vibrant and flourishing. Younger authors like Kole Omotoso and Buchi Emecheta are anchoring their reputations, while established writers like Wole Soyinka and Ngugi expand their literary output. New themes are being introduced, and the audience for African prose is steadily growing. Academic institutions throughout Europe and the United States offer African literature courses, and in many cases African writers are invited to lecture. It seems clear that contemporary authors are preserving Africa's complex history—extending the tradition of Africa's early writers and their *griot* ancestors—and sharing the continent's rich culture with generations worldwide.

HISTORY AND CRITICISM

Awoonor, Kofi. *The Breast of the Earth: A Survey of the History, Culture and Literature of Africa South of the Sahara.* 1975. NOK 1983 $17.50 text ed. pap. $6.95. Ghanian author Awoonor's "comments on contemporary African writing are often brilliant, and his characterization of the modern African intellectual is certain to provoke controversy" (*Choice*).

Beier, Ulli. *An Introduction to African Literature.* Longman 2d ed. text ed. 1980 pap. $10.95. Insightful essays by major African and non-African authors that examine African novels, drama, poetry, and the oral tradition.

Brown, Lloyd W. *Women Writers in Black Africa. Contributions in Women's Studies* Greenwood 1981 lib. bdg. $29.95. This pioneer work focuses on five of Africa's most popular female novelists: Ama Ata Aidoo, Buchi Emecheta, Bessie Head, Flora Nwapa, and Efua Sutherland.

Burness, Donald, comp. *Critical Perspectives on Lusophone Literature from Africa.* Three Continents 1981 $24.00 pap. $14.00. Covers writing from Angola, Mozambique, Guinea-Bissau, Cape Verde, and São Tomé-Príncipe. Includes essays on specific writers and general literary movements; important literary journals are also noted.

Chinweizu and others. *Toward the Decolonization of African Literature.* Howard Univ. Pr. 1982 vol. 1 $12.95 pap. $7.95. "The attacks on Eurocentric writers and critics are free-swinging and sometimes outrageous, but the basic thesis has much validity, and the book is a healthy antidote to the often second-rate writing about contemporary African literature . . ." (*Choice*).

Dathorne, O. R. *African Literature in the Twentieth Century.* Univ. of Minnesota Pr. 1976 pap. $6.50. An extensive survey of African literature in French, English, and Portuguese, as well as several indigenous languages.

Gérard, Albert S. *Four African Literatures: Xhosa, Sotho, Zulu, Amharic.* Univ. of California Pr. 1971 $43.75. Covers a neglected area of African literature. "An admirable literary history and critical study . . ." (*LJ*).

Herdeck, Donald E., ed. *African Authors: A Companion to Black African Writing, 1300–1973.* Gale 1973 vol. 1 $64.00. This pioneering work includes lengthy biographies of more than 500 authors and critical discussions of their writings.

Jablow, Alta. *Yes and No: The Intimate Folklore of Africa.* Greenwood repr. of 1961 ed. 1973 lib. bdg. $17.75. "Particularly delightful, and relatively little known to non-Africans, are the dilemma stories, which pose ethical and moral . . . problems. . . . Jablow has selected excellent examples from the oral traditions of many peoples of Africa's western bulge. Her book will not only instruct scholars and specialists but also entertain general readers" (*LJ*).

Jahn, Janheinz. *Neo-African Literature: A History of Black Writing.* Grove (Evergreen Bks.) 1961 pap. $3.95. Jahn was a pioneer and leading critic in the introduction of African literature to an international audience.

Jordan, A. C. *Towards an African Literature: The Emergence of Literary Form in Xhosa. Perspectives on Southern Africa Ser.* Univ. of California Pr. 1973 $24.00. Jordan was a prominent Xhosa scholar. Included are Xhosa folktales and proverbs along with commentaries on their origins and social functions.

Killam, G. D., ed. *African Writers on African Writing. Studies in African Lit.* Heinemann text ed. 1973 pap. $8.50. "A collection of sixteen previously published essays by fourteen of Africa's best-known creative writers . . ." (*Choice*).

Larson, Charles R. *The Emergence of African Fiction.* Three Continents rev. ed. 1972 $15.00 pap. $5.00. Broad survey of the African novel, with a strong concentration on Nigerian novelists. Addresses the frequent issue of judging African literature from a Eurocentric perspective. Excellent bibliography.

Moore, Gerald. *Twelve African Writers.* Indiana Univ. Pr. 1980 $22.50. An excellent introduction to 12 of Africa's most significant contemporary authors from French- and English-speaking countries. Updated and extended edition of Moore's *Seven African Writers.*

Nkosi, Lewis. *Tasks and Masks: An Introduction to African Literature. African Lit. Studies* Longman text ed. 1982 $30.00 pap. $9.95. South African author Nkosi is a leading critic of African literature. This work is a highly readable, perceptive review of the growth of sub-Saharan literature within its social, historical, and ideological context. Among the topics explored are language, négritude, and South African protest writings.

Obiechina, Emmanuel. *Culture, Tradition and Society in the West African Novel. African Studies* Cambridge Univ. Pr. 1975 $45.00 pap. $12.95. A valuable study that concentrates on twentieth-century prose. Examines the effects of mass media, the rise of the middle class, and cultural nationalism on the works of African authors, such as Achebe, Soyinka, and Gabriel Okara.

Roscoe, Adrian A. *Mother Is Gold: A Study in West African Literature.* Cambridge Univ. Pr. 1971 pap. $13.95. "The book attempts a broad historical perspective and sets the writing into both its socio-linguistic and aesthetic contexts" (*Choice*).

Schmidt, Nancy J. *Children's Books on Africa and Their Authors: An Annotated Bibliography. African Bibliography Ser.* Holmes & Meier (Africana) text ed. 1975 $32.50. Contains more than 800 annotated entries arranged by author, along with a subject, title, and series index. Highly recommended.

Walker, Barbara K., and Warren S. Walker, eds. *Nigerian Folk Tales.* 1961. Shoe String (Archon) 2d ed. rev. 1980 $17.50. Delightful collection of Yoruba folktales with comparative commentary by the editors.

Zell, Hans M., ed. *A New Reader's Guide to African Literature.* Holmes & Meier (Africana) text ed. 1983 $39.50 pap. $27.75. Lists 3,091 works by black African authors south of the Sahara writing in English, French, and Portuguese, along with criticisms and essays. The most comprehensive book available on the subject.

ABRAHAMS, PETER. 1919–

Born in Johannesburg, South Africa, Abrahams emigrated to England at age 20, a refugee from apartheid. His bestselling autobiography, *Tell Freedom*, is limited to his years in South Africa and focuses on his experiences as a mulatto. It is one of the earliest books by an African published in England. Critics generally agree that Abrahams's novel *Mine Boy*, a vivid picture of the life of an African miner, is his finest work. Other important books are *Wild Conquest* (1950, o.p.), about the Great Boer Trek, and *A Wreath for Udomo* (1956), a roman à clef, in which Abrahams foretells, with sophisticated narrative skill, the downfall of a hero generally thought to be Ghana's Kwama Nkrumah. *This Island, Now* (1967, o.p.), his latest critically acclaimed work, is set against the backdrop of a black-ruled Caribbean island seething with political and racial tensions. Abrahams currently lives with his family in Jamaica, West Indies.

BOOKS BY ABRAHAMS

Mine Boy. 1946. *African Writers Ser.* Heinemann text ed. 1963 pap. $3.50
Path of Thunder. Chatham repr. of 1948 ed. 1975 $8.95
Tell Freedom. 1954. Faber 1982 $4.95
A Wreath for Udomo. AMS Pr. repr. of 1956 ed. $32.00; *African-Amer. Lib.* Macmillan 1971 pap. $1.95
The Fury of Rachel Monette. Pocket Bks. 1982 pap. $3.50
Tongues of Fire. Pocket Bks. 1985 pap. $3.95
The View from Coyaba. Faber 1985 $19.95 pap. $8.95

ACHEBE, CHINUA. 1930–

Africa's most popular novelist is Chinua Achebe of Nigeria. He achieved international notoriety with his first novel, *Things Fall Apart*, and since then his name has been in the forefront of modern African literature. A recipient of numerous awards and fellowships, Achebe also has been considered for the Nobel Prize in literature. He has written four novels, a number of short stories, children's books, literary and critical essays, and poetry.

Achebe began writing during the Nigerian Civil War. As an active participant in the war, he lacked the extended time needed for narrative writing, so he chose poetry as a more expedient mode of expression. In 1972, he was awarded the Commonwealth Poetry Prize for *Beware, Soul Brother, and Other Poems*, a poignant reflection of the Nigerian Civil War. He is also coauthor of *The Insider: Stories of War and Peace from Nigeria* (o.p.).

Achebe's works have been translated into more than 25 languages, and his books are required in many comparative literature courses throughout Africa, Europe, and the United States. Considered among Africa's first generation of writers (those published in the 1950s and 1960s), Achebe is best known for his appealingly simple, though memorable, novels imbued with his Ibo traditions, and folklore, especially proverbs. According to Achebe, "proverbs are the palm oil with which words are eaten."

He has no equal in terms of realistically portraying the traditional aspects of his culture, as *Things Fall Apart* illustrates so well. Achebe is the acknowledged doyen of the culture-conflict theme; he has written so vividly on the subject that his name is practically synonymous with it. *No Longer at Ease*, a sequel to *Things Fall Apart*, takes up the plight of what was then referred to as the "been-to" African, a term used to describe Africans who had lived abroad and then returned home, many with Western ways. *Arrow of God*, Achebe's third novel, is considered his most complex and difficult, mainly because of its treatment of religion in Ibo society.

Achebe's latest novel, *A Man of the People*, is a political work set in an imaginary country that resembles modern Nigeria. The book is harshly critical of the political leadership of postindependence Africa. Hailed as prophetic, the novel's publication coincided with the overthrow of the then current Nigerian government.

In 1953, Chinua Achebe received his B.A. degree from the University College at Ibadan. After graduation, he pursued a successful broadcasting career, and served as director of external broadcasting for Nigeria from 1961 to 1966. He has studied and lectured widely in Africa and the United States, and since 1971 has been the editor of *Okike: An African Journal of New Writing*. Achebe currently teaches literature at the University of Nigeria, Nsukka.

BOOKS BY ACHEBE

Things Fall Apart. 1959. Astor-Honor $11.95 pap. $6.95; Fawcett 1978 pap. $2.50; *African Writers Ser.* Heinemann pap. $3.00
No Longer at Ease. 1961. Astor-Honor $11.95 pap. $6.95; Fawcett 1977 pap. $2.25; *African Writers Ser.* Heinemann text ed. 1981 pap. $4.00

Arrow of God. 1964. Doubleday (Anchor) 1982 pap. $4.95

Chike and the River. Cambridge Univ. Pr. text ed. 1966 $2.95

A Man of the People. 1966. Doubleday (Anchor) 1967 pap. $3.50

Beware, Soul Brother, and Other Poems. African Writers Ser. Heinemann text ed. 1972
  pap. $5.50

(and John Iroaganachi). *How the Leopard Got His Claws.* Okpaku 1974 $5.95

The Trouble with Nigeria. Heinemann 1984 text ed. pap. $4.00

(and Catherine L. Innes, eds.). *African Short Stories. African Writers Ser.* Heinemann
  text ed. 1985 pap. $5.00

BOOKS ABOUT ACHEBE

Innes, Catherine L., and Bernth Lindfors, eds. *Critical Perspectives on Chinua Achebe.*
  Three Continents 1978 $24.00 pap. $14.00

Killam, G. D. *The Novels of Chinua Achebe.* Holmes & Meier (Africana) 1969 $9.50
  pap. $6.50

Njoku, Benedict C. *The Four Novels of Chinua Achebe: A Critical Study.* Peter Lang
  text ed. 1984 pap. $20.00

Wren, Robert M. *Achebe's World: The Historical and Cultural Context of Chinua
  Achebe's Novels.* Three Continents 1980 $22.00 pap. $10.00

ARMAH, AYI KWEI. 1939–

Ayi Kwei Armah was born in Takoradi, Ghana. He was educated in
Ghana and received a degree in social studies from Harvard University. He
has taught at several universities in Africa and the United States. He currently lives in Dakar, Senegal. In his semiautobiographical novel *Fragments*
(o.p.), Armah illustrates the difficulties of an intellectual in a culture oriented toward material possessions.

In 1980, Robert Fraser wrote of Armah: "From his . . . emergence in 1968
as the author of . . . *The Beautyful Ones Are Not Yet Born*, Armah has been
seen as a startling writer, a fearless and unpredictable enfant terrible at
drastic odds with the literary establishment. The sense of shock with which
his first book was greeted was, however, decidedly more of a reaction to its
content and imagery than its form" (*The Novels of Ayi Kwei Armah*).

BOOKS BY ARMAH

The Beautyful Ones Are Not Yet Born. 1968. *African Writers Ser.* Heinemann text ed.
  1969 pap. $4.00. Deals with political corruption in a newly independent African
  nation. Accra is the setting for this highly symbolic novel, which is generally felt
  to be about the last years of Nkrumah's government.

Two Thousand Seasons. 1973. Third World 1980 $10.00 pap. $6.95. A mythical tone
  penetrates *Two Thousand Seasons*, ". . . a reconstruction of a thousand years of
  African history, organized around the question 'What happened to the Way?'
  The Way is the rule of reciprocity: of giving, receiving and returning the gift" (Simon Simonse, *Research in African Literature*).

AWOONOR, KOFI. 1935–

Born in Wheta, Ghana, Awoonor is an internationally recognized poet
whose work has been widely translated and anthologized. He also writes
novels and plays. In 1976 the Ghanaian government jailed Awoonor for politi-

cal reasons. At the time of his arrest, he was on a one-year sabbatical from the State University of New York at Stony Brook. His arrest raised an international protest. During his incarceration, Awoonor wrote *The House by the Sea*, a piercing collection of poetry reflecting on his ten months in jail.

His first novel, *This Earth, My Brother*, is a highly acclaimed allegorical work set in postindependence Africa of a lawyer's search for meaning and identity in life.

BOOKS BY AWOONOR

This Earth, My Brother. 1971. *African Writers Ser.* Heinemann 1972 text ed. pap.
    $5.00
Guardian of the Sacred Word: Ewe Poetry. NOK 1974 text ed. $10.00 pap. $3.95
The House by the Sea. Greenfield Review Pr. 1978 $3.00
*The Breast of the Earth: A Survey of the History, Culture and Literature of Africa South
    of the Sahara.* 1975. NOK 1983 $17.50 text ed. pap. $6.95

BÂ, MARIAMA. 1929–1981

The promising but short literary career of Mariama Bâ ended with her death in 1981, just as her second novel, *Le Chant écarlate*, was about to be published. Like that of her Nigerian contemporary Buchi Emecheta, Bâ's writing challenges many of the prevalent stereotypes that reinforce African women's acceptance of their "place" in society.

It is Bâ's first book, *So Long a Letter*, that will assure her a permanent place in African literature. Written in an epistolary style, from one female friend to another, *So Long a Letter* is a deeply moving account of a Muslim woman's innermost feelings and emotional survival, following her husband's decision to take a second, and much younger, wife. The novel has been translated into more than 15 languages and has received international acclaim. In 1980 Mariama Bâ received the Noma Award for the best novel published in Africa.

BOOK BY BÂ

So Long a Letter. 1979. Trans. by Modupe Bode Thomas, *African Writers Ser.* Heinemann text ed. 1981 pap. $6.00

BETI, MONGO. 1932–

Beti was born in Yaoundé, Cameroon; his early education was in local schools, followed by studies at the Sorbonne. He currently teaches in France and is also the director of the journal *Peuples Noirs, Peuples Africans*, founded in 1978.

Beti wrote his first novel, *Ville Cruelle* (o.p.), under the pseudonym Eza Boto. A favorite theme of Beti is the failure of colonial missionary efforts in Africa. He speaks not so much against Christianity as against the futile Europeanization of Africans in the name of religion. *The Poor Christ of Bomba*, his best-known work, is written as a diary. The novel is a satire of Christian religion in precolonial Cameroon.

BOOKS BY BETI

The Poor Christ of Bomba. 1956. Heinemann 1971 pap. $5.50
Mission to Kala. 1957. *African Writers Ser.* Heinemann text ed. 1964 pap. $3.50
King Lazarus. Trans. by Peter Green, *African Writers Ser.* Heinemann text ed. 1970
    pap. $4.50
Perpetua and the Habit of Unhappiness. African Writers Ser. Heinemann text ed. 1978
    pap. $6.50
Remember Ruben. Three Continents 1981 pap. $7.00

COETZEE, J(ACOBUS) M. 1940–

J. M. Coetzee is among the best-known white South African novelists of
his generation. He has published four novels, to much critical acclaim. Born
in Cape Town, Coetzee was educated as a computer scientist and linguist.
He received his M.A. in 1963 from the University of Cape Town, and his
Ph.D. from the University of Texas in 1969. Coetzee is a forceful writer, who
relies heavily on details. His works have a universal appeal, although they
are generally set in South Africa.

Coetzee currently teaches at the University of Cape Town. When asked
during an interview whether the threat of banning or censorship affected
the process of writing, he replied, "Definitely not. I think you act as if it
didn't exist while you're writing" (*PW*).

BOOKS BY COETZEE

In the Heart of the Country (From the Heart of the Country). 1976. Penguin 1982 pap.
    $4.95. A slender, taut book, it "purports to be the diary of a hysterical spinster
    on an isolated . . . sheep farm . . . consumed by loneliness . . . and her love/
    hate relationship with her patriarchal father" (*World Literature Today*).
Waiting for the Barbarians. 1980. Penguin 1982 pap. $4.95
Life and Times of Michael K. Penguin 1985 pap. $5.95; Viking 1984 $13.95. "As in his
    previous novel, *Waiting for the Barbarians*, Mr. Coetzee's landscapes of suffering
    are defined by the little-by-little art of moral disclosures . . . his stories might be
    about everyone and anyplace. At the same time they defy the vice of abstrac-
    tion; they are engrossed in the minute and the concrete. [He] has rewritten the
    travail of Huck's insight, but from Nigger Jim's point of view, and set it in a
    country more terrible . . ." (Cynthia Ozick, *N.Y. Times*).
Dusklands. Penguin 1985 pap. $5.95. Consists of two novellas, *The Vietnam Project*
    and *The Narrative of Jacobus Coetzee.*

EKWENSI, CYPRIAN. 1921–

Born in Minna, Nigeria, Ekwensi was educated in Nigeria, Ghana, and at
London's Chelsea School of Pharmacy. A popular novelist, Ekwensi has frequently stated that he writes for the masses. One of his earliest works was a
highly successful romantic novella, *When Love Whispers* (o.p.), published in
1948. Filled with moralistic and sentimental overtones, it typifies Onitsha
market literature, a genre that is very popular among the masses, especially
in Nigeria and Ghana.

Ekwensi's reputation as a novelist was established with *People of the City*,
published in 1954. Urban decay (political corruption, squalor, and over-

crowding) is the dominant thematic thread running through this book as well as many of Ekwensi's other works. In due course, Ekwensi became known as Africa's first urban novelist.

In *Jagua Nana*, perhaps Ekwensi's best-known work, he skillfully weaves into the story vivid scenes of Lagos nightlife, against a backdrop of political intrigue. This book earned Ekwensi high praise in Africa and abroad (it has been translated into more foreign languages than any of his other books), but it also elicited considerable controversy, especially in Nigeria. Some Nigerians were so incensed by Ekwensi's graphic literary passages that they called for the banning of the book. Their actions were, however, unsuccessful.

Although Ekwensi is known as a chronicler (as well as a critic) of city life, he is by no means one dimensional. *Burning Grass*, for example, is a sensitive look at the migratory patterns of the Fulani cattlemen of northern Nigeria. Ekwensi's firsthand knowledge of traditional rural African culture surfaces in this work. He also writes children's books and literary articles. In addition, his impact is broader than one might at first suspect, as is evidenced by his being awarded the Dag Hammarskjold International Prize in literature in 1968.

Although his critics continue to accuse him of inconsistencies and contradictions, he is undoubtedly a pioneer and major influence in contemporary African literature. Ekwensi's underlying strengths are reflected in his social commitment to the topics he chooses, coupled with their relevance to modern Africa.

BOOKS BY EKWENSI

People of the City. 1953. *African Writers Ser*. Heinemann text ed. 1963 pap. $3.50
The Drummer Boy. Cambridge Univ. Pr. 1960 o.p.
The Passport of Millan Ilia. Cambridge Univ. Pr. 1960 o.p.
Burning Grass: A Story of the Fulani of Northern Nigeria. Heinemann text ed. 1962 pap. $3.50
Lokotown and Other Stories. *African Writers Ser*. Heinemann text ed. 1966 pap. $4.50
Trouble in Form Six. Cambridge Univ. Pr. 1966 o.p.
Beautiful Feathers. *African Writers Ser*. Heinemann text ed. 1971 pap. $3.50
Jagua Nana. *African Writers Ser*. Heinemann text ed. 1975 pap. $4.50. "Unlike *People of the City*, where even the most developed character, Amusa Sango, still remains a shadowy figure, Jagua is very well developed, and the great difference in characterization between the two books is evidence of Ekwensi's growing mastery of the novel" (Ernest Emenyonu *Cyprian Ekwensi*).
Restless City and Christmas Gold. *African Writers Ser*. Heinemann text ed. 1975 pap. $4.50
Survive the Peace. *African Writers Ser*. Heinemann text ed. 1976 pap. $5.50

EMECHETA, BUCHI. 1944–

Buchi Emecheta is probably West Africa's most prolific female novelist. She has published eight novels as well as children's books and numerous articles on African women. The primary focus of her work is the contemporary African woman, torn between traditional and modern social roles.

More than any other West African writer, Emecheta accurately depicts the various social conflicts facing African women today.

Her first novel, *In the Ditch*, was published in London in 1972. Largely autobiographical, it recounts the struggle of Adah, a Nigerian mother of five, who is separated from her husband and living in London. Adah is trying simultaneously to raise a family and earn an advanced degree. In her next book, *Second-Class Citizen*, Emecheta takes her readers back in time to Lagos, where she acquaints us with Adah's early years, marriage, and eventual move to London with her husband and two children. The novel's title derives from the dual discrimination (black, woman) Adah experiences in London.

Emecheta's subsequent novels are all set in Nigeria and usually revolve around a female protagonist boldly challenging cultural traditions. Whether intentional or not, Emecheta has earned the reputation as an outspoken critic of African patriarchal customs. Katherine Frank wrote that "Emecheta's account of African womanhood is an unapologetically feminist one. She exposes and repudiates the feminine stereotypes of male writers such as Achebe, Amadi and others, and reveals the dark underside of their fictional celebrations of the African woman. She explores the psychological and physical toll on women of such things as arranged marriages, polygamy, perpetual pregnancy and childbirth, and widowhood" (*World Literature Written in English*).

BOOKS BY EMECHETA

In the Ditch. 1972. Schocken (Allison & Busby) 1980 pap. $4.95
Second-Class Citizen. Braziller 1975 $6.95 1983 pap. $4.95
The Bride Price: Young Ibo Girl's Love; Conflict of Family and Tradition. Braziller 1976 $6.95 pap. $4.95
The Slave Girl. Braziller 1977 $7.95 pap. $3.95
The Joys of Motherhood. Braziller 1979 $8.95 pap. $4.95
Nowhere to Play. Schocken (Allison & Busby) 1981 $6.95
Destination Biafra. Schocken (Allison & Busby) 1982 $14.95
Double Yoke. Braziller 1983 $12.95
The Moonlight Bride. Braziller 1983 $7.95 pap. $4.95
The Wrestling Match. Braziller 1983 $7.95 pap. $4.95

GORDIMER, NADINE. 1923–

Nadine Gordimer—novelist, short story writer, and essayist—is one of South Africa's best-known authors. Although her novels are highly acclaimed, critics generally agree that her short stories are more revealing of her talent. So many of Gordimer's short stories have been published in the *New Yorker* that she is often referred to as the *New Yorker* writer. Gordimer's dominant theme is South Africa's apartheid policy. She uses her white, middle-class background as the backdrop for many of her stories. "It is not the blacks that Gordimer writes with most authority about, however, but the whites. She is the supreme chronicler of their awakening, or of the failure of their awakening" (Leon Wieseltier, *Salma-gundi*). Gordimer's skillful narration of South Africa's political climate vis-à-vis its racial situation is strikingly evident in *Selected Stories*.

Like her short stories, Gordimer's novels almost always deal with the daily tensions of life in a segregated society. All of her novels except *A Guest of Honour* are set in South Africa. In *A Guest of Honour*, she explores the problems of a newly independent African country through the experiences of a former British administrator.

BOOKS BY GORDIMER

The Conservationist. Penguin 1983 pap. $4.95; Viking 1975 $12.95
Selected Stories. 1975. Penguin 1983 pap. $5.95; Viking 1976 $11.95. "Arranged in a
    chronological order that reveals both her personal and artistic development,
    [this book] shows . . . Gordimer's awareness that Africa has changed. The thirty-
    one stories were written between the ages of twenty and fifty, during a period in
    which the society itself has aged, sharpened, and grown less amenable. The per-
    spective given to her readers is, therefore, historical—in the sense that the peo-
    ple, situations, relationships and moments she describes are unique in the his-
    tory of South Africa" (Ethel W. Githii, *Critique: Studies in Modern Fiction*).
A Soldier's Embrace. Viking 1980 $8.95
Burger's Daughter. Penguin 1981 pap. $4.95; Viking 1979 $10.95
July's People. Penguin 1982 pap. $4.95; Viking 1981 $10.95
A Guest of Honour. Penguin 1983 pap. $8.95
Something Out There. Viking 1983 $15.95
A World of Strangers. Penguin repr. 1984 pap. $6.95

HEAD, BESSIE. 1937–1986

Born in South Africa, Bessie Head wrote from neighboring Botswana, where she lived in exile since 1964. A hallmark of Head's writing, which is set in her adopted country, is unvarnished candor—tradition and customs notwithstanding.

Like her female contemporaries, Head was also deeply concerned about the role of women in African societies. This is an important theme in her writing, and she addressed it with the same frankness and incisiveness as she did other salient issues affecting present-day Africa. In her volume of short stories, *The Collector of Treasures*, Head offers fresh insights into the traditional and contemporary status of women in Botswana, reflecting pre- and postindependence influences.

Another major concern of Head is Africa's economic stagnation, a topic she explores in her first novel, *When Rain Clouds Gather* (o.p.). The protagonist is a South African exile who introduces modern farming techniques to villagers in a remote area of Botswana, despite the opposition of the village chief, a traditionalist. Her second novel, *Maru*, centers on the delicate subject of caste and color prejudice among particular ethnic groups in Botswana.

In Head's semiautobiographical novel *A Question of Power*, the main character, Elizabeth, is, like the author, a "coloured" South African exile in Botswana. She suffers a nervous breakdown ". . . and the narrative is actually a description of the events as they unfold within her mind and of the relationship between these internal events and the world outside" (Lloyd W. Brown, *Women Writers in Black Africa*). "Bessie Head depicts African life with a deep personal commitment and a lyrical flair that gives it a delightful tilt into fantasy" (*N.Y. Times Bk. Review*).

BOOKS BY HEAD

Maru. African Writers Ser. Heinemann text ed. 1972 pap. $4.50
A Question of Power. African Writers Ser. Heinemann text ed. 1974 pap. $5.50
The Collector of Treasures. African Writers Ser. Heinemann text ed. 1977 pap. $5.00
Serowe: Village of the Rain-Wind. African Writers Ser. Heinemann text ed. 1981 pap.
   $6.00

LAYE, CAMARA. 1928–1980

Camara Laye, a pioneer in modern African literature and one of the continent's major novelists, died in exile in 1980. Since the late 1960s, he had been living in Senegal as the guest of President (and noted poet) Léopold Sédar Senghor. Born in the Guinean city of Kouroussa, Laye was raised in a deeply traditional African setting. After completing technical school in Conakry, he continued his education in France. In between odd jobs, and as a way of coping with loneliness, Laye began writing remembrances of his childhood days in Guinea. The result was *L'enfant noir*, an autobiographical novel considered by many critics to be one of the best portraits of traditional African life ever written, despite criticism from African nationalists. "African nationalists had no time for a novel describing the happy life of a child in Central Guinea. For them, the important thing was commitment to the pressing and immediate problems of gaining African independence from European tutelage . . ." (A. C. Brench, *African Literature Today*). Nevertheless, Laye's reputation as a major novelist remains firmly intact, as witnessed by the continuous acclaim of his books.

His next publication, *Le regard du roi* (o.p.), is a much more ambitious and complex work. Full of symbolism, this novel is generally regarded as an ingenious allegory about man's search for God. Laye cleverly weaves humor and mysticism throughout the book. Reviewers often compare the white protagonist's wandering throughout Africa to the quest for the holy grail. "*Le regard du roi* . . . has been one of the most frequently discussed works in African fiction" (Gerald Moore).

In 1966, Laye published *Dramouss (A Dream of Africa)* (o.p.)—a sequel to *L'enfant noir*—which explores the postindependence politics of Guinea. This work was viewed as politically provocative and ". . . led to Laye's forced exile from Guinea to Senegal" (Charles R. Larson).

While living in exile, Laye was working with the Dakar-based Institut Français d'Afrique Noire (I.F.A.N.), collecting and editing the folktales and songs of his Malinke people. His last work, *Le maître de la parole: Kouma Lafolo Kuoma (The Guardian of the Word)*, narrated by a *griot*, is about the great Mali emperor Sundiata. At his death, Laye was working on a political novel called *The Exiles*, which was never published.

BOOKS BY LAYE

L'enfant noir. 1953. Trans. by Joyce Hutchinson, Cambridge Univ. Pr. text ed. 1966
   pap. $6.50
The Dark Child. Trans. by James Kirkup and others, Farrar 1954 pap. $5.25
The Guardian of the Word. Trans. by James Kirkup and others, Random 1984 pap.
   $7.95

MPHAHLELE, EZEKIEL (ES'KIA). 1919–

Born in South Africa, Mphahlele left in 1957, after the government
banned him from teaching because of his active protest against its "Bantu
education" policy. A compassionate and perceptive writer, he is a highly respected critic of African literature. Mphahlele frequently analyzes intellectual and social developments in contemporary Africa for journals in the
United States and abroad. Short stories, anthologies, novels, and an autobiography are all part of Mphahlele's repertoire. According to his biographer,
Ursula A. Barnett, Mphahlele "has been closely associated with every phase
of black South African literature and often gave it direction or led the way."

Mphahlele came to the forefront of African writers with the publication of
his highly acclaimed autobiography, *Down Second Avenue,* which is also a
powerful social commentary on black life in South Africa. Another important work is *The African Image* (1962, o.p.), a collection of essays that deals
specifically "with the literary image created by black and white alike, the
world over—to explain African and Negro life" (Jacket).

Mphahlele's odyssey from Johannesburg took him to several African countries and to Europe before he eventually came to the United States, where
he received a Ph.D. in 1968 from the University of Denver. He taught English at the University of Pennsylvania from 1974 until 1977, when, to the
amazement of many of his friends and colleagues, he gave up the security of
a full professorship and returned to South Africa. Commenting on the problems of writers in exile he said: "You have this kind of spiritual, mental
ghetto you live in. It's crippling. . . . But you still have the freedom of vision which you would have not had in South Africa, and your experiences in
exile have also contributed to your growth" (*Studies in Black Literature*).

Mphahlele currently teaches at the Center for African Studies at Witwa-
tersrand University, Soweto. The government has lifted the ban on some of
his works; *Down Second Avenue* can be purchased, but his first novel, *The
Wanderers* (1971, o.p.), is still on the banned list. Critic Martin Tucker calls
the book "a lyric cry of pain for the many rootless black exiles who wander
across the African continent searching for a new home."

Chirundu (o.p.), Mphahlele's first major creative piece since his return to
South Africa, focuses on the rise and fall of the minister of transportation
and public works in an imaginary African country.

BOOKS BY MPHAHLELE

Down Second Avenue: Growing Up in a South African Ghetto. Peter Smith 1959
   $14.25
In Corner B. Northwestern Univ. Pr. 1967 $6.95

NGUGI WA THIONG'O (NGUGI, JAMES). 1938–

Ngugi is one of several Africans who have been imprisoned because of the political nature of their writing. Novelist, essayist, and playwright, he is Kenya's best-known writer and "East Africa's most articulate social commentator" (Bernth Lindfors). An outspoken nationalist with a decidedly Marxist perspective, Ngugi consistently focuses on colonial and postcolonial issues in modern-day Kenya.

His first publication, *Weep Not, Child,* is a penetrating account of the Mau Mau uprising. This was the first English-language novel by an East African. Two subsequent works, *The River Between* and *A Grain of Wheat,* are sensitive novels about Kenya's Kikuyu people caught between the old and the new Africa.

One of Ngugi's prime concerns is the language issue in Africa, especially the paucity of reading materials in indigenous African languages. He believes that "an African writer should write in a language that will allow him to communicate effectively with peasants and workers in Africa—in other words, he should write in an African language" (*Research in African Literature*). In 1977 Ngugi took a major step in this direction by writing and producing a play in Kikuyu, his mother tongue. *Ngaahika Ndeenda (I Will Marry When I Want)* "depicts social, economic and religious exploitation [of workers and peasants] in the Kikuyu highlands" (Ngugi). The play attracted a large number of peasants from throughout the region, jubilant that they could follow the dialogue. The government, fearful that the play was encouraging political criticism, banned it, and in 1978 sentenced Ngugi to a year in prison, a ruling that provoked a tremendous outcry from an international circle of artists.

Ngugi's confinement did not stop his writing politically provocative pieces, as his later novel *Petals of Blood* attests. Critics gave it mixed reviews, complaining that the work was difficult to follow. The novel's underlying theme, as viewed by critic Charles R. Larson, is "political unrest in post-independence Kenya, and what Ngugi considers the failure of the new black elite (political and business) to live up to the pre-independence expectations" (*World Literature Today*).

Born in Limuru, Kenya, Ngugi attended missionary and Kikuyu schools. In 1964 he graduated from Uganda's Makere College and pursued advanced work at the University of Leeds. He later taught in the United States for a brief period. From 1972 until his detention in 1978, he headed the literature department at the University of Nairobi. Since his release, Ngugi has remained in Kenya, devoting all his time to writing, including children's books.

BOOKS BY NGUGI

Weep Not, Child. African Writers Ser. Heinemann text ed. 1964 $3.50
The River Between. African Writers Ser. Heinemann text ed. 1965 pap. $4.00
The Black Hermit. African Writers Ser. Heinemann text ed. 1968 pap. $3.50
A Grain of Wheat. African Writers Ser. Heinemann text ed. 1968 pap. $4.00
The Trial of Dedan Kimathi. African Writers Ser. Heinemann text ed. 1977 pap. $4.50

Mtawa Mweusi. Heinemann text ed. 1978 pap. $2.50

Petals of Blood. Dutton 1978 pap. $8.95

Detained: A Writer's Prison Diary. African Writers Ser. Heinemann text ed. 1981 pap.
$7.50

Writers in Politics. Studies in African Lit. Heinemann text ed. 1981 $25.00 pap. $10.00

I Will Marry When I Want. African Writers Ser. Heinemann text ed. 1982 pap. $5.50

Devil on the Cross. Heinemann 1982 $21.00 pap. $6.00

Barrell of a Pen: Resistance to Repression in Neo-Colonial Kenya. Africa Research 1983
$15.95 text ed. pap. $6.95

NWAPA, FLORA. 1931–

A pioneer among contemporary African authors, Flora Nwapa is the first Nigerian woman to publish a novel, *Efuru*. This landmark book, published in 1966, explores a subject quite important in Nwapa's writing, although very unusual in African literature as a whole—the unconventional African woman. Nwapa's heroines are generally independent-minded women who often flout established customs. In *Efuru*, for example, the protagonist agrees to marry without payment of the customary bride-price, an extremely important tradition in many African societies.

Motherhood is the theme of Nwapa's second novel, *Idu*. By skillfully using traditional Ibo dialogue, she gives dimension and credibility to her characters, while simultaneously sensitizing her readers to the importance of motherhood in African culture.

Nwapa's novels have received mixed reviews, the complaint being an alleged lack of imagination. However, for exposing the myth of the acquiescent African woman, none can dispute Nwapa's historical impact on African letters.

Books by Nwapa

Efuru. African Writers Ser. Heinemann text ed. 1966 pap. $4.00

Idu. African Writers Ser. Heinemann text ed. 1970 pap. $4.00

OKIGBO, CHRISTOPHER. 1932–1967

Okigbo was an Ibo who was strongly committed to the Biafran cause. Already distinguished as one of Nigeria's leading poets during his brief literary career, he was killed in action during the Nigerian Civil War. His biographer, S. O. Anozie, says that "Okigbo's poetry is difficult. You feel that a final comprehension is just around the corner, but it is a corner you never reach. . . . Okigbo's poetry is constantly exploring two irregular dimensions of myth . . . myth as a privileged mode of cognition . . . myth and totem are seen as not merely cognitive but affective and even evaluative in a given cultural context—that, for example, of the Ibo-speaking people of Nigeria."

Okigbo was indeed a complex individual, not one who readily gave in to tradition and conformity. He was awarded the first prize for poetry in 1966 at the First Festival of Negro Arts held in Dakar, Senegal. Okigbo rejected the award on the grounds that he did not subscribe to the terms "Negro art" or "African literature." There is a spiritual vein in much of his poetry. "He himself said that 'Heavensgate' was originally conceived as an Easter sequence and that the various sections of the poem represent the various stations of the traveller's Cross" (*Présence Africaine*).

BOOK BY OKIGBO

Labyrinths with Path of Thunder. Holmes & Meier (Africana) 1971 $7.50 pap. $5.50

BOOK ABOUT OKIGBO

Anozie, S. O. *Christopher Okigbo: Creative Rhetoric.* Holmes & Meier (Africana) text ed. 1972 $19.50 pap. $9.75

OMOTOSO, KOLE. 1943–

Born in Akure, Nigeria, Omotoso is one of the most popular and prolific of Africa's so-called new generation of writers. His novels, however, have limited distribution outside of Africa because Omotoso has chosen to publish within the continent, thus making his works accessible to a wider African audience. Two of his works, *The Combat*, which uses the Nigerian Civil War as a backdrop, and *The Edifice*, which concerns the marriage of an African student and an English woman, were published outside Africa.

Described as a revolutionary writer by many critics, Omotoso is intensely concerned with the political and social problems facing contemporary Africa. He writes for Africa's masses, and his style is simple and direct.

BOOKS BY OMOTOSO

The Edifice. African Writers Ser. Heinemann text ed. 1971 pap. $5.00
The Combat. African Writers Ser. Heinemann text ed. 1972 pap. $5.00

OUSMANE, SEMBÈNE (SEMBÈNE, OUSMANE). 1923–

Born in Senegal and recognized primarily as Africa's premier filmmaker, Ousmane is also a highly regarded novelist. His books and films are characteristically political, reflecting his keen sense of social commitment. Ousmane often writes from personal experience. Before embarking on a writing career, he had worked as a manual laborer in Senegal and France, where he was very active in the dock workers' union. Union activities are the backdrop for his third book, *God's Bits of Wood*, which established his reputation as an important literary figure. In it he recounts the 1947–48 strike of African railroad workers in Senegal, highlighting the effects of the strike on traditional African customs.

As a way of reaching a more popular audience, Ousmane turned to filmmaking. He has adapted several of his novels into films; *Xala* is perhaps the best known. This film, along with others by Ousmane, has been either censored or banned in Senegal.

His most recent work, *The Last of the Empire*, is a political novel set in Senegal.

BOOKS BY OUSMANE

God's Bits of Wood. 1962. Trans. by Francis Price, *African Writers Ser.* Heinemann
    text ed. 1981 pap. $4.50
The Money-Order with White Genesis. Trans. by Clive Wake, *African Writers Ser.*
    Heinemann text ed. 1972 pap. $4.50
Xala. Trans. by Clive Wake, Lawrence Hill 1976 consult publisher for information
The Last of the Empire. Trans. by Adrian Adams, *African Writers Ser.* Heinemann text
    ed. 1983 pap. $7.00

OYONO, FERDINAND. 1929–

Born in the Cameroon, Oyono was educated in Africa and France, Provins
and Paris (Law School and National School of Administration). Since 1960,
he has served in the Cameroonian diplomatic corps. His international reputation for humorous, satiric writing rests on his 1956 publication of *Houseboy*, which has been widely translated. The novel, written as a diary of an
African houseboy, bitterly attacks French colonialism in Africa.

BOOKS BY OYONO

Houseboy. 1956. Trans. by John Reed, *African Writers Ser.* Heinemann text ed. 1966
    pap. $4.00
The Old Man and the Medal. 1956. Trans. by John Reed, *African Writers Ser.* Heine-
    mann text ed. 1967 pap. $4.00
Boi. Heinemann text ed. 1978 pap. $3.50

PATON, ALAN. 1903–

A white South African, Alan Paton writes novels, short stories, essays, and
poetry. He was founder and president of the now defunct South African Liberal Party. Paton's best-known work, by far—and maybe the most popular
novel to come out of South Africa—is *Cry, the Beloved Country*, published in
1948. Written in simple cadenced prose, this truly memorable work explores racial tensions in South Africa while simultaneously advocating universal brotherhood. It has been translated into some 20 languages, and,
ironically, has sold more copies in South Africa than any other book excluding the Bible. Both the book and the movie (which starred Canada Lee and
Sidney Poitier) were popular in the United States. The story line revolves
around a Zulu minister's immersion into Johannesburg's underworld as he
searches for his son, who is accused of murdering a white man. This novel
earned Paton the Anisfield-Wolf and Newspaper Guild of New York Awards,
among others.

Paton's prolonged interest in race relations stems from his years as a principal in a Johannesburg reform school for African youth. In an effort to sti-
fle, or at least soften, Paton's condemnation of apartheid, the government re-
voked his passport from 1960 to 1970. However, his racially sensitive novels, and numerous essays written after *Cry, the Beloved Country*, prove that
he is not easily silenced.

"All of Paton's writing, his novels, his short stories, his fiction, his biographies ... and his ... autobiography *Towards the Mountain*, express [his]

consistent concern for the freedom, dignity, and worth of individual human beings—a concern that is based, ultimately, on his Christian convictions" (Edward Callan, *Alan Paton*).

BOOKS BY PATON

Cry, the Beloved Country. 1948. Scribner 1982 pap. $3.95
Too Late the Phalarope. Scribner 1953 pap. $6.95
Tales from a Troubled Land. Scribner repr. 1961 $12.50
The Land and People of South Africa. Harper rev. ed. 1972 $10.89
Knocking on the Door. Scribner 1976 $12.50
Instrument of Thy Peace. Winston Pr. rev. ed. 1982 pap. $6.95
Ah, But Your Land Is Beautiful. Scribner 1982 $12.95 1983 pap. $6.95
Towards the Mountain. 1981. Scribner 1983 $16.95

BOOK ABOUT PATON

Callan, Edward. *Alan Paton. Twayne's World Authors Ser.* G. K. Hall 1972 $14.50

SENGHOR, LÉOPOLD SÉDAR. 1906–

Poet, scholar, and politician, Senghor personifies the ideals of black writers of French expression. World renowned as the apostle of négritude (a literary ideology that extols the cultural values of Africa), he is one of Africa's most famous and revered poets and has often been mentioned as a candidate for the Nobel Prize in literature. Among his multitude of literary honors and degrees, including an honorary doctorate from Oxford University, is his election in 1983 to the Académie Française. Senghor is the first black member in the academy's 349-year history. An architect of Senegalese independence, Senghor reached the pinnacle of his political career in 1960 when he was elected the first president of the independent Republic of Senegal, a position he held until his retirement in 1981.

Born in the small village of Joal, Senegal, Senghor received a government scholarship in 1928 and left for France to study first at the Lycée Louis-le-Grand and then at the Sorbonne, where he received his *diplôme d'études supérieures* in 1932. A teacher in the lycées until World War II, Senghor joined the French Army and was captured by the Germans, who held him prisoner from 1940 to 1942.

Senghor remained in France following the war, and in 1945 his first collection of poems, *Chants d'ombre*, was published. Written mostly during his student days in Paris, the poems have a noticeable négritude tone and reflect Senghor's feelings of cultural alienation and physical isolation from his homeland. Three years later, the landmark volume *Anthologie de la nouvelle póesie nègre et malgache de la langue française*, which was edited by Senghor and included Jean-Paul Sartre's well-known and somewhat controversial preface, was published. The works of many obscure, yet highly talented, Caribbean and African writers, like Birago Diop, Léon-G. Damas, and Jacques Roumain, among others, were celebrated for the first time in this now famous collection.

Senghor's poetry is the quintessential expression of love and respect for African culture. He draws heavily on his African roots to create strikingly visual and in many cases highly sensual poems. "The typical Senghorian themes—nature, woman, Africa, blood—are brought sharply into focus by the vivid tones that define them as sensory experiences as well as living realities" (Sylvia Bâ, *The Concept of Negritude in the Poetry of Léopold Sédar Senghor*). Unfortunately, few of Senghor's works are now available in English.

BOOKS BY SENGHOR

Nocturnes. 1961. *African Writers Ser.* Heinemann text ed. 1969 pap. $5.50
Nocturnes. 1964. Trans. by John Reed and Clive Wake, Okpaku 1971 pap. $2.95
The Foundations of "Africanité" or "Négritude" and "Arabité." French & European Publications 1967 pap. $5.95
Senghor: Prose and Poetry. Ed. by John Reed and Clive Wake, *African Writers Ser.* Heinemann text ed. 1976 pap. $7.50

BOOKS ABOUT SENGHOR

Bâ, Sylvia. *The Concept of Negritude in the Poetry of Léopold Sédar Senghor.* Princeton Univ. Pr. 1973 $28.50
Mezu, Okechukuv S. *The Poetry of Léopold Sédar Senghor.* Fairleigh Dickinson Univ. Pr. 1973 $14.50
Peters, Jonathan A. *A Dance of Masks: Senghor, Achebe, Soyinka.* Three Continents 1978 $18.00 pap. $7.00

SOYINKA, WOLE. 1934–

Wole Soyinka, distinguished playwright, novelist, poet, social critic, and political activist, is one of Africa's foremost literary giants. This Nigerian-born artist "has probably received more awards and honours from prestigious institutions and organizations than any other living African scholar" (*Concord Weekly*). Although his literary oeuvre is indeed varied, Soyinka is known internationally for his politically provocative plays, which invariably are social commentaries on the day-to-day problems of the African people. In a recent interview with Henry Louis Gates, Jr., Soyinka said, "I cannot conceive of my existence without political involvement" (*N.Y. Times Bk. Review*).

Soyinka's political commitment was the cause of his imprisonment (1967–69) during Nigeria's civil war. Accused of treason, he was held in solitary confinement for most of this period. Two of his works, *The Man Died: Prison Notes of Wole Soyinka* and *Poems from Prison*, were secretly written on toilet paper and smuggled out of prison.

Soyinka's pioneering efforts and creative talent have been a major influence on the development of Nigerian drama. In the 1960s he founded two Nigerian theater groups, the 1960 Masks and the Orisun Theatre; his plays have been widely performed in Nigeria and England. His latest dramatic work, *A Play of Giants*, is a parody of African dictators. It premiered in 1984 at the Yale Repertory Theater.

To date Soyinka has published two novels, *The Interpreters*, winner of the 1968 Jock Campbell Literary Award, about a group of young Nigerian intellectuals frustrated by their society, and *Season of Anomy* (o.p.), an allegory on Nigeria's civil war.

When his autobiography was published in 1982, it was hailed by the *N.Y. Times* as one of the 12 best books of the year. *Aké: The Years of Childhood* is a charming memoir of Soyinka's first 11 years, offering insights into Yoruba culture and its influence on his childhood. James Gibbs, a prominent critic of Soyinka, had this to say about *Aké:* "It will intrigue and fascinate a new readership; it will introduce Soyinka to many who cannot see his plays, do not read poetry, and find his novels heavy going" (*Research in African Literature*).

Born in Abeoukuta, Nigeria, Soyinka was educated at the University of Ibadan and in England at the University of London and Leeds University. He has held research and teaching appointments at home and abroad, and until recently was chairman of the theater arts department at the University of Ife, Ile-Ife, Nigeria. He is currently on the faculty of Cornell University.

BOOKS BY SOYINKA

A Dance of the Forest. Oxford 1963 $3.95

The Lion and the Jewel. Oxford 1963 pap. $3.95

The Interpreters. 1965. *African Writers Ser.* Heinemann text ed. 1984 pap. $5.00; Holmes & Meier (Africana) 1972 text ed. $22.50

The Road. Oxford 1965 pap. $3.95

Kongi's Harvest. Oxford 1967 $5.95

(and others). *Palaver: Dramatic Discussion Starters from Africa.* Friendship Pr. 1971 pap. $1.50

Madmen and Specialists. Hill & Wang 1972 pap. $6.95

A Shuttle in the Crypt. Hill & Wang 1972 $6.95

Collected Plays. Oxford 2 vols. 1973–74 pap. ea. $5.95–$7.95

Camwood on the Leaves and Before the Blackout: Plays. 1974. Okpaku 1985 $8.95 pap. $5.95

(ed.). *Poems of Black Africa.* Hill & Wang 1975 $12.95 pap. $4.95

The Bacchae of Euripides: A Communion Rite. Norton 1974 pap. $3.95

Death and the King's Horseman: A Play. Norton 1976 pap. $4.95

Opera Wonyosi. Indiana Univ. Pr. 1981 $12.95 pap. $5.95

Aké: The Years of Childhood. Random 1983 $14.95; Random (Vintage) pap. $6.95

(trans.). *Forest of a Thousand Daemons: A Hunter's Saga.* By D. O. Fagunwa, Random 1983 $12.95

A Play of Giants. Methuen 1984 pap. $6.95

TUTUOLA, AMOS. 1920–

Tutuola was born in Abeokuta, Nigeria. He received his elementary education at a Salvation Army school and later went to Lagos High School. His highly controversial reputation as a novelist is based on his unique writing style, a type of Pidgin English. Tutuola's most popular work by far is his first novel, *The Palm-Wine Drinkard*, an extremely imaginative folktale drawn from Yoruba legends and myths. Claude Wauthier writes of him: "Tutuola is both a Grimm and an Edgar Allan Poe to Africa. In ... *The Palm-Wine Drinkard* there is a journey into the land of the dead where every-

thing is topsy-turvy—a sort of African *Alice through the Looking Glass.*"
Lewis Nkosi described the controversy around Tutuola's writing in *African
Report*: "Europeans were fascinated by Tutuola's very personal use of the
English language. But . . . in Nigeria [readers] argued that Tutuola's un-
grammatical use of English was not experimental and that he simply did
not know any other way to write. Some Africans asked why the English publishers had not properly edited Tutuola's manuscript."

Despite the controversy surrounding Tutuola's "wrong" English, his historical significance as a writer cannot be disputed. "He not only was among
the first black African writers to be published and to win a measure of international recognition, but he was also the first writer to see the possibilities
of the imaginative translation of mythology into English" (O. R. Dathorne,
African Literature in the Twentieth Century). For all the controversy, Tutuola
is a delight to read. His books have been translated into many languages.

BOOKS BY TUTUOLA

The Palm-Wine Drinkard. 1952. Grove 1984 pap. $4.50
The Palm-Wine Drinkard and His Dead Palm-Wine Tapster in the Dead's Town. Green-
    wood repr. of 1953 ed. lib. bdg. $15.00
My Life in the Bush of Ghosts. Grove (Evergreen Bks.) 1962 pap. $6.95
Wild Hunter in the Bush of the Ghosts. Ed. by Bernth Lindfors, Three Continents
    1982 $40.00 pap. $20.00
The Witch-Herbalist of the Remote Town. Faber 1982 pap. $7.95

CHAPTER 21

Middle Eastern Literature

Leo Hamalian

> The old Levant must go on living. Ancient land of symbiosis, with its fric-
> tions, its injustices but also its wealth. Mosaic of cultures and creeds, pre-
> cious for its diversity.
> —NICOLAS SOUDRAY, *The House of the Prophets*

ANCIENT NEAR EASTERN LITERATURE

The term "Near East" usually refers to the lands that border the eastern
Mediterranean; that is, northeastern Africa, southwestern Asia, Asia Minor,
and occasionally the Balkan Peninsula. For the purposes of this section, the
ancient Near East is defined as the area consisting of Egypt, Nubia, Palestine and Syria, Armenia, Asia Minor, Mesopotamia, and the adjoining areas
of northeastern Africa, the Aegean, Iran (Persia), and the Indus Valley during the era between 9000 B.C. and the fourth century B.C., when the course of
history was changed by the conquests of Alexander the Great.

The literature of the ancient Near East comprises works from three
mainstreams of culture: the Mesopotamian-Anatolian, which includes the
Sumerians, the Elamites, the Babylonians, the Assyrians, and the Hittites;
the Syro-Palestinian, which takes in the writings of the Canaanite and Hebrew peoples; and the Egyptian, which was inscribed on stone and papyrus
in what was the earliest written language.

Apart from these alignments in time, place, and language, what justifies
the concept of an ancient Near Eastern literature is its characteristic cluster-
ing around some half dozen major genres and a number of lesser genres.
The former includes myth, epic, historical narrative, "wisdom" literature
such as proverbs and sayings, and meditations, hymns, prayers, omens, and
incantations. The latter includes fables, folktales and legends, lamentations,
songs, autobiography, satire, riddles, and dialogue-debates.

As a rule, a literary work in the ancient Near East was not the creation of
a single individual, but a collective effort, preserved, modified, and re-
copied. The original author faded into obscurity and the work entered the
public realm to serve a social purpose.

Because this literature was produced before literary theory was invented,
it defies easy definition by accepted genres. Thus, the reader does not have
the benefit of literary criticism or theory validated by criteria produced in-

ternally by the cultures in question. Finally, the line between sacred and secular literature is far from clear.

General Background

The following list should serve as an introduction to a literature now perceived as vital to an understanding of society's origins and early heritage.

Chiera, Edward. *They Wrote on Clay: The Babylonian Tablets Speak Today.* Ed. by George G. Cameron, Univ. of Chicago Pr. 1938 $11.00; Univ. of Chicago Pr. (Phoenix Bks.) 1956 pap. $3.50. A sensitive introduction to the world of clay tablets and the environment from which they emanate. For the general reader.

Frankfurt, Henri. *The Intellectual Adventure of Ancient Man: An Essay on Speculative Thought in the Ancient Near East.* Univ. of Chicago Pr. 1977 pap. $10.95. The single comprehensive book that seeks to clarify the first intellectual principles of ancient Near Eastern thought, especially Egyptian and Babylonian. An indispensable adjunct to literary study.

Kirk, G. S. *Myth: Its Meaning and Functions in Ancient and Other Cultures.* Univ. of California Pr. 1970 $31.00 pap. $7.95. A wide-ranging, unconventional exploration of the nature and meaning of myth by a Hellenist who sees beyond the limits of the intellectual borders of ancient Greece; especially interesting chapters on Mesopotamia and Greek-Hurrian-Hittite connections.

Kramer, Samuel N., ed. *Mythologies of the Ancient World.* Doubleday 1961 o.p. This is an absolutely essential volume, with each essay of the highest quality. Of special notice is Rudolf Anthes's essay on mythology in Ancient Egypt, which is a little masterpiece in itself. Other cultures treated are Sumeria, Babylonia, and Assyria by Kramer; Hittite by H. Güterbock; Canaanite by C. Gordon; Iran by M. J. Dresden; and Greece by Michael H. Jameson, along with several from the non-Near Eastern arena.

Collections

Breasted, James H., trans. and ed. *Ancient Records of Egypt.* Russell 5 vols. in 3 1906–07 o.p. Although dated, these volumes still serve as a useful introduction to Egyptian historical writing.

Ceadel, Eric B., ed. *Literatures of the East.* Grove 1959 o.p. The essays on Canaanite, early Arab, Hebrew, and Iranian writings are succinct and authoritative.

Erman, Adolf, ed. *The Ancient Egyptians: A Sourcebook of Their Writings.* 1927. Intro. by William K. Simpson, Harper 1966 o.p. "Remains by far the best selection and translation of Egyptian belles-lettres which has appeared so far. Erman, who was the real creator of scientific Egyptology, also possessed a rare understanding of Egyptian mentality and a profound appreciation of ancient Egyptian psychology. It is fair to say that the book will long continue to hold its high position among anthologies of the kind, and there will be few who are not charmed by it" (William F. Albright). The translations employ archaic English, which occasionally makes the Old Egyptians sound like Old Englishmen, but this should be no impairment to the reader's enjoyment. Simpson has provided an up-to-date introductory essay.

Faulkner, R. O., trans. *The Ancient Egyptian Pyramid Texts.* Oxford 1969 o.p. Designed for use by philologists and students of ancient religion.

Gaster, Theodor H., ed. *The Oldest Stories in the World.* Beacon 1958 pap. $4.95. A very elementary retelling of a number of myths and legends designed for the general reader but probably more appropriate to the young. A useful index of motifs appears at the end.

———. *Thespis: Ritual, Myth, and Drama in the Ancient Near East.* Fwd. by Gilbert Murray, Gordian 2d ed. rev. 1975 $16.00. Lively, imaginative, but controversial.

Lambert, Wilfred G. *Babylonian Wisdom Literature.* Oxford 1960 $55.00. Although specifically limited to wisdom literature, the volume offers translations of many texts.

Luckenbill, D. D. *Ancient Records of Assyria and Babylonia.* Greenwood 2 vols. repr. of 1926–27 ed. 1969 o.p. Still useful as a basic introduction to Assyro-Babylonian historical writing. The translations are seriously in need of modernization in accordance with the progress of Assyriological research. The volume by James B. Pritchard that follows contains some more recent translations of the Assyrian materials.

Pritchard, James B., ed. *Ancient Near Eastern Texts Relating to the Old Testament.* Princeton Univ. Pr. 3d ed. 1955 o.p. Although the intent of the volume is to provide texts bearing upon the Old Testament, the contents represent most of the major works of ancient Near Eastern civilization. A collection of translations by major scholars, it ranges widely into all periods and covers all principal genres and many of the lesser. It is indispensable for the reader who wants to encounter the originals in a scholarly, yet readable form.

Simpson, William K., ed. *The Literature of Ancient Egypt: An Anthology of Stories, Instructions and Poetry.* Yale Univ. Pr. 1973 o.p. Modern translations by foremost Egyptologists.

Individual Texts

In addition to James B. Pritchard's collection, *Ancient Near Eastern Texts*, the reader should consult appreciations and criticisms of regional ancient Near Eastern literature cited above. In this section only easily procurable translations and studies of a few well-known individual works are noted.

Atra-Hasis: The Babylonian Story of the Flood. Trans. and ed. by Wilfred G. Lambert and A. R. Millard, Oxford 1969 o.p. "Ever since the original decipherment of fragments of Babylonian literature some 90 years ago, wide interest has been taken in the flood story, which is related in some way to the Hebrew account in Genesis. Hitherto the only complete Babylonian version has been a digest incorporated in the 'Gilgamesh Epic.' Over the past five years large portions of the full Babylonian account have come to light in which the hero is called Atra-Hasis. This book offers the first edition and translation of the new material, along with improved forms of the 'Sumerian Flood' story (by M. Civil) and the other Babylonian fragments."

The Babylonian Genesis. Trans. by Alexander Heidel, Univ. of Chicago Pr. (Phoenix Bks.) 2d ed. 1963 $3.95. "A careful . . . translation and interpretation of the 'Enuma-Elish' [Babylonian Creation Story] and related texts. The book also contains a long chapter on the Old Testament parallels found in the Akkadian [Assyro-Babylonian] 'creation' texts, which is quite detailed and informative. . . ."

The Book of the Dead: The Papyrus of Ani in the British Museum. 1895. Trans. and ed. by E. A. Wallis Budge, Dover 1967 $4.95. Almost a century old, and since publication technically refined, this book remains an accessible introduction to the burial ritual texts of the Middle Kingdom Egyptians and their successors.

The Epic of Gilgamesh. Trans. by N. K. Sanders, Penguin 1960 $2.50. A prose version

that is aesthetically less satisfying than the translation into poetry that Pritchard includes in his collection cited above.

The Gilgamesh Epic and Old Testament Parallels. Ed. by A. Heidel, Univ. of Chicago
Pr. (Phoenix Bks.) 1946 pap. $3.75. The first two chapters contain fully anno-
tated translations of the Gilgamesh Epic, the Sumerian account of the deluge
from Nippur, the Atra-Hasis Epic, Berossus's account of the deluge, the story of
Ishtar's descent into the underworld, the myth about Nergal and Ereshkigal,
and an Assyrian prince's vision of the underworld (probably the origin of the
Greek Hades and the Christian Hell).

ARABIC LITERATURE

Arabic is the major living language of the five-branched Hamido-Semitic
family, and the primary tongue of more than one hundred million people.
The vehicle of Muhammad the Prophet's message, it was carried by conquest and spread by civilization over a vast area stretching from Morocco
and Spain in the West through India and Indonesia in the East. Since the
Koran was written in Arabic, it has also been the language of religious education wherever Islam has prevailed.

Literary Arabic differs from the spoken language, especially in regions
where literacy lags, and is a unifying element in the Arab world and in Islamic civilization. Arabic literature is unparalleled in extent, perhaps because all writings in the Arabic language, whether composed by Arabs or
non-Arabs, are considered part of Arabic literature.

According to most Arabists, Arabic literature falls into six periods, but for
the reader's purposes it may be divided into two broad categories: the classical and the modern. The classical is characterized by the proverbs and poetry (or *quasidah*, a highly formalized form of ode) of the nomads of the
northern desert. The modern opens with the nineteenth-century renaissance
(*Annah-dah Al-Adabiyah*) in Syria, Lebanon, and Egypt. It was stimulated
by growing contacts with the West and fed by a renewed interest in the
great classical past. Since the sixteenth century, the freer environment of
Egypt has made that country the focus of the renaissance. When the Ottoman Empire crumbled after World War I, the movement spread to other
Arab lands and came to a full flowering as the Arab countries gained their
independence during the years following World War II.

The novel and the drama, literary forms largely unfamiliar to the Arab
world, took shape under the impact of European works made available by
nineteenth-century translations into Arabic, but the short story, the essay,
and the new verse forms had their roots in classical Arabic literature. The
confrontation between Arab tradition and modern attitudes put Arabic literature as well as Arab society on a new course. The present trends in Arabic poetry began after the establishment of Israel. To some extent, the anti-Western
sentiment that has prevailed as a consequence of the Palestinian disaster has
led to a conscious discarding of Western themes. The romanticism of the earlier poetry is all but gone, and the younger poets have turned increasingly to
free verse to convey their concern with social and political issues. Current

practitioners of the art have dropped all the technical restraints of prosody and have been expressing themselves in prose poetry. Perhaps the least expected development in the still-patriarchal society of the Arabs is the emergence between 1948 and 1978 of at least a dozen dazzling poets who are carrying on the Arab woman's 1,300-year-old tradition of self-expression within the male-dominated culture.

Background

Gibb, Hamilton A. *Studies on the Civilization of Islam*. Ed. by Stanford J. Shaw and William R. Polk, Princeton Univ. Pr. repr. of 1962 ed. 1982 $31.00 pap. $11.50. Contains excellent articles on interpretation of Islamic history, political thought, religion, and Arabic literature.

Mernissi, Fatima. *Beyond the Veil: Male-Female Dynamics in a Modern Muslim Society: 1976*. Halsted Pr. text ed. pap. $6.95; Schenkman text ed. 1975 pap. $9.95. Useful as background to novels of contemporary Arab life.

History and Criticism

Abdel, Farouk W. *Modern Egyptian Drama: An Anthology. Studies in Middle Eastern Lit*. Bibliotheca Islamica 1974 o.p. The author has provided a good 40-page introduction to the subject; translations follow from *The Sultan's Dilemma* by Tawfiq Al-Hakim, *The New Arrival* by Mikhail Roman, *A Journey Outside the Wall* by Rashad Rushdi, and *The Farfoors* by Yūsuf Idrīs.

Altoma, Salih. *Modern Arabic Literature: A Bibliography of Articles, Books, Dissertations and Translations in English*. Asian Studies Research Institute 1975 o.p. This useful bibliography lists 850 items. There are no annotations, but the work is essential as a starting point for researchers.

Birds through a Ceiling of Alabaster: Three Abbasid Poets. Trans. with intro. by G. B. H. Wightman and A. Y. al-Udhari, *Penguin Class. Ser*. 1976 pap. $1.95. This has a brief but interesting introduction to Arabic poetry and the difficulties of translating it. The translators deliberately used present-day English in an attempt to convey the tone of poems by Ibn al-Ahnaf, Ibn al-Mu'tazz, and al-Ma'arri. For popular, nonscholarly reading.

Boullata, Issa. *Critical Perspectives in Modern Arabic Literature*. Three Continents 1980 pap. $15.00

Deeb, Kamal Abu, ed. *Al-Jurra-Ni's Theory of Poetic Imagery*. Humanities Pr. text ed. 1959 $42.50

Gibb, H. A. R. *Arabic Literature: An Introduction*. 1926. Oxford 1974 o.p. Gibb was perhaps the outstanding English Arabist of the twentieth century, and this book, although dated in some respects, remains the best account in small compass of Arabic literature from pre-Islamic times through the 'Abbāsid era. Modern literature is not included.

Hamori, Andras. *On the Art of Medieval Arabic Literature*. Princeton Univ. Pr. 1974 o.p. The author applies modern literary criticism to three main subjects. He starts by tracing the changes that occurred in poetic genres from pre-Islamic times through the tenth century; in the second section he analyzes the techniques used to provide coherence in poetry; and in the third he examines the structure of two tales from the *Arabian Nights*. The sections on poetry are innovative and should be useful to advanced students of Arabic.

Al- Jayyusi, Salma al- Khadra. *Trends and Movements in Modern Arabic Poetry*. Humanities Pr. 2 vols. text ed. 1977 $50.75. A comprehensive study intended for the specialist, but suitable for the general reader as well.

Kilpatrick, Hilary. *The Modern Egyptian Novel*. International Learning System text ed. 1974 $10.00. The author studies and traces specific topics in Egyptian prose from Haykal's "Zaynab" up to 1968. The book can serve as a reference work for biographical and bibliographic information.

Le Gassick, Trevor J. *Major Themes in Modern Arabic Thought: An Anthology*. Univ. of Michigan Pr. text ed. 1979 $12.50. Good introduction, with representations from a large number of works.

Lichtenstadter, Ilse. *Introduction to Classical Arabic Literature*. Twayne 1974 o.p. Notable for its discussion of "polite letters" (correspondence) and "how-to-do-it" manuals that gave rise to a bureaucratic secretarial class known as *kuttab* (scribes) in the eighth and ninth centuries.

Nicholson, R. A. *A Literary History of the Arabs*. Cambridge Univ. Pr. 1969 $17.50 pap. $5.75. The standard in-depth work (English) on classical Arabic belles-lettres up to the fall of Baghdad in 1258. Contains a wealth of information not found in other surveys.

Zwettler, Michael. *The Oral Tradition of Classical Arabic Poetry*. Ohio State Univ. Pr. 1978 o.p. Argues persuasively that early Arabic poetry represents the culminating point in a long tradition of development and transmission from poet to reciter, followed by the later process of recording a version in written form. Important for its own sake but also because it foreshadowed another oral phenomenon, namely the Koran itself.

Collections

Arberry, A. J., trans. *Arabic Poetry*. Cambridge Univ. Pr. 1965 o.p. Includes translation of the famous elegy written by the poetess al-Khansa for her brother Sakhr slain in battle.

Boullata, Issa J., ed. *Women of the Fertile Crescent: An Anthology of Arab Women's Poems*. Three Continents 1978 $20.00 pap. $10.00. Modern poetry by thirteen Arab women.

Clifford, William, and Daniel Milton, eds. *A Treasury of Modern Asian Stories*. New Amer. Lib. $2.95

Compton, Linda Fish, ed. *Andalusian Lyrical Poetry and Old Spanish Love Songs*. New York Univ. Pr. 1976 o.p. Poetry exhibiting many of the features associated with the tradition of "courtly love" and "troubadours" (a word of Arabic origin meaning "singers").

Hamalian, Leo, and John D. Yohannan, eds. *New Writing from the Middle East*. New Amer. Lib. 1978 pap. $2.95; Ungar 1978 $18.50. Collection of stories, poems, and plays from Armenia, Egypt, Iran, Israel, Jordan, Lebanon, Syria, and Turkey, all written after World War II. "Not a dull page in the over five hundred that make up this unique anthology" (*Choice*).

Haywood, John, ed. *Modern Arabic Literature, 1800–1970*. St. Martin's 1971 $10.95. Extracts in translation, with an editor's introduction.

Johnson-Davies, Denys, trans. *Egyptian Short Stories*. Three Continents 1978 $10.00 pap. $6.00 "Partly because they have had one of the longest cultural and intellectual connections with the West, it is the Egyptians who have given form and structure to story-telling as an Arab literary art."

———. *Modern Arabic Short Stories*. Heinemann 1976 pap. $6.00. This volume contains 20 translations of such high quality that they give the reader the impression that the stories were originally written in English. As A. J. Arberry has pointed out, this collection indicates the way Arab men and women view the modern world.

Khouri, Mounah A., and Hamid Algar, eds. *An Anthology of Modern Arabic Poetry.* Univ. of California Pr. 1974 o.p. This work contains a short but excellent introduction on the development of modern poetry. Selections (text and translation) from poets are carefully arranged in chronological order. Short biographical sketches are given. This work is essential for tracing, understanding, and appreciating modern poetry.

Kritzeck, James, ed. *Anthology of Islamic Literature.* New Amer. Lib. 1969 pap. $5.95. Covers the period between the rise of Muhammad and the Age of the Caliphs to the Ottoman poetry at the end of the eighteenth century. Geared to the general reader, not to the specialist.

———. *Modern Islamic Literature.* Holt 1970 $10.00. Selections from the outstanding Muslim writers, from 1800 to present. Off-beat excerpts from Agha Khan, the Shah of Iran, Abdul Nasser, King Abdullah of Jordan (on Lawrence of Arabia), and a contemporary Egyptian account of the "opening" of the Muslim world by Napoleon.

Maḥfūẓ, 'Najīb. *God's World: An Anthology of Short Stories.* Trans. by Akef Abadir and Roger Allen, *Studies in Middle Eastern Lit.* Bibliotheca Islamica 1973 pap. $11.95. Translations of 20 stories by one of the leading Egyptian authors.

Nicholson, Reynold A., trans. *Translations of Eastern Poetry and Prose.* Greenwood repr. of 1922 ed. lib. bdg. $18.75. Excellent for early and middle Arabic writing.

Wahab, Farouk W. *Modern Egyptian Drama.* Bibliotheca Islamica 1974 $25.00

General Reading

Awwad, Tewfiq Yussef. *Death in Beirut.* Three Continents 1978 $12.00 pap. $8.00. A novel about love against the background of the tragic civil war.

Barakat, Halim. *Days of Dust.* Trans. by Trevor J. Le Gassick and Awdat al Ta'ir Ila'l'bahr, intro. by Edward W. Said, pref. by Jacques Berque, Three Continents 2d ed. repr. of 1974 ed. 1983 $18.00 pap. $8.00

Ghanim, Fathi. *The Man Who Lost His Shadow.* Heinemann text ed. 1980 pap. $6.00

Habibi, Emile. *The Secret Life of Saeed, the Ill-Fated Pessimist: The Ill-Fated Pessoptimist (A Palestinian Who Became a Citizen of Israel).* Vantage 1982 $8.95. Combining fact and fantasy, this comic novel depicts the life of a Palestinian who becomes a citizen of Israel. "Saeed's tale is seen as one of defeat and humility; yet his stupidity, candour, and lack of malice endear him to the reader and make his essential tragedy all the more poignant" (Trevor J. Le Gassick). Habibi, an Arab Christian and a founding member of the Israeli Community party, has been elected to the Knesset three times.

Hussain, Taha. *An Egyptian Childhood.* Three Continents 1980 pap. $6.00. Autobiographical.

Hussein, M. Kamal. *City of Wrong.* Trans. by Kenneth Cragg, Seabury 1959 o.p.

Rifaat, Alifa. *Distant View of a Minaret and Other Stories.* Trans. by Denys Johnson-Davies, Merrimack 1984 $12.95. Rifaat depicts lives of futility, isolation, and unsatisfied desire. In "My World of the Unknown," a frustrated woman abandons conventional values and religion in favor of intercourse with phallically shaped female djinn.

Wormhoudt, Arthur, trans. *The Diwan of Al'Asha*. Wormhoudt 1984 pap. $6.50. One of Wormhoudt's translations from classical and medieval Arabic.

ADONIS (ALI AHMED SAID). 1930–

Ali Ahmed Said was born near Tartus in northern Syria, not far from the mythical birthplace of the god whose name he adopted as a pen name. He moved to Beirut in 1956 and became the editor of *Sh'ir*, the poetry review he helped to found. Educated at the Sorbonne and the author of a two-volume anthology of classical Arabic poetry, he was, until Lebanon went up in flames, an influential voice in the social and intellectual life of the Arab world. He has been a critic and editor of the journal *Mawaquif*. Among his published collections not yet translated into English are *The Book of Changes* and *The Stage and the Mirrors*.

BOOK BY ADONIS

The Blood of Adonis. Trans. by Samuel Hazo, Univ. of Pittsburgh Pr. 1971 o.p.

AL-HAKIM, TAWFIQ. 1902–1976?

Tawfiq Al-Hakim was the undisputed pioneer of dramatic writing in Arabic. "With his natural talent, his wide reading in French, his close study of the techniques of European theatre . . . his interest in the problems of language—most pertinent in a culture where the written language differs so much from the spoken—with these attributes he gave to the Egyptian theatre the foundations of respectability it needed" (Denys Johnson-Davies). Born in Alexandria, he studied law in Paris and spent time with writers there. In 1928, he was appointed an attorney to the public prosecutor in the provinces of Egypt, and his experiences there inspired his novel *The Maze of Justice* (o.p.). He resigned from government service and devoted himself completely to writing.

BOOKS BY AL-HAKIM

The Tree Climber. Trans. by Denys Johnson-Davies, Oxford 1969 o.p.
Fate of a Cockroach and Other Plays. Three Continents 1980 $15.00 pap. $7.00. Representative of Al-Hakim's writing, these plays range from romance to domestic comedy.

IBRAHIM, SANALLAH. 1937–

Born in Cairo and trained as a lawyer, Ibrahim chose a career of journalism. He was imprisoned for five years (1959–64) because of his political activities. In 1968, he went to Lebanon, then to East Berlin, and later to Moscow, where he studied cinema.

BOOK BY IBRAHIM

The Smell of It. Heinemann text ed. 1971 pap. $3.50; Three Continents 1971 $12.00 pap. $7.00

IDRĪS, YŪSUF. 1927–

Idrīs was born in an Egyptian village, practiced medicine for a while, was imprisoned several times for political activism in the 1950s, and then devoted himself entirely to writing. Although recently he has been writing for the stage, he is regarded as Egypt's foremost craftsman in the short story. In his psychologically penetrating tales, death and forbidden erotic love are handled in a poetic, almost surrealistic style.

BOOKS BY IDRĪS

The Cheapest Nights. Three Continents 1978 $10.00 pap. $7.00
In the Eye of the Beholder: Tales of Egyptian Life from the Writings of Yūsef Idrīs. Bibliotheca Islamica 1978 $20.00 pap. $11.95

JUBRAN (GIBRAN), KHALIL. 1883–1931

Poet, philosopher, and artist, Jubran was born near the Cedars of Lebanon. The millions of Arabic-speaking peoples familiar with his writings regard him as the foremost poet of his age. His fame and influence spread beyond the Middle East, and *The Prophet*, his masterpiece, has sold more than four million copies in the United States alone. In the United States, where he lived during the last 20 years of his life, he began to write in English.

BOOKS BY JUBRAN

Secrets of the Heart. Citadel 1978 pap. $5.95. A collection of poems, stories, and meditations that convey the heart of Jubran's spiritual vision.
The Broken Wings. Citadel 1965 pap. $2.95
Spirit Rebellious. Trans. by A. Ferris, Philosophical Lib. 1947 o.p.
The Prophet. 1923 Knopf $7.95; Random $7.95

KANAFANI, GHASSAN. 1936–1972

Kanafani was born in Acre and worked for a time in Kuwait as a teacher. He edited a daily newspaper in Beirut until he was blown up by a bomb placed in his car. His novels, short stories, and one play are interwoven with the tragedy of the Palestinian refugees.

BOOK BY KANAFANI

Men in the Sun. Intro. by Denys Johnson-Davies, Three Continents 1978 pap. $7.00

MAḤFŪẒ, 'NAJĪB. 1911–

The son of a Cairo merchant, Maḥfūẓ studied philosophy at the university there and began his writing career with several historical novels. In 1945, he completed the first of his novels depicting the life of the Egyptian middle class in Cairo. The author of more than 25 works of fiction, he is regarded as the foremost novelist in the Arab world.

BOOKS BY MAḤFŪẒ

God's World: An Anthology of Short Stories. Trans. by Akef Abadir and Roger Allen, *Studies in Middle Eastern Lit.* Bibliotheca Islamica 1973 pap. $11.95. A representation of the short stories.

Children of Gebelawi. Three Continents 1981 pap. $9.00
Midaq Alley. Three Continents 1974 o.p.
Miramar. Three Continents 1978 pap. $8.00
Mirrors: A Novel. Trans. by Roger Allen, *Studies in Middle Eastern Lit.* Bibliotheca
     Islamica 1977 $20.00 pap. $11.95

SALIH, AL-TAYIB. 1929–

Salih was born in northern Sudan and educated in Khartoum and London. He originally intended to follow a career in agriculture but instead has worked in broadcasting, for a time as head of drama for the BBC's Arabic Service.

BOOKS BY SALIH

The Wedding of Zein. Heinemann text ed. 1969 pap. $6.00; Three Continents 1978
     $10.00 pap. $7.00. "These stories are interesting . . . because they show what happens when a considerable sophistication and resourcefulness of technique is applied to traditional storytelling material" (*The Guardian*).
Season of Migration to the North. Heinemann text ed. 1969 pap. $5.00; Three Continents 1978 $7.00. In this complex novel, a brilliant Sudanese student of an earlier generation is seduced and ultimately destroyed by his obsession with the values and freedom of British life.

ARMENIAN LITERATURE

Armenian literature is one of the most distinctive in the Middle East. Having begun as the independent expression of a nation newly converted to Christianity, it flourishes today in such different environments as the Soviet Union, the Middle East, France, and the United States, where there has been a literary renaissance inspired to a large extent by the literary quarterly *Ararat*.

Geographically, Armenia is a tiny republic in the Soviet Union, the Caucasian remnant of a once-mighty empire. Elsewhere in the Middle East, Armenians constitute a significant cultural minority. Beyond geography, Armenia is a state of thousands of people who fled the Turkish terror of 1915 and who put down new roots in Europe, Latin America, Canada, and the United States.

Armenian literature has an impressive heritage, based on Armenia's adoption of Christianity as a state religion in A.D. c.301, and the invention of the Armenian alphabet (based on the Greek) a century later. Not unexpectedly, Armenian oral literature is older than the written, and folk poetry had flourished among proto-Armenians for at least 300 years before Mashtots (c.400). Perhaps the most remarkable piece of oral literature to survive is the epic of David of Sassoun, "discovered" in 1873 by an Armenian clergyman, Garegin Servantstian.

After the political collapse of Greater Armenia in the eleventh century, the literature divided itself into eastern and western branches based on dialect. This split has persisted into modern times. Following a period of literary decadence in the fifteenth century, recovery began in the sixteenth century with the rise of popular bards or troubadours. By the eighteenth century, the spoken language—and secular themes—emerged alongside the *grapar* (church language) and theological or classical themes. By the first decade of the twentieth century, Armenian literature had become secularized.

In 1915, the Ottoman Empire's decision to deport the entire Armenian population of Turkey to the desert of Syria resulted in the death of countless Armenians, among them the writers responsible for the literary renaissance at the turn of the century. The novel became a vehicle for moral, social, and political aspirations of a newly awakened nationalism among Armenians. During the Stalinist purges of the 1930s, a number of Armenian writers were arrested for political "deviationism" and either jailed or deported to Siberia.

Despite this setback, Armenian literature flowered for a third time in the twentieth century. Although the publication of books in Soviet Armenia has flourished, perhaps as never before, Armenian writers are reluctantly leaving their Middle Eastern roots for a more secure life elsewhere.

Background

Baliozian, Ara, ed. *Armenia Observed*. Ararat Pr. 1979 $10.95 pap. $5.95. An anthology of the experiences and impressions of noted writers from Pushkin to Michael Arlen, gathered during visits to Armenia, both Turkish and Russian.

Hamalian, Leo. *Burn after Reading*. Ararat Pr. 1978 pap. $4.95. A collection of personal essays that provide an appreciation of the Middle Eastern temperament.

History and Criticism

Baliozian, Ara. *The Armenians*. Ararat Pr. 1980 pap. $5.95. Aimed at the general reader, this study of Armenian history and culture (religion, language, all arts) is concise, readable, and inexpensive—perhaps the best introduction to Armenia available.

Hamalian, Leo. *As Others See Us: The Armenian Image in Literature*. Ararat Pr. 1980 $9.95 pap. $5.95. A study of the image of the Armenian in Western fiction and travel literature. Contains a concise history of Armenia and a bibliography.

——, ed. *The View from Ararat: Twenty-five Years of Armenian-American Writing*. Ararat Pr. $15.00 pap. $7.50. Includes reviews and criticism of books about Armenia by Armenians. Well-written articles on every phase of Armenian history and cultural life, both in Armenia and in the diaspora.

Collections

Boyajian, Zabelle C. *Armenian Legends and Poems*. Columbia Univ. Pr. 1916 o.p. This volume includes selections of early legends in prose and a wide range of translations in verse of medieval and modern poetry, some being traditional folk songs, others by known authors. Contains a valuable essay on Armenian epics, folk songs, and medieval poetry by Aram Raffi (son of the famous novelist).

Der Hovanessian, Diana, and Marzbed Margossian, eds. *Anthology of Armenian Poetry*. Columbia Univ. Pr. 1978 $27.50 text ed. pap. $14.00. Spanning more than 20 centuries and including pagan fragments, this extraordinary collection presents the full, poignant world of Armenian poetry hitherto unavailable in English. Among the riches included in this volume are the mystical chants of Grigor Naregatsi, the love songs of Nahabed Kouchag, and the troubadour Sayat Nova.

Downing, Charles. *Armenian Folk-Tales and Fables*. Ed. by William Papas, Oxford 1972 $14.95. The selections fall into three categories: fables, folktales, and proverbs.

Etmekjian, James, ed. *Anthology of Western Armenian Literature*. Caravan 1980 $30.00

Hoogasian-Villa, Susan. *One Hundred Armenian Tales and Their Folkloristic Significance*. Wayne State Univ. Pr. 1982 $19.95 pap. $11.95. A valuable collection of folktales as told by Armenian immigrants to the United States.

Samuelian, Thomas J., ed. *Classical Armenian Culture: Influences and Creativity*. Scholars Pr. 1982 $17.50 pap. $13.00. Essays about influences and creativity in the course of Armenian literature.

Samuelian, Thomas J., and Michael E. Stone. *Medieval Armenian Culture*. Scholars Pr. 1984 $23.50 pap. $15.75. Fifteen essays on Armenian literature of the period.

Surmelian, Leon. *Apples of Immortality: Folk Tales of Armenia*. Greenwood repr. of 1968 ed. 1983 $39.95. A collection of charming folktales that reveal the folk wisdom of the Armenian peasantry.

Tolegian, Aram. *Armenian Poetry Old and New*. Wayne State Univ. Pr. 1979 $18.95. Bilingual text sampling the richness of 16 centuries of the Armenian poetic tradition. Contains the complete text of the Hovhannes Toumanian version of "David of Sassoun."

———. *We of the Mountains*. Progressive 1972 o.p. A collection of short stories by 19 writers of different generations, outlook, and style.

ANTREASSIAN, ANTRANIG. 1908–

Now residing in California, Antreassian is among the few Armenian writers in the United States who has created a corpus of work in his own language.

BOOK BY ANTREASSIAN

The Cup of Bitterness. Trans. by Jack Antreassian, Ashod 1979 pap. $4.95. A collection of eight stories concerned with survivors of Turkish persecution who, though they escaped death, bear the psychic damage of the holocaust all their lives.

BARONIAN, HAGOP. 1842–1891

Armenia's foremost satirist, Baronian was born and educated in Edirne but was active mainly in Istanbul. Although both his family and health were poor, he managed to write hugely popular plays, such as *Brother Balthazar*, and satiric sketches before he died of tuberculosis at age 50.

BOOKS BY BARONIAN

The Honorable Beggars. Trans. by Jack Antreassian, Ashod 1980 pap. $4.95. A satire on avarice, about a man who visits Constantinople and finds himself the target of endless schemes to separate him from his money.

The Perils of Politeness. Trans. by Jack Antreassian, intro. by Michael Kermian,

Ashod 1983 pap. $7.50. A satire on the torments people suffer in the name of politeness. Set in Constantinople a century ago, the episodes are disquieting reflections of experiences today.

CHARENTS, EGHISHE. 1897–1937

Modern Armenia's most brilliant poet, Charents was caught up in the Communist Revolution until he fell out of favor in the 1930s. He died in a Soviet prison.

BOOK BY CHARENTS

Land of Fire. Trans. by Diana Der Hovanessian and Marzbed Margossian, Ardis 1985 $25.00

DAVID OF SASSOUN. Late medieval period

The deeds of David of Sassoun were repeated orally in the Armenian countryside, but not written down until the late nineteenth century.

BOOKS ABOUT DAVID OF SASSOUN

Daredevils of Sassoun. Trans. by Leon Surmelian, Swallow 1954 o.p. The Armenian saga of the twelfth century rendered into stirring prose by a skilled novelist, with a substantial introduction setting the epic in its historical and political context.
David of Sassoun: The Armenian Folk Epic in Four Cycles. Trans. and ed. by Artin K. Shalian, Ohio Univ. Pr. 1964 o.p. This is a translation of the Armenian text by the poet Hovhannes Toumanian and covers the third cycle only, of which David is the hero. The complete epic consists of four cycles in rhythmic prose, each describing the exploits of a succeeding generation of legendary heroes from the wild regions of Sassoun, southwest of Lake Van (near Iran), who defend their homeland against foreign tyrants. David is the hero of the third generation and has become, especially in Soviet Armenia, a symbol of patriotic valor.

GABOUDIGIAN, SYLVA. 1920–

One of Armenia's most famous contemporary poets, Gaboudigian has been translated into more than 20 languages. She survived revolution and terror to write more than 500 lyric poems, which stand as an intimate autobiography.

BOOK BY GABOUDIGIAN

Lyrical Poetry of Sylva Gaboudigian. Dorrance 1981 $5.95. First English translation of poems celebrating the love of country and compatriots.

ISSAHAKIAN, AVEDICK. 1875–1957

Issahakian's work includes legends, short stories, political essays, an unfinished novel, prose cameos, and memoirs, but he is best known for his poems recited as popular songs. In 1895, he was imprisoned for political activities. *Songs and Hurts* (o.p.), his first book, appeared in 1896. Again accused of conspiring against the czar, he was exiled to Odessa and jailed. He escaped to Paris, then returned to Armenia for four years. After another absence, he returned again in 1936, remaining there until his death. He is one of Armenia's best-loved poets.

BOOK BY ISSAHAKIAN

Scent Smile and Sorrow: Selected Verse, 1891–1957. Ed. by E. B. Chrakian, Lib. of Armenian 1975 pap. $5.75

KOUCHAG, NAHABED. d.1592

A tombstone in an Armenian village (Karagonis) gives the date of Kouchag's death. Nothing more is known about him except that he wrote poetry. (Until scholars recently settled the question, it was thought that the work attributed to him was anonymous folk poetry.) His lyricism, simplicity, and candor illuminate a dark period in Armenian history. Kouchag's verse is not overburdened with grief like most modern Armenian poets, nor do all his poems always praise God like the work of his religious contemporaries. He knows pathos and love and mixes them gracefully in his verse.

BOOK BY KOUCHAG

Come Sit Beside Me and Listen to Kouchag. Trans. by Diana Der Hovanessian, Ashod 1984 pap. $6.00. These medieval poems are marvelously rendered into idiomatic English by an outstanding poet.

ODIAN, YERVANT. 1869–1926

Sickly as a child, Odian was educated at home. He established his reputation with a novella, *The Victim of Love,* at age 23. He barely escaped the murderous persecutions of 1896 and fled to exile (memorably recounted in *Twelve Years Away from Constantinople*). In other books and in articles he exposed the abuses of the political parties, criticized Turkish policies, and attacked the oppressive influence of landlords and *pashas.* A survivor of the 1915 death marches, he spent his last disillusioned days in Egypt.

BOOK BY ODIAN

Comrade Panchoonie. Trans. by Jack Antreassian, St. Vartan's 1977 $8.95. A rollicking satire of a would-be revolutionary who bungles almost everything connected with his mission of reviving national consciousness. "Panchoonie" literally means "has nothing [upstairs]." The illustrations by Alexander Saroukhian are excellent.

SHIRVANZADEH (pseud. of Alexander Movsessian). 1858–1935

Regarded as the father of eastern Armenian realism, both fiction and drama, Shirvanzadeh was born in Shirvan, Azerbaijan, and had little formal education. He worked as an accountant in the oil city of Baku and his novel *Chaos* (o.p.) describes the early days of the oil industry. He lived in Paris (1905–10), in the United States for seven years, and returned to Russia in 1926, where he died of alcoholism. His plays, adapted from his novels, are still widely performed and have been turned into successful films and operas. He had a bitter vision of society, depicting it as dominated by greed, superstition, puritanism, and gossip.

BOOKS BY SHIRVANZADEH

For the Sake of Honor. DOAC 1976 o.p.

Evil Spirit. DOAC 1980 $6.95 pap. $4.95. Both translations, *For the Sake of Honor* and *Evil Spirit*, are competent, idiomatic, and witty, by a playwright and professor of theater, Nishan Parlakian.

TEKEYAN, VAHAN. 1878–1948

Born and educated in Constantinople, Tekeyan developed into the outstanding poet of his milieu. Besides his own books, he published translations of French symbolist poetry and Shakespearean sonnets (the sonnet remained his favorite form). During the 1896 persecutions, he escaped to Europe. He returned briefly to Turkey but left again to settle in Egypt, where he was active in Armenian political life and editor of the Armenian newspaper *Arev* (*Sun*).

BOOK BY TEKEYAN

Sacred Wrath: The Selected Poems of Vahan Tekeyan. Trans. by Diana Der Hovanessian and Marzbed Margossian, Ashod 1982 $12.50 pap. $7.50. Brilliant translations of a brilliant poet.

YESSAYAN, ZABEL. 1878–1943

Zabel Yessayan (who Gostan Zarian would call "the national turkey-hen") was born in Constantinople to a prosperous family who educated her at the Sorbonne. She lived and worked in Arab-speaking countries and Europe before settling permanently in Yerevan, the capital of Armenia. An erudite scholar, an influential teacher, and a versatile author, she wrote in French and Armenian an autobiography based on her early life, eyewitness accounts of the 1909 massacres of Armenians, literary criticism, and travel impressions (the last reveals a full commitment to the Soviet regime). For her passionate defense of the writers accused of deviationism and anti-government agitation in the mid-thirties, she too was arrested and banished. She died amid mysterious circumstances. Her unfinished *magnum opus*, a long novel about her Zorba-like uncle, awaits translation into English.

BOOK BY YESSAYAN

The Gardens of Silihdar and Other Writings. Trans. by Ara Baliozian, Ashod Pr. 1982 pap. $7.50. Selections from the fiction, satire, autobiography, and travel impressions of Soviet Armenia of a woman much admired in her own time and still avidly read today by Armenians.

ZARIAN, GOSTAN. 1885–1969

Lawrence Durrell called Zarian "a wild and roguish literary man of almost mythological quality." Picasso and Marc Chagall illustrated his books and the Italian composer Respighi set his poems to music. Born in the Caucasus and educated in France and Italy, he became a noted poet, editor, teacher, journalist, and storyteller. Multilingual, he produced a body of vari-

ous work unmatched by any Armenian writer, except possibly his friend
WILLIAM SAROYAN.

BOOKS BY ZARIAN

The Traveller & His Road. Trans. by Ara Baliozian, Ashod 1981 pap. $5.95. Sparkling
encounters with the people of the Caucasus, based on a diary covering the critical years 1922–25. The introduction is informative, the historical and literary
notes useful to the general reader, and the translation swift, crisp, and graceful.
Bancoop and the Bones of the Mammoth. Trans. by Ara Baliozian, Ashod 1982 pap.
$7.50. Further travels through Turkey and Europe, brimming over with pene-
trating meditations on the role of the artist in society, the decline of the West,
and the Armenian "situation" in diaspora. Also provocative portraits and lively
impressions of such eminent writers as Eghishe Charents (whose work in translation Ashod Press published in 1986) and Shirvanzadeh.

ZAROUKIAN, ANTRANIK. 1913–

Zaroukian grew up in an Armenian orphanage and received his schooling
in Aleppo and Beirut. As a young man he worked as editor and teacher. In
1942, he began publishing *Nayiri*, a journal on Armenian letters and public
life. After the outbreak of the Lebanese civil war, the journal appeared ir-
regularly, ceasing altogether in 1983. Zaroukian now lives in Paris with his
wife and daughter. His books include *Tragic Writers*, *The Astray* (a satiric
novel), and *Sails*, a collection of poetry.

BOOK BY ZAROUKIAN

Men without Childhood. Trans. by Elise Bayizian and Marzbed Margossian, Ashod
1985 pap. $10.00. The story of thousands of children who were orphaned by the
massacres, haunted forever by the bitter past, and effectively denied a normal
childhood.

ZOHRAB, KRIKOR. 1861–1915

Author, lawyer, and statesman, Krikor Zohrab was a prominent and respected figure in both Turkish and Armenian life of the late nineteenth and
early twentieth centuries. When he fiercely opposed the Ottoman plan to deport Armenians into the desert, he was murdered by the police along with
200 other leaders of the Armenian community as a prelude to mass killings.
Although born in affluent circumstances, he knew how poor people lived
their wretched lives, and his stories touch on their tragedies and occasional
pleasures with sympathy and sensitivity.

BOOKS BY ZOHRAB

Voice of Conscience. Intro. by Michael Kermian, DOAC 1983 $10.00. Stories of ordi-
nary people of Turkey, immersed in their fears, conflicts, and small joys. Excellent introduction by Kermian that makes clear Zohrab's virtues as a man and a
writer.
Zohrab: An Introduction. Trans. by Ara Baliozian, NAASR 1985 consult publisher for
information.

PERSIAN (IRANIAN) LITERATURE

Like Armenian, Persian is an Indo-European language. It is the official language of Iran and widely spoken in Afghanistan. Beginning with the Achaemenid Dynasty (559–529 B.C.), the Persians have made brilliant contributions to the progress of world civilization, and their achievements in the areas of lyric poetry, epic narrative, and mystical imagery are no less impressive. Although little is known about Achaemenid literature (the term "Persian literature" is usually restricted to the prose and poetry written after the Islamic conquest of Iran in the seventh century), its major monument is the Behistun rock inscriptions (cuneiform), which record the deeds of Darius the Great (521–485 B.C.). That there may have existed an extensive religious literature is suggested by the surviving fragments of the *Avesta*, the sacred text of the Zoroastrians produced about 1000 B.C.

The Middle Persian period of the third to the ninth centuries had a varied literature. The Arab conquest of Iran caused profound shifts in Persian language and literature. Arabic script replaced the ideograms of Aramaic, many Arabic words passed into the new language, and certain forms of literature underwent modification. The most far-reaching change, however, was the defeat of Zoroastrian fire worship by Islam. Iran came to identify itself with the Shi'ite branch of Islam (which regards Ali as Muhammad's successor and ignores the first three caliphs).

Under the patronage of the Seljuk Turks in the eleventh century, many great authors flourished. By this time, Persian poetry had been colored with the tenets and images of Islamic mysticism known as Sufism, which provided the background and imagery of the greatest Persian poetry of the following two centuries.

The nineteenth century witnessed a quickening tempo of changes in society and literary expression, but it was not until 1920 that the truly modern turn in prose and poetry was taken. Prose, relegated to a secondary role in the past, now became the dominant medium of literary expression.

The modern revolt against classical Persian poetry was somewhat retarded by a more persistent strength in the tradition. Like prose, it has been perhaps too self-conscious. In the opinion of some critics, it has been a literature of ideas rather than of experience, but there are signs that this trend may now be reversing itself.

Although the Persian branch of Islam produced a very powerful religious drama, the *tazia*, serious drama has come to Iran through translations of European works. On the other hand, a long tradition of comic and satiric theater, originating in puppetry and court entertainments known as *tamash*, was revived during the constitutional struggle in the late nineteenth century and reasserted itself in the wake of Reza Shah's abdication in 1941. With the resurgence of the monarchy after 1953, censorship curtailed much of this activity except in the bland versions performed in the *chai-khanehs* (teahouses).

The future of all Iranian literature will depend on the degree of independence granted to literary artists by the intensely religious regime. Freethinking Iranians may have to develop their art in diaspora.

History and Criticism

Baraheni, Reza. *The Crowned Cannibals: Writings on Repression in Iran.* Random (Vintage) 1977 pap. $3.95. Once a prisoner of the secret police, the leading critic and novelist of Iran writes about the situation of writers in his country and the problems of nationality groups and women, and chronicles the nation's "torture industry." A stunning and shattering book. Introduction by E. L. Doctorow.

Bashiri, Iraj. *The Fiction of Sādiq Hidāyat.* Mazda 1984 $17.95 pap. $12.00. This revision of Hidāyat's *Ivory Tower* (1974) stresses the importance of the covert details in Hidāyat's life and points out his debt to Indian sources as well as the Bible.

Bosworth, Clifford E. *The Later Ghaznavids: Splendor and Decay—The Dynasty in Afghanistan and Northern India.* Columbia Univ. Pr. text ed. 1977 $25.00. One of the Iranian dynasties to arise after the collapse of the Abbāsid Caliphate, the Ghaznavids (rulers of what today is Afghanistan) were great patrons of literature. Poets were encouraged, and the greatest was Firdawsī, whose *Shahnamah* (*Books of Kings*) is accepted without question as *the* Iranian epic. Matthew Arnold drew upon it for his "Sohrab and Rustum." During the reign of the Ghaznavids, significant cultural exchange took place between the Indian and the Islamic worlds, and Persian became the court language of most of India until the British came.

Browne, Edward G. *A Literary History of Persia.* Cambridge Univ. Pr. 4 vols. 1928 ea. $70.00. This is among the most valuable works in English on the subject. Browne's love of Iran and its people makes him a sensitive interpreter of Persian life and literature. He includes numerous texts and translations and carries his narrative down to 1924. The Islamic era receives the most attention.

Hekmat, Forough, and Yann Lovelock. *Folk Tales of Ancient Persia.* Caravan 1974 o.p. This volume, one of the UNESCO Collection of Representative Works, Asian Series, contains eight folktales from ancient Persia, preserving part of the oral storytelling tradition of present-day Iran.

Hillman, Michael C., ed. *The Blind Owl Forty Years After.* Univ. of Texas Pr. 1978 o.p. Sixteen essays, ranging from the influence of Freud on Hidāyat to the influence of Buddhism and the structure of the novel (*The Blind Owl*) that many critics regard as the masterpiece of all Persian fiction.

Rypka, J. *History of Iranian Literature.* Trans. by Hope P. Van Popta, ed. by Karl Jahn, Kluwer Academic rev. & enl. ed. 1968 $79.00. Done with the collaboration of many scholars, this was originally written in Czech by one of the most accomplished of Iranologists. The present English edition was translated from the German, with revisions. It is an excellent, in-depth account of the subject that uses the results of Russian research not usually available to English readers. In addition to Persian literature, it covers Tajik literature, folk literature, Persian literature in India, and Judeo-Persian literature. A good index and bibliography increase the book's value as a reference tool.

Storey, Charles A. *Persian Literature: A Bio-Bibliography Survey.* 1953. Verry 1970 o.p. This monumental work was not completed by the time of Storey's death. Intended to be the essential reference work for advanced researchers, the work is to be continued by G. M. Meridith-Owens. So far, only the section on Qu'ranic literature, history, and biography; astronomy and astrology; geography; and medicine have been printed.

Yohannan, John D. *Persian Poetry in England and America: A Two Hundred Year History. Persian Studies Ser.* Caravan 1977 lib. bdg. $40.00. A detailed study of the interpretation of Persian and English literatures.

Collections

Bowen, J. C. *Poems from the Persian.* Humanities Pr. repr. of 1948 ed. text ed. 1964 $8.50. Good translations of the classical Persian poets from Firdawsī to Qulzum, with useful introductions to the life and work of each.

Hamalian, Leo, and John D. Yohannan. *New Writing from the Middle East.* New Amer. Lib. 1978 pap. $2.95. Previously unpublished (in English) works of Alavi, Baraheni, Farzan, Golshiri, Shamlu, and Saedi, with an excellent introduction by Yohannan.

Isaque, M. *Four Eminent Poetesses of Iran.* Gordon 1976 lib. bdg. $59.95

Kamshad, Hassan. *Modern Persian Prose Literature.* Cambridge Univ. Pr. 1966 $48.00. This contains the best discussion in English of contemporary Persian prose literature. Kamshad gives a good historical background, settles the question of the identity of the Persian translator of Morier's *Hajji Baba*, and analyzes the principal authors of the twentieth century. The second part of the book provides an analysis of the life and work of Ṣādiq Hidāyat. There is an excellent general bibliography and an extensive list of Hidāyat's work.

Karii-Hakkak, Ahmad, trans. *An Anthology of Modern Persian Poetry.* Caravan 1983 $20.00

Levy, Reuben. *An Introduction to Persian Literature.* Columbia Univ. Pr. 1969 $25.00; Greenwood repr. of 1923 ed. 1974 lib. bdg. $24.75. This is a still-useful survey (excellent for its small compass) of the principal authors and main features of the subject up to the modern period, where the coverage is weak. Several brief translations are given.

Pound, Omar. *Arabic and Persian Poems.* New Directions 1970 pap. $7.50. Excellent translations by the son of Ezra Pound.

Sharma, Nasira, ed. *Echoes of Iranian Revolution: Poems of Revolt and Liberation, 1979.* Advent text ed. 1979 $11.95. Poems of revolt and liberation ably translated.

Southgate, Minoo, ed. and trans. *Modern Persian Short Stories.* Three Continents 1980 $20.00 pap. $9.00

General Reading

Achmad, Jala. *The School Principal.* Bibliotheca Islamica 1983 pap. $11.95. A moving novel about the poverty and hardship of village life in Iran.

Baraheni, Reza. *God's Shadow.* Indiana Univ. Pr. 1976 $15.00. Originally composed in Persian and translated by the poet himself, this collection of poems is a haunting and harrowing reflection on the author's incarceration in an Iranian prison during the reign of the late shah. Baraheni writes unsparingly about torture, sadism, and homosexual rape as part of daily prison existence.

'ALAVĪ, BEZORG (or BOZORG). 1907–

Cofounder of the Tudeh (Communist party) in Iran, 'Alavī was jailed during the 1930s for his political views. Since 1941, he has lived in East Germany, where he had both literary and academic standing. He has written three volumes of short stories, a novel (*Her Eyes*, o.p.), and in German, a history of Persian literature. "The Lead Soldier" is considered one of the best short stories written in Persian.

BOOK BY 'ALAVĪ

The Prison Papers of Bozorg Alavī: A Literary Odyssey. Syracuse Univ. Pr. 1985 $28.00

'AṬṬĀR, FARĪD AL-DĪN. 1142–c.1229

Little accurate information is known about 'Aṭṭār, one of the great Sufi poets of Iran. An apothecary and physician, he had many works attributed to him; the two best known are *The Conference of the Birds* and *Muslim Saints and Mystics*.

BOOKS BY 'AṬṬĀR

The Conference of the Birds. 1917. Trans. by C. S. Nott, Shambhala 1971 pap. $2.95;
    Weiser $3.95. An allegory in rhymed couplets in which birds on a pilgrimage undergo the seven stages of the mystic's path to the truth.
Muslim Saints and Mystics. Trans. by A. J. Arberry, Routledge & Kegan 1973 $13.25

BEHRANGI, SAMAD. 1939–1968

Behrangi was born in Tabriz (Azerbaijan) and taught in the rural village schools of the Turkish North before devoting himself wholly to writing stories that would honestly portray the inhuman plight of the poor and their children. He drowned at age 29 while swimming in a swift river. His pioneering stories, his strong social consciousness, and his sympathy for the downtrodden place him in the forefront of contemporary Persian writers.

BOOK BY BEHRANGI

The Little Black Fish and Other Modern Persian Stories. Trans. by Mary Hooglund and
    Eric Hooglund, Three Continents 1982 pap. $7.00. These five stories look into
    the lives of powerless individuals, particularly children, who must not only face
    grinding poverty, but must also struggle to survive in a society indifferent to
    their suffering. The realism of these stories is rendered more poetic by the simple and everyday language, itself an innovation in Persian prose. Thomas Ricks
    supplies an illuminating commentary.

FARROKHZAD, FOROUGH. 1935–1967

Before her untimely death at age 32, Forough Farrokhzad published five volumes of poetry that made her a major figure in modern Persian letters, one who defied social restraint and taboo to express her innermost feelings about love, sex, society, and self with a candor unprecedented in the history of Persian literature. Born in Tehran to an upper middle-class family, she was married at age 16 to a man she did not love. A year later she gave birth to a son, her only child, of whom she lost custody when she was divorced in 1954. She was killed in an auto accident by an "innocent murderer" (her term).

BOOK BY FARROKHZAD

Another Birth. Three Continents 1981 pap. $10.00. Selections from each of her five collections through which one can trace the development of her style and thought, from the personal and often introspective scope of her earlier poems to the broader social vision and transcendental view of universal questions in her later work. Included are excerpts from interviews and letters, analytical essays on two of her major poems by A. Davaran and H. Javadi, and a bibliography of criticism.

FIRDAWSĪ. c.934–c.1020

Firdawsī was born to a family of landowners near Tus, where his tomb is now a national shrine. Beyond that, little is known about the author of the greatest epic of Persia. He won immortality through his *Shahnamah*, an epic of unique literary and historic importance in Iran. Composed of more than 50,000 couplets, it is a vast collection of Indo-European and Iranian legends and history strung together by the poet's skill. Rustum's exploits are central to this work, and MATTHEW ARNOLD's (see Vol. 1) poem, "Sohrab and Rustum" is based on the tragic encounter between the warrior hero and his son.

BOOKS BY FIRDAWSĪ

The Epic of Kings: Shah-nama. Routledge 1973 $30.00
Suhrab and Rustam: A Poem from the Shah-namah of Firdausi. Trans. by James Atkinson, Scholars' Facsimiles 1972 o.p. Facsimile reproduction, with an introduction by Leonard R. N. Ashley, of the 1814 Calcutta edition.

HIDĀYAT, ṢĀDIQ. 1903–1951

Critics regard Ṣādiq Hidāyat among the outstanding writers of the twentieth century. Known primarily for his short stories, he was influenced by Poe and Kafka. His stories plumb the depth of human motivation and seek out the meaning of life. In his work a deep pessimism emerges, which he himself could not overcome and which led him to suicide.

BOOK BY HIDĀYAT

The Blind Owl. Grove 1958 pap. $1.95. *The Blind Owl (Būf-i Kūr)* was first published in India in 1937. Most readers find the translation morbid and depressing, but agree that Hidāyat's work of self-analysis is a masterpiece. D. P. Costello's translation appeared first in 1958.

NIẒĀMĪ, GANJAVĪ. c.1141–1209

Niẓāmī is poorly represented in English. The most popular of his works is *The Story of Layla and Majun.*

BOOK BY NIẒĀMĪ

The Story of Layla and Majun. Trans. and ed. by R. Gelpke, Shambhala 1978 pap.
    $8.95

OMAR KHAYYAM. c.1021–1122

Known in Iran as a leading mathematician, Omar gained literary importance through certain quatrains that were translated by Edward FitzGerald. The *Rubā'iyāt* is justly famous in English translation. Others besides
FitzGerald have tried their hand at translating it. Bowens's is a good example of competent and pleasing work. Robert Graves's effort caused well-
founded adverse comment by orientalist scholars.

BOOKS BY OMAR KHAYYAM

The Ruba'iyat of Omar Khayyam. Trans. by Edward FitzGerald, 1859 Grosset 1971
    o.p. Numerous paperback editions are available.
A New Selection from the Rubaiyat of Omar Khayyam. Trans. and ed. by John Bowen,
    Humanities Pr. text ed. 1976 $12.75. Rendered into English verse by Bowen,
    with a literal translation of each Persian quatrain by A. J. Arberry.

RŪMĪ, JALĀL AL-DĪN. 1207–1273

The greatest Sufi poet, Rūmī was born in Balkh and settled in Anatolia
(Turkey) after years of travel. His major work, the *Masnavi*, stands as one of
the great complete expressions of Islamic mysticism. There are countless
studies of his work in Persian.

BOOKS BY RŪMĪ

Discourses of Rūmī. Trans. by A. J. Arberry, Weiser 1972 o.p. This is Rūmī's famous
    poetic treatise on Sufism, the *Fihi Ma Fihi.*
Mystical Poems of Rūmī: Second Selection—Poems 201–400. Trans. by A. J. Arberry,
    Persian Heritage Ser. Caravan 1983 $20.00; Univ. of Chicago Pr. (Phoenix Bks.)
    1974 $12.50 pap. $7.95. A stream of rapturous lyric poems, many written in the
    name of a wandering dervish, Shams al-Din of Tabriz, who aroused Rūmī's pas-
    sionate devotion.

TURKISH LITERATURE

Turkish is one of the languages spoken from Sinkiang to Skopje. By convention, the word "Turkish" is applied most properly to the language and literature of the Ottoman Turks and their descendants in modern Turkey. Thus
one may speak of Ottoman Turkish literature (c.1400–1920) and modern
Turkish literature from 1920 to the present.

The native traditions that fed contemporary Turkish literature were threefold: the classical or Divan poetry of the Ottomans, modeled on Arab and
Persian forms and intended for a court elite; religious literature connected
with the *tekkes,* or cells of practicing mystics; and oral folk tradition, nationalistic and democratic in its impulse, which antedated the first two.

The republic of Kemal Ataturk, by at once ridding the country of both the caliphate and the sultanate in the 1920s, paved the way for the ascendancy of the folk tradition. Under the reform government, the new Turkish culture had no quarrel with a return of poetry to its native syllabic meters and away from the quantitative meters of Arabo-Persian verse that had shaped the Divan tradition. It did not oppose, either, the attempt to purify the Turkish language of its foreign borrowings.

The nineteenth-century dominance of French literature has been shared, perhaps displaced, in the twentieth century by British and American influences. But from the West came not only the winds of ideological change, but also the concept of the writer as an autonomous agent who has the right to create a literature of no social significance whatsoever. These antithetical forces give contemporary Turkish literature a pendular movement between elitist and populist poles.

The outstanding figure in Turkish poetry of this century is Nazim Hikmet, who brought to Turkish literature both the free-style verse of the Soviet poet Mayakovsky and the revolutionary doctrines of the Marxist thinkers, but it was left to Fazil Hüsnü Dağlarca, the most talented poet of the post-World War II period, to effect a kind of synthesis of these popular trends.

The criticism of society has been perhaps even stronger in contemporary fiction than in poetry, and many novelists and short-story writers have run afoul of the government for their political views. The preeminence of the "committed" writers of fiction has been challenged, though not successfully thus far, by a more cosmopolitan school concerned mainly with avant-garde techniques of narration adapted from Joyce and other Western writers given to experiment.

The traditional drama of Turkey is the *karagöz*, or shadow play, a genre imported from Egypt in the sixteenth century. An analogous theater of unknown origin, the *Orta Oyunu* (sometimes called the Turkish *commedia dell'arte*) used human actors instead of puppets, but like the *karagöz*, relied heavily on broad humor. These two traditions have barely survived into the modern era, but their absurd and nonrealistic elements have to some extent been embodied in the drama that has developed under Western influence. Contemporary theater emerged during the nineteenth century, first with successful translations of Molière into the Turkish vernacular, then with adaptations of Western forms to native themes and situations. But the fact remains in modern Turkey that no playwright, native or foreign, has enjoyed as wide a fame as Shakespeare in translation.

History and Criticism

Bombaci, Alessio. *The History of Turkish Literature*. Trans. by Kathleen Burrill, Columbia Univ. Pr. 1975 o.p. The only reliable, detailed survey of Turkish literature up to World War II.

Durrell, Lawrence. *Prospero's Cell*. Penguin 1978 pap. $3.95. Contains a marvelous account of a *karagöz* performance.

Rathbun, Carole. *The Village in the Turkish Novel and Short Story, 1920 to 1955.* Mouton text ed. 1972 $37.00. A scholarly but readable analysis of a most important theme in recent fiction. The work of ten Turkish authors form the basis of this excellent study.

Collections

Contemporary Turkish Literature: Fiction and Poetry. Ed. by Talât Halman, Fairleigh Dickinson Univ. Pr. 1981 $39.50. First truly representative anthology of modern Turkish writing in English translation. It offers excerpts from novels, short stories, poetry, and aphorisms by outstanding authors, from 1923, when the republic was founded, until the late 1970s. The editor's introduction illuminates the significant aspects and the historical background of contemporary Turkish literature.

Tales of the Hodja. Retold by Charles Downing, Oxford 1970 o.p. Delightfully illustrated by William Paps, these tales about the celebrated Nareddin (or Nasr-ed-Din, meaning "Helper of Faith") will entertain both young and old.

ANDAY, MELIH CEVDAT. 1915–

Poet, playwright, novelist, essayist, translator, and critic, Anday has been published extensively in Europe and the Soviet Union, as well as in England. In 1971, UNESCO referred to him as "one of the world's foremost literary figures" and published a volume of his selected poems in French.

BOOK BY ANDAY

Rain One Step Away. Trans. by Talât Halman and Brian Swann, Charioteer 1980 $7.50

DAĞLARCA, FAZIL HÜSNÜ. 1914–

Born in Istanbul and educated in military schools, Dağlarca pursued a military career until 1950. He then worked in various ministries through 1959, when he left government service to found a publishing house and devote himself to literature.

Dağlarca's poems have appeared in all the leading Turkish journals, and he has published more than 40 books, including at least 27 volumes of poetry. His poems are distinguished by a skillful and unusual use of language. His style seems to be genuinely Turkish, not revealing direct foreign influences. His style and themes have gradually evolved, but since 1950 with the work "Toprak Ana" ("Mother Earth") he has pursued social realism.

BOOK BY DAĞLARCA

Selected Poems. Trans. by Talât Halman, Univ. of Pittsburgh Pr. 1969 pap. $2.95. These are good translations.

EDIP, HALIDE. 1884–1964

Halide Edip was born in Istanbul and educated at the American Girls College. She taught in various capacities from 1903 to 1917 and entered political and cultural affairs during World War I. She was an active participant in the Struggle for National Independence.

After a long sojourn in England (1936–39), Edip returned to Turkey and served as professor of English literature at Istanbul University from 1940 to 1950. She was the first Turkish woman to hold professional rank. From 1950 to 1954 she was a member of the National Assembly.

Edip, the outstanding Turkish woman of the twentieth century, is known primarily for her novels and memoirs. Of her 20-odd volumes, the most popular deal with the events of the War for Independence. Several have been translated into foreign languages and some have been the basis of motion pictures.

BOOKS BY EDIP

Memoirs of Halide Edip. Ayer repr. of 1926 ed. 1972 $32.00. Essential reading because so much of twentieth-century Turkey is reflected in the life of this leading female personality.
Turkey Faces West. Arno repr. of 1915 ed. $15.00

HIKMET, NAZIM. 1902–1963

Nazim Hikmet was born in Salonika. After participating in the Struggle for National Independence, he taught school for a brief period and then studied economics and sociology in Moscow (1922–34). After returning to Turkey he worked as a journalist and in a film studio. He was in continual trouble with the Turkish authorities during the thirties because of his adherence to communism, and in 1938 he was sentenced to a 20-year term in prison. Released in 1950—partly because of world opinion—he left Turkey and lived in exile until his death in 1963.

Hikmet's poetry (he also wrote plays) represents a complete break with the traditional heritage and a full acceptance of occidental models. Much of his work was inspired outside of Turkey and reached a universal dimension; nevertheless, the land and people of Turkey figure prominently as sources of inspiration. He has been especially well received in France via translation. Ironically, most of his work has appeared in Turkey only since his death.

BOOKS BY HIKMET

Selected Poems. Trans. by Taner Baybars, Grossman 1967 o.p. A representative selection from his work.
Things I Didn't Know I Loved. Trans. by Randy Blasing and Mutlu Konuk, Persea $3.95. Without question, one of the most important books of this century. "What emerges [from these poems] is his human *presence;* the strongest impression that we get from his poetry is the sense of Hikmet as a person. And it is the controlling figure of Hikmet's personality—playful, optimistic, and capable of child-like joy—that enables his poetry to remain open, public, and committed to change without ever becoming programmatic" (Mutlu Konuk). The title poem is one of the great statements in any language, in any form.
Human Landscapes. Trans. by Randy Blasing and Mutlu Konuk, fwd. by Denise Levertov, Persea 1982 $9.95. An epic novel in verse, a wonderful read.

The Epic of Sheik Beddreddin and Other Poems. Trans. by Randy Blasing and Mutlu
   Konuk, Persea 1980 $10.00 pap. $5.95

KEMAL, YAŞAR. 1922–

Yaşar Kemal was born in the Turkish village of Gokceli. After finishing
his secondary education, he worked in various jobs in southern Anatolia,
gaining a deep knowledge of the folklore of the region. Kemal's first volume
of short stories was issued in 1952, and since then more than 15 volumes
have appeared. His novels, short stories, and reportage deal with Anatolian
themes.

BOOKS BY KEMAL

Memed, My Hawk. Trans. by Edouard Roditi, British Bk. Ctr. 1961 o.p. Probably his
   most popular novel; it has been translated into at least 23 languages. This is a
   translation of Vol. 1 of the original (1955) edition, titled *Ince Memed (They Burn
   the Thistles).*
Anatolian Tales. Trans. by Thilda Kemal, British Bk. Ctr. 1969 o.p.
They Burn the Thistles. Trans. by Margaret E. Platon, British Bk. Ctr. 1973 o.p. A
   translation of Vol. 2 of *Ince Memed.*
Iron Earth, Copper Sky. Trans. by Thilda Kemal, British Bk. Ctr. 1974 o.p. A prize-
   winning drama, originally titled *Yer Demir, Gok Baker.*
The Lords of Akchasz: Murder in the Ironsmiths' Market. Trans. by Thilda Kemal, Mor-
   row 1980 $15.00
Seagull. Pantheon 1981 $11.95

NESIN, AZIZ. 1915–

After serving as a career officer for several years, Turkey's most popular
humorist became a columnist in 1944 and edited a series of satiric publications. He was jailed several times for his political views.

BOOK BY NESIN

Istanbul Boy. Trans. by Joseph Jacobson, Univ. of Texas Pr. 2 pts. 1977–79 pap. ea.
   $5.95–$6.95

CHAPTER 22

The Literature of the Indian Subcontinent

Robin Lewis and Sangita Advani

> The reader of any book about India should remember as he closes it that he
> has visited only one of the Indias.
>
> —E. M. FORSTER

The sprawling landmass of the Indian subcontinent—actually the countries
of India, Pakistan, Bangladesh, Nepal, and Sri Lanka—is both a mighty geographical entity and a space in the human mind. Its place in the popular
Western imagination is characterized by apparent ambivalence and contradiction. On the one hand, there is the stereotypical image of India, the second most populous country in the world, with its teeming millions and the
accompanying associations of poverty and hunger. On the other hand, there
is the mystique of India as the womb of the world, the embodiment of traditional Eastern wisdom, a place to seek one's self among gurus and individuals of the likes of Mahatma Gandhi.

A newer and more perplexing image is that of modern India, the world's
largest democracy, charting its course of industrialization and technological development. How can the Western perspective of India encompass holy
men and Indian rope tricks, and also the established reality of India's nuclear power and its space satellites? Ironically, such seemingly contradictory views point to the only possible answer: the most significant aspect of
the history of the Indian subcontinent is its tremendous diversity, reflected
in a kaleidoscope of different peoples, cultures, economies, religions, and
languages. Indeed, India is a tapestry of such varied threads that to speak
only of some, rather than of many, is to speak in half-truths.

A vivid example of this great diversity is the issue of language. Sir George
Grierson, a British scholar, spent the first quarter of the twentieth century
compiling a monumental linguistic survey of the region, listing a staggering
total of 225 principal languages and dialects. Officially, the Indian Constitution recognizes some 15 languages stemming from two separate roots, the
Indo-European and the Dravidian. Belonging to the former is Sanskrit, the
language of ancient India and its sacred texts, from which the following languages have been derived, much as French and Italian trace their origins to
Latin: Hindi, Punjabi, Kashmiri, and Sindhi (the languages of northern In-

dia and also of several provinces of Pakistan); Assamese, Bengali—also the main language of Bangladesh—and Oriya (the languages of the eastern region); and Gujarati and Marathi (spoken in the western areas). The languages of southern India, derived from Dravidian roots, are Tamil, with a tradition as old as Sanskrit, and other closely related languages such as Telugu, Kannada, and Malayalam. In addition, Nepali and its dialects are spoken in Nepal, a mountain kingdom stretching across the Himalayas, while in Pakistan, although Urdu is the official tongue, the majority speak either Sindhi, Punjabi, Pashto, or Baluchi. In the island nation of Sri Lanka (formerly Ceylon), Sinhalese and Tamil are the two major languages. Interestingly enough, it is English—the legacy of more than 200 years of British rule over most of the region—that is the one language commonly spoken and understood by people of all the various areas, making it the subcontinent's unofficial "link language." The subcontinent's potential, from a literary perspective alone, is unprecedented. Contained in this enormous expanse of diverse cultures and peoples is the raw material, the text if you will, of virtually every human experience.

If it is true that the subcontinent is made up of different threads, then it is equally true that these are not isolated strands, but interwoven fibers that give it a vibrant and integrated texture that glories in its variety. This notion of "unity-in-diversity" is a theme that echoes repeatedly through the annals of Indian art, religion, drama, and literature. Perhaps that is why India, to the West, often seems exasperatingly elusive, defying definition. Take the case of the divine love of the god Krishna and the cowherdess Rādhā. What is normally sung in a Hindu temple becomes a poet's love song in the twelfth-century Sanskrit poet Jayadeva's work, the *Gītagovinda*. Even today its verses are enacted through dance, music, and drama, and are also expressed in Indian miniature painting and sculpture. Another case in point is the impact of Islam on Hindu culture—the result was a reformation in medieval Hinduism in the form of the *bhakti* movement, as well as a new religion, Sikhism, which borrowed its central philosophical concepts from both Islam and Hinduism. Other creations of this cultural synthesis were a new language, Urdu, and an exquisite artistic and architectural style that reached its zenith under the Mughal emperors in the sixteenth and seventeenth centuries, giving the world such monuments as the Taj Mahal. The inexorable fact remains that underlying the rich diversity of India is a unifying way of life that transcends the disparities of ethnicity and religion—the unique, indefinable quality, the "Indianness," of a multifaceted but shared heritage.

GENERAL REFERENCE WORKS AND ANTHOLOGIES

The books in this section provide the reader with a general overview of Indian literature from the ancient through the modern periods. They also give the relevant background information about the historical, sociopolitical, religious, and philosophical milieus that gave rise to the literary works. The anthologies, in turn, are meant to give the reader a first, fleeting glimpse into the subject material.

Clark, T. W., ed. *The Novel in India: Its Birth and Development.* Univ. of California Pr. 1970 $33.00

Deshpande, Gauri. *An Anthology of Indo-English Poetry.* Ind-US text ed. 1975 pap. $2.50

Dimock, Edward C., Jr., et al. *The Literatures of India: An Introduction.* Univ. of Chicago Pr. (Phoenix Bks.) 1978 pap. $6.95

Gargi, Balwant. *Folk Theatre of India.* Univ. of Washington Pr. 1966 o.p.

Harrex, S. C. *The Fire and the Offering: The English Language Novel of India.* Ind-US 2 vols. 1977–78 ea. $16.00

Kabīr, Humayun, ed. *Green and Gold: Stories and Poems from Bengal.* Greenwood repr. 1970 o.p. This is an anthology devoted to contemporary Bengali short stories and poems by 32 well-known contemporary authors, including Amiya Chakravarty, Jibanananda Das, Humayun Kabīr, and others.

Misra, Vidya Viswas, ed. *Modern Hindi Poetry: An Anthology.* Trans. by Leonard Nathan and others, pref. by Josephine Miles, intro. by S. H. Vatsyayan, Indiana Univ. Pr. 1965 o.p. Some of the works of the finest modern Hindi poets are presented in this book in translation.

Mukherjee, Meenakshi, ed. *Considerations: Twelve Studies in Indo-Anglican Writings.* South Asia Bks. 1977 $8.00

Natwar-Singh, K., ed., *Tales from Modern India.* Macmillan 1966 o.p. An anthology of short stories by contemporary Indian writers, including Tagore, Saratchandra Chatterjee, Premchand, Bhave, T. S. Pillai, and others.

Obeyesekere, Ranjini, and Chitra Fernando, eds. *Anthology of Modern Writing from Sri Lanka.* Univ. of Arizona Pr. 1981 $12.95 pap. $6.50

Roadarmel, Gordon C., ed. and trans. *Modern Hindi Short Stories.* Univ. of California Pr. 1975 pap. $2.85. Offers readers an excellent sampling of the riches of the contemporary Hindi short story. This is a rich genre, and the stories here have been chosen with care.

Williams, Haydn Moore. *Studies in Modern Indian Fiction in English.* Ind-US 2 vols. 1975 $24.00 pap. $15.00

ANCIENT INDIAN LITERATURE

The Epics: The Rāmāyana, the Māhabhārata, and the Bhagavad Gītā

[SEE ALSO Volume 4]

The *Rāmāyana* and the *Māhabhārata* are the two great epic poems of India. The vast storehouse of myths, legends, and moral teaching that comprises the two texts has been reworked over the centuries and has provided the Indian people with the material for artistic productions of every kind, as well as coloring every aspect of their lives. They have thus given Indian society a stock of more or less common cultural ideals, as well as a treasury of tales and legends known to all. It is this shared inheritance from the epics that is one of the threads that binds together the vastly disparate peoples of India.

The *Rāmāyana*, dated between the second century B.C. and the second century A.D., is traditionally ascribed to Vālmīki, who is considered the first poet of the Sanskrit language. Written in verse, the story is woven around King Rāma and his consort, Sītā, who provide ideal models of behavior, while their story, the *Rāmāyana*, is the central text for the worship of Rāma in Vaishnavism and popular Hinduism.

The *Māhabhārata*, dated between the seventh century B.C. and the fourth century A.D., has an encyclopedic text that centers on a fight for succession to a kingdom between two groups of cousins. To this basic story is added a vast amount of other material—didactic texts (*shastras*), religious and philosophical treatises (the *Bhagavad Gītā*), and unrelated myths and stories.

A relatively late addition to the core of the works of the *Māhabhārata*, the *Bhagavad Gītā* is a religious and philosophical text in the form of a dialogue between Krishna and Arjuna about *dharma*, or man's rightful duty. The *Gītā*, written in verse, is a fundamental text of Hinduism, and it influenced the thought of Mahatma Gandhi and Thoreau, among others.

THE RĀMĀYANA

Buck, William. *Rāmāyana.* Intro. by B. A. van Nooten, New Amer. Lib. 1978 pap. $3.50; Univ. of California Pr. 1976 $19.95 pap. $7.95. Vālmīki's *Rāmāyana* retold in English prose.

Goldman, Robert, trans. *The Rāmāyana of Vālmīki: Balakanda.* Princeton Univ. Pr. vol. 1 1984 $37.50. This is the first volume of an ongoing, scholarly translation of the *Rāmāyana*.

Lal, P., trans. *The Rāmāyana of Vālmīki.* Advent 1981 pap. $14.50

Narayan, R. K. *The Rāmāyana of R. K. Narayan: A Shortened Modern Prose Version of the Indian Epic, Suggested by the Tamil Version of Kamban.* Penguin 1977 pap. $4.95; Viking 1972 $13.95. This work is based on the Tamil version of the epic written by a poet called Kamban in the eleventh century, who, in reinterpreting Vālmīki's Sanskrit text, stuck closely to the original. Tamil is a Dravidian language of great antiquity, with its own literature and culture, spoken by more than 40 million people who live in southern India and Sri Lanka.

THE MĀHABHĀRATA

Buck, William. *Māhabhārata.* Intro. by B. A. van Nooten, Univ. of California Pr. 1974 pap. $7.95

Lal, P. *The Māhabhārata of Vyāsa.* Advent text ed. 1980 pap. $14.50. Condensed from Sanskrit and transliterated into English.

Van Buitenen, J. A. B., ed. and trans. *The Māhabhārata.* Univ. of Chicago Pr. 3 vols. 1973–78 $36.00. This scholarly work is a complete rendering of the first five books of this massive epic.

THE BHAGAVAD GĪTĀ (THE SONG OF THE LORD)

Edgerton, Franklin. *The Bhagavad Gītā.* Harvard Univ. Pr. 1944 pap. $5.95

Miller, Barbara Stoler, trans. *The Bhagavad Gītā: Krishna's Counsel in Time of War.* Bantam 1986 in progress

Other Ancient Writings

Burton, Richard, and F. F. Arbuthnot, trans. and eds. *The Kāma Sūtra of Vātsyāyana: The Classic Hindu Treatise on Love and Social Conduct.* Allen & Unwin 1963 $8.50. The *Kāma Sūtra* (*Aphorisms on Love*) is a famous Hindu treatise attributed to Vātsyāyana, who lived c.300. *Kāma*—the pursuit of love and pleasure— is one of the traditional Hindu ends of man. The *Kāma Sūtra* yields invaluable information about the social mores and conditions of classical ancient India.

Coulson, Michael, trans. *Three Sanskrit Plays.* Penguin Class. Ser. 1981 pap. $8.95. This translation includes three of the best plays by the famous Sanskrit dramatists Kālidāsa, Vishākhadatta, and Bhavabhūti.

Edgerton, Franklin, ed. *The Panchatantra Reconstructed.* Amer. Oriental Ser. Kraus 2 vols. repr. of 1924 ed. 1965 $56.00. A famous collection of didactic animal fables used to teach worldly wisdom to princes. It is the source of the many similar stories that are to be found in the Middle East and Europe.

Hart, George L., III. *The Poems of Ancient Tamil: Their Milieu and Their Sanskrit Counterparts.* Univ. of California Pr. 1975 $36.00. A sophisticated work for readers who are familiar with the subject.

Ingalls, Daniel H., trans. *Sanskrit Poetry from Vidyākara's "Treasury."* Harvard Univ. Pr. (Belknap Pr.) 1968 $18.50 pap. $7.95. This collection of exquisitely rendered poems is from the *Treasury of Well-Turned Verse* compiled by the famous poet Vadyākara in eleventh-century Bengal. These poems, translated from Sanskrit, are concerned largely with love and nature, but also include humorous sketches, poems about gods and heroes, epigrams, panegyrics, and realistic vignettes of village and farm life in ancient India.

Lal, P., trans. and ed. *Great Sanskrit Plays in Modern Translation.* New Directions 1957 $15.00. This volume offers modern translations of five of the best Sanskrit plays, written between the fourth and ninth centuries, including the famous *Shakuntalā* of Kālidāsa. It is interesting to note that *Shakuntalā* inspired the "Prelude in the Theatre" of Goethe's *Faust*. The German romantics were greatly influenced by Indian literature, and this influence survives in the Western literary tradition today.

Merwin, W. S., and J. Moussaieff Masson, trans. *Classical Sanskrit Love Poetry.* Columbia Univ. Pr. 1977 $21.00

Miller, Barbara Stoler, trans. *The Hermit and the Love-Thief: Sanskrit Poems of Bhartrihari and Bilhana.* Columbia Univ. Pr. 1978 $22.00 pap. $9.50. An anthology of selections belonging to the genre of the Sanskrit fragmentary lyric. It includes selections from the *Caurapañcāśikā* (*Fantasies of a Love Thief*), attributed to Bilhana, a poet who lived in the eleventh century. Each verse is a remembered moment of love voiced by a separated lover attempting to evoke his absent mistress.

——. *Love Song of the Dark Lord: Jayadeva's Gītagovinda.* Columbia Univ. Pr. 1977 $21.00 pap. $9.50. Jayadeva's twelfth-century dramatic lyrical poem focuses on the god Krishna's love for the cowherdess Rādhā, which is considered by many to be an allegory of the human soul's love for God. The *Gītagovinda* is a unique work in Indian literature and a source of religious inspiration in both medieval and contemporary Vaishnavism (the worship of the god Vishnu). Its verses are popular in song, dance, and painting even today.

Siegel, Lee. *Fires of Love, Waters of Peace: Passion and Renunciation in Indian Culture.* Univ. of Hawaii Pr. text ed. 1983 $12.50. An introduction to Sanskrit love

poetry and religious verse, with translations of selected excerpts from the works
of the court poet Amaru and the philosopher Shankara.

Van Buitenen, J. A. B., trans. *Tales of Ancient India*. Univ. of Chicago Pr. (Phoenix
Bks.) 1969 pap. $5.95. This is a selection of popular tales from Sanskrit story col-
lections.

———. *Two Plays of Ancient India*. Columbia Univ. Pr. 1968 $30.00. The two ancient
plays translated in this book vividly illustrate the fact that ancient Indian drama
represents a highly stylized tradition that achieved exuberant life and rich variety. *The Little Clay Cart*, ascribed to Sudraka (c.400), is a tale of romance and villainy, intermingled with a whole range of subplots. The play abounds in humor,
including malapropian speech, and ends on a note of Buddhist compassion and
charity. *The Minister's Seal*, ascribed to Prince Vishākhadatta (sixth century),
represents the semihistorical or political play genre of Indian drama.

KĀLIDĀSA. 376–c.454?

The Indian dramatist and poet Kālidāsa is regarded as the most remarkable figure in classical Sanskrit literature. Two of his most famous
plays are *Shakuntalā* and *Meghadūta*. *Shakuntalā*, named after the
play's heroine, is a romantic tale in verse, telling of two lovers who are separated by adversity and later reunited by happy chance. *Meghadūta*, or *The
Cloud Messenger*, is an exquisite love poem, rich in powerful imagery.
Kālidāsa's plays had a profound impact on later Indian writings and
also influenced the works of a number of Western writers.

BOOKS BY KĀLIDĀSA

The Theatre of Memory: Three Plays of Kālidāsa. Trans. and ed. by Barbara Stoler
Miller and others, Columbia Univ. Pr. 1984 $30.00 pap. $12.00

The Transport of Love: The Meghadūta of Kālidāsa. Trans. by Leonard Nathan, Univ.
of California Pr. 1976 $18.00 pap. $3.95

MEDIEVAL LITERATURE: THE BHAKTI MOVEMENT

A striking feature of medieval India was the great upsurge and spread of devotional or *bhakti* movements that swept across northern India and down the
Gangetic plain into Bengal from about the fourteenth through the seventeenth centuries. This popular movement of saint-singers of philosophical
and religious songs had begun much earlier (in the fourth to ninth centuries)
in the South, with the writings of the Tamil Ālvār saints, then spreading to
the Kannada-speaking areas through the works of Basavanna. The late thirteenth century saw it ignite in Maharashtra with an interpretation of the
Bhagavad Gītā by the saint Jnānesvara; other saints of Maharashtra were
Tukarām and Eknath. By the fifteenth century, the movement had spread to
the Hindi-speaking areas and the whole of northern India; some of the best-
known poets are Kabīr, Sūr Dās, and Tulsīdās, and in Bengal,
Chandidās, Vidyāpati, and Chaitanya. Two of the most famous women
saints were Mīrābai, from Rajasthan, and Lalla, from Kashmir. The saint-
teachers who went about making the whole countryside resound with their

songs, popular to this day, had a common theme threading through their different philosophies. The first characteristic of the *bhakti* movement was devotion to a personal god, usually a form of Vishnu or Shiva. In addition, there was a belief in monotheism and the equality of all human beings, irrespective of caste, social status, or creed, reflecting the egalitarianism of Islam, with which the *bhakti* movement had also come into contact. The saints, usually ordinary folk, wrote in the accessible vernacular languages rather than in the esoteric Sanskrit of the priests. The *bhakti* movement thus achieved a unique transformation of the older, ritual-bound Hinduism.

Bhattacharya, Deben, trans. *The Love Songs of Chandidās: The Rebel Poet-Priest of Bengal.* Grove 1970 o.p. In the tradition of other great Bengali poets, Jayadeva, Vidyāpati, and, most recently, Tagore, Chandidās (c.fifteenth century) wrote of love, focusing on the traditional Bengali interest in Rādhā and Krishna, the great divine lovers of Indian worship and legend. The evocative songs, with their balladic tone, are sung by Bengali folk singers even today, and are an important contribution to the *bhakti* movement.

———. *The Love Songs of Vidyāpati.* Grove 1963 pap. $12.50. Vidyāpati was a fourteenth-century Bengali poet who wrote in Maithili, a regional language of eastern India. In the tradition of the earlier, important Sanskrit poem, the *Gītagovinda of Jayadeva*, Vidyāpati's songs focus on the love of Krishna and Rādhā, the major love figures of Indian mythology, art, and literature. This volume contains 100 of his poems in translation, along with an illuminating introduction and a series of 31 plates that show how analogous themes were illustrated in Indian miniature painting.

———. *Songs of the Bards of Bengal.* Grove 1970 pap. $4.95. The name *Baul* has been given to a small group of wandering poets and musicians from the village of Bengal. These songs are a *Baul*'s way of coming to terms with God and love, life and death, society and the individual. In keeping with the *Baul* tradition, which is a revolt against conventional Islam and Hinduism, these troubadourlike songs are iconoclastic yet classical in their lyrics.

Dimock, Edward C., Jr., and Denise Levertov, trans. *In Praise of Krishna: Songs from the Bengali.* Univ. of Chicago Pr. (Phoenix Bks.) 1981 $4.95. These allegorical poems on the love of Rādhā and Krishna, ranging from the twelfth to the seventeenth centuries, include the works of Vidyāpati and the great Vaishnava *bhakti* poets such as Chaitanya and Chandidās.

———. *The Thief of Love: Bengali Tales from Court and Village.* Univ. of Chicago Pr. (Phoenix Bks.) 1975 pap. $3.95. A collection of tales that have become part of Bengali folklore.

Hawley, John S. *Sūr Dās: Poet, Singer, Saint.* Univ. of Washington Pr. text ed. 1984 $25.00. An illuminating glimpse into the work of the blind sixteenth-century poet-singer Sūr Dās, who wrote moving devotional songs in praise of Krishna.

Hess, Linda, and Shukdev Singh, trans. *The Bijak of Kabīr.* North Point Pr. pap. $12.50. Kabīr, a low-caste weaver from Banaras, was in many respects the pioneer of Hindi devotional verse, using the vernacular to popularize religious themes drawn from both Hindu and mystical Islamic (Sūfī) traditions. Numerous couplets and didactic sayings are attributed to Kabīr and constitute much of the folk wisdom of India. This book is a remarkably accurate translation of Kabīr's most authoritative work. Hess's introduction and notes explore Kabīr's work, place it in its original context, and elucidate its meaning for modern times.

Ramanujan, A. K., trans. *Hymns for the Drowning: Poems for Vishnu by Nammālvār.* Princeton Univ. Pr. 1982 $21.00 pap. $7.50. Eighty-three poems by Nammālvār, celebrated Ālvār saint-poet of the ninth century, are presented here in translation from the Tamil. These devotional hymns and love poems addressed to Vishnu are among the earliest *bhakti* texts.

———. *The Interior Landscape: Love Poems from a Classical Tamil Anthology.* Indiana Univ. Pr. 1967 $1.95. The poems come from one of the earliest surviving texts of Tamil poetry, the *Ku runtokai*, an anthology of love lyrics probably recorded during the first three centuries A.D. These wonderful translations serve as an introduction for Western readers to an unfamiliar and fascinating literary tradition. An essay on Tamil poetry explains its techniques and enhances the reader's pleasure in these poems.

———. *Poems of Love and War: From the Eight Anthologies and the Ten Songs of Classical Tamil.* Columbia Univ. Pr. 1985 $27.50 pap. $12.50

———. *Speaking of Shiva.* Penguin Class. Ser. 1973 pap. $3.95. This is a collection of *vachanas* or free-verse lyrics written between the tenth and twelfth centuries by four major Kannada poet-saints of the great *bhakti* reform movement. The poems are lyrical expressions of love for the god Shiva. These passionate, personal and fiercely monotheistic verses possess a timeless and universal appeal.

EARLY MODERN PERIOD: THE FLOWERING OF URDU LANGUAGE AND LITERATURE

While there had been an Islamic presence in the Indian subcontinent since the eighth century, the literary and cultural influence of Islam manifested itself only in the eleventh and twelfth centuries, then flourishing in the thirteenth century, when there was a great influx of Muslims into India. The religious and cultural ideals of the Muslims in India found expression in many languages—Arabic, Persian, Turkish, and the regional Indian languages—but more so in a newly transformed language, Urdu (literally "camp"), a mixture of Hindustani, Persian, and Arabic loanwords. The literature began to develop in the sixteenth century around the courts of Golconda and Bijapur in the Deccan, and later on in Aurangabad, until in the eighteenth century it reached Delhi itself, from where it spread to Lucknow.

The milieu of Urdu literature is that of Muslim court culture and Sūfī religion. The major literary form of the first three centuries was poetry; prose began only in the nineteenth century. The poets pursued many genres: the *qasīda*, a poem praising the ruler or patron; the *hajw*, derogatory verse; the *shahar-āshob*, laments over a destroyed city; and the *marsiya*, elegiac verse, often in praise of the martyrdom of Hasan and Husain. The most important genres, however, were the *masnavī*, whose subject matter was very wide and free, and the *ghazal*, a unique blend of love poetry and the mystical experience. Urdu is spoken and written by both Muslims and non-Muslims in modern India; it is the official language of Pakistan.

Ali, Ahmed, ed. and trans. *The Golden Tradition: An Anthology of Urdu Poetry.* Columbia Univ. Pr. 1973 $28.00 pap. $10.00. This wonderful anthology provides specimens of Urdu poetry from the fourteenth to the beginning of the twentieth centuries. It also includes representative selections from 15 poets of the eighteenth and nineteenth centuries, the most creative period in this literature. The works of the most renowned poets such as Mīr and Ghālib are well represented. The introduction surveys the literary and philosophical background and also contains a comparative study of Urdu and English poetic movements.

Russell, Ralph, and Khurshidul Islam. *Three Mughal Poets: Mīr, Saudā, Mīr Hasan.* Harvard Univ. Pr. 1968 $18.50. These three great Urdu poets all lived in Delhi in the eighteenth century during the unsettling, often violence-ridden period of the decay of the Mughal Empire. Saudā wrote poems in all the main classical forms but it is his satiric, Rabelaisian, and astonishingly resourceful poems, for which he was renowned, that are considered here. Mīr Hasan also wrote in all the classical forms and excelled in one, the *masnavī*, a long narrative poem in rhymed couplets, often telling a love story. His most famous poem in this form, "The Enchanting Story," is examined here, a poem rich in magical imagery and simile. Mīr, perhaps the greatest of the three, is one of the greatest love poets of world literature. His favorite form was the *ghazal*, a subtle and difficult one, which the authors discuss in detail, giving numerous examples.

Sadiq, Muhammad. *A History of Urdu Literature.* Oxford 2d ed. 1984 $39.95. This is an in-depth survey of the history of the Urdu language and its literature.

GHĀLIB, MIRZA ASADULLAH KHAN. 1797–1869

Ghālib, poet and litterateur, was the last major literary figure produced by Mughal India before the Empire was swept away by the British after the Mutiny of 1857. He wrote in both Urdu and Persian, in both prose and verse, raising to new heights the form of the *ghazal*, loosely translated as "love poem" but in fact far transcending it. He is the greatest and most loved classical Urdu poet of India and Pakistan.

BOOKS BY GHĀLIB

Ghazals of Ghālib: Versions from the Urdu. Ed. by Aijaz Ahmad, Columbia Univ. Pr. 1971 $24.00. This book contains both literal translations of some of the best-known couplets of Ghālib as well as lyric transcreations of the *ghazals* exquisitely rendered by some fine twentieth-century English poets, among them W. S. Merwin and Adrienne Rich.

Ghālib, 1797–1869: Life and Letters. Ed. by Ralph Russell and Khurshidul Islam, Harvard Univ. Pr. vol. 1 1969 $25.00. This is an elucidating and near-complete reconstruction of Ghālib's life. The authors allow the poet to speak through his own words by including numerous excerpts from his letters and writings. The introduction, comments, and bibliography enrich the reader's understanding of the poet.

BOOK ABOUT GHĀLIB

Russell, Ralph, ed. *Ghālib: The Poet and His Age.* Harper 1972 o.p. This book is a collection of papers by various scholars presented at the centenary celebrations of Ghālib at London's School of Oriental and African Studies in 1969. They provide a good background to the life and times of the poet.

MODERN AND CONTEMPORARY LITERATURE

Ali, Ahmed. *Twilight in Delhi.* Ind-US 2d ed. 1974 pap. $3.50; Oxford 1985 pap. $13.95. This novel is an elegy for the dying Muslim culture of Delhi, depicted through the relationship of one middle-class Muslim family with other such families in early twentieth-century Delhi. Woven into the novel are fragments of Urdu poetry that highlight the evocative, nostalgic, and melancholic mood of the story.

Anand, Mulk Raj. *Across the Black Waters.* Ind-US 1980 pap. $5.95. This is the second of a trilogy of novels tracing the fortunes of a Punjabi peasant.

———. *Untouchable.* Ind-US 1983 pap. $5.00. Anand's first and most successful novel, describing an eventful day in the life of a young sweeper from a northern Indian cantonment town.

Anantha Murthy, U. R. *Samskara: A Rite for a Dead Man.* Trans. by A. K. Ramanujan. Oxford 1976 pap. $4.95. This novel yields remarkable insights into the workings of a small community of Brahmins in southern India. This is considered one of the true masterpieces of modern Indian fiction.

Bandyopadhyaya, Manik. *Boatman of the Padma.* 1948. Trans. by Hirendranath Mukerjee, Ind-US 1977 o.p. A moving and gripping piece of eastern Bengali village life. It tells of the joys and sorrows of the lives of the boatmen who ply the Padma, Bengal's mightiest river, making a precarious living by scouring its waters for the silver fish prized at every Bengali table.

———. *The Puppet's Tale.* 1936. Trans. by Sachindralal Ghosh, Ind-US 1968 o.p. Written by one of the great modern Bengali writers, this novel, which deals with the clash of traditional and modern values in a Bengali village, is considered Bandyopadhyaya's masterpiece.

Banerji, Bibhutibhushan. *Pather Panchali: Song of the Road.* Trans. by T. W. Clark and Tarapada Mukherji, Indiana Univ. Pr. 1969 $10.00. This is the first English translation of the famous Bengali novel that was the basis for Satyajit Ray's award-winning film of the same title. Totally captivating in its immediacy, this portrayal of Bengali village people and their day-to-day life is presented through the eyes of a small boy and his sister. Banerji ranks as one of the greatest twentieth-century prose writers in Bengali, along with Rabindranath Tagore and Saratchandra Chatterji, and his fame, in great measure, rests on the lasting appeal of this one work.

Basheer, Vaikom Muhammad. *Me Grandad 'ad an Elephant: Three Stories of Muslim Life in South India.* Trans. by R. E. Asher and A. C. Chandersekaran, Edinburgh Univ. Pr. 1980 o.p. Out of the three stories in this book, Basheer's most lauded work is "Me Grandad 'ad an Elephant." It is a skillfully and intricately constructed story, full of humor and wit; at the same time it is an evocative love story, giving readers an insight into an ordinary Kerala Muslim's ideas on life, God, destiny, and human existence.

Bhandari, Mannu. *The Great Feast.* Trans. by Richard Alan Williams, Ind-US 1981 o.p. A scathing indictment of contemporary Indian politics, revealing how politicians exploit the poor and the downtrodden; as such, it marks a significant departure from the established genres of Hindu fiction.

Das, Jibanananda. *Banalata Sen.* Trans. by P. Lal, Ind-US text ed. 1975 pap. $4.00. Four different versions of translations of the poetry of Jibanananda Das, one of the foremost modern Bengali poets.

Desani, G. V. *All about H. Hatterr.* Intro. by Anthony Burgess, Farrar rev. ed. 1970

$5.95. A daringly experimental "Joycean" novel, blending Western and Indian narrative forms in a show of stylistic virtuosity.

Devkota, Laxmiprasad. *Nepali Visions, Nepali Dreams: The Poems of Laxmiprasad Devkota*. Trans. by David Rubin, Columbia Univ. Pr. 1980 $23.00. This volume presents an extended essay on the Nepalese poet Devkota's life and career, along with exquisite translations of 45 poems ranging from short lyrics to lengthy philosophical and satiric works. This is the first collection in English of Devkota's complex, vigorous poetry.

Faiz, Ahmed Faiz. *Poems by Faiz*. Trans. by Victor Kiernan, Allen & Unwin 1971 o.p. Faiz, a foremost Urdu poet, was the leader of the Progressive Movement, a socio-literary movement that advocated that literature should be put to the service of ameliorating social ills. This volume presents some of his best works, and it gives the literal Urdu and its transliteration into English, as well as an English translation of the Urdu text. There is also a detailed introduction. The entire volume was compiled under the guidance of Faiz.

Gokhale, Namita. *Paro: Dreams of Passion*. Merrimack 1985 $12.95. Gokhale's first novel offers readers a trenchant insight into the chic, sophisticated, and fast-paced lives of the Bombay elite.

Joshi, Arun. *The Foreigner*. Ind-US 1972 pap. $3.25. Arun Joshi is a novelist interested in existential dilemmas and the theme of alienation. He depicts the problems of post-independence Indian society and the implications of the East-West encounter.

———. *The Strange Case of Billy Biswas*. Ind-US 1974 pap. $3.50

Markandaya, Kamala. *Handful of Rice*. Crowell 1966 $10.53

———. *Nectar in a Sieve*. New Amer. Lib. (Signet Class.) pap. $2.95

———. *Shalimar*. Harper 1983 $15.34. An original and provocative novel, full of echoes from E. M. Forster and Shakespeare.

Mehta, Rama. *Inside the Haveli*. Ind-US 1977 pap. $4.25. The author, a sociologist by training, has portrayed the tradition-bound, male-dominated lives of those women who today still continue to live in purdah in Rajasthan, secluded from outside society.

Rao, Raja. *Kanthapura*. New Directions 1967 $7.95. A fine evocation of the Gandhian age, this is the story of a small southern Indian village caught in the storm of the freedom struggle of the 1930s and completely transformed by it.

Rushdie, Salman. *Midnight's Children*. Avon 1982 pap. $4.95; Knopf 1981 $14.95. This novel, winner of the Booker Prize, is a brilliant, phantasmagoric saga of the birth of independent India, symbolized by the birth of the hero at the precise moment of independence. Rushdie's novel has been proclaimed the most exciting and original novel on India to appear in a long time.

———. *Shame*. Knopf 1983 $13.95; Random (Vintage) 1984 pap. $7.95. This is a brilliant fable about Pakistan, a country seen as made up, arbitrarily sundered from India in 1947. As in his earlier work, Rushdie's language is mythical and dreamlike in its tone, enmeshing the reader in a bewildering, fantastical spell.

Sahgal, Nayantara. *Storm in Chandigarh*. Ind-US 1969 o.p. This political story about the division of the Punjab into the two states of Harayana and Punjab consists of thinly disguised portrayals of politicians of the day. The author is a well-regarded novelist from a distinguished lineage: She is the niece of the late Prime Minister Nehru, and the cousin—and, during the "Emergency," a bitter enemy—of the late Indira Gandhi.

Sen, Samar. *The Complete Poems of Samar Sen*. Trans. by Pritish Nandy, Ind-US 1975 $11.00 text ed. pap. $4.80. Sen, whose brief poetic career spanned only ten years, was nevertheless a major influence in modern Bengali poetry. His sharp, searching poems have been ably translated by Pritish Nandy, one of India's foremost young poets.

Sidhwa, Bapsi. *The Bride.* St. Martin's 1983 $12.95. Set against the backdrop of Partition in 1947, this is a stirring psychological novel revealing the tough lives of the tribal people who live in the rugged mountains of Afghanistan and Pakistan.

———. *The Crow Eaters.* St. Martin's 1982 $10.95. A brilliant first novel that offers a rare glimpse into the world of the Parsis, one of India's and Pakistan's most influential minority communities.

Singh, Khushwant. *The Train to Pakistan (Mano Majra).* Greenwood repr. of 1956 ed. 1975 lib. bdg. $35.00; Grove 1981 pap. $3.25. This moving and action-filled novel tells of the impact of Partition on a small village on the Indo-Pakistani border.

Tendulkar, Vijay. *Sakharam Binder.* Trans. by Shanta Shahane and Kumud Mehta, Ind-US 1973 o.p. This important work, a play that generated much controversy, is a realistic tragicomic portrayal of the interrelationships that exist between men and women of the so-called lower classes. The main character is a Casanova who drinks and womanizes without any sense of guilt and laughs at puritanical hypocrisy. The play offers insights into the oppressive conditions that tyrannize women in India.

Vaid, Krishna B. *Steps in Darkness.* Ind-US 1972 pap. $2.75; Viking 1962 $3.50. Written by an Indian professor and translated by him from the original Hindi, this is a naturalistic novel about a small, poor Hindu household in urban India. It expresses the hero's search for happiness despite the constant bickering in his family.

DESAI, ANITA. 1937–

Anita Desai is one of the finest Indian novelists writing in English today, and her books have achieved a wide readership both in India and in the West. Her language is lucid and evocative, her technique detailed and well crafted. Two of her works, *Clear Light of Day* and *In Custody*, were nominated for England's prestigious Booker Prize.

BOOKS BY DESAI

Fire on the Mountain. Harper 1977 $12.45; Penguin 1983 pap. $3.95. This novel offers a poignant glimpse into the interior life of a highly accomplished wife and mother who has chosen to retreat from society by spending her last years high up in a mountain town. The sudden, unexpected intrusion of her introverted great-grandchild results in many changes in the life of the old woman, thrusting on her all the pain of shattering disillusionment and self-discovery.

Games at Twilight. Harper 1980 $9.95; Penguin 1983 pap. $3.95. Eleven short stories, each a delightful miniature encapsulating the unique atmosphere of urban Indian life.

Clear Light of Day. Harper 1980 $12.45; Penguin 1982 pap. $4.95. The plot of the novel unfolds through the eyes of two sisters who explore their lives from the Partition riots of 1947 to the present. What emerges is an exquisitely written portrait of a middle-class Hindu family confronting an increasingly problematic world and the breakup of their illusions about themselves.

In Custody. 1984. Harper 1985 $16.95. This novel is woven around an impoverished college lecturer with a sullen, disappointed wife, who sees a way to escape from the hopelessness of his daily life when he is asked to interview India's greatest

Urdu poet for a literary magazine. This is a sad, bitter, funny novel full of the everyday colors and sounds of India, with some truly memorable scenes of comic catastrophe.

GANDHI, MOHANDAS K(ARAMCHAND). 1869–1948.

[SEE Volume 4.]

IQBAL, SIR MUHAMMAD. c.1873–1936

Iqbal was one of the most popular Urdu poet-philosophers of the twentieth century, urging through his writing the spiritual regeneration of Islam based on the love of Man and God. He was also an active political leader, championing the concept of a separate state for Indian Muslims, the country that later came to be called Pakistan. Thus he is revered as Pakistan's national poet and is acclaimed both there and in India. The book listed below contains papers presented by 17 scholars from various countries elucidating the many aspects of Iqbal's career.

BOOK ABOUT IQBAL

Iqbal: Poet Philosopher of Pakistan. Ed. by Hafeez Malik, Columbia Univ. Pr. 1971 $27.00

JHABVALA, RUTH PRAWER. 1927–

Jhabvala is one of the best novelists of India writing in English. Born in Germany of Polish parents, she was educated in London, married a Parsi architect, and lived in Delhi, the setting of many of her novels. Presently residing in New York, she is also noted for her film scripts.

BOOKS BY JHABVALA

The Householder. 1960. Norton 1977 pap. $2.95. This witty and perceptive novel focuses on a newlywed couple in modern Delhi.
How I Became a Holy Mother and Other Short Stories. Harper 1979 pap. $2.50. A collection of nine short stories, ranging over the castes and communities of India, from the beautiful mountains to the sophisticated Westernized elite of Bombay.
Travelers (A New Dominion). Harper 1973 o.p. A witty, sardonic look at a variety of Western "seekers" in India, this novel evokes some of the cross-cultural confusion of the relationship between East and West.

NARAYAN, R. K. 1906–

R. K. Narayan is one of the few Indian writers in English who has achieved a wide readership in the United States and the United Kingdom, as well as in his native India. His novels, dramas of middle-class life, are enacted in Malgudi, an imaginary small town in southern India, which comes to be felt as a living ambience in his fiction. Through the microcosm of Malgudi, Narayan explores in depth a panorama of human traits and values, manifested in a wide range of characters. For example, *The Bachelor of Arts* is the story of a sensitive youth caught in a conflict between Western ideas of love and marriage instilled in him by his education and the traditional social milieu in which he lives. *The Dark Room* explores the predicament of the traditional Hindu wife, while *The Guide* portrays the unwilling transformation of a guide into a half-reluctant and half-purposeful guru or holy teacher. In *The Financial Expert*, we see the rise and fall of an obscure middleman who ekes out a living by sitting in front of a bank and helping illiterate villagers with their loans; this novel is a revealing study of the cash nexus in modern life. *The Vendor of Sweets* shows how the village of Malgudi is altered by the clash of different generations and values, as a street vendor, a staunch Gandhian, is confronted by the mores of his son, who has just returned from the United States. The reader's encounter with Narayan's multifaceted world of Malgudi is consequently rich, witty, and tragicomic. In it, more often than not, we find startling glimpses of ourselves.

BOOKS BY NARAYAN

Swami and Friends. 1935. Univ. of Chicago Pr. 1980 lib. bdg $13.00 pap. $6.95

The Bachelor of Arts. 1937. Intro. by Graham Greene, Univ. of Chicago Pr. 1980 $13.00 pap. $6.95

The Dark Room. 1938. Univ. of Chicago Pr. 1981 lib. bdg $15.00 pap. $4.50

The English Teacher. 1946. Univ. of Chicago Pr. 1980 pap. $6.95

Mr. Sampath: The Printer of Malgudi. 1949. Univ. of Chicago Pr. 1981 lib. bdg $15.00 pap. $4.50

The Financial Expert. 1952. Univ. of Chicago Pr. 1981 lib. bdg $15.00 pap. $4.50

Waiting for the Mahatma. Michigan State Univ. Pr. 1955 $6.00; Univ. of Chicago Pr. repr. of 1955 ed. 1981 lib. bdg $15.00 pap. $4.50

The Guide: A Novel. 1958. Penguin 1980 pap. $5.95

The Man-Eater of Malgudi. 1962. Penguin 1983 pap. $4.95

The Vendor of Sweets. 1967. Avon 1971 pap. $1.45; Penguin 1983 pap. $4.95

The Painter of Signs. Penguin 1983 pap. $4.95; Viking 1976 $11.95

A Tiger for Malgudi. Penguin 1984 pap. $4.95; Viking 1983 $14.75

NEHRU, JAWAHARLAL. 1889–1964

[SEE Volume 3, Chapter 10.]

NIRALA. ?–1961

Nirala, known as "the Strange One," was one of the most extraordinary of the experimental poets who, in the early part of the twentieth century, created a genuine renaissance in Hindi literature. A legendary figure in his lifetime, Nirala published ten volumes of verse between 1923 and his death. The exquisite translations listed below include the best and most representative poems from each phase in his career.

BOOK BY NIRALA

A Season on the Earth: Selected Poems of Nirala. Trans. by David Rubin, Columbia Univ. Pr. 1977 $23.00 pap. $10.00

PILLAI, THAKAZHI SIVASANKARA. 1914–

A lawyer, Pillai was born in the state of Kerala on the southwestern coast of India, which serves as the setting for much of his powerful writing.

BOOKS BY PILLAI

Chemmeen. 1956. Trans. by Narayana Menon, *Writing in Asia Ser.* Heinemann text ed. 1978 pap. $5.50; Ind-US 1964 pap. $3.50. With the moving simplicity of a classic tale, *Chemmeen* unfolds a story of devotion, greed, and sacrifice; of a taboo violated; and of retribution.

The Unchaste. Trans. by M. K. Bhaskaran, Ind-US 1971 pap. $2.10. A trenchant comment on women's predicament in Indian society.

Scavenger's Son. Trans. by R. E. Asher, Ind-US 1975 pap. $2.50

Rungs of the Ladder. Trans. by C. Paul Verghese, Ind-US 1976 pap. $3.50. This novel is set in the former state of Travancore. The hero of the novel comes to town in search of a job. The story is a cutting comment on the men and women who are making the climb to the top—simple folk corrupted by the lure of power in contemporary Indian political life.

PREMCHAND (pseud. of Dhanpat Rai Srivastava). 1880–1936

Premchand is the greatest figure in twentieth-century Hindi literature. *Godaan*, written in 1936 and set in rural India, is his last and most widely acclaimed novel. Some of his finest work is in his short stories.

BOOKS BY PREMCHAND

The Gift of a Cow: A Translation of the Hindi Novel, Godaan. Trans. by Gordon C. Roadarmel. Indiana Univ. Pr. 1968 o.p.

The World of Premchand: Selected Stories of Premchand. Trans. by David Rubin, Indiana Univ. Pr. 1971 o.p. Filled with compassion and indignation, these stories offer an incomparable panorama of northern Indian life in tradition-bound villages and cities, caught in the turmoil of the independence movement. The stories also offer devastating satire on the cruelty and pride of the privileged classes.

TAGORE, SIR RABINDRANATH (also Ravindranatha Thakura). 1861–1941 (NOBEL PRIZE 1913)

Rabindranath Tagore, hailed by Mahatma Gandhi as "the Great Sentinel," was one of those versatile men of his age who touched and enriched modern Indian life in many ways. Poet, dramatist, novelist, short-story writer, musical composer, painter, thinker, educator, nationalist freedom fighter, and internationalist—such were the various roles that Tagore played with uniform distinction during his long and fruitful career. He wrote primarily in Bengali, but also creatively translated some of his works into English with such success that his very first effort, *Gitanjali*, won him the Nobel Prize for literature, making him the only Indian writer ever to win this distinction. Tagore also founded a university, Shantiniketan, which is based on traditional Indian notions of learning; Indira Gandhi, India's late prime minister, was one of its students.

BOOKS BY TAGORE

Gitanjali: Collection of Prose Translations Made by the Author from the Original Bengali. 1912. Intro. by William Butler Yeats, Macmillan 1971 pap. $3.95. The central theme in the 100-odd pieces in *Gitanjali*, Tagore's finest achievement in English verse, is the poet's mystical and devotional quest. The poems were originally written in Bengali by Tagore and translated into English by him.

Hungry Stones and Other Stories. AMS Pr. repr. of 1916 ed. $14.50

The Housewarming, and Other Selected Writings. Trans. by Mary Lago and Tarun Gupta, Greenwood repr. of 1965 ed. 1977 lib. bdg. $24.75. A collection of 19 stories, 3 plays including *The Housewarming*, 6 prose sketches, and 5 narrative poems.

A Tagore Reader. Ed. by Amiya Chakravarty, Beacon 1966 pap. $12.95. A collection of whole pieces and excerpts from Tagore's works, including letters, travel notes, drama, short stories, poems, criticism, and philosophy. This is probably the best introduction to Tagore's writing.

The Broken Nest. Trans. by Mary Lago and Supriya Sen, Univ. of Missouri Pr. 1971 o.p. This novel, which vividly dramatizes the clash of traditional and modern values in Calcutta, is among Tagore's finest works.

BOOK ABOUT TAGORE

Lago, Mary M. *Rabindranath Tagore. Twayne's World Authors Ser.* G. K. Hall 1976 lib. bdg. $14.50

CHAPTER 23

Chinese Literature

Marsha L. Wagner

Man has sorrows and joys, separation and reunion;
The moon has light and shadow; it waxes and wanes—
This imperfection has been since ancient time.
Would that we could live a long life
And together share the moonlight a thousand miles away!
—SU TUNG-P'O, *Tz'u* poem to the tune *Shui-tiao ko-t'ou*

China possesses one of the major literary traditions in the world, with a history of more than 3,000 years. The primary reasons for its preservation over so long a period are threefold: the use of printing from the twelfth century onward, the practice of collecting and reproducing libraries, and, most importantly, an unbroken cultural tradition based above all on the Chinese script as a language medium independent of dialect differences. As the literary language became increasingly removed from the spoken, and thus less vital, literature took a natural turn toward imitation. Indeed, after the formative classical period beginning with Confucius, the literary history of China becomes one of imitation of different models, especially in the prose form. In poetry, vernacular folk songs often exerted strong influence on literary form. Fiction and spoken drama were the only forms of literary prose in which the vernacular language was employed until recent times. It was to this *pai-hua* that the twentieth-century literary revolutionaries turned.

The principal genre of Chinese literature is poetry; early folk songs established the *shih* form that crystallized during the Han dynasty. The Three Kingdoms and Six Dynasties from the third through the sixth centuries were a period of preparation for the great literary ages of T'ang and Sung. Confucianism lost much of its earlier intellectual sway to philosophical Taoism. The most famous writers of the period are remembered for their poetry, which began to show the elaborate and circumscribed forms culminating in the *lü-shih*, the regulated poem of the T'ang period. The short story, which was also to find perfection during the T'ang, began to develop in its two major categories, the supernatural and the historical tale. Prose and verse literature as developed during the T'ang, Five Dynasties, and Sung periods of the seventh through twelfth centuries remained the models until the twentieth century. In the characteristic short poetry of the period, there was a tendency toward an allusive style, intellectualism and erudition. The *tz'u* form, a song lyric written in irregular meter to conform to the rhythm of a particular tune, first appeared during the T'ang dynasty, was extended during the Sung, and was related to the *ch'ü* form, which was used for the verse portions of the great Yüan dramas. In the prose writing of the time, there was a movement toward a simpler style, a turning back to the "old" style (*ku-wen*) of the classical and Han periods, used particularly in T'ang short stories, which were to become the chief thematic sources of the Yuan drama. The novel appeared in complete form during the Ming and Ch'ing dynasties, including *The Romance of the Three Kingdoms*, *The Golden Lotus*, *The Dream of the Red Chamber*, and *Water Margin*. Contacts with the West during the nineteenth and twentieth centuries influenced cultural and literary trends as well as political events. Changes in language, style, and theme during this period have been more violent than at any earlier time of political change in China. Since the turn of the century, Chinese literature has been written with consistently close attention to social and political relevance.

HISTORY AND CRITICISM

Arlington, Lewis C. *Chinese Drama*. Ayer repr. of 1930 ed. $42.00
———, ed. *Famous Chinese Plays*. Trans. by Harold Acton, Russell repr. of 1937 ed. 1963 $22.50
Ayling, Alan, and Duncan Mackintosh, eds. and trans. *A Collection of Chinese Lyrics*. 1956. Vanderbilt Univ. Pr. rev. ed. 1967 o.p. "A conscientious labour of love and a pioneering venture in a neglected field" (*TLS*).
———. *Further Collection of Chinese Lyrics*. Vanderbilt Univ. Pr. 1970 $14.95
Birch, Cyril, ed. *Studies in Chinese Literary Genres*. Univ. of California Pr. 1975 $32.00
———, ed. and trans. *An Anthology of Chinese Literature*. Grove (Evergreen) 2 vols. 1965–72 pap. ea. $12.95–$17.50. "The first true anthology in English of Chinese literature. [It] is enjoyable, informative, and . . . readable to the student and general reader alike" (*LJ*). With historical and literary commentary.
Birrell, Anne, trans. *New Songs from a Jade Terrace: An Anthology of Early Chinese Love Poetry*. Allen & Unwin 1982 $28.50
Bishop, John L., ed. *Studies in Chinese Literature*. Harvard-Yenching Institute Studies Harvard Univ. Pr. 1965 pap. $8.50
Chai, Ch'u, and Winberg Chai, eds. and trans. *A Treasury of Chinese Literature: A New Prose Anthology Including Fiction and Drama*. 1965. Hawthorne o.p. Selected pieces connected by commentary, offering details not easily found elsewhere. The section on drama is especially valuable.
Chang, H. C., ed. *Chinese Literature I: Popular Fiction and Drama*. Columbia Univ. Pr. 1982 pap. $13.00. An anthology of short stories and excerpts from the best-known plays and novels. Each selection is well translated and fully annotated.
———, ed. *Chinese Literature II: Nature Poetry*. Columbia Univ. Pr. 1977 $13.00
———, ed. *Chinese Literature III: Tales of the Supernatural. Chinese Lit. in Translation Ser.* Columbia Univ. Pr. 1983 $20.00
Chang, Kang-i S. *The Evolution of Chinese Tz'u Poetry: From Late T'ang to Northern Sung*. Princeton Univ. Pr. 1980 $26.00

Ch'en, C. J. *Poems of Solitude*. Abelard-Schuman 1960 o.p. Translations of poems from the Six Dynasties period.

Cheng, François. *Chinese Poetic Writing: With an Anthology of T'ang Poetry*. Trans. by Jerome P. Seaton, Indiana Univ. Pr. 1983 $25.00 pap. $12.95

Chow, Tse-tsung. *May Fourth Movement: Intellectual Revolution in Modern China. East Asian Ser.* Harvard Univ. Pr. 1960 $30.00 pap. $9.95. A detailed analysis of the main intellectual currents in China during the 1915–1923 period. Chapter 11, "The Literary Revolution," discusses the development of twentieth-century Chinese prose writing.

Crump, J. I. *Songs from Xanadu: Studies in Mongol Dynasty Song Poetry (San Ch'u). Michigan Monographs in Chinese Studies* Univ. of Michigan Ctr. for Chinese Studies 1983 pap. $10.00. Analysis of Yuan dynasty *san-ch'u* poetry, with Chinese texts and English translation of poems discussed.

Davis, A. R., ed. *The Penguin Book of Chinese Verse: Poets Series*. Trans. by Robert Kotewall and Norman L. Smith, Penguin 1975 pap. $2.50

De Bary, William T., ed. *Sources of Chinese Tradition. Records of Civilization, Sources and Studies and Introduction to Oriental Classics Ser.* Columbia Univ. Pr. 2 vols. 1960 pap. $14.00. Chinese classics well translated, with chronological charts and helpful introductory notes.

Duke, Michael S. *Blooming and Contending: Chinese Literature in the Post Mao Era. Studies in Chinese Literature and Society* Indiana Univ. Pr. 1985 $22.50. A survey of the most important literary events in the People's Republic of China from 1977 to 1982.

——, ed. *Contemporary Chinese Literature*. Sharpe 1985 $35.00 pap. $14.95

Fairbank, John K., Edwin O. Reischauer, and Albert M. Craig. *East Asia*. Houghton Mifflin 2 vols. 1960–65 ea. $13.95

Fitzgerald, Charles P. *China: A Short Cultural History*. Praeger 3d ed. 1954 pap. $4.95

Fletcher, W. J. B. *Gems of Chinese Verse and More Gems of Chinese Poetry*. Paragon repr. of 1919 ed. bilingual ed. 1966 o.p. Includes well-known masterpieces of the T'ang dynasty.

Frankel, Hans H. *The Flowering Plum and the Palace Lady: Interpretations of Chinese Poetry*. Yale Univ. Pr. 1976 $27.50 pap. $8.95. Translation and discussion arranged by theme.

Frodsham, J. D., and Ch'eng Hsi. *An Anthology of Chinese Verse: Han Wei Chin and the Northern and Southern Dynasties*. Oxford 1967 o.p. The most comprehensive selection of poetry from this period in English.

Fung, Sydney S. *Twenty-Five T'ang Poets: Index to English Translations*. Fwd. by Stephen Owen, Univ. of Washington Pr. 1984 $75.00. An index of 207 volumes published between 1902 and 1981, with approximately 4,000 poems and 12,000 entries of English translation.

Fusek, Lois, trans. *Among the Flowers: A Translation of the Tenth-Century Anthology of Tz'u Lyrics, the Hua Chien Chi. Translations from the Oriental Classics Ser.* Columbia Univ. Pr. 1982 $30.00 pap. $12.50. "Fusek's rendition captures elegantly the flavors of both the folk and literary lyrics, written in one of the most confusing periods of Chinese history" (*World Literature Today*).

Gibbs, Donald A., and C. C. Rand. *A Bibliography of Studies and Translations of Modern Chinese Literature, 1918–1942. East Asian Monographs* Harvard Univ. Pr. 1975 $25.00. A comprehensive guide to nearly all English translations of modern Chinese literature with identification of the Chinese original from which the translation was made. Includes references to studies of each author.

Giles, Herbert A., and Liu Wu-chi. *A History of Chinese Literature*. Richard West repr.

of 1923 ed. 1973 $40.00; Tuttle 1973 pap. $5.95; Ungar 1967 $14.50. A popular history for many years. "Liu's account of modern Chinese drama is the first in any Western language.... A valuable handbook" (*LJ*). "The prose volume remains to this day the only one of its kind" (*Choice*).

Goldman, Merle. *China's Intellectuals*. Harvard Univ. Pr. text ed. 1981 $20.00

——. *Literary Dissent in Communist China*. Atheneum repr. of 1971 ed. text ed. pap. $3.75; *East Asian Ser*. Harvard Univ. Pr. 1967 $20.00. An investigation of the conflict between the Chinese Communist party and China's writers in the 1940s and 1950s. "It sheds much light on one aspect of the Chinese situation that has been largely neglected" (*N.Y. Times*).

——, ed. *Modern Chinese Literature in the May Fourth Era: A Social Science Research Council Study*. *East Asian Ser*. Harvard Univ. Pr. 1977 $25.00 1985 text ed. pap. $9.95

Graham, A. C., trans. *Poems of the Late T'ang*. Penguin Class. Ser. 1977 pap. $4.95. "Recommended for undergraduate students of poetry, comparative literature, and Far Eastern studies" (*Choice*).

Gunn, Edward M., trans. and ed. *Twentieth-Century Chinese Drama: An Anthology*. Indiana Univ. Pr. 1983 $27.50 pap. $15.00. "Translations flow smoothly and are of high quality. A valuable addition to Chinese literature collections, as well as collections in world drama" (*LJ*).

——. *Unwelcome Muse: Chinese Literature in Shanghai and Peking 1937–1945*. Columbia Univ. Pr. 1980 $25.00. Literary activities in China under the Japanese occupation.

Hanan, Patrick. *The Chinese Short Story: Studies in Dating, Authorship, and Composition*. *Harvard-Yenching Monograph Ser*. Harvard Univ. Pr. text ed. 1973 $18.50. Authoritative, with technical analysis.

——. *The Chinese Vernacular Story*. *East Asian Ser*. Harvard Univ. Pr. text ed. 1981 $18.50. The most important work on Chinese short fiction.

Hegel, Robert E. *The Novel in Seventeenth-Century China*. Columbia Univ. Pr. 1981 $26.00. "Essential reading for anyone seriously interested in the traditional Chinese novel" (*Ming Studies*).

Hegel, Robert E., and Richard C. Hessney, eds. *Expressions of Self in Chinese Literature*. *Studies in Oriental Culture* Columbia Univ. Pr. 1985 $35.00 pap. $15.00. Twelve essays by well-known scholars.

Hightower, James Robert. *Topics in Chinese Literature: Outlines and Bibliographies*. *Harvard-Yenching Institute Studies* Harvard Univ. Pr. 3d ed. rev. 1962 o.p. A concise and authoritative guide.

Hsia, Chih-tsing. *The Classic Chinese Novel: A Critical Introduction*. *Studies in Chinese Literature and Society* Indiana Univ. Pr. repr. of 1968 ed. 1981 $17.50 pap. $7.95. Summary and analysis of China's six greatest premodern novels. "*The Classic Chinese Novel*, for its painstaking research, its impeccable scholarship, . . . and its fund of invaluable insights, is a classic in itself" (*Journal of Asian Studies*).

——. *A History of Modern Chinese Fiction*. Yale Univ. Pr. 2d ed. rev. 1961 $34.00. The first serious study in English, providing a practical acquaintance with the writing itself by means of copious passages of translations from representative novels and stories.

Hsu, Kai-yu, ed. and trans. *Twentieth-Century Chinese Poetry: An Anthology*. Cornell Univ. Pr. repr. of 1963 ed. 1970 pap. $12.95. "Easily the best work in English concerning China since the end of World War II, this is an indispensable book for all libraries" (*LJ*). The work of more than 50 poets has been beautifully translated. The editor gives dates of both poets and poems wherever possible, together with excellent biographical and critical introductions.

Hsu, Kai-yu, and Ting Wang, eds. *Literature of the People's Republic of China. Chinese Lit. in Translation Ser.* Indiana Univ. Pr. 1980 $37.50 pap. $10.95. "An enterprising anthology with a wide range" (*N. Y. Review of Bks.*)

Hsu, Vivian Ling. *Born of the Same Roots: Stories of Modern Chinese Women. Chinese Lit. in Translation Ser.* Indiana Univ. Pr. 1981 $27.50 pap. $10.95

Huang, Joe C. *Heroes and Villains in Communist China: The Contemporary Chinese Novel as a Reflection of Life.* Universe 1974 $17.50. The first full-fledged study of the Communist Chinese novel.

Hucker, Charles O. *China to 1850: A Short History.* Stanford 1978 pap. $3.95

Isaacs, Harold R., ed. *Re-Encounters in China: Notes of a Journey in a Time Capsule.* Sharpe 1985 $19.95. "Among the visitors to the People's Republic of China who have presented their versions of China in recent years, Isaacs is among the sharpest, most readable, and most compelling" (*LJ*).

———. *Straw Sandals: Chinese Stories of Social Realism.* Intro. by Harold R. Isaacs, MIT 1974 pap. $5.95. A collection of 23 short stories, a play, and a poem, assembled in 1934 with the guidance of two outstanding modern Chinese writers, Lu Hsün and Mao Tun. Well translated, with biographical information on 16 chosen authors.

Jenner, W. J., ed. *Modern Chinese Stories.* Trans. by W. J. Jenner and Gladys Yang, Oxford 1974 pap. $8.95

Kao, Karl S., ed. *Classical Chinese Tales of the Supernatural and the Fantastic: Selections from the Third to the Tenth Century.* Indiana Univ. Pr. 1985 $27.50

Kinkley, Jeffrey C., ed. *After Mao: Chinese Literature and Society, 1978–1981. East Asian Monographs* Harvard Univ. Pr. text ed. 1985 pap. $14.00. Analysis of popular literature in the People's Republic of China by seven contributors.

Klemer, D. J., ed. *Chinese Love Poems.* Doubleday 1959 $6.95

Knechtges, David R., ed. and trans. *Rhapsodies on Metropolises and Capitals.* Vol. 1 in *Wen Xuan, or Selection of Refined Literature.* Princeton Univ. Pr. 1982 $50.00

Lau, Joseph S., ed. *The Unbroken Chain: An Anthology of Taiwan Fiction Since 1926. Chinese Lit. in Translation Ser.* Indiana Univ. Pr. 1984 $25.00. "Represents a major contribution to the ever-growing corpus of modern Chinese literature in translation" (*World Lit. Today*).

Lau, Joseph S., and Leo Ou-fan Lee, eds. *Modern Chinese Stories and Novellas, 1919–1949. Modern Asian Lit. Ser.* Columbia Univ. Pr. 1981 $40.00 pap. $17.00. "The most comprehensive . . . anthology of Republican era fiction available in English today. . . . The quality of the translations surpasses the levels achieved in any of the anthologies of Chinese fiction or criticism produced in recent years" (*Journal of Asian Studies*).

Lau, Joseph S., and Timothy A. Ross, eds. *Chinese Stories from Taiwan, 1960–1970.* Columbia Univ. Pr. 1976 $30.00 pap. $15.00

Lee, Leo Ou-fan. *The Romantic Generation of Modern Chinese Writers. East Asian Ser.* Harvard Univ. Pr. text ed. 1973 $18.50

Liang, Ch'i-ch'ao. *Intellectual Trends in the Ch'ing Period (Ch'ing Tai Hsueh Shu Kai Lun).* Trans. by Immanuel C. Y. Hsu and Benjamin I. Schwartz, fwd. by Benjamin I. Schwartz, *East Asian Ser.* Harvard Univ. Pr. 1959 $8.95. A lively portrayal of the intellectual developments in China under the Ch'ing (or Manchu) dynasty, which ruled from 1644 to 1912.

Lin, Julia C. *Modern Chinese Poetry: An Introduction. Washington Pap. Ser.* Univ. of

Washington Pr. 1972 $15.00 pap. $6.95. Translations of twentieth-century poetry with extensive commentary by the author.

Link, Perry. *Roses and Thorns: The Second Blooming of the Hundred Flowers in Chinese Fiction, 1979–80*. Univ. of California Pr. 1984 lib. bdg. $32.00

——, ed. *Stubborn Weeds: Popular and Controversial Chinese Literature After the Cultural Revolution. Chinese Lit. in Translation Ser.* Indiana Univ. Pr. repr. 1984 $25.00 pap. $10.95. "High quality . . . and immensely readable translations" (*Choice*).

Liu, James J. Y. *The Art of Chinese Poetry.* Univ. of Chicago Pr. 1962 pap. $10.00. A careful study by a professor of Chinese at Stanford University.

——. *Chinese Theories of Literature.* Univ. of Chicago Pr. (Phoenix Bks.) 1979 pap. $4.95. Examines the range of Chinese literary criticism using the author's own categories and Western comparisons.

——. *Major Lyricists of the Northern Sung, 960–1126, A.D.* Princeton Univ. Pr. 1974 $22.00

Liu, Tsun-yan, ed. *Chinese Middlebrow Fiction.* Univ. of Washington Pr. 1983 $35.00. An anthology of popular fiction from the eighteenth, nineteenth, and early twentieth centuries.

Liu, Wu-chi. *An Introduction to Chinese Literature.* Indiana Univ. Pr. 1966 $20.00 pap. $7.95. "Poetry in different forms is the main topic of the first part of the book. The popular novel of the Yuan and the Ming dynasties is treated extensively. The contemporary literary scene is given selective coverage. . . . On the whole . . . a valuable contribution" (*LJ*).

Liu, Wu-chi, and Irving Yucheng Lo, eds. *Sunflower Splendor: Three Thousand Years of Chinese Poetry.* Doubleday (Anchor) 1975 pap. $8.95; Indiana Univ. Pr. 1976 $17.50

Ma, Y. W., and Joseph S. Lau, eds. *Traditional Chinese Stories: Themes and Variations.* Columbia Univ. Pr. 1978 $42.00 pap. $16.00. "A major contribution to the body of excellent translations of fiction in readily available anthologies. . . . These are translations one can read with confidence and a good measure of enjoyment" (*Journal of Asian Studies*).

Mackerras, Colin. *The Chinese Theatre in Modern Times: From 1840 to the Present Day.* Univ. of Massachusetts Pr. 1975 $17.50

Mair, Victor H. *Tunhuang Popular Narratives. Cambridge Studies in Chinese History, Lit. and Institutions* 1984 $59.50

McDougall, Bonnie S., ed. *Popular Chinese Literature and Performing Arts in the People's Republic of China, 1949–1979.* Univ. of California Pr. 1984 lib. bdg. $32.50. A collection of fine essays on written and performed Chinese literature since 1949 by leading experts in the field.

McNaughton, William, ed. *Chinese Literature: An Anthology from the Earliest Times to the Present Day.* Tuttle 1974 pap. $11.75

Meserve, Walter J., and Ruth I. Meserve, eds. *Modern Literature from China.* New York Univ. Pr. 1974 $20.00

Meskill, John. *An Introduction to Chinese Civilization.* Columbia Univ. Pr. 1973 $17.50

Nieh, Hualing, ed. *Literature of the Hundred Flowers. Modern Asian Lit. Ser.* Columbia Univ. Pr. 2 vols. 1981 $80.00. Presents the literature of the late 1950s in the context of political criticism.

Nienhauser, William H., Jr., and Stephen H. West, eds. *The Indiana Companion to Traditional Chinese Literature.* Indiana Univ. Pr. 1985 $75.00. A monumental reference work on Chinese literature before 1911, compiled by almost 200 contributors, including more than 500 entries on specific writers, works, genres, styles, and movements, as well as general essays, cross-references, and indexes.

Owen, Stephen. *The Great Age of Chinese Poetry: The High T'ang.* Yale Univ. Pr. 1980 $42.00. The most scholarly work available in English on the period of China's greatest poetry.

———. *The Poetry of Meng Chiao and Han Yü.* Yale Univ. Pr. 1975 $27.50. A fine study of two pivotal poets from the late eighth and early ninth centuries.

———. *The Poetry of the Early T'ang.* Yale Univ. Pr. 1977 $33.00. The only scholarly treatment of this transitional period.

Palandri, Angela C. Y. Jung, trans. and ed. *Modern Verse from Taiwan.* Univ. of California Pr. 1972 $28.50

Payne, Robert, ed. *The White Pony: An Anthology of Chinese Poetry from the Earliest Times to the Present Day.* New Amer. Lib. 1974 o.p. Comprehensive and authoritative.

Perng, Ching-hsi. *Double Jeopardy: A Critique of Seven Yuan Courtroom Dramas.* Univ. of Michigan Pr. 1978 pap. $6.00

Plaks, Andrew, ed. *Chinese Narrative: Critical and Theoretical Essays.* Princeton Univ. Pr. 1977 $43.00

Prusek, Jaroslav. *Chinese History and Literature: Collections of Studies.* Kluwer Academic 1970 $53.00

Prusek, Jaroslav, and Leo Ou-fan Lee, eds. *The Lyrical and the Epic: Studies of Modern Chinese Literature.* Indiana Univ. Pr. 1970 $22.50

Rexroth, Kenneth, trans. *One Hundred Poems from the Chinese.* New Directions 1970 $6.00 pap. $4.95

Rexroth, Kenneth, and Ling Chung, trans. and eds. *The Orchid Boat: Women Poets of China.* New Directions 1982 pap. $5.95

Rickett, Adele A., ed. *Chinese Approaches to Literature from Confucius to Liang Ch'ich'ao.* Princeton Univ. Pr. 1978 $32.00

Roberts, Moss, ed. and trans. *Chinese Fairy Tales and Fantasies.* Pantheon 1979 $11.95 1980 pap. $5.95

Schlepp, Wayne. *San-ch'ü: Its Technique and Imagery.* Univ. of Wisconsin Pr. 1970 $19.50. A study of the dominant verse of the Yuan dynasty.

Scott, A. C. *Literature and Arts in Twentieth-Century China.* Greenwood repr. of 1963 ed. 1982 lib. bdg. $23.50; Peter Smith $8.50

Shih, Chung-wen. *The Golden Age of Chinese Drama: Yüan Tsa Chü.* Princeton Univ. Pr. 1975 $35.00. A study of the 171 extant plays of the peak of Chinese drama in the Yuan period (1260–1368).

Siu, Helen, and Zelda Stern, eds. *Mao's Harvest: Voices from China's New Generation.* Oxford 1983 $17.95 pap. $10.95

Soong, Stephen C., ed. *Song without Music: Chinese Tz'u Poetry.* Univ. of Washington Pr. 1981 $21.95

———. *Trees on the Mountain: An Anthology of New Chinese Writing.* Univ. of Washington Pr. 1985 $35.00. Recent essays, fiction, poetry, and drama from the People's Republic of China, Taiwan, and Hong Kong, in English translation.

Tsien, Tsuen-hsuin. *Written on Bamboo and Silk: The Beginnings of Chinese Books and Inscriptions.* Univ. of Chicago Pr. 1962 o.p. How Chinese writing developed and how it was used from ancient times to the emergence of the age of printing; an indispensable book.

Wagner, Marsha L. *The Lotus Boat: The Origins of Chinese Tz'u Poetry in T'ang Popular Culture. Studies in Oriental Culture* Columbia Univ. Pr. 1984 $25.00. A study of poetry from Tun-huang manuscripts and literati anthologies.

Waley, Arthur. *Translations from the Chinese.* Random (Vintage) 1971 pap. $1.95. Includes "170 Chinese Poems" and "More Translations from the Chinese."

———, ed. *Chinese Poems.* Allen & Unwin 1982 pap. $5.95. An accessible selection of some of Waley's best translations of classical Chinese poems, with a large sampling of Po Chu-yi.

Wang, Chi-chen, trans. *Traditional Chinese Tales.* Greenwood repr. of 1944 ed. lib. bdg. $22.50. A collection of 20 Chinese stories from the sixth to the sixteenth centuries, covering most aspects of this genre in China.

Watson, Burton, trans. *Chinese Lyricism: Shih Poetry from the Second to Twelfth Century.* Columbia Univ. Pr. 1971 $22.50 pap. $12.50. Translations with helpful discussions of major works by major poets during the 1,500 years when poetry dominated Chinese literature.

———. *Early Chinese Literature.* Columbia Univ. Pr. 1962 $28.50 pap. $9.50. A capable survey of the formative stages of Chinese history, philosophy, and poetry (covering the approximate period 1000 B.C.–100 A.D.)

———, ed. *The Columbia Book of Chinese Poetry: From Early Times to the Thirteenth Century. Translations from the Oriental Classics Ser.* Columbia Univ. Pr. 1984 $19.95. "This gathering of translations is the surest, clearest, most comprehensive presentation of Chinese poetry yet" (Gary Snyder).

Yang, Hsien-yi, and Gladys Yang, trans. *The Courtesan's Jewel Box: Chinese Stories of the Xth-XVIIth Centuries.* Cheng & Tsui 1981 $12.50

Yip, Wai-lim. *Chinese Poetry: Major Modes and Genres.* Univ. of California Pr. 1976 $37.00. Idiosyncratic translations, with an introduction expounding the author's "radical" view of the simplicity of Chinese verse.

Yoshikawa, Kōjirō. *An Introduction to Sung Poetry.* Trans. by Burton Watson, *Harvard-Yenching Monograph Ser.* Harvard Univ. Pr. 1967 $12.50. Well-written discussion of an important period.

AI CH'ING (AI QING). 1910–

China's greatest living poet, Ai Ch'ing first practiced painting and studied in France. After a period with the Communists in Yenan after 1941, he was visible until 1957. From 1957 until 1977, he wrote no poetry, but he has re-emerged since the Cultural Revolution as a leading figure.

BOOKS BY AI CH'ING

The Black Eel. Trans. by Yang Xianyi and Robert C. Friend, China Bks. 1982 pap. $2.95

Selected Poems of Ai Qing. Ed. by Eugene C. Eoyang, Indiana Univ. Pr. bilingual ed. 1983 $27.50 pap. $10.95. More than 50 poems written from 1936 to 1981. "[Ai Qing's] work is emotional, direct and honest.... His voice is more collective than individualistic ... despite the personal vision that informs his poems" (*World Lit. Today*).

THE BOOK OF SONGS (SHIH CHING)

This is China's earliest collection of poetry, including folk songs gathered in the sixth century B.C. from various regions of China, ranging from long ballads recounting legendary history to short songs of such aspects of daily life as love, work, and laments. This anthology of 305 songs had a lasting influence on the style and themes of traditional Chinese poetry.

Shih Ching: The Classic Anthology Defined by Confucius. Trans. by Ezra Pound, Harvard Univ. Pr. 1954 pap. $4.95. Imaginative translations, not always literally accurate.

The Book of Songs. 1937. Trans. by Arthur Waley, Grove (Evergreen) 1960 pap. $9.95. Faithful and felicitous translations of all 305 songs.

BOOKS ABOUT THE BOOK OF SONGS

Dobson, W. A. *The Language of the Book of Songs.* Univ. of Toronto Pr. 1968 $30.00

Wang, C. H. *The Bell and the Drum: A Study of Shih Ching as Formulaic Poetry.* Univ. of California Pr. 1975 $31.00

CHEN JO-HSI. 1938–

Chen Jo-hsi is a Taiwan-born, American-educated Chinese woman who spent seven years during the Cultural Revolution living in the People's Republic of China.

BOOK BY CHEN JO-HSI

The Execution of Mayor Yin and Other Stories from the Great Proletarian Cultural Revolution. Trans. by Nancy Ing and Howard Goldblatt, intro. by Simon Leys, Indiana Univ. Pr. 1978 $15.95 pap. $6.96. Eight stories written in 1974–1976 after Chen's experiences living through the Cultural Revolution. "The people of China transcend its politics, and it is their power of survival that Chen Jo-hsi ultimately celebrates" (*N.Y. Review of Bks*).

CHIANG K'UEI. 1155?–1235?

A writer of *tz'u* poetry, Chiang K'uei was particularly admired for his knowledge of music.

BOOK ABOUT CHIANG K'UEI

Lin, Shuen Fu. *The Transformation of a Chinese Lyrical Tradition: Chiang K'uei and Southern Sung Tz'u Poetry.* Princeton Univ. Pr. 1978 $28.00

CH'IEN CHUNG-SHU (QIAN ZHONGSHU). 1911–

A major scholar and critic, who earned his B. Litt. degree at Oxford University, Ch'ien Chung-shu later taught English literature and wrote literary criticism of Chinese literature at the Academy of Social Sciences in Peking.

BOOK BY CH'IEN CHUNG-SHU

Fortress Besieged. 1947. Trans. by Jeanne Kelly and Nathan K. Mao, *Chinese Lit. in Translation Ser.* Indiana Univ. Pr. 1980 $17.50. Ch'ien's greatest novel, *Fortress Besieged*, was reissued in China in 1980, and it became a bestseller.

BOOK ABOUT CH'IEN CHUNG-SHU

Huters, Theodore. *Qian Zhongshu. Twayne's World Authors Ser.* G. K. Hall 1982 lib. bdg. $19.95

CH'Ü YÜAN (CHU YUAN). 343?–278 B.C.

Ch'ü Yüan was China's first major individual poet, a virtuous official in the southern state of Ch'u who was slandered and exiled from court. He described his grief in a long elegiac poem, the *Li Sao (Encountering Sorrow)*. He is attributed with writing—or perhaps merely collecting and editing— other songs with a shamanistic ritual background from the Ch'u region of southern China into the highly influential collection, the *Ch'u Tz'u*.

BOOKS BY CH'Ü YÜAN

Ch'u Tz'u: The Songs of the South. Oxford 1959 o.p.
The Nine Songs: A Study of Shamanism in Ancient China. Trans. by Arthur Waley, City Lights 2d ed. repr. of 1955 ed. 1973 pap. $3.95

FAN CH'ENG-TA. 1126–1193

One of the four Masters of Southern Sung Poetry, Fan is best known for rural nature poetry.

BOOK ABOUT FAN CH'ENG-TA

Bullett, Gerald. *The Golden Years of Fan Ch'eng-ta*. Cambridge Univ. Pr. 1946 o.p.

FENG MENG-LUNG. 1574–1646

Feng Meng-lung collected and edited short stories into several major anthologies, and perhaps made some significant revisions himself.

BOOK BY FENG MENG-LUNG

Stories from a Ming Collection. Trans. by Cyril Birch, Greenwood repr. of 1959 ed. 1978 lib. bdg. $22.50; trans. by Cyril Birch, Grove (Evergreen) 1968 pap. $5.95. Six selected stories from *Stories Old and New*, published in the early 1620s, as edited by Feng Meng-lung.

HAN SHAN. fl. early 8th century?

Han Shan, which means "Cold Mountain," is the place where an anonymous poet of uncertain dates during the T'ang dynasty settled to pursue an ascetic Buddhist life after renouncing worldly ambitions. His poems, said to have been scrawled on the rocks of the mountainside, were collected with an undated preface written by Lu-ch'iu Yin, a T'ang dynasty official. These accessible poems concern the poet's spiritual quest in nature.

BOOK BY HAN SHAN

Cold Mountain: One Hundred Poems by the T'ang Poet Han Shan. Trans. by Burton Watson, Columbia Univ. Pr. repr. of 1962 ed. 1970 pap. $8.50

HAN YÜ. 768–824

A prominent scholar, writer, and teacher with a checkered career, Han Yü is most famous as a prose writer who advocated a return to the ancient style (*ku-wen*) in order to revitalize the language.

BOOK BY HAN YÜ

Han Yü's Poetische Werke. Trans. by Erwin Von Zach, Harvard Univ. Pr. 1962 o.p.

HSIAO HUNG (XIAO HONG). 1911–1941

A woman writer from Heilongjiang province whose short novels and stories give vivid accounts of the poverty and oppression of peasant life in northern China.

BOOKS BY HSIAO HUNG

The Field of Life and Death and Tales of Hulan River. Trans. by Howard Goldblatt and Ellen Yeung, *Chinese Lit. in Translation Ser.* Indiana Univ. Pr. 1979 $14.95. Two short autobiographical novels.
Selected Stories of Xiao Hong. Trans. by Howard Goldblatt, China Bks. 1982 pap. $3.95

HSIAO KANG (also LIANG CHIEN-WEN TI). 505–555

Hsiao Kang, the crown prince of the Liang dynasty from 531 to 549, ruled as emperor Chien-wen of the Liang from 549 until 551. He was active in literary salons, commissioned the collection of 655 love poems published under the title *New Songs from the Jade Terrace (Yü-t'ai hsin-yung)*, and wrote many of his own compositions.

BOOK ABOUT HSIAO KANG

Marney, John. *Liang Chien Wen Ti. Twayne's World Authors Ser.* G. K. Hall 1976 lib. bdg. $15.95

HU SHIH. 1891–1962

This scholar was educated at Columbia and Cornell universities and taught for many years at the Peking National University. He served as Chinese Ambassador to the United States from 1938 to 1942, and from 1958 until his death was president of the Academia Sinica. He was a strong promoter of the use of the vernacular in Chinese literature, and was one of the literary reformers of the May Fourth Movement.

BOOKS BY HU SHIH

China's Own Critics. Commentary by Wei Wang Ching, Hyperion Conn repr. of 1931 ed. 1981 $19.75
Chinese Renaissance. Paragon repr. 2d ed. 1963 o.p.
The Development of the Logical Method in Ancient China. Krishna lib. bdg. $79.95

BOOK ABOUT HU SHIH

Grieder, Jerome B. *Hu Shih and the Chinese Renaissance: Liberalism in the Chinese Revolution, 1917–1937. East Asian Ser.* Harvard Univ. Pr. 1970 $25.00

JUAN CHI. 210–263

Called one of the Seven Sages of the Bamboo Grove, Juan Chi was an eccentric poet who resigned from politics, criticized the complex political intrigues of his day, and withdrew to a more private investigation of neo-Taoism.

BOOK ABOUT JUAN CHI

Holzman, Donald. *Poetry and Politics: The Life and Works of Juan Chi (A.D. 210–263).*
Cambridge Univ. Pr. 1976 o.p.

KAO CH'I. 1336–1374

An important historian of the Yuan period, Kao Ch'i is regarded as the best early Ming poet for his wit, empathy, and mastery of the traditional verse forms.

BOOK ABOUT KAO CH'I

Mote, F. W. *The Poet Kao Ch'i, 1336–1374.* Princeton Univ. Pr. 1962 o.p.

KAO SHIH. 702?–765

Kao Shih was a High T'ang poet, best known for his poetry in the "heroic" mode, describing military life and natural scenery at remote border outposts.

BOOK ABOUT KAO SHIH

Chan, Marie. *Kao Shih. Twayne's World Authors Ser.* G. K. Hall 1978 lib. bdg. $16.95

KUAN HAN-CH'ING (GUAN HANQING). c.1220–c.1300

Like many intellectuals during the Yuan dynasty, Kuan Han-ch'ing did not serve the government, but turned to writing plays in the *tsa-chü* form of five acts with interspersed arias. Kuan is the major playwright of this Golden Age of Chinese drama: 18 of his 60 plays are extant, and he is also known for light songs in the *ch'u* form.

BOOK BY KUAN HAN-CH'ING

Selected Plays of Kuan Han-ch'ing. Trans. by Yang Hsien-yi and Gladys Yang, China Bks. 1978 $6.95

LAO SHE (also LAO SHEH) (pseud. of Ch'ing-ch'un). 1899–1966

Born in Peking of Manchu descent, Lao She was the only major twentieth-century writer from North China. He resided in England and later in the United States, and was heavily influenced by Western writing, especially that of DICKENS (see Vol. 1). A victim of the Cultural Revolution, Lao She had been a master of fictional social criticism, often in satiric style.

BOOKS BY LAO SHE

Beneath the Red Banner. Trans. by Don J. Cohn, *Panda Ser.* China Bks. 1982 pap.
$4.95. Short stories by Lao She.
Camel Xiangzi. Pref. by Shi Ziaoqing, Indiana Univ. Pr. 1981 $20.00 pap. $6.95. Lao
She's greatest novel, also known as *Rickshaw Boy.*
Cat Country: A Satirical Novel of China in the 1930's. Trans. by William A. Lyell, Jr.,
Ohio State Univ. Pr. 1970 $8.00
Rickshaw: The Novel Lo-t'o Hsiangtzu. Trans. by Jean M. James, Univ. of Hawaii Pr.
text ed. 1979 $12.00 pap. $5.95

BOOK ABOUT LAO SHE

Vohra, Ranbir. *Lao She and the Chinese Revolution. East Asian Monographs* Harvard Univ. Pr. 1974 $20.00

LI CH'ING-CHAO. 1084–c.1151

The first well-known Chinese woman poet, Li Ch'ing-chao wrote *tz'u* poetry about her happy marriage under the Northern Sung dynasty, the tragedy of the Jurchen invasion, and her nostalgia in exile in the South, with striking colloquialism, melodious effects, and direct physicality.

BOOK BY LI CH'ING-CHAO

Li Ch'ing-chao: Complete Poems. Ed. by Kenneth Rexroth and Ling Chung, New Directions 1979 $12.95 pap. $4.95

BOOK ABOUT LI CH'ING-CHAO

Hu, P'in-ch'ing. *Li Ch'ing-chao.* Twayne 1966 o.p.

LI HO. 791–817

A brilliant young man excluded from official success and plagued by poor health, Li Ho wrote complex allusive poetry with eccentric imagery and thinly veiled social criticism, which appears strikingly "modern" today. He died at age 26.

BOOK BY LI HO

Poems of Li Ho, 791–817. Trans. by J. D. Frodsham, *Oxford Lib. of East Asian Lit. Ser.* 1970 $24.95

LI PO. 701–762

One of China's best-known poets, Li Po came from mysterious origins in Central Asia and traveled widely throughout China. He was a favorite of the "Brilliant Emperor" Hsuan-tsung for a brief period. Li Po is admired for his lyrical and imaginative poetry celebrating nature, wine, human sentiments, and Taoist transcendence.

BOOKS BY LI PO

Poems by Li Po. Trans. by Elling O. Eide, Anvil Pr. 1983 o.p.
The Works of Li Po the Chinese Poet. Trans. by Shigeyoshi Obata, Paragon repr. of 1922 ed. 1966 o.p.

BOOK ABOUT LI PO

Waley, Arthur. *The Poetry and Career of Li Po. Ethical and Religious Class. of East and West Ser.* Allen & Unwin 1951 $13.50

LI SHANG-YIN. 813–858

Unsuccessful in his official career, Li Shang-yin wrote ambiguous poems, often describing clandestine love affairs. His innovative imagery influenced many later poets.

BOOK ABOUT LI SHANG-YIN

Liu, James J. *The Poetry of Li Shang-yin, Ninth Century Baroque Chinese Poet.* Univ. of Chicago Pr. 1969 $18.00

LI YÜ. 1611–1680

Li Yü, a playwright, novelist, poet, and essayist born in Kiangsu province, can be considered representative of the intellectual world of the late Ming period. His work reflects his unorthodox views and Bohemian way of life.

BOOK BY LI YÜ

Jou Pu Tuan, The Prayer Mat of Flesh: A 17th Century Erotic Moral Novel. Trans. by Richard Martin, Grove (Evergreen) 1967 o.p. R. H. Van Gulik, the Dutch authority on Chinese Ming erotic literature, had this to say about the story of the sensual adventures of a student in seventeenth-century China: "From the literary point of view, this book is, after the *Chin-p'ing-mei*, the best Ming erotic novel. It is written in a fluent elegant style, interspersed with good poetry, witty dialogues, and clever character sketches. Although it abounds in obscene passages, they are often combined with philosophical disquisitions on the frailty of human nature; this tends to soften the stark realism of the erotic scene."

LIN YUTANG. 1895–1976

Lin Yutang, born in China, lived in New York, then in Cannes, France. Early in 1954 he was appointed chancellor of the new Chinese University in Singapore, but because of a disagreement with the trustees on policy, he and his staff left early in 1955 before the university opened its doors. He helped immeasurably in developing an understanding between East and West. A product of an ancient civilization, with both a classical and modern educational background, he writes an idiomatic, sparkling English in the best essay tradition. The earlier books are notable for their wisdom, wit, and humor. Unfortunately, *My Country and My People* (1935) is now out of print. He has edited *The Wisdom of India* (1942, o.p.) and edited and translated *The Importance of Understanding* (1960, o.p.).

BOOKS BY LIN YUTANG

(and Hu Shih). *China's Own Critics.* Commentary by Wei Wang Ching, Hyperion Conn repr. of 1931 ed. 1981 $19.75

History of the Press and Public Opinion in China. Greenwood repr. of 1936 ed. 1968 lib. bdg. $18.75

Moment in Peking. International Specialized Bk. 1980 pap. $12.75. This and *A Leaf in a Storm* (o.p.) are Lin Yutang's best-known novels.

Between Tears and Laughter. Essay Index Repr. Ser. Ayer repr. of 1943 ed. $15.00

Vermilion Gate. Greenwood repr. of 1953 ed. 1972 lib. bdg. $24.75; International Specialized Bk. 1980 pap. $9.75

Imperial Peking: Seven Centuries of China. 1961. Dufour o.p. With an essay on the art of Peking by Peter C. Swann. A gracefully written account of the 1,000-year history and the near-mythical beauty of the great city.

LIU T'IEH-YÜN (aka LIU TIEYUN, LIU NGO, LIU E, LIU O). 1857–1909

A physician, miner, entrepreneur, and collector of oracle bones, who suffered exile and disappointment, Liu T'ieh-yün wrote a powerful allegorical and autobiographical novel.

BOOKS BY LIU T'IEH-YÜN

The Travels of Lao Can. Trans. by Yanq Xianyi and Gladys Yang, China Bks. 1983 pap. $3.95

The Travels of Lao Ts'an. Trans. and annotated by Harold Shadick, Cornell Univ. Pr. 1966 $15.00. "Since the novel translated here may be justly characterized as one of the greatest novels in the Chinese literary tradition, it is fortunate that it has been put into English by so competent a hand as the professor of Chinese literature at Cornell University. Written in the years 1904–1907 by a Chinese scholar and official of unusual versatility and skill, these Travels throw a powerful light on both the bright and dark aspects of Chinese officialdom in the closing years of the Manchu dynasty" (*U.S. Quarterly Bk. Review*).

LIU TSUNG-YÜAN. 773–819

A master essayist, Liu Tsung-yüan also wrote poetry while in exile in the south of China.

BOOK ABOUT LIU TSUNG-YÜAN

Nienhauser, William H., Jr., and others. *Liu Tsung-yüan. Twayne's World Authors Ser.* G. K. Hall 1973 lib. bdg. $16.95; *Twayne's World Authors Ser.* Irvington 1971 $15.95

LO KUAN-CHUNG. c.1330–1400

Very little is known of this writer, author of *The Romance of the Three Kingdoms,* one of China's most famous novels, a fictional account of historical episodes of the third century A.D.

BOOKS BY LO KUAN-CHUNG

The Romance of the Three Kingdoms. Translations from the Oriental Class. Series. Columbia Univ. Pr. 1968 $29.00. A complete translation by Moss Roberts is in progress.

Romance of the Three Kingdoms. Trans. by C. H. Brewitt-Taylor, intro. by Roy A. Miller, Tuttle 2 vols. 1969 $37.50

LU HSÜN (LU XUN) (pseud. of Chou Shu-jen). 1881–1936

A writer, essayist, translator, poet, and literary theorist and critic, Lu Hsün was born in Chekiang province of an educated family. A participant in the May Fourth (1919) Movement, he was a founding member of the League of Left-Wing Writers in 1930. He translated a number of European works of literature and theoretical studies on art and literature into Chinese, and helped to introduce modern art to China. The extent of his work and his high standards laid the foundation for modern Chinese literature, and he is still considered China's greatest twentieth-century writer in the People's Republic of China. The stories are satiric, unflinchingly realistic, disturbing, and brilliantly crafted in tone and style.

BOOKS BY LU HSÜN

A Brief History of Chinese Fiction. China Bks. $12.95; trans. by Yang Hsien-yi and Gladys Yang, Hyperion Conn repr. of 1959 ed. 1973 $27.50. An able translation of Lu Hsün's most important scholarly work and the first of its kind to be published in China.

Ah Q, and Others: Selected Stories of Lu Hsun. Trans. by Chi Chen Wang, *Short Story Index Repr. Ser.* Ayer repr. of 1941 ed. $17.00; trans. by Wang Chi-chen, Greenwood repr. of 1941 ed. 1971 lib. bdg. $24.75. Eleven of Lu Hsün's best stories, including his most famous, "The True Story of Ah Q."

The Complete Stories of Lu Xun: Call to Arms: Wandering. Trans. by Gladys Yang, Indiana Univ. Pr. 1982 $20.00 pap. $6.95. Standard translations of twenty-five stories from Lu Hsün's two original volumes, *Call to Arms* and *Wandering.* "Here at last Lu Xun's creative writing is faithfully and fully presented in English; this volume should be on the reading list for any course on Chinese or world literature of the twentieth century" (*World Lit. Today*).

Selected Stories of Lu Hsün. Trans. by Yang Hsien-yi and Gladys Yang, *Norton Lib.* repr. 1977 pap. $6.95. Nineteen of Lu Hsün's best-known stories, written 1918–1926.

Silent China: Selected Writings of Lu Xun. Trans. and ed. by Gladys Yang, Oxford 1974 pap. $2.95

Wild Grass. China Bks. 1974 pap. $2.50. A collection of all of Lu Hsün's prose poems.

LU YU. 1125–1210

One of the four Masters of Southern Sung Poetry, Lu Yu was frustrated by being forced to divorce his beloved wife and by setbacks in his political career. He wrote more than 10,000 poems, mostly on themes of personal emancipation.

BOOKS BY LU YU

The Old Man Who Does as He Pleases: Poems and Prose. Trans. by Burton Watson, *Translations from the Oriental Classics Ser.* Columbia Univ. Pr. 1973 $16.00

The Rapier of Lu. Trans. by Clara M. Candlin, Paragon o.p.

MAO TSE-TUNG (MAO ZEDONG). 1893–1976

Born into a prosperous peasant family in Hunan province, Mao first came into contact with revolutionary writings in the decade of the 1910s. He was present at the founding of the Communist party in 1921, and has been the most influential leader in China since 1935. President of the People's Republic from 1949 to 1959, he was later chairman of the Communist party. As a result of his education, he had a great command of classical Chinese; this, together with his sense of history, casts his poetry in the traditional style.

BOOKS BY MAO TSE-TUNG

Mao Papers: Anthology and Bibliography. Ed. by Jerome Ch'en, Oxford 1970 $11.95

Ten Poems and Lyrics by Mao Tse-tung. Trans. by Hui Ming Wang, Univ. of Massachusetts Pr. 1975 $8.00 pap. $3.95

Talks at the Yenan Forum on Literature and Art. China Bks. 1965 $1.00. Mao gives his definition of the cultural policies of the Communist party, summing up at the same time Chinese discussions of the revolutionary literature of the preceding 20 years. He states that literature and art must support other revolutionary activities.

BOOKS ABOUT MAO TSE-TUNG

Ch'en, Jerome. *Mao and the Chinese Revolution.* Oxford 1967 pap. $6.95. This book is one of the three standard biographies of Mao. "The poems are translated with an unusual degree of sensitivity for the nuances and subtleties that are characteristic of Chinese poetry" (C. T. Hu, *SR*).

Schram, Stuart R. *Mao Tse-tung.* Simon & Schuster 1967 o.p.

MAO TUN (MAO DUN) (pseud. of Shen Yen-ping). 1896–1981

One of modern China's best and most representative novelists, Mao Tun was an active member of the Literary Research Organization, a writers' group founded in 1920 to foster a "literature of humanity," depicting society and its ills. He was Minister of Culture for the People's Republic of China from 1949 to 1966. His novels protesting exploitation of workers and peasants and advocating change by revolution have established him as a prominent literary figure in Communist China. "Among all the novelists sympathetic to the extreme left Mao Tun was artistically outstanding" (A. C. Scott).

BOOKS BY MAO TUN

Midnight. Trans. by Hsu Meng-hsiung and A. C. Barnes, China Bks 1980 $15.95. This novel, written in 1930–1931, is Mao Tun's greatest work, a picture of life in Shanghai in 1930.

Spring Silkworms and Other Stories. Trans. by Sidney Shapiro, AMS Pr. repr. of 1956 ed. $24.50; trans. by Sidney Shapiro, Cheng & Tsui 2d ed. 1979 $6.95; China Bks. 2d ed. 1980 $9.95. Thirteen short stories dealing primarily with life in the countryside and written between 1930 and 1936.

MEI YAO-CH'EN. 1002–1060

A scholar-official who influenced early Sung poetry through his fine poems of personal emotion and social reality, Mei Yao-ch'en's poems are notable for their simple diction and plain style.

BOOK ABOUT MEI YAO-CH'EN

Chaves, Jonathan. *Mei Yao-ch'en and the Development of Early Sung Poetry. Studies in Oriental Culture* Columbia Univ. Pr. 1976 $23.00

MENG HAO-JAN. 689–740

More than 200 poems survive by Meng Hao-jan, a recluse who never passed the civil service examination but described his travels and the pleasures of a simple life in seclusion through delicately evocative poems.

BOOKS ABOUT MENG HAO-JAN

Frankel, Hans, trans. *Biographies of Meng Hao-jan*. 1952. Univ. of California Pr. 1961
    o.p.
Kroll, Paul W. *Meng Hao Jan. Twayne's World Authors Ser.* G. K. Hall 1981 lib. bdg.
    $16.95

OU-YANG HSIU. 1007–1072

A great scholar, essayist, and conservative statesman who advocated an-
cient-style prose and colloquialism in poetry.

BOOK ABOUT OU-YANG HSIU

Liu, James T. *Ou-yang Hsiu: An Eleventh-century Neo-Confucianist*. Stanford Univ.
    Pr. 1967 o.p. "A remarkable contribution to the intellectual and political history
    of the 11th century, sophisticated, well-written, balanced and stimulating" (*Jour-
    nal of Asian History*).

PA CHIN (BA JIN) (pseud. of Li Fei-kan). 1904–

Pa Chin, a novelist, short-story writer, and translator, spent the years
1927–1929 in France. His novels, for which he is best known, express two
major themes: an attack on the traditional patriarchal family, such as the
one into which he was born, and a defense of young revolutionaries fighting
for a better future for mankind. He has been criticized since 1949, most recently during the Cultural Revolution, but has now been "rehabilitated."

BOOK BY PA CHIN

Family. 1931. Trans. by Sidney Shapiro, Doubleday (Anchor) 1972 pap. $5.50. Chin's
    most popular novel, which forms a trilogy with two succeeding novels, *Spring*
    (1937) and *Autumn* (1940), altogether known as *Turbulent Currents*. An autobio-
    graphical account of painful generation gaps as China struggled to modernize in
    the early twentieth century.

BOOKS ABOUT PA CHIN

Lang, Olga. *Pa Chin and His Writings: Chinese Youth between Two Revolutions. East
    Asian Ser.* Harvard Univ Pr. 1967 o.p.
Mao, Nathan K. *Pa Chin. Twayne's World Authors Ser.* G. K. Hall 1978 $16.95

PO CHÜ-YI (also PO CHÜ-I). 772–846

Po Chü-yi was a literatus and official who wrote often in the straightforward style of folk songs (*yüeh-fu*) and felt an important role of poetry was social criticism. Because of his sympathy for ordinary people and his simplicity of style, his poetry was widely popular in China and was also the best-
known Chinese poetry in Japan.

BOOKS BY PO CHÜ-YI

Lament Everlasting. Trans. by Howard S. Levy, Oriental Bk. Store 1962 pap. $7.00
Translations from Po Chü-i's Collected Works. Trans. by Howard S. Levy, Oriental Bk.
    Store 4 vols. ea. $18.00–$42.00

BOOK ABOUT PO CHÜ-YI

Waley, Arthur. *The Life and Times of Po Chü-i.* Allen & Unwin 1949 o.p.

ROU SHI. 1901–1931

A committed political writer of short fiction, Rou Shi was killed in 1931 for his political activities.

BOOK BY ROU SHI

Threshold of Spring. China Bks. 1981 pap. $2.95

SHIH NAI-AN (SHI NAI'AN). fl. before 1400

A Chinese writer who is traditionally assumed to be the author of the romance *Shui-hu chuan,* he is also one of the greatest writers of Chinese popular literature. Nearly all that is known of his life is that he lived at the turn of the Yuan-Ming periods, in or near Hangchow.

BOOKS BY SHI NAI-AN

All Men Are Brothers. Trans. by Pearl S. Buck, Crowell repr. of 1933 ed. 1968 vol. 1 $10.00

Outlaws of the Marsh. Trans. by Luo Guanzhong and Sidney Shapiro, Indiana Univ. Pr. 2 vols. 1981 $37.50. "What Mr. Shapiro has done . . . is to make a readable novel as readable in English as it has been, for hundreds of years, in Chinese" (*Wall Street Journal*).

Water Margin. China Bks. 1963 $15.95

BOOK ABOUT SHIH NAI-AN

Irwin, Richard G. *Evolution of a Chinese Novel: Shui Hu Chuan. Harvard-Yenching Institute Studies* Harvard Univ. Pr. 1953 pap. $6.50

SU TUNG-P'O (also SU SHIH). 1037–1101

A towering figure, influential in politics, literature, and art theory, Su Tung-p'o was exiled 12 times for bold criticism of political policy. He was both philosophical and deeply concerned with the welfare of the common people. Su is remembered for his spontaneity in poetry, painting, and calligraphy; his wit and self-irony; and his all-around creative genius.

BOOKS BY SU TUNG-P'O

The Prose Poetry of Su Tung-p'o. Trans. by Cyril Le Gros Clark, Paragon repr. of 1935 ed. 1964 o.p.

Su Tung-p'o: Selections from a Sung Dynasty Poet. Trans. by Burton Watson, Columbia Univ. Pr. 1965 $18.00 pap. $11.00

BOOK ABOUT SU TUNG-P'O

Lin Yutang. *The Gay Genius: The Life and Times of Su Tungpo.* Greenwood repr. of 1948 ed. lib. bdg. $24.75

T'ANG HSIEN-TZU (TANG XIAN-ZU). 1550–1617

A contemporary of Shakespeare, T'ang Hsien-tzu was a minor official who wrote brilliant dramas in the long *ch'uan-ch'i* form. His masterpiece, *The Peony Pavilion*, combines social criticism with a dreamlike search for ideals in love and personal freedom.

BOOK BY T'ANG HSIEN-TZU

The Peony Pavilion (Mudan Ting). Trans. by Cyril Birch, *Chinese Lit. in Translation Ser.* Indiana Univ. Pr. 1980 $25.00. "A translation which captures the scope and spirit of . . . one of China's greatest achievements of dramatic and literary art" (*World Lit. Today*).

T'AO CH'IEN (also T'AO YÜAN-MING). 365–427

One of China's most beloved nature poets, T'ao Ch'ien resigned from his official position and claimed to abandon all worldly ambitions to return to the fields and gardens that he celebrated in his unadorned nature poetry, which was for centuries admired and imitated for its spontaneity and sincerity.

BOOK BY T'AO CH'IEN

The Poetry of T'ao Ch'ien. Ed. by James R. Hightower, Oxford $24.95

BOOK ABOUT T'AO CH'IEN

Davis, A. R. *T'ao Yüan-ming: His Works and Their Meaning.* Cambridge Univ. Pr. 2 vols. 1984 $125.00

TING LING (DING LING). 1904–1986

China's best-known twentieth-century woman writer, Ting Ling early joined the Chinese Communist party and consistently struggled against women's oppression, though she was for many years in exile for her bold statement of these views. Her short stories, such as *The Diary of Miss Sophia*, appear in many anthologies.

BOOK ABOUT TING LING

Feuerwerker, Yi-tse Mei. *Ding Ling's Fiction. East Asian Ser.* Harvard Univ. Pr. text ed. 1982 $20.00

TS'AO CHIH. 192–232

The third son of a notorious warlord, Ts'ao Chih was disappointed that his elder brother gained the throne of the state of Wei at the fall of the Han dynasty. He wrote poetry of loss and lament, and is best known for establishing a new level of poetic self-expression.

BOOK BY TS'AO CHIH

Worlds of Dust and Jade. Ed. and trans. by George W. Kent, Philosophical Lib. 1969 $3.95

TS'AO HSÜEH-CH'IN (CAO XUEQIN) (also TS'AO CHAN [CAO ZHAN]). 1715–1763

Born into a wealthy aristocratic clan that for three generations controlled China's textile monopoly in Nanking, Ts'ao Hsüeh-ch'in grew up in a large, extended family. When he was 13, in 1728, the Yung-cheng emperor, threatened by aristocratic strength, confiscated the family property and the family moved to Peking and spent the rest of their lives in poverty. Ts'ao Hsüeh-ch'in, with editorial assistance from his relatives, composed the brilliant long novel, known as *The Dream of the Red Chamber* (1792) and also as *The Story of the Stone*, which is both a nostalgic re-creation of that golden world of his childhood and a Buddhist and Taoist warning that worldly achievements and material possessions are vain and unenduring. The last 40 chapters of the 120-chapter novel were written or edited by a second author, Kao O (Gao E or Kao Ngo), who more or less followed Ts'ao Hsüeh-ch'in's original intentions.

BOOKS BY TS'AO HSÜEH-CH'IN

The Dream of the Red Chamber. Intro. by Franz Kuhn, Greenwood repr. of 1958 ed. 1975 lib. bdg. $37.50

The Story of the Stone (The Dream of the Red Chamber). Trans. by David Hawkes, *Chinese Lit. in Translation Ser.* Indiana Univ. Pr. 4 vols. ea. $25.00 set $92.00. A superb complete translation into idiomatic English notable for its virtuosity in capturing the distinctions of tone and nuance, in both prose and verse sections. "One of the great translations of this century. No other single book tells us so much about Chinese civilization" (*Bulletin of the School of Oriental and African Studies*).

BOOKS ABOUT TS'AO HSÜEH-CH'IN

Knoerle, Jeanne. *The Dream of the Red Chamber: A Critical Study. East Asian Ser.* Indiana Univ. Pr. 1973 o.p.

Miller, Lucien. *Masks of Fiction in Dream of the Red Chamber: Myth, Mimesis, and Persona.* Univ. of Arizona Pr. 1975 $7.95

Plaks, Andrew H. *Archetype and Allegory in The Dream of the Red Chamber.* Princeton Univ. Pr. 1975 $31.00

TS'AO YÜ (CAO YU) (pseud. of Wan Chia-bao). 1910–

Ts'ao Yü is China's greatest living playwright, known for his satirical plays of social criticism. He visited the United States after the Cultural Revolution, and his play *Peking Man* was produced in New York City.

BOOKS BY TS'AO YÜ

Sunrise: A Play in Four Acts. 1935. Trans. by A. C. Barnes, Cheng & Tsui 1978 $4.95

Thunderstorm. Trans. by Liang Tso and A. C. Barnes, Cheng & Tsui 3d ed. 1978 $4.95; China Bks. 1978 $6.95

BOOK ABOUT TS'AO YÜ

Hu, John Y. *Ts'ao Yü. Twayne's World Authors Ser.* G. K. Hall lib. bdg. $15.95

TU FU. 719–770

Regarded as China's greatest poet, Tu Fu is outstanding for his passion, his social concern, and his achievements as a poetic craftsman. Though he never passed official examinations and held only minor posts, Tu Fu wrote prolifically of his patriotic concern for the nation's welfare and his own search for the most suitable way to be true to himself and to serve society. His poetry is complex, polished, and emotionally powerful.

BOOKS BY TU FU

Tu Fu's Gedichte. Trans. by Erwin Von Zach, ed. by James R. Hightower, *Harvard-Yenching Institute Studies* Harvard Univ. Pr. 2 vols. 1952 pap. $20.00

Tu Fu: China's Greatest Poet. Trans. by William Hung, Russell repr. of 1952 ed. 1969 $15.00. Prose translations of 374 poems, with background on the poet's life and times.

A Little Primer of Tu Fu. Trans. with interpretations by David Hawkes, Oxford 1967 $10.25

BOOK ABOUT TU FU

Davis, A. R. *Tu Fu.* Twayne 1971 o.p.

WANG SHIH-CHENG. 1526–1590

Many novels were written during the Ming dynasty (1368–1644), but the names of their authors have rarely been preserved. *The Golden Lotus* has been attributed to Wang Shih-cheng, although some scholars believe it was written later, in the closing years of the Ming dynasty. Pearl Buck called it "the greatest novel of physical love which China has produced." The *Saturday Review* said, "This extraordinary book . . . plunges the reader into the midst of Chinese society as it existed during the first quarter of the twelfth century . . . when official corruption was rampant and political chaos imminent. It records the amorous exploits and grisly end of a wealthy merchant . . . and the criminal exploits and ghastly death of Golden Lotus, the merchant's Fifth Lady. . . . It records much besides, with a wealth of detail that makes the pages bustle with life; much that will seem strange to today's readers, and much that will seem strangely familiar to them." *Flower Shadows Behind the Curtain* (o.p.) is considered by some to be the sequel, written perhaps 20 years later either by the same author or by one whose command of his medium equals that of the original novelist. Some of the same characters appear, some appear in reincarnations.

BOOK BY WANG SHIH-CHENG

The Golden Lotus: A Translation of the Chinese Novel, Chin P'ing Mei. Trans. by Clement Egerton, Routledge & Kegan 4 vols. 1972 $80.00

WANG SHIH-FU. fl. 13th century

The life story of this famous Chinese playwright, a native of Peking, is unknown. It is thought that he wrote 14 plays, of which only three have survived.

BOOK BY WANG SHIH-FU

The Romance of the Western Chamber. Trans. by T. C. Lai and E. Gamarekian, *Writing in Asia Ser.* Heinemann text ed. 1979 $10.95 pap. $3.25. This is the most famous Chinese play of all times, and has entered the repertoire of Western theaters. Its theme of the tragic lovers has been repeated in numerous Chinese ballads and plays from the fourteenth century to the present.

WANG WEI. 701–761

Poet, painter, musician, and successful statesman, Wang Wei was a leading literatus of the brilliant Golden Age of the T'ang period. He is best known for the simple yet evocative imagery in his court poetry and nature poetry.

BOOKS BY WANG WEI

Hiding the Universe. Trans. by Wai Lim Yip, Small Pr. Dist. 1972 $12.50 pap. $4.95
Poems of Wang Wei. Trans. by G. W. Robinson, *Penguin Class. Ser.* 1974 pap. $4.95
The Poetry of Wang Wei: New Translations and Commentary. Trans. by Pauline Yu, *Chinese Lit. in Translation Ser.* Indiana Univ. Pr. 1980 $27.50 pap. $9.95

BOOKS ABOUT WANG WEI

Wagner, Marsha L. *Wang Wei. Twayne's World Authors Ser.* G. K. Hall 1981 lib. bdg. $16.95
Walmsley, Lewis C., and Dorothy W. Walmsley. *Wang Wei: The Painter Poet.* Tuttle $6.60

WEI CHUANG. 836–910

An early writer of erotic *tz'u* poetry, Wei Chuang also composed a dramatic political narrative poem entitled *The Lament of the Lady of Ch'in* to protest the Huang Ch'ao rebellion of 881.

BOOK BY WEI CHUANG

The Song-Poetry of Wei Chuang. Trans. and intro. by John Timothy Wixted, Arizona State Univ., Ctr. for Asian Studies text ed. 1979 pap. $6.00

WU CH'ENG-EN. 1500–1582

A novelist and poet from Kiangsu province, Wu spent part of his life as district governor and master of ceremonies in the regent's palace in Nanking before returning to his home and his writing.

BOOK BY WU CH'ENG-EN

The Journey to the West. Trans. by Anthony C. Yu, Univ. of Chicago Pr. 4 vols. 1977–84 pap. ea. $12.50. A novel full of wit and allegory, *Journey to the West* is based on the historical 16-year pilgrimage of the Chinese Buddhist monk Hsuan-tsang to India and his return. The magical monkey is one of the most memorable characters. This is the most faithful and felicitous translation.

BOOK ABOUT WU CH'ENG-EN

Dudbridge, Glen. *The Hsi-yu chi: A Study of Antecedents to the Sixteenth-century Chinese Novel.* Cambridge Univ. Pr. 1970 $25.00

YANG WAN-LI. 1124–1206

One of the four Masters of Southern Sung Poetry, Yang Wan-li is recognized for his colloquial style.

BOOK BY YANG WAN-LI

Heaven My Blanket, Earth My Pillow. Trans. by Jonathan Chaves, Weatherhill 1975 $7.95 pap. $4.95

BOOK ABOUT YANG WAN-LI

Schmidt, J. D. *Yang Wan-li.* G. K. Hall 1976 o.p.

CHAPTER 24

Japanese Literature

Jacqueline Mueller

> Japanese literature has about as long a history as English literature, and
> contains works in as wide a variety of genres as may be found in any coun-
> try. It includes some of the world's longest novels and shortest poems, plays
> which are miracles of muted suggestion and others filled with the most ex-
> travagant bombast.
>
> —DONALD KEENE, *Anthology of Japanese Literature*

When Donald Keene wrote the above statement in 1955, he also expressed
the hope that Japanese literature would receive more recognition and understanding from the reading public. In the 30 years since, the amount of literature available in English translation has increased dramatically and is
readily accessible, proof of its inherent interest and literary merit.

A brief survey of major genres will reveal the diversity of this literature.
In poetry there are the 31-syllable poem, called the *waka* in classical times
and the *tanka* in modern form; the 17-syllable poem, the *haiku*; and *renga*,
or linked verse. There is also free verse. In drama, in addition to modern
works, there are the spectacular *kabuki*; the evocative and minimalist medieval drama, *nō* or *noh*, and its comic complement, *kyōgen*; and the puppet
theater, termed *bunraku* or *jōruri*. In prose Japan has a rich premodern tradition of romances (*monogatari*), fables (*setsuwa*), diaries (*nikki*), and a great
body of modern novels and short stories.

It is worth remembering that just as Japanese literature has been influenced by Western literature in the modern period, so has Western literature
been influenced by Japanese works. The Irish poet and dramatist WILLIAM
BUTLER YEATS (see Vol. 1) was strongly attracted by the sense of myth embodied in *noh* plays and their symbolism and actually wrote some plays in
imitation of them. The imagism of the American poet EZRA POUND (see Vol.
1) was influenced in part by haiku, in which the image is central. One
should note, too, that in America today, there are groups of serious English-
language haiku poets who work at their art.

Many who are curious about Japanese literature may find it rewarding to
read something about Japanese culture. Two of the many works available
are H. Paul Varley's *Japanese Culture* and Edwin O. Reischauer's *Japan: The
Story of a Nation.*

Lastly, a suggestion to the reader of modern Japanese literature who is interested in a particular author but can find little by him or her in the library or bookstore. Many authors have been fond of the short story, and these works, when translated, either go into anthologies or are separately published in periodicals. In either case, one may consult Yukio Fujino, ed., *Modern Japanese Literature in Translation: A Bibliography*. The work is unannotated, and the translations are not limited to those in Western languages, but the coverage is good.

Note: The editors have followed the Japanese practice of giving a person's surname first. In addition, the reader should be aware that the Japanese also often replace given names with pen names, and frequently refer to an author by a pen name rather than a surname. This chapter uses the most commonly accepted English versions of an author's name, but the reader is advised that other variations may exist elsewhere in print.

HISTORY AND CRITICISM

General and Prose

Keene, Donald. *Dawn to the West: Japanese Literature in the Modern Era*. Holt 2 vols. 1984 vol. 1 $60.00 vol. 2 $40.00. Detailed and authoritative study of modern Japanese literature. Comprehensive, except that writers whose careers are still in progress have been omitted. The first volume deals with fiction and the second with poetry, drama, and criticism.

————. *Japanese Literature: An Introduction for Western Readers*. Grove (Evergreen Bks.) 1955 pap. $2.25. A brief but informative work. Basic reading for the beginner.

————. *World within Walls: Japanese Literature of the Pre-Modern Era 1600–1867*. Grove (Evergreen Bks.) 1979 pap. $9.50; Holt 1976 $22.95. Eminently readable, either as a whole or on the basis of a single chapter, which can be read as a complete study of a given genre or author.

Kimball, Arthur G. *Crisis in Identity and Contemporary Japanese Novels*. Tuttle 1972 $6.00. Short essays on works, almost all available in translation, by significant postwar writers. Included is "Syllabus: A Suggested Reading Course."

Konishi, Ji'ichi. *A History of Japanese Literature: The Archaic and Ancient Ages*. Trans. by Aileen Gatten, Princeton Univ. Pr. 1984 vol. 1 $50.00 pap. $19.50. A complex work—valuable not only to the student of early Japanese literature but to the comparativist as well for its emphasis on the interrelation among Chinese, Korean, and Japanese literatures.

Marks, Alfred H., and Barry D. Bort. *Guide to Japanese Prose. Asian Lit. Bibliography Ser.* G. K. Hall 2d ed. 1984 lib. bdg. $29.95. Somewhat dated as a bibliography, but useful for a brief history and plot summaries.

Miyoshi, Masao. *Accomplices of Silence: The Modern Japanese Novel*. Univ. of California Pr. 1975 $26.50. A penetrating study, by a scholar of both Western and Japanese literature, of the way in which fundamental differences in language and the concept of the individual have given the modern Japanese novel distinctive features. Concentrates on works available in good translations.

Petersen, Gwen Boardman. *The Moon in the Water: Understanding Tanizaki, Kawabata and Mishima*. Univ. of Hawaii Pr. 1979 $15.95. A study of three widely translated authors. Useful analysis but sometimes idiosyncratic in dealing with hidden images and meanings. For the experienced reader.

Rimer, J. Thomas. *Modern Japanese Fiction and Its Traditions: An Introduction.* Princeton Univ. Pr. 1978 $30.00. A thought-provoking work that invites readers to understand works of both traditional and modern literature in terms of Japanese literary values.

Ueda, Makoto. *Literary and Art Theories in Japan.* Pr. of Western Reserve Univ. 1967 o.p. A valuable investigation of premodern aesthetics and poetics. The greater part of the work deals with literature. Citations of primary sources with interpretations. Appended are short biographies of the subjects of the study.

———. *Modern Japanese Writers and the Nature of Literature.* Stanford Univ. Pr. 1976 $22.50. The work and literary thought of eight authors widely available in translation.

Drama

Bowers, Faubion. *Japanese Theatre.* Fwd. by Joshua Logan, Greenwood repr. of 1952 ed. 1976 lib. bdg. $24.75; Tuttle 1974 pap. $6.95. A classic work. Includes plot summaries and excerpts from plays. At the end are translations of three kabuki plays. Genres other than kabuki are also discussed.

Ernst, Earle. *The Kabuki Theatre.* Univ. of Hawaii Pr. repr. of 1956 ed. text ed. 1974 pap. $5.95. With the nonspecialist in mind, the author often uses Western drama as a point of reference. A standard work.

Fenollosa, Ernest F., and Ezra Pound. *The Classic Noh Theatre of Japan.* Greenwood repr. of 1959 ed. 1977 lib. bdg. $45.00. An early study with translations, distinguished by the stature of the authors.

Kincaid, Zoe. *Kabuki: The Popular Stage of Japan.* Ayer repr. of 1925 ed. $25.00. An evocative and entertaining account of the history and performing tradition of kabuki by a devoted amateur who spent 12 years in Japan attending performances and discussing the genre with scholars and actors.

Leiter, Samuel L. *Kabuki Encyclopedia: An English Language Adaptation of Kabuki Jiten.* Greenwood 1979 lib. bdg. $45.00. Valuable for understanding terminology and for numerous plot summaries. Helpful cross-references and index. Especially useful is the "Subject Guide to Main Entries," in which, for instance, the reader can look up "Props" and find relevant entries without any knowledge of kabuki or Japanese.

Pronko, Leonard C. *Guide to Japanese Drama.* Asian Lit. Bibliography Ser. G. K. Hall 2d ed. 1984 lib. bdg. $29.95. Supplies a good short history as well as bibliographies and plot summaries.

Scott, A. C. *Puppet Theatre of Japan.* Tuttle 1973 pap. $5.50. A brief but useful introduction to the genre. Includes summaries of ten popular plays and a glossary of terms.

Verse

Brower, Robert H., and Earl Miner. *Japanese Court Poetry.* Stanford Univ. Pr. 1961 $35.00. The definitive work on the subject, distinguished by excellent translations and analyses as well as a detailed history. Helpful glossary of terms and index.

Miner, Earl. *An Introduction to Japanese Court Poetry.* Stanford Univ. Pr. 1968 $12.50 pap. $5.95. The basic book on Japanese verse from the seventh century to 1500.

Valuable for its description of the values of the society that produced the verse and its forms and conventions. Also discusses major poetic themes.

————. *Japanese Linked Poetry: An Account with Translations of Renga and Haikai Sequences.* Princeton Univ. Pr. 1978 $36.00 pap. $12.50. Divided equally between a study of the development and conventions of *renga* and haikai and translations of several important poetic sequences. As a study of the poetic forms that came to displace court poetry, it complements Brower and Miner's *Japanese Court Poetry.*

Rimer, J. Thomas, and Robert E. Morrell. *Guide to Japanese Poetry. Asian Lit. Bibliography Ser.* G. K. Hall 2d ed. 1984 lib. bdg. $29.95. A well-organized introduction to the various forms of Japanese verse.

Ueda, Makoto. *Modern Japanese Poets and the Nature of Literature.* Stanford Univ. Pr. 1983 $28.50. A study of eight major poets, all of whom have had some of their work translated into English. In addition to an analysis of their poetry and literary thought, Ueda quotes these poets' writings about poetry. Includes a bibliography of translations of their poetry and articles about them.

ANTHOLOGIES

General and Prose

Hibbett, Howard. *Contemporary Japanese Literature: An Anthology of Fiction, Film and Other Writing since 1945.* Knopf 1977 pap. $12.95. This is primarily an anthology of prose, but also includes drama, poetry, and the film scripts for two well-known movies. A well-rounded selection that gives introductions for each of the works included.

Keene, Donald, ed. *Anthology of Japanese Literature: Earliest Era to Mid-Nineteenth Century.* Grove (Evergreen Bks.) 1955 pap. $7.95. Still the basic anthology of premodern Japanese literature, with helpful essays and good translations. Genres other than prose are also included.

————. *Modern Japanese Literature: An Anthology.* Grove (Evergreen Bks.) 1956 pap. $12.50. A continuation and companion volume to Keene's *Anthology of Japanese Literature.* Covers various genres from 1871 to 1949.

Kobayashi, Takiji. *The Cannery Boat and Other Japanese Short Stories.* AMS Pr. repr. of 1933 ed. $12.50; Greenwood repr. of 1933 ed. 1968 lib. bdg. $24.75. A major anthology of proletarian literature with many stories by Kobayashi, who was murdered by the police for his leftist activities. Neither the stories nor the anonymous translations are great literature, but they represent an important element of prewar writing.

Morris, Ivan, ed. *Modern Japanese Stories: An Anthology.* Tuttle 1977 pap. $8.50. Short stories from 1910 to 1954, each with its own introduction. Good general introduction.

Saeki, Shoichi, comp. *The Catch and Other War Stories (The Shadow of Sunrise: Selected Stories of Japan and the War).* 1966. Kodansha 1981 pap. $4.95. As explained in the introduction, "They are stories of human events that only occur during and as a result of that overwhelmingly human event called war. And though ultimately and universally human, they are at the same time intrinsically Japanese."

Tanaka, Yukiko, and Elizabeth Hanson, eds. *This Kind of Woman: Ten Stories by Japanese Women Writers, 1960–1976.* Putnam (Perigee) 1984 pap. $9.95; Stanford Univ. Pr. 1982 $18.75. The general introduction provides a brief history of literature by women. Each translation is preceded by an article about the author and her work.

Drama

Brandon, James R. *Kabuki: Five Classic Plays*. Harvard Univ. Pr. 1975 $27.50. Excellent translations that capture the vigor and poetic yet colloquial force of this genre. The introduction, stage directions, and photographs add to the appreciation of the plays. Glossary of terms is appended.

Keene, Donald, ed. *Twenty Plays of the Nō Theatre*. Columbia Univ. Pr. 1970 $30.00 pap. $13.50. The major "modern" anthology of *nō* plays in that it draws on current scholarship. The translations, by various contributors, are of high literary quality, unburdened by extensive annotations. Helpful introduction, "The Conventions of the Nō Drama," by the editor.

Takaya, Ted T., trans. *Modern Japanese Drama: An Anthology*. Columbia Univ. Pr. 1980 $28.00 pap. $14.00. The introduction supplies a helpful outline of the development of modern Japanese drama. Footnotes are selectively added to enhance the reader's understanding of Japanese terms and literary or historical allusions.

Waley, Arthur. *The Nō Plays of Japan*. Grove (Evergreen Bks.) 1957 pap. $7.95; Tuttle 1976 pap. $7.25. Graceful translations by a major translator of Japanese literature.

Verse

Henderson, Harold G., trans. *An Introduction to Haiku: An Anthology of Poems and Poets from Bashō to Shiki*. Anchor Literary Lib. Doubleday 1958 pap. $4.95. The translator's aim is to present a poet's best poems and others that will give the reader a sense of the poet's art. Interspersed with commentary.

Levy, Howard S., trans. *Japan's Best-Loved Poetry Classic: Hyakunin Isshu*. Oriental Bk. Store 3d ed. rev. 1976 vol. 1 $15.00 pap. $8.00. The most widely known collection of poetry in Japan. It is memorized by many as it forms part of a game based on matching the first and second halves of the poems. An anthology of 100 poems, each by a different classical poet.

Rexroth, Kenneth, and Ikuko Atsumi, trans. *Women Poets of Japan (The Burning Heart: Women Poets of Japan)*. New Directions 1982 pap. $5.95. Verse in various forms from the seventh century to the present. At the end are brief biographies of the poets and a concise but helpful survey of poetry by women in Japan. Both of the translators are poets in their own right.

Sato, Hiroaki, and Burton Watson, trans. and eds. *From the Country of Eight Islands*. Intro. by J. Thomas Rimer, Doubleday (Anchor) 1981 pap. $11.95; Univ. of Washington Pr. 1981 $22.50. A remarkably complete and diversified anthology of poetry from antiquity to the present by two distinguished translators. Appended are a glossary of terms, brief biographies of major poets, and an index of poets.

ANONYMOUSLY AND COLLECTIVELY COMPOSED CLASSICS

Chūshingura: A Puppet Play by Takeda Izumo, Miyoshi Shōraku and Namiki Senryū. Trans. by Donald Keene, Columbia Univ. Pr. 1971 $25.00 pap. $10.00. First performed in 1748, this is probably the most popular of Japanese plays. It is a tale of vendetta, based on an actual event.

Kitagawa, Hiroshi, and Bruce T. Tsuchida, trans. *The Tale of the Heike: Heike Monogatari.* Fwd. by Edward G. Seidensticker, Columbia Univ. Pr. 2 vols. 1975 $52.50 pap. $9.95. The greatest of the medieval war tales, it depicts the late twelfth-century conflict between the Minamoto and Taira clans. Along with battles there are touching personal stories and throughout the Buddhist notion of the impermanence of things and the notion that the proud (the Taira) are bound to fall. Originally transmitted orally, this tale probably acquired written form in the late fourteenth century.

Kojiki. Trans. by Donald L. Philippi, Columbia Univ. Pr. 1977 $24.00. Completed in 712, Japan's first history and a major source of its mythology. Helpful notes and appendixes elucidate the text.

Kokinshū: A Collection of Poems Ancient and Modern. Trans. by Laurel R. Rodd and Mary C. Henkinius, Princeton Univ. Pr. 1984 $40.00. The first imperially commissioned anthology of court poetry in the *waka* form and the model for many to follow, completed in 905. Major topics are love and the seasons. The vernacular preface by Ki Tsurayuki contains the first analysis of the poetics of verse in Japanese.

The Manyōshū: The Nippon Gakujutsu Shinkōkai Translation of One Thousand Poems. Fwd. by Donald Keene, Columbia Univ. Pr. 1969 pap. $14.50. Translation of 1,000 of the more than 4,000 poems in the first extant anthology of Japanese verse traditionally dated at 759. The foreword notes that the introduction and some of the attributions of authorship are flawed by prewar biases. The same may be said of some of the biographical notes. This is, however, still the standard translation and is generally sound in its scholarship. Important not only for the quality of the poetry but for the variety of genres and authors.

McCullough, Helen C., ed. and trans. *Yoshitsune: A Fifteenth-Century Japanese Chronicle (Gikeiki).* Stanford Univ. Pr. 1966 $22.50. Set in the same world as *The Tale of the Heike*, this fifteenth-century work deals with the adventures and tragedy of Minamoto no Yoshitsune. A good story, well translated, and like *Heike*, a major source of material for later works.

A Tale of Flowering Fortunes: Annals of Japanese Aristocratic Life in the Heian Period. Trans. by William H. McCullough and Helen C. McCullough, Stanford Univ. Pr. 2 vols. 1980 $62.50. A portrait of an age, rich in detail. The notes and appendixes form a fine introduction to the institutions and culture of the time.

Tales of Ise: Lyrical Episodes from Tenth-Century Japan (Ise Monogatari). Trans. by Helen C. McCullough, Stanford Univ. Pr. 1968 $20.00. The introduction sets this poem-tale in the context of the court culture of its time. The subject is the loves of the famous ninth-century poet Ariwara no Narihira. Inherently attractive, this work was a major source of material for later writers.

Tales of Times Now Past: Sixty-Two Stories from a Medieval Japanese Collection (Konjaku Monogatari). Trans. by Marian Ury, Univ. of California Pr. 1979 $11.95. Selections from a collection of fables about India, China, and Japan. The themes may be either Buddhist or secular, but the stories are entertaining. An important example of the *setsuwa* (fable) genre.

ABE KŌBŌ (pseud. of Abe Kimifusa). 1924–

A major figure in the contemporary literary scene, Abe is known both as a novelist and a playwright. His themes are fairly constant—deracination, alienation, and the loss of personal identity in oppressive urban life. He brings these themes to literary life through a powerful imagination and dark humor.

BOOKS BY ABE

The Woman in the Dunes. Trans. by E. Dale Saunders, Random (Vintage) 1972 pap. $4.95

The Man Who Turned into a Stick: Three Related Plays. Trans. by Donald Keene, Columbia Univ. Pr. 1975 $9.00. The drama of alienation and deracination.

The Box Man. Trans. by E. Dale Saunders, Putnam (Perigee) 1981 pap. $4.95

Inter Ice Age Four. Trans. by E. Dale Saunders, Putnam (Perigee) 1981 pap. $4.95. "The future gives a verdict of guilty to this usual continuity of daily life. I consider the problem an especially important theme in these critical times. Thus I decided to grasp the image of a future that intrudes on the present, a future that sits in judgement" (Author's Postscript). The mechanism for this judgment is a computer.

AKUTAGAWA RYŪNOSUKE. 1892–1927

Akutagawa is best known as a writer of short stories and for his vivid imagination and narrative skills. For material for many of his works he drew on medieval fables. He rejected the vogue for confessional literature until the last years of his life, when his mental stability declined. His mother had gone insane shortly before his birth, and this fact had always haunted him. The works written shortly before his suicide suggest that life no longer made any sense to him.

BOOKS BY AKUTAGAWA

Exotic Japanese Stories. Trans. by Takashi Kojima and John McVittie, ed. by John McVittie and Arthur Pell, Liveright 1964 $6.95 1972 pap. $4.95. A generous anthology of 17 short stories. Each one has an introductory note. The supplementary notes at the end of the work are also helpful.

"Rashōmon" and Other Stories. Trans. by Takashi Kojima, intro. by Howard Hibbett, Liveright 1970 pap. $3.95. A collection of six stories including "In a Grove," on which the famous Kurosawa movie *Rashōmon* is primarily based.

Kappa: A Satire. Trans. by Geoffrey Bowmas, Tuttle 1971 pap. $5.25. A tale of mythical creatures called Kappas who live in a world that on the surface is the opposite of the human world. This is a dark satire, reflecting many of the author's personal fears and the stresses of life in prewar Japan.

BOOK ABOUT AKUTAGAWA

Yu, Beongcheon. *Akutagawa: An Introduction.* Wayne State Univ. Pr. 1972 $9.95. A study of the life, work, and thought of Akutagawa. Includes a chronology, index, and bibliography of stories available in English translation.

ARIYOSHI SAWAKO. 1931–

Ariyoshi Sawako is a novelist concerned with social issues, the position of women among them, although some of her earlier works were less topical. Her recent novels have been bestsellers in Japan.

BOOKS BY ARIYOSHI

The Doctor's Wife. Trans. by Wakako Hironaka and Ann Siller Konstant, Kodansha 1978 pap. $4.25. Mother and wife in conflict for possession of Hanaoka Seishū, a historical figure who discovered anesthesia at the beginning of the nineteenth century.

The Twilight Years. Trans. by Mildred Tahara, Kodansha 1984 $14.95. A story of a woman who selflessly cares for her ailing and senile father-in-law while dealing with her other family responsibilities. A moving work.

BASHŌ (pseud. of Matsuo Munefusa; also Matsuo Bashō). 1644–1694

The greatest of Japan's haiku poets and the greatest poet of his age, Bashō raised this genre from a mediocre entertainment to serious verse and contributed greatly to its poetics. He traveled widely and his journeys are recorded in his lyrical poetic diaries. He had numerous disciples, and haiku has remained a vigorous form of poetry to the present.

BOOKS BY BASHŌ

A Haiku Journey: Bashō's "The Narrow Road to the Far North" and Selected Haiku. Trans. by Dorothy Britton, Kodansha 1982 $23.50 pap. $4.25. Primarily a photographic essay intended to illustrate Bashō's masterpiece, *Oku no Hosomichi*, although the accompanying translation reads well.

The Monkey's Straw Raincoat and Other Poetry of the Bashō School. Trans. by Earl Miner and Odagiri Hiroko, Princeton Univ. Pr. 1981 $36.00. The greater part of this work is a translation of Bashō's *Sarumino*, which, like *Oku no Hosomichi*, is a poetic travel diary. The introduction presents this genre to the reader and explains how to read it. Annotations are helpful but unobtrusive. Included are an index of critical terms and a biographical index of poets represented in this work.

The Narrow Road to the Deep North and Other Travel Sketches. Trans. by Nobuyuki Yuasa, *Penguin Class. Ser.* 1974 pap. $3.95. In addition to *Oku no Hosomichi*, this collection includes translations of *Nozarashi Kikō (The Records of a Weather-Exposed Skeleton)*, *Kashima Mōde (A Visit to the Kashima Shrine)*, *Oi no Kobumi (The Records of a Travel-worn Satchel)*, and *Sarashina Kikō (A Visit to Sarashina Village)*. Bashō's travel diaries in serviceable translations. Some annotations.

BOOK ABOUT BASHŌ

Ueda, Makoto. *Matsuo Bashō.* Kodansha 1983 pap. $4.95. A thorough but readable study of the life and work of Bashō. The bibliography includes a list of works in English translation. Also includes a chronology of Bashō's life and a map showing the various journeys he made.

CHIKAMATSU MONZAEMON. 1653–1724

Widely regarded as the greatest dramatist of the Edo period, Chikamatsu wrote for both the kabuki stage and the puppet theater. He gradually abandoned the former because the actors often took liberties with his lines. His plays fall into two major groups, historical and domestic dramas. A dominant theme of the latter, which were sometimes based on contemporary events, is the conflict between duty (*giri*) and human feelings (*ninjō*). Some of his finest plays are domestic works, often consisting of the lyrical depiction of ill-fated loves. Chikamatsu's language is rich and reflects his knowledge of the classics, both Japanese and Chinese, and Buddhism. His plays are still widely read and performed.

BOOK BY CHIKAMATSU

Major Plays of Chikamatsu. Trans. by Donald Keene, Columbia Univ. Pr. 1961 $30.00. Works by the finest writer for the puppet theater in an excellent translation. The introduction, which deals specifically with Chikamatsu, also contains information about the puppet theater in general.

DAZAI OSAMU (pseud. of Tsushima Shūji). 1909–1948

Dazai was born into a wealthy family and spent his youth as a dilettante and something of a rake. Around 1933 he began to think seriously about writing, but his life was complicated by drug addiction, a string of affairs, and two attempts at suicide. The end of the war brought a certain change in Dazai, and he produced his two finest works, listed below, even though his own life was coming to an end because of alcoholism and tuberculosis. He did not wait for nature to take its course and committed suicide with a mistress. His was a tortured existence, but his talent and sense of style are unmistakable.

BOOKS BY DAZAI

The Setting Sun. Trans. by Donald Keene, New Directions 1968 pap. $4.95
No Longer Human. Trans. by Donald Keene, New Directions 1973 pap. $5.95

ENCHI FUKIMO. 1905–

The daughter of a philologist and classicist, Enchi had a fine education in language and literature. Coming to maturity at a time of social and political turmoil, she supported the proletarian movement by writing topical plays, but later turned to the novel and short story. Her early output was hampered by illness, prewar repression, and the war itself. In her recent works she has been concerned with the psychology and sexuality of women.

BOOKS BY ENCHI

The Waiting Years. Trans. by John Bester, Kodansha 1971 $8.95 1980 pap. $5.95. A compelling portrait of a woman who is able to retain her integrity and power despite years of abuse and infidelity by her husband.
Masks. Trans. by Juliet Winters Carpenter, Knopf 1983 $11.95; Random (Vintage) pap. $5.95

ENDŌ SHŪSAKU. 1923–

Endō's writing, which has won him many literary prizes, is distinguished by his concern with moral and religious themes. The author himself is Roman Catholic and has often been linked to Graham Greene.

BOOKS BY ENDŌ

The Sea and Poison: A Novel. Trans. with an intro. by Michael Gallagher, Taplinger 1980 $8.95

Silence. Trans. by William Johnston, Taplinger 1980 pap. $5.95
The Samurai. Trans. by Van C. Gessel, Harper 1982 $12.45; Random (Vintage) 1984
      pap. $7.95

FUTABATEI SHIMEI (HASEGAWA TATSUNOSUKE). 1864–1909

As a young man, Futabatei Shimei studied Russian literature and later became a prolific translator and essayist. He also worked on finding an appropriate language for literature, which had long been written in a classical
style divorced from spoken Japanese.

BOOK BY FUTABATEI

Japan's First Modern Novel: "Ukigumo" of Futabatei Shimei. Trans. and ed. by Mar-
      leigh Grayer Ryan, Greenwood repr. 1983 $39.75. As an early work of modern fic-
      tion, it is notable for its realism and the development of three-dimensional char-
      acters.

HIGUCHI ICHIYŌ (HIGUCHI NATSUKO). 1872–1896

Ichiyō was the leading woman writer of the Meiji period and an inspiration to those who followed. Her family was never wealthy and was often in
great poverty. Her education, too, was limited, but her talent and determination compensated for this. She wrote numerous poems, but is best known
for her short stories and diary. A major theme is that people are denied happiness because of their circumstances in life, something that was true of
Ichiyō herself. Just when she had finally attained recognition of her talents,
she died of tuberculosis at age 24.

BOOK ABOUT ICHIYŌ

Danly, Robert L. *In the Shade of Spring Leaves: The Life and Writings of Higuchi
      Ichiyō, a Woman of Letters in Meiji Japan.* Yale Univ. Pr. 1981 $27.50 1983 pap.
      $10.95. A scholarly yet personal interpretation of Ichiyō's life that quotes heav-
      ily and effectively from her diary and the writings of those who knew her. Danly
      nevertheless steers clear of hagiography. His study, valuable of itself, is comple-
      mented by a translation of five of her stories. The bibliography includes a list of
      works that have been translated into Western languages.

IBUSE MASUJI. 1898–

The son of middle-class landowners, Ibuse grew up in the country, for
which he always retained a special feeling. While in college in Tokyo, the
center of literary life, he majored in French literature but also read the
works of Russian authors such as Chekhov and Tolstoy. His first works,
short stories, appeared at this time. Many are in the form of the I-novel but
are written from a relatively detached point of view. In the 1920s, he entered the proletarian literature movement but later turned to the writing of
historical novels and works intended to capture the flavor of various regions
of Japan. His style is spare and generally marked by dry, sometimes dark,
humor.

BOOK BY IBUSE

Black Rain: A Novel. Trans. by John Bester, Kodansha 1980 pap. $5.25. A novelization of the experiences of a real person, Shigematsu Shizume, who was in the vicinity of Hiroshima when the atom bomb was dropped. Rather than comment, the author observes events through Shigematsu, who is concerned that his niece will be unable to find a husband. She is outwardly healthy, but there is a rumor that she has radiation sickness. Despite the serious subject matter, Ibuse occasionally leavens it with touches of humor, as with accounts of bureaucratic incompetence, or observations of beauty, even in small things.

IHARA SAIKAKU (pseud. of Hirayama Togo; also Ibara Saikaku). 1642–1693

A prolific writer of haiku, Saikaku is better known now as a writer of fiction about the life of the townspeople in his native Osaka. His style is marked by detachment and wit. His major themes are the search for love and/or wealth, and the effect this has on the lives of people. Saikaku was a keen observer, and the overall tone of his works, although often picaresque, is satiric.

BOOKS BY SAIKAKU

Five Women Who Loved Love. Trans. by William T. De Bary, Tuttle 1955 pap. $5.95. The introduction and essay offer helpful studies of Saikaku's life and works.

The Life of an Amorous Man. Trans. by Hamada Kengi, Tuttle 1963 pap. $5.95. Notable as Saikaku's first major work and for its portrayal of the world of courtesans.

This Scheming World. Trans. by Masanori Takatsuka and David C. Stubbs, Tuttle 1965 pap. $4.25

The Life of an Amorous Woman and Other Writings. Ed. and trans. by Ivan Morris, New Directions 1969 pap. $8.95. A Saikaku reader, this book contains selections from *Five Women Who Chose Love, The Life of an Amorous Woman, The Eternal Storehouse of Japan,* and *Reckonings That Carry Men Through the World.* Useful introduction and appendixes about the sources of Saikaku's stories, money, and the hierarchy of courtesans. Notes to the stories and a topical index to those notes make this work a study of Saikaku's life and time.

Some Final Words of Advice. Trans. by Peter Nosco, Tuttle 1980 $12.00. The more pessimistic and detached side of Saikaku comes out in this posthumously published work.

IZUMI SHIKIBU. fl. c.1000

One of the most accomplished poets of her time, Izumi is known for the wild course of her love life. In addition to being twice married, she was in succession mistress to two princes who were brothers. The younger one, Astumichi, was her true love, and her diary is a fictionalized account of their affair. Little else is known of her life, but she left behind about 1,500 poems, which were often included in later anthologies.

BOOK BY IZUMI

The Izumi Shikibu Diary: A Romance of the Heian Court. Tr. by Edwin A. Cranston, Harvard Univ. Pr. 1969 $20.00. This work is also translated by Earl Miner in

Japanese Poetic Diaries. Both translations are good, with Cranston's the more scholarly in form.

KAWABATA YASUNARI. 1889–1972 (NOBEL PRIZE 1968)

Kawabata is Japan's only Nobel laureate in literature and undoubtedly one of its finest novelists. He was well versed in both Japanese and Western literature. His best works are distinguished by his sensitivity to his characters and the use of elliptical images, which has invited comparisons to linked verse (*renga*) or haiku, where the association of images is important. For all of his talent and success, Kawabata does not appear to have been a happy man. Knowledgeable in the classics and in Buddhism, he felt a sense of loss and impermanence, as if this world held no particular place for him. Despite this, he was active in literary circles and was the patron of another major author, Yukio Mishima. Yet as he grew older, Kawabata suffered increasingly from insomnia and one night took his own life, not leaving a word to explain his act.

BOOKS BY KAWABATA

The Master of Go. Trans. by Edward G. Seidensticker, Putnam (Perigee) 1981 pap. $4.95

Snow Country (Yukiguni). Trans. with an intro. by Edward G. Seidensticker, Putnam (Perigee) 1981 pap. $5.95. "It is not by chance that Kawabata Yasunari has chosen a hot-spring geisha for the heroine and the dark snow country for the setting. . . . Darkness and wasted beauty run like a ground bass through his major work, and in *Snow Country* we feel most strongly the cold loneliness of the Kawabata world" (Introduction).

The Sound of the Mountain (Yama no Oto). Trans. by Edward G. Seidensticker, Putnam (Perigee) pap. $5.95. A richly imagistic story of aging and the premonition of death, set in contemporary life. Viewed by many as Kawabata's finest work.

Thousand Cranes (Sembazuru). Trans. by Edward G. Seidensticker, Putnam (Perigee) 1981 pap. $5.95. A tale of complicated human relations variously linked to the tea ceremony and its utensils.

KENKŌ YOSHIDA. c.1283–c.1352

Famous as a poet and essayist, Kenkō obtained a position at court in 1301, but by 1313 had become a recluse for reasons that are unclear. He was strongly convinced that he was living in an age of decay, and his poetry, which survives in an anthology that he compiled, was in the vein of a conservative school that rejected innovation and urged preservation of past traditions. His *Essays in Idleness* is one of the more important works of classical literature.

BOOK BY KENKŌ

Essays in Idleness: The Tsurezuregusa of Kenkō. Trans. by Donald Keene, Columbia Univ. Pr. 1967 pap. $10.00. A collection of essays of greatly varying length on various topics.

KI TSURAYUKI. d.945 or 946

Tsurayuki is best known as a poet and as the author of *The Tosa Diary*. In both respects he was a pioneer. As a poet, he was the primary compiler of the *Kokinshū* (905), the premier anthology of court poetry. In its vernacular preface, as opposed to the one in Chinese written by someone else, he made the first statement about the poetics of verse in Japanese. He was greatly esteemed as a poet and calligrapher in his own time and has been venerated since.

BOOK BY TSURAYUKI

The Tosa Diary (Tosa Nikki). 935. AMS Pr. repr. of 1912 ed. $11.45; trans. by William N. Porter, Tuttle repr. of 1912 ed. 1981 $9.75. The first diary in vernacular Japanese by a man in the persona of a woman, because the custom of the time was for men to keep diaries in Chinese. An interesting account of life and travel in tenth-century Japan and a moving personal record.

KOBAYASHI ISSA (pseud. of Kobayashi Nobuyuki). 1763–1827

An important haiku poet of the Edo period, Issa wrote in the style of Bashō, but cultivated a particular simplicity of expression and emotion. His was a life of hardship filled with personal tragedies, and yet his writings reveal an unexpected streak of humor. His literary output was not large but is divided between collections of haiku and diaries based either on his travels throughout Japan or events in his family life.

BOOK BY ISSA

The Year of My Life: A Translation of Issa's "Oraga Haru." Trans. by Nobuyuki Yuasa, Univ. of California Pr. rev. ed. 1973 $17.50. Valuable as one of the few English-language studies of Issa and as a translation of a major work in which he describes the death of a daughter with moving lyricism.

MISHIMA YUKIO (pseud. of Kimitake Hiraoka). 1925–1970

Mishima was a writer of the aesthetic, master of a rich vocabulary and ornate style. He was versed in the Japanese classics and also well read in Western literature. His talent was precocious and he soon received recognition for it. He was a prolific writer and his work includes plays and criticism, as well as the novels for which he is best known in the West. His literature was generally apolitical in content and tone. Part of Mishima's aesthetic was the feudal period notion of the double way of the warrior and scholar. He also viewed the physical body as an aesthetic object and developed a muscular physique.

Impelled by the notion of the way of the warrior, he founded in 1968 the Shield Society, a private military group whose goal was to defend the idea of the emperor, as distinct from the reigning emperor, and to restore Japan to a "pure" spiritual state. He continued to work on the *Sea of Fertility*, which he viewed as his last literary testament. On the day that he delivered the manuscript of the last volume to his publisher, he went, armed and in uniform, to the local headquarters of the Self-Defense Forces. Taking a hostage, he had soldiers assembled and urged them to change their values and join his cause. He then committed ritual suicide along with another member of the Shield Society. This kind of death had also long been part of his aesthetic.

BOOKS BY MISHIMA

Confessions of a Mask. 1949. Trans. by Meredith Weatherby, New Directions 1968 pap. $5.25. The author's confessional account of growing up and self-discovery. An important work for understanding his life and writings.

Five Modern Nō Plays. Trans. by Donald Keene, Tuttle 1957 pap. $7.50. Traditional plays in imaginatively modern settings.

The Sea of Fertility:

Spring Snow. Trans. by Michael Gallagher, Washington Square Pr. 1975 pap. $2.95. The tragic love of two young aristocrats, Kiyoaki and Satoko, beautifully detailed. Within the tetralogy, which takes its name from one of the arid seas on the moon, this work introduces the character of Honda, Kiyoaki's friend, and the fact that Kiyoaki has an unusual group of three moles under his left arm. Honda will use this as a clue to discover subsequent reincarnations of his friend.

Runaway Horses. Trans. by Michael Gallagher, Knopf 1973 $11.95; Washington Square Pr. 1975 pap. $3.50. The action takes place 20 years after *Spring Snow.* Honda is now a judge, and the man with the mark is Isao, a young right-wing terrorist who plays out one of Mishima's personal fantasies.

The Temple of Dawn. Trans. by E. Dale Saunders and Cecilia Segawa Seigle, Knopf 1973 $12.95; Washington Square Pr. 1975 pap. $3.95. The first part of this work is set in Bangkok and India in 1941, where Honda is looking for the next reincarnation. He thinks it is a mysterious Thai princess who claims she is really Japanese. They meet in Japan after the war and one of Honda's tasks is to discover if she has the mark.

The Decay of the Angel. Trans. by Edward G. Seidensticker, Washington Square Pr. 1974 pap. $3.95. Mishima's last work. Honda has adopted the latest reincarnation, a youth named Tōru. Honda anticipates that, like the others, Tōru will die young. At the anticipated time, something does happen and he begins to display the five signs of the decay of an angel as described in Buddhism. Honda, too, must face his own decline as he grows old.

The Temple of the Golden Pavilion. Trans. by Ivan Morris, Putnam (Perigee) 1981 pap. $5.95. One of Mishima's most popular works, this is based on the true story of a mentally disturbed acolyte who burned down the Golden Pavilion. He narrates the story, explaining how he came to commit the arson.

BOOKS ABOUT MISHIMA

Nathan, John. *Mishima: A Biography.* Little, Brown 1974 pap. $3.95. A relatively detached study of Mishima but a valuable source of information. Controversial figures need more than a single biographer.

Scott-Stokes, Henry. *The Life and Death of Yukio Mishima.* Farrar 1974 $10.00 pap. $8.95. Like the Nathan book, a serious study of Mishima with a somewhat greater emphasis on his literary career and writings.

MORI ŌGAI (pseud. of Mori Rintarō). 1862–1922

Born into a family of physicians, Ōgai had a traditional education in the Chinese classics and was also well read in Japanese. While in medical school, he studied German and later spent four years in Germany studying medicine. During that time he read German and other Western literature. He eventually became the head of the medical division of the Army Ministry.

His literary production, which was often interrupted by official duties, falls into three main groups: 1909–1912, semiautobiographical fiction; 1912–1916, historical literature; and lastly, biography. He was also an able translator. With the exception of his early romantic works, his writing is marked by an austerity of tone.

BOOKS BY ŌGAI

The Historical Literature of Mori Ōgai. Ed. by David Dilworth and J. Thomas Rimer, Univ. of Hawaii Pr. 2 vols. 1977 ea. $14.95. The title of this set is apt: historical literature, not historical fiction. Ōgai wrote about real people and real events and researched his subjects, as the notes at the end of each volume indicate. He was, however, a superb stylist, and these stories make good reading.

Vita Sexualis. Trans. by Kazuji Ninomiya and Sanford Goldstein, Tuttle 1972 pap. $4.95. A philosophical look by the author at the development of his sexual awareness and the place of sexual desire in life. Although not devoid of humor, this is a serious work that was also intended to chide writers of the naturalist school for their relentless scrutiny of their own lives to the exclusion of other subjects.

The Wild Geese (Gan). Trans. by Kingo Ochiai and Sanford Goldstein, Tuttle 1974 pap. $4.25

BOOK ABOUT ŌGAI

Bowring, Richard John. *Mori Ōgai and the Modernization of Japanese Culture.* Cambridge Univ. Pr. 1979 $47.50. An in-depth study of Ōgai as an individual, a writer, and a thinker at a time of great intellectual and cultural flux in Japan. Bowring quotes extensively from Ōgai's writings, literary and other, and creates a coherent portrait of a complex and sensitive man struggling to deal with the difficulties of his day.

THE MOTHER OF FUJIWARA MICHITSUNA. d.955

Although of middling rank, the mother of Fujiwara Michitsuna was said to have been one of the three great beauties of her day. Like most women of her time, her personal name is not known. Her only real joy in married life seems to have been her son, and her diary reveals an acerbic personality.

BOOK BY THE MOTHER OF FUJIWARA MICHITSUNA

The Gossamer Years: Diary of a Noblewoman of Heian Japan (Kagerō Nikki). Trans. by Edward G. Seidensticker, Tuttle 1974 pap. $5.50. An engrossing work, ably translated. The introduction analyzes the work and explains how a noblewoman of the tenth century might have lived.

MURASAKI SHIKIBU (pseud.). fl. c.1000

Little is known of Murasaki Shikibu's life beyond what she tells in her diary. Even the name by which she is known is a sobriquet. Among her ancestors were men of literary talent. She married and had a daughter but was widowed in 1001. In that same decade she entered the service of an empress. Her literary reputation may have been a factor in her appointment, and she must have had substantial patronage, because the paper needed for writing a novel was rare and expensive. Her *Tale of Genji* is generally considered the greatest work in Japanese literature. Nothing is known of her life after 1013.

BOOKS BY MURASAKI

Murasaki Shikibu: Her Diary and Poetic Memoirs. Trans. by Richard Bowring, Princeton Univ. Pr. 1982 $27.50. A brief study of Murasaki's life and an annotated translation of the works contained. Annotations, although scholarly, are often very interesting and are an aid to understanding the content and context of these works. Helpful appendixes and good index.

The Tale of Genji. Trans. by Edward G. Seidensticker, Knopf 1978 pap. $13.95; trans. by Arthur Waley, Modern Lib. $8.95. Love would appear to be the main subject, but in fact the author probes human frailty, the evanescence of things, and spiritual concerns. Both translations listed are great, and the reader's choice will be determined by stylistic preferences. Waley's rich prose gives the romance an Edwardian setting but his translation is not complete and does not reflect modern scholarship. Seidensticker's version is up-to-date in this respect and complete. His is also a felicitous translation, but the style is relatively terse.

BOOK ABOUT MURASAKI

Puette, William J. *Guide to The Tale of Genji by Murasaki Shikibu.* Tuttle 1983 $13.50. Of particular use for chapter summaries and for the names of characters as given in the Waley and Seidensticker translations (see above).

NAGAI KAFŪ (NAGAI SŌKICHI). 1879–1959

Born into a wealthy family, Kafū developed an early interest in Edo period literature and culture. He disliked formal education and dropped out of school to enjoy popular entertainments, such as kabuki, and the pleasure quarters, which, in his youth, still retained some of the aura of the preceding age. In his writings, which included novels, essays, and short stories, he revealed a great nostalgia for the vanishing "old" Tokyo, and in his style he looked to the nineteenth century for models. It is fortunate that most of his writing was done before the Great Tokyo Earthquake of 1923, which put an end to the world he loved.

BOOK BY KAFŪ

Geisha in Rivalry (Udekurabe). Trans. by Kurt Meissner and Ralph Friedrich, Tuttle 1963 pap. $5.75. The denizens of the pleasure quarters observed. Loosely plotted but evocative and sometimes picaresque.

BOOK ABOUT KAFŪ

Seidensticker, Edward G. *Kafū the Scribbler: The Life and Writings of Nagai Kafū, 1879–1959.* Stanford Univ. Pr. 1965 $27.50. A book by a man in love with Tokyo about an author who was in love with the city. Valuable not only as a study but because almost one-half of the book is made up of translations of works by Kafū.

NATSUME SŌSEKI (pseud. of Natsume Kinnosuke). 1867–1916

Sōseki's works have been extremely popular since the beginning of his literary career and remain so today. The works of his contemporary, Mori Ōgai, while greatly respected and in some ways of equal significance, have not attracted as wide a readership. Sōseki began his career as a scholar of English literature and, after a period of teaching, was sent to Britain by the government in 1900. Poorly funded and isolated, he found his years abroad painful and exhibited neurotic behavior. On his return to Japan he resumed teaching, but left it in 1907 for writing. As his fame grew he acquired disciples who were to become part of the next generation of writers. Despite poor health in the last years of his life, Sōseki continued to write an average of one novel a year.

BOOKS BY SŌSEKI

Botchan. 1906. Trans. by Alan Turney, Kodansha 1972 $6.95 pap. $3.95. An early example of Sōseki's concern with the alienated intellectual.

Kokoro: A Novel by Natsume Sōseki. 1914. Trans. with a fwd. by Edwin McClellan, Regnery-Gateway 1957 pap. $4.95. A novella centering about a young man whose father is dying and an enigmatic older man. Through their conversations and correspondence, Sōseki explores themes of trust and betrayal, innocence and its loss.

And Then: Natsume Sōseki's Novel "Sore Kara." Afterword and bibliography by Norma Moore Field, Louisiana State Univ. Pr. 1978 $25.00; Putnam (Perigee) 1982 pap. $6.95. One of Sōseki's most popular novels.

Wayfarer: Kōjin. Trans. with an intro. by Beongcheon Yu, Wayne State Univ. Pr. 1967 $12.95; Putnam (Perigee) 1982 pap. $6.95. The most memorable figure in this complex work is the character of the narrator's brother. Initially insecure and suspicious, even of his wife, he becomes increasingly confused. Although lonely, he cannot trust, love, or believe in anything. One of Sōseki's studies of deracination in modern society.

Mon: The Gate. Trans. by Francis Mathy, Putnam (Coward) 1982 $13.95; Putnam (Perigee) pap. $5.95

Sanshirō: A Novel by Natsume Sōseki. Trans. with a critical essay by Jay Rubin, Putnam (Perigee) 1982 pap. $5.95. A story about a country boy in Tokyo, an innocent with illusions that the reader knows are bound to be dashed and whose innocence is lost to the realities of life. Rubin's essay relates *Sanshirō* to Sōseki's other writings and examines both themes and symbols.

The Three-Cornered World (Kusamakura). Trans. by Alan Turney, Putnam (Perigee) 1982 pap. $4.95. A quotation from Sōseki at the front of the work states that "an artist is a person who lives in the triangle which remains after the angle we may call common sense has been removed from this four-cornered world."

BOOK ABOUT SŌSEKI

McClellan, Edwin. *Two Japanese Novelists: Sōseki and Tōson.* Univ. of Chicago Pr. 1969 o.p. "Of all the writers of their time, these two were probably the most influential. Nowhere in the world has the autobiographical novel flourished as it has since Tōson's time. And perhaps much of the suspicion that still lingers there toward the imaginative storyteller is owing to his influence. On the other hand, it is equally likely that had Sōseki never lived, there would have been less audacity in Japanese fiction today" (Preface).

NIJŌ, LADY. late 13th–early 14th century

Of good birth, little is known of Lady Nijō's life apart from what she recounts in her diary. It covers the years from 1271, when she was 14 and became a concubine, through her expulsion from court in 1283, to 1306, when she had already turned to a life of religion. She was a keen observer of life both at the court and elsewhere and produced a document that depicts aristocratic life giving way to the mores of the rising warrior class.

Book by Nijō

Lady Nijō's Own Story: The Candid Diary of a 13th-Century Japanese Imperial Court Concubine. Trans. by Wilfrid Whitehouse and Eizo Yanagisawa, Tuttle 1974 pap. $9.50

ŌE KENZABURŌ. 1935–

A winner of numerous literary prizes, Ōe came to manhood during the war and occupation. In college, he studied Jean-Paul Sartre and absorbed many popular leftist ideas. These influences appear in his early writings, which often deal with (then) contemporary issues. With the birth of his deformed son, father and son became the new material for his literature. A blend of the personal and the political, backed by a powerful and poetic imagination, continues to distinguish Ōe's work.

Books by Ōe

A Personal Matter. Trans. by John Nathan, Grove 1968 pap. $6.95. A semiautobiographical account, in the existential vein, of the author's reaction to the birth of his deformed son.
The Silent Cry. Trans. by John Bester, Kodansha 1974 $10.00 1981 pap. $4.95. The subjective and objective sides of the author, in the form of two brothers, in a hallucinatory visit to their childhood home and a dark past. Also an engrossing mystery.

SEI SHŌNAGON. fl. late 10th century

This woman is known only by her sobriquet at court. She was in the service of an empress, about whom she writes with adulation, but apart from what she records in *The Pillow Book*, which is not autobiographical, little is known of her life. It does, however, reveal an educated, sensitive, and vivacious woman who held herself in high esteem and was popular at court. *The Pillow Book* is a classic of the *zuihitsu* or miscellany genre.

Book by Sei Shōnagon

The Pillow Book of Sei Shōnagon (Makura no Sōshi). Trans. by Ivan Morris, *Penguin Class. Ser.* 1971 pap. $4.95. Written with wit and translated with style, *The Pillow Book* includes lists of things that the author liked or disliked, spontaneous observations, anecdotes of court life, and miscellaneous tales, some of her own invention. The Penguin edition omits the lists of things, some appendixes, and the glossary-index found in the out-of-print Columbia University Press edition, but is valuable nonetheless.

SHIGA NAOYA. 1883–1971

Shiga is best known for his short stories and as a writer of confessional works about himself and his family and friends, with whom he was often in conflict. Although he lived to be almost 90, he wrote very little from the late thirties on.

BOOK BY SHIGA

A Dark Night's Passing (An'ya Kōro). Trans. by Edwin McClellan, Kodansha 1980 pap. $6.95. Shiga's only novel and one of his last significant literary works. A major theme is the issue of reconciliation.

BOOK ABOUT SHIGA

Sibley, William F. *The Shiga Hero*. Univ. of Chicago Pr. 1979 $18.00. ". . . one finds the most prominent recurring themes to be obsessive memories of childhood, fantasies of murder and parricide . . . a deeply ambivalent attraction to alternately protective and destructive older women, and ultimately the death wish . . ." (Author's Introduction). Shiga and his works psychoanalyzed. The book also contains translations of ten of his short stories.

SHIMAZAKI TŌSON (SHIMAZAKI HARUKI). 1872–1943

Shimazaki Tōson began his literary career as a romantic poet but later switched to prose. After writing *The Broken Commandment*, which is widely regarded as his masterpiece and a major work of modern Japanese realism, he turned to writing autobiographical novels. The best of these is *The Family*. His last work was a long historical novel, *Yoake Mae (Before the Dawn)*, in which he depicted the tragic effects on his father of the transition from feudal to modern Japan.

BOOKS BY TŌSON

The Broken Commandment (Hakai). Trans. by Kenneth Strong, Columbia Univ. Pr. 1977 pap. $9.50. A good portrait of the age, with fine psychological studies, marred only by a contrived ending.

The Family (Ie). Trans. with an intro. by Cecilia Segawa Seigle, Columbia Univ. Pr. 1977 pap. $12.50. The problems of life encountered by an extended family living in several households. The translator's introduction contains a brief biography of Tōson and general information about the actual families involved and their relation to the characters in the novel. There is also a discussion of the style and thematic content of the work.

BOOK ABOUT TŌSON

McClellan, Edwin. *Two Japanese Novelists: Sōseki and Tōson*. Univ. of Chicago Pr. 1969 o.p.

TANIZAKI JUN'ICHIRŌ. 1886–1965

Tanizaki is best known as a novelist, but was also a prolific writer of short stories, many of which have been translated. He has often been termed a decadent writer because of his preoccupation with women, whom he portrayed as a manifest danger as well as an irresistible attraction. Such a view, far from detracting from the quality of his works, infuses them with an intense sensuality, which is well served by Tanizaki's rich prose and superb ability as a storyteller. His life and, to an extent, his writing were changed by the Great Tokyo Earthquake of 1923. He moved from devastated Tokyo to the less earthquake-prone Kansai area, where the more traditional aspects of Japanese life still existed. His love of this "old" Japan is an element in many of his works.

BOOKS BY TANIZAKI

The Makioka Sisters (Sasame Yuki). 1946–49. Trans. by Edward G. Seidensticker, Knopf 1957 $15.00; Putnam (Perigee) 1981 pap. $9.95. Widely regarded as Tanizaki's masterpiece. A nostalgic but objective look at the elegant decline of an Osaka merchant family and the passing of an age. Also a story of four sisters, two married and two unmarried.

Diary of a Mad Old Man. 1961. Trans. by Howard Hibbett, Putnam (Perigee) 1981 pap. $4.95. One of Tanizaki's later works, written when he was in his seventies. On one level it is the story of an ill and impotent old man attracted to his daughter-in-law and on another a fine study of old age.

In Praise of Shadows. Trans. by Thomas Harper and Edward G. Seidensticker, Lette's Island Bks. 1977 pap. $3.95. An essay on Japanese aesthetics that argues for the implicit and unstated over the explicit.

Seven Japanese Tales. Trans. by Howard Hibbett, Putnam (Perigee) 1981 pap. $7.95. A collection of major short stories written between 1910 and 1959.

Some Prefer Nettles. Trans. by Edward G. Seidensticker, Putnam (Perigee) 1981 pap. $5.95. The story of a man in a failing marriage who is torn between the allure of the West, as represented by a Eurasian prostitute, and traditional Japan, in the person of his father-in-law's mistress.

UEDA AKINARI. 1734–1809

An adopted child, Ueda ran the family business and also worked as a doctor before he became a full-time writer. In writing *Ugetsu Monogatari*, for which he is probably best known, he drew on both Chinese and Japanese classical traditions and produced a work known for its elegant diction. He was also respected as a *waka* poet and as a scholar of ancient Japanese literature.

BOOK BY UEDA

Tales of Moonlight and Rain: Japanese Gothic Tales (Ugetsu Monogatari). Trans. by Kengi Hamada, Columbia Univ. Pr. 1971 $16.50. An entertaining collection of tales of the supernatural by a master of the genre.

YOSA BUSON (TANIGUCHI BUSON). 1716–1784

Along with Bashō and Issa, Buson was one of the three great haiku poets of the Edo period. He is equally famous as a painter. His poetry was in the style of Bashō, but was distinguished by a particular lyricism and romantic subjectivity. Although more prolific than Bashō, Buson is still underrepresented in English translation.

BOOK ABOUT BUSON

Haiku Master Buson. Trans. by Yuki Sawa and Edith M. Shiffert, Heian 1978 pap. $8.50. The first and as yet only book in English about Buson. In addition to a literary and biographical study of Buson and translations of his work, this book includes selections from writings about Buson by one of his disciples.

CHAPTER 25

Southeast Asian and Korean Literature

David R. Claussenius

> To study with comprehension the literature of the East is very greatly to in-
> crease one's horizon and enjoyment. History has repeatedly shown that a re-
> naissance of learning and artistic creation follows the discovery or rediscov-
> ery of alien cultures. The toil of our early Humanists fertilized and fructified
> all the national literatures of Europe. . . . As the books of Asia reach a wider
> and wider audience, it is reasonable to look forward to a splendid rebirth of
> our Western letters. New literary theories, new forms of expression, new sub-
> jects in plenty await the delighted exploitation of future writers. At this point
> of time we can do no more than call attention to the treasures lying at hand.
> —A. J. ARBERRY, Introduction to *Literatures of the East*

Although Southeast Asia is considered a distinct geographical region, the
civilization, language, and literature of each country have developed as a result of different influences, both in the premodern and modern periods. Buddhism, Hinduism, and Islam, adapted in varying ways to indigenous beliefs,
customs, and settings, are reflected in the classical literature of each state
in the region.

With the exception of Thailand, colonization of Southeast Asian countries
by various Western powers in the nineteenth and twentieth centuries directly affected official languages of instruction and indirectly the literary
languages. Indeed, the common bond among the Southeast Asian nations
can be said to be the predominance of external influences on their historical, political, and cultural lives.

Although the region has received much political attention in recent years,
translation of its literature into English has not kept pace. Much that exists
is scattered in journals and unpublished manuscripts or is available only
abroad. The colonial heritage is again reflected in the concentration of translations in the languages of former colonial powers, especially in the cases of
Cambodia and Laos. To attempt to bridge this gap for the English reader,
and by way of introduction to the literature, a number of bibliographies
and anthologies have been published.

BIBLIOGRAPHIES

Brandon, James R. *Theater in Southeast Asia.* 1967. Harvard Univ. Pr. 1974 pap. $8.95. Including bibliographies, descriptions of major genres, and extracts, this first survey of contemporary Southeast Asian theater "discusses four distinct but interrelated aspects of theater in eight Southeast Asian countries: the cultural setting and development of theater genres; the performing arts and production methods; the theater as a social institution; and the theater as a communication medium" (*LJ*).

Chee, Tham Seong, ed. *Essays on Literature and Society in Southeast Asia.* Ohio Univ. Pr. 1981 $20.00 pap. $15.00. A valuable collection of analytical accounts describing the modern literature of Burma, Cambodia, Indonesia, Malaysia, the Philippines, Singapore, Thailand, and Vietnam. Each essay is accompanied by a select bibliography.

Embree, John F., and Lillian Ota Dotson. *Bibliography of the Peoples and Cultures of Mainland Southeast Asia.* 1950. Russell 1972 o.p. Despite its age, this bibliography is the best such work available, with excellent sections on folklore, language, and literature.

Hall, D. G. *A History of Southeast Asia.* St. Martin's 4th ed. 1981 $37.50 pap. $15.95. This detailed and accurate chronology with maps, illustrations, bibliography, and index has made this history an excellent basic reference work on Southeast Asian studies. No other single volume contains as much information.

Jenner, Philip N. *Southeast Asian Literatures in Translation: A Preliminary Bibliography.* Univ. of Hawaii Pr. 1972 o.p. An invaluable reference source that draws together bibliographic information on the diverse and scattered literature of all the Southeast Asian nations. All languages into which the literature has been translated are covered.

José, F. Sionil, ed. *Asian PEN Anthology.* Taplinger 1967 $7.50. The 27 stories and 31 poems by more than 40 authors included in this collection give "an excellent indication of the contemporary literary scene" (*Choice*).

Saito, Shiro, ed. *Southeast Asian Research Tools.* Univ. of Hawaii Pr. 9 vols. 1979 o.p. Each of the country volumes (Brunei, Burma, Cambodia, Indonesia, Laos, Malaysia, the Philippines, Singapore, Thailand, and Vietnam) is divided into two sections, one listing reference works by form, and the second a listing by broad subject area. The first section covers bibliographies and periodicals, with annotations for all works listed. One of the most ambitious and exhaustive undertakings for Southeast Asia.

Shimer, Dorothy Blair, ed. *The Mentor Book of Modern Asian Literature: From the Khyber Pass to Fuji.* New Amer. Lib. 1969 o.p. A valuable anthology, including critical commentary and biographical notes on the authors.

Yeo, Robert, ed. *ASEAN Short Stories.* Heinemann text ed. 1981 pap. $7.50. This anthology includes 21 contemporary stories representing Indonesia, Malaysia, the Philippines, Singapore, and Thailand.

Zong, In-Sob. *A Guide to Korean Literature.* Hollym 1983 $22.00

BURMESE LITERATURE

Although Burma is linguistically and ethnically linked to China, from the eleventh-century founding of the first powerful Burmese kingdom at Pagan until the colonial period of the nineteenth and twentieth centuries, its cultural life was dominated by India. Burma's classical literature was in great part an expression of the religious and philosophical concepts of Indian Buddhism. Popular animist beliefs in spirits (*nat*) and other supernatural beings are barely visible in the written literature. The earliest surviving records are twelfth-century stone inscriptions, and the earliest literary texts date from the mid-fifteenth century. Poetry was the principal genre until the eighteenth century, taking the form of *pyo*, long religious poems on Buddhist themes written by Buddhist monks. It was not until the late eighteenth century, under Thai influence, that literature of entertainment, popular dramas (*pyo-zat*), and long poems (*yagan*) on increasingly secular themes began to appear. Prose remained at the service of the court and the cloister, primarily because printing did not become widespread until the late nineteenth century.

The Great Chronicle (*Maha Ya-zawin-gyi*) by U. Kala (1678?–1738?) was the first full-scale historical work in Burmese prose, and it was incorporated into *The Glass Palace Chronicle* (*Hmannān Ya-zawin-gyi*), the official history compiled in 1830 by a group of royal scholars. By the time of British annexation in 1886, court dominance had lost sway in literature for the public, and new forms of verse, drama, and the short story had been introduced.

Translations of Burmese literary works remain, in general, scattered. The *Journal of the Burma Research Society* and the *Guardian* magazine, both published in Rangoon, have over the years included articles and translations of works by many twentieth-century authors, such as Ma Ma Lei, Dagon Taya, and Theip-pan Maung Wa. Two other journals are significant for their inclusion of Burmese literature. The *Journal of Forward*, also published in Rangoon, contains numerous works of Tet Toe, an important literary critic in Burma. Also to be found in both the *Guardian* and *Forward* are the extensive writings of Pearl Aung and Kenneth Ba Sein on Burmese folk literature. Godfrey E. Harvey's *History of Burma* includes information on literature. *Old Burma-Early Pagan* by Gordon H. Luce and others (o.p.) is the definitive work on the archaeology and art of Pagan, with many references to Hindu-Buddhist literature. John F. Cady's *History of Modern Burma* is an excellent treatment of the modern period. J. Badgley, "Intellectuals and the National Vision: The Burmese Case" in *Asian Survey*, August 1979, is an important review. Badgley surveys 32 representative works written between 1936 and 1962 by 24 authors—novels, biographies, and political commentaries are included—a valuable treatment for its factual content and probing analysis.

Bode, Mabel Haynes. *The Pali Literature of Burma*. AMS Pr. repr. of 1909 ed. $15.00. This slim volume gives an excellent treatment of the evolution of Pali literature in Burmese society.

Cady, John F. *Contacts with Burma, 1935–1949: Personal Account*. Ohio Univ. Pr. 1983 pap. $9.00

The Glass Palace Chronicle of the Kings of Burma. Trans. by Pe Maung Tin and Gordon H. Luce, AMS Pr. repr. of 1923 ed. 1975 o.p.

Gray, James, ed. *Ancient Proverbs and Maxims from Burmese Sources: The Niti Literature of Burma*. AMS Pr. repr. of 1886 ed. $17.50

Htin, Aung Maung. *Burmese Drama: A Study with Translations of Burmese Plays.* Greenwood repr. of 1957 ed. 1978 lib. bdg. $21.00. *The Water Carrier,* by U. Ponnya, three other dramas, and extracts from several other plays. Htin has also edited *Burmese Folk Tales* (o.p.) and *Burmese Law Tales: The Legal Element in Burmese Folklore* (o.p.).

————. *Burmese Monk's Tales.* Columbia Univ. Pr. 1966 o.p. A Burmese writer, dramatist, and translator, Htin has also served as a correspondent for the *London Times.* These tales are modern didactic stories, forming a new subgenre of Burmese literature.

Lustig, R. F., ed. *Burmese Classical Poems.* Paragon repr. 1968 o.p. An excellent collection originally published in 1966 by the *Rangoon Gazette.*

Pe, U. Hla, ed. *Burmese Proverbs.* Paragon repr. 1962 o.p. Originally published in London in the *UNESCO Collection of Representative Works: Burmese Series,* this is the best available work on the subject.

Selected Short Stories of Thein Pe Myint. Trans. by Patricia M. Milne, *Cornell Univ. Southeast Asia Program* 1973 $4.00. A Burmese politician, writer, and journalist, many of whose short stories chronicle his own life.

INDONESIAN AND MALAYSIAN LITERATURE

Malaysia and Indonesia comprise what has traditionally been referred to in the West as the Malay Peninsula and Archipelago. Although more than 200 languages, most with no written literature, are spoken in the area, Malay, now called Bahasa Malaysia and Bahasa Indonesia, is the *lingua franca* in both nations, and, taking precedence over Javanese, Sundanese, and Balinese, is the dominant literary language. The spread of Islam into the region between the fourteenth and sixteenth centuries lent the classical version of the Malay language (written in Arabic script) and its literature (rhythmical, long-winded, and well suited to religion and romance) its distinctive character. There is a considerable Hindu-derived, although Muslim-influenced, literature, due to Hindu influence in early Java, the Malacca straits, and still today in Bali. This influence is reflected in versions of the *Rāmāyana,* the *Māhabhārata,* and romance cycles, which have provided the plots of the Javanese *wayang* shadow plays. Together with folk literature, of which the *pantun,* a quatrain adapted to love poetry and songs, has long been the most popular verse form, histories and picaresque novels and the Persian-derived *sha'ir* verse form were the major literary genres of premodern Malay.

Nationalist sentiments, first in the Netherlands East Indies and later in Malaya, led to the founding of a teachers' training college in Minangkabau, Sumatra, which undertook the development of a modern literary language based on classical Malay and influenced by Dutch grammar and vocabulary, and to the establishment in Batavia of the *Balai Pustaka* (Hall of Books), which sponsored the publication of Malay translations of European works. These events spurred the development of a new literary language. The modernization of the language has today reached a point where Bahasa Malaysia and Bahasa Indonesia have few essential differences except in the area of spelling; adoption of uniform spelling is a stated goal of the two nations. Among many outstanding monographs on the history and culture of the Malaysian world are *The Golden Chersonese and the Way Thither*, by Isabella L. Bird, a perceptive popular history; *The Malays: A Cultural History*, by Richard O. Winstedt; and *The Story of the Dutch East Indies*, by Bernard H. Vlekke. The last two are standard historical treatments.

Indonesian Literature

Ali, Ahmed. *The Flaming Earth: Poems from Indonesia, Karachi*. Friends of the Indonesian People Society 1949 o.p. A selection of some of the best Indonesian poetry to appear between 1945 and 1949, including renderings of works by Chairil Anwar and Rivai Apin. As far as literary impact, this is one of the most successful anthologies of Indonesian poetry in English to appear.

Anwar, Chairil. *The Complete Poetry and Prose of Chairil Anwar*. State Univ. of New York Pr. 1970 $27.00 pap. $14.95. Anwar, who died in 1949, lived only 27 years, but is still regarded as modern Indonesia's most outstanding writer. The corpus of his work includes some 75 original poems and several dozen translations or adaptations.

Aveling, Harry. *Contemporary Indonesian Poetry*. Univ. of Queensland Pr. 1975 $14.95 pap. $8.50

——. *A Thematic History of Indonesian Poetry, 1920 to 1974*. Northern Illinois Univ. Center for Southeast Asian Studies 1974 o.p.

Brandon, James R., ed. *On Thrones of Gold: Three Javanese Shadow Plays*. Harvard Univ. Pr. 1970 $25.00

Freidus, Alberta Joy. *Sumatran Contributions to the Development of Indonesian Literature, 1920–1942*. Univ. of Hawaii Pr. text ed. 1977 $7.50

Hendon, Rufus S. *Six Indonesian Short Stories*. Yale Univ. Southeast Asia Studies 1968 $5.50

Johns, Anthony H. *Cultural Options and the Role of Tradition: A Collection of Essays on Modern Indonesian and Malaysian Literature*. Australia National Univ. Pr. text ed. 1979 pap. $6.95

Lubis, Mochtar. *A Road with No End*. Trans. by Anthony H. Johns, Regnery-Gateway 1970 o.p.

——. *Twilight in Djakarta*. Trans. by Claire Holt, Vanguard 1964 o.p. Lubis, one of Indonesia's outstanding modern novelists, is also a political journalist.

McVey, Ruth T., ed. *Indonesia*. Survey of World Culture Ser. Human Relations Area Files 1962 o.p. Particularly good is the chapter "Genesis of Modern Literature" by Anthony H. Johns.

Multatuli. *Max Havelaar: Or the Coffee Auctions of the Dutch Trading Company*. Univ. of Massachusetts Pr. 1982 lib. bdg. $17.50 pap. $11.00. A historical novel.

Pane, Armijn. *Shackles*. Trans. by John McGlynn, intro. by William H. Frederick, Ohio Univ. Pr. 1985 $9.00. Probably the best-known Indonesian novel and generally considered the first fully modern novel written in Indonesia.

Peacock, James L. *Rites of Modernization: Symbolic and Social Aspects of Indonesian Proletarian Drama*. Univ. of Chicago Pr. 1968 $22.00

Raffel, Burton. *Anthology of Modern Indonesian Poetry*. State Univ. of New York Pr. 1968 pap. $12.95

——. *The Development of Modern Indonesian Poetry*. State Univ. of New York Pr. 1967 $34.50

Sick, Marguerite. *Favourite Stories from Indonesia*. Heinemann bilingual ed. text ed. 1981 pap. $2.50

Simatupang, Iwan. *The Pilgrim*. Heinemann text ed. 1975 pap. $5.00

Simatupang, T. B. *Report from Banaran: The Story of the Experiences of a Soldier during the War of Independence*. Cornell Univ. Southeast Asia Program 1972 pap. $6.50

Teeuw, A. *Modern Indonesian Literature*. Martinus Nijhoff 1967 o.p. Provides an extensive historical coverage of prewar literature and postwar literature.

Toer, Pramoedya Ananta. *The Fugitive*. Trans. by Harry Aveling, Humanities Pr. 1976 o.p. One of the greatest of Indonesian writers, Toer was born in Java in 1925 and is a writer of revolution. The majority of his themes are related to the revolutionary fight against the Dutch, British, and Japanese.

Tur, Pramudya. *Child of All Nations*. Trans. by Max Lane, Penguin 1979 pap. $6.95

——. *This Earth of Mankind*. Penguin 1979 pap. $6.95

Wagner, Frits A. *Indonesia: The Art of an Island Group*. Crown 1959 o.p. A broad, sensitive history, well illustrated, concerned with literature, politics, economics, and sociology, as well as the art history that is the book's primary emphasis.

Ward, Philip. *Indonesian Traditional Poetry*. Oleander 1975 $13.50

Malaysian Literature

Abdullah, Bin Abdul Kadir. *Hikayat Abdullah*. Ed. by A. H. Hill, Oxford 1970 o.p. The first modern book published in Malaya. Abdullah, who was clerk to Sir Stamford Raffles, broke with tradition in this autobiography by writing about current conditions in Malaya, in particular Malaysian contacts with Europeans.

Geddes, W. R. *Nine Dayak Nights*. Oxford 1957 o.p. This volume of translations includes the epic *The Story of Kichapi*.

Knappert, Jan. *Malay Myths and Legends*. Heinemann text ed. 1981 pap. $7.95

Osman, Muhammad Taib. *An Introduction to the Development of Modern Malay Language and Literature*. Eastern Univ. Pr. 1961 o.p.

Rice, Oliver, and Abdullah Majid Asraf, trans. *Modern Malay Verse, 1946–1961*. Intro. by James Kirkup, Oxford 1963 o.p. This is the best anthology of contemporary Malaysian poetry.

Sejarah Melayu; or Malay Annals. 1952. Trans. and ed. by C. C. Brown, intro. by C. C. Roolvink, Oxford 1970 $10.50. One of the finest of all Malaysian classics, and one of the most important historical works concerned with Malaysia.

Skeat, Walter W. *Fables and Folk-Tales from an Eastern Forest*. 1901. Norwood $10.00. Includes 26 tales from the Malay Peninsula.

Sweeney, Amin. *Authors and Audiences in Traditional Malay Literature*. Univ. Pr. of Amer. text ed. 1983 pap. $7.00. A well-documented treatise refuting the earlier interpretations of Malaysian literature by Richard O. Winstedt.

——. *Malay Shadow Puppets: The Wayang Siam of Kelantan*. Oxford 1980 o.p.

Winstedt, Richard O. *A History of Classical Malay Literature*. 1961. Oxford 2d ed. 1969 o.p. This outstanding work includes a good bibliography.

KOREAN LITERATURE

No history of Korean literature can be written without acknowledging the strong influence of Chinese culture in premodern Korea. Indeed, until the mid-fifteenth century, the use of Chinese characters was standard practice in Korean literature. Among the most important examples of early Korean work extant is a group of 45 poems written in Chinese between the seventh and fourteenth centuries. In the 1440s, a group of scholars under royal patronage devised a new Korean alphabet. The first work published in this new alphabet was "Yong Pi O Ch'on Ka" ("The Song of the Dragons Flying to Heaven"), a long poem in praise of the founders of the Yi dynasty.

The literature that has received a great amount of critical attention consists of poems from the late sixteenth to the early nineteenth centuries called *sijo*, a form of lyric poem with prescribed versification. Early prose, or *sosol*, is generally in the novel form, and many of the extant examples are translations and imitations of Chinese works. Foremost are two novels by Kim Man-jung, *Sa-ssi Namjong ki* (*A Korean Classic: The Story of Mrs. Sah's Journey to the South*) and *Kuun mong* (*A Nine Cloud Dream*). Both were written in Chinese and later translated into Korean.

Twentieth-century Korean literature is characterized by a movement to break away from classical traditions, both in style and theme. Among the outstanding modern writers are Yi Kwangsu and Kim Tongin, both prodigious producers of novels and short stories, and Kim Sowol, author of "The Azaleas," one of the most popular modern Korean poems. It should be noted that although Korean publishers have issued a number of English translations of Korean literary works both in the form of anthologies and separate pieces under the aegis of the Korean National Commission for UNESCO and the Korean Center of the International PEN, materials published in the United States have until quite recently concentrated on Korean history and politics.

Bang, Im, and Yi Ryuk. *Korean Folk Tales: Imps, Ghosts and Fairies*. Trans. by James S. Gale, Tuttle 1962 pap. $4.95

Barkan, Stanley H., comp. *South Korean Poets of Resistance*. Trans. by Won Ko, Cross Cultural Review 1980 $10.00 pap. $4.00

Kim, Chong-un, ed. *Postwar Korean Short Stories: An Anthology*. Univ. of Hawaii Pr. text ed. 1983 $18.00

Ko, Won, trans. *Contemporary Korean Poetry*. Univ. of Iowa Pr. 1970 $6.95

Koh, Chang-soo, trans. *Best Loved Poems of Korea: Selected for Foreigners*. Hollym $9.95

Lee, Peter H. *The Silence of Love: Twentieth-Century Korean Poetry*. Univ. of Hawaii Pr. text ed. 1980 $17.95 pap. $8.95

————. *Songs of Flying Dragons*. Harvard Univ. Pr. text ed. 1975 $20.00

————, ed. *Anthology of Korean Literature: From Early Times to the Nineteenth Century*. Univ. of Hawaii Pr. text ed. 1981 pap. $12.00

Sym, Myung-Ho. *The Making of Modern Korean Poetry: Foreign Influences and Native Creativity*. Univ. of Hawaii Pr. text ed. 1982 $18.00

Zong, In-Sob, trans. and ed. *Folk Tales from Korea*. Grove (Everyman's) 1979 $6.95

MONGOLIAN LITERATURE

European scholars long thought that Mongolian literature consisted almost entirely of translations, mainly of Buddhist works. Now, however, there is evidence of a rich tradition of oral and written literature as early as the thirteenth century. The earliest work extant, *The Secret History of the Mongols*, dates from that time and is devoted principally to the life of Genghis Khan. It contains narrative and alliterative verse and is an important source on early Mongolian culture. Historical writing underwent a revival in the seventeenth century and consisted primarily of chronicles written under Lamaist influence. Folktales, fantastic and historical, and lyric poetry, mostly in the form of folk songs, epics, and stories, comprised the bulk of the literature of entertainment that developed by the eighteenth century. The Revolution of 1921 saw a break in the literary tradition, with much writing thereafter becoming an instrument of political persuasion. Much of the work on Mongolian literature has taken place abroad, especially by such scholars as Paul Pelliot, Nicholas Poppe, and Walter Heissig. The most important work of the modern period is B. Rintchen's historical novel *Dawn on the Steppes*, which is not currently available in English.

Cleaves, Francis W., trans. and ed. *The Secret History of the Mongols, for the First Time, Done into English out of the Original Tongue, and Provided with an Exegetical Commentary.* Harvard Univ. Pr. 1982 $20.00; North Point Pr. 1984 pap. $14.00

Poppe, Nicholas. *The Diamond Sutra: Three Mongolian Versions of the Vajracchedika Prajnaparamita.* International Publishing 1971 o.p.

Rasipungsuy. *Bolor Erike: Mongolian Chronicle in Five Parts.* Harvard Univ. Pr. pap. $32.50

Schwartz, Henry G., trans. and ed. *Mongolian Short Stories.* Washington State Univ. Pr. 1974 o.p.

Waley, Arthur. *The Secret History of the Mongols and Other Pieces.* 1964 o.p.

PHILIPPINE LITERATURE

The various migrations to and occupations of the Philippine archipelago throughout its history have led to a diversity of languages and cultural influences in its literature. The migration of the Malayo-Polynesian peoples introduced Tagalog, Ilokano, and Bisayan as major languages. Few examples remain today of the poetry, usually oral, proverbs, love songs, and ballads of the period prior to the Spanish Conquest in the mid-sixteenth century. The Spaniards introduced a new language and a romanized alphabet, as well as new literary forms and themes. Spanish chivalric tales were freely adapted, in particular by the Tagalog poet Francisco Balagtas in his *Florante at Laura*, first published in 1838 (o.p.). Roman Catholic liturgy was the basis for indigenous biblical stories and choral chanting. The popular *moro-moro* plays were based on Spanish models, their most common plot being conflict between Christians and Moors. The U.S. occupation of the Philippines from 1898 to 1943 saw the adoption of English as the official medium of instruction and therefore as the literary language of a number of modern writers. One of the most prominent of these is José Garcia Villa, a novelist, short story writer, and poet.

Translations of Philippine literature into English have appeared mostly under Filipino imprint. These include *Pen Short Stories*, edited by Francisco Arcellona (o.p.), and *The Authentic Voice of Poetry*, edited by Ricardo Demetillo (o.p.). For an excellent overview of contemporary Philippine literature, consult *Literature and Society, Cross-Cultural Perspectives: A Project of the Philippine-American Educational Foundation*, by Roger J. Bresnahan.

Agacoili, T. D., ed. *Philippine Writings: An Anthology.* Greenwood repr. of 1953 ed. 1971 lib. bdg. $17.75

Bulosan, Carlos. *American Is in the Heart.* Univ. of Washington Pr. 4th ed. 1973 pap. $8.95. A stirring autobiographical account of the author's travels on the West Coast, from the canneries in Alaska to the farm fields in California.

———. *The Laughter of My Father.* Harcourt 1942 o.p. Bulosan's first publication is a collection of short stories portraying rural life in the Philippines.

Casper, Leonard. *New Writing from the Philippines: A Critique.* Syracuse Univ. Pr. 1966 $15.95

Galdon, Joseph A., ed. *Essays on the Philippine Novel in English.* Cellar 1980 $16.00 pap. $6.75

González, Nestor Vicente Madali. *The Bamboo Dancers.* Ohio Univ. Pr. 1961 $8.95. González is a Filipino writer and poet writing in English and currently teaching at the California State University at Hayward.

———. *Mindoro and Beyond: Twenty-One Stories.* Univ. of Hawaii Pr. text ed. 1979 $15.00 pap. $8.50. An appendix, "In the Workshop of Time and Tide," provides a helpful history of Philippine literature from the 1600s until contemporary times with an extensive bibliography.

Hosillo, Lucila V. *Philippine-American Literary Relations.* Oriole Eds. 1969 o.p.

Joaquin, Nick. *Tropical Baroque: Four Manileño Theatricals.* Univ. of Queensland Pr. text ed. 1982 $18.00 pap. $9.50

———. *Tropical Gothic.* Univ. of Queensland Pr. 1972 $14.95 pap. $8.50. A Filipino poet, essayist, and journalist, Joaquin is considered one of the giants of modern Filipino literature. Made famous by his short story "Three Generations" (1940), he wrote essays for the Philippines Free Press under the name Quijano de Manila. A great deal of his writing is scattered among periodical publications.

Rizal, José y Alonso. *Lost Eden (Noli Me Tangere).* 1887. Trans. by Leon M. Guerrero, Greenwood repr. of 1961 ed. 1968 lib. bdg. $20.25. Rizal, Filipino national hero and writer who wrote in Spanish, died in 1896. Both his poetic and prose works, including *Noli Me Tangere*, his first novel, express the rising nationalistic feeling of the Philippine middle class of the late nineteenth century. *Noli Me Tangere* was prohibited by the censor when it was published, and many copies found in the Philippines were burned.

———. *Subversive (El Filibusterismo).* Trans. by Leon M. Guerrero, Norton 1968 pap. $1.95. Originally published in London under the title *El Filibusterismo*, this sequel to *Noli Me Tangere* is sharply critical of the Spanish colonizers, but less successful as writing.

Rosca, Ninotachka. *The Monsoon Collection.* Univ. of Queensland Pr. text ed. 1983 $16.50 pap. $8.95. Collection of contemporary short stories written both in the Philippines and the United States during the period 1975–79.

Roseburg, Arturo G., ed. *Pathways to Philippine Literature in English: Anthology with Biographical and Critical Introductions.* Alemar-Phoenix 1966 o.p. Provides an excellent source of biographical sketches of 12 major Philippine writers with ample excerpts of their writings.

Santos, Bienvenido N. *Scent of Apples: A Collection of Stories*. Univ. of Washington
    Pr. 1979 pap. $8.95. Similar to Bulosan in autobiographical nature, Santos por-
    trays life as an immigrant on the East Coast prior to World War II.
Yabes, Leopoldo. *Philippine Literature in English*. Krishna lib. bdg. $79.95

THAI LITERATURE

The classical literature of Thailand, like its culture, is a synthesis of Hindu
and Buddhist influences, native attitudes, and settings. The earliest Siamese literature dates from the mid-thirteenth century and takes the form of
historical inscriptions, didactic poetry, and moral sayings. During the classical period, which extended to the nineteenth century, the play, including
court and popular drama, shadow plays of various types, and stories based
on the Rama legend, coexisted with more secular lengthy historical poems
and epic romances concerned with Thai heroes. The seventeenth-century
love poetry by Si Prat is particularly noteworthy. As the output of traditional poetic literature declined, prose became the dominant literary medium in the post-1850 period; popular forms of elegies, lyrics, folk songs,
and tales continue to the present day.

Although English translations of Thai literature are increasing in recent
years, little of the work of outstanding Thai writers, such as Si Prat, Kikrit
Pramoj, and Sunthorn Bhu, has been published in the United States. As
background to Thai civilization, two books are worthy of mention: *Thailand: Society and Politics*, by J. L. S. Girling, and *Study in Thailand: The
Analyses of Knowledge, Approaches and Prospects in Anthropology, Art, History, and Political Science*, edited by Eliezar B. Ayal.

Cadet, J. M., trans. *The Rāmakien: The Thai Epic Myth*. Kodansha 1970 $31.00. Based
    on the Indian *Rāmāyana*, but probably patterned after a Javanese version, the
    Rāmakien is the longest and most famous epic of premodern Thailand.
Draskau, Jennifer, ed. and trans. *Taw and Other Thai Stories*. Heinemann text ed.
    1975 pap. $6.50
Jones, Robert B. *An Introduction to Thai Literature*. Cornell Univ. Southeast Asia Pro-
    gram 1970 $7.00
Jones, Robert B., and others. *Thai Cultural Reader*. Cornell Univ. Pr. repr. of 1970 ed.
    1976 $7.50
Jumsai, M. L. Manich. *History of Thai Literature: Including Laos, Shans, Khanti,
    Ahom and Yunnan-nanchao*. Paragon repr. 1975 o.p. The best history of Thai lit-
    erature available, written by the author of several histories of Thailand.
Khon Khai, Khamman. *The Teachers of Mad Dog Swamp*. Trans. and intro. by Gehan
    Wijeyewardene, Univ. of Queensland Pr. text ed. 1982 $18.00 pap. $9.50. An in-
    teresting example of a contemporary Thai novel that was made into a film, *Ru-
    ral School Teachers*. Includes a glossary.
Manuet Banhān, Phya, ed. *Siamese Tales Old and New: The Four Riddles and Other
    Stories*. Trans. by Reginald LeMay, Folcroft repr. of 1930 ed. 1974 lib. bdg.
    $25.00. These tales express the Thais' outlook on life, their capacity for humor,
    philosophical values, and the place of magic and superstition in their lives. The
    translator was formerly judge of the International Court in Bangkok.

Masavisut, Nitayan, ed. *Thai PEN Anthology: Short Stories and Poems of Social Consciousness*. PEN 1984 consult publisher for price
Pramoj, Seni M. R. *Interpretative Translations of Thai Poets*. Thai Watana Panich 1978 o.p. Originally published in 1965 for private distribution, this work has become increasingly popular as one of the few works on Thai poets in English. Each section includes the original Thai poem followed by a romanized script and then English translation. Each poet is introduced by a short biographical sketch.
Rama, King, II. *Sang Thong: A Dance-Drama from Thailand*. Trans. by Fern S. Ingersoll, Tuttle 1972 o.p.
Soonsawad, Thong-In, trans. *Thai Poets*. Paragon repr. 1968 o.p.
Srinawk, Khamsing. *The Politician and Other Stories*. Trans. by Domnern Garden, intro. by Michael Smithies, Oxford 1973 o.p.
Wray, Elizabeth, and others. *Ten Lives of Buddha: Siamese Temple Paintings and Jataka Tales*. Wetherhill 1972 $20.00. Jataka tales are stories based on the birth of Buddha.

VIETNAMESE LITERATURE

The pervasive influence of Chinese tradition, rules, and characters that was the style of prose and verse until the nineteenth century made Chinese influence in Vietnam the strongest in Southeast Asia. By the thirteenth century, a system of writing Vietnamese in Chinese-style characters called *chu nom* had developed. *Nom* literature gradually assumed a manner distinctive from Chinese forms and reached its height of excellence at the beginning of the nineteenth century. Its decline thereafter is in part attributable to the development, by seventeenth-century Christian missionaries, of a romanized script, *quoc ngu* (now universally used), which spread after French colonization. Among the poetic genres most common in both the classical and folk literatures of Vietnam are the *luc bat* (six- and eight-syllable lines alternating) and the *truyen*, which was normally in the form of verse novels or verse romances and was especially popular in the eighteenth century. Although studies and translations of Vietnamese literature have been primarily published in French, U.S. involvement has produced many historical and political monographs in English.

Balaban, John T., trans. and ed. *Ca Dao Vietnam: Bilingual Anthology of Vietnamese Folk Poetry*. Unicorn Pr. 1980 $15.00 pap. $6.00
Binh, Tran Bu. *The Red Earth: A Vietnamese Memoir of Life on a Colonial Rubber Plantation*. Trans. by John Spragens, Ohio Univ. Pr. 1984 pap. $9.00
Hollenbeck, Peter, and others. *Vietnam Literature Anthology: A Balanced Perspective*. Amer. Poetry & Lit. Pr. 1984 $11.95 pap. $7.95
Marr, David G., ed. *Reflections from Captivity*. Ohio Univ. Pr. 1978 $12.00. Translations of Phan Boi Chau, Nguc Trung Thu, Ho Chi Minh, and Nhat Ky Trong Tu.
Monigold, Glen W., trans. and ed. *Folktales from Vietnam*. Peter Pauper 1964 o.p.
Nguyen, Du. *Tale of Kieu: The Classic Vietnamese Verse Novel*. Trans. and ed. by Huynh Sanh Thong, pref. by Gloria Emerson, historical background by Alexander Woodside, Yale bilingual ed. 1983 $17.50. In the *truyen* form, this long narrative poem is considered the greatest epic in the Vietnamese language. The au-

thor was a poet and the son of a high government official. This, his major work, was completed in 1820, the year of his death.

Nguyen, Khac Vien, and Ngoc Huu, trans. and eds. *Vietnamese Literature*. Hanoi Foreign Languages Publishing House 1983 consult publisher for price. An authoritative anthology of Vietnamese literature from the tenth century to the twentieth century representing a condensation from a four-volume set.

Nguyen, Ngoc Bich, and others, trans. and eds. *A Thousand Years of Vietnamese Poetry*. Knopf 1975 o.p.

Raffel, Burton, trans. *From the Vietnamese: Ten Centuries of Poetry*. October 1968 $4.95 pap. $1.95

Thong, Huynh Sanh, trans. and ed. *The Heritage of Vietnamese Poetry*. Yale Univ. Pr. 1979 $22.50. This ambitious anthology goes a long way toward filling the gap of Vietnamese poetry translated into English. The 475 poems range from the tenth century through the early part of the French colonial period. Includes an introduction, notes, biographical sketches, index, and bibliography.

Vo-Dinh. *The Toad Is the Emperor's Uncle: Animal Folktales from Vietnam*. Doubleday 1970 o.p.

Name Index

In addition to authors, this index includes the names of persons mentioned in connection with titles of books written, whether they appear in introductory essays, general bibliographies at the beginnings of chapters, discussions under main headings, or "Books About" sections. Persons mentioned in passing—to indicate friendships, relationships, and so on—are generally not indexed. Editors are not indexed unless there is no specific author given; such books include anthologies, bibliographies, yearbooks, and the like. Translators, writers of introductions, forewords, afterwords, etc., are not indexed except for those instances where the translator seems as closely attached to a title as the real author, e.g., FitzGerald's translation of the *Rubáiyát of Omar Khayyám*. Main name headings appear in boldface as do the page numbers on which the main entries appear.

Title Index

Titles of all books discussed in *The Reader's Adviser* are indexed here, except broad generic titles such as "Complete Works," "Selections," "Poems," "Correspondence." Also omitted is any title listed with a main-entry author that includes that author's name, e.g., *Collected Prose of T. S. Eliot*, and titles under "Books About," e.g., *Eliot's Early Years* by Lyndall Gordon. The only exception to this is Shakespeare (Volume 2), where all works by and about him are indexed. To locate all titles by and about a main-entry author, the user should refer to the Name Index for the author's primary listing (given in boldface). Whenever the name of a main-entry author is part of a title indexed here, the page reference is to a section other than the primary listing. In general, subtitles are omitted. When two or more identical titles by different authors appear, the last name of each author is given in parentheses following the title.

Subject Index

This index provides detailed, multiple-approach access to the subject content of the volume, employing the subject headings as entry terms. Arrangement is alphabetical. Where subjects involve both literary forms and national literatures, entries are grouped first by form and then by country. Collective terms for authors are included, e.g., *Artists*, *Dramatists*, *Economists*, but the reader is reminded to use the Name Index to locate individual writers.